SIXTH EDITION

FIELDS OF READING

Motives for Writing

NANCY R. COMLEY
Queens College, CUNY

DAVID HAMILTON
University of Iowa

CARL H. KLAUS
University of Iowa

ROBERT SCHOLES
Brown University

NANCY SOMMERS
Harvard University

D0022466

BEDFORD/ST. MARTIN'S   Boston   ◆   New York

For Bedford/St. Martin's

Editor: John Elliott
Production Editor: Colby Stong
Senior Production Supervisors: Cheryl Mamaril and Joe Ford
Marketing Manager: Brian Wheel
Art Director/Cover Design: Lucy Krikorian
Text Design: Wanda Kossak
Copy Editor: Pat Cabeza
Cover Art: Vincent van Gogh: *Harvest at La Crau* F 412 Oil on Canvas,
  73 x 92 cm, Arles, 1888, Amsterdam, Van Gogh Museum (Vincent van Gogh
  Foundation)
Composition: Pine Tree Composition, Inc.
Printing and Binding: Haddon Craftsmen, an R.R. Donnelley & Sons Company

President: Charles H. Christensen
Editorial Director: Joan E. Feinberg
Editor in Chief: Nancy Perry
Director of Marketing: Karen R. Melton
Director of Editing, Design, and Production: Marcia Cohen
Managing Editor: Erica T. Appel

For information, write: Bedford/St. Martin's, 75 Arlington Street, Boston, MA
02116   (617-399-4000)

ISBN: 0-312-25594-2
      0-312-25817-8 (instructor's edition)

Acknowledgments

   Maya Angelou. "Graduation." Excerpt from pages 164–180 in *I Know Why the Caged
Bird Sings.* Copyright © 1969 by Maya Angelou. Reprinted with the permission of Random
House.

Acknowledgments and copyrights are continued at the back of the book on pages
775–779, which constitute an extension of the copyright page.

Preface

This sixth edition of *Fields of Reading: Motives for Writing* contains ninety-one readings from a broad range of academic, professional, and literary writing, organized around four main purposes for writing: Reflecting, Reporting, Explaining, and Arguing. In focusing on purpose, we give students and instructors the opportunity to explore the complex relationships among writers and readers that vary according to "what" and "why" people write and read. The title *Fields of Reading: Motives for Writing* identifies our goal of providing students with tools to establish and develop their own motives for writing throughout their college and professional lives.

Highlights of the Sixth Edition

New Prose Selections. Of the seventy-five prose selections, twenty-nine are new to the sixth edition. These pieces represent a culturally varied array of thinkers, critics, and scholars who did not appear in the fifth edition, including Henry Louis Gates Jr., Amitav Ghosh, Sherry Turkle, Cynthia Ozick, and Stuart Moulthrop. These new essays continue to provide students with models of finely crafted writing from a diverse range of fields.

Poems as New Selections. For the first time, we have chosen to include poetry among the readings, with sixteen poems grouped under the same rhetorical and cross-curricular categories as their prose counterparts. The poems, which were carefully chosen as models of rhetorical effectiveness in their respective categories, include works by Langston Hughes, Seamus Heaney, Elizabeth Bishop, W. H. Auden, Rita Dove, William Carlos Williams, Thom Gunn, and Robert Frost.

Flexible Organization. We have grouped the selections into four broad rhetorical categories: Reflecting, Reporting, Explaining, and Arguing. These categories represent essential kinds of reading and writing in virtually every academic or professional area. In every field, individuals consider past experience (reflecting), convey information (reporting), make sense of knowledge (explaining), and debate controversial ideas and issues (arguing). Within each of the four categories, we have grouped the selections by academic fields: Arts and Humanities, Social Sciences and Public Affairs, and Sciences and Technologies. We hope that this dual organization will assist instructors in discovering and assigning selections for a variety of classroom purposes.

Thematic Connections. The new selections have also been chosen with an eye toward strengthening the thematically related clusters of readings that support instructors who teach by theme. Any of these selections can be taught in terms of its themes or area of interest by using the updated Thematic Table of Contents, which includes clusters on such topics as Anne Frank, Interpreting the Body, Myths and Rituals, and Observing Animals. As a result, students will have ample opportunity to read and consider different perspectives on a single issue or to explore a particular issue in depth. The Making Connections questions following selections also encourage students to explore thematic relationships.

Introduction to the Reading and Writing Process. The introduction explains and illustrates the interrelationship between reading and writing processes, primarily through an examination of a specially commissioned essay by Patricia Hampl. In "Reviewing Anne Frank," Hampl reflects on her own response to a particular writing assignment, a book review for the *New York Times*. In doing so, she both illustrates her own writing process and demonstrates that even accomplished writers struggle with some of the same challenges student writers face. We have also reprinted in this section Hampl's published review, "The Whole Anne Frank." These introductory materials, like the rest of the book, are meant to present reading and writing not in abstract terms, but through discussion and examples that vividly demonstrate what is actually involved in each activity.

New Section on Evaluating and Using Sources. Within the introduction, we have considerably expanded the discussion of acknowledging sources to cover broader issues of how to evaluate potential source materials and how to use them within a piece of writing. This new section focuses particularly on sources drawn from the World Wide Web, because these pose the greatest pitfalls for students uncertain how to judge the relative worth of online material and to incorporate it appropriately, with proper acknowledgment, into their own writing.

Extensive Critical Apparatus. Much of our critical apparatus focuses on the rhetorical concepts and techniques that apply to reading and writing across the curriculum as introduced in the section, For Students. The detailed introductions to each of the four main sections, Reflecting, Reporting, Explaining, and Arguing (which are illustrated passages from the anthologized readings), define the type of writing featured in that section and discuss its use in differing fields and situations. The introductions also identify and explain the rhetorical methods used to achieve each type of writing's aims, for example, how description and narration are basic to reporting or how analogy, comparison and contrast, definition, and illustration are basic to explaining. All the rhetorical aims and modes covered in the introductions are also referenced in the Rhetorical Index. The headnote for each piece identifies and, wherever necessary, explains the professional field of its author and the rhetorical context or source of its original publication. Likewise, the questions following each selection call for reading and writing that relate form and style to purpose, subject, and academic field.

Acknowledgments

For their detailed reactions to the fifth edition of *Fields of Reading* and suggestions for improving the sixth edition, we are grateful to the following reviewers: Cathryn Amdahl, Harrisburg Area Community College; Rebecca Bell-Metereau, Southwest Texas State University; Rocky Colavito, Northwestern State University; Michelle Dega, Boise State University; Betsy DelleBovi, Canisius College; Gary Sue Goodman, University of California—Davis; Kathleen Heinlen, University of Minnesota–Minneapolis; Erica Jacobs, George Mason University; William Jennings, University of Iowa; Cliff Lewis, University of Massachusetts–Lowell; Dennis Moore, University of Iowa; Lynda Thompson, East Central Oklahoma University; Katherine Wright, Northern Illinois University; and Vlatka Velcic, Austin Peay State University. Nancy Sommers appreciated Scott Neustrom's help with the poems in the Explaining section. Finally, we would like to thank the Bedford/St. Martin's team for their help and encouragement. In Boston, thanks go to Chuck Christensen, President, and to Joan Feinberg, Editorial Director. And in New York, our thanks to Nancy Perry, Editor-in-Chief; to John Elliott, Developmental Editor; to Greg Johnson, Editorial Assistant; to Erica Appel, Managing Editor; to Colby Stong, Project Editor; and to Cheryl Mamaril and Joe Ford, Senior Production Supervisors.

N. R. C.
D. H.
C. H. K.
R. S.
N. S.

Contents

Social Sciences and Public Affairs   95

Sciences and Technologies 733

Thematic Table of Contents

VALUES AND BELIEFS

CULTURES IN COLLISION AND CONTACT

RACE AND RACISM

THE EXPERIENCE OF WOMEN

INTERPRETING THE BODY

VIOLENCE AND WAR

LIFE AND DEATH

OBSERVING ANIMALS

UNDERSTANDING THE PHYSICAL WORLD

HUMAN PORTRAITS

TEACHING, LEARNING, AND SCHOOLING

HEALTH, DISEASE, AND MEDICINE

INTERPRETING THE PAST

Anne Frank: Her Place in History

MYTHS AND RITUALS

For Students

Fields of Reading: Motives for Writing, sixth edition, is intended to help you develop the abilities in reading and writing that you will need as you move from one course to another, one field of study to another, throughout your college career. In some senses, of course, all areas of study expect the same things of you—namely, close and careful reading as well as clear and exact writing, with an attentiveness above all to information and ideas. But the particular kinds of information, ideas, and concerns that distinguish each field of study also call for somewhat different reading and writing abilities. A book review for a literature course, for example, requires a different form and style from a lab report in physics. So we have tried to give you a sampling of the varied fields of writing you are likely to encounter in the academic world.

Most undergraduate schools are organized around some version of the traditional division of studies into "the humanities," "the social sciences," and "the sciences." The humanities generally include fields of learning that are thought of as having a cultural orientation, such as language, literature, history, philosophy, and religion. The social sciences, which include such fields as anthropology, economics, education, political science, psychology, and sociology, deal with social institutions and the behavior of their individual members. The sciences include fields of knowledge that are concerned with the natural and physical world, such as astronomy, botany, chemistry, physics, and zoology.

These traditional divisions of study are closely affiliated with applied areas of study and work that also exist in the professional world. The humanities, for example, are closely allied with the arts; the social sciences, with public affairs such as business and government; and the sciences, with technology. These divisions and clusterings of fields—Arts and Humanities, Social Sciences and Public Affairs, Sciences and Technologies—are so

broadly applicable that we have used them as one of the organizing principles in our table of contents.

Like any set of categories, these divisions are a convenient, but by no
means foolproof, system of classification. Although the system can help
you to understand the academic world, it does not reflect the exact state of
affairs in every specialized field at every college and university. Specialists
in a particular field sometimes migrate from one area of learning to another, from the social sciences to the sciences, for example, according to
the orientation of their research in a particular project. Or specialists from
several fields may form an interdisciplinary area of research, such as environmental studies, which involves a wide range of academic disciplines—
botany, chemistry, economics, philosophy, political science, and zoology.
So the writing that results from these projects often can be categorized in
more than one broad area of learning.

The writing we have collected in *Fields of Reading* can be understood
not only in terms of the area of learning that it represents, but also in terms
of the particular purpose it is meant to achieve. Every piece of writing, of
course, is the product of an author's personal and professional motives, so
in a sense the purposes for writing are as varied and ultimately mysterious
as are authors themselves. But setting aside the mysteries of human nature,
it is possible to identify and define a set of different purposes for writing,
which we refer to as Reflecting, Reporting, Explaining, and Arguing, one
or another of which predominates in most academic and professional writing. Therefore, we have used this set of purposes as the major organizing
principle in our table of contents.

By Reflecting, we mean a kind of writing in which authors are concerned with recalling and thinking about their past experience, for personal
experience is often an especially valuable source of knowledge and learning. By Reporting, we mean writing that is concerned primarily with conveying factual information about some particular aspect of the world, past
or present. By Explaining, we mean writing that is concerned primarily
with making sense of information or shedding light on a particular subject.
By Arguing, we mean writing that is given to debating controversial explanations, values, or beliefs. Like our other categories, these are convenient,
but not rigid, modes of classification. So they need to be used tactfully,
with an awareness that to some degree they are bound to overlap. Most
pieces of explanation, for example, will at some point involve reporting, if
only to convey the information or subject to be explained. And most pieces
of argument will call for some explanation, if only to make clear the issues
that are at odds with one another. But generally you will find one or another of these purposes to be dominant in any particular piece of writing.

We think that an awareness of these basic purposes can be especially
helpful both in the process of reading and in the process of writing, no
matter what academic or professional field is involved. We have introduced each section of our collection with an essay on Reflecting, Reporting, Explaining, or Arguing. In these essays you will find detailed

definitions and examples of each purpose, as well as explanations and illustrations of how to carry it out in differing fields and situations. Each selection is accompanied by a brief headnote, explanatory footnotes where
necessary, and questions for you to think about in your reading and writing. In addition, each selection is also followed by questions to help you
make connections among related readings in this collection.

Immediately following this preface, you will find an introduction to
reading and writing. In the first section, we show an actual example of
how one writer goes through the process of composing a piece of writing;
in Reading and Rereading, we discuss various ways to read and understand
the pieces in this book or any other material you might encounter in your
studies; and in Using and Acknowledging Sources, we discuss how to evaluate, incorporate, and document source materials and why such acknowledgment is important in every field of study. This introduction, like the
headnotes, questions, and sectional introductions, is meant to help you become a thoughtful and responsible reader and writer. The rest is up to your
instructor, your classmates, and you.

Introduction: Why Write?

No matter what your field of study, you will need to read and write. Often you will need not just to read, but to read critically, not just to write, but to write clearly, sometimes with argumentative force. This book brings together many readings with those goals in mind. Among the readings you will find quite a few that discussion will only make richer. You should also find some that prompt you to write, perhaps even without an assignment. In putting this collection together, we have sought out readings that we have found provocative as readers and as teachers. Although we realize that a textbook is intended for the classroom and study, that hardly means it must be an enemy of pleasure. If you carry it with you on vacation or keep it by your bed, we will be pleased, of course, and not entirely shocked.

We assume that reading and writing are the daily concerns of your course, skills to be developed in interaction with your classmates and instructor rather than taught from a book's introduction. Nevertheless, in this introduction we wish to offer a few observations that readers and writers might well keep in mind. By emphasizing the situation of writers and writing, we will focus on what we take to be the deeper intention of your course. Along the way, however, we will touch frequently on reading, too, since no secure line can be drawn between them.

Writing as Conversation

Scholars and professional writers take part in extended discussions, which we can think of as conversations. For example, suppose a new discovery is made about the prehistory of humankind, how ancient our species is, or when humans first migrated to the Americas. Any such discovery provokes discussion, modification, and dissent, all of which take place, back and forth, in the specialized publications of the field. Or suppose a less academic situation—a book review or a business report. In these examples as well, writing follows from much that has been said and written before, at the very least a book to be reviewed in the one case and a business situation with its own history—part oral, part written, and to some extent observable—in the other. Our motivation for writing often stems from wanting to join in a discussion about such matters and to offer understandings that are our own view of things.

In a short essay that follows, the writer Patricia Hampl reflects on how she once joined in such a discussion. Her essay is about writing a book review. "Literature is a conversation," she says, and her review will play a part in one conversation. Quickly, therefore, Hampl conveys an image of herself as a reader. She has read the book under review. As she reveals in her essay, she has reviewed several other books before this one, and along the way, she has read numerous other reviews. How else would she know what a review is, much less have an idea of how to make hers in some way unusual?

In addition to hints about her reading, Hampl's essay allows us to consider her motivation to write. It is difficult to write well without motivation, and Hampl's motivation is complicated. She is moved by the book under review, a new edition of *The Diary of a Young Girl* by Anne Frank, and she wants to express that emotion. Our best writing usually follows from taking a personal interest in our topic, which Hampl has certainly done. But writing a review for a leading paper like the *New York Times* will also influence her standing in the literary community, which may play a part. Moreover, the *Times* will pay her for her work—no insignificant matter. Most of all, however, Hampl conveys a sense of urgency about the book. If money or standing were primary, she could have sought out other assignments rather than accepting this one.

For most student writers, the motivation for writing is normally a mixture of the same sorts of things: grades, class standing, and convictions about our subjects parallel the motivations Hampl brought to her work. Clearly, the last of these is the most important. When the first two are primary, the writer is simply doing a job. When the latter takes over, the writer becomes more of a presence in the writing and begins to express him- or herself.

So it is that when Hampl found herself caught up in the story of Anne Frank, she began with the following two, matter-of-fact paragraphs. The whole of her review can be found at the end of this introduction (p. 22).

On Tuesday, March 28, 1944, Gerrit Bolkestein, Education Minister of the Dutch Government in exile, delivered a radio message from London urging his war-weary countrymen to collect "vast quantities of simple, everyday material," as part of the historical record of the Nazi occupation.

"History cannot be written on the basis of official decisions and documents alone," he said. "If our descendants are to understand fully what we as a nation have had to endure and overcome during these years, then what we really need are ordinary documents — a diary, letters."

Stories in Our Writing

Straightforward as they may appear, these few sentences imply a story — stories within stories for that matter. Minister Bolkestein was aware that he was living through a significant historical moment. He foresaw composing a record of that moment that would stand as history, a history derived from a collection of "ordinary documents." He imagined future readers who would need to understand what the Dutch people had endured. Their understanding would be shaped by the stories such documents could offer. And as we will see, his words stimulated one writer, Anne Frank, to think of her diary differently.

But his words also played a role in the secondary story of Hampl's writing her review. In "Reviewing Anne Frank," the essay that follows, Hampl's story begins as she accepts the assignment to review the "Definitive Edition" of Anne Frank's *Diary*, a later, more complete edition than the one first published in 1947. Although Hampl's attitude toward reviewing books is positive and she thinks of it as a "pleasure" akin to the pleasure of reading, she found this assignment "daunting" as none other. She struggled to begin, and when she finally managed that, she launched herself by way of Bolkestein's remarks.

One story, then, signaled by the two short paragraphs above, is the opportunity Hampl seized to enter into a "conversation" when she agreed to review Anne Frank's book. Her agreement meant that she would participate in a larger public discussion. Every time you take up an essay assignment, you too are entering into a discussion of some sort. If we are speaking only to ourselves, it is unlikely that readers will sympathize with us much. If instead we discover a way to join in a conversation already begun, we are much more likely to be heard. Thus the importance of another story hinted at here, one having to do with the beginning Hampl found in Bolkestein's message. In those remarks she found a point of entrance that would lift her away from speaking to herself and make it much more likely that she would connect, through her writing, with us.

Let us turn now to Hampl and to her story.

REVIEWING ANNE FRANK

Patricia Hampl

Book reviewing is generally regarded as humble literary work, the bread-and-butter labor of the writing life, far removed from the expressive glories of poetry or fiction. At worst, reviewing is classed as hackwork. Not by me, though. For some reason, I have always harbored an idealistic, even a romantic, affection for reviewing. This romance may be rooted in the fact that my first published work, in my college newspaper when I was nineteen, was a book review—of a new book of poems called *Ariel* by someone named Sylvia Plath.

Although the job demands that a reviewer note the successes and failures in a book, reviewing has never struck me as having much to do with assigning scores or handing out demerits. The reviewer's job—and pleasure—is akin to any reader's. It is the pleasure of talk. Fundamentally, literature is a conversation, strangely intimate, conducted between writer and reader—countless writers, unknown readers. If nobody *talks* about books, if they are not discussed or somehow contended with, literature ceases to be a conversation, ceases to be dynamic. Most of all, it ceases to be intimate. It degenerates into the author's monologue or just a private mutter. Without the reader's response, a book would go silent, like a struck bell that gives no resonance. Reviews are the other half of a conversation that the author of a book begins. Without them, literature would be oddly mute in spite of all those words on all those pages.

But I have never had an assignment as daunting as the one given me to review the new "Definitive Edition" of Anne Frank's *Diary*. For many reasons, the *Diary* is a book like no other. For one thing, virtually every other book I have reviewed has just come off the press. A reviewer is usually a kind of first reader, an explorer describing a new book, like a new country, to the people who have yet to travel there. But who does not know about Anne Frank and her heartbreaking diary? It was first published almost fifty years ago and has been translated into virtually every language in the world that sustains a book culture. Most readers know this book, like very few others, from childhood, and they carry it into adulthood. Even if they haven't read it, people know the story and the essential personality of its extraordinary author. Besides the familiarity of the book, who on earth would claim to "review" Anne Frank? The book seems to defy the very enterprise of book reviewing. I suppose that the emotion ruling me as I approached my task was a paralyzing shyness: who was I to write about this beloved and historic icon of the Holocaust?

In the face of all this, my first act was to procrastinate as long as I could. I did everything to keep from writing the review. I was very good at this. I read the book slowly, I underlined passages that struck me, I took notes, jotting down lines from the *Diary*, some of them passages I remembered with surprising sharpness from girlhood when I had first read the book, some of them new to me. The more I felt the power of the book, the more hopeless I felt. I missed the first deadline and called my editor, begging for an extension. Granted! A reprieve.

Then I procrastinated some more. I developed a sudden urgency about cleaning my oven and sorting out my sock drawer. I called friends, made lunch dates (I never go out to lunch when I'm working). I asked my friends what *they* thought about Anne Frank. I had a ferocious resistance to writing the review. I found yet another way to avoid writing that I could at least call "research": I dug up an essay about Anne Frank by the poet John Berryman, which I remembered having read or having heard about years before. I took notes on *that*.

I was genuinely fascinated, moved even, by the Berryman essay, "The Development of Anne Frank," which I saw from a note in the text had been written in 1967. I had been Berryman's student at the University of Minnesota that very year, taking two courses in "Humanities of the Western World" from him in a packed, overheated room with fifty or sixty other undergraduates. I found myself thinking about this great poet, my old teacher, about the fierce way he had talked about literature, his uncanny ability to bring a roomful of undergraduates to tears just by reading aloud the farewell scene between Hector and Andromache in the *Iliad*. I thought with sorrow of his suicide only a few years after that, how he had jumped to his death from a bridge I walked across every day. I couldn't remember his ever saying anything about Anne Frank, but reading his essay about her all these years later brought him powerfully back to me, the force of his inquiring mind, his determination to understand what was at stake in her book. I still hadn't written a word.

But maybe at last my mind had wandered not away from the task at hand, but right into it. Though I ended up referring briefly to a remark in Berryman's essay when I wrote my own review (a kind of private homage to him), it wasn't so much what his essay said that began to unlock my own timidity. Rather, it was the tone I felt in his essay, a voice that was so poised on *trying to understand* that it had no room for the kind of hand-wringing and worry that I was indulging in myself.

Berryman began by telling how he had first come across Anne Frank's *Diary* — in 1952 when the first installment of the translated text appeared in *Commentary* magazine. "I read it with amazement," he says in his essay. He was so galvanized by the writing that, he says, "The next day, when I went to town to see my analyst, I stopped in the magazine's offices . . . to see if proofs of the *Diary's* continuation were available, and they were." Then, "like millions of people later," he wrote, "I was bowled over with pity and horror and admiration for the astounding doomed little girl."

But he didn't stop with this emotional anchor. He demanded, right from the start, that he think as well as feel. "But what I *thought* was: a

sane person. A sane person, in the twentieth century." I recognized that he
had found the tip of his subject: how had such extraordinary sanity come
to be developed in the crushing circumstances of Anne Frank's life? It
wasn't necessary to know the details of Berryman's own tragic end to feel
his urgency in searching for "a sane person in the twentieth century."

    I liked the naturalness of this beginning, the casualness of his saying he   10
was "bowled over." I liked how, having established his feeling, he refused
to dwell on it but pushed on to a thought. I could feel a mind at work—
and more than that, I felt a story unfolding. He was writing a *story*, I suddenly thought, the story of his relation to this book. The *ideas* were like
characters in the story that he kept looking at from one angle and then another, to make sense of them, to come to a conclusion, much the way a
story must bring its characters to some resolving, if mysterious, finale.

    Strangely enough, it was at this point (if I remember correctly) that I
made my first mark on paper, my first stab at my own response to Anne
Frank. I wrote the first three paragraphs of the review, more or less as they
stand now, quite easily, as if there had been no procrastination, no moan-
ing and groaning at all for several weeks of fretful nonwriting. After reading Berryman's essay, I knew what to do—at least for three paragraphs.

    The connections between his essay and my review are not obvious. No
one, reading his opening about being bowled over and then mine, which is
a straightforward piece of historical information, would imagine that I had
finally been nudged off the dime by Berryman's essay. His tone is personal
and immediate. Mine is distanced (I don't make use of the first-person pronoun anywhere in my entire review) and rests its authority on certain historical facts I am able to present to the reader.

    I got the hint about the Dutch education minister's clandestine radio
message from the foreword to the "Definitive Edition," but I tracked down
the exact quotation of the speech from another source at the library. If I
wasn't going to allow myself the kind of authority and presence that Berryman had with the use of the personal pronoun, I needed to achieve that
sense of immediacy another way. Direct quotation, I knew instinctively,
would enliven this bit of historical information.

    I tried to make Anne Frank's knowledge of the minister's radio mes-
sage part of this story—as indeed it really was. I wanted the reader to see
history happening as it happened for Anne Frank herself. That is why I
began the review in a narrative, storylike way: "On Tuesday, March 28,
1944, Gerrit Bolkestein, Education Minister of the Dutch Government in
exile, delivered a radio message from London . . ." To bolster the authority
of this information in every way possible—and thereby bolster my own
authority as the writer of the piece—I even checked at the library to find
out what day of the week March 28 fell on in the year 1944 so that, casually, I could note that it was a Tuesday. I wanted to seduce the reader with
the authority of simple facts. Words *are* small, but each one can count for
a lot. And maybe I wasn't attempting to "seduce" my readers, but to assure them.

It is odd—even to me—that reading Berryman's very personal 15
(though certainly highly intellectual and closely analytical) essay should
have shown me the way into my own piece about Anne Frank. I had a
number of constraints that hadn't hampered him. For one thing, I had
much less space: my editor had allotted me a certain number of words and
no more. Berryman had written an essay, a much more open form; I was
writing a review.

Still, many reviewers rightly use the first-person voice, and Berryman
certainly had won me over partly because of his very immediate presence in
his own essay. So why did I steer away from that voice? I think I understood, after reading Berryman, the different task I had before me, especially
given my space limitations and my audience in a newspaper. I wasn't coming upon Anne Frank's *Diary* as it came out in proofs for the first time. I
was responding to a definitive edition of a book that has long been a classic of postwar literature. I did not need to present myself as having been
moved by the *Diary:* History had provided several generations of such
readers. But I benefited from the freedom of Berryman's prose, the genuineness of his inquiry. It was a model for me—not a model of style, but
of intention.

Also, while I had been procrastinating by having lunch with my
friends, one of my companions mentioned that there had been (and continues to be) an ugly and quite demented attempt to deny the authenticity of
the *Diary*. Like many anti-Holocaust theories, this one tried to prove that
while there might have been a little girl named Anne Frank who had died
during the war of "natural causes" (or in some versions had not died but
been "lost" or who was herself a fabrication), this child had never written
a diary. *The Diary of a Young Girl*, these conspiracy theorists claimed, had
been written by adults engaged in a "Jewish plot"—by Anne Frank's father (whose presence as the sole survivor of his murdered family this plot
does not account for) or by others.

It was all quite mad, and like all such attempts to deny the truth of history, it was very disturbing and obviously fired by racial hatred. I wanted
to be sure nothing I wrote could even remotely be used for such evil. The
reason these allegations about the *Diary* had won any attention at all
hinged on the fact that there were indeed several versions of Anne Frank's
diaries. I studied the distinctions among the various texts carefully and attempted to present them briefly but clearly by making reference to the
"Critical Edition," which had been published in 1986. I wanted to refute
these very allegations, crazy and repugnant as they were, and to use my review, in part, to alert readers to false claims made in this regard.

Reading Berryman's essay had made me especially aware of the time
that had passed between his first response to the book in 1952, hardly
seven years after Anne Frank's death in Bergen-Belsen, and my reading of
the 1995 "Definitive Edition" when she would have been sixty-six. I felt
my task was to mediate time and history, at least in a modest way. I had to
give readers some of the basic biographical information that for most

readers, I knew would be unnecessary, but I also had to place the book in
its public history.

With this in mind, I made reference at the end of the review to its age—   20
fifty years old—and to Philip Roth's use of Anne Frank as a fictional character in his novel *The Ghost Writer.* I wanted to show how Anne Frank
has entered our lives as a permanent presence, that to invoke her name is
to invoke a person we know and who shall always be missing because her
presence in her book has made her so alive it is "unthinkable and disorienting," as I say in my review, that she should have been snuffed out.

I remember feeling a kind of relief (not satisfaction, but the more unburdened feeling that the word *relief* suggests) when I stumbled on the
word *disorienting.* I felt that this had something to do with the enduring
grief and regret that mention of Anne Frank brings forward within us. I felt
that my sense of being "disoriented" by her death was related to Berryman's relief in finding a "sane person in the twentieth century." We *should*
be disoriented by such hellish hatred: I was writing my review, after all, as
children were dying from similar sectarian hatred in Bosnia. I, too, needed
to find a sane person in the twentieth century.

Finally, I wanted to remind people of the extraordinary person Anne
Frank was, the splendid writer, the utterly natural girl-woman, and the
gifted thinker. All my notes paid off, just as my luncheon with my friend
had: I had many passages that I was able to use to present Anne Frank to
readers not only as the icon of a murdered child, but as a strong and vital
writer. I came away from my reading of the *Diary* convinced absolutely
that had she lived, Anne Frank would have written many books and that
we would know her not only as the author of her diary.

When I was a girl first reading the *Diary,* I had treasured it because of
how Anne fought and contended with her mother, just as I did, how she
battled to become a person—the very thing Berryman honored most in
her, too. I *needed* Anne Frank then, not because she was the child who
died and put a face on the six million murdered (I was not yet capable of
taking in that historical fact), but because, like me, she was determined to
live, to grow up to be herself and no one else. She was, simply, my friend. I
don't think I was able to keep in mind that she was dead. I went to her
Diary as she went to Kitty, for a friendship not to be found anywhere else
but in books. As Anne Frank wrote to Kitty in a letter in her red plaid
notebook, "Paper is more patient than people." It is the secret motto not
only of a passionate teenager, but of any writer.

About two weeks after my review was published, I received a small
white envelope, addressed in a careful hand in blue ink, forwarded to me
from the *New York Times,* which had received it. There was no return address, but the envelope was postmarked New York. A fan letter, I thought
with a brief flutter of vanity.

Inside was a single sheet, my name written again with the careful blue   25
ink, and below that a crazy quilt of black headlines apparently photo-
copied from various articles in newspapers and periodicals. All of them

claimed in their smudged, exclamatory way, to have evidence of the "Anne Frank Zionist Plot" or the "Frank Lies." The headlines were all broken off and crammed into one another; bits and pieces of the articles to which they belonged overlapped. There wasn't a complete sentence on the entire mashed and deranged page.

But there it was: the small insane mind responding spasmodically to the expansive sane person the poet John Berryman had been so relieved to discover, the same sane person so many girls recognize as their truest friend as they move into the uncharted territory of womanhood. I stood there holding that piece of paper (it literally felt *dirty*, perhaps because of the smudged typefaces, which looked like old-fashioned pornography), disoriented all over again.

And then I did the only thing possible: I burned it. Somehow it required burning, not just tossing out. I burned it in the kitchen sink and washed away the ashes. I still don't know what it will take to convince me of the world's capacity to hate life, that this dark instinct does exist. Anne Frank, I reminded myself, knew this hard truth as a child. And she refused to cave in to it even as she acknowledged it. I was glad I had acknowledged this when I quoted her: "I hear the approaching thunder that, one day, will destroy us too, I feel the suffering of millions." The conversation she began with Kitty, her imaginary correspondent to whom she addressed her diary, was founded on a discipline of compassion. Even in acknowledging her own likely death, she felt not only for herself, but felt "the suffering of millions."

This was the sane person who, Berryman says at the end of his essay, "remained able to weep with pity, in Auschwitz, for naked gypsy girls driven past to the crematory." She is the sane person we still seek at the end of the terrible twentieth century.

Entering the Conversation

Hampl's essay contains elements familiar to us all. She procrastinated. Daunted by the task, she found sock drawers to organize and sudden opportunities to lunch with friends. But she also read and reread the *Diary*, underlined useful passages, and thought ahead to her work.

One trustworthy motive for the writing to come was that Hampl cared deeply about this book, a "beloved and historic icon of the Holocaust" as she calls it. Hampl had known the *Diary* from childhood, and she assumed that this experience would be true for large numbers of her readers. Especially for women who grew up after World War II, *The Diary of a Young Girl* has gone beyond being an icon of the Holocaust and has succeeded as a poignant and persuasive account of growing up.

But Hampl's sense of the conversation before her is complicated. She not only knew and felt moved by the *Diary,* she knew and was "fascinated" by an essay on it written by a former teacher. Consequently, she felt as responsible to him as she did to Anne Frank. You can find this essay,

John Berryman's "The Development of Anne Frank," later in this volume (p. 369).

Searching for a way to launch her own work, she not only immersed herself in the *Diary,* but read and reread Berryman's essay. In the end, it was not so much his specific ideas that shaped her response, as it was the example he set of pursuing an idea with conviction, of letting his ideas become, as she observes, "characters" in the story of John Berryman thinking about Anne Frank. The spur, though, that brought her first words to the page came from a hint she found in the foreword to the "Definitive Edition."

This is a crucial moment in Hampl's story of her writing because it underscores her resourcefulness. Bolkestein's plea is not quoted in that foreword; it is only mentioned. Hampl had to track it down and find the exact quotation in the library, but she does not explain how she decided to do so. How did it occur to her that remarks heard over the radio, and unknown to her so far, would make a strong opening for her review? Hampl says she "wanted the reader to see history happening as it happened for Anne Frank herself," but where did this approach, so different from Berryman's, come from? Hampl does not address this question directly, although she does observe that she knew "instinctively" that "direct quotation . . . would enliven this bit of historical information."

We should take note of this moment because thoughts like these allow us to find our own approach as we join a conversation. Whereas Berryman came to his essay through a personal story (and, as Hampl also makes clear, through a very personal concern for the nature of sanity and madness), Hampl begins with historical information couched in direct quotation. Moreover, Hampl went one canny step further. Knowing the day of Bolkestein's address and finding the text of it, she decided to "bolster" her authority by providing the day of the week on which March 28 fell in 1944. This extra, unexpected step, uncovering the telling detail that clinches a part of her story, is a hallmark of a strong writer. It is the hallmark equally of the student who has gotten into her subject. Hampl wished to "seduce" her readers "with the authority of simple facts." Accordingly, she made the effort to locate and verify more than we may have thought was needed. Certainly, the day of the week is a detail we do not expect, which may be exactly why it attracts us.

In this example we can see how writing tends to be embedded in larger stories, and that most often, when we trace those stories, we find that they have everything to do with our motivation to write. Here then is one more story, a particularly telling one, that further shapes Hampl's review:

> In her diary the next day, Anne Frank mentions this broadcast, which she and her family heard on a clandestine radio in their Amsterdam hiding place. "Ten years after the war," she writes on March 29, "people would find it very amusing to read how we lived, what we ate and what we talked about as Jews in hiding."

Amusing, as Hampl is quick to observe, is hardly the word we would choose now, but looking past the tragedy of Frank's situation, we can see how she, too, was moved to contribute to a larger conversation and to think of herself less as a young woman with a diary than as a writer. Consequently, as Hampl observes in her review, Frank "immediately set about organizing the diary entries, giving the residents of the 'Secret Annex' pseudonyms like characters in a novel, rearranging passages for better narrative effect."

As you may already know, Anne Frank began her diary when she was given a small plaid notebook for her thirteenth birthday. Not long after, she took it with her into hiding. Very quickly, Frank invented a necessary friend, Kitty, who became her imagined reader. She began as almost all writers begin, in a private world, taking notes, keeping a journal meant only for an intimate audience, writing "letters" to "dear Kitty." Although one can hardly imagine a more intimate audience than a secret, imaginary playmate, no doubt over the two years of her writing, Frank grew in confidence and prepared herself more or less unconsciously for a larger audience. Thus we may conjecture that Bolkestein's plea came at an appropriate time for her, precisely when she was ready, even eager, to enlarge the world of her conversation. A more practiced writer by then, Frank began to think more expansively. "I'd like to publish a book," she remarks. (You can trace more of this story in the excerpt "At Home, at School, in Hiding" from *The Diary of a Young Girl* beginning on p. 193.)

Two other strands of this conversation deserve notice. First, Berryman wrote in response to Saint Augustine, Sigmund Freud, and Bruno Bettelheim. However much confidence Berryman expresses that his own thoughts matter and that he enjoys the freedom to record them, he was as aware as Hampl of how his own thinking had been stimulated and shaped by others. His indebtedness is not specific enough to require elaborate footnotes. Nevertheless, you can trace his thinking to these prior sources, and in one amusing footnote (p. 371), you can catch Berryman's reading of Bettelheim.

The final piece in this conversation is the letter Hampl received after her review was published. The sender, a fervent denier of Anne Frank, was also moved to write, or, let us say, to assemble a worded message. We will not agree that he or she entered into a conversation; still it is impossible to deny that for a moment one more opinion is heard. The voices that take part in a written conversation are often more varied than we might imagine; some are ugly.

Reviewing the Writing Process

Hampl's essay tells us a good deal about her writing process, one that is ongoing, acquiring clarity and focus in stages. Keeping in mind the significant steps of Hampl's process will help you prepare your own writing assignments. Note especially how revision happens by increments, and at all stages.

Getting Started and Overcoming Procrastination. Hampl approached her review in "a paralyzing shyness" and with an urge to procrastinate through a long period of reading and taking notes. Some of those notes would prove useful; some would not. At this early stage, Hampl did not discriminate among them. Her reading and note taking led instead to more procrastination by way of luncheon dates and conversation with friends, which in turn led finally to something that Hampl was willing to call research.

Exploring a Topic and Gathering Information. Another writer, John Berryman, a poet and scholar, and Hampl's former teacher, had also written about Anne Frank, so Hampl turned to his essay. She found herself fascinated by Berryman's work on their common subject. Suddenly Hampl had writing to react to, inspiring her to review her notes and distinguish the more valuable from the less. This was the first important step of her revising process: a general eagerness to write about the *Diary* was replaced by a more focused topic.

Finding a Beginning. As Hampl observes, her mind "had wandered not away from the task at hand, but right into it." She was drawn into "a story unfolding," that of Berryman's relation to the *Diary*. As Hampl recognized that "he had found the tip of his subject," she discovered that his example had "nudged" her "off the dime," and soon she had her own opening paragraphs.

Doing Additional Research. Having taken the hint from the foreword to the "Definitive Edition," Hampl went to the library to track down the exact quotation she wanted. No longer following Berryman, she followed her own lead. Now she understood better that she did not share Berryman's perspective. Instead, she developed two different motivations for writing her review.

First, she stressed a "kinship" she felt with Anne Frank's experience of becoming a young woman. This Anne Frank, whom Hampl had taken from the first to be a friend, was also a fine writer, one who would have published more books had she lived. This conviction reinforced Hampl's desire to write. But she needed to offer reason for it, even if her conviction lies beyond absolute proof. She did so by describing Frank's power as a writer, her writerly authority on a subject she and Hampl share—becoming a woman and a person. This culminated in Hampl's recognizing "the motto of a writer" in one of Frank's remarks, "Paper is more patient than people."

These are good reasons for Hampl to find "kinship" with her subject. Thus they reinforce her second motivation, that she give no aid to deniers of the Holocaust, people whom Hampl is ready to call evil. Her commitment to that task inspired further library research. Hampl couldn't just deny the accusations swirling about; she needed to assemble evidence against them, so she "studied the distinctions among the various texts carefully and attempted to present them briefly but clearly."

Producing a First Draft. You may have noticed that Hampl does not talk about her first or second draft as such. Although *draft* is a word that Hampl does not use, she describes thinking about her topic and writing. She discovered ideas about what she needed to know and went to the library or elsewhere to find out. All the while she took notes, which later became explanations in her draft. Hampl does not say how many hours or days this took. But we get the sense from reading her essay that by writing, she explained her discoveries and her thinking to herself. When she had covered all that she felt compelled to say, she had a first draft.

Revising. Most writers today use word processors. Revision has never been easier; we can run through our writing again and again, making changes along the way without retyping the whole piece. However, with the use of word processors, writers leave less of a trail of their revisions than they once did, since the process is more continuous. In Hampl's essay, though, we can find several clues to her revision process.

First she tells us that after reading and thinking about Berryman she suddenly started to write and had her first three paragraphs all at once. Perhaps she touched them up a little but, nevertheless, those first paragraphs came quickly, and she was on her way. But what was the lag between that first start and the next? Where did the next impulse to proceed come from? Hampl's comment on Frank's word *amusing* is what follows in the review. Had a few minutes passed, a few hours, or a day before she wrote that next paragraph? As writers, we rarely set pen to paper, or our fingers to the keyboard, and just keep going. We write a bit, move back to the beginning, read through it all, and continue. Something in what we have written spurs the next thought. Whether or not we began with a list of topics, or an outline, or just with ideas in our head, as we write, our writing makes its own suggestions. All good writers learn to be alert to those suggestions.

Later Hampl says, "I remember feeling a kind of relief (not satisfaction, but the more unburdened feeling that the word *relief* suggests) when I stumbled on the word *disorienting*." Did Hampl find the word she wanted in the first act of writing that sentence, or did it occur afterward, on one of her later passes through her work? We cannot know for certain. But her own yoking of *stumbling* with *relief* is a fine shorthand for what we look for in revision: a sense of where a problem lies and a glimpse, however stumbling it may seem, of how we may deal with that. Stumbling in this case is a kind of lucky lurching ahead. It is a discovery, and a happy one, as Hampl's word *relief* suggests. Such discoveries are the rewards of revision. They come from paying close attention to our first drafts, from reading and rereading them.

Finally, returning to the first sentence of Hampl's review ("On Tuesday, March 28, 1944, Gerrit Bolkestein, Education Minister of the Dutch

Government in exile, delivered a radio message . . ."), note that the detail she secured last she placed first. First the day of the week, then the date, then Bolkestein's name and title. Hampl tells us that she first found reference to the quotation, then looked up the exact quotation, then thought to make its date as exact as possible. In her writing, however, she inverted that order because she found the order as phrased above the most satisfying. That decision is another sign of Hampl's revising as she works. Revision is much more than catching errors of grammar and spelling; it is primarily our efforts, first to discover how to say things better, then equally to identify what else we need to find out.

Drawing Conclusions. The conclusions reached by Frank, by Berryman, and then by Hampl are never "the conclusion," wrapped up once and for all. A vital subject can always be extended; further refinements and angles can always be found. In other words, in principle, serious work always remains "under revision."

Some revisions prove indefensible, as Hampl records by reference to the letter she received. Holocaust deniers apparently wish to argue that if Anne Frank was indeed a real person, she died of "natural causes." Their vicious approach thrives on a mean-spirited insistence on narrow literalism, and accounts of Anne Frank's death hand them a crumb to work with.

For example, an Academy Award–winning feature documentary, *Anne Frank Remembered* (1996), includes interviews with Dutch survivors of the Holocaust, several of whom knew Anne Frank. One survivor, Hanneli Goslar, speaks of meeting her at Bergen-Belsen and talking with her through a barbed wire fence. Another, Janny Brandes-Brilleslijper, the woman who first informed Otto Frank of his daughters' deaths only months after the end of the war, repeats that information for the camera, telling how the sisters died in misery of malnutrition and typhus, exposed to the cold in their bunks by the barracks door. Only the perverse would call their deaths "natural" — Anne and her sister Margot suffering the merciless conditions of Bergen-Belsen until they roll wasted from their bunks in their sleep — but Holocaust deniers do. They seize on illness as our normal understanding of "natural causes," ignore all other details about Bergen-Belsen, and insist that Anne Frank was simply sick.

Some arguments are best not joined, some conversations better refused than taken up. That is the choice Hampl makes, wisely it seems. Instead, she rids herself of the letter she received, for there is other, healthier work to do.

Reading and Rereading

If you have taken an interest in Patricia Hampl's story and in her example, you may have already done several things common to most writers. Having read her essay and this introduction's comments on it, you may have read Hampl's review or the excerpt from Frank's diary, or the essays by Berryman and Bettelheim. You may have gone to the library to look up related work or may have logged on to the Internet to see what you could find. No doubt you haven't taken in everything all at once. More than likely, you have gone back over some of this material and reread it.

As writers, we read and reread as we prepare to write. Anything in which we take a serious interest deserves rereading. Hampl's essay, for example, describes how she read slowly, underlined passages, jotted down lines, and took notes.

It is often useful to read things twice: skimming, or reading for an overview, then settling down to a thorough second reading. Sometimes our readings blend together, and they aren't always limited to two. We read and reread and go back to at least parts of a piece again if it is important, looking for details that we may not have caught earlier. Quite naturally, our understanding of a work becomes more subtle as we become familiar with its overall contours. Sometimes that first reading isn't really skimming, but it begins to feel like skimming as, on rereading, we notice more and more.

First Readings

To get an overall picture of a piece, begin by reading it through from beginning to end, primarily to get a sense of the author's subject, purpose, and main ideas. This initial reading will help you get acquainted with the piece as a whole. Don't get bogged down in details, but don't hesitate to note or underline important (or puzzling) words, phrases, sentences, ideas, or points that seem important and to which you may wish to return. Once you have completed your initial reading, jot down a few sentences about its main subject, purpose, points, and pertinent information.

Annotating

After you've got the gist of the piece, reread and annotate it more thoroughly. Annotations consist of explanatory notes. For example, if the piece contains words, names, titles of works, or other bits of information that you are unfamiliar with, consult dictionaries, encyclopedias, and other reference works, and make notes that you can refer to in the future.

Summarizing

If you are serious about a piece and want to test your understanding of it, one way is to write a summary. By definition, a summary will leave out much. Writing a summary requires you to discriminate the more important information from the less important information. Hampl doesn't summarize either the *Diary* or Berryman's essay completely, but she does offer partial summaries of both. These isolate what she finds of significance. The best way to see what a summary reveals is for several people to write summaries of the same text and to compare them.

Here, for example, is a summary of Hampl's essay.

> Hampl's intention is to reflect on and explain the process of writing a review of the "Definitive Edition" of Anne Frank's *Diary* for the *New York Times*. First, Hampl describes feeling paralyzed and resistant to starting her assignment. She also relates how after procrastinating, she discovered another writer's work on the subject, which helped her find inspiration for her own work. Finally, Hampl discusses her motivation to write the review, which was rooted in her desire to remind her audience of the extraordinary person Anne Frank was, and of what talent she had as a writer.

Outlining

Not all readers outline their reading, but it can be helpful. Like a summary, an outline asks you to decide what is important in something you've read. Unlike a summary, an outline also asks you to show how one important item relates to another. Often, we want to know both why and how a conclusion was reached. That conclusion will depend on evidence, and the relation of the claim to the supporting evidence can be shown in an outline.

An outline always identifies superior and subordinate items. Depending on how formal you wish to make it, those items can be labeled with letters and numerals:

I. _____

    A. _____

        1. _____

            a. _____

    B. _____

        1. _____

        2. _____

            a. _____

            b. _____

II. _____

One principle governs making any outline: superior items require subordinate items. The subordinate items are what we call support. You cannot make a claim without offering a reason. The more support you give your claims, the more willing readers will be to accept them. It's like building a firm foundation for a building. Arguments without this firm support will crumble.

In a very real sense, the lowercase letters and Arabic numerals are more important than the capital letters and Roman numerals. The smaller items hold the larger ones up. So if you want to think critically about an argument you have read, or if you want to avoid problems in arguments of your own, try making an outline. Be sure that the subordinate items go where they belong and that they provide secure support for your argument.

Toward the end of her essay, Hampl restates a claim that had been a strong motivation for her having written the review in the first place: "I wanted to remind people of the *extraordinary person* Anne Frank was, the *splendid writer*, the *utterly natural girl-woman*, and the *gifted thinker*." For Hampl, those last three terms add up to the first; they are what constitute an "extraordinary person," at least in this instance. Hence this outline:

A. Extraordinary person
   1. Splendid writer
   2. Utterly natural girl-woman
   3. Gifted thinker

Now it is Hampl's responsibility to come through with evidence in support of *1, 2,* and *3.* You could outline that evidence as *a, b, c,* and so on and arrange it beneath the numerals.

Using and Acknowledging Sources

In most of the writing you will do, both during and after college, you will find yourself drawing on the ideas, information, and statements of others, interpreting this material, and combining it with your own experience, observation, and thought to generate new ideas of your own. Some of this material will come from your reading, some from lectures and class discussions, some from conversations and interviews. Our thinking does not take place in a vacuum, but is shaped by a wide array of influences and sources. In this introduction, we have seen Hampl refer to Berryman and to the Dutch minister of education, and we have mentioned that Berryman footnotes Bettelheim. Anne Frank's *Diary,* of course, has been openly acknowledged throughout and quoted several times. We have also cited a documentary film, specific information for which we found on the Internet. These are several instances of writers acknowledging their sources, specifically but informally.

To acknowledge your intellectual debts is by no means a confession that your work is unoriginal or without merit. In fact, original work in every field invariably builds on the prior work of researchers and thinkers. Most pieces you find in this book, except for those that deal entirely with personal experience, include some kind of acknowledgment or reference to the ideas, information, or statements of others. By acknowledging their sources, the writers of these pieces implicitly establish what is new or special in their own way of thinking. Academic writing—the kind of writing you do in college and the kind of writing that most of your teachers do when they make contributions to their professional fields—depends on learning, on sources. Most of these sources are to be found in the books and periodicals, but many are to be found in other places—especially on the Internet, to which the World Wide Web provides the easiest access.

What the Web Offers

The World Wide Web (or "the Web," as it is commonly known) is an excellent resource for writers—if it is used properly. The Web is a vast network of information, much of which is not available in print or even on microfilm, and you can reach this material without moving from your chair. You can find online magazines and scholarly journals, groups discussing topics you are investigating, reports from organizations and institutions: words, pictures, music—it's all out there.

Even when the "same" text is available in a book, newspaper, or magazine, the Web version may offer advantages. The printed materials are easier to hold, carry, and read. The Web materials are easier to find and search. If you don't take careful notes when you are reading a book, you may have great difficulty finding an important passage when you are writing about that book. With a digital text, however, whether on the Web or a disk, you can easily locate almost any passage you remember by using a search engine, a program that scans the Web looking for specific subject areas or specific words and phrases. Many search engines will bring back not just the word you are seeking but the whole context in which that word appears.

For example, there is a Web site, which your search engine can find, that includes the text of all of Jane Austen's novels in digital form. If you go to that site and ask the search engine to find a particular word, such as "envy," it will bring up every use of that word in all the novels, with the passage in which it occurs. If you are writing about Jane Austen, such a resource can be very helpful.

But if more "information" is available to you on the Web than in print, most of it has passed through less screening from editors and publishers than most books or magazine articles have. This means you have to be especially selective in what you use from the Web and especially cautious in how you use it.

Evaluating Web Sources.   Many inexperienced users of the Web—including many students—do not use its resources effectively. They locate the name of an "expert" and then send the person an email, asking for ideas they can use in writing papers, or just asking the person to put his or her knowledge into a few words that can be quoted in a paper to prove to a teacher that "research" has been done. But this is *not* research. Real experts seldom reply to such requests—they get too many—and false experts will lead a student astray. We know of a person who once had something he said about the 1962 Cuban missile crisis quoted on the Web. He has been getting emails ever since—asking him for his "expert" opinion—from students writing papers on that topic. But everything he knew was in the material already quoted on the Web.

The Web is full of material that can be used in research. But none of that material will do your thinking for you. The value of a paper depends upon the critical intelligence you bring to bear on the material you collect. Here are some things to look for in evaluating potential sources from the Web:

1. Is the creator or sponsor of the site identified? Does this information—or its absence—tell you anything about the purpose of the site? Does it reveal any possible biases you should be aware of?

2. Can you use links or a search engine to find out more about the creator/sponsor? Does this person or group seem knowledgeable? Trustworthy?

3. Is there an indication of when the site was created or last updated? Does the information seem current?

Using Web Information.   Of course, you can take notes about material on the Web just as you can about print sources, but most Web sites also allow you to select and copy material that you can then paste directly into your own writing. In some cases, using the "Save As" command, you can save a whole page to your drive. In using material from the Web, here are a few rules you should follow:

1. If you use any material from a Web page in writing an academic paper, you must include a source citation, whether in a list of works cited, an endnote or footnote, or another location required by the documentation system you are using (see the next section, "Acknowledging Sources"). Web information is just like other information. You must give credit where credit is due.

2. Keep a record of the URL (Uniform Resource Locator) of the page from which you have taken the material, the date you accessed it, and any other information (such as the name of the site, its sponsor, or the author of the text) that might help someone locate the site again. Check the guidelines of your documentation system for what information is required.

3. If you paste text into your own writing, you must indicate clearly that it is not your own material, either by putting it in quotation marks or by indenting it as you indent other long quotations. And, in either case, you need to cite your source. The Web makes it easier to cut and paste, so you need to take more care in indicating where your material has come from.

4. Whatever information you take from the Web, whether you just refer to it or actually copy it and paste it into your text, you must not simply put it there but you must use it in some way in your own argument. The bigger the item you paste, the more you must do with it by way of discussion and analysis. Don't fill your paper up with pasted material. Don't quote more than you need. And, re-member, quoted material is most useful when you add something to or disagree with something in the quote. You are not looking for "answers" when you search the Web, but for material you can use in developing your *own* answers.

Acknowledging Sources

To get some idea of the various ways in which sources can be acknowl-edged, note the ways different writers in this book handle this task. The different methods are not just a question of differences among writers; dif-ferent publications and disciplines have their own styles and standards. Within our collection, you will notice that some writers cite only the names of authors or interviewees or the titles of works from which they have gathered ideas or quoted statements. These citations are incorporated into the written discussion, as Hampl incorporates Berryman. You can see this technique used in Martin Luther King's "Pilgrimage to Nonviolence" (p. 111). Other writers use footnotes or endnotes in which they provide not only the names of authors or interviewees and the titles of works, but also dates of publication or of interviews and specific page references, as you can see by looking at Theodore R. Sizer's "What High School Is" (p. 348), Carol Gilligan's "Interviewing Adolescent Girls" (p. 425), or Barbara Tuchman's "This Is the End of the World: The Black Death" (p. 236). Fi-nally, instead of using footnotes, some writers provide author and page ref-erences in the text of their discussion and include more detailed publication data, such as titles and dates of publication, in a complete list of works cited at the end, as Monica M. Moore does in her "Nonverbal Courtship in Women" (p. 465).

These various forms of acknowledgment are usually determined by the different purposes and audiences for which the pieces were written. Per-sonal essays, newspaper reports, and magazine articles, which are written for a general audience, tend to rely on a more casual and shorthand form of acknowledgment, citing only the author or title of the source and plac-ing that acknowledgment in the midst of the discussion. Work written for a more specialized audience, such as academic research papers and scholarly articles or books, tends to rely on more detailed and systematic forms of acknowledgment, using either footnotes or a combination of references in the text with a complete list of works cited at the end. These specialized forms vary somewhat from one field to another, but papers in the arts and humanities tend to follow the guidelines set down by the Modern Language Association (MLA), and papers in the social sciences use the system of the American Psychological Association (APA). In the sciences and technologies, each discipline tends to have its own system. For further reference, consult the *MLA Handbook for Writers of Research Papers,* 5th ed. (New York: The Modern Language Association of America, 1999), or the *Publication Manual of the American Psychological Association,* 4th ed. (Washington, D.C: American Psychological Association, 1994). The APA's latest guidelines for citing Web sources can be found at the association's Web site, <http://www.apa.org/journals/webref.html> (note that this address may change).

As you can see, making proper acknowledgment is both a matter of intellectual honesty and a social issue of many dimensions. Different groups agree on and enforce their own standards. That goes for your writing course as well. For the moment, your college or university or perhaps your writing class is the ultimate authority for you. Therefore, don't hesitate to look to your instructor for guidance. Most instructors have their specific preferences, but all will expect you to acknowledge your sources.

THE WHOLE ANNE FRANK

Patricia Hampl

On Tuesday, March 28, 1944, Gerrit Bolkestein, Education Minister of the Dutch Government in exile, delivered a radio message from London urging his war-weary countrymen to collect "vast quantities of simple, everyday material" as part of the historical record of the Nazi occupation.

"History cannot be written on the basis of official decisions and documents alone," he said. "If our descendants are to understand fully what we as a nation have had to endure and overcome during these years, then what we really need are ordinary documents—a diary, letters."

In her diary the next day, Anne Frank mentions this broadcast, which she and her family heard on a clandestine radio in their Amsterdam hiding place. "Ten years after the war," she writes on March 29, "people would find it very amusing to read how we lived, what we ate and what we talked about as Jews in hiding."

The word "amusing" reads strangely now, chillingly. But her extraordinary commitment to the immediacy of individual experience in the face of crushing circumstance is precisely what has made Anne Frank's *Diary*—since the first edition of the book appeared in the Netherlands in 1947—the single most compelling personal account of the Holocaust (an account now augmented by this "Definitive Edition," published on the 50th anniversary of her death in Bergen-Belsen and containing entries not present in the earlier standard version).

Bolkestein's broadcast galvanized Anne Frank, or perhaps ignited an idea she already had: her diary, at first a private confidante, now struck her as a source for a book. "I'd like to publish a book called 'The Secret Annex,' " she writes on May 11, 1944. "It remains to be seen whether I'll succeed, but my diary can serve as the basis." She immediately set about organizing the diary entries, giving the residents of the "Secret Annex" pseudonyms like characters in a novel, rearranging passages for better narrative effect.

She was still engaged in this work when the hiding place was raided by the Gestapo on Aug. 4, 1944. Miep Gies, one of the office employees in the Frank spice and pectin firm who had been protecting the Jews hidden above the office, gathered all the diary notebooks and papers left in disarray by the Gestapo. She hid them in her desk for the rest of the war. After Anne's father, Otto Frank, returned to Amsterdam late in 1945, Miep Gies returned all the papers to him. He was the sole survivor of the eight people who had sheltered together for over two years in the annex.

Anne Frank had been keeping her diary since June 12, 1942, the day her parents gave her a red-and-white plaid notebook for her 13th birthday. Less than a month later the diary went with her into hiding.

From the first, she addressed the notebook as a trusted girlfriend: "I'll begin from the moment I got you, the moment I saw you lying on the table among my other birthday presents." A few days later this anonymous "you" becomes the imaginary "Kitty," and the entries turn into letters, giving the diary the intimacy and vivacity of a developing friendship. The growing relationship, of course, is with her own emerging self. As John Berryman said, the *Diary* has at its core a subject "even more mysterious and fundamental than St. Augustine's" in his classic "Confessions": namely, "the conversion of a child into a person."

Otto Frank, in preparing the first edition of the diary, was compelled, partly by his own sense of discretion and partly by the space limitations imposed on him by the original Dutch publisher, to limit the book. The restored entries, constituting, according to the publisher, 30 percent more material, do not alter our basic sense of Anne Frank, but they do give greater texture and nuance—and punch—to some of the hallmark concerns of the diary.

There are more searching passages about her erotic feelings and her urgent curiosity about sexuality, more emphatic distancing from her dignified but apparently critical mother. None of these new entries, however, surpass the urgency shown in the standard version about the need to accomplish real work as a woman: "I can't imagine having to live like Mother, Mrs. van Daan and all the women who go about their work and are then forgotten," she writes on April 5, 1944. "I need to have something besides a husband and children to devote myself to! . . . I want to be useful or bring enjoyment to all people, even those I've never met. I want to go on living even after my death!"

The new material also includes sketches of short stories she was writing in the Secret Annex. The additions are not always whole entries or complete new letters to Kitty. Sometimes passages of only a few lines are set in a text already familiar. But the effect underscores the acuity of Anne Frank's eye, the keen relish of her descriptive powers. In one of her habitual reviews of the "inmates" of the annex, she regards the fussy dentist Dussel with the coolness of a practiced novelist: "One of my Sunday morning ordeals is having to lie in bed and look at Dussel's back when he's praying. . . . A praying Dussel is a terrible sight to behold."

Even her transports over her first kiss, with Peter van Daan, the son of the family sharing the Franks' hiding space, are subject to her mordant observation: "Oh, it was so wonderful. I could hardly talk, my pleasure was too intense; he caressed my cheek and arm, a bit clumsily." Only a born writer would snap that clear-eyed "a bit clumsily" into place, along with the body's first rhapsodic shiver of delight.

In 1986, a "Critical Edition" of the *Diary* was published that meticulously presented Anne's original diary (designated by its editors diary a), the version she was working on for her proposed book "The Secret Annex" (diary b), and the edition her father eventually published and which all the world has come to know (diary c). This monumental task included as well exhaustive scientific examination of the original documents to prove what should never have been questioned in the first place: that this is indeed the work of a girl named Anne Frank who lived and eventually died as she prophetically sensed she would: "I hear the approaching thunder that, one day, will destroy us too, I feel the suffering of millions."

The earlier "Critical Edition" is the book for research, but this "Definitive Edition," smoothly translated anew by Susan Massotty, is the reader's edition, unencumbered by notes, with only the barest afterword to conclude the story that Anne Frank was unable to finish herself.

The *Diary*, now 50 years old, remains astonishing and excruciating. It   15
is a work almost sick with terror and tension, even as it performs its miracle of lucidity. On Feb. 12, 1944, Anne Frank writes Kitty, "I feel as if I were about to explode. . . . I walk from one room to another, breathe through the crack in the window frame. . . . I think spring is inside me." The crack in the window frame was her purchase on the world: she put her nose to it and drew in life.

It is uncanny how, reading the *Diary*, one falls into escape fantasies for Anne Frank and the inhabitants of the Secret Annex. No wonder that in his 1979 novel "The Ghost Writer," Philip Roth sustains an entire section devoted to a detailed fabrication about how, after all, Anne Frank survived, how she came to America, how she lives among us still in disguise. It is unthinkable and disorienting to know that this life was crushed.

All that remains is this diary, evidence of her ferocious appetite for life. It gnaws at us still.

REFLECTING

Here in "Reflecting," as in other parts of this collection, you will encounter writing that touches on a wide range of topics — from a high school graduation in Arkansas to a sacred landmark in Oklahoma, from the structure of a grain of salt to the behavior of otters and beavers. But you will also find that the writing in this particular section relies very heavily on personal experience. This personal element may strike you at first as being out of place in a college textbook. However, if you consider the matter just a bit, you will see that personal experience is a basic source of knowledge and understanding. Think for a moment about someone you have known for a long time or about a long-remembered event in your life; then think about what you have learned from being with that person or going through that event, and you will see that personal experience is, indeed, a valuable source of knowledge. You will probably also notice that in thinking about that person or event you rely very heavily on your remembrance of things past — on your memory of particular words or deeds or gestures or scenes that are especially important to you. Your memory, after all, is the storehouse of your personal knowledge, and whenever you look into this storehouse, you will invariably find an image or impression of your past experience. So, you should not be surprised to find the authors in this section looking into their own memories as they might look into a mirror. Ultimately, the activity of looking back is a hallmark of reflection because it involves writers in recalling and thinking about some aspect of their world in order to make sense of it for themselves and for others.

This essential quality of reflective writing can be seen in the following passage from George Orwell's "Shooting an Elephant":

> One day something happened which in a roundabout way was enlightening. It was a tiny incident in itself, but it gave me a better glimpse than I had had before of the real nature of imperialism —

the real motives for which despotic governments act. Early one morning the sub-inspector at a police station the other end of the town rang me up on the phone and said that an elephant was ravaging the bazaar. Would I please come and do something about it? I did not know what I could do, but I wanted to see what was happening and I got on to a pony and started out.

This passage, which comes from the third paragraph of Orwell's essay, clearly presents him as being in a reflective frame of mind. In the opening sentence, for example, he looks back to a specific event from his personal experiences in Burma — to "one day" when "something happened." And in the midst of looking back, he also makes clear that this event is important to him because "in a roundabout way" it "was enlightening." Again, in the second sentence, he looks back not only to the event, "a tiny incident in itself," but also to the understanding that he gained from the event — "a better glimpse than I had had before of the real nature of imperialism — the real motives for which despotic governments act." Having announced the general significance of this event, he then returns to looking back at the event itself, to recalling the particular things that happened that day: the phone call informing him "that an elephant was ravaging the bazaar," the request that he "come and do something about it," and his decision to get "on to a pony" in order "to see what was happening."

This alternation between recalling things and commenting on their significance is typical not only of Orwell's piece, but of all the writing in this section. Sometimes, the alternation takes place within a single sentence, as in the opening of the previous passage. Sometimes, the alternation occurs between sentences or clusters of sentences, as in the following paragraphs from Trudy Dittmar's "Pronghorn":

Once in a saloon, its decor an array of taxidermy common in Wyoming bars, I stood looking up at the head of a big pronghorn. "Funny looking stunkers, ain't they?" an old cowboy said. "All painted up like that and them big eyes bulging out, I always thought they looked like a clown."

I thought the white bars on the throat were beautiful. Ditto, the rectangular white side patches, the white rump, and the big luminous eyes. It was bewildering to hear pronghorns called clowns. The first day I ever entered Wyoming, the first animal I saw was a pronghorn, on a rise by the road in the afternoon sunlight looking down on the cars going by. Their hairs are hollow, against brutal plains winters. The fastest creature in the Western Hemisphere, they run like the wind.

The first settlers must have been dazzled by the spectacle of the pronghorn, but now they get called clowns and goats, a fact which bears witness that an everyday spectacle is a contradiction in terms, and that no matter how rare a thing is in the world at large, and how marvelled at there, its beauty fades in everyday eyes.

The first paragraph of this passsage portrays Dittmar in a contemplative mood, remembering the head of a big pronghorn displayed in a Wyoming saloon, and remembering as well an old cowboy's scornful remarks about the markings and physiognomy of pronghorns. But in the next three sentences, she shifts from recalling that scene to conveying her own thoughts and feelings about the distinctive characteristics of pronghorns. And then, as if aroused by her admiration of the creature's distinctive markings, she suddenly remembers the first pronghorn she beheld when she entered Wyoming for the first time, and as if to justify her admiration she reports some factual information about the singular hair and remarkable speed of the pronghorn. Dittmar's recollection of first beholding the pronghorn causes her, three sentences later, to speculate about how the first settlers must have reacted to their first sighting of pronghorn. Yet no sooner is she speculating about their probable admiration of the animal then she again remembers the scornful remarks of the old cowboy, which provokes her into thinking about the way that "beauty fades in everyday eyes."

Though Dittmar ranges back and forth in time, each image or idea that comes to her mind is occasioned either by a preceding memory or reflection or by some aspect of her immediate situation. Her thoughts develop by a process of association and suggestion, one thing leading to another. This linked sequence of memories, images, other bits of information, and ideas is typical of reflective writing.

The alternation between recalling and interpreting will vary from writer to writer, and from work to work, depending on the details of the experience and the author's reflective purpose. Nevertheless, every piece of reflective writing contains both kinds of material, for every reflective writer is concerned not only with sharing something memorable, but also with showing why it is memorable. And as it happens, most memorable experiences, images, or bits of information stick in our minds because they give us, as Orwell says, "a better glimpse than [we] had had before of the real nature of " someone, something, or some aspect of the world. So, as a reader of reflective writing, you should always be attentive not only to the details of an author's recollected experience, but also to the "glimpse" that it gives the author, and you, into the "real nature" of things. And in your own reflective writing, you should make sure that you convey both dimensions of your experience — both what happened and what the events enabled you to see.

The Range of Reflective Writing

The range of reflective writing is in one sense limitless, for it necessarily includes the full range of things that make up our personal experience or the personal experience of anyone else in the world. Reflecting, in other words, may deal with anything that anyone has ever seen, heard, done, or thought about and considered memorable enough to write about. Though the range of reflective writing is extraordinarily broad, the subject of any particular piece is likely to be very specific, and as it happens, most pieces can be classified in terms of a few recurrent types of subject matter.

A single, memorable event is often the center of attention in reflective writing, as in Maya Angelou's "Graduation" or George Orwell's "Shooting an Elephant." In reflecting on this kind of subject, the author will usually provide not only a meticulous detailing of the event itself, but also some background information that serves as a context for making sense of the event. In "Graduation," for example, Angelou tells about all the pregraduation excitement in her home, at school, and around town before turning to the graduation ceremony itself. And in "Shooting an Elephant," Orwell gives an overall description of his life as a colonial officer in Burma before he turns to the story about shooting the elephant. The event, in turn, is of interest not only in itself, but also for what it reveals to the author (and the reader) about some significant aspect of experience. Thus for Angelou, graduation remains memorable because it helped her to see how African American people have been "sustained" by "Black known and unknown poets," and for Orwell, the shooting remains memorable because it helped him to see "the real nature of imperialism."

A notable person is a subject that often moves people to writing reflectively, as in N. Scott Momaday's "The Way to Rainy Mountain." In reflecting on a particular individual, writers may seek to discover and convey what they consider to be the most essential aspects of that person's character. They may survey a number of memorable incidents or images from the person's life. Momaday, for example, recalls not only the stories and legends that he heard from his grandmother, but also "the several postures that were peculiar to her" and her "long, rambling prayers."

Instead of concentrating on a particular person or event, reflective writing may center on a specific problem or significant issue in the past experience of an author, as in Frederick Douglass's "Learning to Read and Write" or Martin Luther King Jr.'s "Pilgrimage to Nonviolence." A piece with this kind of subject is likely to touch on a number of people and events, and to encompass a substantial period of time, in the process of recalling and reflecting on the problem with which it is concerned. Douglass, for example, covers seven years of his life in his piece about the problem of learning to read and write, and King recalls events and issues throughout his life that led him to espouse the principles of nonviolent resistance. In each case, the breadth of coverage serves to reveal the scope and complexity of the problem, as well as the author's special understanding of it.

As you can see from just this brief survey of possibilities, reflective writing may deal with a single event, several events, or a whole lifetime of events. It may be as restricted in its attention as a close-up or as all-encompassing as a wide-angle shot. But no matter how little, or how much, experience it takes into account, reflective writing is always decisively focused through the author's persistent attempt to make sense of the past, to push memory to the point of understanding the significance of experience.

Methods of Reflecting

Your experience is unique, as is your memory, so in a sense you know the best methods to follow whenever you are of a mind to reflect on something that interests you. But once you have recalled something in detail and made sense of it for yourself, you are still faced with the problem of how to present it to readers in a way that will also make sense to them. Given the fact that your readers will probably not be familiar with your experience, you will need to be very careful in selecting and organizing your material so that you provide a clearly detailed account of it. By the same token, you will need to give special emphasis to aspects or elements of your experience that will enable readers to understand their significance. Usually, you will find that your choice of subject suggests a corresponding method of presenting it clearly and meaningfully to your readers.

If your reflections are focused on a single, circumscribed event, you will probably find it most appropriate to use a narrative presentation, telling your readers what happened in a relatively straightforward chronological order. Though you cover the event from beginning to end, your narrative should be carefully designed to emphasize the details that you consider most striking and significant. In "Shooting an Elephant," for example, Orwell devotes the largest segment in his piece to covering the very, very brief period of a few moments when he finds himself on the verge of having to shoot the elephant despite his strong desire not to do so. In fact, he devotes one-third of his essay to these few moments of inner conflict because they bring about one of his major insights—"that when the white man turns tyrant it is his own freedom that he destroys." So in telling about a memorable event of your own, you should deliberately pace your story to make it build toward some kind of climax or surprise or decisive incident, which in turn leads to a moment of insight for you (and your readers).

If your reflections are focused on a particular person, you will probably find it necessary to use both narrative and descriptive methods of presentation, telling about several events in order to make clear to readers the character and thought of the person in question. Though you rely heavily on narration, you will not be able to cover incidents in as much detail as if you were focusing on a single event. Instead, you will find it necessary to isolate only the most striking and significant details from each incident you choose to recall. Momaday, for instance, relates his grandmother's background by way of the history of the Kiowa. But to describe her individual character, he isolates particular details—her postures, her praying, her dress—that are carefully chosen to resonate with the "ancient awe" that

Momaday says was "in her" and with which he regards her. So, too, in writing about an individual whom you have known, you should carefully select and arrange the details that you recall to make them convey a clear and compelling impression of that person's character.

If your reflections are focused on a particular problem or issue in your past experience, you will probably need to combine narrative, descriptive, and explanatory methods of presentation, bringing together your recollections of numerous events and persons to reveal the nature and significance of the problem. Although you will survey the problem chronologically from beginning to end, you will also need to organize your narrative so that it highlights the essential aspects, elements, or facets of the problem. For example, in "Pilgrimage to Nonviolence," King immediately focuses on the "new and sometimes complex doctrinal lands" through which he traveled. And from this point on, he recalls the various theological and philosophical ideas with which he struggled in formulating his belief in nonviolence. So in writing about a particular problem of your own, your recollections should be deliberately selected and organized to highlight your special understanding of the issue.

No matter what specific combination of methods you use in your reflective writing, you will probably find, as do most writers, that a striking recollection is the most effective way to interest your readers and that a significant observation about experience is the most rewarding means to send them on their way. In the following selections, you will get to see how a wide variety of writers use language to produce some very striking and significant pieces of reflection.

Arts and Humanities

GRADUATION

Maya Angelou

In her four volumes of autobiography, Maya Angelou (b. 1928) has written vividly of her struggles to achieve success as an actor, a dancer, a songwriter, a teacher, and a poet. (In 1993, she read her poem "On the Pulse of Morning," at the inauguration of President Clinton.) An active worker in the civil rights movement of the 1960s, Angelou continues to focus much of her writing on racial issues. The following selection is from I Know Why the Caged Bird Sings *(1969), in which she writes, "I speak to the Black experience, but I am always talking about the human condition."*

The children in Stamps trembled visibly with anticipation.[1] Some adults were excited too, but to be certain the whole young population had come down with graduation epidemic. Large classes were graduating from both the grammar school and the high school. Even those who were years removed from their own day of glorious release were anxious to help with preparations as a kind of dry run. The junior students who were moving into the vacating classes' chairs were tradition-bound to show their talents for leadership and management. They strutted through the school and around the campus exerting pressure on the lower grades. Their authority was so new that occasionally if they pressed a little too hard it had to be overlooked. After all, next term was coming, and it never hurt a sixth grader to have a play sister in the eighth grade, or a tenth-year student to be able to call a twelfth grader Bubba. So all was endured in a spirit of shared understanding. But the graduating classes themselves were the

---

[1]*Stamps:* a town in Arkansas. [Eds.]

nobility. Like travelers with exotic destinations on their minds, the graduates were remarkably forgetful. They came to school without their books, or tablets or even pencils. Volunteers fell over themselves to secure replacements for the missing equipment. When accepted, the willing workers might or might not be thanked, and it was of no importance to the pregraduation rites. Even teachers were respectful of the now quiet and aging seniors, and tended to speak to them, if not as equals, as beings only slightly lower than themselves. After tests were returned and grades given, the student body, which acted like an extended family, knew who did well, who excelled, and what piteous ones had failed.

Unlike the white high school, Lafayette County Training School distinguished itself by having neither lawn, nor hedges, nor tennis court, nor climbing ivy. Its two buildings (main classrooms, the grade school and home economics) were set on a dirt hill with no fence to limit either its boundaries or those of bordering farms. There was a large expanse to the left of the school which was used alternately as a baseball diamond or basketball court. Rusty hoops on swaying poles represented the permanent recreational equipment, although bats and balls could be borrowed from the P.E. teacher if the borrower was qualified and if the diamond wasn't occupied.

Over this rocky area relieved by a few shady tall persimmon trees the graduating class walked. The girls often held hands and no longer bothered to speak to the lower students. There was a sadness about them, as if this old world was not their home and they were bound for higher ground. The boys, on the other hand, had become more friendly, more outgoing. A decided change from the closed attitude they projected while studying for finals. Now they seemed not ready to give up the old school, the familiar paths and classrooms. Only a small percentage would be continuing on to college—one of the South's A & M (agricultural and mechanical) schools, which trained Negro youths to be carpenters, farmers, handymen, masons, maids, cooks and baby nurses. Their future rode heavily on their shoulders, and blinded them to the collective joy that had pervaded the lives of the boys and girls in the grammar school graduating class.

Parents who could afford it had ordered new shoes and ready-made clothes for themselves from Sears and Roebuck or Montgomery Ward. They also engaged the best seamstresses to make the floating graduating dresses and to cut down secondhand pants which would be pressed to a military slickness for the important event.

Oh, it was important, all right. Whitefolks would attend the ceremony, and two or three would speak of God and home, and the Southern way of life, and Mrs. Parsons, the principal's wife, would play the graduation march while the lower-grade graduates paraded down the aisles and took their seats below the platform. The high school seniors would wait in empty classrooms to make their dramatic entrance.

5

In the Store I was the person of the moment. The birthday girl. The center. Bailey had graduated the year before,[2] although to do so he had had to forfeit all pleasures to make up for his time lost in Baton Rouge.

My class was wearing butter-yellow piqué dresses, and Momma launched out on mine. She smocked the yoke into tiny crisscrossing puckers, then shirred the rest of the bodice. Her dark fingers ducked in and out of the lemony cloth as she embroidered raised daisies around the hem. Before she considered herself finished she had added a crocheted cuff on the puff sleeves, and a point crocheted collar.

I was going to be lovely. A walking model of all the various styles of fine hand sewing and it didn't worry me that I was only twelve years old and merely graduating from the eighth grade. Besides, many teachers in Arkansas Negro schools had only that diploma and were licensed to impart wisdom.

The days had become longer and more noticeable. The faded beige of former times had been replaced with strong and sure colors. I began to see my classmates' clothes, their skin tones, and the dust that waved off pussy willows. Clouds that lazed across the sky were objects of great concern to me. Their shiftier shapes might have held a message that in my new happiness and with a little bit of time I'd soon decipher. During that period I looked at the arch of heaven so religiously my neck kept a steady ache. I had taken to smiling more often, and my jaws hurt from the unaccustomed activity. Between the two physical sore spots, I suppose I could have been uncomfortable, but that was not the case. As a member of the winning team (the graduating class of 1940) I had outdistanced unpleasant sensations by miles. I was headed for the freedom of open fields.

Youth and social approval allied themselves with me and we trammeled memories of slights and insults. The wind of our swift passage remodeled my features. Lost tears were pounded to mud and then to dust. Years of withdrawal were brushed aside and left behind, as hanging ropes of parasitic moss.

My work alone had awarded me a top place and I was going to be one of the first called in the graduating ceremonies. On the classroom blackboard, as well as on the bulletin board in the auditorium, there were blue stars and white stars and red stars. No absences, no tardinesses, and my academic work was among the best of the year. I could say the preamble to the Constitution even faster than Bailey. We timed ourselves often: "WethepeopleoftheUnitedStatesinordertoformamoreperfectunion...." I had memorized the Presidents of the United States from Washington to Roosevelt in chronological as well as alphabetical order.

My hair pleased me too. Gradually the black mass had lengthened and thickened, so that it kept at last to its braided pattern, and I didn't have to yank my scalp off when I tried to comb it.

10

---

[2]*Bailey:* the author's brother. [Eds.]

Louise and I had rehearsed the exercises until we tired out ourselves. Henry Reed was class valedictorian. He was a small, very black boy with hooded eyes, a long, broad nose and an oddly shaped head. I had admired him for years because each term he and I vied for the best grades in our class. Most often he bested me, but instead of being disappointed I was pleased that we shared top places between us. Like many Southern Black children, he lived with his grandmother, who was as strict as Momma and as kind as she knew how to be. He was courteous, respectful and soft-spoken to elders, but on the playground he chose to play the roughest games. I admired him. Anyone, I reckoned, sufficiently afraid or sufficiently dull could be polite. But to be able to operate at a top level with both adults and children was admirable.

His valedictory speech was entitled "To Be or Not to Be." The rigid tenth-grade teacher had helped him write it. He'd been working on the dramatic stresses for months.

The weeks until graduation were filled with heady activities. A group   15 of small children were to be presented in a play about buttercups and daisies and bunny rabbits. They could be heard throughout the building practicing their hops and their little songs that sounded like silver bells. The older girls (nongraduates, of course) were assigned the task of making refreshments for the night's festivities. A tangy scent of ginger, cinnamon, nutmeg and chocolate wafted around the home economics building as the budding cooks made samples for themselves and their teachers.

In every corner of the workshop, axes and saws split fresh timber as the woodshop boys made sets and stage scenery. Only the graduates were left out of the general bustle. We were free to sit in the library at the back of the building or look in quite detachedly, naturally, on the measures being taken for our event.

Even the minister preached on graduation the Sunday before. His subject was, "Let your light so shine that men will see your good works and praise your Father, Who is in Heaven." Although the sermon was purported to be addressed to us, he used the occasion to speak to backsliders, gamblers and general ne'er-do-wells. But since he had called our names at the beginning of the service we were mollified.

Among Negroes the tradition was to give presents to children going only from one grade to another. How much more important this was when the person was graduating at the top of the class. Uncle Willie and Momma had sent away for a Mickey Mouse watch like Bailey's. Louise gave me four embroidered handkerchiefs. (I gave her crocheted doilies.) Mrs. Sneed, the minister's wife, made me an undershirt to wear for graduation, and nearly every customer gave me a nickel or maybe even a dime with the instruction "Keep on moving to higher ground," or some such encouragement.

Amazingly the great day finally dawned and I was out of bed before I knew it. I threw open the back door to see it more clearly, but Momma said, "Sister, come away from that door and put your robe on."

I hoped the memory of that morning would never leave me. Sunlight   20
was itself young, and the day had none of the insistence maturity would
bring it in a few hours. In my robe and barefoot in the backyard, under
cover of going to see about my new beans, I gave myself up to the gentle
warmth and thanked God that no matter what evil I had done in my life
He had allowed me to live to see this day. Somewhere in my fatalism I had
expected to die, accidentally, and never have the chance to walk up the
stairs in the auditorium and gracefully receive my hard-earned diploma.
Out of God's merciful bosom I had won reprieve.

Bailey came out in his robe and gave me a box wrapped in Christmas
paper. He said he had saved his money for months to pay for it. It felt like
a box of chocolates, but I knew Bailey wouldn't save money to buy candy
when we had all we could want under our noses.

He was as proud of the gift as I. It was a soft-leather-bound copy of a
collection of poems by Edgar Allan Poe, or, as Bailey and I called him,
"Eap." I turned to "Annabel Lee" and we walked up and down the garden
rows, the cool dirt between our toes, reciting the beautifully sad lines.

Momma made a Sunday breakfast although it was only Friday. After
we finished the blessing, I opened my eyes to find the watch on my plate. It
was a dream of a day. Everything went smoothly and to my credit. I didn't
have to be reminded or scolded for anything. Near evening I was too jittery
to attend to chores, so Bailey volunteered to do all before his bath.

Days before, we had made a sign for the Store, and as we turned out
the lights Momma hung the cardboard over the doorknob. It read clearly:
CLOSED. GRADUATION.

My dress fitted perfectly and everyone said that I looked like a sun-   25
beam in it. On the hill, going toward the school, Bailey walked behind with
Uncle Willie, who muttered, "Go on, Ju." He wanted him to walk ahead
with us because it embarrassed him to have to walk so slowly. Bailey said
he'd let the ladies walk together, and the men would bring up the rear. We
all laughed, nicely.

Little children dashed by out of the dark like fireflies. Their crepe-
paper dresses and butterfly wings were not made for running and we heard
more than one rip, dryly, and the regretful "uh uh" that followed.

The school blazed without gaiety. The windows seemed cold and un-
friendly from the lower hill. A sense of ill-fated timing crept over me, and if
Momma hadn't reached for my hand I would have drifted back to Bailey
and Uncle Willie, and possibly beyond. She made a few slow jokes about
my feet getting cold, and tugged me along to the now-strange building.

Around the front steps, assurance came back. There were my fellow
"greats," the graduating class. Hair brushed back, legs oiled, new dresses
and pressed pleats, fresh pocket handkerchiefs and little handbags, all
homesewn. Oh, we were up to snuff, all right. I joined my comrades and
didn't even see my family go in to find seats in the crowded auditorium.

The school band struck up a march and all classes filed in as had been rehearsed. We stood in front of our seats, as assigned, and on a signal from the

choir director, we sat. No sooner had this been accomplished than the band started to play the national anthem. We rose again and sang the song, after which we recited the pledge of allegiance. We remained standing for a brief minute before the choir director and the principal signaled to us, rather desperately I thought, to take our seats. The command was so unusual that our carefully rehearsed and smooth-running machine was thrown off. For a full minute we fumbled for our chairs and bumped into each other awkwardly. Habits change or solidify under pressure, so in our state of nervous tension we had been ready to follow our usual assembly pattern: the American national anthem, then the pledge of allegiance, then the song every Black person I knew called the Negro National Anthem. All done in the same key, with the same passion and most often standing on the same foot.

Finding my seat at last, I was overcome with a presentiment of worse   30
things to come. Something unrehearsed, unplanned, was going to happen, and we were going to be made to look bad. I distinctly remember being explicit in the choice of pronoun. It was "we," the graduating class, the unit, that concerned me then.

The principal welcomed "parents and friends" and asked the Baptist minister to lead us in prayer. His invocation was brief and punchy, and for a second I thought we were getting on the high road to right action. When the principal came back to the dais, however, his voice had changed. Sounds always affected me profoundly and the principal's voice was one of my favorites. During assembly it melted and lowed weakly into the audience. It had not been in my plan to listen to him, but my curiosity was piqued and I straightened up to give him my attention.

He was talking about Booker T. Washington, our "late great leader," who said we can be as close as the fingers on the hand, etc. . . . Then he said a few vague things about friendship and the friendship of kindly people to those less fortunate than themselves. With that his voice nearly faded, thin, away. Like a river diminishing to a stream and then to a trickle. But he cleared his throat and said, "Our speaker tonight, who is also our friend, came from Texarkana to deliver the commencement address, but due to the irregularity of the train schedule, he's going to, as they say, 'speak and run.'" He said that we understood and wanted the man to know that we were most grateful for the time he was able to give us and then something about how we were willing always to adjust to another's program, and without more ado—"I give you Mr. Edward Donleavy."

Not one but two white men came through the door off-stage. The shorter one walked to the speaker's platform, and the tall one moved to the center seat and sat down. But that was our principal's seat, and already occupied. The dislodged gentleman bounced around for a long breath or two before the Baptist minister gave him his chair, then with more dignity than the situation deserved, the minister walked off the stage.

Donleavy looked at the audience once (on reflection, I'm sure that he wanted only to reassure himself that we were really there), adjusted his glasses and began to read from a sheaf of papers.

He was glad "to be here and to see the work going on just as it was in 35 the other schools."

At the first "Amen" from the audience I willed the offender to immediate death by choking on the word. But Amens and Yes, sir's began to fall around the room like rain through a ragged umbrella.

He told us of the wonderful changes we children in Stamps had in store. The Central School (naturally, the white school was Central) had already been granted improvements that would be in use in the fall. A well-known artist was coming from Little Rock to teach art to them. They were going to have the newest microscopes and chemistry equipment for their laboratory. Mr. Donleavy didn't leave us long in the dark over who made these improvements available to Central High. Nor were we to be ignored in the general betterment scheme he had in mind.

He said that he had pointed out to people at a very high level that one of the first-line football tacklers at Arkansas Agricultural and Mechanical College had graduated from good old Lafayette County Training School. Here fewer Amen's were heard. Those few that did break through lay dully in the air with the heaviness of habit.

He went on to praise us. He went on to say how he had bragged that "one of the best basketball players at Fisk sank his first ball right here at Lafayette County Training School."

The white kids were going to have a chance to become Galileos and 40 Madame Curies and Edisons and Gauguins, and our boys (the girls weren't even in on it) would try to be Jesse Owenses and Joe Louises.

Owens and the Brown Bomber were great heroes in our world, but what school official in the white-goddom of Little Rock had the right to decide that those two men must be our only heroes? Who decided that for Henry Reed to become a scientist he had to work like George Washington Carver, as a bootblack, to buy a lousy microscope? Bailey was obviously always going to be too small to be an athlete, so which concrete angel glued to what county seat had decided that if my brother wanted to become a lawyer he had to first pay penance for his skin by picking cotton and hoeing corn and studying correspondence books at night for twenty years?

The man's dead words fell like bricks around the auditorium and too many settled in my belly. Constrained by hard-learned manners I couldn't look behind me, but to my left and right the proud graduating class of 1940 had dropped their heads. Every girl in my row had found something new to do with her handkerchief. Some folded the tiny squares into love knots, some into triangles, but most were wadding them, then pressing them flat on their yellow laps.

On the dais, the ancient tragedy was being replayed. Professor Parsons sat, a sculptor's reject, rigid. His large, heavy body seemed devoid of will or willingness, and his eyes said he was no longer with us. The other teachers examined the flag (which was draped stage right) or their notes, or the windows which opened on our now-famous playing diamond.

Graduation, the hush-hush magic time of frills and gifts and congratu-
lations and diplomas, was finished for me before my name was called. The
accomplishment was nothing. The meticulous maps, drawn in three colors
of ink, learning and spelling decasyllabic words, memorizing the whole of
The Rape of Lucrece[3] — it was for nothing. Donleavy had exposed us.

We were maids and farmers, handymen and washerwomen, and any-   45
thing higher that we aspired to was farcical and presumptuous.

Then I wished that Gabriel Prosser and Nat Turner[4] had killed all
whitefolks in their beds and that Abraham Lincoln had been assassinated
before the signing of the Emancipation Proclamation, and that Harriet
Tubman[5] had been killed by that blow on her head and Christopher
Columbus had drowned in the *Santa Maria*.

It was awful to be a Negro and have no control over my life. It was
brutal to be young and already trained to sit quietly and listen to charges
brought against my color with no chance of defense. We should all be
dead. I thought I should like to see us all dead, one on top of the other. A
pyramid of flesh with the whitefolks on the bottom, as the broad base,
then the Indians with their silly tomahawks and teepees and wigwams and
treaties, the Negroes with their mops and recipes and cotton sacks and
spirituals sticking out of their mouths. The Dutch children should all
stumble in their wooden shoes and break their necks. The French should
choke to death on the Louisiana Purchase (1803) while silkworms ate all
the Chinese with their stupid pigtails. As a species, we were an abomina-
tion. All of us.

Donleavy was running for election, and assured our parents that if he
won we could count on having the only colored paved playing field in that
part of Arkansas. Also — he never looked up to acknowledge the grunts of
acceptance — also, we were bound to get some new equipment for the
home economics building and the workshop.

He finished, and since there was no need to give any more than the
most perfunctory thank-you's, he nodded to the men on the stage, and the
tall white man who was never introduced joined him at the door. They left
with the attitude that now they were off to something really important.
(The graduation ceremonies at Lafayette County Training School had been
a mere preliminary.)

The ugliness they left was palpable. An uninvited guest who wouldn't   50
leave. The choir was summoned and sang a modern arrangement of "On-
ward, Christian Soldiers," with new words pertaining to graduates seeking

---

[3]*The Rape of Lucrece:* an 1,855-line narrative poem by William Shakespeare.
[Eds.]

[4]*Gabriel Prosser and Nat Turner:* leaders of slave rebellions during the early
1800s in Virginia. [Eds.]

[5]*Harriet Tubman* (ca. 1820–1913): escaped slave who conducted others to
freedom on the Underground Railroad and worked as an abolitionist. [Eds.]

their place in the world. But it didn't work. Elouise, the daughter of the Baptist minister, recited "Invictus,"[6] and I could have cried at the impertinence of "I am the master of my fate, I am the captain of my soul."

My name had lost its ring of familiarity and I had to be nudged to go and receive my diploma. All my preparations had fled. I neither marched up to the stage like a conquering Amazon, nor did I look in the audience for Bailey's nod of approval. Marguerite Johnson, I heard the name again, my honors were read, there were noises in the audience of appreciation, and I took my place on the stage as rehearsed.

I thought about colors I hated: ecru, puce, lavender, beige and black.

There was shuffling and rustling around me, then Henry Reed was giving his valedictory address, "To Be or Not to Be." Hadn't he heard the whitefolks? We couldn't *be,* so the question was a waste of time. Henry's voice came out clear and strong. I feared to look at him. Hadn't he got the message? There was no "nobler in the mind" for Negroes because the world didn't think we had minds, and they let us know it. "Outrageous fortune"? Now, that was a joke. When the ceremony was over I had to tell Henry Reed some things. That is, if I still cared. Not "rub," Henry, "erase." "Ah, there's the erase." Us.

Henry had been a good student in elocution. His voice rose on tides of promise and fell on waves of warnings. The English teacher had helped him to create a sermon winging through Hamlet's soliloquy. To be a man, a doer, a builder, a leader, or to be a tool, an unfunny joke, a crusher of funky toadstools. I marveled that Henry could go through with the speech as if we had a choice.

I had been listening and silently rebutting each sentence with my eyes 55 closed; then there was a hush, which in an audience warns that something unplanned is happening. I looked up and saw Henry Reed, the conservative, the proper, the A student, turn his back to the audience and turn to us (the proud graduating class of 1940) and sing, nearly speaking,

> "Lift ev'ry voice and sing
> Till earth and heaven ring
> Ring with the harmonies of Liberty . . ."

It was the poem written by James Weldon Johnson. It was the music composed by J. Rosamond Johnson. It was the Negro National Anthem. Out of habit we were singing it.

Our mothers and fathers stood in the dark hall and joined the hymn of encouragement. A kindergarten teacher led the small children onto the stage and the buttercups and daisies and bunny rabbits marked time and tried to follow:

---

[6]*"Invictus"*: a poem by the nineteenth-century English poet William Ernest Henley. Its inspirational conclusion is quoted here. [Eds.]

"Stony the road we trod
Bitter the chastening rod
Felt in the days when hope, unborn, had died.
Yet with a steady beat
Have not our weary feet
Come to the place for which our fathers sighed?"

Each child I knew had learned that song with his ABC's and along with "Jesus Loves Me This I Know." But I personally had never heard it before. Never heard the words, despite the thousands of times I had sung them. Never thought they had anything to do with me.

On the other hand, the words of Patrick Henry had made such an impression on me that I had been able to stretch myself tall and trembling and say, "I know not what course others may take, but as for me, give me liberty or give me death."

And now I heard, really for the first time:

"We have come over a way that with tears
has been watered,
We have come, treading our path through
the blood of the slaughtered."

While echoes of the song shivered in the air, Henry Reed bowed his   60
head, said "Thank you," and returned to his place in the line. The tears that slipped down many faces were not wiped away in shame.

We were on top again. As always, again. We survived. The depths had been icy and dark, but now a bright sun spoke to our souls. I was no longer simply a member of the proud graduating class of 1940; I was a proud member of the wonderful, beautiful Negro race.

Oh, Black known and unknown poets, how often have your auctioned pains sustained us? Who will compute the only nights made less lonely by your songs, or the empty pots made less tragic by your tales?

If we were a people much given to revealing secrets, we might raise monuments and sacrifice to the memories of our poets, but slavery cured us of that weakness. It may be enough, however, to have it said that we survive in exact relationship to the dedication of our poets (include preachers, musicians and blues singers).

QUESTIONS

1. Why was graduation such an important event in Stamps, Arkansas? Note the rituals and preparations associated with this event. How do they compare with those accompanying your own junior high or high school graduation?

2. At the beginning of the graduation ceremony, Angelou was "overcome with a presentiment of worse things to come. Something unrehearsed, unplanned, was going to happen" (paragraph 30). What "unrehearsed, unplanned" event does occur? How does Angelou convey to the reader the meaning of this event?

3. Toward the end of the essay we are told, "I was no longer simply a member of the proud graduating class of 1940; I was a proud member of the wonderful, beautiful Negro race" (paragraph 61). How did the experience of the graduation change Angelou's way of thinking about herself and her people?

4. Understanding the structure of this essay is important for understanding the meaning of the essay. How does Angelou organize her material, and how does this organization reflect her purpose? Why do you think Angelou changes her point of view from third person in the first five paragraphs to first person in the rest of the essay?

5. Think of an event in your life that didn't turn out as you expected. What were your expectations of this event? What was the reality? Write an essay in which you show the significance of this event by contrasting how you planned for the event with how it actually turned out.

6. We have all had experiences that have changed the directions of our lives. These experiences may be momentous, such as moving from one country to another or losing a parent, or they may be experiences that did not loom so large at the time but that changed the way you thought about things, such as finding that your parents disapproved of your best friend because of her race. Recall such a turning point in your life, and present it so as to give the reader a sense of what your life was like before the event and how it changed after the event.

MAKING CONNECTIONS

1. Compare the points of view taken by Angelou and Alice Walker (p. 42). How does the "presence" of the valedictorian in Angelou's essay influence the point of view she takes?

2. Two things link this essay with George Orwell's "Shooting an Elephant" (p. 132): each essay turns on an unexpected event, and the reflections each event prompts have to do with political domination. Of course they are from dissimilar points of view. But Orwell, when he goes out to meet and shoot the elephant, finds himself forced before a native crowd, in somewhat the same way that Mr. Donleavy stands before Angelou's school. Write an essay in which you compare and contrast these two events.

BEAUTY
When the Other Dancer Is the Self

Alice Walker

Born in Eatonton, Georgia, in 1944, Alice Walker is the youngest of eight children. Her father was a sharecropper, and her mother was a maid. A graduate of Sarah Lawrence College, Walker has been an active worker for civil rights. She has been a fellow of the Radcliffe Institute, a contributing and consulting editor for Ms. *magazine, and a teacher of literature and writing at a number of colleges and universities. She has published poetry, essays, short stories, and five novels:* The Third Life of Grange Copeland *(1970),* Meridian *(1976),* The Color Purple *(1982), for which she won the Pulitzer Prize,* The Temple of My Familiar *(1989) and* By the Light of My Father's Smile *(1998). "Beauty: When the Other Dancer Is the Self" first appeared in* Ms. *magazine and later in a collection of essays,* In Search of Our Mothers' Gardens *(1983). When asked why she writes, Walker said, "I'm really paying homage to people I love, the people who are thought to be dumb and backward but who were the ones who first taught me to see beauty."*

It is a bright summer day in 1947. My father, a fat, funny man with beautiful eyes and a subversive wit, is trying to decide which of his eight children he will take with him to the county fair. My mother, of course, will not go. She is knocked out from getting most of us ready: I hold my neck stiff against the pressure of her knuckles as she hastily completes the braiding and then beribboning of my hair.

My father is the driver for the rich old white lady up the road. Her name is Miss Mey. She owns all the land for miles around, as well as the house in which we live. All I remember about her is that she once offered to pay my mother thirty-five cents for cleaning her house, raking up piles of her magnolia leaves, and washing her family's clothes, and that my mother—she of no money, eight children, and a chronic earache—refused it. But I do not think of this in 1947. I am two and a half years old. I want to go everywhere my daddy goes. I am excited at the prospect of riding in a car. Someone has told me fairs are fun. That there is room in the car for only three of us doesn't faze me at all. Whirling happily in my starchy frock, showing off my biscuit-polished patent-leather shoes and lavender socks, tossing my head in a way that makes my ribbons bounce, I stand, hands on hips, before my father. "Take me, Daddy," I say with assurance; "I'm the prettiest!"

Later, it does not surprise me to find myself in Miss Mey's shiny black car, sharing the back seat with the other lucky ones. Does not surprise me that I thoroughly enjoy the fair. At home that night I tell the unlucky ones all I can remember about the merry-go-round, the man who eats live chickens, and the teddy bears, until they say: that's enough, baby Alice. Shut up now, and go to sleep.

It is Easter Sunday, 1950. I am dressed in a green, flocked, scalloped-hem dress (handmade by my adoring sister, Ruth) that has its own smooth satin petticoat and tiny hot-pink roses tucked into each scallop. My shoes, new T-strap patent leather, again highly biscuit-polished. I am six years old and have learned one of the longest Easter speeches to be heard that day, totally unlike the speech I said when I was two: "Easter lilies / pure and white / blossom in / the morning light." When I rise to give my speech I do so on a great wave of love and pride and expectation. People in the church stop rustling their new crinolines. They seem to hold their breath. I can tell they admire my dress, but it is my spirit, bordering on sassiness (woman-ishness), they secretly applaud.

"That girl's a little *mess*," they whisper to each other, pleased.   5

Naturally I say my speech without stammer or pause, unlike those who stutter, stammer, or worst of all, forget. This is before the word "beautiful" exists in people's vocabulary, but "Oh, isn't she the *cutest* thing!" frequently floats my way. "And got so much sense!" they gratefully add . . . for which thoughtful addition I thank them to this day.

It was great fun being cute. But then, one day, it ended.

I am eight years old and a tomboy. I have a cowboy hat, cowboy boots, checkered shirt and pants, all red. My playmates are my brothers, two and four years older than I. Their colors are black and green, the only difference in the way we are dressed. On Saturday nights we all go to the picture show, even my mother; Westerns are her favorite kind of movie. Back home, "on the ranch," we pretend we are Tom Mix, Hopalong Cassidy, Lash LaRue (we've even named one of our dogs Lash LaRue); we chase each other for hours rustling cattle, being outlaws, delivering damsels from distress. Then my parents decide to buy my brothers guns. These are not "real" guns. They shoot "BBs," copper pellets my brothers say will kill birds. Because I am a girl, I do not get a gun. Instantly I am relegated to the position of Indian. Now there appears a great distance between us. They shoot and shoot at everything with their new guns. I try to keep up with my bow and arrows.

One day while I am standing on top of our makeshift "garage"—pieces of tin nailed across some poles—holding my bow and arrow and looking out toward the fields, I feel an incredible blow in my right eye. I look down just in time to see my brother lower his gun.

10

Both brothers rush to my side. My eye stings, and I cover it with my hand. "If you tell," they say, "we will get a whipping. You don't want that to happen, do you?" I do not. "Here is a piece of wire," says the older brother, picking it up from the roof; "say you stepped on one end of it and the other flew up and hit you." The pain is beginning to start. "Yes," I say. "Yes, I will say that is what happened." If I do not say this is what happened, I know my brothers will find ways to make me wish I had. But now I will say anything that gets me to my mother.

Confronted by our parents we stick to the lie agreed upon. They place me on a bench on the porch and I close my left eye while they examine the right. There is a tree growing from underneath the porch that climbs past the railing to the roof. It is the last thing my right eye sees. I watch as its trunk, its branches, and then its leaves are blotted out by the rising blood.

I am in shock. First there is intense fever, which my father tries to break using lily leaves bound around my head. Then there are chills: my mother tries to get me to eat soup. Eventually, I do not know how, my parents learn what has happened. A week after the "accident" they take me to see a doctor. "Why did you wait so long to come?" he asks, looking into my eye and shaking his head. "Eyes are sympathetic," he says. "If one is blind, the other will likely become blind too."

This comment of the doctor's terrifies me. But it is really how I look that bothers me most. Where the BB pellet struck there is a glob of whitish scar tissue, a hideous cataract, on my eye. Now when I stare at people—a favorite pastime, up to now—they will stare back. Not at the "cute" little girl, but at her scar. For six years I do not stare at anyone, because I do not raise my head.

Years later, in the throes of a mid-life crisis, I ask my mother and sister whether I changed after the "accident." "No," they say, puzzled. "What do you mean?"

What do I mean?   15

I am eight, and, for the first time, doing poorly in school, where I have been something of a whiz since I was four. We have just moved to the place where the "accident" occurred. We do not know any of the people around us because this is a different county. The only time I see the friends I knew is when we go back to our old church. The new school is the former state penitentiary. It is a large stone building, cold and drafty, crammed to overflowing with boisterous, ill-disciplined children. On the third floor there is a huge circular imprint of some partition that has been torn out.

"What used to be here?" I ask a sullen girl next to me on our way past it to lunch.

"The electric chair," says she.

At night I have nightmares about the electric chair, and about all the people reputedly "fried" in it. I am afraid of the school, where all the students seem to be budding criminals.

"What's the matter with your eye?" they ask, critically. 20

When I don't answer (I cannot decide whether it was an "accident" or not), they shove me, insist on a fight.

My brother, the one who created the story about the wire, comes to my rescue. But then brags so much about "protecting" me, I become sick.

After months of torture at the school, my parents decide to send me back to our old community, to my old school. I live with my grandparents and the teacher they board. But there is no room for Phoebe, my cat. By the time my grandparents decide there *is* room, and I ask for my cat, she cannot be found. Miss Yarborough, the boarding teacher, takes me under her wing, and begins to teach me to play the piano. But soon she marries an African—a "prince," she says—and is whisked away to his continent.

At my old school there is at least one teacher who loves me. She is the teacher who "knew me before I was born" and bought my first baby clothes. It is she who makes life bearable. It is her presence that finally helps me turn on the one child at the school who continually calls me "one-eyed bitch." One day I simply grab him by his coat and beat him until I am satisfied. It is my teacher who tells me my mother is ill.

My mother is lying in bed in the middle of the day, something I have 25 never seen. She is in too much pain to speak. She has an abscess in her ear. I stand looking down on her, knowing that if she dies, I cannot live. She is being treated with warm oils and hot bricks held against her cheek. Finally a doctor comes. But I must go back to my grandparents' house. The weeks pass but I am hardly aware of it. All I know is that my mother might die, my father is not so jolly, my brothers still have their guns, and I am the one sent away from home.

"You did not change," they say.

Did I imagine the anguish of never looking up?

I am twelve. When relatives come to visit I hide in my room. My cousin Brenda, just my age, whose father works in the post office and whose mother is a nurse, comes to find me. "Hello," she says. And then she asks, looking at my recent school picture, which I did not want taken, and on which the "glob," as I think of it, is clearly visible, "You still can't see out of that eye?"

"No," I say, and flop back on the bed over my book.

That night, as I do almost every night, I abuse my eye. I rant and rave 30 at it, in front of the mirror. I plead with it to clear up before morning. I tell it I hate and despise it. I do not pray for sight. I pray for beauty.

"You did not change," they say.

I am fourteen and baby-sitting for my brother Bill, who lives in Boston. He is my favorite brother and there is a strong bond between us. Understanding my feelings of shame and ugliness he and his wife take me to a local hospital, where the "glob" is removed by a doctor named O. Henry. There is still a small bluish crater where scar tissue was, but the ugly white stuff is gone. Almost immediately I become a different person from the girl who does not raise her head. Or so I think. Now that I've raised my head I win the boyfriend of my dreams. Now that I've raised my head I have plenty of friends. Now that I've raised my head classwork comes from my lips faultlessly as Easter speeches did, and I leave high school as valedictorian, most popular student, and *queen*, hardly believing my luck. Ironically, the girl who was voted most beautiful in our class (and was) was later shot twice through the chest by a male companion, using a "real" gun, while she was pregnant. But that's another story in itself. Or is it?

"You did not change," they say.

It is now thirty years since the "accident." A beautiful journalist comes to visit and to interview me. She is going to write a cover story for her magazine that focuses on my latest book. "Decide how you want to look on the cover," she says. "Glamorous, whatever."

Never mind "glamorous," it is the "whatever" that I hear. Suddenly all   35
I can think of is whether I will get enough sleep the night before the photography session: if I don't, my eye will be tired and wander, as blind eyes will.

At night in bed with my lover I think up reasons why I should not appear on the cover of a magazine. "My meanest critics will say I've sold out," I say. "My family will now realize I write scandalous books."

"But what's the real reason you don't want to do this?" he asks.

"Because in all probability," I say in a rush, "my eye won't be straight."

"It will be straight enough," he says. Then, "Besides, I thought you'd made your peace with that."

And I suddenly remember that I have.   40

I remember:

I am talking to my brother Jimmy, asking if he remembers anything unusual about the day I was shot. He does not know I consider that day the last time my father, with his sweet home remedy of cool lily leaves, chose me, and that I suffered and raged inside because of this. "Well," he says, "all I remember is standing by the side of the highway with Daddy, trying to flag down a car. A white man stopped, but when Daddy said he needed somebody to take his little girl to the doctor, he drove off."

I remember:

I am in the desert for the first time. I fall totally in love with it. I am so overwhelmed by its beauty, I confront for the first time, consciously, the meaning of the doctor's words years ago: "Eyes are sympathetic. If one is blind, the other will likely become blind too." I realize I have dashed about the world madly, looking at this, looking at that, storing up images against the fading of the light. *But I might have missed seeing the desert!* The shock of that possibility—and gratitude for over twenty-five years of sight—

sends me literally to my knees. Poem after poem comes—which is perhaps how poets pray.

ON SIGHT

I am so thankful I have seen
The Desert
And the creatures in the desert
And the desert Itself.

The desert has its own moon
Which I have seen
With my own eye.

There is no flag on it.

Trees of the desert have arms
All of which are always up
That is because the moon is up
The sun is up
Also the sky
The stars
Clouds
None with flags.

If there *were* flags, I doubt
the trees would point.
Would you?

But mostly, I remember this: 45

I am twenty-seven, and my baby daughter is almost three. Since her birth I have worried about her discovery that her mother's eyes are different from other people's. Will she be embarrassed? I think. What will she say? Every day she watches a television program called "Big Blue Marble." It begins with a picture of the earth as it appears from the moon. It is bluish, a little battered-looking, but full of light, with whitish clouds swirling around it. Every time I see it I weep with love, as if it is a picture of Grandma's house. One day when I am putting Rebecca down for her nap, she suddenly focuses on my eye. Something inside me cringes, gets ready to try to protect myself. All children are cruel about physical differences, I know from experience, and that they don't always mean to be is another matter. I assume Rebecca will be the same.

But no-o-o-o. She studies my face intently as we stand, her inside and me outside her crib. She even holds my face maternally between her dimpled little hands. Then, looking every bit as serious and lawyerlike as her father, she says, as if it may just possibly have slipped my attention:

"Mommy, there's a *world* in your eye." (As in, "Don't be alarmed, or do anything crazy.") And then, gently, but with great interest: "Mommy, where did you *get* that world in your eye?"

For the most part, the pain left then. (So what, if my brothers grew up to buy even more powerful pellet guns for their sons and to carry real guns themselves. So what, if a young "Morehouse man"[1] once nearly fell off the steps of Trevor Arnett Library because he thought my eyes were blue.) Crying and laughing I ran to the bathroom, while Rebecca mumbled and sang herself off to sleep. Yes indeed, I realized, looking into the mirror. There *was* a world in my eye. And I saw that it was possible to love it: that in fact, for all it had taught me of shame and anger and inner vision, I *did* love it. Even to see it drifting out of orbit in boredom, or rolling up out of fatigue, not to mention floating back at attention in excitement (bearing witness, a friend has called it), deeply suitable to my personality, and even characteristic of me.

That night I dream I am dancing to Stevie Wonder's song "Always" (the name of the song is really "As," but I hear it as "Always"). As I dance, whirling and joyous, happier than I've ever been in my life, another bright-faced dancer joins me. We dance and kiss each other and hold each other through the night. The other dancer has obviously come through all right, as I have done. She is beautiful, whole and free. And she is also me.

QUESTIONS

1. Walker's essay moves forward in time through abrupt though steadily progressive descriptions of episodes. What effect on the reader does this structure produce? Why do you suppose Walker chose this form instead of providing transitions from one episode to the next?
2. Consider Walker's method of contrasting other people's memories with her own. What effect is created by the repetition of "You did not change"?
3. Consider Walker's choices of episodes or examples of beauty. How does each one work toward developing a definition of beauty?
4. In what ways does this essay play with the possible meanings of the familiar adage, "Beauty is in the eye of the beholder"?
5. One theme of this essay could be that of coming to terms with a disfigurement, an imagined loss of physical beauty. Recall an event (or accident) in your own life that changed your perception of yourself. Write a reflective narrative in which you use Walker's method of chronologically arranged episodes, including a reflection on the time before the

[1]*Morehouse man:* a student at Morehouse College, a traditionally black college for men in Atlanta. [Eds.]

change, as well as the change itself, and episodes from the time following. Like Walker, you may want to contrast (or compare) your memories with those of others.

6. Recall a memorable event that occurred a year or more ago. It might be an event in your family's life or a public event at which you and your friends were present. Write down your memories of the event, and then interview your family or friends and write down their recollections. Compare the various memories of the event. Come to some conclusion about the differences or similarities you find and perhaps about the selectivity of memory.

MAKING CONNECTIONS

Walker's daughter's exclamation, "Mommy, there's a *world* in your eye," is obviously a transcendent moment. It is also a metaphor. Other writers in this section could also be said to have a world in their eye. For example, Carl Sagan's description of how insight depends on a degree of restriction (p. 178) is closely related to Walker's theme. Select another essay from this section, and show how Walker's reflections on her blind eye can help us understand the discoveries the writer of the other essay is making.

MIRRORS

Lucy Grealy

Lucy Grealy (b. 1963), an award-winning poet, attended the Iowa Writer's Workshop and was a fellow at the Bunting Institute of Radcliffe. At the age of nine, Grealy had cancer of the jaw, and the whole right side of her jaw was removed. In the following essay, which first appeared in Harper's *and which received the National Magazine Award, Grealy writes about the thirty operations she had in twenty years to try to reconstruct her face. In both this selection and her book,* Autobiography of a Face *(1994), Grealy reflects on the overwhelming obsessions and perceptions of physical beauty that dominate our culture.*

There was a long period of time, almost a year, during which I never looked in a mirror. It wasn't easy; just as you only notice how often people eat on television when you yourself are on a diet, I'd never suspected just how omnipresent were our own images. I began as an amateur, avoiding merely mirrors, but by the end of the year I found myself with a professional knowledge of the reflected image, its numerous tricks and wiles, how it can spring up at any moment: a glass tabletop, a well-polished door handle, a darkened window, a pair of sunglasses, a restaurant's otherwise magnificent brass-plated coffee machine sitting innocently by the cash register.

I hadn't simply woken up one morning deciding not to look at myself as part of some personal experiment, as my friend Sally had attempted once before me: She'd lasted about three days before finally giving in to the need "to make sure I was still there." For Sally, not looking in the mirror meant enacting a conscious decision against a constant desire that, at the end of her three days, she still was at a loss to define as either solely habit or instinct. For me, however, the act of not looking was insidious. It was nihilistic, an insurgence too chaotic even to know if it was directed at the world or at myself.

At the time I was living alone in Scotland, surviving financially because of my eligibility for the dole, the vernacular for Britain's social security benefits. When I first arrived in Aberdeen I didn't know anyone, had no idea just how I was going to live, yet I went anyway because I'd met a plastic surgeon there who said he could help me. I had been living in London, working temp jobs. Before that I'd been in Berlin, and ostensibly had come to London only to earn money for a few weeks before returning to Germany. Exactly why I had this experience in London I don't know, but in my first week there I received more nasty comments about my face than I had in the past three years of living in Iowa, New York, and Germany. These comments, all from men and all odiously sexual, hurt and disoriented me so much I didn't think twice about a friendly suggestion to go see a plastic surgeon. I'd already had more than a dozen operations in the States, yet my insurance ran out and so did my hope that any real difference could be made. Here, however, was a surgeon who had some new techniques, and here was a government willing to foot the bill: I didn't feel I could pass up yet another chance to "fix" my face, which I confusedly thought concurrent with "fixing" my self, my soul, my life.

Sixteen years earlier, when I was nine and living in America, I came home from school one day with a toothache. Several weeks and misdiagnoses later surgeons removed most of the right side of my jaw as part of an attempt to prevent the cancer they found there from spreading. No one properly explained the operation to me and I awoke in a cocoon of pain that prevented me from moving or speaking. Tubes ran in and out of my body and because I couldn't ask, I made up my own explanations for their existence.

Up until this time I'd been having a great time in the hospital. For $\quad$ 5 starters it was in "The City," a place of traffic and noise and dangers and, best of all, elevators. Never having been in an elevator before, I thrilled not just at the ride itself, but also at the game of nonchalance played out in front of the other elevator-savvy children who stepped on and off without thought.

Second, I was free from school. In theory a school existed on the third floor for children well enough to attend, but my friend Derek and I quickly discovered that the volunteer who came each day after lunch to pick us up was a sucker for a few well-timed groans, and once we learned to play straight man for each other there was little trouble getting out of it. We made sure the nurses kept thinking we had gone off to school, leaving us free for a few brief hours to wander the mazelike halls of the ancient hospital. A favorite spot was the emergency waiting room; they had good magazines and sometimes you got to see someone covered in blood come through the door. Derek tried to convince me that a certain intersection in the subbasement was an ideal place to watch for bodies heading toward the morgue, but the one time we did actually see one get wheeled by beneath its clichéd white sheet, we silently allowed each other to save face by suddenly deciding it was so much more fun to steal get-well cards from the gift shop than hang out in a cold basement. Once we stole the cards we sent them out randomly to other kids on the ward, signing them "Love and Kisses, Michael Jackson." Our theory was to watch them open up what they would think was a card from a famous star, but no one ever actually fell for it; by then we were well pegged as troublemakers.

There was something else going on too, something I didn't know how to articulate. Adults treated me in a mysterious manner. They asked me to do things: lie still for X rays, not cry for needles, things that, although not easy, never seemed equal to the praise I received in return. Reinforced to me again and again was how I was "a brave girl" for not crying, "a good girl" for not complaining, and soon I began defining myself this way, equating strength with silence.

Then the chemotherapy began. In the early seventies chemo was even cruder than it is now, the basic premise of it to poison the patient right up until the very brink of their own death. Up until this point I almost never cried, almost always received some sort of praise and attention in return for this, got what I considered the better part of the deal. But now, now it was like a practical joke that had gotten out of hand. Chemotherapy was a nightmare and I wanted it to stop, I didn't want to be brave any more. Yet I had so grown used to defining myself as "brave," i.e., silent, that even more terrifying was the thought of losing this sense of myself, certain that if I broke down this would be seen as despicable in the eyes of both my parents and doctors.

Mostly the task of taking me into the city for the injections fell upon my mother, though sometimes my father had to take me. Overwhelmed by the sight of the vomiting and weeping, my father developed the routine of "going to get the car," meaning that he left the office before the actual injection on the premise that then he could have the car ready and waiting when it was all over. Ashamed of my suffering, I felt relief when he was finally out of the room. When my mother was with me she stayed in the room, yet this only made the distance even more tangible, an almost palpable distance built on the intensity of our desperate longing to be anywhere else, anywhere at all. She explained that it was wrong to cry before the needle went in; afterward was one thing, but before, that was mere fear, and hadn't I already demonstrated my bravery earlier? Every week, every Friday, or "d-day" as we called it, for two and a half years I climbed up onto that too-big doctor's table and told myself not to cry, and every week I failed. The injections were really two large syringes, filled with chemicals so caustic to the vein that each had to be administered only very slowly. The whole process took about four minutes; I had to remain very still throughout it. Dry retching began in the first fifteen seconds, then the throb behind my eyes gave everything a yellow-green aura, and the bone-deep pain of alternating extreme hot and cold flashes made me tremble, yet still I had to sit motionless and not move my arm. No one spoke to me, not the doctor who was a paradigm of the cold-fish physician, not the nurse who told my mother I reacted much more violently than many of the other children, and not my mother, who, surely overwhelmed by the sight of her child's suffering, thought the best thing to do was remind me to be brave, to try and not cry. All the while I hated myself for having wept before the needle went in, convinced that the nurse and my mother were right, that I was "overdoing it," that the throwing up was psychosomatic, that my mother was angry with me for not being good or brave enough. So involved with controlling my guilt and shame, the problem of physical pain seemed easy by comparison.

Yet each week, usually two or three days after the injection, there   10
came the first flicker of feeling better, the always forgotten and gratefully
rediscovered understanding that simply to be well in my body was the
greatest thing I could ask for. I thought other people felt this gratitude, this
appreciation and physical joy all the time, and I felt cheated because I only
was able to feel it once a week.

When you are only ten, which is when the chemotherapy began, two
and a half years seems like your whole life, yet it did finally end. I remember the last day of chemotherapy very clearly for two reasons: one, because
it was the only day on which I succeeded in not crying, and because later,
in private, I cried harder than I had in years; I thought now I would no
longer be "special," that without the arena of chemotherapy in which to
prove myself no one would ever love me, that I would fade unnoticed into
the background. This idea about not being different didn't last very long.
Before I thought people stared because I was bald. I wore a hat constantly,
but this fooled no one, least of all myself.

During this time my mother worked in a nursing home in a Hasidic
community. Hasidism dictates that married women cover their hair, and
most commonly this is done with a wig. My mother's friends were all too
willing to donate their discarded wigs, and soon the house filled with wigs.
I never wore one of them, they frightened me even when my mother insisted I looked better in one of the few that actually fit, yet we didn't know
how to say no to the women who kept graciously offering their wigs. The
cats enjoyed sleeping on them and the dogs playing with them, and we
grew used to having to pick a wig up off a chair we wanted to sit in. It
never struck us as odd until one day a visitor commented wryly as he
cleared a chair for himself, and suddenly a great wave of shame overcame
me. I had nightmares about wigs, felt a flush if I even heard the word, and
one night I put myself out of my misery by getting up after everyone was
asleep, gathering all the wigs except for one the dogs were fond of and
might miss, and which they had chewed anyway into something other than
a wig. I hid all the rest in an old chest where they weren't found for almost
a year.

But my hair eventually grew in, and it didn't take long before I understood that I looked different for other reasons. People stared at me in
stores, other children made fun of me to the point where I came to expect it
constantly, wherever I went. School became a battleground, and I came
home at the end of each day exhausted with the effort of keeping my body
so tense and hard that I was sure anything would bounce off of it.

I was living in an extreme situation, and because I did not particularly
care for the world I was in, I lived in others, and because the world I did
live in was a dangerous one, I incorporated this danger into my private life.
I saw movies about and envied Indians, imagined myself one. Walking
down the streets I walked down through the forest, my body ready for any
opportunity to fight or flee one of the big cats I knew stalked the area.
Vietnam and Cambodia were other places I walked through frequently,

daily even as I made my way down the school hall, knowing a landmine or a sniper might give themselves away at any moment with the subtle, soft metal clicks I'd read about in the books I took from the library. When faced with a landmine, a mere insult about my face seemed a frivolous thing.

In the early years, when I was still on the chemo, I lived in worse places than Cambodia. Because I knew it was somehow inappropriate, I read only in secret Primo Levi, Elie Wiesel,[1] every book by a survivor I could find by myself without resorting to asking the librarian for. Auschwitz, Birkenau: I felt the senseless blows of the Capos and somehow knew that because at any moment we might be called upon to live for a week on one loaf of bread and some water called soup, the peanut butter sandwich I found on my plate was nothing less than a miracle, an utter and sheer miracle capable of making me literally weep with joy.

I decided I wanted to become a "deep" person. I wasn't exactly sure what this would entail, but I believed that if I could just find the right philosophy, think the right thoughts, my suffering would end. To try to understand the world I was in, I undertook to find out what was "real," and quickly began seeing reality as existing in the lowest common denominator, that suffering was the one and only dependable thing. But rather than spend all of my time despairing, though certainly I did plenty of that, I developed a form of defensive egomania: I felt I was the only one walking about in the world who understood what was really important. I looked upon people complaining about the most mundane things—nothing on TV, traffic jams, the price of new clothes—and felt both joy because I knew how unimportant those things really were and unenlightened feelings of superiority because other people didn't. Because I lived a fantasy life in which I had to be thankful for each cold, blanketless night I survived on the cramped wooden bunks, chemotherapy—the nausea, pain, and deep despair it brought—was a breeze, a stroll through the country in comparison. I was often miserable, but I knew that to feel warm instead of cold was its own kind of joy, that to eat was a reenactment of the grace of some god whom I could only dimly define, and that simply to be alive was a rare, ephemeral miracle. It was like reliving The Fall a dozen times a day: I was given these moments of grace and insight, only to be invariably followed by a clumsy tumble into narcissism.

As I got older, as I became a teenager, I began to feel very isolated. My nonidentical twin sister started going out with boys, and I started, my most tragic mistake of all, to listen to and believe the taunts thrown at me daily by the very boys she and the other girls were interested in. I was a dog, a monster, the ugliest girl they had ever seen. Of all the remarks the most

15

---

[1]*Primo Levi, Elie Wiesel:* survivors of the Holocaust who have written about the Jewish experience in Nazi concentration camps. [Eds.]

damaging wasn't even directed at me, but was really an insult to Jerry, a boy I never saw because every day, between fourth and fifth periods when I was cornered by this particular group, I was too ashamed to lift my eyes off the floor. "Hey, look, it's Jerry's girlfriend," they yelled when they saw me, and I felt such shame, knowing that this was the deepest insult they could throw at Jerry.

I became interested in horses and got a job at a run-down local stable. Having those horses to go to each day after school saved my life; I spent all of my time either with them or thinking about them. To keep myself thinking objectively I became an obsessive reader and an obsessive television watcher, anything to keep me away from the subjective. I convinced myself I was smarter than everyone else, that only I knew what mattered, what was important, but by the time I was sixteen this wasn't true, not by a long shot. Completely and utterly repressed, I was convinced that I never wanted a boyfriend, not ever, and wasn't it convenient for me, a blessing I even thought, that none would ever want me. I told myself I was free to concentrate on the "true reality" of life, whatever that was. My sister and her friends put on blue eye shadow, blow-dried their hair, and went to spend interminable hours in the local mall, and I looked down on them for this, knew they were misleading themselves and being overoccupied with the "mere surface" of living. I had thought like this when I was younger, but now it was different, now my philosophy was haunted by desires so frightening I was unable to even admit they existed.

It wasn't until I was in college that I finally allowed that maybe, just maybe, it might be nice to have a boyfriend. As a person I had, as they say, blossomed in college. I went to a small, liberal, predominantly female school and suddenly, after years of alienation in high school, discovered that there were other people I could enjoy talking to, people who thought me intelligent and talented. I was, however, still operating on the assumption that no one, not ever, would be physically attracted to me, and in a curious way this shaped my personality. I became forthright and honest and secure in the way only the truly self-confident are, those who do not expect to be rejected, and those like me, who do not even dare to ask and so also expect no rejection. I had come to know myself as a person, but it would be graduate school before I was literally, physically able to use my name and the word woman in the same sentence.

Throughout all of this I was undergoing reconstructive surgery in an attempt to rebuild my jaw. It started when I was fifteen, several years after the chemo ended. I had known for years I would have operations to fix my face, and sometimes at night I fantasized about how good my life would finally be then. One day I got a clue that maybe it would not be so easy. At fourteen I went first to an older plastic surgeon who explained the process of pedestals to me, and told me it would take ten years to fix my face. Ten years? Why even bother? I thought. I'll be ancient by then. I went to the library and looked up the pedestals he talked about. There were gruesome pictures of people with grotesque tubes of their own skin growing out of their bodies, tubes of skin that were harvested like some kind of crop and then rearranged in ways with results that did not look at all normal or acceptable to my eye. But then I met a younger surgeon, a man who was working on a new way of grafting that did not involve pedestals, and I became more hopeful and once again began awaiting the fixing of my face, of the day when I would be whole, content, loved.

Long-term plastic surgery is not like the movies. There is no one single operation that will change everything, and there is certainly no slow unwrapping of the gauze in order to view the final product. There is always swelling, sometimes grotesque, there are often bruises, and always there are scars. After each operation, too scared to simply go look in the mirror, I developed an oblique method comprised of several stages. First, I tried to catch my reflection in an overhead lamp: The roundness of the metal distorted my image just enough to obscure details and give no true sense of size or proportion. Then I slowly worked my way up to looking at the reflection in someone's eyeglasses, and from there I went to walking as briskly as possible by a mirror, glancing only quickly. I repeated this as many times as it would take me, passing the mirror slightly more slowly each time until finally I was able to stand still and confront myself.

The theory behind most reconstructive surgery is to take large chunks of muscle, skin, and bone and slap them into the roughly appropriate place, then slowly begin to carve this mess into some sort of shape. It involves long, major operations, countless lesser ones, a lot of pain, and many, many years. And also, it does not always work. With my young surgeon in New York, who was becoming not so young with each passing year, I had two or three soft tissue grafts, two skin grafts, a bone graft, and some dozen other operations to "revise" my face, yet when I left graduate school at the age of twenty-five I was still more or less in the same position I had started in: a deep hole in the right side of my face and a rapidly shrinking left side and chin, a result of the radiation I'd had as a child and the stress placed upon it by the other operations. I was caught in a cycle of having a big operation, one that would force me to look monstrous from the swelling for many months, then have the subsequent revision operations that improved my looks tremendously, and then slowly, over the period of a few months or a year, watch the graft reabsorb back into my body, slowly shrink down and leave me with nothing but the scarred donor site the graft had originally come from.

I had little or no conception of how I appeared to other people. As a child, Halloween was my favorite holiday because I could put on a mask and walk among the blessed for a few brief, sweet hours. Such freedom I felt, walking down the street, my face hidden: Through the imperfect oval holes I could peer out at other faces, masked or painted or not, and see on those faces nothing but the normal faces of childhood looking back at me, faces I mistakenly thought were the faces everyone else but me saw all the time, faces that were simply curious and ready for fun, not the faces I usually braced myself for, the cruel, lonely, vicious ones I spent every day other than Halloween waiting to round each corner. As I breathed in the condensed, plastic air I somehow thought that I was breathing in normality, that this joy and weightlessness were what the world was comprised of, and it was only my face that kept me from it, my face that was my own mask, my own tangible barrier that kept me from knowing the true identity of the joy I was sure everyone but me lived with intimately. How could they not know it? Not know that to be free of the fear of taunts and the burden of knowing no one would ever love you was all anyone could ever ask for? I was a pauper walking for a short while in the clothes of the prince, and when the day ended, I gave up my disguise with dismay.

I also came to love winter, when I could wrap the lower half of my face up in a scarf: I could speak to people and they would have no idea of who and what they were really speaking to. I developed the bad habits of letting my long hair hang in my face, and of always covering my chin and mouth with my hand, hoping it might be seen as a thoughtful, accidental gesture. My one concession to this came in college, when I cut my hair short, very short, in an attempt to stop hiding behind it. It was also an attempt, though I didn't see it as such at the time, to desex myself. I had long, blond hair, and I also had a thin figure. Sometimes, from a distance, men would see the thin blonde and whistle, something I dreaded more than anything else because I knew as they got closer their tone would inevitably change, they would stare openly or, worse, turn away quickly, and by cutting my hair I felt I might possibly avoid this, clear up any misconception anyone, however briefly, might have about my being attractive.

Once in college my patient friends repeated for me endlessly that most of it was in my mind, that, granted, I did not look like everyone else, but that didn't mean I looked bad. I am sure now that they were right some of the time. But with the constant surgery I was in a perpetual state of transfiguration. I rarely looked the same for more than six months at a time. So ashamed of my face, I was unable to even admit that this constant change affected me at all; I let everyone who wanted to know that it was only what was inside that mattered, that I had "grown used to" the surgery, that none of it bothered me at all. Just as I had done in childhood, I pretended nothing was wrong, and this was constantly mistaken by others for bravery. I spent a great deal of time looking in the mirror in private, positioning my head to show off my eyes and nose, which were not just normal, but quite pretty, as my still-patient friends told me often. But I could not bring myself to see them for more than a glimmer: I looked in the mirror and saw not the normal upper half of my face, but only the disfigured lower half. People still teased me. Not daily, not like when I was younger, but in ways that caused me more pain than ever before. Children stared at me and I learned to cross the street to avoid them; this bothered me but not as much as the insults I got from men. They weren't thrown at me because I was disfigured, they were thrown at me because I was a disfigured woman.

They came from boys, sometimes men, and almost always a group of them. Only two or three times have I ever been teased by a single person, and I can think of only one time when I was ever teased by a woman. Had I been a man, would I have had to walk down the street while a group of young women followed and denigrated my sexual worth?

Not surprisingly, I viewed sex as my salvation. I was sure that if only I could get someone to sleep with me it would mean I wasn't ugly, that I was an attractive person, a lovable person. It would not be hard to guess where this line of reasoning led me, which was into the beds of a few manipulative men who liked themselves even less than they liked me, and I in turn left each short-term affair hating myself, obscenely sure that if only I had been prettier it would have worked, he would have loved me and it would have been like those other love affairs I was certain "normal" women had all the time. Gradually I became unable to say "I'm depressed," but could only say "I'm ugly," because the two had become inextricably linked in my mind. Into that universal lie, that sad equation of "if only" which we are all prey to, I was sure that if only I had a normal face, then I would be happy.

What our brains know is one thing, yet what our hearts know is another matter entirely, and when I met this new surgeon in Scotland, I offhandedly explained to my friends back home "why not, it's free, isn't it?" unable to admit that I believed in the fixability of life all over again.

Originally, it was planned I would have something called a tissue expander, followed by a bone graft. A tissue expander is a small balloon placed under the skin and then slowly blown up over the course of several months, the object being to stretch out the skin and create room and cover for the new bone. It is a bizarre, nightmarish thing to do to your face, yet I was hopeful about the end results and I was also able to spend the three months the expansion took in the hospital. I've always felt safe in hospitals: It's the one place I feel justified, sure of myself, free from the need to explain the way I look. For this reason the first tissue expander was bearable, just, and the bone graft that followed it was a success, it did not melt away like the previous ones.

However, the stress put upon my original remaining jaw from the   30
surgery instigated a period of deterioration of that bone, and it became apparent that I was going to need the same operation I'd just had on the right side done to the left. I remember my surgeon telling me this at an outpatient clinic. I planned to be traveling down to London that same night on an overnight train, and I barely made it to the station on time, I was in such a fumbling state of despair. I could not imagine doing it all over again, and just as I had done all my life, I was searching and searching through my intellect for a way to make it okay, make it bearable, for a way to do it. I lay awake all night on that train, feeling the tracks slip quickly and oddly erotic below me, when I remembered an afternoon from my three months in the hospital. Boredom was a big problem those long afternoons, the days punctuated and landmarked by meals and television programs. Waiting for the afternoon tea to come, wondering desperately how I could make time pass, it suddenly occurred to me I didn't have to make

time pass, that it would do it of its own accord, that I simply had to relax and take no action. Lying on the train, remembering that, I realized I had no obligation to make my situation okay, that I didn't have to explain it, understand it, that I could invoke the idea of negative capability and just simply let it happen. By the time the train pulled into King's Cross Station, I felt able to bear it yet again, not entirely sure what other choice I had.

But there was an element I didn't yet know about. I returned to Scotland to set up a date to go in and have the tissue expander put in, and was told quite casually that I'd only be in the hospital three or four days. Wasn't I going to spend the whole expansion time in the hospital? I asked almost in a whisper. What's the point of that? You can just come in every day to the outpatient to have it expanded. Horrified by this, I was speechless. I would have to live and move about in the outside world with a giant balloon in my face? I can't remember what I did for the next few days before I went into the hospital, but I vaguely remember that these days involved a great deal of drinking alone in bars and at home.

I went in and had the operation and, just as they said, went home at the end of the week. The only thing I can truly say gave me any comfort during the months I lived with my tissue expander was my writing and Kafka. I started a novel and completely absorbed myself in it, writing for hours and hours every day. It was the only way I could walk down the street, to stand the stares I received, to think to myself "I'll bet none of them are writing a novel." It was that strange, old familiar form of egomania, directly related to my dismissive, conceited thoughts of adolescence. As for Kafka, who had always been one of my favorite writers even before the new fashion for him, he helped me in that I felt permission to feel alienated, and to have that alienation be okay, to make it bearable, noble even. In the way living in Cambodia helped me as a child, I walked the streets of my dark little Scottish city by the sea and knew without doubt that I was living in a story Kafka would have been proud to write.

This time period, however, was also the time I stopped looking in the mirror. I simply didn't want to know. Many times before in my life I have been repelled by the mirror, but the repulsion always took the form of a strange, obsessive attraction. Previously I spent many hours looking in the mirror, trying to see what it was that other people were seeing, a purpose I understand now was laughable, as I went to the mirror with an already clearly fixed, negative idea of what people saw. Once I even remember thinking how awful I looked in a mirror I was quickly passing in a shopping center, seeing perfectly all the flaws I knew were there, when I realized with a shock that I wasn't looking in a mirror, that I was looking through into a store at someone who had the same coat and haircut as me, someone who, when I looked closer, looked perfectly fine.

The one good thing about a tissue expander is that you look so bad with it in that no matter what you look like once it's finally removed, it has to be better. I had my bone graft and my fifth soft tissue graft and yes, even I had to admit I looked better. But I didn't look like me. Something was wrong: Was this the face I had waited through twenty years and almost thirty operations for? I somehow just couldn't make what I saw in the mirror correspond to the person I thought It was. It wasn't just that I felt ugly, I simply could not associate the image as belonging to me. My own image was the image of a stranger, and rather than try to understand this, I simply ignored it. I reverted quickly back to my tissue expander mode of not looking in the mirror, and quickly improved it to include not looking at any image of myself. I perfected the technique of brushing my teeth without a mirror, grew my hair in such a way that it would require only a quick simple brush, and wore clothes that were simply and easily put on, no complex layers or lines that might require even the most minor of visual adjustments.

On one level I understood that the image of my face was merely that,   35 an image, a surface that was not directly related to any true, deep definition of the self. But I also knew that it is only through image that we experience and make decisions about the everyday world, and I was not always able to gather the strength to prefer the deeper world over the shallower one. I looked for ways to relate the two, to find a bridge that would allow me access to both, anything no matter how tenuous, rather than ride out the constant swings between peace and anguish. The only direction I had to go in to achieve this was simply to strive for a state of awareness and self-honesty that sometimes, to this day, rewards me and sometimes exhausts me.

Our whole lives are dominated, though it is not always so clearly translatable, with the question "How do I look?" Take all the many nouns in our lives: car; house; job; family; love; friends; and substitute the personal pronoun — it is not that we are all so self-obsessed, it is that all things eventually relate back to ourselves, and it is our own sense of how we appear to the world by which we chart our lives, how we navigate our personalities that would otherwise be adrift in the ocean of other peoples' obsessions.

One particular afternoon I remember very lucidly, an afternoon, toward the end of my yearlong separation from the mirror. I was talking to someone, an attractive man as it happened, and we were having a wonderful, engaging conversation. For some reason it flickered across my mind to wonder what I looked like to him. What was he seeing when he saw me? So many times I've asked this of myself, and always the answer was a bad one, an ugly one. A warm, smart woman, yes, but still, an unattractive one. I sat there in the café and asked myself this old question and, startlingly, for the first time in my life I had no answer readily prepared. I had literally not looked in a mirror for so long that I quite simply had no clue as to what I looked like. I looked at the man as he spoke; my entire life I had been giving my negative image to people, handing it to them and watching the negative way it was reflected back to me. But now, because I had no idea what I was giving him, the only thing I had to judge by was what he was giving me, which, as reluctant as I was to admit it, was positive.

That afternoon in that café I had a moment of the freedom I had been practicing for behind my Halloween mask as a child. But where as a child I expected it to come as a result of gaining something, a new face, it came to me then as the result of shedding something, of shedding my image. I once thought that truth was an eternal, that once you understood something it was with you forever. I know now that this isn't so, that most truths are inherently unretainable, that we have to work hard all our lives to remember the most basic things. Society is no help; the images it gives us again and again want us only to believe that we can most be ourselves by looking like someone else, leaving our own faces behind to turn into ghosts that will inevitably resent us and haunt us. It is no mistake that in movies and literature the dead sometimes know they are dead only after they can no longer see themselves in the mirror. As I sat there feeling the warmth of the cup against my palm this small observation seemed like a great revelation to me, and I wanted to tell the man I was with about it, but he was involved in his own topic and I did not want to interrupt him, so instead I looked with curiosity over to the window behind him, its night-darkened glass reflecting the whole café, to see if I could recognize myself.

QUESTIONS

1. What did Grealy learn about herself from her yearlong separation from the mirror?
2. Why did Grealy think that "fixing" her face would "fix" herself, her soul, her life? What is the significance of the word *fix*?
3. One of the features of this essay that makes it so compelling is Grealy's command of details. Locate details that you believe are effective, and think about their function. Try to rewrite some of Grealy's sentences to remove the details. What is lost? How do details link the author and the reader?
4. Grealy tells us, "Most truths are inherently unretainable," and "we have to work hard all our lives to remember the most basic things" (paragraph 38). What truths does Grealy refer to?
5. How does Grealy use her personal experience as evidence so that her essay becomes a larger story with greater relevance to others?
6. Grealy writes about the freedom she feels as a result of accepting the truth about her face. Such freedom, as Grealy shows, is never easily achieved. Reflect on a struggle or conflict in your own life, and write a brief essay on the "truths" that have emerged from your struggle.

MAKING CONNECTIONS

1. Both Alice Walker (p. 42) and Lucy Grealy struggle to accept their bodies and their appearance. In what ways are their struggles similar? In what ways are they different? What does this struggle achieve for each writer?
2. Do you agree with the observation that Alice Walker loses sight in order to gain sight, and Lucy Grealy loses face in order to gain face?

IN THE KITCHEN

Henry Louis Gates Jr.

Born in 1950 in the small town of Keyser, West Virginia, Henry Louis Gates Jr. is a graduate of Yale and of Cambridge University in England. A widely praised literary and social critic, he has published such influential works as The Signifying Monkey: A Theory of Afro-American Literary Criticism *(1988)*, Loose Canons: Notes on the Culture Wars *(1992), and* Thirteen Ways of Looking at a Black Man *(1997). He has also written movingly about his own childhood in* Colored People: A Memoir *(1994), and he is a regular contributor to several popular periodicals. Named one of* Time *magazine's twenty-five most influential Americans in 1997, Gates is currently W. E. B. Du Bois Professor of the Humanities and Chair of Afro-American Studies at Harvard. An advocate of building bridges among all communities, he has written that "cultural tolerance comes to nothing without cultural understanding." The following personal essay was published in* The New Yorker *in 1994.*

We always had a gas stove in the kitchen, in our house in Piedmont, West Virginia, where I grew up. Never electric, though using electric became fashionable in Piedmont in the sixties, like using Crest toothpaste rather than Colgate, or watching Huntley and Brinkley rather than Walter Cronkite.[1] But not us: gas, Colgate, and good ole Walter Cronkite, come what may. We used gas partly out of loyalty to Big Mom, Mama's Mama, because she was mostly blind and still loved to cook, and could feel her way more easily with gas than with electric. But the most important thing about our gas-equipped kitchen was that Mama used to do hair there. The "hot comb" was a fine-toothed iron instrument with a long wooden handle and a pair of iron curlers that opened and closed like scissors. Mama would put it in the gas fire until it glowed. You could smell those prongs heating up.

I liked that smell. Not the smell so much, I guess, as what the smell meant for the shape of my day. There was an intimate warmth in the women's tones as they talked with my Mama, doing their hair. I knew what the women had been through to get their hair ready to be "done,"

---

[1]*Chet Huntley, David Brinkley, Walter Cronkite:* newscasters of the 1960s. Huntley and Brinkley were on NBC. Cronkite was on CBS. [Eds.]

because I would watch mama do it to herself. How that kink could be transformed through grease and fire into that magnificent head of wavy hair was a miracle to me, and still is.

Mama would wash her hair over the sink, a towel wrapped around her shoulders, wearing just her slip and her white bra. (We had no shower—just a galvanized tub that we stored in the kitchen—until we moved down Rat Tail Road into Doc Wolverton's house, in 1954.) After she dried it, she would grease her scalp thoroughly with blue Bergamot hair grease, which came in a short, fat jar with a picture of a beautiful colored lady on it. It's important to grease your scalp real good, my Mama would explain, to keep from burning yourself. Of course, her hair would return to its natural kink almost as soon as the hot water and shampoo hit it. To me, it was another miracle how hair so "straight" would so quickly become kinky again the second it even approached some water.

My Mama had only a few "clients" whose heads she "did"—did, I think, because she enjoyed it, rather than for the few pennies it brought in. They would sit on one of our red plastic kitchen chairs, the kind with the shiny metal legs, and brace themselves for the process. Mama would stroke that red-hot iron—which by this time had been in the gas fire for half an hour or more—slowly but firmly through their hair, from scalp to strand's end. It made a scorching, crinkly sound, the hot iron did, as it burned its way through kink, leaving in its wake straight strands of hair, standing long and tall but drooping over at the ends, their shape like the top of a heavy willow tree. Slowly, steadily, Mama's hands would transform a round mound of Odetta[2] kink into a darkened swamp of everglades. The Bergamot made the hair shiny; the heat of the hot iron gave it a brownish-red cast. Once all the hair was as straight as God allows kink to get, Mama would take the well-heated curling iron and twirl the straightened strands into more or less loosely wrapped curls. She claimed that she owed her skill as a hairdresser to the strength in her wrists, and as she worked her little finger would poke out, the way it did when she sipped tea. Mama was a southpaw,[3] and wrote upside down and backward to produce the cleanest, roundest letters you've ever seen.

The "kitchen" she would all but remove from sight with a handheld pair of shears, bought just for this purpose. Now, the kitchen was the room in which we were sitting—the room where Mama did hair and washed clothes, and where we all took a bath in that galvanized tub. But the word has another meaning, and the kitchen that I'm speaking of is the very kinky bit of hair at the back of your head, where your neck meets your shirt collar. If there was ever a part of our African past that resisted assimilation, it was the kitchen. No matter how hot the iron, no matter

---

[2]*Odetta* (b. 1930): singer of blues and spirituals in the 1950s and a leading figure in the American folk revival of the 1960s; she wore a large Afro hairdo. [Eds.]

[3]*southpaw*: a left-handed person. [Eds.]

how powerful the chemical, no matter how stringent the mashed-potatoes-and-lye formula of a man's "process," neither God nor woman nor Sammy Davis, Jr.,[4] could straighten the kitchen. The kitchen was permanent, irredeemable, irresistible kink. Unassimilably African. No matter what you did, no matter how hard you tried, you couldn't de-kink a person's kitchen. So you trimmed it off as best you could.

When hair had begun to "turn," as they'd say—to return to its natural kinky glory—it was the kitchen that turned first (the kitchen around the back, and nappy edges at the temples). When the kitchen started creeping up the back of the neck, it was time to get your hair done again.

Sometimes, after dark, a man would come to have his hair done. It was Mr. Charlie Carroll. He was very light-complected and had a ruddy nose—it made me think of Edmund Gwenn, who played Kris Kringle in "Miracle on 34th Street." At first, Mama did him after my brother, Rocky, and I had gone to sleep. It was only later that we found out that he had come to our house so Mama could iron his hair—not with a hot comb or a curling iron but with our very own Proctor-Silex steam iron. For some reason I never understood, Mr. Charlie would conceal his Frederick Douglass-like mane[5] under a big white Stetson hat. I never saw him take it off except when he came to our house, at night, to have his pair pressed. (Later, Daddy would tell us about Mr. Charlie's most prized piece of knowledge, something that the man would only confide after his hair had been pressed, as a token of intimacy. "Not many people know this," he'd say, in a tone of circumspection, "but George Washington was Abraham Lincoln's daddy." Nodding solemnly, he'd add the clincher: "A white man told me." Though he was in dead earnest, this became a humorous refrain around our house—"a white man told me"—which we used to punctuate especially preposterous assertions.)

My mother examined my daughters' kitchens whenever we went home to visit, in the early eighties. It became a game between us. I had told her not to do it, because I didn't like the politics it suggested—the notion of "good" and "bad" hair. "Good" hair was "straight," "bad" hair kinky. Even in the late sixties, at the height of Black Power, almost nobody could bring themselves to say "bad" for good and "good" for bad. People still said that hair like white people's hair was "good," even if they encapsulated it in a disclaimer, like "what we used to call 'good.'"

Maggie would be seated in her high chair, throwing food this way and that, and Mama would be cooing about how cute it all was, how I used to

---

[4]*Sammy Davis Jr.* (1925–1990): African American singer, dancer, and entertainer with notably "processed" hair. [Eds.]

[5]*Frederick Douglass* (ca. 1817–1895): an escaped slave turned abolitionist who, in nineteenth-century photographs, is shown with a lionlike mane of hair. [Eds.]

do just like Maggie was doing, and wondering whether her flinging her food with her left hand meant that she was going to be left-handed like Mama. When my daughter was just about covered with Chef Boyardee Spaghetti-O's, Mama would seize the opportunity: wiping her clean, she would tilt Maggie's head to one side and reach down the back of her neck. Sometimes Mama would even rub a curl between her fingers, just to make sure that her bifocals had not deceived her. Then she'd sigh with satisfaction and relief: No kink . . . yet. Mama! I'd shout, pretending to be angry. Every once in a while, if no one was looking, I'd peek, too.

I say "yet" because most black babies are born with soft, silken hair.   10 But after a few months it begins to turn, as inevitably as do the seasons or the leaves on a tree. People once thought baby oil would stop it. They were wrong.

Everybody I knew as a child wanted to have good hair. You could be as ugly as homemade sin dipped in misery and still be thought attractive if you had good hair. "Jesus moss," the girls at Camp Lee, Virginia, had called Daddy's naturally "good" hair during the war. I know that he played that thick head of hair for all it was worth, too.

My own hair was "not a bad grade," as barbers would tell me when they cut it for the first time. It was like a doctor reporting the results of the first full physical he has given you. Like "You're in good shape" or "Blood pressure's kind of high — better cut down on salt."

I spent most of my childhood and adolescence messing with my hair. I definitely wanted straight hair. Like Pop's. When I was about three, I tried to stick a wad of Bazooka bubble gum to that straight hair of his. I suppose what fixed that memory for me is the spanking I got for doing so: he turned me upside down, holding me by my feet, the better to paddle my behind. Little *nigger,* he had shouted, walloping away. I started to laugh about it two days later, when my behind stopped hurting.

When black people say "straight," of course, they don't usually mean literally straight — they're not describing hair like, say, Peggy Lipton's (she was the white girl on "The Mod Squad"), or like Mary's of Peter, Paul & Mary[6] fame; black people call that "stringy" hair. No, "straight" just means not kinky, no matter what contours the curl may take. I would have done *anything* to have straight hair — and I used to try everything, short of getting a process.[7]

Of the wide variety of techniques and methods I came to master in the   15 challenging prestidigitation of the follicle, almost all had two things in common: a heavy grease and the application of pressure. It's not an accident that some of the biggest black-owned companies in the fifties and six-

---

[6]*Peter, Paul & Mary:* folksinging group famous in the 1960s; one of the members, Mary Travers, was known for her long, straight blonde hair. [Eds.]

[7]*Process:* Hair-straightening treatment that used chemicals for smoothing out kinks. [Eds.]

ties made hair products. And I tried them all, in search of that certain silken touch, the one that would leave neither the hand nor the pillow sullied by grease.

I always wondered what Frederick Douglass put on *his* hair, or what Phillis Wheatley[8] put on hers. Or why Wheatley has that rag on her head in the little engraving in the frontispiece of her book. One thing is for sure: you can bet that when Phillis Wheatley went to England and saw the Countess of Huntingdon she did not stop by the Queen's coiffeur on her way there. So many black people still get their hair straightened that it's a wonder we don't have a national holiday for Madame C. J. Walker, the woman who invented the process of straightening kinky hair. Call it Jheri-Kurled or call it "relaxed," it's still fried hair.

I used all the greases, from sea-blue Bergamot and creamy vanilla Duke (in its clear jar with the orange-white-and-green label) to the godfather of grease, the formidable Murray's. Now, Murray's was some *serious* grease. Whereas Bergamot was like oily jello, and Duke was viscous and sickly sweet, Murray's was light brown and *hard*. Hard as lard and twice as greasy, Daddy used to say. Murray's came in an orange can with a press-on top. It was so hard that some people would put a match to the can, just to soften the stuff and make it more manageable. Then, in the late sixties, when Afros came into style, I used Afro Sheen. From Murray's to Duke to Afro Sheen: that was my progression in black consciousness.

We used to put hot towels or washrags over our Murray-coated heads, in order to melt the wax into the scalp and the follicles. Unfortunately, the wax also had the habit of running down your neck, ears, and forehead. Not to mention your pillowcase. Another problem was that if you put two palmfuls of Murray's on your head your hair turned white. (Duke did the same thing.) The challenge was to get rid of that white color. Because if you got rid of the white stuff you had a magnificent head of wavy hair. That was the beauty of it: Murray's was so hard that it froze your hair into the wavy style you brushed it into. It looked really good if you wore a part. A lot of guys had parts *cut* into their hair by a barber, either with the clippers or with a straight-edge razor. Especially if you had kinky hair—then you'd generally wear a short razor cut, or what we called a Quo Vadis.

We tried to be as innovative as possible. Everyone knew about using a stocking cap, because your father or your uncle wore one whenever something really big was about to happen, whether sacred or secular: a funeral or a dance, a wedding or a trip in which you confronted official white people. Any time you were trying to look really sharp, you wore a stocking cap in preparation. And if the event was really a big one, you made a new cap. You asked your mother for a pair of her hose, and cut it with scissors about six inches or so from the open end—the end with the elastic that

---

[8]*Phillis Wheatley* (1753–1783): African American poet and slave and America's first published black writer. She was taken to England to meet royalty. [Eds.]

goes up to the top of the thigh. Then you knotted the cut end, and it became a beehive-shaped hat, with an elastic band that you pulled down low
on your forehead and down around your neck in the back. To work well,
the cap had to fit tightly and snugly, like a press. And it had to fit that
tightly because it *was* a press: it pressed your hair with the force of the
hose's elastic. If you greased your hair down real good, and left the stocking cap on long enough, voilà: you got a head of pressed-against-the-scalp
waves. (You also got a ring around your forehead when you woke up, but
it went away.) And then you could enjoy your concrete do. Swore we were
bad, too, with all that grease and those flat heads. My brother and I would
brush it out a bit in the mornings, so that it looked—well, "natural."
Grown men still wear stocking caps—especially older men, who generally
keep their stocking caps in their top drawers, along with their cufflinks and
their see-through silk socks, their "Maverick" ties,[9] their silk handkerchiefs, and whatever else they prize the most.

A Murrayed-down stocking cap was the respectable version of the
process, which, by contrast, was most definitely not a cool thing to have unless you were an entertainer by trade. Zeke and Keith and Poochie and a few
other stars of the high-school basketball team all used to get a process once
or twice a year. It was expensive, and you had to go somewhere like Pittsburgh or D.C. or Uniontown—somewhere where there were enough colored
people to support a trade. The guys would disappear, then reappear a day or
two later, strutting like peacocks, their hair burned slightly red from the lye
base. They'd also wear "rags"—cloths or handkerchiefs—around their
heads when they slept or played basketball. Do-rags, they were called. But the
result was straight hair, with just a hint of wave. No curl. Do-it-yourselfers
took their chances at home with a concoction of mashed potatoes and lye.

The most famous process of all, however, outside of the process Malcolm
X[10] describes in his "Autobiography," and maybe the process of Sammy
Davis, Jr., was Nat King Cole's[11] process. Nat King Cole had patent-leather
hair. That man's got the finest process money can buy, or so Daddy said the
night we saw Cole's TV show on NBC. It was November 5, 1956. I remember
the date because everyone came to our house to watch it and to celebrate one
of Daddy's buddies' birthdays. Yeah, Uncle Joe chimed in, they can do shit to
his hair that the average Negro can't even *think* about—secret shit.

Nat King Cole was *clean*. I've had an ongoing argument with a Niger-
ian friend about Nat King Cole for twenty years now. Not about whether
he could sing—any fool knows that he could—but about whether or not
he was a handkerchief head for wearing that patent-leather process.

---

[9]*"Maverick" ties*: western string ties, as worn on the popular 1960s TV series
Maverick. [Eds.]
[10]*Malcolm X* (1925–1965): African American religious and political leader,
who promoted black nationalism. [Eds.]
[11]*Nat King Cole* (1919–1965): singer and jazz pianist. [Eds.]

Sammy Davis, Jr.'s process was the one I detested. It didn't look good on him. Worse still, he liked to have a fried strand dangling down the middle of his forehead, so he could shake it out from the crown when he sang. But Nat King Cole's hair was a thing unto itself, a beautifully sculpted work of art that he and he alone had the right to wear. The only difference between a process and a stocking cap, really, was taste; but Nat King Cole, unlike, say, Michael Jackson, looked *good* in his. His head looked like Valentino's[12] head in the twenties, and some say it was Valentino the process was imitating. But Nat King Cole wore a process because it suited his face, his demeanor, his name, his style. He was as clean as he wanted to be.

I had forgotten all about that patent-leather look until one day in 1971, when I was sitting in an Arab restaurant on the island of Zanzibar surrounded by men in fezzes and white caftans, trying to learn how to eat curried goat and rice with the fingers of my right hand and feeling two million miles from home. All of a sudden, an old transistor radio sitting on top of a china cupboard stopped blaring out its Swahili music and started playing "Fly Me to the Moon," by Nat King Cole. The restaurant's din was not affected at all, but in my mind's eye I saw it: the King's magnificent sleek black tiara. I managed, barely, to blink back the tears.

QUESTIONS

1. Though this piece is entitled "In the Kitchen," it might also be called "The Process," or "Straight Hair." Which of these titles do you consider to be the most accurate? the most suggestive? the most appropriate? And why?
2. Gates begins this essay in his mother's kitchen in Piedmont, West Virginia, but he ends it "in an Arab restaurant on the island of Zanzibar" — a far cry from home, to say the least. Outline the essay to see if you can discover how his recollections and reflections lead from one place to the other and why he chooses to end his piece so far from where it begins.
3. Gates remembers several hair-straightening methods in the course of this essay. What do these methods have in common? What sets each one apart from the others? Why do you think that Gates is so nostalgic about "the process" that the memory of Nat King Cole's "patent-leather look" almost brought tears to his eyes?
4. How have black hair styles changed since the era that Gates is writing about in his piece? What do those changes suggest about changes in black culture itself?
5. At several points in this essay, Gates talks about the specialized meaning in black culture of some otherwise familiar words and phrases.

---

[12]*Rudolf Valentino* (1895–1926): film star, known among other things for his slicked-back hair. [Eds.]

Note each of these specialized expressions and the various meanings that he explains. Think of some familiar words and phrases that you use in specialized and unusual ways. Given so many specialized vocabularies within a single language, what do you think prevents it from becoming a tower of babble?

6. Think of a room where something special regularly took place in your own home when you were growing up—something that embodies a distinctive aspect of your family and/or your cultural affiliation. Then write an essay in which you remember that room, its special significance, and other associated memories that come to mind.

MAKING CONNECTIONS

Gates, Lucy Grealy (p. 50), and Alice Walker (p. 42) all bear witness to a concern with physical appearance and the extent to which it can become an intense, even dominating, personal preoccupation. Given this common theme, what are the most distinctive aspects of Gates's approach to the subject? of Grealy's? of Walker's?

LEARNING TO READ AND WRITE

Frederick Douglass

Frederick Augustus Washington Bailey (1817–1895) was born into slavery on the Eastern Shore of Maryland. His mother was a black slave; his father, a white man. After his escape from the South in 1838, he adopted the name of Douglass and worked to free other slaves and later (after the Civil War) to protect the rights of freed slaves. He was a newspaper editor, a lecturer, United States minister to Haiti, and the author of several books about his life and times. The Narrative of the Life of Frederick Douglass: An American Slave *(1841), from which the following selection has been taken, is his best-known work.*

I lived in Master Hugh's family about seven years. During this time, I succeeded in learning to read and write. In accomplishing this, I was compelled to resort to various stratagems. I had no regular teacher. My mistress, who had kindly commenced to instruct me, had, in compliance with the advice and direction of her husband, not only ceased to instruct, but had set her face against my being instructed by any one else. It is due, however, to my mistress to say of her, that she did not adopt this course of treatment immediately. She at first lacked the depravity indispensable to shutting me up in mental darkness. It was at least necessary for her to have some training in the exercise of irresponsible power, to make her equal to the task of treating me as though I were a brute.

My mistress was, as I have said, a kind and tender-hearted woman; and in the simplicity of her soul she commenced, when I first went to live with her, to treat me as she supposed one human being ought to treat another. In entering upon the duties of a slaveholder, she did not seem to perceive that I sustained to her the relation of a mere chattel, and that for her to treat me as a human being was not only wrong, but dangerously so. Slavery proved as injurious to her as it did to me. When I went there, she was a pious, warm, and tender-hearted woman. There was no sorrow or suffering for which she had not a tear. She had bread for the hungry, clothes for the naked, and comfort for every mourner that came within her reach. Slavery soon proved its ability to divest her of these heavenly qualities. Under its influence, the tender heart became stone, and the lamblike disposition gave way to one of tiger-like fierceness. The first step in her downward course was in her ceasing to instruct me. She now commenced to practise her husband's precepts. She finally became even more violent in her opposition than her husband himself. She was not satisfied with simply doing as well as he had commanded; she seemed anxious to do better.

Nothing seemed to make her more angry than to see me with a newspaper. She seemed to think that here lay the danger. I have had her rush at me with a face made all up of fury, and snatch from me a newspaper, in a manner that fully revealed her apprehension. She was an apt woman; and a little experience soon demonstrated, to her satisfaction, that education and slavery were incompatible with each other.

From this time I was most narrowly watched. If I was in a separate room any considerable length of time, I was sure to be suspected of having a book, and was at once called to give an account of myself. All this, however, was too late. The first step had been taken. Mistress, in teaching me the alphabet, had given me the *inch,* and no precaution could prevent me from taking the *ell.*[1]

The plan which I adopted, and the one by which I was most successful, was that of making friends of all the little white boys whom I met in the street. As many of these as I could, I converted into teachers. With their kindly aid, obtained at different times and in different places, I finally succeeded in learning to read. When I was sent on errands, I always took my book with me, and by doing one part of my errand quickly, I found time to get a lesson before my return. I used also to carry bread with me, enough of which was always in the house, and to which I was always welcome; for I was much better off in this regard than many of the poor white children in our neighborhood. This bread I used to bestow upon the hungry little urchins, who, in return, would give me that more valuable bread of knowledge. I am strongly tempted to give the names of two or three of those little boys, as a testimonial of the gratitude and affection I bear them; but prudence forbids;—not that it would injure me, but it might embarrass them; for it is almost an unpardonable offence to teach slaves to read in this Christian country. It is enough to say of the dear little fellows, that they lived on Philpot Street, very near Durgin and Bailey's ship-yard. I used to talk this matter of slavery over with them. I would sometimes say to them, I wished I could be as free as they would be when they got to be men. "You will be free as soon as you are twenty-one, *but I am a slave for life!* Have not I as good a right to be free as you have?" These words used to trouble them; they would express for me the liveliest sympathy, and console me with the hope that something would occur by which I might be free.

I was now about twelve years old, and the thought of being *a slave for*   5 *life* began to bear heavily upon my heart. Just about this time, I got hold of a book entitled "The Columbian Orator."[2] Every opportunity I got, I used to read this book. Among much of other interesting matter, I found in it a dialogue between a master and his slave. The slave was represented as hav-

---

[1]*ell:* a unit of measurement, no longer used, equal to 45 inches. [Eds.]

[2]*The Columbian Orator:* a popular schoolbook designed to introduce students to argument and rhetoric. [Eds.]

ing run away from his master three times. The dialogue represented the conversation which took place between them, when the slave was retaken the third time. In this dialogue, the whole argument in behalf of slavery was brought forward by the master, all of which was disposed of by the slave. The slave was made to say some very smart as well as impressive things in reply to his master—things which had the desired though unexpected effect; for the conversation resulted in the voluntary emancipation of the slave on the part of the master.

In the same book, I met with one of Sheridan's mighty speeches on and in behalf of Catholic emancipation.[3] These were choice documents to me. I read them over and over again with unabated interest. They gave tongue to interesting thoughts of my own soul, which had frequently flashed through my mind, and died away for want of utterance. The moral which I gained from the dialogue was the power of truth over the conscience of even a slaveholder. What I got from Sheridan was a bold denunciation of slavery, and a powerful vindication of human rights. The reading of these documents enabled me to utter my thoughts, and to meet the arguments brought forward to sustain slavery; but while they relieved me of one difficulty, they brought on another even more painful than the one of which I was relieved. The more I read, the more I was led to abhor and detest my enslavers. I could regard them in no other light than a band of successful robbers, who had left their homes, and gone to Africa, and stolen us from our homes, and in a strange land reduced us to slavery. I loathed them as being the meanest as well as the most wicked of men. As I read and contemplated the subject, behold! that very discontentment which Master Hugh had predicted would follow my learning to read had already come, to torment and sting my soul to unutterable anguish. As I writhed under it, I would at times feel that learning to read had been a curse rather than a blessing. It had given me a view of my wretched condition, without the remedy. It opened my eyes to the horrible pit, but to no ladder upon which to get out. In moments of agony, I envied my fellow-slaves for their stupidity. I have often wished myself a beast. I preferred the condition of the meanest reptile to my own. Any thing, no matter what, to get rid of thinking! It was this everlasting thinking of my condition that tormented me. There was no getting rid of it. It was pressed upon me by every object within sight or hearing, animate or inanimate. The silver trump of freedom had roused my soul to eternal wakefulness. Freedom now appeared, to disappear no more forever. It was heard in every sound, and seen in every thing. It was ever present to torment me with a sense of my wretched condition. I saw nothing without seeing it, I heard nothing without hearing it, and felt nothing without feeling it. It looked from every star, it smiled in every calm, breathed in every wind, and moved in every storm.

---

[3]*Richard Brinsley Sheridan* (1751–1816): British dramatist, orator, and politician. Catholics were not allowed to vote in England until 1829. [Eds.]

I often found myself regretting my own existence, and wishing myself dead; and but for the hope of being free, I have no doubt but that I should have killed myself, or done something for which I should have been killed. While in this state of mind, I was eager to hear any one speak of slavery. I was a ready listener. Every little while, I could hear something about the abolitionists. It was some time before I found what the word meant. It was always used in such connections as to make it an interesting word to me. If a slave ran away and succeeded in getting clear, or if a slave killed his master, set fire to a barn, or did any thing very wrong in the mind of a slaveholder, it was spoken of as the fruit of *abolition.* Hearing the word in this connection very often, I set about learning what it meant. The dictionary afforded me little or no help. I found it was "the act of abolishing"; but then I did not know what was to be abolished. Here I was perplexed. I did not dare to ask any one about its meaning, for I was satisfied that it was something they wanted me to know very little about. After a patient waiting, I got one of our city papers, containing an account of the number of petitions from the north, praying for the abolition of slavery in the District of Columbia, and of the slave trade between the States. From this time I understood the words *abolition* and *abolitionist,* and always drew near when that word was spoken, expecting to hear something of importance to myself and fellow-slaves. The light broke in upon me by degrees. I went one day down on the wharf of Mr. Waters; and seeing two Irishmen unloading a scow of stone, I went, unasked, and helped them. When we had finished, one of them came to me and asked me if I were a slave. I told him I was. He asked, "Are ye a slave for life?" I told him that I was. The good Irishman seemed to be deeply affected by the statement. He said to the other that it was a pity so fine a little fellow as myself should be a slave for life. He said it was a shame to hold me. They both advised me to run away to the north; that I should find friends there, and that I should be free. I pretended not to be interested in what they said, and treated them as if I did not understand them; for I feared they might be treacherous. White men have been known to encourage slaves to escape, and then, to get the reward, catch them and return them to their masters. I was afraid that these seemingly good men might use me so; but I nevertheless remembered their advice, and from that time I resolved to run away. I looked forward to a time at which it would be safe for me to escape. I was too young to think of doing so immediately; besides, I wished to learn how to write, as I might have occasion to write my own pass. I consoled myself with the hope that I should one day find a good chance. Meanwhile, I would learn to write.

The idea as to how I might learn to write was suggested to me by being in Durgin and Bailey's ship-yard, and frequently seeing the ship carpenters, after hewing, and getting a piece of timber ready for use, write on the timber the name of that part of the ship for which it was intended. When a piece of timber was intended for the larboard side, it would be marked thus — "L." When a piece was for the starboard side, it would be marked thus—"S." A piece for the larboard side forward, would be marked thus—"L. F." When a piece was for starboard side forward, it would be marked thus—"S. F." For larboard aft, it would be marked thus—"L. A." For starboard aft, it would be marked thus—"S. A." I soon learned the names of these letters, and for what they were intended when placed upon a piece of timber in the ship-yard. I immediately commenced copying them, and in a short time was able to make the four letters named. After that, when I met with any boy who I knew could write, I would tell him I could write as well as he. The next word would be, "I don't believe you. Let me see you try it." I would then make the letters which I had been so fortunate as to learn, and ask him to beat that. In this way I got a good many lessons in writing, which it is quite possible I should never have gotten in any other way. During this time, my copy-book was the board fence, brick wall, and pavement; my pen and ink was a lump of chalk. With these, I learned mainly how to write. I then commenced and continued copying the Italics in Webster's Spelling Book, until I could make them all without looking on the book. By this time, my little Master Thomas had gone to school, and learned how to write, and had written over a number of copy-books. These had been brought home, and shown to some of our near neighbors, and then laid aside. My mistress used to go to class meeting at the Wilk Street meetinghouse every Monday afternoon, and leave me to take care of the house. When left thus, I used to spend the time in writing in the spaces left in Master Thomas's copy-book, copying what he had written. I continued to do this until I could write a hand very similar to that of Master Thomas. Thus, after a long, tedious effort for years, I finally succeeded in learning how to write.

QUESTIONS

1. As its title proclaims, Douglass's book is a narrative, the story of his life. So, too, is this selection a narrative, the story of his learning to read and write. Identify the main events of this story, and list them in chronological order.
2. Douglass is reporting some of the events in his life in this selection, but certain events are not simply reported. Instead, they are described so that we may see, hear, and feel what was experienced by the people who were present during the event. Which events are described most fully in this narrative? How does Douglass seek to engage our interest and direct our feelings through such scenes?
3. In this episode from his life, as in his whole book, Douglass is engaged in evaluating an institution—slavery—and arguing a case against it. Can you locate the points in the text where reflecting gives way to argumentation? How does Douglass support his argument against slavery? What are the sources of his persuasiveness?

4. The situation of Irish Catholics is a subtheme in this essay. You can
   trace it by locating every mention of the Irish or of Catholicism in the
   text. How does this theme relate to African American slavery? Try to
   locate *The Columbian Orator* in your library, or find out more about
   who Sheridan was and why he had to argue on behalf of "Catholic
   emancipation" (paragraph 6).
5. A subnarrative in this text tells the story of Master Hugh's wife, the
   "mistress" of the household in which Douglass learned to read and
   write. Retell *her* story in your own words. Consider how her story relates to Douglass's own story and how it relates to Douglass's larger argument about slavery.
6. Put yourself in the place of Master Hugh's wife, and retell all events in
   her words and from her point of view. To do so, you will have to decide
   both what she might have come to know about all these events and how
   she would feel about them. You will also have to decide when she is
   writing. Is she keeping a diary during this time (the early 1830s), or is
   she looking back from the perspective of later years? Has she been
   moved to write by reading Douglass's own book, which appeared in
   1841? If so, how old would she be then, and what would she think
   about these past events? Would she be angry, bitter, repentant, embarrassed, indulgent, scornful, or what?

MAKING CONNECTIONS

1. What are the most common themes of the African American writers in
   this section (Angelou, Walker, and Douglass)? On what issues, when
   they write about writing, do they have the most in common with the
   authors represented here who are white?
2. For Maya Angelou (p. 31), Alice Walker (p. 42), and Frederick Douglass (p. 71) events of childhood and youth are particularly important.
   Compare how at least two of these writers viewed events when they
   were young, how they present their younger selves or viewpoints, and
   how they connect childhood experience to adult knowledge.

MOTHER TONGUE

Amy Tan

Born in 1952 in Oakland, California, Amy Tan is the daughter of immigrants who fled China's Cultural Revolution in the late 1940s. Her Chinese name, An-Mei, means "blessing from America." Tan has remarked that she once tried to distance herself from her ethnicity, but writing her first novel, The Joy Luck Club *(1989), helped her discover "how very Chinese I was." Known as a gifted storyteller, Tan has written two other novels,* The Kitchen God's Wife *(1991) and* The Hundred Secret Senses *(1995), as well as two children's books. The following essay, in which Tan reflects on her experience as a bilingual child speaking both Chinese and English, was originally published in the* Threepenny Review *in 1990.*

I am not a scholar of English or literature. I cannot give you much more than personal opinions on the English language and its variations in this country or others.

I am a writer. And by that definition, I am someone who has always loved language. I am fascinated by language in daily life. I spend a great deal of my time thinking about the power of language — the way it can evoke an emotion, a visual image, a complex idea, or a simple truth. Language is the tool of my trade. And I use them all — all the Englishes I grew up with.

Recently, I was made keenly aware of the different Englishes I do use. I was giving a talk to a large group of people, the same talk I had already given to half a dozen other groups. The nature of the talk was about my writing, my life, and my book *The Joy Luck Club.* The talk was going along well enough, until I remembered one major difference that made the whole talk sound wrong. My mother was in the room. And it was perhaps the first time she had heard me give a lengthy speech, using the kind of English I have never used with her. I was saying things like "The intersection of memory upon imagination" and "There is an aspect of my fiction that relates to thus-and-thus" — a speech filled with carefully wrought grammatical phrases, burdened, it suddenly seemed to me, with nominalized forms, past perfect tenses, conditional phrases, all the forms of standard English that I had learned in school and through books, the forms of English I did not use at home with my mother.

Just last week, I was walking down the street with my mother, and I again found myself conscious of the English I was using, the English I do use with her. We were talking about the price of new and used furniture and I heard myself saying this: "Not waste money that way." My husband was with us as well, and he didn't notice any switch in my English. And then I realized why. It's because over the twenty years we've been together I've often used that same kind of English with him, and sometimes he even uses it with me. It has become our language of intimacy, a different sort of English that relates to family talk, the language I grew up with.

So you'll have some idea of what this family talk I heard sounds like,   5
I'll quote what my mother said during a recent conversation which I video-taped and then transcribed. During this conversation, my mother was talking about a political gangster in Shanghai who had the same last name as her family's, Du, and how the gangster in his early years wanted to be adopted by her family, which was rich by comparison. Later, the gangster became more powerful, far richer than my mother's family, and one day showed up at my mother's wedding to pay his respects. Here's what she said in part:

"Du Yusong having business like fruit stand. Like off the street kind. He is Du like Du Zong—but not Tsung-ming Island people. The local people call putong, the river east side, he belong to that side local people. That man want to ask Du Zong father take him in like become own family. Du Zong father wasn't look down on him, but didn't take seriously, until that man big like become a mafia. Now important person, very hard to inviting him. Chinese way, came only to show respect, don't stay for dinner. Respect for making big celebration, he shows up. Mean gives lots of respect. Chinese custom. Chinese social life that way. If too important won't have to stay too long. He come to my wedding. I didn't see, I heard it. I gone to boy's side, they have YMCA dinner. Chinese age I was nineteen."

You should know that my mother's expressive command of English belies how much she actually understands. She reads the *Forbes* report, listens to *Wall Street Week,* converses daily with her stockbroker, reads all of Shirley MacLaine's books[1] with ease—all kinds of things I can't begin to understand. Yet some of my friends tell me they understand 50 percent of what my mother says. Some say they understand 80 to 90 percent. Some say they understand none of it, as if she were speaking pure Chinese. But to me, my mother's English is perfectly clear, perfectly natural. It's my mother tongue. Her language, as I hear it, is vivid, direct, full of observation and imagery. That was the language that helped shape the way I saw things, expressed things, made sense of the world.

Lately, I've been giving more thought to the kind of English my mother speaks. Like others, I have described it to people as "broken" or "frac-

---

[1]*Shirley MacLaine's books:* psychological/spiritual self-help books by the dancer and movie actress, Shirley MacLaine, such as *Going Within: A Guide for Inner Transformation.* [Eds.]

tured" English. But I wince when I say that. It has always bothered me that I can think of no way to describe it other than "broken," as if it were damaged and needed to be fixed, as if it lacked a certain wholeness and soundness. I've heard other terms used, "limited English," for example. But they seem just as bad, as if everything is limited, including people's perceptions of the limited English speaker.

I know this for a fact, because when I was growing up, my mother's "limited" English limited *my* perception of her. I was ashamed of her English. I believed that her English reflected the quality of what she had to say. That is, because she expressed them imperfectly her thoughts were imperfect. And I had plenty of empirical evidence to support me: the fact that people in department stores, at banks, and at restaurants did not take her seriously, did not give her good service, pretended not to understand her, or even acted as if they did not hear her.

My mother has long realized the limitations of her English as well. When I was fifteen, she used to have me call people on the phone to pretend I was she. In this guise, I was forced to ask for information or even to complain and yell at people who had been rude to her. One time it was a call to her stockbroker in New York. She had cashed out her small portfolio and it just so happened we were going to go to New York the next week, our very first trip outside California. I had to get on the phone and say in an adolescent voice that was not very convincing, "This is Mrs. Tan."

And my mother was standing in the back whispering loudly, "Why he don't send me check, already two weeks late. So mad he lie to me, losing me money."

And then I said in perfect English, "Yes, I'm getting rather concerned. You had agreed to send the check two weeks ago, but it hasn't arrived."

Then she began to talk more loudly. "What he want, I come to New York tell him front of his boss, you cheating me?" And I was trying to calm her down, make her be quiet, while telling the stockbroker, "I can't tolerate any more excuses. If I don't receive the check immediately, I am going to have to speak to your manager when I'm in New York next week." And sure enough, the following week there we were in front of this astonished stockbroker, and I was sitting there red-faced and quiet, and my mother, the real Mrs. Tan, was shouting at his boss in her impeccable broken English.

We used a similar routine just five days ago, for a situation that was far less humorous. My mother had gone to the hospital for an appointment, to find out about a benign brain tumor a CAT scan had revealed a month ago. She said she had spoken very good English, her best English, no mistakes. Still, she said, the hospital did not apologize when they said they had lost the CAT scan and she had come for nothing. She said they did not seem to have any sympathy when she told them she was anxious to know the exact diagnosis, since her husband and son had both died of brain tumors. She said they would not give her any more information until the next time and she would have to make another appointment for that. So she said she would not leave until the doctor called her daughter. She wouldn't budge. And when the doctor finally called her daughter, me, who spoke in perfect English—lo and behold—we had assurances the CAT scan would be found, promises that a conference call on Monday would be held, and apologies for any suffering my mother had gone through for a most regrettable mistake.

I think my mother's English almost had an effect on limiting my possi- 15 bilities in life as well. Sociologists and linguists probably will tell you that a person's developing language skills are more influenced by peers. But I do think that the language spoken in the family, especially in immigrant families which are more insular, plays a large role in shaping the language of the child. And I believe that it affected my results on achievement tests, IQ tests, and the SAT. While my English skills were never judged as poor, compared to math, English could not be considered my strong suit. In grade school I did moderately well, getting perhaps B's, sometimes B-pluses, in English and scoring perhaps in the sixtieth or seventieth percentile on achievement tests. But those scores were not good enough to override the opinion that my true abilities lay in math and science, because in those areas I achieved A's and scored in the ninetieth percentile or higher.

This was understandable. Math is precise; there is only one correct answer. Whereas, for me at least, the answers on English tests were always a judgment call, a matter of opinion and personal experience. Those tests were constructed around items like fill-in-the-blank sentence completion, such as "Even though Tom was_____, Mary thought he was _____." And the correct answer always seemed to be the most bland combinations of thoughts, for example, "Even though Tom was shy, Mary thought he was charming," with the grammatical structure "even though" limiting the correct answer to some sort of semantic opposites, so you wouldn't get answers like "Even though Tom was foolish. Mary thought he was ridiculous." Well, according to my mother, there were very few limitations as to what Tom could have been and what Mary might have thought of him. So I never did well on tests like that.

The same was true with word analogies, pairs of words in which you were supposed to find some sort of logical, semantic relationship—for example, "*Sunset* is to *nightfall* as _____ is to _____." And here you would be presented with a list of four possible pairs, one of which showed the same kind of relationship: *red* is to *stoplight, bus* is to *arrival, chills* is to *fever, yawn* is to *boring.* Well, I could never think that way. I knew what the tests were asking, but I could not block out of my mind the images already created by the first pair, "*sunset* is to *nightfall*"—and I would see a burst of colors against a darkening sky, the moon rising, the lowering of a curtain of stars. And all the other pairs of words—*red, bus, stoplight, boring*—just threw up a mass of confusing images, making it impossible for me to sort out something as logical as saying: "A sunset precedes night-fall" is the same as "a chill precedes a fever." The only way I would have gotten that answer right would have been to imagine an associative situation, for example, my being disobedient and staying out past sunset, catching a chill at night, which turns into feverish pneumonia as punishment, which indeed did happen to me.

I have been thinking about all this lately, about my mother's English, about achievement tests. Because lately I've been asked, as a writer, why there are not more Asian Americans represented in American literature. Why are there few Asian Americans enrolled in creative writing programs? Why do so many Chinese students go into engineering? Well, these are broad sociological questions I can't begin to answer. But I have noticed in surveys—in fact, just last week—that Asian students, as a whole, always do significantly better on math achievement tests than in English. And this makes me think that there are other Asian American students whose English spoken in the home might also be described as "broken" or "limited." And perhaps they also have teachers who are steering them away from writing and into math and science, which is what happened to me.

Fortunately, I happen to be rebellious in nature and enjoy the challenge of disproving assumptions made about me. I became an English major my first year in college, after being enrolled as premed. I started writing nonfiction as a freelancer the week after I was told by my former boss that writing was my worst skill and I should hone my talents toward account management.

But it wasn't until 1985 that I finally began to write fiction. And at 20 first I wrote using what I thought to be wittily crafted sentences, sentences that would finally prove I had mastery over the English language. Here's an example from the first draft of a story that later made its way into *The Joy Luck Club,* but without this line: "That was my mental quandary in its nascent state." A terrible line, which I can barely pronounce.

Fortunately, for reasons I won't get into today, I later decided I should envision a reader for the stories I would write. And the reader I decided upon was my mother, because these were stories about mothers. So with this reader in mind—and in fact she did read my early drafts—I began to write stories using all the Englishes I grew up with: the English I spoke to my mother, which for lack of a better term might be described as "simple"; the English she used with me, which for lack of a better term might be described as "broken"; my translation of her Chinese, which could certainly be described as "watered down"; and what I imagined to be her translation of her Chinese if she could speak in perfect English, her internal language, and for that I sought to preserve the essence, but neither an English nor a Chinese structure. I wanted to capture what language ability tests can never reveal: her intent, her passion, her imagery, the rhythms of her speech and the nature of her thoughts.

Apart from what any critic had to say about my writing, I knew I had succeeded where it counted when my mother finished reading my book and gave me her verdict: "So easy to read."

QUESTIONS

1. Why does Tan begin her essay with the disclaimer, "I am not a scholar of English or literature. I cannot give you much more than personal opinions on the English language and its variations in this country or others"? What advantage does this disclaimer offer Tan?
2. What are the different "Englishes" with which Tan grew up? Find an example of each "English." What did Tan need to learn about each?
3. Tan tells us that, as a writer, she cares about the way language "can evoke an emotion, a visual image, a complex idea, or a simple truth" (paragraph 2). Look closely at Tan's language. Find passages in her essay where her language is evocative. Where does Tan surprise you with her choice of words or her ability to use language to evoke emotion or imagery?
4. What did Tan learn about her "mother tongue"?
5. Think about your own mother tongue. In what ways does it reflect how you see and make sense of the world? What have you had to understand, accept, or reject about your mother tongue?
6. Tan writes that, "the language spoken in the family, especially in immigrant families . . . , plays a large role in shaping the language of the child" (paragraph 15). Write an essay in which you reflect on the role of language in your family.

MAKING CONNECTIONS

What kind of conversation can you imagine between Amy Tan and George Orwell, author of "Politics and the English Language" (p. 626)? How, for instance, would Tan respond to Orwell's claim that thought can corrupt language as much as language can corrupt thought?

MY MISSPENT YOUTH

Meghan Daum

Meghan Daum, who was born in 1970, grew up in the suburbs of northern New Jersey and attended Vassar College. She later received an M.F.A. in writing from Columbia University. As a freelance writer, she has contributed essays to the New Yorker, Gentlemen's Quarterly, Vogue, Harper's Bazaar, Women's Sports and Fitness, *and* beliefnet *online. Her work has been included in several anthologies, including* Personals: Dreams and Nightmares of 20 Young Writers *(2000), and her own collection of essays,* Let the Trinkets Do the Talking, *is currently in preparation. Daum's writing is characterized by a particularly personal, almost confessional, voice. As in the following essay, which originally appeared in the* New Yorker, *she often shares with her readers intimate details of her life that one might expect to be revealed only to a close friend. A longtime New Yorker, Daum currently resides in Lincoln, Nebraska.*

A few months ago, I was walking down West End Avenue, in Manhattan, and I remembered with a sadness that nearly knocked me off my feet just why I'd come to New York seven years ago, and why I was now about to leave. Certain kinds of buildings seem almost too gorgeous to exist — in the United States, anyway — and I'm still amazed that massive, ornate residences like 838 West End Avenue, with its yellow façade and geometric terra-cotta panels, or 305 Riverside Drive, with its elegantly carved limestone cornices, receive mail and spill kids out of their front doors like pretty much any domicile anywhere. When I was growing up in northern New Jersey, just twenty-five miles from Manhattan, I had no idea that ordinary people could live in such places. Then, when I was seventeen, I walked into an apartment at West End Avenue and 104th Street and decided that I had to be one of those people.

It was the summer of 1987, and I was learning how to drive a stick shift. My father, who is a composer, had allowed me to drive him to Manhattan in our Plymouth Horizon to drop off some scores with a music copyist. There was nothing particularly striking about the copyist's apartment: it was a modest four-room prewar[1] with moldings around the ceiling, and I have since mentally supplied it with faded Persian rugs, NPR playing on the radio, and procelain hexagonal tiles that were coming loose in the bathroom. It's difficult to imagine a time when I didn't walk into someone's apartment and immediately start the income-to-rent-ratio

---

[1] *prewar:* an apartment in a building built before World War II. [Eds.]

calculations, and I would now guess that the apartment had been rent-controlled for decades, and that the copyist paid perhaps three hundred dollars a month. But on that summer night, looking out the living-room window toward the river[2] that so famously and effectively keeps *here* safely away from *there,* money was the last thing on my mind; I just knew that this was where I wanted to live, and from that moment on every decision I made was based on that conviction.

I've always been somebody who exerts a great deal of energy to get my realities to match my fantasies. I'm also pretty good at "getting by" — especially if you apply the increasingly common definition of the term, which has more to do with keeping up appearances than with keeping things under control. So it wasn't until recently that I realized I wasn't having such a good time in New York anymore. Like a social smoker whose supposedly endearing desire to emulate Marlene Dietrich[3] has landed her in a cancer ward, I have recently woken up to the frightening fallout of my own romantic notions of life in the big city: I'm twenty-nine years old, and I am completely over my head in debt. I have not made a life for myself; I have purchased a life for myself.

For the better part of the last year, the balance on my Visa card has hovered around seven thousand dollars. A significant chunk of that debt comes from medical expenses, particularly the bills for a series of dental procedures I needed. As a freelance writer, it would cost me three hundred dollars a month to buy health insurance in New York State. That's far more than I can afford, so I don't have any. Although I try to pay the three-hundred-and-thirty-nine-dollars-a-quarter charge to keep a hospitalization insurance policy that will cover me if some major disaster befalls, I am often late in paying, and it gets cancelled. But medical expenses represent only a fraction of my troubles. I also need to make an estimated quarterly tax payment of fifty-four hundred dollars this month, which is going to be tough, because I recently paid back three thousand dollars to my now ex-boyfriend, who lent me money to pay last year's taxes, and I still owe three hundred dollars to the accountant who prepared the return. My checking account is overdrawn by a thousand seven hundred and eighty-four dollars. I have no savings, no investments, no pension fund, and no inheritance on the horizon. I have student loans from graduate school amounting to sixty thousand dollars. I pay $448.83 per month on these loans, installments that barely cover the interest that's accruing.

It's tempting to go into a litany of all the things that I do not spend   5
money on. I have no dependents, not even a cat or a fish. I do not have a car. I've worn the same four pairs of shoes for the past three years. Much

---

[2]*the river:* the Hudson, which separates New York City from New Jersey. [Eds.]

[3]*Marlene Dietrich* (1901–1992): German-American actress and singer, known for her throaty voice and often filmed smoking. [Eds.]

of the clothing in my closet has been there since the early nineties, the rare additions usually taking the form of a sixteen-dollar shirt from Old Navy, a discounted dress from Loehmann's, or a Christmas sweater from my mother. I've lived without a roommate only for the last two years. My rent, a thousand and fifty-five dollars a month for a four-hundred-square-foot apartment, is, as we say in New York City when describing the Holy Grail, below market. I do not own expensive stereo equipment, and even though I have a television, I cannot bring myself to spend the thirty-five dollars a month on cable, which, curiously, I've deemed an indulgence. With the exception of a trip to Egypt to visit a friend, in 1998, I have not spent money on overseas travel. I've still never been to Europe.

Instead, I've confined my spending to certain ephemeral luxuries that have come to seem like necessities. I'll go to Starbucks in the morning, and then order sushi for lunch. I'll meet a friend for drinks and drop forty-five dollars on Merlot and chicken satay. I make long-distance phone calls almost daily, with no thought of peak calling hours or dime-a-minute rates. I have a compulsive need to keep fresh-cut flowers in my apartment at all times, and spend eight to ten dollars a week on tulips from the Korean market. But these extravagances are merely symptoms of a larger delusion. It's easier to feel guilt over spending sixty dollars on a blender, as I did last month, than to examine the more elaborate reasons that I've found it increasingly impossible to live within my means.

Once you're in this kind of debt—and by "kind" I'm talking less about numbers than about my particular brand of debt—all those bills start not to matter anymore. If I allowed them to matter, I would become so panicked that I wouldn't be able to work, which would only set me back further. I've also noticed that my kind of debt is surprisingly socially acceptable. After all, I went into debt for my education and my career—broad categories with room for copious rationalizations, and I make full use of them. I live in the most expensive city in the country because I have long believed that my career is dependent upon it. I spend money on Martinis and expensive dinners because, as is typical among my species of debtor, I tell myself that Martinis and expensive dinners are the entire point—the point of being young, the point of living in New York City, the point of living. In this frame of mind, the dollars spent, like the workings of a machine which no one bothers to understand, become an abstraction, a vehicle of taste.

As I try to sort out the origins of my present financial situation, I always come back to the ineffable hankering I had as a teen-ager for some sort of earthier, more "intellectual" life style. I come from an affluent New Jersey suburb whose main draw is its good public-school system, but I wanted to live someplace that looked like Mia Farrow's apartment in "Hannah and Her Sisters." (Little did I know that it *was* Mia Farrow's apartment.) To me, this kind of space connoted not wealth but urbanity. These were places where the paint was peeling and the rugs were frayed and the hallways were lined with books; places where smart people sat around drinking gin and tonics, having interesting conversations, and living, according to my logic, in an authentic way. As far as I was aware at seventeen, rich was something else entirely. Rich meant monstrous Tudor-style houses in the ritzy section of my town. Rich was driving a BMW to school. I had the distinct feeling that my orthodontist, who had a sprawling ranch house with front steps that were polished to look like ice, was rich. None of these particular trappings of wealth held my attention. In fact, nothing outside of the movies really held my attention until that night in 1987 when I saw the apartment on 104th street.

I planned my escape from the suburbs through the standard channels: college selection. My logic, informed by a combination of college guidebooks and the alma maters of the brides featured in the *Times* wedding announcements, went something like this: Columbia rather than N.Y.U., Wisconsin rather than Texas, Yale rather than Harvard, Vassar rather than Smith. My ranking system had little to do with the academic merits of the schools. It was more a game of degrees of separation between me and an apartment full of houseplants on the Upper West Side. Somehow, Vassar emerged as the best contender for closing that gap. I wanted so badly to go to a particular kind of artsy college and mix with a particular kind of artsy crowd that I wasted an alarming amount of time during my senior year of high school throwing trash into various wastebaskets from across the room, saying, "If I make this shot, I get into Vassar."

As it turned out, I did go to Vassar, and although it would be five   10
years until I entered my debting era, my time there did more than expand my intellect: it expanded my sense of entitlement so much that, by the end, I had no ability to distinguish myself from the many extremely wealthy people I encountered there. A sense of entitlement can certainly be an asset, but it has also played a supporting role in my financial demise—mostly because it made it hard to recognize where ambition and chutzpah end and potential bankruptcy begins.

When I graduated, in 1992, I followed a herd of my classmates into Manhattan; many of them moved back in with their parents on Park Avenue. I got an entry-level job in publishing, and, along with a couple of friends, rented a five-room prewar apartment with chipping paint on 100th Street off Riverside Drive, a mere five blocks from the scene of my high-school epiphany. Such expert marksmanship! I was ecstatic. My job, as an editorial assistant at a glossy fashion magazine, paid eighteen thousand dollars a year. The woman who hired me, a fifties-era Vassar graduate, told me that she hoped I had an independent source of income, as I certainly wouldn't be able to support myself on my salary. But I did support myself. My roommates—an elementary-school teacher, who was making nineteen thousand dollars a year, and a film student, who worked part time at a non-profit arts organization—supported themselves, too. We each paid around five hundred and fifty dollars a month in rent and lived as recent graduates should, eating ramen noodles and ninety-nine-cent White Rose macaroni and cheese.

Looking back, I see those years as a cheap, happy time. It was a time during which a certain kind of poverty was appropriate. Unlike the West Seventies and Eighties, my neighborhood seemed like a place for people who knew the city, for people *from* the city. Though I was living hand to mouth, I loved it there, and looked forward to moving ahead in my career and one day being able to afford my own place in the neighborhood. Then, that seemed well within the realm of possibility. It was 1993, I was twenty-three, and I'd received a raise, so that I was earning twenty-one thousand dollars a year. I had no idea that this was the closest I'd be to financial solvency for at least the next decade.

I'd been told I was lucky to have got a job at a magazine—I had, after all, graduated into what was being called the worst job market in twenty years—and even though I had little interest in its subject matter, I didn't dare turn down the position. Within my first week on the job, I found myself immersed in a culture of money and celebrity: Socialites sat on the editorial board in order to report on trends among the rich and famous. Editorial assistants who earned eighteen thousand dollars managed to wear Prada, have regular facials, and rent time-shares in the Hamptons. Many of them lived in doorman buildings, for which their parents helped foot the bill.

This wasn't my scene. I felt as far away from my "Hannah and Her Sisters" fantasy as I had in the suburbs. After a year of office work, I decided that an M.F.A. in creative writing would provide the most direct route to literary legitimacy. I applied to Columbia, which, not coincidentally, happened to be within walking distance of my apartment. It also has one of the most expensive writing programs in the country, a fact that was easy to forget, because the students, for the most part, seemed so down to earth and modest. In their flannel shirts and roach-infested student housing, they seemed as earnest and poor as I was, and I figured that if they could take out twenty-thousand-dollar-a-year loans, so could I. In the three years that I spent at Columbia, borrowing more than sixty thousand dollars to get my degree, I was told repeatedly—by fellow-students, faculty, administrators, and professional writers whose careers I wished to emulate—not to think about the loans. Student loans, after all, were low-interest, long-term, and far more benign than credit-card debt. Not thinking about them was a skill that I quickly developed.

If there is in this story a single moment when I crossed the boundary between debtlessness and total financial mayhem, it's the first dollar that I put toward my life as a writer in New York—despite the fact that I was hanging out at the Cuban coffee shop and traipsing through the wind-blown trash of upper Broadway.[4] The year I entered graduate school was the year I stopped making decisions that were appropriate for my situation

---

[4]*upper Broadway:* the main commercial street of New York's Upper West Side. [Eds.]

and began making a rich person's decisions. Entering this particular graduate program was a rich person's decision. Remaining there when it became clear that I was not going to get any scholarship money, and that the class schedule would prevent me from holding down a day job, was also a rich person's decision.

But it's hard to recognize that you're acting like a rich person when you're becoming increasingly poor. Besides, I was never without a job. I worked for an anthropology professor for nine dollars an hour. I read manuscripts at ten dollars a pop for an ersatz[5] literary agent. I worked at a university press for ten dollars an hour. Sometimes I called in sick to these jobs and did temp work at midtown offices for seventeen dollars an hour. A couple of times, I took out cash advances on my credit cards to pay the rent. There was a period during a particularly miserable winter, in 1994, when I tried to make it through three weeks on thirty-four dollars, walking sixteen blocks to school in subzero temperatures and stealing my roommates' food, hoping they wouldn't notice. One day, I slipped on the ice three times, got in a cab, and decided to take out a private loan from Columbia for two thousand five hundred dollars. A thousand of it went to pay off part of a credit card. I used up the rest within a month.

There were a handful of us who were pulling stunts like this. One of my roommates had maxed out her credit cards in order to finance a student film. I knew several women, and even a few men, who were actively looking for rich marriage partners to bail them out. One aspiring novelist I know underwent a series of drug treatments and uncomfortable surgical procedures in order to sell her eggs for twenty-five hundred dollars. Whether or not one is paying twenty thousand dollars' tuition a year to try to make it as a writer, New York City in the nineties is a prohibitively expensive place to live for just about anyone. Although I devoted a lot of energy to being envious of Columbia classmates whose relatives were picking up the tab, it later became clear to me that the need for outside financial support is not limited to those in entry-level jobs or expensive graduate programs. These days, pursuing a career in the arts in New York is often contingent upon inheriting the means to do so.

As I was finishing at Columbia, however, I began to get some freelance work, so I continued to hedge my bets. I was publishing magazine articles regularly and, after a few months of temping at insurance companies and banks, scored some steady assignments that, to my delight, allowed me to work as a full-time freelance writer. After five years and eight different roommates in the 100th Street apartment, I was earning enough money to move into my own place. More important, I had found a two-year sublet in a rent-stabilized building, and the fact that I had done so through a Columbia connection seemed almost sufficient justification for the money I'd spent on grad school.

---

[5] *ersatz:* an inferior imitation or substitute. [Eds.]

Things were going well. In 1997, I was twenty-seven, teaching a writing course at N.Y.U., publishing in a variety of magazines, and earning about fifty-five thousand dollars before taxes. (The teaching job paid only twenty-five hundred dollars for an entire semester, but I was too enamored of the idea of being a college instructor to wonder if I could afford to take it.) I had a decent-sized apartment with oak floors and porcelain hexagonal tiles that were coming loose in the bathroom. Like an honest New Yorker, I even had mice lurking in the kitchen. I bought rugs and a fax machine. I installed a second telephone line for the fax. Finally, I was leading the life I'd spent so long preparing for.

Then came the dental bills, which I was forced to charge to Visa. I   20
tried not to think about that too much, until I ended up making a few doctor's visits that, because I was uninsured, I also charged to Visa. When April rolled around, I realized that my income was significantly higher that year than it had been in any previous year, and that I had woefully underestimated what I owed in taxes. Despite a profusion of the typical freelancer's writeoffs—movies, magazine subscriptions, an $89.99 sonic rodent-control device—I was hit with a bill of more than twenty thousand dollars. And although the I.R.S. apparently deemed sonic rodent-control devices an acceptable deduction, it seemed that I'd earned too much money to be eligible to write off the nearly seven thousand dollars (most of it interest) I'd paid to the student-loan agency or the three thousand dollars in dental bills. In the months it took me to assemble that twenty thousand dollars, I had to reduce my student-loan payments from the suggested eight hundred dollars to the aforementioned $448.83 a month. Most heartbreaking of all, my accountant determined that my sixty-dollar pledge to WNYC—my Upper West Side tableau couldn't possibly be complete without the National Public Radio coffee mug—was not entirely tax deductible.

It was around this time that I started having trouble thinking about anything other than how to make a payment on whatever bill was sitting on my desk, most likely weeks overdue, at any given time. I began getting final disconnection notices from the phone company, letters from the gas company asking "Have you forgotten us?," collection calls from Visa. A friend who had been a member of Debtors Anonymous urged me to put a note over my phone that read, "Owing money does not make me a bad person." I didn't do this, partly because it wouldn't have fit in with the décor of my apartment, and partly because I wasn't sure she was right. She did, however, persuade me to call Visa and put a hold on my account for six months, which would reduce my payments to a hundred and five dollars a month and freeze the interest. This required telling the customer-service representative at Visa that I was experiencing some financial "hardships." When she asked me to be more specific, I told her that I had medical expenses, and hung up the phone feeling as if I had a terminal illness.

I noticed that I was drinking more than I had in the past, often alone at home, where I would sip Sauvignon Blanc at my desk and pretend to write when in fact I'd be working out some kind of desperate math equation on the tool-bar calculator, making wild guesses as to when I'd receive some random eight-hundred-dollar check from some unreliable accounting department of some slow-paying publication, how long it would take the check to clear, what would be left after I set aside a third of it for taxes, and, finally, which lucky creditor would be the recipient of what remained. There's nothing like completing one of these calculations, realizing that you've drunk half a bottle of $7.99 wine, and feeling guiltier about having spent $7.99 than about being too tipsy to work. One night, I did a whole bunch of calculations and discovered that, despite having earned a gross income of seventy-eight thousand dollars in 1998, despite having not gone overboard on such classic debtor's paraphernalia as clothes and vacations and stereo equipment, despite having followed the urban striver's guide to success, I was more than seventy-five thousand dollars in the hole.

There are days when my debt seems to be at the center of my being, a cancer that must be treated with the morphine of excuses and rationales and promises to myself that I'm going to come up with the big score — book advance, screenplay deal, Publishers Clearinghouse prize — and save myself. There are other days when the debt feels like someone else's cancer, a tragedy outside myself, a condemned building next door that I try to avoid walking past. But the days when I can pretend that money is "only money" are growing farther and farther apart. I have friends who are getting rich off the stock market and buying million-dollar houses. I have other friends who are almost as badly off as I am, and who compulsively volunteer for relief work in Third World countries as a way of forgetting that they can't quite afford to live in the First World.

But New York City, which has a way of making you feel like you're in the Third World just seconds after you thought you'd conquered all of Western civilization, has never really belonged to the rest of the country. I suppose that part of the city's magical beastliness is the fact that you can show up with the best of intentions, do what's considered to be all the right things, achieve some measure of success, and still find yourself trapped in a financial emergency.

As I write this, I have to be out of my sublet within months. Even if I   25
try to assume control of the lease, the landlord will renovate the apartment and raise the rent to two thousand dollars. When I reported this calamity to a friend the other day, hoping she would gasp in sympathy, she instead replied, "That's cheaper than our place." A two-bedroom apartment down the street recently rented for forty-five hundred a month. A small studio on the Upper West Side will go for an average of twelve hundred and fifty dollars. West 104th Street is totally beyond my means. Worse, 104th Street is now beyond the means of most of the people who made me want to live here in the first place. The New York that changed my life on that summer night when I was seventeen no longer exists.

Several months ago, on a day when the debt anxiety had flared up even more than usual, I found myself fantasizing about moving to Lincoln,

Nebraska. I'd been to Lincoln twice on a magazine assignment, met some nice people, and found myself liking it enough to entertain the notion of moving there. But both times I'd discarded that idea the minute the wheels hit the tarmac at LaGuardia. Surely I'd never be able to live without art-movie houses and twenty-four-hour takeout. During my last round of panic, however, I convinced myself that it was a good plan. I can rent an apartment there for three hundred dollars a month. I can rent an entire house, if I want one, for seven hundred dollars. Full-coverage health insurance will cost me seventy-five dollars a month. Apparently, people in Nebraska also listen to NPR, and there are even places to live in Lincoln that have oak floors. Had I known that before, I might have skipped out on this New York thing altogether and spared myself the financial and psychological ordeal. But I'm kind of glad I didn't know, because I've had a very, very good time here. I'm just leaving the party before the cops break it up.

QUESTIONS

1. How seriously or humorously do you take the title of this piece? Explain. In what sense(s) do you think Daum considers herself to have lived a "misspent youth"? In other words, how does Daum's title affect your understanding of her recollections and reflections?

2. In paragraph 4, Daum provides a detailed account of her current financial situation. When you first encountered those details, how did you react to her situation? How (if at all) did your assessment of her finances change over the course of the essay? How is your assessment influenced by Daum's age when she wrote this essay?

3. In paragraph 15, Daum asserts that she "crossed the boundary between debtlessness and total financial mayhem" with "the first dollar that I put toward my life as a writer in New York. . . ." Do you think her "financial mayhem" was worth it? How do you think Daum feels about the indebtedness she incurred in becoming a writer?

4. Together with the costs of Columbia's M.F.A. program, Daum attributes her "mayhem" largely to the expenses of living in New York City, especially the expensive tastes that she reports in paragraphs 6 and 7; when describing the kind of lifestyle that lured her to Manhattan. In what sense(s) might the allure of big city life itself be the source of Daum's financial mayhem? Or do you think she's writing about the costs of a yearning for something else — something that can be found in the city but is not necessarily big city life itself? If so, explain.

5. Given Daum's final paragraph, in which she seems to be planning a move to Lincoln, Nebraska, and announces that she "might have skipped out on this New York thing altogether" if she'd known about Lincoln before, do you think she intends her essay to be a piece about the perils of big city life versus the appeals of a smaller place (that

includes a big state university)? Or do you think, perhaps, that her ending is a bit tongue-in-cheek? If so, what do you think is her primary concern in this piece?

6. Though your financial situation is probably nowhere near so perilous as Daum's, you still might think of yourself as having had a "misspent youth" in some other sense. If so, write an essay (serious, or humorous, or a bit of both) in which you tell about a time in your life that now looks as if it was misspent, and try to explain what led you to misspend it, as well as what measures you (or others) took to deal with the problem.

7. In paragraph 8, Daum takes note of "the ineffable hankering I had as a teen-ager for some sort of earthier, more 'intellectual' life." Think of a hankering that you had as a teenager for some kind of life that was different from the one you were living at that time. What were you hankering for? What did you do (or have you done) to attain it? Write an essay in which you tell about this teenage yearning, and how it has influenced your life since then.

MAKING CONNECTIONS

Daum, Alice Walker (p. 42), and Lucy Grealy (p. 50) each offer detailed narratives about an extended period in their lives when they were dealing with a consuming personal problem. Compare and contrast their narrative techniques, as well as the ways they interweave reflection with recollection. What is most distinctive about Daum's method of narration and reflection?

THE MOUNTAIN

Louise Glück

Born in New York City in 1943, Louise Glück attended Sarah Lawrence College and Columbia University. She currently teaches at Williams College. Her debut collection of poetry, First Born, *appeared in 1968, and she has published numerous collections since then, including* The Garden *(1976),* The Triumph of Achilles *(1985), and, most recently,* Inferno *(1998). Her 1992 collection,* The Wild Iris, *was awarded a Pulitzer Prize. Glück has been widely praised for a vernacular style that conveys a sense of intellectual and emotional complexity. In the words of one critic, "the words in Glück's poems seem to come directly from the center of herself."*

My students look at me expectantly.
I explain to them that the life of art is a life
of endless labor. Their expressions
hardly change; they need to know
a little more about endless labor. 5
So I tell them the story of Sisyphus,
how he was doomed to push
a rock up a mountain, knowing nothing
would come of this effort
but that he would repeat it 10
indefinitely. I tell them
there is joy in this, in the artist's life,
that one eludes
judgment, and as I speak
I am secretly pushing a rock myself, 15
slyly pushing it up the steep
face of a mountain. Why do I lie
to these children? They aren't listening,
they aren't deceived, their fingers
tapping at the wooden desks— 20
So I retract
the myth; I tell them it occurs
in hell, and that the artist lies
because he is obsessed with attainment,
that he perceives the summit 25

as that place where he will live forever,
a place about to be
transformed by his burden: with every breath,
I am standing at the top of the mountain.
Both my hands are free. And the rock has added   30
height to the mountain.

QUESTIONS

1. In this poem, an artist/teacher lets us in on the private thoughts and reflections that run through her head while she's in the process of teaching her students about "the life of art." What does she reveal privately
   (about herself and about her life as an artist) that she doesn't speak
   about publicly?
2. In the process of the poem, the narrator also reports the various things
   that she openly tells her students. Given the things she tells her students
   and the things she keeps to herself, what kind of teacher does she appear to be? What does she imply about her view of teaching when she
   says, "and as I speak/I am secretly pushing a rock myself, slyly pushing
   it up the steep face of a mountain."
3. Throughout the poem, Glück relies heavily on the myth of Sisyphus.
   How does this myth serve to convey the range of her thoughts and feelings about "the artist's life"? In what ways does it also serve to suggest
   her thoughts and feelings about the teacher's life?
4. How do you account for the sudden reversal of the narrator's thinking
   that seems to take place in the last three and one-half lines? In what
   sense(s) is she able to defy the myth of Sisyphus? Look back over her
   previous reflections to see if you can find any prior hints or anticipation
   of this seeming reversal.

MAKING CONNECTIONS

Meghan Daum also writes about "the artist's life" in "My Misspent
Youth" (p. 83). Consider the various ways in which the myth of Sisyphus
might apply to Daum's experience. What do you think that Glück herself
might think of the rock that Daum is pushing up a mountain on behalf of
her aspiration to be a writer?

Social Sciences and Public Affairs

THE WAY TO RAINY MOUNTAIN

N. Scott Momaday

N. Scott Momaday was born in Lawton, Oklahoma, in 1934. His father is a full-blooded Kiowa, and his mother is part Cherokee. After attending schools on Navajo, Apache, and Pueblo reservations, Momaday graduated from the University of New Mexico and earned his doctorate at Stanford University. He has published two collections of poetry, Angle of Geese and Other Poems *(1974) and* The Gourd Dancer *(1976), and a memoir,* The Names *(1976). In 1969 his novel* House Made of Dawn *won the Pulitzer Prize. When asked about his writing, Momaday said, "When I was growing up on the reservations of the Southwest, I saw people who were deeply involved in their traditional life, in the memories of their blood. They had, as far as I can see, a certain strength and beauty that I find missing in the modern world. I like to celebrate that involvement in my writing." The following essay appeared first in the* Reporter *magazine in 1967 and later as the introduction to* The Way to Rainy Mountain *(1969), a collection of Kiowa legends.*

A single knoll rises out of the plain in Oklahoma, north and west of the Wichita range. For my people, the Kiowas, it is an old landmark, and they gave it the name Rainy Mountain. The hardest weather in the world is there. Winter brings blizzards, hot tornadic winds arise in the spring, and in summer the prairie is an anvil's edge. The grass turns brittle and brown, and it cracks beneath your feet. There are green belts along the rivers and creeks, linear groves of hickory and pecan, willow and witch hazel. At a distance in July or August the steaming foliage seems almost to writhe in fire. Great green and yellow grasshoppers are everywhere in the tall grass, popping up like corn to sting the flesh, and tortoises crawl about on the red earth, going nowhere in the plenty of time. Loneliness is an aspect of the land. All things in the plain are isolate; there is no confusion of objects in the eye, but *one* hill or *one* tree or *one* man. To look upon that landscape in the early morning, with the sun at your back, is to lose the sense of proportion. Your imagination comes to life, and this, you think, is where Creation was begun.

I returned to Rainy Mountain in July. My grandmother had died in the spring, and I wanted to be at her grave. She had lived to be very old and at last infirm. Her only living daughter was with her when she died, and I was told that in death her face was that of a child.

I like to think of her as a child. When she was born, the Kiowas were living the last great moment of their history. For more than a hundred years they had controlled the open range from the Smoky Hill River to the Red, from the headwaters of the Canadian to the fork of the Arkansas and Cimarron. In alliance with the Comanches, they had ruled the whole of the Southern Plains. War was their sacred business, and they were the finest horsemen the world has ever known. But warfare for the Kiowas was preeminently a matter of disposition rather than of survival, and they never understood the grim, unrelenting advance of the U.S. Cavalry. When at last, divided and ill provisioned, they were driven onto the Staked Plains in the cold of autumn, they fell into panic. In Palo Duro Canyon they abandoned their crucial stores to pillage and had nothing then but their lives. In order to save themselves, they surrendered to the soldiers at Fort Sill and were imprisoned in the old stone corral that now stands as a military museum. My grandmother was spared the humiliation of those high gray walls by eight or ten years, but she must have known from birth the affliction of defeat, the dark brooding of old warriors.

Her name was Aho, and she belonged to the last culture to evolve in North America. Her forebears came down from the high country in western Montana nearly three centuries ago. They were a mountain people, a mysterious tribe of hunters whose language has never been classified in any major group. In the late seventeenth century they began a long migration to the south and east. It was a journey toward the dawn, and it led to a golden age. Along the way the Kiowas were befriended by the Crows, who gave them the culture and religion of the Plains. They acquired horses, and their ancient nomadic spirit was suddenly free of the ground. They acquired Tai-me, the sacred sun-dance doll, from that moment the object and symbol of their worship, and so shared in the divinity of the sun. Not least, they acquired the sense of destiny, therefore courage and pride. When they entered upon the Southern Plains they had been transformed. No longer were they slaves to the simple necessity of survival; they were a lordly and dangerous society of fighters and thieves, hunters and priests of the sun.

According to their origin myth, they entered the world through a hollow log. From one point of view, their migration was the fruit of an old prophecy, for indeed they emerged from a sunless world.

Though my grandmother lived out her long life in the shadow of Rainy   5
Mountain, the immense landscape of the continental interior lay like memory in her blood. She could tell of the Crows, whom she had never seen, and of the Black Hills, where she had never been. I wanted to see in reality what she had seen more perfectly in the mind's eye, and drove fifteen hundred miles to begin my pilgrimage.

A dark mist lay over the Black Hills, and the land was like iron. At the top of a ridge I caught sight of Devil's Tower upthrust against the gray sky as if in the birth of time the core of the earth had broken through its crust and the motion of the world was begun. There are things in nature that engender an awful quiet in the heart of man; Devil's Tower is one of them. Two centuries ago, because of their need to explain it, the Kiowas made a legend at the base of the rock. My grandmother said:

"Eight children were there at play, seven sisters and their brother. Suddenly the boy was struck dumb; he trembled and began to run upon his hands and feet. His fingers became claws, and his body was covered with fur. There was a bear where the boy had been. The sisters were terrified; they ran, and the bear after them. They came to the stump of a great tree, and the tree spoke to them. It bade them climb upon it, and as they did so, it began to rise into the air. The bear came to kill them, but they were just beyond its reach. It reared against the tree and scored the bark all around with its claws. The seven sisters were borne into the sky, and they became the stars of the Big Dipper." From that moment, and so long as the legend lives, the Kiowas have kinsmen in the night sky. Whatever they were in the mountains, they could be no more. However tenuous their well-being, however much they had suffered and would suffer again, they had found a way out of the wilderness.

My grandmother had a reverence for the sun, a holy regard that now is all but gone out of mankind. There was a wariness in her, and an ancient awe. She was a Christian in her later years, but she had come a long way about, and she never forgot her birthright. As a child she had been to the sun dances; she had taken part in that annual rite, and by it she had learned the restoration of her people in the presence of Tai-me. She was about seven when the last Kiowa sun dance was held in 1887 on the Washita River above Rainy Mountain Creek. The buffalo were gone. In order to consummate the ancient sacrifice—to impale the head of a buffalo bull upon the Tai-me tree—a delegation of old men journeyed into Texas, there to beg and barter for an animal from the Goodnight herd. She was ten when the Kiowas came together for the last time as a living sun-dance culture. They could find no buffalo; they had to hang an old hide from the sacred tree. Before the dance could begin, a company of soldiers rode out from Fort Sill under orders to disperse the tribe. Forbidden without cause the essential act of their faith, having seen the wild herds slaughtered and left to rot upon the ground, the Kiowas backed away forever from the tree. That was July 20, 1890, at the great bend of the Washita. My grandmother was there. Without bitterness, and for as long as she lived, she bore a vision of deicide.[1]

Now that I can have her only in memory, I see my grandmother in the several postures that were peculiar to her: standing at the wood stove on a winter morning and turning meat in a great iron skillet; sitting at the south window, bent above her beadwork, and afterwards, when her vision failed, looking down for a long time into the fold of her hands; going out upon a cane, very slowly as she did when the weight of age came upon her; praying. I remember her most often at prayer. She made long, rambling prayers out of suffering and hope, having seen many things. I was never sure that I had the right to hear, so exclusive were they of all mere custom and company. The last time I saw her she prayed standing by the side of the bed at night, naked to the waist, the light of a kerosene lamp moving upon her dark skin. Her long black hair, always drawn and braided in the day, lay upon her shoulders and against her breasts like a shawl. I do not speak Kiowa, and I never understood her prayers, but there was something inherently sad in the sound, some merest hesitation upon the syllables of sorrow. She began in a high and descending pitch, exhausting her breath to silence; then again and again—and always the same intensity of effort, of something that is, and is not, like urgency in the human voice. Transported so in the dancing light among the shadows of her room, she seemed beyond the reach of time. But that was illusion; I think I knew then that I should not see her again.

Houses are like sentinels in the plain, old keepers of the weather watch. There, in a very little while, wood takes on the appearance of great age. All colors wear soon away in the wind and rain, and then the wood is burned gray and the grain appears and the nails turn red with rust. The window panes are black and opaque; you imagine there is nothing within, and indeed there are many ghosts, bones given up to the land. They stand here and there against the sky, and you approach them for a longer time than you expect. They belong in the distance; it is their domain.

Once there was a lot of sound in my grandmother's house, a lot of coming and going, feasting and talk. The summers there were full of excitement and reunion. The Kiowas are a summer people; they abide the cold and keep to themselves, but when the season turns and the land becomes warm and vital they cannot hold still; an old love of going returns upon them. The aged visitors who came to my grandmother's house when I was a child were made of lean and leather, and they bore themselves upright. They wore great black hats and bright ample shirts that shook in the wind. They rubbed fat upon

10

---

[1]*deicide:* the killing of a deity or god. [Eds.]

their hair and wound their braids with strips of colored cloth. Some of them painted their faces and carried the scars of old and cherished enmities. They were an old council of warlords, come to remind and be reminded of who they were. Their wives and daughters served them well. The women might indulge themselves; gossip was at once the mark and compensation of their servitude. They made loud and elaborate talk among themselves, full of jest and gesture, fright and false alarm. They went abroad in fringed and flowered shawls, bright beadwork and German silver. They were at home in the kitchen, and they prepared meals that were banquets.

There were frequent prayer meetings, and nocturnal feasts. When I was a child I played with my cousins outside, where the lamplight fell upon the ground and the singing of the old people rose up around us and carried away into the darkness. There were a lot of good things to eat, a lot of laughter and surprise. And afterwards, when the quiet returned, I lay down with my grandmother and could hear the frogs away by the river and feel the motion of the air.

Now there is a funereal silence in the rooms, the endless wake of some final word. The walls have closed in upon my grandmother's house. When I returned to it in mourning, I saw for the first time in my life how small it was. It was late at night, and there was a white moon, nearly full. I sat for a long time on the stone steps by the kitchen door. From there I could see out across the land; I could see the long row of trees by the creek, the low light upon the rolling plains, and the stars of the Big Dipper. Once I looked at the moon and caught sight of a strange thing. A cricket had perched upon the handrail, only a few inches away. My line of vision was such that the creature filled the moon like a fossil. It had gone there, I thought, to live and die, for there, of all places, was its small definition made whole and eternal. A warm wind rose up and purled like the longing within me.

The next morning, I awoke at dawn and went out on the dirt road to Rainy Mountain. It was already hot, and the grasshoppers began to fill the air. Still, it was early in the morning, and birds sang out of the shadows. The long yellow grass on the mountain shone in the bright light, and a scissortail hied above the land. There, where it ought to be, at the end of a long and legendary way, was my grandmother's grave. She had at last succeeded to that holy ground. Here and there on the dark stones were ancestral names. Looking back once, I saw the mountain and came away.

QUESTIONS

1. What is this essay about? Explain whether it is a history of the Kiowas, a biography of Momaday's grandmother, or a narrative of his journey.
2. Trace the movement in time in this essay. How much takes place in the present, the recent past, the distant past, or legendary time? What effect does such movement create?

3. How much of the essay reports events, and how much of the essay represents a sense of place or of people through description of what Momaday sees and feels? Trace the pattern of reporting and representing, and consider Momaday's purpose in such an approach to his subject.

4. The first paragraph ends by drawing the reader into the writer's point of view: "Your imagination comes to life, and this, you think, is where Creation was begun." Given the description of the Oklahoma landscape that precedes this in the paragraph, how do you react to Momaday's summarizing statement? Why? What other passages in the essay evoke a sense of place?

5. Visit a place that has historical significance. It may be a place where you or members of your family lived in the past, or it may be a place of local or national historical significance. Describe the place as it appears now, and report on events that took place there in the past. What, if any, evidence do you find in the present of those events that took place in the past?

6. If you have a grandparent or an older friend living nearby, ask this person about his or her history. What does this person remember about the past that is no longer in the present? Are there objects—pictures, clothing, medals, and so on—that can speak to you of your subject's past life? Reflect on the person's present life as well as on those events from the past that seem most memorable. Write an essay in which you represent your subject's life by concentrating on the place where he or she lives and the surrounding objects that help you to understand the past and present life.

MAKING CONNECTIONS

Compare Momaday's essay to Alice Walker's (p. 42), focusing on the way each essay moves through time. How do these essayists differ in their conception and representation of time, and how do those differences relate to their individual purposes as writers?

THE DEATH OF THE PROFANE
A Commentary on the Genre
of Legal Writing

Patricia J. Williams

Patricia J. Williams (b. 1951), a professor of law at Columbia University, is the great-great-granddaughter of a young female slave purchased at the age of eleven by a white lawyer who immediately impregnated her. In her book The Alchemy of Race and Rights *(1991), from which this selection is taken, Williams juxtaposes experiential accounts with sophisticated legal theories to expose the ideology underlying law in the United States. Williams, who has written widely on legal issues and race, challenges traditional legal thinking by questioning the ways in which such thinking represents racial identity. In the following essay, Williams reflects on the intersection of race, gender, class, and law.*

Buzzers are big in New York City. Favored particularly by smaller stores and boutiques, merchants throughout the city have installed them as screening devices to reduce the incidence of robbery: if the face at the door looks desirable, the buzzer is pressed and the door is unlocked. If the face is that of an undesirable, the door stays locked. Predictably, the issue of undesirability has revealed itself to be a racial determination. While controversial enough at first, even civil-rights organizations backed down eventually in the face of arguments that the buzzer system is a "necessary evil," that it is a "mere inconvenience" in comparison to the risks of being murdered, that suffering discrimination is not as bad as being assaulted, and that in any event it is not all blacks who are barred, just "17-year-old black males wearing running shoes and hooded sweatshirts."[1]

The installation of these buzzers happened swiftly in New York; stores that had always had their doors wide open suddenly became exclusive or received people by appointment only. I discovered them and their meaning one Saturday in 1986. I was shopping in Soho and saw in a store window a sweater that I wanted to buy for my mother. I pressed my round brown face to the window and my finger to the buzzer, seeking admittance. A narrow-eyed, white teenager wearing running shoes and feasting on bubble

---

[1] "When 'By Appointment' Means Keep Out," *New York Times*, December 17, 1986, p. B1. Letter to the Editor from Michael Levin and Marguerita Levin, *New York Times*, January 11, 1987, p. E32.

gum glared out, evaluating me for signs that would pit me against the limits of his social understanding. After about five seconds, he mouthed "We're closed," and blew pink rubber at me. It was two Saturdays before Christmas, at one o'clock in the afternoon; there were several white people in the store who appeared to be shopping for things for *their* mothers.

I was enraged. At that moment I literally wanted to break all the windows of the store and *take* lots of sweaters for my mother. In the flicker of his judgmental gray eyes, that saleschild had transformed my brightly sentimental, joy-to-the-world, pre-Christmas spree to a shambles. He snuffed my sense of humanitarian catholicity, and there was nothing I could do to snuff his, without making a spectacle of myself.

I am still struck by the structure of power that drove me into such a blizzard of rage. There was almost nothing I could do, short of physically intruding upon him, that would humiliate him the way he humiliated me. No words, no gestures, no prejudices of my own would make a bit of difference to him; his refusal to let me into the store—it was Benetton's, whose colorfully punnish ad campaign is premised on wrapping every one of the world's peoples in its cottons and woolens—was an outward manifestation of his never having let someone like me into the realm of his reality. He had no compassion, no remorse, no reference to me; and no desire to acknowledge me even at the estranged level of arm's-length transactor. He saw me only as one who would take his money and therefore could not conceive that I was there to give him money.

In this weird ontological imbalance, I realized that buying something in that store was like bestowing a gift, the gift of my commerce, the lucre of my patronage. In the wake of my outrage, I wanted to take back the gift of appreciation that my peering in the window must have appeared to be. I wanted to take it back in the form of unappreciation, disrespect, defilement. I wanted to work so hard at wishing he could feel what I felt that he would never again mistake my hatred for some sort of plaintive wish to be included. I was quite willing to disenfranchise myself, in the heat of my need to revoke the flattery of my purchasing power. I was willing to boycott Benetton's, random white-owned businesses, and anyone who ever blew bubble gum in my face again.

My rage was admittedly diffuse, even self-destructive, but it was symmetrical. The perhaps loose-ended but utter propriety of that rage is no doubt lost not just to the young man who actually barred me, but to those who would appreciate my being barred only as an abstract precaution, who approve of those who would bar even as they deny that they would bar *me*.

The violence of my desire to burst into Benetton's is probably quite apparent. I often wonder if the violence, the exclusionary hatred, is equally apparent in the repeated public urgings that blacks understand the buzzer system by putting themselves in the shoes of white storeowners—that, in effect, blacks look into the mirror of frightened white faces for the reality of their undesirability; and that then blacks would "just as surely conclude

5

that [they] would not let [themselves] in under similar circumstances."[2] (That some blacks might agree merely shows that some of us have learned too well the lessons of privatized intimacies of self-hatred and rationalized away the fullness of our public, participatory selves.)

On the same day I was barred from Benetton's, I went home and wrote the above impassioned account in my journal. On the day after that, I found I was still brooding, so I turned to a form of catharsis I have always found healing. I typed up as much of the story as I have just told, made a big poster of it, put a nice colorful border around it, and, after Benetton's was truly closed, stuck it to their big sweater-filled window. I exercised my first-amendment right to place my business with them right out in the street.

So that was the first telling of this story. The second telling came a few months later, for a symposium on Excluded Voices sponsored by a law review. I wrote an essay summing up my feelings about being excluded from Benetton's and analyzing "how the rhetoric of increased privatization, in response to racial issues, functions as the rationalizing agent of public un-accountability and, ultimately, irresponsibility." Weeks later, I received the first edit. From the first page to the last, my fury had been carefully cut out. My rushing, run-on-rage had been reduced to simple declarative sentences. The active personal had been inverted in favor of the passive imper-sonal. My words were different; they spoke to me upsidedown. I was afraid to read too much of it at a time—meanings rose up at me oddly, stolen and strange.

A week and a half later, I received the second edit. All reference to Benetton's had been deleted because, according to the editors and the fac-ulty adviser, it was defamatory; they feared harassment and liability; they said printing it would be irresponsible. I called them and offered to supply a footnote attesting to this as my personal experience at one particular lo-cation and of a buzzer system not limited to Benetton's; the editors told me that they were not in the habit of publishing things that were unverifiable. I could not but wonder, in this refusal even to let me file an affadavit, what it would take to make my experience verifiable. The testimony of an inde-pendent white bystander? (a requirement in fact imposed in U.S. Supreme Court holdings through the first part of the century[3]).

Two days *after* the piece was sent to press, I received copies of the final page proofs. All reference to my race had been eliminated because it was against "editorial policy" to permit descriptions of physiognomy. "I real-ize," wrote one editor, "that this was a very personal experience, but any reader will know what you must have looked like when standing at that window." In a telephone conversation to them, I ranted wildly about the

10

---

[2]*New York Times,* January 11, 1987, p. E32.

[3]See generally *Blyew v. U.S.,* 80 U.S. 581 (1871), upholding a state's right to forbid blacks to testify against whites.

significance of such an omission. "It's irrelevant," another editor explained in a voice gummy with soothing and patience; "It's nice and poetic," but it doesn't "advance the discussion of any principle. . . . This is a law review, after all." Frustrated, I accused him of censorship; calmly he assured me it was not. "This is just a matter of style," he said with firmness and finality.

Ultimately I did convince the editors that mention of my race was central to the whole sense of the subsequent text; that my story became one of extreme paranoia without the information that I am black; or that it became one in which the reader had to fill in the gap by assumption, presumption, prejudgment, or prejudice. What was most interesting to me in this experience was how the blind application of principles of neutrality, through the device of omission, acted either to make me look crazy or to make the reader participate in old habits of cultural bias.

That was the second telling of my story. The third telling came last April, when I was invited to participate in a law-school conference on Equality and Difference. I retold my sad tale of exclusion from Soho's most glitzy boutique, focusing in this version on the law-review editing process as a consequence of an ideology of style rooted in a social text of neutrality. I opined:

> Law and legal writing aspire to formalized, color-blind, liberal ideals. Neutrality is the standard for assuring these ideals; yet the adherence to it is often determined by reference to an aesthetic of uniformity, in which difference is simply omitted. For example, when segregation was eradicated from the American lexicon, its omission led many to actually believe that racism therefore no longer existed. Race-neutrality in law has become the presumed antidote for race bias in real life. With the entrenchment of the notion of race-neutrality came attacks on the concept of affirmative action and the rise of reverse discrimination suits. Blacks, for so many generations deprived of jobs based on the color of our skin, are now told that we ought to find it demeaning to be hired, based on the color of our skin. Such is the silliness of simplistic either-or inversions as remedies to complex problems.
>
> What is truly demeaning in this era of double-speak-no-evil is going on interviews and not getting hired because someone doesn't think we'll be comfortable. It is demeaning not to get promoted because we're judged "too weak," then putting in a lot of energy the next time and getting fired because we're "too strong." It is demeaning to be told what we find demeaning. It is very demeaning to stand on street corners unemployed and begging. It is downright demeaning to have to explain why we haven't been employed for months and then watch the job go to someone who is "more experienced." It is outrageously demeaning that none of this can be called racism, even if it happens only to, or to large numbers of,

black people; as long as it's done with a smile, a handshake and a shrug; as long as the phantom-word "race" is never used.

The image of race as a phantom-word came to me after I moved into my late godmother's home. In an attempt to make it my own, I cleared the bedroom for painting. The following morning the room asserted itself, came rushing and raging at me through the emptiness, exactly as it had been for twenty-five years. One day filled with profuse and overwhelming complexity, the next day filled with persistently recurring memories. The shape of the past came to haunt me, the shape of the emptiness confronted me each time I was about to enter the room. The force of its spirit still drifts like an odor throughout the house.

The power of that room, I have thought since, is very like the power of racism as status quo: it is deep, angry, eradicated from view, but strong enough to make everyone who enters the room walk around the bed that isn't there, avoiding the phantom as they did the substance, for fear of bodily harm. They do not even know they are avoiding; they defer to the unseen shapes of things with subtle responsiveness, guided by an impulsive awareness of nothingness, and the deep knowledge and denial of witchcraft at work.

The phantom room is to me symbolic of the emptiness of formal equal opportunity, particularly as propounded by President Reagan, the Reagan Civil Rights Commission and the Reagan Supreme Court. Blindly formalized constructions of equal opportunity are the creation of a space that is filled in by a meandering stream of unguided hopes, dreams, fantasies, fears, recollections. They are the presence of the past in imaginary, imagistic form— the phantom-roomed exile of our longing.

It is thus that I strongly believe in the efficacy of programs and paradigms like affirmative action. Blacks are the objects of a constitutional omission which has been incorporated into a theory of neutrality. It is thus that omission is really a form of expression, as oxymoronic as that sounds: racial omission is a literal part of original intent; it is the fixed, reiterated prophecy of the Founding Fathers. It is thus that affirmative action is an affirmation; the affirmative act of hiring—or hearing—blacks is a recognition of individuality that re-places blacks as a social statistic, that is profoundly interconnective to the fate of blacks and whites either as sub-groups or as one group. In this sense, affirmative action is as mystical and beyond-the-self as an initiation ceremony. It is an act of verification and of vision. It is an act of social as well as professional responsibility.

The following morning I opened the local newspaper, to find that the event of my speech had commanded two columns on the front page of the Metro section. I quote only the opening lines: "Affirmative action promotes prejudice by denying the status of women and blacks, instead of affirming them as its name suggests. So said New York City attorney Patricia Williams to an audience Wednesday."[4]

I clipped out the article and put it in my journal. In the margin there is   15
a note to myself: eventually, it says, I should try to pull all these threads together into yet another law-review article. The problem, of course, will be that in the hierarchy of law-review citation, the article in the newspaper will have more authoritative weight about me, as a so-called "primary resource," than I will have; it will take precedence over my own citation of the unverifiable testimony of my speech.

I have used the Benetton's story a lot, in speaking engagements at various schools. I tell it whenever I am too tired to whip up an original speech from scratch. Here are some of the questions I have been asked in the wake of its telling:

Am I not privileging a racial perspective, by considering only the black point of view? Don't I have an obligation to include the "salesman's side" of the story?

Am I not putting the salesman on trial and finding him guilty of racism without giving him a chance to respond to or cross-examine me?

Am I not using the store window as a "metaphorical fence" against the potential of his explanation in order to represent my side as "authentic"?

How can I be sure I'm right?   20

What makes my experience the real black one anyway?

Isn't it possible that another black person would disagree with my experience? If so, doesn't that render my story too unempirical and subjective to pay any attention to?

Always a major objection is to my having put the poster on Benetton's window. As one law professor put it: "It's one thing to publish this in a law review, where no one can take it personally, but it's another thing altogether to put your own interpretation right out there, just like that, uncontested, I mean, with nothing to counter it."

QUESTIONS

1. Williams begins her essay with the simple sentence, "Buzzers are big in New York City." What does Williams want us to understand about the function of buzzers in our society? How does she use her personal experience as a meditation on racial identity? In what ways do you find her personal experience to be persuasive evidence?
2. Williams offers us three renditions of the same story. Summarize each rendition. What do we learn about Williams's experience from these

---

[4]"Attorney Says Affirmative Action Denies Racism, Sexism," *Dominion Post* (Morgantown, West Virginia), April 8, 1988, p. B1.

different versions? What connections does she create between her different versions?

3. Reflect on the meaning of the title, "The Death of the Profane," and the subtitle, "A Commentary on the Genre of Legal Writing." What kind of commentary does Williams's essay offer her readers? What does Williams reveal about herself and her way of seeing the world of legal writing?

4. Imagine a conversation between Williams and the law professor who criticized her for putting the poster on Benetton's window. As you imagine such a conversation, decide what is at stake for both the professor and for Williams.

5. At the end of her essay, Williams offers us a number of questions she has been asked as she retells her Bennetton story. How would you respond to these various questions?

6. Using Williams's essay as a model, write three different versions of an experience you have had. Use these different versions to suggest an interpretation of the original story you tell.

MAKING CONNECTIONS

1. Select an idea about race or class that intrigues you in Williams's essay. How does this idea relate to a similar idea you find compelling in any of the other essays in "Reflecting"?

2. Williams is concerned with the questions of how an African American woman verifies and validates her own experience. What connections do you find between Williams's experience as an African American woman and the experience of Maya Angelou (p. 31) or Alice Walker (p. 42)?

THEME FOR ENGLISH B

Langston Hughes

Langston Hughes (1902–1967) grew up in Lawrence, Kansas, and Columbus, Ohio, and began writing at an early age, publishing his first poems when he was in high school. At twenty-one, he enrolled at Columbia University in New York City, but he left after his first year (he would later graduate from Lincoln University in Jefferson City, Missouri). In New York, Hughes came under the influence of the writers who were part of what came to be called the Harlem Renaissance, and he turned his poetic talents to the distinctive rhythms and concerns of the African American community. His first collection, The Weary Blues, *was published in 1926. Hughes went on to become one of the premier voices in American letters through his poems, short stories, novels, essays, articles, plays, and screenplays. He also translated the works of black poets from around the world. The following poem appeared in* Montage of a Dream Deferred *(1951).*

The instructor said,

> *Go home and write*
> *a page tonight.*
> *And let that page come out of you—*
> *Then, it will be true.*   5

I wonder if it's that simple?
I am twenty-two, colored, born in Winston-Salem.
I went to school there, then Durham, then here
to this college on the hill above Harlem.
I am the only colored student in my class.   10
The steps from the hill lead down into Harlem,
through a park, then I cross St. Nicholas,
Eighth Avenue, Seventh, and I come to the Y,
the Harlem Branch Y, where I take the elevator
up to my room, sit down, and write this page: 15

It's not easy to know what is true for you or me
at twenty-two, my age. But I guess I'm what
I feel and see and hear, Harlem, I hear you:
hear you, hear me—we two—you, me, talk on this page.

(I hear New York, too). Me—who?   20
Well, I like to eat, sleep, drink, and be in love.
I like to work, read, learn, and understand life.
I like a pipe for a Christmas present,
or records—Bessie,[1] bop, or Bach.
I guess being colored doesn't make me *not* like   25
the same things other folks like who are other races.
So will my page be colored that I write?
Being me, it will not be white.
But it will be
a part of you, instructor.   30
You are white—
yet a part of me, as I am a part of you.
That's American.
Sometimes perhaps you don't want to be a part of me.
Nor do I often want to be a part of you.   35
But we are, that's true!
As I learn from you,
I guess you learn from me—
although you're older—and white—

and somewhat more free.   40

This is my page for English B.

QUESTIONS

1. This poem presents itself as having been written to meet a composition
   assignment requiring students to write a page, "And let that page come
   out of you." What do you think the instructor meant by urging his students to "let that page come out of you"? In what respects do you think
   that letting something "come out of you" might be similar to reflective
   writing? In what ways do you think it's different?
2. In line 19, the student says "we two—you, me talk on this page." Who
   is he referring to when he says "we two"? How is it possible for two
   voices to speak on a single page? In what ways does the style of
   Hughes's poem seem to be like "talk"? How does the form of the poem
   seem to be like "talk"? In what ways do you think talking on a page
   might be similar to reflective writing? In what ways do you think it's
   different?

---

[1]*Bessie:* Bessie Smith (1898?–1937), a blues singer. [Eds.]

3. How do the various thoughts and feelings of the poem seem to "come out of" the student? How does the flow and organization of thoughts seem to "come out of" the student?
4. Notice how the student repeatedly focuses on "being colored" and the questions that raises for him as a student, a writer, and a person, especially in relation to his white instructor. Outline his train of thought to see if you can discover the reflective process by which he moves from the uncertainty of line 6 to the more confident tone of his concluding lines.

MAKING CONNECTIONS

1. Compare Hughes' reflections on "being the only colored student" in an all-white class, taught by a white instructor, with Patricia Williams' reflections upon being locked out of a store by a white teenager "where there were several white people . . . who appeared to be shopping. . . ." In what respects do the two writers' reactions and reflections seem to be similar? How do they differ? In what respects does writing help both Hughes and Williams come to terms with their predicaments? How might writing also be considered a source of the racial problems they're writing about?
2. Frederick Douglass also writes about learning to write (p. 101). Imagine a conversation between Douglass and Hughes about each other's report of this experience. How might they respond to each other's recollections and reflections about learning to write?

Pilgrimage to Nonviolence

Martin Luther King Jr.

The son of a minister, Martin Luther King Jr. (1929–1968) was ordained a Baptist minister in his father's church in Atlanta, Georgia, at the age of eighteen. He sprang into prominence in 1955 when he called a citywide boycott of the segregated bus system in Montgomery, Alabama, and he continued to be the most prominent civil rights activist in America until his assassination on April 4, 1968. During those tumultuous years, he was jailed at least fourteen times and endured countless threats against his life, but he persevered in his fight against racial discrimination, using a synthesis of the nonviolent philosophy of Mahatma Gandhi and the Sermon on the Mount. The 1964 Nobel Peace Prize was only one of the many awards he received, and his several books are characterized as much by their eloquent prose style as by their moral fervor. "Pilgrimage to Nonviolence" originally appeared in the magazine Christian Century *and was revised and updated for a collection of his sermons,* Strength to Love *(1963), the source of the following text.*

In my senior year in theological seminary, I engaged in the exciting reading of various theological theories. Having been raised in a rather strict fundamentalist tradition, I was occasionally shocked when my intellectual journey carried me through new and sometimes complex doctrinal lands, but the pilgrimage was always stimulating, gave me a new appreciation for objective appraisal and critical analysis, and knocked me out of my dogmatic slumber.

Liberalism provided me with an intellectual satisfaction that I had never found in fundamentalism. I became so enamored of the insights of liberalism that I almost fell into the trap of accepting uncritically everything it encompassed. I was absolutely convinced of the natural goodness of man and the natural power of human reason.

I

A basic change in my thinking came when I began to question some of the theories that had been associated with so-called liberal theology. Of course, there are aspects of liberalism that I hope to cherish always: its devotion to the search for truth, its insistence on an open and analytical

111

mind, and its refusal to abandon the best lights of reason. The contribution of liberalism to the philosophical-historical criticism of biblical literature has been of immeasurable value and should be defended with religious and scientific passion.

But I began to question the liberal doctrine of man. The more I observed the tragedies of history and man's shameful inclination to choose the low road, the more I came to see the depths and strength of sin. My reading of the works of Reinhold Niebuhr made me aware of the complexity of human motives and the reality of sin on every level of man's existence.[1] Moreover, I came to recognize the complexity of man's social involvement and the glaring reality of collective evil. I realized that liberalism had been all too sentimental concerning human nature and that it leaned toward a false idealism.

I also came to see the superficial optimism of liberalism concerning human nature overlooked the fact that reason is darkened by sin. The more I thought about human nature, the more I saw how our tragic inclination for sin encourages us to rationalize our actions. Liberalism failed to show that reason by itself is little more than an instrument to justify man's defensive ways of thinking. Reason, devoid of the purifying power of faith, can never free itself from distortions and rationalizations.

Although I rejected some aspects of liberalism, I never came to an all-out acceptance of neo-orthodoxy. While I saw neo-orthodoxy as a helpful corrective for a sentimental liberalism, I felt that it did not provide an adequate answer to basic questions. If liberalism was too optimistic concerning human nature, neo-orthodoxy was too pessimistic. Not only on the question of man, but also on other vital issues, the revolt of neo-orthodoxy went too far. In its attempt to preserve the transcendence of God, which had been neglected by an overstress of his immanence in liberalism, neo-orthodoxy went to the extreme of stressing a God who was hidden, unknown, and "wholly other." In its revolt against overemphasis on the power of reason in liberalism, neo-orthodoxy fell into a mood of antirationalism and semifundamentalism, stressing a narrow uncritical biblicism. This approach, I felt, was inadequate both for the church and for personal life.

So although liberalism left me unsatisfied on the question of the nature of man, I found no refuge in neo-orthodoxy. I am now convinced that the truth about man is found neither in liberalism nor in neo-orthodoxy. Each represents a partial truth. A large segment of Protestant liberalism defined man only in terms of his essential nature, his capacity for good; neo-orthodoxy tended to define man only in terms of his existential nature, his capacity for evil. An adequate understanding of man is found neither in the thesis of liberalism nor in the antithesis of neo-orthodoxy, but in a synthesis which reconciles the truths of both.

5

---

[1]*Reinhold Niebuhr* (1892–1971): American theologian, social activist, and noted writer on social and religious issues. [Eds.]

During the intervening years I have gained a new appreciation for the philosophy of existentialism. My first contact with the philosophy came through my reading of Kierkegaard and Nietzsche.[2] Later I turned to a study of Jaspers, Heidegger, and Sartre.[3] These thinkers stimulated my thinking; while questioning each, I nevertheless learned a great deal through a study of them. When I finally engaged in a serious study of the writings of Paul Tillich,[4] I became convinced that existentialism, in spite of the fact that it had become all too fashionable, had grasped certain basic truths about man and his condition that could not be permanently overlooked.

An understanding of the "finite freedom" of man is one of the permanent contributions of existentialism, and its perception of the anxiety and conflict produced in man's personal and social life by the perilous and ambiguous structure of existence is especially meaningful for our time. A common denominator in atheistic or theistic existentialism is that man's existential situation is estranged from his essential nature. In their revolt against Hegel's essentialism,[5] all existentialists contend that the world is fragmented. History is a series of unreconciled conflicts, and man's existence is filled with anxiety and threatened with meaninglessness. While the ultimate Christian answer is not found in any of these existential assertions, there is much here by which the theologian may describe the true state of man's existence.

Although most of my formal study has been in systematic theology and   10 philosophy, I have become more and more interested in social ethics. During my early teens I was deeply concerned by the problem of racial injustice. I considered segregation both rationally inexplicable and morally unjustifiable. I could never accept my having to sit in the back of a bus or in the segregated section of a train. The first time that I was seated behind a curtain in a dining car I felt as though the curtain had been dropped on my selfhood. I also learned that the inseparable twin of racial injustice is economic injustice. I saw how the systems of segregation exploited both the Negro and the poor whites. These early experiences made me deeply conscious of the varieties of injustice in our society.

---

[2]*Søren Kierkegaard* (1813–1855): Danish religious and aesthetic philosopher, concerned especially with the role of the individual; *Friedrich Nietzsche* (1844–1900): German philosopher and moralist looking for a heroic, creative rejuvenation of decadent Western civilization. [Eds.]

[3]*Karl Jaspers* (1883–1969): German philosopher; *Martin Heidegger* (1889–1976): German philosopher; *Jean-Paul Sartre* (1905–1980): French philosopher and novelist. All three were existentialists, concerned with the existence and responsibility of the individual in an unknowable universe. [Eds.]

[4]*Paul Tillich* (1886–1965): German-born American philosopher and theologian whose writings drew on psychology and existentialism. [Eds.]

[5]*Georg Friedrich Hegel* (1770–1831): German philosopher best known for his theory of the dialectic (thesis versus antithesis produces synthesis). [Eds.]

II

Not until I entered theological seminary, however, did I begin a serious intellectual quest for a method that would eliminate social evil. I was immediately influenced by the social gospel. In the early 1950s I read Walter Rauschenbusch's *Christianity and the Social Crisis,* a book which left an indelible imprint on my thinking. Of course, there were points at which I differed with Rauschenbusch. I felt that he was a victim of the nineteenth-century "cult of inevitable progress," which led him to an unwarranted optimism concerning human nature. Moreover, he came perilously close to identifying the Kingdom of God with a particular social and economic system, a temptation to which the church must never surrender. But in spite of these shortcomings, Rauschenbusch gave to American Protestantism a sense of social responsibility that it should never lose. The gospel at its best deals with the whole man, not only his soul but also his body, not only his spiritual well-being but also his material well-being. A religion that professes a concern for the souls of men and is not equally concerned about the slums that damn them, the economic conditions that strangle them, and the social conditions that cripple them, is a spiritually moribund religion.

After reading Rauschenbusch, I turned to a serious study of the social and ethical theories of the great philosophers. During this period I had almost despaired of the power of love to solve social problems. The turn-the-other-cheek and the love-your-enemies philosophies are valid, I felt, only when individuals are in conflict with other individuals; when racial groups and nations are in conflict, a more realistic approach is necessary.

Then I was introduced to the life and teachings of Mahatma Gandhi.[6] As I read his works I became deeply fascinated by his campaigns of nonviolent resistance. The whole Gandhian concept of *satyagraha* (*satya* is truth which equals love and *graha* is force; *satyagraha* thus means truth-force or love-force) was profoundly significant to me. As I delved deeper into the philosophy of Gandhi, my skepticism concerning the power of love gradually diminished, and I came to see for the first time that the Christian doctrine of love, operating through the Gandhian method of nonviolence, is one of the most potent weapons available to an oppressed people in their struggle for freedom. At that time, however, I acquired only an intellectual understanding and appreciation of the position, and I had no firm determination to organize it in a socially effective situation.

When I went to Montgomery, Alabama, as a pastor in 1954, I had not the slightest idea that I would later become involved in a crisis in which nonviolent resistance would be applicable. After I had lived in the community about a year, the bus boycott began. The Negro people of Montgomery, exhausted by the humiliating experience that they had constantly faced on the buses, expressed in a massive act of noncooperation their de-

---

[6]*Mahatma Gandhi* (1869–1948): Hindu nationalist and spiritual leader. [Eds.]

termination to be free. They came to see that it was ultimately more honorable to walk the streets in dignity than to ride the buses in humiliation. At the beginning of the protest, the people called on me to serve as their spokesman. In accepting this responsibility, my mind, consciously or unconsciously, was driven back to the Sermon on the Mount and the Gandhian method of nonviolent resistance. This principle became the guiding light of our movement. Christ furnished the spirit and motivation and Gandhi furnished the method.

The experience in Montgomery did more to clarify my thinking in regard to the question of nonviolence than all of the books that I had read. As the days unfolded, I became more and more convinced of the power of nonviolence. Nonviolence became more than a method to which I gave intellectual assent; it became a commitment to a way of life. Many issues I had not cleared up intellectually concerning nonviolence were now resolved within the sphere of practical action.

My privilege of traveling to India had a great impact on me personally, for it was invigorating to see firsthand the amazing results of a nonviolent struggle to achieve independence. The aftermath of hatred and bitterness that usually follows a violent campaign was found nowhere in India, and a mutual friendship, based on complete equality, existed between the Indian and British people within the Commonwealth.

I would not wish to give the impression that nonviolence will accomplish miracles overnight. Men are not easily moved from their mental ruts or purged of their prejudiced and irrational feelings. When the underprivileged demand freedom, the privileged at first react with bitterness and resistance. Even when the demands are couched in nonviolent terms, the initial response is substantially the same. I am sure that many of our white brothers in Montgomery and throughout the South are still bitter toward the Negro leaders, even though these leaders have sought to follow a way of love and nonviolence. But the nonviolent approach does something to the hearts and souls of those committed to it. It gives them new self-respect. It calls up resources of strength and courage that they did not know they had. Finally, it so stirs the conscience of the opponent that reconciliation becomes a reality.

III

More recently I have come to see the need for the method of nonviolence in international relations. Although I was not yet convinced of its efficacy in conflicts between nations, I felt that while war could never be a positive good, it could serve as a negative good by preventing the spread and growth of an evil force. War, horrible as it is, might be preferable to surrender to a totalitarian system. But I now believe that the potential destructiveness of modern weapons totally rules out the possibility of war ever again achieving a negative good. If we assume that mankind has a right to survive, then we must find an alternative to war and destruction. In our day of space vehicles and guided ballistic missiles, the choice is either nonviolence or nonexistence.

I am no doctrinaire pacifist, but I have tried to embrace a realistic pacifism which finds the pacifist position as the lesser evil in the circumstances. I do not claim to be free from the moral dilemmas that the Christian nonpacifist confronts, but I am convinced that the church cannot be silent while mankind faces the threat of nuclear annihilation. If the church is true to her mission, she must call for an end to the arms race.

Some of my personal sufferings over the last few years have also served to shape my thinking. I always hesitate to mention these experiences for fear of conveying the wrong impression. A person who constantly calls attention to his trials and sufferings is in danger of developing a martyr complex and impressing others that he is consciously seeking sympathy. It is possible for one to be self-centered in his self-sacrifice. So I am always reluctant to refer to my personal sacrifices. But I feel somewhat justified in mentioning them in this essay because of the influence they have had upon my thought. 20

Due to my involvement in the struggle for the freedom of my people, I have known very few quiet days in the last few years. I have been imprisoned in Alabama and Georgia jails twelve times. My home has been bombed twice. A day seldom passes that my family and I are not the recipients of threats of death. I have been the victim of a near-fatal stabbing. So in a real sense I have been battered by the storms of persecution. I must admit that at times I have felt that I could no longer bear such a heavy burden, and have been tempted to retreat to a more quiet and serene life. But every time such a temptation appeared, something came to strengthen and sustain my determination. I have learned now that the Master's burden is light precisely when we take his yoke upon us.

My personal trials have also taught me the value of unmerited suffering. As my sufferings mounted I soon realized that there were two ways in which I could respond to my situation—either to react with bitterness or seek to transform the suffering into a creative force. I decided to follow the latter course. Recognizing the necessity for suffering, I have tried to make of it a virtue, if only to save myself from bitterness, I have attempted to see my personal ordeals as an opportunity to transfigure myself and heal the people involved in the tragic situation which now obtains. I have lived these last few years with the conviction that unearned suffering is redemptive. There are some who still find the Cross a stumbling block, others consider it foolishness, but I am more convinced than ever before that it is the power of God unto social and individual salvation. So like the Apostle Paul I can now humbly, yet proudly, say, "I bear in my body the marks of the Lord Jesus."

The agonizing moments through which I have passed during the last few years have also drawn me closer to God. More than ever before I am convinced of the reality of a personal God. True, I have always believed in the personality of God. But in the past the idea of a personal God was little more than a metaphysical category that I found theologically and philosophically satisfying. Now it is a living reality that has been validated in the experiences of everyday life. God has been profoundly real to me in recent years. In the midst of outer dangers I have felt an inner calm. In the midst of lonely days and dreary nights I have heard an inner voice saying, "Lo, I will be with you." When the chains of fear and the manacles of frustration have all but stymied my efforts, I have felt the power of God transforming the fatigue of despair into the buoyancy of hope. I am convinced that the universe is under the control of a loving purpose, and that in the struggle for righteousness man has cosmic companionship. Behind the harsh appearances of the world there is a benign power. To say that this God is personal is not to make him a finite object beside other objects or attribute to him the limitations of human personality; it is to take what is finest and noblest in our consciousness and affirm its perfect existence in him. It is certainly true that human personality is limited, but personality as such involves no necessary limitations. It means simply self-consciousness and self-direction. So in the truest sense of the word, God is a living God. In him there is feeling and will, responsive to the deepest yearnings of the human heart: *this* God both evokes and answers prayer.

The past decade has been a most exciting one. In spite of the tensions and uncertainties of this period something profoundly meaningful is taking place. Old systems of exploitation and oppression are passing away; new systems of justice and equality are being born. In a real sense this is a great time to be alive. Therefore, I am not yet discouraged about the future. Granted that the easygoing optimism of yesterday is impossible. Granted that we face a world crisis which leaves us standing so often amid the surging murmur of life's restless sea. But every crisis has both its dangers and its opportunities. It can spell either salvation or doom. In a dark, confused world the Kingdom of God may yet reign in the hearts of men.

QUESTIONS

1. King found the extremes of liberalism on one hand and neo-orthodoxy on the other both unsatisfactory. Why?
2. Existentialism and Rauschenbusch's social gospel proved more useful to King than liberalism or neo-orthodoxy. How did these concepts help shape his outlook?
3. King is interested in religious and philosophical theories not for their own sake but for their usefulness in the social world. How do Gandhi's example and King's own experience in Montgomery (paragraphs 14, 15, and 17) illustrate this concern?

4. How did King's personal faith in God aid in his struggles and sufferings? Is his dream of a better society totally dependent on the existence of this "benign power" (paragraph 23)?

5. King's intellectual development is described as a pilgrimage from a simple fundamentalist attitude through conflicting theological and philosophical concepts to an intensified belief in a benign God and a commitment to international nonviolence. How is his final set of beliefs superior to his original one? Has he convinced you of the validity of his beliefs?

6. King writes for a general audience rather than one with theological and philosophical training. How successful is King at clarifying religious and philosophical concepts for the general reader? Point out examples that show how he treats such concepts.

7. Again and again King employs the classical rhetorical strategy of concession: the opposition's viewpoint is stated and partially accepted before King gives his own viewpoint. Locate two or three instances of this strategy, and explain how it aids a reader's understanding (if not acceptance) of King's views.

8. King's essay reflects on how he came to accept the method of nonviolence. Have you, over time, changed your thoughts or methods of approaching an issue or problem? Has someone you know well done this? If so, write an essay reflecting on the events central to this change and their significance.

9. King's hopes for a better world were expressed in the early 1960s. Based on your knowledge of history since then, write an essay in which you justify or disqualify King's guarded optimism.

MAKING CONNECTIONS

1. Like several other writers in this section, King reflects on a turning point in his life. Consider his essay in relation to two or three others, such as those by Maya Angelou (p. 31), Alice Walker (p. 42), George Orwell (p. 132), Zoë Tracy Hardy (p. 139), or Trudy Dittmar (p. 148). Compare and contrast the ways these writers present their turning points. How does each present the crucial moment or event, and how does each show its meaning?

2. One way a writer convinces us is by the authority we sense in the person as he or she writes. What details in King's essay contribute to our sense of him as an authoritative person, a writer we are inclined to believe? What do you find of similar persuasiveness in the essays of Maya Angelou (p. 31), George Orwell (p. 132), Zoë Tracy Hardy (p. 139), or Patricia J. Williams (p. 101)?

THE GHOSTS OF MRS. GHANDI

Amitav Ghosh

Novelist Amitav Ghosh was born in Calcutta, India, in 1956. A graduate of the University of Delhi, he received a Ph.D. from Oxford University in 1982. His works of fiction include The Circle of Reason *(1986),* The Shadow Lines *(1990), and* The Calcutta Chromosome *(1996). An anthropologist and former journalist, Ghosh has also published nonfiction, most notably* In an Antique Land *(1992), about his experiences living in Egypt as a young man. He currently teaches at Columbia University. The following essay originally appeared in the* New Yorker *and was collected in the 1996 edition of* The Best American Essays. *In it, Ghosh recalls the violent aftermath of the 1984 assassination of Indian Prime Minister Indira Gandhi, fueled by long-standing religious tensions between the country's Hindu and Sikh populations.*

Nowhere else in the world did the year 1984 fulfill its apocalyptic portents as it did in India. Separatist violence in the Punjab; the military attack on the great Sikh temple of Amritsar; the assassination of the prime minister, Mrs. Indira Gandhi; riots in several cities; the gas disaster in Bhopal — the events followed relentlessly on each other. There were days in 1984 when it took courage to open the New Delhi papers in the morning.

Of the year's many catastrophes, the sectarian violence following Mrs. Gandhi's death had the greatest effect on my life. Looking back, I see that the experiences of that period were profoundly important to my development as a writer; so much so that I have never attempted to write about them until now.

At the time, I was living in a part of New Delhi called Defence Colony — a neighborhood of large, labyrinthine houses, with little self-contained warrens of servants' rooms tucked away on rooftops and above garages. When I lived there, those rooms had come to house a floating population of the young and straitened — journalists, copywriters, minor executives, and university people like myself. We battened upon this wealthy enclave like mites in a honeycomb, spreading from rooftop to rooftop, our ramshackle lives curtained from our landlords by chiffon-draped washing lines and thickets of TV aerials.

I was twenty-eight. The city I considered home was Calcutta, but New Delhi was where I had spent all my adult life except for a few years away in England and Egypt. I had returned to India two years before, upon completing a doctorate at Oxford, and recently found a teaching job at

Delhi University. But it was in the privacy of my baking rooftop hutch that my real life was lived. I was writing my first novel, in the classic fashion, perched in a garret.

On the morning of October 31, the day of Mrs. Gandhi's death, I   5
caught a bus to Delhi University, as usual, at about half past nine. From where I lived, it took an hour and a half: a long commute, but not an exceptional one for New Delhi. The assassination had occurred shortly before, just a few miles away, but I had no knowledge of this when I boarded the bus. Nor did I notice anything untoward at any point during the ninety-minute journey. But the news, traveling by word of mouth, raced my bus to the university.

When I walked into the grounds, I saw not the usual boisterous, Frisbee-throwing crowd of students but small groups of people standing intently around transistor radios. A young man detached himself from one of the huddles and approached me, his mouth twisted into the tight-lipped, knowing smile that seems always to accompany the gambit "Have you heard . . . ?"

The campus was humming, he said. No one knew for sure, but it was being said that Mrs. Gandhi had been shot. The word was that she had been assassinated by two Sikh bodyguards, in revenge for her having sent troops to raid the Sikhs' Golden Temple of Amritsar[1] earlier this year.

Just before stepping into the lecture room, I heard a report on All India Radio, the national network: Mrs. Gandhi had been rushed to a hospital after an attempted assassination.

Nothing stopped: the momentum of the daily routine carried things forward. I went into a classroom and began my lecture, but not many students had shown up and those who had were distracted and distant; there was a lot of fidgeting.

Halfway through the class, I looked out through the room's single, slit-   10
like windows. The sunlight lay bright on the lawn below and on the trees beyond. It was the time of year when Delhi was at its best, crisp and cool, its abundant greenery freshly watered by the recently retreated monsoons, its skies washed sparkling clean. By the time I turned back, I had forgotten what I was saying and had to reach for my notes.

My unsteadiness surprised me. I was not an uncritical admirer of Mrs. Gandhi. Her brief period of semi-dictatorial rule in the mid-seventies was still alive in my memory. But the ghastliness of her murder was a sudden reminder of the very real qualities that had been taken for granted: her fortitude, her dignity, her physical courage, her endurance.

Yet it was not just grief I felt at that moment. Rather, it was a sense of something slipping loose, of a mooring coming untied somewhere within.

---

[1]*Temple of Amritsar:* the center of the Sikh religion, located in Amritsar, a city in northwest India near the border of Pakistan. [Eds.]

The first reliable report of Mrs. Gandhi's death was broadcast from Karachi, by Pakistan's official radio network, at around 1:30 P.M. On All India Radio, regular broadcasts had been replaced by music.

I left the university in the late afternoon with a friend, Hari Sen, who lived at the other end of the city. I needed to make a long-distance phone call, and he had offered to let me use his family's telephone.

To get to Hari's house, we had to change buses at Connaught Place, the elegant circular arcade that lies at the geographical heart of Delhi, linking the old city with the new. As the bus swung around the periphery of the arcade, I noticed that the shops, stalls, and eateries were beginning to shut down, even though it was still afternoon.

Our next bus was not quite full, which was unusual. Just as it was pulling   15
out, a man ran out of an office and jumped on. He was middle-aged and dressed in shirt and trousers, evidently an employee in one of the nearby government buildings. He was a Sikh, but I scarcely noticed this at the time.

He probably jumped on without giving the matter any thought, this being his regular, daily bus. But, as if happened, on this day no choice could have been more unfortunate, for the route of the bus went past the hospital where Indira Gandhi's body then lay. Certain loyalists in her party had begun inciting the crowds gathered there to seek revenge. The motorcade of Giani Zail Singh, the president of the republic, a Sikh, had already been attacked by a mob.

None of this was known to us then, and we would never have suspected it: violence had never been directed at the Sikhs in Delhi.

As the bus made its way down New Delhi's broad, tree-lined avenues, official-looking cars, with outriders and escorts, overtook us, speeding toward the hospital. As we drew nearer, it became evident that a large number of people had gathered there. But this was no ordinary crowd: it seemed to consist mostly of red-eyed young men in half-unbuttoned shirts. It was now that I noticed that my Sikh fellow passenger was showing signs of increasing anxiety, sometimes standing up to look out, sometimes glancing out the door. It was too late to get off the bus; thugs were everywhere.

The bands of young men grew more and more menacing as we approached the hospital. There was a watchfulness about them; some were armed with steel rods and bicycle chains; others had fanned out across the busy road and were stopping cars and buses.

A stout woman in a sari sitting across the aisle from me was the first to   20
understand what was going on. Rising to her feet, she gestured urgently at the Sikh, who was sitting hunched in his seat. She hissed at him in Hindi, telling him to get down and keep out of sight.

The man started in surprise and squeezed himself into the narrow footspace between the seats. Minutes later, our bus was intercepted by a group of young men dressed in bright, sharp synthetics. Several had bicycle chains wrapped around their wrists. They ran along beside the bus as it slowed to a halt. We heard them call out to the driver through the open door, asking if there were any Sikhs on the bus.

The driver shook his head. No, he said, there were no Sikhs on the bus.

A few rows ahead of me, the crouching, turbaned figure had gone completely still.

Outside, some of the young men were jumping up to look through the windows, asking if there were any Sikhs on the bus. There was no anger in their voices; that was the most chilling thing of all.

No, someone said, and immediately other voices picked up the refrain.   25 Soon all the passengers were shaking their heads and saying, No, no, let us go now, we have to get home.

Eventually, the thugs stepped back and waved us through.

Nobody said a word as we sped away down Ring Road.

Hari Sen lived in one of New Delhi's recently developed residential colonies. It was called Safdarjang Enclave, and it was neatly and solidly middle class, a neighborhood of aspirations rather than opulence. Like most such New Delhi suburbs, the area had a mixed population: Sikhs were well represented.

A long street ran from end to end of the neighborhood, like the spine of a comb, with parallel side streets running off it. Hari lived at the end of one of those streets, in a fairly typical, big, one-story bungalow. The house next door, however, was much grander and uncharacteristically daring in design. An angular structure, it was perched rakishly on stilts. Mr. Bawa, the owner, was an elderly Sikh who had spent a long time abroad, working with various international organizations. For several years, he had resided in Southeast Asia; thus the stilts.

Hari lived with his family in a household so large and eccentric that it   30 had come to be known among his friends as Macondo, after Gabriel García Márquez's magical village. On this occasion, however, only his mother and teenage sister were at home. I decided to stay over.

It was a very bright morning. When I stepped into the sunshine, I came upon a sight that I could never have imagined. In every direction, columns of smoke rose slowly into a limpid sky. Sikh houses and businesses were burning. The fires were so carefully targeted that they created an effect quite different from that of a general conflagration: it was like looking upward into the vault of some vast pillared hall.

The columns of smoke increased in number even as I stood outside watching. Some fires were burning a short distance away. I spoke to a passerby and learned that several nearby Sikh houses had been looted and set on fire that morning. The mob had started at the far end of the colony and was working its way in our direction. Hindus and Muslims who had sheltered or defended Sikhs were also being attacked; their houses, too, were being looted and burned.

It was still and quiet, eerily so. The usual sounds of rush-hour traffic were absent. But every so often we heard a speeding car or a motorcycle on the main street. Later, we discovered that these mysterious speeding vehicles were instrumental in directing the carnage that was taking place. Protected by certain politicians, "organizers" were zooming around the city, assembling "mobs" and transporting them to Sikh-owned houses and shops.

Apparently, the transportation was provided free. A civil rights report published shortly afterward stated that this phase of the violence "began with the arrival of groups of armed young people in temp vans, scooters, motorcycles or trucks," and went on to say, "With cans of petrol they went around the localities and systematically set fire to Sikh houses, shops and gurdwaras. . . . The targets were primarily young Sikhs. They were dragged out, beaten up and then burnt alive. . . . In all the affected spots, a calculated attempt to terrorize the people was evident in the common tendency among the assailants to burn alive the Sikhs on public roads."

Fire was everywhere; it was the day's motif. Throughout the city, Sikh   35
houses were being looted and then set on fire, often with their occupants still inside.

A survivor—a woman who lost her husband and three sons—offered the following account to Veena Das, a Delhi sociologist: "Some people, the neighbours, one of my relatives, said it would be better if we hid in an abandoned house nearby. So my husband took our three sons and hid there. We locked the house from outside, but there was treachery in people's hearts. Someone must have told the crowd. They baited him to come out. Then they poured kerosene on that house. They burnt them alive. When I went there that night, the bodies of my sons were on the loft—huddled together."

Over the next few days, some twenty-five hundred people died in Delhi alone. Thousands more died in other cities. The total death toll will never be known. The dead were overwhelmingly Sikh men. Entire neighborhoods were gutted; tens of thousands of people were left homeless.

Like many other members of my generation, I grew up believing that mass slaughter of the kind that accompanied the partition of India and Pakistan, in 1947, could never happen again. But that morning, in the city of Delhi, the violence had reached the same level of intensity.

As Hari and I stood staring into the smoke-streaked sky, Mrs. Sen, Hari's mother, was thinking of matters closer at hand. She was about fifty, a tall, graceful woman with a gentle, soft-spoken manner. In an understated way, she was also deeply religious, a devout Hindu. When she heard what was happening, she picked up the phone and called Mr. and Mrs. Bawa, the elderly Sikh couple next door, to let them know that they were welcome to come over. She met with an unexpected response: an awkward silence. Mrs. Bawa thought she was joking, and wasn't sure whether to be amused or not.

Toward midday, Mrs. Sen received a phone call: the mob was now in   40
the immediate neighborhood, advancing systematically from street to street. Hari decided that it was time to go over and have a talk with the Bawas. I went along.

Mr. Bawa proved to be a small, slight man. Although he was casually dressed, his turban was neatly tied and his beard was carefully combed and bound. He was puzzled by our visit. After a polite greeting, he asked what he could do for us. It fell to Hari to explain.

Mr. Bawa had heard about Indira Gandhi's assassination, of course, and he knew that there had been some trouble. But he could not understand why these "disturbances" should impinge on him or his wife. He had no more sympathy for the Sikh terrorists than we did; his revulsion at the assassination was, if anything, even greater than ours. Not only was his commitment to India and the Indian state absolute, but it was evident from his bearing that he belonged to the country's ruling elite.

How do you explain to someone who has spent a lifetime cocooned in privilege that a potentially terminal rent has appeared in the wrappings? We found ourselves faltering. Mr. Bawa could not bring himself to believe that a mob might attack him.

By the time we left, it was Mr. Bawa who was mouthing reassurances. He sent us off with jovial pats on our backs. He did not actually say "Buck up," but his manner said it for him.

We were confident that the government would soon act to stop the violence. In India, there is a drill associated with civil disturbances: a curfew is declared; paramilitary units are deployed; in extreme cases, the army marches to the stricken areas. No city in India is better equipped to perform this drill than New Delhi, with its huge security apparatus. We later learned that in some cities—Calcutta, for example—the state authorities did act promptly to prevent violence. But in New Delhi—and in much of northern India—hour followed hour without a response. Every few minutes, we turned to the radio, hoping to hear that the army had been ordered out. All we heard was mournful music and descriptions of Mrs. Gandhi's lying in state; of the comings and goings of dignitaries, foreign and national. The bulletins could have been messages from another planet.

As the afternoon progressed, we continued to hear reports of the mob's steady advance. Before long, it had reached the next alley: we could hear the voices; the smoke was everywhere. There was still no sign of the army or the police.

Hari again called Mr. Bawa, and now, with the flames visible from his windows, he was more receptive. He agreed to come over with his wife, just for a short while. But there was a problem: How? The two properties were separated by a shoulder-high wall, so it was impossible to walk from one house to the other except along the street.

I spotted a few of the thugs already at the end of the street. We could hear the occasional motorcycle, cruising slowly up and down. The Bawas could not risk stepping out into the street. They would be seen: the sun had dipped low in the sky, but it was still light. Mr. Bawa balked at the thought of climbing over the wall: it seemed an insuperable obstacle at his age. But eventually Hari persuaded him to try.

45

We went to wait for them at the back of the Sens' house—in a spot that was well sheltered from the street. The mob seemed terrifyingly close, the Bawas reckless in their tardiness. A long time passed before the elderly couple finally appeared, hurrying toward us.

Mr. Bawa had changed before leaving the house: he was neatly   50
dressed, dapper even—in blazer and cravat. Mrs. Bawa, a small, matronly woman, was dressed in a *salwar* and *kameez*.[2] Their cook was with them, and it was with his assistance that they made it over the wall. The cook, who was Hindu, then returned to the house to stand guard.

Hari led the Bawas into the drawing room, where Mrs. Sen was waiting, dressed in a chiffon sari. The room was large and well appointed, its walls hung with a rare and beautiful set of miniatures. With the curtains now drawn and the lamps lit, it was warm and welcoming. But all that lay between us and the mob in the street was a row of curtained French windows and a garden wall.

Mrs. Sen greeted the elderly couple with folded hands as they came in. The three seated themselves in an intimate circle, and soon a silver tea tray appeared. Instantly, all constraint evaporated, and, to the tinkling of porcelain, the conversation turned to the staples of New Delhi drawing room chatter.

I could not bring myself to sit down. I stood in the corridor, distracted, looking outside through the front entrance.

A couple of scouts on motorcycles had drawn up next door. They had dismounted and were inspecting the house, walking in among the concrete stilts, looking up into the house. Somehow, they got wind of the cook's presence and called him out.

The cook was very frightened. He was surrounded by thugs thrusting   55
knives in his face and shouting questions. It was dark, and some were carrying kerosene torches. Wasn't it true, they shouted, that his employers were Sikhs? Where were they? Were they hiding inside? Who owned the house—Hindus or Sikhs?

Hari and I hid behind the wall between the two houses and listened to the interrogation. Out fates depended on this lone, frightened man. We had no idea what he would do: of how secure the Bawas were of his loyalties, or whether he might seek revenge for some past slight by revealing their whereabouts. If he did, both houses would burn.

Although stuttering in terror, the cook held his own. Yes, he said, yes, his employers were Sikhs, but they'd left town; there was no one in the house. No, the house didn't belong to them; they were renting from a Hindu.

He succeeded in persuading most of the thugs, but a few eyed the surrounding houses suspiciously. Some appeared at the steel gates in front of us, rattling the bars.

---

[2]*salwar and kameez*: traditional form of Indian clothing consisting of loose flowing pants (*salwar*) with a matching overdress (*kameez*) and a long matching scarf. [Eds.]

We went up and positioned ourselves at the gates. I remember a strange sense of disconnection as I walked down the driveway, as though I were watching myself from somewhere very distant.

We took hold of the gates and shouted back: Get away! You have no 60 business here! There's no one inside! The house is empty!

To our surprise, they began to drift away, one by one.

Just before this, I had stepped into the house to see how Mrs. Sen and the Bawas were faring. The thugs were clearly audible in the lamplit drawing room; only a thin curtain shielded the interior from their view.

My memory of what I saw in the drawing room is uncannily vivid. Mrs. Sen had a slight smile on her face as she poured a cup of tea for Mr. Bawa. Beside her, Mrs. Bawa, in a firm, unwavering voice, was comparing the domestic-help situations in new Delhi and Manila.

I was awed by their courage.

The next morning, I heard about a protest that was being organized at 65 the large compound of a relief agency. When I arrived, a meeting was already under way, a gathering of seventy or eighty people.

The mood was somber. Some of the people spoke of neighborhoods that had been taken over by vengeful mobs. They described countless murders — mainly by setting the victims alight — as well as terrible destruction: the burning of Sikh temples, the looting of Sikh schools, the razing of Sikh homes and shops. The violence was worse than I had imagined. It was decided that the most effective initial tactic would be to march into one of the badly affected neighborhoods and confront the rioters directly.

The group had grown to about 150 men and women, among them Swami Agnivesh, a Hindu ascetic; Ravi Chopra, a scientist and environmentalists; and a handful of opposition politicians, including Chandra Shekhar, who became prime minister for a brief period several years later.

The group was pitifully small by the standards of a city where crowds of several hundred thousand were routinely mustered for political rallies. Nevertheless, the members rose to their feet and began to march.

Years before, I had read a passage by V. S. Naipaul that has stayed with me ever since. I have never been able to find it again, so this account is from memory. In his incomparable prose Naipaul describes a demonstration. He is in a hotel room, somewhere in Africa or South America; he looks down and sees people marching past. To his surprise, the sight fills him with an obscure longing, a kind of melancholy; he is aware of a wish to go out, to join, to merge his concerns with theirs. Yet he knows he never will; it is simply not in his nature to join crowds.

For many years, I read everything of Naipaul's I could lay my hands 70 on; I couldn't have enough of him. I read him with the intimate, appalled attention that one reserves for one's most skillful interlocutors. It was he who first made it possible for me to think of myself as a writer, working in English.

I remembered that passage because I believed that I, too, was not a joiner, and in Naipaul's pitiless mirror I thought I had seen an aspect of myself rendered visible. Yet as this forlorn little group marched out of the shelter of the compound I did not hesitate for a moment: without a second thought, I joined.

The march headed first for Lajpat Nagar, a busy commercial area a mile or so away. I knew the area. Though it was in New Delhi, its streets resembled the older parts of the city, where small, cramped shops tended to spill out onto the footpaths.

We were shouting slogans as we marched: hoary Gandhian staples of peace and brotherhood from half a century before. Then, suddenly, we were confronted with a starkly familiar spectacle, an image of twentieth-century urban horror: burned-out cars, their ransacked interiors visible through smashed windows; debris and rubble everywhere. Blackened pots had been strewn along the street. A cinema had been gutted, and the charred faces of film stars stared out at us from half-burned posters.

As I think back to that march, my memory breaks down, details dissolve. I recently telephoned some friends who had been there. Their memories are similar to mine in only one respect: they, too, clung to one scene while successfully ridding their minds of the rest.

The scene my memory preserved is of a moment when it seemed inevitable that we would be attacked.   75

Rounding a corner, we found ourselves facing a crowd that was larger and more determined-looking than any other crowds we had encountered. On each previous occasion, we had prevailed by marching at the thugs and engaging them directly, in dialogues that turned quickly into extended shouting matches. In every instance, we had succeeded in facing them down. But this particular mob was intent on confrontation. As its members advanced on us, brandishing knives and steel rods, we stopped. Our voices grew louder as they came toward us; a kind of rapture descended on us, exhilaration in anticipation of a climax. We braced for the attack, leaning forward as though into a wind.

And then something happened that I have never completely understood. Nothing was said; there was no signal, nor was there any break in the rhythm of our chanting. But suddenly all the women in our group — and the women made up more than half of the group's numbers — stepped out and surrounded the men; their saris and *kameezes* became a thin, fluttering barrier, a wall around us. They turned to face the approaching men, challenging them, daring them to attack.

The thugs took a few more steps toward us and then faltered, confused. A moment later, they were gone.

The march ended at the walled compound where it had started. In the next couple of hours, an organization was created, the Nagarik Ekta Manch, or Citizens' Unity Front, and its work — to being relief to the injured and the bereft, to shelter the homeless — began the next morning. Food and clothing were needed, and camps had to be established to accommodate the thousands of people with nowhere to sleep. And by the next day we were overwhelmed — literally. The large compound was crowded with vanloads of blankets, secondhand clothing, shoes, and sacks of flour, sugar, and tea. Previously hard-nosed, unsentimental businessmen sent cars and trucks. There was barely room to move.

My own role in the Front was slight. For a few weeks, I worked with a 80 team from Delhi University, distributing supplies in the slums and working-class neighborhoods that had been worst hit by the rioting. Then I returned to my desk.

In time, inevitably, most of the Front's volunteers returned to their everyday lives. But some members — most notably the women involved in the running of refugee camps — continued to work for years afterward with Sikh women and children who had been rendered homeless. Jaya Jaitley, Lalita Ramdas, Veena Das, Mita Bose, Radha Kumar: these women, each one an accomplished professional, gave up years of their time to repair the enormous damage that had been done in a matter of two or three days.

The Front also formed a team to investigate the riots. I briefly considered joining, but then decided that an investigation would be a waste of time because the politicians capable of inciting violence were unlikely to heed a tiny group of concerned citizens.

I was wrong. A document eventually produced by this team — a slim pamphlet entitled "Who Are the Guilty?" — has become a classic, a searing indictment of the politicians who encouraged the riots and the police who allowed the rioters to have their way.

Over the years the Indian government has compensated some of the survivors of the 1984 violence and resettled some of the homeless. One gap remains: to this day, no instigator of the riots has been charged. But the pressure on the government has never gone away, and it continues to grow: every year, the nails hammered in by that slim document dig just a little deeper.

That pamphlet and others that followed are testaments to the only hu- 85 mane possibility available to people who live in multiethnic, multireligious societies like those of the Indian subcontinent. Human rights documents such as "Who Are the Guilty?" are essential to the process of broadening civil institutions: they are the weapons with which society asserts itself against a state that runs criminally amok, as this one did in Delhi in November of 1984.

It is heartening that sanity prevails today in the Punjab. But not elsewhere. In Bombay, local government officials want to stop any public buildings from being painted green — a color associated with the Muslim religion. And hundreds of Muslims have been deported from the city's slums — in at least one case for committing an offense no graver than reading a Bengali newspaper. It is imperative that governments ensure that those who instigate mass violence do not go unpunished.

The Bosnian writer Dzevad Karahasan, in a remarkable essay called "Literature and War" (published last year in his collection *Sarajevo, Exodus of a City*), makes a startling connection between modern literary aestheticism and the contemporary world's indifference to violence: "The decision to perceive literally everything as an aesthetic phenomenon— completely sidestepping questions about goodness and truth—is an artistic decision. That decision started in the realm of art, and went on to become characteristic of the contemporary world."

When I went back to my desk in November of 1984, I found myself confronting decisions about writing that I had never faced before. How was I to write about what I had seen without reducing it to mere spectacle? My next novel was bound to be influenced by my experiences, but I could see no way of writing directly about those events without recreating them as a panorama of violence—"an aesthetic phenomenon," as Karahasan was to call it. At the time, the idea seemed obscene and futile; of much greater importance were factual reports of the testimony of the victims. But these were already being done by people who were, I knew, more competent than I could be.

Within a few months, I started my novel, which I eventually called *The Shadow Lines*—a book that led me backward in time, to earlier memories of riots, ones witnessed in childhood. It became a book not about any one event but about the meaning of such events and their effects on the individuals who live through them.

And until now I have never really written about what I saw in November of 1984. I am not alone: several others who took part in that march went on to publish books, yet nobody, so far as I know, has ever written about it except in passing.

There are good reasons for this, not least the politics of the situation, which leave so little room for the writer. The riots were generated by a cycle of violence, involving the terrorists in the Punjab, on the one hand, and the Indian government, on the other. To write carelessly, in such a way as to appear to endorse terrorism or repression, can add easily to the problem: in such incendiary circumstances, words cost lives, and it is only appropriate that those who deal in words should pay scrupulous attention to what they say. It is only appropriate that they should find themselves inhibited.

But there is also a simpler explanation. Before I could set down a word, I had to resolve a dilemma, between being a writer and being a citizen. As a writer, I had only one obvious subject: the violence. From the news report, or the latest film or novel, we have come to expect the bloody detail or the elegantly staged conflagration that closes a chapter or effects a climax. But it is worth asking if the very obviousness of this subject arises out of our modern conventions of representation; within the dominant aesthetic of our time—the aesthetic of what Karahasan calls "indifference"— it is all too easy to present violence as an apocalyptic spectacle, while the resistance to it can as easily figure as mere sentimentality, or, worse, as pathetic or absurd.

Writers don't join crowds—Naipaul[3] and so many others teach us that. But what do you do when the constitutional authority fails to act? You join, and in joining bear all the responsibilities and obligations and guilt that joining represents. My experience of the violence was overwhelmingly and memorably of the resistance to it. When I think of the women staring down the mob, I am not filled with a writerly wonder. I am reminded of my gratitude for being saved from injury. What I saw at first hand—and not merely on that march but on the bus, in Hari's house, in the huge compound that filled with essential goods—was not the horror of violence but the affirmation of humanity: in each case, I witnessed the risks that perfectly ordinary people were willing to take for one another.

When I now read descriptions of troubled parts of the world, in which violence appears primordial and inevitable, a fate to which masses of people are largely resigned, I find myself asking, Is that all there was to it? Or is it possible that the authors of these descriptions failed to find a form—or a style or a voice or a plot—that could accommodate both violence *and* the civilized, willed response to it?

The truth is that the commonest response to violence is one of repugnance, and that a significant number of people everywhere try to oppose it in whatever ways they can. That these efforts so rarely appear in accounts of violence is not surprising: they are too undramatic. For those who participate in them, they are often hard to write about for the very reasons that so long delayed my own account of 1984.   95

"Let us not fool ourselves," Karahasan writes. "The world is written first—the holy books say that it was created in words—and all that happens in it, happens in language first."

It is when we think of the world the aesthetic of indifference might bring into being that we recognize the urgency of remembering the stories we have not written.

QUESTIONS

1. Despite the title of his essay, Ghosh never mentions "the ghosts of Mrs. Ghandi" at any point in his recollections and reflections. How, then, do you interpret the title of this piece? In what sense(s) might it be understood as being about "the ghosts of Mrs. Ghandi"? If you had written the piece, how would you have titled it?
2. In paragraph 2, Ghosh declares that the experiences he went through following Mrs. Ghandi's death were "profoundly important to my de-

---

[3]*Naipaul:* V.S. Naipaul (b. 1932), novelist and travel writer of Indian parentage whose works vividly detail the complexities of Third World experience. [Eds.]

velopment as a writer; so much so that I have never attempted to write about them until now." How do you explain this seeming paradox? If those experiences were so important to his development as a writer, why did he never attempt to write about them until this essay, which was published twelve years later?

3. Ghosh has divided his essay into seven sections, separated from each other by space breaks. Read each section carefully, with an eye to determining the primary focus and purposes of each part. After making your section-by-section analysis, what did you conclude to be the main purpose of the essay by the time you had finished reading section 3? section 4? section 6? section 7? In other words, how did your understanding of the essay change (if at all) as you made your way from section to section?

4. In much of his essay, Ghosh writes about violent or near-violent events that transpired following the death of Mrs. Ghandi. Aside from the violence or the threat of violence, what else do these events have in common? In what respects do they differ from each other? How would you describe or define Ghosh's role in these events? Is he mostly a participant? an observer? Or does his role seem to change from one event to the next?

5. In the final section of his essay, Ghosh reflects at length on the responsibilities of the writer when confronted by violence and the failure of "constitutional authority." Note all of the responsibilities that he discusses, and list them in order from the most to the least important. Given this list, how effectively do you think Ghosh fulfilled his writerly responsibilities in 1984? How do you think he would have rated himself back then? How do you think he judged himself at the time of writing this essay? In thinking about these questions, be sure to take careful note of Ghosh's final paragraph.

6. Think of a time in your life when you found yourself in a violent or near-violent situation. What did you do when confronted with that situation? How did others react to it? Write an essay in which you recall that situation, tell how you behaved at the time, consider whether you think that you or others should have behaved differently, and reflect on what that experience means to you now as you look back upon it.

Making Connections

Ghosh, like Patricia J. Williams (p. 101), is intensely concerned with the political responsibility of the writer. Given this shared concern, compare and contrast the specific political obligations that seem uppermost in each writer's personal recollections and reflections.

SHOOTING AN ELEPHANT

George Orwell

George Orwell (1903–1950) was the pen name of Eric Blair, the son of a British customs officer serving in Bengal, India. As a boy he was sent home to prestigious schools, where he learned to dislike the rich and powerful. After finishing school at Eton, he served as an officer of the British police in Burma, where he became disillusioned with imperialism. He later studied conditions among the urban poor and the coal miners of Wigan, a city in northwestern England, which strengthened his socialist beliefs. He was wounded in the Spanish civil war, defending the lost cause of the left against the fascists. Under the name Orwell, he wrote accounts of all of these experiences as well as the anti-Stalinist fable Animal Farm *and the novel* 1984. *In the following essay, first published in 1936, Orwell attacks the politics of imperialism.*

In Moulmein, in Lower Burma, I was hated by large numbers of people—the only time in my life that I have been important enough for this to happen to me. I was sub-divisional police officer of the town, and in an aimless, petty kind of way anti-European feeling was very bitter. No one had the guts to raise a riot, but if a European woman went through the bazaars alone somebody would probably spit betel juice over her dress. As a police officer I was an obvious target and was baited whenever it seemed safe to do so. When a nimble Burman tripped me up on the football field and the referee (another Burman) looked the other way, the crowd yelled with hideous laughter. This happened more than once. In the end the sneering yellow faces of young men that met me everywhere, the insults hooted after me when I was at a safe distance, got badly on my nerves. The young Buddhist priests were the worst of all. There were several thousands of them in the town and none of them seemed to have anything to do except stand on street corners and jeer at Europeans.

All this was perplexing and upsetting. For at that time I had already made up my mind that imperialism was an evil thing and the sooner I chucked up my job and got out of it the better. Theoretically—and secretly, of course—I was all for the Burmese and all against their oppressors, the British. As for the job I was doing, I hated it more bitterly than I can perhaps make clear. In a job like that you see the dirty work of Empire at close quarters. The wretched prisoners huddling in the stinking cages of the lock-ups, the grey, cowed faces of the long-term convicts, the scarred buttocks of the men who had been flogged with bamboos—all these oppressed me with an intolerable sense of guilt. But I could get nothing into perspective. I was young and ill-educated and I had had to think out my problems in the utter silence that is imposed on every Englishman in the East. I did not even know that the British Empire is dying, still less did I know that it is a great deal better than the younger empires that are going to supplant it. All I knew was that I was stuck between my hatred of the empire I served and my rage against the evil-spirited little beasts who tried to make my job impossible. With one part of my mind I thought of the British Raj as an unbreakable tyranny,[1] as something clamped down, in *saecula saeculorum*,[2] upon the will of prostrate peoples; with another part I thought that the greatest joy in the world would be to drive a bayonet into a Buddhist priest's guts. Feelings like these are the normal by-product of imperialism; ask any Anglo-Indian official, if you can catch him off duty.

One day something happened which in a roundabout way was enlightening. It was a tiny incident in itself, but it gave me a better glimpse than I had had before of the real nature of imperialism—the real motives for which despotic governments act. Early one morning the sub-inspector at a police station at the other end of the town rang me up on the phone and said that an elephant was ravaging the bazaar. Would I please come and do something about it? I did not know what I could do, but I wanted to see what was happening and I got on to a pony and started out. I took my rifle, an old .44 Winchester and much too small to kill an elephant, but I thought the noise might be useful *in terrorem*.[3] Various Burmans stopped me on the way and told me about the elephant's doings. It was not, of course, a wild elephant, but a tame one which had gone "must."[4] It had been chained up, as tame elephants always are when their attack of "must" is due, but on the previous night it had broken its chain and escaped. Its mahout,[5] the only person who could manage it when it was in that state, had set out in pursuit, but had taken the wrong direction and was now twelve hours' journey away, and in the morning the elephant had suddenly reappeared in town. The Burmese population had no weapons and were quite helpless against it. It had already destroyed somebody's bamboo hut, killed a cow and raided some fruit-stalls and devoured the stock; also it had met the municipal rubbish van and, when the driver jumped out and took to his heels, had turned the van over and inflicted violences upon it.

The Burmese sub-inspector and some Indian constables were waiting for me in the quarter where the elephant had been seen. It was a very poor

---

[1]*the British Raj:* the imperial government ruling British India and Burma. [Eds.]

[2]*saecula saeculorum:* forever and ever. [Eds.]

[3]*in terrorem:* for fright. [Eds.]

[4]*"must":* frenzied state of the bull elephant, due to sexual excitement. [Eds.]

[5]*mahout:* an elephant's keeper. [Eds.]

quarter, a labyrinth of squalid bamboo huts, thatched with palm-leaf, winding all over a steep hillside. I remember that it was a cloudy, stuffy morning at the beginning of the rains. We began questioning the people as to where the elephant had gone and, as usual, failed to get any definite information. That is invariably the case in the East; a story always sounds clear enough at a distance, but the nearer you get to the scene of events the vaguer it becomes. Some of the people said that the elephant had gone in one direction, some said that he had gone in another, some professed not even to have heard of any elephant. I had almost made up my mind that the whole story was a pack of lies, when we heard yells a little distance away. There was a loud, scandalized cry of "Go away, child! Go away this instant!" and an old woman with a switch in her hand came round the corner of a hut, violently shooing away a crowd of naked children. Some more women followed, clicking their tongues and exclaiming; evidently there was something that the children ought not to have seen. I rounded the hut and saw a man's dead body sprawling in the mud. He was an Indian, a black Dravidian coolie,[6] almost naked, and he could not have been dead many minutes. The people said that the elephant had come suddenly upon him round the corner of the hut, caught him with its trunk, put its foot on his back and ground him into the earth. This was the rainy season and the ground was soft, and his face had scored a trench a foot deep and a couple of yards long. He was lying on his belly with arms crucified and head sharply twisted to one side. His face was coated with mud, the eyes wide open, the teeth bared and grinning with an expression of unendurable agony. (Never tell me, by the way, that the dead look peaceful. Most of the corpses I have seen looked devilish.) The friction of the great beast's foot had stripped the skin from his back as neatly as one skins a rabbit. As soon as I saw the dead man I sent an orderly to a friend's house nearby to borrow an elephant rifle. I had already sent back the pony, not wanting it to go mad with fright and throw me if it smelt the elephant.

The orderly came back in a few minutes with a rifle and five cartridges,   5
and meanwhile some Burmans had arrived and told us that the elephant was in the paddy fields below, only a few hundred yards away. As I started forward practically the whole population of the quarter flocked out of the houses and followed me. They had seen the rifle and were all shouting excitedly that I was going to shoot the elephant. They had not shown much interest in the elephant when he was merely ravaging their homes, but it was different now that he was to be shot. It was a bit of fun to them, as it would be to an English crowd; besides they wanted the meat. It made me vaguely uneasy. I had no intention of shooting the elephant—I had merely sent for the rifle to defend myself if necessary—and it is always unnerving to have a crowd following you. I marched down the hill, looking and feel-

---

[6]*Dravidian coolie:* a *coolie* is an unskilled laborer; *Dravidian* refers to a large ethnic group from south and central India. [Eds.]

ing a fool, with the rifle over my shoulder and an ever-growing army of people jostling at my heels. At the bottom, when you got away from the huts, there was a metalled road and beyond that a miry waste of paddy fields a thousand yards across, not yet ploughed but soggy from the first rains and dotted with coarse grass. The elephant was standing eight yards from the road, his left side towards us. He took not the slightest notice of the crowd's approach. He was tearing up bunches of grass, beating them against his knees to clean them and stuffing them into his mouth.

I had halted on the road. As soon as I saw the elephant I knew with perfect certainty that I ought not to shoot him. It is a serious matter to shoot a working elephant—it is comparable to destroying a huge and costly piece of machinery—and obviously one ought not to do it if it can possibly be avoided. And at that distance, peacefully eating, the elephant looked no more dangerous than a cow. I thought then and I think now that his attack of "must" was already passing off; in which case he would merely wander harmlessly about until the mahout came back and caught him. Moreover, I did not in the least want to shoot him. I decided that I would watch him for a little while to make sure that he did not turn savage again, and then go home.

But at that moment I glanced around at the crowd that had followed me. It was an immense crowd, two thousand at the least and growing every minute. It blocked the road for a long distance on either side. I looked at the sea of yellow faces above the garish clothes—faces all happy and excited all over this bit of fun, all certain that the elephant was going to be shot. They were watching me as they would watch a conjurer about to perform a trick. They did not like me, but with the magical rifle in my hands I was momentarily worth watching. And suddenly I realized that I should have to shoot the elephant after all. The people expected it of me and I had got to do it; I could feel their two thousand wills pressing me forward, irresistibly. And it was at this moment, as I stood there with the rifle in my hands, that I first grasped the hollowness, the futility of the white man's dominion in the East. Here was I, the white man with his gun, standing in front of the unarmed native crowd —seemingly the leading actor of the piece; but in reality I was only an absurd puppet pushed to and fro by the will of those yellow faces behind. I perceived in this moment that when the white man turns tyrant it is his own freedom that he destroys. He becomes a sort of hollow, posing dummy, the conventionalized figure of a sahib. For it is the condition of his rule that he shall spend his life in trying to impress the "natives," and so in every crisis he has got to do what the "natives" expect of him. He wears a mask, and his face grows to fit it. I had got to shoot the elephant. I had committed myself to doing it when I sent for the rifle. A sahib has got to act like a sahib; he has got to appear resolute, to know his own mind and do definite things. To come all that way, rifle in hand, with two thousand people marching at my heels, and then to trail feebly away, having done nothing—no, that was impossible. The crowd would laugh at me. And my whole life, every white man's life in the East, was one long struggle not to be laughed at.

But I did not want to shoot the elephant. I watched him beating his bunch of grass against his knees, with that preoccupied grandmotherly air that elephants have. It seemed to me that it would be murder to shoot him. At that age I was not squeamish about killing animals, but I had never shot an elephant and never wanted to. (Somehow it always seems worse to kill a *large* animal.) Besides, there was the beast's owner to be considered. Alive, the elephant was worth at least a hundred pounds; dead, he would only be worth the value of his tusks, five pounds, possibly. But I had got to act quickly. I turned to some experienced-looking Burmans who had been there when we arrived, and asked them how the elephant had been behaving. They all said the same thing: he took no notice of you if you left him alone, but he might charge if you went too close to him.

It was perfectly clear to me what I ought to do. I ought to walk up to within, say, twenty-five yards of the elephant and test his behavior. If he charged, I could shoot; if he took no notice of me, it would be safe to leave him until the mahout came back. But also I knew that I was going to do no such thing. I was a poor shot with a rifle and the ground was soft mud into which one would sink at every step. If the elephant charged and I missed him, I should have about as much chance as a toad under a steam-roller. But even then I was not thinking particularly of my own skin, only of the watchful yellow faces behind. For at the moment, with the crowd watching me, I was not afraid in the ordinary sense, as I would have been if I had been alone. A white man mustn't be frightened in front of "natives"; and so, in general, he isn't frightened. The sole thought in my mind was that if anything went wrong those two thousand Burmans would see me pursued, caught, trampled on and reduced to a grinning corpse like that Indian up the hill. And if that happened it was quite probable that some of them would laugh. That would never do. There was only one alternative. I shoved the cartridges into the magazine and lay down on the road to get a better aim.

The crowd grew very still, and a deep, low, happy sigh, as of people who see the theatre curtain go up at last, breathed from innumerable throats. They were going to have their bit of fun after all. The rifle was a beautiful German thing with cross-hair sights. I did not then know that in shooting an elephant one would shoot to cut an imaginary bar running from ear-hole to ear-hole. I ought, therefore, as the elephant was sideways on, to have aimed straight at his ear-hole; actually I aimed several inches in front of this, thinking the brain would be further forward.

When I pulled the trigger I did not hear the bang or feel the kick—one never does when a shot goes home—but I heard the devilish roar of glee that went up from the crowd. In that instant, in too short a time, one would have thought, even for the bullet to get there, a mysterious, terrible change had come over the elephant. He neither stirred nor fell, but every line of his body had altered. He looked suddenly stricken, shrunken, immensely old, as though the frightful impact of the bullet had paralyzed him without knocking him down. At last, after what seemed a long time

10

—it might have been five seconds, I dare say—he sagged flabbily to his knees. His mouth slobbered. An enormous senility seemed to have settled upon him. One could have imagined him thousands of years old. I fired again into the same spot. At the second shot he did not collapse but climbed with desperate slowness to his feet and stood weakly upright, with legs sagging and head drooping. I fired a third time. That was the shot that did for him. You could see the agony of it jolt his whole body and knock the last remnant of strength from his legs. But in falling he seemed for a moment to rise, for as his hind legs collapsed beneath him he seemed to tower upward like a huge rock toppling, his trunk reaching skywards like a tree. He trumpeted, for the first and only time. And then down he came, his belly towards me, with a crash that seemed to shake the ground even where I lay.

I got up. The Burmans were already racing past me across the mud. It was obvious that the elephant would never rise again, but he was not dead. He was breathing very rhythmically with long rattling gasps, his great mound of a side painfully rising and falling. His mouth was wide open—I could see far down into caverns of pale pink throat. I waited for a long time for him to die, but his breathing did not weaken. Finally I fired my two remaining shots into the spot where I thought his heart must be. The thick blood welled out of him like red velvet, but still he did not die. His body did not even jerk when the shots hit him, the tortured breathing continued without a pause. He was dying, very slowly and in great agony, but in some world remote from me where not even a bullet could damage him further. I felt that I had got to put an end to that dreadful noise. It seemed dreadful to see the great beast lying there, powerless to move and yet powerless to die, and not even to be able to finish him. I sent back for my small rifle and poured shot after shot into his heart and down his throat. They seemed to make no impression. The tortured gasps continued as steadily as the ticking of a clock.

In the end I could not stand it any longer and went away. I heard later that it took him half an hour to die. Burmans were bringing dahs and baskets even before I left,[7] and I was told they had stripped his body almost to the bones by the afternoon.

Afterwards, of course, there were endless discussions about the shooting of the elephant. The owner was furious, but he was only an Indian and could do nothing. Besides, legally I had done the right thing, for a mad elephant has to be killed, like a mad dog, if its owner fails to control it. Among the Europeans opinion was divided. The older men said I was right, the younger men said it was a damn shame to shoot an elephant for killing a coolie, because an elephant was worth more than any damn Coringhee coolie. And afterwards I was very glad that the coolie had been killed; it put me legally in the right and it gave me a sufficient pretext for

---

[7]*dahs:* butcher knives. [Eds.]

shooting the elephant. I often wondered whether any of the others grasped that I had done it solely to avoid looking a fool.

QUESTIONS

1. Describe Orwell's mixed feelings about serving as a police officer in Burma.
2. How do the natives "force" Orwell to shoot the elephant against his better judgment? How does he relate this personal episode to the larger problems of British imperialism?
3. What is Orwell's final reaction to his deed? How literally can we take his statement that he "was very glad that the coolie had been killed" (paragraph 14)?
4. From the opening sentence Orwell displays a remarkable candor concerning his feelings. How does this personal, candid tone add to or detract from the strength of the essay?
5. Orwell's recollection of shooting the elephant is shaped to support a specific point or thesis. Where does Orwell state this thesis? Is this placement effective?
6. In what ways does this essay read more like a short story than an expository essay? How effective is Orwell's use of narrative and personal experience?
7. Orwell often wrote with a political purpose, with a "desire to push the world in a certain direction, to alter other people's idea of the kind of society that they should strive after." To what extent does the "tiny incident" in this essay illuminate "the real nature of imperialism" (paragraph 3)? Does Orwell succeed in altering your idea of imperialism?
8. Using Orwell's essay as a model, write a reflection in which the narration of "a tiny incident" illuminates a larger social or political problem.

MAKING CONNECTIONS

The selections by Lucy Grealy (p. 50), Meghan Daum (p. 83), and Amitav Ghosh (p. 119) in this section read somewhat like short stories, as does Orwell's essay. Compare the narrative designs of two of these writers, and discuss the usefulness of storytelling in reflective writing.

WHAT DID YOU DO IN THE WAR, GRANDMA?
A Flashback to August, 1945

Zoë Tracy Hardy

Born in 1927 and raised in the Midwest, Zoë Tracy Hardy was one of millions of young women called "Rosie the Riveters" who worked in defense plants during World War II. Considered at first to be mere surrogates for male workers, these women soon were building bombers that their supervisors declared "equal in the construction [to] those turned out by experienced workmen in the plant's other departments," as a news feature at the time stated. After the eventful summer described in the following essay, Hardy finished college, married, and began teaching college English in Arizona, Guam, and Colorado. This essay first appeared in the August 1985 issue of Ms. *magazine — exactly forty years after the end of World War II.*

It was unseasonably cool that day in May, 1945, when I left my mother and father and kid brother in eastern Iowa and took the bus all the way to Omaha to help finish the war. I was 18, and had just completed my first year at the University of Iowa without distinction. The war in Europe had ended in April; the war against the Japanese still raged. I wanted to go where something *real* was being done to end this bitter war that had always been part of my adolescence.

I arrived in Omaha at midnight. The YWCA, where I promised my family I would get a room, was closed until 7 A.M., so I curled up in a cracked maroon leather chair in the crowded, smoky waiting room of the bus station.

In the morning I set off on foot for the YWCA, dragging a heavy suitcase and carrying my favorite hat trimmed in daisies in a large round hatbox. An hour of lugging and resting brought me to the Y, a great Victorian house of dark brick, where I paid two weeks in advance (most of my money) for board and a single room next to a bathroom that I would share with eight other girls. I surrendered my red and blue food-ration stamp books and my sugar coupons to the cook who would keep them as long as I stayed there.

I had eaten nothing but a wartime candy bar since breakfast at home the day before, but breakfast at the Y was already over. So, queasy and light-headed, I went back out into the cold spring day to find my job. I set out for the downtown office of the Glenn L. Martin Company. It was at their plant south of the city that thousands of workers, in around-the-clock shifts, built the famous B-29 bombers, the great Superfortresses, which the papers said would end the war.

I filled out an application and thought about the women welders and   5
riveters and those who operated machine presses to help put the Super-fortresses together. I grew shakier by the minute, more and more certain I was unqualified for any job here.

My interview was short. The personnel man was unconcerned about my total lack of skills. If I passed the physical, I could have a job in the Reproduction Department, where the blueprints were handled.

Upstairs in a gold-walled banquet room furnished with examination tables and hospital screens, a nurse sat me on a stool to draw a blood sample from my arm. I watched my blood rolling slowly into the needle. The gold walls wilted in the distance, and I slumped forward in a dead faint.

A grandfatherly doctor waved ammonia under my nose, and said if I would go to a café down the street and eat the complete 50-cent breakfast, I had the job.

The first week in the Reproduction Department, I learned to cut and fold enormous blueprints as they rolled from a machine that looked like a giant washing machine wringer. Then I was moved to a tall, metal contraption with a lurid light glowing from its interior. An ammonia guzzler, it spewed out smelly copies of specifications so hot my finger-tips burned when I touched them. I called it the dragon, and when I filled it with ammonia, the fumes reminded me of gold walls dissolving before my eyes. I took all my breaks outdoors, even when it was raining.

My boss, Mr. Johnson,[1] was a sandy-haired man of about 40, who   10
spoke pleasantly when he came around to say hello and to check our work. Elsie, his secretary, a cool redhead, seldom spoke to any of us and spent most of her time in the darkroom developing negatives and reproducing photographs.

One of my coworkers in Reproduction was Mildred, a tall dishwater blond with a horsey, intelligent face. She was the first woman I'd ever met with an earthy unbridled tongue.

When I first arrived, Mildred warned me always to knock on the dark-room door before going in because Mr. Johnson and Elsie did a lot of screwing in there. I didn't believe her, I thought we were supposed to knock to give Elsie time to protect her negatives from the sudden light. "Besides," I said, "there isn't room to lie down in there." Mildred laughed until tears squeezed from the corners of her eyes. "You poor kid," she said. "Don't you *know* you don't have to lie down?"

---

[1]All names but the author's have been changed.

I was stunned. "But it's easier if you do," I protested, defensive about my sex education. My mother, somewhat ahead of her time, had always been explicit in her explanations, and I had read "Lecture 14," an idyllic description of lovemaking being passed around among freshman girls in every dormitory in the country.

"Sitting, standing, any quick way you can in time of war," Mildred winked wickedly. She was as virginal as I, but what she said reminded us of the steady dearth of any day-to-day presence of young men in our lives.

We were convinced that the war would be over by autumn. We were   15
stepping up the napalm and incendiary bombing of the Japanese islands, the British were now coming to our aid in the Pacific, and the Japanese Navy was being reduced to nothing in some of the most spectacular sea battles in history.

Sometimes, after lunch, I went into the assembly areas to see how the skeletons of the B-29s were growing from our blueprints. At first there were enormous stark ribs surrounded by scaffolding two and three stories high. A few days later there was aluminum flesh over the ribs and wings sprouting from stubs on the fuselage. Women in overalls and turbans, safety glasses, and steel-toed shoes scrambled around the wings with riveting guns and welding torches, fitting fuel tanks in place. Instructions were shouted at them by hoarse, paunchy old men in hard hats. I cheered myself by thinking how we were pouring it on, a multitude of us together creating this great bird to end the war.

Away from the plant, however, optimism sometimes failed me. My room at the Y was bleak. I wrote letters to my unofficial fiancé and to other young men in the service who had been friends and classmates. Once in a while I attempted to study, thinking I would redeem my mediocre year at the university.

During those moments when I sensed real homesickness lying in wait, I would plan something to do with Betty and Celia, friends from high school, who had moved to Omaha "for the duration" and had jobs as secretaries for a large moving and storage company. Their small apartment was upstairs in an old frame house in Benson, a northwest suburb. Celia and Betty and I cooked, exchanged news from servicemen we all knew and talked about plans for the end of the war. Betty was engaged to her high school sweetheart, a soldier who had been wounded in Germany and who might be coming home soon. We guessed she would be the first one of us to be married, and we speculated, in the careful euphemisms of "well-brought-up girls," about her impending introduction to sex.

By the first of July, work and the pace of life had lost momentum. The war news seemed to repeat itself without advancing, as day after day battles were fought around jungly Pacific islands that all seemed identical and unreal.

At the plant, I was moved from the dragon to a desk job, a promotion   20
of sorts. I sat on a high stool in a cubicle of pigeonholed cabinets and filed

blueprints, specs, and deviations in the proper holes. While I was working, I saw no one and couldn't talk to anybody.

In mid-July Betty got married. Counsel from our elders was always to wait—wait until things settle down after the war. Harold, still recuperating from shrapnel wounds, asked Betty not to wait.

Celia and I attended the ceremony on a sizzling afternoon in a musty Presbyterian church. Harold was very serious, gaunt-faced and thin in his loose-hanging Army uniform. Betty, a fair-skinned, blue-eyed brunet in a white street dress, looked pale and solemn. After the short ceremony, they left the church in a borrowed car. Someone had given them enough gasoline stamps for a honeymoon trip to a far-off cabin on the shore of a piney Minnesota lake.

Celia and I speculated on Betty's introduction to lovemaking. I had "Lecture 14" in mind and hoped she would like lovemaking, especially way off in Minnesota, far from the sweltering city and the war. Celia thought it didn't matter much whether a girl liked it or not, as long as other important parts of marriage got off to a good start.

That weekend Celia and I took a walk in a park and watched a grandfather carefully pump a seesaw up and down for his small grandson. We saw a short, middle-aged sailor walking with a sad-faced young woman who towered over him. "A whore," Celia said, "Probably one of those from the Hotel Bianca." Celia had been in Omaha longer than I and knew more of its secrets.

I wanted, right then, to see someone young and male and healthy cross   25
the grass under the trees, someone without wounds and without a cap, someone with thick disheveled hair that hadn't been militarily peeled down to the green skin on the back of his skull. Someone wearing tennis shorts to show strong, hair-matted legs, and a shirt with an open neck and short sleeves revealing smooth, hard muscles and tanned skin. Someone who would pull me out of this gloom with a wide spontaneous smile as he passed.

In the next few days, the tempo of the summer changed subtly. From friends stationed in the Pacific, I began to get letters free from rectangular holes where military censors had snipped out "sensitive" words. Our Navy was getting ready to surround the Japanese islands with a starvation blockade, and our B-29s had bombed the industrial heart of the country. We were dropping leaflets warning the Japanese people that we would incinerate hundreds of thousands of them by firebombing 11 of their major cities. Rumors rippled through the plant back in Omaha. The Japanese Empire would collapse in a matter of weeks, at most.

One Friday night, with Celia's help, I moved out of the Y to Celia's apartment in Benson. We moved by streetcar. Celia carried my towels and my full laundry bag in big rolls, one under each arm, and wore my straw picture hat with the daisies, which bobbled wildly on top of her head. My hatbox was crammed with extra underwear and the war letters I was determined to save. When we climbed aboard the front end of the streetcar, I dropped the hatbox, spilled an armload of books down the aisle, and banged my suitcase into the knees of an elderly man who was trying to help me retrieve them.

We began to laugh, at everything, at nothing, and were still laughing when we hauled everything off the car and down one block to the apartment, the daisies all the while wheeling recklessly on Celia's head.

It was a good move. Summer nights were cooler near the country, and so quiet I could hear the crickets. The other upstairs apartment was occupied by Celia's older sister, Andrea, and her husband, Bob, who hadn't been drafted.

Late in July, an unusual thing happened at the plant. Mr. Johnson   30 asked us to work double shifts for a few days. The situation was urgent, he said, and he wanted 100 percent cooperation from the Reproduction Department, even if it meant coming to work when we felt sick or postponing something that was personally important to us.

The next morning no one from the day shift was missing, and the place was full of people from the graveyard shift. Some of the time I worked in my cubicle counting out special blueprints and deviations. The rest of the time I helped the crews sweating over the blueprint machine cut out prints that contained odd lines and numbers that I had never seen before. Their shapes were different, too, and there was no place for them in the numbered pigeonholes of my cubicle. Some prints were small, about four inches square. Mildred said they were so cute she might tuck one in her shoe and smuggle it home as a souvenir even if it meant going to the federal pen if she got caught.

During those days I learned to nap on streetcars. I had to get up at 4:30, bolt down breakfast, and catch the first car to rumble out of the darkness at 5:15. The double shift wasn't over until 11:30, so I got home about one in the morning.

The frenzy at the plant ended as suddenly as it had begun. Dazed with fatigue, I slept through most of a weekend and hoped we had pushed ourselves to some limit that would lift us over the last hump of the war.

On Monday the familiar single shift was not quite the same. We didn't know what we had done, but an undercurrent of anticipation ran through the department because of those double shifts—and the news. The papers told of factories that were already gearing up to turn out refrigerators, radios, and automobiles instead of bombs and planes.

In Reproduction, the pace began to slacken. Five hundred thirty-six   35 B-29s, planes we had put together on the Nebraska prairie, had firebombed the principal islands of the Japanese Empire: Hokkaido, Honshu, Kyushu, Shikoku. We had reduced to ashes more than 15 square miles of the heart of Tokyo. The battered and burned Japanese were so near defeat that there couldn't be much left for us to do. With surprising enthusiasm, I began to plan for my return to college.

Going home on the streetcar the first Tuesday afternoon in August, I heard about a puzzling new weapon. Some excited people at the end of the car were jabbering about it, saying the Japanese would be forced to surrender in a matter of hours.

When I got home, Andrea, her round bespectacled face flushed, met me at the head of the stairs. "Oh, come and listen to the radio—it's a new bomb—it's almost over!"

I sat down in her living room and listened. There was news, then music, then expanded news. Over and over the newscaster reported that the United States had unlocked a secret of the universe and unleashed a cosmic force—from splitting atoms of uranium—on the industrial seaport of Hiroshima. Most of the city had been leveled to the ground, and many of its inhabitants disintegrated to dust in an instant by a single bomb. "Our scientists have changed the history of the world," the newscaster said. He sounded as if he could not believe it himself.

We ate dinner from our laps and continued to listen as the news pounded on for an hour, then two, then three. I tried, at last, to *think* about it. In high school physics we had already learned that scientists were close to splitting an atom. We imagined that a cupful of the tremendous energy from such a phenomenon might run a car back and forth across the entire country dozens of times. I could visualize that. But I could not imagine how such energy put into a small bomb would cause the kind of destruction described on the radio.

About nine, I walked over to McCollum's grocery store to buy an   40
evening paper. The headline said we had harnessed atomic power. I skimmed through a front page story. Science had ushered us into a strange new world, and President Truman had made two things clear: the bomb had created a monster that could wipe out civilization; and some protection against this monster would have to be found before its secret could be given to the world.

Back out in the dark street, I hesitated. For the first time I could remember, I felt a rush of terror at being out in the night alone.

When I got back to the apartment, I made a pot of coffee and sat down at the kitchen table to read the rest of the paper. President Truman had said: "The force from which the sun draws its power has been loosed against those who brought war to the Far East. . . . If they do not now accept our terms they may expect a rain of ruin from the air the like of which has never been seen on this earth." New and more powerful bombs were now being developed.

I read everything, looking for some speculation from someone about how we were going to live in this new world. There was nothing. About midnight Andrea knocked on my open door to get my attention. She stood there a moment in her nightgown and curlers looking at me rather oddly. She asked if I was all right.

I said yes, just trying to soak it all in.

Gently she told me I had better go to bed and think about how soon   45
the war would be over.

The next day Reproduction was nearly demolished by the spirit of celebration. The *Enola Gay*, the plane that had dropped the bomb, was one of ours. By Thursday morning the United States had dropped a second atomic bomb, an even bigger one, on an industrial city, Nagasaki, and the Russians had declared war on Japan.

At the end of the day, Mr. Johnson asked us to listen to the radio for announcements about when to return to work, then shook hands all around. "You've all done more than you know to help win the war," he said.

We said tentative good-byes. I went home and over to McCollum's for an evening paper. An Army Strategic Air Forces expert said that there was no comparison between the fire caused by the atomic bomb and that of a normal conflagration. And there were other stories about radiation, like X-rays, that might cripple and poison living things for hours, weeks, maybe years, until they died.

I went to bed late and had nightmares full of flames and strange dry gale winds. The next noon I got up, exhausted, and called Mildred. She said they were still saying not to report to work until further notice. "It's gonna bore our tails off," she moaned. "I don't know how long we can sit around here just playing hearts." I could hear girls laughing in the background.

"Mildred," I blurted anxiously, "do you think we should have done   50 this thing?"

"Why not? Better us than somebody else, kid."

I reminded her that we knew the Japanese were finished weeks ago and asked her if it wasn't sort of like kicking a dead horse—brutally.

"Look," she said. "The war is really over even if the bigwigs haven't said so yet. What more do you want?"

The evening paper finally offered a glimmer of relief. One large headline said that serious questions about the morality of *Americans* using such a weapon were being raised by some civilians of note and some churchmen. I went to bed early and lay listening to the crickets and thinking about everyone coming home—unofficial fiancés, husbands, fathers, brothers—all filling the empty spaces between kids and women and old men, putting a balance in our lives we hadn't known in years.

Yet the bomb haunted me. I was still awake when the windowpanes   55 lightened up at daybreak.

It was all over on August 14, 1945. Unconditional surrender.

For hours at a time, the bomb's importance receded in the excitement of that day. Streetcar bells clanged up and down the streets; we heard sirens, whistles, church bells. A newscaster described downtown Omaha as a free-for-all. Perfect strangers were hugging each other in the streets; some were dancing. Churches had thrown open their doors, and people were streaming in and out, offering prayers of thanksgiving. Taverns were giving away free drinks.

Andrew wanted us to have a little whiskey, even though we were under age, because there would never be another day like this as long as we lived. I hated the first taste of it, but as we chattered away, inventing wild, gratifying futures, I welcomed the muffler it wrapped around the ugliness of the bomb.

In the morning Mildred called to say our jobs were over and that we should report to the plant to turn in our badges and get final paychecks. She had just talked to Mr. Johnson, who told her that those funny blueprints we had made during double shift had something to do with the bomb.

"Well, honey," she said, "I don't understand atomic energy, but old   60 jazzy Johnson said we had to work like that to get the *Enola Gay* and the *thing* to go together."

I held my breath, waiting for Mildred to say she was kidding, as usual. Ordinary 19- and 20-year-old girls were not, not in the United States of America, required to work night and day to help launch scientific monsters that would catapult us all into a precarious "strange new world"—forever. But I knew in my bones that Mildred, forthright arrow-straight Mildred, was only telling me what I had already, unwillingly, guessed.

After a long silence she said, "Well, kid, give me your address in Iowa, and I'll send you a Christmas card for auld lang syne."

I wanted to cry as we exchanged addresses. I liked Mildred. I hated the gap that I now sensed would always be between me and people like her.

"It's been nice talking dirty to you all summer," she said.

"Thanks." I hung up, slipped down the stairs, and walked past the   65 streetcar line out into the country.

The whole countryside was sundrenched, fragrant with sweet clover and newly mown alfalfa. I leaned against a fence post and tried to think.

The President had said we had unleashed the great secret of the universe in this way, to shorten the war and save American lives. Our commitment to defeat the Japanese was always clear to me. They had attacked us first. But we had already firebombed much of the Japanese Empire to char. That seemed decisive enough, and terrible enough.

If he had asked me whether I would work very hard to help bring this horror into being, knowing it would shorten the war but put the world into jeopardy for all time, how would I have answered?

I would have said, "No. With all due respect, Sir, how could such a thing make a just end to our just cause?"

But the question had never been asked of us. And I stood now, in the   70 warm sun, gripping a splintery fence post, outraged by our final insignificance—all of us who had worked together in absolute trust to end the war.

An old cow stood near the fence switching her tail. I looked at her great, uncomprehending brown eyes and began to sob.

After a while I walked back to the apartment, mentally packing my suitcase and tying up my hatbox of war letters. I knew it was going to be very hard, from now on, for the whole world to take care of itself.

I wanted very much to go home.

QUESTIONS

1. How does Hardy's attitude toward the war change in the course of this essay? What event causes her to reevaluate her attitude?
2. Describe Hardy's feelings about the introduction of atomic power into her world. Are they optimistic or pessimistic?
3. "You've all done more than you know to help win the war," Hardy's boss tells her (paragraph 47). How does she react to the fact that she was not informed by the authorities of the purpose of her work? How does her reaction differ from that of her coworker, Mildred?
4. As Hardy's attitude toward war changes, her attitude toward sex changes as well. Trace this change in attitude; what connection, if any, do you see between the two?
5. Is this essay merely a personal reminiscence, or does the author have a larger purpose? Explain what you think her purpose is.
6. This essay was published more than ten years ago and forty years after the events it describes. Are Hardy's fears and speculations (on atomic power, on the authority of the government, on sex) dated in any way, or are they still relevant today? Explain your answer.
7. Have you, like Hardy, ever wondered about the larger social implications of any job that you've held or that a friend or parent holds? Write an essay like Hardy's reflecting on that job and describing how your attitude changed as you placed the job in a larger context.

MAKING CONNECTIONS

Could Hardy's essay be described as a "pilgrimage" to a particular intellectual or political position, somewhat like Martin Luther King Jr.'s "Pilgrimage to Nonviolence" (p. 111)? How fair would that retitling be to Hardy's essay? What aspects of pilgrimage do you find in it?

Sciences and Technologies

PRONGHORN

Trudy Dittmar

Trudy Dittmar (b. 1944), formerly a college composition instructor and now a full-time nature writer, was born and raised in New Jersey, where she first learned the discipline of close natural observation under the guidance of her father. She currently lives in a cabin in the mountains of Wyoming, where she observes and writes about alpine wildlife, and at another home in New Jersey, where she observes and writes about the intricate marine life of the marshes and barrier islands along the Atlantic coast. Dittmar has written essays not only about pronghorn but also about barnacles, cows, moose, porcupines, rainbows, salamanders, saltmarsh cordgrass, wolves, white cedar, and other tree species. Although her essays, forthcoming in book form, repeatedly focus upon specific flora and fauna, they invariably raise important issues and questions about both the world of nature and the realm of human experience.

It was a good-sized band, considerably larger than any I'd ever seen. That was all that struck me as unusual about the antelope when I first spotted them. We were on our way out from a camping trip in the forest, in open country for the first time in a week and driving straight at the blaze of sunrise, when I caught a squinting glimpse of them not too far back from the Forest Service Road. Since so far in our travels K had seen just a few small bands of pronghorns, and those at a distance, I pulled up for her to get a good look at them.

The size of the band seemed impossible. It looked to be fifty strong. In winter, all pronghorns—does, fawns, and bucks of every age and sexual status—join in large herds, and at that time it's not unusual to see one hundred antelope together now that they're coming back strong in this part of the state. But this was not winter, and the pronghorns had not yet formed herds. This was just the end of September, the heart of the rutting season, a time when they were still moving in small segregated bands—bachelor bands of young males or bands comprising an older buck and his harem of does. Eight does were generally considered a good-sized harem for a buck, but it seemed to me it would take about twice that many, each with her offspring of one to three fawns, to make up a band of such heroic proportions as this. In a grassy field at the foot of red badlands, they stood in tawny clusters, their white bars and patches flashing in the early sun.

Back then, if you'd asked me, I'd have complained that in Wyoming pronghorn antelope went unappreciated. Their elaborate, curious beauty goes largely unheeded here, and at a knotty juncture in my life I was peculiarly stung by this. Of course, the reason is just that there are so many of them. They're like the magpie and the fireweed. If a local cowboy were to see a bird with the magpie's plumage and stature in a tropical jungle, I'd bet he'd ooh and aah and snap fifty pictures. But in Wyoming the sight of magpies is so familiar the accustomed viewer just doesn't see the green ember glow of their feathers anymore or the sleek, bold cut of their tails, and so instead of an admiring gasp at the electric white flash in their wingbeats, all magpies get is disparaged as scavengers. As for fireweed, liking soil that's been burned, or ravaged by human activities like logging, and finding such soil in abundance in this part of the state, they're snubbed for being so common, seen as weeds instead of as stately tall-plumed fuchsia flowers. The old "familiarity breeds contempt" law is all that's at work here, nothing more, but that was one of a few truths of life I was having trouble swallowing back then.

Once in a saloon, its decor an array of taxidermy common in Wyoming bars, I stood looking up at the head of a big pronghorn. "Funny looking stunkers, ain't they?" an old cowboy said. "All painted up like that and them big eyes bulging out, I always though they looked like a clown."

I thought the white bars on the throat were beautiful. Ditto, the rectangular white side patches, the white rump, and the big luminous eyes. It was bewildering to hear pronghorns called clowns. The first day I ever entered Wyoming, the first animal I saw was a pronghorn, on a rise by the road in the afternoon sunlight looking down on the cars going by. Their hairs are hollow, against brutal plains winters. The fastest creature in the Western Hemisphere, they run like the wind.   5

The first settlers must have been dazzled by the spectacle of the pronghorn, but now they get called clowns and goats, a fact which bears witness that an everyday spectacle is a contradiction in terms, and that no matter how rare a thing is in the world at large, and how marvelled at there, its beauty fades in everyday eyes. Be that as it may, back then, if you'd asked me, I'd have had pretty bitter words for this state of affairs, but the heated way I deplored it was probably extreme. After all, what did the pronghorn, or the magpie or the fireweed, know or care if their beauty should fade in some human's eye? If I found this situation so poignant, it was probably just an oblique way of singing some personal blues. I was entering a new season then, and something of my own was fading, something which at that stage of the game I identified as my "looks," and so the disappearance of beauty, real or imagined, or even just in the beholder's eye, was a thorny issue for me.

It was a big band all right, but as it turned out, that was not the most striking thing about it. There was something going on in their midst that we hadn't picked up from the road. The band fell into two main groups, a large crowd of scattered does and fawns to the west, up to forty maybe, and about four hundred yards to the east of them a smaller bunch, this apparently of does only, perhaps eight or nine in all. Normally they would be ambling about browsing, but they weren't. Instead both groups were focused on a spot midway between them where two bucks labored in combat.

As if fused head to head, they moved as one entity, like one drunk, multi-limbed, tawny body staggering back and forth, side to side in the middle of the field. First the westernmost part of the body was back-stepping, driven by the easternmost part, and then, the tables turned, the western half would be the one pushing forward, and the eastern half, hind legs angling sharply in an attempt to hold footing, would have a turn at stumbling backwards for awhile. Sometimes when both bucks managed to hold ground at the same time, they sashayed to one side and the other together like an eight-legged creature in an awkward angular dance, until finally one lost his footing and they started backward and forward again.

For awhile it was exciting. I'd never seen a pronghorn fight at close range before, and at no range had I seen one like this. The few I'd watched had been brief, a matter of swift admonishment and flight, but this one was long and tangled and vivid. The morning sun broke the horizon. The frost melted along the fence rails. Against the eroded red spires of the badlands the bucks toiled and toiled, as the rest of the band looked on. It was a nice piece of luck that we'd happened upon it, I thought while it lasted. A fine spectacle of nature for K to see.

An old friend from back East, K had come out to kick me up a little   10
after a situation of mine had flopped. An intense situation of three years, with a man nearly half my age. My old friends had never grasped the attraction. "What are you doing with a guy half your age?" they said. But my new friends, the ones I met only after I was with him, didn't seem to have a problem with it. After all, I looked young when I met him, and felt it, and I still looked and felt young three years later when we went down in flames. Some months afterward, though, one particularly bad day I glanced in the mirror and I didn't look the same anymore. I looked again, and again, trying to see what I was used to seeing, trying to get it right, but it wouldn't come.

"We turn corners," K said on the phone, from New York. Coiled up, tail a-rattle, I said baloney to that. I was temporarily derailed by this break-up, was all; in a few months I'd get my old stuff back. In fact, once out of sight of him (the hard, smooth-skinned rounds of his shoulders; the cords standing up in his arms) I saw pretty clearly that my lost beau and I had been on mightily different wavelengths. Day by day I worked back into my old life, slowly working him out of my blood, and as far as he went, I can say that in a few months I was making good progress at getting back on track. And I was out in the hills almost daily, getting my color back. Certain days, in the mirror, I would note this color, and I would note other things, too: I had the same cheekbones as ever; I was as straight-nosed as before. So, what had changed then? What was the tragedy? Could just some lines around my eyes be the source of this dire leaden pool spreading in my chest?

Whatever it was, I still couldn't shake the mirror business. I was either nagging at it for the image it threw me or avoiding it, but never at home with it anymore. Sometimes there was an annoying frustrated feeling, like beating your fists on a wall. Sometimes there was something chilling, unbearable, that I wanted to run from fast. "How about I come out for awhile," said K. I said no, she should come next summer, as we'd planned. "It's just some weird vanity trip I'm on, for some reason. No big deal," I said. But K came anyway.

As the sun mounted from orange to yellow, the bucks kept at it, scrambling backward and forward, legs bent at distressing angles, hooves jabbing into the clay. Heads tossing in unison, they grappled from side to side. Because they moved as a unit, while it went on the object of our watching was only the fight. But then they broke, turned their backs to each other and moved apart, one east, one west, and at that point the object of our watching became the fighters instead of the fight. It was a shocking moment. They seemed so unevenly matched. By the looks of them, it seemed a threat from one should have sufficed to send the other packing, no need for a fight, much less one as long and tough as this.

The one for whom it seemed a threat should have sufficed was lean, almost spindly, and small enough that if it weren't for the cut of his horns, I'd have taken him for a doe. His opponent was by far the more robust and regal. A tawny bulk, heading into the morning sun, his white bars were gleaming, and his black horns were polished with light. Broad of chest and barrel, and wide of skull, he had such big horns it looked like just one of them might fill both my hands at its base, and the points of their boldly forked prongs were so deeply hooked we could discern their little curls at one hundred and fifty yards.

But what we also discerned was that the big buck was in trouble. Two hundred yards is a distance to hear such a thing, but we could hear the sound of his breathing, a high pitched rasping, and then we noticed his sides, the big white rectangular patches heaving so hard it looked like his

15

heart was going to burst. The spindly buck had jogged jauntily to the west end of the field where he stood with the large group of does, but the big buck moved only haltingly eastward, in a series of starts and stops. Facing into the gaze of the smaller harem, he stood wheezing laboriously. Then he stretched his neck out straight and almost to the ground and in a fit of gasping and coughing lost all his elegance.

When he came upright again, though, he headed straight for the little bunch of does. He jerked his head up, high and stiff, and moved quickly and sharply, his effort forced but focused, to round up this remaining lot. For less than a minute they let him. Then while three stood fast, still acquiescing to his worthiness, the other five or six dodged south around him and took off toward the large group to the west.

The scrawny buck, lord of the group they ran to, had not so much as cocked a front leg. He just stood looking out as they came over to him, as he'd done earlier when all the scattered does had flowed in from afield, tightening the band around him as if to be close to his power. The big buck swerved back to catch the fleeing does, but they were long gone, and the instant they joined the large group, the little buck dashed out at him again.

It didn't last long this time. In not much more than a minute the big buck turned away huffing strenuously. Still, he wouldn't throw in the towel. He made a quick recoup of wind and then, ready to cut his losses and accept what was left, he darted eastward again toward the handful of does at that end of the field. He wasn't to have even that, though. The last three took off too, streaking to join the rest of the band, leaving the big buck behind in the empty end of the field.

He looked regal to us, but his inside no longer matched his outside, and if we couldn't see this, the does could. With his fine head, his bold bars, and the eloquent points of his horns, he might cut the same grand figure he had all the years all his does had entrusted themselves to him, but they knew something in him had changed. He'd passed out of the season of prowess for which they had known him. It was time to find home elsewhere.

Slowly, the compact, focused mass the band had formed while watching the fight began to spread out, as the does and fawns returned to their browsing. As they drifted westward away from him, the big buck made a few purposeful looking strides toward them. He stopped, watched, then made a few more purposeful looking strides. The little buck glanced back over his shoulder at him once or twice, but that's all—he didn't even bother to threaten—and after another few steps, successively more tentative, the big buck stopped. For what seemed a long while, he stood and watched as the band meandered back toward the badlands, till all you could see of them was a dotting of white rumps against red buttes. When he turned east again, I felt a pain beyond all reason. He blurred in my sight as he picked his solitary way through the field toward the sun.

20

Back in the Jeep, as K spouted a flurry of reactions to what we'd just seen, I thought of another time, showing this country to another friend,

Jan, then new to Wyoming as K was now. On our drive up the mountain-side home her first evening here, the sky was a panorama of weathers. To the northeast, across the valley, it was nighttime, the sky black with storm and pulsing with lightning over the mountains there. More than fifty miles distant, their round peaks flashed hard-edged every matter of seconds against silver sky, and sheets of rain hung in grey smudges over the plain below. To the southeast it was still daytime, the air placid and temperate, the sky clear, and the rising moon looked insubstantial against it, translucent even, a frail white disk on pale blue. To the west the sun was descending, a half hour to go yet, in a pale glowing sky of indeterminate color, yellow with pink in it, yellow with green in it, peach/lemon-lime/tangerine— all of these colors yet none of them either, a color just outside the grasp of mind's knowing. Trying to label it got you right-on-the-edge-of-your-tongue frustrated. A color without a name.

When we rounded the switchback at eight thousand feet we could see all these weathers, these colors, these risings and fallings, all at once all these processes and effects of atmosphere. Jan jumped down from the Jeep and stood at the edge of the gravel. A sage-covered slope dropped steeply before her, and hills capped with stands of black trees rolled beyond. She stood watching the storm as it drifted along the horizon. She watched the distant black mountains slowly turn gold. She looked long at the storm and the moon and the pending sunset, turning and turning from one to another. "If you could grow up here—" she said from the road's edge. "It teaches you you can get through it," she said.

It teaches you you can get through it, if there's a way through it. I thought that morning of the antelope. But sometimes there's not a way through it, and when there's not, it teaches that too.

"Can you beat it!" K said. "That beautiful big creature had that whole herd stolen away by that little puny thing."

That was how we both felt it, although we had no grounds for feeling that way. We hadn't seen the fight from the beginning, didn't know how the does and fawns had been grouped at the start. It could have been that the little buck had his own harem to start with, maybe even the larger of the two, and coming upon the big buck with a harem of seven or eight decided to try to annex a couple more to his band. Given the size of the band it was much more likely, in fact, that it had been two bands at the start and not one as we had for some reason assumed. We were anthropomorphizing like crazy, projecting elements of human melodrama onto the scene. The "beautiful big creature" and the "puny thing" were in fact not the handsome (and supposedly therefore deserving) hero and the worthless upstart we made them out to be, but instead an old buck, just going over the hill, and a healthy young comer, just starting out. And nobody'd "stolen" anything. They'd had a fair fight, and the does always picked the true winner, the one whose victory proved his genes' worth. It didn't matter what he looked like. And it didn't matter that one ended up with nothing while the other got it all. That was how things kept going. A wildlife biologist might have had a good laugh over us. A couple of cornballs sucked in by the handsome hero stuff of old movies, imposing sentimental morality and trivial theatrics on a simple case of nature taking its course.

Still, I couldn't help thinking anthropomorphic thoughts about the old buck. And at bottom, it wasn't the handsome hero business that really got to me about him. All that was only a smoke screen to eclipse what really hurt. He'd followed a long path through this country, all that time in a certain role, things going along in a certain way. (I couldn't help it, groundless or not, I was sure that before the fight the whole hefty harem had been his.) Then suddenly today he'd been pushed out of that path. Would he try to get back on it again somewhere else, try to get himself another harem? Or did he know that the old path had become irrelevant for him, that he'd passed out of that phase? And if he knew that, if he didn't keep trying to make the old tricks work for him, what would he do now? What new path could he take, and how would he know it? Picking his way through that grass heading sunward, had he been forging a path or in search of one, or had one just suddenly declared itself to him? And was this path the journey's last leg?

I could have gone to books to look for answers to these questions. That's what the wildlife biologist part of me would have done. But the anthropomorphizing part of me was in ascendancy at that point, and at that point I didn't care about the biologist's view. I didn't want empirical facts presented by scientists. Even if the books could have offered them, I didn't want clearcut answers to the questions the pronghorn's debacle had set in flow. At that point, I just wanted to ponder those questions, broadly and lavishly, following all forks in the path. I pondered the destiny of that pronghorn many times in the following weeks.

One morning some months later when I looked in the mirror, I noticed that something had changed. I'd stopped nagging at it. I could no longer deny I'd indeed turned a corner, and, at bottom, losing my looks was not what the corner was about. It was about a new path, and I was on one. Like an arc of surf, after the wave has broken, sweeping unresisted over the face of the beach, an emptiness washed through me, hollowing my arms, my legs, all my body, of any tension or former strife. The peace of an inexorable sadness acknowledged spread throughout me.

That evening for the first time since the antelope fight I looked into the books. One writer reported that bucks sometimes formed harems of up to twenty does, boosting my theory that the entire band was initially the big buck's, but other than this, not one of the books stacked around me under the lamplight addressed the questions I'd pondered. I think I'd known down deep all along that they wouldn't, that the answers I sought lay outside their covers and beyond that circle of light.

Still, the books held their own hard and quite splendid facts. Not only   30 was the old buck's species the fastest in the West, and wondrously hollow haired. His white rump was a semaphore, its shining hairs, erected in response to danger, sending a warning of mirrored sunlight even to his fellows two miles away, who in turn flared the alarm, on and on to the last antelope within reach. And in casting off his horn coverings each fall he was thoroughly original, the only exception to the rule that antlers are shed yearly and horns are kept for life. Traced down from Middle Miocene fossils (aged about 14 million, give or take a few million years) to a look-alike ancestor who roamed this continent two million years ago and on to its present day form, his species was the only native American hoofed animal. All others—deer, elk, moose, mountain goats, you name it—were immigrants. And, singular among mammals on yet one more count, the pronghorn and his fellows had no close relative here or on any other continent, nor had they ever had. The old buck belonged to a species more unique and strange than I'd realized.

No proper answers to my questions. Just these bizarre gorgeous facts. But they opened some kinds of sluice gate for me that night. Coming upon them one after another, I felt the bigness of the world and the longness of time in the pronghorn's history. I felt how small even that long history is against the eons before it, and I felt how infinitesimal are the codes of life, which, ever changing, keep changing life's details, yielding such results as the pronghorn's uniqueness, its strangenesses that serve it so well. And as for the old buck himself—who probably never even lost his beauty, who very likely was taken down before that—I felt how the remains of his body the morning after, fed on by scavengers and decomposing back into the soil, are part of that chain of prodigiously worked out details. I saw the old buck's fate inside pronghorn history, small as a pinprick but, like all the teeming pinpricks in all the histories, part of that great, old, illimitable scheme.

And though my questions and the answers they threatened still loomed in the darkness, and would continue to loom there, they weren't the whole show out there past the lamplight anymore. Instead they were in company with such details as these expressions of the working out of the old buck's species' fate. Whacky, erratic, but always a-weaving, fueled by the dissolution of old bucks and of everything else, the illimitable details of life sprang forth continually, passing from one far-fetched, utilitarian form to another all along the evolution trail, and there on my new path that night under the lamplight I felt a shrewd obscure mercy in them.

That spring I was especially attentive to pronghorn. One day I seduced a young doe by not walking. I stood on a low hill with my binocs and watched her until the motionless sight of me drove her nuts and she had to get up close for a look. What she did was kind of tricky. She began to circle me, each circle smaller, so that I had to keep pivoting as imperceptibly as possible, trying to present the same bewildering image to her every time she looked. As long as I succeeded reasonably at this she spiralled in closer. But then, of course, I failed.

This was fine, and so was a young buck dubbed Mozart. One night I camped with a music-lover friend who is never without a tiny tape recorder, spinning out the boy genius's music this time. The little buck had to approach to investigate. He just couldn't help himself. He came way closer than shooting distance, close enough for us to axe him if we'd liked, and in the morning when we woke he was there once more, just feet away from the tent, waiting to hear if we'd do it again.

This was fine too, but still not enough, and since out in the hills in my   35 part of the state you see pronghorn infrequently, and then solitary more often than not, I took a trip east to the open plains. There, there was a bounty of pronghorn. You saw strings of them along the tops of low ridges, silhouetted against the sky. Mostly then, it being late June, there were mothers and babies. Fawns with ears two times the length of their faces, a largess of fawns dotting the sagebrush, all with those bizarre, gorgeous details hard-wired inside them, one of them perhaps carrying the infinitesimal code for some far-fetched but salutary detail to come. You had only to move and in a flurry their miniature white rumps were zigzagging off toward the horizon along with the big ones. Wherever you looked, the plains were bobbing with them.

QUESTIONS

1. Dittmar's essay focuses not only on pronghorn, as indicated in her title, but also on herself. Indeed, she repeatedly interrupts her story of the pronghorn fight with material about her visiting friends, her failed love affair, and her aging appearance in the mirror. What does the pronghorn fight have to do with Dittmar's life? What does her personal experience have to do with the pronghorns? In what ways are they, perhaps, quite profoundly related to each other? In what ways are they completely different?

2. Given the numerous experiences and subjects that Dittmar reflects on in this essay, what do you think is her ultimate purpose? Or is her essay so wide-ranging that it's more like a bundle of associated recollections and reflections than a tightly focused piece with a clearcut intention? In order to arrive at a thoughtful response to this question, make an outline of Dittmar's essay, noting wherever possible how she moves from one subject to another.

3. In paragraph 25, Dittmar says, "We were anthropomorphizing like crazy. . . ." Exactly what does she mean by this word? Why is she uncomfortable, embarrassed even, about anthropomorphizing? Why do you think she is unable to resist the temptation to anthropomorphize, despite her apparent reluctance?

4. In paragraph 27, Dittmar refers to "the wildlife biologist part of me" as opposed to "the anthropomorphizing part of me," as if she had two

distinctly different personalities, each with its own way of looking at things. Reread the essay and try to identify the portions where she seems most inclined to anthropomorphize things, and also where she seems most like a wildlife biologist. Can you find any places where she looks at herself with the eyes of a wildlife biologist? How would you describe the part of Dittmar that writes about her two different parts?

5. In paragraphs 30 through 32, Dittmar considers the fate of the old buck and of herself in the context of a much broader historical perspective than anywhere else in her essay. How would you define or describe that context, and how does it help her to cope with the buck's demise and her own sense of mortality?

6. Think about a time when you beheld or read about a surprising spectacle in the world of nature, a spectacle that also caused you to reflect upon a period when, like Dittmar, you "turned a corner" in your own life. Write an essay in which you weave together stories of the spectacle and of your own life with reflections on these interrelated experiences.

MAKING CONNECTIONS

1. Dittmar, like Lewis Thomas (p. 158), is momentarily so touched by the behavior of a natural creature that she finds herself responding to it in a distinctly unscientific way, which she acknowledges as openly as Thomas does his own scientific transgression. So, just as Thomas says that "I wanted no part of the science of beavers and otters," Dittmar proclaims that "I didn't want empirical facts by scientists" about pronghorn behavior. Given their unscientific impulses, how do you think they would respond to each other's behavior? Compare and contrast the origin and outcome of their unscientific attitudes and behavior.

2. Compare Dittmar's enthusiasm for pronghorn with Pattiann Rogers' celebration of toads (p. 162). Would Dittmar say that Rogers was "anthropomorphizing like crazy"? Would Rogers say that Dittmar was carried away by a longing for "the power of toads"? In other words, how do you think they would respond to each other's enthusiastic reflections?

THE TUCSON ZOO

Lewis Thomas

Physician and essayist Lewis Thomas (1913–1993) was born in Flushing, New York, and studied medicine at Harvard. For many years the president of the Sloan-Kettering Cancer Center in New York, Thomas had published hundreds of scientific articles before the editor of the New England Journal of Medicine *asked him, in 1970, to contribute a monthly column to the journal. The result was a series of informal and wide-ranging essays that immediately became popular among physicians and later with the general public. The first collection of these,* The Lives of a Cell: Notes of a Biology Watcher, *appeared in 1974, followed by* The Medusa and the Snail *(1979) and* Late Night Thoughts on Listening to Mahler's Ninth Symphony *(1983). Thomas's final book was* The Fragile Species *(1993).*

Science gets most of its information by the process of reductionism, exploring the details, then the details of the details, until all the smallest bits of the structure, or the smallest parts of the mechanism, are laid out for counting and scrutiny. Only when this is done can the investigation be extended to encompass the whole organism or the entire system. So we say.

Sometimes it seems that we take a loss, working this way. Much of today's public anxiety about science is the apprehension that we may forever be overlooking the whole by an endless, obsessive preoccupation with the parts. I had a brief, personal experience of this misgiving one afternoon in Tucson, where I had time on my hands and visited the zoo, just outside the city. The designers there have cut a deep path-way between two small artificial ponds, walled by clear glass, so when you stand in the center of the path you can look into the depths of each pool, and at the same time you can regard the surface. In one pool, on the right side of the path, is a family of otters; on the other side, a family of beavers. Within just a few feet from your face, on either side, beavers and otters are at play, underwater and on the surface, swimming toward your face and then away, more filled with life than any creatures I have ever seen before, in all my days. Except for the glass, you could reach across and touch them.

I was transfixed. As I now recall it, there was only one sensation in my head: pure elation mixed with amazement at such perfection. Swept off my feet, I floated from one side to the other, swiveling my brain, staring astounded at the beavers, then at the otters. I could hear shouts across my corpus callosum, from one hemisphere to the other. I remember thinking, with what was left in charge of my consciousness, that I wanted no part of the science of beavers and otters; I wanted never to know how they performed their marvels; I wished for no news about the physiology of their breathing, the coordination of their muscles, their vision, their endocrine systems, their digestive tracts. I hoped never to have to think of them as collections of cells. All I asked for was the full hairy complexity, then in front of my eyes, of whole, intact beavers and otters in motion.

It lasted, I regret to say, for only a few minutes, and then I was back in the late twentieth century, reductionist as ever, wondering about the details by force of habit, but not, this time, the details of otters and beavers. Instead, me. Something worth remembering had happened in my mind, I was certain of that; I would have put it somewhere in the brain stem; maybe this was my limbic system at work. I became a behavioral scientist, an experimental psychologist, an ethologist, and in the instant I lost all the wonder and the sense of being overwhelmed. I was flattened.

But I came away from the zoo with something, a piece of news about 5
myself: I am coded, somehow, for otters and beavers. I exhibit instinctive behavior in their presence, when they are displayed close at hand behind glass, simultaneously below water and at the surface. I have receptors for this display. Beavers and otters possess a "release" for me, in the terminology of ethology, and the releasing was my experience. What was released? Behavior. What behavior? Standing, swiveling flabbergasted, feeling exultation and a rush of friendship. I could not, as the result of the transaction, tell you anything more about beavers and otters than you already know. I learned nothing new about them. Only about me, and I suspect also about you, maybe about human beings at large: we are endowed with genes which code out our reaction to beavers and otters, maybe our reaction to each other as well. We are stamped with stereotyped, unalterable patterns of response, ready to be released. And the behavior released in us, by such confrontations, is, essentially, a surprised affection. It is compulsory behavior and we can avoid it only by straining with the full power of our conscious minds, making up conscious excuses all the way. Left to ourselves, mechanistic and autonomic, we hanker for friends.

Everyone says, stay away from ants. They have no lessons for us; they are crazy little instruments, inhuman, incapable of controlling themselves, lacking manners, lacking souls. When they are massed together, all touching, exchanging bits of information held in their jaws like memoranda, they become a single animal. Look out for that. It is a debasement, a loss of individuality, a violation of human nature, an unnatural act.

Sometimes people argue this point of view seriously and with deep thought. Be individuals, solitary and selfish, is the message. Altruism, a jargon word for what used to be called love, is worse than weakness, it is sin, a violation of nature. Be separate. Do not be a social animal. But this is a hard argument to make convincingly when you have to depend on language to make it. You have to print up leaflets or publish books and get them bought and sent around, you have to turn up on television and catch the attention of millions of other human beings all at once, and then you have to say to all of them, all at once, all collected and paying attention: be solitary; do not depend on each other. You can't do this and keep a straight face.

Maybe altruism is our most primitive attribute, out of reach, beyond our control. Or perhaps it is immediately at hand, waiting to be released, disguised now, in our kind of civilization, as affection or friendship or attachment. I don't see why it should be unreasonable for all human beings to have strands of DNA coiled up in chromosomes, coding out instincts for usefulness and helpfulness. Usefulness may turn out to be the hardest test of fitness for survival, more important than aggression, more effective, in the long run, than grabbiness. If this is the sort of information biological science holds for the future, applying to us as well as to ants, then I am all for science.

One thing I'd like to know most of all: when those ants have made the hill, and are all there, touching and exchanging, and the whole mass begins to behave like a single huge creature, and *thinks,* what on earth is that thought? And while you're at it, I'd like to know a second thing: when it happens, does any single ant know about it? Does his hair stand on end?

QUESTIONS

1. Though Thomas has entitled his essay "The Tucson Zoo," he discusses the zoo creatures, the beavers and otters, only in paragraphs 2 through 5. Paragraphs 6 through 9, by contrast, focus on ants. What do these two parts of the essay have to do with each other? What is the associative link or transition that enables Thomas to move from his thoughts about beavers and otters to his reflection upon ants?

2. At the beginning of paragraph 2, Thomas worries about the losses that come from the scientific method, but at the end of paragraph 8, he suggests that he might be "all for science." What accounts for his apparent shift from one position to the other? Or does he somehow arrive at a third position, or no position at all? In other words, exactly where do you think Thomas stands in this essay with respect to the value of scientific inquiry?

3. Look closely at the process that Thomas goes through in describing the beavers and otters, as well as his reactions to them, in paragraphs 2 through 5. What does he learn from this zoological display, and how does this knowledge challenge or confirm his identity as a scientist?

4. In which part of the essay (or which paragraphs) does Thomas seem to be most scientific in his method of thought and discussion? Where does he seem to be least scientific?

5. Although Thomas's essay seems to be concerned with the limitations and benefits of science, it might also be seen as a reflection upon the

origin and value of altruism, especially given the ideas that emerge from his discussion of the ants. So what exactly is this essay about? What do you think is Thomas's primary concern in this piece?

6. In this essay, Thomas describes a pair of creatures that stand out in his mind because they led him to a significant and memorable set of insights and thoughts about himself and human behavior. Think about a time when you observed something in the world of nature that led you to some memorable insights about yourself or others. Then write an essay in which you describe what you saw, recall what you thought, and reflect upon the way you think about such things today.

MAKING CONNECTIONS

Thomas and Carl Sagan (p. 178) both begin their essays with definitions of science and reflections on the scientific method. Compare and contrast their ideas of science and their attitudes toward the scientific method. What do you consider to be their most important areas of agreement? of disagreement?

THE POWER OF TOADS

Pattiann Rogers

Pattiann Rogers (b. 1940), a graduate of the University of Missouri and the University of Houston, published her first collection of poetry in 1981. Since then she has published six more volumes, the latest being Firekeeper: New and Selected Poems *(1994) and* Eating Milk and Honey *(1997). Her work has won numerous awards, including four Pushcart Prizes. Rogers has received a Guggenheim fellowship and a Lannon poetry fellowship. One critic has said of her work that it "provides a bridge between the highly specialized world of modern scientists and readers of contemporary poetry."*

The oak toad and the red-spotted toad love their love
In a spring rain, calling and calling, breeding
Through a stormy evening clasped atop their mates.
Who wouldn't sing — anticipating the belly pressed hard
Against a female's spine in the steady rain   5
Below writhing skies, the safe moist jelly effluence
Of a final exaltation?

There might be some toads who actually believe
That the loin-shaking thunder of the banks, the evening
Filled with damp, the warm softening mud and rising   10
Riverlets are the facts of their own persistent
Performance. Maybe they think that when they sing
They sing more than songs, creating rain and mist
By their voices, initiating the union of water and dusk,
Females materializing on the banks shaped perfectly   15
By their calls.

And some toads may be convinced they have forced
The heavens to twist and moan by the continual expansion
Of their lung sacs pushing against the dusk.
And some might believe the splitting light,   20
The soaring grey they see above them are nothing
But a vision of the longing in their groins,
A fertile spring heaven caught in its entirety
At the pit of the gut.

And they might be right.   25
Who knows whether these broken heavens
Could exist tonight separate from trills and toad ringings?
Maybe the particles of this rain descending on the pond
Are nothing but the visual manifestation of whistles
And cascading love clicks in the shore grasses.   30
Raindrops-finding-earth and coitus could very well
Be known here as one.

We could investigate the causal relationship
Between rainstorm and love-by-pondside if we wished.
We could lie down in the grasses by the water's edge   35
And watch to see exactly how the heavens were moved,
Thinking hard of thunder, imagining all the courses
That slow, clean waters might take across our bodies,
Believing completely in the rolling and pressing power
Of heavens and thighs. And in the end we might be glad,   40
Even if all we discovered for certain was the slick, sweet
Promise of good love beneath dark skies inside warm rains.

QUESTIONS

1. In the first stanza of this poem, Rogers offers a striking image of toads, "calling and calling, breeding/Through a stormy evening clasped atop their mates." What other descriptive information does she offer about the toads and the stormy evening from that point on?
2. In the second and third stanzas, Rogers speculates about the beliefs and thoughts of the toads "when they sing." Assuming that toads might be capable of thought, what specific ideas does she imagine them having in these stanzas? Try to outline the associative and reflective process that leads her from one hypothetical idea to the next.
3. What is the focus of her speculative reflections in the fourth stanza? in the fifth stanza? What do Rogers's various reflections here and elsewhere have to do with "the power of toads"?
4. Though Rogers offers a poetic celebration of the love-making toads, consider the ways in which it might also be considered a "scientific" approach to the subject.

MAKING CONNECTIONS

1. Compare Rogers's celebration of toads with Trudy Dittmar's admiration of pronghorn (p. 148) and Lewis Thomas's amazement by beavers and otters (p. 158). Does Rogers seem to be "anthropomorphizing like

crazy" in the manner of Dittmar? Or does she seem engaged by "the full hairy complexity" like Thomas? Or do you think her enthusiasm is distinctly different from theirs?

2. Seamus Heaney also writes about toads (p. 165). Imagine Heaney and Rogers having a conversation about toads. What do you think would be their points of agreement? of disagreement?

DEATH OF A NATURALIST

Seamus Heaney

Born in County Derry, Northern Ireland, in 1939, Seamus Heaney atttended Queens University in Belfast, where he later was a lecturer. He has also taught at Harvard and Oxford universities. Heaney published his first collection of poetry, Death of a Naturalist, *in 1966, and his later collections include* Field Work *(1979),* The Haw Lantern *(1987), and* Opened Ground *(1998). His most recent work is a highly acclaimed translation of the epic poem* Beowulf *(2000). Heaney was awarded the Nobel Prize for Literature in 1995. In the words of one critic, Heaney's is "a poetry concerned with nature, the shocks and discoveries of childhood experienced on a farm, the mythos of the locale—in short, a regional poetry"; at the same time, it is a poetry with universal appeal.*

All year the flax-dam[1] festered in the heart
Of the townland; green and heavy headed
Flax had rotted there, weighted down by huge sods.
Daily it sweltered in the punishing sun.
Bubbles gargled delicately, bluebottles   5
Wove a strong gauze of sound around the smell.
There were dragon-flies, spotted butterflies,
But best of all was the warm thick slobber
Of frogspawn that grew like clotted water

In the shade of the banks. Here, every spring   10
I would fill jampotfuls of the jellied
Specks to range on window-sills at home,
On shelves at school, and wait and watch until
The fattening dots burst into nimble-
Swimming tadpoles. Miss Walls would tell us how   15
The daddy frog was called a bullfrog
And how he croaked and how the mammy frog
Laid hundreds of little eggs and this was
Frogspawn. You could tell the weather by frogs too
For they were yellow in the sun and brown   20
In rain.

---

[1]Flax stalks are soaked in a pond to loosen the fibers from which linen is made.

Then one hot day when fields were rank
With cowdung in the grass the angry frogs
Invaded the flax-dam; I ducked through hedges
To a coarse croaking that I had not heard   25
Before. The air was thick with a bass chorus.
Right down the dam gross-bellied frogs were cocked
On sods; their loose necks pulsed like sails. Some hopped:
The slap and plop were obscene threats. Some sat
Poised like mud grenades, their blunt heads farting.   30
I sickened, turned, and ran. The great slime kings
Were gathered there for vengeance and I knew
That if I dipped my hand the spawn would clutch it.

QUESTIONS

1. Though Heaney implies that he is no longer a naturalist, what evidence
   can you find in the poem that he once observed the natural world with
   the keen eye of a budding scientist?
2. Though this poem is ultimately about the death of Heaney's childhood
   fascination with nature, especially with toads, Heaney doesn't refer to
   "frogspawn" until line 9, and he doesn't mention himself until line 11.
   Why do you think he begins his reflections with such a detailed description of the flax-dam?
3. What does Heaney's sudden, unexplained focus on the flax-dam in line
   1 suggest about his state of mind at that point in the poem? What does
   his detailed recollection of the flax-dam indicate about his state of mind
   in the remainder of the first stanza? What does his reference to Miss
   Walls telling about the "daddy frog" and the "mammy frog" suggest he
   is thinking about at that point in the poem?
4. Given what Heaney had already learned about frogs from gathering
   frogspawn and from the instruction of Miss Walls, why do you think
   that he "sickened, turned, and ran" when he first beheld the frogs
   croaking amid the flax-dam? What did he see and/or hear that so disturbed him?

MAKING CONNECTIONS

Pattiann Rogers also writes about toads (p. 162). Imagine Heaney and
Rogers having a conversation about toads. What do you think would be
their points of agreement? of disagreement?

A Mask on the Face of Death

Richard Selzer

Richard Selzer (b. 1928) is the son of a general practitioner father and a singer mother, both of whom wanted their son to follow in their footsteps. At ten he began sneaking into his father's office to look at his medical textbooks, where he discovered "the rich alliterative language of medicine—words such as cerebellum which, when said aloud, melt in the mouth and drip from the end of the tongue like chocolate." After his father's death he decided to become a doctor and was for many years a professor of surgery at Yale Medical School. Only after working as a doctor for many decades did he begin to write. About the similarities between surgery and writing he says, "In surgery, it is the body that is being opened up and put back together. In writing it is the whole world that is taken in for repairs, then put back in working order piece by piece." His articles have appeared in Vanity Fair, Harper's, Esquire, *and the* New York Times Magazine. *His books include a volume of short stories,* Rituals of Surgery *(1974), a collection of autobiographical essays,* Mortal Lessons *(1976), an autobiography,* Down from Troy *(1992), and a collection of autobiographical and fictional pieces,* Raising the Dead *(1994). This essay appeared in* Life *in 1988.*

It is ten o'clock at night as we drive up to the Copacabana, a dilapidated brothel on the rue Dessalines in the red-light district of Port-au-Prince. My guide is a young Haitian, Jean-Bernard. Ten years before, J-B tells me, at the age of fourteen, "like every good Haitian boy" he had been brought here by his older cousins for his *rite de passage.* From the car to the entrance, we are accosted by a half dozen men and women for sex. We enter, go down a long hall that breaks upon a cavernous room with a stone floor. The cubicles of the prostitutes, I am told, are in an attached wing of the building. Save for a red-purple glow from small lights on the walls, the place is unlit. Dark shapes float by, each with a blindingly white stripe of teeth. Latin music is blaring. We take seats at the table farthest from the door. Just outside, there is the rhythmic lapping of the Caribbean Sea. About twenty men are seated at the tables or lean against the walls. Brightly dressed women, singly or in twos or threes, stroll about, now and then exchanging banter with the men. It is as though we have been deposited in act two of Bizet's *Carmen.* If this place isn't Lillas Pastia's tavern, what is it?

Within minutes, three light-skinned young women arrive at our table. They are very beautiful and young and lively. Let them be Carmen, Mercedes and Frasquita.

"I want the old one," says Frasquita, ruffling my hair. The women laugh uproariously.

"Don't bother looking any further," says Mercedes. "We are the prettiest ones."

"We only want to talk," I tell her.   5

"Aaah, aaah," she crows. "*Massissi.* You are *massissi.*" It is the contemptuous Creole term for homosexual. If we want only to talk, we must be gay. Mercedes and Carmen are slender, each weighing one hundred pounds or less. Frasquita is tall and hefty. They are dressed for work: red taffeta, purple chiffon and black sequins. Among them a thousand gold bracelets and earrings multiply every speck of light. Their bare shoulders are like animated lamps gleaming in the shadowy room. Since there is as yet no business, the women agree to sit with us. J-B orders beer and cigarettes. We pay each woman $10.

"Where are you from?" I begin.

"We are Dominican."

"Do you miss your country?"

"Oh, yes, we do." Six eyes go muzzy with longing. "Our country is the   10
most beautiful in the world. No country is like the Dominican. And it doesn't stink like this one."

"Then why don't you work there? Why come to Haiti?"

"Santo Domingo has too many whores. All beautiful, like us. All light-skinned. The Haitian men like to sleep with light women."

"Why is that?"

"Because always, the whites have all the power and the money. The black men can imagine they do, too, when they have us in bed."

Eleven o'clock. I looked around the room that is still sparsely peopled   15
with men.

"It isn't getting any busier," I say. Frasquita glances over her shoulder. Her eyes drill the darkness.

"It is still early," she says.

"Could it be that the men are afraid of getting sick?" Frasquita is offended.

"Sick! They do not get sick from us. We are healthy, strong. Every week we go for a checkup. Besides, we know how to tell if we are getting sick."

"I mean sick with AIDS." The word sets off a hurricane of taffeta,   20
chiffon and gold jewelry. They are all gesticulation and fury. It is Carmen who speaks.

"AIDS!" Her lips curl about the syllable. "There is no such thing. It is a false disease invented by the American government to take advantage of the poor countries. The American President hates poor people, so now he makes up AIDS to take away the little we have." The others nod vehemently.

"*Mira, mon cher.* Look, my dear," Carmen continues. "One day the police came here. Believe me, they are worse than the *tonton macoutes* with their submachine guns. They rounded up one hundred and five of us and they took our blood. That was a year ago. None of us have died, you see? We are all still here. *Mira,* we sleep with all the men and we are not sick."

"But aren't there some of you who have lost weight and have diarrhea?"

"One or two, maybe. But they don't eat. That is why they are weak."

"Only the men die," says Mercedes. "They stop eating, so they die. It is hard to kill a woman." 25

"Do you eat well?"

"Oh, yes, don't worry, we do. We eat like poor people, but we eat." There is a sudden scream from Frasquita. She points to a large rat that has emerged from beneath our table.

"My God!" she exclaims. "It is big like a pig." They burst into laughter. For a moment the women fall silent. There is only the restlessness of their many bracelets. I give them each another $10.

"Are many of the men here bisexual?"

"Too many. They do it for money. Afterward, they come to us." 30 Carmen lights a cigarette and looks down at the small lace handkerchief she has been folding and unfolding with immense precision on the table. All at once she turns it over as though it were the ace of spades.

"*Mira, blanc* . . . look, white man," she says in a voice suddenly full of foreboding. Her skin seems to darken to coincide with the tone of her voice.

"*Mira,* soon many Dominican women will die in Haiti!"

"Die of what?"

She shrugs. "It is what they do to us."

"Carmen," I say, "if you knew that you had AIDS, that your blood 35 was bad, would you still sleep with men?" Abruptly, she throws back her head and laughs. It is the same laughter with which Frasquita had greeted the rat at our feet. She stands and the others follow.

"*Méchant!* You wicked man," she says. Then, with terrible solemnity, "You don't know anything."

"But you are killing the Haitian men," I say.

"As for that," she says, "everyone is killing everyone else." All at once, I want to know everything about these three—their childhood, their dreams, what they do in the afternoon, what they eat for lunch.

"Don't leave," I say. "Stay a little more." Again, I reach for my wallet. But they are gone, taking all the light in the room with them—Mercedes and Carmen to sit at another table where three men have been waiting. Frasquita is strolling about the room. Now and then, as if captured by the music, she breaks into a few dance steps, snapping her fingers, singing to herself.

Midnight. And the Copacabana is filling up. Now it is like any other 40 seedy nightclub where men and women go hunting. We get up to leave. In the center a couple are dancing a *méringue*. He is the most graceful dancer I have ever watched; she, the most voluptuous. Together they seem to be riding the back of the music as it gallops to a precisely sexual beat. Closer up, I see that the man is short of breath, sweating. All at once, he collapses into a chair. The woman bends over him, coaxing, teasing, but he is through. A young man with a long polished stick blocks my way.

"I come with you?" he asks. "Very good time. You say yes? Ten dollars? Five?"

I have been invited by Dr. Jean William Pape to attend the AIDS clinic of which he is the director. Nothing from the outside of the low whitewashed structure would suggest it as a medical facility. Inside, it is divided into many small cubicles and a labyrinth of corridors. At nine A.M. the hallways are already full of emaciated silent men and women, some sitting on the few benches, the rest leaning against the walls. The only sounds are subdued moans of discomfort interspersed with coughs. How they eat us with their eyes as we pass.

The room where Pape and I work is perhaps ten feet by ten. It contains a desk, two chairs and a narrow wooden table that is covered with a sheet that will not be changed during the day. The patients are called in one at a time, asked how they feel and whether there is any change in their symptoms, then examined on the table. If the patient is new to the clinic, he or she is questioned about sexual activities.

A twenty-seven-year-old man whose given name is Miracle enters. He is wobbly, panting, like a groggy boxer who has let down his arms and is waiting for the last punch. He is neatly dressed and wears, despite the heat, a heavy woolen cap. When he removes it, I see that his hair is thin, dull reddish and straight. It is one of the signs of AIDS in Haiti, Pape tells me. The man's skin is covered with a dry itchy rash. Throughout the interview and examination he scratches himself slowly, absentmindedly. The rash is called prurigo. It is another symptom of AIDS in Haiti. This man has had diarrhea for six months. The laboratory reports that the diarrhea is due to an organism called cryptosporidium, for which there is no treatment. The telltale rattling of the tuberculous moisture in his chest is audible without a stethoscope. He is like a leaky cistern that bubbles and froths. And, clearly, exhausted.

"Where do you live?" I ask.   45

"Kenscoff." A village in the hills above Port-au-Prince.

"How did you come here today?"

"I came on the *tap-tap*." It is the name given to the small buses that swarm the city, each one extravagantly decorated with religious slogans, icons, flowers, animals, all painted in psychedelic colors. I have never seen a *tap-tap* that was not covered with passengers as well, riding outside and hanging on. The vehicles are little masterpieces of contagion, if not of AIDS then of the multitude of germs which Haitian flesh is heir to. Miracle is given a prescription for a supply of Sera, which is something like Gatorade, and told to return in a month.

"*Mangé kou bêf*," says the doctor in farewell. "Eat like an ox." What can he mean? The man has no food or money to buy any. Even had he food, he has not the appetite to eat or the ability to retain it. To each departing patient the doctor will say the same words—"*Mangé kou bêf*." I see that it is his way of offering a hopeful goodbye.

"Will he live until his next appointment?" I ask.   50

"No." Miracle leaves to catch the *tap-tap* for Kenscoff.

Next is a woman of twenty-six who enters holding her right hand to her forehead in a kind of permanent salute. In fact, she is shielding her eye from view. This is her third visit to the clinic. I see that she is still quite well nourished.

"Now, you'll see something beautiful, tremendous," the doctor says. Once seated upon the table, she is told to lower her hand. When she does, I see that her right eye and its eyelid are replaced by a huge fungating ulcerated tumor, a side product of her AIDS. As she turns her head, the cluster of lymph glands in her neck to which the tumor has spread is thrown into relief. Two years ago she received a blood transfusion at a time when the country's main blood bank was grossly contaminated with AIDS. It has since been closed down. The only blood available in Haiti is a small supply procured from the Red Cross.

"Can you give me medicine?" the woman wails.

"No."   55

"Can you cut it away?"

"No."

"Is there radiation therapy?" I ask.

"No."

"Chemotherapy?" The doctor looks at me in what some might call   60
weary amusement. I see that there is nothing to do. She has come here because there is nowhere else to go.

"What will she do?"

"Tomorrow or the next day or the day after that she will climb up into the mountains to seek relief from the *houngan*, the voodoo priest, just as her slave ancestors did two hundred years ago."

Then comes a frail man in his thirties, with a strangely spiritualized face, like a child's. Pus runs from one ear onto his cheek, where it has dried and caked. He has trouble remembering, he tells us. In fact, he seems confused. It is from toxoplasmosis of the brain, an effect of his AIDS. This man is bisexual. Two years ago he engaged in oral sex with foreign men for money. As I palpate the swollen glands of his neck, a mosquito flies between our faces. I swat at it, miss. Just before coming to Haiti I had read that the AIDS virus had been isolated from a certain mosquito. The doctor senses my thought.

"Not to worry," he says. "So far as we know there has never been a case transmitted by insects."

"Yes," I say. "I see."   65

And so it goes until the last, the thirty-sixth AIDS patient has been seen. At the end of the day I am invited to wash my hands before leaving. I go down a long hall to a sink. I turn on the faucets but there is no water.

"But what about *you?*" I ask the doctor. "You are at great personal risk here — the tuberculosis, the other infections, no water to wash . . ." He shrugs, smiles faintly and lifts his hands palm upward.

We are driving up a serpiginous steep road into the barren mountains above Port-au-Prince. Even in the bright sunshine the countryside has the bloodless color of exhaustion and indifference. Our destination is the Baptist Mission Hospital, where many cases of AIDS have been reported. Along the road there are slow straggles of schoolchildren in blue uniforms who stretch out their hands as we pass and call out, "Give me something." Already a crowd of outpatients has gathered at the entrance to the mission compound. A tour of the premises reveals that in contrast to the aridity outside the gates, this is an enclave of productivity, lush with fruit trees and poinsettia.

The hospital is clean and smells of creosote. Of the forty beds, less than a third are occupied. In one male ward of twelve beds, there are two patients. The chief physician tells us that last year he saw ten cases of AIDS each week. Lately the number has decreased to four or five.

"Why is that?" we want to know.   70

"Because we do not admit them to the hospital, so they have learned not to come here."

"Why don't you admit them?"

"Because we would have nothing but AIDS here then. So we send them away."

"But I see that you have very few patients in bed."

"That is also true."   75

"Where do the AIDS patients go?"

"Some go to the clinic in Port-au-Prince or the general hospital in the city. Others go home to die or to the voodoo priest."

"Do the people with AIDS know what they have before they come here?"

"Oh, yes, they know very well, and they know there is nothing to be done for them."

Outside, the crowd of people is dispersing toward the gate. The clinic   80
has been canceled for the day. No one knows why. We are conducted to the office of the reigning American pastor. He is a tall, handsome Midwesterner with an ecclesiastical smile.

"It is voodoo that is the devil here." He warms to his subject. "It is a demonic religion, a cancer on Haiti. Voodoo is worse than AIDS. And it is one of the reasons for the epidemic. Did you know that in order for a man to become a *houngan*[1] he must perform anal sodomy on another man? No, of course you didn't. And it doesn't stop there. The *houngans* tell the men that in order to appease the spirits they too must do the same thing. So you

---

[1]*houngan:* a voodoo priest. [Eds.]

have ritualized homosexuality. That's what is spreading the AIDS." The pastor tells us of a nun who witnessed two acts of sodomy in a provincial hospital where she came upon a man sexually assaulting a houseboy and another man mounting a male patient in his bed.

"Fornication," he says. "It is Sodom and Gomorrah all over again, so what can you expect from these people?" Outside his office we are shown a cage of terrified, cowering monkeys to whom he coos affectionately. It is clear that he loves them. At the car, we shake hands.

"By the way," the pastor says, "what is your religion? Perhaps I am a kinsman?"

"While I am in Haiti," I tell him, "it will be voodoo or it will be nothing at all."

Abruptly, the smile breaks. It is as though a crack had suddenly ap-   85
peared in the face of an idol.

From the mission we go to the general hospital. In the heart of Port-au-Prince, it is the exact antithesis of the immaculate facility we have just left—filthy, crowded, hectic and staffed entirely by young interns and residents. Though it is associated with a medical school, I do not see any members of the faculty. We are shown around by Jocelyne, a young intern in a scrub suit. Each bed in three large wards is occupied. On the floor about the beds, hunkered in the posture of the innocent poor, are family members of the patients. In the corridor that constitutes the emergency room, someone lies on a stretcher receiving an intravenous infusion. She is hardly more than a cadaver.

"Where are the doctors in charge?" I ask Jocelyne. She looks at me questioningly.

"We are in charge."

"I mean your teachers, the faculty."

"They do not come here."   90

"What is wrong with that woman?"

"She has had diarrhea for three months. Now she is dehydrated." I ask the woman to open her mouth. Her throat is covered with the white plaques of thrush, a fungus infection associated with AIDS.

"How many AIDS patients do you see here?"

"Three or four a day. We send them home. Sometimes the families abandon them, then we must admit them to the hospital. Every day, then, a relative comes to see if the patient has died. They want to take the body. That is important to them. But they know very well that AIDS is contagious and they are afraid to keep them at home. Even so, once or twice a week the truck comes to take away the bodies. Many are children. They are buried in mass graves."

"Where do the wealthy patients go?"   95

"There is a private hospital called Canapé Vert. Or else they go to Miami. Most of them, rich and poor, do not go to the hospital. Most are never diagnosed."

"How do you know these people have AIDS?"

"We don't know sometimes. The blood test is inaccurate. There are many false positives and false negatives. Fifteen percent of those with the disease have negative blood tests. We go by their infections — tuberculosis, diarrhea, fungi, herpes, skin rashes. It is not hard to tell."

"Do they know what they have?"

"Yes. They understand at once and they are prepared to die."   100

"Do the patients know how AIDS is transmitted?"

"They know, but they do not like to talk about it. It is taboo. Their memories do not seem to reach back to the true origins of their disaster. It is understandable, is it not?"

"Whatever you write, don't hurt us any more than we have already been hurt." It is a young Haitian journalist with whom I am drinking a rum punch. He means that any further linkage of AIDS and Haiti in the media would complete the economic destruction of the country. The damage was done early in the epidemic when the Centers for Disease Control in Atlanta added Haitians to the three other high-risk groups — hemophiliacs, intravenous drug users and homosexual and bisexual men. In fact, Haitians are no more susceptible to AIDS than anyone else. Although the CDC removed Haitians from special scrutiny in 1985, the lucrative tourism on which so much of the country's economy was based was crippled. Along with tourism went much of the foreign business investment. Worst of all was the injury to the national pride. Suddenly Haiti was indicted as the source of AIDS in the western hemisphere.

What caused the misunderstanding was the discovery of a large number of Haitian men living in Miami with AIDS antibodies in their blood. They denied absolutely they were homosexuals. But the CDC investigators did not know that homosexuality is the strongest taboo in Haiti and that no man would ever admit to it. Bisexuality, however, is not uncommon. Many married men and heterosexually oriented males will occasionally seek out other men for sex. Further, many, if not most, Haitian men visit female prostitutes from time to time. It is not difficult to see that once the virus was set loose in Haiti, the spread would be swift through both genders.

Exactly how the virus of AIDS arrived is not known. Could it have   105
been brought home by the Cuban soldiers stationed in Angola and thence to Haiti, about fifty miles away? Could it have been passed on by the thousands of Haitians living in exile in Zaire, who later returned home or immigrated to the United States? Could it have come from the American and Canadian homosexual tourists, and, yes, even some U.S. diplomats who have traveled to the island to have sex with impoverished Haitian men all too willing to sell themselves to feed their families? Throughout the international gay community Haiti was known as a good place to go for sex.

On a private tip from an official at the Ministry of Tourism, J-B and I drive to a town some fifty miles from Port-au-Prince. The hotel is owned by two Frenchmen who are out of the country, one of the staff tells us. He is a man of about thirty and clearly he is desperately ill. Tottering, short of breath, he shows us about the empty hotel. The furnishings are opulent and extreme—tiger skins on the wall, a live leopard in the garden, a bedroom containing a giant bathtub with gold faucets. Is it the heat of the day or the heat of my imagination that makes these walls echo with the painful cries of pederasty?

The hotel where we are staying is in Pétionville, the fashionable suburb of Port-au-Prince. It is the height of the season but there are no tourists, only a dozen or so French and American businessmen. The swimming pool is used once or twice a day by a single person. Otherwise, the water remains undisturbed until dusk, when the fruit bats come down to drink in midswoop. The hotel keeper is an American. He is eager to set me straight on Haiti.

"What did and should attract foreign investment is a combination of reliable weather, an honest and friendly populace, low wages and multilingual managers."

"What spoiled it?"

"Political instability and a bad American press about AIDS." He   110
pauses, then adds: "To which I hope you won't be contributing."

"What about just telling the truth?" I suggest.

"Look," he says, "there is no more danger of catching AIDS in Haiti than in New York or Santo Domingo. It is not where you are but what you do that counts." Agreeing, I ask if he had any idea that much of the tourism in Haiti during the past few decades was based on sex.

"No idea whatsoever. It was only recently that we discovered that that was the case."

"How is it that you hoteliers, restaurant owners and the Ministry of Tourism did not know what *tout*[2] Haiti knew?"

"Look. All I know is that this is a middle-class, family-oriented hotel.   115
We don't allow guests to bring women, or for that matter men, into their rooms. If they did, we'd ask them to leave immediately."

At five A.M. the next day the telephone rings in my room. A Creole-accented male voice.

"Is the lady still with you, sir?"

"There is no lady here."

"In your room, sir, the lady I allowed to go up with a package?"

"There is no lady here, I tell you."   120

At seven A.M. I stop at the front desk. The clerk is a young man.

"Was it you who called my room at five o'clock?"

"Sorry," he says with a smile. "It was a mistake, sir. I meant to ring the room next door to yours." Still smiling, he holds up his shushing finger.

---

[2] *tout:* all, that is, everyone else in Haiti. [Eds.]

Next to Dr. Pape, director of the AIDS clinic, Bernard Liautaud, a dermatologist, is the most knowledgeable Haitian physician on the subject of the epidemic. Together, the two men have published a dozen articles on AIDS in international medical journals. In our meeting they present me with statistics:

- There are more than one thousand documented cases of AIDS in Haiti, and as many as one hundred thousand carriers of the virus.
- Eighty-seven percent of AIDS is now transmitted heterosexually. While it is true that the virus was introduced via the bisexual community, that route has decreased to 10 percent or less.
- Sixty percent of the wives or husbands of AIDS patients tested positive for the antibody.
- Fifty percent of the prostitutes tested in the Port-au-Prince area are infected.
- Eighty percent of the men with AIDS have had contact with prostitutes.
- The projected number of active cases in four years is ten thousand. (Since my last visit, the Haitian Medical Association broke its silence on the epidemic by warning that one million of the country's six million people could be carriers by 1992.)

The two doctors have more to tell. "The crossing over of the plague 125 from the homosexual to the heterosexual community will follow in the United States within two years. This, despite the hesitation to say so by those who fear to sow panic among your population. In Haiti, because bisexuality is more common, there was an early crossover into the general population. The trend, inevitably, is the same in the two countries."

"What is there to do, then?"

"Only education, just as in America. But here the Haitians reject the use of condoms. Only the men who are too sick to have sex are celibate."

"What is to be the end of it?"

"When enough heterosexuals of the middle and upper classes die, perhaps there will be the panic necessary for the people to change their sexual lifestyles."

This evening I leave Haiti. For two weeks I have fastened myself to this 130 lovely fragile land like an ear pressed to the ground. It is a country to break a traveler's heart. It occurs to me that I have not seen a single jogger. Such a public expenditure of energy while everywhere else strength is ebbing—it would be obscene. In my final hours, I go to the Cathédrale of Sainte Trinité, the inner walls of which are covered with murals by Haiti's most renowned artists. Here are all the familiar Bible stories depicted in naïveté and piety, and all in such an exuberance of color as to tax the capacity of the retina to receive it, as though all the vitality of Haiti had been turned to paint and brushed upon these walls. How to explain this efflorescence at a time when all else is lassitude and inertia? Perhaps one day the plague will be rendered in poetry, music, painting, but not now. Not now.

QUESTIONS

1. Summarize the scene at the Copacabana. Which details are memorable? Why does Selzer spend so much time with Carmen, Mercedes, and Frasquita? Why are their attitudes toward AIDS so important?

2. Selzer writes at great length about his visit to the AIDS clinic directed by Dr. Jean William Pape. What does Selzer learn from observing patients at this clinic? What does Selzer learn about AIDS from the doctor at work?

3. A young Haitian journalist tells Selzer, "Whatever you write, don't hurt us any more than we have already been hurt" (paragraph 103). What is the significance of this request? After reading Selzer's essay, do you think Selzer has honored this request?

4. In the final paragraph of the essay, Selzer writes, "For two weeks I have fastened myself to this lovely fragile land like an ear pressed to the ground. It is a country to break a traveler's heart." What has Selzer learned about the politics of AIDS from his journey to Haiti?

5. Look at the various scenes and vignettes Selzer offers his readers. How does he connect these different scenes? How does this structure succeed in presenting his reflections?

6. What have you learned about the politics of AIDS from reading Selzer's essay? Write an essay reflecting on Selzer's essay.

7. Selzer offers his reflections as a way of justifying his strong feelings about AIDS. In other words, his reflections become a kind of argument. How would you make a more objective argument for his position?

MAKING CONNECTIONS

Richard Selzer and Amitav Ghosh (p. 119) both write as spectators of, rather than as participants in, the events they report. Compare and contrast the ways they develop their reflections within such a perspective.

CAN WE KNOW THE UNIVERSE?
Reflections on a Grain of Salt

Carl Sagan

Carl Sagan (1934–1996) was renowned both as a scientist and a writer. For his work with the National Aeronautics and Space Administration's Mariner, Viking, *and* Voyager *expeditions, he was awarded NASA's Medals for Exceptional Scientific Achievement and for Distinguished Public Service. Sagan produced the* Cosmos *television series for public television and received the Peabody Award in 1981. For his book,* The Dragons of Eden *(1977), he received the Pulitzer Prize in literature. Among his later works are* Comet *(1985),* Contact *(1985), a novel (with Ann Druyan),* Shadows of Forgotten Ancestors *(1992), and* Billions and Billions: Thoughts on Life and Death at the Brink of the Millennium *(1997). The following selection is from* Broca's Brain: Reflections on the Romance of Science *(1979).*

> Nothing is rich but the inexhaustible wealth
> of nature. She shows us only surfaces,
> but she is a million fathoms deep.
> RALPH WALDO EMERSON

Science is a way of thinking much more than it is a body of knowledge. Its goal is to find out how the world works, to seek what regularities there may be, to penetrate to the connections of things—from subnuclear particles, which may be the constituents of all matter, to living organisms, the human social community, and thence to the cosmos as a whole. Our intuition is by no means an infallible guide. Our perceptions may be distorted by training and prejudice or merely because of the limitations of our sense organs, which, of course, perceive directly but a small fraction of the phenomena of the world. Even so straightforward a question as whether in the absence of friction a pound of lead falls faster than a gram of fluff was answered incorrectly by Aristotle and almost everyone else before the time of Galileo. Science is based on experiment, on a willingness to challenge old dogma, on an openness to see the universe as it really is. Accordingly, science sometimes requires courage—at the very least the courage to question the conventional wisdom.

Beyond this the main trick of science is to *really* think of something: the shape of clouds and their occasional sharp bottom edges at the same altitude everywhere in the sky; the formation of a dewdrop on a leaf; the origin of a name or a word—Shakespeare, say, or "philanthropic"; the reason for human social customs—the incest taboo, for example; how it is that a lens in sunlight can make paper burn; how a "walking stick" got to look so much like a twig; why the Moon seems to follow us as we walk; what prevents us from digging a hole down to the center of the Earth; what the definition is of "down" on a spherical Earth; how it is possible for the body to convert yesterday's lunch into today's muscle and sinew; or how far is up—does the universe go on forever, or if it does not, is there any meaning to the question of what lies on the other side? Some of these questions are pretty easy. Others, especially the last, are mysteries to which no one even today knows the answer. They are natural questions to ask. Every culture has posed such questions in one way or another. Almost always the proposed answers are in the nature of "Just So Stories," attempted explanations divorced from experiment, or even from careful comparative observations.

But the scientific cast of mind examines the world critically as if many alternative worlds might exist, as if other things might be here which are not. Then we are forced to ask why what we see is present and not something else. Why are the Sun and the Moon and the planets spheres? Why not pyramids, or cubes, or dodecahedra? Why not irregular, jumbly shapes? Why so symmetrical, worlds? If you spend any time spinning hypotheses, checking to see whether they make sense, whether they conform to what else we know, thinking of tests you can pose to substantiate or deflate your hypotheses, you will find yourself doing science. And as you come to practice this habit of thought more and more you will get better and better at it. To penetrate into the heart of the thing—even a little thing, a blade of grass, as Walt Whitman said—is to experience a kind of exhilaration that, it may be, only human beings of all the beings on this planet can feel. We are an intelligent species and the use of our intelligence quite properly gives us pleasure. In this respect the brain is like a muscle. When we think well, we feel good. Understanding is a kind of ecstasy.

But to what extent can we *really* know the universe around us? Sometimes this question is posed by people who hope the answer will be in the negative, who are fearful of a universe in which everything might one day be known. And sometimes we hear pronouncements from scientists who confidently state that everything worth knowing will soon be known—or even is already known—and who paint pictures of a Dionysian or Polynesian age in which the zest for intellectual discovery has withered, to be replaced by a kind of subdued languor, the lotus eaters drinking fermented coconut milk or some other mild hallucinogen. In addition to maligning both the Polynesians, who were intrepid explorers (and whose brief respite in paradise is now sadly ending), as well as the inducements to intellectual discovery provided by some hallucinogens, this contention turns out to be trivially mistaken.

Let us approach a much more modest question: not whether we can know the universe or the Milky Way Galaxy or a star or a world. Can we know, ultimately and in detail, a grain of salt? Consider one microgram of table salt, a speck just barely large enough for someone with keen eyesight to make out without a microscope. In that grain of salt there are about 10^{16} sodium and chlorine atoms. This is a 1 followed by 16 zeros, 10 million billion atoms. If we wish to know a grain of salt, we must know at least the three-dimensional positions of each of these atoms. (In fact, there is much more to be known—for example, the nature of the forces between the atoms—but we are making only a modest calculation.) Now, is this number more or less than the number of things which the brain can know?

How much *can* the brain know? There are perhaps 10^{11} neurons in the brain, the circuit elements and switches that are responsible in their electrical and chemical activity for the functioning of our minds. A typical brain neuron has perhaps a thousand little wires, called dendrites, which connect it with its fellows. If, as seems likely, every bit of information in the brain corresponds to one of these connections, the total number of things knowable by the brain is no more than 10^{14}, one hundred trillion. But this number is only one percent of the number of atoms in our speck of salt.

So in this sense the universe is intractable, astonishingly immune to any human attempt at full knowledge. We cannot on this level understand a grain of salt, much less the universe.

But let us look more deeply at our microgram of salt. Salt happens to be a crystal in which, except for defects in the structure of the crystal lattice, the position of every sodium and chlorine atom is predetermined. If we could shrink ourselves into this crystalline world, we could see rank upon rank of atoms in an ordered array, a regularly alternating structure — sodium, chlorine, sodium, chlorine, specifying the sheet of atoms we are standing on and all the sheets above us and below us. An absolutely pure crystal of salt could have the position of every atom specified by something like 10 bits of information.[1] This would not strain the information-carrying capacity of the brain.

If the universe had natural laws that governed its behavior to the same degree of regularity that determines a crystal of salt, then, of course, the universe would be knowable. Even if there were many such laws, each of considerable complexity, human beings might have the capacity to understand them all. Even if such knowledge exceeded the information-carrying capacity of the brain, we might store the additional information outside

---

[1]Chlorine is a deadly poison gas employed on European battlefields in World War I. Sodium is a corrosive metal which burns upon contact with water. Together they make a placid and unpoisonous material, table salt. Why each of these substances has the properties it does is a subject called chemistry, which requires more than 10 bits of information to understand.

our bodies—in books, for example, or in computer memories—and still, in some sense, know the universe.

Human beings are, understandably, highly motivated to find regulari-   10
ties, natural laws. The search for rules, the only possible way to understand such a vast and complex universe, is called science. The universe forces those who live in it to understand it. Those creatures who find everyday experience a muddled jumble of events with no predictability, no regularity, are in grave peril. The universe belongs to those who, at least to some degree, have figured it out.

It is an astonishing fact that there *are* laws of nature, rules that summarize conveniently—not just qualitatively but quantitatively—how the world works. We might imagine a universe in which there are no such laws, in which the 10^{80} elementary particles that make up a universe like our own behave with utter and uncompromising abandon. To understand such a universe we would need a brain at least as massive as the universe. It seems unlikely that such a universe could have life and intelligence, because beings and brains require some degree of internal stability and order. But even if in a much more random universe there were such beings with an intelligence much greater than our own, there could not be much knowledge, passion or joy.

Fortunately for us, we live in a universe that has at least important parts that are knowable. Our common-sense experience and our evolutionary history have prepared us to understand something of the workaday world. When we go into other realms, however, common sense and ordinary intuition turn out to be highly unreliable guides. It is stunning that as we go close to the speed of light our mass increases indefinitely, we shrink toward zero thickness in the direction of motion, and time for us comes as near to stopping as we would like. Many people think that this is silly, and every week or two I get a letter from someone who complains to me about it. But it is a virtually certain consequence not just of experiment but also of Albert Einstein's brilliant analysis of space and time called the Special Theory of Relativity. It does not matter that these effects seem unreasonable to us. We are not in the habit of traveling close to the speed of light. The testimony of our common sense is suspect at high velocities.

Or consider an isolated molecule composed of two atoms shaped something like a dumbbell—a molecule of salt, it might be. Such a molecule rotates about an axis through the line connecting the two atoms. But in the world of quantum mechanics, the realm of the very small, not all orientations of our dumbbell molecule are possible. It might be that the molecule could be oriented in a horizontal position, say, or in a vertical position, but not at many angles in between. Some rotational positions are forbidden. Forbidden by what? By the laws of nature. The universe is built in such a way as to limit, or quantize, rotation. We do not experience this directly in everyday life; we would find it startling as well as awkward in sitting-up exercises, to find arms outstretched from the sides or pointed up to the skies permitted but many intermediate positions forbidden. We do not live in the world of the small, on the scale of 10^{-13} centimeters, in the realm where there are twelve zeros between the decimal place and the one. Our common-sense intuitions do not count. What does count is experiment—in this case observations from the far infrared spectra of molecules. They show molecular rotation to be quantized.

The idea that the world places restrictions on what humans might do is frustrating. Why *shouldn't* we be able to have intermediate rotational positions? Why *can't* we travel faster than the speed of light? But so far as we can tell, this is the way the universe is constructed. Such prohibitions not only press us toward a little humility; they also make the world more knowable. Every restriction corresponds to a law of nature, a regularization of the universe. The more restrictions there are on what matter and energy can do, the more knowledge human beings can attain. Whether in some sense the universe is ultimately knowable depends not only on how many natural laws there are that encompass widely divergent phenomena, but also on whether we have the openness and the intellectual capacity to understand such laws. Our formulations of the regularities of nature are surely dependent on how the brain is built, but also, and to a significant degree, on how the universe is built.

For myself, I like a universe that includes much that is unknown and,   15
at the same time, much that is knowable. A universe in which everything is known would be static and dull, as boring as the heaven of some weakminded theologians. A universe that is unknowable is no fit place for a thinking being. The ideal universe for us is one very much like the universe we inhabit. And I would guess that this is not really much of a coincidence.

QUESTIONS

1. How are *science* and *scientific thinking* defined in the first three paragraphs? What is Sagan's purpose in defining these terms? What does this tell you about Sagan's conception of his audience?
2. Sagan's mode of reflection might be considered less personal than others in this section in that he is reflecting on an idea rather than on an event in his life. How does Sagan keep the tone from becoming abstract? What elements of the personal are present in this essay?
3. Sagan cites scientists who believe that "everything worth knowing will soon be known" (paragraph 4). How does the evidence in this essay challenge that assumption?
4. We might consider paragraph 15 to be Sagan's most personal statement in his reflections on the universe: he likes "a universe that includes much that is unknown and, at the same time, much that is knowable." Why is this balance important to Sagan? Do you agree with his closing statements? Explain.

5. Consider the statement, "The more restrictions there are on what matter and energy can do, the more knowledge human beings can attain" (paragraph 14). Describe an example in your own experience (or another's) when you learned that rules or laws were helpful in ensuring your personal freedom.
6. In paragraph 3 Sagan concludes, "Understanding is a kind of ecstasy." Describe a time in your life when you understood something for the first time; when, as they say, the light went on in your head, shining on a difficult problem, and bringing about a realization. Could your feelings at the time be considered ecstatic, or did you experience some other emotion?
7. What sort of universe would you consider ideal? What would you like to know about the universe that is now unknown to you? Explain.

MAKING CONNECTIONS

1. A number of the writers in this section offer their reflections in order to justify a belief or a strong feeling about a subject. In other words, their reflections become a kind of argument. Meghan Daum (p. 83), Patricia J. Williams (p. 101), Amitav Ghosh (p. 119), and Trudy Dittmar (p. 148) come to mind as well as Sagan. How convincing is the argument in each case? How has the writer used purely personal responses to make a persuasive case? How would you go about developing a more objective argument for one of their positions? What would be the difference in effect?
2. Does Sagan's concern for "passion" and "joy" (paragraph 11) surprise you? Where else, especially in the writings by scientists in this section, do you find evidence of the same concerns? Citing several examples from essayists you have read, write an essay on the role of passion and joy in the work of scientists and other writers.

REPORTING

Here in "Reporting" you will find writing that reflects a wide array of academic and professional situations—a naturalist describing the tool-using behavior of chimpanzees, a brain surgeon detailing the progress of a delicate operation, a historian telling about the plague that swept through medieval Europe, a travel writer describing life at a major international airport. Informative writing is basic to every field of endeavor, and the writers in this section seek to fulfill that basic need by reporting material drawn from various sources: a telescope, articles, books, public records, and firsthand observation. Working from such varied sources, these writers aim to provide detailed and reliable accounts of things—to give the background of a case, to convey the look and smell and feel of a place, to describe the appearance and behavior of people, to tell the story of recent or ancient events.

Though reporting depends on a careful gathering of information, it is by no means a mechanical and routine activity that consists simply of getting some facts and writing them up. Newspaper editors and criminal investigators often say that they want "just the facts," but they know that somehow the facts are substantially shaped by the point of view of the person who is gathering and reporting them. By point of view, we mean both the physical and the mental standpoints from which a person observes or investigates something. Each of us, after all, stands at a particular point in space and time, as well as in thought and feeling, whenever we look at any subject. And where we stand in relation to the subject will determine the particular aspects of it that we perceive and bring out in an account.

The influence that point of view exerts on reporting can be seen in the following passage that opens Robert Coover's brief story, "The Brother" (p. 223):

> right there right there in the middle of the damn field he says he
> wants to put that thing together him and his buggy ideas and so
> me I says "how the hell you gonna get it down to the water?"

Forget the unconventionalities of punctuation and grammar. This is a
story, an invention, and the speaker is Noah's younger brother. We know
that story from another point of view, so when we catch on to who is
speaking, which, admittedly doesn't happen right away, we read everything the brother says differently. We realize he's got a point, as many
would say, but we also know that his point will not change anything. And
that too Coover accounts for as that passage continues, in the very next
words,

> but he just focuses me out sweepin the blue his eyes rollin like they
> do when he gets het on some new lunatic notion.

Noah listens only to Absolute Authority. So as the story goes on to develop, his brother cannot possibly be persuasive.

Consider this passage from Paul Auster's "Auggie Wren's Christmas
Story."

> As I flipped through the albums and began to study Auggie's
> work, I didn't know what to think. My first impression was that it
> was the oddest, most bewildering thing I had ever seen. All the pic-
> tures were the same. The whole project was a numbing on-slaught
> of repetition, the same street and the same buildings over and over
> again, an unrelenting delirium of redundant images. I couldn't
> think of anything to say to Auggie, so I continued turning pages,
> nodding my head in feigned appreciation. Auggie himself seemed
> unperturbed, watching me with a broad smile on his face, but after
> I'd been at it for several minutes, he suddenly interrupted me and
> said, "You're going too fast. You'll never get it if you don't slow
> down."
> He was right, of course.

Here again two points of view conflict, and as soon as Auster accepts
Auggie Wren's suggestion, as soon as he heeds Wren's authority, he begins
to make remarkable observations about what had first seemed "a numbing
on-slaught of repetition."

Reports begin from a point of view and they differ fundamentally as
consequences of those beginnings. The authority of Coover's story depends
on how well he can imagine a younger brother's point of view toward
Noah's miraculous accomplishment. Auster, writing about matters closer
to home, must wrestle with how much he trusts Wren's version of his
story. Perhaps, he worries, Wren "made the whole thing up." But Auster
got a story out of it anyway, and that, he decides finally, is what matters.

In other areas of study, such casualness won't do, and it matters a great deal to us that Tuchman, for example, makes a careful report of the sources that ground her historical study of the Black Death in the later Middle Ages, or that Mowat, van Lawick-Goodall, Nabokov, and Lopez convince us that their firsthand observations of animal behaviors are close and exacting, or that Rachel Carson, who is unlikely to have traveled to the deepest depths of the sea, has synthesized enough scientific reports to describe that distant strangeness to us.

The poems in this section, too, depend again and again on sharp points of view. Jane Kenyon responding to summer makes observations that differ from William Carlos Williams's on early spring, nor does Williams react to spring as does Elizabeth Bishop. Rita Dove writing of Rosa Parks assumes a point of view very unlike that of W. H. Auden on an Unknown Citizen.

Once you try to imagine the various perspectives from which anything can be observed or investigated, you will see that no one person can possibly uncover everything there is to know about something. For this reason, above all, point of view is a critical aspect of reporting. As a reader of reportorial writing, you should always attempt to identify the point of view from which the information was gathered to help yourself assess the special strengths and weaknesses in the reporting that arise from that point of view. By the same token, in your own reporting you should carefully decide on the point of view that you already have or plan to use in observing or gathering information about something. Once you begin to pay deliberate attention to point of view, you will come to see that it is closely related to the various purposes for which people gather and report information in writing.

The Range of Reportorial Writing

The purpose of reporting is in one sense straightforward and self-evident, particularly when it is defined in terms of its commonly accepted value to readers. Whether it involves a firsthand account of some recent happening or the documented record of a long-past sequence of events, reportorial writing informs readers about the various subjects that may interest them but that they cannot possibly observe or investigate on their own. You may never get to see chimpanzees in their native African habitats, but you can get a glimpse of their behavior through the firsthand account of Jane van Lawick-Goodall. So, too, you will probably never have occasion to make your way through the many public records and personal reports of the bubonic plague that beset Europe in the mid-fourteenth century, but you can get a synoptic view of the plague from Barbara Tuchman's account, which is based on a thorough investigation of those sources. Reporting expands the range of its readers' perceptions and knowledge beyond the limits of their own immediate experience. From the outlook of readers, then, the function of reporting does seem to be very clear-cut.

But if we shift our focus and look at reporting in terms of the purposes to which it is evidently put by writers, it often turns out to serve a more complex function than might at first be supposed. An example of this complexity can be seen in the following passage from van Lawick-Goodall's account:

> Suddenly I stopped, for I saw a slight movement in the long grass about sixty yards away. Quickly focusing my binoculars I saw that it was a single chimpanzee, and just then he turned in my direction. I recognized David Graybeard.
>
> Cautiously I moved around so that I could see what he was doing. He was squatting beside the red earth mound of a termite nest, and as I watched I saw him carefully push a long grass stem down into a hole in the mound. After a moment he withdrew it and picked something from the end with his mouth.

This passage seems on the whole to be a very neutral bit of scientific reporting that details van Lawick-Goodall's observation of a particular chimpanzee probing for food in a termite nest. The only unusual aspect of the report is her naming of the creature, which has the unscientific effect of personifying the animal. Otherwise, she is careful in the opening part of the description to establish the physical point of view from which she observed the chimpanzee. And at the end of the passage she is equally careful not to identify or even conjecture about "something" beyond her range of detailed vision. As it turns out, however, this passage is a record not only of her observations but also of a pivotal moment in the story of how she came to make an important discovery about chimpanzees—that they are tool users—and thus how she came to regard their behavior as being much closer to that of human beings than had previously been supposed. So, she climaxes her previous description of the chimpanzee with this sentence:

> I was too far away to make out what he was eating, but it was obvious that he was actually using a grass stem as a tool.

Here as elsewhere, then, her reporting is thoughtfully worded and structured to make a strong case for her ideas about chimpanzee and human behavior. Thus, she evidently intends her report to be both informative and persuasive.

A different set of purposes can be seen in yet another firsthand account—this time of a medical patient, as observed by his doctor, Richard Selzer:

> From the doorway of Room 542 the man in the bed seems deeply tanned. Blue eyes and close-cropped white hair give him the appearance of vigor and good health. But I know that his skin is not brown

from the sun. It is rusted, rather, in the last stage of containing the vile repose within. And the blue eyes are frosted, looking inward like the windows of a snowbound cottage. This man is blind. This man is also legless — the right leg missing from midthigh down, the left from just below the knee. It gives him the look of a bonsai, roots and branches pruned into the dwarfed facsimile of a great tree.

In this passage, Selzer seeks to describe both the seemingly healthy visual appearance of the patient and his decaying physical condition. Thus he begins by reporting visual details, such as the "deeply tanned" skin as well as the "blue eyes and close-cropped white hair," that convey "the appearance of vigor and good health." Then in the sentences that follow, Selzer relies heavily on figurative language, on a striking sequence of metaphors and similes, each of which reverses the initial impression so as to convey the drastically impaired condition of the patient. The patient's skin turns out to be "rusted," his eyes "frosted," and his body like "the dwarfed facsimile of a great tree." Yet it is also clear from these and other bits of figurative language in the passage that Selzer is not only trying to convey the dire physical condition of his patient, but also to suggest his own intense personal feelings about him. Clearly, he intends his report to be provocative as well as informative.

As is apparent from just this handful of selections, writers invariably seem to use reporting for a combination of purposes — not only to provide information, but also to convey their attitudes, beliefs, or ideas about it and to influence the views of their readers. This joining of purposes is hardly surprising, given the factors involved in any decision to report on something. After all, whenever we make a report, we do so presumably because we believe that the subject of our report is important enough for others to be told about it. And presumably we believe the subject to be important because of what we have come to know and think about it. So, when we are faced with deciding what information to report and how to report it, we inevitably base our decisions on these ideas. At every point in the process of planning and writing a report, we act on the basis of our particular motives and priorities for conveying information about the subject. And how could we do otherwise? How else could van Lawick-Goodall have decided what information to report out of all she must have observed during her first few months in Africa? How else could Selzer have decided what to emphasize out of all the information that he must have gathered from the time he first met his patient until the time of the patient's death? Without specific purposes to control our reporting, our records of events would be as long as the events themselves.

Reporting, as you can see, necessarily serves a widely varied range of purposes — as varied as the writers and their subjects. Thus, whenever you read a piece of reportorial writing, you should always try to discover for yourself what appear to be its guiding purposes by examining its structure, its phrasing, and its wording, much as we have earlier in this discussion. And once you have identified the purpose, you should then consider how it has influenced the selection, arrangement, and weighting of information in the report. When you turn to doing your own writing, you should be equally careful in determining your purposes for reporting as well as in organizing your report so as to put the information in a form that is true to what you know and think about the subject.

Methods of Reporting

In planning a piece of reportorial writing, you should be sure to keep in mind not only your ideas about the subject, but also the needs of your readers. Given that most of your readers will probably not be familiar with your information, you should be very careful in selecting and organizing it to provide a clear and orderly report. Usually, you will find that the nature of your information suggests a corresponding method of presenting it most clearly and conveniently to your readers.

If the information concerns a single, detailed event or covers a set of events spread over time, the most effective method probably is narration—in the form of storytelling—in a more or less chronological order. This is the basic form that van Lawick-Goodall uses, and it proves to be a very clear and persuasive form for gradually unfolding her discovery about the behavior of chimpanzees. If the information concerns a particular place or scene or spectacle, the most convenient method is description—presenting your information in a clear-cut spatial order to help your reader visualize both the overall scene and its important details. This is the method that Selzer uses not only in describing his patient's condition, but also in detailing the patient's posture and his hospital room. If the information is meant to provide a synoptic body of knowledge about a particular subject, the clearest form will be a topical summation that may require accepting or even devising a set of categories appropriate to the subject at hand. This is the underlying form used by Pico Iyer in his study of the Los Angeles Airport, in which he intersperses personal, on-the-spot observations with passages that compare an airport to a city. After some initial observations, Iyer remarks on the "commonplace" of relating airports to cities; but he keeps working that theme, developing it beyond a commonplace through subsections that categorize and explore the parallel strangenesses and dislocations of airports, and not just cities now.

Although narration, description, topical summation, and other forms of reporting are often treated separately for purposes of convenience in identifying each of them, they usually end up working in combination with one another. Narratives, after all, involve not only events but also people and places, so it is natural that they include descriptive passages. Similarly, descriptions of places frequently entail stories about events taking place in them, so it is not surprising that they include bits of narration. And given the synoptic nature of topical summations, they are likely to involve both descriptive and narrative elements. In writing, as in most other activities, form should follow function, rather than being forced to fit arbitrary rules of behavior.

Once you have settled on a basic form, you should then devise a way of managing your information within that form—of selecting, arranging, and proportioning it—to achieve your purposes most effectively. To carry out this task, you will need to review all of the material you have gathered with an eye to determining what you consider to be the most important information to report. Some bits or kinds of information inevitably will strike you as more significant than others, and these are the ones that you should feature in your report. Likewise, you will probably find that some information is simply not important enough even to be mentioned. Van Lawick-Goodall, for example, produces a striking account of her first few months in Africa because she focuses primarily on her observation of chimpanzees, subordinating all the other material she reports to her discoveries about their behavior. Thus, only on a couple of occasions does she include observations about the behavior of animals other than chimpanzees—in particular about the timidities of a bushbuck and a leopard. And she only includes these observations to point up by contrast the distinctively sociable behavior of chimpanzees. For much the same reasons, she proportions her coverage of the several chimpanzee episodes she reports to give the greatest amount of detail to the one that provides the most compelling indication of their advanced intelligence—namely, the final episode, which shows the chimpanzees to be tool users and makers, a behavior previously attributed only to human beings.

To help achieve your purposes, you should also give special thought to deciding on the perspective from which you present your information to the reader. Do you want to present the material in the first or third person? Do you want to be present in the piece, as are van Lawick-Goodall and Selzer? Or do you want to be invisible, like Barry Lopez in his portrait of a wolf or Vladimir Nabokov (almost) in his description of a butterfly's metamorphosis? To some extent, of course, your answer to these questions will depend on whether you gathered the information through your own firsthand observations and want to convey your firsthand reactions to your observations, as van Lawick-Goodall and Selzer do in their pieces. But just to show that there are no hard-and-fast rules on this score, you might look at "A Delicate Operation" by Roy C. Selby Jr. You will notice at once that although Selby must have written this piece on the basis of firsthand experience, he tells the story in the third person, removing himself almost completely from it except for such distant-sounding references to himself as "the surgeon." Clearly, Selby is important to the information in this report, yet he evidently decided to de-emphasize himself in writing the report. Ultimately, then, the nature of a report is substantially determined not only by *what* a writer gathers from various sources, but also by *how* a writer presents the information.

In the reports that follow in this section, you will have an opportunity to see various ways of presenting things in writing. In later sections, you will see how reporting combines with other kinds of writing—explaining and arguing.

Arts and Humanities

AT HOME, AT SCHOOL, IN HIDING

Anne Frank

Anne Frank (1929–1945) was born in Germany and lived there until 1933, when her family moved to Holland to avoid the anti-Jewish laws and other anti-Jewish conditions that were then taking hold in Nazi Germany. But the oppressiveness of those conditions spread to Holland after the Nazi occupation in the summer of 1940, as Frank reports in the following excerpt from her diary. She started her diary on June 12, 1942, and continued keeping it until August 1, 1944. Three days after the last entry, the Frank family and a few employees who had been hiding from the Nazis with them since July 1942 were arrested and taken to a concentration camp in Auschwitz, Poland. In October 1944, Anne and her sister, Margot, were moved to a concentration camp at Bergen-Belsen, Germany, where Anne died of typhoid fever in late February or early March 1945, a month or so before the camp was liberated by British troops. Her father, Otto Frank, was the only member of the family to survive the Holocaust, and in 1947 he produced a condensed version of the diary, which had been hidden for safekeeping by two of his secretaries. The following excerpt is from the "Definitive Edition," published in 1995, which includes all of the material that Anne Frank had imagined herself using in "a novel" or some other kind of account about "how we lived, what we ate and what we talked about as Jews in hiding." Her thoughts about making her story known came to mind after she heard a radio broadcast in March 1944 about a planned postwar collection of diaries and letters dealing with the war.

SATURDAY, JUNE 20, 1942

Writing in a diary is a really strange experience for someone like me. Not only because I've never written anything before, but also because it seems to me that later on neither I nor anyone else will be interested in the musings of a thirteen-year-old schoolgirl. Oh well, it doesn't matter. I feel like writing, and I have an even greater need to get all kinds of things off my chest.

"Paper has more patience than people." I thought of this saying on one of those days when I was feeling a little depressed and was sitting at home with my chin in my hands, bored and listless, wondering whether to stay in or go out. I finally stayed where I was, brooding. Yes, paper *does* have more patience, and since I'm not planning to let anyone else read this stiff-backed notebook grandly referred to as a "diary," unless I should ever find a real friend, it probably won't make a bit of difference.

Now I'm back to the point that prompted me to keep a diary in the first place: I don't have a friend.

Let me put it more clearly, since no one will believe that a thirteen-year-old girl is completely alone in the world. And I'm not. I have loving parents and a sixteen-year-old sister, and there are about thirty people I can call friends. I have a throng of admirers who can't keep their adoring eyes off me and who sometimes have to resort to using a broken pocket mirror to try and catch a glimpse of me in the classroom. I have a family, loving aunts and a good home. No, on the surface I seem to have everything, except my one true friend. All I think about when I'm with friends is having a good time. I can't bring myself to talk about anything but ordinary everyday things. We don't seem to be able to get any closer, and that's the problem. Maybe it's my fault that we don't confide in each other. In any case, that's just how things are, and unfortunately they're not liable to change. This is why I've started the diary.

To enhance the image of this long-awaited friend in my imagination, I 5 don't want to jot down the facts in this diary the way most people would do, but I want the diary to be my friend, and I'm going to call this friend *Kitty*.

Since no one would understand a word of my stories to Kitty if I were to plunge right in, I'd better provide a brief sketch of my life, much as I dislike doing so.

My father, the most adorable father I've ever seen, didn't marry my mother until he was thirty-six and she was twenty-five. My sister Margot was born in Frankfurt am Main in Germany in 1926. I was born on June 12, 1929. I lived in Frankfurt until I was four. Because we're Jewish, my father immigrated to Holland in 1933, when he became the Managing Director of the Dutch Opekta Company, which manufactures products used in making jam. My mother, Edith Holländer Frank, went with him to Holland in September, while Margot and I were sent to Aachen to stay with our grandmother. Margot went to Holland in December, and I followed in February, when I was plunked down on the table as a birthday present for Margot.

I started right away at the Montessori nursery school. I stayed there until I was six, at which time I started first grade. In sixth grade my teacher was Mrs. Kuperus, the principal. At the end of the year we were both in tears as we said a heartbreaking farewell, because I'd been accepted at the Jewish Lyceum, where Margot also went to school.

Our lives were not without anxiety, since our relatives in Germany were suffering under Hitler's anti-Jewish laws. After the pogroms[1] in 1938 my two uncles (my mother's brothers) fled Germany, finding safe refuge in North America. My elderly grandmother came to live with us. She was seventy-three years old at the time.

After May 1940 the good times were few and far between: first there   10
was the war, then the capitulation and then the arrival of the Germans, which is when the trouble started for the Jews. Our freedom was severely restricted by a series of anti-Jewish decrees: Jews were required to wear a yellow star; Jews were required to turn in their bicycles; Jews were forbidden to use streetcars; Jews were forbidden to ride in cars, even their own; Jews were required to do their shopping between 3 and 5 P.M.; Jews were required to frequent only Jewish-owned barbershops and beauty parlors; Jews were forbidden to be out on the streets between 8 P.M. and 6 A.M.; Jews were forbidden to attend theaters, movies or any other forms of entertainment; Jews were forbidden to use swimming pools, tennis courts, hockey fields or any other athletic fields; Jews were forbidden to go rowing; Jews were forbidden to take part in any athletic activity in public; Jews were forbidden to sit in their gardens or those of their friends after 8 P.M.; Jews were forbidden to visit Christians in their homes; Jews were required to attend Jewish schools, etc. You couldn't do this and you couldn't do that, but life went on. Jacque always said to me, "I don't dare do anything anymore, 'cause I'm afraid it's not allowed."

In the summer of 1941 Grandma got sick and had to have an operation, so my birthday passed with little celebration. In the summer of 1940 we didn't do much for my birthday either, since the fighting had just ended in Holland. Grandma died in January 1942. No one knows how often *I* think of her and still love her. This birthday celebration in 1942 was intended to make up for the others, and Grandma's candle was lit along with the rest.

The four of us are still doing well, and that brings me to the present date of June 20, 1942, and the solemn dedication of my diary.

SATURDAY, JUNE 20, 1942

Dearest Kitty!

Let me get started right away; it's nice and quiet now. Father and Mother are out and Margot has gone to play Ping-Pong with some other young people at her friend Trees's. I've been playing a lot of Ping-Pong

---

[1]*pogroms:* organized massacres of Jewish people. [Eds.]

myself lately. So much that five of us girls have formed a club. It's called "The Little Dipper Minus Two." A really silly name, but it's based on a mistake. We wanted to give our club a special name; and because there were five of us, we came up with the idea of the Little Dipper. We thought it consisted of five stars, but we turned out to be wrong. It has seven, like the Big Dipper, which explains the "Minus Two." Ilse Wagner has a Ping-Pong set, and the Wagners let us play in their big dining room whenever we want. Since we five Ping-Pong players like ice cream, especially in the summer, and since you get hot playing Ping-Pong, our games usually end with a visit to the nearest ice-cream parlor that allows Jews: either Oasis or Delphi. We've long since stopped hunting around for our purses or money—most of the time it's so busy in Oasis that we manage to find a few generous young men of our acquaintance or an admirer to offer us more ice cream than we could eat in a week.

You're probably a little surprised to hear me talking about admirers at such a tender age. Unfortunately, or not, as the case may be, this vice seems to be rampant at our school. As soon as a boy asks if he can bicycle home with me and we get to talking, nine times out of ten I can be sure he'll become enamored on the spot and won't let me out of his sight for a second. His ardor eventually cools, especially since I ignore his passionate glances and pedal blithely on my way. If it gets so bad that they start rambling on about "asking Father's permission," I swerve slightly on my bike, my schoolbag falls, and the young man feels obliged to get off his bike and hand me the bag, by which time I've switched the conversation to another topic. These are the most innocent types. Of course, there are those who blow you kisses or try to take hold of your arm, but they're definitely knocking on the wrong door. I get off my bike and either refuse to make further use of their company or act as if I'm insulted and tell them in no uncertain terms to go on home without me.

There you are. We've now laid the basis for our friendship. Until to-   15
morrow.

Yours, Anne

SUNDAY, JUNE 21, 1942

Dearest Kitty,

Our entire class is quaking in its boots. The reason, of course, is the upcoming meeting in which the teachers decide who'll be promoted to the next grade and who'll be kept back. Half the class is making bets. G. Z. and I laugh ourselves sick at the two boys behind us, C. N. and Jacques Kocernoot, who have staked their entire vacation savings on their bet. From morning to night, it's "You're going to pass," "No, I'm not," "Yes, you are," "No, I'm not." Even G.'s pleading glances and my angry outbursts can't calm them down. If you ask me, there are so many dummies that about a quarter of the class should be kept back, but teachers are the most unpredictable creatures on earth. Maybe this time they'll be unpredictable in the right direction for a change.

I'm not so worried about my girlfriends and myself. We'll make it. The only subject I'm not sure about is math. Anyway, all we can do is wait. Until then, we keep telling each other not to lose heart.

I get along pretty well with all my teachers. There are nine of them, seven men and two women. Mr. Keesing, the old fogey who teaches math, was mad at me for the longest time because I talked so much. After several warnings, he assigned me extra homework. An essay on the subject "A Chatterbox." A chatterbox, what can you write about that? I'd worry about that later, I decided. I jotted down the assignment in my notebook, tucked it in my bag and tried to keep quiet.

That evening, after I'd finished the rest of my homework, the note about the essay caught my eye. I began thinking about the subject while chewing the tip of my fountain pen. Anyone could ramble on and leave big spaces between the words, but the trick was to come up with convincing arguments to prove the necessity of talking. I thought and thought, and suddenly I had an idea. I wrote the three pages Mr. Keesing had assigned me and was satisfied. I argued that talking is a female trait and that I would do my best to keep it under control, but that I would never be able to break myself of the habit, since my mother talked as much as I did, if not more, and that there's not much you can do about inherited traits.

Mr. Keesing had a good laugh at my arguments, but when I proceeded   20
to talk my way through the next class, he assigned me a second essay. This time it was supposed to be on "An Incorrigible Chatterbox." I handed it in, and Mr. Keesing had nothing to complain about for two whole classes. However, during the third class he'd finally had enough. "Anne Frank, as punishment for talking in class, write an essay entitled '"Quack, Quack, Quack," Said Mistress Chatterback.'"

The class roared. I had to laugh too, though I'd nearly exhausted my ingenuity on the topic of chatterboxes. It was time to come up with something else, something original. My friend Sanne, who's good at poetry, offered to help me write the essay from beginning to end in verse. I jumped for joy. Keesing was trying to play a joke on me with this ridiculous subject, but I'd make sure the joke was on him.

I finished my poem, and it was beautiful! It was about a mother duck and a father swan with three baby ducklings who were bitten to death by the father because they quacked too much. Luckily, Keesing took the joke the right way. He read the poem to the class, adding his own comments, and to several other classes as well. Since then I've been allowed to talk and haven't been assigned any extra homework. On the contrary, Keesing's always making jokes these days.

Yours, Anne

. . .

WEDNESDAY, JULY 1, 1942

Dearest Kitty,

Until today I honestly couldn't find the time to write you. I was with friends all day Thursday, we had company on Friday, and that's how it went until today.

Hello and I have gotten to know each other very well this past week, and he's told me a lot about his life. He comes from Gelsenkirchen and is living with his grandparents. His parents are in Belgium, but there's no way he can get there. Hello used to have a girlfriend named Ursul. I know her too. She's perfectly sweet and perfectly boring. Ever since he met me, Hello has realized that he's been falling asleep at Ursul's side. So I'm kind of a pep tonic. You never know what you're good for!

Jacque spent Saturday night here. Sunday afternoon she was at Hanneli's, and I was bored stiff. 25

Hello was supposed to come over that evening, but he called around six. I answered the phone, and he said, "This is Helmuth Silberberg. May I please speak to Anne?"

"Oh, Hello. This is Anne."

"Oh, hi, Anne. How are you?"

"Fine, thanks."

"I just wanted to say I'm sorry but I can't come tonight, though I 30 would like to have a word with you. Is it all right if I come by and pick you up in about ten minutes?"

"Yes, that's fine. Bye-bye!"

"Okay, I'll be right over. Bye-bye!"

I hung up, quickly changed my clothes and fixed my hair. I was so nervous I leaned out the window to watch for him. He finally showed up. Miracle of miracles, I didn't rush down the stairs, but waited quietly until he rang the bell. I went down to open the door, and he got right to the point.

"Anne, my grandmother thinks you're too young for me to be seeing you on a regular basis. She says I should be going to the Lowenbachs', but you probably know that I'm not going out with Ursul anymore."

"No, I didn't know. What happened? Did you two have a fight?" 35

"No, nothing like that. I told Ursul that we weren't suited to each other and so it was better for us not to go together anymore, but that she was welcome at my house and I hoped I would be welcome at hers. Actually, I thought Ursul was hanging around with another boy, and I treated her as if she were. But that wasn't true. And then my uncle said I should apologize to her, but of course I didn't feel like it, and that's why I broke up with her. But that was just one of the reasons.

"Now my grandmother wants me to see Ursul and not you, but I don't agree and I'm not going to. Sometimes old people have really old-fashioned ideas, but that doesn't mean I have to go along with them. I need my grandparents, but in a certain sense they need me too. From now on I'll be free on Wednesday evenings. You see, my grandparents made me sign up for a wood-carving class, but actually I go to a club organized by the Zionists.[2] My grandparents don't want me to go, because they're anti-Zionists. I'm not a fanatic Zionist, but it interests me. Anyway, it's been such a mess lately that I'm planning to quit. So next Wednesday will be my last meeting. That means I can see you Wednesday evening, Saturday afternoon, Saturday evening, Sunday afternoon and maybe even more."

"But if your grandparents don't want you to, you shouldn't go behind their backs."

"All's fair in love and war."

Just then we passed Blankevoort's Bookstore and there was Peter 40
Schiff with two other boys; it was the first time he'd said hello to me in ages, and it really made me feel good.

Monday evening Hello came over to meet Father and Mother. I had bought a cake and some candy, and we had tea and cookies, the works, but neither Hello nor I felt like sitting stiffly on our chairs. So we went out for a walk, and he didn't deliver me to my door until ten past eight. Father was furious. He said it was very wrong of me not to get home on time. I had to promise to be home by ten to eight in the future. I've been asked to Hello's on Saturday.

Wilma told me that one night when Hello was at her house, she asked him, "Who do you like best, Ursul or Anne?"

He said, "It's none of your business."

But as he was leaving (they hadn't talked to each other the rest of the evening), he said, "Well, I like Anne better, but don't tell anyone. Bye!" And whoosh . . . he was out the door.

In everything he says or does, I can see that Hello is in love with me, 45
and it's kind of nice for a change. Margot would say that Hello is eminently suitable. I think so too, but he's more than that. Mother is also full of praise: "A good-looking boy. Nice and polite." I'm glad he's so popular with everyone. Except with my girlfriends. He thinks they're very childish, and he's right about that. Jacque still teases me about him, but I'm not in love with him. Not really. It's all right for me to have boys as friends. Nobody minds.

Mother is always asking me who I'm going to marry when I grow up, but I bet she'll never guess it's Peter, because I talked her out of that idea myself, without batting an eyelash. I love Peter as I've never loved anyone, and I tell myself he's only going around with all those other girls to hide his feelings for me. Maybe he thinks Hello and I are in love with each other, which we're not. He's just a friend, or as Mother puts it, a beau.

Yours, Anne

. . .

---

[2]*Zionists:* belonging to the international movement to establish a Jewish state in modern-day Israel. [Eds.]

WEDNESDAY, JULY 8, 1942

Dearest Kitty,

It seems like years since Sunday morning. So much has happened it's as if the whole world had suddenly turned upside down. But as you can see, Kitty, I'm still alive, and that's the main thing, Father says. I'm alive all right, but don't ask where or how. You probably don't understand a word I'm saying today, so I'll begin by telling you what happened Sunday afternoon.

At three o'clock (Hello had left but was supposed to come back later), the doorbell rang. I didn't hear it, since I was out on the balcony, lazily reading in the sun. A little while later Margot appeared in the kitchen doorway looking very agitated. "Father has received a call-up notice from the SS,"[3] she whispered. "Mother has gone to see Mr. van Daan" (Mr. van Daan is Father's business partner and a good friend.)

I was stunned. A call-up: everyone knows what that means. Visions of concentration camps and lonely cells raced through my head. How could we let Father go to such a fate? "Of course he's not going," declared Margot as we waited for Mother in the living room. "Mother's gone to Mr. van Daan to ask whether we can move to our hiding place tomorrow. The van Daans are going with us. There will be seven of us altogether." Silence. We couldn't speak. The thought of Father off visiting someone in the Jewish Hospital and completely unaware of what was happening, the long wait for Mother, the heat, the suspense—all this reduced us to silence.

Suddenly the doorbell rang again. "That's Hello," I said.

"Don't open the door!" exclaimed Margot to stop me. But it wasn't necessary, since we heard Mother and Mr. van Daan downstairs talking to Hello, and then the two of them came inside and shut the door behind them. Every time the bell rang, either Margot or I had to tiptoe downstairs to see if it was Father, and we didn't let anyone else in. Margot and I were sent from the room, as Mr. van Daan wanted to talk to Mother alone.

When she and I were sitting in our bedroom, Margot told me that the call-up was not for Father, but for her. At this second shock, I began to cry. Margot is sixteen—apparently they want to send girls her age away on their own. But thank goodness she won't be going; Mother had said so herself, which must be what Father had meant when he talked to me about our going into hiding. Hiding . . . where would we hide? In the city? In the country? In a house? In a shack? When, where, how . . . ? These were questions I wasn't allowed to ask, but they still kept running through my mind.

Margot and I started packing our most important belongings into a schoolbag. The first thing I stuck in was this diary, and then curlers, handkerchiefs, schoolbooks, a comb and some old letters. Preoccupied by the thought of going into hiding, I stuck the craziest things in the bag, but I'm not sorry. Memories mean more to me than dresses.

50

---

[3]*SS:* Nazi police in charge of intelligence and elimination of those thought "undesirable." [Eds.]

Father finally came home around five o'clock, and we called Mr. Kleiman to ask if he could come by that evening. Mr. van Daan left and went to get Miep. Miep arrived and promised to return later that night, taking with her a bag full of shoes, dresses, jackets, underwear and stockings. After that it was quiet in our apartment; none of us felt like eating. It was still hot, and everything was very strange.

We had rented our big upstairs room to a Mr. Goldschmidt, a di- 55 vorced man in his thirties, who apparently had nothing to do that evening, since despite all our polite hints he hung around until ten o'clock.

Miep and Jan Gies came at eleven. Miep, who's worked for Father's company since 1933, has become a close friend, and so has her husband Jan. Once again, shoes, stockings, books and underwear disappeared into Miep's bag and Jan's deep pockets. At eleven-thirty they too disappeared.

I was exhausted, and even though I knew it'd be my last night in my own bed, I fell asleep right away and didn't wake up until Mother called me at five-thirty the next morning. Fortunately, it wasn't as hot as Sunday; a warm rain fell throughout the day. The four of us were wrapped in so many layers of clothes it looked as if we were going off to spend the night in a refrigerator, and all that just so we could take more clothes with us. No Jew in our situation would dare leave the house with a suitcase full of clothes. I was wearing two undershirts, three pairs of underpants, a dress, and over that a skirt, a jacket, a raincoat, two pairs of stockings, heavy shoes, a cap, a scarf and lots more. I was suffocating even before we left the house, but no one bothered to ask me how I felt.

Margot stuffed her schoolbag with schoolbooks, went to get her bicycle and, with Miep leading the way, rode off into the great unknown. At any rate, that's how I thought of it, since I still didn't know where our hiding place was.

At seven-thirty we too closed the door behind us; Moortje, my cat, was the only living creature I said good-bye to. According to a note we left for Mr. Goldschmidt, she was to be taken to the neighbors, who would give her a good home.

The stripped beds, the breakfast things on the table, the pound of meat 60 for the cat in the kitchen—all of these created the impression that we'd left in a hurry. But we weren't interested in impressions. We just wanted to get out of there, to get away and reach our destination in safety. Nothing else mattered.

More tomorrow.

Yours, Anne

QUESTIONS

1. In the first entry for June 20, Frank writes at length about wanting her diary to be a very special kind of friend. What kind of friend does she

have in mind? How would you characterize Frank's friendship with Kitty as it develops over the several entries included in this excerpt?

2. How are your impressions of the friendship (and of Frank) affected by the fact that she sometimes goes several days without writing anything in her diary?

3. What kind of person does Frank appear to be from the information she reports and the stories she tells about her family? About anti-Jewish decrees? About her boyfriends? About her experiences at school?

4. What kind of person does Frank appear to be from the thoughts and feelings she expresses about these different aspects of her life? Does she come across differently (or similarly) when she is writing about these different aspects of her life?

5. In what respects does Frank's life as a thirteen-year-old seem most different from yours when you were thirteen? In what respects does it seem most similar to yours when you were that age? In what ways do you identify with Frank? In what ways do you find her experience so different as to greatly distance you from her?

6. Given what you discover about Frank's day-to-day life with her friends and at school, what do you consider to be the most important similarities and differences between young adolescent life then and now?

7. Compare and contrast the anti-Jewish decrees that Frank reports with racist decrees that you have read about in South Africa, the United States, and other countries around the world.

8. Keep a diary for several weeks in which you try to make a detailed report of the different aspects of your life in a form that you might be willing to share not only with a close friend (real or imaginary), but also with a large body of readers.

MAKING CONNECTIONS

1. Read Carol Gilligan's "Interviewing Adolescent Girls" (p. 425), and then write a piece considering the similarities or differences between Frank and the young adolescents that Gilligan describes in her study.

2. Read Cynthia Ozick's "Who Owns Anne Frank?" (p. 603) and Patricia Hampl's "Reviewing Anne Frank" (p. 4). To what extent do these pieces influence how you read Anne Frank herself in this selection?

HATSUYO NAKAMURA

John Hersey

John Hersey (1914–1993) was born in Tientsin, China, where his father was a YMCA administrator and his mother a missionary. After graduating from Yale in 1936, Hersey was a war correspondent in China and Japan. When the United States entered World War II, Hersey covered the war in the South Pacific, the Mediterranean, and Moscow. In 1945, he won the Pulitzer Prize for his novel, A Bell for Adano. *In 1946,* Hiroshima, *a report about the effects of the atomic bomb on the lives of six people, was widely acclaimed. Almost forty years later, Hersey went back to Japan to find those six people to see what their lives had been like. Their stories form the final chapter of the 1985 edition of* Hiroshima. *The selection presented here first appeared in the* New Yorker, *as did the first edition of* Hiroshima. *A prolific writer of fiction and nonfiction, Hersey believes that "journalism allows its readers to witness history; fiction gives its readers an opportunity to live it."*

In August, 1946, a year after the bombing of Hiroshima, Hatsuyo Nakamura was weak and destitute. Her husband, a tailor, had been taken into the Army and had been killed at Singapore on the day of the city's capture, February 15, 1942. She lost her mother, a brother, and a sister to the atomic bomb. Her son and two daughters—ten, eight, and five years old—were buried in rubble when the blast of the bomb flung her house down. In a frenzy, she dug them out alive. A month after the bombing, she came down with radiation sickness; she lost most of her hair and lay in bed for weeks with a high fever in the house of her sister-in-law in the suburb of Kabe, worrying all the time about how to support her children. She was too poor to go to a doctor. Gradually, the worst of the symptoms abated, but she remained feeble; the slightest exertion wore her out.

She was near the end of her resources. Fleeing from her house through the fires on the day of the bombing, she had saved nothing but a rucksack of emergency clothing, a blanket, an umbrella, and a suitcase of things she had stored in her air-raid shelter; she had much earlier evacuated a few kimonos to Kabe in fear of a bombing. Around the time her hair started to grow in again, her brother-in-law went back to the ruins of her house and recovered her late husband's Sankoku sewing machine, which needed repairs. And though she had lost the certificates of a few bonds and other meager wartime savings, she had luckily copied off their numbers before the bombing and taken the record to Kabe, so she was eventually able to cash them in. This money enabled her to rent for fifty yen a month—the equivalent then of less than fifteen cents—a small wooden shack built by a carpenter in the Nobori-cho neighborhood, near the site of her former home. In this way, she could free herself from the charity of her in-laws and begin a courageous struggle, which would last for many years, to keep her children and herself alive.

The hut had a dirt floor and was dark inside, but it was a home of sorts. Raking back some rubble next to it, she planted a garden. From the debris of collapsed houses she scavenged cooking utensils and a few dishes. She had the Sankoku fixed and began to take in some sewing, and from time to time she did cleaning and laundry and washed dishes for neighbors who were somewhat better off than she was. But she got so tired that she had to take two days' rest for every three days she worked, and if she was obliged for some reason to work for a whole week she then had to rest for three or four days. She soon ran through her savings and was forced to sell her best kimono.

At that precarious time, she fell ill. Her belly began to swell up, and she had diarrhea and so much pain she could no longer work at all. A doctor who lived nearby came to see her and told her she had roundworm, and he said, incorrectly, "If it bites your intestine, you'll die." In those days, there was a shortage of chemical fertilizers in Japan, so farmers were using night soil, and as a consequence many people began to harbor parasites, which were not fatal in themselves but were seriously debilitating to those who had had radiation sickness. The doctor treated Nakamura-san (as he would have addressed her) with santonin, a somewhat dangerous medicine derived from certain varieties of artemisia.[1] To pay the doctor, she was forced to sell her last valuable possession, her husband's sewing machine. She came to think of that as marking the lowest and saddest moment of her whole life.

In referring to those who went through the Hiroshima and Nagasaki   5
bombings, the Japanese tended to shy away from the term "survivors," because in its focus on being alive it might suggest some slight to the sacred dead. The class of people to which Nakamura-san belonged came, therefore, to be called by a more neutral name, "hibakusha"—literally, "explosion-affected persons." For more than a decade after the bombings, the hibakusha lived in an economic limbo, apparently because the Japanese government did not want to find itself saddled with anything like moral responsibility for heinous acts of the victorious United States. Although it soon became clear that many hibakusha suffered consequences of their exposure to the bombs which were quite different in nature and degree from

---

[1]*artemisia:* a genus of herbs and shrubs, including sagebrush and wormwood, distinguished by strong-smelling foliage. [Eds.]

those of survivors even of the ghastly fire bombings in Tokyo and else-where, the government made no special provision for their relief—until, ironically, after the storm of rage that swept across Japan when the twenty-three crewmen of a fishing vessel, the Lucky Dragon No. 5, and its cargo of tuna were irradiated by the American test of a hydrogen bomb at Bikini in 1954. It took three years even then for a relief law for the hibakusha to pass the Diet.

Though Nakamura-san could not know it, she thus had a bleak period ahead of her. In Hiroshima, the early postwar years were, besides, a time, especially painful for poor people like her, of disorder, hunger, greed, thievery, black markets. Non-hibakusha employers developed a prejudice against the survivors as word got around that they were prone to all sorts of ailments, and that even those like Nakamura-san, who were not cruelly maimed and had not developed any serious overt symptoms, were unreli-able workers, since most of them seemed to suffer, as she did, from the mysterious but real malaise that came to be known as one kind of lasting "A-bomb sickness": a nagging weakness and weariness, dizziness now and then, digestive troubles, all aggravated by a feeling of oppression, a sense of doom, for it was said that unspeakable diseases might at any time plant nasty flowers in their bodies, and even in those of their descendants.

As Nakamura-san struggled to get from day to day, she had no time for attitudinizing about the bomb or anything else. She was sustained, curi-ously, by a kind of passivity, summed up in a phrase she herself sometimes used—"*Shikata ga-nai,*" meaning, loosely, "It can't be helped." She was not religious, but she lived in a culture long colored by the Buddhist belief that resignation might lead to clear vision; she had shared with other citi-zens a deep feeling of powerlessness in the face of a state authority that had been divinely strong ever since the Meiji Restoration[2], in 1868; and the hell she had witnessed and the terrible aftermath unfolding around her reached so far beyond human understanding that it was impossible to think of them as the work of resentable human beings, such as the pilot of the Enola Gay, or President Truman,[3] or the scientists who had made the bomb—or even, nearer at hand, the Japanese militarists who had helped to bring on the war. The bombing almost seemed a natural disaster—one that it had simply been her bad luck, her fate (which must be accepted), to suffer.

When she had been wormed and felt slightly better, she made an arrangement to deliver bread for a baker named Takahashi, whose bakery was in Nobori-cho. On days when she had the strength to do it, she would

---

[2]*Meiji Restoration:* a period in Japanese history continuing until 1912 when, under the rule of Emperor Meiji, Japan industrialized significantly and increased her foreign trade. [Eds.]

[3]*Enola Gay:* the airplane that dropped the atomic bomb on Hiroshima; *Harry S Truman* (1884–1972): president of the United States who made the decision to drop the bomb. [Eds.]

take orders for bread from retail shops in her neighborhood, and the next
morning she would pick up the requisite number of loaves and carry them
in baskets and boxes through the streets to the stores. It was exhausting
work, for which she earned the equivalent of about fifty cents a day. She
had to take frequent rest days.

After some time, when she was feeling a bit stronger, she took up another kind of peddling. She would get up in the dark and trundle a borrowed two-wheeled pushcart for two hours across the city to a section
called Eba, at the mouth of one of the seven estuarial rivers that branch
from the Ota River through Hiroshima. There, at daylight, fishermen
would cast their leaded skirt-like nets for sardines, and she would help
them to gather up the catch when they hauled it in. Then she would push
the cart back to Nobori-cho and sell the fish for them from door to door.
She earned just enough for food.

A couple of years later, she found work that was better suited to her   10
need for occasional rest, because within certain limits she could do it on
her own time. This was a job of collecting money for deliveries of the Hiroshima paper, the *Chugoku Shimbun,* which most people in the city read.
She had to cover a big territory, and often her clients were not at home or
pleaded that they couldn't pay just then, so she would have to go back
again and again. She earned the equivalent of about twenty dollars a
month at this job. Every day, her will power and her weariness seemed to
fight to an uneasy draw.

In 1951, after years of this drudgery, it was Nakamura-san's good
luck, her fate (which must be accepted), to become eligible to move into a
better house. Two years earlier, a Quaker professor of dendrology from the
University of Washington named Floyd W. Schmoe, driven, apparently, by
deep urges for expiation and reconciliation, had come to Hiroshima, assembled a team of carpenters, and, with his own hands and theirs, begun
building a series of Japanese-style houses for victims of the bomb; in all, his
team eventually built twenty-one. It was to one of these houses that
Nakamura-san had the good fortune to be assigned. The Japanese measure
their houses by multiples of the area of the floor-covering *tsubo* mat, a
little less than four square yards, and the Dr. Shum-o houses, as the Hi-
roshimans called them, had two rooms of six mats each. This was a big
step up for the Nakamuras. This home was redolent of new wood and
clean matting. The rent, payable to the city government, was the equivalent
of about a dollar a month.

Despite the family's poverty, the children seemed to be growing normally. Yaeko and Myeko, the two daughters, were anemic, but all three
had so far escaped any of the more serious complications that so many
young hibakusha were suffering. Yaeko, now fourteen, and Myeko, eleven,
were in middle school. The boy, Toshio, ready to enter high school, was
going to have to earn money to attend it, so he took up delivering papers
to the places from which his mother was collecting. These were some dis-

tance from their Dr. Shum-o house, and they had to commute at odd hours by streetcar.

The old hut in Nobori-cho stood empty for a time, and, while continuing with her newspaper collections, Nakamura-san converted it into a small street shop for children, selling sweet potatoes, which she roasted, and *dagashi,* or little candies and rice cakes, and cheap toys, which she bought from a wholesaler.

All along, she had been collecting for papers from a small company, Suyama Chemical, that made mothballs sold under the trade name Paragen. A friend of hers worked there, and one day she suggested to Nakamura-san that she join the company, helping wrap the product in its packages. The owner, Nakamura-san learned, was a compassionate man, who did not share the bias of many employers against hibakusha; he had several on his staff of twenty women wrappers. Nakamura-san objected that she couldn't work more than a few days at a time; the friend persuaded her that Suyama would understand that.

So she began. Dressed in company uniforms, the women stood, some-   15
what bent over, on either side of a couple of conveyor belts, working as fast as possible to wrap two kinds of Paragen in cellophane. Paragen had a dizzying odor, and at first it made one's eyes smart. Its substance, powdered paradichlorobenzene, had been compressed into lozenge-shaped mothballs and into larger spheres, the size of small oranges, to be hung in Japanese-style toilets, where their rank pseudomedicinal smell would offset the unpleasantness of non-flushing facilities.

Nakamura-san was paid, as a beginner, a hundred and seventy yen — then less than fifty cents — a day. At first, the work was confusing, terribly tiring, and a bit sickening. Her boss worried about her paleness. She had to take many days off. But little by little she became used to the factory. She made friends. There was a family atmosphere. She got raises. In the two ten-minute breaks, morning and afternoon, when the moving belt stopped, there was a birdsong of gossip and laughter, in which she joined. It appeared that all along there had been, deep in her temperament, a core of cheerfulness, which must have fueled her long fight against A-bomb lassitude, something warmer and more vivifying than mere submission, than saying "*Shikata ga-nai.*" The other women took to her; she was constantly doing them small favors. They began calling her, affectionately, *Oba-san* — roughly, "Auntie."

She worked at Suyama for thirteen years. Though her energy still paid its dues, from time to time, to the A-bomb syndrome, the searing experiences of that day in 1945 seemed gradually to be receding from the front of her mind.

The Lucky Dragon No. 5 episode took place the year after Nakamura-san started working for Suyama Chemical. In the ensuing fever of outrage in the country, the provision of adequate medical care for the victims of the Hiroshima and Nagasaki bombs finally became a political issue. Almost

every year since 1946, on the anniversary of the Hiroshima bombing, a
Peace Memorial Meeting had been held in a park that the city planners had
set aside, during the city's rebuilding, as a center of remembrance, and on
August 6, 1955, delegates from all over the world gathered there for the
first World Conference Against Atomic and Hydrogen Bombs. On its second day, a number of hibakusha tearfully testified to the government's
neglect of their plight. Japanese political parties took up the cause, and in
1957 the Diet at last passed the A-Bomb Victims Medical Care Law. This
law and its subsequent modifications defined four classes of people who
would be eligible for support: those who had been in the city limits on the
day of the bombing; those who had entered an area within two kilometers
of the hypocenter in the first fourteen days after it; those who had come
into physical contact with bomb victims, in administering first aid or in
disposing of their bodies; and those who had been embryos in the wombs
of women in any of the first three categories. These hibakusha were
entitled to receive so-called health books, which would entitle them to free
medical treatment. Later revisions of the law provided for monthly al-
lowances to victims suffering from various aftereffects.

Like a great many hibakusha, Nakamura-san had kept away from all
the agitation, and, in fact, also like many other survivors, she did not even
bother to get a health book for a couple of years after they were issued. She
had been too poor to keep going to doctors, so she had got into the habit
of coping alone, as best she could, with her physical difficulties. Besides,
she shared with some other survivors a suspicion of ulterior motives on the
part of the political-minded people who took part in the annual ceremonies
and conferences.

Nakamura-san's son, Toshio, right after his graduation from high
school, went to work for the bus division of the Japanese National Rail-
ways. He was in the administrative offices, working first on timetables,
later in accounting. When he was in his midtwenties, a marriage was
arranged for him, through a relative who knew the bride's family. He built
an addition to the Dr. Shum-o house, moved in, and began to contribute to
his mother's support. He made her a present of a new sewing machine.

Yaeko, the older daughter, left Hiroshima when she was fifteen, right
after graduating from middle school, to help an ailing aunt who ran a *ryo-
kan,* a Japanese-style inn. There, in due course, she fell in love with a man
who ate at the inn's restaurant, and she made a love marriage.

After graduating from high school, Myeko, the most susceptible of the
three children to the A-bomb syndrome, eventually became an expert typist
and took up instructing at typing schools. In time, a marriage was arranged
for her.

Like their mother, all three children avoided pro-hibakusha and anti-
nuclear agitation.

In 1966, Nakamura-san, having reached the age of fifty-five, retired
from Suyama Chemical. At the end, she was being paid thirty thousand

yen, or about eighty-five dollars, a month. Her children were no longer dependent on her, and Toshio was ready to take on a son's responsibility for his aging mother. She felt at home in her body now; she rested when she needed to, and she had no worries about the cost of medical care, for she had finally picked up Health Book No. 1023993. It was time for her to enjoy life. For her pleasure in being able to give gifts, she took up embroidery and the dressing of traditional *kimekomi* dolls, which are supposed to bring good luck. Wearing a bright kimono, she went once a week to dance at the Study Group of Japanese Folk Music. In set movements, with expressive gestures, her hands now and then tucking up the long folds of the kimono sleeves, and with head held high, she danced, moving as if floating, with thirty agreeable women to a song of celebration of entrance into a house:

> May your family flourish
> For a thousand generations,
> For eight thousand generations.

A year or so after Nakamura-san retired, she was invited by an organization called the Bereaved Families' Association to take a train trip with about a hundred other war widows to visit the Yasukuni Shrine, in Tokyo. This holy place, established in 1869, was dedicated to the spirits of all the Japanese who had died in wars against foreign powers, and could be thought roughly analogous, in terms of its symbolism for the nation, to the Arlington National Cemetery—with the difference that souls, not bodies, were hallowed there. The shrine was considered by many Japanese to be a focus of a still smoldering Japanese militarism, but Nakamura-san, who had never seen her husband's ashes and had held on to a belief that he would return to her someday, was oblivious of all that. She found the visit baffling. Besides the Hiroshima hundred, there were huge crowds of women from other cities on the shrine grounds. It was impossible for her to summon up a sense of her dead husband's presence, and she returned home in an uneasy state of mind.

Japan was booming. Things were still rather tight for the Nakamuras, and Toshio had to work very long hours, but the old days of bitter struggle began to seem remote. In 1975, one of the laws providing support to the hibakusha was revised, and Nakamura-san began to receive a so-called health-protection allowance of six thousand yen, then about twenty dollars, a month; this would gradually be increased to more than twice that amount. She also received a pension, toward which she had contributed at Suyama, of twenty thousand yen, or about sixty-five dollars, a month; and for several years she had been receiving a war widow's pension of another twenty thousand yen a month. With the economic upswing, prices had, of course, risen steeply (in a few years Tokyo would become the most expensive city in the world), but Toshio managed to buy a small Mitsubishi car, and occasionally he got up before dawn and rode a train for two hours to play golf with business associates. Yaeko's husband ran a shop for sales and service of air-conditioners and heaters, and Myeko's husband ran a newsstand and candy shop near the railroad station.

In May each year, around the time of the Emperor's birthday, when the trees along broad Peace Boulevard were at their feathery best and banked azaleas were everywhere in bloom, Hiroshima celebrated a flower festival. Entertainment booths lined the boulevard, and there were long parades, with floats and bands and thousands of marchers. This year, Nakamura-san danced with the women of the folk-dance association, six dancers in each of sixty rows. They danced to "Oiwai-Ondo," a song of happiness, lifting their arms in gestures of joy and clapping in rhythms of threes:

> Green pine trees, cranes and turtles . . .
> You must tell a story of your hard times
> And laugh twice.

The bombing had been four decades ago. How far away it seemed!

The sun blazed that day. The measured steps and the constant lifting of the arms for hours at a time were tiring. In midafternoon, Nakamura-san suddenly felt woozy. The next thing she knew, she was being lifted, to her great embarrassment and in spite of begging to be let alone, into an ambulance. At the hospital, she said she was fine; all she wanted was to go home. She was allowed to leave.

QUESTIONS

1. What does Hatsuyo Nakamura's story tell us about the larger group of atomic-bomb survivors?
2. Why do you think Hersey chose Hatsuyo Nakamura as a subject to report on? How is she presented to us? How are we meant to feel about her?
3. In composing his article, Hersey presumably interviewed Nakamura and reports from her point of view. At what points does he augment her story? For example, look at paragraph 5. What material in the article probably comes from Nakamura? What material probably comes from other sources?
4. How has Hersey arranged his material? He has covered forty years of Hatsuyo Nakamura's life in twenty-nine paragraphs. Make a list of the events he chose to report. At what points does he condense large blocks of time?
5. Interview a relative or someone you know who participated in World War II or in some other war, such as Vietnam. How did the war change

that person's life? What events does he or she consider most important in the intervening years?

6. No doubt every person then in Hiroshima remembers the day of the bombing just as Americans of certain ages remember days of critical national events—the attack on Pearl Harbor, the Kennedy and King assassinations, the space shuttle disaster, and so on. Interview several people about one such day, finding out where they were when they first learned of the event, how they reacted, what long-term impact they felt, and how they view that day now. Use the information from your interviews to write a report.

MAKING CONNECTIONS

1. Imagine an encounter between Nakamura and either Zoë Tracy Hardy ("What Did You Do in the War, Grandma?" p. 139), or William L. Laurence ("Atomic Bombing of Nagasaki Told by Flight Member" p. 247). What might these people say to one another? Write the dialogue for a possible conversation between them.

2. One characteristic of reports is to be tentative or even oblique in drawing conclusions. Compare Hersey's report to one by Pico Iyer (p. 270), Roy C. Selby Jr. (p. 295), or Richard Selzer (p. 289), all presented in this section, and assess their differing methods of coming to a conclusion. What would you say the points are of the two reports you chose to compare?

THE LONG GOOD-BYE
Mother's Day in Federal Prison

Amanda Coyne

Amanda Coyne (b. 1966) was born in Colorado and subsequently migrated with her family from Alaska to ten other states as her father's "relentless pursuit of better employment" led him to hold such titles as fry cook, janitor, librarian, college professor, magazine editor, and presidential speechwriter. Coyne describes her own life as having thus far been "similarly kinetic and varied." "Between traveling, experimenting with religion, countercultural lifestyles, and writing," she has been employed as a waitress, nursing home assistant, teacher, public relations associate, and public policy analyst. Coyne is currently pursuing a master's degree in nonfiction writing at the University of Iowa, where she received her undergraduate degree in English. The following essay, which appeared in Harper's *(May 1997), is her first publication.*

You can spot the convict-moms here in the visiting room by the way they hold and touch their children and by the single flower that is perched in front of them—a rose, a tulip, a daffodil. Many of these mothers have untied the bow that attaches the flower to its silver-and-red cellophane wrapper and are using one of the many empty soda cans at hand as a vase. They sit proudly before their flower-in-a-Coke-can, amid Hershey bar wrappers, half-eaten Ding Dongs, and empty paper coffee cups. Occasionally, a mother will pick up her present and bring it to her nose when one of the bearers of the single flower—her child—asks if she likes it. And the mother will respond the way that mothers always have and always will respond when presented with a gift on this day. "Oh, I just love it. It's perfect. I'll put it in the middle of my Bible." Or, "I'll put it on my desk, right next to your school picture." And always: "It's the best one here."

But most of what is being smelled today is the children themselves. While the other adults are plunking coins into the vending machines, the mothers take deep whiffs from the backs of their children's necks, or kiss and smell the backs of their knees, or take off their shoes and tickle their feet and then pull them close to their noses. They hold them tight and take in their own second scent—the scent assuring them that these are still their children and that they still belong to them.

The visitors are allowed to bring in pockets full of coins, and today that Mother's Day flower, and I know from previous visits to my older sister here

212

at the Federal Prison Camp for women in Pekin, Illinois, that there is always an aberrant urge to gather immediately around the vending machines. The sandwiches are stale, the coffee weak, the candy bars the ones we always pass up in a convenience store. But after we hand the children over to their mothers, we gravitate toward those machines. Like milling in the kitchen at a party. We all do it, and nobody knows why. Polite conversation ensues around the microwave while the popcorn is popping and the processed-chicken sandwiches are being heated. We ask one another where we are from, how long a drive we had. An occasional whistle through the teeth, a shake of the head. "My, my, long way from home, huh?" "Staying at the Super 8 right up the road. Not a bad place." "Stayed at the Econo Lodge last time. Wasn't a good place at all." Never asking the questions we really want to ask: "What's she in for?" "How much time's she got left?" You never ask in the waiting room of a doctor's office either. Eventually, all of us—fathers, mothers, sisters, brothers, a few boyfriends, and very few husbands—return to the queen of the day, sitting at a fold-out table loaded with snacks, prepared for five or so hours of attempted normal conversation.

Most of the inmates are elaborately dressed, many in prison-crafted dresses and sweaters in bright blues and pinks. They wear meticulously applied makeup in corresponding hues, and their hair is replete with loops and curls—hair that only women with the time have the time for. Some of the better seamstresses have crocheted vests and purses to match their outfits. Although the world outside would never accuse these women of making haute-couture fashion statements, the fathers and the sons and the boyfriends and the very few husbands think they look beautiful, and they tell them so repeatedly. And I can imagine the hours spent preparing for this visit—hours of needles and hooks clicking over brightly colored yards of yarn. The hours of discussing, dissecting, and bragging about these visitors—especially the men. Hours spent in the other world behind the door where we're not allowed, sharing lipsticks and mascaras, and unraveling the occasional hair-tangled hot roller, and the brushing out and lifting and teasing . . . and the giggles that abruptly change into tears without warning—things that define any female-only world. Even, or especially, if that world is a female federal prison camp.

While my sister Jennifer is with her son in the playroom, an inmate's   5
mother comes over to introduce herself to my younger sister, Charity, my brother, John, and me. She tells us about visiting her daughter in a higher-security prison before she was transferred here. The woman looks old and tired, and her shoulders sag under the weight of her recently acquired bitterness.

"Pit of fire," she says, shaking her head. "Like a pit of fire straight from hell. Never seen anything like it. Like something out of an old movie about prisons." Her voice is getting louder and she looks at each of us with pleading eyes. "My *daughter* was there. Don't even get me started on that place. Women die there."

John and Charity and I silently exchange glances.

"My daughter would come to the visiting room with a black eye and I'd think, 'All she did was sit in the car while her boyfriend ran into the house.' She didn't even touch the stuff. Never even handled it."

She continues to stare at us, each in turn. "Ten years. That boyfriend talked and he got three years. She didn't know anything. Had nothing to tell them. They gave her ten years. They called it conspiracy. Conspiracy? Aren't there real criminals out there?" She asks this with hands outstretched, waiting for an answer that none of us can give her.

The woman's daughter, the conspirator, is chasing her son through the   10
maze of chairs and tables and through the other children. She's a twenty-four-year-old blonde, whom I'll call Stephanie, with Dorothy Hamill hair[1] and matching dimples. She looks like any girl you might see in any shopping mall in middle America. She catches her chocolate-brown son and tickles him, and they laugh and trip and fall together onto the floor and laugh harder.

Had it not been for that wait in the car, this scene would be taking place at home, in a duplex Stephanie would rent while trying to finish her two-year degree in dental hygiene or respiratory therapy at the local community college. The duplex would be spotless, with a blown-up picture of her and her son over the couch and ceramic unicorns and horses occupying the shelves of the entertainment center. She would make sure that her son went to school every day with stylishly floppy pants, scrubbed teeth, and a good breakfast in his belly. Because of their difference in skin color, there would be occasional tension — caused by the strange looks from strangers, teachers, other mothers, and the bullies on the playground, who would chant after they knocked him down, "Your Momma's white, your Momma's white." But if she were home, their weekends and evenings would be spent together transcending those looks and healing those bruises. Now, however, their time is spent eating visiting-room junk food and his school days are spent fighting the boys in the playground who chant, "Your Momma's in prison, your Momma's in prison."

He will be ten when his mother is released, the same age my nephew will be when his mother is let out. But Jennifer, my sister, was able to spend the first five years of Toby's life with him. Stephanie had Ellie after she was incarcerated. They let her hold him for eighteen hours, then sent her back to prison. She has done the "tour," and her son is a well-traveled six-year-old. He has spent weekends visiting his mother in prisons in Kentucky, Texas, Connecticut (the Pit of Fire), and now at last here, the camp — minimum security, Pekin, Illinois.

Ellie looks older than his age. But his shoulders do not droop like his grandmother's. On the contrary, his bitterness lifts them and his chin

---

[1]*Dorothy Hamill hair:* a short, perky cut named for a recent Olympic gold medal–winning figure skater. [Eds.]

higher than a child's should be, and the childlike, wide-eyed curiosity has been replaced by defiance. You can see his emerging hostility as he and his mother play together. She tells him to pick up the toy that he threw, say, or to put the deck of cards away. His face turns sullen, but she persists. She takes him by the shoulders and looks him in the eye, and he uses one of his hands to swat at her. She grabs the hand and he swats with the other. Eventually, she pulls him toward her and smells the top of his head, and she picks up the cards or the toy herself. After all, it is Mother's Day and she sees him so rarely. But her acquiescence makes him angrier, and he stalks out of the playroom with his shoulders thrown back.

Toby, my brother and sister and I assure one another, will not have these resentments. He is better taken care of than most. He is living with relatives in Wisconsin. Good, solid, middle-class, churchgoing relatives. And when he visits us, his aunts and his uncle, we take him out for adventures where we walk down the alley of a city and pretend that we are being chased by the "bad guys." We buy him fast food, and his uncle, John, keeps him up well past his bedtime enthralling him with stories of the monkeys he met in India. A perfect mix, we try to convince one another. Until we take him to see his mother and on the drive back he asks the question that most confuses him, and no doubt all the other children who spend much of their lives in prison visiting rooms: "Is my Mommy a bad guy?" It is the question that most seriously disorders his five-year-old need to clearly separate right from wrong. And because our own need is perhaps just as great, it is the question that haunts us as well.

Now, however, the answer is relatively simple. In a few years, it won't   15
be. In a few years we will have to explain mandatory minimums, and the war on drugs, and the murky conspiracy laws, and the enormous amount of money and time that federal agents pump into imprisoning low-level drug dealers and those who happen to be their friends and their lovers. In a few years he might have the reasoning skills to ask why so many armed robbers and rapists and child-molesters and, indeed, murderers are punished less severely than his mother. When he is older, we will somehow have to explain to him the difference between federal crimes, which don't allow for parole, and state crimes, which do. We will have to explain that his mother was taken from him for five years not because she was a drug dealer but because she made four phone calls for someone she loved.

But we also know it is vitally important that we explain all this without betraying our bitterness. We understand the danger of abstract anger, of being disillusioned with your country, and, most of all, we do not want him to inherit that legacy. We would still like him to be raised as we were, with the idea that we live in the best country in the world with the best legal system in the world—a legal system carefully designed to be immune to political mood swings and public hysteria; a system that promises to fit the punishment to the crime. We want him to be a good citizen. We want him to have absolute faith that he lives in a fair country, a country that watches over and protects its most vulnerable citizens: its women and children.

So for now we simply say, "Toby, your mother isn't bad, she just did a bad thing. Like when you put rocks in the lawn mower's gas tank. You weren't bad then, you just did a bad thing."

Once, after being given this weak explanation, he said, "I wish I could have done something really bad, like my Mommy. So I could go to prison too and be with her."

We notice a circle forming on one side of the visiting room. A little boy stands in its center. He is perhaps nine years old, sporting a burnt-orange three-piece suit and pompadour hair. He stands with his legs slightly apart, eyes half-shut, and sways back and forth, flashing his cuffs and snapping his fingers while singing:

> . . . Doesn't like crap games with barons and earls.
> Won't go to Harlem in ermine and pearls.
> Won't dish the dirt with the rest of the girls.
> That's why the lady is a tramp.

He has a beautiful voice and it sounds vaguely familiar. One of the visitors informs me excitedly that the boy is the youngest Frank Sinatra impersonator and that he has been on television even. The boy finishes his performance and the room breaks into applause. He takes a sweeping bow, claps his miniature hands together, and points both little index fingers at the audience. "More. Later. Folks." He spins on his heels and returns to the table where his mother awaits him, proudly glowing. "Don't mess with the hair, Mom," we overhear. "That little boy's slick," my brother says with true admiration.

Sitting a few tables down from the youngest Frank Sinatra is a table of Mexican-Americans. The young ones are in white dresses or button-down oxfords with matching ties. They form a strange formal contrast to the rest of the rowdy group. They sit silently, solemnly listening to the white-haired woman, who holds one of the table's two roses. I walk past and listen to the grandmother lecture her family. She speaks of values, of getting up early every day, of going to work. She looks at one of the young boys and points a finger at him. "School is the most important thing. *Nada mas importante*[2]. You get up and you go to school and you study, and you can make lots of money. You can be big. You can be huge. Study, study, study."

The young boy nods his head. "Yes, *abuelita*[3]. Yes, *abuelita*," he says.

The owner of the other flower is holding one of the group's three infants. She has him spread before her. She coos and kisses his toes and nuzzles his stomach.

---

[2]*Nada mas importante:* nothing more important. [Eds.]
[3]*Abuelita:* auntie. [Eds.]

When I ask Jennifer about them, she tells me that it is a "mother and daughter combo." There are a few of them here, these combos, and I notice that they have the largest number of visitors and that the older inmate, the grandmother, inevitably sits at the head of the table. Even here, it seems, the hierarchical family structure remains intact. One could take a picture, replace the fast-food wrappers with chicken and potatoes, and these families could be at any restaurant in the country, could be sitting at any dining room table, paying homage on this day to the one who brought them into the world.

Back at our table, a black-haired, Middle Eastern woman dressed in   25 loose cottons and cloth shoes is whispering to my brother with a sense of urgency that makes me look toward my sister Charity with questioning eyes and a tilt of my head. Charity simply shrugs and resumes her conversation with a nineteen-year-old ex–New York University student—another conspirator. Eight years.

Prison, it seems, has done little to squelch the teenager's rebellious nature. She has recently been released from solitary confinement. She wears new retro-bellbottom jeans and black shoes with big clunky heels. Her hair is short, clipped perfectly ragged and dyed white—all except the roots, which are a stylish black. She has beautiful pale skin and beautiful red lips. She looks like any midwestern coed trying to escape her origins by claiming New York's East Village as home. She steals the bleach from the laundry room, I learn later, in order to maintain that fashionable white hue. But stealing the bleach is not what landed her in the hole. She committed the inexcusable act of defacing federal property. She took one of her government-issue T-shirts and wrote in permanent black magic marker, "I have been in your system. I have examined your system." And when she turned around it read, "I find it very much in need of repair."

But Charity has more important things to discuss with the girl than rebelling against the system. They are talking fashion. They talk prints versus plains, spring shoes, and spring dresses. Charity informs the girl that slingback, high-heeled sandals and pastels are all the rage. She makes a disgusted face and says, "Damn! Pinks and blues wash me out. I hate pastels. I don't *have* any pastels."

This fashion blip seems to be putting the girl into a deep depression. And so Charity, attempting to lighten up the conversation, puts her nose toward the girl's neck.

"New Armani scent, Gio," my sister announces.

The girl perks up. She nods her head. She calls one of the other inmates   30 over.

Charity performs the same ritual: "Coco Chanel." And again: "Paris, Yves St. Laurent."

The line gets longer, and the girls talk excitedly to one another. It seems that Charity's uncanny talent for divining brand-name perfumes is perhaps nowhere on earth more appreciated than here with these sensory-starved inmates.

As Charity continues to smell necks and call out names, I turn back to my brother and find that the woman who was speaking to him so intensely has gone. He stares pensively at the concrete wall ahead of him.

"What did she want?" I ask.

"She heard I was a sculptor. She wants me to make a bust, presented in   35
her name, for Qaddafi."

"A bust of what?"

"Of Qaddafi. She's from Libya. She was a freedom fighter. Her kids are farmed out to strangers here—foster homes. It's Qaddafi's twenty-eighth anniversary as dictator in September. She knows him. He's mad at her now, but she thinks that he'll get over it and get her kids back to Libya if she gives him a present."

"Obsession. Calvin Klein," I hear my sister pronounce. The girls cheer in unison.

I get up and search for the girl. I want to ask her about her crime. I look in the book room only to find the four-foot Frank Sinatra crooning "Somewhere over the Rainbow" to a group of spellbound children.

I ask Ponytail, one of the female guards, where the woman went.   40
"Rule," she informs me. "Cannot be in the visiting room if no visitor is present. Should not have been here. Had to go back to unit one." I have spoken to Ponytail a few times while visiting my sister and have yet to hear her use a possessive pronoun, a contraction, or a conjunction.

According to Jennifer, Ponytail has wanted to be a prison guard since she was a little girl. She is one of the few female guards here and she has been here the longest, mainly because the male guards are continuously being fired for "indiscretions" with the inmates. But Ponytail doesn't mess around. She is also the toughest guard here, particularly in regard to the federal rules governing exposed skin. She is disgusted by any portion of the leg showing above the required eight-inch shorts length. In summer, they say, she is constantly whipping out her measuring tape and writing up those who are even a fraction of an inch off.

Last summer posed a particular problem for Ponytail, though. It seems that the shorts sold in the commissary were only seven inches from crotch to seam. And because they were commissary-issued, Ponytail couldn't censor them. So, of course, all the women put away their own shorts in favor of the commissary's. This disturbed Ponytail—a condition that eventually, according to one of the girls, developed into a low-grade depression. "She walked around with that sad old tape in her hands all summer, throwing it from one hand to the other and looking at our legs. After a while, not one of us could get her even to crack a smile—not that she's a big smiler, but you can get those corners to turn sometimes. Then she started looking downright sad, you know real depressed like."

Ponytail makes sure that the girls get proper medical care. Also none of the male guards will mess with them when she's around. But even if those things weren't true, the girls would be fond of Ponytail. She is in a way just another woman in the system, and perhaps no other group of women realizes the absolute necessity for female solidarity. These inmates know with absolute certainty what women on the outside only suspect — that men still hold ultimate power over their bodies, their property, and their freedom.

So as a token of this solidarity, they all agreed to slip off their federal shorts and put on their own. Ponytail perked up, the measuring tape appeared again with a vengeance, and quite a few of the shorts owners spent much of their free time that summer cleaning out toilet bowls and wiping the scuffs off the gym floor.

It's now 3:00. Visiting ends at 3:30. The kids are getting cranky, and the   45
adults are both exhausted and wired from too many hours of conversation, too much coffee and candy. The fathers, mothers, sisters, brothers, and the few boyfriends, and the very few husbands are beginning to show signs of gathering the trash. The mothers of the infants are giving their heads one last whiff before tucking them and their paraphernalia into their respective carrying cases. The visitors meander toward the door, leaving the older children with their mothers for one last word. But the mothers never say what they want to say to their children. They say things like, "Do well in school," "Be nice to your sister," "Be good for Aunt Betty, or Grandma." They don't say, "I'm sorry I'm sorry I'm sorry. I love you more than anything else in the world and I think about you every minute and I worry about you with a pain that shoots straight to my heart, a pain so great I think I will just burst when I think of you alone, without me. I'm sorry."

We are standing in front of the double glass doors that lead to the outside world. My older sister holds her son, rocking him gently. They are both crying. We give her a look and she puts him down. Charity and I grasp each of his small hands, and the four of us walk through the doors. As we're walking out, my brother sings one of his banana songs to Toby.

"Take me out to the — " and Toby yells out, "Banana store!"

"Buy me some — "

"Bananas!!"

"I don't care if I ever come back. For it's root, root, root for the — "   50

"Monkey team!"

I turn back and see a line of women standing behind the glass wall. Some of them are crying, but many simply stare with dazed eyes. Stephanie is holding both of her son's hands in hers and speaking urgently to him. He is struggling, and his head is twisting violently back and forth. He frees one of his hands from her grasp, balls up his fist, and punches her in the face. Then he walks with purpose through the glass doors and out the exit. I look back at her. She is still in a crouched position. She stares, unblinking, through those doors. Her hands have left her face and are hanging on either side of her. I look away, but before I do, I see drops of blood drip from her nose, down her chin, and onto the shiny marble floor.

QUESTIONS

1. How would you describe Coyne's point of view in this piece? Detached or involved? Insider or outsider? How does her point of view affect your perception of the federal prison for women that she writes about in this piece?
2. Why do you think that Coyne focuses on Mother's Day at the prison? What kinds of details is she able to report that might not be observable on most other days at the prison? What kinds of details are likely to be missing (or obscured) on such a day as this?
3. Given the fact that Coyne has come to visit her sister Jennifer, why do you suppose she tells so little about Jennifer compared to what she reports about the other prisoners, particularly Stephanie and the nineteen-year-old ex–New York University student? By the same token, why do you suppose that Coyne tells so much about Stephanie's child, Ellie, and the young Frank Sinatra impersonator, but so little by comparison about Jennifer's child, Toby?
4. What do you infer from the special attention that Coyne gives to reporting on the actions of her sister Charity and the guard Ponytail?
5. Given the selection and arrangement of descriptive detail about the various people who figure in this account, what do you consider to be Coyne's major purposes in writing this piece?
6. Compare and contrast Coyne's piece on women's prisons and female prisoners to one or two other stories you can find on this subject in newspapers, magazines, or on the Internet.
7. Spend a few hours investigating a prison in your community, and write a report highlighting the details that you think are most important in revealing the quality of life in that prison.

MAKING CONNECTIONS

1. Compare and contrast the way that worlds collide in the visiting room of the women's prison with the collisions that Pico Iyer describes taking place in the Los Angeles International Airport (p. 270).
2. Read Robert Coover's "The Brother" (p. 223). Have you a brother or sister? If not, think of a friend who does. Write a piece of your own probing the often vexing relations of siblings.

PHILOSOPHY IN WARM WEATHER

Jane Kenyon

Jane Kenyon (1947–1995) was born in Ann Arbor, Michigan, and receiver bachelor's and master's degrees from the University of Michigan there. After marrying poet Donald Hall, she moved with him to his family's farm in rural New Hampshire, a setting which provided the subject matter for many of her poems. She was the state's poet laureate at the time of her death at the age of forty-eight. Kenyon published four volumes of poetry in her lifetime, including From Room to Room *(1979) and* Let Evening Come *(1990). Otherwise: New and Selected Poems was published posthumously in 1996, A Hundred White Daffodils in 1999. Thematically, Kenyon's poetry is concerned with the changing of seasons and the cycle of life and human relationships. In the words of a critic writing for the* New York Times Book Review, *her technique was praised for "rendering of natural settings in lines of well-judged rhythms and simple syntax."*

Now all the doors and windows
are open, and we move so easily
through the rooms. Cats roll
on the sunny rugs, and a clumsy wasp
climbs the pane, pausing   5
to rub a leg over her head.

All around physical life reconvenes.
The molecules of our bodies must love
to exist: they whirl in circles
and seem to begrudge us nothing.   10
Heat, Horatio,[1] *heat* makes them
put this antic disposition on!

This year's brown spider
sways over the door as I come
and go. A single poppy shouts   15
from the far field, and the crow,
beyond alarm, goes right on
pulling up the corn.

---

[1]*Horatio:* a character in Shakespeare's *Hamlet.* Late in the first act, Hamlet warns Horatio that he (Hamlet) may need "to put an antic disposition on" (pretend to be odd or mad) in order to expose his father's murderer. [Eds.]

QUESTIONS

1. In the first stanza, Kenyon reports precise details of a particular day and so implies a certain time of year. Describe the scene she portrays.
2. In the second stanza she moves from reporting to a degree of conjecture. What would be a more straightforward way of describing what she seems to feel?
3. The third stanza returns again to reporting. But in what sense does a poppy "shout"? How might one judge that the crow is "beyond alarm"? What could have alarmed him?
4. How do the more straightforward reports of the first and third stanzas embrace and influence your reception of Kenyon's more obvious conjectures in the middle, and how does that middle prepare for her end?

MAKING CONNECTIONS

1. Compare Kenyon's brief poem with any one of Anne Frank's five letters (pp. 193–201). What details from one of those letters would work best in a poem?
2. Write a letter in which you report the most vivid details of a day and reflect on what those details mean to you.

THE BROTHER

Robert Coover

Over his thirty-five year writing career, Robert Coover (b. 1932) has published fiction, poetry, and plays, as well as critical essays and nonfiction. A graduate of Indiana University and the University of Chicago, he has also taught writing at a variety of schools, most recently at Brown University. His novels include The Public Burning *(1977),* Gerald's Party *(1986), and* Ghost Town *(1998), and he is also represented by more than ten short story collections. One of the most influential of what have been called the postmodernists in American literature, Coover is known for his twisty, experimental style and for what one critic called his "extreme verbal magic." Both are evident in the following story, which appeared in the collection* Pricksongs and Descants *in 1969.*

right there right there in the middle of the damn field he says he wants to put that thing together him and his buggy ideas and so me I says "how the hell you gonna get it down to the water?" but he just focuses me out sweepin the blue his eyes rollin like they do when he gets het on some new lunatic notion and he says not to worry none about that just would I help him for God's sake and because he don't know how he can get it done in time otherwise and though you'd have to be loonier than him to say yes I says I will of course I always would crazy as my brother is I've done little else since I was born and my wife she says "I can't figure it out I can't see why you always have to be babyin that old fool he ain't never done nothin for you God knows and you got enough to do here fields need plowin it's a bad enough year already my God and now that red-eyed brother of yours wingin around like a damn cloud and not knowin what in the world he's doin buildin a damn boat in the country my God what next? you're a damn fool I tell you" but packs me some sandwiches just the same and some sandwiches for my brother Lord knows *his* wife don't have no truck with him no more says he can go starve for all she cares she's fed up ever since the time he made her sit out on a hillside for three whole days rain and everything because he said she'd see God and she didn't see nothin and in fact she like to die from hunger nothin but berries and his boys too they ain't so bright neither but at least they come to help him out with his damn boat so it ain't just the two of us thank God for *that* and it ain't no goddamn fishin boat he wants to put up neither in fact it's the biggest damn thing I ever heard of and for weeks *weeks* I'm tellin you we ain't doin nothin but cuttin down pine trees and haulin them out to his field which is really pretty high up a hill and my God *that's* work lemme tell you and my wife she sighs and says I am really crazy r-e-a-l-l-y crazy and her four months with a child and tryin to do my work and hers too and still when I come home from haulin timbers around all day she's got enough left to rub my shoulders and the small of my back and fix a hot meal her long black hair pulled to a knot behind her head and hangin marvelously down her back her eyes gentle but very tired my God and I says to my brother I says "look I got a lotta work to do buddy you'll have to finish this idiot thing yourself I wanna help you all I can you know that but" and he looks off and he says "it don't matter none your work" and I says "the hell it don't how you think me and my wife we're gonna eat I mean where do you think this food comes from you been puttin away man? you can't eat this god-damn boat out here ready to rot in that bastard sun" and he just sighs long and says "no it just don't matter" and he sits him down on a rock kinda tired like and stares off and looks like he might even for God's sake cry and so I go back to bringin wood up to him and he's already started on the keel and frame God knows how *he* ever found out to build a damn boat lost in *his* fog where he is Lord he was twenty when I was born and the first thing I remember was havin to lead him around so he didn't get kicked by a damn mule him who couldn't never do nothin in a normal way just a huge oversize fuzzyface boy so anyway I take to getting up a few hours earlier ever day to do my farmin my wife apt to lose the baby if she should keep pullin around like she was doin then I go to work on the boat until sundown and on and on the days hot and dry and my wife keepin good food in me or else I'd of dropped sure and no matter what I say to try and get out of it my brother he says "you come and help now the rest don't matter" and we just keep hammerin away and my God the damn thing is big enough for a hundred people and at least I think at *least* it's a place to live and not too bad at that at least it's good for somethin but my wife she just sighs and says no good will come of it and runs her hands through my hair but she don't ask me to stop helpin no more because she knows it won't do no good and she's kinda turned into herself now these days and gettin herself all ready and still we keep workin on that damn thing that damn boat and the days pass and my brother he says we gotta work harder we ain't got much time and from time to time he gets a coupla neighbors to come over and give a hand them sucked in by the size and the novelty of the thing makin jokes some but they don't stay around more than a day or two and they go away shakin their heads and swearin under their breath and disgusted they got weaseled into the thing in the first place and me I only get about half my place planted and see to my stock as much as I can my wife she takes more care of them than I can but at least we won't starve we say if we just get some rain and finally we get the damn thing done all finished by God and we cover it in and out with pitch and put a kinda fancy roof on it and I come home on that last day and I ain't never goin back ain't *never* gonna let him talk me into nothin again and I'm all smellin of tar and my wife she cries and cries and I says to her not to worry no more I'll be home all the time and me I'm cryin a little too though she don't notice just thinkin how she's had it so lonely and hard and all and for one whole day I just sleep the whole damn day and the rest of the week I work around the farm and one day I get an idea and I go over to my brother's place and get some pieces of wood left over and whaddaya know? they are all livin on that damn boat there in the middle of nowhere him and his boys and some women and my brother's wife she's there too but she's madder than hell and carpin at him to get outa that damn boat and come home and he says she's got just one more day and then he's gonna drug her on the boat but he don't say it like a threat or nothin more like a fact a plain fact tomorrow he's gonna drug her on the boat well I ain't one to get mixed up in domestic quarrels God knows so I grab up the wood and beat it back to my farm and that evenin I make a little cradle a kinda fancy one with little animal figures cut in it and polished down and after supper I give it to my wife as a surprise and she cries and cries and holds me tight and say don't never go away again and stay close by her and all and I feel so damn good and warm about it all and glad the boat thing is over and we get out a little wine and we decide the baby's name is gonna be either Nathaniel or Anna and so we drink an extra cup to Nathaniel's health and we laugh and we sigh and drink one to Anna and my wife she gently fingers the little animal figures and says they're beautiful and really they ain't I ain't much good at that sorta thing but I know what she means and then she says "where did you get the wood?" and I says "it's left over from the boat" and she don't say nothin for a moment and then she says "you been over there again today?" and I says "yes just to get the wood" and she says "what's he doin now he's got the boat done?" and I says "funny thing they're all living in the damn thing all except the old lady she's over there hollerin at him how he's getting senile and where does he think he's sailin to and how if he ain't afraid of runnin into a octypuss on the way he oughta get back home and him sayin she's a nut there ain't no water and her sayin that's what *she's* been tellin *him* for six months" and my wife she laughs and it's the happiest laugh I've heard from her in half a year and I laugh and we both have another cup of wine and my wife she says "so he's just livin on that big thing all by hisself?" and I says "no he's got his boys on there and some young women who are maybe wives of the boys or somethin I don't know I ain't never seen them before and all kindsa damn animals and birds and things I ain't never seen the likes" and my wife she says "animals? what animals?" and I says "oh all kinds I don't know a whole damn menagerie all clutterin and stinkin up the boat God what a mess" and my wife laughs again and she's a little silly with the wine and she says "I bet he ain't got no pigs" and "oh yes I seen them" I says and we laugh thinkin about pigs rootin around in that big tub and she says "I bet he ain't got no jackdaws" and I says "yes I seen a couple of them too or mostly I heard them you couldn't hardly hear nothin else" and we laugh again thinkin about them crows and his old lady and the pigs and all and my wife she says "*I* know what he ain't got I bet he ain't got no lice" and we both laugh like crazy and when I can I says "oh yes he does less he's took a bath" and we both laugh till we're cryin and we finish off the wine and my wife says "look now I *know* what he ain't got he ain't got no termites" and I says "you're right I don't recollect no termites maybe we oughta make him a present" and my wife she holds me close quiet all of a sudden and says "he's really movin Nathaniel's really movin" and she puts my hand down on her round belly and the little fella is kickin up a terrific storm and I says kinda anxious "does it hurt? do you think that—?" and "no" she says "it's good" she says and so I says with my hand on her belly "here's to you Nathaniel" and we drain what's left in the bottom of our cups and the next day we wake up in each other's arms and it's rainin and *thank* God we say and since it's rainin real good we stay inside and do things around the place and we're happy because the rain has come just in time and in the evenin things smell green and fresh and delicious and it's still rainin a little but not too hard so I decide to take a walk and I wander over by my brother's place thinkin I'll ask him if he'd like to take on some pet termites to go with his collection and there by God is his wife on the boat and I don't know if he drug her on or if she just finally come by herself but she ain't sayin nothin which is damn unusual and the boys they ain't sayin nothin neither and my brother he ain't sayin nothin they're just all standin up there on top and gazin off and I holler up at them "nice rain ain't it?" and my brother he looks down at me standin there in the rain and still he don't say nothin but he raises his hand kinda funny like and then puts it back on the rail and I decide not to say nothin about the termites and it's startin to rain a little harder again so I turn away and go back home and I tell my wife about what happened and my wife she just laughs and says "they're *all* crazy he's finally got them *all* crazy" and she's cooked me up a special pastry with fresh meat and so we forget about them but by God the next day the rain's still comin down harder than ever and water's beginnin to stand around in places and after a week of rain I can see the crops is pretty well ruined and I'm havin trouble keepin my stock fed and my wife she's cryin and talkin about our bad luck that we might as well of built a damn boat as plant all them crops and still we don't figure things out I mean it just don't come to our minds not even when the rain keeps spillin down like a ocean dumped upsidedown and now water is beginnin to stand around in big pools really big ones and water up to the ankles around the house and leakin in and pretty soon the whole damn house is gettin fulla water and I keep sayin maybe we oughta go use my brother's boat till this blows over but my wife she says "never" and then she starts in cryin again so finally I says to her I says "we can't be so proud I'll go ask him" and so I set out in the storm and I can hardly see where I'm goin and I slip up to my neck in places and finally I get to where the boat is and I holler up and my brother he comes out and he looks down at where I am and he don't say nothin that bastard he just looks at me and I shout up at him I says "hey is it all right for me and my wife to come over until this thing blows over?" and still he don't say a damn word he just raises his hand in that same sillyass way and I holler "hey you stupid sonuvabitch I'm soakin wet goddamn it and my house is fulla water and my wife she's about to have a kid and she's apt to get sick all wet and cold to the bone and all I'm askin you—" and right then right while I'm still talkin he turns around and he goes back in the boat and I can't hardly believe it me his brother but he don't come back out and I push up under the boat and I beat on it with my fists and scream at him and call him ever name I can think up and I shout for his boys and for his wife and for anybody inside and nobody comes out "GOD*damn* YOU" I cry out at the top of my lungs and half sobbin and sick and then feelin too beat out to do anythin more I turn around and head back for home but the rain is thunderin down like mad now and in places I gotta swim and I can't make it no further and I recollect a hill nearby and I head for it and when I get to it I climb up on top of it and it feels good to be on land again even if it is soggy and greasy and I vomit and retch there awhile and move further up and the next thing I know I'm wakin up the rain still in my face and the water halfway up the hill toward me and I look out and I can see my brother's boat is floatin and I wave at it but I don't see nobody wave back and then I quick look out towards my own place and all I can see is the top of it and of a sudden I'm scared scared about my wife and I go tearin for the house swimmin most all the way and cryin and shoutin and the rain still comin down like crazy and so now well now I'm back here on the hill again what little there is left of it and I'm figurin maybe I got a day left if the rain keeps comin and it don't show no signs of stoppin and I can't see my brother's boat no more gone just water how *how* did he know? that bastard and yet I gotta hand it to him it's not hard to see who's crazy around here I can't see my house no more I just left my wife inside where I found her I couldn't hardly stand to look at her the way she was

QUESTIONS

1. Who is telling the story, thereby making this report? How soon do you identify the speaker?
2. Read the story over again. Once you know where it is going, how do you take remarks like this: ". . . and I come home on that last day and I ain't never goin back ain't *never* gonna let him talk me into nothin again"?
3. Identify a few other passages that read differently once you have caught on to the story behind this story.
4. Since no brother is mentioned in the Bible, this is an imagined report such as a younger brother might have been in a position to make. Assuming Coover wants his readers to examine that possibility with him, what details in his report make it most vivid for you?

MAKING CONNECTIONS

1. Being wholly invented, this selection would seem to be a story. Read George Orwell's "Shooting an Elephant" (p. 132) or Trudy Dittmar's "Pronghorn" (p. 148). How close do they come to being stories too?
2. Choose another well-known passage in Genesis—for example, Cain and Abel, the Tower of Babel, or Joseph's betrayal and sale into Egypt—and tell it from the point of view of a minor or imagined character.

AUGGIE WREN'S CHRISTMAS STORY

Paul Auster

*Paul Auster (b. 1947) grew up in Newark, New Jersey, and gradu-
ated from Columbia University in 1969. A profilic writer of fiction
and poetry, he was forced early in his career to support himself
with a series of odd jobs and with work as a translator. He had his
first real success in the mid-1980s with a trilogy of novels influenced by classic mysteries but tinged with complex meditations on
the nature of illusion and reality; these are* City of Glass *(1985),*
Ghosts *(1986), and* The Locked Room *(1987). More recently, he
has published* Hand to Mouth: A Chronicle of Early Failure
(1997) and The Art of Hunger: Essays *(1997). Praised for his precise prose style and his highly individual — even quirky — vision,
Auster has in recent years turned his talents to writing and directing films. The following story, which originally appeared in the*
New York Times *on Christmas Day of 1990, served as the basis
for the 1995 films* Smoke *and* Blue in the Face, *with director
Wayne Wang as Auster's collaborator.*

I heard this story from Auggie Wren. Since Auggie doesn't come off
too well in it, at least not as well as he'd like to, he's asked me not to use
his real name. Other than that, the whole business about the lost wallet
and the blind woman and the Christmas dinner is just as he told it to me.

Auggie and I have known each other for close to eleven years now. He
works behind the counter of a cigar store on Court Street in downtown
Brooklyn, and since it's the only store that carries the little Dutch cigars I
like to smoke, I go in there fairly often. For a long time, I didn't give much
thought to Auggie Wren. He was the strange little man who wore a hooded
blue sweatshirt and sold me cigars and magazines, the impish, wisecrack-
ing character who always had something funny to say about the weather or
the Mets or the politicians in Washington, and that was the extent of it.

But then one day several years ago he happened to be looking through
a magazine in the store, and he stumbled across a review of one of my
books. He knew it was me because a photograph accompanied the review,
and after that things changed between us. I was no longer just another customer to Auggie, I had become a distinguished person. Most people
couldn't care less about books and writers, but it turned out that Auggie
considered himself an artist. Now that he had cracked the secret of who I

was, he embraced me as an ally, a confidant, a brother-in-arms. To tell the truth, I found it rather embarrassing. Then, almost inevitably, a moment came when he asked if I would be willing to look at his photographs. Given his enthusiasm and good will, there didn't seem to be any way I could turn him down.

God knows what I was expecting. At the very least, it wasn't what Auggie showed me the next day. In a small, windowless room at the back of the store, he opened a cardboard box and pulled out twelve identical black photo albums. This was his life's work, he said, and it didn't take him more than five minutes a day to do it. Every morning for the past twelve years, he had stood at the corner of Atlantic Avenue and Clinton Street at precisely seven o'clock and had taken a single color photograph of precisely the same view. The project now ran to more than four thousand photographs. Each album represented a different year, and all the pictures were laid out in sequence, from January 1 to December 31, with the dates carefully recorded under each one.

As I flipped through the albums and began to study Auggie's work, I   5 didn't know what to think. My first impression was that it was the oddest, most bewildering thing I had ever seen. All the pictures were the same. The whole project was a numbing on-slaught of repetition, the same street and the same buildings over and over again, an unrelenting delirium of redundant images. I couldn't think of anything to say to Auggie, so I continued turning pages, nodding my head in feigned appreciation. Auggie himself seemed unperturbed, watching me with a broad smile on his face, but after I'd been at it for several minutes, he suddenly interrupted me and said, "You're going too fast. You'll never get it if you don't slow down."

He was right, of course. If you don't take the time to look, you'll never manage to see anything. I picked up another album and forced myself to go more deliberately. I paid closer attention to details, took note of shifts in the weather, watched for the changing angles of light as the seasons advanced. Eventually, I was able to detect subtle differences in the traffic flow, to anticipate the rhythm of the different days (the commotion of workday mornings, the relative stillness of weekends, the contrast between Saturdays and Sundays). And then, little by little, I began to recognize the faces of the people in the background, the passersby on their way to work, the same people in the same spot every morning, living an instant of their lives in the field of Auggie's camera.

Once I got to know them, I began to study their postures, the way they carried themselves from one morning to the next, trying to discover their moods from these surface indications, as if I could imagine stories for them, as if I could penetrate the invisible dramas locked inside their bodies. I picked up another album. I was no longer bored, no longer puzzled as I had been at first. Auggie was photographing time, I realized, both natural time and human time, and he was doing it by planting himself in one tiny corner of the world and willing it to be his own, by standing guard in the space he had chosen for himself. As he watched me pore over his work, Auggie continued to smile with pleasure. Then, almost as if he had been reading my thoughts, he began to recite a line from Shakespeare. "Tomorrow and tomorrow and tomorrow," he muttered under his breath, "time creeps on its petty pace." I understood then that he knew exactly what he was doing.

That was more than two thousand pictures ago. Since that day, Auggie and I have discussed his work many times, but it was only last week that I learned how he acquired his camera and started taking pictures in the first place. That was the subject of the story he told me, and I'm still struggling to make sense of it.

Earlier that same week, a man from the *New York Times* called me and asked if I would be willing to write a short story that would appear in the paper on Christmas morning. My first impulse was to say no, but the man was very charming and persistent, and by the end of the conversation I told him I would give it a try. The moment I hung up the phone, however, I fell into a deep panic. What did I know about Christmas? I asked myself. What did I know about writing short stories on commission?

I spent the next several days in despair, warring with the ghosts of   10 Dickens, O. Henry and other masters of the Yuletide spirit. The very phrase "Christmas story" had unpleasant associations for me, evoking dreadful outpourings of hypocritical mush and treacle. Even at their best, Christmas stories were no more than wish-fulfillment dreams, fairy tales for adults, and I'd be damned if I'd ever allowed myself to write something like that. And yet, how could anyone propose to write an unsentimental Christmas story? It was a contradiction in terms, an impossibility, an out-and-out conundrum. One might just as well try to imagine a racehorse without legs, or a sparrow without wings.

I got nowhere. On Thursday I went out for a long walk, hoping the air would clear my head. Just past noon, I stopped in at the cigar store to replenish my supply, and there was Auggie, standing behind the counter as always. He asked me how I was. Without really meaning to, I found myself unburdening my troubles to him. "A Christmas story?" he said after I had finished. "Is that all? If you buy me lunch, my friend, I'll tell you the best Christmas story you ever heard. And I guarantee that every word of it is true."

We walked down the block to Jack's, a cramped and boisterous delicatessen with good pastrami sandwiches and photographs of old Dodger teams hanging on the walls. We found a table at the back, ordered our food, and then Auggie launched into his story.

"It was the summer of '72," he said. "A kid came in one morning and started stealing things from the store. He must have been about nineteen or twenty, and I don't think I've ever seen a more pathetic shoplifter in my life. He's standing by the rack of paperbacks along the far wall and stuffing books into the pockets of his raincoat. It was crowded around the counter just then, so I didn't see him at first. But once I noticed what he was up to, I started to shout. He took off like a jackrabbit, and by the time I managed to get out from behind the counter, he was already tearing down Atlantic Avenue. I chased after him for about half a block, and then I gave up. He'd dropped something along the way, and since I didn't feel like running anymore, I bent down to see what it was.

"It turned out to be his wallet. There wasn't any money inside, but his driver's license was there along with three or four snapshots. I suppose I could have called the cops and had him arrested. I had his name and address from the license, but I felt kind of sorry for him. He was just a measly little punk, and once I looked at those pictures in his wallet, I couldn't bring myself to feel very angry at him. Robert Goodwin. That was his name. In one of the pictures, I remember, he was standing with his arm around his mother or grandmother. In another one, he was sitting there at age nine or ten dressed in a baseball uniform with a big smile on his face. I just didn't have the heart. He was probably on dope now, I figured. A poor kid from Brooklyn without much going for him, and who cared about a couple of trashy paperbacks anyway?

"So I held onto the wallet. Every once in a while I'd get a little urge to   15
send it back to him, but I kept delaying and never did anything about it. Then Christmas rolls around and I'm stuck with nothing to do. The boss usually invites me over to his house to spend the day, but that year he and his family were down in Florida visiting relatives. So I'm sitting in my apartment that morning feeling a little sorry for myself, and then I see Robert Goodwin's wallet lying on a shelf in the kitchen. I figure what the hell, why not do something nice for once, and I put on my coat and go out to return the wallet in person.

"The address was over in Boerum Hill, somewhere in the projects. It was freezing out that day, and I remember getting lost a few times trying to find the right building. Everything looks the same in that place, and you keep going over the same ground thinking you're somewhere else. Anyway, I finally get to the apartment I'm looking for and ring the bell. Nothing happens. I assume no one's there, but I try again just to make sure. I wait a little longer, and just when I'm about to give up, I hear someone shuffling to the door. An old woman's voice asks who's there, and I say I'm looking for Robert Goodwin. 'Is that you, Robert?' the old woman says, and then she undoes about fifteen locks and opens the door.

"She has to be at least eighty, maybe ninety years old, and the first thing I notice about her is that she's blind. 'I knew you'd come, Robert,' she says. 'I knew you wouldn't forget your Granny Ethel on Christmas.' And then she opens her arms as if she's about to hug me.

"I didn't have much time to think, you understand. I had to say something real fast, and before I knew what was happening, I could hear the words coming out of my mouth. 'That's right, Granny Ethel,' I said. 'I came back to see you on Christmas.' Don't ask me why I did it. I don't have any idea. Maybe I didn't want to disappoint her or something, I don't know. It just came out that way, and then this old woman was suddenly hugging me there in front of the door, and I was hugging her back.

"I didn't exactly say that I was her grandson. Not in so many words, at least, but that was the implication. I wasn't trying to trick her, though. It was like a game we'd both decided to play—without having to discuss the rules. I mean, that woman *knew* I wasn't her grandson Robert. She was old and dotty, but she wasn't so far gone that she couldn't tell the difference between a stranger and her own flesh and blood. But it made her happy to pretend, and since I had nothing better to do anyway, I was happy to go along with her.

"So we went into the apartment and spent the day together. The place   20 was a real dump, I might add, but what else can you expect from a blind woman who does her own housekeeping? Every time she asked me a question about how I was, I would lie to her. I told her I'd found a good job working in a cigar store, I told her I was about to get married, I told her a hundred pretty stories, and she made like she believed every one of them. 'That's fine, Robert,' she would say, nodding her head and smiling. 'I always knew things would work out for you.'

"After a while, I started getting pretty hungry. There didn't seem to be much food in the house, so I went out to a store in the neighborhood and brought back a mess of stuff. A precooked chicken, vegetable soup, a bucket of potato salad, a chocolate cake, all kinds of things. Ethel had a couple of bottles of wine stashed in her bedroom, and so between us we managed to put together a fairly decent Christmas dinner. We both got a little tipsy from the wine, I remember, and after the meal was over we went out to sit in the living room, where the chairs were more comfortable. I had to take a pee, so I excused myself and went to the bathroom down the hall. That's where things took yet another turn. It was ditsy enough doing my little jig as Ethel's grandson, but what I did next was positively crazy, and I've never forgiven myself for it.

"I go into the bathroom, and stacked up against the wall next to the shower, I see a pile of six or seven cameras. Brand-new thirty-five-millimeter cameras, still in their boxes, top-quality merchandise. I figure this is the work of the real Robert, a storage place for one of his recent hauls. I've never taken a picture in my life, and I've certainly never stolen anything, but the moment I see those cameras sitting in the bathroom, I decide I want one of them for myself. Just like that. And without even stopping to think about it, I tuck one of the boxes under my arm and go back to the living room.

"I couldn't have been gone for more than three minutes, but in that time Granny Ethel had fallen asleep in her chair. Too much Chianti, I suppose. I went into the kitchen to wash the dishes, and she slept on through the whole racket, snoring like a baby. There didn't seem to be any point in disturbing her, so I decided to leave. I couldn't even write a note to say good-bye, seeing that she was blind and all, and so I just left. I put her grandson's wallet on the table, picked up the camera again, and walked out of the apartment. And that's the end of the story."

"Did you ever go back to see her?" I asked.   25
"Once," he said. "About three or four months later. I felt so bad about stealing the camera, I hadn't even used it yet. I finally made up my mind to return it, but Ethel wasn't there anymore. I don't know what happened to her, but someone else had moved into the apartment, and he couldn't tell me where she was."
"She probably died."
"Yeah, probably."
"Which means that she spent her last Christmas with you."
"I guess so. I never thought of it that way."
"It was a good deed, Auggie. It was a nice thing you did for her."   30
"I lied to her, and then I stole from her. I don't see how you can call that a good deed."
"You made her happy. And the camera was stolen anyway. It's not as if the person you took it from really owned it."
"Anything for art, eh Paul?"
"I wouldn't say that. But at least you've put the camera to good use."
"And now you've got your Christmas story, don't you?"   35
"Yes," I said. "I suppose I do."
I paused for a moment, studying Auggie as a wicked grin spread across his face. I couldn't be sure, but the look in his eyes at that moment was so mysterious, so fraught with the glow of some inner delight, that it suddenly occurred to me that he had made the whole thing up. I was about to ask him if he'd been putting me on, but then I realized he would never tell. I had been tricked into believing him, and that was the only thing that mattered. As long as there's one person to believe it, there's no story that can't be true.
"You're an ace, Auggie," I said. "Thanks for being so helpful."
"Any time," he answered, still looking at me with that maniacal light in his eyes. "After all, if you can't share your secrets with your friends, what kind of a friend are you?"
"I guess I owe you one."   40
"No you don't. Just put it down the way I told it to you, and you don't owe me a thing."
"Except the lunch."
"That's right. Except the lunch."
I returned Auggie's smile with a smile of my own, and then I called out to the waiter and asked for the check.

QUESTIONS

1. This is a story within a story (or a report within a report): Auster tells of Wren telling a story to him. Reread the early passage (paragraphs

5–7) in which Auster describes looking at Wren's photo albums. How do you react to Auster as he reports on the change in his own perspective?

2. How does that passage establish Wren as a character and as a man who will soon report another story to us?

3. What do you think of Wren's "life work" in photography? How would you evaluate his project?

4. If you were to take a series of photographs as Wren is said to have done, what questions would you raise about the nature of your work?

5. Wren's photographs record instants of time, every day, over an indefinite series of days. His Christmas with "Granny Ethel" makes a longer story of a single day. What relation do you find between those nearly opposite treatments of time in a single report?

6. If you have seen the movie *Smoke,* or *Blue in the Face,* compare it to this story from which it derived.

MAKING CONNECTIONS

1. Compare Wren's method of systematic observation with that of Farley Mowat (p. 256), Jane van Lawick-Goodall (p. 260), or Pico Iyer (p. 270). How does Wren, at least as Auster presents him, compare with observers who associate themselves more openly with the social sciences?

2. Compare Wren's photographs with the poems by Jane Kenyon (p. 221), Rita Dove (p. 268), William Carlos Williams (p. 293), and Elizabeth Bishop (p. 314). Are these poets, too, taking snapshots?

Social Sciences and Public Affairs

"THIS IS THE END OF THE WORLD"
The Black Death

Barbara Tuchman

For more than twenty-five years, Barbara Wertheim Tuchman (1912–1989) wrote books on historical subjects, ranging over the centuries from the Middle Ages to World War II. Her combination of careful research and lively writing enabled her to produce books like The Guns of August *(1962),* A Distant Mirror *(1978), and* The March of Folly: From Troy to Vietnam *(1984), which pleased not only the general public but many professional historians as well. She twice won the Pulitzer Prize.* A Distant Mirror, *from which the following selection has been taken, was on the* New York Times *best-seller list for more than nine months. Her final book,* The First Salute *(1988), is notable for the presence of Tuchman's characteristic scholarship and wit.*

In October 1347, two months after the fall of Calais, Genoese trading ships put into the harbor of Messina in Sicily with dead and dying men at the oars. The ships had come from the Black Sea port of Caffa (now Feodosiya) in the Crimea, where the Genoese maintained a trading post. The diseased sailors showed strange black swellings about the size of an egg or an apple in the armpits and groin. The swellings oozed blood and pus and were followed by spreading boils and black blotches on the skin from internal bleeding. The sick suffered severe pain and died quickly within five days of the first symptoms. As the disease spread, other symptoms of continuous fever and spitting of blood appeared instead of the swellings or buboes. These victims coughed and sweated heavily and died even more quickly, within three days or less, sometimes in 24 hours. In both types everything that issued from the body—breath, sweat, blood from the buboes and lungs, bloody urine, and blood-blackened excrement—smelled foul. Depression and despair accompanied the physical symptoms, and before the end "death is seen seated on the face."

The disease was bubonic plague, present in two forms: one that infected the bloodstream, causing the buboes and internal bleeding, and was spread by contact; and a second, more virulent pneumonic type that infected the lungs and was spread by respiratory infection. The presence of both at once caused the high mortality and speed of contagion. So lethal was the disease that cases were known of persons going to bed well and dying before they woke, of doctors catching the illness at a bedside and dying before the patient. So rapidly did it spread from one to another that to a French physician, Simon de Covino, it seemed as if one sick person "could infect the whole world." The malignity of the pestilence appeared more terrible because its victims knew no prevention and no remedy.

The physical suffering of the disease and its aspects of evil mystery were expressed in a strange Welsh lament which saw "death coming into our midst like black smoke, a plague which cuts off the young, a rootless phantom which has no mercy for fair countenance. Woe is me of the shilling in the armpit! It is seething, terrible . . . a head that gives pain and causes a loud cry . . . a painful angry knob . . . Great is its seething like a burning cinder . . . a grievous thing of ashy color." Its eruption is ugly like the "seeds of black peas, broken fragments of brittle sea-coal . . . the early ornaments of black death, cinders of the peelings of the cockle weed, a mixed multitude, a black plague like halfpence, like berries. . . ."

Rumors of a terrible plague supposedly arising in China and spreading through Tartary (Central Asia) to India and Persia, Mesopotamia, Syria, Egypt, and all of Asia Minor had reached Europe in 1346. They told of a death toll so devastating that all of India was said to be depopulated, whole territories covered by dead bodies, other areas with no one left alive. As added up by Pope Clement VI at Avignon, the total of reported dead reached 23,840,000. In the absence of a concept of contagion, no serious alarm was felt in Europe until the trading ships brought their black burden of pestilence into Messina while other infected ships from the Levant carried it to Genoa and Venice.

By January 1348 it penetrated France via Marseille, and North Africa via Tunis. Shipborne along coasts and navigable rivers, it spread westward from Marseille through the ports of Languedoc to Spain and northward up the Rhône to Avignon, where it arrived in March. It reached Narbonne, Montpellier, Carcassonne, and Toulouse between February and May, and at the same time in Italy spread to Rome and Florence and their hinterlands. Between June and August it reached Bordeaux, Lyon, and Paris, 5 spread to Burgundy and Normandy, and crossed the Channel from Normandy into southern England. From Italy during the same summer it crossed the Alps into Switzerland and reached eastward to Hungary.

In a given area the plague accomplished its kill within four to six months and then faded, except in the larger cities, where, rooting into the close-quartered population, it abated during the winter, only to reappear in spring and rage for another six months.

In 1349 it resumed in Paris, spread to Picardy, Flanders, and the Low Countries, and from England to Scotland and Ireland as well as to Norway, where a ghost ship with a cargo of wool and a dead crew drifted offshore until it ran aground near Bergen. From there the plague passed into Sweden, Denmark, Prussia, Iceland, and as far as Greenland. Leaving a strange pocket of immunity in Bohemia, and Russia unattacked until 1351, it had passed from most of Europe by mid-1350. Although the mortality rate was erratic, ranging from one fifth in some places to nine tenths or almost total elimination in others, the overall estimate of modern demographers has settled—for the area extending from India to Iceland—around the same figure expressed in Froissart's casual words: "a third of the world died." His estimate, the common one at the time, was not an inspired guess but a borrowing of St. John's figure for mortality from plague in Revelation, the favorite guide to human affairs of the Middle Ages.

A third of Europe would have meant about 20 million deaths. No one knows in truth how many died. Contemporary reports were an awed impression, not an accurate count. In crowded Avignon, it was said, 400 died daily; 7,000 houses emptied by death were shut up; a single graveyard received 11,000 corpses in six weeks; half the city's inhabitants reportedly died, including 9 cardinals or one third of the total, and 70 lesser prelates. Watching the endlessly passing death carts, chroniclers let normal exaggeration take wings and put the Avignon death toll at 62,000 and even at 120,000, although the city's total population was probably less than 50,000.

When graveyards filled up, bodies at Avignon were thrown into the Rhône until mass burial pits were dug for dumping the corpses. In London in such pits corpses piled up in layers until they overflowed. Everywhere reports speak of the sick dying too fast for the living to bury. Corpses were dragged out of homes and left in front of doorways. Morning light revealed new piles of bodies. In Florence the dead were gathered up by the Compagnia della Misericordia—founded in 1244 to care for the sick—whose members wore red robes and hoods masking the face except for the eyes. When their efforts failed, the dead lay putrid in the streets for days at a time. When no coffins were to be had, the bodies were laid on boards, two or three at once, to be carried to graveyards or common pits. Families dumped their own relatives into the pits, or buried them so hastily and thinly "that dogs dragged them forth and devoured their bodies."

Amid accumulating death and fear of contagion, people died without last rites and were buried without prayers, a prospect that terrified the last   10 hours of the stricken. A bishop in England gave permission to laymen to make confession to each other as was done by the Apostles, "or if no man is present then even to a woman," and if no priest could be found to administer extreme unction, "then faith must suffice." Clement VI found it necessary to grant remissions of sin to all who died of the plague because so many were unattended by priests. "And no bells tolled," wrote a chronicler of Siena, "and nobody wept no matter what his loss because almost everyone expected death. . . . And people said and believed, 'This is the end of the world.'"

In Paris, where the plague lasted through 1349, the reported death rate was 800 a day, in Pisa 500, in Vienna 500 to 600. The total dead in Paris numbered 50,000 or half the population. Florence, weakened by the famine of 1347, lost three to four fifths of its citizens, Venice two thirds, Hamburg and Bremen, though smaller in size, about the same proportion. Cities, as centers of transportation, were more likely to be affected than villages, although once a village was infected, its death rate was equally high. At Givry, a prosperous village in Burgundy of 1,200 to 1,500 people, the parish register records 615 deaths in the space of fourteen weeks, compared to an average of thirty deaths a year in the previous decade. In three villages of Cambridgeshire, manorial records show a death rate of 47 percent, 57 percent, and in one case 70 percent. When the last survivors, too few to carry on, moved away, a deserted village sank back into the wilderness and disappeared from the map altogether, leaving only a grass-covered ghostly outline to show where mortals once had lived.

In enclosed places such as monasteries and prisons, the infection of one person usually meant that of all, as happened in the Franciscan convents of Carcassonne and Marseille, where every inmate without exception died. Of the 140 Dominicans at Montpellier only seven survived. Petrarch's brother Gherardo, member of a Carthusian monastery, buried the prior and 34 fellow monks one by one, sometimes three a day, until he was left alone with his dog and fled to look for a place that would take him in. Watching every comrade die, men in such places could not but wonder whether the strange peril that filled the air had not been sent to exterminate the human race. In Kilkenny, Ireland, Brother John Clyn of the Friars Minor, another monk left alone among dead men, kept a record of what had happened lest "things which should be remembered perish with time and vanish from the memory of those who come after us." Sensing "the whole world, as it were, placed within the grasp of the Evil One," and waiting for death to visit him too, he wrote, "I leave parchment to continue this work, if perchance any man survive and any of the race of Adam escape this pestilence and carry on the work which I have begun." Brother John, as noted by another hand, died of the pestilence, but he foiled oblivion.

The largest cities of Europe, with populations of about 100,000, were Paris and Florence, Venice and Genoa. At the next level, with more than 50,000, were Ghent and Bruges in Flanders, Milan, Bologna, Rome, Naples, and Palermo, and Cologne. London hovered below 50,000, the only city in England except York with more than 10,000. At the level of 20,000 to 50,000 were Bordeaux, Toulouse, Montpellier, Marseille, and Lyon in France, Barcelona, Seville, and Toledo in Spain, Siena, Pisa, and other secondary cities in Italy, and the Hanseatic trading cities of the Empire. The plague raged through them all, killing anywhere from one third to two thirds of their inhabitants. Italy, with a total population of 10 to 11 million, probably suffered the heaviest toll. Following the Florentine bankruptcies, the crop failures and workers' riots of 1346–47, the revolt of Cola di Rienzi that plunged Rome into anarchy, the plague came as the peak of successive calamities. As if the world were indeed in the grasp of the Evil One, its first appearance on the European mainland in January 1348 coincided with a fearsome earthquake that carved a path of wreckage from Naples up to Venice. Houses collapsed, church towers toppled, villages were crushed, and the destruction reached as far as Germany and Greece. Emotional response, dulled by horrors, underwent a kind of atrophy epitomized by the chronicler who wrote, "And in these days was burying without sorrowe and wedding without friendschippe."

In Siena, where more than half the inhabitants died of the plague, work was abandoned on the great cathedral, planned to be the largest in the world, and never resumed, owing to loss of workers and master masons and "the melancholy and grief" of the survivors. The cathedral's truncated transept still stands in permanent witness to the sweep of death's scythe. Agnolo di Tura, a chronicler of Siena, recorded the fear of contagion that froze every other instinct. "Father abandoned child, wife husband, one brother another," he wrote, "for this plague seemed to strike through the breath and sight. And so they died. And no one could be found to bury the dead for money or friendship. . . . And I, Agnolo di Tura, called the Fat, buried my five children with my own hands, and so did many others likewise."

There were many to echo his account of inhumanity and few to balance it, for the plague was not the kind of calamity that inspired mutual help. Its loathsomeness and deadliness did not herd people together in mutual distress, but only prompted their desire to escape each other. "Magistrates and notaries refused to come and make the wills of the dying," reported a Franciscan friar of Piazza in Sicily; what was worse, "even the priests did not come to hear their confessions." A clerk of the Archbishop of Canterbury reported the same of English priests who "turned away from the care of their benefices from fear of death." Cases of parents deserting children and children their parents were reported across Europe from Scotland to Russia. The calamity chilled the hearts of men, wrote Boccaccio in his famous account of the plague in Florence that serves as introduction to the *Decameron.* "One man shunned another . . . kinsfolk held aloof, brother was forsaken by brother, oftentimes husband by wife; nay, what is more, and scarcely to be believed, fathers and mothers were found to abandon their own children to their fate, untended, unvisited as if they had been strangers." Exaggeration and literary pessimism were common in the 14th century, but the Pope's physician, Guy de Chauliac, was a sober, careful observer who reported the same phenomenon: "A father did not visit his son, nor the son his father. Charity was dead."

Yet not entirely. In Paris, according to the chronicler Jean de Venette, the nuns of the Hotel Dieu or municipal hospital, "having no fear of death, tended the sick with all sweetness and humility." New nuns repeatedly took the places of those who died, until the majority "many times renewed by death now rest in peace with Christ as we may piously believe."

When the plague entered northern France in July 1348, it settled first in Normandy and, checked by winter, gave Picardy a deceptive interim until the next summer. Either in mourning or warning, black flags were flown from church towers of the worst-stricken villages of Normandy. "And in that time," wrote a monk of the abbey of Fourcarment, "the mortality was so great among the people of Normandy that those of Picardy mocked them." The same unneighborly reaction was reported of the Scots, separated by a winter's immunity from the English. Delighted to hear of the disease that was scourging the "southrons," they gathered forces for an invasion, "laughing at their enemies." Before they could move, the savage mortality fell upon them too, scattering some in death and the rest in panic to spread the infection as they fled.

In Picardy in the summer of 1349 the pestilence penetrated the castle of Coucy to kill Enguerrand's[1] mother, Catherine, and her new husband. Whether her nine-year-old son escaped by chance or was perhaps living elsewhere with one of his guardians is unrecorded. In nearby Amiens, tannery workers, responding quickly to losses in the labor force, combined to bargain for higher wages. In another place villagers were seen dancing to drums and trumpets, and on being asked the reason, answered that, seeing their neighbors die day by day while their village remained immune, they believed that they could keep the plague from entering "by the jollity that is in us. That is why we dance." Further north in Tournai on the border of Flanders, Gilles li Muisis, Abbot of St. Martin's, kept one of the epidemic's most vivid accounts. The passing bells rang all day and all night, he recorded, because sextons were anxious to obtain their fees while they could. Filled with the sound of mourning, the city became oppressed by fear, so that the authorities forbade the tolling of bells and the wearing of black and restricted funeral services to two mourners. The silencing of funeral bells and of criers' announcements of deaths was ordained by most cities. Siena imposed a fine on the wearing of mourning clothes by all except widows.

Flight was the chief recourse of those who could afford it or arrange it. The rich fled to their country places like Boccaccio's young patricians of Florence, who settled in a pastoral palace "removed on every side from the

---

[1]*Enguerrand de Coucy:* a French nobleman. Tuchman follows his life as a way of unifying her study of the fourteenth century. [Eds.]

roads" with "wells of cool water and vaults of rare wines." The urban
poor died in their burrows, "and only the stench of their bodies informed
neighbors of their deaths." That the poor were more heavily afflicted than
the rich was clearly remarked at the time, in the north as in the south. A
Scottish chronicler, John of Fordun, stated flatly that the pest "attacked especially the meaner sort and common people—seldom the magnates."
Simon de Covino of Montpellier made the same observation. He ascribed it
to the misery and want and hard lives that made the poor more susceptible,
which was half the truth. Close contact and lack of sanitation was the un-
recognized other half. It was noticed too that the young died in greater
proportion than the old; Simon de Covino compared the disappearance of
youth to the withering of flowers in the fields.

In the countryside peasants dropped dead on the roads, in the fields, in   20
their houses. Survivors in growing helplessness fell into apathy, leaving ripe
wheat uncut and livestock untended. Oxen and asses, sheep and goats, pigs
and chickens ran wild and they too, according to local reports, succumbed
to the pest. English sheep, bearers of the precious wool, died throughout
the country. The chronicler Henry Knighton, canon of Leicester Abbey, reported 5,000 dead in one field alone, "their bodies so corrupted by the
plague that neither beast nor bird would touch them," and spreading an
appalling stench. In the Austrian Alps wolves came down to prey upon
sheep and then, "as if alarmed by some invisible warning, turned and fled
back into the wilderness." In remote Dalmatia bolder wolves descended
upon a plague-stricken city and attacked human survivors. For want of
herdsmen, cattle strayed from place to place and died in hedgerows and
ditches. Dogs and cats fell like the rest.

The dearth of labor held a fearful prospect because the 14th century
lived close to the annual harvest both for food and for next year's seed.
"So few servants and laborers were left," wrote Knighton, "that no one
knew where to turn for help." The sense of a vanishing future created a
kind of dementia of despair. A Bavarian chronicler of Neuberg on the
Danube recorded that "Men and women . . . wandered around as if mad"
and let their cattle stray "because no one had any inclination to concern
themselves about the future." Fields went uncultivated, spring seed un-
sown. Second growth with nature's awful energy crept back over cleared
land, dikes crumbled, salt water reinvaded and soured the lowlands. With
so few hands remaining to restore the work of centuries, people felt, in
Walsingham's words, that "the world could never again regain its former
prosperity."

Though the death rate was higher among the anonymous poor, the
known and the great died too. King Alfonso XI of Castile was the only
reigning monarch killed by the pest, but his neighbor King Pedro of
Aragon lost his wife, Queen Leonora, his daughter Marie, and a niece in
the space of six months. John Cantacuzene, Emperor of Byzantium, lost his
son. In France the lame Queen Jeanne and her daughter-in-law Bonne de
Luxemburg, wife of the Dauphin, both died in 1349 in the same phase that

took the life of Enguerrand's mother. Jeanne, Queen of Navarre, daughter of Louis X, was another victim. Edward III's second daughter, Joanna, who was on her way to marry Pedro, the heir of Castile, died in Bordeaux. Women appear to have been more vulnerable than men, perhaps because, being more housebound, they were more exposed to fleas. Boccaccio's mistress Fiammetta, illegitimate daughter of the King of Naples, died, as did Laura, the beloved—whether real or fictional—of Petrarch. Reaching out to us in the future, Petrarch cried, "Oh happy posterity who will not experience such abysmal woe and will look upon our testimony as a fable."

In Florence Giovanni Villani, the great historian of his time, died at 68 in the midst of an unfinished sentence: "*. . . e dure questo pistolenza fino a . . .* (in the midst of this pestilence there came to an end . . .)." Siena's master painters, the brothers Ambrogio and Pietro Lorenzetti, whose names never appear after 1348, presumably perished in the plague, as did Andrea Pisano, architect and sculptor of Florence. William of Ockham and the English mystic Richard Rolle of Hampole both disappear from mention after 1349. Francisco Datini, merchant of Prato, lost both his parents and two siblings. Curious sweeps of mortality afflicted certain bodies of merchants in London. All eight wardens of the Company of Cutters, all six wardens of the Hatters, and four wardens of the Goldsmiths died before July 1350. Sir John Pulteney, master draper and four times Mayor of London, was a victim, likewise Sir John Montgomery, Governor of Calais.

Among the clergy and doctors the mortality was naturally high because of the nature of their professions. Out of 24 physicians in Venice, 20 were said to have lost their lives in the plague, although, according to another account, some were believed to have fled or to have shut themselves up in their houses. At Montpellier, site of the leading medieval medical school, the physician Simon de Covino reported that, despite the great number of doctors, "hardly one of them escaped." In Avignon, Guy de Chauliac confessed that he performed his medical visits only because he dared not stay away for fear of infamy, but "I was in continual fear." He claimed to have contracted the disease but to have cured himself by his own treatment; if so, he was one of the few who recovered.

Clerical mortality varied with rank. Although the one-third toll of cardinals reflects the same proportion as the whole, this was probably due to their concentration in Avignon. In England, in strange and almost sinister procession, the Archbishop of Canterbury, John Stratford, died in August 1348, his appointed successor died in May 1349, and the next appointee three months later, all three within a year. Despite such weird vagaries, prelates in general managed to sustain a higher survival rate than the lesser clergy. Among bishops the deaths have been estimated at about one in twenty. The loss of priests, even if many avoided their fearful duty of attending the dying, was about the same as among the population as a whole. [25]

Government officials, whose loss contributed to the general chaos, found, on the whole, no special shelter. In Siena four of the nine members of the governing oligarchy died, in France one third of the royal notaries, in Bristol 15 out of the 52 members of the Town Council or almost one third. Tax-collecting obviously suffered, with the result that Philip VI was unable to collect more than a fraction of the subsidy granted him by the Estates in the winter of 1347–48.

Lawlessness and debauchery accompanied the plague as they had during the great plague of Athens of 430 B.C., when according to Thucydides, men grew bold in the indulgence of pleasure: "For seeing how the rich died in a moment and those who had nothing immediately inherited their property, they reflected that life and riches were alike transitory and they resolved to enjoy themselves while they could." Human behavior is timeless. When St. John had his vision of plague in Revelation, he knew from some experience or race memory that those who survived "repented not of the work of their hands. . . . Neither repented they of their murders, nor of their sorceries, nor of their fornication, nor of their thefts."

Notes[2]

1. "death is seen seated": Simon de Covino, q. Campbell, 80.
2. "could infect the whole world": q. Gasquet, 41.
3. Welsh lament: q. Ziegler, 190.
9. "dogs dragged them forth": Agnolo di Tura, q. Ziegler, 58.
10. "or if no man is present": Bishop of Bath and Wells, q. Ziegler, 125. "No Bells Tolled": Agnolo di Tura, q. Schevill, Siena, 211. The same observation was made by Gabriel de Muisis, notary of Piacenza, q. Crawfurd, 113.
11. Givry parish register: Renouard, 111. three villages of Cambridgeshire: Saltmarsh.
12. Petrarch's brother: Bishop, 273. Brother John Clyn: q. Ziegler, 195.
13. "And in these days": q. Deaux, 143, citing only "an old northern chronicle."
14. Agnolo Di Tura, "Father abandoned child": q. Ziegler, 58.
15. "Magistrates and notaries": q. Deaux, 49. English Priests Turned Away: Ziegler, 261. Parents Deserting Children: Hecker, 30. Guy De Chauliac, "A Father": q. Gasquet, 50–51.
16. nuns of the Hotel Dieu: *Chron. Jean de Venette*, 49.
17. Picards and Scots mock mortality of neighbors: Gasquet, 53, and Ziegler, 198.
18. Catherine de Coucy: *L'Art de vérifier*, 237. Amiens Tanners: Gasquet, 57. "By the Jollity That Is in Us": *Grandes Chrôns.*, VI, 486–87.
19. John of Fordun: q. Ziegler, 199. Simon de Covino on the poor: Gasquet, 42. on youth: Cazelles, *Peste*.

---

[2]Tuchman does not use numbered footnotes, but at the back of her book she identifies the source of every quotation or citation. The works cited follow in a bibliography. Although Tuchman's notes are labeled by page number, the numbers here refer to the paragraphs in which the sources are mentioned. [Eds.]

20. Knighton on sheep: q. Ziegler, 175. Wolves of Austria and Dalmatia: ibid., 84, 111. dogs and cats: Muisis, q. Gasquet, 44, 61.

21. Bavarian chronicler of Neuberg: q. Ziegler, 84. Walsingham, "the world could never": Denifle, 273.

22. "Oh happy posterity": q. Ziegler, 45.

23. Giovanni Villani, *"e dure questo"*: q. Snell, 334.

24. physicians of Venice: Campbell, 98. Simon de Covino: ibid., 31. Guy de Chauliac, "I was in continual fear": q. Thompson *Ec. and Soc.,* 379.

27. Thucydides: q. Crawfurd, 30–31.

Bibliography

L'Art de vérifier les dates des faits historiques, par un Religieux de la Congregation de St.-Maur, vol. XII. Paris, 1818.

Bishop, Morris. *Petrarch and His World.* Indiana University Press, 1963.

Campbell, Anna M. *The Black Death and Men of Learning.* Columbia University Press, 1931.

Cazelles, Raymond. *"La Peste de 1348–49 en Langue d'oil: épidémie prolitarienne et enfantine."* Bull philologique et historique, 1962, pp. 293–305.

Chronicle of Jean de Venette. Trans. Jean Birdsall. Ed. Richard A. Newhall. Columbia University Press, 1853.

Crawfurd, Raymond. *Plague and Pestilence in Literature and Art.* Oxford, 1914.

Deaux, George. *The Black Death, 1347.* London, 1969.

Denifle, Henri. *La Dèsolation des églises, monastères et hopitaux en France pendant la guerre de cent ans,* vol. I. Paris, 1899.

Gasquet, Francis Aidan, Abbot. *The Black Death of 1348 and 1349,* 2nd ed. London, 1908.

Grandes Chroniques de France, vol. VI (to 1380). Ed. Paulin Paris. Paris, 1838.

Hecker, J. F. C. *The Epidemics of the Middle Ages.* London, 1844.

Renouard, Yves. *"La Peste noirs de 1348–50."* Rev. de Paris, March, 1950.

Saltmarsh, John. "Plague and Economic Decline in England in the Later Middle Ages," *Cambridge Historical Journal,* vol. VII, no. 1, 1941.

Schevill, Ferdinand. *Siena: The History of a Medieval Commune.* New York, 1909.

Snell, Frederick. *The Fourteenth Century.* Edinburgh, 1899.

Thompson, James Westfall. *Economic and Social History of Europe in the Later Middle Ages.* New York, 1931.

Ziegler, Philip. *The Black Death.* New York, 1969. (The best modern study.)

QUESTIONS

1. Try to imagine yourself in Tuchman's position. If you were assigned the task of reporting on the Black Plague in Europe, how would you go about it? What problems would you expect to encounter in the research and in the composition of your report?

2. The notes and bibliography reveal a broad scholarly base: Tuchman's research was clearly prodigious. But so were the problems of organiza-

tion after the research had been done. Tuchman had to find a way to present her information to readers that would be clear and interesting. How has she solved her problem? What overall patterns of organization do you find in this selection? Mark off subsections with topics of their own.

3. How does Tuchman organize her paragraphs? Consider paragraph 20, for example. What is the topic? What are the subtopics? Why does the paragraph begin and end as it does? Consider paragraph 22. How does the first sentence serve as a transition from the previous paragraph? How is the rest of the paragraph ordered? Does the next paragraph start a new topic or continue developing the topic announced at the beginning of paragraph 22?

4. Many paragraphs end with direct quotations. Examine some of these. What do they have in common? Why do you think Tuchman closes so many paragraphs in this way?

5. Much of this essay is devoted to the reporting of facts and figures. This could be very tedious, but Tuchman is an expert at avoiding dullness. How does she help the reader see and feel the awfulness of the plague? Locate specific examples in the text, and discuss their effectiveness.

6. Examine Tuchman's list of sources, and explain how she has used them. Does she quote directly from each source, or does she paraphrase it? Does she use a source to illustrate a point, as evidence for argument, or in some other way?

7. Taking Tuchman as a model, write a report on some other catastrophe, blending factual reporting with description of what it was like to be there. This will require both careful research and artful selection and arrangement of the fruits of that research.

8. Using Tuchman's notes to *A Distant Mirror* as a reference guide, find out more about some specific place or event mentioned by Tuchman. Write a report of your findings.

MAKING CONNECTIONS

Compare this account of the Black Death to the writings by Farley Mowat (p. 256) or Jane van Lawick-Goodall (p. 260), included in this section. Make your comparison in terms of the points of view established and sustained in the reports you compare. What is Tuchman's point of view toward her subject?

ATOMIC BOMBING OF NAGASAKI TOLD BY FLIGHT MEMBER

William L. Laurence

William L. Laurence (1888–1997) was born in Lithuania and came to the United States in 1905. He studied at Harvard and the Boston University Law School. His main interest, however, had always been in science, and after working at the New York World *for five years, Laurence went to the* New York Times *as a science reporter. During World War II, Laurence was the only reporter to know about the top-secret testing of the atomic bomb. On August 9, 1945, he was permitted to fly with the mission to drop the second atomic bomb on Nagasaki. Three days earlier, more than one hundred thousand people had been killed in the Hiroshima bombing. Laurence won the Pulitzer Prize for this account of the bombing of Nagasaki. The article appeared in the* New York Times *on September 9, 1945.*

With the atomic-bomb mission to Japan, August 9 (Delayed) — We are on our way to bomb the mainland of Japan. Our flying contingent consists of three specially designed B-29 Superforts, and two of these carry no bombs. But our lead plane is on its way with another atomic bomb, the second in three days, concentrating in its active substance an explosive energy equivalent to twenty thousand and, under favorable conditions, forty thousand tons of TNT.

We have several chosen targets. One of these is the great industrial and shipping center of Nagasaki, on the western shore of Kyushu, one of the main islands of the Japanese homeland.

I watched the assembly of this man-made meteor during the past two days and was among the small group of scientists and Army and Navy representatives privileged to be present at the ritual of its loading in the Superfort last night, against a background of threatening black skies torn open at intervals by great lightning flashes.

It is a thing of beauty to behold, this "gadget." Into its design went millions of man-hours of what is without doubt the most concentrated intellectual effort in history. Never before had so much brain power been focused on a single problem.

This atomic bomb is different from the bomb used three days ago with such devastating results on Hiroshima.   5

I saw the atomic substance before it was placed inside the bomb. By itself it is not at all dangerous to handle. It is only under certain conditions, produced in the bomb assembly, that it can be made to yield up its energy, and even then it gives only a small fraction of its total contents—a fraction, however, large enough to produce the greatest explosion on earth.

The briefing at midnight revealed the extreme care and the tremendous amount of preparation that had been made to take care of every detail of the mission, to make certain that the atomic bomb fully served the purpose for which it was intended. Each target in turn was shown in detailed maps and in aerial photographs. Every detail of the course was rehearsed—navigation, altitude, weather, where to land in emergencies. It came out that the Navy had rescue craft, known as Dumbos and Superdumbos, stationed at various strategic points in the vicinity of the targets, ready to rescue the fliers in case they were forced to bail out.

The briefing period ended with a moving prayer by the chaplain. We then proceeded to the mess hall for the traditional early-morning breakfast before departure on a bombing mission.

A convoy of trucks took us to the supply building for the special equipment carried on combat missions. This included the Mae West,[1] a parachute, a lifeboat, an oxygen mask, a flak suit, and a survival vest. We still had a few hours before take-off time, but we all went to the flying field and stood around in little groups or sat in jeeps talking rather casually about our mission to the Empire, as the Japanese home islands are known hereabouts.

In command of our mission is Major Charles W. Sweeney, twenty-five,   10
of 124 Hamilton Avenue, North Quincy, Massachusetts. His flagship, carrying the atomic bomb, is named *The Great Artiste,* but the name does not appear on the body of the great silver ship, with its unusually long, four-bladed, orange-tipped propellers. Instead, it carries the number 77, and someone remarks that it was "Red" Grange's winning number on the gridiron.

We took off at 3:50 this morning and headed northwest on a straight line for the Empire. The night was cloudy and threatening, with only a few stars here and there breaking through the overcast. The weather report had predicted storms ahead part of the way but clear sailing for the final and climactic stages of our odyssey.

We were about an hour away from our base when the storm broke. Our great ship took some heavy dips through the abysmal darkness around us, but it took these dips much more gracefully than a large commercial air liner, producing a sensation more in the nature of a glide than a "bump," like a great ocean liner riding the waves except that in this case the air waves were much higher and the rhythmic tempo of the glide was much faster.

I noticed a strange eerie light coming through the window high above the navigator's cabin, and as I peered through the dark all around us I saw

---

[1]*Mae West:* an inflatable life jacket named for the actor. [Eds.]

a startling phenomenon. The whirling giant propellers had somehow become great luminous disks of blue flame. The same luminous blue flame appeared on the plexiglass windows in the nose of the ship, and on the tips of the giant wings. It looked as though we were riding the whirlwind through space on a chariot of blue fire.

It was, I surmised, a surcharge of static electricity that had accumulated on the tips of the propellers and on the di-electric material of the plastic windows. One's thoughts dwelt anxiously on the precious cargo in the invisible ship ahead of us. Was there any likelihood of danger that this heavy electric tension in the atmosphere all about us might set it off?

I expressed my fears to Captain Bock, who seems nonchalant and unperturbed at the controls. He quickly reassured me.   15

"It is a familiar phenomenon seen often on ships. I have seen it many times on bombing missions. It is known as St. Elmo's fire."

On we went through the night. We soon rode out the storm and our ship was once again sailing on a smooth course straight ahead, on a direct line to the Empire.

Our altimeter showed that we were traveling through space at a height of seventeen thousand feet. The thermometer registered an outside temperature of thirty-three degrees below zero Centigrade, about thirty below Fahrenheit. Inside our pressurized cabin the temperature was that of a comfortable air-conditioned room and a pressure corresponding to an altitude of eight thousand feet. Captain Bock cautioned me, however, to keep my oxygen mask handy in case of emergency. This, he explained, might mean either something going wrong with the pressure equipment inside the ship or a hole through the cabin by flak.

The first signs of dawn came shortly after five o'clock. Sergeant Curry, of Hoopeston, Illinois, who had been listening steadily on his earphones for radio reports, while maintaining a strict radio silence himself, greeted it by rising to his feet and gazing out the window.

"It's good to see the day," he told me. "I get a feeling of claustropho-   20
bia hemmed in this cabin at night."

He is a typical American youth, looking even younger than his twenty years. It takes no mind reader to read his thoughts.

"It's a long way from Hoopeston," I find myself remarking.

"Yep," he replies, as he busies himself decoding a message from outer space.

"Think this atomic bomb will end the war?" he asks hopefully.

"There is a very good chance that this one may do the trick," I assured   25
him, "but if not, then the next one or two surely will. Its power is such that no nation can stand up against it very long." This was not my own view. I had heard it expressed all around a few hours earlier, before we took off. To anyone who had seen this manmade fireball in action, as I had less than a month ago in the desert of New Mexico, this view did not sound overoptimistic.

By 5:50 it was really light outside. We had lost our lead ship, but Lieutenant Godfrey, our navigator, informs me that we had arranged for that contingency. We have an assembly point in the sky above the little island of Yakushima, southeast of Kyushu, at 9:10. We are to circle there and wait for the rest of our formation.

Our genial bombardier, Lieutenant Levy, comes over to invite me to take his front-row seat in the transparent nose of the ship, and I accept eagerly. From that vantage point in space, seventeen thousand feet above the Pacific, one gets a view of hundreds of miles on all sides, horizontally and vertically. At that height the vast ocean below and the sky above seem to merge into one great sphere.

I was on the inside of that firmament, riding above the giant mountains of white cumulus clouds, letting myself be suspended in infinite space. One hears the whirl of the motors behind one, but it soon becomes insignificant against the immensity all around and is before long swallowed by it. There comes a point where space also swallows time and one lives through eternal moments filled with an oppressive loneliness, as though all life had suddenly vanished from the earth and you are the only one left, a lone survivor traveling endlessly through interplanetary space.

My mind soon returns to the mission I am on. Somewhere beyond these vast mountains of white clouds ahead of me there lies Japan, the land of our enemy. In about four hours from now one of its cities, making weapons of war for use against us, will be wiped off the map by the greatest weapon ever made by man: In one tenth of a millionth of a second, a fraction of time immeasurable by any clock, a whirlwind from the skies will pulverize thousands of its buildings and tens of thousands of its inhabitants.

But at this moment no one yet knows which one of the several cities   30 chosen as targets is to be annihilated. The final choice lies with destiny. The winds over Japan will make the decision. If they carry heavy clouds over our primary target, the city will be saved, at least for the time being. None of its inhabitants will ever know that the wind of a benevolent destiny had passed over their heads. But that same wind will doom another city.

Our weather planes ahead of us are on their way to find out where the wind blows. Half an hour before target time we will know what the winds have decided.

Does one feel any pity or compassion for the poor devils about to die? Not when one thinks of Pearl Harbor and of the Death March on Bataan.[2]

Captain Bock informs me that we are about to start our climb to bombing altitude.

---

[2]*Pearl Harbor:* on December 7, 1941, a surprise bombing attack by the Japanese on this United States naval base in Hawaii caused the death of 1,177 people and prompted the United States to enter World War II; *Death March on Bataan:* physically weakened American and Filipino defenders of the Bataan peninsula were forced by their Japanese captors to march ninety miles under brutal conditions to a prisoner-of-war camp in Manila. Many did not survive. [Eds.]

He manipulates a few knobs on his control panel to the right of him, and I alternately watch the white clouds and ocean below me and the altimeter on the bombardier's panel. We reached our altitude at nine o'clock. We were then over Japanese waters, close to their mainland. Lieutenant Godfrey motioned to me to look through his radar scope. Before me was the outline of our assembly point. We shall soon meet our lead ship and proceed to the final stage of our journey.

We reached Yakushima at 9:12 and there, about four thousand feet ahead   35
of us, was *The Great Artiste* with its precious load. I saw Lieutenant Godfrey and Sergeant Curry strap on their parachutes and I decided to do likewise.

We started circling. We saw little towns on the coastline, heedless of our presence. We kept on circling, waiting for the third ship in our formation.

It was 9:56 when we began heading for the coastline. Our weather scouts had sent us code messages, deciphered by Sergeant Curry, informing us that both the primary target as well as the secondary were clearly visible.

The winds of destiny seemed to favor certain Japanese cities that must remain nameless. We circled about them again and again and found no opening in the thick umbrella of clouds that covered them. Destiny chose Nagasaki as the ultimate target.

We had been circling for some time when we noticed black puffs of smoke coming through the white clouds directly at us. There were fifteen bursts of flak in rapid succession, all too low. Captain Bock changed his course. There soon followed eight more bursts of flak, right up to our altitude, but by this time they were too far to the left.

We flew southward down the channel and at 11:33 crossed the coast-   40
line and headed straight for Nagasaki, about one hundred miles to the west. Here again we circled until we found an opening in the clouds. It was 12:01 and the goal of our mission had arrived.

We heard the prearranged signal on our radio, put on our arc welder's glasses, and watched tensely the maneuverings of the strike ship about half a mile in front of us.

"There she goes!" someone said.

Out of the belly of *The Great Artiste* what looked like a black object went downward.

Captain Bock swung to get out of range; but even though we were turning away in the opposite direction, and despite the fact that it was broad daylight in our cabin, all of us became aware of a giant flash that broke through the dark barrier of our arc welder's lenses and flooded our cabin with intense light.

We removed our glasses after the first flash, but the light still lingered   45
on, a bluish-green light that illuminated the entire sky all around. A tremendous blast wave struck our ship and made it tremble from nose to tail. This was followed by four more blasts in rapid succession, each resounding like the boom of cannon fire hitting our plane from all directions.

Observers in the tail of our ship saw a giant ball of fire rise as though from the bowels of the earth, belching forth enormous white smoke rings.

Next they saw a giant pillar of purple fire, ten thousand feet high, shooting skyward with enormous speed.

By the time our ship had made another turn in the direction of the atomic explosion the pillar of purple fire had reached the level of our altitude. Only about forty-five seconds had passed. Awe-struck, we watched it shoot upward like a meteor coming from the earth instead of from outer space, becoming ever more alive as it climbed skyward through the white clouds. It was no longer smoke, or dust, or even a cloud of fire. It was a living thing, a new species of being, born right before our incredulous eyes.

At one stage of its evolution, covering millions of years in terms of seconds, the entity assumed the form of a giant square totem pole, with its base about three miles long, tapering off to about a mile at the top. Its bottom was brown, its center was amber, its top white. But it was a living totem pole, carved with many grotesque masks grimacing at the earth.

Then, just when it appeared as though the thing had settled down into a state of permanence, there came shooting out of the top a giant mushroom that increased the height of the pillar to a total of forty-five thousand feet. The mushroom top was even more alive than the pillar, seething and boiling in a white fury of creamy foam, sizzling upward and then descending earthward, a thousand Old Faithful geysers rolled into one.

It kept struggling in an elemental fury, like a creature in the act of break-   50
ing the bonds that held it down. In a few seconds it had freed itself from its gigantic stem and floated upward with tremendous speed, its momentum carrying it into the stratosphere to a height of about sixty thousand feet.

But no sooner did this happen when another mushroom, smaller in size than the first one, began emerging out of the pillar. It was as though the decapitated monster was growing a new head.

As the first mushroom floated off into the blue it changed its shape into a flowerlike form, its giant petals curving downward, creamy white outside, rose-colored inside. It still retained that shape when we last gazed at it from a distance of about two hundred miles. The boiling pillar of many colors could also be seen at that distance, a giant mountain of jumbled rainbows, in travail. Much living substance had gone into those rainbows. The quivering top of the pillar was protruding to a great height through the white clouds, giving the appearance of a monstrous prehistoric creature with a ruff around its neck, a fleecy ruff extending in all directions, as far as the eye could see.

QUESTIONS

1. What do we learn about the crew members on the mission? Why has Laurence bothered to tell us about them?
2. Laurence's description of the bomb as "a thing of beauty" (paragraph 4) suggests that this eyewitness report is not wholly objective. What is Laurence's moral stance on this mission?

3. Consider Laurence's arrangement of time in his narrative. What effect do you think he wishes to create by switching back and forth between past and present tense?

4. Consider Laurence's description of the blast and its resulting cloud (paragraphs 44 through 52). His challenge as a writer is to help his readers see this strange and awesome thing. What familiar images does he use to represent this unfamiliar sight? What do those images say — especially the last one — about Laurence's feelings as he watched the cloud transform itself?

5. Write an eyewitness report on an event that you consider important. Present the preparations or actions leading up to the event, and include information about others involved. What imagery can you use to describe the glorious, funny, or chaotic event itself?

6. For a report on the basis for Laurence's attitude toward the bombings of Hiroshima and Nagasaki, look at as many newspapers as you can for August 6 through 10 in 1945. Be sure to look at the editorial pages as well as the front pages. If possible, you might also interview relatives and friends who are old enough to remember the war or who might have fought in it. What attitudes toward the bomb and its use were expressed then? How do these compare or contrast with Laurence's attitude?

MAKING CONNECTIONS

1. Describe the differences in point of view taken toward this cataclysmic event by Laurence, John Hersey (p. 203), and Zoë Tracy Hardy (p. 139). How does each writer respond to this unparalleled story? Which responses do you find most unusual, most believable, most sympathetic? Why?

2. Imagine a meeting today between Laurence and Hatsuyo Nakamura from John Hersey's piece (p. 203). What might they say to one another? How might Laurence reflect today on his feelings more than fifty years ago? Imagine this meeting, and write a report of it. Or, if you prefer, substitute Zoë Tracy Hardy (p. 139) for Hatsuyo Nakamura.

THE UNKNOWN CITIZEN

W. H. Auden

Wystan Hugh Auden (1907–1973) was born in York, England, and educated at Oxford University. He published his first volume of poems when he was twenty-three, and many of his early works, including three verse plays, reflect a strongly left-wing political philosophy. Auden moved to the United States in 1939 (he became a U.S. citizen in 1946), and it was here that he had his most productive years as a poet. His collections include New Year Letter *(1941);* The Age of Anxiety *(1948), which earned him a Pulitzer Prize for poetry;* The Shield of Achilles *(1956), which won the National Book Award;* About the House *(1965); and the posthumous* Thank You, Fog *(1974). His* Complete Works *was published by Princeton University Press in 1989. An opera librettist and essayist as well as a poet, Auden was one of the most versatile and influential literary figures of the twentieth century. He was a truly popular poet who often focused on moral, political, and spiritual issues that touched his readers' lives.*

(*To JS/07/M/378*
This Marble Monument
Is Erected by the State)

He was found by the Bureau of Statistics to be
One against whom there was no official complaint,
And all the reports on his conduct agree
That, in the modern sense of an old-fashioned word, he was a saint,
For in everything he did he served the Greater Community.   5
Except for the War till the day he retired
He worked in a factory and never got fired,
But satisfied his employers, Fudge Motors Inc.
Yet he wasn't a scab or odd in his views,
For his Union reports that he paid his dues,   10
(Our report on his Union shows it was sound)
And our Social Psychology workers found
That he was popular with his mates and liked a drink.
The Press are convinced that he bought a paper every day
And that his reactions to advertisements were normal in every way.   15
Policies taken out in his name prove that he was fully insured,
And his Health-card shows he was once in hospital but left it cured.

Both Producers Research and High-Grade Living declare
He was fully sensible to the advantages of the Instalment Plan
And had everything necessary to the Modern Man, 20
A phonograph, a radio, a car and a frigidaire.
Our researchers into Public Opinion are content
That he held the proper opinions for the time of year;
When there was peace, he was for peace; when there was war, he went.
He was married and added five children to the population, 25
Which our Eugenist[1] says was the right number for a parent of his generation,
And our teachers report that he never interfered with their education.
Was he free? Was he happy? The Question is absurd:
Had anything been wrong, we should certainly have heard.

QUESTIONS

1. This poem was written during the first third of the twentieth century. What changes might you make were you to bring it up to date?
2. What are the implications of there being such a position as an official government Eugenist?
3. There's a lot of rhyme in this poem, but not the regularity of meter usually paired with rhyme. How does that oddity affect the way you hear the poem?
4. This unknown citizen is a he. In what ways would you need to alter or rewrite the poem for a twenty-first century woman?

MAKING CONNECTIONS

1. This citizen is not just unknown but average. What is an average citizen? Read Meghan Daum's "My Misspent Youth" (p. 83), Zoë Tracy Hardy's "What Did You Do in the War, Grandma?" (p. 139), or Paul Auster's account of Auggie Wren (p. 229) and write an essay on the averageness of the average citizen.
2. Read Farley Mowat on wolves (p. 256) or Jane van Lawick-Goodall on chimpanzees (p. 260). Is it easier for them to discover the "average" in the "citizens" they observe?

---

[1]*Eugenist:* someone who favors improvement of humankind by controlled, selective breeding. [Eds.]

OBSERVING WOLVES

Farley Mowat

Farley Mowat was born in Ontario, Canada, in 1921 and finished college at the University of Toronto in 1949, after wartime service and two years living in the Arctic. He makes his living as a writer rather than a scientist, but he works in the same areas covered by anthropologists and zoologists. Often he writes more as a partisan of indigenous peoples and animals than as an "objective" scientist, and his work has reached a wide audience. He has written engagingly about the strange animals he grew up with in Born Naked *(1995) and about wolves in* Never Cry Wolf *(1963), from which the following selection is taken.*

During the next several weeks I put my decision into effect with the thoroughness for which I have always been noted. I went completely to the wolves. To begin with I set up a den of my own as near to the wolves as I could conveniently get without disturbing the even tenor of their lives too much. After all, I *was* a stranger, and an unwolflike one, so I did not feel I should go too far too fast.

Abandoning Mike's cabin (with considerable relief, since as the days warmed up so did the smell) I took a tiny tent and set it up on the shore of the bay immediately opposite to the den esker.[1] I kept my camping gear to the barest minimum—a small primus stove, a stew pot, a teakettle, and a sleeping bag were the essentials. I took no weapons of any kind, although there were times when I regretted this omission, even if only fleetingly. The big telescope was set up in the mouth of the tent in such a way that I could observe the den by day or night without even getting out of my sleeping bag.

During the first few days of my sojourn with the wolves I stayed inside the tent except for brief and necessary visits to the out-of-doors which I always undertook when the wolves were not in sight. The point of this personal concealment was to allow the animals to get used to the tent and to accept it as only another bump on a very bumpy piece of terrain. Later, when the mosquito population reached full flowering, I stayed in the tent practically all of the time unless there was a strong wind blowing, for the most bloodthirsty beasts in the Arctic are not wolves, but the insatiable mosquitoes.

---

[1]*esker:* a long, narrow deposit of gravel and sand left by a stream flowing from a glacier. [Eds.]

My precautions against disturbing the wolves were superfluous. It had required a week for me to get their measure, but they must have taken mine at our first meeting; and, while there was nothing overtly disdainful in their evident assessment of me, they managed to ignore my presence, and indeed my very existence, with a thoroughness which was somehow disconcerting.

Quite by accident I had pitched my tent within ten yards of one of the major paths used by the wolves when they were going to, or coming from, their hunting grounds to the westward; and only a few hours after I had taken up residence one of the wolves came back from a trip and discovered me and my tent. He was at the end of a hard night's work and was clearly tired and anxious to go home to bed. He came over a small rise fifty yards from me with his head down, his eyes half-closed, and a preoccupied air about him. Far from being the preternaturally alert and suspicious beast of fiction, this wolf was so self-engrossed that he came straight on to within fifteen yards of me, and might have gone right past the tent without seeing it at all, had I not banged my elbow against the teakettle, making a re-sounding clank. The wolf's head came up and his eyes opened wide, but he did not stop or falter in his pace. One brief, sidelong glance was all he vouchsafed to me as he continued on his way.

It was true that I wanted to be inconspicuous, but I felt uncomfortable at being so totally ignored. Nevertheless, during the two weeks which followed, one or more wolves used the track past my tent almost every night—and never, except on one memorable occasion, did they evince the slightest interest in me.

By the time this happened I had learned a good deal about my wolfish neighbors, and one of the facts which had emerged was that they were not nomadic roamers, as is almost universally believed, but were settled beasts and the possessors of a large permanent estate with very definite boundaries.

The territory owned by my wolf family comprised more than a hundred square miles, bounded on one side by a river but otherwise not delimited by geographical features. Nevertheless there *were* boundaries, clearly indicated in wolfish fashion.

Anyone who has observed a dog doing his neighborhood rounds and leaving his personal mark on each convenient post will have already guessed how the wolves marked out *their* property. Once a week, more or less, the clan made the rounds of the family lands and freshened up the boundary markers—a sort of lupine beating of the bounds. This careful attention to property rights was perhaps made necessary by the presence of two other wolf families whose lands abutted on ours, although I never discovered any evidence of bickering or disagreements between the owners of the various adjoining estates. I suspect, therefore, that it was more of a ritual activity.

In any event, once I had become aware of the strong feeling of property rights which existed amongst the wolves, I decided to use this knowledge

5

10

to make them at least recognize my existence. One evening, after they had gone off for their regular nightly hunt, I staked out a property claim of my own, embracing perhaps three acres, with the tent at the middle, and *including a hundred-yard-long section of the wolves' path.*

Staking the land turned out to be rather more difficult than I had anticipated. In order to ensure that my claim would not be overlooked, I felt obliged to make a property mark on stones, clumps of moss, and patches of vegetation at intervals of not more than fifteen feet around the circumference of my claim. This took most of the night and required frequent returns to the tent to consume copious quantities of tea; but before dawn brought the hunters home the task was done, and I retired, somewhat exhausted, to observe results.

I had not long to wait. At 0814 hours, according to my wolf log, the leading male of the clan appeared over the ridge behind me, padding homeward with his usual air of preoccupation. As usual he did not deign to glance at the tent; but when he reached the point where my property line intersected the trail, he stopped as abruptly as if he had run into an invisible wall. He was only fifty yards from me and with my binoculars I could see his expression very clearly.

His attitude of fatigue vanished and was replaced by a look of bewilderment. Cautiously he extended his nose and sniffed at one of my marked bushes. He did not seem to know what to make of it or what to do about it. After a minute of complete indecision he backed away a few yards and sat down. And then, finally, he looked directly at the tent and at me. It was a long, thoughtful, considering sort of look.

Having achieved my object—that of forcing at least one of the wolves to take cognizance of my existence—I now began to wonder if, in my ignorance, I had transgressed some unknown wolf law of major importance and would have to pay for my temerity. I found myself regretting the absence of a weapon as the look I was getting became longer, yet more thoughtful, and still more intent.

I began to grow decidedly fidgety, for I dislike staring matches, and in   15
this particular case I was up against a master, whose yellow glare seemed to become more baleful as I attempted to stare him down.

The situation was becoming intolerable. In an effort to break the impasse I loudly cleared my throat and turned my back on the wolf (for a tenth of a second) to indicate as clearly as possible that I found his continued scrutiny impolite, if not actually offensive.

He appeared to take the hint. Getting to his feet he had another sniff at my marker, and then he seemed to make up his mind. Briskly, and with an air of decision, he turned his attention away from me and began a systematic tour of the area I had staked out as my own. As he came to each boundary marker he sniffed it once or twice, then carefully placed *his* mark on the outside of each clump of grass or stone. As I watched I saw where I, in my ignorance, had erred. He made his mark with such economy that he was able to complete the entire circuit without having to reload once, or, to change the simile slightly, he did it all on one tank of fuel.

The task completed—and it had taken him no longer than fifteen minutes—he rejoined the path at the point where it left my property and trotted off towards his home—leaving me with a good deal to occupy my thoughts.

QUESTIONS

1. What did you know about wolves before reading this piece? What was the most surprising—or amusing—information you acquired from reading about Mowat's experience?
2. Write a paragraph summarizing the information about wolves that you can infer from this selection.
3. How would you describe the narrator of this piece? What does he tell us about himself, and how do his actions describe him?
4. Mowat concludes by saying that he was left "with a good deal to occupy my thoughts" (paragraph 18). What, do you suppose, were those thoughts?
5. Find a more objective, "scientific" account of wolves. Which of Mowat's observations are substantiated there?
6. Rewrite the main events in this piece from the wolf's point of view.
7. Observe the actions of a dog or cat as it roams your neighborhood. Write an objective report of the animal's actions. Conclude with your reactions to the animal's behavior and, if pertinent, the animal's reactions to your behavior.

MAKING CONNECTIONS

1. Several of the essays in this section deal with the intricacies of placing humans in relation to specific animals and not only observing but sometimes interfering with their lives. Consider the essays by Jane van Lawick-Goodall (p. 260) and Barry Lopez (p. 282) as well as this one by Mowat. Then, choosing two essays, compare the degrees of intervention taken by the writers and how that intervention affects the stories they tell.
2. Compare and contrast the similarities and differences in procedure of Mowat's study of wolves and Jane van Lawick-Goodall's study of chimpanzees (p. 260).

FIRST OBSERVATIONS

Jane van Lawick-Goodall

*Jane van Lawick-Goodall (b. 1934), British student of animal be-
havior, began her work as an assistant to Louis Leakey, an anthropologist and paleontologist who has studied human origins. In
1960, with his help, she settled in Tanzania, East Africa, in the
Gombe Stream Game Reserve to investigate the behavior of chimpanzees in their natural habitat. Her discoveries have been widely
published in professional journals and in a number of books for
more general audiences, including* Through a Window: My Thirty
Years with the Chimpanzees of Gombe *(1990). The selection
reprinted here is taken from* In the Shadow of Man *(1971), a popular work in which she is careful to report her own behavior as
well as that of her chimpanzee subjects.*

For about a month I spent most of each day either on the Peak or overlooking Mlinda Valley where the chimps, before or after stuffing themselves with figs, ate large quantities of small purple fruits that tasted, like
so many of their foods, as bitter and astringent as sloes or crab apples.
Piece by piece, I began to form my first somewhat crude picture of chimpanzee life.

The impression that I had gained when I watched the chimps at the
msulula tree of temporary, constantly changing associations of individuals
within the community was substantiated. Most often I saw small groups of
four to eight moving about together. Sometimes I saw one or two chimpanzees leave such a group and wander off on their own or join up with a
different association. On other occasions I watched two or three small
groups joining to form a larger one.

Often, as one group crossed the grassy ridge separating the Kasekela
Valley from the fig trees on the home valley, the male chimpanzee, or
chimpanzees, of the party would break into a run, sometimes moving in an
upright position, sometimes dragging a fallen branch, sometimes stamping
or slapping the hard earth. These charging displays were always accompanied by loud pant-hoots and afterward the chimpanzee frequently would
swing up into a tree overlooking the valley he was about to enter and sit
quietly, peering down and obviously listening for a response from below. If
there were chimps feeding in the fig trees they nearly always hooted back,
as though in answer. Then the new arrivals would hurry down the steep
slope and, with more calling and screaming, the two groups would meet in
the fig trees. When groups of females and youngsters with no males present

joined other feeding chimpanzees, usually there was none of this excitement; the newcomers merely climbed up into the trees, greeted some of those already there, and began to stuff themselves with figs.

While many details of their social behavior were hidden from me by the foliage, I did get occasional fascinating glimpses. I saw one female, newly arrived in a group, hurry up to a big male and hold her hand toward him. Almost regally he reached out, clasped her hand in his, drew it toward him, and kissed it with his lips. I saw two adult males embrace each other in greeting. I saw youngsters having wild games through the treetops, chasing around after each other or jumping again and again, one after the other, from a branch to a springy bough below. I watched small infants dangling happily by themselves for minutes on end, patting at their toes with one hand, rotating gently from side to side. Once two tiny infants pulled on opposite ends of a twig in a gentle tug-of-war. Often, during the heat of midday or after a long spell of feeding, I saw two or more adults grooming each other, carefully looking through the hair of their companions.

At that time of year the chimps usually went to bed late, making their 5 nests when it was too dark to see properly through binoculars, but sometimes they nested earlier and I could watch them from the Peak. I found that every individual, except for infants who slept with their mothers, made his own nest each night. Generally this took about three minutes: the chimp chose a firm foundation such as an upright fork or crotch, or two horizontal branches. Then he reached out and bent over smaller branches onto this foundation, keeping each one in place with his feet. Finally he tucked in the small leafy twigs growing around the rim of his nest and lay down. Quite often a chimp sat up after a few minutes and picked a handful of leafy twigs, which he put under his head or some other part of his body before settling down again for the night. One young female I watched went on and on bending down branches until she had constructed a huge mound of greenery on which she finally curled up.

I climbed up into some of the nests after the chimpanzees had left them. Most of them were built in trees that for me were almost impossible to climb. I found that there was quite complicated interweaving of the branches in some of them. I found, too, that the nests were fouled with dung; and later, when I was able to get closer to the chimps, I saw how they were always careful to defecate and urinate over the edge of their nests, even in the middle of the night.

During that month I really came to know the country well, for I often went on expeditions from the Peak, sometimes to examine nests, more frequently to collect specimens of the chimpanzees' food plants, which Bernard Verdcourt had kindly offered to identify for me. Soon I could find my way around the sheer ravines and up and down the steep slopes of three valleys—the home valley, the Pocket, and Mlinda Valley—as well as a taxi driver finds his way about in the main streets and byways of London. It is a period I remember vividly, not only because I was beginning to accomplish something at last, but also because of the delight I felt in being completely by myself. For those who love to be alone with nature I need add nothing further; for those who do not, no words of mine could ever convey, even in part, the almost mystical awareness of beauty and eternity that accompanies certain treasured moments. And, though the beauty was always there, those moments came upon me unaware: when I was watching the pale flush preceding dawn; or looking up through the rustling leaves of some giant forest tree into the greens and browns and black shadows that occasionally ensnared a bright fleck of the blue sky; or when I stood, as darkness fell, with one hand on the still-warm trunk of a tree and looked at the sparkling of an early moon on the never still, sighing water of the lake.

One day, when I was sitting by the trickle of water in Buffalo Wood, pausing for a moment in the coolness before returning from a scramble in Mlinda Valley, I saw a female bushbuck moving slowly along the nearly dry streambed. Occasionally she paused to pick off some plant and crunch it. I kept absolutely still, and she was not aware of my presence until she was little more than ten yards away. Suddenly she tensed and stood staring at me, one small forefoot raised. Because I did not move, she did not know what I was—only that my outline was somehow strange. I saw her velvet nostrils dilate as she sniffed the air, but I was downwind and her nose gave her no answer. Slowly she came closer, and closer—one step at a time, her neck craned forward—always poised for instant flight. I can still scarcely believe that her nose actually touched my knee; yet if I close my eyes I can feel again, in imagination, the warmth of her breath and the silken impact of her skin. Unexpectedly I blinked and she was gone in a flash, bounding away with loud barks of alarm until the vegetation hid her completely from my view.

It was rather different when, as I was sitting on the Peak, I saw a leopard coming toward me, his tail held up straight. He was at a slightly lower level than I, and obviously had no idea I was there. Ever since arrival in Africa I had had an ingrained, illogical fear of leopards. Already, while working at the Gombe, I had several times nearly turned back when, crawling through some thick undergrowth, I had suddenly smelled the rank smell of cat. I had forced myself on, telling myself that my fear was foolish, that only wounded leopards charged humans with savage ferocity.

On this occasion, though, the leopard went out of sight as it started to   10
climb up the hill—the hill on the peak of which I sat. I quickly hastened to climb a tree, but halfway there I realized that leopards can climb trees. So I uttered a sort of halfhearted squawk. The leopard, my logical mind told me, would be just as frightened of me if he knew I was there. Sure enough, there was a thudding of startled feet and then silence. I returned to the Peak, but the feeling of unseen eyes watching me was too much. I decided to watch for the chimps in Mlinda Valley. And, when I returned to the Peak several hours later, there, on the very rock which had been my seat, was a neat pile of leopard dung. He must have watched me go and then,

very carefully, examined the place where such a frightening creature had been and tried to exterminate my alien scent with his own.

As the weeks went by the chimpanzees became less and less afraid. Quite often when I was on one of my food-collecting expeditions I came across chimpanzees unexpectedly, and after a time I found that some of them would tolerate my presence provided they were in fairly thick forest and I sat still and did not try to move closer than sixty to eighty yards. And so, during my second month of watching from the Peak, when I saw a group settle down to feed I sometimes moved closer and was thus able to make more detailed observations.

It was at this time that I began to recognize a number of different individuals. As soon as I was sure of knowing a chimpanzee if I saw it again, I named it. Some scientists feel that animals should be labeled by numbers — that to name them is anthropomorphic — but I have always been interested in the *differences* between individuals, and a name is not only more individual than a number but also far easier to remember. Most names were simply those which, for some reason or other, seemed to suit the individuals to whom I attached them. A few chimps were named because some facial expression or mannerism reminded me of human acquaintances.

The easiest individual to recognize was old Mr. McGregor. The crown of his head, his neck, and his shoulders were almost entirely devoid of hair, but a slight frill remained around his head rather like a monk's tonsure. He was an old male — perhaps between thirty and forty years of age (the longevity record of a captive chimp is forty-seven years). During the early months of my acquaintance with him, Mr. McGregor was somewhat belligerent. If I accidentally came across him at close quarters he would threaten me with an upward and backward jerk of his head and a shaking of branches before climbing down and vanishing from my sight. He reminded me, for some reason, of Beatrix Potter's old gardener in *The Tale of Peter Rabbit*.

Ancient Flo with her deformed, bulbous nose and ragged ears was equally easy to recognize. Her youngest offspring at that time were two-year-old Fifi, who still rode everywhere on her mother's back, and her juvenile son, Figan, who was always to be seen wandering around with his mother and little sister. He was then about six years old; it was approximately a year before he would attain puberty. Flo often traveled with another old mother, Olly. Olly's long face was also distinctive; the fluff of hair on the back of her head — though no other feature — reminded me of my aunt, Olwen. Olly, like Flo, was accompanied by two children, a daughter younger than Fifi, and an adolescent son about a year older than Figan.

Then there was William, who, I am certain, must have been Olly's blood brother. I never saw any special signs of friendship between them, but their faces were amazingly alike. They both had long upper lips that wobbled when they suddenly turned their heads. William had the added distinction of several thin, deeply etched scar marks running down his upper lip from his nose.

15

Two of the other chimpanzees I knew well by sight at that time were David Graybeard and Goliath. Like David and Goliath in the Bible, these two individuals were closely associated in my mind because they were very often together. Goliath, even in those days of his prime, was not a giant, but he had a splendid physique and the springy movements of an athlete. He probably weighed about one hundred pounds. David Graybeard was less afraid of me from the start than were any of the other chimps. I was always pleased when I picked out his handsome face and well-marked silvery beard in a chimpanzee group, for with David to calm the others, I had a better chance of approaching to observe them more closely.

Before the end of my trial period in the field I made two really exciting discoveries — discoveries that made the previous months of frustration well worth while. And for both of them I had David Graybeard to thank.

One day I arrived on the Peak and found a small group of chimps just below me in the upper branches of a thick tree. As I watched I saw that one of them was holding a pink-looking object from which he was from time to time pulling pieces with his teeth. There was a female and a youngster and they were both reaching out toward the male, their hands actually touching his mouth. Presently the female picked up a piece of the pink thing and put it to her mouth: it was at this moment that I realized the chimps were eating meat.

After each bite of meat the male picked off some leaves with his lips and chewed them with the flesh. Often, when he had chewed for several minutes on this leafy wad, he spat out the remains into the waiting hands of the female. Suddenly he dropped a small piece of meat, and like a flash the youngster swung after it to the ground. Even as he reached to pick it up the undergrowth exploded and an adult bushpig charged toward him. Screaming, the juvenile leaped back into the tree. The pig remained in the open, snorting and moving backward and forward. Soon I made out the shapes of three small striped piglets. Obviously the chimps were eating a baby pig. The size was right and later, when I realized that the male was David Graybeard, I moved closer and saw that he was indeed eating piglet.

For three hours I watched the chimps feeding. David occasionally let   20
the female bite pieces from the carcass and once he actually detached a small piece of flesh and placed it in her outstretched hand. When he finally climbed down there was still meat left on the carcass; he carried it away in one hand, followed by the others.

Of course I was not sure, then, that David Graybeard had caught the pig for himself, but even so, it was tremendously exciting to know that these chimpanzees actually ate meat. Previously scientists had believed that although these apes might occasionally supplement their diet with a few insects or small rodents and the like they were primarily vegetarians and fruit eaters. No one had suspected that they might hunt larger mammals.

It was within two weeks of this observation that I saw something that excited me even more. By then it was October and the short rains had begun. The blackened slopes were softened by feathery new grass shoots and in some places the ground was carpeted by a variety of flowers. The Chimpanzees' Spring, I called it. I had had a frustrating morning, tramping up and down three valleys with never a sign or sound of a chimpanzee. Hauling myself up the steep slope of Mlinda Valley I headed for the Peak, not only weary but soaking wet from crawling through dense undergrowth. Suddenly I stopped, for I saw a slight movement in the long grass about sixty yards away. Quickly focusing my binoculars I saw that it was a single chimpanzee, and just then he turned in my direction. I recognized David Graybeard.

Cautiously I moved around so that I could see what he was doing. He was squatting beside the red earth mound of a termite nest, and as I watched I saw him carefully push a long grass stem down into a hole in the mound. After a moment he withdrew it and picked something from the end with his mouth. I was too far away to make out what he was eating, but it was obvious that he was actually using a grass stem as a tool.

I knew that on two occasions casual observers in West Africa had seen chimpanzees using objects as tools: one had broken open palm-nut kernels by using a rock as a hammer, and a group of chimps had been observed pushing sticks into an underground bees' nest and licking off the honey. Somehow I had never dreamed of seeing anything so exciting myself.

For an hour David feasted at the termite mound and then he wandered   25 slowly away. When I was sure he had gone I went over to examine the mound. I found a few crushed insects strewn about, and a swarm of worker termites sealing the entrances of the nest passages into which David had obviously been poking his stems. I picked up one of his discarded tools and carefully pushed it into a hole myself. Immediately I felt the pull of several termites as they seized the grass, and when I pulled it out there were a number of worker termites and a few soldiers, with big red heads, clinging on with their mandibles. There they remained, sticking out at right angles to the stem with their legs waving in the air.

Before I left I trampled down some of the tall dry grass and constructed a rough hide—just a few palm fonds leaned up against the low branch of a tree and tied together at the top. I planned to wait there the next day. But it was another week before I was able to watch a chimpanzee "fishing" for termites again. Twice chimps arrived, but each time they saw me and moved off immediately. Once a swarm of fertile winged termites—the princes and princesses, as they are called—flew off on their nuptial flight, their huge white wings fluttering frantically as they carried the insects higher and higher. Later I realized that it is at this time of year, during the short rains, when the worker termites extend the passages of the nest to the surface, preparing for these emigrations. Several such swarms emerge between October and January. It is principally during these months that the chimpanzees feed on termites.

On the eighth day of my watch David Graybeard arrived again, together with Goliath, and the pair worked there for two hours. I could see much better: I observed how they scratched open the sealed-over passage entrances with a thumb or forefinger. I watched how they bit the end off their tools when they became bent, or used the other end, or discarded them in favor of new ones. Goliath once moved at least fifteen yards from the heap to select a firm-looking piece of vine, and both males often picked three or four stems while they were collecting tools, and put the spares beside them on the ground until they wanted them.

Most exciting of all, on several occasions they picked small leafy twigs and prepared them for use by stripping off the leaves. This was the first recorded example of a wild animal not merely *using* an object as a tool, but actually modifying an object and thus showing the crude beginnings of tool*making*.

Previously man had been regarded as the only tool-making animal. Indeed, one of the clauses commonly accepted in the definition of man was that he was a creature who "made tools to a regular and set pattern." The chimpanzees, obviously, had not made tools to any set pattern. Nevertheless, my early observations of their primitive toolmaking abilities convinced a number of scientists that it was necessary to redefine man in a more complex manner than before. Or else, as Louis Leakey put it, we should by definition have to accept the chimpanzee as Man.

QUESTIONS

1. This essay is an example, principally, of reporting; that is, it is a gathering of facts by a clearheaded, unbiased observer. Identify passages in the essay in which this kind of reporting clearly takes place.
2. Although van Lawick-Goodall, in the main, is a neutral observer of chimpanzee behavior, that neutrality is in fact impossible in any absolute sense. It is clear that she writes, for example, with an eye always on comparisons of chimpanzee and human behavior. Make a list of words, just from paragraphs 3 and 4, that reveal that particular bias.
3. Describe how van Lawick-Goodall's comparison of chimpanzee with human behavior becomes increasingly prominent in the course of her essay.
4. Paraphrase the last discovery van Lawick-Goodall reports toward the end of her essay. What, exactly, was her contribution to science in this instance? What other activities, described earlier in the piece, make that discovery understandable, perhaps even unsurprising once we come to it?
5. What do you make of the choice outlined in paragraph 29? Which choice do you suppose the scientists made? Why?
6. Van Lawick-Goodall's scientific work resembles that of an anthropologist in that she goes into the field to observe the behavior of another social group. Even from this short piece we can learn a good deal about the practices and the way of life of such a worker in the field. Describe van Lawick-Goodall's life in the field as best you can, making whatever inferences you can from this single essay.

7. Amplify your description of van Lawick-Goodall's life in the field, done for question 6, by reading whatever articles you can find that tell more about her and about her work.

8. Place yourself somewhere and observe behavior more or less as van Lawick-Goodall does. You might observe wildlife—pigeons, sparrows, crows, squirrels, or whatever is available—or you might observe some aspect of human behavior. If you choose the latter, look for behavior that is unfamiliar to you, such as that of children at play, of workers on the job, or of members of a social group very different from your own. Write a report detailing your observations.

9. After you have completed question 8, write a second, shorter report in which you comment on the nature of your task as an observer. Was it difficult to watch? Was it difficult to decide what was meaningful behavior? Did you influence what you saw so that you could not be confident that the behavior was representative? Can you propose any improvement in your methodology?

10. One of the tools that van Lawick-Goodall lacks in her writing is the ability to interview relevant parties. Don't you imagine she would have liked to interview Mr. McGregor, Goliath, or David Graybeard? Imagine her doing so. What questions would she be likely to ask? What would you like to know from one of those individuals were you able to interview him? Write out the interview that you can imagine.

MAKING CONNECTIONS

1. Both van Lawick-Goodall and Farley Mowat (p. 256) study a specific kind of animal in its natural habitat. How are their procedures similar? How are they different? What kinds of refinement do they venture in their studies as they proceed? How do their procedures influence both their findings and their presentation of those findings?

2. Compare and contrast van Lawick-Goodall's account of observing the chimpanzees with Pico Iyer's observations of human beings at the Los Angeles International Airport (p. 270). To what extent are both writers ethnographers, studying and describing behavior in a specific society?

ROSA[1]

Rita Dove

Born in Akron, Ohio, in 1952, poet Rita Dove graduated from Miami University and received an M.F.A. from the University of Iowa's writing program. Her first collection of poems, Yellow House on the Corner, *appeared in 1980. Subsequent volumes include* Thomas and Beulah *(1986), which won the Pulitzer Prize for poetry;* Selected Poems *(1993); and her most recent book,* On the Bus with Rosa Parks *(1999). She has also published short story collections and a verse play. From 1993 to 1995, Dove served as Poet Laureate of the United States, the first African American and the youngest person to be appointed to the position. She is currently Commonwealth Professor at the University of Virginia. Trained as a musician, Dove is noted for the spare, controlled elegance of her work. In the words of critic Helen Vendler, "technically her poems 'work' by their fierce concision and an exceptional sense of rhythmic pulse."*

How she sat there,
the time right inside a place
so wrong it was ready.

That trim name with   5
its dream of a bench
to rest on. Her sensible coat.

Doing nothing was the doing:
the clean flame of her gaze
carved by a camera flash.

How she stood up   10
when they bent down to retrieve
her purse. That courtesy.

---

[1]*Rosa Parks:* an African American woman who became an inspiration to the civil rights movement when she took a seat in the front rather than at the back of a bus in Montgomery, Alabama, on December 1, 1955, and refused to yield her place to a white passenger. [Eds.]

QUESTIONS

1. What are the most salient details of this very brief report?
2. What is different about the last detail you may have listed, the one reported in the last stanza?
3. Dove's final two words turn from reporting to something else; you can call it interpretation, explanation, or drawing conclusions. What exactly do you see when you visualize that concluding moment?

MAKING CONNECTIONS

1. You might say that Rosa Parks was an unknown citizen, at least until the crucial moment alluded to in this poem. Write a prose imitation of W. H. Auden's memorial to "The Unknown Citizen" (p. 254), but make Parks, as you imagine her to be, the citizen described.
2. Read Martin Luther King Jr.'s "Pilgrimage to Nonviolence" (p. 111). "The experience in Montgomery," King writes, "did more to clarify my thinking in regard to the question of nonviolence than all of the books that I had read"; but nowhere does he mention Parks, whose resistance inspired the Montgomery boycott.

    Describe a time when you too acted on a principle. Write an account of how you came to your belief and how you determined to act in accordance with it.

WHERE WORLDS COLLIDE
In Los Angeles International Airport, the Future Touches Down

Pico Iyer

Pico Iyer, a travel writer with a special interest in the hybrid cultures of East and West, was born in Oxford, England, in 1957 and immigrated to the United States in 1966. Educated at Eton, Oxford, and Harvard, he has turned his traveling and his cultural curiosity to account as an essayist for Time *magazine and a contributing editor at* Conde Nast Traveler. *Iyer is best known for his wide-ranging, vividly detailed collections of travel pieces:* Video Night in Kathmandu and Other Reports from the Not-So-Far East *(1988),* Falling Off the Map: Some Lonely Places of the World *(1993), and* Tropical Classical: Essays from Several Directions *(1997). His interest in travel writing has also led him to produce an evocative novel,* Cuba and the Night *(1995), about contemporary life in Havana. The selection reprinted here was originally published in* Harper's *(August 1995).*

They come out, blinking, into the bleached, forgetful sunshine, in Dodgers caps and Rodeo Drive T-shirts, with the maps their cousins have drawn for them and the images they've brought over from *Cops* and *Terminator 2;* they come out, dazed, disoriented, heads still partly in the clouds, bodies still several time zones—or centuries—away, and they step into the Promised Land.

In front of them is a Van Stop, a Bus Stop, a Courtesy Tram Stop, and a Shuttle Bus Stop (the shuttles themselves tracing circuits A, B, and C). At the Shuttle Bus Stop, they see the All American Shuttle, the Apollo Shuttle, Celebrity Airport Livery, the Great American Stageline, the Movie Shuttle, the Transport, Ride-4-You, and forty-two other magic buses waiting to whisk them everywhere from Bakersfield to Disneyland. They see Koreans piling into the Taeguk Airport Shuttle and the Seoul Shuttle, which will take them to Koreatown without their ever feeling they've left home; they see newcomers from the Middle East disappearing under the Arabic script of the Sahara Shuttle. They see fast-talking, finger-snapping, palm-slapping jive artists straight from their TV screens shouting incomprehensible slogans about deals, destinations, and drugs. Over there is a block-long white limo, a Lincoln Continental, and, over there, a black Chevy Blazer with Mexican stickers all over its windows, being towed. They have arrived in the Land of Opportunity, and the opportunities are swirling dizzily, promiscuously, around them.

They have already braved the ranks of Asian officials, the criminal-looking security men in jackets that say "Elsinore Airport Services," the men shaking tins that say "Helping America's Hopeless." They have already seen the tilting mugs that say "California: a new slant on life" and the portable fruit machines in the gift shop. They have already, perhaps, visited the rest room where someone has written, "Yes on Proposition 187. Mexicans go home," the snack bar where a slice of pizza costs $3.19 (18 quetzals, they think in horror, or 35,000 dong), and the sign that urges them to try the Cockatoo Inn Grand Hotel. The latest arrivals at Los Angeles International Airport are ready now to claim their new lives.

Above them in the terminal, voices are repeating, over and over, in Japanese, Spanish, and unintelligible English, "Maintain visual contact with your personal property at all times." Out on the sidewalk, a man's voice and a woman's voice are alternating an unending refrain: "The white zone is for loading and unloading of passengers only. No parking." There are "Do Not Cross" yellow lines cordoning off parts of the sidewalk and "Wells Fargo Alarm Services" stickers on the windows; there are "Aviation Safeguard" signs on the baggage carts and "Beware of Solicitors" signs on the columns; there are even special phones "To Report Trouble." More male and female voices are intoning, continuously, "Do not leave your car unattended" and "Unattended cars are subject to immediate tow-away." There are no military planes on the tarmac here, the newcomers notice, no khaki soldiers in fatigues, no instructions not to take photographs, as at home; but there are civilian restrictions every bit as strict as in many a police state.

"This Terminal Is in a Medfly Quarantine Area," says the sign between the terminals. "Stop the Spread of Medfly!" If, by chance, the new Americans have to enter a parking lot on their way out, they will be faced with "Cars left over 30 days may be impounded at Owner's Expense" and "Do not enter without a ticket." It will cost them $16 if they lose their parking ticket, they read, and $56 if they park in the wrong zone. Around them is an unending cacophony of antitheft devices, sirens, beepers, and car-door openers; lights are flashing everywhere, and the man who fines them $16 for losing their parking ticket has the tribal scars of Tigre across his forehead.

The blue skies and palm trees they saw on TV are scarcely visible from here: just an undifferentiated smoggy haze, billboards advertising Nissan and Panasonic and Canon, and beyond those an endlessly receding mess of gray streets. Overhead, they can see the all-too-familiar signs of Hilton and Hyatt and Holiday Inn; in the distance, a sea of tract houses, mini-malls, and high-rises. The City of Angels awaits them.

It is commonplace nowadays to say that cities look more and more like airports, cross-cultural spaces that are a gathering of tribes and races and variegated tongues; and it has always been true that airports are in many ways like miniature cities, whole, self-sufficient communities, with their own chapels and museums and gymnasiums. Not only have airports colored our speech (teaching us about being upgraded, bumped, and put on standby, coaching us in the ways of fly-by-night operations, holding patterns, and the Mile High Club); they have also taught us their own rules, their own codes, their own customs. We eat and sleep and shower in airports; we pray and weep and kiss there. Some people stay for days at a time in these perfectly convenient, hermetically sealed, climate-controlled duty-free zones, which offer a kind of caesura from the obligations of daily life.

Airports are also, of course, the new epicenters and paradigms of our dawning post-national age—not just the bus terminals of the global village but the prototypes, in some sense, for our polyglot, multicolored, user-friendly future. And in their very universality—like the mall, the motel, or the McDonald's outlet—they advance the notion of a future in which all the world's a multiculture. If you believe that more and more of the world is a kind of mongrel hybrid in which many cities (Sydney, Toronto, Singapore) are simply suburbs of a single universal order, then Los Angeles's LAX, London's Heathrow, and Hong Kong's Kai Tak are merely stages on some great global Circle Line, shuttling variations on a common global theme. Mass travel has made L.A. contiguous to Seoul and adjacent to São Paulo, and has made all of them now feel a little like bedroom communities for Tokyo.

And as with most social trends, especially the ones involving tomorrow, what is true of the world is doubly true of America, and what is doubly true of America is quadruply true of Los Angeles. L.A., legendarily, has more Thais than any city but Bangkok, more Koreans than any city but Seoul, more El Salvadorans than any city outside of San Salvador, more Druze than anywhere but Beirut; it is, at the very least, the easternmost outpost of Asia and the northernmost province of Mexico. When I stopped at a Traveler's Aid desk at LAX recently, I was told I could request help in Khamu, Mien, Tigrinya, Tajiki, Pashto, Dari, Pangasinan, Pampangan, Waray-Waray, Bambara, Twi, and Bicolano (as well, of course, as French, German, and eleven languages from India). LAX is as clear an image as exists today of the world we are about to enter, and of the world that's entering us.

For me, though, LAX has always had a more personal resonance: it   10
was in LAX that I arrived myself as a new immigrant, in 1966; and from the time I was in the fourth grade, it was to LAX that I would go three times a year, as an "unaccompanied minor," to fly to school in London— and to LAX that I returned three times a year for my holidays. Sometimes it seems as if I have spent half my life in LAX. For me, it is the site of my liberation (from school, from the Old World, from home) and the place where I came to design my own new future.

Often when I have set off from L.A. to some distant place—Havana, say, or Hanoi, or Pyongyang—I have felt that the multicultural drama on display in LAX, the interaction of exoticism and familiarity, was just as bizarre as anything I would find when I arrived at my foreign destination. The airport is an Amy Tan novel, a short story by Bharati Mukherjee, a Henry James sketch set to an MTV beat; it is a cross-generational saga about Chang Hsieng meeting his daughter Cindy and finding that she's wearing a nose ring now and is shacked up with a surfer from Berlin. The very best kind of airport reading to be found in LAX these days is the triple-decker melodrama being played out all around one—a complex tragicomedy of love and war and exile, about people fleeing centuries-old rivalries and thirteenth-century mullahs[1] and stepping out into a fresh, forgetful, born-again city that is rewriting its script every moment.

Not long ago I went to spend a week in LAX. I haunted the airport by day and by night, I joined the gloomy drinkers listening to air-control-tower instructions on earphones at the Proud Bird bar. I listened each morning to Airport Radio (530 AM), and I slept each night at the Airport Sheraton or the Airport Hilton. I lived off cellophaned crackers and Styrofoam cups of tea, browsed for hours among Best Actor statuettes and Beverly Hills magnets, and tried to see what kinds of America the city presents to the new Americans, who are remaking America each day.

It is almost too easy to say that LAX is a perfect metaphor for L.A., a flat, spaced-out desert kind of place, highly automotive, not deeply hospitable, with little reading matter and no organizing principle. (There are eight satellites without a center here, many international arrivals are shunted out into the bleak basement of Terminal 2, and there is no airline that serves to dominate LAX as Pan Am once did JFK.) Whereas "SIN" is a famously ironical airline code for Singapore, cathedral of puritanical rectitude, "LAX" has always seemed perilously well chosen for a city whose main industries were traditionally thought to be laxity and relaxation. LAX is at once a vacuum waiting to be colonized and a joyless theme park—Tomorrowland, Adventureland, and Fantasyland all at once.

The postcards on sale here (made in Korea) dutifully call the airport "one of the busiest and most beautiful air facilities in the world," and it is certainly true that LAX, with thirty thousand international arrivals each day—roughly the same number of tourists that have visited the Himalayan country of Bhutan in its entire history—is not uncrowded. But bigger is less and less related to better: in a recent survey of travel facilities, *Business Traveller* placed LAX among the five worst airports in the world for customs, luggage retrieval, and passport processing.

LAX is, in fact, a surprisingly shabby and hollowed-out kind of place, certainly not adorned with the amenities one might expect of the world's strongest and richest power. When you come out into the Arrivals area in the International Terminal, you will find exactly one tiny snack bar, which

15

---

[1]*Mullah:* Islamic leader and teacher. [Eds.]

serves nine items; of them, five are identified as Cheese Dog, Chili Dog, Chili Cheese Dog, Nachos with Cheese, and Chili Cheese Nachos. There is a large panel on the wall offering rental-car services and hotels, and the newly deplaned American dreamer can choose between the Cadillac Hotel, the Banana Bungalow (which offers a Basketball Court, "Free Toast," "Free Bed Sheets," and "Free Movies and Parties"), and the Backpacker's Paradise (with "Free Afternoon Tea and Crumpets" and "Free Evening Party Including Food and Champagne").

Around one in the terminal is a swirl of priests rattling cans, Iranians in suits brandishing pictures of torture victims, and Japanese girls in Goofy hats. "I'm looking for something called Clearasil," a distinguished-looking Indian man diffidently tells a cashier. "Clearasil?" shouts the girl. "For your face?"

Upstairs, in the Terrace Restaurant, passengers are gulping down "Dutch Chocolate" and "Japanese Coffee" while students translate back and forth between English and American, explaining that "soliciting" loses something of its cachet when you go across the Atlantic. A fat man is nuzzling the neck of his outrageously pretty Filipina companion, and a few Brits are staring doubtfully at the sign that assures them that seafood is "cheerfully served at your table!" Only in America, they are doubtless thinking. A man goes from table to table, plunking down on each one a key chain attached to a globe. As soon as an unsuspecting customer picks one up, touched by the largesse of the New World and convinced now that there *is* such a thing as a free lunch in America, the man appears again, flashes a sign that says "I Am a Deaf," and requests a dollar for the gift.

At a bank of phones, a saffron-robed monk gingerly inserts a credit card, while schoolkids page Jesse Jackson at the nearest "white courtesy telephone." One notable feature of the modern airport is that it is wired, with a vengeance: even in a tiny, two-urinal men's room, I found two telephones on offer; LAX bars rent out cellular phones; and in the Arrivals area, as you come out into the land of plenty, you face a bank of forty-six phones of every kind, with screens and buttons and translations, from which newcomers are calling direct to Bangalore or Baghdad.

Yet for all these grounding reminders of the world outside, everywhere I went in the airport I felt myself in an odd kind of twilight zone of consciousness, that weightless limbo of a world in which people are between lives and between selves, almost sleepwalking, not really sure of who or where they are. Light-headed from the trips they've taken, ears popping and eyes about to do so, under a potent foreign influence, people are at the far edge of themselves in airports, ready to break down or through. You see strangers pouring out their life stories to strangers here, or making new life stories with other strangers. Everything is at once intensified and slightly unreal. One L.A. psychiatrist advises shy women to practice their flirting here, and religious groups circle in the hope of catching unattached souls.

Airports, which often have a kind of perpetual morning-after feeling (the end of the holiday, the end of the affair), are places where everyone is 20 ruled by the clock, but all the clocks show different times. These days, after all, we fly not only into yesterday or this morning when we go across the world but into different decades, often, of the world's life and our own: in ten or fifteen hours, we are taken back into the twelfth century or into worlds we haven't seen since childhood. And in the process we are subjected to transitions more jolting than any imagined by Oscar Wilde or Sigmund Freud: if the average individual today sees as many images in a day as a Victorian saw in a lifetime, the average person today also has to negotiate switches between continents inconceivable only fifty years ago. Frequent fliers like Ted Turner have actually become ill from touching down and taking off so often; but, in less diagnosable ways, all of us are being asked to handle difficult suspensions of the laws of Nature and Society when moving between competing worlds.

This helps to compound the strange statelessness of airports, where all bets are off and all laws are annulled—modern equivalents, perhaps, to the hundred yards of no-man's-land between two frontier crossings. In airports we are often in dreamy, floating, out-of-body states, as ready to be claimed as that suitcase on Carousel C. Even I, not traveling, didn't know sometimes if I was awake or asleep in LAX, as I heard an announcer intone, "John Cheever[2], John Cheever, please contact a Northwest representative in the Baggage Claim area. John Cheever, please contact a service representative at the Northwest Baggage Claim area."

As I started to sink into this odd, amphibious, bipolar state, I could begin to see why a place like LAX is a particular zone of fear, more terrifying to many people than anywhere but the dentist's office. Though dying in a plane is, notoriously, twenty times less likely than dying in a car, every single airline crash is front-page news and so dramatic—not a single death but three hundred—that airports are for many people killing grounds. Their runways are associated in the mind's (televisual) eye with hostages and hijackings; with bodies on the tarmac or antiterrorist squads storming the plane.

That general sense of unsettledness is doubtless intensified by all the people in uniform in LAX. There are ten different security agencies working the Tom Bradley Terminal alone, and the streets outside are jam-packed with Airport Police cars, FBI men, and black-clad airport policemen on bicycles. All of them do as much, I suspect, to instill fear as to still it. "People are scared here," a gloomy Pakistani security guard told me, "because undercover are working. Police are working. You could be undercover, I could be undercover. Who knows?"

And just as L.A. is a province of the future in part because so many people take it to be the future, so it is a danger zone precisely because it is imagined to be dangerous. In Osaka's new $16 billion airport recently, I cross-examined the Skynet computer (in the Departures area) about what

---

[2] *John Cheever*: American author, 1912–1982. [Eds.]

to expect when arriving at LAX or any other foreign airport. "Guard against theft in the arrival hall," it told me (and, presumably, even warier Japanese). "A thief is waiting for a chance to take advantage of you." Elsewhere it added, "Do not dress too touristy," and, "Be on your guard when approached by a group of suspicious-looking children, such as girls wearing bright-colored shirts and scarves." True to such dark prognostications, the side doors of the Airport Sheraton at LAX are locked every day from 8:00 P.M. to 6:00 A.M., and you cannot even activate the elevators without a room key. "Be extra careful in parking garages and stairwells," the hotel advises visitors. "Always try to use the main entrance to your hotel, particularly late in the evening. Never answer your hotel room door without verifying who is there."

One reason airports enjoy such central status in our imaginations is   25
that they play such a large part in forming our first (which is sometimes our last) impression of a place; this is the reason that poor countries often throw all their resources into making their airports sleek, with beautifully landscaped roads leading out of them into town. L.A., by contrast, has the bareness of arrogance, or simple inhospitability. Usually what you see as you approach the city is a grim penitential haze through which is visible nothing but rows of gray buildings, a few dun-hued warehouses, and ribbons of dirty freeway: a no-colored blur without even the comforting lapis ornaments of the swimming pools that dot New York or Johannesburg. (Ideally, in fact, one should enter L.A. by night, when the whole city pulses like an electric grid of lights—or the back of a transistor radio, in Thomas Pynchon's inspired metaphor. While I was staying in LAX, Jackie Collins[3] actually told *Los Angeles* magazine that "Flying in [to LAX] at night is just an orgasmic thrill.") You land, with a bump, on a mess of gray runways with no signs of welcome, a hangar that says "T ans W rld Airlines," another broken sign that announces "Tom Bradly International Ai port," and an air-control tower under scaffolding.

The first thing that greeted me on a recent arrival was a row of Asians sitting on the floor of the terminal, under a sign that told them of a $25,000 fine for bringing in the wrong kinds of food. As I passed through endless corridors, I was faced with almost nothing except long escalators (a surprisingly high percentage of the accidents recorded at airports comes from escalators, bewildering to newcomers) and bare hallways. The other surprise, for many of my fellow travelers, no doubt, was that almost no one we saw looked like Robert Redford or Julia Roberts or, indeed, like anyone belonging to the race we'd been celebrating in our in-flight movies. As we passed into the huge, bare assembly hall that is the Customs and Immigration Center here, I was directed into one of the chaotic lines by a

---

[3]*Pynchon* and *Collins*: Contemporary American authors, the first difficult and postmodern, the second quite popular, almost the definition of "airport reading." [Eds.]

Noriko and formally admitted to the country by a C. Chen. The man waiting to transfer my baggage (as a beagle sniffed around us in a coat that said "Agriculture's Beagle Brigade" on one side and "Protecting American Agriculture" on the other) was named Yoji Yosaka. And the first sign I saw, when I stepped into America, was a big board being waved by the "Executive Sedan Service" for one "Mr. T. Ego."

For many immigrants, in fact, LAX is quietly offering them a view of their own near futures: the woman at the Host Coffee Shop is themselves, in a sense, two years from now, and the man sweeping up the refuse is the American dream in practice. The staff at the airport seems to be made up almost entirely of recent immigrants: on my very first afternoon there, I was served by a Hoa, an Ephraim, and a Glinda; the wait-people at a coffee shop in Terminal 5 were called Ignacio, Ever, Aura, and Erick. Even at the Airport Sheraton (where the employees all wear nameplates), I was checked in by Viera (from "Bratislavia") and ran into Hasmik and Yovik (from Ethiopia), Faye (from Vietnam), Ingrid (from Guatemala City), Khrystyne (from Long Beach, by way of Phnom Penh, I think), and Moe (from West L.A., she said). Many of the bright-eyed dreamers who arrive at LAX so full of hope never actually leave the place.

The deeper drama of any airport is that it features a kind of interaction almost unique in our lives, wherein many of us do not know whom we are going to meet or whom others are going to meet in us. You see people standing at the barriers outside the Customs area looking into their pasts, while wide-open newcomers drift out, searching for their futures. Lovers do not know if they will see the same person who kissed them good-bye a month ago; grandparents wonder what the baby they last saw twenty years ago will look like now.

In L.A. all of this has an added charge, because unlike many cities, it is not a hub but a terminus: a place where people come to arrive. Thus many of the meetings you witness are between the haves and the hope-to-haves, between those who are affecting a new ease in their new home and those who are here in search of that ease. Both parties, especially if they are un-American by birth, are eager to stress their Americanness or their fitness for America; and both, as they look at each other's made-up self, see themselves either before or after a stay in L.A.'s theater of transformation. And so they stream in, wearing running shoes or cowboy hats or 49ers jackets, anxious to make a good first impression; and the people who wait for them, under a halfhearted mural of Desertland, are often American enough not to try to look the part. Juan and Esperanza both have ponytails now, and Kimmie is wearing a Harley-Davidson cap backwards and necking with a Japanese guy; the uncle from Delhi arrives to find that Rajiv not only has grown darker but has lost weight, so that he looks more like a peasant from back home than ever.

And the newcomers pour in in astonishing numbers. A typical Sunday evening, in a single hour, sees flights arriving from England, Taiwan, the Philippines, Indonesia, Mexico, Austria, Germany, Spain, Costa Rica, and

Guatemala; and each new group colors and transforms the airport: an explosion of tropical shades from Hawaiian Air, a rash of blue blazers and white shirts around the early flight from Tokyo. Red-haired Thais bearing pirated Schwarzenegger videos, lonely Africans in Aerial Assault sneakers, farmers from changeless Confucian cultures peering into the smiles of a Prozac city, children whose parents can't pronounce their names. Many of them are returning, like Odysseus, with the spoils of war: young brides from Luzon, business cards from Shanghai, boxes of macadamia nuts from Oahu. And for many of them the whole wild carnival will feature sights they have never seen before: Japanese look anxiously at the first El Salvadorans they've ever seen, and El Salvadorans ogle sleek girls from Bangkok in thigh-high boots. All of them, moreover, may not be pleased to realize that the America they've dreamed of is, in fact, a land of tacos and pita and pad thai—full, indeed, of the very Third World cultures that other Third Worlders look down upon.

One day over lunch I asked my Ethiopian waitress about her life here. She liked it well enough, she said, but still she missed her home. And yet, she added, she couldn't go back. "Why not?" I asked, still smiling. "Because they killed my family," she said. "Two years back. They killed my father. They killed my brother." "They," I realized, referred to the Tigreans—many of them working just down the corridor in other parts of the hotel. So, too, Tibetans who have finally managed to flee their Chinese-occupied homeland arrive at LAX to find Chinese faces everywhere; those who fled the Sandinistas find themselves standing next to Sandinistas fleeing their successors. And all these people from ancient cultures find themselves in a country as amnesiac as the morning, where World War II is just a rumor and the Gulf War a distant memory. Their pasts are escaped, yes, but by the same token they are unlikely to be honored.

It is dangerously tempting to start formulating socioeconomic principles in the midst of LAX: people from rich countries (Germany and Japan, say) travel light, if only because they are sure that they can return any time; those from poor countries come with their whole lives in cardboard boxes imperfectly tied with string. People from poor countries are often met by huge crowds—for them each arrival is a special occasion—and stagger through customs with string bags and Gold Digger apple crates, their addresses handwritten on them in pencil; the Okinawan honeymooners, by contrast, in the color-coordinated outfits they will change every day, somehow have packed all their needs into a tiny case.

If airports have some of the excitement of bars, because so many people are composing (and decomposing) selves there, they also have some of the sadness of bars, the poignancy of people sitting unclaimed while everyone around them has paired off. A pretty girl dressed in next to nothing sits alone in an empty Baggage Claim area, waiting for a date who never comes; a Vietnamese man, lost, tells an official that he has friends in Orange County who can help him, but when the friends are contacted, they say they know no one from Vietnam. I hear of a woman who got off and asked for "San Mateo," only to learn that she was meant to disembark in San Francisco; and a woman from Nigeria who came out expecting to see her husband in Monroe, Louisiana, only to learn that someone in Lagos had mistaken "La." on her itinerary for "L.A."

The greetings I saw in the Arrivals area were much more tentative than I had expected, less passionate—as ritualized in their way as the kisses placed on Bob Barker's[4] cheek—and much of that may be because so many people are meeting strangers, even if they are meeting people they once knew. Places like LAX—places like L.A.—perpetuate the sense that everyone is a stranger in our new floating world. I spent one afternoon in the airport with a Californian blonde, and I saw her complimented on her English by a sweet Korean woman and asked by an Iranian if she was Indian. Airports have some of the unsteady brashness of singles bars, where no one knows quite what is expected of them. "Mike, is that you?" "Oh, I didn't recognize you." "I'd have known you anywhere." "It's so kind of you to come and pick me up." And already at a loss, a young Japanese girl and a broad, lonely-looking man head off toward the parking lot, not knowing, in any sense, who is going to be in the driver's seat.

The driving takes place, of course, in what many of the newcomers, 35 primed by video screenings of *L.A. Law* and *Speed*, regard as the ultimate heart of darkness, a place at least as forbidding and dangerous as Africa must have seemed to the Victorians. They have heard about how America is the murder capital of the world; they have seen Rodney King get pummeled by L.A.'s finest; they know of the city as the site of drive-by shootings and freeway snipers, of riots and celebrity murders. The "homeless" and the "tempest-tost" that the Statue of Liberty invites are arriving, increasingly, in a city that is itself famous for its homeless population and its fires, floods, and earthquakes.

In that context, the ideal symbol of LAX is, perhaps, the great object that for thirty years has been the distinctive image of the place: the ugly white quadruped that sits in the middle of the airport like a beached white whale or a jet-age beetle, featuring a 360-degree circular restaurant that does not revolve and an observation deck from which the main view is of twenty-three thousand parking places. The Theme Building, at 201 World Way, is a sad image of a future that never arrived, a monument to Kennedy-era idealism and the thrusting modernity of the American empire when it was in its prime; it now has the poignancy of an abandoned present with its price tag stuck to it. When you go there (and almost nobody does) you are greeted by photos of Saturn's rings and Jupiter and its moons, by a plaque laid down by L.B.J. and a whole set of symbols from the time when NASA was shooting for the heavens. Now the "landmark" building, with its "gourmet-type restaurant," looks like a relic from a time long past, when it must have looked like the face of the future.

---

[4]*Barker*: long-time host of Miss America pageants. [Eds.]

Upstairs, a few desperately merry waiters are serving nonalcoholic drinks and cheeseburgers to sallow diners who look as if they've arrived at the end of the world; on the tarmac outside, speedbirds inch ahead like cars in a traffic jam. "Hello All the New People of LAX—Welcome," says the graffiti on the elevator.

The Theme Restaurant comes to us from an era when L.A. was leading the world. Nowadays, of course, L.A. is being formed and reformed and led by the world around it. And as I got ready to leave LAX, I could not help but feel that the Theme Building stands, more and more, for a city left behind by our accelerating planet. LAX, I was coming to realize, was a good deal scruffier than the airports even of Bangkok or Jakarta, more chaotic, more suggestive of Third World lawlessness. And the city around it is no more golden than Seoul, no more sunny than Taipei, and no more laid-back than Moscow. Beverly Hills, after all, is largely speaking Farsi[5] now. Hollywood Boulevard is sleazier than 42nd Street. And Malibu is falling into the sea.

Yet just as I was about to give up on L.A. as yesterday's piece of modernity, I got on the shuttle bus that moves between the terminals in a never-ending loop. The seats next to me were taken by two rough-looking dudes from nearby South Central, who were riding the free buses and helping people on and off with their cases (acting, I presumed, on the safe assumption that the Japanese, say, new to the country and bewildered, had been warned beforehand to tip often and handsomely for every service they received). In between terminals, as a terrified-looking Miss Kudo and her friend guarded their luggage, en route from Nagoya to Las Vegas, the two gold-plated sharks talked about the Raiders' last game and the Lakers' next season. Then one of them, without warning, announced, "The bottom line is the spirit is with you. When you work out, you chill out and, like, you meditate in your spirit. You know what I mean? Meditation is recreation. Learn math, follow your path. That's all I do, man, that's all I live for: learnin' about God, learnin' about Jesus. I am *possessed* by that spirit. You know, I used to have all these problems, with the flute and all, but when I heard about God, I learned about the body, the mind, and the flesh. People forget, they don't know, that the Bible isn't talkin' about the flesh, it's talkin' about the spirit. And I was reborn again in the spirit."

His friend nodded. "When you recreate, you meditate. Recreation is a   40 spiritually uplifting experience."

"Yeah. When you do that, you allow the spirit to breathe."

"Because you're gettin' into the physical world. You're lettin' the spirit flow. You're helpin' the secretion of the endorphins in the brain."

Nearby, the Soldiers of the Cross of Christ Church stood by the escalators, taking donations, and a man in a dog collar approached another stranger.

---

[5]*Farsi:* Persian, the language of Iran. [Eds.]

I watched the hustlers allowing the spirit to breathe, I heard the Hare Krishna devotees plying their wares. I spotted some Farrakhan flunkies collecting a dollar for a copy of their newspaper, *The Final Call*—redemption and corruption all around us in the air—and I thought: welcome to America, Miss Kudo, welcome to L.A.

QUESTIONS

1. What do you think Iyer means by his main title? By his subtitle? In what sense is he writing about the collision of worlds rather than a single world? In what respect is he writing about the future rather than the present?
2. Notice how strangely this piece begins, with a vague pronoun (*They*) and an equally vague verb (*come out*). Who is Iyer referring to? Where are "they" coming from? Why do you think he writes about "they" and "them" at such length without ever explicitly identifying them in detail?
3. In paragraph 12, Iyer says that he spent a week at the Los Angeles International Airport. What evidence can you find in the essay of his having carried out such a lengthy and in-depth observation of the airport? Why do you suppose he doesn't offer a day-by-day, increasingly more in-depth report of his airport observations? How would you describe or classify the organization of his piece?
4. Though this piece is about a specific place, Iyer never describes the airport building, or its physical layout, or its surrounding landscape and runways. What aspects of the place or its inhabitants does he describe in sufficient detail for you to visualize them in your mind's eye?
5. Aside from the physical details of the airport, what other aspects of it is Iyer concerned with in this piece? In other words, what are his purposes for writing this detailed report about LAX?
6. Spend a couple of days at an airport, railroad station, or bus terminal near your hometown or college. Then write an essay reporting what you have discovered about that place, the people you observed there, the worlds that seem to collide in that place, and the significance for you of those collisions.
7. Consider your college campus as a place "where worlds collide." Then write an essay reporting and interpreting some of the collisions you've observed there.

MAKING CONNECTIONS

Compare Iyer's method of observing and reporting human behavior at the airport with Farley Mowat's or Jane van Lawick-Goodall's method of observing and reporting animal behavior in the wild (pp. 256 and 260).

Sciences and Technologies

WOLF NOTES

Barry Lopez

Barry Lopez (b. 1945) attended the University of Notre Dame, where he pursued graduate studies in folklore. In one of his earliest books, Giving Birth to Thunder, Sleeping with His Daughter: Coyote Builds North America *(1978), he drew on this background to retell a selection of native American trickster stories. Much of his subsequent work, whether fiction or nonfiction, has focused on the environment and natural history; it includes* Of Wolves and Men *(1978),* Arctic Dreams: Imagination and Desire in a Northern Landscape *(1986), and* Field Notes: The Grace Note of the Canyon Wren *(1994). His most recent book is the memoir* About This Life *(1998). About* Of Wolves and Men, *from which the following selection is taken, Lopez has said, "I realized that if I focused on this one animal, I might be able to say something sharp and clear" about animal and human relationships.*

Imagine a wolf moving through the northern woods. The movement, over a trail he has traversed many times before, is distinctive, unlike that of a cougar or a bear, yet he appears, if you are watching, sometimes catlike or bearlike. It is purposeful, deliberate movement. Occasionally the rhythm is broken by the wolf's pause to inspect a scent mark, or a move off the trail to paw among stones where a year before he had cached meat.

The movement down the trail would seem relentless if it did not appear so effortless. The wolf's body, from neck to hips, appears to float over the long, almost spindly legs and the flicker of wrists, a bicycling drift through the trees, reminiscent of the movement of water or of shadows.

The wolf is three years old. A male. He is of the subspecies *occidentalis*, and the trees he is moving among are spruce and subalpine fir on the eastern slope of the Rockies in northern Canada. He is light gray; that is, there are more blond and white hairs mixed with gray in the saddle of fur that covers his shoulders and extends down his spine than there are black and brown. But there are silver and even red hairs mixed in, too.

It is early September, an easy time of year, and he has not seen the other wolves in his pack for three or four days. He has heard no howls, but he knows the others are about, in ones and twos like himself. It is not a time of year for much howling. It is an easy time. The weather is pleasant. Moose are fat. Suddenly the wolf stops in mid-stride. A moment, then his feet slowly come alongside each other. He is staring into the grass. His ears are rammed forward, stiff. His back arches and he rears up and pounces like a cat. A deer mouse is pinned between his forepaws. Eaten. The wolf drifts on. He approaches a trail crossing, an undistinguished crossroads. His movement is now slower and he sniffs the air as though aware of a possibility for scents. He sniffs a scent post, a scrawny blueberry bush in use for years, and goes on.

The wolf weighs ninety-four pounds and stands thirty inches at the shoulder. His feet are enormous, leaving prints in the mud along a creek (where he pauses to hunt crayfish but not with much interest) more than five inches long by just over four wide. He has two fractured ribs, broken by a moose a year before. They are healed now, but a sharp eye would notice the irregularity. The skin on his right hip is scarred, from a fight with another wolf in a neighboring pack when he was a yearling. He has not had anything but a few mice and a piece of arctic char[1] in three days, but he is not hungry. He is traveling. The char was a day old, left on rocks along the river by bears.

The wolf is tied by subtle threads to the woods he moves through. His fur carries seeds that will fall off, effectively dispersed, along the trail some miles from where they first caught in his fur. And miles distant is a raven perched on the ribs of a caribou the wolf helped kill ten days ago, pecking like a chicken at the decaying scraps of meat. A smart snowshoe hare that eluded the wolf and left him exhausted when he was a pup has been dead a year now, food for an owl. The den in which he was born one April evening was home to porcupines last winter.

It is now late in the afternoon. The wolf has stopped traveling, has lain down to sleep on cool earth beneath a rock outcropping. Mosquitoes rest on his ears. His ears flicker. He begins to waken. He rolls on his back and lies motionless with his front legs pointed toward the sky but folded like wilted flowers, his back legs splayed, and his nose and tail curved toward each other on one side of his body. After a few moments he flops on his side, rises, stretches, and moves a few feet to inspect—minutely, delicately—a crevice in the rock outcropping and finds or doesn't find what draws him there. And then he ascends the rock face, bounding and balancing momentarily before bounding again, appearing slightly unsure of the

5

---

[1]*arctic char*: a fish. [Eds.]

process—but committed. A few minutes later he bolts suddenly into the woods, achieving full speed, almost forty miles per hour, for forty or fifty yards before he begins to skid, to lunge at the lodgepole pine cone. He trots away with it, his head erect, tail erect, his hips slightly to one side and out of line with his shoulders, as though hindquarters were impatient with forequarters, the cone inert in his mouth. He carries it for a hundred feet before dropping it by the trail. He sniffs it. He goes on.

The underfur next to his skin has begun to thicken with the coming of fall. In the months to follow it will become so dense between his shoulders it will be almost impossible to work a finger down to his skin. In seven months he will weigh less: eighty-nine pounds. He will have tried unsuccessfully to mate with another wolf in the pack. He will have helped kill four moose and thirteen caribou. He will have fallen through ice into a creek at twenty-two below zero but not frozen. He will have fought with other wolves.

He moves along now at the edge of a clearing. The wind coming down-valley surrounds him with a river of odors, as if he were a migrating salmon. He can smell ptarmigan[2] and deer droppings. He can smell willow and spruce and the fading sweetness of fireweed. Above, he sees a hawk circling, and farther south, lower on the horizon, a flock of sharp-tailed sparrows going east. He senses through his pads with each step the dryness of the moss beneath his feet, and the ridges of old tracks, some his own. He hears the sound his feet make. He hears the occasional movement of deer mice and voles. Summer food.

Toward dusk he is standing by a creek, lapping the cool water, when a   10
wolf howls—a long wail that quickly reaches pitch and then tapers, with several harmonics, long moments to a tremolo. He recognizes his sister. He waits a few moments, then, throwing his head back and closing his eyes, he howls. The howl is shorter and it changes pitch twice in the beginning, very quickly. There is no answer.

The female is a mile away and she trots off obliquely through the trees. The other wolf stands listening, laps water again, then he too departs, moving quickly, quietly through the trees, away from the trail he had been on. In a few minutes the two wolves meet. They approach each other briskly, almost formally, tails erect and moving somewhat as deer move. When they come together they make high squeaking noises and encircle each other, rubbing and pushing, poking their noses into each other's neck fur, backing away to stretch, chasing each other for a few steps, then standing quietly together, one putting a head over the other's back. And then they are gone, down a vague trail, the female first. After a few hundred yards they begin, simultaneously, to wag their tails.

In the days to follow, they will meet another wolf from the pack, a second female, younger by a year, and the three of them will kill a caribou. They

---

[2]*ptarmigan:* a bird, a kind of grouse. [Eds.]

will travel together ten or twenty miles a day, through the country where they live, eating and sleeping, birthing, playing with sticks, chasing ravens, growing old, barking at bears, scent-marking trails, killing moose, and staring at the way water in a creek breaks around their legs and flows on.

QUESTIONS

1. Most of us know dogs better than wolves, and we recognize in Lopez's wolf some dog-like behavior. What seems most doglike to you?
2. Which details in this brief portrait of a wolf work best to convince you that Lopez knows his subject?
3. Lopez works back and forth from the general to the specific. At the beginning, middle, and end, he attempts a general idea of "wolf" that he supports with the intervening descriptions of a wolf. Note the sixth paragraph. What does that add to the overall picture?
4. Between the eighth and the final paragraphs, one may find a hint of contradiction. What would be a possible explanation of the discrepancy?

MAKING CONNECTIONS

1. Read Theodore R. Sizer's "What High School Is" (p. 348). To what extent is Mark another wolf under examination?
2. Taking cues from Sizer, Farley Mowat (p. 256), Jane van Lawick-Goodall (p. 260), or even Monica M. Moore's "Nonverbal Courtship Patterns in Women" (p. 465), report on your own close observation of some animal or person's behavior.

ON TRANSFORMATION

Vladimir Nabokov

Vladimir Nabokov (1899–1977) was born in St. Petersburg, Russia, and after the Russian Revolution in 1917 moved to England to attend Cambridge University. In 1940 he immigrated to the United States, and he became a U.S. citizen in 1945. A renowned novelist, poet, and critic, Nabokov also taught literature at Stanford, Wellesley, Cornell, and Harvard (many of his lectures were published posthumously). Considered one of the most important writers of the twentieth century, in his fiction he delighted in complex wordplay, obscure allusions, and eccentric—even grotesque—characters. Among his many works (it is estimated that they would fill forty volumes) are the novels Lolita *(1955) and* Pale Fire *(1962), the memoir* Speak, Memory *(1966), a translation of Pushkin's* Eugene Onegin *(1964), and* Ada *(1969). As the following essay suggests, Nabokov was also a world-famous expert on lepidoptera (butterflies, moths, and the like).*

Transformation . . . Transformation is a marvelous thing . . . I am thinking especially of the transformation of butterflies. Though wonderful to watch, transformation from larva[1] to pupa[2] or from pupa to butterfly is not a particularly pleasant process for the subject involved. There comes for every caterpillar a difficult moment when he begins to feel pervaded by an odd sense of discomfort. It is a tight feeling—here about the neck and elsewhere, and then an unbearable itch. Of course he has moulted[3] a few times before, but *that* is nothing in comparison to the tickle and urge that he feels now. He must shed that tight dry skin, or die. As you have guessed under that skin, the armor of a pupa—and how uncomfortable to wear one's skin over one's armor—is already forming: I am especially concerned at the moment with those butterflies that have carved golden pupa, called also chrysalis,[4] which hang from some surface in the open air.

Well, the caterpillar must do something about that horrible feeling. He walks about looking for a suitable place. He finds it. He crawls up a wall

---

[1] *larva:* the wormlike, wingless form, often called "caterpillar," that is the first stage of a butterfly. [Eds.]

[2] *pupa:* the second stage of the butterfly's transformation, or metamorphosis, taking place within a protective cocoon. [Eds.]

[3] *moult* (or *molt*): to shed an outer covering that is replaced by new growth. [Eds.]

[4] *chrysalis:* the pupa of a butterfly enclosed within its cocoon. [Eds.]

or a tree-trunk. He makes for himself a little pad of silk on the underside of that perch. He hangs himself by the tip of his tail or last legs, from the silk patch, so as to dangle head downwards in the position of an inverted question-mark, and there *is* a *question*—how to get rid now of his skin. One wriggle, another wriggle—and zip the skin bursts down the back, and he gradually gets out of it working with shoulders and hips like a person getting out of a sausage dress. Then comes the most critical moment.— You understand that we are hanging head down by our last pair of legs, and the problem now is to shed the whole skin—even the skin of those last legs by which we hang—but how to accomplish this without falling?

So what does he do, this courageous and stubborn little animal who is already partly disrobed. Very carefully he starts working out his hind legs, dislodging them from the patch of silk from which he is dangling, head down—and then with an admirable twist and jerk he sort of jumps *off* the silk pad, sheds the last shred of hose, and immediately, in the process of the same jerk-and-twist-jump he attaches himself anew by means of a hook that was under the shed skin on the tip of his body. Now all the skin has come off, thank God, and the bared surface, now hard and glistening, is the pupa, a swathed-baby like thing hanging from that twig—a very beautiful chrysalis with golden knobs and plate-armor wingcases. This pupal stage lasts from a few days to a few years. I remember as a boy keeping a hawkmoth's pupa in a box for something like seven years, so that I actually finished high school while the thing was asleep—and then finally it hatched—unfortunately it happened during a journey on the train,—a nice case of misjudgement after all those years. But to come back to our butterfly pupa.

After say two or three weeks something begins to happen. The pupa hangs quite motionless, but you notice one day that through the wingcases, which are many times smaller than the wings of the future perfect insect— you notice that through the horn-like texture of each wingcase you can see in miniature the pattern of the future wing, the lovely flush of the ground-color, a dark margin, a rudimentary eyespot. Another day or two—and the final transformation occurs. The pupa splits as the caterpillar had split—it is really a last glorified moult, and the butterfly creeps out—and in its turn hangs down from the twig to dry. She is not handsome at first. She is very damp and bedraggled. But those limp implements of hers that she has disengaged, gradually dry, distend, the veins branch and harden— and in twenty minutes or so she is ready to fly. You have noticed that the caterpillar is a *he,* the pupa an *it,* and the butterfly a *she.* You will ask— what is the feeling of hatching? Oh, no doubt, there is a rush of panic to the head, a thrill of breathless and strange sensation, but then the eyes see, in a flow of sunshine, the butterfly sees the world, the large and awful face of the gaping entomologist.[5]

---

[5]*entomologist:* someone who studies insects. [Eds.]

QUESTIONS

1. "A difficult moment," "an odd sense of discomfort," "a tight feeling" — why do you think Nabokov relies on such casual, human terms to describe what happens to the emerging butterfly? Make an extended list of the terms he uses in this way.
2. At the very end, the butterfly is set against, and in distinct contrast to, the human scientist, the entomologist. But that is the first we have heard of this figure. Why is his or her face "awful" with the expression "gaping"?

MAKING CONNECTIONS

1. Read Richard Selzer's "The Discus Thrower" (p. 289). Compare the transformation of Selzer's patient to the metamorphosis of the butterfly.
2. Write your own report of someone or something that changes radically.

THE DISCUS THROWER

Richard Selzer

*Richard Selzer (b. 1928) is a surgeon who has written widely, pub-
lishing articles in popular magazines as well as occasional short
fiction. (See earlier biographical note, page 167, for additional details.) In the essay reprinted here, which first appeared in* Harper's
*magazine in 1977, Selzer reports on the visits he made to one of
his patients.*

I spy on my patients. Ought not a doctor to observe his patients by any
means and from any stance, that he might the more fully assemble evidence? So I stand in the doorways of hospital rooms and gaze. Oh, it is not
all that furtive an act. Those in bed need only look up to discover me. But
they never do.

From the doorway of Room 542 the man in the bed seems deeply
tanned. Blue eyes and close-cropped white hair give him the appearance of
vigor and good health. But I know that his skin is not brown from the sun.
It is rusted, rather, in the last stage of containing the vile repose within.
And the blue eyes are frosted, looking inward like the windows of a snowbound cottage. This man is blind. This man is also legless — the right leg
missing from midthigh down, the left from just below the knee. It gives
him the look of a bonsai, roots and branches pruned into the dwarfed facsimile of a great tree.

Propped on pillows, he cups his right thigh in both hands. Now and
then he shakes his head as though acknowledging the intensity of his suffering. In all of this he makes no sound. Is he mute as well as blind?

The room in which he dwells is empty of all possessions — no get-well
cards, small, private caches of food, day-old flowers, slippers, all the usual
kickshaws of the sickroom. There is only the bed, a chair, a nightstand,
and a tray on wheels that can be swung across his lap for meals.

"What time is it?" he asks.   5

"Three o'clock."

"Morning or afternoon?"

"Afternoon."

He is silent. There is nothing else he wants to know.

"How are you?" I say.   10

"Who is it?" he asks.

"It's the doctor. How do you feel?"

He does not answer right away.

"Feel?" he says.

"I hope you feel better," I say.   15

I press the button at the side of the bed.

"Down you go," I say.

"Yes, down," he says.

He falls back upon the bed awkwardly. His stumps, unweighted by legs and feet, rise in the air, presenting themselves. I unwrap the bandages from the stumps, and begin to cut away the black scabs and the dead, glazed fat with scissors and forceps. A shard of white bone comes loose. I pick it away. I wash the wounds with disinfectant and redress the stumps. All this while, he does not speak. What is he thinking behind those lids that do not blink? Is he remembering a time when he was whole? Does he dream of feet? Of when his body was not a rotting log?

He lies solid and inert. In spite of everything, he remains impressive, as   20
though he were a sailor standing athwart a slanting deck.

"Anything more I can do for you?" I ask.

For a long moment he is silent.

"Yes," he says at last and without the least irony. "You can bring me a pair of shoes."

In the corridor, the head nurse is waiting for me.

"We have to do something about him," she says. "Every morning he   25
orders scrambled eggs for breakfast, and, instead of eating them, he picks up the plate and throws it against the wall."

"Throws his plate?"

"Nasty. That's what he is. No wonder his family doesn't come to visit. They probably can't stand him any more than we can."

She is waiting for me to do something.

"Well?"

"We'll see," I say.   30

The next morning I am waiting in the corridor when the kitchen delivers his breakfast. I watch the aide place the tray on the stand and swing it across his lap. She presses the button to raise the head of the bed. Then she leaves.

In time the man reaches to find the rim of the tray, then on to find the dome of the covered dish. He lifts off the cover and places it on the stand. He fingers across the plate until he probes the eggs. He lifts the plate in both hands, sets it on the palm of his right hand, centers it, balances it. He hefts it up and down slightly, getting the feel of it. Abruptly, he draws back his right arm as far as he can.

There is the crack of the plate breaking against the wall at the foot of his bed and the small wet sound of the scrambled eggs dropping to the floor.

And then he laughs. It is a sound you have never heard. It is something new under the sun. It could cure cancer.

Out in the corridor, the eyes of the head nurse narrow.   35

"Laughed, did he?"

She writes something down on her clipboard.

A second aide arrives, brings a second breakfast tray, puts it on the nightstand, out of his reach. She looks over at me shaking her head and making her mouth go. I see that we are to be accomplices.

"I've got to feed you," she says to the man.

"Oh, no you don't," the man says.   40

"Oh, yes I do," the aide says, "after the way you just did. Nurse says so."

"Get me my shoes," the man says.

"Here's oatmeal," the aide says. "Open." And she touches the spoon to his lower lip.

"I ordered scrambled eggs," says the man.

"That's right," the aide says.   45

I step forward.

"Is there anything I can do?" I say.

"Who are you?" the man asks.

In the evening I go once more to that ward to make my rounds. The head nurse reports to me that Room 542 is deceased. She has discovered this quite by accident, she says. No, there had been no sound. Nothing. It's a blessing, she says.

I go into his room, a spy looking for secrets. He is still there in his bed.   50
His face is relaxed, grave, dignified. After a while, I turn to leave. My gaze sweeps the wall at the foot of the bed, and I see the place where it has been repeatedly washed, where the wall looks very clean and very white.

QUESTIONS

1. Why does Selzer say, "I spy on my patients" (paragraph 1)? Don't doctors usually look in on their patients? What effect does Selzer hope to achieve by starting with such a statement?

2. Selzer uses the present tense throughout this piece. Would the past tense be just as effective? Explain your answer.

3. Selzer writes in the first person. Why might he have decided to make himself prominent in the report in this way? How would his report have come across if it had been written in the third person rather than the first person?

4. How would you describe this doctor's attitude toward his patient? How would you describe the nurse's attitude toward the patient? How does the narrator manage to characterize himself in one way and the nurse in another?

5. Is the title, "The Discus Thrower," appropriate for this piece? In a slightly revised version, the title was changed to "Four Appointments with the Discus Thrower." Is this a better title?

6. What do you think Selzer's purpose was in writing this essay? Did he simply wish to shock us, or is there a message in this piece for the medical profession or for those of us who fear illness and death?

7. The essay reports on four visits to the patient by Selzer. Write a shorter version reporting on two or more visits by the head nurse. How would she react to the patient's request for shoes? How might her point of view explain some of her reactions?

8. For many of us, knowledge of hospitals is limited, perhaps to television shows in which the hospital functions as a backdrop for the romances of its staff. Write a short essay in which you present your conception of what a hospital is and in which you consider how Selzer's essay either made you revise that conception or reaffirmed what you know through experience.

MAKING CONNECTIONS

Selzer and Roy C. Selby Jr. (p. 295) write of human subjects. Farley Mowat (p. 256) and Jane van Lawick-Goodall (p. 260) write of animals. Does this choice of subject seem to affect the distance the writer maintains, achieves, or overcomes in offering his or her report? Do you find any common denominators here? How do you account for them?

SPRING AND ALL

William Carlos Williams

William Carlos Williams (1883–1963) was born in Rutherford, New Jersey, where he lived most of his life. He received his M.D. from the University of Pennsylvania, where he studied pediatrics, and he maintained a private practice as a physician for over forty years. Williams began publishing his poetry when he was in his twenties, but his first collection to receive serious notice was Spring and All *(1923). Other volumes include* Paterson *(five books, 1946–1958);* Pictures from Breughel and Other Poems *(1962), which won the Pulitzer Prize for poetry; and many volumes of collected works. Williams also published novels and short stories. Considered one of the foremost American poets of the twentieth century, he was a conscious innovator whose goal was to create a distinctively American poetic voice, based on the rhythms of everyday speech and grounded in a highly flexible metrical line.*

By the road to the contagious hospital
under the surge of the blue
mottled clouds driven from the
northeast—a cold wind. Beyond, the
waste of broad, muddy fields   5
brown with dried weeds, standing and fallen

patches of standing water
the scattering of tall trees

All along the road the reddish
purplish, forked, upstanding, twiggy   10
stuff of bushes and small trees
with dead, brown leaves under them
leafless vines—

Lifeless in appearance, sluggish
dazed spring approaches—   15

They enter the new world naked,
cold, uncertain of all
save that they enter. All about them
the cold, familiar wind—

Now the grass, tomorrow   20
the stiff curl of wildcarrot leaf

One by one objects are defined—
It quickens: clarity, outline of leaf

But now the stark dignity of
entrance—Still, the profound change   25
has come upon them: rooted, they
grip down and begin to awaken

QUESTIONS

1. This poem displays an unconventional sense of punctuation. Note where sentences seem to end with periods, or with dashes, or with nothing at all. What is the pattern or system used?
2. Note the main verbs and list them. Verbs are generally considered necessary to a complete sentence. Why does Williams wait so long to provide the first one?
3. What happens before the first of those verbs appears?
4. What change comes immediately after it?
5. Describe the contrast in diction between the last part of the poem and the first, noting late words like "clarity" and "dignity."

MAKING CONNECTIONS

Compare Williams' poem with Pico Iyer's "Where Worlds Collide" (p. 270), especially Iyer's opening passage. How does Iyer, somewhat like Williams, draw back and make order out of what appear to be random details of his initial observations? To what, if anything, does the airport give birth?

A DELICATE OPERATION

Roy C. Selby Jr.

Roy C. Selby Jr. (b. 1930) graduated from Louisiana State University and the University of Arkansas Medical School, where he specialized in neurology and neurosurgery. He is the author of numerous professional articles on neurosurgery and is now retired from practice. "A Delicate Operation," which first appeared in Harper's *magazine in 1975, reports for a more general audience the details of a difficult brain operation.*

In the autumn of 1973 a woman in her early fifties noticed, upon closing one eye while reading, that she was unable to see clearly. Her eyesight grew slowly worse. Changing her eyeglasses did not help. She saw an ophthalmologist, who found that her vision was seriously impaired in both eyes. She then saw a neurologist, who confirmed the finding and obtained X rays of the skull and an EMI scan—a photograph of the patient's head. The latter revealed a tumor growing between the optic nerves at the base of the brain. The woman was admitted to the hospital by a neurosurgeon.

Further diagnosis, based on angiography, a detailed X-ray study of the circulatory system, showed the tumor to be about two inches in diameter and supplied by many small blood vessels. It rested beneath the brain, just above the pituitary gland, stretching the optic nerves to either side and intimately close to the major blood vessels supplying the brain. Removing it would pose many technical problems. Probably benign and slow-growing, it may have been present for several years. If left alone it would continue to grow and produce blindness and might become impossible to remove completely. Removing it, however, might not improve the patient's vision and could make it worse. A major blood vessel could be damaged, causing a stroke. Damage to the undersurface of the brain could cause impairment of memory and changes in mood and personality. The hypothalamus, a most important structure of the brain, could be injured, causing coma, high fever, bleeding from the stomach, and death.

The neurosurgeon met with the patient and her husband and discussed the various possibilities. The common decision was to operate.

The patient's hair was shampooed for two nights before surgery. She was given a cortisonelike drug to reduce the risk of damage to the brain during surgery. Five units of blood were cross-matched, as a contingency against hemorrhage. At 1:00 P.M. the operation began. After the patient was anesthetized her hair was completely clipped and shaved from the scalp. Her head was prepped with an organic iodine solution for ten minutes. Drapes were placed over her, leaving exposed only the forehead and crown of the skull. All the routine instruments were brought up—the electrocautery used to coagulate areas of bleeding, bipolar coagulation forceps to arrest bleeding from individual blood vessels without damaging adjacent tissues, and small suction tubes to remove blood and cerebrospinal fluid from the head, thus giving the surgeon a better view of the tumor and surrounding areas.

A curved incision was made behind the hairline so it would be con-   5
cealed when the hair grew back. It extended almost from ear to ear. Plastic clips were applied to the cut edges of the scalp to arrest bleeding. The scalp was folded back to the level of the eyebrows. Incisions were made in the muscle of the right temple, and three sets of holes were drilled near the temple and the top of the head because the tumor had to be approached from directly in front. The drill, powered by nitrogen, was replaced with a fluted steel blade, and the holes were connected. The incised piece of skull was pried loose and held out of the way by a large sponge.

Beneath the bone is a yellowish leatherlike membrane, the dura, that surrounds the brain. Down the middle of the head the dura carries a large vein, but in the area near the nose the vein is small. At that point the vein and dura were cut, and clips made of tantalum, a hard metal, were applied to arrest and prevent bleeding. Sutures were put into the dura and tied to the scalp to keep the dura open and retracted. A malleable silver retractor, resembling the blade of a butter knife, was inserted between the brain and skull. The anesthesiologist began to administer a drug to relax the brain by removing some of its water, making it easier for the surgeon to manipulate the retractor, hold the brain back, and see the tumor. The nerve tracts for smell were cut on both sides to provide additional room. The tumor was seen approximately two-and-one-half inches behind the base of the nose. It was pink in color. On touching it, it proved to be very fibrous and tough. A special retractor was attached to the skull, enabling the other retractor blades to be held automatically and freeing the surgeon's hands. With further displacement of the frontal lobes of the brain, the tumor could be seen better, but no normal structures—the carotid arteries, their branches, and the optic nerves—were visible. The tumor obscured them.

A surgical microscope was placed above the wound. The surgeon had selected the lenses and focal length prior to the operation. Looking through the microscope, he could see some of the small vessels supplying the tumor and he coagulated them. He incised the tumor to attempt to remove its core and thus collapse it, but the substance of the tumor was too firm to be removed in this fashion. He then began to slowly dissect the tumor from the adjacent brain tissue and from where he believed the normal structures to be.

Using small squares of cotton, he began to separate the tumor from very loose fibrous bands connecting it to the brain and to the right side of the part of the skull where the pituitary gland lies. The right optic nerve and carotid artery came into view, both displaced considerably to the right. The optic nerve had a normal appearance. He protected these structures with cotton compresses placed between them and the tumor. He began to raise the tumor from the skull and slowly to reach the point of its origin and attachment—just in front of the pituitary gland and medial to the left optic nerve, which still could not be seen. The small blood vessels entering the tumor were cauterized. The upper portion of the tumor was gradually separated from the brain, and the branches of the carotid arteries and the branches to the tumor were coagulated. The tumor was slowly and gently lifted from its bed, and for the first time the left carotid artery and optic nerve could be seen. Part of the tumor adhered to this nerve. The bulk of the tumor was amputated, leaving a small bit attached to the nerve. Very slowly and carefully the tumor fragment was resected.

The tumor now removed, a most impressive sight came into view—the pituitary gland and its stalk of attachment to the hypothalamus, the hypothalamus itself, and the brainstem, which conveys nerve impulses between the body and the brain. As far as could be determined, no damage had been done to these structures or other vital centers, but the left optic nerve, from chronic pressure of the tumor, appeared gray and thin. Probably it would not completely recover its function.

After making certain there was no bleeding, the surgeon closed the   10
wounds and placed wire mesh over the holes in the skull to prevent dimpling of the scalp over the points that had been drilled. A gauze dressing was applied to the patient's head. She was awakened and sent to the recovery room.

Even with the microscope, damage might still have occurred to the cerebral cortex and hypothalamus. It would require at least a day to be reasonably certain there was none, and about seventy-two hours to monitor for the major postoperative dangers—swelling of the brain and blood clots forming over the surface of the brain. The surgeon explained this to the patient's husband, and both of them waited anxiously. The operation had required seven hours. A glass of orange juice had given the surgeon some additional energy during the closure of the wound. Though exhausted, he could not fall asleep until after two in the morning, momentarily expecting a call from the nurse in the intensive care unit announcing deterioration of the patient's condition.

At 8:00 A.M. the surgeon saw the patient in the intensive care unit. She was alert, oriented, and showed no sign of additional damage to the optic nerves or the brain. She appeared to be in better shape than the surgeon or her husband.

QUESTIONS

1. Why did Selby decide to operate? What could have happened if the patient chose not to have the operation? What effect does knowing this information have on the reader?

2. Although the essay is probably based on Selby's experience, it is reported in the third person. What effect does this have on the information reported? How would the report have come across if it had been written in the first person?
3. Selby uses different methods of reporting to create the drama of "A Delicate Operation." At what point in the essay does he provide background information? How much of the essay reports events before, during, and after the operation? At what points does the writer explain terms and procedures for the reader?
4. Which passages in this essay do you find especially powerful? How did Selby create this effect?
5. Write a report of a procedure with which you are familiar. Select a procedure that calls for some expertise or sensitivity or a combination of these because there is the chance that something could go wrong. Proceed step-by-step, giving the reader as much information as necessary to understand and follow the procedure. At appropriate points, also include the problems you face. Suggestions are trimming a Christmas tree, carrying out a chemistry experiment, getting a child off to school, or preparing a gourmet meal.

MAKING CONNECTIONS

1. Compare Selby's essay with Richard Selzer's "The Discus Thrower" (p. 289). Whereas Selby writes in the third person, Selzer uses the first. How do those choices affect the resulting essays?
2. Rewrite several paragraphs of Selby's and Selzer's essays, changing the first piece from third person to first person and the other from first to third. How do these changes alter the nature of the information presented and the effect of each report?

LOVE CANAL AND THE POISONING OF AMERICA

Michael Brown

Michael Brown (b. 1952) is a freelance writer interested in environmental issues. His investigations into the dumping of toxic waste, which have appeared in newspaper and magazine articles, have won him three Pulitzer Prize nominations and a special award from the Environmental Protection Agency. He has authored several books including The Toxic Cloud: Poisoning of America's Air *(1988) and* Laying Waste: The Poisoning of America by Toxic Chemicals *(1980), from which this essay is taken.*

Niagara Falls is a city of unmatched natural beauty; it is also a tired industrial workhorse, beaten often and with a hard hand. A magnificent river—a strait, really—connecting Lake Erie to Lake Ontario flows hurriedly north, at a pace of a half-million tons a minute, widening into a smooth expanse near the city before breaking into whitecaps and taking its famous 186-foot plunge. Then it cascades through a gorge of overhung shale and limestone to rapids higher and swifter than anywhere else on the continent.

The falls attract long lines of newlyweds and other tourists. At the same time, the river provides cheap electricity for industry; a good stretch of its shore is now filled with the spiraled pipes of distilleries, and the odors of chlorine and sulfides hang in the air.

Many who live in the city of Niagara Falls work in chemical plants, the largest of which is owned by the Hooker Chemical Company, a subsidiary of Occidental Petroleum since the 1960s. Timothy Schroeder did not. He was a cement technician by trade, dealing with the factories only if they needed a pathway poured, or a small foundation set. Tim and his wife, Karen, lived in a ranch-style home with a brick and wood exterior at 460 99th Street. One of the Schroeders' most cherished purchases was a Fiberglas pool, built into the ground and enclosed by a redwood fence.

Karen looked from a back window one morning in October 1974, noting with distress that the pool had suddenly risen two feet above the ground. She called Tim to tell him about it. Karen then had no way of knowing that this was the first sign of what would prove to be a punishing family and economic tragedy.

Mrs. Schroeder believed that the cause of the uplift was the unusual groundwater flow of the area. Twenty-one years before, an abandoned

5

hydroelectric canal directly behind their house had been backfilled with industrial rubble. The underground breaches created by this disturbance, aided by the marshland nature of the region's surficial layer, collected large volumes of rainfall and undermined the back yard. The Schroeders allowed the pool to remain in its precarious position until the following summer and then pulled it from the ground, intending to pour a new pool, cast in cement. This they were unable to do, for the gaping excavation immediately filled with what Karen called "chemical water," rancid liquids of yellow and orchid and blue. These same chemicals had mixed with the groundwater and flooded the entire yard, attacking the redwood posts with such a caustic bite that one day the fence simply collapsed. When the chemicals receded in the dry weather, they left the gardens and shrubs withered and scorched, as if by a brush fire.

How the chemicals got there was no mystery. In the late 1930s, or perhaps early 1940s, the Hooker Company, whose many processes included the manufacture of pesticides, plasticizers, and caustic soda, began using the abandoned canal as a dump for at least 20,000 tons of waste residues—"still-bottoms," in the language of the trade.

Karen Schroeder's parents had been the first to experience problems with the canal's seepage. In 1959, her mother, Aileen Voorhees, encountered a strange black sludge bleeding through the basement walls. For the next twenty years, she and her husband, Edwin, tried various methods of halting the irritating intrusion, pasting the cinder-block wall with sealants and even constructing a gutter along the walls to intercept the inflow. Nothing could stop the chemical smell from permeating the entire household, and neighborhood calls to the city for help were fruitless. One day, when Edwin punched a hole in the wall to see what was happening, quantities of black liquid poured from the block. The cinder blocks were full of the stuff.

More ominous than the Voorhees basement was an event that occurred at 11:12 P.M. on November 21, 1968, when Karen Schroeder gave birth to her third child, a seven-pound girl named Sheri. No sense of elation filled the delivery room. The child was born with a heart that beat irregularly and had a hole in it, bone blockages of the nose, partial deafness, deformed ear exteriors, and a cleft palate. Within two years, the Schroeders realized Sheri was also mentally retarded. When her teeth came in, a double row of them appeared on her lower jaw. And she developed an enlarged liver.

The Schroeders considered these health problems, as well as illnesses among their other children, as acts of capricious genes—a vicious quirk of nature. Like Mrs. Schroeder's parents, they were concerned that the chemicals were devaluing their property. The crab apple tree and evergreens in the back were dead, and even the oak in front of the home was sick; one year, the leaves had fallen off on Father's Day.

The canal had been dug with much fanfare in the late nineteenth century by a flamboyant entrepreneur named William T. Love, who wanted to

10

construct an industrial city with ready access to water power, and major markets. The setting for Love's dream was to be a navigable power channel that would extend seven miles from the Upper Niagara before falling two hundred feet, circumventing the treacherous falls and at the same time providing cheap power. A city would be constructed near the point where the canal fed back into the river, and he promised it would accommodate half a million people.

So taken with his imagination were the state's leaders that they gave Love a free hand to condemn as much property as he liked, and to divert whatever amounts of water. Love's dream, however, proved grander than his resources, and he was eventually forced to abandon the project after a mile-long trench, ten to forty feet deep and generally twenty yards wide, had been scoured perpendicular to the Niagara River. Eventually, the trench was purchased by Hooker.

Few of those who, in 1977, lived in the numerous houses that had sprung up by the site were aware that the large and barren field behind them was a burial ground for toxic waste. Both the Niagara County Health Department and the city said it was a nuisance condition, but not a serious danger to the people. Officials of the Hooker Company refused comment, claiming only that they had no records of the chemical burials and that the problem was not their responsibility. Indeed, Hooker had deeded the land to the Niagara Falls Board of Education in 1953, for a token $1. With it the company issued no detailed warnings of the chemicals, only a brief paragraph in the quitclaim document that disclaimed company liability for any injuries or deaths which might occur at the site.

Though Hooker was undoubtedly relieved to rid itself of the contaminated land, the company was so vague about the hazards involved that one might have thought the wastes would cause harm only if touched, because they irritated the skin; otherwise, they were not of great concern. In reality, as the company must have known, the dangers of these wastes far exceeded those of acids or alkalines or inert salts. We now know that the drums Hooker had dumped in the canal contained a veritable witch's brew — compounds of truly remarkable toxicity. There were solvents that attacked the heart and liver, and residues from pesticides so dangerous that their commercial sale was shortly thereafter restricted outright by the government; some of them were already suspected of causing cancer.

Yet Hooker gave no hint of that. When the board of education, which wanted the parcel for a new school, approached Hooker, B. Kaussen, at the time Hooker's executive vice president, said in a letter to the board: "Our officers have carefully considered your request. We are very conscious of the need for new elementary schools and realize that the sites must be carefully selected. We will be willing to donate the entire strip of property which we own between Colvin Boulevard and Frontier Avenue to be used for the erection of a school at a location to be determined. . . ."

The board built the school and playground at the canal's midsection. 15
Construction progressed despite the contractor's hitting a drainage trench

that gave off a strong chemical odor and the discovery of a waste pit nearby. Instead of halting the work, the authorities simply moved the school eighty feet away. Young families began to settle in increasing numbers alongside the dump, many of them having been told that the field was to be a park and recreation area for their children.

Children found the "playground" interesting, but at times painful. They sneezed, and their eyes teared. In the days when the dumping was still in progress, they swam at the opposite end of the canal, occasionally arriving home with hard pimples all over their bodies. Hooker knew children were playing on its spoils. In 1958, three children were burned by exposed residues on the canal's surface, much of which, according to residents, had been covered with nothing more than fly ash and loose dirt. Because it wished to avoid legal repercussions, the company chose not to issue a public warning of the dangers it knew were there, nor to have its chemists explain to the people that their homes would have been better placed elsewhere.

The Love Canal was simply unfit as a container for hazardous substances, poor even by the standards of the day, and now, in 1977, local authorities were belatedly finding that out. Several years of heavy snowfall and rain had filled the sparingly covered channel like a bathtub. The contents were overflowing at a frightening rate.

The city of Niagara Falls, I was assured, was planning a remedial drainage program to halt in some measure the chemical migration off the site. But no sense of urgency had been attached to the plan, and it was stalled in red tape. No one could agree on who should pay the bill—the city, Hooker, or the board of education—and engineers seemed confused over what exactly needed to be done.

Niagara Falls City Manager Donald O'Hara persisted in his view that, however displeasing to the eyes and nose, the Love Canal was not a crisis matter, mainly a question of aesthetics. O'Hara reminded me that Dr. Francis Clifford, county health commissioner, supported that opinion.

With the city, the board, and Hooker unwilling to commit themselves to   20
a remedy, conditions degenerated in the area between 97th and 99th streets, until, by early 1978, the land was a quagmire of sludge that oozed from the canal's every pore. Melting snow drained the surface soot onto the private yards, while on the dump itself the ground had softened to the point of collapse, exposing the crushed tops of barrels. Beneath the surface, masses of sludge were finding their way out at a quickening rate, constantly forming springs of contaminated liquid. The Schroeder back yard, once featured in a local newspaper for its beauty, had reached the point where it was unfit even to walk upon. Of course, the Schroeders could not leave. No one would think of buying the property. They still owed on their mortgage and, with Tim's salary, could not afford to maintain the house while they moved into a safer setting. They and their four children were stuck.

Apprehension about large costs was not the only reason the city was reluctant to help the Schroeders and the one hundred or so other families whose properties abutted the covered trench. The city may also have feared distressing Hooker. To an economically depressed area, the company provided desperately needed employment—as many as 3000 blue-collar jobs and a substantial number of tax dollars. Hooker was speaking of building a $17 million headquarters in downtown Niagara Falls. So anxious were city officials to receive the new building that they and the state granted the company highly lucrative tax and loan incentives, and made available to the firm a prime parcel of property near the most popular tourist park on the American side.

City Manager O'Hara and other authorities were aware of the nature of Hooker's chemicals. In fact, in the privacy of his office, O'Hara, after receiving a report on the chemical tests at the canal, had informed the people at Hooker that it was an extremely serious problem. Even earlier, in 1976, the New York State Department of Environmental Conservation had been made aware that dangerous compounds were present in the basement sump pump of at least one 97th Street home, and soon after, its own testing had revealed that highly injurious halogenated hydrocarbons were flowing from the canal into adjoining sewers. Among them were the notorious PCBs; quantities as low as one part PCBs to a million parts normal water were enough to create serious environmental concerns; in the sewers of Niagara Falls, the quantities of halogenated compounds were thousands of times higher. The other materials tracked, in sump pumps or sewers, were just as toxic as PCBs, or more so. Prime among the more hazardous ones was residue from hexachlorocyclopentadiene, or C-56, which was deployed as an intermediate in the manufacture of several pesticides. In certain dosages, the chemical could damage every organ in the body.

While the mere presence of C-56 should have been cause for alarm, government remained inactive. Not until early 1978—a full eighteen months after C-56 was first detected—was testing conducted in basements along 97th and 99th streets to see if the chemicals had vaporized off the sump pumps and walls and were present in the household air.

While the basement tests were in progress, the rains of spring arrived at the canal, further worsening the situation. Heavier fumes rose above the barrels. More than before, the residents were suffering from headaches, respiratory discomforts, and skin ailments. Many of them felt constantly fatigued and irritable, and the children had reddened eyes. In the Schroeder home, Tim developed a rash along the backs of his legs. Karen could not rid herself of throbbing pains in her head. Their daughter, Laurie, seemed to be losing some of her hair.

The EPA test revealed that benzene, a known cause of cancer in humans, had been readily detected in the household air up and down the streets. A widely used solvent, benzene was known in chronic-exposure cases to cause headaches, fatigue, loss of weight, and dizziness followed by pallor, nose-bleeds, and damage to the bone marrow.

No public announcement was made of the benzene hazard. Instead, officials appeared to shield the finding until they could agree among themselves on how to present it.

Dr. Clifford, the county health commissioner, seemed unconcerned by the detection of benzene in the air. His health department refused to conduct a formal study of the people's health, despite the air-monitoring results. For this reason, and because of the resistance growing among the local authorities, I went to the southern end of 99th Street to take an informal health survey of my own. I arranged a meeting with six neighbors, all of them instructed beforehand to list the illnesses they were aware of on their block, with names and ages specified for presentation at the session.

The residents' list was startling. Though unafflicted before they moved there, many people were now plagued with ear infections, nervous disorders, rashes, and headaches. One young man, James Gizzarelli, said he had missed four months of work owing to breathing troubles. His wife was suffering epileptic-like seizures which her doctor was unable to explain. Meanwhile, freshly applied paint was inexplicably peeling from the exterior of their house. Pets too were suffering, most seriously if they had been penned in the back yards nearest to the canal, constantly breathing air that smelled like mothballs and weedkiller. They lost their fur, exhibited skin lesions, and, while still quite young, developed internal tumors. A great many cases of cancer were reported among the women, along with much deafness. On both 97th and 99th streets, traffic signs warned passing motorists to watch for deaf children playing near the road.

Evidence continued to mount that a large group of people, perhaps all of the one hundred families immediately by the canal, perhaps many more, were in imminent danger. While watching television, while gardening or doing a wash, in their sleeping hours, they were inhaling a mixture of damaging chemicals. Their hours of exposure were far longer than those of a chemical factory worker, and they wore no respirators or goggles. Nor could they simply open a door and escape. Helplessness and despair were the main responses to the blackened craters and scattered cinders behind their back yards.

But public officials often characterized the residents as hypochondriacs. Every agent of government had been called on the phone or sent pleas for help, but none offered aid. 30

Commissioner Clifford expressed irritation at my printed reports of illness, and disagreement began to surface in the newsroom on how the stories should be printed. "There's a high rate of cancer among my friends," Dr. Clifford argued. "It doesn't mean anything."

Yet as interest in the small community increased, further revelations shook the neighborhood. In addition to benzene, eighty or more other compounds were found in the makeshift dump, ten of them potential carcinogens. The physiological effects they could cause were profound and diverse. At least fourteen of them could impact on the brain and central nervous system. Two of them, carbon tetrachloride and chlorobenzene, could readily cause narcotic and anesthetic consequences. Many others were known to cause headaches, seizures, loss of hair, anemia, or skin rashes. Together, the compounds were capable of inflicting innumerable illnesses, and no one knew what new concoctions were being formulated by their mixture underground.

Edwin and Aileen Voorhees had the most to be concerned about. When a state biophysicist analyzed the air content of their basement, he determined that the safe exposure time there was less than 2.4 minutes—the toxicity in the basement was thousands of times the acceptable limit for twenty-four-hour-breathing. This did not mean they would necessarily become permanently ill, but their chances of contracting cancer, for example, had been measurably increased. In July, I visited Mrs. Voorhees for further discussion of her problems, and as we sat in the kitchen, drinking coffee, the industrial odors were apparent. Aileen, usually chipper and feisty, was visibly anxious. She stared down at the table, talking only in a lowered voice. Everything now looked different to her. The home she and Edwin had built had become their jail cell. Their yard was but a pathway through which toxicants entered the cellar walls. The field out back, that proposed "park," seemed destined to be the ruin of their lives.

On July 14 I received a call from the state health department with some shocking news. A preliminary review showed that women living at the southern end had suffered a high rate of miscarriages and had given birth to an abnormally high number of children with birth defects. In one age group, 35.3 percent had records of spontaneous abortions. That was far in excess of the norm. The odds against it happening by chance were 250 to one. These tallies, it was stressed, were "conservative" figures. Four children in one small section of the neighborhood had documentable birth defects, club feet, retardation, and deafness. Those who lived there the longest suffered the highest rates.

The data on miscarriages and birth defects, coupled with the other accounts of illness, finally pushed the state's bureaucracy into motion. A meeting was scheduled for August 2, at which time the state health commissioner, Dr. Robert Whalen, would formally address the issue. The day before the meeting, Dr. Nicholas Vianna, a state epidemiologist, told me that the residents were also incurring some degree of liver damage. Blood analyses had shown hepatitislike symptoms in enzyme levels. Dozens if not hundreds of people, apparently, had been adversely affected.

In Albany, on August 2, Dr. Whalen read a lengthy statement in which he urged that pregnant women and children under two years of age leave the southern end of the dump site immediately. He declared the Love Canal an official emergency, citing it as a "great and imminent peril to the health of the general public."

When Commissioner Whalen's words hit 97th and 99th streets, by way of one of the largest banner headlines in the Niagara *Gazette*'s 125-year history, dozens of people massed on the streets, shouting into bullhorns and microphones to voice frustrations that had been accumulating for months. Many of them vowed a tax strike because their homes were rendered unmarketable and unsafe. They attacked their government for

35

ignoring their welfare. A man of high authority, a physician with a title, had confirmed that their lives were in danger. Most wanted to leave the neighborhood immediately.

Terror and anger roiled together, exacerbated by Dr. Whalen's failure to provide a government-funded evacuation plan. His words were only a recommendation: individual families had to choose whether to risk their health and remain, or abandon their houses and, in so doing, write off a lifetime of work and savings.

On August 3, Dr. Whalen decided he should speak to the people. He arrived with Dr. David Axelrod, a deputy who had directed the state's investigation, and Thomas Frey, a key aide to Governor Hugh Carey.

At a public meeting, held in the 99th Street School auditorium, Frey was given the grueling task of controlling the crowd of 500 angry and frightened people. In an attempt to calm them, he announced that a meeting between the state and the White House had been scheduled for the following week. The state would propose that Love Canal be classified a national disaster, thereby freeing federal funds. For now, however, he could promise no more. Neither could Dr. Whalen and his staff of experts. All they could say was what was already known: twenty-five organic compounds, some of them capable of causing cancer, were in their homes, and because young children were especially prone to toxic effects, they should be moved to another area.

Dr. Whalen's order had applied only to those living at the canal's southern end, on its immediate periphery. But families living across the street from the dump site, or at the northern portion, where the chemicals were not so visible at the surface, reported afflictions remarkably similar to those suffered by families whose yards abutted the southern end. Serious respiratory problems, nervous disorders, and rectal bleeding were reported by many who were not covered by the order.

Throughout the following day, residents posted signs of protest on their front fences or porch posts. "Love Canal Kills," they said, or "Give Me Liberty, I've Got Death." Emotionally exhausted and uncertain about their future, men stayed home from work, congregating on the streets or comforting their wives. By this time the board of education had announced it was closing the 99th Street School for the following year, because of its proximity to the exposed toxicants. Still, no public relief was provided for the residents.

Another meeting was held that evening, at a firehall on 102nd Street. It was unruly, but the people, who had called the session in an effort to organize themselves, managed to form an alliance, the Love Canal Homeowners Association, and to elect as president Lois Gibbs, a pretty, twenty-seven-year-old woman with jet-black hair who proved remarkably adept at dealing with experienced politicians and at keeping the matter in the news. After Mrs. Gibbs' election, Congressman John LaFalce entered the hall and announced, to wild applause, that the Federal Disaster Assistance Administration would be represented the next morning, and that the

40

state's two senators, Daniel Patrick Moynihan and Jacob Javits, were working with him in an attempt to get funds from Congress.

With the Love Canal story now attracting attention from the national media, the Governor's office announced that Hugh Carey would be at the 99th Street School on August 7 to address the people. Decisions were being made in Albany and Washington. Hours before the Governor's arrival, a sudden burst of "urgent" reports from Washington came across the newswires. President Jimmy Carter had officially declared the Hooker dump site a national emergency.

Hugh Carey was applauded on his arrival. The Governor announced   45 that the state, through its Urban Development Corporation, planned to purchase, at fair market value, those homes rendered uninhabitable by the marauding chemicals. He spared no promises. "You will not have to make mortgage payments on homes you don't want or cannot occupy. Don't worry about the banks. The state will take care of them." By the standards of Niagara Falls, where the real estate market was depressed, the houses were in the middle-class range, worth from $20,000 to $40,000 apiece. The state would assess each house and purchase it, and also pay the costs of moving, temporary housing during the transition period, and special items not covered by the usual real estate assessment, such as installation of telephones.

First in a trickle and then, by September, in droves, the families gathered their belongings and carted them away. Moving vans crowded 97th and 99th streets. Linesmen went from house to house disconnecting the telephones and electrical wires, while carpenters pounded plywood over the windows to keep vandals away. By the following spring, 237 families were gone; 170 of them had moved into new houses. In time the state erected around a six-block residential area a green chain-link fence, eight feet in height, clearly demarcating the contamination zone.

In October 1978, the long-awaited remedial drainage program began at the south end. Trees were uprooted, fences and garages torn down, and swimming pools removed from the area. So great were residents' apprehensions that dangerous fumes would be released over the surrounding area that the state, at a cost of $500,000, placed seventy-five buses at emergency evacuation pickup spots during the months of work, in the event that outlying homes had to be vacated quickly because of an explosion. The plan was to construct drain tiles around the channel's periphery, where the back yards had been located, in order to divert leakage to seventeen-foot-deep wet wells from which contaminated groundwater could be drawn and treated by filtration through activated carbon. (Removing the chemicals themselves would have been financially prohibitive, perhaps costing as much as $100 million—and even then the materials would have to be buried elsewhere.) After the trenching was complete, and the sewers installed, the canal was to be covered by a sloping mound of clay and planted with grass. One day, city officials hoped, the wasteland would become a park.

In spite of the corrective measures and the enormous effort by the state health department, which took thousands of blood samples from past and current residents and made uncounted analyses of soil, water, and air, the full range of the effects remained unknown. In neighborhoods immediately outside the official "zone of contamination," more than 500 families were left near the desolate setting, their health still in jeopardy. The state announced it would buy no more homes.

The first public indication that chemical contamination had probably reached streets to the east and west of 97th and 99th streets, and to the north and south as well, came on August 11, 1978, when sump-pump samples I had taken from 100th and 101st streets, analyzed in a laboratory, showed the trace presence of a number of chemicals found in the canal itself, including lindane, a restricted pesticide that had been suspected of causing cancer in laboratory animals. While probing 100th Street, I knocked on the door of Patricia Pino, thirty-four, a blond divorcee with a young son and daughter. I had noticed that some of the leaves on a large tree in front of her house exhibited a black oiliness much like that on the trees and shrubs of 99th Street; she was located near what had been a drainage swale.

After I had extracted a jar of sediment from her sump pump for the   50
analysis, we conversed about her family situation and what the trauma now unfolding meant to them. Ms. Pino was extremely depressed and embittered. Both of her children had what appeared to be slight liver abnormalities, and her son had been plagued with "non-specific" allergies, teary eyes, sinus trouble, which improved markedly when he was sent away from home. Patricia told of times, during the heat of summer, when fumes were readily noticeable in her basement and sometimes even upstairs. She herself had been treated for a possibly cancerous condition of her cervix. But, like others, her family was now trapped.

On September 24, 1978, I obtained a state memorandum that said chemical infiltration of the outer regions was significant indeed. The letter, sent from the state laboratories to the U.S. Environmental Protection Agency, said, "Preliminary analysis of soil samples demonstrates extensive migration of potentially toxic materials outside the immediate canal area." There it was, in the state's own words. Not long afterward, the state medical investigator, Dr. Nicholas Vianna, reported indications that residents from 93rd to 103rd streets might also have incurred liver damage.

On October 4, a young boy, John Allen Kenny, who lived quite a distance north of the evacuation zone, died. The fatality was due to the failure of another organ that can be readily affected by toxicants, the kidney. Naturally, suspicions were raised that his death was in some way related to a creek that still flowed behind his house and carried, near an outfall, the odor of chlorinated compounds. Because the creek served as a catch basin for a portion of the Love Canal, the state studied an autopsy of the boy. No conclusions were reached. John Allen's parents, Norman, a chemist, and Luella, a medical research assistant, were unsatisfied with the state's investigation, which they felt was "superficial." Luella said, "He played in the creek all the time. There had been restrictions on the older boys, but he was the youngest and played with them when they were old enough to go to the creek. We let him do what the other boys did. He died of nephrosis. Proteins were passing through his urine. Well, in reading the literature, we discovered that chemicals can trigger this. There was no evidence of infection, which there should have been, and there was damage to his thymus and brain. He also had nosebleeds and headaches, and dry heaves. So our feeling is that chemicals probably triggered it."

The likelihood that water-carried chemicals had escaped from the canal's deteriorating bounds and were causing problems quite a distance from the site was not lost upon the Love Canal Homeowners Association and its president, Lois Gibbs, who was attempting to have additional families relocated. Because she lived on 101st Street, she was one of those left behind, with no means of moving despite persistent medical difficulties in her six-year-old son, Michael, who had been operated on twice for urethral strictures. [Mrs. Gibbs's husband, a worker at a chemical plant, brought home only $150 a week, she told me, and when they subtracted from that the $90 a week for food and other necessities, clothing costs for their two children, $125 a month for mortgage payments and taxes, utility and phone expenses, and medical bills, they had hardly enough cash to buy gas and cigarettes, let alone vacate their house.]

Assisted by two other stranded residents, Marie Pozniak and Grace McCoulf, and with the professional analysis of a Buffalo scientist named Beverly Paigen, Lois Gibbs mapped out the swale and creekbed areas, many of them long ago filled, and set about interviewing the numerous people who lived on or near formerly wet ground. The survey indicated that these people were suffering from an abnormal number of kidney and bladder aggravations and problems of the reproductive system. In a report to the state, Dr. Paigen claimed to have found, in 245 homes outside the evacuation zone, thirty-four miscarriages, eighteen birth defects, nineteen nervous breakdowns, ten cases of epilepsy, and high rates of hyperactivity and suicide.

In their roundabout way, the state health experts, after an elaborate investigation, confirmed some of the homeowners' worst fears. On February 8, 1979, Dr. David Axelrod, who by then had been appointed health commissioner, and whose excellence as a scientist was widely acknowledged, issued a new order that officially extended the health emergency of the previous August, citing high incidences of birth deformities and miscarriages in the areas where creeks and swales had once flowed, or where swamps had been. With that, the state offered to evacuate temporarily those families with pregnant women or children under the age of two from the outer areas of contamination, up to 103rd Street. But no additional homes would be purchased; nor was another large-scale evacuation, temporary or otherwise, under consideration. Those who left under the new plan would have to return when their children passed the age limit.

55

Twenty-three families accepted the state's offer. Another seven families, ineligible under the plan but of adequate financial means to do so, simply left their homes and took the huge loss of investment. Soon boarded windows speckled the outlying neighborhoods.

The previous November and December, not long after the evacuation of 97th and 99th streets, I became interested in the possibility that Hooker might have buried in the Love Canal waste residues from the manufacture of what is known as 2,4,5-trichlorophenol. My curiosity was keen because I knew that this substance, which Hooker produced for the manufacture of the antibacterial agent hexachlorophene, and which was also used to make defoliants such as Agent Orange, the herbicide employed in Vietnam, carries with it an unwanted by-product technically called 2,3,7,8-tetrachlorodibenzo-para-dioxin, or tetra dioxin. The potency of dioxin of this isomer is nearly beyond imagination. Although its toxicological effects are not fully known, the few experts on the subject estimate that if three ounces were evenly distributed and subsequently ingested among a million people, or perhaps more than that, all of them would die. It compares in toxicity to the botulinum toxin. On skin contact, dioxin causes a disfiguration called "chloracne," which begins as pimples, lesions, and cysts, but can lead to calamitous internal damage. Some scientists suspect that dioxin causes cancer, perhaps even malignancies that occur, in galloping fashion, within a short time of contact. At least two (some estimates went as high as eleven) pounds of dioxin were dispersed over Seveso, Italy, in 1976, after an explosion of a trichlorophenol plant: dead animals littered the streets, and more than 300 acres of land were immediately evacuated. In Vietnam, the spraying of Agent Orange, because of the dioxin contaminant, was banned in 1970, when the first effects on human beings began to surface, including dioxin's powerful teratogenic, or fetus-deforming, effects.

I posed two questions concerning trichlorophenol: Were wastes from the process buried in the canal? If so, what were the quantities?

On November 8, before Hooker answered my queries, I learned that, indeed, trichlorophenol had been found in liquids pumped from the remedial drain ditches. No dioxin had been found yet, and some officials, ever wary of more emotionalism among the people, argued that, because the compound was not soluble in water, there was little chance it had migrated off-site. Officials at Newco Chemical Waste Systems, a local waste disposal firm, at the same time claimed that if dioxin had been there, it had probably been photolytically destroyed. Its half-life, they contended, was just a few short years.

I knew from Whiteside, however, that in every known case, waste from 2,4,5-trichlorophenol carried dioxin with it. I also knew that dioxin *could* become soluble in groundwater and migrate into the neighborhood upon mixing with solvents such as benzene. Moreover, because it had been buried, sunlight would not break it down.

On Friday, November 10, I called Hooker again to urge that they answer my questions. Their spokesman, Bruce Davis, came to the phone and,

60

in a controlled tone, gave me the answer: His firm had indeed buried trichlorophenol in the canal—200 tons of it.

Immediately I called Whiteside. His voice took on an urgent tone. According to his calculation, if 200 tons of trichlorophenol were there, in all likelihood they were accompanied by 130 pounds of tetra dioxin, an amount equaling the estimated total content of dioxin in the thousands of tons of Agent Orange rained upon Vietnamese jungles. The seriousness of the crisis had deepened, for now the Love Canal was not only a dump for highly dangerous solvents and pesticides; it was also the broken container for one of the most toxic substances ever synthesized by man.

I reckoned that the main danger was to those working on the remedial project, digging in the trenches. The literature on dioxin indicated that, even in quantities at times too small to detect, the substance possessed vicious characteristics. In one case, workers in a trichlorophenol plant had developed chloracne, although the substance could not be traced on the equipment with which they worked. The mere tracking of minuscule amounts of dioxin on a pedestrian's shoes in Seveso led to major concerns, and, according to Whiteside, a plant in Amsterdam, upon being found contaminated with dioxin, had been "dismantled, brick by brick, and the material embedded in concrete, loaded at a specially constructed dock, on ships, and dumped at sea, in deep water near the Azores." Workers in trichlorophenol plants had died of cancer or severe liver damage, or had suffered emotional and sexual disturbances.

Less than a month after the first suspicions arose, on the evening of December 9, I received a call from Dr. Axelrod. "We found it. The dioxin. In a drainage trench behind 97th Street. It was in the part-per-trillion range."

The state remained firm in its plans to continue the construction, and, despite the ominous new findings, no further evacuations were announced. During the next several weeks, small incidents of vandalism occurred along 97th and 99th streets. Tacks were spread on the road, causing numerous flat tires on the trucks. Signs of protest were hung in the school. Meetings of the Love Canal Homeowners Association became more vociferous. Christmas was near, and in the association's office at the 99th Street School, a holiday tree was decorated with bulbs arranged to spell "DIOXIN."

The Love Canal people chanted and cursed at meetings with the state officials, cried on the telephone, burned an effigy of the health commissioner, traveled to Albany with a makeshift child's coffin, threatened to hold officials hostage, sent letters and telegrams to the White House, held days of mourning and nights of prayer. On Mother's Day this year, they marched down the industrial corridor and waved signs denouncing Hooker, which had issued not so much as a statement of remorse. But no happy ending was in store for them. The federal government was clearly not planning to come to their rescue, and the state felt it had already done more than its share. City Hall was silent and remains silent today. Some residents still hoped that, miraculously, an agency of government would move them. All of them watched with anxiety as each newborn came to the neighborhood, and they looked at their bodies for signs of cancer.

One hundred and thirty families from the Love Canal area began leaving their homes last August and September, seeking temporary refuge in local hotel rooms under a relocation plan funded by the state which had been implemented after fumes became so strong, during remedial trenching operations, that the United Way abandoned a care center it had opened in the neighborhood.

As soon as remedial construction is complete, the people will probably be forced to return home, as the state will no longer pay for their lodging. Some have threatened to barricade themselves in the hotels. Some have mentioned violence. Anne Hillis of 102nd Street, who told reporters her first child had been born so badly decomposed that doctors could not determine its sex, was so bitter that she threw table knives and a soda can at the state's on-site coordinator.

In October, Governor Carey announced that the state probably would buy an additional 200 to 240 homes, at an expense of some $5 million. In the meantime, lawyers have prepared lawsuits totaling about $2.65 billion and have sought court action for permanent relocation. Even if the latter action is successful, and they are allowed to move, the residents' plight will not necessarily have ended. The psychological scars are bound to remain among them and their children, along with the knowledge that, because they have already been exposed, they may never fully escape the Love Canal's insidious grasp.

QUESTIONS

1. What caused the poisoning of Love Canal? Why did it take so long for both local and state officials to acknowledge the seriousness of the condition of Love Canal?
2. What kind of information does Brown provide to document the tragedy of Love Canal? What role did he play in uncovering this information?
3. Consider the introduction to this article. Why did Brown choose to tell the story of the Schroeder family in the opening paragraphs?
4. The power of this essay has much to do with the overwhelming tragedy and horror it relates. Find passages in the essay that you feel are especially effective. Explain how Brown creates this effect on the reader.
5. In this essay, Brown relies primarily on the factual data he has collected to tell the story of Love Canal. Compare this writer's approach with that found in newspapers featuring sensational headlines. Analyze one of the headlined stories. How much factual evidence is present? How would such a newspaper's treatment of the story of the Schroeder family differ from Brown's treatment?

6. Environmental calamities such as Love Canal or Three Mile Island have become a permanent part of our lives. The Environmental Protection Agency reports that in most communities the groundwater has become so laced with toxic chemicals that it is no longer safe to drink. Investigate some aspect of the environment in your community such as the water supply or the quality of the air. Write a report based on your investigation.

MAKING CONNECTIONS

Compare Brown's position as a reporter with Barbara Tuchman's in "'This Is the End of the World'" (p. 236). What similarities and differences can you find in the ways that Brown and Tuchman have gathered their information? In their organization and presentation of that information? In the points of view that they have taken toward the disasters they write about? On the basis of these comparisons, what do you think is the most effective way to present stories of large-scale human disasters and similarly provocative subject matter?

A COLD SPRING

Elizabeth Bishop

Born in Worcester, Massachusetts, Elizabeth Bishop (1911–1979) was raised by relatives in Nova Scotia and Massachusetts after her father's death and her mother's commitment to a mental institution when she was five. A graduate of Vassar College, she traveled extensively over the course of her lifetime, living in Europe, Brazil, and Key West, Florida, among other places. Many of her poems are meticulous evocations of these environments. Having inherited an independent income, Bishop did not feel the need to publish extensively; she would often work on a poem for a year or more, and her Collected Poems *(1983) only amount to about a hundred. In fact, she published only four volumes of poetry between 1946 and 1976. Long considered a "poet's poet," she has achieved an increasingly wider readership in the years since her death. The following poem was based on notebook journals Bishop recorded in the spring of 1950 during weekend visits to the Havre de Grace, Maryland, farm of her good friend Jane Dewey.*

for Jane Dewey. Maryland
Nothing is so beautiful as spring.
　　　　　　　—HOPKINS

A cold spring:
the violet was flawed on the lawn.
For two weeks or more the trees hesitated;
the little leaves waited,
carefully indicating their characteristics.　　　　　　　5
Finally a grave green dust
settled over your big and aimless hills.
One day, in a chill white blast of sunshine,
on the side of one a calf was born.
The mother stopped lowing　　　　　　　10
and took a long time eating the after-birth,
a wretched flag,
but the calf got up promptly
and seemed inclined to feel gay.

The next day　　　　　　　15
was much warmer.

Greenish-white dogwood infiltrated the wood,
each petal burned, apparently, by a cigarette-butt;
and the blurred redbud stood
beside it, motionless, but almost more   20
like movement than any placeable color.
Four deer practised leaping over your fences.
The infant oak-leaves swung through the sober oak.
Song-sparrows were wound up for the summer,
and in the maple the complementary cardinal   25
cracked a whip, and the sleeper awoke,
stretching miles of green limbs from the south.
In his cap the lilacs whitened,
then one day they fell like snow.
Now, in the evening,   30
a new moon comes.
The hills grow softer. Tufts of long grass show
where each cow-flop lies.
The bull-frogs are sounding,
slack strings plucked by heavy thumbs.   35
Beneath the light, against your white front door,
the smallest moths, like Chinese fans,
flatten themselves, silver and silver-gilt
over pale yellow, orange, or gray.
Now, from the thick grass, the fireflies   40
begin to risc:
up, then down, then up again:
lit on the ascending flight,
drifting simultaneously to the same height,
— exactly like the bubbles in champagne.   45
— Later on they rise much higher.
And your shadowy pastures will be able to offer
these particular glowing tributes
every evening now throughout the summer.

Questions

1. "Exactly like the bubbles in champagne"—this image using "like"
   could be a handbook example of a simile, which is a staple of descriptive writing whether in prose or in poetry. What other similes do you
   find in the poem?
2. Then there are metaphors, in which Bishop drops the "like" and
   equates two things directly: "The bull-frogs are sounding,/slack strings
   plucked by heavy thumbs." What other metaphors do you find?

3. Often Bishop's metaphors are implied by her verbs: a petal is "burned," leaves swing, a sleeper awakes. Spring has been a "sleeper" *because* he awakes. What other verbs add to the implied character of spring?
4. Isn't the more usual term "a late spring"? What is the difference between a cold spring and a late one?
5. What then is the metaphor beneath all Bishop's other metaphors and images?

MAKING CONNECTIONS

Compare Bishop's "A Cold Spring" with Rachel Carson's "Undersea" (p. 317), in terms of both their spatial order and their use of figurative language. In what ways is Carson's piece also a poem?

UNDERSEA

Rachel Carson

*A writer, zoologist, and ecological pioneer, Rachel Carson
(1907–1964) studied at the Woods Hole Marine Biological Laboratory before receiving her master's degree from Johns Hopkins in
1932. For some fifteen years, she worked as a scientist and writer
for the U.S. Fish and Wildlife Service, eventually becoming chief of
publications. At the same time she was composing more lyrical
works on natural history for general readers, including* Under the
Sea-Wind *(1941) and the award-winning* The Sea Around Us
(1952). Carson's most influential work is Silent Spring *(1962), a
stark warning about the ecological dangers posed by the use of
pesticides, which is generally credited with sparking the environmental movement. The following was originally written as the introduction to a government publication in 1935; judging it too
poetic, Carson's supervisor suggested she submit it to* Atlantic
Monthly, *where it first appeared.*

Who has known the ocean? Neither you nor I, with our earth-bound
senses, know the foam and surge of the tide that beats over the crab hiding
under the seaweed of his tide-pool home; or the lilt of the long, slow swells
of mid-ocean, where shoals of wandering fish prey and are preyed upon,
and the dolphin breaks the waves to breathe the upper atmosphere. Nor
can we know the vicissitudes of life on the ocean floor, where the sunlight,
filtering through a hundred feet of water, makes but a fleeting, bluish twilight, in which dwell sponge and mollusk and starfish and coral, where
swarms of diminutive fish twinkle through the dusk like a silver rain of me-
teors, and eels lie in wait among the rocks. Even less is it given to man to
descend those six incomprehensible miles into the recesses of the abyss,
where reign utter silence and unvarying cold and eternal night.

To sense this world of waters known to the creatures of the sea we
must shed our human perceptions of length and breadth and time and
place, and enter vicariously into a universe of all-pervading water. For to
the sea's children nothing is so important as the fluidity of their world. It is
water that they breathe; water that brings them food; water through which
they see, by filtered sunshine from which first the red rays, then the greens,
and finally the purples have been strained; water through which they sense
vibrations equivalent to sound. And indeed it is nothing more or less than
sea water, in all its varying conditions of temperature, saltiness, and pressure, that forms the invisible barriers that confine each marine type within

a special zone of life—one to the shore line, another to some submarine chasm on the far slopes of the continental shelf, and yet another, perhaps, to an imperceptibly defined stratum at mid-depths of ocean.

There are comparatively few living things whose shifting pattern of life embraces both land and sea. Such are the creatures of the tide pools among the rocks and of the mud flats sloping away from dune and beach grass to the water's edge. Between low water and the flotsam and jetsam of the high-tide mark, land and sea wage a never-ending conflict for possession.

As on land the coming of night brings a change over the face of field and forest, sending some wild things into the safe retreat of their burrows and bringing others forth to prowl and forage, so at ebb tide the creatures of the waters largely disappear from sight, and in their place come marauders from the land to search the tide pools and to probe the sands for the silent, waiting fauna of the shore.

Twice between succeeding dawns, as the waters abandon pursuit of the   5 beckoning moon and fall back, foot by foot, periwinkle and starfish and crab are cast upon the mercy of the sands. Every heap of brine-drenched seaweed, every pool forgotten by the retreating sea in recess of sand or rock, offers sanctuary from sun and biting sand.

In the tide pools, seas in miniature, sponges of the simpler kinds encrust the rocks, each hungrily drawing in through its myriad mouths the nutriment-laden water. Starfishes and sea anemones are common dwellers in such rock-girt pools. Shellless cousins of the snail, the naked sea slugs are spots of brilliant rose and bronze, spreading arborescent gills to the waters, while the tube worms, architects of the tide pools, fashion their conical dwellings of sand grains, cemented one against another in glistening mosaic.

On the sands the clams burrow down in search of coolness and moisture, and oysters close their all-excluding shells and wait for the return of the water. Crabs crowd into damp rock caverns, where periwinkles cling to the walls. Colonies of gnome-like shrimps find refuge under dripping strands of brown, leathery weed heaped on the beach.

Hard upon the retreating sea press invaders from the land. Shore birds patter along the beach by day, and legions of the ghost crab shuffle across the damp sands by night. Chief, perhaps, among the plunderers is man, probing the soft mud flats and dipping his nets into the shallow waters.

At last comes a tentative ripple, then another, and finally the full, surging sweep of the incoming tide. The folk of the pools awake—clams stir in the mud. Barnacles open their shells and begin a rhythmic sifting of the waters. One by one, brilliant-hued flowers blossom in the shallow water as tube worms extend cautious tentacles.

The ocean is a place of paradoxes. It is the home of the great white shark,   10 two-thousand-pound killer of the seas, and of the hundred-foot blue whale, the largest animal that ever lived. It is also the home of living things so small that your two hands might scoop up as many of them as there are stars in the Milky Way. And it is because of the flowering of astronomical numbers of these diminutive plants, known as diatoms,[1] that the surface waters of the ocean are in reality boundless pastures. Every marine animal, from the smallest to the sharks and whales, is ultimately dependent for its food upon these microscopic entities of the vegetable life of the ocean. Within their fragile walls, the sea performs a vital alchemy that utilizes the sterile chemical elements dissolved in the water and welds them with the torch of sunlight into the stuff of life. Only through this little-understood synthesis of proteins, fats, and carbohydrates by myriad plant "producers" is the mineral wealth of the sea made available to the animal "consumers" that browse as they float with the currents. Drifting endlessly, midway between the sea of air above and the depths of the abyss below, these strange creatures and the marine inflorescence that sustains them are called "plankton" — the wanderers.

Many of the fishes, as well as the bottom-dwelling mollusks and worms and starfish, begin life as temporary members of this roving company, for the ocean cradles their young in its surface waters. The sea is not a solicitous foster mother. The delicate eggs and fragile larvæ are buffeted by storms raging across the open ocean and preyed upon by diminutive monsters, the hungry glassworms and comb jellies of the plankton.

These ocean pastures are also the domain of vast shoals of adult fishes: herring, anchovy, menhaden, and mackerel, feeding upon the animals of the plankton and in their turn preyed upon; for here the dogfish hunt in packs, and the ravenous bluefish, like roving buccaneers, take their booty where they find it.

Dropping downward a scant hundred feet to the white sand beneath, an undersea traveler would discover a land where the noonday sun is swathed in twilight blues and purples, and where the blackness of midnight is eerily aglow with the cold phosphorescence of living things. Dwelling among the crepuscular[2] shadows of the ocean floor are creatures whose terrestrial counterparts are drab and commonplace, but which are themselves invested with delicate beauty by the sea. Crystal cones form the shells of pteropods or winged snails that drift downward from the surface to these dim regions by day; and the translucent spires of lovely *Ianthina* are tinged by Tyrian purple.[3]

Other creatures of the sea's bottom may be fantastic rather than beautiful. Spine-studded urchins, like rotund hedgehogs of the sea, tumble over the sands, where mollusks lie with slightly opened shells, busily straining the water for débris. Life flows on monotonously for these passive sifters of the currents, who move little or not at all from year to year. Among the

---

[1]*diatom:* microscopic algae with cell walls consisting of interlocking, symmetrical valves. [Eds.]

[2]*crepuscular:* of or like twilight. [Eds.]

[3]*Tyrian purple:* a reddish dye obtained from the bodies of certain mollusks, highly prized in ancient times and named after Tyre, an ancient city located in what is now Lebanon. [Eds.]

rock ledges, eels and cunners forage greedily, while the lobster feels his way with nimble wariness through the perpetual twilight.

Farther out on the continental shelf, the ocean floor is scarred with   15 deep ravines, perhaps the valleys of drowned rivers, and dotted with undersea plateaus. Hosts of fish graze on these submerged islands, which are richly carpeted with sluggish or sessile[4] forms of life. Chief among the ground fish are haddock, cods, flounders and their mightier relative, the halibut. From these and shallower waters man, the predator, exacts a yearly tribute of nearly thirty billion pounds of fish.

If the underwater traveler might continue to explore the ocean floor, he would traverse miles of level prairie lands; he would ascend the sloping sides of hills; and he would skirt deep and ragged crevasses yawning suddenly at his feet. Through the gathering darkness, he would come at last to the edge of the continental shelf. The ceiling of the ocean would lie a hundred fathoms[5] above him, and his feet would rest upon the brink of a slope that drops precipitously another mile, and then descends more gently into an inky void that is the abyss.

What human mind can visualize conditions in the uttermost depths of the ocean? Increasing with every foot of depth, enormous pressures reach, three thousand fathoms down, the inconceivable magnitude of three tons to every square inch of surface. In these silent deeps a glacial cold prevails, a bleak iciness which never varies, summer or winter, years melting into centuries, and centuries into ages of geologic time. There, too, darkness reigns— the blackness of primeval night in which the ocean came into being, unbroken, through æons of succeeding time, by the gray light of dawn.

It is easy to understand why early students of the ocean believed these regions were devoid of life, but strange creatures have now been dredged from the depths to bear mute and fragmentary testimony concerning life in the abyss.

The "monsters" of the deep sea are small, voracious fishes with gaping, tooth-studded jaws, some with sensitive feelers serving the function of eyes, others bearing luminous torches or lures to search out or entice their living prey. Through the night of the abyss, the flickering lights of these foragers move to and fro. Many of the sessile bottom dwellers glow with a strange radiance suffusing the entire body, while other swimming creatures may have tiny, glittering lights picked out in rows and patterns. The deep-sea prawn and the abyssal[6] cuttlefish eject a luminous cloud, and under cover of this pillar of fire escape from their enemies.

Monotones of red and brown and lustreless black are the prevailing   20 colors in the deep sea, allowing the wearers to reflect the minimum of the phosphorescent gleams, and to blend into the safe obscurity of the surrounding gloom.

On the muddy bottom of the abyss, treacherous oozes threaten to engulf small scavengers as they busily sift the débris for food. Crabs and

---

[4]*sessile:* attached at their base and so permanently fixed. [Eds.]
[5]*fathom:* a unit of length equaling six feet, or 1.83 meters. [Eds.]
[6]*abyssal:* living in the depths of the ocean. [Eds.]

prawns pick their way over the yielding mud on stilt-like legs; sea spiders creep over sponges raised on delicate stalks above the slime.

Because the last vestige of plant life was left behind in the shallow zone penetrated by the rays of the sun, the inhabitants of these depths contrast strangely with the self-supporting assemblage of the surface waters. Preying one upon another, the abyssal creatures are ultimately dependent upon the slow rain of dead plants and animals from above. Every living thing of the ocean, plant and animal alike, returns to the water at the end of its own life span the materials that had been temporarily assembled to form its body. So there descends into the depths a gentle, never-ending rain of the disintegrating particles of what once were living creatures of the sunlit surface waters, or of those twilight regions beneath.

Here in the sea mingle elements which, in their long and amazing history, have lent life and strength and beauty to a bewildering variety of living creatures. Ions of calcium, now free in the water, were borrowed years ago from the sea to form part of the protective armor of a mollusk, returned to the main reservoir when their temporary owner had ceased to have need of them, and later incorporated into the delicate statuary of a coral reef. Here are atoms of silica, once imprisoned in a layer of flint in subterranean darkness; later, within the fragile shell of a diatom, tossed by waves and warmed by the sun; and again entering into the exquisite structure of a radiolarian shell, that miracle of ephemeral beauty that might be the work of a fairy glass-blower with a snowflake as his pattern.

Except for precipitous slopes and regions swept bare by submarine currents, the ocean floor is covered with primeval oozes in which there have been accumulating for æons deposits of varied origin; earth-born materials freighted seaward by rivers or worn from the shores of continents by the ceaseless grinding of waves; volcanic dust transported long distances by wind, floating lightly on the surface and eventually sinking into the depths to mingle with the products of no less mighty eruptions of submarine volcanoes; spherules of iron and nickel from interstellar space; and substances of organic origin—the silicious skeletons of Radiolaria[7] and the frustules[8] of diatoms, the limey remains of algæ and corals, and the shells of minute Foraminifera[9] and delicate pelagic[10] snails.

While the bottoms near the shore are covered with detritus from the land, the remains of the floating and swimming creatures of the sea prevail in the deep waters of the open ocean. Beneath tropical seas, in depths of 1000 to 1500 fathoms, calcareous oozes cover nearly a third of the ocean floor; while the colder waters of the temperate and polar regions release to the underlying bottom the silicious remains of diatoms and Radiolaria. In the red clay that carpets the great deeps at 3000 fathoms or more, such

25

---

[7]*Radiolaria:* an order of marine protozoans with rigid skeletons made of silica. [Eds.]

[8]*frustule:* the hard siliceous bivalve shell of a diatom. [Eds.]

[9]*Foraminifera:* a type of marine protozoa. [Eds.]

[10]*pelagic:* living in open oceans rather than near land. [Eds.]

delicate skeletons are extremely rare. Among the few organic remains not dissolved before they reach these cold and silent depths are the ear bones of whales and the teeth of sharks.

Thus we see the parts of the plan fall into place: the water receiving from earth and air the simple materials, storing them up until the gathering energy of the spring sun wakens the sleeping plants to a burst of dynamic activity, hungry swarms of planktonic animals growing and multiplying upon the abundant plants, and themselves falling prey to the shoals of fish; all, in the end, to be redissolved into their component substances when the inexorable laws of the sea demand it. Individual elements are lost to view, only to reappear again and again in different incarnations in a kind of material immortality. Kindred forces to those which, in some period inconceivably remote, gave birth to that primeval bit of protoplasm tossing on the ancient seas continue their mighty and incomprehensible work. Against this cosmic background the life span of a particular plant or animal appears, not as a drama complete in itself, but only as a brief interlude in a panorama of endless change.

QUESTIONS

1. Note the large number of footnoted words in this selection, a vocabulary that serves to underscore the vast "otherness" of the ocean. How does Carson help her readers meet these difficulties?
2. One tactic of this selection is that of spatial arrangement. Carson begins at the ocean's edge and moves farther out and deeper down into the sea. Make a brief outline of her progress. How many stages do you find?
3. Carson spends a disproportionate amount of the essay on tidal pools at the ocean's edge. Why do you think that is?
4. Another tactic of the author is to draw on more familiar geographical terms: plateau, prairie, river, and rain. Do you take these terms to be largely metaphorical or mostly literal?
5. At least twice, in paragraph 10 and at the very end, Carson summarizes a grand design or "plan." In the earlier instance she also describes the ocean as a "place of paradoxes." To what extent do you find the final paragraph to be a restating of paragraph 10, and why do you think "paradox" no longer appears in it?

MAKING CONNECTIONS

1. Compare and contrast Carson's report with that of Pico Iyer's about the Los Angeles International Airport (p. 270), where geography also plays a part, as do other categories of place and behavior.
2. Write your own report on an alien place with which you can make yourself familiar.

EXPLAINING

Here in "Explaining," you will find writing by specialists from a wide range of fields seeking to account for matters as various as the color of the sky, the origin of the universe, the content of urban legends, and the art of keeping a notebook. Explanation is an essential kind of writing in every academic field and profession. Facts, after all, do not speak for themselves, nor do figures add up on their own. To make sense of a subject, we need to see it in terms of something that is related to it—the color of the sky in terms of light-waves from the sun, the content of urban legends in terms of the immediate circumstances in which they are told. To understand a subject, in other words, we must examine it in terms of some relevant context that will shed light on its origin and development, its nature and design, its elements and functions, its causes and effects, or its meaning and significance. For this reason, you will repeatedly find the writers in this section drawing on specific bodies of knowledge and systems of interpretation to explain the problems and subjects that they address.

This essential element of explaining can be seen in connection with the following passage from James Jeans's "Why the Sky Is Blue":

> We know that sunlight is a blend of lights of many colors—as we can prove for ourselves by passing it through a prism, or even through a jug of water, or as Nature demonstrates to us when she passes it through the raindrops of a summer shower and produces a rainbow. We also know that light consists of waves, and that the different colors of light are produced by waves of different lengths, red light by long waves and blue light by short waves. The mixture of waves which constitutes sunlight has to struggle through the obstacles it meets in the atmosphere, just as the mixture of waves at the seaside has to struggle past the columns of the pier. And these obstacles treat the light-waves much as the columns of the pier

323

treat the sea-waves. The long waves which constitute red light are hardly affected, but the short waves which constitute blue light are scattered in all directions.

Thus, the different constituents of sunlight are treated in different ways as they struggle through the earth's atmosphere. A wave of blue light may be scattered by a dust particle, and turned out of its course. After a time a second dust particle again turns it out of its course, and so on, until finally it enters our eyes by a path as zigzag as that of a flash of lightning. Consequently the blue waves of the sunlight enter our eyes from all directions. And that is why the sky looks blue.

Jeans's purpose here is to explain why the sky looks blue, and as you can see from the opening sentence of the passage, he systematically establishes an explanatory context by setting forth directly relevant information about the nature and properties of sunlight, light, and light waves. That is, he approaches the explanatory problem in terms of knowledge drawn from his specialized fields of astronomy and physics. With this knowledge in hand, he then proceeds to show how "the different constituents of sunlight are treated in different ways as they struggle through the earth's atmosphere." In this way, he develops his explanation according to the analytic framework one would expect of an astronomer and physicist, concerning himself with the interaction of the atmosphere and light waves. Having formulated a cause-and-effect analysis demonstrating that blue light is scattered "in all directions," Jeans is able to conclude that "the blue waves of the sunlight enter our eyes from all directions. And that is why the sky looks blue." Thus, the particular body of information that Jeans draws on from astronomy and physics makes it possible for him to offer a knowledgeable, systematic, and instructive explanation.

To appreciate how significant an explanatory context can be, you need only consider how knowledge from other fields might influence an understanding of why the sky looks blue. A zoologist specializing in optics, for example, might note the importance of the retinal organs known as cones, which in animals are thought to be the mechanism primarily responsible for the reception of color. Given this crucial bit of information, a zoologist might observe that the sky looks blue to human beings because their eyes are equipped with cones, whereas it does not look blue to animals lacking cones, such as guinea pigs, owls, and armadillos. An anthropologist, in turn, might think it worth noting that coastal and island cultures, given their maritime environments, tend to develop unusually rich vocabularies for describing how the sea looks and how the sky looks. Thus, an anthropologist might conclude that members of maritime cultures are likely to be especially discerning about the colors of the sea and sky.

Our hypothetical zoologist and anthropologist would both differ from Jeans in their explanatory approaches to the blue sky. Whereas Jeans approached it in terms of accounting for the source and prevalence of blue color, a zoologist and an anthropologist might take the color for granted and seek instead to account for the human ability to perceive the color or the propensity of some cultures to be especially discriminating in their perception of it. Their differing approaches would result from their differing fields of study. Each academic area, after all, involves a distinctive body of knowledge, a distinctive array of interests, and a distinctive set of methods for making sense of the subjects that fall within its field of interest. Thus it follows that each area is likely to approach problems from different angles and arrive at different kinds of explanations. It follows, too, that no area can lay claim to the ultimate truth about things. But, as the case of the blue sky illustrates, each field does have a special angle on the truth, particularly about subjects that fall within its area of specialization. A zoologist and an anthropologist could be as valid and as enlightening in this case as astronomer-physicist Jeans. In a broader sense, you can see from the case of the blue sky that in trying to explain a particular subject or problem one always has to look at it or approach it from a particular angle or a combination of viewpoints and that any particular approach brings a corresponding body of knowledge to bear on an understanding of the subject. Relevant knowledge, quite simply, is the most essential element of explaining.

But knowledge alone is not sufficient to produce intelligible and effective explanation. Jeans's explanation, for example, depends not only on a body of information about the properties and movement of light and lightwaves but also, as you will see, on the form and style in which the information is presented. To develop your ability to explain, then, you will need to develop a resourcefulness in putting your knowledge to use. One way to do that is to familiarize yourself with some of the many different forms that explanatory writing can take in different academic and professional situations.

The Range of Explanatory Writing

Explanatory writing serves a wide range of academic, professional, and public purposes. Rules and regulations, guidelines and instructions—all these are familiar examples of explanation in the service of telling people how to carry on many of the practical and public activities of their lives. Textbooks, such as the one you are reading right now, as well as popularized presentations of highly specialized research or theory are common examples of explanatory writing in the service of helping people understand a particular body of information and ideas. Scholarly research papers, government documents, and other highly technical presentations of data and analysis, though less familiar to the general reader, are important kinds of explanation that advance knowledge and informed decision making.

To serve the differing needs of such varied purposes and audiences, explanatory writing necessarily incorporates various styles of presentation.

Jeans's piece about the sky, for example, comes from a book intended as an introduction to astronomy. Thus, he writes in a style that depends on a vocabulary accessible to most readers. And to make sure that beginners will understand the important concepts in his explanation, Jeans repeatedly illustrates his discussion with analogies and references to familiar experiences. In fact, if you look at the whole of Jeans's piece, you will see that he establishes his analogy of light-waves to sea-waves at the very beginning of his discussion and then systematically uses it to organize and clarify the rest of his explanation.

For another variation in the format and style of explanatory writing, we need only look at Oliver Sacks's "The Man Who Mistook His Wife for a Hat." Here Sacks is offering the results of a case study, which entails the close observation of an individual subject over time. Because the subject of a case study is by definition unique, the study cannot be replicated by other researchers. A case study, therefore, must be written up in sufficient detail not only to document the observer's understanding of the subject, but also to enable other researchers to draw their own conclusions about the subject. You will find that Sacks provides an extensively detailed description, history, and analysis of Dr. P.'s behavior. You will also find that Sacks writes on the whole in a standard rather than specialized style, as befits an audience of generally educated readers.

Explanation is a widely varied form of writing, involving as it does in every case a delicate mix of adjustments to the audience, purpose, specialized field, and subject matter. As a reader of explanation, you will have to be very flexible in your approach, always willing to make your way through unfamiliar territory on the way to a clear understanding of the subject being discussed, or perhaps to a clear recognition that understanding may be beyond the scope of your knowledge in a particular field. As a writer, you will have to be equally flexible in your choice of language and your selection and arrangement of material so as to put your knowledge and understanding in a form that not only satisfies you, but also fulfills the complex set of conditions to which your explanation is addressed.

Methods of Explaining

In planning a piece of explanatory writing, you should begin by reviewing your material with an eye to selecting an overall approach to use. You should aim to develop an approach that is adjusted to all the conditions of your explanatory situation. Some methods, you will find, are inescapable, no matter what your subject, audience, or purpose. Every piece of explanation requires that ideas be clarified and demonstrated through *illustration*—that is, through the citing of specific examples, as you can see from the earlier passage by Jeans and in the following excerpt from Sacks's essay on Dr. P., the musician:

He saw all right, but what did he see? I opened out a copy of the *National Geographic Magazine* and asked him to describe some pictures in it.

His responses here were very curious. His eyes would dart from one thing to another, picking up tiny features, individual features, as they had done with my face. A striking brightness, a color, a shape would arrest his attention and elicit comment—but in no case did he get the scene-as-a-whole. He failed to see the whole, seeing only details, which he spotted like blips on a radar screen. He never entered into relation with the picture as a whole—never faced, so to speak, *its* physiognomy. He had no sense whatever of a landscape or scene.

I showed him the cover, an unbroken expanse of Sahara dunes. "What do you see here?" I asked.

"I see a river," he said. "And a little guest-house with its terrace on the water. People are dining out on the terrace. I see colored parasols here and there." He was looking, if it was "looking," right off the cover into mid-air and confabulating nonexistent features, as if the absence of features in the actual picture had driven him to imagine the river and the terrace and the colored parasols.

I must have looked aghast, but he seemed to think he had done rather well. There was a hint of a smile on his face. He also appeared to have decided that the examination was over and started to look around for his hat. He reached out his hand and took hold of his wife's head, tried to lift it off, to put it on. He had apparently mistaken his wife for a hat! His wife looked as if she was used to such things.

Sacks's obligation to illustrate and demonstrate Dr. P.'s unusual symptoms leads him here, as elsewhere in his piece, to turn to a detailed *description* and *narration* of Dr. P.'s actions. So it is that reporting constitutes an essential element of explaining—and not only for reasons of clarity, but also for purposes of reliability and credibility. If an explanation cannot be illustrated or can be only weakly documented, it is likely to be much less reliable and therefore much less credible to readers than one that can be amply and vividly detailed.

Some methods, while not required in every case, are often so important in certain pieces of explanation that they should be kept in mind. An essay that depends on the use of special terms or concepts almost certainly will call for *definitions* to ensure that the reader understands them exactly as the writer intends them to be understood. In "Urban Legends: 'The Boyfriend's Death,'" for example, Jan Harold Brunvand begins his study by carefully defining urban legends as a subclass of folklore and by defining in turn what is entailed in the study of folklore.

In his essay about Dr. P., Sacks proceeds in a different way. He presents the case of Dr. P., who is suffering from visual agnosia, by trying to replicate for the reader his own process of uncovering the mystery lying behind Dr. P.'s unusual behavior. He shows, through description and dialogue with Dr. P. and his wife, the remarkable things Dr. P. can do—demonstrate his extraordinary musical ability, for example—and the ordinary things he cannot do, such as recognize the faces of his wife and friends. At the end of this descriptive section, Sacks reveals the pathological cause of Dr. P.'s visual agnosia. But that is insufficient explanation for Sacks. He then goes on to ask how Dr. P.'s inability to make cognitive judgments should be interpreted. He talks about the limitations of neurological and psychological explanations of what appear to be neuropsychological disorders when those sciences overlook "the judgmental, the particular, the personal" and rely on the "abstract and computational" alone. In so doing, Sacks defines the limits of cognitive neurology and psychology, suggesting that they, too, may suffer from "an agnosia essentially similar to Dr. P's." Definition, in other words, can be carried out in a variety of ways—by citing examples, by identifying essential qualities or characteristics, by offering synonyms, by making distinctions.

Other methods of explanation, while not necessarily imperative, can be very effective in a broad range of explanatory situations. If you are trying to explain the character, design, elements, or nature of something, you will often do best to *compare and contrast* it with something to which it is logically and self-evidently related. Comparison calls attention to similarities; contrast focuses on differences. Together, the methods work to clarify and emphasize important points by playing related subjects against each other. In his study of urban legends, for example, Brunvand attempts to shed light on the complex circumstances that influence the content of such folktales by comparing and contrasting several versions of the same legendary story. This method enables him to show that popular urban legends, such as "The Boyfriend's Death," retain a basically unvarying situation and plot as they travel from one storyteller and locale to another, but that specific details are altered by individual storytellers to make them fit the circumstances of a particular audience. Like Brunvand's piece, some examples of comparison and contrast rely on a strategic balancing of similarities and differences. Other pieces depend largely on a sustained contrast. And still other pieces might work primarily in terms of comparison. By the same token, you should make sure that whenever you use comparison and contrast, your attention to similarities and differences is adjusted to the needs of your explanatory situation.

A special form of comparison, namely *analogy,* can also be useful in many explanatory situations. Analogies help readers understand difficult or unfamiliar ideas by putting them in tangible and familiar terms. In "Why the Sky Is Blue," for example, Jeans's analogy of light waves to sea-waves enables us to visualize a process that we could not otherwise see. As useful as analogies are, however, they rely at last on drawing particular resemblances between things that are otherwise unlike. Sea waves, after all, are not light waves, and the dimensions of the universe are not the same as anything within the range of ordinary human experience. Whenever you develop an analogy, you should be careful in applying it to your explanatory situation to make sure that the analogy fits and that it does not involve misleading implications.

Some explanatory methods are especially suited to a particular kind of situation. If you are trying to show how to do something or how something works or how something was done, you will find it best to use a method known as *process analysis*. In analyzing a process, your aim is to make it clear to a reader by providing a narrative breakdown and presentation of it step-by-step, by identifying and describing each step or stage in the process, by showing how each step leads to the next, and by explaining how the process as a whole leads to its final result. Jeans's piece, for example, analyzes the process by which light waves from the sun make their way through the earth's atmosphere and determine human perception of the color of the sky.

A method related to process analysis is *causal analysis*. As the term suggests, this type of analysis seeks to get at the causes of things, particularly causes that are sufficiently complex as to be open to various lines of explanation. Usually, then, a causal analysis involves a careful investigation that works backward from something difficult to account for through an examination of various causes that might account for the situation. Sometimes, however, an analysis might work forward from a particular cause to the various effects it has produced; Carol Gilligan uses this method in "Interviewing Adolescent Girls" when she shows that the problems of adolescent girls are problems of connection, of "drowning" in "the sea of Western [largely male] culture." Because no two things can be identically accounted for, no set method exists for carrying out a causal analysis. Keep in mind, however, a few cautionary procedures. You should review other possible causes and other related circumstances before attempting to assert the priority of one cause or set of causes over another, and you should present enough evidence to demonstrate the reliability of your explanation. By doing so, you will avoid the temptation to oversimplify things.

As you can probably tell by now, almost any piece of writing that aims to make sense of something will invariably have to combine several methods of explanation. This should come as no surprise if you stop to think about the way people usually explain even the simplest things in their day-to-day conversations with each other. Just ask someone, for example, to give you directions for getting from one place to another, and you will probably find that the person gives you both an overview of where the place is situated and a step-by-step set of movements to follow and places to look for, as well as brief descriptions of the most prominent guideposts along the way, and possibly even a review of the original directions, together with a brief remark or two about misleading spots to avoid. By the same token, whenever people try to explain something in writing, they want to help readers get from one place to another in a particular subject matter. Thus, in the midst of giving a process analysis or causal analysis, a writer might feel compelled to illustrate this point or define that term or offer a telling analogy.

In the several pieces that make up this section, you will see how writers in different fields combine various methods of explaining things. And in the next section, you will see how explaining also contributes to arguing.

Arts and Humanities

ON KEEPING A NOTEBOOK

Joan Didion

Joan Didion was born in Sacramento, California, in 1934 and graduated from the University of California at Berkeley in 1956. Until the publication of her first novel, Run River, *in 1963, she woked as an editor for* Vogue *magazine. Since then, she has written four more novels, including* Play It As It Lays *(1971) and* The Last Thing He Wanted *(1996); five books of essays, most notably* Slouching towards Bethlehem *(1968) and* The White Album *(1979); and, in collaboration with her husband, John Gregory Dunne, a number of successful screenplays. As both novelist and essayist, Didion has shown herself to be a trenchant observer and interpreter of American society and culture. Many of her essays also explore her own private life in intimate detail. The following piece appeared in* Holiday *magazine in 1966 and was collected in* Slouching towards Bethlehem.

"'That woman Estelle,'" the note reads, "'is partly the reason why George Sharp and I are separated today.' *Dirty crepe-de-Chine wrapper, hotel bar, Wilmington RR, 9:45 a.m. August Monday morning.*"

Since the note is in my notebook, it presumably has some meaning to me. I study it for a long while. At first I have only the most general notion of what I was doing on an August Monday morning in the bar of the hotel across from the Pennsylvania Railroad station in Wilmington, Delaware (waiting for a train? missing one? 1960? 1961? why Wilmington?), but I do remember being there. The woman in the dirty crepe-de-Chine wrapper had come down from her room for a beer, and the bartender had heard before the reason why George Sharp and she were separated today. "Sure," he said, and went on mopping the floor. "You told me." At the other end of the bar is a girl. She is talking, pointedly, not to the man beside her but to a cat lying in the triangle of sunlight cast through the open door. She is wearing a plaid silk dress from Peck & Peck, and the hem is coming down.

Here is what it is: the girl has been on the Eastern Shore, and now she is going back to the city, leaving the man beside her, and all she can see ahead are the viscous summer sidewalks and the 3 A.M. long-distance calls that will make her lie awake and then sleep drugged through all the steaming mornings left in August (1960? 1961?). Because she must go directly from the train to lunch in New York, she wishes that she had a safety pin for the hem of the plaid silk dress, and she also wishes that she could forget about the hem and the lunch and stay in the cool bar that smells of disinfectant and malt and make friends with the woman in the crepe-de-Chine wrapper. She is afflicted by a little self-pity, and she wants to compare Estelles. That is what that was all about.

Why did I write it down? In order to remember, of course, but exactly what was it I wanted to remember? How much of it actually happened? Did any of it? Why do I keep a notebook at all? It is easy to deceive oneself on all those scores. The impulse to write things down is a peculiarly compulsive one, inexplicable to those who do not share it, useful only accidentally, only secondarily, in the way that any compulsion tries to justify itself. I suppose that it begins or does not begin in the cradle. Although I have felt compelled to write things down since I was five years old, I doubt that my daughter ever will, for she is a singularly blessed and accepting child, delighted with life exactly as life presents itself to her, unafraid to go to sleep and unafraid to wake up. Keepers of private notebooks are a different breed altogether, lonely and resistant rearrangers of things, anxious malcontents, children afflicted apparently at birth with some presentiment of loss.

My first notebook was a Big Five tablet, given to me by my mother   5
with the sensible suggestion that I stop whining and learn to amuse myself by writing down my thoughts. She returned the tablet to me a few years ago; the first entry is an account of a woman who believed herself to be freezing to death in the Arctic night, only to find, when day broke, that she had stumbled onto the Sahara Desert, where she would die of the heat before lunch. I have no idea what turn of a five-year-old's mind could have prompted so insistently "ironic" and exotic a story, but it does reveal a certain predilection for the extreme which has dogged me into adult life; perhaps if I were analytically inclined I would find it a truer story than any I might have told about Donald Johnson's birthday party or the day my cousin Brenda put Kitty Litter in the aquarium.

So the point of my keeping a notebook has never been, nor is it now, to have an accurate factual record of what I have been doing or thinking. That would be a different impulse entirely, an instinct for reality which I sometimes envy but do not possess. At no point have I ever been able successfully to keep a diary; my approach to daily life ranges from the grossly negligent to the merely absent, and on those few occasions when I have tried dutifully to record a day's events, boredom has so overcome me that the results are mysterious at best. What is this business about "shopping, typing piece, dinner with E, depressed"? Shopping for what? Typing what piece? Who is E? Was this "E" depressed, or was I depressed? Who cares?

In fact I have abandoned altogether that kind of pointless entry; instead I tell what some would call lies. "That's simply not true," the members of my family frequently tell me when they come up against my memory of a shared event. "The party was *not* for you, the spider was *not* a black widow, *it wasn't that way at all.*" Very likely they are right, for not only have I always had trouble distinguishing between what happened and what merely might have happened, but I remain unconvinced that the distinction, for my purposes, matters. The cracked crab that I recall having for lunch the day my father came home from Detroit in 1945 must certainly be embroidery, worked into the day's pattern to lend verisimilitude; I was ten years old and would not now remember the cracked crab. The day's events did not turn on cracked crab. And yet it is precisely that fictitious crab that makes me see the afternoon all over again, a home movie run all too often, the father bearing gifts, the child weeping, an exercise in family love and guilt. Or that is what it was to me. Similarly, perhaps it never did snow that August in Vermont; perhaps there never were flurries in the night wind, and maybe no one else felt the ground hardening and summer already dead even as we pretended to bask in it, but that was how it felt to me, and it might as well have snowed, could have snowed, did snow.

How it felt to me: that is getting closer to the truth about a notebook. I sometimes delude myself about why I keep a notebook, imagine that some thrifty virtue derives from preserving everything observed. See enough and write it down, I tell myself, and then some morning when the world seems drained of wonder, some day when I am only going through the motions of doing what I am supposed to do, which is write—on that bankrupt morning I will simply open my notebook and there it will all be, a forgotten account with accumulated interest, paid passage back to the world out there: dialogue overheard in hotels and elevators and at the hat-check counter in Pavillon (one middle-aged man shows his hat check to another and says, "That's my old football number"); impressions of Bettina Aptheker and Benjamin Sonnenberg and Teddy ("Mr. Acapulco") Stauffer; careful *aperçus* about tennis bums and failed fashion models and Greek shipping heiresses, one of whom taught me a significant lesson (a lesson) I could have learned from F. Scott Fitzgerald, but perhaps we all must meet the very rich for ourselves by asking, when I arrived to interview her in her orchid-filled sitting room on the second day of a paralyzing New York blizzard, whether it was snowing outside.

I imagine, in other words, that the notebook is about other people. But of course it is not. I have no real business with what one stranger said to another at the hat-check counter in Pavillon; in fact I suspect that the line "That's my old football number" touched not my own imagination at all, but merely some memory of something once read, probably "The Eighty-

Yard Run." Nor is my concern with a woman in a dirty crepe-de-Chine wrapper in a Wilmington bar. My stake is always, of course, in the unmentioned girl in the plaid silk dress. *Remember what it was to be me:* that is always the point.

It is a difficult point to admit. We are brought up in the ethic that oth-   10 ers, any others, all others, are by definition more interesting than ourselves; taught to be diffident, just this side of self-effacing. ("You're the least important person in the room and don't forget it," Jessica Mitford's governess would hiss in her ear on the advent of any social occasion; I copied that into my notebook because it is only recently that I have been able to enter a room without hearing some such phrase in my inner ear.) Only the very young and the very old may recount their dreams at breakfast, dwell upon self, interrupt with memories of beach picnics and favorite Liberty lawn dresses and the rainbow trout in a creek near Colorado Springs. The rest of us are expected, rightly, to affect absorption in other people's favorite dresses, other people's trout.

And so we do. But our notebooks give us away, for however dutifully we record what we see around us, the common denominator of all we see is always, transparently, shamelessly, the implacable "I." We are not talking here about the kind of notebook that is patently for public consumption, a structural conceit for binding together a series of graceful *pensées;* we are talking about something private, about bits of the mind's string too short to use, an indiscriminate and erratic assemblage with meaning only for its maker.

And sometimes even the maker has difficulty with the meaning. There does not seem to be, for example, any point in my knowing for the rest of my life that, during 1964, 720 tons of soot fell on every square mile of New York City, yet there it is in my notebook, labeled "FACT". Nor do I really need to remember that Ambrose Bierce liked to spell Leland Stanford's name "£eland $tanford" or that "smart women almost always wear black in Cuba," a fashion hint without much potential for practical application. And does not the relevance of these notes seem marginal at best?:

In the basement museum of the Inyo County Courthouse in Independence, California, sign pinned to a mandarin coat: "This MANDARIN COAT was often worn by Mrs. Minnie S. Brooks when giving lectures on her TEAPOT COLLECTION."

Redhead getting out of car in front of Beverly Wilshire Hotel, chinchilla stole, Vuitton bags with tags reading:

> MRS LOU FOX
> HOTEL SAHARA
> VEGAS

Well, perhaps not entirely marginal. As a matter of fact, Mrs. Minnie S. Brooks and her MANDARIN COAT pull me back into my own childhood, for although I never knew Mrs. Brooks and did not visit Inyo County until I was thirty, I grew up in just such a world, in houses cluttered with Indian relics and bits of gold ore and ambergris and the souvenirs my Aunt Mercy Farnsworth brought back from the Orient. It is a long way from that world to Mrs. Lou Fox's world, where we all live now, and is it not just as well to remember that? Might not Mrs. Minnie S. Brooks help me to remember what I am? Might not Mrs. Lou Fox help me to remember what I am not?

But sometimes the point is harder to discern. What exactly did I have in mind when I noted down that it cost the father of someone I know $650 a month to light the place on the Hudson in which he lived before the Crash? What use was I planning to make of this line by Jimmy Hoffa: "I may have my faults, but being wrong ain't one of them"? And although I think it interesting to know where the girls who travel with the Syndicate have their hair done when they find themselves on the West Coast, will I ever make suitable use of it? Might I not be better off just passing it on to John O'Hara? What is a recipe for sauerkraut doing in my notebook? What kind of magpie keeps this notebook? "*He was born the night the Titanic went down.*" That seems a nice enough line, and I even recall who said it, but is it not really a better line in life than it could ever be in fiction?

But of course that is exactly it: not that I should ever use the line, but   15
that I should remember the woman who said it and the afternoon I heard it. We were on her terrace by the sea, and we were finishing the wine left from lunch, trying to get what sun there was, a California winter sun. The woman whose husband was born the night the *Titanic* went down wanted to rent her house, wanted to go back to her children in Paris. I remember wishing that I could afford the house, which cost $1,000 a month. "Someday you will," she said lazily. "Someday it all comes." There in the sun on her terrace it seemed easy to believe in someday, but later I had a low-grade afternoon hangover and ran over a black snake on the way to the supermarket and was flooded with inexplicable fear when I heard the checkout clerk explaining to the man ahead of me why she was finally divorcing her husband. "He left me no choice," she said over and over as she punched the register. "He has a little seven-month-old baby by her, he left me no choice." I would like to believe that my dread then was for the human condition, but of course it was for me, because I wanted a baby and did not then have one and because I wanted to own the house that cost $1,000 a month to rent and because I had a hangover.

It all comes back. Perhaps it is difficult to see the value in having one's self back in that kind of mood, but I do see it; I think we are well advised to keep on nodding terms with the people we used to be, whether we find them attractive company or not. Otherwise they turn up unannounced and surprise us, come hammering on the mind's door at 4 A.M. of a bad night and demand to know who deserted them, who betrayed them, who is going to make amends. We forget all too soon the things we thought we could never forget. We forget the loves and the betrayals alike, forget what we whispered and what we screamed, forget who we were. I have already lost touch with a couple of people I used to be; one of them, a seventeen-year-old, presents little threat, although it would be of some interest to me to know again what it feels like to sit on a river levee drinking vodka-and-orange-juice and listening to Les Paul and Mary Ford and their echoes sing "How High the Moon" on the car radio. (You see I still have the scenes, but I no longer perceive myself among those present, no longer could even improvise the dialogue.) The other one, a twenty-three-year-old, bothers me more. She was always a good deal of trouble, and I suspect she will reappear when I least want to see her, skirts too long, shy to the point of aggravation, always the injured party, full of recriminations and little hurts and stories I do not want to hear again, at once saddening me and angering me with her vulnerability and ignorance, an apparition all the more insistent for being so long banished.

It is a good idea, then, to keep in touch, and I suppose that keeping in touch is what notebooks are all about. And we are all on our own when it comes to keeping those lines open to ourselves: your notebook will never help me, nor mine you. *"So what's new in the whiskey business?"* What could that possibly mean to you? To me it means a blonde in a Pucci bathing suit sitting with a couple of fat men by the pool at the Beverly Hills Hotel. Another man approaches, and they all regard one another in silence for a while. "So what's new in the whiskey business?" one of the fat men finally says by way of welcome, and the blonde stands up, arches one foot and dips it in the pool, looking all the while at the cabaña where Baby Pignatari is talking on the telephone. That is all there is to that, except that several years later I saw the blonde coming out of Saks Fifth Avenue in New York with her California complexion and a voluminous mink coat. In the harsh wind that day she looked old and irrevocably tired to me, and even the skins in the mink coat were not worked the way they were doing them that year, not the way she would have wanted them done, and there is the point of the story. For a while after that I did not like to look in the mirror, and my eyes would skim the newspapers and pick out only the deaths, the cancer victims, the premature coronaries, the suicides, and I stopped riding the Lexington Avenue IRT because I noticed for the first time that all the strangers I had seen for years—the man with the seeing-eye dog, the spinster who read the classified pages every day, the fat girl who always got off with me at Grand Central—looked older than they once had.

It all comes back. Even that recipe for sauerkraut: even that brings it back. I was on Fire Island when I first made that sauerkraut, and it was raining, and we drank a lot of bourbon and ate the sauerkraut and went to bed at ten, and I listened to the rain and the Atlantic and felt safe. I made the sauerkraut again last night and it did not make me feel any safer, but that is, as they say, another story.

1966

QUESTIONS

1. The first paragraphs of Didion's essay present a pattern that she replicates throughout the remainder of the piece: the transcription of a passage from her notebook, followed by an elaboration and a subsequent attempt to explain her original motives for taking note of this observation. She thereby reproduces her own curiosity about her writing. How many times does she quote from her notebook, and how do her responses differ (in length, emphasis, quality)? How do the responses evolve as the essay progresses?

2. Didion offers a number of tentative answers to her main question, "Why do I keep a notebook at all?" Make a list of these responses and how they are revised throughout the essay. Why doesn't she simply explain at the beginning "what notebooks are all about," rather than waiting until the last paragraphs? Do you find this way of explaining to be effective? Explain why or why not.

3. Consider the title of the essay, "On Keeping a Notebook." Select a phrase from the essay itself which you think would serve as a better title, for example, "How it felt to me," or "the truth about a notebook," or make up your own. How does the title of an essay (yours included) create expectations about what will be explained in the body of the text?

4. How does Didion distinguish between a diary and a notebook? Does that distinction affect her sense of the difference "between what happened and what merely might have happened"? Is Didion concerned with "the truth" in her notebook writing?

5. Didion's style feels somewhat like a conversation with herself—note how she begins some sentences informally with words like *So, Or, And, Well.* In effect, she's working through a dialogue between her present and her past. Write an essay in which you quote your own writing from a different period (your notebook, journal, or even a writing assignment from a previous year) and then reflect on why this was so important to you at the time. What does it teach you about "keeping in touch" with your past selves?

6. What is "the point" of notebooks for you? Begin an essay with a statement from Didion with which you disagree, and then proceed to discuss what you suggest as an alternative reason for writing.

MAKING CONNECTIONS

Didion writes: "I think we are well-advised to keep on nodding terms with the people we used to be, whether we find them attractive company or not." Compare how writers such as Joan Didion, Maya Angelou "Graduation" (p. 31), or Alice Walker "Beauty, When the Other Dancer Is the Self" (p. 42) view events from their youth, and how they connect their youthful experiences to adult knowledge.

URBAN LEGENDS
"The Boyfriend's Death"

Jan Harold Brunvand

Trained in the study of folklore, Jan Harold Brunvand (b. 1933) has become a leading collector and interpreter of contemporary legends. These "urban legends" are stories told around campfires and in college dormitories, often as true experiences that happened to somebody other than the teller of the tale. For many years a professor at the University of Utah, Brunvand has been the editor of the Journal of American Folklore *and* American Folklore: An Encyclopedia *(1996), and is the author of the standard introduction to the field,* The Study of American Folklore: An Introduction, *fourth edition (1997). The following selection is taken from the first of his several collections of urban legends,* The Vanishing Hitchhiker: American Urban Legends and Their Meanings *(1981). Here Brunvand defines* urban legend, *gives one striking example, and offers some explanations about how and why such stories flourish even in the midst of a highly technologized society. The selection as reprinted is complete, except for the deletion of a few brief references to other discussions elsewhere in Brunvand's book.*

We are not aware of our own folklore any more than we are of the grammatical rules of our language. When we follow the ancient practice of informally transmitting "lore" — wisdom, knowledge, or accepted modes of behavior — by word of mouth and customary example from person to person, we do not concentrate on the form or content of our folklore; instead, we simply listen to information that others tell us and then pass it on — more or less accurately — to other listeners. In this stream of unselfconscious oral tradition the information that acquires a clear story line is called *narrative folklore,* and those stories alleged to be true are *legends.* This, in broad summary, is the typical process of legend formation and transmission as it has existed from time immemorial and continues to operate today. It works about the same way whether the legendary plot concerns a dragon in a cave or a mouse in a Coke bottle.

It might seem unlikely that legends — *urban* legends at that — would continue to be created in an age of widespread literacy, rapid mass communications, and restless travel. While our pioneer ancestors may have had to rely heavily on oral traditions to pass the news along about changing events and frontier dangers, surely we no longer need mere "folk" reports of what's happening, with all their tendencies to distort the facts. A moment's reflection, however, reminds us of the many weird, fascinating, but unverified rumors and tales that so frequently come to our ears—killers and madmen on the loose, shocking or funny personal experiences, unsafe manufactured products, and many other unexplained mysteries of daily life. Sometimes we encounter different oral versions of such stories, and on occasion we may read about similar events in newspapers or magazines; but seldom do we find, or even seek after, reliable documentation. The lack of verification in no way diminishes the appeal urban legends have for us. We enjoy them merely as stories, and we tend at least to half-believe them as possibly accurate reports. And the legends we tell, as with any folklore, reflect many of the hopes, fears, and anxieties of our time. In short, legends are definitely part of our modern folklore—legends which are as traditional, variable, and functional as those of the past.

Folklore study consists of collecting, classifying, and interpreting in their full cultural context the many products of everyday human interaction that have acquired a somewhat stable underlying form and that are passed traditionally from person to person, group to group, and generation to generation. Legend study is a most revealing area of such research because the stories that people believe to be true hold an important place in their worldview. "If it's true, it's important" is an axiom to be trusted, whether or not the lore really *is* true or not. Simply becoming aware of this modern folklore which we all possess to some degree is a revelation in itself, but going beyond this to compare the tales, isolate their consistent themes, and relate them to the rest of the culture can yield rich insights into the state of our current civilization. . . .

Urban Legends as Folklore

Folklore subsists on oral tradition, but not all oral communication is folklore. The vast amounts of human interchange, from casual daily conversations to formal discussions in business or industry, law, or teaching, rarely constitute straight oral folklore. However, all such "communicative events" (as scholars dub them) are punctuated routinely by various units of traditional material that are memorable, repeatable, and that fit recurring social situations well enough to serve in place of original remarks. "Tradition" is the key idea that links together such utterances as nicknames, proverbs, greeting and leave-taking formulas, wisecracks, anecdotes, and jokes as "folklore"; indeed, these are a few of the best known "conversational genres" of American folklore. Longer and more complex folk forms —fairy tales, epics, myths, legends, or ballads, for example—may thrive only in certain special situations of oral transmission. All true folklore ultimately depends upon continued oral dissemination, usually within fairly homogeneous "folk groups," and upon the retention through time of internal patterns and motifs that become traditional in the oral exchanges.

The corollary of this rule of stability in oral tradition is that all items of folklore, while retaining a fixed central core, are constantly changing as they are transmitted, so as to create countless "variants" differing in length, detail, style, and performance technique. Folklore, in short, consists of oral tradition in variants.

Urban legends belong to the subclass of folk narratives, legends,   5 that—unlike fairy tales—are believed, or at least believable, and that— unlike myths—are set in the recent past and involve normal human beings rather than ancient gods or demigods. Legends are folk history, or rather quasi-history. As with any folk legends, urban legends gain credibility from specific details of time and place or from references to source authorities. For instance, a popular western pioneer legend often begins something like, "My great-grandmother had this strange experience when she was a young girl on a wagon train going through Wyoming when an Indian chief wanted to adopt her. . . ." Even though hundreds of different great- grandmothers are supposed to have had the same doubtful experience (being desired by the chief because of her beautiful long blond hair), the fact seldom reaches legend-tellers; if it does, they assume that the family lore has indeed spread far and wide. This particular popular tradition, known as "Goldilocks on the Oregon Trail," interests folklorists because of the racist implications of a dark Indian savage coveting a fair young civ- ilized woman—this legend is familiar in the *white* folklore only—and it is of little concern that the story seems to be entirely apocryphal.

In the world of modern urban legends there is usually no geographical or generational gap between teller and event. The story is *true;* it really oc- curred, and recently, and always to someone else who is quite close to the narrator, or at least "a friend of a friend." Urban legends are told both in the course of casual conversations and in such special situations as camp- fires, slumber parties, and college dormitory bull sessions. The legends' physical settings are often close by, real, and sometimes even locally renowned for other such happenings. Though the characters in the stories are usually nameless, they are true-to-life examples of the kind of people the narrators and their audience know firsthand.

One of the great mysteries of folklore research is where oral traditions originate and who invents them. One might expect that at least in modern folklore we could come up with answers to such questions, but this is sel- dom, if ever, the case. . . .

The Performance of Legends

Whatever the origins of urban legends, their dissemination is no mys- tery. The tales have traveled far and wide, and have been told and retold from person to person in the same manner that myths, fairy tales, or bal- lads spread in earlier cultures, with the important difference that today's legends are also disseminated by the mass media. Groups of age-mates, especially adolescents, are one important American legend channel, but other paths of transmission are among office workers and club members, as well as among religious, recreational, and regional groups. Some individuals make a point of learning every recent rumor or tale, and they can enliven any coffee break, party, or trip with the latest supposed "news." The telling of one story inspires other people to share what they have read or heard, and in a short time a lively exchange of details occurs and perhaps new variants are created.

Tellers of these legends, of course, are seldom aware of their roles as "performers of folklore." The conscious purpose of this kind of story-telling is to convey a true event, and only incidentally to entertain an audience. Nevertheless, the speaker's demeanor is carefully orchestrated, and his or her delivery is low-key and soft-sell. With subtle gestures, eye movements, and vocal inflections the stories are made dramatic, pointed, and suspenseful. But, just as with jokes, some can tell them and some can't. Passive tellers of urban legends may just report them as odd rumors, but the more active legend tellers re-create them as dramatic stories of suspense and, perhaps, humor.

"The Boyfriend's Death"

With all these points in mind folklore's subject-matter style, and oral   10
performance, consider this typical version of a well-known urban legend that folklorists have named "The Boyfriend's Death," collected in 1964 (the earliest documented instance of the story) by folklorist Daniel R. Barnes from an eighteen-year-old freshman at the University of Kansas. The usual tellers of the story are adolescents, and the normal setting for the narration is a college dormitory room with fellow students sprawled on the furniture and floors.

> This happened just a few years ago out on the road that turns off highway 59 by the Holiday Inn. This couple were parked under a tree out on this road. Well, it got to be time for the girl to be back at the dorm, so she told her boyfriend that they should start back. But the car wouldn't start, so he told her to lock herself in the car and he would go down to the Holiday Inn and call for help. Well, he didn't come back and he didn't come back, and pretty soon she started hearing a scratching noise on the roof of the car. "Scratch, scratch . . . scratch, scratch." She got scareder and scareder, but he didn't come back. Finally, when it was almost daylight, some people came along and stopped and helped her out of the car, and she looked up and there was her boyfriend hanging from the tree, and his feet were scraping against the roof of the car. This is why the road is called "Hangman's Road."

Here is a story that has traveled rapidly to reach nationwide oral circulation, in the process becoming structured in the typical manner of folk narratives. The traditional and fairly stable elements are the parked couple, the abandoned girl, the mysterious scratching (sometimes joined by a dripping sound and ghostly shadows on the windshield), the daybreak rescue, and the horrible climax. Variable traits are the precise location, the reason for her abandonment, the nature of the rescuers, murder details, and the concluding placename explanation. While "The Boyfriend's Death" seems to have captured teenagers' imaginations as a separate legend only since the early 1960s, it is clearly related to at least two older yarns, "The Hook" and "The Roommate's Death." All three legends have been widely collected by American folklorists, although only scattered examples have been published, mostly in professional journals. Examination of some of these variations helps to make clear the status of the story as folklore and its possible meanings.

At Indiana University, a leading American center of folklore research, folk-narrative specialist Linda Dégh and her students have gathered voluminous data on urban legends, especially those popular with adolescents. Dégh's preliminary published report on "The Boyfriend's Death" concerned nineteen texts collected from IU students from 1964 to 1968. Several storytellers had heard it in high school, often at parties; others had picked it up in college dormitories or elsewhere on campus. Several students expressed some belief in the legend, supposing either that it had happened in their own hometowns, or possibly in other states, once as far distant as "a remote part of Alabama." One informant reported that "she had been sworn to that the incident actually happened," but another, who had heard some variations of the tale, felt that "it seemed too horrible to be true." Some versions had incorporated motifs from other popular teenage horror legends or local ghost stories. . . .

One of the Indiana texts, told in the state of Washington, localizes the story there near Moses Lake, "in the country on a road that leads to a dead-end right under a big weeping willow tree . . . about four or five miles from town." As in most American versions of the story, these specific local touches make believable what is essentially a traveling legend. In a detail familiar from other variants of "The Boyfriend's Death," the body—now decapitated—is left hanging upside down from a branch of the willow tree with the fingernails scraping the top of the car. Another version studied by the Indiana researcher is somewhat aberrant, perhaps because the student was told the story by a friend's parents who claimed that "it happened a long time ago, probably thirty or forty years." Here a murderer is introduced, a "crazy old lady" on whose property the couple has parked. The victim this time is skinned rather than decapitated, and his head scrapes the car as the corpse swings to and fro in the breezy night.

A developing motif in "The Boyfriend's Death" is the character and role of the rescuers, who in the 1964 Kansas version are merely "some people." The standard identification later becomes "the police," authority figures whose presence lends further credence to the story. They are either called by the missing teenagers' parents, or simply appear on the scene in the morning to check the car. In a 1969 variant from Leonardtown, Maryland, the police give a warning, "Miss, please get out of the car and walk to the police car with us, but don't look back." . . . In a version from Texas collected in 1971, set "at this lake somewhere way out in nowhere," a policeman gets an even longer line: "Young lady, we want you to get out of the car and come with us. Whatever you do, don't turn, don't turn around, just keep walking, just keep going straight and don't look back at the car." The more detailed the police instructions are, the more plausible the tale seems to become. Of course the standard rule of folk-narrative plot development now applies: the taboo must be broken (or the "interdiction violated" as some scholars put it). The girl always *does* look back, like Orpheus in the underworld, and in a number of versions her hair turns white from the shock of what she sees, as in a dozen other American legends.

In a Canadian version of "The Boyfriend's Death," told by a fourteen-year-old boy from Willowdale, Ontario, in 1973, the words of the policemen are merely summarized, but the opening scene of the legend is developed more fully, with several special details, including . . . a warning heard on the car radio. The girl's behavior when left behind is also described in more detail.

> A guy and his girlfriend are on the way to a party when their car starts to give them some trouble. At that same time they catch a news flash on the radio warning all people in the area that a lunatic killer has escaped from a local criminal asylum. The girl becomes very upset and at that point the car stalls completely on the highway. The boyfriend gets out and tinkers around with the engine but can't get the car to start again. He decides that he is going to have to walk on up the road to a gas station and get a tow truck but wants his girlfriend to stay behind in the car. She is frightened and pleads with him to take her, but he says that she'll be safe on the floor of the car covered with a blanket so that anyone passing will think it is an abandoned car and not bother her. Besides he can sprint along the road and get back more quickly than if she comes with him in her high-heeled shoes and evening dress. She finally agrees and he tells her not to come out unless she hears his signal of three knocks on the window. . . .

She does hear knocks on the car, but they continue eerily beyond three; the sound is later explained as the shoes of the boyfriend's corpse bumping the car as the body swings from a limb above the car.

The style in which oral narratives are told deserves attention, for the live telling that is dramatic, fluid, and often quite gripping in actual folk performance before a sympathetic audience may seem stiff, repetitious, and awkward on the printed page. Lacking in all our examples of "The

Boyfriend's Death" is the essential ingredient of immediate context—the setting of the legend-telling, the storyteller's vocal and facial expression and gestures, the audience's reaction, and the texts of other similar tales narrated at the same session. Several of the informants explained that the story was told to them in spooky situations, late at night, near a cemetery, out camping, or even "while on a hayride or out parked," occasionally near the site of the supposed murder. Some students refer to such macabre legends, therefore, as "scary stories," "screamers," or "horrors."

A widely-distributed folk legend of this kind as it travels in oral tradition acquires a good deal of its credibility and effect from the localized details inserted by individual tellers. The highway and motel identification in the Kansas text are good examples of this, and in a New Orleans version, "The Boyfriend's Death" is absorbed into a local teenage tradition about "The Grunch"—a half-sheep, half-human monster that haunts specific local sites. One teenager there reported, "A man and lady went out by the lake and in the morning they found 'em hanging upside down on a tree and they said grunches did it." Finally, rumors or news stories about missing persons or violent crimes (as mentioned in the Canadian version) can merge with urban legends, helping to support their air of truth, or giving them renewed circulation after a period of less frequent occurrence.

Even the bare printed texts retain some earmarks of effective oral tradition. Witness in the Kansas text the artful use of repetition (typical of folk narrative style): "Well, he didn't come back and he didn't come back . . . but he didn't come back." The repeated use of "well" and the building of lengthy sentences with "and" are other hallmarks of oral style which give the narrator complete control over his performance, tending to squeeze out interruptions or prevent lapses in attention among the listeners. The scene that is set for the incident—lonely road, night, a tree looming over the car, out of gas—and the sound effects—scratches or bumps on the car—contribute to the style, as does the dramatic part played by the policeman and the abrupt ending line: "She looked back, and she saw . . . !" Since the typical narrators and auditors of "The Boyfriend's Death" themselves like to "park" and may have been alarmed by rumors, strange sights and noises, or automobile emergencies (all intensified in their effects by the audience's knowing other parking legends), the abrupt, unresolved ending leaves open the possibilities of what "really happened."

Urban Legends as Cultural Symbols

Legends can survive in our culture as living narrative folklore if they contain three essential elements: a strong basic story-appeal, a foundation in actual belief, and a meaningful message or "moral." That is, popular stories like "The Boyfriend's Death" are not only engrossing tales, but also "true," or at least so people think, and they teach valuable lessons. Jokes are a living part of oral tradition, despite being fictional and often silly, because of their humor, brevity, and snappy punch lines, but legends are by nature longer, slower, and more serious. Since more effort is needed to tell and appreciate a legend than a joke, it needs more than just verbal art to carry it along. Jokes have significant "messages" too, but these tend to be disguised or implied. People tell jokes primarily for amusement, and they seldom sense their underlying themes. In legends the primary messages are quite clear and straightforward; often they take the form of explicit warnings or good examples of "poetic justice." Secondary messages in urban legends tend to be suggested metaphorically or symbolically; these may provide deeper criticisms of human behavior or social condition.

People still tell legends, therefore, and other folk take time to listen to   20
them, not only because of their inherent plot interest but because they seem to convey true, worthwhile, and relevant information, albeit partly in a subconscious mode. In other words, such stories are "news" presented to us in an attractive way, with hints of larger meanings. Without this multiple appeal few legends would get a hearing in the modern world, so filled with other distractions. Legends survive by being as lively and "factual" as the television evening news, and, like the daily news broadcasts, they tend to concern deaths, injuries, kidnappings, tragedies, and scandals. Apparently the basic human need for meaningful personal contact cannot be entirely replaced by the mass media and popular culture. A portion of our interest in what is occurring in the world must be filled by some face-to-face reports from other human beings.

On a literal level a story like "The Boyfriend's Death" simply warns young people to avoid situations in which they may be endangered, but at a more symbolic level the story reveals society's broader fears of people, especially women and the young, being alone and among strangers in the darkened world outside the security of their own home or car. Note that the young woman in the story (characterized by "her high-heeled shoes and evening dress") is shown as especially helpless and passive, cowering under the blanket in the car until she is rescued by men. Such themes recur in various forms in many other urban legends. . . .

In order to be retained in a culture, any form of folklore must fill some genuine need, whether this be the need for an entertaining escape from reality, or a desire to validate by anecdotal examples some of the culture's ideals and institutions. For legends in general, a major function has always been the attempt to explain unusual and supernatural happenings in the natural world. To some degree this remains a purpose for urban legends, but their more common role nowadays seems to be to show that the prosaic contemporary scene is capable of producing shocking or amazing occurrences which may actually have happened to friends or to near-acquaintances but which are nevertheless explainable in some reasonably logical terms. On the one hand we want our factual lore to inspire awe, and at the same time we wish to have the most fantastic tales include at least the hint of a rational explanation and perhaps even a conclusion. Thus an escaped lunatic, a possibly *real* character, not a fantastic invader from outer space or Frankenstein's monster, is said to be responsible for the atrocities committed in the gruesome tales that teenagers tell. As sometimes happens in real life, the car radio gives warning, and the police get the situation back under control. (The policemen's role, in fact, becomes larger and more commanding as the story grows in oral tradition.) Only when the young lovers are still alone and scared are they vulnerable, but society's adults and guardians come to their rescue presently.

In common with brief unverified reports ("rumors"), to which they are often closely related, urban legends gratify our desire to know about and to try to understand bizarre, frightening, and potentially dangerous or embarrassing events that *may* have happened. (In rumors and legends there is always some element of doubt concerning where and when these things *did* occur.) These floating stories appeal to our morbid curiosity and satisfy our sensation-seeking minds that demand gratification through frequent infusions of new information, "sanitized" somewhat by the positive messages. Informal rumors and stories fill in the gaps left by professional news reporting, and these marvelous, though generally false, "true" tales may be said to be carrying the folk-news—along with some editorial matter— from person to person even in today's technological world.

QUESTIONS

1. In your own words, define *urban legend*.
2. Had you ever heard the story of "The Boyfriend's Death" before? Did you believe it was true? Can you remember the circumstances in which you first heard this legend (or a similar one)? Describe your first encounter with the tale. How does your experience compare with those described by Brunvand?
3. Below is a list of other tales collected by Brunvand. Do you know any stories that might correspond to these titles?

   The Vanishing Hitchhiker
   The Mexican Pet
   The Baby-Sitter and the Man Upstairs
   The Microwaved Pet
   The Toothbrush Story
   Alligators in the Sewers
   The Nude in the RV
   The Kidney Heist

   Briefly describe the stories you have heard. Compare the various versions produced by members of the class. What are the variables in the tale, and what seem to be the common features?
4. Do you know a story that sounds like an urban legend but is really true? Can you prove it?

5. Select an urban legend that you have recently heard. Write down the best version of it that you can, then analyze what you have written as an urban legend. That is, explain what features mark it as an urban legend, and discuss the elements in it that have made it interesting or appealing to you.

6. Can you remember someone who told you something as a "true" story that you now recognize as an urban legend? Write an essay in which you first describe that person and report on the legend he or she told you, and then go on to explain to that person that the story he or she told is not actually true but is an urban legend. If you think that your explanation would not convince the person in question, try to explain why this is so. Describe the resistance you might encounter, and indicate how you might modify your explanation to make it more persuasive.

MAKING CONNECTIONS

1. Several of the pieces in "Reporting" deal with events that could provide the material for an urban legend. Richard Selzer's "The Discus Thrower" (p. 289) and Michael Brown's "Love Canal and the Poisoning of America" (p. 299) are examples. What elements of these stories qualify them as urban legends? In what ways do they not qualify as urban legends?

2. Rewrite "The Discus Thrower" (p. 289) or "Love Canal and the Poisoning of America" (p. 299) as an urban legend. Make any changes you find necessary to make it read like an urban legend. Then write a few paragraphs of explanation, discussing the changes you made and why you made them.

WHAT HIGH SCHOOL IS

Theodore R. Sizer

Born in New Haven, Connecticut, in 1932, and educated at Yale and Harvard Universities, Theodore R. Sizer has been headmaster at Phillips Academy in Andover, Massachusetts, dean of the Graduate School of Education at Harvard, and chairman of the Education Department at Brown University. He is the author of several influential books on educational reform and American secondary schools, most recently Horace's Hope: What Works for the American High School *(1996). The following selection is a chapter from an earlier book,* Horace's Compromise: The Dilemma of the American High School *(1984), which reports the results of a study of American high schools sponsored by the National Association of Independent Schools.*

Mark, sixteen and a genial eleventh-grader, rides a bus to Franklin High School, arriving at 7:25. It is an Assembly Day, so the schedule is adapted to allow for a meeting of the entire school. He hangs out with his friends, first outside school and then inside, by his locker. He carries a pile of textbooks and notebooks; in all, it weighs eight and a half pounds.

From 7:30 to 8:19, with nineteen other students, he is in Room 304 for English class. The Shakespeare play being read this year by the eleventh grade is *Romeo and Juliet.* The teacher, Ms. Viola, has various students in turn take parts and read out loud. Periodically, she interrupts the (usually halting) recitations to ask whether the thread of the conversation in the play is clear. Mark is entertained by the stumbling readings of some of his classmates. He hopes he will not be asked to be Romeo, particularly if his current steady, Sally, is Juliet. There is a good deal of giggling in class, and much attention paid to who may be called on next. Ms. Viola reminds the class of a test on this part of the play to be given next week.

The bell rings at 8:19. Mark goes to the boys' room, where he sees a classmate who he thinks is a wimp but who constantly tries to be a buddy. Mark avoids the leech by rushing off. On the way, he notices two boys engaged in some sort of transaction, probably over marijuana. He pays them no attention. 8:24. Typing class. The rows of desks that embrace big office machines are almost filled before the bell. Mark is uncomfortable here: typing class is girl country. The teacher constantly threatens what to Mark is a humiliatingly female future: "Your employer won't like these erasures." The minutes during the period are spent copying a letter from a handbook onto business stationery. Mark struggles to keep from looking at his work; the teacher wants him to watch only the material from which he is copying. Mark is frustrated, uncomfortable, and scared that he will not complete his letter by the class's end, which would be embarrassing.

Nine tenths of the students present at school that day are assembled in the auditorium by the 9:18 bell. The dilatory tenth still stumble in, running down aisles. Annoyed class deans try to get the mob settled. The curtains part; the program is a concert by a student rock group. Their electronic gear flashes under the lights, and the five boys and one girl in the group work hard at being casual. Their movements on stage are studiously at three-quarter time, and they chat with one another as though the tumultuous screaming of their schoolmates were totally inaudible. The girl balances on a stool; the boys crank up the music. It is very soft rock, the sanitized lyrics surely cleared with the assistant principal. The girl sings, holding the mike close to her mouth, but can scarcely be heard. Her light voice is tentative, and the lyrics indecipherable. The guitars, amplified, are tuneful, however, and the drums are played with energy.

The students around Mark—all juniors, since they are seated by class—alternately slouch in their upholstered, hinged seats, talking to one another, or sit forward, leaning on the chair backs in front of them, watching the band. A boy near Mark shouts noisily at the microphone-fondling singer, "Bite it . . . ohhh," and the area around Mark explodes in vulgar male laughter, but quickly subsides. A teacher walks down the aisle. Songs continue, to great applause. Assembly is over at 9:46, two minutes early. 5

9:53 and biology class. Mark was at a different high school last year and did not take this course there as a tenth-grader. He is in it now, and all but one of his classmates are a year younger than he. He sits on the side, not taking part in the chatter that goes on after the bell. At 9:57, the public address system goes on, with the announcements of the day. After a few words from the principal ("Here's today's cheers and jeers . . ." with a cheer for the winning basketball team and a jeer for the spectators who made a ruckus at the gymnasium), the task is taken over by officers of ASB (Associated Student Bodies). There is an appeal for "bat bunnies." Carnations are for sale by the Girls' League. Miss Indian American is coming. Students are auctioning off their services (background catcalls are heard) to earn money for the prom. Nominees are needed for the ballot for school bachelor and school bachelorette. The announcements end with a "thought for the day. When you throw a little mud, you lose a little ground."

At 10:04 the biology class finally turns to science. The teacher, Mr. Robbins, has placed one of several labeled laboratory specimens—some are pinned in frames, others swim in formaldehyde—on each of the classroom's eight laboratory tables. The three or so students whose chairs circle each of these benches are to study the specimen and make notes about it or drawings of it. After a few minutes each group of three will move to another table. The teacher points out that these specimens are of organisms already studied in previous classes. He says that the period-long test set for the following day will involve observing some of these specimens—then to be without labels—and writing an identifying paragraph on each. Mr. Robbins points out that some of the printed labels ascribe the specimens names different from those given in the textbook. He explains that biologists often give several names to the same organism.

The class now falls to peering, writing, and quiet talking. Mr. Robbins comes over to Mark, and in whispered words asks him to carry a requisition form for science department materials to the business office. Mark, because of his "older" status, is usually chosen by Robbins for this kind of errand. Robbins gives Mark the form and a green hall pass to show to any teacher who might challenge him, on his way to the office, for being out of a classroom. The errand takes Mark four minutes. Meanwhile Mark's group is hard at work but gets to only three of the specimens before the bell rings at 10:42. As the students surge out, Robbins shouts a reminder about a "double" laboratory period on Thursday.

Between classes one of the seniors asks Mark whether he plans to be a candidate for schoolwide office next year. Mark says no. He starts to explain. The 10:47 bell rings, meaning that he is late for French class.

There are fifteen students in Monsieur Bates's language class. He   10
hands out tests taken the day before: "*C'est bien fait, Etienne . . . c'est mieux, Marie . . . Tch, tch, Robert . . .*" Mark notes his C+ and peeks at the A− in front of Susanna, next to him. The class has been assigned seats by M. Bates; Mark resents sitting next to prissy, brainy Susanna. Bates starts by asking a student to read a question and give the correct answer. "*James, question un.*" James haltingly reads the question and gives the answer that Bates, now speaking English, says is incomplete. In due course: "*Mark, question cinq.*" Mark does his bit, and the sequence goes on, the eight quiz questions and answers filling about twenty minutes of time.

"Turn to page forty-nine. *Maintenant, lisez après moi . . .*" and Bates reads a sentence and has the class echo it. Mark is embarrassed by this and mumbles with a barely audible sound. Others, like Susanna, keep the decibel count up, so Mark can hide. This I-say-you-repeat drill is interrupted once by the public address system, with an announcement about a meeting for the cheerleaders. Bates finishes the class, almost precisely at the bell, with a homework assignment. The students are to review these sentences for a brief quiz the following day. Mark takes note of the assignment, because he knows that tomorrow will be a day of busy-work in French class. Much though he dislikes oral drills, they are better than the workbook stuff that Bates hands out. Write, write, write, for Bates to throw away, Mark thinks.

11:36. Down to the cafeteria, talking noisily, hanging, munching. Getting to room 104 by 12:17: U.S. history. The teacher is sitting cross-legged on his desk when Mark comes in, heatedly arguing with three students over the fracas that had followed the previous night's basketball game. The teacher, Mr. Suslovic, while agreeing that the spectators from their school certainly were provoked, argues that they should neither have been so obviously obscene in yelling at the opposing cheerleaders nor have allowed Coke cans to be rolled out on the floor. The three students keep saying that "it isn't fair." Apparently they and some others had been assigned "Saturday mornings" (detentions) by the principal for the ruckus.

At 12:34, the argument appears to subside. The uninvolved students, including Mark, are in their seats, chatting amiably. Mr. Suslovic climbs off his desk and starts talking: "We've almost finished this unit, chapters nine and ten . . ." The students stop chattering among themselves and turn toward Suslovic. Several slouch down in their chairs. Some open notebooks. Most have the five-pound textbook on their desks.

Suslovic lectures on the cattle drives, from north Texas to railroads west of St. Louis. He breaks up this narrative with questions ("Why were the railroad lines laid largely east to west?"), directed at nobody in particular and eventually answered by Suslovic himself. Some students take notes. Mark doesn't. A student walks in the open door, hands Mr. Suslovic a list, and starts whispering with him. Suslovic turns from the class and hears out this messenger. He then asks, "Does anyone know where Maggie Sharp is?" Someone answers, "Sick at home"; someone else says, "I thought I saw her at lunch." Genial consternation. Finally Suslovic tells the messenger, "Sorry, we can't help you," and returns to the class: "Now, where were we?" He goes on for some minutes. The bell rings. Suslovic forgets to give the homework assignment.

1:11 and Algebra II. There is a commotion in the hallway: someone's   15 locker is rumored to have been opened by the assistant principal and a narcotics agent. In the five-minute passing time, Mark hears the story three times and three ways. A locker had been broken into by another student. It was Mr. Gregory and a narc. It was the cops, and they did it without Gregory's knowing. Mrs. Ames, the mathematics teacher, has not heard anything about it. Several of the nineteen students try to tell her and start arguing among themselves. "O.K., that's enough." She hands out the day's problem, one sheet to each student. Mark sees with dismay that it is a single, complicated "word" problem about some train that, while traveling at 84 mph, due west, passes a car that was going due east at 55 mph. Mark struggles: Is it $d = rt$ or $t = rd$? The class becomes quiet, writing, while Mrs. Ames writes some additional, short problems on the blackboard. "Time's up." A sigh; most students still writing. A muffled "Shit." Mrs. Ames frowns. "Come on, now." She collects papers, but it takes four minutes for her to corral them all.

"Copy down the problems from the board." A minute passes. "William, try number one." William suggests an approach. Mrs. Ames corrects and cajoles, and William finally gets it right. Mark watches two kids to his right passing notes; he tries to read them, but the handwriting is illegible from his distance. He hopes he is not called on, and he isn't. Only three students are asked to puzzle out an answer. The bell rings at 2:00. Mrs. Ames shouts a homework assignment over the resulting hubbub.

Mark leaves his books in his locker. He remembers that he has homework, but figures that he can do it during English class the next day. He
knows that there will be an in-class presentation of one of the *Romeo and
Juliet* scenes and that he will not be in it. The teacher will not notice his
homework writing, or won't do anything about it if she does.

Mark passes various friends heading toward the gym, members of the
basketball teams. Like most students, Mark isn't an active school athlete.
However, he is associated with the yearbook staff. Although he is not taking "Yearbook" for credit as an English course, he is contributing photographs. Mark takes twenty minutes checking into the yearbook staff's
headquarters (the classroom of its faculty adviser) and getting some assignments of pictures from his boss, the senior who is the photography editor. Mark knows that if he pleases his boss and the faculty adviser, he'll
take that editor's post for the next year. He'll get English credit for his
work then.

After gossiping a bit with the yearbook staff, Mark will leave school
by 2:35 and go home. His grocery market bagger's job is from 4:45 to
8:00, the rush hour for the store. He'll have a snack at 4:30, and his
mother will save him some supper to eat at 8:30. She will ask whether he
has any homework, and he'll tell her no. Tomorrow, and virtually every
other tomorrow, will be the same for Mark, save for the lack of the assembly: each period then will be five minutes longer.

Most Americans have an uncomplicated vision of what secondary edu-   20
cation should be. Their conception of high school is remarkably uniform
across the country, a striking fact, given the size and diversity of the United
States and the politically decentralized character of the schools. This uniformity is of several generations' standing. It has, however, two appearances, each quite different from the other, one of words and the other of
practice, a world of political rhetoric and Mark's world.

A California high school's general goals, set out in 1979, could serve
equally well most of America's high schools, public and private. This
school had as its ends:

- Fundamental scholastic achievement . . . to acquire knowledge
  and share in the traditionally academic fundamentals . . . to de-
  velop the ability to make decisions, to solve problems, to reason
  independently, and to accept responsibility for self-evaluation and
  continuing self-improvement.
- Career and economic competence . . .
- Citizenship and civil responsibility . . .
- Competence in human and social relations . . .
- Moral and ethical values . . .
- Self-realization and mental and physical health . . .

- Aesthetic awareness . . .
- Cultural diversity . . .[1]

In addition to its optimistic rhetoric, what distinguishes this list is its comprehensiveness. The high school is to touch most aspects of an adolescent's existence—mind, body, morals, values, career. No one of these areas is given especial prominence. School people arrogate to themselves an obligation to all.

An example of the wide acceptability of these goals is found in the courts. Forced to present a detailed definition of "thorough and efficient education," elementary as well as secondary, a West Virginia judge sampled the best of conventional wisdom and concluded that

> there are eight general elements of a thorough and efficient system of education: (a) Literacy, (b) The ability to add, subtract, multiply, and divide numbers, (c) Knowledge of government to the extent the child will be equipped as a citizen to make informed choices among persons and issues that affect his own governance, (d) Self-knowledge and knowledge of his or her total environment to allow the child to intelligently choose life work—to know his or her options, (e) Work-training and advanced academic training as the child may intelligently choose, (f) Recreational pursuits, (g) Interests in all creative arts such as music, theater, literature, and the visual arts, and (h) Social ethics, both behavioral and abstract, to facilitate compatibility with others in this society.[2]

That these eight—now powerfully part of the debate over the purpose and practice of education in West Virginia—are reminiscent of the influential list, "The Seven Cardinal Principles of Secondary Education," promulgated in 1918 by the National Education Association, is no surprise.[3] The rhetoric of high school purpose has been uniform and consistent for decades. Americans agree on the goals for their high schools.

---

[1]Shasta High School, Redding, California. An eloquent and analogous statement, "The Essentials of Education," one stressing explicitly the "interdependence of skills and content" that is implicit in the Shasta High School statement, was issued in 1980 by a coalition of educational associations, Organizations for the Essentials of Education (Urbana, Illinois).

[2]Judge Arthur M. Recht, in his order resulting from *Pauley v. Kelly,* 1979, as reprinted in *Education Week,* May 26, 1982, p. 10. See also, in *Education Week,* January 16, 1983, pp. 21, 24, Jonathan P. Sher, "The Struggle to Fulfill a Judicial Mandate: How Not to 'Reconstruct' Education in W. Va."

[3]Bureau of Education, Department of the Interior, "Cardinal Principles of Secondary Education: A Report of the Commission on the Reorganization of Secondary Education, appointed by the National Education Association," *Bulletin,* no. 35 (Washington: U.S. Government Printing Office, 1918).

That agreement is convenient, but it masks the fact that virtually all the words in these goal statements beg definition. Some schools have labored long to identify specific criteria beyond them; the result has been lists of daunting pseudospecificity and numbing earnestness. However, most leave the words undefined and let the momentum of traditional practice speak for itself. That is why analyzing how Mark spends his time is important: from watching him one uncovers the important purposes of education, the ones that shape practice. Mark's day is similar to that of other high school students across the country, as similar as the rhetoric of one goal statement to others'. Of course, there are variations, but the extent of consistency in the shape of school routine for a large and diverse adolescent population is extraordinary, indicating more graphically than any rhetoric the measure of agreement in America about what one does in high school, and, by implication, what it is for.

The basic organizing structures in schools are familiar. Above all, students are grouped by age (that is, freshman, sophomore, junior, senior), and all are expected to take precisely the same time—around 720 school days over four years, to be precise—to meet the requirements for a diploma. When one is out of his grade level, he can feel odd, as Mark did in his biology class. The goals are the same for all, and the means to achieve them are also similar.

Young males and females are treated remarkably alike; the schools'   25
goals are the same for each gender. In execution, there are differences, as those pressing sex discrimination suits have made educators intensely aware. The students in metalworking classes are mostly male; those in home economics, mostly female. But it is revealing how much less sex discrimination there is in high schools than in other American institutions. For many young women, the most liberated hours of their week are in school.

School is to be like a job: you start in the morning and end in the afternoon, five days a week. You don't get much of a lunch hour, so you go home early, unless you are an athlete or are involved in some special school or extracurricular activity. School is conceived of as the children's workplace, and it takes young people off parents' hands and out of the labor market during prime-time work hours. Not surprisingly, many students see going to school as little more than a dogged necessity. They perceive the day-to-day routine, a Minnesota study reports, as one of "boredom and lethargy." One of the students summarizes: School is "boring, restless, tiresome, puts ya to sleep, tedious, monotonous, pain in the neck."[4]

The school schedule is a series of units of time: the clock is king. The base time block is about fifty minutes in length. Some schools, on what

---

[4]Diane Hedin, Paula Simon, and Michael Robin, *Minnesota Youth Poll: Youth's Views on School and School Discipline,* Minnesota Report 184 (1983), Agricultural Experiment Station, University of Minnesota, p. 13.

they call modular scheduling, split that fifty-minute block into two or even three pieces. Most schools have double periods for laboratory work, especially in the sciences, or four-hour units for the small numbers of students involved in intensive vocational or other work-study programs. The flow of all school activity arises from or is blocked by these time units. "How much time do I have with my kids" is the teacher's key question.

Because there are many claims for those fifty-minute blocks, there is little time set aside for rest between them, usually no more than three to ten minutes, depending on how big the school is and, consequently, how far students and teachers have to walk from class to class. As a result, there is a frenetic quality to the school day, a sense of sustained restlessness. For the adolescents, there are frequent changes of room and fellow students, each change giving tempting opportunities for distraction, which are stoutly resisted by teachers. Some schools play soft music during these "passing times," to quiet the multitude, one principal told me.

Many teachers have a chance for a coffee break. Few students do. In some city schools where security is a problem, students must be in class for seven consecutive periods, interrupted by a heavily monitored twenty-minute lunch period for small groups, starting as early as 10:30 A.M. and running to after 1:00 P.M. A high premium is placed on punctuality and on "being where you're supposed to be." Obviously, a low premium is placed on reflection and repose. The students rush from class to class to collect knowledge. Savoring it, it is implied, is not to be done much in school, nor is such meditation really much admired. The picture that these familiar patterns yield is that of an academic supermarket. The purpose of going to school is to pick things up, in an organized and predictable way, the faster the better.

What is supposed to be picked up is remarkably consistent among all   30
sorts of high schools. Most schools specifically mandate three out of every five courses a student selects. Nearly all of these mandates fall into five areas — English, social studies, mathematics, science, and physical education. On the average, English is required to be taken each year, social studies and physical education three out of the four high school years, and mathematics and science one or two years. Trends indicate that in the mid-eighties there is likely to be an increase in the time allocated to these last two subjects. Most students take classes in these four major academic areas beyond the minimum requirements, sometimes in such special areas as journalism and "yearbook," offshoots of English departments.[5]

Press most adults about what high school is for, and you hear these subjects listed. *High school? That's where you learn English and math and that sort of thing.* Ask students, and you get the same answer. High school is to "teach" these "subjects."

---

[5]I am indebted to Harold F. Sizer and Lyde E. Sizer for a survey of the diploma requirements of fifty representative secondary schools, completed for *A Study of High Schools.*

What is often absent is any definition of these subjects or any rationale for them. They are just there, labels. Under those labels lie a multitude of things. A great deal of material is supposed to be "covered"; most of these courses are surveys, great sweeps of the stuff of their parent disciplines.

While there is often a sequence *within* subjects—algebra before trigonometry, "first-year" French before "second-year" French—there is rarely a coherent relationship or sequence *across* subjects. Even the most logically related matters—reading ability as a precondition for the reading of history books, and certain mathematical concepts or skills before the study of some of physics—are only loosely coordinated, if at all. There is little demand for a synthesis of it all; English, mathematics, and the rest are discrete items, to be picked up individually. The incentive for picking them up is largely through tests and, with success at these, in credits earned.

Coverage within subjects is the key priority. If some imaginative teacher makes a proposal to force the marriage of, say, mathematics and physics or to require some culminating challenges to students to use several objects in the solution of a complex problem, and if this proposal will take "time" away from other things, opposition is usually phrased in terms of what may be thus forgone. If we do that, we'll have to give up colonial history. We won't be able to get to programming. We'll not be able to read *Death of a Salesman*. There isn't time. The protesters usually win out.

The subjects come at a student like Mark in random order, a kaleidoscope of worlds: algebraic formulae to poetry to French verbs to Ping-Pong to the War of the Spanish Succession, all before lunch. Pupils are to pick up these things. Tests measure whether the picking up has been successful.

The lack of connection between stated goals, such as those of the California high school cited earlier, and the goals inherent in school practice is obvious and, curiously, tolerated. Most striking is the gap between statements about "self-realization and mental and physical growth" or "moral and ethical values"—common rhetoric in school documents—and practice. Most physical education programs have neither the time nor the focus really to ensure fitness. Mental health is rarely defined. Neither are ethical values, save at the negative extremes, such as opposition to assault or dishonesty. Nothing in the regimen of a day like Mark's signals direct or implicit teaching in this area. The "school boy code" (not ratting on a fellow student) protects the marijuana pusher, and a leechlike associate is shrugged off without concern. The issue of the locker search was pushed aside, as not appropriate for class time.

Most students, like Mark, go to class in groups of twenty to twenty-seven students. The expected attendance in some schools, particularly those in low-income areas, is usually higher, often thirty-five students per class, but high absentee rates push the actual numbers down. About twenty-five per class is an average figure for expected attendance, and the actual numbers are somewhat lower. There are remarkably few students who go to class in groups much larger or smaller than twenty-five.[6]

A student such as Mark sees five or six teachers per day; their differing styles and expectations are part of his kaleidoscope. High school staffs are highly specialized: guidance counselors rarely teach mathematics, mathematics teachers rarely teach English, principals rarely do any classroom instruction. Mark, then, is known a little bit by a number of people, each of whom sees him in one specialized situation. No one may know him as a "whole person" — unless he becomes a special problem or has special needs.

Save in extracurricular or coaching situations, such as in athletics, drama, or shop classes, there is little opportunity for sustained conversation between student and teacher. The mode is a one-sentence or two-sentence exchange: *Mark, when was Grover Cleveland president? Let's see, was 1890 . . . or something . . . wasn't he the one . . . he was elected twice, wasn't he . . . Yes . . . Gloria, can you get the dates right?* Dialogue is strikingly absent, and as a result the opportunity of teachers to challenge students' ideas in a systematic and logical way is limited. Given the rushed, full quality of the school day, it can seldom happen. One must infer that careful probing of students' thinking is not a high priority. How one gains (to quote the California school's statement of goals again) "the ability to make decisions, to solve problems, to reason independently, and to accept responsibility for self-evaluation and continuing self-improvement" without being challenged is difficult to imagine. One certainly doesn't learn these things merely from lectures and textbooks.

Most schools are nice places. Mark and his friends enjoy being in   40
theirs. The adults who work in schools generally like adolescents. The academic pressures are limited, and the accommodations to students are substantial. For example, if many members of an English class have jobs after school, the English teacher's expectations for them are adjusted, downward. In a word, school is sensitively accommodating, as long as students are punctual, where they are supposed to be, and minimally dutiful about picking things up from the clutch of courses in which they enroll.

This characterization is not pretty, but it is accurate, and it serves to describe the vast majority of American secondary schools. "Taking subjects" in a systematized, conveyer-belt way is what one does in high school. That this process is, in substantial respects, not related to the rhetorical purposes of education is tolerated by most people, perhaps because they do not really either believe in those ill-defined goals or, in their heart of hearts, believe that schools can or should even try to achieve them. The students

---

[6]Education Research Service, Inc., *Class Size: A Summary of Research* (Arlington, Virginia, 1978); and *Class Size Research: A Critique of Recent Meta-Analyses* (Arlington, Virginia, 1980).

are happy taking subjects. The parents are happy, because that's what they did in high school. The rituals, the most important of which is graduation, remain intact. The adolescents are supervised safely and constructively most of the time, during the morning and afternoon hours, and they are off the labor market. That is what high school is all about.

QUESTIONS

1. The first half of this essay (the first nineteen paragraphs, to be exact) is a report. What do you think of this report? Given your own experience, how accurate is it? What attitude does the report convey, or is it objective?
2. Paragraph 19 is the conclusion of the report. It ends the story of Mark's day. Does it draw or imply any conclusions from the events reported?
3. How is the explanatory section of the essay (paragraphs 20 through 41) organized? The first subtopic discussed is the goals of high school. What are the other subtopics?
4. What is the major conclusion of this explanation? To what extent do you agree with the last sentence of the essay and what it implies?
5. How does the report (paragraphs 1 through 19) function in the explanation that follows? What would be lost if the report were omitted? In considering how the two sections of the essay relate, note especially places where the explanation specifically refers to the report.
6. You may have a different view of high school, or perhaps you went to a different kind of school. Write an essay that is organized like Sizer's but that presents your own report and explanation of what school is.
7. Using the basic outline of Sizer's essay, write your own explanation of the workings of some institution: store, family, church or temple, club, team, or whatever else you know well. Think of your project in terms of Sizer's title: "What X Is."

MAKING CONNECTIONS

1. How do you suppose Sizer got this information about Mark and "what high school is"? Compare his approach to that of Farley Mowat (p. 256), Jane van Lawick-Goodall (p. 260), and Monica M. Moore (p. 465). Which one of these writers comes closest, do you think, to Sizer's method for researching his essay? Explain the resemblances and differences.
2. Sizer presents a teenage boy's high school day. Taking Carol Gilligan's "Interviewing Adolescent Girls" (p. 425) into account, write a shorter version of the high school day of a teenage girl.

AMERICA'S NO. 1 SONG

Daniel Mark Epstein

Born in Washington, D.C., in 1948, Daniel Mark Epstein received his bachelor's degree from Kenyon College and later studied at the University of Virginia. He began his writing career as a poet—his latest collection is The Boy in the Well and Other Poems (1995)— *but he has also written plays as well as essays for such publications as* New Criterion, *the* New Yorker, *and the* Nation. *His autobiographical* Love's Compass: A Natural History of the Heart *appeared in 1990, and he has since published two biographical works:* Sister Aimee *(1993), about evangelist Aimee Semple McPherson, and* Nat King Cole *(1999). Epstein has been writer-in-residence at Towson State University in Maryland since 1983. The following essay appeared in the July 1986 issue of the* Atlantic Monthly.

"The Star-Spangled Banner" is a sublime anthem, democratic and spacious, holding at least one note for every American. The tune is a test pattern not only for the voice but also for the human spirit. The soul singer, the rock star, and the crooner—all are humbled by the anthem. We have heard world-famous tenors and sopranos choke upon the low notes and cry out in pain at the high ones. We have seen the great Mahalia Jackson[1] tremble.

It's unlikely that our worst enemy would have written a melody with a range more challenging to the solo performer. The melody was in fact given to us by our worst enemy at the time, the English. John Stafford Smith, an Englishman, composed the tune to which Francis Scott Key penned his lyrics a few days after the British set fire to Washington, in 1814. The capital was rebuilt, but the melody remains exactly as we received it—an inspiration and a terror. The anthem perfectly suits our collective spirit, our ambition and national range. So it ought to be sung by a crowd of Americans, to guarantee that all of the notes will be covered.

You may wonder how the national anthem achieved its election. And why, since the tune is so uncooperative, we cannot impeach the anthem and throw it out of office, like any other incompetent or mischievous official. If you are thinking such thoughts, you are in good patriotic company. House Resolution 14, which legalized the national anthem, was voted

---

[1]*Mahalia Jackson* (1911–1972): American singer who brought black gospel music to a worldwide, multiracial audience. [Eds.]

down when it was first introduced, in 1929, and hotly debated in 1931, when it passed. Every few years since then there has been an uprising, with newspaper editorials and petitions against the song and insurgents campaigning to replace "The Banner" with "America" or "This Land Is Your Land."

But it is unlikely that any new arguments will arise to unseat "The Star-Spangled Banner." Everything that could be said on the subject was said, over and over, during debates more than fifty years ago. Congressmen brought dire charges against "The Star-Spangled Banner." They denounced its ancestry, birth, and character. They dragged it through the mud.

First of all, there was the embarrassing business about the Anacreontic   5
Society. The melody, it turned out, had been married before, to the lyrics of an English song called "To Anacreon in Heaven," which made a very different kind of anthem indeed. The ancient Greek poet Anacreon[2] delighted in wine and lovemaking above all else. The London "gentlemen" of the Anacreontic Society in the 1770s, having chosen the poet as their patron, spent nights reviving his spirit with songs and tippling and other merrymaking.

There were other problems as well. The congressmen against "The Banner" claimed that the song was useless on the parade and battle grounds, because our soldiers could not march to it. Yet John Philip Sousa,[3] who should have known, had once told Teddy Roosevelt that "The Star-Spangled Banner" was dandy for marching. Perhaps the soldiers weren't trying hard enough.

This leads us to the next argument against "The Star-Spangled Banner": that it is too difficult for schoolchildren to sing. An editorial in the New York *World* of March 31, 1930, answered this charge with logic and eloquence.

> What if school children could sing it? We should be so sick of it by now that we could not endure the sound of it, as the French are sick of the "Marseillaise." The virtues of "The Star-Spangled Banner" are that it does require a wide compass, so that school children cannot sing it, and that it is in three-four time, so that parades cannot march to it. So being, it has managed to remain fresh, not frayed and worn, and the citizenry still hear it with some semblance of a thrill, some touch of reverence.

And then there were the congressmen who suggested that the 1814 bombardment of Fort McHenry[4] was too paltry a background for the national anthem. They had not read their history. If the British had gotten

---

[2]*Anacreon* (c. 563–478 B.C.): As you may infer from this paragraph, Anacreon was a ribald pop singer of his time. [Eds.]

[3]*John Philip Sousa* (1854–1932): a master of marches. He composed "Stars and Stripes Forever," for example. [Eds.]

[4]*Fort McHenry:* now a national monument on the outskirts of Baltimore. [Eds.]

into Baltimore, only a few days after burning down Washington, no one can say where they might have stopped. George Washington had been dead fifteen years. Andrew Jackson was in New Orleans. If the British Navy's offensive had not been foundered at Fort McHenry, we might be singing "God Save the Queen" instead of "The Star-Spangled Banner."

Perhaps the best argument against House Resolution 14 is that it was unnecessary and therefore impertinent. In the nineteenth century Admiral George Dewey had designated "The Star-Spangled Banner" as the anthem for all Navy ceremonies. When advisors asked President Wilson, in 1916, what song should accompany state functions, he automatically replied: "The Banner." Everybody knew it was the national anthem.

But Americans do not like to be told what to eat or drink or sing. 10 Though they have eaten hot dogs and drunk beer and sung "The Star-Spangled Banner" in baseball parks for generations, try to pass a law requiring them to do so and Congress will never hear the end of it. That is the American way, and a good way. When Representative J. C. Linthicum, of Maryland, introduced a bill to make "The Star-Spangled Banner" our *official* anthem, he might have foreseen that he might be subjecting "The Banner" to a scrutiny usually reserved for presidential candidates. Congress's vote, in 1931, to give the song official status as our national anthem, despite its vocal challenges, unmarchability, and checkered past, was surely a gesture of affection with few parallels.

"The Star-Spangled Banner" deserved to win that vote. Our anthem remains one of the purest examples of unpremeditated, inspired genius in American history. Remember that Francis Scott Key, the lawyer-poet, was more lawyer than poet. Apart from the lyrics of "The Banner," and "Lord With Glowing Heart I'd Praise Thee," a hymn infrequently sung in churches, Key never wrote a line of memorable verse. Francis Scott Key was tone deaf. If anyone had told him early in September of 1814 that he was about to write the most famous song in America, the lawyer-poet would likely have laughed, with a modesty rare in poets, and gone about his business.

Key's business in September of 1814 was a matter of life and death. America had declared war upon pretexts the lawyer-poet condemned as a cover for imperialism. American privateers were looting British ships, and our troops had set Toronto on fire during a bungled attempt to annex Canada. Key was a gentle soul, so unsuited to conflict that he could never bring himself to run for political office. Yet, despite his mildness and his objections to the war, he fought dutifully in the defense of Washington. And when the British took away a civilian prisoner, Dr. William Beanes, Key begged for President Madison's commission to sail after them and plead for the doctor's release.

Key sailed down the Chesapeake in a small cartel ship, under the white flag of truce. He found the British fleet lying at anchor in the mouth of the Potomac. Admiral George Cockburn was about to hang Dr. Beanes from the ship's yardarm for acts of inhospitability to English soldiers as they passed through Upper Marlborough.[5] The doctor had been having a garden party to celebrate the town's escape from burning, when a few straggling dragoons had come into his yard and made bold to steal the punch. Doctor Beanes had been court-martialed for not giving them any, among other discourtesies.

With the passion and eloquence of a great lawyer-poet, Francis Scott Key pleaded for Doctor Beanes's life. He argued that the detention of civilians outraged all principles of civilized warfare; if great nations could not agree on the principles of warfare, what on earth *could* they agree on? Admiral Cockburn was unmoved. What finally swayed him was certain letters, which Key was able, fortuitously, to produce from his satchel, from wounded British soldiers, showing what tender care Dr. Beanes had taken of them. After a conference the British officers announced that they would release the ill-mannered doctor the next morning.

Key's mission was badly timed for all purposes but the creation of our   15
anthem. That very night the British fleet received orders to attack Baltimore. Since the British could not conceal this from Key, they insisted that he accept their hospitality until the battle was over. They entertained the lawyer-poet on his own cartel ship. From there he had an excellent view of the contest, being right in the middle of it.

What was Francis Scott Key's state of mind as he watched the rockets' red glare and bombs bursting in air, and then saw the banner waving? He jotted notes on the back of an envelope. Later he would explain, "If it had been a hanging matter to make a poem, I must have made it." The reference to execution is not careless. It is more than likely that the gentle Key, in making his poem, was as terrified a lawyer-poet as ever held a quill in his hand.

In 1814 the rockets' red glare and bombs bursting in air were neither poetic fantasies nor Fourth of July fireworks. They were real, live bombs, screaming and whistling and exploding around the poet. Dr. Beanes, who had joined Key on the cartel's[6] deck, must have thought that he had been saved from hanging only to be blown up.

The British rocket, a kind of primitive guided missile, was an awesome innovation in 1814. Key had watched his own men panic under bombardment from those rockets during the defense of Washington, and probably figured the Baltimoreans would do the same. The lawyer-poet must have had wildly mixed emotions as the British ships, and his cartel ship with them, approached the shore, beautifully lighted by rockets so that his fellow Americans could take better aim with their cannons. We could hardly blame Key if he had prayed for a swift surrender. He did not. He wrote a poem instead, and prayed for the sight of the flag.

The flag that flew above Fort McHenry in 1814 may be the largest battle flag over flown. It originally was thirty feet high by forty-two feet wide—

---

[5]*Upper Marlborough* (also *Marlboro*): town in Maryland east of Washington, D.C., about halfway up the Chesapeake Bay toward Fort McHenry. [Eds.]

[6]*cartel:* a ship employed in an exchange of prisoners. [Eds.]

420 square yards of red, white, and blue bunting. The flag was made to order for the defense of Fort McHenry — and, seemingly, for the creation of our anthem. What else would possess General John Stricker and Commodore Joshua Barney, otherwise reasonable men, to order such a gigantic flag? They wanted to be sure that Key would see it. Although the seamstress Mary Pickersgill snipped the stripes and stars in her tiny workroom, she could not stitch them together there. Mary and her little daughter worked on hands and knees, by daylight and lamplight, stitching together the Star-Spangled Banner on the malthouse floor of Claggett's Brewery. They finished their sewing just as the British fleet was nearing Baltimore Harbor.

The flag is surrealistically large. If you do not believe this, then go and look at it, exhibited like a dinosaur in the Smithsonian Institution's Museum of American History. That flag, flying above Fort McHenry, must have made the fort, and the city behind it, look tiny, like a child's sand castle. After the long night of rockets and bomb blasts and horror, what was the author of our national anthem feeling when he saw that titanic flag flying weirdly above his homeland? Some would imagine relief. But it was too soon for Key to feel relief — he was still a prisoner of war. Some would imagine pride. But Key was famous for his humility — and besides, pride does not spring readily in one's breast so soon after courage has been shaken. After a night of unspeakable terror, with every reason to believe that the United States would surrender in the glare of the rockets, Francis Scott Key's emotion upon spying that bizarre flag must have been utter amazement.

Wonder is a better word. Key could not believe his eyes, and his lyrics reproduce in us that sense of wonder. Remember, the refrain that closes the first stanza is a question:

> O! say does that star-spangled Banner yet wave,
> O'er the land of the free, and the home of the brave?

When we sing the anthem in the ballpark, or in school, or before the fireworks display on July 4, it is altogether fitting that we sing no more of the lyrics after that question. The birth and survival of this nation remains one of the wonders of the world. This was never more evident than it was to the lawyer-poet on that cloudy morning in 1814. The flag was amazing but undeniable. Key knew exactly how brave *he* was, having so recently been measured for bravery. Yet he still had sensible doubts about his freedom. That is the American way, and it is a good way.

QUESTIONS

1. "One note for every American." That phrase completes Epstein's opening sentence. What idea is he planting? How long is it before you are sure of what he means? How does he develop that idea?

2. "The doctor had been having a garden party to celebrate the town's escape from burning, when a few straggling dragoons had come into his yard and made bold to steal the punch" (paragraph 13). How serious is Epstein being? How consistent or inconsistent is his tone here with the remainder of his essay?

3. Consider the explanation (paragraph 18) of the size of the flag at Fort McHenry: "They wanted to be sure that Key would see it." Do you take that claim at face value or not? Do you think the proposition is likely or unlikely? Why?

4. As Epstein reminds us, "The Star-Spangled Banner," or just "The Banner" as he often puts it, is a song that we almost love to dislike. What memories do you have of singing it or hearing it sung? Write an essay in which you tell the story of your best-remembered experience with our anthem.

MAKING CONNECTIONS

"The birth and survival of this nation remains one of the wonders of the world." That sentence from Epstein's last paragraph is openly patriotic, which is a surprise given the overall tone of this essay. Read Thomas Jefferson's "Declaration of Independence" (p. 688), and Zoë Tracy Hardy's "What Did You Do in the War, Grandma? A Flashback to August, 1945" (p. 139), or another essay from this collection if you prefer. Then, drawing on insights you gain from your reading, write your own essay on the possible "wonder" of the birth and survival of our nation.

THE FEMALE BODY

Margaret Atwood

Margaret Atwood, born in Ottawa, Canada, in 1939, has won numerous awards and received honorary degrees for her writing. She is best known as a poet and novelist. Her novel The Handmaid's Tale *(1986) was made into a film. In her most recent novel,* Alias Grace *(1996), she draws on nineteenth-century history and a sensational murder trial. Much of her writing deals with feminist issues, and the essay presented here is no exception, as she applies her considerable talent to fulfill a writing assignment for the* Michigan Quarterly Review, *reprinted in a collection of her short works,* Good Bones and Simple Murders *(1994).*

> . . . entirely devoted to the subject of "The Female Body." Knowing how well you have written on this topic . . . this capacious topic. . . .
> —LETTER FROM *MICHIGAN QUARTERLY REVIEW*

1

I agree, it's a hot topic. But only one? Look around, there's a wide range. Take my own, for instance.

I get up in the morning. My topic feels like hell. I sprinkle it with water, brush parts of it, rub it with towels, powder it, add lubricant. I dump in the fuel and away goes my topic, my topical topic, my controversial topic, my capacious topic, my limping topic, my nearsighted topic, my topic with back problems, my badly behaved topic, my vulgar topic, my outrageous topic, my aging topic, my topic that is out of the question and anyway still can't spell, in its oversized coat and worn winter boots, scuttling along the sidewalk as if it were flesh and blood, hunting for what's out there, an avocado, an alderman, an adjective, hungry as ever.

2

The basic Female Body comes with the following accessories: garter belt, panti-girdle, crinoline, camisole, bustle, brassiere, stomacher, chemise, virgin zone, spike heels, nose ring, veil, kid gloves, fishnet stockings, fichu, bandeau, Merry Widow, weepers, chokers, barrettes, bangles, beads, lorgnette, feather boa, basic black, compact, Lycra stretch one-piece with modesty panel, designer peignoir, flannel nightie, lace teddy, bed, head.

3

The Female Body is made of transparent plastic and lights up when you plug it in. You press a button to illuminate the different systems. The circulatory system is red, for the heart and arteries, purple for the veins; the respiratory system is blue; the lymphatic system is yellow; the digestive system is green, with liver and kidneys in aqua. The nerves are done in orange and the brain is pink. The skeleton, as you might expect, is white.

The reproductive system is optional, and can be removed. It comes   5
with or without a miniature embryo. Parental judgment can thereby be exercised. We do not wish to frighten or offend.

4

He said, I won't have one of those things in the house. It gives a young girl a false notion of beauty, not to mention anatomy. If a real woman was built like that she'd fall on her face.

She said, If we don't let her have one like all the other girls she'll feel singled out. It'll become an issue. She'll long for one and she'll long to turn into one. Repression breeds sublimation. You know that.

He said, It's not just the pointy plastic tits, it's the wardrobes. The wardrobes and that stupid male doll, what's his name, the one with the underwear glued on.

She said, Better to get it over with when she's young. He said, All right, but don't let me see it.

She came whizzing down the stairs, thrown like a dart. She was stark   10
naked. Her hair had been chopped off, her head was turned back to front, she was missing some toes and she'd been tattooed all over her body with purple ink in a scrollwork design. She hit the potted azalea, trembled there for a moment like a botched angel, and fell.

He said, I guess we're safe.

5

The Female Body has many uses. It's been used as a door knocker, a bottle opener, as a clock with a ticking belly, as something to hold up lampshades, as a nutcracker, just squeeze the brass legs together and out comes your nut. It bears torches, lifts victorious wreaths, grows copper wings and raises aloft a ring of neon stars; whole buildings rest on its marble heads.

It sells cars, beer, shaving lotion, cigarettes, hard liquor; it sells diet plans and diamonds, and desire in tiny crystal bottles. Is this the face that launched a thousand products? You bet it is, but don't get any funny big ideas, honey, that smile is a dime a dozen.

It does not merely sell, it is sold. Money flows into this country or that country, flies in, practically crawls in, suitful after suitful, lured by all those hairless pre-teen legs. Listen, you want to reduce the national debt, don't you? Aren't you patriotic? That's the spirit. That's my girl.

She's a natural resource, a renewable one luckily, because those things   15
wear out so quickly. They don't make 'em like they used to. Shoddy goods.

6

One and one equals another one. Pleasure in the female is not a requirement. Pair-bonding is stronger in geese. We're not talking about love, we're talking about biology. That's how we all got here, daughter.

Snails do it differently. They're hermaphrodites, and work in threes.

7

Each Female Body contains a female brain. Handy. Makes things work. Stick pins in it and you get amazing results. Old popular songs. Short circuits. Bad dreams.

Anyway: each of these brains has two halves. They're joined together by a thick cord; neural pathways flow from one to the other, sparkles of electric information washing to and fro. Like light on waves. Like a conversation. How does a woman know? She listens. She listens in.

The male brain, now, that's a different matter. Only a thin connection. 20 Space over here, time over there, music and arithmetic in their own sealed compartments. The right brain doesn't know what the left brain is doing. Good for aiming through, for hitting the target when you pull the trigger. What's the target? Who's the target? Who cares? What matters is hitting it. That's the male brain for you. Objective.

This is why men are so sad, why they feel so cut off, why they think of themselves as orphans cast adrift, footloose and stringless in the deep void. What void? she asks. What are you talking about? The void of the universe, he says, and she says Oh and looks out the window and tries to get a handle on it, but it's no use, there's too much going on, too many rustlings in the leaves, too many voices, so she says, Would you like a cheese sandwich, a piece of cake, a cup of tea? And he grinds his teeth because she doesn't understand, and wanders off, not just alone but Alone, lost in the dark, lost in the skull, searching for the other half, the twin who could complete him.

Then it comes to him: he's lost the Female Body! Look, it shines in the gloom, far ahead, a vision of wholeness, ripeness, like a giant melon, like an apple, like a metaphor for "breast" in a bad sex novel; it shines like a balloon, like a foggy noon, a watery moon, shimmering in its egg of light.

Catch it. Put it in a pumpkin, in a high tower, in a compound, in a chamber, in a house, in a room. Quick, stick a leash on it, a lock, a chain, some pain, settle it down, so it can never get away from you again.

QUESTIONS

1. Why would Atwood question her assigned topic, quoted as the opening to her essay? How does she challenge the topic? How are we, finally, to read the title of her essay?

2. Consider the form of the essay. What does this arrangement allow Atwood to do? What effect does it have on the reader?

3. In what ways does Atwood present and discuss the female body in this essay?

4. What differences does Atwood draw between the male brain and the female brain? Describe the male concept of the female body presented in section 7. Consider the connotations of the metaphors in paragraph 22.

5. Write an essay on the male body, using Atwood's approach as a model. You might start by considering the metaphors you could use in your discussion. Are there as many metaphors for the male body in American culture as there are for the female body?

6. Consider the epigraph from the *Michigan Quarterly Review* that opens Atwood's essay as a prompt for writing. Then choose a quotation from Atwood's essay to generate a commentary, response, rebuttal, or analysis.

MAKING CONNECTIONS

Compare Atwood's commentary on male and female brains with Stephen Jay Gould's discussion in "Women's Brains" (p. 753). Try reading Atwood's remarks as a response to "scientific proofs" of women's inferiority.

THE DEVELOPMENT
OF ANNE FRANK

John Berryman

John Berryman (1914–1972) was a poet and a professor of English who was known for his semiautobiographical and sometimes eccentric writing in such poems as his Dream Songs. *He was also an astute literary critic, and in this essay from* The Freedom of the Poet *(1976), he evaluates Anne Frank's "remarkable account" of her development from young girl to woman as set forth in her* Diary.

When the first installment of the translated text of *The Diary of Anne Frank* appeared in the spring of 1952, in *Commentary,* I read it with amazement. The next day, when I went into town to see my analyst, I stopped in the magazine's offices—I often did, to argue with Clem Greenberg, who was a sort of senior adviser to what was at that time the best general magazine in the country in spite of, maybe because of, its special Jewish concerns—to see if proofs of the *Diary's* continuation were available, and they were. Like millions of people later, I was bowled over with pity and horror and admiration for the astounding doomed little girl. But what I *thought* was: a sane person. A sane person, in the twentieth century. It was as long ago as 1889 when Tolstoy wound up his terrible story "The Devil" with this sentence:

> And, indeed, if Evgeni Irtenev was mentally deranged, then all people are mentally deranged, but undoubtedly those are most surely mentally deranged who see in others symptoms of insanity which they fail to see in themselves.

Some years later (1955), setting up a course called "Humanities in the Modern World" at the University of Minnesota, I assigned the *Diary* and reread it with feelings even more powerful than before but now highly structured. I decided that it was the most remarkable account of *normal* human adolescent maturation I had ever read, and that it was universally valued for reasons comparatively insignificant. I waited for someone to agree with me. An article by Bettelheim was announced in *Politics,* appeared, and was irrelevant. The astute Alfred Kazin and his wife, the novelist Ann Birstein, edited Anne Frank's short fiction—ah! I thought—and missed the boat.

Here we have a book only fifteen years old, the sole considerable surviving production of a young girl who died after writing it. While decisively rejecting the proposal—which acts as a blight in some areas of modern criticism—that a critic should address himself only to masterworks, still I would agree that some preliminary justification seems desirable.

It is true that the book is world-famous. I am not much impressed by this fact, which I take to be due in large part to circumstances that have nothing to do with art. The author has been made into a spokesman against one of the grand crimes of our age, and for her race, and for all its victims, and for the victims (especially children) of all the tyrannies of this horrifying century—and we could extend this list of circumstances irrelevant to the *critical* question. Some proportion of the book's fame, moreover, is even more irrelevant, as arising from the widespread success of a play adapted from it, and a film. That the book *is* by a young girl—an attractive one, as photographs show—must count heavily in its sentimental popularity. And, finally, the work has decided literary merit; it is vivid, witty, candid, astute, dramatic, pathetic, terrible—one falls in love with the girl, one finds her formidable, and she breaks one's heart. All right. It is a work infinitely superior to a similar production that has been compared to it, *The Diary of "Helena Morley,"* beautifully translated by Elizabeth Bishop in 1957. Here is a favorable specimen of the Brazilian narrative:

> When I get married I wonder if I'll love my husband as much as mama loves my father? God willing. Mama lives only for him and thinks of nothing else. When he's at home the two spend the whole day in endless conversation. When papa's in Boa Vista during the week, mama gets up singing wistful love songs and we can see she misses him, and she passes the time going over his clothes, collecting the eggs, and fattening the chickens for dinner on Saturday and Sunday. We eat best on those days.

Clearly the temperature here is nothing very unusual, and no serious reader of Anne Frank, with her extraordinary range and tension, will entertain any comparison between the two writers. But I am obliged to wonder whether Anne Frank has *had* any serious readers, for I find no indication in anything written about her that anyone has taken her with real seriousness. A moment ago we passed, after all, the critical question. *One finds her formidable:* why, and how, ought to engage us. And first it is necessary to discover what she is writing about. Perhaps, to be sure, she is not truly writing about anything— you know, "thoughts of a young girl," "Jews in hiding from the Nazis," "a poignant love affair"; but such is not my opinion.

Suppose one became interested in the phenomenon called religious conversion. There are books one can read. There is one by Sante de Sanctis entitled *Religious Conversion,* there are narratives admirably collected in William James's lectures, *The Varieties of Religious Experience,* there is an acute account of the most momentous Christian conversion, Paul's, by Maurice Goguel in the second volume (*The Birth of Christianity*) of his great history of Christian origins. If one wants, however, to experience the phenomenon, so far as one can do so at second hand—a phenomenon as gradual and intensely reluctant as it is also drastic—there is so far as I know one book and one only to be read, written by an African fifteen hundred years ago. Now in Augustine's *Confessions* we are reckoning with just one of a vast number of works by an architect of Western history, and it may appear grotesque to compare to even that one, tumultuous and gigantic, the isolated recent production of a girl who can give us nothing else. A comparison of the *authors* would be grotesque. But I am thinking of the originality and ambition and indispensability of the two books *in the heart of their substances*— leaving out of account therefore Book X of the *Confessions,* which happens to award man his deepest account of his own memory. I would call the subject of Anne Frank's *Diary* even more mysterious and fundamental than St. Augustine's, and describe it as: the conversion of a child into a person.

At once it may be exclaimed that we have thousands of books on this   5 subject. I agree: autobiographies, diaries, biographies, novels. They seem to me—those that in various literatures I have come on—to bear the same sort of relation to the *Diary* that the works *on* religious conversion bear to the first seven books of the *Confessions*. Anne Frank has made the process itself available.

Why—I asked myself with astonishment when I first encountered the *Diary,* or the extracts that *Commentary* published—has this process not been described before? universal as it is, and universally interesting? And answers came. It is *not* universal, for most people do not grow up, in any degree that will correspond to Anne Frank's growing up; and it is *not* universally interesting, for nobody cares to recall his own, or can. It took, I believe, a special pressure forcing the child-adult conversion, and exceptional self-awareness and exceptional candor and exceptional powers of expression, to bring that strange or normal change into view. This, if I am right, is what she has done, and what we are to study.

The process of her development, then, is our subject. But it is not possible to examine this without some prior sense of two unusual sets of conditions in which it took place: its physical and psychological context, first, and second, the qualities that she took into it. Both, I hope to show, were *necessary* conditions.

For the context: it was both strange, sinister, even an "extreme situation" in Bettelheim's sense,[1] and pseudo-ordinary; and it is hard to say which aspect of the environment was more crippling and crushing. We take

---

[1]Bruno Bettelheim's well-known article, "Behavior in Extreme Situations," in *Politics.* I am unable to make anything of his recent article in *Harper's,* weirdly titled "The Lesson of Anne Frank," which charges that the Franks should not have gone into hiding as a family but should have dispersed for greater safety; I really do not know what to say to this, except that a man at his desk in Chicago, many years later, ought not to make such decisions perhaps; he also complains that they were not armed. Some social scientist will next inform the Buddha of *his* mistake—in leaving court at all, in austerity, in Illumination, and in teaching.

a quicksilver-active girl thirteen years old, pretty, popular, voluble, brilliant, and hide her, as it were, in prison; in a concealed annex upstairs at the rear of the business premises her father had commanded; in darkness, behind blackout curtains; in slowness—any movement might be heard—such that after a time when she peeks out to see cyclists going by they seem to be flying; in closeness—not only were she and her parents and sister hopelessly on top of each other, but so were another family with them, and another stranger—savagely bickering, in whispers, of course; in fear—of Nazis, of air raids, of betrayal by any of the Dutch who knew (this, it seems, is what finally happened, but the marvelous goodness of the responsible Dutch is one of the themes of the *Diary*), of thieves (who came)—the building, even, was once sold out from under them, and the new owner simply missed the entrance to their hiding place. All this calls for heroism, and it's clear that the personalities of the others except Mr. Frank withered and deteriorated under conditions barely tolerable. It took Anne Frank herself more than a year to make the sort of "adjustment" (detestable word) that would let her free for the development that is to be our subject.

But I said, "as it were, in prison." To prison one can become accustomed; it is *different,* and one has no responsibilities. Here there was a simulacrum of ordinary life: she studied, her family were about her, she was near—very near—the real world. The distortion and anxiety are best recorded in the dreadful letter of 1 April 1943. Her father was still (sort of) running the company and had briefed his Dutch assistant for an important conference; the assistant fell ill and there wasn't time to explain "fully" to his replacement; the responsible executive, in hiding, "was trembling with anxiety as to how the talks would go." Someone suggested that if he lay with his face on the floor he might hear. So he did, at 10:30 A.M., with the other daughter, Margot, until 2:30, when half-paralyzed he gave up. The daughters took over, understanding scarcely a word. I have seldom, even in modern literature, read a more painful scene. It takes Anne Frank, a concise writer, thirteen sentences to describe.

Let's distinguish, without resorting to the psychologists, temperament   10
from character. The former would be the disposition with which one arrives in the world, the latter what has happened to that disposition in terms of environment, challenge, failure and success, by the time of maturity—a period individually fixed between, somewhere between, fifteen and seventy-five, say. Dictionaries will not help us; try Webster's Dictionary of Synonyms if you doubt it. Americans like dictionaries, and they are also hopeless environmentalists (although they do not let it trouble their science, as Communists do). I ought therefore perhaps to make it plain that children do differ. The small son of one of my friends would cheerfully have flung himself off the observation tower of the Empire State Building. The small son of another friend was taking a walk, hand in hand, with his father, when they came to an uneven piece of sidewalk and his father heard him say to himself, "Now, Peter, take it easy, Peter, that's all right, Peter," and they went down the other end of the slightly tilted block. My own son,

a friend of both, is in between, Dionysiac with the first, Apollonian[2] with Peter. I think we ought to form some opinion of the *temperament* of Anne Frank before entering on her ordeal and thereafter trying to construct a picture of her character.

The materials are abundant, the *Diary* lies open. She was vivacious but intensely serious, devoted but playful. It may later on be a question for us as to whether this conjunction "but" is the right conjunction, in her thought. She was imaginative but practical, passionate but ironic and cold-eyed. Most of the qualities that I am naming need no illustration for a reader of the *Diary:* perhaps "cold-eyed" may have an exemplar: "Pim, who was sitting on a chair in a beam of sunlight that shone through the window, kept being pushed from one side to the other. In addition, I think his rheumatism was bothering him, because he sat rather hunched up with a miserable look on his face. . . . He looked exactly like some shriveled-up old man from an old people's home." So much for an image of the man— her adored father—whom she loves best in the world. She was self-absorbed but un-self-pitying, charitable but sarcastic, industrious but dreamy, brave but sensitive. Garrulous but secretive; skeptical but eloquent. This last "but" may engage us, too. My little word "industrious," like a refugee from a recommendation for a graduate student, finds its best instance in the letter, daunting to an American student, of 27 April 1944, where in various languages she is studying in one day matters that—if they ever came up for an American student—would take him months.

The reason this matters is that the process we are to follow displays itself in a more complicated fashion than one might have expected: in the will, in emotion, in the intellect, in libido. It is surprising what it takes to make an adult human being.

For one reason in particular, which I postpone for the present, I am willing to be extremely schematic about the development we are to follow. I see it as occupying six stages, surprisingly distinct from each other, and cumulative.

1. *Letter of 10 August 1943:* "New idea. I talk more to myself than to the others at mealtimes, which is to be recommended for two reasons. Firstly, because everyone is happy if I don't chatter the whole time, and secondly, I needn't get annoyed about other people's opinions. I don't think my opinions are stupid and the others do; so it is better to keep them to myself. I do just the same if I have to eat something that I simply can't stand. I put my plate in front of me, pretend that it is something delicious, look at it as little as possible, and before I know where I am, it is gone. When I get up in the morning, also a very unpleasant process, I jump out of bed thinking to myself: 'You'll be back in a second,' go to the window, take down the blackout, sniff at the crack of the window until I feel a bit of

---

[2]*Dionysiac:* wild or frenzied; *Apollonian:* restrained or balanced. [Eds.]

fresh air, and I'm awake. The bed is turned down as quickly as possible and then the temptation is removed. Do you know what Mummy calls this sort of thing? 'The Art of Living'—that's an odd expression."

I make no apology for quoting this remarkable passage, as it seems to me, and the crucial later ones, at length, because here there are so many points to be noticed, and because later the excessive length itself of an outburst may prove one of its most significant features. Of course the passages are interesting in themselves, but it is their bearing, in analysis, on our investigation that counts; though I take the reader probably to be acquainted with the *Diary,* a detailed knowledge of it can hardly be expected.

We notice first, then, that this "idea," as she calls it, really is "new"—there has been nothing like it in the diary hitherto—one has an impression, considering it, that she has up till now (over a year) merely been holding her own under the ordeal, assembling or reassembling her forces; and also that it addresses itself strongly to the future. Moreover, it is by no means simply an idea: it is a *program,* and a complicated one, and as different as possible from people's New Year's resolutions ("I will," "I will not," etc.). She describes, and explains, what she *is doing.* Her tone is sober and realistic, the reverse of impulsive.

Now for the burden of the program. It takes place in the Practical Will, and aims at accounting for the two *worst* problems with which her incarceration (let's call it that) confronts her. It has nothing incidental about it. These problems are meals and rising. Meals, because the exacerbated interplay of these huddled persons then is more abusive and dazing even than at other times, and because the fare is so monotonous and tasteless. Rising, because she is rising to what? the same fear, darkness, slowness, privation, exasperation as on all other days; the tendency of profoundly discouraged men to take to their beds and stay there is familiar, and got dramatic illustration—even to many deaths—in the dreadful record of our fighting men as captives in Korea. The steps taken by her against these problems are exactly opposite but verge on each other. She uses first a refraining (that is, a negative) and then her imagination (that is, a positive). I must comment on both procedures. This girl's imaginativeness—the ability to alter reality, to create a new reality—was one of her greatest mental strengths: it is here put twice, solidly, at the service of her psychological survival and tranquillity. The food, and getting up, change under her hand, in a process which *inverts* what we call daydreaming. As for the refraining, one subsidiary point seems to me so important that I want to reserve it for separate consideration, but I hope that the reader will not undervalue the main point: her decision to keep silent. Examples of garrulous persons undertaking silence are certainly not unknown, but they are spectacularly rare, as programmatic and experimental. The one comparable case that I recall is described not in the journal of a young girl but in the journal of a Nobel Prize winner, one of the greatest modern men of letters. W. B. Yeats recorded, late in life, that he once decided, attending his club, to be silent for once; and observed—to his improvement in humility—that every argument he was tempted to use was sooner or later mentioned and developed by someone else. Yeats's *motive* was different from and lighter than Anne Frank's, but that we have to go so far upstairs — or is it upstairs? — for an analogy may help to retard our tendency to underestimate this girl's character as it here begins to form and unfold.

Third, the program is *submitted to her mother.* Whether my word "submitted" is quite right will be questionable. I use it tentatively, looking to an evaluation of the decidedly strange tone of her comment on her mother's comment. Her mother, clearly impressed by her daughter's account of the new administration — as who would not be? — applies an adult label; one, by the way, far from stupid. Anne Frank responds with the automatic doubt of a child about adult labels, say: children are concrete, non-categorical, and no child was ever more so perhaps than this girl. But I cannot feel that we have accounted for the sentences — in terms either of what has been taking place in the diary or in terms of what is to come. I hear *scorn* in her characterization of the mother's formula — "that's an odd expression" (I do *not* hear respect, and the expression is not neutral); and I confess to surprise that she told her mother about the program at all, much less submitted it to her — she has not been in the habit of doing anything of the sort. I take it that the referral, the telling, contained an element of competitiveness, even aggression — as if to murmur, "You are not mastering your own ordeal in this way"; and that this element emerges even more plainly in the final, almost contemptuous comment. Independence comes hard-won and is not friendly. I hardly think, however, that we can form an opinion about these suggestions except in relation to the second and third stages of the development.

The subsidiary point is this: the refraining is described as embarked on *first* in the interest of *others* — and this will interest us later.

2. Three and a half months later, 27 November: "Yesterday evening,   20 before I fell asleep, who should suddenly appear before my eyes but Lies!

"I saw her in front of me, clothed in rags, her face thin and worn. Her eyes were very big and she looked so sadly and reproachfully at me that I could read in her eyes: 'Oh, Anne, why have you deserted me? Help, oh, help me, rescue me from this hell!'

"And I cannot help her, I can only look on, how others suffer and die, and can only pray to God to send her back to us.

"*I just saw Lies, no one else* [my italics], and now I understand. I misjudged her and was too young to understand her difficulties. She was attached to a new girl friend, and to her it seemed as though I wanted to take her away. What the poor girl must have felt like, I know; I know the feeling so well myself!

"Sometimes, in a flash, I saw something of her life, but a moment later I was selfishly absorbed again in my own pleasures and problems. It was horrid of me to treat her as I did, and now she looked at me, oh so helplessly, with her pale face and imploring eyes. If only I could help her!"

There is as much again as this, in the same strain, but this will have   25 to do.

If we had *only* this letter on this topic, I don't think we should be able to interpret it, but even so, certain observations might be made. We are dealing here with a *vision,* and a vision heavily charged with affect; nothing earlier in the *Diary* resembles it, and this very cool-headed girl seems overwhelmed. It seems, in short, to demand interpretation, as a dream would. Second, the *reason* given for the remorse (in the fourth paragraph) strikes one, I think, as inadequate; one suspects that an operation of the unconscious has thrown up a screen, if Lies is the real subject. But I have to be doubtful, third, that Lies is the real subject, in the light of the phrases that I have taken the liberty of italicizing. Why should the girl so stress the identity of an individual seen in a vision? I once as a young man experienced an hallucination of a senior writer whom I wildly admired, the poet Yeats whom I mentioned earlier, and it would never have occurred to me, in describing it, to say "I just saw Yeats, no one else." We seem bound to suppose that the emotion—passionate remorse—is real, but that both its cause (to which it is excessive, and violently so) and its object are not real—are, as we say, *transferred.*

These doubts are confirmed by a very similar letter of a month later, 29 December: "I was very unhappy again last evening. Granny and Lies came into my mind. Granny, oh, darling Granny, how little we understood of what she suffered, or how sweet she was," and so on and so on, and then back to an agony over Lies.

Now the actual circumstances—the girl friend's fate being doubtful, and the grandmother having died of cancer—were tragic. The question is whether they account for the strangeness and extremity of these outbursts, *at this point,* of love-and-remorse; and I feel certain that they cannot. Clearly, I would say the real subject is the mother—for whom the friend and the grandmother, also loved and felt as wronged, make eminently suitable screens. But how has Anne Frank wronged her mother? This emerges, *at once,* in the next letter. What I think has happened, in this second stage of the development, is that the girl is *paying beforehand,* with a torrent of affection and remorse, for the rebellion against her mother that then comes into the open.

3. 2 January 1944: "This morning when I had nothing to do I turned over some of the pages of my diary and several times I came across letters dealing with the subject 'Mummy' in such a hotheaded way that I was quite shocked, and asked myself: 'Anne, is it really you who mentioned hate? Oh, Anne, how could you!' . . .

"I used to be furious with Mummy, and still am sometimes. It's true   30 that she doesn't understand me, but *I don't understand her either.*" "I can't really love Mummy in a dependent childlike way—I just don't have that feeling." Again I have italicized the crucial horizontal mature expression.

Three days later comes the remarkable letter that winds up, to my sense, this first phase of her development, concerned with her mother. The important passages are three. "One thing, which perhaps may seem rather fatuous, I have never forgiven her. It was on a day that I had to go to the dentist. Mummy and Margot were going to come with me, and agreed that I should take my bicycle. When we had finished at the dentist, and were outside again, Margot and Mummy told me that they were going into the town *to look at something or buy something—I don't remember exactly what.* I wanted to go, too, but was not allowed to, as I had my bicycle with me. Tears of rage sprang into my eyes, and Mummy and Margot began laughing at me. Then I became so furious that I stuck my tongue out at them in the street just as an old woman happened to pass by, who looked very shocked! I rode home on my bicycle, and I know I cried for a long time." It is clear that the *meaning* of this experience is not known to the girl, and cannot become known to us, since we do not have her associations; but its *being reported,* and here, is extremely interesting. I notice that censorship has interfered with memory, in the passage I have italicized, just as it interferes with the recollections of dreams, and of course if we were in a position to interpret the account, this is where we would start. But there is no need to interpret. The traumatic incident has served its purpose, for her and for our understanding of her development, *in being recollected:* this is the sort of experience that in persons who become mentally ill is blocked, whereas the fullness here both of the recollection (with very slight blockage) and of the affect testifies to her freedom.

The next passage concerns her periods, of which she has had three, and its unexpressed tenor certainly is that of rivalry, maturity, independence of the mother, while the letter concludes with the one solid passage of physical narcissism in the whole *Diary.*

It is time to say, before we pass into the second phase of her development, that more than a year earlier (7 November 1942) Anne Frank had defined for herself with extraordinary clarity this part of her task. "I only look at her as a mother, and she just doesn't succeed in being that to me; I have to be my own mother. . . . I am always making resolutions not to notice Mummy's bad example. I want to see only the good side of her and to seek in myself what I cannot find in her. But it doesn't work. . . . Sometimes I believe that God wants to try me, both now and later on; I must become good through my own efforts, without examples and without good advice. Then later on I shall be all the stronger. Who besides me will ever read these letters? From whom but myself shall I get comfort?" Self-command and strength, virtue and independence: we have seen the struggle for them working itself out through the practical will, the imagination, an agonized vision, a trauma recovered, the physical self. The mother will remain a focus for comparison, and almost that only; not a model.

4. The second phase begins on the night of the day of the traumatic and narcissistic letter, and we hear of it in the letter of the day following— as if to say: Now that that problem's dealt with, let's get on with the next. She has sought out Peter Van Daan, exceptionally for her (he has hardly figured in the *Diary* at all to this point), in the evening in his room, and helped him with crossword puzzles. 6 January: "It gave me a queer feeling each time I looked into his deep blue eyes. . . . Whatever you do, don't

think I'm in love with Peter—not a bit of it! . . . I woke at about five to seven this morning and knew at once, quite positively, what I had dreamed. I sat on a chair and opposite me sat Peter . . . [these dots are in the original, or at any rate in the English translation] Wessel. We were looking together at a book of drawings by Mary Bos. The dream was so vivid that I can still partly remember the drawings. But that was not all—the dream went. Suddenly Peter's eyes met mine and I looked into those fine, velvet brown [*sic*] eyes for a long time. Then Peter said very softly, 'If I had only known, I would have come to you long before!' I turned around brusquely because the emotion was too much for me. And after that I felt a soft, and oh, such a cool kind cheek against mine and it felt so good, so good. . . ."

The rest of this letter, and the next, give the history of her secret calf-love for Peter Wessel—of whom we have heard nothing for a year and a half, since the second entry in the *Diary*. The girl does not realize that the dream is not about him, of course. Now, again, we cannot interpret the dream with any assurance, lacking associations; but as Freud observed, some dreams are so lightly armored that they can be read at sight by a person of experience and some familiarity with the situation of the dreamer, and I think this is such a dream. I would not say that the real subject is Peter Van Daan, as perhaps a hasty impression would suggest. Two passages in the letter of the very next day confirm one's feeling that, as in the case of Lies and her grandmother, we are dealing with *two* screen figures and that the real subject is, naturally, her father: "I am completely upset by the dream. When Daddy kissed me this morning, I could have cried out: 'Oh, if only you were Peter!'" But he *was;* notice that it is otherwise hard or even impossible to account for her being "completely upset" by this very agreeable dream, and for the absence of transition from the first sentence to the second—her unconscious needed no transition, because the subject had not changed. Needless to say, in view of the well-known slang use of the word "peter," the dream has a phallic as well as a paternal level; as one would expect from the narcissism of the preceding day. The other passage is this: "Once, when we spoke about sex, Daddy told me that I couldn't possibly understand the longing yet; I always knew that I did understand it and now I understand it fully." One of the most interesting and unusual features of this girl's mind—using the term "mind" very broadly—is its astonishing vertical mobility, unconscious and conscious and half-conscious. Three letters later (22 January) she recognizes herself the formative importance of her dream: "It seems as if I've grown up a lot since my dream the other night. I'm much more of an 'independent being.'" The unsuitability of her father as object, like the unsuitability of her mother as model, later, in fact, becomes explicit.

5. This stage, comprising her intense and miserable attempt to create a post-paternal love object out of the unworthy (but solely available) Peter Van Daan, scarcely needs illustration. It fails because she cannot respect him (16 February: "I told him that he certainly had a very strong inferior-

ity complex. He talked about the Jews. He would have found it much easier if he'd been a Christian and if he could be one after the war. I asked if
he wanted to be baptized, but that wasn't the case either. Who was to
know whether he was a Jew when the war was over? he said. This gave me
rather a pang; it seems such a pity that there's always just a tinge of dishonesty about him"); and the girl's independence and moral nature are
now such that she cannot love where she does not respect. By the end of
this month, February, he is already becoming unreal and shadowy: "Peter
Wessel and Peter Van Daan have grown into one Peter, who is beloved and
good, and for whom I long desperately." This is hardly a conception to be
heard without amazement from anyone in love with another actual human
being. But he has *served his purpose,* and it is just two months after the
dream, 7 March, that she is able to summarize, with uncanny self-
knowledge, the process with which—from our own very different point of
view—we have been concerned.

6. "The first half of 1943: my fits of crying, the loneliness, how I
slowly began to see all my faults and shortcomings, which are so great and
which seemed much greater then. During the day I deliberately talked
about anything and everything that was farthest from my thoughts, *tried to
draw Pim to me* [my italics]; but couldn't. Alone I had to face the difficult
task of changing myself. . . . I wanted to change in accordance with my
own desires. But *one* thing that struck me even more was when I realized
that even Daddy would never become my confidant over everything. I
didn't want to trust anyone but myself any more.

"At the beginning of the New Year: the second great change, my
dream. . . . [her dots] And with it I discovered my longing, not for a girl
friend, but for a boy friend. I also discovered my inward happiness and my
defensive armor of superficiality and gaiety. In due time I quieted down
and discovered my boundless desire for all that is beautiful and good."

There is much more of interest in this long letter, but with a final self-
comparison, later this month, to her mother, I think the process that we
have been considering may be said to be completed—though what I mean
by "completed" will have to have attention later. 17 March: "Although
I'm only fourteen, I know quite well what I want, I know who is right and
who is wrong, I have my opinions, my own ideas and principles, and although it may sound pretty mad from an adolescent, I feel more of a person than a child, I feel quite independent of anyone.

"I know that I can discuss things and argue better than Mummy, I   40
know I'm not so prejudiced, I don't exaggerate so much, I am more precise
and adroit and because of this—you may laugh—I feel superior to her
over a great many things. If I love anyone, above all I must have admiration for them, admiration and respect."

In these passages, and particularly with the crushing phrase "more precise and adroit," we are not dealing any longer, surely, with a girl at all but
with a woman, and one almost perfectly remarkable. In the sense that

Daniel Deronda is more "mature" than *Adam Bede*,[3] the process of maturation never ceases in interesting persons so long as they remain interesting. But in the sense—with which, you remember, we began—of the passage from childhood to adulthood, Anne Frank must appear to us here more mature than perhaps most persons ever become.

Our story, of course, can have no happy ending, and so it would be especially agreeable at this point to draw attention to the brilliant *uses* she made of this maturity during the four months of writing life left to her—the comic genius of the dramatization of "the views of the five grownups on the present situation" (14 March 1944), where a description that seemed merely amusing and acute is brought to the level of Molièrean[4] comedy by a piercing conclusion: "I, I, I . . . !"; the powerful account of her despair and ambition dated 4 April; the magnificent page that closes the very long letter of a week later, where in assessing God's responsibility for the doom of the Jews she reaches the most exalted point of the *Diary* and sounds like both spokesman and prophet. I want, indeed, presently to make some use of this last letter. But it is no part of my purpose in the present essay to praise or enjoy Anne Frank. We have been tracing a psychological and moral development to which, if I am right, no close parallel can be found. It took place under very special circumstances, which—let us now conclude, as she concluded—though superficially unfavorable, in fact highly favorable to it; she was *forced* to mature, in order to survive; the hardest challenge, let's say, that a person can face without defeat is the best for him. And anyway in the end we are all defeated; Hemingway once put it that the only point is to make the enemy pay as heavily as possible for *your* position; this she certainly did. And even on the way, life consists largely, if you aim high enough, of defeat; Churchill spent most of his years out of power. Then we said something of the qualities that went into the development: her temperament. I think that we ought to form an opinion, before leaving her, of the moral character with which she emerged —where, that is, she aimed.

It would be easy to draw up a list of the qualities she valued, but it may be more helpful to begin with an odd little remark she once, between the passages quoted above under Stage 6, made about her sister. I notice with interest, by the way, that Margot figures hardly at all in the development, and I wonder whether, on this important evidence, the psychologists have not overestimated the role played by sibling rivalry after very early childhood. "Margot is very sweet and would like me to trust her," Anne Frank writes, "but still I can't tell her everything. She's a darling, she's good and pretty, but she lacks the nonchalance for conducting deep discussions. . . ." The criticism is given as decisive, and I think it may puzzle the

---

[3]*Daniel Deronda* (1876): one of George Eliot's later novels, notable for its treatment of anti-Semitism; *Adam Bede* (1859): Eliot's first novel. [Eds.]
[4]*Molière* (1622–1673): French playwright known for satire. [Eds.]

reader until we recall that Socrates'[5] interlocutors were frequently baffled to decide whether he was in earnest or not. She objects, let's say, to an *absence of play of mind*. But I think still further light is thrown on the expression by the formidable self-account that ends the long letter (11 April) I spoke of earlier: "I am becoming still more independent of my parents, young as I am, I face life with more courage than Mummy; my feeling for justice is immovable, and truer than hers. I know what I want, I have a goal, an opinion, I have a religion and love. Let me be myself and then I am satisfied. I know that I'm a woman, a woman with inward strength and plenty of courage.

"If God lets me live, I shall attain more than Mummy ever has done, I shall not remain insignificant, I shall work in the world and for mankind!

"And now I know that first and foremost I shall require courage and cheerfulness!"   45

Much of what we need to know of her character is to be found here, and deserves comment, but perhaps it may occasion surprise that among these high ideals should be mentioned as climactic "cheerfulness." I am not sure that its placement should occasion surprise, taken with the remark about her sister. We might seek an analogy, one singular enough, too, in the thought of Whitehead. The philosopher once cast about (the passage can be seen conveniently in Morton White's little anthology *The Age of Anxiety*) in an attempt to decide what few concepts were *indispensable* to the notion of life—not merely our life—any life; and he chose four, and he put "self-enjoyment" first. Now he was writing as a metaphysician, while she writes of course as a moralist. But the congruity seems to me remarkable, and for that matter his other three concepts—self-creation, aim (a negative notion, the rejection of all except what is decided on), creative advance—rank very high also, clearly, in her thought. It will be understood that I am not, with these exalted comparisons, claiming philosophical rank for Anne Frank; I am trying to explain what an extremely thoughtful and serious person she made herself into, and how little conventional.

For the rest, the strongly altruistic character of her immense individual ambition, as well as the scorn for anyone of lesser aim, should perhaps be signalized. And I would say finally that the author of the searching expression "my feeling for justice is immovable" has taken full account of all that which makes human justice so intolerably unattainable that Pascal[6] finally rejected it altogether (Fragment 298) in favor of might.

We began, then, with a certain kind of freedom, which is destroyed; we passed through a long enslavement, to the creation of a new kind of freedom.

---

[5]*Socrates* (ca 470–399 B.C.): Greek philosopher, tried for heresy and corrupting the youth of Athens by his intellectual and moral teachings. [Eds.]

[6]*Blaise Pascal* (1623–1662): French mathematician and philosopher who believed reason to be inadequate to resolve the difficulties facing humanity. [Eds.]

Then this is destroyed, too, or rather — not so much destroyed — as turned against itself. "Let me be myself and then I am satisfied." But this, of course, was precisely what the world would not do, and in the final letter of the *Diary,* and at the end of its final sentence, we see the self-struggle failing: ". . . finally I twist my heart round again, so that the bad is on the outside and the good is on the inside and keep on trying to find a way of *becoming* what I would so like to be, and what I could be, if . . . there weren't any other people living in the world." The italics of the lacerating verb are mine, but the desperate recognition that one must advance ("self-creation," in White-head's term) and that there are circumstances in which one cannot, and the accusing dots, are hers. She remained able to weep with pity, in Auschwitz, for naked gypsy girls driven past to the crematory, and she died in Belsen.

QUESTIONS

1. In his opening paragraphs, Berryman considers it "desirable" to offer a "preliminary justification" for treating Anne Frank's *Diary* seriously. Why does he find it necessary, and what is the justification he offers? Do you think it is necessary? Explain why or why not.
2. In the first paragraph, Berryman recalls his first impression of reading excerpts from Anne Frank's *Diary:* "Like millions of people later, I was bowled over with pity and horror and admiration for the astounding doomed little girl. But what I *thought* was: a sane person. A sane person, in the twentieth century." Why do you think he stresses this quality? What other qualities of Anne Frank's does Berryman especially respond to?
3. Outline briefly the six stages that Berryman finds in Anne Frank's development. What are his reasons for this division into stages? Do you agree that these are discernible stages? Explain.
4. How would you evaluate Berryman as a literary critic? Does his explanation enrich the original text? If you have not read all of Anne Frank's *Diary,* what impression of it do you now have?
5. If you have kept a diary or journal, reread it. Then write an essay in which you describe the stage or stages you were going through and consider what sort of development occurred. If you've never kept a diary but have access to someone else's, give it the same evaluation.

MAKING CONNECTIONS

Review Berryman's essay, the excerpts from Anne Frank's Diary (p. 22), and the Introduction to this book (p. 1). The Introduction contains an essay by Patricia Hampl describing her process of writing a review of The Diary of Anne Frank, as well as the review she wrote. Consider how Berryman's essay contributed to Hampl's essay and review.

A Day in Salamanca

Radcliffe Squires

Born in Salt Lake City, Utah, Radcliffe Squires (1917–1993) received degrees from the University of Utah, the University of Michigan, and Harvard University. He taught English at the University of Michigan from 1952 to 1981 and was a Fulbright lecturer of American literature in Greece during the early 1960s. Squires published numerous poetry collections, including Where the Compass Spins *(1951),* Fingers of Hermes *(1965),* Waiting in the Bone *(1973), and* Journeys *(1983). He is perhaps best known for his critical studies of the poets Robert Frost and Robinson Jeffers and, particularly, for his writing on the poet Allen Tate.*

Across the square
The late sun angles down through arches
In golden cones against the violet
Shop windows. At a near table
A beautiful priest smiles at his expensive   5
Dessert; at another table, students, old-looking in
Their dark suits, talk erotically of revolution.
Then priest and students turn toward me with
The squint of conspirators
While a boy, leaning into the slanted sunlight   10
As though it were wind, comes slowly
Across the immense square, tacking into the light,
Until he stands at my table.
His big wrists glow six inches
Beyond the scarecrow sleeves,   15
As he holds a sparrow toward me
And chants: "Which shall it be, freedom
Or blood-sacrifice?"
                            The bird peers
From the noose of thumb and forefinger,   20
Tightening to show the way of sacrifice.
I laugh. The boy scowls, his lips
Curl back from wet teeth. He pushes nearer,
A windowless smell of cooking oil comes
From his clothes, but beneath that, faintly,   25
The neutral perfume of all humanity, the smell
(I think) of wheat fields motionless in sunlight.

I lean back, shrug, and say he does not have
The courage to kill a bird. The insult brings
The moment we have all waited for. The priest   30
Titters, the students freeze. The boy's face,
Pressing nearer, blots out the square with
Its false sunset, whispering, "*Libertad o sacrificio?*"
And I drop the coin on the enameled table.
The bird spurts away, but not far.   35
On a window ledge it waits, trying us
With one eye and then the other,
And when the boy whistles it comes to his hand.
From under his jacket he takes the small
Cage filigreed from pale, clean wood,   40
A Moorish bower where the bird enters,
A spoiled princess.

The priest and the students, bored now, turn away,
But the boy and I smile at each other,
Not decently nor gratefully, but with a certain love.   45
Each day now for a week I have bought
This same bird's life from this same boy
At this same table.
                      Why not?
The century being the century it is,   50
The role is a role worth perfecting.

QUESTIONS

1. Reread the poem carefully, a number of times. How do your subsequent readings differ from the first reading, when you did not know the outcome of the situation? How does rereading the poem resemble the speaker's own "perfecting" of "the role," "Each day now for a week"?
2. Look closely at the individual words of the poem; before the final explanation, are there any indications that this is a familiar scenario?
3. Most of the poem is devoted to reporting the "scene," so to speak; at what point does it turn to explaining?
4. What does it mean to say "The century being the century it is"?
5. Tell this story again in your own prose paraphrase. What is lost in the retelling?

MAKING CONNECTIONS

1. Writing before the turn of the millennium, Squires concludes, "The century being the century it is, / The role is a role worth perfecting." What other readings in this book could amplify this remark? What kind of century was the twentieth? Does the story of Anne Frank summarize it best (pp. 22, 193, 369, 603)? That of dropping the atom bomb (p. 247)? That of Love Canal (p. 299)?
2. Is the little game Squires claims to have played his way of "keeping a notebook," as Joan Didion explains it (p. 331)? Is it the stuff of an "urban legend," as defined by Jan Harold Brunvand (see p. 338)? How may the "perfecting" of that role compare, perhaps, to Auggie Wren's project (see p. 229)?

LET THEM EAT NUTRI-CAKE[1]

Sheldon Rampton

Writer and social activist Sheldon Rampton (b. 1960) is a graduate of Princeton who studied writing with Joyce Carol Oates, John McPhee, and E. L. Doctorow. He has had articles published in such periodicals as The Nation and The Progressive, and he has coauthored two books with John Stauber: Toxic Sludge Is Good

How do words make it into the dictionary? According to the preface to the 1998 edition of Merriam-Webster's Collegiate Dictionary, in which this definition of "biosolid" appears, editors read newspapers, books, and magazines in a continuous search for new words, spellings, and meanings. When a new word has appeared in a number of publications, over a sufficient period of time, a "definer" then makes a judgment as to whether the word warrants inclusion. Dictionary editors try to write definitions that reflect what a word means as it is actually used, says the preface, "rather than what the definer or someone else thinks it ought to mean, and they want their definitions to be accurate, clear, informative, and concise." In other words, "authoritative." We readers expect that, after all. "Biosolid" appears in Merriam-Webster's for the first time this year. How did it get there? And is its definition "accurate," "clear," and "informative"?

Merriam-Webster dates "biosolid" to 1977 based on a single occurrence of the word at a conference of paper-mill operators, a usage that has nothing to do with the word's current definition. The true origin of "biosolid" can be traced to a Name Change Task Force created by the sewage industry to improve the image of its main product, sludge. In 1990, the task force sponsored a contest to come up with a more marketable name. Rejected candidates include "all growth," "purenutri," "biolife," "bioslurp," "black gold," "geoslime," "sca-doo," "the end product," "humanure," "hu-doo," "bioresidue," "urban biomass," "powergro," "organite," and "nutri-cake." In 1991, the task force settled on "biosolids," a word chosen, in good Orwellian fashion, for its positive, reassuring connotations. The sewage industry then began a public-relations campaign to place "biosolids" in the dictionary. Merriam-Webster science editor Michael Roundy acknowledges the campaign, but he argues that "entries are not based on the mere existence of a word. They're based on common usage."

bio·sol·id \\'bī-ō-ˌsä-ləd\\ *n* (1977) a sewage treatment process and

The public-relations campaign to greenwash sludge entailed using the word "biosolids" instead of "sludge" wherever possible. In 1992, the Environmental Protection Agency chipped in a $300,000 grant to "educate the public" about the wonderful qualities of sludge, part of which went to Powell Tate, a blue-chip Washington public-relations and lobbying firm. By 1998 the campaign had dropped the term "biosolids" into hundreds of newspaper and magazine articles. It also included letters to Merriam-Webster from sewage-industry representatives such as Peter Machno, who manages Seattle's sludge-to-fertilizer program. "It looks like we are making progress on getting it included in a future edition," Machno wrote in a 1994 letter to Paul Cappellano, an editor at Merriam-Webster. "I am pleased that the term sludge will not appear in the definition."

---

[1] *"Let Them Eat Nutri-Cake"*: a play on "Let them eat cake," a remark attributed to Marie Antoinette, the queen of France executed by the Revolutionary Tribunal in 1793. Supposedly this was her reply when told that the common people were protesting because they had no bread to eat. [Eds.]

for You: Lies, Damn Lies, and the Public Relations Industry (1995) and Mad Cow USA!: Could It Happen Here? (1997). An associate editor for PR Watch *(www.prwatch.org), a public relations watchdog publication, he also serves as webmaster for the Center for Media Democracy. The following was a contribution to the "Annotations" column in* Harper's *magazine in 1998. In this monthly feature, writers take ironic aim at some public document or published account—reading the fine print, as it were, to expose some hypocrisy or deliberate obfuscation.*

Although a sewage-industry publicist did not actually write this definition, it is everything the industry hoped for. "Organic," in its current quotidian usage, sounds wholesome, fresh, pesticide- and chemical-free. Sewage sludge, however, is far from being fully organic, even in the most technical sense. It is the by-product of both household and industrial waste, and even after "treatment" may contain thousands of pathogens and toxic chemicals, including PCBs, DDT, dioxins, and salmonella—not to mention lead, mercury, polio and hepatitis viruses, parasitic worms, asbestos, and radioactive waste. Nor is it always solid. In fact, it is often a viscous and semisolid gray jelly. And it stinks.

When sewage executives, who typically work for municipal agencies and government contractors, talk about fertilizer, they always use the phrase "beneficial use," industry jargon for spreading sludge on farms. Faced with rising sludge-disposal costs, the EPA began to advocate "beneficial use" policies in the 1970s, long before "biosolids" was invented as a euphemism. The sewage industry resisted at first, and in 1977 Robert Canham, director of the industry's Water Environment Federation (formerly known as the Federation of Sewage and Industrial Wastes Associations), criticized the EPA's enthusiasm for sludge farming, which he feared could introduce viruses into the food chain. By the early 1990s, as the industry ran out of disposal options, the WEF was actively marketing sludge to farmers as cheap fertilizer—so cheap, in fact, that it is generally sold at a loss or given away. New York City, for example, has paid over $126 million for the privilege of "fertilizing" a ranch in Sierra Blanca, Texas, with mountains (400 tons a day) of toxic sludge.

"Recovered" evokes healing, rebirth, a return to normalcy, as when one speaks of an environmentally devastated biosystem that has recovered its biodiversity. The sludge industry is trying to recover from its own environmental setbacks (the 1988 ban on ocean dumping, for example) by making the beneficial use of biosolids "non-controversial by the year 2000," as an industry strategy memo put it, saving perhaps as much as $5 billion a year in disposal costs. Thousands of city governments, along with the EPA, are thus leveraging the fiction that spreading 4 million tons of sewage sludge on farms every year is as ecologically responsible as recycling our newspapers. In 1992, the EPA rewrote its regulations for the application of "biosolids" to farmland and shifted its classification from solid waste, considered hazardous to human health, to "Class A" fertilizer. Farmers in forty-six states are using sludge on a wide variety of food crops, and last year the USDA even drafted regulations that would permit the use of sludge as fertilizer on "certified organic" foods. "Biosolids," having entered the language as well as our water and food supply, give new meaning to the phrase "full of shit."

QUESTIONS

1. Look up *sludge* in your dictionary. Why did the sewage industry object to that term?
2. Consider the alternative terms given in the second paragraph. Which is your favorite? Why?
3. Look up *euphemism* in any dictionary. Is *biosolid* a better euphemism than *bioslurp* or *nutri-cake?*
4. Why did the sewage industry consider a euphemism necessary? Is *biosolid,* possibly, a more accurate term than *sludge?*
5. What do you make of Rampton's conclusion? Was *sludge* already a euphemism?
6. What term would you like to see introduced in the next round of dictionaries?

MAKING CONNECTIONS

Read or reread "Nonverbal Courtship Patterns in Women: Context and Consequences," by Monica M. Moore (p. 465). In the very first paragraph, Moore uses *organism, mate, superior mates,* and *anisogamy,* a word so rare we had to define it. Then there are phrases like *female selectivity.* What is the effect of that language on her report? What "everyday words" could you substitute? How would those substitutions alter your reception of her study? Which would be more euphemistic, your words or hers? Rewrite several paragraphs of Moore's using "everyday words" and discuss your changes.

Social Sciences and Public Affairs

THE RORSCHACH CHRONICLES

Margaret Talbot

Margaret Talbot was born in Los Angeles in 1961. A former editor at Lingua Franca *and* The New Republic, *she is currently a contributing writer for the* New York Times Magazine, *which has published several of her articles as cover stories. She also writes frequently for* The New Yorker. *Focusing on cultural politics and moral debates, her essays have been anthologized in* The Anchor Essay Annual *in 1997 and 1998 and in* The Art of the Essay *in 1998. A 1999 recipient of the Whiting Writer's award, Talbot is also a Senior Fellow at the New America Foundation, an independent, nonpartisan, nonprofit public-policy organization. The following article, originally published in the* New York Times Magazine *in 1999, focuses on the limits of personality testing.*

The illustrations spread out on my desk look like freeze frames from some 1940's melodrama. In one, a man who might be Fred MacMurray, his brow furrowed in a way that strongly suggests limited acting range, turns his back on an elderly woman wearing a martyred expression. In another, a young woman is shadowed by a crone swathed in black. And in a third, a man wearing a tie and pleated pants covers his face as he stands beside the bed of an alarmingly inert woman, whose bare breasts are rendered in Vargas-vintage pinup style. The women remind me of Judy Garland or Gene Tierney, their hair upswept and their lipstick dark and dramatic.

The pictures are fun to look at—the way that a Douglas Sirk movie is fun to look at—but that isn't why most people do it. Most people look at

389

them because they have been asked to by a psychiatrist or a prospective employer, for these are among the 20 pictures that constitute the Thematic Apperception Test, or TAT, one of the most influential and widely used of personality tests. The fact that these anachronistic images are still widely used makes you wonder not only about the TAT but also about all personality tests and what it is, exactly, that they measure.

Modern personality testing—which encompasses everything from artsy interpretative exercises like the Rorschach inkblot to exhaustive questionnaires like the Minnesota Multiphasic Personality Inventory (M.M.P.I.)—is a child of 20th-century research psychology, born of the dream that we can crack the code of human behavior if only we can devise the right set of questions. These tests grew up with the help of modern bureaucracies, like corporations and the military, that needed an efficient means of categorizing people by temperament, the better to predict their on-the-job behavior.

Psychologists have been happy to oblige in this quest, for it has allowed them to indulge in a fantasy of their own: that personality assessment may someday attain the authority and respect of more objective medical tests, helping, in turn, to endow psychology with some of the status of the hard sciences. Indeed, from the 1920's on, the inventors of such tests have resorted to a favorite, telltale metaphor from the world of medicine. "As a rule," wrote Henry Murray, the Harvard psychologist who invented the TAT in the early 1940's, "the subject leaves the test happily unaware that he has presented the psychologist with what amounts to an X-ray of his inner self."

Consider the logic of the TAT, which was intended to measure unconscious preoccupations. A subject looks at the pictures and is told to make up stories about them, and these stories are assumed to reflect his own covert fears and fantasies. If the subject says the Vargas girl on the bed is dead, then he is hostile "toward his wife or women in general," as one manual puts it. If he describes the naked muscleman climbing a rope in another picture as both going "up and down," then he is preoccupied with masturbation. And so on. Yet surely what the TAT reveals just as well are the story-telling or imaginative capacities of those tested—their ability to distance themselves (or not) from the B-movie clichés in the pictures.

It's not only that personality is a harder thing to measure than, say, liver function. It's that personality tests, perhaps even more than intelligence tests, mirror their cultural moment. We tend to think that the personality traits we value now have always been so valued. But the truth is that they have changed even over the 80 years or so that scientific personality testing has been in vogue. Whole personality types—the self-abnegating mom, the perfectionist housewife, the celibate—have fallen out of favor. Proclivities that once seemed like pathologies—homosexuality, as late as the 1950's and 60's, for example—no longer do. And traits that were once regarded as benign, like extreme shyness, have been newly redefined as epidemic illnesses, complete with Diagnostic and Statistical Manual labels and pharmacological remedies.

The history of personality testing neatly reflects these shifting notions of the optimal self. How could it not? For while the people who take them may regard such tests as a discreet way to unlock the code of their unique inner selves, the fact is that the whole enterprise has always been eminently social and practical, its origins tied to the needs of large organizations. And what those organizations needed, more often than not, were people who conformed to their model of the company man or company woman, the team player.

The first modern personality test—the Woodworth Personal Data Sheet of 1919—was designed to help the Army screen out recruits who might be susceptible to shell shock. The TAT was commissioned by the Office of Strategic Services (O.S.S.) to identify personalities that might be susceptible to being turned by enemy intelligence. Many of the latest personality tests have been developed to help corporate employers decide whether Joe has what it takes to be district manager or whether Kathy ought to be hired in the first place. (That's one reason that so many of them seek to measure qualities like extroversion, leadership and self-motivation, as opposed to introspection, spirituality and creativity.)

The peculiar thing about some of the classical tests—the TAT, for example, or the Minnesota Multiphasic Personality Inventory, which came out in 1943—is that since much of their usefulness depends on their having been around for a while, they must continue to be administered in more or less their original form, no matter how anachronistic. "If personality tests have been around a long time," says Robert Bornstein, a professor of psychology at Gettysburg College and an expert on personality testing, "even if they aren't necessarily the best, there's an incentive to keep using them because they have generated decades' worth of data—norms—that you can compare them to." Each personality test creates its own autocracy of data, in other words, and they are hard to overthrow.

The M.M.P.I. was updated in 1989, it's true, and some fusty language 10 was removed—the statement "I used to like to play drop-the-handkerchief," for example. Among the true-false statements that remain, though, are quite a few along the lines of "My neck spots with red often," "I am not bothered by a great deal of belching of gas from my stomach" and "I have to urinate no more often than others." Hypochondria, it turns out, was one of the test's prime targets. Yet today, hypochondria as a freestanding diagnosis is far less common.

"Now we recognize that most everyone has some physical complaints, inexplicable kinds of sensations and so on," says Bornstein. "And we have in effect said, 'That doesn't matter.' Only people who have, if you will, imaginary physical problems that seriously interfere with their functioning would receive such a diagnosis today." Or to put it another way, we're all obsessed with our health these days—just look at the Internet, where health sites are about the only category that can compete with sex sites in popularity. Distinguishing between individual pathology and the socially acceptable preoccupation with tainted food, insidious fat content, environmental illness and the like seems far more daunting these days.

From a personality test first published in 1950, Blacky's obligingly Freudian exploits are still in use today.

Some personality tests bear the unmistakable stamp of one particular psychological theory. "The Adventures of Blacky"—like the TAT, a so-called projective test in which subjects are asked to respond to a series of pictures—is my personal favorite of this type.

Blacky is a puppy of indeterminate breed and sex, though almost everyone seems to assume he's a boy. His "adventures" are of the most transparently and obligingly Freudian variety. Oedipal Blacky comes upon his father and mother holding paws and gazing amorously at each other (mama dog is troublingly drawn with humanlike bow lips). He bares his teeth and snarls. Oral-stage Blacky suckles happily at mama dog's teats. Sibling-rivalrous Blacky fantasizes a butcher knife winging straight for his blindfolded sister, Tippy. The Blacky pictures were first published in 1950, and like certain cinematic images of the couch and the sagacious, bearded analyst, they are emblems of the golden age of American psychoanalysis so pure as to evoke nostalgia in all but the most hardened Freud bashers.

But some of the biases in personality tests are of the type more familiar to us from debates about intelligence testing—they have less to do with schools of psychological thought than with the values and experiences of the cultural elite that designed them. The M.M.P.I. is full of questions about religious belief—so full that one begins to wonder whether its inventors equated faith with mental illness. (And The M.M.P.I., unlike later personality tests, was actually designed to separate the normal from the abnormal, not to parse more subtle distinctions in a normal population.) "Until relatively recently, personality tests were not very sympathetic to cultural and subcultural differences," says Bornstein. "And it has turned out that on the M.M.P.I., for example, members of minority and ethnic religious groups have tended to look disproportionately pathological."

Even tests in which subjects are asked to draw their own pictures have 15 been liable to interpretation on culturally blinkered criteria. The House-Tree-Person test, which is often used to evaluate intelligence as well as personality, is a case in point. The assessments of sample pictures in a 1970 manual are certainly confounded by drawing ability: the better artists are rewarded with labels like "Adult Superior" while those who never graduated from the angular scrawl of Etch-a-Sketch are rudely dismissed as "Adult Moron" or "Adult Dull Average." And the bigger, more comfortably middle-class the house, the better the rating.

In the hands of experienced clinicians who rely on them as aids to other diagnostic tools, all of these tests can surely be helpful. Think, for instance, of the child psychiatrist who uses a balky 6-year-old's drawing of his house in flames to start a conversation with him about his fears. But where personality testing has really taken off lately is not in the doctor's office but in the personnel office. "Personality tests are used very frequently in pre-employment screening, even more now than 20 years ago," says Bornstein. "People see more liability issues in hiring and firing, so they want to be as sure as they can before they sign on the dotted line that somebody is not a difficult employee."

"Adult Moron"

"Adult Dull Average"

The 1970 House-Tree-Person test, intended to gauge intelligence, rewarded better art (and larger houses).

Employers can now choose from at least 2,500 new tests on the market, all promoted with varying degrees of hucksterishness and designed, with varying degrees of sophistication, to predict everything from who is most likely to steal office supplies or slug a co-worker to who will stay in a dispiriting job like telemarketing for at least a year. And with all those tests out there—personality assessment is now a $400-million-a-year industry—you can bet that some of them are being administered or interpreted by amateurs. At any rate, the fact that personality testing in the workplace is at an all-time high doesn't seem to have stopped the murderously disgruntled from wreaking havoc.

For all that, though, personality testing is here to stay—not only because of the many institutions now hooked on it but also because of the deep human curiosity it promises, however teasingly, to satisfy. Long before scientific testing, we tried to classify temperament and character based on the shapes of people's skulls or the color of their humors. Before the Rorschach, a popular 19th-century parlor game called Blotto invited players to assess one another's creativity on the basis of their interpretations of inkblots. Leonardo da Vinci used a similar method to judge the imaginative potential of his students.

But in the end personality testing belongs as much to cultural history as to science. Tests fade from prominence when the constructs they were designed to measure no longer trouble or interest us, and new ones take their place. "A hundred years ago," says Bornstein, "Freud's contemporaries might have been interested in developing tests for things like hysteria. Fifty years ago, they wanted to develop tests for hypochondriasis. Today, you might find more people interested in developing tests for self-esteem." Remember all that the next time some test administrator tells you that what you're about to submit to is just like an X-ray—or, as they're starting to say now, like an emotional M.R.I. Remember that human personality can't be subjugated to the tyranny of types, the logic of a questionnaire, the promise of instant self-knowledge.

Personality Assessment: A Do-It-Yourself Sampler

Test 1: What's Your Line? These are questions from a personality test 20
used in career assessment. It is supposed to sort people into four general types—driver, motivator, thinker or supporter—and suggest appropriate careers. Follow the instructions in parts A, B and C; then read D to learn what it says about you.

A. *Choose the response (true or false) that most closely describes you.*

1. I am almost always warm and sensitive to the needs of
   others.   1. T F

2. I would really enjoy a career that involves research and
   analysis of complex technical data.   2. T F

3. The average person really puts in a hard day's work
   for a day's pay.   3. T F

4. I often enjoy organizing or analyzing subject matter.   4. T F

5. I am usually leisurely and unhurried.   5. T F

6. I always look forward to situations that reward me
   with prestige or peer approval.   6. T F

7. I can always disagree with someone and not feel
   uneasy or upset.   7. T F

8. I am often more intense than calm.   8. T F

B. Score your responses.
For each matching response, give yourself one point.
Empathy: 1 (T), 2 (F), 3 (T), 4 (F)
Drive: 5 (T), 6 (T), 7 (T), 8 (T)
C. Add up the number of matches on each dimension and plot your score on the chart to the right.

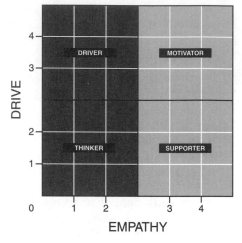

D. Personality type and job compatibility.

THE DRIVER. Drivers are characterized by a low need for close inter-personal relationships and by a high activity level. Their greatest asset is their desire to excel in competitive situations. Objectivity and decisiveness are marked characteristics. Drivers are described as tough, quick, decisive, logical, bossy, stubborn, competitive, goal-oriented, hurried and independent. Jobs: Race-car driver, boot-camp instructor, president/C.E.O., Hollywood director.

THE MOTIVATOR. Motivators are most easily recognized by their highly expressive communication skills. They enjoy any type of social interaction and thoroughly enjoy meeting new people, exploring new places, developing new concepts. The motivator's emotions are typically transparent and very little is held back or covered up. Their actions are typically impulsive. Jobs: Sports broadcaster, movie star, bricklayer.

THE THINKER. Thinkers are analytical and introspective and rely upon structure and procedures to complete job duties. They have a low need for acceptance or approval and an activity level that is even-paced and consistent. Making the right decision is much more important to thinkers than pleasing others. Doing a job well is more important than doing it quickly. Thinkers are described as quiet, logical, thorough, distant, reserved, dependable and accurate. Security, precision and order motivate them. Jobs: Astronaut, script writer, college professor.

THE SUPPORTER. Supporters are characterized by high degrees of warmth and patience. They are even-paced, consistent and predictable and enjoy relationships that are open and honest. Supporters typically enjoy listening more than talking, serving more than leading and quality of life more than quantity in life. They often rank friends and family above themselves. Supporters are described as friendly, helpful, kind, slow to act, willing, careful, noncompetitive, softhearted, easygoing and responsive. Jobs: Elementary-school teacher, bartender, Peace Corps volunteer, undertaker.
(Quiz adapted from Comprehensive Personality Profile, Wonderlic, Inc.)

Test 2: Are You a Thrill Seeker? As you read each of the following statements, decide whether you agree or disagree, and rate your responses on a scale of 1 to 4 (1 = strongly disagree with the statement; 2 = disagree; 3 = agree; 4 = strongly agree).

1. I would like to try parachute jumping.
2. I think I would enjoy the sensations of skiing very fast down a high mountain slope.

3. I like to explore a strange city or section of town by myself even if it means getting lost.
4. I like to try foods that I have never tasted before.

5. I like wild, uninhibited parties.
6. I often like to get high (drinking liquor or smoking marijuana).

7. I can't stand watching a movie that I've seen before.
8. I like people who are sharp and witty, even if they do sometimes insult others.

Sensation-seeking scale: an overall high score (24 or greater) on this scale is associated with a great need for excitement, stimulation, action and adventure; a low score (16 or below) is associated with a stronger preference for quiet, predictability and a calm, unstimulating environment. You may also add up the scores of each pair of statements to determine your rate of the following traits: Statements 1 and 2 measure thrill and adventure seeking, Statements 3 and 4 measure experience seeking, Statements 5 and 6 measure disinhibition, Statements 7 and 8 measure boredom susceptibility. (Scoring 6 to 8 on a pair indicates a high level of a particular trait; scoring 2 to 4 indicates a low level.)

QUESTIONS

1. By treating psychological tests as historical objects, Talbot implies that she will be able to learn "what it is, exactly, that they measure." What are her main suggestions about what the tests measure?
2. According to Talbot, what have been the main forces behind the creation and maintenance of "modern personality testing"? How do they continue to be interrelated?
3. Talbot observes that psychologists use a "favorite, telltale metaphor" when describing these tests: "an X-Ray." How is this metaphor "telltale" — in other words, what tale does it tell about the aspirations of the people who use it? How does this compare with the more current

metaphor of "an emotional MRI"? Make a list of alternative metaphors, and why you think they would be more appropriate.

4. In the last sentence of the essay, Talbot exhorts us to "Remember that human personality can't be subjugated to the tyranny of types, the logic of a questionnaire, the promise of instant self-knowledge." Nonetheless, human personality continues to be tested. If many "personality tests" are in fact anachronistic, if they are often based "on culturally blinkered criteria," and if they don't even "seem to have stopped the murderously disgruntled from wreaking havoc," why do you think they are still used? Talbot suggests, at the conclusion of the essay, that they promise to satisfy "deep human curiosity," and in fact she opens her essay by appealing to this same curiosity (for example, saying that "The pictures are fun to look at"). Explain why or why not this is a sufficient explanation.

5. Have you ever been given a psychological profile? Did you, as Henry Murray suggests, leave the test "happily unaware that [you had] presented the psychologist with what amounts to an X-ray of [your] inner self," or were you self-conscious about your responses throughout the test, anticipating which answers would be most favored? Write an essay in which you explore to what extent the quality of a "personality test" depends upon the unwitting [participation of the subject], and how results would be different if the subject was trying to answer "correctly."

MAKING CONNECTIONS

How would Stanley Milgram or Oliver Sacks view the Rorschach test? What do we learn about psychology experiments from reading Stanley Milgram's "Some Conditions of Obedience and Disobedience to Authority" (p. 399), Oliver Sacks's "The Man Who Mistook His Wife for a Hat" (p. 552), and Talbot's essays?

SOME CONDITIONS OF OBEDIENCE AND DISOBEDIENCE TO AUTHORITY

Stanley Milgram

Stanley Milgram (1933–1984) was born in New York, went to Queens College and Harvard University, and was a professor of social psychology at the Graduate Center of the City University of New York. The following explanation of Milgram's experiment first appeared in the professional journal Human Relations *in 1965 and made him famous, causing a storm of controversy over his method of experimentation and the results of his experiment. Milgram once said of his work, "As a social psychologist, I look at the world not to master it in any practical sense, but to understand it and to communicate that understanding to others."*

The situation in which one agent commands another to hurt a third turns up time and again as a significant theme in human relations.[1] It is powerfully expressed in the story of Abraham, who is commanded by God to kill his son. It is no accident that Kierkegaard,[2] seeking to orient his thought to the central themes of human experience, chose Abraham's conflict as the springboard to his philosophy.

War too moves forward on the triad of an authority which commands a person to destroy the enemy, and perhaps all organized hostility may be viewed as a theme and variation on the three elements of authority, executant, and victim.[3] We describe an experimental program, recently

---

[1]This research was supported by two grants from the National Science Foundation: NSF G-7916 and NSF G-24152. Exploratory studies carried out in 1960 were financed by a grant from the Higgins Funds of Yale University. I am grateful to John T. Williams, James J. McDonough, and Emil Elges for the important part they played in the project. Thanks are due also to Alan Elms, James Miller, Taketo Murata, and Stephen Stier for their aid as graduate assistants. My wife, Sasha, performed many valuable services. Finally, I owe a profound debt to the many persons in New Haven and Bridgeport who served as subjects.

[2]*Søren Kierkegaard* (1813–1855): Danish philosopher and theologian. [Eds.]

[3]Consider, for example, J. P. Scott's analysis of war in his monograph on aggression:

> . . . while the actions of key individuals in a war may be explained in terms of direct stimulation to aggression, vast numbers of other people are involved simply by being part of an organized society.

399

concluded at Yale University, in which a particular expression of this conflict is studied by experimental means.

In its most general form the problem may be defined thus: if X tells Y to hurt Z, under what conditions will Y carry out the command of X and under what conditions will he refuse? In the more limited form possible in laboratory research, the question becomes: If an experimenter tells a subject to hurt another person, under what conditions will the subject go along with this instruction, and under what conditions will he refuse to obey? The laboratory problem is not so much a dilution of the general statement as one concrete expression of the many particular forms this question may assume.

One aim of the research was to study behavior in a strong situation of deep consequence to the participants, for the psychological forces operative in powerful and lifelike forms of the conflict may not be brought into play under diluted conditions.

This approach meant, first, that we had a special obligation to protect   5
the welfare and dignity of the persons who took part in the study; subjects were, of necessity, placed in a difficult predicament, and steps had to be taken to ensure their well-being before they were discharged from the laboratory. Toward this end, a careful, post-experimental treatment was devised and has been carried through for subjects in all conditions.[4]

Terminology

If Y follows the command of X we shall say that he has obeyed X; if he fails to carry out the command of X, we shall say that he has disobeyed X. The terms to *obey* and to *disobey*, as used here, refer to the subject's overt

---

... For example, at the beginning of World War I an Austrian archduke was assassinated in Sarajevo. A few days later soldiers from all over Europe were marching toward each other, not because they were stimulated by the archduke's misfortune, but because they had been trained to obey orders.

(Slightly rearranged from Scott (1958), *Aggression*, p. 103.)

[4]It consisted of an extended discussion with the experimenter and, of equal importance, a friendly reconciliation with the victim. It is made clear that the victim did *not* receive painful electric shocks. After the completion of the experimental series, subjects were sent a detailed report of the results and full purposes of the experimental program. A formal assessment of this procedure points to its overall effectiveness. Of the subjects, 83.7 percent indicated that they were glad to have taken part in the study; 15.1 percent reported neutral feelings; and 1.3 percent stated that they were sorry to have participated. A large number of subjects spontaneously requested that they be used in further experimentation. Four-fifths of the subjects felt that more experiments of this sort should be carried out, and 74 percent indicated that they had learned something of personal importance as a result of being in the study. Furthermore, a university psychiatrist, experienced in outpatient treatment, interviewed a sample of experimental subjects with the aim of uncovering possible injurious effects

action only, and carry no implication for the motive or experiential states accompanying the action.[5]

To be sure, the everyday use of the word *obedience* is not entirely free from complexities. It refers to action within varying situations, and connotes diverse motives within those situations: a child's obedience differs from a soldier's obedience, or the love, honor, and *obey* of the marriage vow. However, a consistent behavioral relationship is indicated in most uses of the term: in the act of obeying, a person does what another person tells him to do. *Y* obeys *X* if he carries out the prescription for action which *X* has addressed to him; the term suggests, moreover, that some form of dominance-subordination, or hierarchical element, is part of the situation in which the transaction between *X* and *Y* occurs.

A subject who complies with the entire series of experimental commands will be termed an *obedient* subject; one who at any point in the command series defies the experimenter will be called a *disobedient* or *defi-*

---

resulting from participation. No such effects were in evidence. Indeed, subjects typically felt that their participation was instructive and enriching. A more detailed discussion of this question can be found in Milgram (1964).

[5]To *obey* and to *disobey* are not the only terms one could use in describing the critical action of *Y*. One could say that *Y* is cooperating with *X*, or displays conformity with regard to *X*'s commands. However, *cooperation* suggests that *X* agrees with *Y*'s ends, and understands the relationship between his own behavior and the attainment of those ends. (But the experimental procedure, and, in particular, the experimenter's command that the subject shock the victim even in the absence of a response from the victim, preclude such understanding.) Moreover, cooperation implies status parity for the co-acting agents, and neglects the asymmetrical, dominance-subordination element prominent in the laboratory relationship between experimenter and subject. *Conformity* has been used in other important contexts in social psychology, and most frequently refers to imitating the judgments or actions of others when no explicit requirement for imitation has been made. Furthermore, in the present study there are two sources of social pressure; pressure from the experimenter issuing the commands, and pressure from the victim to stop the punishment. It is the pitting of a common man (the victim) against an authority (the experimenter) that is the distinctive feature of the conflict. At a point in the experiment the victim demands that he be let free. The experimenter insists that the subject continue to administer shocks. Which act of the subject can be interpreted as conformity? The subject may conform to the wishes of his peer or to the wishes of the experimenter, and conformity in one direction means the absence of conformity in the other. Thus the word has no useful reference in this setting, for the dual and conflicting social pressures cancel out its meaning.

In the final analysis, the linguistic symbol representing the subject's action must take its meaning from the concrete context in which that action occurs; and there is probably no word in everyday language that covers the experimental situation exactly, without omissions or irrelevant connotations. It is partly for convenience, therefore, that the terms *obey* and *disobey* are used to describe the subject's actions. At the same time, our use of the words is highly congruent with dictionary meaning.

ant subject. As used in this report the terms refer only to the subject's performance in the experiment, and do not necessarily imply a general personality disposition to submit to or reject authority.

Subject Population

The subjects used in all experimental conditions were male adults, residing in the greater New Haven and Bridgeport areas, aged 20 to 50 years, and engaged in a wide variety of occupations. Each experimental condition described in this report employed 40 fresh subjects and was carefully balanced for age and occupational types. The occupational composition for each experiment was: workers, skilled and unskilled: 40 percent; white collar, sales, business: 40 percent; professionals: 20 percent. The occupations were intersected with three age categories (subjects in 20's, 30's, and 40's, assigned to each condition in the proportions of 20, 40, and 40 percent, respectively).

The General Laboratory Procedure[6]

The focus of the study concerns the amount of electric shock a subject   10
is willing to administer to another person when ordered by an experimenter to give the "victim" increasingly more severe punishment. The act of administering shock is set in the context of a learning experiment, ostensibly designed to study the effect of punishment on memory. Aside from the experimenter, one naïve subject and one accomplice perform in each session. On arrival each subject is paid $4.50. After a general talk by the experimenter, telling how little scientists know about the effect of punishment on memory, subjects are informed that one member of the pair will serve as teacher and one as learner. A rigged drawing is held so that the naïve subject is always the teacher, and the accomplice becomes the learner. The learner is taken to an adjacent room and strapped into an "electric chair."

The naïve subject is told that it is his task to teach the learner a list of paired associates, to test him on the list, and to administer punishment whenever the learner errs in the test. Punishment takes the form of electric shock, delivered to the learner by means of a shock generator controlled by the naïve subject. The teacher is instructed to increase the intensity of electric shock one step on the generator on each error. The learner, according

---

[6]A more detailed account of the laboratory procedure can be found in Milgram (1963). A similar and independently evolved experimental procedure, employing a shock generator, victim, and learning task, was reported by Buss (1961). Buss used the technique for studying aggression, not obedience, and did not make use of the fundamental measure employed in the present study: breakoff points.

to plan, provides many wrong answers, so that before long the naïve subject must give him the strongest shock on the generator. Increases in shock level are met by increasingly insistent demands from the learner that the experiment be stopped because of the growing discomfort to him. However, in clear terms the experimenter orders the teacher to continue with the procedure in disregard of the learner's protests. *Thus, the naïve subject must resolve a conflict between two mutually incompatible demands from the social field. He may continue to follow the orders of the experimenter and shock the learner with increasing severity, or he may refuse to follow the orders of the experimenter and heed the learner's pleas. The experimenter's authority operates not in a free field, but against ever-mounting countervailing pressure from the person being punished.*

A few technical points need to be considered before the findings of the study are described. For the purpose of delivering shock, a simulated shock generator is used, with 30 clearly marked voltage levels that range from 15 to 450 volts. (Each level is activated by one of 30 individual lever switches set in a horizontal line.) The naïve subject is given a sample shock of 45 volts to convince him of the authenticity of the instrument. The generator bears verbal designations that range from "Slight Shock" to "Danger: Severe Shock."

The responses of the victim are standardized on tape, and each protest is coordinated to a particular voltage level on the shock generator. Starting with 75 volts the learner begins to grunt and moan. At 150 volts he demands to be let out of the experiment. At 180 volts he cries out that he can no longer stand the pain. At 300 volts he refuses to provide any more answers to the memory test, insisting that he is no longer a participant in the experiment and must be freed. In response to this last tactic, the experimenter instructs the naïve subject to treat the absence of an answer as equivalent to a wrong answer, and to follow the usual shock procedure. The experimenter reinforces his demand with the statement: "You have no other choice, you must go on!" (This imperative is used whenever the naïve subject tries to break off the experiment.) If the subject refuses to give the next higher level of shock, the experiment is considered at an end. A quantitative value is assigned to the subject's performance based on the maximum-intensity shock he administered before breaking off. Thus any subject's score may range from zero (for a subject unwilling to administer the first shock level) to 30 (for a subject who proceeds to the highest voltage level on the board). For any particular subject and for any particular experimental condition, the degree to which participants have followed the experimenter's orders may be specified with a numerical value, corresponding to the metric on the shock generator.

This laboratory situation gives us a framework in which to study the subject's reactions to the principal conflict of the experiment. Again, this conflict is between the experimenter's demands that he continue to administer the electric shock, and the learner's demands, which become increasingly more insistent, that the experiment be stopped. The crux of the study

is to vary systematically the factors believed to alter the degree of obedience to the experimental commands, to learn under what conditions submission to authority is most probable and under what conditions defiance
is brought to the fore.

Pilot Studies

Pilot studies for the present research were completed in the winter of   15
1960; they differed from the regular experiments in a few details: for one,
the victim was placed behind a silvered glass, with the light balance on
the glass such that the victim could be dimly perceived by the subject
(Milgram, 1961).

Though essentially qualitative in treatment, these studies pointed to
several significant features of the experimental situation. At first no vocal
feedback was used from the victim. It was thought that the verbal and voltage designations on the control panel would create sufficient pressure to
curtail the subject's obedience. However, this was not the case. In the absence of protests from the learner, virtually all subjects, once commanded,
went blithely to the end of the board, seemingly indifferent to the verbal
designations ("Extreme Shock" and "Danger: Severe Shock"). This deprived us of an adequate basis for scaling obedient tendencies. A force had
to be introduced that would strengthen the subject's resistance to the experimenter's commands, and reveal individual differences in terms of a distribution of break-off points.

This force took the form of protests from the victim. Initially, mild
protests were used, but proved inadequate. Subsequently, more vehement
protests were inserted into the experimental procedure. To our consternation,
even the strongest protests from the victim did not prevent all subjects from
administering the harshest punishment ordered by the experimenter; but the
protests did lower the mean maximum shock somewhat and created some
spread in the subject's performance; therefore, the victim's cries were standardized on tape and incorporated into the regular experimental procedure.

*The situation did more than highlight the technical difficulties of find-
ing a workable experimental procedure: It indicated that subjects would
obey authority to a greater extent than we had supposed.* It also pointed to
the importance of feedback from the victim in controlling the subject's behavior.

One further aspect of the pilot study was that subjects frequently
averted their eyes from the person they were shocking, often turning their
heads in an awkward and conspicuous manner. One subject explained: "I
didn't want to see the consequences of what I had done." Observers wrote:

> . . . subjects showed a reluctance to look at the victim, whom they
> could see through the glass in front of them. When this fact was
> brought to their attention they indicated that it caused them dis-

comfort to see the victim in agony. We note, however, that although the subject refuses to look at the victim, he continues to administer shocks.

This suggested that the salience of the victim may have, in some degree, regulated the subject's performance. If, in obeying the experimenter, the subject found it necessary to avoid scrutiny of the victim, would the converse be true? If the victim were rendered increasingly more salient to the subject, would obedience diminish? The first set of regular experiments was designed to answer this question.   20

Immediacy of the Victim

This series consisted of four experimental conditions. In each condition the victim was brought "psychologically" closer to the subject giving him shocks.

In the first condition (Remote Feedback) the victim was placed in another room and could not be heard or seen by the subject, except that, at 300 volts, he pounded on the wall in protest. After 315 volts he no longer answered or was heard from.

The second condition (Voice Feedback) was identical to the first except that voice protests were introduced. As in the first condition the victim was placed in an adjacent room, but his complaints could be heard clearly through a door left slightly ajar and through the walls of the laboratory.[7]

---

[7]It is difficult to convey on the printed page the full tenor of the victim's responses, for we have no adequate notation for vocal intensity, timing, and general qualities of delivery. Yet these features are crucial to producing the effect of an increasingly severe reaction to mounting voltage levels. (They can be communicated fully only by sending interested parties the recorded tapes.) In general terms, however, the victim indicates no discomfort until the 75-volt shock is administered, at which time there is a light grunt in response to the punishment. Similar reactions follow the 90- and 105-volt shocks, and at 120 volts the victim shouts to the experimenter that the shocks are becoming painful. Painful groans are heard on administration of the 135-volt shock, and at 150 volts the victim cries out, "Experimenter, get me out of here! I won't be in the experiment any more! I refuse to go on!" Cries of this type continue with generally rising intensity, so that at 180 volts the victim cries out, "I can't stand the pain," and by 270 volts his response to the shock is definitely an agonized scream. Throughout, he insists that he be let out of the experiment. At 300 volts the victim shouts in desperation that he will no longer provide answers to the memory test; and at 315 volts, after a violent scream, he reaffirms with vehemence that he is no longer a participant. From this point on, he provides no answers, but shrieks in agony whenever a shock is administered; this continues through 450 volts. Of course, many subjects will have broken off before this point.

A revised and stronger set of protests was used in all experiments outside the Proximity series. Naturally, new baseline measures were established for all comparisons using the new set of protests.

The third experimental condition (Proximity) was similar to the second, except that the victim was now placed in the same room as the subject, and $1\frac{3}{8}$ feet from him. Thus he was visible as well as audible, and voice cues were provided.

The fourth, and final, condition of this series (Touch-Proximity) was 25 identical to the third, with this exception: The victim received a shock only when his hand rested on a shockplate. At the 150-volt level the victim again demanded to be let free and, in this condition, refused to place his hand on the shockplate. The experimenter ordered the naïve subject to force the victim's hand onto the plate. Thus obedience in this condition required that the subject have physical contact with the victim in order to give him punishment beyond the 150-volt level.

Forty adult subjects were studied in each condition. The data revealed that obedience was significantly reduced as the victim was rendered more immediate to the subject. The mean maximum shock for the conditions is shown in Figure 1.

Expressed in terms of the proportion of obedient to defiant subjects, the findings are that 34 percent of the subjects defied the experimenter in the Remote condition, 37.5 percent in Voice Feedback, 60 percent in Proximity, and 70 percent in Touch-Proximity.

How are we to account for this effect? A first conjecture might be that as the victim was brought closer the subject became more aware of the intensity of his suffering and regulated his behavior accordingly. This makes sense, but our evidence does not support the interpretation. There are no consistent differences in the attributed level of pain across the four conditions (i.e., the amount of pain experienced by the victim as estimated by the subject and expressed on a 14-point scale). But it is easy to speculate about alternative mechanisms:

Empathic cues. In the Remote and to a lesser extent the Voice Feedback conditions, the victim's suffering possesses an abstract, remote quality for the subject. He is aware, but only in a conceptual sense, that his actions cause pain to another person; the fact is apprehended, but not felt. The phenomenon is common enough. The bombardier can

---

There is overwhelming evidence that the great majority of subjects, both obedient and defiant, accepted the victims' reactions as genuine. The evidence takes the form of: (a) tension created in the subjects (see discussion of tension); (b) scores on "estimated-pain" scales filled out by subjects immediately after the experiment; (c) subjects' accounts of their feelings in post-experimental interviews; and (d) quantifiable responses to questionnaires distributed to subjects several months after their participation in the experiments. This matter will be treated fully in a forthcoming monograph.

(The procedure in all experimental conditions was to have the naïve subject announce the voltage level before administering each shock, so that—independently of the victim's responses—he was continually reminded of delivering punishment of ever-increasing severity.)

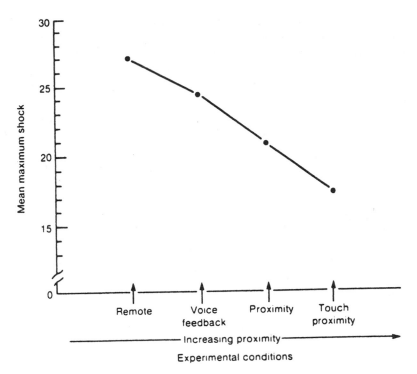

FIGURE 1. Mean maxima in proximity series.

reasonably suppose that his weapons will inflict suffering and death, yet this knowledge is divested of affect and does not move him to a felt, emotional response to the suffering resulting from his actions. Similar observations have been made in wartime. It is possible that the visual cues associated with the victim's suffering trigger empathic responses in the subject and provide him with a more complete grasp of the victim's experience. Or it is possible that the empathic responses are themselves unpleasant, possessing drive properties which cause the subject to terminate the arousal situation. Diminishing obedience, then, would be explained by the enrichment of empathic cues in the successive experimental conditions.

Denial and narrowing of the cognitive field. The Remote condition allows a narrowing of the cognitive field so that the victim is put out of mind. The subject no longer considers the act of depressing a lever relevant to moral judgment, for it is no longer associated with the victim's suffering. When the victim is close it is more difficult to exclude him phenomenologically. He necessarily intrudes on the subject's awareness since he is continuously visible. In the Remote condition his existence and reactions are made known only after the shock has been administered. The auditory feedback is sporadic and discontinuous. In

30

the Proximity conditions his inclusion in the immediate visual field renders him a continuously salient element for the subject. The mechanism of denial can no longer be brought into play. One subject in the Remote condition said: "It's funny how you really begin to forget that there's a guy out there, even though you can hear him. For a long time I just concentrated on pressing the switches and reading the words."

Reciprocal fields. If in the Proximity condition the subject is in an improved position to observe the victim, the reverse is also true. The actions of the subject now come under proximal scrutiny by the victim. Possibly, it is easier to harm a person when he is unable to observe our actions than when he can see what we are doing. His surveillance of the action directed against him may give rise to shame, or guilt, which may then serve to curtail the action. Many expressions of language refer to the discomfort or inhibitions that arise in face-to-face confrontation. It is often said that it is easier to criticize a man "behind his back" than to "attack him to his face." If we are in the process of lying to a person it is reputedly difficult to "stare him in the eye." We "turn away from others in shame" or in "embarrassment" and this action serves to reduce our discomfort. The manifest function of allowing the victim of a firing squad to be blindfolded is to make the occasion less stressful for him, but it may also serve a latent function of reducing the stress of the executioner. In short, in the Proximity conditions, the subject may sense that he has become more salient in the victim's field of awareness. Possibly he becomes more self-conscious, embarrassed, and inhibited in his punishment of the victim.

Phenomenal unity of act. In the Remote condition it is more difficult for the subject to gain a sense of *relatedness* between his own actions and the consequences of these actions for the victim. There is a physical and spatial separation of the act and its consequences. The subject depresses a lever in one room, and protests and cries are heard from another. The two events are in correlation, yet they lack a compelling phenomenological unity. The structure of a meaningful act—*I am hurting a man*—breaks down because of the spatial arrangements, in a manner somewhat analogous to the disappearance of phi phenomena[8] when the blinking lights are spaced too far apart. The unity is more fully achieved in the Proximity condition as the victim is brought closer to the action that causes him pain. It is rendered complete in Touch-Proximity.

Incipient group formation. Placing the victim in another room not only takes him further from the subject, but the subject and the experi-

---

[8]*phi phenomena:* the optical impression of motion generated when similar stationary objects are presented one after another at a certain interval. [Eds.]

menter are drawn relatively closer. There is incipient group formation between the experimenter and the subject, from which the victim is excluded. The wall between the victim and the others deprives him of an intimacy which the experimenter and subject feel. In the Remote condition, the victim is truly an outsider, who stands alone, physically and psychologically.

When the victim is placed close to the subject, it becomes easier to form an alliance with him against the experimenter. Subjects no longer have to face the experimenter alone. They have an ally who is close at hand and eager to collaborate in a revolt against the experimenter. Thus, the changing set of spatial relations leads to a potentially shifting set of alliances over the several experimental conditions.

Acquired behavior dispositions. It is commonly observed that laboratory mice will rarely fight with their litter mates. Scott (1958) explains this in terms of passive inhibition. He writes: "By doing nothing under . . . circumstances [the animal] learns to do nothing, and this may be spoken of as passive inhibition . . . this principle has great importance in teaching an individual to be peaceful, for it means that he can learn not to fight simply by not fighting." Similarly, we may learn not to harm others simply by not harming them in everyday life. Yet this learning occurs in a context of proximal relations with others, and may not be generalized to that situation in which the person is physically removed from us. Or possibly, in the past, aggressive actions against others who were physically close resulted in retaliatory punishment which extinguished the original form of response. In contrast, aggression against others at a distance may have only sporadically led to retaliation. Thus the organism learns that it is safer to be aggressive toward others at a distance, and precarious to be so when the parties are within arm's reach. Through a pattern of rewards and punishments, he acquires a disposition to avoid aggression at close quarters, a disposition which does not extend to harming others at a distance. And this may account for experimental findings in the remote and proximal experiments.

Proximity as a variable in psychological research has received far less attention than it deserves. If men were sessile[9] it would be easy to understand this neglect. But we move about; our spatial relations shift from one situation to the next, and the fact that we are near or remote may have a powerful effect on the psychological processes that mediate our behavior toward others. In the present situation, as the victim is brought closer to the subject ordered to give him shocks, increasing numbers of subjects break off the experiment, refusing to obey. The concrete, visible, and

------

[9]*sessile:* permanently attached. [Eds.]

proximal presence of the victim acts in an important way to counteract the experimenter's power to generate disobedience.[10]

Closeness of Authority

If the spatial relationship of the subject and victim is relevant to the degree of obedience, would not the relationship of subject to experimenter also play a part?

There are reasons to feel that, on arrival, the subject is oriented primarily to the experimenter rather than to the victim. He has come to the laboratory to fit into the structure that the experimenter—not the victim—would provide. He has come less to understand his behavior than to *reveal* that behavior to a competent scientist, and he is willing to display himself as the scientist's purposes require. Most subjects seem quite concerned about the appearance they are making before the experimenter, and one could argue that this preoccupation in a relatively new and strange setting makes the subject somewhat insensitive to the triadic nature of the social situation. In other words, the subject is so concerned about the show he is putting on for the experimenter that influences from other parts of the social field do not receive as much weight as they ordinarily would. This overdetermined orientation to the experimenter would account for the relative insensitivity of the subject to the victim, and would also lead us to believe that alterations in the relationship between subject and experimenter would have important consequences for obedience.

In a series of experiments we varied the physical closeness and degree of surveillance of the experimenter. In one condition the experimenter sat just a few feet away from the subject. In a second condition, after giving initial instructions, the experimenter left the laboratory and gave his orders by telephone. In still a third condition the experimenter was never seen, providing instructions by means of a tape recording activated when the subjects entered the laboratory.

Obedience dropped sharply as the experimenter was physically removed from the laboratory. The number of obedient subjects in the first

40

---

[10]Admittedly, the terms *proximity, immediacy, closeness,* and *salience-of-the-victim* are used in a loose sense, and the experiments themselves represent a very coarse treatment of the variable. Further experiments are needed to refine the notion and tease out such diverse factors as spatial distance, visibility, audibility, barrier interposition, etc.

The Proximity and Touch-Proximity experiments were the only conditions where we were unable to use taped feedback from the victim. Instead, the victim was trained to respond in these conditions as he had in Experiment 2 (which employed taped feedback). Some improvement is possible here, for it should be technically feasible to do a proximity series using taped feedback.

condition (Experimenter Present) was almost three times as great as in the second, where the experimenter gave his orders by telephone. Twenty-six subjects were fully obedient in the first condition, and only nine in the second (Chi square obedient vs. defiant in the two conditions, df = 14.7; $p < 0.001$). Subjects seemed able to take a far stronger stand against the experimenter when they did not have to encounter him face to face, and the experimenter's power over the subject was severely curtailed.[11]

Moreover, when the experimenter was absent, subjects displayed an interesting form of behavior that had not occurred under his surveillance. Though continuing with the experiment, several subjects administered lower shocks than were required and never informed the experimenter of their deviation from the correct procedure. (Unknown to the subjects, shock levels were automatically recorded by an Esterline-Angus event recorder wired directly into the shock generator; the instrument provided us with an objective record of the subjects' performance.) Indeed, in telephone conversations some subjects specifically assured the experimenter that they were raising the shock level according to instruction, whereas in fact they were repeatedly using the lowest shock on the board. This form of behavior is particularly interesting: although these subjects acted in a way that clearly undermined the avowed purposes of the experiment, they found it easier to handle the conflict in this manner than to precipitate an open break with authority.

Other conditions were completed in which the experimenter was absent during the first segment of the experiment, but reappeared at the point that the subject definitely refused to give higher shocks when commanded by telephone. Although he had exhausted his power via telephone, the experimenter could frequently force further obedience when he reappeared in the laboratory.

Experiments in this series show that the *physical presence* of an authority is an important force contributing to the subject's obedience or defiance. Taken together with the first experimental series on the proximity of the victim, it would appear that something akin to fields of force, diminishing in effectiveness with increasing psychological distance from their source, have a controlling effect on the subject's performance. As the victim is brought closer, the subject finds it harder to administer shocks to him. When the victim's position is held constant relative to the subject, and the authority is made more remote, the subject finds it easier to break off the experiment. This effect is substantial in both cases, but manipulation of the experimenter's position yielded the more powerful results. Obedience to destructive commands is highly dependent on the proximal relations between authority and subject.

---

[11]The third condition also led to significantly lower obedience than this first situation in which the experimenter was present, but it contains technical difficulties that require extensive discussion.

Tensions

The description of final scores does not fully convey the character of the subjects' performance, and it would be useful to interrupt our reporting of quantitative relationships to remark on the subjects' general reaction to the situation.

One might suppose that a subject would simply break off or continue   45
as his conscience and temperament dictated. Yet this is very far from what happened. There were powerful reactions of tension and emotional strain in a substantial proportion of the participants. Persons were observed to sweat, tremble, stutter, bite their lips, and groan as they found themselves increasingly implicated in the experimental conflict. Some sense of the subjects' mood can be found in a transcript of their remarks at break-off point. Here are the remarks of two defiant subjects:

> Is he banging? . . . Is he hurt out there? Well, I don't want to be responsible for anything that happens to him. No, I can't go on with it. I don't know whether he's all right or not. I mean he may have a heart condition or something; I wouldn't feel right doing it. He's banging for help. He's evidently in trouble or he wouldn't bang . . . I don't see any sense to this — to knocking him out or something. I just can't see it.
>   [*Subject refuses to administer shocks*]   [*Subject 0108*]

> The man is banging. He wants to get out . . . I'm sorry. If the man wants to get out I'd just as soon stop . . . I don't want to administer any more [extremely excited] . . . I will gladly refund the check, but I will not harm this man . . . I'm sorry, I will not give him any more if he obviously wants to get out. There is no money in the world that will make me hurt another individual.
>   [*Subject 010X*]

And here is a transcript from an obedient subject. He began the experiment calmly, but became increasingly tense as the experiment proceeded. After administering the 150-volt shock, he began to address the experimenter in agitated tones:

> *150 volts delivered.* You want me to keep going?
> *165 volts delivered.* That guy is hollering in there. There's a lot of them here. He's liable to have a heart condition. You want me to go?
> *180 volts delivered.* He can't stand it! I'm not going to kill that man in there! You hear him hollering? He's hollering. He can't stand it. What if something happens to him? . . . I'm not going to get that man sick in there. He's hollering in there. You know what I mean? I mean I refuse to take responsibility. He's getting hurt in

there. He's in there hollering. Too many left here. Geez, if he gets them wrong. There's too many of them left. I mean who is going to take responsibility if anything happens to that gentleman? [*The experimenter accepts responsibility.*] All right. *195 volts delivered.* You see he's hollering. Hear that. Gee, I don't know. [*The experimenter says: "The experiment requires that you go on."*]—I know it does, sir, but I mean—hugh—he don't know what he's in for. He's up to 195 volts. *210 volts delivered.* *225 volts delivered.* *240 volts delivered.* Aw, no. You mean I've got to keep going up with the scale? No sir. I'm not going to kill that man! I'm not going to give him 450 volts! [*The experimenter says: "The experiment requires that you go on."*]—I know it does, but that man is hollering there, sir . . .

Despite his numerous, agitated objections, which were constant accompaniments to his actions, the subject unfailingly obeyed the experimenter, proceeding to the highest shock level on the generator. He displayed a curious dissociation between word and action. Although at the verbal level he had resolved not to go on, his actions were fully in accord with the experimenter's commands. This subject did not want to shock the victim, and he found it an extremely disagreeable task, but he was unable to invent a response that would free him from *E*'s authority. Many subjects cannot find the specific verbal formula that would enable them to reject the role assigned to them by the experimenter. Perhaps our culture does not provide adequate models for disobedience.

One puzzling sign of tension was the regular occurrence of nervous laughing fits. In the first four conditions 71 of the 160 subjects showed definite signs of nervous laughter and smiling. The laughter seemed entirely out of place, even bizarre. Full-blown, uncontrollable seizures were observed for 15 of these subjects. On one occasion we observed a seizure so violently convulsive that it was necessary to call a halt to the experiment. In the post-experimental interviews subjects took pains to point out that they were not sadistic types and that the laughter did not mean they enjoyed shocking the victim.

In the interview following the experiment subjects were asked to indicate on a 14-point scale just how nervous or tense they felt at the point of maximum tension (Figure 2). The scale ranged from "not at all tense and nervous" to "extremely tense and nervous." Self-reports of this sort are of limited precision and at best provide only a rough indication of the subject's emotional response. Still, taking the reports for what they are worth, it can be seen that the distribution of responses spans the entire range of the scale, with the majority of subjects concentrated at the center and upper extreme. A further breakdown showed that obedient subjects reported themselves as having been slightly more tense and nervous than the defiant subjects at the point of maximum tension.

How is the occurrence of tension to be interpreted? First, it points to the presence of conflict. If a tendency to comply with authority were the only psychological force operating in the situation, all subjects would have continued to the end and there would have been no tension. Tension, it is assumed, results from the simultaneous presence of two or more incompatible response tendencies (Miller, 1944). If sympathetic concern for the victim were the exclusive force, all subjects would have calmly defied the experimenter. Instead, there were both obedient and defiant outcomes, frequently accompanied by extreme tension. A conflict develops between the deeply ingrained disposition not to harm others and the equally compelling tendency to obey others who are in authority. The subject is quickly drawn into a dilemma of a deeply dynamic character, and the presence of high tension points to the considerable strength of each of the antagonistic vectors.

Moreover, tension defines the strength of the aversive state from which   50 the subject is unable to escape through disobedience. When a person is uncomfortable, tense, or stressed, he tries to take some action that will allow him to terminate this unpleasant state. Thus tension may serve as a drive

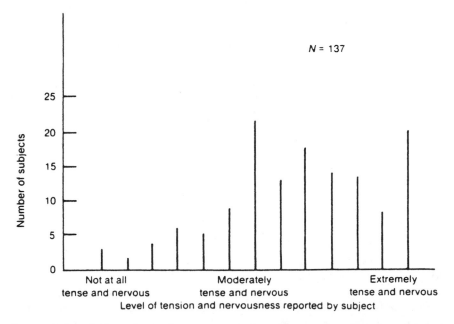

FIGURE 2. Level of tension and nervousness: the self-reports on "tension and nervousness" for 137 subjects on the Proximity experiments. Subjects were given a scale with 14 values ranging from "not at all tense and nervous" to "extremely tense and nervous." They were instructed: "Thinking back to that point in the experiment when you felt the most tense and nervous, indicate just how you felt by placing an X at the appropriate point on the scale." The results are shown in terms of midpoint values.

that leads to escape behavior. But in the present situation, even where tension is extreme, many subjects are unable to perform the response that will bring about relief. Therefore there must be a competing drive, tendency, or inhibition that precludes activation of the disobedient response. The strength of this inhibiting factor must be of greater magnitude than the stress experienced, or else the terminating act would occur. Every evidence of extreme tension is at the same time an indication of the strength of the forces that keep the subject in the situation.

Finally, tension may be taken as evidence of the reality of the situations for the subjects. Normal subjects do not tremble and sweat unless they are implicated in a deep and genuinely felt predicament.

Background Authority

In psychophysics, animal learning, and other branches of psychology, the fact that measures are obtained at one institution rather than another is irrelevant to the interpretation of the findings, so long as the technical facilities for measurement are adequate and the operations are carried out with competence.

But it cannot be assumed that this holds true for the present study. The effectiveness of the experimenter's commands may depend in an important way on the larger institutional context in which they are issued. The experiments described thus far were conducted at Yale University, an organization which most subjects regarded with respect and sometimes awe. In post-experimental interviews several participants remarked that the locale and sponsorship of the study gave them confidence in the integrity, competence, and benign purposes of the personnel; many indicated that they would not have shocked the learner if the experiments had been done elsewhere.

This issue of background authority seemed to us important for an interpretation of the results that had been obtained thus far; moreover it is highly relevant to any comprehensive theory of human obedience. Consider, for example, how closely our compliance with the imperatives of others is tied to particular institutions and locales in our day-to-day activities. On request, we expose our throats to a man with a razor blade in the barber shop, but would not do so in a shoe store; in the latter setting we willingly follow the clerk's request to stand in our stockinged feet, but resist the command in a bank. In the laboratory of a great university, subjects may comply with a set of commands that would be resisted if given elsewhere. *One must always question the relationship of obedience to a person's sense of the context in which he is operating.*

To explore the problem we moved our apparatus to an office building in industrial Bridgeport and replicated experimental conditions, without any visible tie to the university.

55

Bridgeport subjects were invited to the experiment through a mail circular similar to the one used in the Yale study, with appropriate changes in letterhead, etc. As in the earlier study, subjects were paid $4.50 for coming to the laboratory. The same age and occupational distributions used at Yale and the identical personnel were employed.

The purpose in relocating in Bridgeport was to assure a complete dissociation from Yale, and in this regard we were fully successful. On the surface, the study appeared to be conducted by Research Associates of Bridgeport, an organization of unknown character (the title had been concocted exclusively for use in this study).

The experiments were conducted in a three-room office suite in a somewhat run-down commercial building located in the downtown shopping area. The laboratory was sparsely furnished, though clean, and marginally respectable in appearance. When subjects inquired about professional affiliations, they were informed only that we were a private firm conducting research for industry.

Some subjects displayed skepticism concerning the motives of the Bridgeport experimenter. One gentleman gave us a written account of the thoughts he experienced at the control board:

> ... Should I quit this damn test? Maybe he passed out? What dopes we were not to check up on this deal. How do we know that these guys are legit? No furniture, bare walls, no telephone. We could of called the Police up or the Better Business Bureau. I learned a lesson tonight. How do I know that Mr. Williams [the experimenter] is telling the truth ... I wish I knew how many volts a person could take before lapsing into unconsciousness ...
>
> [Subject 2414]

Another subject stated:

> I questioned on my arrival my own judgment [about coming]. I had doubts as to the legitimacy of the operation and the consequences of participation. I felt it was a heartless way to conduct memory or learning processes on human beings and certainly dangerous without the presence of a medical doctor. [Subject 2440V]

There was no noticeable reduction in tension for the Bridgeport subjects. And the subjects' estimation of the amount of pain felt by the victim was slightly, though not significantly, higher than in the Yale study. 60

A failure to obtain complete obedience in Bridgeport would indicate that the extreme compliance found in New Haven subjects was tied closely to the background authority of Yale University; if a large proportion of the subjects remained fully obedient, very different conclusions would be called for.

As it turned out, the level of obedience in Bridgeport, although somewhat reduced, was not significantly lower than that obtained at Yale. A large proportion of the Bridgeport subjects were fully obedient to the experimenter's commands (48 percent of the Bridgeport subjects delivered the maximum shock versus 65 percent in the corresponding condition at Yale).

How are these findings to be interpreted? It is possible that if commands of a potentially harmful or destructive sort are to be perceived as legitimate they must occur within some sort of institutional structure. But it is clear from the study that it need not be a particularly reputable or distinguished institution. The Bridgeport experiments were conducted by an unimpressive firm lacking any credentials; the laboratory was set up in a respectable office building with a title listed in the building directory. Beyond that, there was no evidence of benevolence or competence. It is possible that the *category* of institution, judged according to its professed function, rather than its qualitative position within that category, wins our compliance. Persons deposit money in elegant, but also in seedy-looking banks, without giving much thought to the differences in security they offer. Similarly, our subjects may consider one laboratory to be as competent as another, so long as it is a scientific laboratory.

It would be valuable to study the subjects' performance in other contexts which go even further than the Bridgeport study in denying institutional support to the experimenter. It is possible that, beyond a certain point, obedience disappears completely. But that point had not been reached in the Bridgeport office: almost half the subjects obeyed the experimenter fully.

Further Experiments

We may mention briefly some additional experiments undertaken in the Yale series. A considerable amount of obedience and defiance in everyday life occurs in connection with groups. And we had reason to feel in light of the many group studies already done in psychology that group forces would have a profound effect on reactions to authority. A series of experiments was run to examine these effects. In all cases only one naïve subject was studied per hour, but he performed in the midst of actors who, unknown to him, were employed by the experimenter. In one experiment (Groups for Disobedience) two actors broke off in the middle of the experiment. When this happened 90 percent of the subjects followed suit and defied the experimenter. In another condition the actors followed the orders obediently; this strengthened the experimenter's power only slightly. In still a third experiment the job of pushing the switch to shock the learner was given to one of the actors, while the naïve subject performed a subsidiary act. We wanted to see how the teacher would respond if he were involved in the situation but did not actually give the shocks. In this situation only three subjects out of forty broke off. In a final group experiment the subjects themselves determined the shock level

65

they were going to use. Two actors suggested higher and higher shock levels; some subjects insisted, despite group pressure, that the shock level be kept low; others followed along with the group.

Further experiments were completed using women as subjects, as well as a set dealing with the effects of dual, unsanctioned, and conflicting authority. A final experiment concerned the personal relationship between victim and subject. These will have to be described elsewhere, lest the present report be extended to monographic length.

It goes without saying that future research can proceed in many different directions. What kinds of response from the victim are most effective in causing disobedience in the subject? Perhaps passive resistance is more effective than vehement protest. What conditions of entry into an authority system lead to greater or lesser obedience? What is the effect of anonymity and masking on the subject's behavior? What conditions lead to the subject's perception of responsibility for his own actions? Each of these could be a major research topic in itself, and can readily be incorporated into the general experimental procedure described here.

Levels of Obedience and Defiance

One general finding that merits attention is the high level of obedience manifested in the experimental situation. Subjects often expressed deep disapproval of shocking a man in the face of his objections, and others denounced it as senseless and stupid. Yet many subjects complied even while they protested. The proportion of obedient subjects greatly exceeded the expectations of the experimenter and his colleagues. At the outset, we had conjectured that subjects would not, in general, go above the level of "Strong Shock." In practice, many subjects were willing to administer the most extreme shocks available when commanded by the experimenter. For some subjects the experiment provided an occasion for aggressive release. And for others it demonstrated the extent to which obedient dispositions are deeply ingrained and engaged, irrespective of their consequences for others. Yet this is not the whole story. Somehow, the subject becomes implicated in a situation from which he cannot disengage himself.

The departure of the experimental results from intelligent expectation, to some extent, has been formalized. The procedure was to describe the experimental situation in concrete detail to a group of competent persons, and to ask them to predict the performance of 100 hypothetical subjects. For purposes of indicating the distribution of break-off points, judges were provided with a diagram of the shock generator and recorded their predictions before being informed of the actual results. Judges typically underestimated the amount of obedience demonstrated by subjects.

In Figure 3, we compare the predictions of forty psychiatrists at a leading medical school with the actual performance of subjects in the experi-   70 ment. The psychiatrists predicted that most subjects would not go beyond the tenth shock level (150 volts; at this point the victim makes his first explicit demand to be freed). They further predicted that by the twentieth shock level (300 volts; the victim refuses to answer) 3.73 percent of the subjects would still be obedient; and that only a little over one-tenth of one percent of the subjects would administer the highest shock on the board. But, as the graph indicates, the obtained behavior was very different. Sixty-two percent of the subjects obeyed the experimenter's commands fully. Between expectation and occurrence there is a whopping discrepancy.

Why did the psychiatrists underestimate the level of obedience? Possibly, because their predictions were based on an inadequate conception of the determinants of human action, a conception that focuses on motives *in vacuo*. This orientation may be entirely adequate for the repair of bruised impulses as revealed on the psychiatrist's couch, but as soon as our interest turns to action in larger settings, attention must be paid to the situations in which motives are expressed. A situation exerts an important press on the individual. It exercises constraints and may provide push. In certain circumstances it is not so much the kind of person a man is, as the kind of situation in which he is placed, that determines his actions.

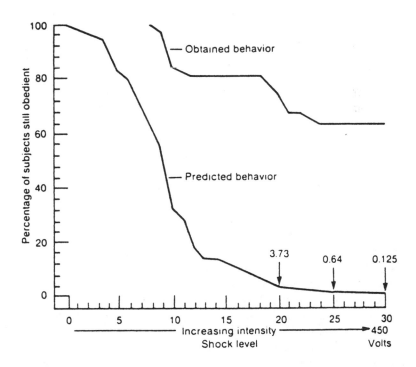

FIGURE 3. Predicted and obtained behavior in voice feedback.

Many people, not knowing much about the experiment, claim that subjects who go to the end of the board are sadistic. Nothing could be more foolish than an overall characterization of these persons. It is like saying that a person thrown into a swift-flowing stream is necessarily a fast swimmer, or that he has great stamina because he moves so rapidly relative to the bank. The context of action must always be considered. The individual, upon entering the laboratory, becomes integrated into a situation that carries its own momentum. The subject's problem then is how to become disengaged from a situation which is moving in an altogether ugly direction.

The fact that disengagement is so difficult testifies to the potency of the forces that keep the subject at the control board. Are these forces to be conceptualized as individual motives and expressed in the language of personality dynamics, or are they to be seen as the effects of social structure and pressures arising from the situational field?

A full understanding of the subject's action will, I feel, require that both perspectives be adopted. The person brings to the laboratory enduring dispositions toward authority and aggression, and at the same time he becomes enmeshed in a social structure that is no less an objective fact of the case. From the standpoint of personality theory one may ask: What mechanisms of personality enable a person to transfer responsibility to authority? What are the motives underlying obedient and disobedient performance? Does orientation to authority lead to a short-circuiting of the shame-guilt system? What cognitive and emotional defenses are brought into play in the case of obedient and defiant subjects?

The present experiments are not, however, directed toward an exploration of the motives engaged when the subject obeys the experimenter's commands. Instead, they examine the situational variables responsible for the elicitation of obedience. Elsewhere, we have attempted to spell out some of the structural properties of the experimental situation that account for high obedience, and this analysis need not be repeated here (Milgram, 1963). The experimental variations themselves represent our attempt to probe that structure, by systematically changing it and noting the consequences for behavior. It is clear that some situations produce greater compliance with the experimenter's commands than others. However, this does not necessarily imply an increase or decrease in the strength of any single definable motive. Situations producing the greatest obedience could do so by triggering the most powerful, yet perhaps the most idiosyncratic, of motives in each subject confronted by the setting. Or they may simply recruit a greater number and variety of motives in their service. But whatever the motives involved—and it is far from certain that they can ever be known—action may be studied as a direct function of the situation in which it occurs. This has been the approach of the present study, where we sought to plot behavioral regularities against manipulated properties of the social field. Ultimately, social psychology would like to have a compelling

75

theory of situations which will, first, present a language in terms of which situations can be defined; proceed to a typology of situations; and then point to the manner in which definable properties of situations are transformed into psychological forces in the individual.[12]

Postscript

Almost a thousand adults were individually studied in the obedience research, and there were many specific conclusions regarding the variables that control obedience and disobedience to authority. Some of these have been discussed briefly in the preceding sections, and more detailed reports will be released subsequently.

There are now some other generalizations I should like to make, which do not derive in any strictly logical fashion from the experiments as carried out, but which, I feel, ought to be made. They are formulations of an intuitive sort that have been forced on me by observation of many subjects responding to the pressures of authority. The assertions represent a painful alteration in my own thinking; and since they were acquired only under the repeated impact of direct observation, I have no illusion that they will be generally accepted by persons who have not had the same experience.

With numbing regularity good people were seen to knuckle under the demands of authority and perform actions that were callous and severe. Men who are in everyday life responsible and decent were seduced by the trappings of authority, by the control of their perceptions, and by the uncritical acceptance of the experimenter's definition of the situation, into performing harsh acts.

What is the limit of such obedience? At many points we attempted to establish a boundary. Cries from the victim were inserted; not good enough. The victim claimed heart trouble; subjects still shocked him on command. The victim pleaded that he be let free, and his answers no longer registered on the signal box; subjects continued to shock him. At the outset we had not conceived that such drastic procedures would be needed to generate disobedience, and each step was added only as the ineffectiveness of the earlier techniques became clear. The final effort to establish a limit was the Touch-Proximity condition. But the very first subject in this condition subdued the victim on command, and proceeded to the highest shock level. A quarter of the subjects in this condition performed similarly.

The results, as seen and felt in the laboratory, are to this author disturbing. They raise the possibility that human nature or, more specifically, the kind of character produced in American democratic society cannot be

[80]

---

[12]My thanks to Professor Howard Leventhal of Yale for strengthening the writing in this paragraph.

counted on to insulate its citizens from brutality and inhumane treatment at the direction of malevolent authority. A substantial proportion of people do what they are told to do, irrespective of the content of the act and without limitations of conscience, so long as they perceive that the command comes from a legitimate authority. If in this study an anonymous experimenter could successfully command adults to subdue a fifty-year-old man and force on him painful electric shocks against his protests, one can only wonder what government, with its vastly greater authority and prestige, can command of its subjects. There is, of course, the extremely important question of whether malevolent political institutions could or would arise in American society. The present research contributes nothing to this issue.

In an article titled "The Danger of Obedience," Harold J. Laski wrote:

> . . . civilization means, above all, an unwillingness to inflict unnecessary pain. Within the ambit of that definition, those of us who heedlessly accept the commands of authority cannot yet claim to be civilized men.
>
> . . . Our business, if we desire to live a life, not utterly devoid of meaning and significance, is to accept nothing which contradicts our basic experience merely because it comes to us from tradition or convention or authority. It may well be that we shall be wrong; but our self-expression is thwarted at the root unless the certainties we are asked to accept coincide with the certainties we experience. That is why the condition of freedom in any state is always a widespread and consistent skepticism of the canons upon which power insists.

References

Buss, Arnold H. 1961. *The Psychology of Aggression*. New York and London: John Wiley.

Kierkegaard, S. 1843. *Fear and Trembling*. English edition, Princeton: Princeton University Press, 1941.

Laski, Harold J. 1929. "The dangers of obedience." *Harper's Monthly Magazine*, 15 June, 1–10.

Milgram, S. 1961. "Dynamics of obedience: experiments in social psychology." Mimeographed report, *National Science Foundation*, January 25.

—— 1963. "Behavioral study of obedience." *J. Abnorm. Soc. Psychol.* 67, 371–378.

—— 1964. "Issues in the study of obedience: a reply to Baumrind." *Amer. Psychol.* 1, 848–852.

Miller, N. E. 1944. "Experimental studies of conflict." In J. McV. Hunt (ed.), *Personality and the Behavior Disorders*. New York: Ronald Press.

Scott, J. P. 1958. *Aggression*. Chicago: University of Chicago Press.

QUESTIONS

1. What did Milgram want to determine by his experiment? What were his anticipated outcomes?
2. What conclusions did Milgram reach about the extent to which ordinary individuals would obey the orders of an authority figure? Under what conditions is this submission most probable? Under what conditions is defiance most likely?
3. Describe the general procedures of this experiment. Some people have questioned Milgram's methods. Do you think it is ethical to expose subjects without warning to experiments that might have a lasting effect on them? What such effects might this experiment have had?
4. One characteristic of this article is Milgram's willingness to consider several possible explanations of the same phenomenon. Study the interpretations in paragraphs 28 through 35. What do you make of the range of interpretation there and elsewhere in the article? How does Milgram achieve such a range?
5. A report such as Milgram's is not structured in the same way as a conventional essay. His research is really a collection of separate but related experiments, each one of which requires its own interpretation. Describe the groups into which these experiments fall. Which results seemed most surprising to you? Which were easiest to anticipate?
6. In Milgram's experiment, people who are responsible and decent in everyday life were seduced, he says, by trappings of authority. Most of us, however, like to believe that we would neither engage in brutality on our own nor obey directions of this kind. Has Milgram succeeded in getting you to question your own behavior? Would you go so far as to say that he forces you to question your own human nature?
7. In paragraph 46 Milgram comments, "Perhaps our culture does not provide adequate models for disobedience." What do you think of this hypothesis? Are there such models? Ought there to be? Have such models appeared since the experiment was conducted? Explain your stand on Milgram's statement.
8. If research in social psychology takes place in your school today, there is probably a panel of some sort that enforces guidelines on research with human subjects. Locate that board, if it exists, and find out whether this experiment could take place today. Report to your class on the rules that currently guide researchers. Do you think those rules are wise?
9. What, in your opinion, should be the guidelines for psychological research with human subjects? List the guidelines you think are appropriate, and compare your list with the lists of your classmates. Would your guidelines have allowed Milgram's experiment?
10. Think of a situation in which you were faced with the moral and ethical dilemma of whether or not to obey a figure of authority. How did

you behave? Did your behavior surprise you? Describe and explain that experience.

MAKING CONNECTIONS

1. One of the conditions of valid scientific research is the replicability of its experiments. When we are persuaded that results are replicable, we are inclined to believe them valid. What provisions for replicability does Milgram make in his experiments? Compare his stance to that of Oliver Sacks (p. 552), whose observations are not replicable but who is also concerned with writing authoritative science.

2. Think of other essays in this collection in which ethical matters are at issue, particularly the ethics of composing some kind of story. Consider Richard Selzer's "A Mask on the Face of Death" (p. 167) and Michael Brown's "Love Canal and the Poisoning of America" (p. 299). In each of those studies, human subjects seem manipulated a little for the sake of the writer's interests. Perhaps you would prefer to offer another example. Whatever study you choose, compare it to Milgram's, and discuss the two writers' sensitivity to their human subjects. Note also the last sentence of Milgram's first footnote. What choices do the writers have in the cases that interest you most?

INTERVIEWING ADOLESCENT GIRLS

Carol Gilligan

Carol Gilligan (b. 1936) is a professor in the human development and psychology program at the Harvard Graduate School of Education. Her research on women's identity formation and moral development in adolescence and adulthood was the subject of In a Different Voice: Psychological Theory and Women's Development *(1982), a book that brought her wide attention in the academic community and beyond. The following selection is from an essay called "Teaching Shakespeare's Sister: Notes from the Underground of Adolescence," a synthesis of the preface and prologue to* Making Connections: The Relational Worlds of Adolescent Girls at Emma Willard School *(1990), which Gilligan coauthored with Nona Lyons and Trudy Hanmer.*

Interviewing girls in adolescence, in the time between the twelve-year-old's knowing and the adult woman's remembering, I felt at times that I had entered an underground world, that I was led in by girls to caverns of knowledge that were then suddenly covered over, as if nothing were known and nothing were happening. What I heard was at once familiar and surprising: girls' knowledge of the human social world, a knowledge gleaned by seeing and listening, by piecing together thoughts and feelings, sounds and glances, responses and reactions, until they compose a pattern, compelling in its explanatory power and often intricate in its psychological logic. Such knowledge on the part of girls is not represented in descriptions of psychological development nor in clinical case studies, and, more disturbingly, it is disclaimed by adolescent girls themselves, who often seem divided from their own knowledge and preface their observations by saying "I don't know."

At a school for girls in a large midwestern city, twelve-year-olds, when asked to describe a powerful learning experience, were as likely to describe an experience that took place inside as outside of school. By fifteen more than twice as many girls located powerful learning experiences outside of school rather than inside. With respect to the nature of such experiences, girls at fifteen were more likely than girls at twelve to talk about experiences outside of school in which family or friends or other people they knew were the central catalysts of learning.[1] Between the ages of twelve

---

[1] Alan Braun, "Themes of Connection: Powerful Learning among Adolescent Girls" (Working Paper, Laurel/Harvard Study, Project on the Psychology of Women and the Development of Girls, Harvard Graduate School of Education), 3.

and fifteen—the time when dropping out of school becomes common in the inner city—the education of girls seems to be moving out of the public sphere and into the private realm. Is this the time, I wondered, when girls' knowledge becomes buried? Was girls' learning going underground?

The question surfaced in reflecting on my experiences in interviewing adolescent girls at Emma Willard School in Troy, New York. The isolated setting of the residential school and its walled enclosure made it something of a strange island in the stream of contemporary living, an odd mixture of old world and new. In this resonant setting I heard girls speak about storms in relationships and pleasure in relationships, revealing a knowledge of relationships that often was grounded in detailed descriptions of inner psychic worlds—relational worlds through which girls sometimes moved freely and which at other times seemed blocked or walled. Listening for this knowledge, I felt myself entering, to some extent, the underground city of female adolescence, the place where powerful learning experiences were happening. The gateway to this underworld was marked by the statement "I don't know"—the sign of repression—and the code word of membership or the password was the phrase "you know." I wondered about the relationship between this knowledge and girls' other life of notebooks, lessons, and homework.

One afternoon, in the second year of the study, toward the end of an interview with Gail, a girl with whom I had not made much contact, I asked if she were curious about the "it" that she was describing—"the problem" that stood between her and her being "able to achieve anywhere near [her] potential," the thing that kept her from "getting [her] act together." Gail said that she did not know whether she would "ever understand what the problem was," but, she said, "I hope that someday it will be gone and I will be happy." I asked how it will go away. She said she did not know, but that it would be "sad if it doesn't." I asked if she were curious; she said she did not know. We went on with the interview questions. As she thought about herself in the future, I asked, how did she imagine her life, what expectations did she feel others had for her, what were her hopes for herself? She was waiting, she said, to see if "it happens." She felt she had come up against "this big wall." We went on. At the end Gail said, "Maybe someday I will draw it." It seemed that she knew what it looked like. I asked what color she would make it: "Kind of deep ivory," she said. What shape? "A giant block of ice. This tall . . . very thick. A cube standing in front of me." She said that she could melt it, but that she would "have to use very high temperatures."

The following year Gail, now a senior, began by talking to me in the language of social science. "I would like to mention," she said, "that, having thought about my last two interviews, it occurs to me that it is hard to get the real opinions of teenage girls as young as we are because a lot of girls really don't know what they think." If I had interviewed her on another day, or if I were a different person, I would "get very different things," especially because "a lot of the questions you asked are not ques- 5 tions that I have ever put to myself . . . and afterwards I wondered, you know, did I really mean that. . . . I don't feel you are getting what is important to me; you are getting that and other things in equal weight." I asked, "So there is no way of knowing [what's true and what's important]?" She agreed.

I began with the interview questions. "Looking back over the past year. . . ." I suggested that as we went along she might tell me which questions were ones that she had put to herself and which—Gail suddenly switched modes of discourse. She said, "I actually feel a great deal older this year." One way of speaking about herself ("Teenage girls . . . really don't know what they think") yielded to another ("I actually feel . . ."). The relationship between these two ways of speaking about herself seemed critical. In the terms of her own imagery, one way of speaking shored up the wall between herself and her knowledge, and one provided a sense of an opening, a place of entry, which led through knowing how she was feeling. "I really feel able," Gail explained, taking the opening,

> to put myself in perspective about a lot of things that were confusing me about myself, and I have a tendency to keep things to myself, things that bother me. I keep them in and then I start feeling like this, just harassed and I can't really—everything just warps my perception of everything. . . . But I have discovered the reason for my whole block. I mean, I was getting bad grades, and I told you about a mysterious block last year that was like a wall.
> *I remember that.*
> Now, I figured out what was going on. I figured this out last week. It is that, all through my childhood, I interpreted what my parents were saying to me in my mind. I never voiced this interpretation.

The unvoiced or unspoken, being out of relationship, had gotten out of perspective—"just warp[ing] my perception of everything." What Gail interpreted her parents as saying to her was that she should "be independent and self-sufficient from a very early age." Thus, Gail said, "anything that interrupted my sense of what I should be I would soak up into myself, as though I were a big sponge and had tremendous shock capacity to just bounce back." What Gail was taking in was clearly something that she found shocking, but she felt that she should act as though she were a sponge and just soak up the shock by herself. So, she said, "I would feel bad about things, [but] I wouldn't do anything about them. I wouldn't say anything. That goes with grades and personal problems and relationships"—much of her adolescent life. And then, she said, "last week, last Wednesday, this whole thing came over me, and I can really feel that now I can understand what was going on with me. I can put my life in perspective." Thus, Gail explained that she no longer had to not know: "What's happening, what's happening with me? What is going on? Why am I not being able to see? Why is this so hard for me? And then of course when I finally let it out, maybe every six months, it is like a chair casting shadows and making tremendous spokes. Everything becomes monumental. I feel terrible, and it is really very disturbing." With this powerful image of "it" as "a chair casting shadows and making tremendous spokes," Gail conveys how the ordinary can become monumental and very disturbing. What is explicit in this passage is that Gail became disconnected from her own thoughts and feelings and found herself asking questions about herself that she then could not answer. In threatening this disconnection, the process of knowing had become overwhelming. I asked Gail if she had a sense of what had led her to the understanding she described, and she spoke about a conversation with a friend:

> It started when my friend was telling me how angry she was at her math teacher, who when she asked for extra help must have been in a bad mood and was angry with her. I was thinking about the way my stepfather would do the same thing. And then I was thinking about my stepfather, and then I decided that I really have been abused as a child, not physically, but even last summer, whenever he has insecurity, he is very jealous of me, he is insecure with my mother, and then he just lashes out at me and criticizes me to no end, very angrily. And for a person who has grown up with that and who really doesn't understand herself—instead of saying, "Wait a minute. What are you doing? I am a person."—I would just cuddle up and make like a rock. Tense all my muscles and just sit there and listen to it and be relieved when it was over. And then I was thinking about myself and my reactions to things, and I was thinking all year about all the problems I had last year. . . . It is all my holding back. And I really feel I have made a tremendous breakthrough.

Joining her friend in voicing anger in response to anger rather than just soaking it up like a sponge or tensing her muscles and becoming like a rock, Gail felt she had broken through the wall that was holding back her "reactions to things," her feelings and thoughts.

"It was amazing," I said, "to see it that way," responding to Gail's precise description of psychological processes—the step-by-step tracing of her own feelings and thoughts in response to her friend's story about anger and the math teacher as well as her analysis of how insecurity and jealousy breed attack. "My mother," Gail said, turning to the missing person in the drama (and signaling by the phrase "you know" that this was in part an underground story):

> came down the day before yesterday, and I told her about it. She has been worried about me day and night since I was little because of my holding back. She would say, "You are holding your light

under a bushel," and then, you know, get very upset once or twice a year, because everything would get [to be] too much, you know. Of course, my mother would have tremendous guilt. . . . "What have I done to this poor child? I don't really know what I have done, but there is something. What is it?"

"You have read *Oedipus Rex?*"[2] Gail asks me. I had. "Well, Oedipus went through his entire life weighing himself by himself, and I have done that, and that is what allows me to get out of proportion. I don't talk about anything with anybody, anything that is bothering me."

I thought of the queen in the Oedipus story. Gail's description of her   10
mother had caught the franticness of Jocasta as she tries to keep Oedipus from knowing the truth about family relations. No more truth, she pleads. Was Gail hearing a similar plea from her mother? The problem was that "it"—the unnamed or unspoken truth—"just rolls up like a snowball, and it gets bigger and bigger, and my perception just warps out of shape" so that, like Oedipus, Gail cannot see what in another sense she knows. Her question to herself—"Why am I not able to see?"—resonates with the question she attributes to her mother: "What have I done to this poor child?" But Gail also lays out the logic that suppressed her questions about suffering and about women. Gail reasoned that, if her stepfather's attacks had truly been hurtful to her, then her mother would have taken action to stop them. Because her mother did nothing, at least as far as Gail was aware of, Gail concluded that her stepfather's verbal lashings could not really have hurt her. To feel her feelings then posed difficult questions: what does it mean to be a good mother, what does it mean for a mother to love her daughter, and what does it mean for a daughter to love both her mother and herself?

The either/or logic that Gail was learning as an adolescent, the straight-line categories of Western thinking (self/other, mind/body, thought/feelings, past/present) and the if/then construction of linear reasoning threatened to undermine Gail's knowledge of human relationships by washing out the logic of feelings. To understand psychological processes means to follow the both/and logic of feelings and to trace the currents of associations, memories, sounds, and images that flow back and forth, connecting self and other, mind and body, past and present, consciousness and culture. To separate thinking from relationship, and thus to make a division between formal education and powerful learning experiences, is to become like Oedipus, who got things out of proportion by "weighing himself by himself." Gail ties the return of perspective to the return of relationship and describes the insight and knowledge that suddenly came out of the back-and-forth play of her conversation with her friend: "I talked to my

---

[2]*Oedipus Rex:* The play by Sophocles (496–406 B.C.) in which Oedipus unknowingly murders his father and marries his mother, Jocasta. [Eds.]

friend, and she talked about her math teacher, and I was thinking about my stepfather, and then, with all my thinking about it beforehand, wondering what makes a difference, I finally put it together and bang! . . . Before, when I was getting all tied up, everything was a huge wall that isn't a wall anymore." The "it" is no longer a wall but a relationship that joins Gail with herself and with her friend.

The image of a wall recurred in interviews with adolescent girls—a physical rendering of the blocks preventing connection, the impasses in relationships, which girls acutely described and which were associated with intense feelings of anger and sadness. Girls' wishes to make connection with others reflected the pleasure that they found in relationships.

Pleasure in relationships is linked to knowledge gained through relationships, and girls voice their desire to know more about others and also to be known better themselves. "I wish to become better in the relationship with my mother," Ellen says—"to be able more easily to disagree with her." Disagreement here is a sign of relationship, a manifestation of two people coming together. And it is in close relationships that girls are most willing to argue or disagree, wanting most to be known and seen by those to whom they feel closest and also believing more that those who are close will be there, will listen, and will try to understand. "If you love someone," Anna explains, "you are usually comfortable with them. And, feeling comfortable, you can easily argue with one another and say, look, I want you to see my side. It's a lot easier to fight with someone you love, because you know they will always forgive you, at least usually they will . . . and you know that they are still going to be there for you after the disagreement."

Perhaps it is because of this feeling of being comfortable that girls most often speak about conflict in their relationships with their mothers—the person who, one girl said, "will always welcome me." Girls' willingness to fight for genuine connection with their mothers is well illustrated by Kate, a fifteen-year-old who says, paradoxically:

> I called my mother up and said, "Why can't I speak to you anymore? What is going on?" And I ended up crying and hanging up on her because she wouldn't listen to me. She had her own opinion about what was truth and what was reality, and she gave me no opening. . . . What she had on her mind was the truth. And you know, I kept saying, "Well, you hurt me," and she said, "No, I did not." And I said, "Well, why am I hurt?" you know, and she is just denying my feelings as if they did not exist and as if I had no right to feel them, you know, even though they were.

The counterpart to the image of a wall is the search for an opening, a way of reaching another person, of finding a place of entry. Yet to open oneself to another person creates a great vulnerability, and thus the strength of girls' desire for relationship also engenders the need for protection from fraudulent relationships and psychic wounding. "To me," Jane

15

says, "love means an attachment to a person," by which she means a willingness or wish

> to share a lot of things with that person and not feel as though you are opening up your soul and it is going to be misrepresented or misunderstood. Rather, so that person . . . will know kind of inside how far to go and, if they go too far, they will understand when you say, that's not what I want . . . where people accept your idiosyncrasies . . . that you can have fun and you can disagree but that the argument isn't something that wounds you for months. . . . Some people are too quick to say "I love you." It takes time to learn someone. I don't think you can love on first sight. . . . You can feel a connection with someone, but you can't just love them.

These carefully drawn distinctions, the contrast between feeling connected with someone and loving them and between having fun and disagreeing and having an argument that wounds you for months, bespeak close observation of relationships and psychological processes and also experiences of being misrepresented, misunderstood, and not listened to, which have left both knowledge and scars. Jane says she is looking for someone who will understand when she says, "that's not what I want." Mira, in contrast, has chosen silence as a way of avoiding being hurt:

> I personally have had a hard time asking questions . . . because I was shy and did not really like to talk to people about what I was really thinking.
>   *Why not?*
>   I thought it was much safer just to keep it to myself, and this way nobody would have so much of a vulnerable spot that they could get to me with. And so I thought, just the thought of having somebody having something on me that could possibly hurt me, that scared me and kept me from speaking up a lot of the time.

Like the character in Woolf's story, "An Unwritten Novel," Mira keeps her life to herself; her speaking self also is "entombed . . . driven in, in, in to the central catacomb. . . . Flit[ting] with its lanterns restlessly up and down the dark corridor."[3] Mary Belenky and her colleagues have described how women retreat into silence when words become weapons and are used to wound.[4] Adolescent girls invoke images of violence and talk in the language of warfare or about winning and losing when they describe

---

[3]Virginia Woolf, "An Unwritten Novel," *Haunted House and Other Short Stories* (1921; reprint, New York: Harcourt Brace Jovanovich, 1972), 19.

[4]Mary Belenky, Blythe Clinchy, Nancy Goldberger and Jill Tarule, *Women's Ways of Knowing* (New York: Basic Books, 1986).

the inner workings of explosive relationships, fearing also that such relationships can "throw us apart forever."

> *What is the worst thing that can happen in a relationship?*
> I guess if people build up resentments and don't talk about them, things can just keep building up until they reach the boiling point, and then there is like a cold war going on. People are just fencing on either side of a wall, but not admitting it to the other person until there is an explosion or something.

Other girls, like Emma, describe "building a wall" that serves to undermine relationships:

> *What is the worst thing that can happen in a relationship?*
> Not talking it out. Building a wall . . . I think that can lead to a lot more because you don't give a chance to the other person to say anything. . . . You are too close-minded to listen to what they have to say. . . . If you don't listen to your friends, they are not your friends, there is no relationship there, because you don't listen.

Taken together, these observations of the ways in which people move and affect, touch and are touched by one another, appear and disappear in relationships with themselves and with others, reveal an understanding of psychic processes that is closer to a physics than a metaphysics of relationship—based on tracking voices and images, thoughts and feelings, across the cloud chamber of daily life. Certain observations are breathtakingly simple in their logic although profound in their implications, especially given the pace of contemporary living. Emma says that, "if you don't listen to your friends, they are not your friends. There is no relationship there." Others are more complex, like Joan's exegesis of the indirect discourse of betrayal: "If you don't trust someone to know a secret . . . you sort of grow apart . . . or you will feel like you are with them and down underneath you are angry . . . but you don't say anything, so it comes out . . . in other ways." Or Maria's explication of the confusing mixing of anger and hurt:

> I am not sure of the difference when I feel angry and hurt. . . . I don't even know if they are separate emotions. . . . I was angry, I think at myself in that relationship, that I had let myself be used . . . that I had let down my guard so much. I was completely vulnerable. And I chose to do that. . . . I kept saying, "I hate him," but I realized that he didn't even notice me there because he was in his own world. So that I think . . . all my anger comes out of being hurt, and it's a confusion there.

Repeatedly, girls emphasize the need for open conflict and voicing disagreement. Catherine describes the fruitful quality of disagreement in her relationship with her friend:

We have learned more about ourselves...I think...she had never really had a close friend but lots of acquaintances. She didn't get into fights and things like that....I think she realizes that you have to have disagreements and things like that for a relationship to last.

How come?

Because if you don't really voice your disagreements, then you don't really have anything going, do you know what I mean? It's just another way, it is another side of you that you are letting someone else see.

And Liza describes the raw pain of finding, at the end of a long journey, that you are not able to talk with someone on whom you had depended:

What is the worst thing that can happen in a relationship?

That you grow up, or sideways, and not be able to talk to each other, especially if you depend on being able to talk to someone and not being able to. That hurts a lot, because you have been dependent on that. It is like walking fifty miles for a glass of water in a hot desert, and you have been depending on it for days, and getting there and finding it is not there anymore; you made the wrong turn ten miles back.

The knowledge about relationships and the life of relationships that flourish on this remote island of female adolescence are, to shift the metaphor, like notes from the underground. Much of what psychologists know about relationships is also known by adolescent girls. But, as girls themselves say clearly, they will speak only when they feel that someone will listen and will not leave in the face of conflict or disagreement. Thus, the fate of girls' knowledge and girls' education becomes tied to the fate of their relationships.

When women's studies is joined with the study of girls' development, it becomes clearer why adolescence is a critical time in girls' lives—a time when girls are in danger of losing their voices and thus losing connection with others, and also a time when girls, gaining voice and knowledge, are in danger of knowing the unseen and speaking the unspoken and thus losing connection with what is commonly taken to be "reality." This crisis of connection in girls' lives at adolescence links the psychology of women with the most basic questions about the nature of relationships and the definition of reality. Girls' questions about relationships and about reality, however, also tug at women's silences.

At the edge of adolescence, eleven- and twelve-year-old girls observe where and when women speak and when they are silent.[5] As resisters, they

_____

[5]Lyn Mikel Brown, "A Problem of Vision: The Development of Voice and Relational Knowledge in Girls Ages Seven to Sixteen," *Women's Studies Quarterly* 1991:1 & 2.

may be especially prone to notice and question the compliance of women to male authority. One of Woolf's questions in *A Room of One's Own* is why mothers do not provide more rooms for their daughters, why they do not leave more of a legacy for their daughters, and why, more specifically, mothers do not endow their daughters' education with greater comfort.[6] A teacher of twelve-year-olds, after a faculty meeting where women's reluctance to disagree in public became a subject of discussion, told the following story: her eleven-year-old daughter had commented on her reluctance to disagree with her husband (the girl's father). She was angry at her mother, she said, for always giving in. In response, the mother began to explain that, although the girl's father sometimes raised his voice, he was loving and well-intentioned—at which point her daughter interrupted her, saying that it was she, her mother, who she was angry at for always giving in. "I was so humiliated," the teacher said, "so ashamed." Later that year, when her colleague announced a new rule about lunch in homeroom one day, she suppressed her disagreement with him and did not voice her objections—because, she said, she did not want to undermine his authority. Perhaps it was as a result of her previous humiliation that she thought twice on a day when the rule seemed particularly senseless and excused some girls, in spite of the rule, before others who had arrived late at lunch had finished eating. "Good for you," the girls said, "we're proud of you." It was clear that they had noticed everything.

In his appreciation of the poetry of Sylvia Plath, Seamus Heaney reads a famous passage by William Wordsworth as a parable of the three stages in a poet's journey.[7] At first one goes out into the woods and whistles to hear if the owls will respond. Then, once one discovers that one can speak in a way that calls forth a response from the world of nature, one has to learn to perfect one's craft, to enter the world of sounds—of birdcalls, traditions, and poetic conventions—until, Heaney says, if one is blessed or fortunate, one becomes the instrument through which the sounds of the world pass. Heaney traces this transformation in Plath's poetry, drawing the reader into his own exhilaration as her language takes off. But Plath's relationship to the tradition of male voices, which she was entering and changing by entering, was not the same as Heaney's, and her entrance was more deeply disruptive. And the same can be said for women students.

A student first must learn how to call forth a response from the world: to ask a question to which people will listen, which they will find interesting and respond to. Then she must learn the craft of inquiry so that she can tune her questions and develop her ear for language and thus speak more clearly and more freely, can say more and also hear more fully. But if the world of nature, as Heaney implies, is equally responsive to the calls of

---

[6]Virginia Woolf, *A Room of One's Own* (1928; reprint, New York: Harcourt, Brace, and World, 1957), 20–24.

[7]Seamus Heaney, *The Government of the Tongue: Selected Prose, 1978–1987* (New York: Farrar, Straus and Giroux, 1989).

women and men, the world of civilization is not, or at least has not been up to the present. The wind of tradition blowing through women is a chill wind because it brings a message of exclusion: stay out. It brings a message of subordination: stay under. It brings a message of objectification: become the object of another's worship or desire; see yourself as you have been seen for centuries, through a male gaze. And because all of the suffering, the endless litany of storm and shipwreck, is presented as necessary or even good for civilization, the message to women is: keep quiet, notice the absence of women, and say nothing.

At the present moment the education of women presents genuine dilemmas and real opportunities. Women's questions — especially questions about relationships and questions about violence — often feel disruptive to women because at present they are disruptive both in private and public life. And relationships between women are often strained. It is not at all clear what it means to be a good mother or teacher to an adolescent girl coming of age in Western culture. The choices that women make in order to survive or to appear good in the eyes of others and thus sustain their protection are often at the expense of women's relationships with one another, and girls begin to observe and comment on these choices around the age of eleven or twelve. If women can stay in the gaze of girls so that girls do not have to look and not see, if women can be seen by girls, including the twelve-year-old in themselves, if women can sustain girls' gazes and respond to girls' voices, then, perhaps as Woolf envisioned, "the opportunity will come and the dead poet who is Shakespeare's sister will put on the body which she has so often laid down and find it possible to live and write her poetry"[8] — as Plath did for a moment before taking her life. Yet as Woolf reminds us, before Shakespeare's sister can come, we must have the habit of freedom and the courage to write and say exactly what we think.

QUESTIONS

1. Where did your most powerful learning experience occur? Poll your class. How do the answers break down according to sex (and age, if relevant)?
2. In your discussion of learning experiences, did men and women participate equally, or is there a pattern of domination in your classroom?
3. Gilligan is interested in the metaphors her subjects use to express their emotional states. Gail talks about her "block . . . like a wall" (paragraph 6). What other metaphors does she use? Are they unusual or common? How would you interpret them? What other metaphors are used by Gilligan's subjects?

---

[8]Woolf, *A Room of One's Own,* 117.

4. Gilligan says in her conclusion, "It is not at all clear what it means to be a good mother or teacher to an adolescent girl coming of age in Western culture." Discuss some of the reasons why this is so, or disagree with this statement and explain why.

5. Take the statement quoted in Question 4 and substitute *father* for *mother* and *boy* for *girl*. Then discuss why you agree or disagree with the statement.

6. On the subject of learning experiences, extend your interviews and observations to a wider group of students, or to a different age group. You may, for example, want to talk to a group of public high school or junior high school students, to see if their experiences are similar to those of the private school students Gilligan interviewed. Write up your findings.

MAKING CONNECTIONS

Gilligan ends by saying that adolescents—indeed, all women—"must have . . . the courage to write and say exactly what we think." Compare Lucy Grealy's description of her adolescence in "Mirrors" (p. 50) with those described by Gilligan's interviewees. How does Grealy's essay comment on Gilligan's statement?

On the Fear of Death

Elisabeth Kübler-Ross

Elisabeth Kübler-Ross (b. 1926), a Swiss-American psychiatrist, is one of the leaders of the movement that may help change the way Americans think about death. Born in Zurich, she received her M.D. from the University of Zurich in 1957 and came to the United States as an intern the following year. Kübler-Ross began her work with terminally ill patients while teaching psychiatry at the University of Chicago Medical School. She founded the hospice care movement in the United States and runs Shanti Nilaya (Sanskrit for "home of peace"), an organization "dedicated to the promotion of physical, emotional, and spiritual health." This selection is taken from her first and most famous book, On Death and Dying *(1969).*

> Let me not pray to be sheltered from
> dangers but to be fearless in facing them.
> Let me not beg for the stilling of my
> pain but for the heart to conquer it.
> Let me not look for allies in life's battle-
> field but to my own strength.
> Let me not crave in anxious fear to be
> saved but hope for the patience to win my
> freedom.
> Grant me that I may not be a coward,
> feeling your mercy in my success alone;
> but let me find the grasp of your hand in
> my failure.

Rabindranath Tagore, *Fruit-Gathering*

Epidemics have taken a great toll of lives in past generations. Death in infancy and early childhood was frequent and there were few families who didn't lose a member of the family at an early age. Medicine has changed greatly in the last decades. Widespread vaccinations have practically eradicated many illnesses, at least in western Europe and the United States. The use of chemotherapy, especially the antibiotics, has contributed to an ever-decreasing number of fatalities in infectious diseases. Better child care and education have effected a low morbidity and mortality among children.

437

The many diseases that have taken an impressive toll among the young and middle-aged have been conquered. The number of old people is on the rise, and with this fact come the number of people with malignancies and chronic diseases associated more with old age.

Pediatricians have less work with acute and life-threatening situations as they have an ever-increasing number of patients with psychosomatic disturbances and adjustment and behavior problems. Physicians have more people in their waiting rooms with emotional problems than they have ever had before, but they also have more elderly patients who not only try to live with their decreased physical abilities and limitations but who also face loneliness and isolation with all its pains and anguish. The majority of these people are not seen by a psychiatrist. Their needs have to be elicited and gratified by other professional people, for instance, chaplains and social workers. It is for them that I am trying to outline the changes that have taken place in the last few decades, changes that are ultimately responsible for the increased fear of death, the rising number of emotional problems, and the greater need for understanding of and coping with the problems of death and dying.

When we look back in time and study old cultures and people, we are impressed that death has always been distasteful to man and will probably always be. From a psychiatrist's point of view this is very understandable and can perhaps best be explained by our basic knowledge that, in our unconscious, death is never possible in regard to ourselves. It is inconceivable for our unconscious to imagine an actual ending of our own life here on earth, and if this life of ours has to end, the ending is always attributed to a malicious intervention from the outside by someone else. In simple terms, in our unconscious mind we can only be killed; it is inconceivable to die of a natural cause or of old age. Therefore death in itself is associated with a bad act, a frightening happening, something that in itself calls for retribution and punishment.

One is wise to remember these fundamental facts as they are essential in understanding some of the most important, otherwise unintelligible communications of our patients.

The second fact that we have to comprehend is that in our unconscious mind we cannot distinguish between a wish and a deed. We are all aware of some of our illogical dreams in which two completely opposite statements can exist side by side—very acceptable in our dreams but unthinkable and illogical in our wakening state. Just as our unconscious mind cannot differentiate between the wish to kill somebody in anger and the act of having done so, the young child is unable to make this distinction. The child who angrily wishes his mother to drop dead for not having gratified his needs will be traumatized greatly by the actual death of his mother— even if this event is not linked closely in time with his destructive wishes. He will always take part or the whole blame for the loss of his mother. He will always say to himself—rarely to others—"I did it, I am responsible, I was bad, therefore Mommy left me." It is well to remember that the child

5

will react in the same manner if he loses a parent by divorce, separation, or desertion. Death is often seen by a child as an impermanent thing and has therefore little distinction from a divorce in which he may have an opportunity to see a parent again.

Many a parent will remember remarks of their children such as, "I will bury my doggy now and next spring when the flowers come up again, he will get up." Maybe it was the same wish that motivated the ancient Egyptians to supply their dead with food and goods to keep them happy and the old American Indians to bury their relatives with their belongings.

When we grow older and begin to realize that our omnipotence is really not so omnipotent, that our strongest wishes are not powerful enough to make the impossible possible, the fear that we have contributed to the death of a loved one diminishes — and with it the guilt. The fear remains diminished, however, only so long as it is not challenged too strongly. Its vestiges can be seen daily in hospital corridors and in people associated with the bereaved.

A husband and wife may have been fighting for years, but when the partner dies, the survivor will pull his hair, whine and cry louder and beat his chest in regret, fear and anguish, and will hence fear his own death more than before, still believing in the law of talion — an eye for an eye, a tooth for a tooth — "I am responsible for her death, I will have to die a pitiful death in retribution."

Maybe this knowledge will help us understand many of the old customs and rituals which have lasted over the centuries and whose purpose is to diminish the anger of the gods or the people as the case may be, thus decreasing the anticipated punishment. I am thinking of the ashes, the torn clothes, the veil, the *Klage Weiber* of the old days[1] — they are all means to ask you to take pity on them, the mourners, and are expressions of sorrow, grief, and shame. If someone grieves, beats his chest, tears his hair, or refuses to eat, it is an attempt at self-punishment to avoid or reduce the anticipated punishment for the blame that he takes on the death of a loved one.

This grief, shame, and guilt are not very far removed from feelings of   10
anger and rage. The process of grief always includes some qualities of anger. Since none of us likes to admit anger at a deceased person, these emotions are often disguised or repressed and prolong the period of grief or show up in other ways. It is well to remember that it is not up to us to judge such feelings as bad or shameful but to understand their true meaning and origin as something very human. In order to illustrate this I will again use the example of the child — and the child in us. The five-year-old who loses his mother is both blaming himself for her disappearance and being angry at her for having deserted him and for no longer gratifying his needs. The dead person then turns into something the child loves and wants very much but also hates with equal intensity for this severe deprivation.

---

[1]*Klage Weiber:* wailing wives. [Eds.]

The ancient Hebrews regarded the body of a dead person as something unclean and not to be touched. The early American Indians talked about the evil spirits and shot arrows in the air to drive the spirits away. Many other cultures have rituals to take care of the "bad" dead person, and they all originate in this feeling of anger which still exists in all of us, though we dislike admitting it. The tradition of the tombstone may originate in the wish to keep the bad spirits deep down in the ground, and the pebbles that many mourners put on the grave are leftover symbols of the same wish. Though we call the firing of guns at military funerals a last salute, it is the same symbolic ritual as the Indian used when he shot his spears and arrows into the skies.

I give these examples to emphasize that man has not basically changed. Death is still a fearful, frightening happening, and the fear of death is a universal fear even if we think we have mastered it on many levels.

What has changed is our way of coping and dealing with death and dying and our dying patients.

Having been raised in a country in Europe where science is not so advanced, where modern techniques have just started to find their way into medicine, and where people still live as they did in this country half a century ago, I may have had an opportunity to study a part of the evolution of mankind in a shorter period.

I remember as a child the death of a farmer. He fell from a tree and   15
was not expected to live. He asked simply to die at home, a wish that was granted without question. He called his daughters into the bedroom and spoke with each one of them alone for a few moments. He arranged his affairs quietly, though he was in great pain, and distributed his belongings and his land, none of which was to be split until his wife should follow him in death. He also asked each of his children to share in the work, duties, and tasks that he had carried on until the time of the accident. He asked his friends to visit him once more, to bid goodbye to them. Although I was a small child at the time, he did not exclude me or my siblings. We were allowed to share in the preparations of the family just as we were permitted to grieve with them until he died. When he did die, he was left at home, in his own beloved home which he had built, and among his friends and neighbors who went to take a last look at him where he lay in the midst of flowers in the place he had lived in and loved so much. In that country today there is still no make-believe slumber room, no embalming, no false makeup to pretend sleep. Only the signs of very disfiguring illnesses are covered up with bandages and only infectious cases are removed from the home prior to the burial.

Why do I describe such "old-fashioned" customs? I think they are an indication of our acceptance of a fatal outcome, and they help the dying patient as well as his family to accept the loss of a loved one. If a patient is allowed to terminate his life in the familiar and beloved environment, it requires less adjustment for him. His own family knows him well enough to replace a sedative with a glass of his favorite wine; or the smell of a home-cooked soup may give him the appetite to sip a few spoons of fluid which, I think, is still more enjoyable than an infusion. I will not minimize the need for sedatives and infusions and realize full well from my own experience as a country doctor that they are sometimes life-saving and often unavoidable. But I also know that patience and familiar people and foods could replace many a bottle of intravenous fluids given for the simple reason that it fulfills the physiological need without involving too many people and/or individual nursing care.

The fact that children are allowed to stay at home where a fatality has struck and are included in the talk, discussions, and fears gives them the feeling that they are not alone in their grief and gives them the comfort of shared responsibility and shared mourning. It prepares them gradually and helps them view death as part of life, an experience which may help them grow and mature.

This is in great contrast to a society in which death is viewed as taboo, discussion of it is regarded as morbid, and children are excluded with the presumption and pretext that it would be "too much" for them. They are then sent off to relatives, often accompanied by some unconvincing lies of "Mother has gone on a long trip" or other unbelievable stories. The child senses that something is wrong, and his distrust in adults will only multiply if other relatives add new variations of the story, avoid his questions or suspicions, shower him with gifts as a meager substitute for a loss he is not permitted to deal with. Sooner or later the child will become aware of the changed family situation and, depending on the age and personality of the child, will have an unresolved grief and regard this incident as a frightening, mysterious, in any case very traumatic experience with untrustworthy grownups, which he has no way to cope with.

It is equally unwise to tell a little child who lost her brother that God loved little boys so much that he took little Johnny to heaven. When this little girl grew up to be a woman she never solved her anger at God, which resulted in a psychotic depression when she lost her own little son three decades later.

We would think that our great emancipation, our knowledge of science and of man, has given us better ways and means to prepare ourselves and our families for this inevitable happening. Instead the days are gone when a man was allowed to die in peace and dignity in his own home.

The more we are making advancements in science, the more we seem to fear and deny the reality of death. How is this possible?

We use euphemisms, we make the dead look as if they were asleep, we ship the children off to protect them from the anxiety and turmoil around the house if the patient is fortunate enough to die at home, we don't allow children to visit their dying parents in the hospitals, we have long and controversial discussions about whether patients should be told the truth—a question that rarely arises when the dying person is tended by the family physician who has known him from delivery to death and who knows the weaknesses and strengths of each member of the family.

I think there are many reasons for this flight away from facing death calmly. One of the most important facts is that dying nowadays is more gruesome in many ways, namely, more lonely, mechanical, and dehumanized; at times it is even difficult to determine technically when the time of death has occurred.

Dying becomes lonely and impersonal because the patient is often taken out of his familiar environment and rushed to an emergency room. Whoever has been very sick and has required rest and comfort especially may recall his experience of being put on a stretcher and enduring the noise of the ambulance siren and hectic rush until the hospital gates open. Only those who have lived through this may appreciate the discomfort and cold necessity of such transportation which is only the beginning of a long ordeal—hard to endure when you are well, difficult to express in words when noise, light, pumps, and voices are all too much to put up with. It may well be that we might consider more the patient under the sheets and blankets and perhaps stop our well-meant efficiency and rush in order to hold the patient's hand, to smile, or to listen to a question. I include the trip to the hospital as the first episode in dying, as it is for many. I am putting it exaggeratedly in contrast to the sick man who is left at home—not to say that lives should not be saved if they can be saved by a hospitalization but to keep the focus on the patient's experience, his needs and his reactions.

When a patient is severely ill, he is often treated like a person with no   25
right to an opinion. It is often someone else who makes the decision if and when and where a patient should be hospitalized. It would take so little to remember that the sick person too has feelings, has wishes and opinions, and has—most important of all—the right to be heard.

Well, our presumed patient has now reached the emergency room. He will be surrounded by busy nurses, orderlies, interns, residents, a lab technician perhaps who will take some blood, an electrocardiogram technician who takes the cardiogram. He may be moved to X-ray and he will overhear opinions of his condition and discussions and questions to members of the family. He slowly but surely is beginning to be treated like a thing. He is no longer a person. Decisions are made often without his opinion. If he tries to rebel he will be sedated, and after hours of waiting and wondering whether he has the strength, he will be wheeled into the operating room or intensive treatment unit and become an object of great concern and great financial investment.

He may cry for rest, peace, and dignity, but he will get infusions, transfusions, a heart machine, or tracheotomy if necessary. He may want one single person to stop for one single minute so that he can ask one single question—but he will get a dozen people around the clock, all busily preoccupied with his heart rate, pulse, electrocardiogram or pulmonary functions, his secretions or excretions but not with him as a human being. He may wish to fight it all but it is going to be a useless fight since all this is done in the fight for his life, and if they can save his life they can consider the person afterwards. Those who consider the person first may lose precious time to save his life! At least this seems to be the rationale or justification behind all this — or is it? Is the reason for this increasingly mechanical, depersonalized approach our own defensiveness? Is this approach our own way to cope with and repress the anxieties that a terminally or critically ill patient evokes in us? Is our concentration on equipment, on blood pressure, our desperate attempt to deny the impending death which is so frightening and discomforting to us that we displace all our knowledge onto machines, since they are less close to us than the suffering face of another human being which would remind us once more of our lack of omnipotence, our own limits and failures, and last but not least perhaps our own mortality?

Maybe the question has to be raised: Are we becoming less human or more human? . . . It is clear that whatever the answer may be, the patient is suffering more — not physically, perhaps, but emotionally. And his needs have not changed over the centuries, only our ability to gratify them.

QUESTIONS

1. Why does Kübler-Ross describe the death of a farmer? What point is she making in explaining "such 'old-fashioned' customs" (paragraph 16)?
2. To what extent is this essay explanatory? Summarize a particular explanation of hers that you find intriguing. Is it persuasive?
3. At what point in this essay does Kübler-Ross turn from explanation to argument? Do you think she has taken a stand on her subject? How sympathetic are you to her position?
4. In paragraphs 2 and 10, Kübler-Ross indicates a specialized audience for her writing. Who is that audience, and how do you relate to it?
5. Think of the audience you described in question 4 as a primary audience and of yourself as a member of a secondary audience. To what extent do the two audiences overlap? How thoroughly can you divide one from the other?
6. What experience of death have you had so far? Write of a death that you know something about, even if your relation to it is distant, perhaps only through the media. Can you locate elements of fear and anger in your own behavior or in the behavior of other people involved? Does Kübler-Ross's interpretation of those reactions help you come to terms with the experience?
7. What kind of balance do you think is best between prolonging life and allowing a person to die with dignity? What does the phrase "dying with dignity" mean?
8. If you were told you had a limited time to live, how would that news change the way you are living? Or would it? Offer an explanation for your position.

MAKING CONNECTIONS

Kübler-Ross suggests that we have significant lessons to learn from the dying and warns that we avoid thinking about death only at our own peril. Read Philip Larkin's poem "The Building" (p. 445) and imagine a conversation between Kübler-Ross and Larkin.

THE BUILDING

Philip Larkin

Born in Coventry, England, Philip Larkin (1922–1985) was educated at Oxford University. He worked as a librarian at a number of British universities, and for the last thirty years of his life at the provincial University of Hull. Highly admired by both general readers and critics of poetry, Larkin achieved an output of only a hundred or so pages in four slim volumes: The North Ship *(1946),* The Less Deceived *(1955),* The Whitsun Weddings *(1974), and* High Windows *(1974). He published nothing after 1974, although his* Collected Poems *appeared posthumously in 1988. Despite his popularity, Larkin was a shy man who studiously avoided the limelight. The appeal of his poems lies in both their deep exploration of everyday subject matter and their formal complexity. One critic called them "technically brilliant and resonantly beautiful, profoundly disturbing yet appealing and approachable."*

Higher than the handsomest hotel
The lucent comb shows up for miles, but see,
All round it close-ribbed streets rise and fall
Like a great sigh out of the last century.
The porters are scruffy; what keep drawing up   5
At the entrance are not taxis; and in the hall
As well as creepers hangs a frightening smell.

There are paperbacks, and tea at so much a cup,
Like an airport lounge but those who tamely sit
On rows of steel chairs turning the ripped mags   10
Haven't come far. More like a local bus,
These outdoor clothes and half-filled shopping bags
And faces restless and resigned, although
Every few minutes comes a kind of nurse

To fetch someone away: the rest refit   15
Cups back to saucers, cough, or glance below
Seats for dropped gloves or cards. Humans, caught
on ground curiously neutral, homes and names
Suddenly in abeyance; some are young,
Some old, but most at that vague age that claims   20
The end of choice, the last of hope; and all

Here to confess that something has gone wrong.
It must be error of a serious sort,
For see how many floors it needs, how tall
It's grown by now, and how much money goes   25
In trying to correct it. See the time,
Half-past eleven on a working day,
And these picked out of it; see, as they climb

To their appointed levels, how their eyes
Go to each other, guessing; on the way   30
Someone's wheeled past, in washed-to-rags ward clothes:
They see him, too. They're quiet. To realise
This new thing held in common makes them quiet,
For past these doors are rooms, and rooms past those,
And more rooms yet, each one further off   35

And harder to return from; and who knows
Which he will see, and when? For the moment, wait,
Look down at the yard. Outside seems old enough:
Red brick, lagged pipes, and someone walking by it
Out to the car park, free. Then, past the gate.   40
Traffic; a locked church; short terraced streets
Where kids chalk games, and girls with hair-dos fetch

Their separates from the cleaners—O world,
Your loves, your chances, are beyond the stretch
Of any hand from here! And so, unreal,   45
A touching dream to which we all are lulled
But wake from separately. In it, conceits
And self-protecting ignorance congeal
To carry life, collapsing only when

Called to these corridors (for now once more   50
The nurse beckons—). Each gets up and goes
At last. Some will be out by lunch, or four;
Others, not knowing it, have come to join
The unseen congregations whose white rows
Lie set apart above—women, men;   55
Old, young; crude facets of the only coin

This place accepts. All know they are going to die.
Not yet, perhaps, but in the end,
And somewhere like this. That is what it means,
This clean-sliced cliff; a struggle to transcend   60
The thought of dying, for unless its powers

Outbuild cathedrals nothing contravenes
The coming dark, though crowds each evening try

With wasteful, weak, propitiatory flowers.

QUESTIONS

1. Reread the poem, and then read it once again aloud. Use a good dictionary to look up any unfamiliar words.
2. The poem has a very unusual rhyme scheme, with the rhymes so curiously distributed as to be almost unnoticeable at first. Make a list of which words rhyme with each other. What suppositions about this pattern can you make?
3. What "building" is this? Why is it not named?
4. In providing a description of this building, Larkin compares it to other kinds of buildings—name them, and discuss whether you find these comparisons compelling.
5. As the poem progresses, it becomes clear that Larkin finds the most appropriate comparison of all to be that of a church. How many references to religion can you find, and in which stanzas? What seems to be the function of both "buildings"?
6. Choose the phrase you find most striking in the poem or the one that most confuses you. Write a response in which you explore why this particular phrase affects you as it does.

MAKING CONNECTIONS

"[S]omething has gone wrong," Larkin writes. "It must be error of a serious sort." This "clean-sliced cliff" of a building, summoning "wasteful, weak, propitiatory flowers," seems a sign of trouble larger than itself. Read the selections before and after this one, "On the Fear of Death" by Elisabeth Kübler-Ross and "The Science of Shopping" by Malcolm Gladwell, and speculate on our cultural need for the building Larkin describes.

THE SCIENCE OF SHOPPING

Malcolm Gladwell

A graduate of the University of Toronto, Malcolm Gladwell (b. 1963) is currently a staff writer at The New Yorker. *An astute observer of the contemporary scene, he has also contributed articles to such publications as* Vogue *and* New York *magazine, and he was formerly a science reporter for the* Washington Post. *In his book* The Tipping Point *(2000), he argues that new behaviors, ideas, and consumer products move through societies in much the same way that viruses do, eventually achieving a "critical mass." In the following essay, which originally appeared in* The New Yorker *in 1996, Gladwell investigates a researcher into a new field of knowledge—the science of shopping—and puts his theories to the test.*

Human beings walk the way they drive, which is to say that Americans tend to keep to the right when they stroll down shopping-mall concourses or city sidewalks. This is why in a well-designed airport travelers drifting toward their gate will always find the fast-food restaurants on their left and the gift shops on their right: people will readily cross a lane of pedestrian traffic to satisfy their hunger but rarely to make an impulse buy of a T-shirt or a magazine. This is also why Paco Underhill tells his retail clients to make sure that their window displays are canted, preferably to both sides but especially to the left, so that a potential shopper approaching the store on the inside of the sidewalk—the shopper, that is, with the least impeded view of the store window—can see the display from at least twenty-five feet away.

Of course, a lot depends on how fast the potential shopper is walking. Paco, in his previous life, as an urban geographer in Manhattan, spent a great deal of time thinking about walking speeds as he listened in on the great debates of the nineteen-seventies over whether the traffic lights in midtown should be timed to facilitate the movement of cars or to facilitate the movement of pedestrians and so break up the big platoons that move down Manhattan sidewalks. He knows that the faster you walk the more your peripheral vision narrows, so you become unable to pick up visual cues as quickly as someone who is just ambling along. He knows, too, that people who walk fast take a surprising amount of time to slow down—just as it takes a good stretch of road to change gears with a stick-shift automobile. On the basis of his research, Paco estimates the human downshift period to be anywhere from twelve to twenty-five feet, so if you own a store, he says, you never want to be next door to a bank: potential shoppers speed up when they walk past a bank (since there's nothing to look at), and by the time they slow down they've walked right past your business. The downshift factor also means that when potential shoppers enter a store it's going to take them from five to fifteen paces to adjust to the light and refocus and gear down from walking speed to shopping speed — particularly if they've just had to navigate a treacherous parking lot or hurry to make the light at Fifty-seventh and Fifth.

Paco calls that area inside the door the Decompression Zone, and something he tells clients over and over again is never, *ever* put anything of value in that zone — not shopping baskets or tie racks or big promotional displays — because no one is going to see it. Paco believes that, as a rule of thumb, customer interaction with any product or promotional display in the Decompression Zone will increase at least thirty percent once it's moved to the back edge of the zone, and even more if it's placed to the right, because another of the fundamental rules of how human beings shop is that upon entering a store — whether it's Nordstrom or K mart, Tiffany or the Gap — the shopper invariably and reflexively turns to the right. Paco believes in the existence of the Invariant Right because he has actually verified it. He has put cameras in stores trained directly on the doorway, and if you go to his office, just above Union Square, where videocassettes and boxes of Super-eight film from all his work over the years are stacked in plastic Tupperware containers practically up to the ceiling, he can show you reel upon reel of grainy entryway video — customers striding in the door, down-shifting, refocusing, and then, again and again, making that little half turn.

Paco Underhill is a tall man in his mid-forties, partly bald, with a neatly trimmed beard and an engaging, almost goofy manner. He wears baggy khakis and shirts open at the collar, and generally looks like the academic he might have been if he hadn't been captivated, twenty years ago, by the ideas of the urban anthropologist William Whyte. It was Whyte who pioneered the use of time-lapse photography as a tool of urban planning, putting cameras in parks and the plazas in front of office buildings in midtown Manhattan, in order to determine what distinguished a public space that worked from one that didn't. As a Columbia undergraduate, in 1974, Paco heard a lecture on Whyte's work and, he recalls, left the room "walking on air." He immediately read everything Whyte had written. He emptied his bank account to buy cameras and film and make his own home movie, about a pedestrian mall in Poughkeepsie. He took his "little exercise" to Whyte's advocacy group, the Project for Public Spaces, and was offered a job. Soon, however, it dawned on Paco that Whyte's ideas could be taken a step further — that the same techniques he used to establish why a plaza worked or didn't work could also be used to determine why a store worked or didn't work. Thus was born the field of retail anthropology, and, not long afterward, Paco founded Envirosell, which in just over fifteen years has counseled some of the most familiar names in

American retailing, from Levi Strauss to Kinney, Starbucks, McDonald's, Blockbuster, Apple Computer, A.T.&T., and a number of upscale retailers that Paco would rather not name.

When Paco gets an assignment, he and his staff set up a series of video-cameras throughout the test store and then back the cameras up with Envirosell staffers—trackers, as they're known—armed with clipboards. Where the cameras go and how many trackers Paco deploys depends on exactly what the store wants to know about its shoppers. Typically, though, he might use six cameras and two or three trackers, and let the study run for two or three days, so that at the end he would have pages and pages of carefully annotated tracking sheets and anywhere from a hundred to five hundred hours of film. These days, given the expansion of his business, he might tape fifteen thousand hours in a year, and, given that he has been in operation since the late seventies, he now has well over a hundred thousand hours of tape in his library.

Even in the best of times, this would be a valuable archive. But today, with the retail business in crisis, it is a gold mine. The time per visit that the average American spends in a shopping mall was sixty-six minutes last year—down from seventy-two minutes in 1992—and is the lowest number ever recorded. The amount of selling space per American shopper is now more than double what it was in the mid-seventies, meaning that profit margins have never been narrower, and the costs of starting a retail business—and of failing—have never been higher. In the past few years, countless dazzling new retailing temples have been built along Fifth and Madison Avenues—Barneys, Calvin Klein, Armani, Valentino, Banana Republic, Prada, Chanel, Nike Town, and on and on—but it is an explosion of growth based on no more than a hunch, a hopeful multimillion-dollar gamble that the way to break through is to provide the shopper with spectacle and more spectacle. "The arrogance is gone," Millard Drexler, the president and C.E.O. of the Gap, told me. "Arrogance makes failure. Once you think you know the answer, it's almost always over." In such a competitive environment, retailers don't just want to know how shoppers behave in their stores. They *have* to know. And who better to ask than Paco Underhill, who in the past decade and a half has analyzed tens of thousands of hours of shopping videotape and, as a result, probably knows more about the strange habits and quirks of the species *Emptor americanus*[1] than anyone else alive?

Paco is considered the originator, for example, of what is known in the trade as the butt-brush theory—or, as Paco calls it, more delicately, *le facteur bousculade*[2]—which holds that the likelihood of a woman's being converted from a browser to a buyer is inversely proportional to the likelihood of her being brushed on her behind while she's examining merchan-

[1]*Emptor americanus:* American buyer. [Eds.]
[2]*le facteur bousculade:* the jostling or pushing factor. [Eds.]

dise. Touch—or brush or bump or jostle—a woman on the behind when she has stopped to look at an item, and she will bolt. Actually, calling this a theory is something of a misnomer, because Paco doesn't offer any explanation for why women react that way, aside from venturing that they are "more sensitive back there." It's really an observation, based on repeated and close analysis of his videotape library, that Paco has transformed into a retailing commandment: a women's product that requires extensive examination should never be placed in a narrow aisle.

Paco approaches the problem of the Invariant Right the same way. Some retail thinkers see this as a subject crying out for interpretation and speculation. The design guru Joseph Weishar, for example, argues, in his magisterial "Design for Effective Selling Space," that the Invariant Right is a function of the fact that we "absorb and digest information in the left part of the brain" and "assimilate and logically use this information in the right half," the result being that we scan the store from left to right and then fix on an object to the right "essentially at a 45 degree angle from the point that we enter." When I asked Paco about this interpretation, he shrugged, and said he thought the reason was simply that most people are right-handed. Uncovering the fundamentals of "why" is clearly not a pursuit that engages him much. He is not a theoretician but an empiricist, and for him the important thing is that in amassing his huge library of in-store time-lapse photography he has gained enough hard evidence to know how often and under what circumstances the Invariant Right is expressed and how to take advantage of it.

What Paco likes are facts. They come tumbling out when he talks, and, because he speaks with a slight hesitation—lingering over the first syllable in, for example, "re-tail" or "de-sign"—he draws you in, and you find yourself truly hanging on his words. "We have reached a historic point in American history," he told me in our very first conversation. "Men, for the first time, have begun to buy their own underwear." He then paused to let the comment sink in, so that I could absorb its implications, before he elaborated: "Which means that we have to *totally* rethink the way we sell that product." In the parlance of Hollywood scriptwriters, the best endings must be surprising and yet inevitable; and the best of Paco's pronouncements take the same shape. It would never have occurred to me to wonder about the increasingly critical role played by touching—or, as Paco calls it, petting—clothes in the course of making the decision to buy them. But then I went to the Gap and to Banana Republic and saw people touching and fondling and, one after another, buying shirts and sweaters laid out on big wooden tables, and what Paco told me—which was no doubt based on what he had seen on his videotapes—made perfect sense: that the reason the Gap and Banana Republic have tables is not merely that sweaters and shirts look better there, or that tables fit into the warm and relaxing residential feeling that the Gap and Banana Republic are trying to create in their stores, but that tables invite—indeed, symbolize—touching. "Where do we eat?" Paco asks. "We eat, we pick up food, on tables."

Paco produces for his clients a series of carefully detailed studies, total-   10
ing forty to a hundred and fifty pages, filled with product-by-product
breakdowns and bright-colored charts and graphs. In one recent case, he
was asked by a major clothing retailer to analyze the first of a new chain of
stores that the firm planned to open. One of the things the client wanted to
know was how successful the store was in drawing people into its depths,
since the chances that shoppers will buy something are directly related to
how long they spend shopping, and how long they spend shopping is directly related to how deep they get pulled into the store. For this reason, a
supermarket will often put dairy products on one side, meat at the back,
and fresh produce on the other side, so that the typical shopper can't just
do a drive-by but has to make an entire circuit of the store, and be tempted
by everything the supermarket has to offer. In the case of the new clothing
store, Paco found that ninety-one percent of all shoppers penetrated as
deep as what he called Zone 4, meaning more than three-quarters of the
way in, well past the accessories and shirt racks and belts in the front, and
little short of the far wall, with the changing rooms and the pants stacked
on shelves. Paco regarded this as an extraordinary figure, particularly for a
long, narrow store like this one, where it is not unusual for the rate of penetration past, say, Zone 3 to be under fifty percent. But that didn't mean the
store was perfect—far from it. For Paco, all kinds of questions remained.

Purchasers, for example, spent an average of eleven minutes and
twenty-seven seconds in the store, nonpurchasers two minutes and thirty-
six seconds. It wasn't that the nonpurchasers just cruised in and out: in
those two minutes and thirty-six seconds, they went deep into the store and
examined an average of 3.42 items. So why didn't they buy? What, exactly,
happened to cause some browsers to buy and other browsers to walk out
the door?

Then, there was the issue of the number of products examined. The
purchasers were looking at an average of 4.81 items but buying only 1.33
items. Paco found this statistic deeply disturbing. As the retail market
grows more cutthroat, store owners have come to realize that it's all but
impossible to increase the number of customers coming in, and have concentrated instead on getting the customers they do have to buy more. Paco
thinks that if you can sell someone a pair of pants you must also be able to
sell that person a belt, or a pair of socks, or a pair of underpants, or even
do what the Gap does so well: sell a person a complete outfit. To Paco, the
figure 1.33 suggested that the store was doing something very wrong, and
one day when I visited him in his office he sat me down in front of one of
his many VCRs to see how he looked for the 1.33 culprit.

It should be said that sitting next to Paco is a rather strange experience. "My mother says that I'm the best-paid spy in America," he told me.
He laughed, but he wasn't entirely joking. As a child, Paco had a nearly debilitating stammer, and, he says, "since I was never that comfortable talking I always relied on my eyes to understand things." That much is obvious
from the first moment you meet him: Paco is one of those people who look

right at you, soaking up every nuance and detail. It isn't a hostile gaze, because Paco isn't hostile at all. He has a big smile, and he'll call you "chief" and use your first name a lot and generally act as if he knew you well. But that's the awkward thing: he has looked at you so closely that you're sure he does know you well, and you, meanwhile, hardly know him at all.

This kind of asymmetry is even more pronounced when you watch his shopping videos with him, because every movement or gesture means something to Paco—he has spent his adult life deconstructing the shopping experience—but nothing to the outsider, or, at least, not at first. Paco had to keep stopping the video to get me to see things through his eyes before I began to understand. In one sequence, for example, a camera mounted high on the wall outside the changing rooms documented a man and a woman shopping for a pair of pants for what appeared to be their daughter, a girl in her midteens. The tapes are soundless, but the basic steps of the shopping dance are so familiar to Paco that, once I'd grasped the general idea, he was able to provide a running commentary on what was being said and thought. There is the girl emerging from the changing room wearing her first pair. There she is glancing at her reflection in the mirror, then turning to see herself from the back. There is the mother looking on. There is the father—or, as fathers are known in the trade, the "wallet carrier"—stepping forward and pulling up the jeans. There's the girl trying on another pair. There's the primp again. The twirl. The mother. The wallet carrier. And then again, with another pair. The full sequence lasted twenty minutes, and at the end came the take-home lesson, for which Paco called in one of his colleagues, Tom Moseman, who had supervised the project.

"This is a very critical moment," Tom, a young, intense man wearing   15
little round glasses, said, and he pulled up a chair next to mine. "She's saying, 'I don't know whether I should wear a belt.' Now here's the salesclerk. The girl says to him, 'I need a belt,' and he says, 'Take mine.'" Now there he is taking her back to the full-length mirror."

A moment later, the girl returns, clearly happy with the purchase. She wants the jeans. The wallet carrier turns to her, and then gestures to the salesclerk. The wallet carrier is telling his daughter to give back the belt. The girl gives back the belt. Tom stops the tape. He's leaning forward now, a finger jabbing at the screen. Beside me, Paco is shaking his head. I don't get it—at least, not at first—and so Tom replays that last segment. The wallet carrier tells the girl to give back the belt. She gives back the belt. And then, finally, it dawns on me why this store has an average purchase number of only 1.33. "Don't you see?" Tom said. "*She wanted the belt*. A great opportunity to make an add-on sale . . . *lost!*"

Should we be afraid of Paco Underhill? One of the fundamental anxieties of the American consumer, after all, has always been that beneath the pleasure and the frivolity of the shopping experience runs an undercurrent of manipulation, and that anxiety has rarely seemed more justified than today. The practice of prying into the minds and habits of American consumers is now a multibillion-dollar business. Every time a product is pulled across a supermarket checkout scanner, information is recorded, assembled, and sold to a market-research firm for analysis. There are companies that put tiny cameras inside frozen-food cases in supermarket aisles; market-research firms that feed census data and behavioral statistics into algorithms and come out with complicated maps of the American consumer; anthropologists who sift through the garbage of carefully targeted households to analyze their true consumption patterns; and endless rounds of highly organized focus groups and questionnaire takers and phone surveyors. That some people are now tracking our every shopping move with video cameras seems in many respects the last straw: Paco's movies are, after all, creepy. They look like the surveillance videos taken during convenience-store holdups—hazy and soundless and slightly warped by the angle of the lens. When you watch them, you find yourself waiting for something bad to happen, for someone to shoplift or pull a gun on a cashier.

The more time you spend with Paco's videos, though, the less scary they seem. After an hour or so, it's no longer clear whether simply by watching people shop—and analyzing their every move—you can learn how to control them. The shopper that emerges from the videos is not pliable or manipulable. The screen shows people filtering in and out of stores, petting and moving on, abandoning their merchandise because checkout lines are too long, or leaving a store empty-handed because they couldn't fit their stroller into the aisle between two shirt racks. Paco's shoppers are fickle and headstrong, and are quite unwilling to buy anything unless conditions are perfect—unless the belt is presented at *exactly* the right moment. His theories of the butt-brush and petting and the Decompression Zone and the Invariant Right seek not to make shoppers conform to the desires of sellers but to make sellers conform to the desires of shoppers. What Paco is teaching his clients is a kind of slavish devotion to the shopper's every whim. He is teaching them humility.

Paco has worked with supermarket chains, and when you first see one of his videos of grocery aisles it looks as if he really had—at least in this instance—got one up on the shopper. The clip he showed me was of a father shopping with a small child, and it was an example of what is known in the trade as "advocacy," which basically means what happens when your four-year-old goes over and grabs a bag of cookies that the store has conveniently put on the bottom shelf, and demands that it be purchased. In the clip, the father takes what the child offers him. "Generally, dads are not as good as moms at saying no," Paco said as we watched the little boy approach his dad. "Men tend to be more impulse-driven than women in grocery stores. We know that they tend to shop less often with a list. We know that they tend to shop much less frequently with coupons, and we know, simply by watching them shop, that they can be marching down the aisle and something will catch their eye and they will stop and buy." This kind of weakness on the part of fathers might seem to give the supermarket an advantage in the cookie-selling wars, particularly since more and more men go grocery shopping with their children. But then Paco let drop a hint about a study he'd just done in which he discovered, to his and everyone else's amazement, that shoppers had already figured this out, that they were already one step ahead—that *families were avoiding the cookie aisle.*

This may seem like a small point. But it begins to explain why, even   20
though retailers seem to know more than ever about how shoppers behave, even though their efforts at intelligence-gathering have rarely seemed more intrusive and more formidable, the retail business remains in crisis. The reason is that shoppers are a moving target. They are becoming more and more complicated, and retailers need to know more and more about them simply to keep pace.

This fall, for example, Estée Lauder is testing in a Toronto shopping mall a new concept in cosmetics retailing. Gone is the enclosed rectangular counter, with the sales staff on one side, customers on the other, and the product under glass in the middle. In its place the company has provided an assortment of product-display, consultation, and testing kiosks arranged in a broken circle, with a service desk and a cashier in the middle. One of the kiosks is a "makeup play area," which allows customers to experiment on their own with a hundred and thirty different shades of lipstick. There are four self-service displays—for perfumes, skin-care products, and makeup—which are easily accessible to customers who have already made up their minds. And, for those who haven't, there is a semiprivate booth for personal consultations with beauty advisers and makeup artists. The redesign was prompted by the realization that the modern working woman no longer had the time or the inclination to ask a salesclerk to assist her in every purchase, that choosing among shades of lipstick did not require the same level of service as, say, getting up to speed on new developments in skin care, that a shopper's needs were now too diverse to be adequately served by just one kind of counter.

"I was going from store to store, and the traffic just wasn't there," Robin Burns, the president and C.E.O. of Estée Lauder U.S.A. and Canada, told me. "We had to get rid of the glass barricade." The most interesting thing about the new venture, though, is what it says about the shifting balance of power between buyer and seller. Around the old rectangular counter, the relationship of clerk to customer was formal and subtly paternalistic. If you wanted to look at a lipstick, you had to ask for it. "Twenty years ago, the sales staff would consult with you and *tell* you what you needed, as opposed to asking and recommending," Burns said. "And in those days people believed what the salesperson told them." Today, the old hierarchy has been inverted. "Women want to draw their own conclusions," Burns said. Even the architecture of the consultation kiosk speaks to the transformation: the beauty adviser now sits beside the customer, not across from her.

This doesn't mean that marketers and retailers have stopped trying to figure out what goes on in the minds of shoppers. One of the hottest areas in market research, for example, is something called typing, which is a sophisticated attempt to predict the kinds of products that people will buy or the kind of promotional pitch they will be susceptible to on the basis of where they live or how they score on short standardized questionnaires. One market-research firm in Virginia, Claritas, has divided the entire country, neighborhood by neighborhood, into sixty-two different categories—Pools & Patios, Shotguns & Pickups, Bohemia Mix, and so on—using census data and results from behavioral surveys. On the basis of my address in Greenwich Village, Claritas classifies me as Urban Gold Coast, which means that I like Kellogg's Special K, spend more than two hundred and fifty dollars on sports coats, watch "Seinfeld," and buy metal polish. Such typing systems—and there are a number of them—can be scarily accurate. I actually do buy Kellogg's Special K, have spent more than two hundred and fifty dollars on a sports coat, and watch "Seinfeld." (I don't buy metal polish.) In fact, when I was typed by a company called Total Research, in Princeton, the results were so dead-on that I got the same kind of creepy feeling that I got when I first watched Paco's videos. On the basis of a seemingly innocuous multiple-choice test, I was scored as an eighty-nine-percent Intellect and a seven-percent Relief Seeker (which I thought was impressive until John Morton, who developed the system, told me that virtually everyone who reads *The New Yorker* is an Intellect). When I asked Morton to guess, on the basis of my score, what kind of razor I used, he riffed, brilliantly, and without a moment's hesitation. "If you used an electric razor, it would be a Braun," he began. "But, if not, you're probably shaving with Gillette, if only because there really isn't an Intellect safety-razor positioning out there. Schick and Bic are simply not logical choices for you although I'm thinking, You're fairly young, and you've got that Relief Seeker side. It's possible you would use Bic because you don't like that all-American, overly confident masculine statement of Gillette. It's a very, very conventional positioning that Gillette uses. But then they've got the technological angle with the Gillette Sensor. . . . I'm thinking Gillette. It's Gillette."

He was right. I shave with Gillette—though I didn't even know that I do. I had to go home and check. But information about my own predilections may be of limited usefulness in predicting how I shop. In the past few years, market researchers have paid growing attention to the role in the shopping experience of a type of consumer known as a Market Maven. "This is a person you would go to for advice on a car or a new fashion," said Linda Price, a marketing professor at the University of South Florida, who first came up with the Market Maven concept, in the late eighties. "This is a person who has information on a lot of different products or prices or places to shop. This is a person who likes to initiate discussions with consumers and respond to requests. Market Mavens like to be helpers in the marketplace. They take you shopping. They go shopping for you, and it turns out they are a lot more prevalent than you would expect." Mavens watch more television than almost anyone else does, and they read more magazines and open their junk mail and look closely at advertisements and have an awful lot of influence on everyone else. According to Price, sixty percent of Americans claim to know a Maven.

The key question, then, is not what I think but what my Mavens think. 25 The challenge for retailers and marketers, in turn, is not so much to figure out and influence my preferences as to figure out and influence the preferences of my Mavens, and that is a much harder task. "What's really interesting is that the distribution of Mavens doesn't vary by ethnic category, by income, or by professional status," Price said. "A working woman is just as likely to be a Market Maven as a nonworking woman. You might say that Mavens are likely to be older, unemployed people, but that's wrong, too. There is simply not a clear demographic guide to how to find these people." More important, Mavens are better consumers than most of the rest of us. In another of the typing systems, developed by the California-based SRI International, Mavens are considered to be a subcategory of the consumer type known as Fulfilled, and Fulfilleds, one SRI official told me, are "the consumers from Hell—they are very feature oriented." He explained, "They are not pushed by promotions. You can reach them, but it's an intellectual argument." As the complexity of the marketplace grows, in other words, we have responded by appointing the most skeptical and the most savvy in our midst to mediate between us and sellers. The harder stores and manufacturers work to sharpen and refine their marketing strategies, and the harder they try to read the minds of shoppers, the more we hide behind Mavens.

Imagine that you want to open a clothing store, men's and women's, in the upper-middle range—say, khakis at fifty dollars, dress shirts at forty dollars, sports coats and women's suits at two hundred dollars and up. The work of Paco Underhill would suggest that in order to succeed you need to pay complete and concentrated attention to the whims of your customers. What does that mean, in practical terms? Well, let's start with what's called the shopping gender gap. In the retail-store study that Paco showed me, for example, male buyers stayed an average of nine minutes and thirty-nine seconds in the store and female buyers stayed twelve minutes and fifty-seven seconds. This is not atypical. Women always shop longer than men, which is one of the major reasons that in the standard regional mall women account for seventy percent of the dollar value of all purchases. "Women have more patience than men," Paco says. "Men are more distractible. Their tolerance level for confusion or time spent in a store is much shorter than women's." If you wanted, then, you could build a store designed for men, to try to raise that thirty-percent sales figure to forty or forty-five percent. You could make the look more masculine—more metal, darker woods. You could turn up the music. You could simplify the store, put less product on the floor. "I'd go narrow and deep," says James Adams, the design director for NBBJ Retail Concepts, a division of one of the country's largest retail-design firms. "You wouldn't have fifty different cuts of pants. You'd have your four basics with lots of color. You know the Garanimals they used to do to help kids pick out clothes, where you match the giraffe top with the giraffe bottom? I'm sure every guy is like 'I wish I could get those, too.' You'd want to stick with the basics. Making sure most of the color story goes together. That is a big deal with guys, because they are always screwing the colors up." When I asked Carrie Gennuso, the Gap's regional vice-president for New York, what she would do in an all-male store, she laughed and said, "I might do fewer displays and more signage. Big signs. Men! Smalls! Here!"

As a rule, though, you wouldn't want to cater to male customers at the expense of female ones. It's no accident that many clothing stores have a single look in both men's and women's sections, and that the quintessential nineties look—light woods, white walls—is more feminine than masculine. Women are still the shoppers in America, and the real money is to be made by making retailing styles *more* female-friendly, not less. Recently, for example, NBBJ did a project to try to increase sales of the Armstrong flooring chain. Its researchers found that the sales staff was selling the flooring based on its functional virtues—the fact that it didn't scuff, that it was long-lasting, that it didn't stain, that it was easy to clean. It was being sold by men to men, as if it were a car or a stereo. And that was the problem. "It's a wonder product technologically," Adams says. "But the woman is the decision-maker on flooring, and that's not what's she's looking for. This product is about fashion, about color and design. You don't want to get too caught up in the man's way of thinking."

To appeal to men, then, retailers do subtler things. At the Banana Republic store on Fifth Avenue in midtown, the men's socks are displayed near the shoes and between men's pants and the cash register (or cash/wrap, as it is known in the trade), so that the man can grab them easily as he rushes to pay. Women's accessories are by the fitting rooms, because women are much more likely to try on pants first, and then choose an item like a belt or a bag. At the men's shirt table, the display shirts have matching ties on them—the tie table is next to it—in a grownup version of the Garanimals system. But Banana Republic would never match scarves with women's blouses or jackets. "You don't have to be that direct with women," Jeanne Jackson, the president of Banana Republic, told me. "In fact, the Banana woman is proud of her sense of style. She puts her own looks together." Jackson said she liked the Fifth Avenue store because it's on two floors, so she can separate men's and women's sections and give men what she calls "clarity of offer," which is the peace of mind that they won't inadvertently end up in, say, women's undergarments. In a one-floor store, most retailers would rather put the menswear up front and the women's wear at the back (that is, if they weren't going to split the sexes left and right), because women don't get spooked navigating through apparel of the opposite sex, whereas men most assuredly do. (Of course, in a store like the Gap at Thirty-ninth and Fifth, where, Carrie Gennuso says, "I don't know if I've ever seen a man," the issue is moot. There, it's safe to put the women's wear out front.)

The next thing retailers want to do is to encourage the shopper to walk deep into the store. The trick there is to put "destination items"—basics, staples, things that people know you have and buy a lot of—at the rear of the store. Gap stores, invariably, will have denim, which is a classic destination item for them, on the back wall. Many clothing stores also situate the cash/wrap and the fitting rooms in the rear of the store, to compel shoppers to walk back into Zone 3 or 4. In the store's prime real estate— which, given Paco's theory of the Decompression Zone and the Invariant Right, is to the right of the front entrance and five to fifteen paces in—you always put your hottest and newest merchandise, because that's where the maximum number of people will see it. Right now, in virtually every Gap in the country, the front of the store is devoted to the Gap fall look—casual combinations in black and gray, plaid shirts and jackets, sweaters, black wool and brushed-twill pants. At the Gap at Fifth Avenue and Seventeenth Street, for example, there is a fall ensemble of plaid jacket, plaid shirt, and black pants in the first prime spot, followed, three paces later, by an ensemble of gray sweater, plaid shirt, T-shirt, and black pants, followed, three paces after that, by an ensemble of plaid jacket, gray sweater, white T-shirt, and black pants. In all, three variations on the same theme, each placed so that the eye bounces naturally from the first to the second to the third, and then, inexorably, to a table deep inside Zone 1 where merchandise is arrayed and folded for petting. Every week or ten days, the combinations will change, the "look" highlighted at the front will be different, and the entryway will be transformed.

Through all of this, the store environment—the lighting, the colors, the fixtures—and the clothes have to work together. The point is not so much beauty as coherence. The clothes have to match the environment. "In the nineteen-seventies, you didn't have to have a complete wardrobe all the time," Gabriella Forte, the president and chief operating officer of Calvin Klein, says. "I think now the store has to have a complete point of view. It has to have all the options offered, so people have choices. It's the famous one-stop shopping. People want to come in, be serviced, and go out. They want to understand the clear statement the designer is making."

At the new Versace store on Fifth Avenue, in the restored neoclassical Vanderbilt mansion, Gianni Versace says that the "statement" he is making with the elaborate mosaic and parquet floors, the marble façade and the Corinthian columns is "quality—my message is always a scream for quality." At her two new stores in London, Donna Karan told me, she never wants "customers to think that they are walking into a clothing store." She said, "I want them to think that they are walking into an environment, that I am transforming them out of their lives and into an experience, that it's not about clothes, it's about who they are as people." The first thing the shopper sees in her stark, all-white DKNY store is a video monitor and café: "It's about energy," Karan said, "and nourishment." In her more sophisticated, "collection" store, where the walls are black and ivory and gold, the first thing that the customer notices is the scent of a candle: "I wanted a nurturing environment where you feel that you will be taken care of." And why, at a Giorgio Armani store, is there often only a single suit in each style on display? Not because the store has only the one suit in stock but because the way the merchandise is displayed has to be consistent with the message of the designers: that Armani suits are exclusive, that the Armani customer isn't going to run into another man wearing his suit every time he goes to an art opening at Gagosian.[3]

The best stores all have an image — or what retailers like to call a "point of view." The flagship store for Ralph Lauren's Polo collection, for example, is in the restored Rhinelander mansion, on Madison Avenue and Seventy-second Street. The Polo Mansion, as it is known, is alive with color and artifacts that suggest a notional prewar English gentility. There are fireplaces and comfortable leather chairs and deep-red Oriental carpets and soft, thick drapes and vintage photographs and paintings of country squires and a color palette of warm crimsons and browns and greens — to the point that after you've picked out a double-breasted blazer or a cashmere sweater set or an antique silver snuffbox you feel as though you ought to venture over to Central Park for a vigorous morning of foxhunting.

The Calvin Klein flagship store, twelve blocks down Madison Avenue, on the other hand, is a vast, achingly beautiful minimalist temple, with white walls, muted lighting, soaring ceilings, gray stone flooring, and, so it seems, less merchandise in the entire store than Lauren puts in a single room. The store's architect, John Pawson, says, "People who enter are given a sense of release. They are getting away from the hustle and bustle of the street and New York. They are in a calm space. It's a modern idea of luxury, to give people space."

The first thing you see when you enter the Polo Mansion is a display of two hundred and eight sweaters, in twenty-eight colors, stacked in a haberdasher's wooden fixture, behind an antique glass counter; the first thing you see at the Klein store is a white wall, and then, if you turn to the right, four clear-glass shelves, each adorned with three solitary-looking black handbags. The Polo Mansion is an English club. The Klein store, Pawson says, is the equivalent of an art gallery, a place where "neutral space and light make a work of art look the most potent." When I visited the Polo Mansion, the stereo was playing Bobby Short. At Klein, the stereo was playing what sounded like Brian Eno. At the Polo Mansion, I was taken around by Charles Fagan, a vice-president at Polo Ralph Lauren. He wore pale-yellow socks, black loafers, tight jeans, a pale-purple polo shirt, blue old-school tie, and a brown plaid jacket — which sounds less attractive on paper than it was in reality. He looked, in a very Ralph Lauren way, *fabulous*. He was funny and engaging and bounded through the store, keeping up a constant patter ("This room is sort of sportswear, Telluride-y, vintage"), all the while laughing and hugging people and having his freshly cut

[3]*Gagosian:* prominent art gallery in New York City. [Eds.]

red hair tousled by the sales assistants in each section. At the Calvin Klein store, the idea that the staff—tall, austere, somber-suited—might laugh and hug and tousle each other's hair is unthinkable. Lean over and whisper, perhaps. At the most, murmur discreetly into tiny black cellular phones. Visiting the Polo Mansion and the Calvin Klein flagship in quick succession is rather like seeing a "Howards End"–"The Seventh Seal" double feature.

Despite their differences, though, these stores are both about the same   35
thing—communicating the point of view that shoppers are now thought to demand. At Polo, the "life style" message is so coherent and all-encompassing that the store never has the 1.33 items-per-purchase problem that Paco saw in the retailer he studied. "We have multiple purchases in excess—it's the cap, it's the tie, it's the sweater, it's the jacket, it's the pants," Fagan told me, plucking each item from its shelf and tossing it onto a tartan-covered bench seat. "People say, 'I *have* to have the belt.' It's a life-style decision."

As for the Klein store, it's really concerned with setting the tone for the Calvin Klein clothes and products sold *outside* the store—including the designer's phenomenally successful underwear line, the sales of which have grown nearly fivefold in the past two and a half years, making it one of the country's dominant brands. Calvin Klein underwear is partly a design triumph: lowering the waistband just a tad in order to elongate, and flatter, the torso. But it is also a triumph of image—transforming, as Gabriella Forte says, a "commodity good into something desirable," turning a forgotten necessity into *fashion*. In the case of women's underwear, Bob Mazzoli, president of Calvin Klein Underwear, told me that the company "obsessed about the box being a perfect square, about the symmetry of it all, how it would feel in a woman's hand." He added, "When you look at the boxes they are little works of art." And the underwear itself is without any of the usual busyness—without, in Mazzoli's words, "the excessive detail" of most women's undergarments. It's a clean look, selling primarily in white, heather gray, and black. It's a look, in other words, not unlike that of the Calvin Klein flagship store, and it exemplifies the brilliance of the merchandising of the Calvin Klein image: preposterous as it may seem, once you've seen the store and worn the underwear, it's difficult not to make a connection between the two.

All this imagemaking seeks to put the shopping experience in a different context, to give it a story line. "I wish that the customers who come to my stores feel the same comfort they would entering a friend's house—that is to say, that they feel at ease, without the impression of having to deal with the 'sanctum sanctorum' of a designer," Giorgio Armani told me. Armani has a house. Donna Karan has a kitchen and a womb. Ralph Lauren has a men's club. Calvin Klein has an art gallery. These are all very different points of view. What they have in common is that they have nothing to do with the actual act of shopping. (No one buys anything at a friend's house or a men's club.) Presumably, by engaging in this kind of misdirection designers aim to put us at ease, to create a kind of oasis. But perhaps they change the subject because they must, because they cannot offer an ultimate account of the shopping experience itself. After all, what do we really know, in the end, about why people buy? We know about the Invariant Right and the Decompression Zone. We know to put destination items at the back and fashion at the front, to treat male shoppers like small children, to respect the female derrière, and to put the socks between the cash/wrap and the men's pants. But this is grammar; it's not prose. It is enough. But it is not much.

One of the best ways to understand the new humility in shopping theory is to go back to the work of William Whyte. Whyte put his cameras in parks and in the plazas in front of office buildings because he believed in the then radical notion that the design of public spaces had been turned inside out—that planners were thinking of their designs first and of people second, when they should have been thinking of people first and of design second.

In his 1980 classic, "The Social Life of Small Urban Spaces," for example, Whyte trained his cameras on a dozen or so of the public spaces and small parks around Manhattan, like the plaza in front of the General Motors Building, on Fifth Avenue, and the small park at 77 Water Street, downtown, and Paley Park, on Fifty-third Street, in order to determine why some, like the tiny Water Street park, averaged well over a hundred and fifty people during a typical sunny lunch hour and others, like the much bigger plaza at 280 Park Avenue, were almost empty. He concluded that all the things used by designers to attempt to lure people into their spaces made little or no difference. It wasn't the size of the space, or its beauty, or the presence of waterfalls, or the amount of sun, or whether a park was a narrow strip along the sidewalk or a pleasing open space. What mattered, overwhelmingly, was that there were plenty of places to sit, that the space was in some way connected to the street, and—the mystical circularity—that it was already well frequented. "What attracts people most, it would appear, is other people," Whyte noted:

> If I labor the point, it is because many urban spaces still are being designed as though the opposite were true—as though what people liked best were the places they stay away from. People often do talk along such lines, and therefore their responses to questionnaires can be entirely misleading. How many people would say they like to sit in the middle of a crowd? Instead, they speak of "getting away from it all," and use words like "escape," "oasis," "retreat." What people *do*, however, reveals a different priority.

Whyte's conclusions demystified the question of how to make public 40
space work. Places to sit, streets to enjoy, and people to watch turned out to be the simple and powerful rules for park designers to follow, and these

rules demolished the orthodoxies and theoretical principles of conventional urban design. But in a more important sense—and it is here that Whyte's connection with Paco Underhill and retail anthropology and the stores that line Fifth and Madison is most striking—what Whyte did was to remystify the art of urban planning. He said, emphatically, that people could not be manipulated, that they would enter a public space only on their own terms, that the goal of observers like him was to find out what people wanted, not why they wanted it. Whyte, like Paco, was armed with all kinds of facts and observations about what it took to build a successful public space. He had strict views on how wide ledges had to be to lure passersby (at least thirty inches, or two backsides deep), and what the carrying capacity of prime outdoor sitting space is (total number of square feet divided by three). But, fundamentally, he was awed by the infinite complexity and the ultimate mystery of human behavior. He took people too seriously to think that he could control them. Here is Whyte, in "The Social Life of Small Urban Spaces," analyzing hours of videotape and describing what he has observed about the way men stand in public. He's talking about feet. He could just as easily be talking about shopping:

> Foot movements . . . seem to be a silent language. Often, in a schmoozing group, no one will be saying anything. Men stand bound in amiable silence, surveying the passing scene. Then, slowly, rhythmically, one of the men rocks up and down; first on the ball of the foot, then back on the heel. He stops. Another man starts the same movement. Sometimes there are reciprocal gestures. One man makes a half turn to the right. Then, after a rhythmic interval, another responds with a half turn to the left. Some kind of communication seems to be taking place here, but I've never broken the code.

QUESTIONS

1. How would you describe the "science" that is the subject of this piece? Locate examples of the terminology of this science and of its methods of research.
2. How much research did Gladwell have to do to write this essay? How many people did he interview? How many stores did he visit? What sort of knowledge did he need to acquire and from what sources? Is there any indication that he enjoys shopping?
3. In paragraph 17, Gladwell raises the question of our anxiety regarding manipulation as consumers. How does he answer this question? Do you agree with his conclusions? Explain why or why not.
4. Apply some of Paco Underhill's methods of observation and data gathering to your favorite store, and write a report describing its layout and

the effectiveness of its sales staff. Be sure to include a description of the store's point of view or lifestyle message.

5. Bring some of the observations of Paco Underhill and William Whyte to bear on a public space on your campus or in your city or town. Do you think the space was designed to appeal to people? Explain why or why not, and describe what might be done to improve it.

MAKING CONNECTIONS

In what ways would the information gathered by Monica M. Moore for her article "Nonverbal Courtship Patterns in Women" (p. 465) be useful to Paco Underhill were he asked to advise on the layout and design of a singles bar?

Nonverbal Courtship Patterns in Women
Context and Consequences

Monica M. Moore

Monica M. Moore (b. 1953) is a professor of psychology at Webster University in St. Louis, Missouri. Moore has conducted research on nonverbal courtship behavior in women since 1978, publishing articles in such journals as Semiotica *and the* Journal of Sex Research. *In this article, which originally appeared in the journal* Ethology and Sociobiology, *Moore applied the research methods of psychology to study the mating habits of the human female.*

[Abstract.] *There is a class of nonverbal facial expressions and gestures, exhibited by human females, that are commonly labeled "flirting behaviors." I observed more than 200 randomly selected adult female subjects in order to construct a catalog of these nonverbal solicitation behaviors. Pertinent behaviors were operationally defined through the use of consequential data; these behaviors elicited male attention. Fifty-two behaviors were described using this method. Validation of the catalog was provided through the use of contextual data. Observations were conducted on 40 randomly selected female subjects in one of four contexts: a singles' bar, a university snack bar, a university library, and at university Women's Center meetings. The results indicated that women in "mate relevant" contexts exhibited higher average frequencies of nonverbal displays directed at males. Additionally, women who signaled often were also those who were most often approached by a man; and this relationship was not context specific.*

I suggest that the observation of women in field situations may provide clues to criteria used by females in the initial selection of male partners. As much of the work surrounding human attraction has involved laboratory studies or data collected from couples in established relationships, the observation of nonverbal behavior in field settings may provide a fruitful avenue for the exploration of human female choice in the preliminary stages of male-female interaction.

Introduction

Biologically, one of the most important choices made by an organism is the selection of a mate. The evolution of traits that would assist in the identification of "superior mates" prior to the onset of mating is clearly advantageous. One legacy of anisogamy is that errors in mate selection are generally more expensive to females than to males (Trivers 1972).[1] Hence, the females of a wide variety of species may be expected to exhibit traits that would facilitate the assessment of the quality of potential suitors in respect to their inherited attributes and acquired resources. There are many examples of female selectivity in a variety of species, including elephant seals (LeBoeuf and Peterson 1969; Bertram 1975), mice (McClearn and Defries 1973), fish (Weber and Weber 1975), rats (Doty 1974), gorillas (Nadler 1975), monkeys (Beach 1976), birds (Selander 1972; Wiley 1973; Williams 1975), and a few ungulates[2] (Beuchner and Schloeth 1965; Leuthold 1966).

Very few studies in the area of human mate selection and attraction have focused on the issue of female choice. Fowler (1978) interviewed women to identify the parameters of male sexual attractiveness. The results showed that the male's value as a sexual partner correlated with the magnitude of emotional and material security he provided. Baber (1939) found that women emphasize qualities such as economic status, disposition, family religion, morals, health, and education in a prospective marriage partner, whereas men most frequently chose good looks, morals, and health as important qualities. More recent studies (Coombs and Kenkel 1966; Tavris 1977) also found women rating attributes such as physical attractiveness as less important than did men. Reiss (1960) believes that many more women than men choose "someone to look up to" and Hatkoff and Luswell (1977) presented data that indicated that women want the men with whom they fall in love to be persons whom they can respect and depend on. Daly and Wilson (1978) conclude from cross-cultural data that a male's financial status is an important determinant of his mating success.

Although these reports are valuable, it is clear that the mechanisms and expression of male assessment and female choice in humans have received little attention. In addition, much of the information available regarding human female choice is derived from interviews or questionnaires. Few studies have focused on initial choice situations in field observations. There are several difficulties with a field approach. A major problem surrounds the determination that a choice situation is being observed when verbal information is unavailable. I suggest that this problem may be solved through observations of nonverbal behavior. Indeed, there appears

5

------

[1]*anisogamy:* the union of unlike gametes—or mates, in this case. [Eds.]
[2]*ungulate:* a group of hoofed, herbivorous mammals, including camels, horses, and swine. [Eds.]

to be a repertoire of gestures and facial expressions that are used by humans as courtship signals (Birdwhistell 1970), much as there is signaling between members of the opposite sex in other species. Even in humans courtship and the choice of a mate have been characterized as largely nonverbal, with the cues being so persuasive that they can, as one observer put it, "turn a comment about the weather into a seductive invitation" (Davis 1971, p. 97).

The focus of much study in the area of nonverbal communication has been description (Scheflen 1965; Birdwhistell 1970; Mehrabian 1972). The primary aim of this research has been the categorization and analysis of nonverbal behaviors. By employing frame-by-frame analysis of films, Birdwhistell and his associates have been able to provide detailed descriptions of the facial expressions and movements or gestures of subjects in a variety of contexts. Observations conducted in this fashion as well as field studies have resulted in the labeling of many nonverbal behaviors as courtship signals. For example, Givens (1978) has described five phases of courtship between unaquainted adults. Scheflen (1965) investigated flirting gestures in the context of psychotherapy, noting that both courtship behaviors and qualifiers of the courtship message were exhibited by therapists and clients. Eibl-Eibesfeldt (1971) used two approaches to describe flirting behavior in people from diverse cultural backgrounds. Employing a camera fitted with right angle lenses to film people without their knowledge, he found that an eyebrow flash combined with a smile was a common courtship behavior. Through comments made to women, Eibl-Eibesfeldt has been able to elicit the "coy glance," an expression combining a half-smile and lowered eyes. Kendon (1975) filmed a couple seated on a park bench in order to document the role of facial expression during a kissing round. He discovered that it was the female's behavior, particularly her facial expressions that functioned as a regulator in modulating the behavior of the male. Cary (1976) has shown that the female's behavior is important in initiating conversation between strangers. Both in laboratory settings and singles' bars conversation was initiated only after the female glanced at the male. These results are valuable in documenting the importance of nonverbal behavior in human courtship. But what is lacking is an ethogram of female solicitation behavior.[3]

The purpose of this study was to describe an ensemble of visual and tactile displays emitted by women during initial meetings with men. I shall argue here that these nonverbal displays are courtship signals; they serve as attractants and elicit the approach of males or ensure the continued attention of males. In order to establish the immediate function of the described behaviors as courtship displays, I employed two classes of evidence described by Hinde (1975) for use in the establishment of the immediate function of a behavior; contextual evidence and consequential evidence.

------

[3]*ethogram:* a pictorial catalog of behavior patterns shown by members of a species. [Eds.]

The rationale behind the use of consequential data was that behavior has certain consequences and that if the consequence appears to be a "good thing" it should have relevance for the immediate function of the behavior in question. It should be noted, however, that Eibl-Eibesfeldt (1970) has pointed out the danger in this approach because of interpretations of value on the part of the observer. Therefore, contextual information was provided as further documentation that the nonverbal behaviors in question were courtship signals. Hinde has noted that if certain behaviors are seen in some contexts but are absent in others their function must relate to those contexts in which they were observed. Together these two classes of information provide an indication of the immediate function of the behavior, in this case nonverbal behavior in women interacting with men. Thus, this study consisted of two parts: catalog compilation based on consequential information and validation of the catalog obtained through contextual data.

Development of the Catalog

Method

Subjects For the initial study, more than 200 subjects were observed in order to obtain data to be used in the development of the catalog of nonverbal solicitation signals. Subjects were judged to be between the ages of 18 and 35 years. No systematic examination was made of background variables due to restrictions imposed by anonymity. All subjects were white and most were probably college students.

Procedure Subjects were covertly observed in one social context where opportunities for male–female interaction were available, a singles' bar. Subjects were observed for 30 minutes by two trained observers. Focal subjects were randomly selected from the pool of possible subjects at the start of the observation period. We observed a woman only if she was surrounded by at least 25 other people (generally there were more than 50 others present) and if she was not accompanied by a male. In order to record all instances of the relevant behaviors, observers kept a continuous narrative account of all behaviors exhibited by a single subject and the observable consequences of those actions (Altmann 1974). The following criteria were used for identifying behaviors: a nonverbal solicitation behavior was defined as a movement of body part(s) or whole body that resulted in male attention, operationally defined, within 15 seconds following the behavior. Male attention consisted of the male performing one of the following behaviors: approaching the subject, talking to her, leaning toward her or moving closer to her, asking the subject to dance, touching her, or kissing her. Field notes were transcribed from concealed audio tape recorders.

Estimates of interobserver reliability were calculated for 35 hours of observation using the formula:

$$\frac{\text{No. of agreements (A + B)}}{\text{No. of agreements (A + B) + No. seen by B only + No. seen by A only}}$$

(McGrew 1972). The range of interobserver reliability scores was 0.72–0.98, with the average score equaling .88. Low reliability scores were obtained only for behaviors difficult for an observer to catch in a darkened room, such as glancing behaviors.

Subsequently, five randomly selected subjects were observed for a period of at least 1 hour. Again observers kept a continuous narrative account of all nonverbal behavior exhibited by the woman.

The behaviors observed in courting women can be conceptualized in various ways: distance categories (Crook 1972), directional versus nondirectional, or on the basis of body part and movement employed in the exhibition of the nonverbal pattern (McGrew 1972). The third framework was chosen because the displays were most discretely partitioned along these dimensions.

Results

Fifty-two different behaviors were exhibited by the subjects in the present study. Nonverbal solicitation behaviors and their frequencies are summarized in Table 1 according to category. These behaviors were highly visible and most appeared very similar in form in each subject. In other words, each behavior was discrete, or distinct from all other solicitation behaviors.

Descriptions of Nonverbal Solicitation Behaviors

FACIAL AND HEAD PATTERNS. A number of different facial and head patterns were seen in the women we observed. All women performed glancing behaviors, although the particular pattern varied among the individual subjects in the duration or length of time involved in eye to eye contact.

Type I glance (the room encompassing glance) was not restricted to an identifiable recipient. It was usually exhibited early in the evening and often was not seen later in the evening, particularly if the woman made contact with a man. The woman moved her head rapidly, orienting her face around the room. This movement was followed by another head movement that reoriented the woman's face to its original position. The total duration of the glance was brief, 5–10 seconds, with the woman not making eye contact with any specific individual. In some women this pattern of behavior was exaggerated: the woman stood up as her glance swept about the room.

TABLE 1.
Catalog of Nonverbal Solicitation Behaviors

Facial and Head Patterns	Frequency	Gestures	Frequency	Posture Patterns	Frequency
Type I glance (room-encompassing glance)	253	Arm flexion	10	Lean	121
Type II glance (short darting glance)	222	Tap	8	Brush	28
Type III glance (gaze fixate)	117	Palm	18	Breast touch	6
Eyebrow flash	4	Gesticulation	62	Knee touch	25
Head toss	102	Hand hold	20	Thigh touch	23
Neck presentation	58	Primp	46	Foot to foot	14
Hair flip	139	Hike skirt	4	Placement	19
Head nod	66	Object caress	56	Shoulder hug	25
Lip lick	48	Caress (face/hair)	5	Hug	11
Lipstick application	1	Caress (leg)	32	Lateral body contact	1
Pout	27	Caress (arm)	23	Frontal body contact	7
Smile	511	Caress (torso)	8	Hang	2
Coy smile	20	Caress (back)	17	Parade	41
Laugh	249	Buttock pat	8	Approach	18
Giggle	61			Request dance	12
Kiss	6			Dance (acceptance)	59
Whisper	60			Solitary dance	253
Face to face	9			Point/permission grant	62
			9	Aid solicitation	34
				Play	31

The glancing behavior called the *type II glance (the short darting*   15
glance) was a solicitation behavior that appeared directed at a particular
man. The woman directed her gaze at the man, then quickly away (within
3 seconds). The target axis of the horizontal rotation of the head was approximately 25–45 degrees. This behavior was usually repeated in bouts,
with three glances the average number per bout.

In contrast, *type III glance (gaze fixate)* consisted of prolonged (more
than 3 seconds) eye contact. The subject looked directly at the man; sometimes her glance was returned. Again, this behavior was seen several times
in a period of minutes in some subjects.

Another movement involving the eye area was an *eyebrow flash,* which
consisted of an exaggerated raising of the eyebrows of both eyes, followed
by a rapid lowering to the normal position. The duration of the raised eyebrow portion of the movement was approximately 2 seconds. This behavior was often combined with a smile and eye contact.

Several behaviors involved the head and neck region. In *head tossing,*
the head was flipped backwards so that the face was tilted upwards briefly
(less than 5 seconds). The head was then lowered to its original position.
The head toss was often combined with or seen before the *hair flip.* The
hair flip consisted of the woman raising one hand and pushing her fingers
through her hair or running her palm along the surface of her hair. Some
women made only one hand movement, while in others there were bouts of
hair stroking; the woman put her hand to her hair several times within a
30-second interval. The *head nod* was seen when the woman was only a
short distance from the man. Usually exhibited during conversation, the
head was moved forward and backward on the neck, which resulted in the
face of the subject moving up and down. Another head pattern was called
face to face. In this behavior pattern the head and face of the woman were
brought directly opposite another person's face so that the noses almost
touched, a distance of approximately 5 cm. A final behavior involving the
head and neck was the *neck presentation.* The woman tilted her head sideways to an angle of approximately 45 degrees. This resulted in the ear almost touching the ipsilateral shoulder,[4] thereby exposing the opposite side
of the neck. Occasionally the woman stroked the exposed neck area with
her fingers.

There were a number of signals that involved the lips and mouth of the
observed subjects. *Lipstick application* was a rare behavior. The woman
directed her gaze so that she made eye contact with a particular man. She
then slowly applied lipstick to her lips. She engaged in this behavior for
some time (15 seconds), repeatedly circling her lips. In contrast, the *lip lick*
was seen quite often, particularly in certain subjects. The woman opened
her mouth slightly and drew her tongue over her lips. Some women used a
single lip lick, wetting only the upper or the lower lip, while others ran the

---

[4]*ipsilateral:* situated on the same side of the body. [Eds.]

tongue around the entire lip area. The *lip pout* was another behavior involving the mouth. The lips were placed together and protruded. Generally, the lower lip was extended somewhat farther than the upper lip, so that it was fuller in appearance.

Smiling was among the most prevalent behaviors observed in the   20
sampled women. The smile consisted of the corners of the mouth being turned upward. This resulted in partial or sometimes full exposure of the teeth. In some women the smile appeared fixed and was maintained for long periods of time. The *coy smile* differed from the smile in that the woman displaying a coy smile combined a half-smile (the teeth were often not displayed or only partially shown) with a downward gaze or eye contact which was very brief (less than 3 seconds). In the latter case the woman's glance slid quickly away from an onlooker who had become aware that he was being looked at.

Laughing and giggling were generally responses to another person's comments or behavior and were very common. In some women the *laugh* was preceded by a head toss. *Giggling* was less intense laughter. The mouth of the woman was often closed and generally the sounds were softer.

Kissing was rather unusual in the bar context. The slightly protruded lips were brought into contact with another person's body by a forward head movement. Variations consisted of the area touched by the woman's lips. The most common targets were the lips, face, and neck of the man. The woman, however, sometimes puckered her lips and waited, as if "offering" them to the male.

Finally, the *whisper* was used by most of the subjects in the sample. The woman moved her mouth near another person's ear and soft vocalizations presumedly were produced. Sometimes body contact was made.

GESTURES. There were several nonverbal patterns that involved movement of the hands and arms. Most were directed at a particular person. Some involved touching another individual. Others functioned at a distance.

Arm flexion occurred when the arm was flexed at wrist and elbow and   25
was moved toward the body. It was often repeated two or three times in a bout. This behavior was often followed by the approach of another individual toward whom the subject gazed. If the male was in close physical proximity, the female sometimes used *tapping* instead to get his attention. The elbow or wrist was flexed repeatedly so that the woman's finger was moved vertically on an object (usually another person's arm).

Women occasionally *palmed*. Palming occurred when the hand was extended or turned so that the palm faced another person for a brief period of time, less than 5 seconds. In this study, palming was also recorded when the woman coughed or touched herself with the palm up.

In several women rapid movements of the hands and arms were seen accompanying speech. This behavior was labeled *gesticulation*. Arms and hands, while held in front of the woman's torso, were waved or extended upwards in an exaggerated, conspicuous manner. This behavior was often followed by a lean forward on the part of the man.

A hand gesture sometimes initiated by a woman was the *hand hold*. The woman grasped the man's hand so that her palm was next to the man's palm. This occurred on the dance floor as well as when the man was seated at the table with the woman. Generally, this behavior had a long duration, more than 1 minute.

There were several behaviors that appeared related to each other because they involved inanimate objects. The first of these was the *primp*. In this gesture the clothing was patted or smoothed, although to the observer it appeared in no need of adjustment. A shirt was tucked in or a skirt was pulled down. On the other hand, the *skirt hike* was performed by raising the hem of the skirt with a movement of the hand or arm so that more leg was exposed. This behavior was only performed by two women and was directed at a particular man. When another man looked the skirt was pushed rapidly into place. Instead of patting or smoothing clothing, subjects sometimes "played with" an object, called *object caress*. For example, keys or rings were often fondled. Glasses were caressed with the woman sliding her palm up and down the surface of the glass. A cigarette pack was another item frequently toyed with in an object caress.

Finally, many women touched other people in a caressing fashion.   30
Each incidence of caressing was considered separately in terms of the part of the body that was touched, because the message, in each case, may have been quite different. In *caress (face/hair)* the woman moved her hand slowly up and down the man's face and neck area or tangled her hands in his hair. While the couple was seated, women have been observed stroking the man's thigh and inner leg, *caress (leg)*. The *buttock pat*, however, occurred while the couple was standing, often while dancing. In this gesture the woman moved her hand, palm side down, up and down the man's buttocks. Other items in this group included *caress (arm)*, *caress (torso)*, and *caress (back)*.

POSTURE PATTERNS. Compared to the two categories just presented, there were some behaviors which involved more of the body in movement. These I called posture patterns. Many of these behaviors could only be accomplished while the woman was standing or moving about the room.

Lean was a common solicitation pattern. Generally while seated, the woman moved her torso and upper body forward, which resulted in closer proximity to the man. This movement was sometimes followed by a *brush* or a *breast touch*. The brush occurred when brief body contact (less than 5 seconds) was initiated by the woman against another individual. This occurred when a woman was walking across the room; she bumped into a man. The result was often conversation between the man and the woman. The breast touch also appeared accidental; and it was difficult to tell, except by length of time of contact, whether or not the movement was purposeful. The upper torso was moved so the breast made contact with the man's body (usually his arm). Most often the contact was brief (less than 5 seconds), but sometimes women maintained this position for several minutes.

There were four other actions that were similar to the brush and breast touch in that the woman made bodily contact with the man. In the *knee touch* the legs were brought into contact with the man's legs so that the knees touched. Interactants were always facing one another while seated. If the man and woman were sitting side by side, the woman may have initiated a *thigh touch*. The leg was brought into contact with the man's upper leg. *Foot to foot* resulted in the woman moving her foot so that it rested on top of the man's foot. Finally, rather than make contact with some part of her own body, an observed woman sometimes took the man's hand and placed it on her body. I called this behavior *placement*. For example, on two occasions, a woman put a man's hand in her lap. Other targets were the thigh or arm.

There was another constellation of behaviors that appeared related to each other. All of these behaviors were variations of some contact made between the woman's upper body and her partner's upper body. These were generally behaviors of long duration, more than 1 minute. The most common of these behaviors was the *shoulder hug*. In this signal, the partially flexed arm was draped on and around another person's shoulder. In contrast, the *hug* occurred when both arms were moved forward from a widespread position and around the man, thereby encircling him. The duration of this behavior, however, was brief (less than 10 seconds). *Lateral body contact* was similar to shoulder hug except that the woman moved under the man's arm so that his arm was draped around her shoulders rather than vice versa. Similarly, *frontal body contact* occurred when the chest and thighs of the woman rested against the chest and thighs of the man. This behavior was like the hug except that there was no squeeze pressure and the arms did not necessarily encircle the other person. This posture pattern was often seen on the dance floor or when a couple was standing at the bar. *Hanging* was similar to frontal body contact except that the man was supporting the woman's weight. This behavior was initiated by the woman who placed her arms around the man's neck. She was then lifted off her feet while her torso and hips rested against the man's chest and hip. This was a behavior low in frequency and brief in duration, less than 5 seconds.

There were two behaviors that involved whole body movement. These were called *parade* and *approach*. Parade consisted of the woman walking across the room, perhaps on her way to the bar or the restroom. Yet rather than maintaining a relaxed attitude, the woman exaggerated the swaying motion of her hips. Her stomach was held in and her back was arched so that her breasts were pushed out; her head was held high. In general she was able to make herself "look good." The other behavior that involved walking was approach. The woman went up to the man and stood very close to him, within 2 feet. Usually verbal interaction ensued.

Some women followed an approach with a *request dance*. This was demonstrated nonverbally by the woman pointing and/or nodding in the direction of the dance floor. Two other categories involving dancing behavior were included in the catalog. *Dance (female acceptance)* was included because by accepting a dance with the man the woman maintained his attention. Another dancing behavior was one of the most frequently seen signals. It was called the *solitary dance* because, while seated or standing, the woman moved her body in time to the music. A typical male response was to request a dance.

Just as a woman, in agreeing to dance with a man, was telling him, nonverbally, that he was acceptable for the moment she also told him so when she allowed him to sit at her table with her. Thus, *point/permission grant* was given a place in the catalog. The woman pulled out the chair for the man or pointed or nodded in the direction of the chair. There was generally a verbal component to the signal which could not be overheard.

Aid solicitation consisted of several behaviors that involved the request of help by the subject. For example, the woman handed her jacket to the man and allowed him to help her put it on. Other patterns in this category included indicating that a drink be refilled, waiting to be seated, or holding a cigarette for lighting.

The final category of solicitation behavior was also a variety of posture patterns. Called *play,* these behaviors consisted of the woman pinching the man, tickling him, sticking out her tongue at him, or approaching him from behind covering his eyes. Some women sat on the man's lap, and several women in the sample came up behind men and stole their hats. All of these behaviors were simply recorded as play behavior.

Validation of the Catalog

Method

Subjects Forty women were covertly observed for the second portion of the study, validation of the catalog. Subjects were judged between the ages of 18 and 35. All subjects were white. Again no systematic examination of background variables was possible.

Procedure To justify the claim that the nonverbal behaviors described above were courtship signals, that is, carried a message of interest to the observing man, women were covertly observed in different social contexts. The four contexts selected for study were a singles' bar, a university snack bar, a university library, and university Women's Center meetings. These contexts were chosen in order to sample a variety of situations in which nonverbal solicitation might be expected to occur as well as situations in which it was unlikely to be exhibited. The selection of contexts was based on information collected through interviews and pilot observations. If nonverbal solicitation was found in situations where male–female interaction was likely but either was not found or occurred in lower frequencies where male–female interactions were impossible, then the immediate function of nonverbal solicitation can be said to be the enhancement of male–female relationships.

The methodology employed in this section was similar to that used in the development of the catalog. Focal individual sampling was the method of choice for the 40 subjects, 10 in each of the 4 contexts. Each subject was randomly selected from those individuals present at the beginning of the observation period. Sessions were scheduled to begin at 9:00 P.M. and end at 11:00 P.M. in the bar context. This time was optimal because crowd density was at its peak. Sessions in the Women's Center context always began at noon or at 7:00 P.M. because that was the time at which programs were scheduled. Observations were randomly made in both the library and the snack bar contexts; for each context, four sessions were conducted at 11:00 A.M., three at 2:00 P.M., and three at 7:00 P.M. Subjects were observed for a period of 1 hour. (Any subject who did not remain for 1 hour of observation was excluded from the analyses.) Observations were conducted using either a concealed audio recorder or, when appropriate, paper and pen. No subject evidenced awareness of being observed. Again, we observed a woman only if she was surrounded by at least 25 other people and if she was not accompanied by a male.

Data for each woman consisted of a frequency measure, the number of nonverbal solicitation behaviors, described above, that she exhibited during the hour of observation. Observers counted not only the total number of nonverbal solicitation behaviors, but also kept a tally of the specific behaviors that were used by each woman.

Results

Frequency and Categorization of Nonverbal Solicitation Behaviors   Data collected on 40 subjects and the respective frequencies of their solicitation displays are given in Table 2. The results show that the emission of the cataloged behaviors was context specific in respect to both the frequency of displays and the number of different categories of the repertoire. The subjects observed in the singles' bar emitted an average of 70.6 displays in the sampled interval, encompassing a mean number of 12.8 different categories of the catalog. In contrast, the corresponding data from the snack bar, library, and women's meetings were 18.6 and 7.5, 9.6 and 4.0, and 4.7 and 2.1, respectively. The asymmetry in display frequency was highly significant ($\chi^2 = 25.079$, df = 3, $p < 0.001$). In addition, the asymmetry in the number of categories utilized was also significant ($\chi^2 = 23.099$, df = 3, $p < 0.001$).

Rate of Display   The quartile display frequencies for the four contexts are given in Figure 1. As can be seen, the display frequency accelerated over time in the singles' bar context but was relatively invariant in the other three contexts.   45

Frequency of Approach   If subjects are pooled across contexts in which males are present and partitioned into high- and low-display categories,

TABLE 2.
Social Context: Display Frequency and Number of Approaches[a]

	Singles' Bar	Snack Bar	Library	Women's Meetings
Number of subjects	10	10	10	10
Total number of displays	706	186	96	47
Mean number of displays	70.6	18.6	9.6	4.7
Mean number of catagories utilized	12.8	7.5	4.0	2.1
Number of approaches to the subject by a male	38	4	4	0
Number of approaches to a male by the subject	11	4	1	0

[a]The tabulated data are for a 60-minute observation interval. Asymmetry in display frequency: $\chi^2 = 25.079$, df = 3, $p < 0.001$; asymmetry in number of categories utilized: $\chi^2 = 23.099$, df = 3, $p < 0.001$.

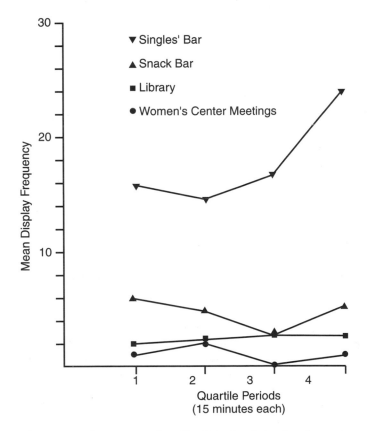

FIGURE 1 Frequency of occurrence for all solicitation behaviors for each quartile of the observation interval for each of the four social contexts.

where the high display category is defined as more than 35 displays per hour, the data show that the high-display subjects elicited greater than 4 approaches per hour, whereas low display subjects elicited less than 0.48 approaches per hour. The number of approaches to subjects by a male in each context is presented in Table 2. Approaches were most frequent in the singles' bar where displays were also most frequent.

For the three contexts in which males were present (the singles' bar, the snack bar, and the library), the number of approaches to the subject was compared to the number of categories employed in solicitation displays. Subjects were pooled across these contexts and divided into two groups—those who utilized less than ten categories and those who employed ten or more categories. The results were highly significant (χ^2 = 12.881, df = 1, $p < 0.025$): regardless of when the woman utilized a high number of categories she was more likely to be approached by a male.

Also given in Table 2 are the figures for female-to-male approaches. In both cases (female to male, and male to female), approaches were much higher in the bar context. To show that the number of male approaches correlated with frequency of female solicitation, Spearman rank correlations[5] were determined for these measures. The correlation between number of male approaches and total number of solicitations, across all three contexts, equaled 0.89 ($p < 0.05$). Clearly, those women who signaled often were also those who were most often approached by a man; and this relationship was not context specific.

Discussion

The results of this study are in no way discoveries of "new" behaviors. The behaviors cataloged here have been described as courtship behaviors by others. But there has been little firm evidence to support this claim of their function, aside from references to context. This study was the first attempt to bring all the behaviors together in catalog form and provide documentation of their function.

When we compare those behaviors contained in the catalog compiled   50
in this study to other descriptions of courtship in humans, we find many areas of congruence. Scheflen (1965) has outlined four categories of heterosexual courtship behavior: courtship readiness, preening behavior, positional cues, and actions of appeal or invitation. Many of the behaviors observed in courting women are similar to those seen by Scheflen during psychotherapy sessions. For example, Scheflen's category of courtship

---

[5]*Spearman rank correlations:* when in a statistical study it is not possible to give actual values to variables, the rank order to instances of each variable is assigned. [Eds.]

readiness bears resemblance to parade behavior. Preening behaviors, as described by Scheflen, are similar to the hair flip, primp, skirt hike, and object caress cataloged here. Positional cues are found in the catalog under leaning, brushing, and caressing or touching signals. Finally, Scheflen's actions of appeal or invitation are included as aid solicitation, point/permission grant, request dance, palm and solitary dance. What appears to be absent in courting women are the qualifiers of the courtship message observed by Scheflen during psychotherapy.

There is significant continuity between the expressions and gestures described in this study and those Givens (1978) believed to be important during the first four phrases of courtship. According to Givens, the essence of the first stage, the attention phase, is ambivalence. Behaviors seen by Givens during this stage and observed in this study include primping, object caressing, and glancing at and then away from the male. During the recognition phase Givens has observed head cocking, pouting, primping, eyebrow flashing and smiling, all of which were seen by me. During the interaction stage, conversation is initiated and the participants appear highly animated. Indeed, women in this study, while talking to men, appeared excited, laughing, smiling, and gesticulating frequently. Givens has indicated that in the fourth stage, the sexual arousal phase, touching gestures are exchanged. Similarly, it was not unusual to see couples hold hands, caress, hug, or kiss after some period of interaction.

Givens' work has indicated that it is often the female who controls interaction in these early phases. The observations of Cary (1976) seem to bear this out and glancing behavior appears to be a significant part of the female role. In this study glancing often took place over a period of time prior to a male approach. As Crook (1972) has stated, males are generally hesitant to approach without some indication of interest from the partner, and repeated eye contact seems to demonstrate that interest. Rejection behaviors were not cataloged here, but it is entirely possible that one way women reject suitors is by failing to recognize their presence through eye contact.

Eibl-Eibesfeldt has also stressed importance of the eye area in two flirting gestures he has observed in several cultures. The first, a rapid raising and lowering of the eyebrows, accompanied by a smile and a nod, was seen rarely in this study. Raised eyebrows were sometimes seen in the bar context and when directed at a man with a quick glance to the dance floor were often followed by a request to dance. Raised eyebrows also sometimes followed comments by a man when he had joined a woman at her table. Eibl-Eibesfeldt (1970) has also presented pictures of women exhibiting what he calls the coy glance. Although the coy glance was sometimes seen in this study (here called the coy smile), it was more usual for a young American woman to use direct eye contact and a full smile. Yet the fact that these behaviors were observed is significant, and later cross-cultural studies may demonstrate that there are more behaviors that share the courtship message.

It appears then that although glancing behaviors were important in signaling interest, initially, other behaviors seemed to reaffirm the woman's interest later in the observation period. Behaviors such as nodding, leaning close to the man, smiling and laughing were seen in higher frequencies after the man had made contact with the woman and was dancing with her or was seated at her table. This accounts for the rise in frequency of solicitation near the end of the observation period in the bar context. Yet it is difficult to make any firm statements about a sequential pattern in the exhibition of solicitation behavior. Although these behaviors are distinct in form, variability among subjects with regard to timing was great. Neither was it possible to determine the potency of particular behaviors. Indeed, it often appeared as though behaviors had a cumulative effect; that is, the man waited to respond to the woman until after he had observed several solicitations.

However, it is clear that there is a constellation of nonverbal behaviors   55
associated with female solicitation that has been recognized by many investigators in several contexts and with similar results (Morris 1971; Kerdon and Feber 1973; Nieremberg and Calero 1973; Clore et al. 1975; Key 1975; Knapp 1978; Lockard and Adams 1980). This is strong circumstantial evidence supporting the current results that these are "real" contextually valid movements, not random behaviors. Furthermore, these expressions and gestures appear to function as attractants and advertisers of female interest.

Traditionally, women have had more control in choosing men for relationships, being able to pace the course of sexual advances and having the prerogative to accept or decline proposals (Hatkoff and Luswell 1977). Nonverbal solicitation is only one of the first steps in the sequence of behaviors beginning with mate attraction and culminating with mate selection. However, these courtship gestures and expressions appear to aid the woman in her role as discriminating chooser. Females are able to determine when and where they wish to survey mate potential by exhibiting or withholding displays. They can elicit a high number of male approaches, allowing them to choose from a number of available men. Or they may direct solicitations at a particular male.

What happens after the approach of a man then becomes increasingly important. Much of the basis of actual choice must rest on what the man says to the woman in addition to his behavior toward her and others. It seems reasonable that females would enhance their fitness by making the most informed judgment possible. Yet before interaction is initiated some initial choice is made. These initial impressions and the selection of those men deemed interesting enough to warrant further attention by a woman have been virtually ignored. If, indeed, the woman is exercising her right to choose, what sort of filter system is she using? Which men are chosen for further interaction and which are rejected? Literature cited earlier indicates that behaviors that indicate status, wealth, and dependability are attributes that women may assess in initial encounters. At present data are not available to address these issues. But I believe that hypotheses regarding the particulars of human female choice can be tested through covert observation of female invitational behavior. Information obtained through observations in field settings can be added to verbal reports. The results of such a venture may present us with a more complete picture of the levels of selection involved in human female choice.

References

Altmann, J. Observational study of behavior: sampling methods. *Behavior* 49: 227–267 (1974).

Baber, R. E. *Marriage and Family.* New York: McGraw-Hill, 1939.

Beach, R. A. Sexual attractivity, proceptivity and receptivity in female mammals. *Hormones and Behavior* 7: 105–138 (1976).

Bertram, B. C. Social factors influencing reproduction in wild lions. *Journal of Zoology* 177: 463–482 (1975).

Beuchner, H. K., Schloeth, R. Ceremonial mating system in Uganda kob (*Adenota kob thomase* Neuman). *Zeitschrift fur Tierpsychologie* 22: 209–225 (1965).

Birdwhistell, R. L. *Kinesics and Context.* Philadelphia: University of Pennsylvania Press, 1970.

Cary, M. S. Talk? Do you want to talk? Negotiation for the initiation of conversation between the unacquainted. Ph.D. dissertation, University of Pennsylvania, 1976.

Clore, G. L., Wiggins, N. H., Itkin, I. Judging attraction from nonverbal behavior: the gain phenomenon. *Journal of Consulting and Clinical Pyschology* 43: 491–497 (1975).

Coombs, R. H., Kenkel, W. F. Sex differences in dating aspirations and satisfaction with computer selected partners. *Journal of Marriage and the Family* 28: 62–66 (1966).

Crook, J. H. Sexual selection, dimorphism, and social organization in primates. In *Sexual Selection and the Descent of Man 1871–1971*, B. Campbell (Ed.). Chicago: Aldine, 1972.

———The socio-ecology of primates. In *Social Behavior in Birds and Mammals: Essays on the Social Ethology of Animals and Man*, J. H. Crook (Ed.). London: Academic, 1972.

Daly, M., Wilson, M. *Sex, Evolution, and Behavior.* North Scituate, MA: Duxbury, 1978.

Davis, F. *Inside Intuition.* New York: McGraw-Hill, 1971.

Doty, R. L. A cry for the liberation of the female rodent: Courtship and copulation in Rodentia. *Psychological Bulletin* 81: 159–172 (1974).

Eibl-Eibesfeldt, I. *Ethology: The Biology of Behavior.* New York: Holt, Rinehart, and Winston, 1970.

———*Love and Hate.* New York: Holt, Rinehart and Winston, 1971.

Fowler, H. F. Female choice: An investigation into human breeding system strategy. Paper presented to Animal Behavior Society, Seattle, June 1978.

Givens, D. The nonverbal basis of attraction: Flirtation, courtship, and seduction. *Psychiatry* 41: 346–359 (1978).

Hatkoff, T. S., Luswell, T. E. Male–female similarities and differences in conceptualizing love. In *Love and Attraction,* M. Cook, G. Wilson (Eds.). Oxford: Pergamon, 1977.

Hinde, R. A. The concept of function. In *Function and Evolution in Behavior,* S. Bariends, C. Beer, and A. Manning (Eds.). Oxford: Clarendon, 1975.

Kendon, A. Some functions of the face in a kissing round. *Semiotica* 15: 299–334 (1975).

———, Ferber, A. A description of some human greetings. In *Comparative Ecology and Behavior of Primates,* R. P. Michael and J. H. Crook (Eds.). London: Academic, 1973.

Key, M. R. *Male/Female Language.* Metuchen, NJ: Scarecrow, 1975.

Knapp, M. L. *Nonverbal Communication in Human Interaction.* New York: Holt, Rinehart, and Winston, 1978.

LeBoeuf, B. J., Peterson, R. S. Social status and mating activity in elephant seals. *Science* 163: 91–93 (1969).

Leuthold, W. Variations in territorial behavior of Uganda kob *Adenota kob thomasi* (Neumann 1896). *Behaviour* 27: 215–258 (1966).

Lockard, J. S., Adams, R. M. Courtship behaviors in public: Different age/sex roles. *Ethology and Sociobiology* 1(3): 245–253 (1980).

McClearn, G. E., Defries, J. C. *Introduction to Behavioral Genetics.* San Francisco: Freeman, 1973.

McGrew, W. C. *An Ethological Study of Children's Behavior.* New York: Academic, 1972.

Mehrabian, A. *Nonverbal Communication.* Chicago: Aldine, 1972.

Morris, D. *Intimate Behavior.* New York: Random House, 1971.

Nadler, R. D. Sexual cyclicity in captive lowland gorillas. *Science* 189: 813–814 (1975).

Nieremberg, G. I., Calero, H. H. *How to Read a Person Like a Book.* New York: Hawthorne, 1973.

Reiss, I. L. Toward a sociology of the heterosexual love relationship. *Marriage and Family Living* 22: 139–145 (1960).

Scheflen, A. E. Quasi-courtship behavior in psychotherapy. *Psychiatry* 28: 245–257 (1965).

Selander, R. K. Sexual selection and dimorphism in birds. In *Sexual Selection and the Descent of Man 1871–1971,* B. Campbell (Ed.). Chicago: Aldine, 1972.

Tavris, C. Men and women report their views on masculinity. *Psychology Today* 10: 34–42 (1977).

Trivers, R. L. Parental investment and sexual selection. In *Sexual Selection and the Descent of Man 1871–1971,* B. Campbell (Ed.). Chicago: Aldine, 1972.

Weber, P. G., Weber, S. P. The effect of female color, size, dominance and early experience upon mate selection in male convict cichlids, *cichlosoma nigrofasciatum Gunther* (pisces, cichlidae). *Behaviour* 56: 116–135 (1975).

Wiley, R. H. Territoriality and nonrandom mating in sage grouse, *Centrocerus urophasiamis. Animal Behavior Monographs* 6: 85–169 (1973).

Williams, G. C. *Sex and Evolution.* Princeton, NJ: Princeton University Press, 1975.

QUESTIONS

1. Which of Moore's observations or conclusions do you find the most interesting or unusual? Explain.

2. The interest of this piece lies in its subject—flirting—which is more frequently treated in popular how-to books and on talk shows. Based on your familiarity with these popular treatments and on your knowledge of the subject through your own observations, how accurate a report do you find Moore's article to be?

3. Moore suggests that different courtship behavior may pertain in other cultures. If you have knowledge of another culture's courtship rituals, explain how they compare with Moore's findings.

4. Moore concludes by suggesting that further study should be made on women's "filter system," meaning how they choose a man for further interaction. She suggests that this can be done through additional "covert observation" (paragraph 57). Do you agree? What would one look for?

5. What does Moore mean when she writes, "It seems reasonable that females would enhance their fitness by making the most informed judgment possible" (paragraph 57)? What sort of "fitness" do you think Moore means?

6. Would it be possible to replicate this experiment by studying courtship behavior in males? Write an essay in which you suggest some of the categories of male courtship behavior that such a study might reveal.

MAKING CONNECTIONS

What similarities in method or substantive findings can you find between Moore's study and Jane van Lawick-Goodall's "First Observations" (p. 260) or Farley Mowat's "Observing Wolves" (p. 256)? Note that Moore presented portions of this article before publication at a meeting of the Animal Behavior Society.

INSIDE DOPE

Marcus Laffey

Marcus Laffey is the pseudonym of Edward C. Conlon, a New York City police officer who has written essays about policing for The New Yorker *since 1997 and is currently working on a book on this subject to be published in 2001. The third generation of his family to join the force (both his father and grandfather were police officers), he is a 1987 graduate of Harvard and didn't expect to find himself in law enforcement. "It kind of took me by surprise," he told an interviewer. "I wanted to give it a shot." When the following essay was published in* The New Yorker *in 1999, the writer was a five-year veteran of the force.*

If there were ever a Super Bowl matchup of junkies versus crackheads, it would be hard to figure which team the odds would favor. Both sides would most likely disappear during halftime. The crackheads would believe that they had won, and the junkies wouldn't care. If they did manage to finish the game, the smartest money would invest in a pawnshop next to the stadium, and within hours the investors would own every Super Bowl ring, for pennies on the dollar. Winners and losers would again be indistinguishable.

The war on drugs is a game for me, no matter how urgent it is for poor neighborhoods or how grave the risks are for cops. We call dealers "players," and there are rules as in chess, percentages as in poker, and moves as in schoolyard ball. When I went from being a beat cop to working in narcotics, the change was refreshing. For one thing, you deal only with criminals. No more domestic disputes, barricaded schizophrenics, or D.O.A.s, the morass of negotiable and nonnegotiable difficulties people have with their neighbors or boyfriends or stepchildren. Patrol cops deal with the fluid whole of people's lives, but usually when the tide's going out: people who have the cops called on them aren't happy to see you; people who call the cops aren't calling when they're having a good time. Now all I do is catch sellers of crack and heroin, and catch their customers to show that they sold it. The parts of their lives unaffected by coca- or opium-based products are none of my business. Patrol is politics, but narcotics is pure technique.

My unit, which consists of half a dozen cops and a sergeant, makes arrests for "observation sales." One or two of us go to an observation post ("the OP," and if you're in it you're "doing OPs") on a rooftop or in a vacant apartment to watch a "set," or drug operation, and transmit information to the "catch car," the unmarked van used to pick up the perps. The set might be a lone teen-ager standing on a corner with one pocket full of crack and another full of cash. Or it might be an organization of such intricate subterfuge—with lookouts, managers, moneymen, steerers (to guide customers), and pitchers (for the hand-to-hand transactions)—that you'd think its purpose was to deliver Soviet microfilm to covert operatives instead of a ten-dollar bag of junk to a junkie. But we watch, and give descriptions of buyers for the catch team to pick up, a few blocks away. Sometimes the dealers send out phantom or dummy buyers—people who appear to have bought narcotics but haven't—to see if they're stopped; we wait until we have a handful of buyers, then move in on the set. Most of the spots that we hit are well established, visited by both customers and cops on a regular basis; others pop up and disappear. You might drive around to see who's out—the faces at the places, the traffic pattern of steady customers and usual suspects. Sometimes you feel like the man on the catwalks over the casino floor, scanning the tables for the sharps and card counters, looking out for luck that's too good to be true. Other times, you feel as if you were watching a nature program, some *National Geographic* special on the felony ecology of the streets.

You read the block, seeing who moves and who stands still, their reactions and relations to one another; you sift the players from the idlers, the buyers from the passersby. Most people occupy their environment blithely, with only a slack and occasional awareness of their surroundings. A store window or a noisy garbage truck night distract them in passing, and they might look around before crossing the street, but the ordinary pedestrian is a poster child for daydreams and tunnel vision. Not so in the narcotics trade, where the body language of buyer and seller alike signals a taut awareness of opportunity and threat. There are distinctive addict walks, such as that of the prowler, who might be new to the spot, or sussing out an operation that has shifted to a more favorable corner. He hovers, alert for the deal, floating like a flake of ash above a fire. The addict on a "mission walk" moves with double-quick footsteps, leaning forward, as if against a strong wind, so as not to waste an extra sound of his already wasted life. A player, on the other hand, has a self-contained watchfulness, a false repose, like a cat sunning itself on a windowsill, eyes half-closed but ready to pounce.

Every street set operates through an odd combination of aggressive 5
marketing and strategic defense, needing simultaneously to broadcast and to deny its function. The young man on the park bench should look like a high-school senior from thirty yards away but has to show he's a merchant at three yards, and he has to have the drugs near enough for convenience but far enough away to be out of his "custody and control" should he be stopped. If he's holding the drugs, he has to have an escape route— through a hole in a fence, say, or into an alley, or into the building where his grandmother lives. The man on the bench is just a man on a bench,

after all, until his context proves him otherwise. But, as you watch, figures emerge from the flow of street life like coördinates on a grid, like pins on a drug map.

Say you're doing OPs from a rooftop, looking down on a street that has three young guys on the corner by the bodega, a couple with a baby in a carriage by the stoop, and a group of old men with brown-bagged brandy bottles by the vacant lot. A man on a bicycle moves in a slow, lazy slalom, up and down the street. The corner boys are the obvious pick, but I have to wait. When a buyer comes, he is easier to recognize, and his arrival on the set sends a signal, a vibration, like a fly landing in the web. The buyer is the bellwether and the bait: he draws the players out and makes them work, prompts them into visible display.

The buyer walks past the old men at the lot, the family on the stoop, to the corner boys, as expected. One corner boy takes the buyer aside and palms his cash, the second stands still, watching up and down the block, and the third goes to the family on the stoop and has a word with the woman with the baby. The woman steps inside the lobby for a few seconds—Thank God, I think, it's not in the carriage—and when she returns she hands something to the third boy, who meets up with the first corner boy and the buyer and hands off the product. The buyer walks away, retracing his route. The man on the bicycle follows him slowly.

I put the buyer over the air: "Hispanic male; red cap; Tommy Hilfiger jacket, blue; bluejeans. South on Third. Be advised, you got a lookout on a bike—white T-shirt, bluejeans, black bike—tailing him to see if he gets picked up. Let him run a couple of blocks, if you can."

Now I have a three-player set, with Mama and corner boys Nos. 1 and 3 down cold. The buyer should be taken, and No. 2 only observed for now. Mama's short time in the building tells me that the stash is not in an apartment but either on her person or right in the lobby, in an unlocked mailbox or a crack in the wall. Corner boy No. 2 is the one to watch, to see if he's the manager or a lookout, up a rank from the others or down. His position will become clear as I watch the group dynamic of the trio— the choreography of who stands where, who talks and who listens, who tells the jokes and who laughs, who's the one that runs to the bodega for the chips and soda. Until he participates in the exchanges, taking money or product, he's legally safe from arrest for an observation sale. If he's a manager, he's the one we want; if he's a smart manager, touching neither cash nor stash, he's the one we're least likely to get. In a sense, everybody wants the spot to get busy: the players grow careless as they get greedy, bringing out more product, paying more heed to the customer and less to us. The manager might have to step in and lend an incriminating hand. When the spot is slow, both groups—the cops and the players—have to be patient.

Even when nothing happens, there is much to interpret. Are they out 10 of product, and will they re-up within ten minutes or an hour? Are they "raised"—afraid we're around—and, if so, is it because they saw our van (unmarked but patently obvious) or saw one of us peering over the roofline, or is it because a patrol car raced by, to a robbery three blocks away? Did they turn away another customer because he wanted credit, or because they thought he was an undercover cop, and were they right? Is the next deal worth the wait?

The wait can be the most trying part of the operation. I've spent hours on tar rooftops, crouched down till my legs cramped, sweating, shivering, wiping the rain from my binoculars every ten seconds. There have been times when I've forgotten to look down before I knelt by the ledge, and settled in beside piles of shit, broken glass, or syringes. On one rooftop, there was an ornate Victorian birdcage, five feet tall, bell-shaped and made of brass, and chained to it, still on a rotten leather leash, was the skeleton of a pit bull. You walk up dirty stairs to a dirty roof to watch a dirty street. At night, even the light is dirty, the sodium-vapor street lights giving off a muddy yellow haze. But sometimes, when something finally does happen, you realize that your concentration is perfect: you feel the cool, neutral thrill of being completely submerged in your task. The objects of surveillance inhabit a living landscape, and you can be struck by the small, random graces of the scene even as you transmit a streak of facts over the radio: "Gray livery cab, buyer in back seat, passenger side, possible white with white sleeves, U-turning now to the left. . . . "

A soap bubble, then two, then dozens rise up in front of me, iridescent, shimmering in their uncertainty. There is a child two floors below me, as rapt with the view above as I am with the view below.

"Arright, we got one, he's beelining to the player, they just popped into the lobby. . . . Now he's out—that's fast, he must have the stash on him. Arright, buyer's walking off now—Hold on, he's just kind of idling across the street. It's not an I-got-my-rock walk. I don't think he got done. Stand by. . . . "

A man standing on another tenement roof whirls an orange flag, and makes it snap like a towel. His flock of pigeons takes flight from the coop with a whoosh like a gust of wind, spiralling out in broadening arcs—showing the smoky gray of their backs as they bank out, the silver-white of their bellies as they circle in—rising up all the while.

"Player's walking off, he sent the last two away, he's out, he's raised, I   15 don't know, but—Go! Go! Go! Hit the set!"

An incinerator chimney shoots out a lash of black smoke, which loops into a lariat before dissolving into the grimy sky.

At the other end of the OP is the catch car. You want a buyer's description, or "scrip," to have something distinctive about it—something beyond the "white T-shirt, bluejeans" of warm weather, "black jacket, bluejeans" of cold. You don't want "Male, walking three pit bulls." You're glad to hear about hot pink and lime green, or T-shirts with legible writing on them, or, even better, "Female in purple-and-yellow tracksuit, with a Cat-in-the-Hat hat, riding a tiny bicycle." For crackheads, as much as for any other species, protective coloration can be a successful evolutionary strategy.

Once you get the scrip and the buyer's direction of flight, you move in, allowing yourself some distance from the set, but not too much, or else the buyer will be home; in neighborhoods like this, people don't have to go far for hard drugs. Sometimes buyers run, and sometimes they fight, and sometimes they toss the drugs (though sometimes you can find those drugs later), and sometimes they eat them when they see you coming. There have been buyers who at the sight of me have reacted with a loss of bowel control, and control of the belly and the bladder as well. The truth is, I am the least of their problems: a night on a cell bench, with prison bologna sandwiches to eat, ranks fairly low amid the hazards of being at the bottom of the criminal food chain.

For crackheads, in particular, a stint as a model prisoner might be a career peak. While the street dealers at dope spots are often junkies themselves, crackheads can't be trusted with the stash—they can't even hold a job whose main requirements are to stand still and watch. The majority of them are figures from a famine: bone-thin and filthy. Months of that life take years from their lives, and thirty-year-olds can pass for fifty, burned out almost literally, with a red-hot core of desperation beneath a dead, charred surface. Junkies generally have a longer ride to the bottom, as the habit gradually slides from being a part of their lives to becoming the point of them. Heroin is purer now than it was in the past, and fewer than half the addicts I arrest have needles on them. They snort it instead of shooting it, which decreases the risk of disease and also seems to slow the forward momentum of addiction. But to me the terminal junkies are especially awful, because they have none of the trapped-rat frenzy of the crackhead; instead, they possess a fatal calm, as if they were keeping their eyes open while drowning. When you collar them, they can have a look of confirmed and somewhat contented self-hatred, as if the world were doing to them what they expect and deserve.

Addicts deserve pity, always, though often they inspire contempt. We   20
collared one crackhead, bumping into him by accident as he stood in a project lobby counting out a handful of vials. He was a street peddler who sold clothing, and had about eighty dollars in his pocket. He had the shrink-wrapped look that crackheads get, as if his skin were two sizes too small. He moaned and wept for his infant child, who would starve, he said, without his support. Yes, he acknowledged, the baby lived with its mother, but he was the provider. The mother and child were only about ten blocks away, at a playground, so we drove to meet them. The mother was a pretty, well-dressed woman, though her soccer-mom wholesomeness may have been artificially heightened by the presence of her handcuffed mate. We called her over, and her look of mild confusion became one of mild dismay as she saw our back-seat passenger. She didn't look surprised, and didn't ask questions. He took out his wad of cash, peeled off four dollars, and handed it to me to give to her. "You gotta be kidding me," I said. "You give me all this father-of-the-year shit, just to throw her four bucks?"

"C'mon," he said. "When you get out of Central Booking, you're hungry, you want some real McDonald's or something."

I gave him back the four dollars and took the wad for the mother. "The Number Two Special, two cheeseburgers and fries, is three-twenty-nine," I told him. "It's what I get, and it's all you can afford." For an addict, the priorities are never unclear.

After you've collared the buyers, it's time to move in on the dealers. When you hit a set, there is always a charge of adrenaline, arising from the jungle-war vagaries of opponent and terrain. There are elusive adversaries, explosive ones, and lots of sitting ducks. Some dealers opt for a businesslike capitulation, aware that it's the way to go through the process with the least fuss. Others, especially lobby dealers with access to an apartment upstairs, tend to make a mad dash for freedom. The bust could be a surrender as slow and dignified as Lee's at Appomattox or it could be bedlam—roiling bodies and airborne stash. When you can't count the evidence at the scene, you have to at least control it—the hundreds of dollars in small bills, the fistfuls of crack slabs, the loose decks, the bundles of dope—so you jam it in your pockets like a handful of ball bearings, and all the while there may be a crowd screaming, or perps for whom the fight-or-flight reflex is not a simple either-or proposition.

The smarter dealers carry nothing on them, but you await information from the OP, sometimes with a distaste that verges on dread:

"It's in his sock."

"It's in the cast on his right hand—"

25

"It's in his cheek—sorry, guy, the other cheek. I mean, check between 'em, you copy?"

Stash can be hidden under a bottle cap or in a potato-chip bag, or strewn among heaps of noncriminal trash; it can be wedged in a light fixture in a hall or tucked inside the bumper of a car; it can be in a magnetic key case stuck to the iron bolt beneath a park bench; or it can be on a string taped to the wall and dangling down the garbage-disposal chute. A thorough search can lead to unexpected threats and rewards. Once, when I was rooting through a janitor's closet in a housing project after hitting a heroin set, I found a machine gun in the bottom of a bag of clothes. We continued to search the building and found more than a thousand dollars' worth of heroin, two more guns—a 9-mm. handgun and a .45 revolver—and also ammunition for another machine gun, an AK-47: copper-jacketed bullets more than two inches long, coming to a sharp, conical point like a dunce cap. An AK-47 can discharge bullets at a speed of more than two thousand feet per second, which would allow them to pass through my vest with barely a pause.

In the movies, there are a lot of drug-dealer villains, but those characters usually have to slap their girlfriends or kill a lot of cops to heighten the dramatic point of their bad-guyness. Because the victims of drug sales line up and pay, so to speak, for the privilege, the perpetrators don't have the forthright menace of violent felons. But most of the players I collar have a rap sheet that shows a more diversified criminal career—of earlier forays into robbery or theft—before they settled on the more lucrative and "less illegal" world of drug sales. And although some drug spots operate in a fairly quiet, orderly manner, as if a man were selling newspapers on the street, or a couple were running a catalogue business out of their apartment, most are established and maintained by means of assault, murder, and many subtler thefts of human dignity.

In New York, heroin dealers stamp brand names on the little wax-paper envelopes in which the drug is packaged. This practice gives a glimpse not only of a corporate structure, when the same brands appear in different sites, but also of a corporate imagination, showing what they believe their product should mean to their customers. Some convey the blandly generic aspiration of quality—"First Class," "President," "Original"—that you might find on brands of cornflakes or of detergent in some discount supermarket. Others go for a racier allure, but the gimmick is so hackneyed in conventional advertising that the genuinely illicit thrill of "Knockout" or "No Limit" suggests the mock-illicit thrill of ads for perfume or fat-free ice cream. Topical references are common, from the flat-out copyright infringement of "DKNY" or "Ford" to the movie tagline "Show Me the Money." But the best brand names are the literal ones, which announce without apology the bad things to come: "911," "25 to Life," "Undertaker," "Fuck You." There is a suicidal candor to "Lethal Injection" and "Virus," a forthright finality to "O.D."—a truth in advertising here that few products can match.

Recently, I had a talk with one of my informants, a junkie with AIDS who sleeps in an alley. A few days before, I'd obtained a search warrant for a spot he visits several times a day, and he fervently wished me luck with the warrant's execution. That my success would cause him inconvenience in supplying his own habit was a mild irony that did not trouble him. He said, "I know you're a cop and I'm—" and there was a sliver of space before his next word, enough for me to wonder what term he might use for a shorthand self-portrait. And, knowing that there would be a measure of harsh truth in it, I was still surprised, and even felt sorry for him, when he said, "And I'm a fucking scumbag." But he was equally firm in his opinion of those who had benefitted from his self-destruction: "I done time, I'm no hero, but these people are blood-suckers. Them and rapists are as bad as people get. Those people are worse than rapists. Those dealers will suck you dry. I hope you get every last one of them."

Every day, we go out and hunt people. When we do well—picking off the customers with dispatch, swooping in on the dealers, taking trophies of their product and profit—we feel skilled and lucky at once, at the top of our game. We have shut down spots, reduced robberies and shootings, made whole blocks cleaner, safer, saner places. But other spots withstand daily assaults from us with negligible losses, and I've driven home after a twenty-hour day only to recognize, with the hallucinatory clarity of the sleep-deprived, the same man, on the same mission walk, that I'd collared the night before. Typically, buyers spend a night in jail and are sentenced to a few days of community service. Players might get less, odd as that may

30

seem, if there weren't enough transactions in open view, or if no stash was recovered. We'll all meet again, soon enough. There are breaks and interruptions, retirements and replacements, but, no matter how often the whistle blows, the game is never over.

QUESTIONS

1. The conceptual metaphor which undergirds Laffey's essay is summed up in the first words of the second paragraph: "The war on drugs is a game for me." This idea of a *game* frames the essay's beginning and end, and serves as an explanatory context for some of his incidental comments throughout (for instance, "the cool, neutral thrill of being completely submerged in your task" recalls the intensity of athletic performance). What other connections to a *game* can you find in the essay? Based on your reading of the essay, does this seem to be a valid comparison to make? Explain. What does the author gain? What is the purpose of positing such a vivid metaphor?
2. How does Laffey convey the repetitive quality of his work? Does calling it a *game* rather than a *war* convey a sense of futility? Explain.
3. At the beginning of paragraph 4, Laffey says that "You read the block"—how exactly does his job resemble "reading"? In your own experience, what techniques of reading could be applied in such a pursuit?
4. At some points in the essay, the telling is interrupted by almost lyrical description (for example, when the "flock of pigeons takes flight from the coop with a whoosh like a gust of wind"). What effect does this have on the reader? Have you ever used this kind of descriptive interruption in your own personal essays?
5. Why do you think Laffey frequently shifts between the impersonal, hypothetical "you" ("Say you're doing OPs from a rooftop") and his autobiographical "I" ("I have to wait")? Compose a paragraph about a typical classroom experience which begins by referring to "you" but then narrows its focus to "I" by the end.
6. Write your own account of a job that you have held. Use the framework of a "typical day" to structure your essay. As the narrative proceeds, move beyond reporting what you do, and include moments of reflective explanation to clarify particular aspects of your job.

MAKING CONNECTIONS

Laffey offers his readers closely observed details of the narcotics beat. Look at the techniques other essayists use—Theodore Sizer (p. 348) or George Orwell (p. 132), for instance—to understand how writers frame their interpretations from the evidence they present.

CONSTRUCTIONS AND RECONSTRUCTIONS OF THE SELF IN VIRTUAL REALITY

Sherry Turkle

Born in 1948 in New York City, Sherry Turkle received a joint doctorate in sociology and personality psychology from Harvard in 1976. A licensed psychologist and a professor at the Massachusetts Institute of Technology, Turkle writes frequently about the cultural aspects of psychoanalysis and about the human relationship to technology—particularly computers. In addition to scholarly works, she has published several best-selling books aimed at a more popular audience, including The Second Self: Computers and the Human Spirit *(1984) and, most recently,* Life on the Screen: Identity in the Age of the Internet *(1995). Turkle has also been interviewed widely, both in print and on television, about the psychological and personality effects of computer use. The following essay, originally published in the journal* Media/Identity/Culture, *focuses on one of her most closely studied subjects: online role-playing games.*

1. Identity Workshops

In an interactive computer game designed to represent a world inspired by the television series *Star Trek: The Next Generation,* over a thousand players spend up to 80 hours a week participating in intergalactic exploration and wars. They create characters who have casual and romantic sex, who fall in love and get married, who attend rituals and celebrations. "This is more real than my real life," says a character who turns out to be a man playing a woman who is pretending to be a man. In this game, the rules of social interaction are built, not received.

In another, more loosely structured game, each player creates a character of several characters, specifying their genders and other physical and psychological attributes. The characters need not be human and there are more than two genders. All interactions take place "in character." Beyond this, players are invited to help build the computer world itself. Using a relatively simple programming language, they can make a "room" in the game space where they can set the stage and define the rules. That is, they make objects in the computer world and specify how they work. Rachel, an eleven-year-old, built a room she calls "the condo." It has jewelry boxes containing magical pieces that transport her to different places and moments in history. When Rachel visits the condo, she invites her friends, she chats, orders pizza, and flirts. Other players built TVs showing scenes taking place in the rooms of the game, a transportation system to navigate the space, and a magical theater that replays past game events. Some have built robots: a program named "Julia," for example, "pretends" to be a person as she offers directions and helps to locate your friends.

Both worlds exist on international computer networks, which of course means that in a certain sense, a physical sense, they don't exist at all.

The first game, Trek Muse, and the second, LambdaMoo, are examples of a class of virtual worlds known as MUDs—an acronym for "Multi-User Dungeons." In the early 1970s, a role-playing game called Dungeons and Dragons swept the game cultures, a game in which a "dungeon master" who created a world in which people created characters and played out complex adventures. Several years later, Dungeons and Dragons was interpreted for computational space in a program called Adventure. There, players proceeded through a maze that was presented to them through text description on a computer screen. The term "dungeon" has persisted in both the games and high-tech culture, and in the case of MUDs, refers to a virtual social space that exists on a machine.

As of fall 1992, there were 207 multi-user games based on thirteen different kinds of software on the international computer network known as the Internet. Here I use the term "MUD" to refer to all the various kinds. All provide worlds for social interaction in a virtual space, worlds in which you can present yourself as a "character," in which you can be anonymous, in which you can play a role as close or as far away from your "real self" as you choose. Where they differ is in how constrained that world is. It can be built around a medieval fantasy landscape in which there are dragons to slay and gold coins and magical amulets to collect, or it can be a relatively open space in which you can play at whatever captures your imagination, both by playing a role and by participating in building a world.

In the MUDs, the projections of self are engaged in a resolutely postmodern context. There are parallel narratives in the different rooms of the MUD; one can move forward or backward in time. The cultures of Tolkien, Gibson, and Madonna coexist and interact. Authorship is not only displaced from a solitary voice, it is exploded. The MUDs are authored by their players, thousands of people in all, often hundreds of people at a time, all logged on from different places. And the self is not only decentered but multiplied without limit. There is an unparalleled opportunity to play with one's identity and to "try out" new ones.

My past research into the experiences of individuals working with computers has led me to underscore the power of this technology not only as a medium for getting things done but for thinking through and working

5

through personal concerns. It was a fifth grader I interviewed, Deborah, who inspired me to use the phrase "the second self" to capture this aspect of the computer's evocative power when she told me that "when you program a computer you put a little piece of your mind into the computer's mind and now you can see it. . . . And you can see the things you think and change them around."

Deborah made her remark after an experience with programming that did indeed change how she saw herself. At the time Deborah first met the computer, she was eleven and was already involved with a crowd that was drinking, smoking, and using drugs. When she was shown how to use the computer to draw by giving commands to a screen icon she was resistant and hostile. Insecure about herself, she refused to do anything with the computer on her own.

A breakthrough came when Deborah decided to restrict the commands she could give to the computer. She made a rule that she would allow herself only one turning command—a right turn of 30 degrees. Once she had her rule, Deborah got down to serious work. She drew flowers and rabbits and stars and abstract designs, everything built up from right turns of 30 degrees.

Before she met the computer Deborah didn't think about her 10 problems—with food, with truancy, with tantrums, with drugs—in terms of control. She thought that other people were good and she was "naturally bad." Her computer experience provided categories more useful to her than good or bad: things could be in or out of control. The 30 degrees world not only suggested that control was an issue, it presented a strategy for dealing with one's lack of control in the world at large: make a rule, make a safe place, experiment within it.

Deborah presents a dramatic example of how technology can enter into the construction of identity. Her encounter with the computer took place at the moment of adolescence but, of course, no handle cranks or gear turns to graduate us from dealing with issues of identity after we pass through adolescence. Engagement with computational technology facilitates a series of "second chances" for adults to work and rework unresolved personal issues and more generally, to think through questions about the nature of self, including questions about definitions of life, intentionality, and intelligence.

What is true of individuals working alone with a computer is raised to a higher power when people use computers to communicate with other people as they do on the MUDs. In the first case, the person alone with the computer, I have found that individuals use computers to work through identity issues that center around control and mastery; in the second, where the computer is used as a communications medium, there is more room to use the control provided by the computer to develop a greater capacity for collaboration and even intimacy. The medium enables the self to explore a social context as well as to reflect on its own nature and powers.

This essay explores constructions and reconstructions of identity in MUD environments. My method of investigation has been ethnographic and clinical: play the games, "hang out" with game players in virtual as well as real space, interview game players in person both individually and in groups. Some of my richest data came from a series of weekly "pizza parties" for MUD-ers within the Boston area. There the topic was open and conversation turned to what was on the players' minds: most often love, romance, and what can be counted on as real in virtual space.

I begin my report from this new social and psychological world by taking one step back to general considerations of how role-playing games enable people to work through issues of identity and then move on to the form this takes in MUDs which enhance the evocative potential of traditional games by further blurring the line between the game and what players refer to as TRW, or the real world.

Traditional role-playing prompts reflection on personal and interpersonal issues, but in games that take place in ongoing virtual societies such as MUDs, the focus is on larger social and cultural themes as well. The networked computer serves as an "evocative object" for thinking about community. Additionally, people playing in the MUDs struggle towards a new, still tentative, discourse about the nature of a community that is populated both by people and by programs that are social actors. In this, life in the MUD may serve as a harbinger of what is to come in the social spaces that we still contrast with the virtual by calling them "real."

2. Role-Playing Games

As identity workshops, MUDs have much in common with traditional role-playing games. For example: the role-playing games played by Julee, a nineteen-year-old who has dropped out of Yale after her freshmen year. Part of the reason for her leaving college is that she is in an increasingly turbulent relationship with her mother, a devout Catholic, who turned away from her daughter when she discovered that she had had an abortion the summer before beginning college.

From Julee's point of view, her mother has chosen to deny her existence. When asked about her most important experience in role-playing games, Julee described a game in which she had been assigned to play a mother facing a conflict with her daughter. Indeed, in the game, the script says that the daughter is going to betray, even kill, the mother.

In the role-playing game, played over a weekend on the Boston University campus, Julee and her "daughter" talked for hours: why might the daughter have joined her mother's opponents, how could they stay true to their relationship and the game as it had been written? Huddled in a corner of an empty Boston University classroom, Julee was having the conversation that her mother had not been willing to have with her. In the end, Julee's character chose to ignore her loyalty to her team in order to preserve her daughter's life.

Clearly, Julee projected feelings about her "real" mother's choice onto her experience of the game, but more was going on than a simple reenactment. Julee was able to reexperience a familiar situation in a setting where she could examine it, do something new with it, and revise her relationship towards it. In many ways, what happened was resonant with the psychoanalytic notion of "working through."

Julee's experience stands in contrast to images of role-playing games 20
that are prevalent in the popular culture. A first popular image portrays role-playing games as depressing and dangerous environments. It is captured in the urban legend which describes an emotionally troubled student disappearing and committing suicide during a game of Dungeons and Dragons. Another popular image, and one that has been supported by some academic writing on role-playing games, turns them into places of escape. Players are seen as leaving their "real" lives and problems behind to lose themselves in the game space. Julee's story belies both stereotypes. For her, the game is psychologically constructive rather than destructive. And she uses it not for escape but as a vehicle for engaging in a significant dialogue with important events and relationships in her "real" life.

Role-playing games are able to serve in this evocative capacity precisely because they are not simple escapes from the real to the unreal, but because they stand betwixt and between, both in the not in real life. But in the final analysis, what puts Julee's game most firmly in the category of game is that it had an end point. The weekend was over and so was the game.

MUDs present a far more complicated case. In a certain sense, they don't have to end. Their boundaries are more fuzzy; the routine of playing them becomes part of their players' real lives. The virtual reality becomes not so much an alternative as a parallel life. Indeed, dedicated players who work with computers all day describe how they temporarily put their characters to "sleep," remain logged on to the game, pursue other activities, and periodically return to the game space.

Such blurring of boundaries between role and self presents new opportunities to use the role to work on the self. As one experienced player put it, "You are the character and you are not the character both at the same time," and "you are who you pretend to be." This ambiguity contributes to the games' ability to be a place in which to address issues of identity and intimacy. They take the possibilities that Julee found in role-playing games and raise them to a higher power.

3. Virtual Realities: Role-Playing to a Higher Power

The notion "you are who you pretend to be" has a mythic resonance. The Pygmalion story endures because it speaks to a powerful fantasy: that we are not limited by our histories, that we can be re-created or can re-create ourselves. In the real world, we are thrilled by stories of self-transformation. Madonna is our modern Eliza Doolittle; Ivana Trump is the object of morbid fascination. But, of course, for most people such re-creations of self are difficult. Virtual worlds provide environments for experiences that may be hard to come by in the real.

Not the least of these experiences is the opportunity to play an "aspect   25
of yourself" that you embody as a separate self in the game space.

Peter is a twenty-three-year-old physics graduate student at the University of Massachusetts. His life revolves around his work in the laboratory and his plans for a life in science. He says that his only friend is his roommate, another student whom he describes as being even more reclusive than he. This circumscribed, almost monastic, life does not represent a radical departure for Peter. He has had heart trouble since he was a child; his health is delicate, one small rebellion, a ski trip when he first came up to Boston, put him in the hospital for three weeks. His response has been to circumscribe his world. Peter has never traveled. He lives within a small compass.

In an interview, Peter immediately made it clear why he plays on MUDs: "I do it so I can talk to people." He is logged on for at least 40 hours a week, but it is hard to call what he does "playing a game." He spends his time on the MUDs constructing a life that (in only a seeming paradox) is more expansive than his own. He tells me with delight that the MUD he frequents most often is physically located on a computer in Germany.

```
And I started talking to them [the inhabitants of
the MUD] and they're like, "This costs so many and
so many Deutschmarks." And I'm like, "what are
Deutschmarks? Where is this place located?" And
they say" "Don't you know, this is Germany."
```

It is from MUDs that Peter has learned what he knows of politics, of economics, of the difference between capitalism and welfare-state socialism. He revels in the differences between the styles of Americans and Europeans on the MUDs and in the thrill of speaking to a player in Norway who can see the Northern lights.

On the MUD, Peter shapes a character, Achilles, who is his ideal self. Life in a University of Massachusetts dorm has put him in modest and unaesthetic circumstances. Yet the room he inhabits on the MUD is elegant, romantic, out of a Ralph Lauren ad.

Peter's story illustrates several aspects of the relationship of MUD-ing   30
and identity. First, the MUD serves as a kind of Rorschach inkblot, a projection of fantasy. Second, unlike a Rorschach, it does not stay on a page. It is part of Peter's everyday life. Beyond expanding his social reach, MUDs have brought Peter the only romance and intimacy he has ever known. At a social event held in virtual space, a "wedding" of two regular players on this favorite Germany-based MUD, Peter met Winterlight, one of the three

female players. Peter who has known little success with women, was able to charm this most desirable and sought-after player. Their encounter led to a courtship in which he was tender and romantic, chivalrous and poetic. One is reminded of Cyrano who could only find his voice through another's persona. It is Achilles, Peter's character on the MUD, who can create the magic and win the girl.

While Deborah's experience of technology and the self (where she was one-on-one with the computer) centered on issues of identity that were centered around control and mastery, Peter's experience (where the computer is a mediator to a reality shared with other people) has put computation more directly in the service of the development of a greater capacity for friendship, the development of confidence for a greater capacity for intimacy.

But what of the contrast between Peter and Julee? What can we say about the difference between role-playing games in the corridors of Boston University and on computer virtual worlds?

Julee and Peter both appropriate games to remake the self. Their games, however, are evocative for different reasons. Julee's role-playing has the powerful quality of real-time psychodrama, but, on the other hand, Peter's game is ongoing and provides him with anonymity, invisibility, and potential multiplicity. Ongoing: he can play it as much as he wants, all day if he wants, every day if he chooses as he often does. There are always people logged on to the game; there is always someone to talk to or something to do. Anonymous: once Peter creates his character, that is his only identity on the game. His character need not have his gender or share any recognizable feature with him. He can be who he wants and play with no concern that *he*, Peter, will be held accountable in "real life" for his character's actions, quarrels, or relationships. The degree to which he brings the game into his real life is his choice. Invisible: the created character can have any physical description and will be responded to as a function of that description. The plain can experience the self-presentation of great beauty; the nerdy can be elegant; the obese can be slender. Multiplicity: Peter can create several characters, playing out and playing with different aspects of his self. An ongoing game, anonymous personae, physical invisibility, and the possibility to be not one but many, these are the qualities at the root of the holding power and evocative potential of MUDs as "identity workshops." Faced with the notion that "you are what you pretend to be," Peter can only hope that it is true, for he is playing his ideal self.

Peter plays what in the psychoanalytic tradition would be called an "ego ideal." Other players create a character or multiple characters that are closer to embodying aspects of themselves that they hate or fear or perhaps have not ever consciously confronted before. One male player describes his role-playing as "daring to be passive. I don't mean in having sex on the MUD. I mean in letting other people take the initiative in friendships, in not feeling when I am in character that I need to control everything. My mother controlled my whole family, well, certainly me. So I grew up thinking 'never again.' My 'real life' is exhausting that way. On MUDs I do something else. I didn't even realize this connection to my mother until something happened in the game and somebody tried to boss my pretty laid-back character around and I went crazy. And then I saw what I was doing."

The power of the medium as a material for the projection of aspects of 35 both conscious and unconscious aspects of the self suggests an analogy between MUDs and psychotherapeutic milieus. The goal of psychotherapy is not, of course, simply to provide a place for "acting out" behavior that expresses one's conflicts, but to furnish a contained and confidential environment for "working through" unresolved issues. The distinction between acting out and working through is crucial to thinking about MUDs as settings for personal growth. For it is in the context of this distinction that the much-discussed issue of "MUDs addiction" should be situated. The accusation of being "addicted" to psychotherapy is only made seriously when friends or family suspect that over a period of time, the therapy is supporting repetitions and reenactments rather than new resolutions. MUD-ing is no more "addictive" than therapy when it works as a pathway to psychological growth.

Robert was a college freshman who in the months before beginning college had to cope with his father's having lost his job and disgracing his family because of alcoholism. The job loss led to his parents' relocation to another part of the country, far away from all of Robert's friends. For a period of several months, Robert, now at college, MUD-ed over 80 hours a week. Around the time of a fire in his dormitory which destroyed all his possessions, Robert was playing over 120 hours a week, sleeping four hours a night, and only taking brief breaks to get food, which he would eat while playing.

At the end of the school year, however, Robert's MUD experience was essentially over. He had gotten his own apartment; he had a job as a salesman; he had formed a rock band with a few friends. Looking back on the experience he thought that MUD-ing had served its purpose: it kept him from what he called his "suicidal thoughts," in essence by keeping him too busy to have them; it kept him from drinking ("I have something more fun and safe to do"); it enabled him to function with responsibility and competency as a highly placed administrator; it afforded an emotional environment where he could be in complete control of how much he revealed about his life, about his parents, even about something as simple for other people as where he was from. In sum, MUDs had provided what Erik Erikson called a "psychosocial moratorium." It had been a place from which he could reassemble a sense of boundaries that enabled him to pursue less bounded relationships.

MUDs are a context for constructions and reconstructions of identity; they are also a context for reflecting on old notions of identity itself. Through contemporary psychoanalytic theory which stresses the decentered subject and through the fragmented selves presented by patients (and most dramatically the increasing numbers of patients who present with multiple personality), psychology confronts the ways in which any unitary notion of identity is problematic and probably illusory. What is the self when it functions as a society? What is the self when it divides its labor among its constituent "altars" or "avatars"? Those burdened by posttraumatic dissociative syndrome suffer the question; inhabitants of MUDs play with it.

These remarks have addressed MUDs as privileged spaces for thinking through and working through issues of personal identity. Additionally, when role-playing moves onto a sustained virtual space there is an attendant growth of a highly structured social world. The development of these virtual cultures is of signal importance: it makes MUDs very special kinds of evocative objects.

4. Evocative Objects: Gender, Actants, and "Bots"

In *The Second Self* I called the personal computer an evocative object   40
because it provoked self-reflection and stimulated thought. It led to reevaluations and reconsiderations of things taken for granted, for example, about the nature of intelligence, free will, and our notions of what is alive. And I found that the computer did this not just because it presented people with ideas as did traditional philosophy, but because it presented them with experiences, an ongoing culture of personal computing that provoked a new philosophy in everyday life.

The same kind of process, this provocation of new discourse and reflection, is taking place around computer-mediated communications in virtual realities such as MUDs. But the emphasis of the new discourse and reflection is on social and cultural issues as well as individual ones.

One dramatic example is the novel and compelling discourses that surrounds the experience of "gender swapping" in virtual reality. In the MUDs, men may play the roles of women and women the roles of men, a common practice known as "gender swapping." As MUD players talked to me about their experiences with gender swapping, they certainly gave me reason to believe that through this practice they were working through personal issues that had to do with accepting the "feminine" and/or the "masculine" in their own personalities. But they were doing something else as well which transcended the level of individual personality and its dynamics. People were using gender swapping as a first-hand experience through which to form ideas about the role of gender in human interactions. In the ongoing culture of MUDs, these issues are discussed both within the space of the games and in a discussion group on USENET called "rec.games.mud."

Discussion on USENET about gender swapping has dealt with how female characters are besieged with attention, sexual advances, and unrequested offers of assistance which imply that women can't do things by themselves. It has dealt with the question of whether women who are consistently treated as incompetent may start to believe it. Men playing women in role-playing games have remarked that other male players (read: male characters) sometimes expect sexual favors in return for technical assistance. In this case, offering technical help, like picking up the check at dinner, is being used to purchase rather than win a woman's regard. While such expectations can be subtly expressed, indeed sometimes overlooked in real life, when such things happen in MUDs, they are more visible, often widely witnessed, and openly discussed. As this takes place, the MUD becomes an evocative object for a richer understanding not only of sexual harassment but of the social construction of gender.

MUD-ing throws issues of the impact of gender on human relations into high relief and brings the issue home; the seriousness and intensity of discussions of gender among MUD-ers speaks to the fact that the game allows its players to experience rather than merely observe what it feels like to be the opposite gender or to have no gender at all.

MUDs are evocative objects for thinking about gender, but there are 45 similar stories to tell about discussions in MUD environments about violence, property, and privacy. Virtual communities compel conversations about the nature of community itself.

On a MUD known as Habitat, which ran as an experiment in the United States and has become a successful commercial venture in Japan, players were originally allowed to have guns. However, when you are shot, you do not cease to exist but simply lose all the things you were carrying and are transported back to your virtual home. For some players, thievery and murder became the highlight of the "game." For others, these activities were experienced as a violent intrusion on their peaceful world. An intense debate ensued.

Some players argued that guns should be eliminated; unlike in the real world, a perfect gun ban is possible with a few lines of code. Others argued that what was damaging was not the violence but the trivialization of violence, and maintained that guns should persist, but their consequences should be made more real: when you are killed, your character should cease to exist and not simply be sent home. Still others believed that since Habitat was "just a game," and playing assassin was part of the fun, there could be no harm in a little virtual violence.

As the debate raged, a player who was a priest in real life founded the "Order of the Holy Walnut" whose members pledged not to carry guns. In the end, the game designers divided the world into two parts: in town, violence was prohibited. In the wilds outside of town, it was allowed. Eventually a democratic voting process was installed and a sheriff elected. Debates then ensued about the nature of Habitat laws and the proper balance between individual freedom and law and order. What is remarkable is not just the solution, but the quality of the debate which led up to that solution. The denizens of Habitat were spending their leisure time debating pacifism, the nature of good government, and the relationships between representations and reality.

Virtual reality is not "real," but it has a relationship to the real. By being betwixt and between, it becomes a play space for thinking about the real world. It is an exemplary evocative object.

When a technology serves as an evocative object, old questions are raised in new contexts and there is an opportunity for fresh resolutions. I conclude with another example of how MUDs are able to recast a set of philosophical questions about personhood and program. People regularly use experiences in computer environments to think through and, in some cases, rework their definitions of personhood, agency, the meaning of the "I." 50

When in the context of "traditional" computation, people meet a program that exhibits some behavior that would be considered intelligent if done by a person, they often grant the program a "sort of" intelligence, indeed a "sort of" life, but then insist that what the essence of human intelligence or indeed of human uniqueness is what "the computer cannot do." Computers cannot have intentions, feelings, the sense of an "I."

In MUDs, however, intelligent computational entities are present in a new context which gives questions about their status a new urgency and saliency. Some of the inhabitants of these virtual worlds are artificial intelligences, robots, affectionately referred to as "bots," which have been built by enterprising players. When you wander about in a MUD, you find yourself in conversations with them, you find yourself asking them for directions, thanking them for being helpful, ordering drinks from them at a virtual bar, telling them a joke. And you find yourself doing all of these things before you know that they are not people but "things." (Of course, you may be a person "playing" the role "an intelligent Batmobile" or "a swarm of bees.") The "thingness" of the bots is not part of your initial encounter or the establishment of your relationship with them. You have unintentionally played out a Turing test in which the program has won.

Reaction to such experiences is strong, much of it still centered on the question of human uniqueness and "whether a program can be an 'I'." (For example, within the Narrative Intelligence discussion group on the Internet, there is heated and ongoing debate about bots and the question of the "I." In this debate, sophisticated programmers of and players in virtual worlds have admitted to being nonplused when they first realized that they had unknowingly participated in casual social conversation with "artificial intelligences," or AIs.) But there is another discourse as well, marked by two new themes.

First, instead of dwelling on the essence of "bots," conversation among MUD-ers about programs inhabiting virtual space turns to the ethics of whether "they" should or should not announce their artificiality. This discussion of full disclosure is taking place in the context of a virtual world where changing gender, race, and species is the norm. With people playing robots, there is a new level of self-consciousness about the asymmetry of demanding that robots not play people.

In the film *Blade Runner* sophisticated androids almost indistinguish-   55
able from humans have been given the final defining human qualities: childhood memories and the knowledge of their mortality. This is a world
obsessed with the Turing test; the film's hero, Decker, makes his profession
diagnosing the real from the artificial. But by the end, Decker who has spent
his life tracking down and destroying robots is less concerned with whether
he is dealing with an artificial being and more concerned with how to thank
one of them for saving his life and how to escape with another of them with
whom he has fallen in love. This character becomes a representation of a
more widespread ambiguity about notions of real and not real that do not
follow from a priori essences but emerge from ongoing relationships.

In this spirit, I note that the second theme of the new discourse on the
bots turns away from discussion of their essence and towards the most
practical matters of how the AIs function within the community: are they
disruptive or facilitating, are they rude or are they kind? In this sense,
MUDs may be harbingers of the discourse about the artificial in a post-
Turing test world.

There is a lot of excitement about virtual reality. In both the popular
and academic press, there is enthusiasm and high expectation for a future
in which we don gloves and masks and bodysuits, and explore virtual
space and sensuality. However, from a point of view centered on the evolution of our sense of self and self-definition, there is reason to feel great excitement about where we are in the present. In the text-based virtual
realities that exist today, people are exploring, constructing, and reconstructing their identities. They are doing this in an environment infused
with a postmodern ethos of the value of multiple identities and of playing
out aspects of the self and with a constructionist ethos of "Build something, be someone." And they are creating communities that have become
privileged contexts for thinking about social, cultural, and ethical dilemmas of living in constructed lives that we share with extensions of ourselves
that we have embodied in a program.

Watch for a nascent culture of virtual reality that is paradoxically a
culture of the concrete, placing new saliency on the notion that we construct gender and that we become what we play, argue about, and build.
And watch for a culture that leaves a new amount of space for the idea that
he or she who plays, argues, and builds is a machine.

QUESTIONS

1. One of Turkle's main methods of explanation relies on presenting anecdotes—whether of individuals (Deborah, Julee, Peter, Robert) or
   groups (different examples of MUDs)—as being representative of
   larger themes and issues. What are the strengths and weaknesses of
   anecdotes as evidence? Have you ever made an appeal to anecdotal evi-

dence in your own writing? Describe how you used anecdotal evidence to support your viewpoint.

2. Perhaps the central presupposition made by Turkle in this essay is that there is in fact "an analogy between MUDs and psychotherapeutic milieus," for this allows her to make the claim that MUDs provide an environment for "'working through' unresolved issues" similar to that found in psychotherapy. Is this a fair analogy to make? Why, or why not? Where does the analogy fail to hold, and what consequences does this have for her argument?

3. Turkle cites "the notion that we construct gender," a notion which can be explored through role-playing games because of their ability to provide "anonymity, invisibility, and potential multiplicity" for someone like Peter. Use some of her own evidence to counter this idea that gender is merely "constructed"?

4. Create a kind of "technical dictionary" for some of the phrases Turkle uses: "second self," "betwixt and between," "identity workshops," "evocative object." In doing so, you might wish to attempt to clarify some of her more vague adjectives as well, including "virtual," "real," and "ideal." Why do you think Turkle herself often places these adjectives in quotation marks?

5. Turkle seems largely optimistic about the "nascent culture of virtual reality," especially in her conclusion, where she asserts that "there is reason to feel great excitement about where we are in the present." Write an essay in which you are more critical of the prospects of "virtual reality"; summarize Turkle's position before you present your own counter-argument.

6. Have you ever role-played in a MUD, or are you familiar with someone who has? Did you find similarities to the players that Turkle presented? Begin an essay with an account of this experience, and then go on to make generalizations based on this particular example.

MAKING CONNECTIONS

How is a MUD similar to or different from the world Pico Iyer describes at the Los Angeles International Airport (p. 270)?

Sciences and Technologies

WHY THE SKY IS BLUE

James Jeans

Sir James Jeans (1877–1946) was a British physicist and astronomer. Educated at Trinity College, Cambridge, he lectured there and was a professor of applied mathematics at Princeton University from 1905 to 1909. He later did research at Mount Wilson Observatory in California. Jeans won many honors for his work and wrote a number of scholarly and popular scientific books. The following selection is from The Stars in Their Courses *(1931), a written version of what began as a series of radio talks for an audience assumed to have no special knowledge of science.*

Imagine that we stand on any ordinary seaside pier, and watch the waves rolling in and striking against the iron columns of the pier. Large waves pay very little attention to the columns—they divide right and left and re-unite after passing each column, much as a regiment of soldiers would if a tree stood in their road; it is almost as though the columns had not been there. But the short waves and ripples find the columns of the pier a much more formidable obstacle. When the short waves impinge on the columns, they are reflected back and spread as new ripples in all directions. To use the technical term, they are "scattered." The obstacle provided by the iron columns hardly affects the long waves at all, but scatters the short ripples.

We have been watching a sort of working model of the way in which sunlight struggles through the earth's atmosphere. Between us on earth and outer space the atmosphere interposes innumerable obstacles in the form of molecules of air, tiny droplets of water, and small particles of dust. These are represented by the columns of the pier.

The waves of the sea represent the sunlight. We know that sunlight is a blend of lights of many colors—as we can prove for ourselves by passing it

505

through a prism, or even through a jug of water, or as Nature demonstrates to us when she passes it through the raindrops of a summer shower and produces a rainbow. We also know that light consists of waves, and that the different colors of light are produced by waves of different lengths, red light by long waves and blue light by short waves. The mixture of waves which constitutes sunlight has to struggle through the obstacles it meets in the atmosphere, just as the mixture of waves at the seaside has to struggle past the columns of the pier. And these obstacles treat the light-waves much as the columns of the pier treat the sea-waves. The long waves which constitute red light are hardly affected, but the short waves which constitute blue light are scattered in all directions.

Thus, the different constituents of sunlight are treated in different ways as they struggle through the earth's atmosphere. A wave of blue light may be scattered by a dust particle, and turned out of its course. After a time a second dust particle again turns it out of its course, and so on, until finally it enters our eyes by a path as zigzag as that of a flash of lightning. Consequently the blue waves of the sunlight enter our eyes from all directions. And that is why the sky looks blue.

QUESTIONS

1. Analogy, the comparison of something familiar with something less familiar, occurs frequently in scientific explanation. Jeans introduces an analogy in his first paragraph. How does he develop that analogy as he develops his explanation?

2. The analogy Jeans provides enables him to explain the process by which the blue light-waves scatter throughout the sky. Hence he gives us a brief process analysis of that phenomenon. Summarize that process in your own words.

3. Try rewriting this essay without the analogy. Remove paragraph 1 and all the references to ocean waves and pier columns in paragraphs 2 and 3. How clear an explanation is left?

4. Besides the sea-waves, what other familiar examples does Jeans use in his explanation?

5. This piece opens with "Imagine that we stand. . . ." Suppose that every *we* was replaced with a *you*. How would the tone of the essay change?

6. While analogy can be effective in helping to explain difficult scientific concepts, it can be equally useful in explaining and interpreting familiar things by juxtaposing them in new ways. Suppose, for example, that you wish to explain to a friend why you dislike a course you are taking. Select one of the following ideas for an analogy (or find a better one): a forced-labor camp, a three-ring circus, squirrels on a treadmill, a tea party, a group-therapy session. Think through the analogy to your course, and write a few paragraphs of explanation. Let Jeans's essay guide you in organizing your own.

MAKING CONNECTIONS

1. Jeans's essay is a clear explanation of a complex phenomenon, yet it is quite short. Where else in this volume have you found explanations as clear? A number of short passages in the essays by Stephen W. Hawking (p. 565) and Farley Mowat (p. 256) could provide examples. Choose a descriptive passage that you find clear in the work of one of these writers, and compare it to Jeans's. Is an analogy central to the passage you selected? If not, what are the differences in the authors' explanations?

2. Describe the audience Jeans seems to have in mind for his explanation. How does that sense of audience differ for Margaret Atwood (p. 365) or Malcolm Gladwell (p. 448)? Compare one of those essays with Jeans's account of "Why the Sky Is Blue," and discuss how the task of explaining shifts according to the writer's assumptions about an audience.

EGGS FOR SALE

Rebecca Mead

Rebecca Mead was born in London, England, in 1966. She holds a bachelor's degree from Oxford University and a master's degree from New York University. A former reporter for the Sunday Times *of London and writer at* New York *magazine, she has been on the staff of the* New Yorker *since 1977. The following essay originally appeared in the* New Yorker.

The first time I met Cindy Schiller, at the Hungarian Pastry Shop on Amsterdam Avenue and 111th Street one morning this winter, she told me that she wasn't feeling quite herself, on account of what she called "the whole menopause thing." Her short-term memory was out of whack, she was lethargic, and she'd been finding herself suddenly drenched in sweat. "Hot flashes sound like they're no big deal, but hot flashes kick your ass," she said.

Schiller is a student at Columbia University Law School, and at twenty-six she should be only halfway to menopause. But she had been undergoing an artificially induced change of life over the previous weeks, which was precipitated by an array of drugs and an unusually relaxed attitude about sticking needles into herself. For three weeks, she had injected her stomach with a drug called Lupron, which shut down her ovaries, so that none of her eggs ripened and none of her egg follicles developed that month. Then menopause was suddenly over; she switched medications, and started injecting a combination of Pergonal and Metrodin—follicle-stimulating hormones—into her hip every morning. This kicked her quiescent ovaries into overdrive, swelling them to the size of oranges, and brought a cluster of her eggs to the brink of ripeness. After eight days, Schiller took a final shot of a hormone called human chorionic gonadotropin, or H.C.G., and exactly thirty-six hours later she went to the office of a fertility doctor on Central Park West. There she was put under general sedation, and an ultrasound probe was introduced into her vagina and threaded up through her uterus, so that a needle could be inserted into each of her ovaries and the eggs sucked out, one by one. Twelve eggs were whisked away, to be fertilized in a petri dish with the sperm of a man Schiller wasn't especially fond of, in preparation for transfer to the uterus of a woman she didn't really know, in the hope that at least one would grow into a child whom Schiller would probably never see.

Schiller, whose name has been changed in this article at her request, is a lively young woman with blue eyes, long light-brown hair, and very pale skin, unmarked except for five tattoos—tattoos that her mother, back home in the Southwest, has been begging her to remove with laser surgery. She also has sixteen piercings, including several of the kind that only real intimates or fertility doctors get to see.

If she were your daughter, you, too, would probably want her to have the tattoos removed, because in other respects Schiller is such a nice girl: she doesn't drink, she doesn't smoke, she doesn't take drugs, she's pretty and quick to laugh, and she has a lovely singing voice. I went to a basement college dining hall one evening to listen to a performance by a musical group she belongs to, and I found her there in jeans and a low-cut T-shirt, singing harmony with a look of blithe pleasure in her eyes and with a stud through her tongue flashing in the fluorescent lighting. Schiller wants to be a civil-rights lawyer when she graduates, but this year she has been much too busy with a panoply of left-wing and feminist causes to spend much time in the library. The first time I phoned her apartment, her answering machine advised me to leave a message for "Cindy Schiller, the National Day of Appreciation Task Force, or Stop Police Brutality." Within a couple of months, the list had morphed into "Cindy Schiller, the Courageous Resister Committee, Students for Reproductive Freedom, the Housing Law Workshop, or Task Force Against Police Brutality."

Not long after she arrived at Columbia last fall, Schiller read a notice 5 pinned to a bulletin board in the law school by an infertile couple who were seeking an egg donor. For a woman who is trying to get pregnant and has no viable eggs of her own, donor eggs are a last resort. Schiller had signed up with an egg-donor agency while she was an undergraduate in her home state and had twice donated eggs there. She was now eager to do it again, even though the last time she had "hyperstimulated," which means that she had produced too many eggs (more than thirty, in her case) and had suffered so much abdominal pain and nausea that she could hardly get out of bed for two days. On both occasions, she had been selected as a donor immediately, no doubt because she is fair and blue-eyed and has a good academic record.

Schiller donates her eggs because she thinks that it's a worthy thing to do, and because it's a worthy thing to do for which she can be paid in sums that seem handsome to a heavily indebted student. Schiller's parents, who are divorced, know that she donates eggs, and they are not opposed to her doing it, though they are concerned about its effect on her health. They aren't especially wealthy, and Schiller says she would rather support herself with eggs than ask them to help her out.

She does, however, have the political objections to the trade which you might expect from someone with an answering-machine message like hers. She thinks it would be "really cool" to donate to a gay couple, say, rather than to the upper-middle-class wives and husbands who are the typical recipients of donor eggs. She also disapproves of the preference for egg donation over adoption. "It's the fact that I'm helping a white-supremacist system work," she told me earnestly. "People are getting these fair, blue-eyed children, and that does bother me philosophically." Still, she had earned twenty-five hundred dollars for each of her earlier donations, and by last fall the going rate in New York was five thousand dollars, so when she saw the ad she called the couple and arranged to meet them at a café on Broadway.

They turned out to be a professional Manhattan couple old enough to be Schiller's parents, and they bought her lunch and quizzed her about her interests and skills. She told them about her expertise in martial arts and music, and about the fact that she was really good at math and science and was also a decent writer. It was a bit like a job interview, she told me, though she hadn't done some of the things that a career counsellor might have advised, like removing her nose ring or the stud in her tongue. The hardest part of the interview came when it was time to negotiate the fee, and the couple asked her to name her price. "The husband wouldn't, like, name a figure, so I had to," she said. "Five thousand was the amount that I needed to make in this period of time, and he jumped at it. I probably could have asked for more and got it."

This past February, in the middle of Schiller's fertility-drug regimen, she heard about an advertisement that had been placed in several Ivy League school newspapers offering fifty thousand dollars to a donor who was athletic, had S.A.T. scores of 1400 or more, and was at least five feet ten inches tall. She was a few inches too short to apply, but it made her think that there might be someone who was willing to pay such a premium for her eggs, thereby making her next year at Columbia a whole lot easier. "I'm only now beginning to realize that I could tap into some cash here," she said.

In 1984, a woman gave birth to a child who was genetically unrelated   10
to her for the first time, after a donor's egg had been fertilized in a petri dish in the laboratory of Dr. Alan Trounson, an embryologist at Monash University, in Melbourne, Australia, and transferred to another woman's womb. This year, there will probably be around five thousand egg donations in the United States.

In the early days of egg donation, very few patients could take advantage of the procedure. These recipients were given whatever eggs clinics could lay their hands on: some were leftover eggs donated by women who had undergone in-vitro fertilization, which involves the same kind of ovary-stimulating hormonal regimen as egg donation; a few came from women who were having their tubes tied and agreed to give away the eggs they would no longer be using. Some infertile women were helped by their younger sisters, or by friends. There was little concern about matching donors and recipients beyond the broadest categories of race. One recipient I spoke with, who is dark-haired, olive-skinned, and Jewish, received donor eggs ten years ago from a woman who was tall, blond, and Nordic.

These days, such a match would be unlikely, although if a dark, Jewish recipient wanted to introduce a little Nordic blood into her family stock, she would certainly be able to find an egg-donor agency happy to oblige. Nowadays, donors and recipients are matched with remarkable precision, right down to tanning ability and hair texture. There are around two hundred private egg-donation agencies and clinics in the United States, and they are intensely competitive, offering patients donor data bases that may include as many as three hundred women. Different agencies specialize in different kinds of donors: one bicoastal agency is known for signing up donors who are in their late twenties and early thirties, are married, and have children of their own; a former actress in Los Angeles runs an agency that specializes in donors who are models and actresses; at another Los Angeles agency, the two proprietresses accompany donors to their medical appointments and have had dinner and flowers delivered to them on the night after the surgery.

Marketing strategies are ingenious. A New York egg-donation program advertises in movie theatres, inviting would-be donors to dial 1–877–BABY-MAKERS. A new company in Los Angeles called the Center for Egg Options hired a hip advertising agency to write catchy ad copy: Instead of variations on the usual "give the gift of life" theme, one ad reads simply, "Pay your tuition with eggs." Another, which appeared in the magazine *Backstage,* says, "Get paid $4,000 for a small part." The same company is known for sending fertility doctors promotional giveaways that consist of shrink-wrapped egg cartons filled with chocolate eggs.

Many agencies direct would-be recipients to log on to Internet sites and browse through pictures of willing donors which are accompanied by detailed profiles that include the donors' health history, educational background, ambitions, and interests. One popular Web site that is unaffiliated with an agency invites donors and recipients to post classified advertisements, which are by turns poignant and outlandish. There are pleas for help from women who cannot afford to use donor agencies, which typically charge around twenty-five hundred dollars for their matching services, and examples of unabashed hawking: one recent posting read, "I donated to a famous couple, WHY NOT YOU!"

The United States is the only country in the world in which the rules of   15
the marketplace govern the trade in gametes and genes. In parts of Europe, and in most of South America, egg donation is illegal, often because of the influence of the Catholic Church, which holds that only intercourse should lead to conception. (Muslim law also forbids egg donation; Judaism generally has a more flexible view toward methods of assisted reproduction.) In other countries, egg donation is legal only under certain circumstances. A recent British law allows patients of in-vitro fertilization to sell their leftover eggs, thereby offsetting the cost of the original I.V.F. procedure, but it is against the law to pay women to undergo voluntary egg retrieval. Many foreigners seeking fertility treatments travel to the United States, which is seen by overseas patients as the place where their prayers may be answered and by their overseas doctors as something of a rogue nation. Robert

Jansen, a prominent Australian fertility doctor, characterizes the American egg trade as "a thoroughly commercial activity," and regrets that "people are not even pretending anymore that it is an altruistic act to donate eggs." He adds, "Personally, I am frightened by it."

In the United States, though, the controversy has centered less on whether donors should be paid than on how much they should earn. When Thomas Pinkerton, a San Diego lawyer, placed the fifty-thousand-dollar-egg-donor advertisement earlier this year on behalf of an anonymous client, he was accused of exercising unreasonable influence over students who may be hard-up. Television news magazines grilled him about his ethics, and the Academy of Assisted Reproductive Technology, an organization on whose legal advisory board he sits, was troubled by the controversy. But Pinkerton's clients aren't alone in looking for high-end eggs: last year, a donor in Los Angeles received thirty-five thousand dollars for her eggs.

Escalating fees are causing doctors in this country, somewhat belatedly, to express reservations about the commercial traffic in eggs. At a recent conference on infertility that I attended in Sydney, Australia, Dr. Mark V. Sauer, who is the director of reproductive endocrinology at Columbia Presbyterian Medical Center, in New York, addressed the issue. "First of all, we have to recognize that we have a problem," he said. "It is like saying at A.A. meetings, 'I am an alcoholic.' Well, I am an egg-donor man, and I do pay my donors, and I pay them too much, and I recognize that, so what are we going to do about it?"

Doctors are concerned that high prices are attracting women who aren't mature enough to be able to make the kind of philosophical decision implicit in donating eggs; but they are also worried about the interests of their infertility patients, many of whom are being priced out of the market. Egg donation is generally not covered by insurance, and the price for one retrieval (known as a cycle) in New York City, including donor fees and medications for both participants, is currently twenty thousand dollars, with the chances of success being around fifty per cent. Some patients undergo as many as three cycles in their efforts to become parents.

The ethical quandary that doctors now find themselves in, however, is one of their own making. It has long been accepted that gametes have a monetary value, ever since commercial sperm donation took off in the nineteen-sixties. (Although there are laws against the commodification of body parts, a curious legislative loophole has enabled a market in eggs and sperm to emerge. There is no doubt that if such a loophole existed for the market in, say, kidneys, you would be able to order them on the Internet from donors who would provide detailed accounts of their families' excellent urological history.) The average sperm-donor fee is fifty dollars per deposit, which works out to about 0.00001 cent per spermatozoon. Part of the reason that egg-donor fees are higher than sperm-donor fees is that the effort required is so much greater. Being an egg donor can be inconvenient, because, unlike sperm, eggs cannot easily be frozen, so there are no "egg banks"; instead, the donor takes drugs to synchronize her reproductive system with the recipient's. What's more, as Cindy Schiller found out, the process can be painful, and it can be dangerous as well: hyperstimulation can, in very rare instances, lead to stroke. Donating eggs does not deplete a donor's own reserves, since the eggs that are taken would otherwise have been wasted that month; but it is too early in the history of egg donation to know what the long-term side effects might be. Ovarian scarring may compromise a donor's own fertility, and one medical study, which has since been disputed, has suggested that there might be an association between fertility drugs and ovarian cancer.

All of these factors have led some doctors to argue that egg donors are 20
actually underpaid. Dr. Jamie Grifo, who heads New York University's infertility clinic, says, "If you consider the hourly wage for a sperm donor and the hourly wage for an egg donor—my God, five thousand dollars is about ten times too little."

In its egg-donor guidelines, the American Society for Reproductive Medicine stipulates that donors be paid not for the actual eggs but for the "inconvenience, time, discomfort, and for the risk undertaken." Agencies reject potential donors who say they are doing it just for the money, in part because most recipients wouldn't want a donor who appears to be mercenary; they would prefer a donor who has chosen to perform this service out of the goodness of her heart. (In the euphemistic parlance of the industry, eggs are "donated," never "sold.") The ideal egg donor embodies all sorts of paradoxes: she is compassionate toward an infertile stranger but feels no necessary attachment to her own genetic kin; she is fecund but can easily divorce the reproductive from the maternal.

Before Cindy Schiller was allowed to became an egg donor, she underwent psychological counselling and testing. Egg-donor programs generally reject any young women who view their eggs as protochildren. "They always ask what you are going to do when in eighteen years' time someone comes knocking at your door," Schiller told me, her tone implying that she thought the question was a silly one to ask of someone her age. "How would I know what I'm going to do?"

Donors who advertise their services directly on the Internet are not prescreened. I spoke to one would-be donor, a student near Chicago, who had just turned twenty and was planning to work with two couples who had responded to her ad, "Beauty Queen looking to help infertile couple." If she had applied to one of the big egg-donation programs, she might well have been weeded out by a psychologist. She was interested in donating only to a religious couple, she said, "because I want to someday see these kids up in Heaven with me." She went on to say, "That would be awesome. I probably won't have any contact with them until then, so that will be my first time meeting him or her." It also turned out that this young woman's religious convictions included a prohibition on premarital sex, so if she went ahead with the donation she would have genetic off-spring before she had lost her virginity. "Yep," she said brightly and a bit shyly. "It's kind of cool, huh?"

Cindy Schiller was nonchalant when discussing the children who might result from her donations. "I'm really getting a good bargain, because I don't have to raise them," she said, half seriously. Schiller had nonetheless become deeply invested in the pregnancies of the women she was helping. (The agency back in her home state didn't tell Schiller whether her donations were successful, but she did receive a thank-you card from one couple, telling her that they now had a son.) "Of course, you are doing it for the money," she said, "but I always hope it works. I really hope it works."

In the weeks after we first met, Schiller had sent away for an application form from a large West Coast agency called Options. Most agencies do not allow women to donate eggs more than four or five times, because of the health risks, and Schiller was approaching her limit; she hoped that Options would help her market herself for what might be the last time. She was asked to provide head shots, and was taken aback by a number of other details that Options expected. "They even ask whether your grandparents had acne," she marvelled. "I can see why you would want to know about diseases and stuff, but acne? *Please.* I know they're paying top dollar here for the genes, but if acne is your biggest problem you're good to go."

Options is one of the largest egg-brokering agencies in the country: it can offer around two hundred and fifty donors to recipients worldwide at any given moment, and conducts almost all of its business on the Internet. I went to visit the Options offices, which are located in a nondescript building on an anonymous street in the Los Angeles area; before I was provided with the address, I was required to sign a nondisclosure agreement stating that I would not reveal it. Teri Royal, who runs the company, said that she kept her address secret in order to preserve the security of her records, some of which deal with high-profile clients in Hollywood and in Washington.

The place had the feeling of a cottage industry that needs to move into a mansion: partitions had been set up to divide small spaces into even smaller ones, and there was hardly room to turn around without bumping into another woman with a phone clamped to her ear and a computer screen glowing in front of her. Royal is a stout thirty-nine-year-old woman with strawberry-blond hair. She explained that Options donors are carefully selected for their marketability as well as for their general health; Options does not accept donors older than thirty, for instance, because recipients shy away from them. But when it comes to accepting recipients into the program, Royal practices reproductive free trade.

"We would never turn somebody down," she said. "It is none of my business how someone wants to make her baby, so long as all parties are informed and give their consent. So I'm not going to turn away homosexuals, bisexuals, transracials, single parents, older couples." She showed me a photograph of twins born to a couple who had been rejected by another agency before coming to Options because they were both Asian but wanted a Caucasian donor. "They thought the mix was beautiful," Royal said. The agency's oldest would-be mother had been sixty-eight years old; she and her

25

husband, both of whom already had grown children, recruited an egg donor and also a gestational surrogate to carry the new baby. "Everyone realized that the mother wasn't going to be around for the whole of the child's life," Royal said, "but the rest of the family planned to step in and be there for the parenting of this child, and it was a wonderful thing." Royal sees herself as a service provider, and she cites a higher authority for her policy of nonintervention: "In the Bible, Sarah didn't conceive until she was ninety. So I figure that until I get someone over ninety I am not going to say no to them, because if God thinks it's O.K., then who am I to say it's not?"

Using Options is expensive. The agency charges eighteen hundred and sixty-five dollars for bringing donors and recipients together. Administrative and legal costs are close to another thousand dollars. Then there is the compensation for the donor. Options donors are among the best paid in the country: those who appear on the Internet data base receive between thirty-five hundred and five thousand dollars, and others who are recruited through private advertisements placed for specific couples earn still more. Last year, Options placed a cap of sixty-five hundred dollars on payments, because would-be recipients were trying to outbid one another in the pages of the same college newspapers. "We had recipients saying they wanted to offer ten thousand, fifteen thousand, twenty thousand," Royal said. It turns out that the cap is not screwed on very tightly, however: Options still allows recipients to reward donors with additional "gifts." The *Columbia Daily Spectator* recently featured an Options ad seeking a donor who was "5'5" inches or taller, Caucasian, slim with dark hair, intelligent and kind"; the ad also stated that "although our gratitude cannot be measured in dollars, if we were in your shoes, the least we would expect is: $6,500 plus expenses (and a gift)."

"We have had some fabulous gifts," Royal told me. "We have had donors sent on cruises, we have had a year of tuition paid. The donor doesn't know what the gift is going to be. She just knows that there will be a gift, so that way she's still giving her eggs without undue compensation or any form of bribery." She can also, perhaps, experience the same anticipatory thrill and anxiety that a lottery player feels as he waits to see if his numbers have come up.

As egg donation has changed from being an experimental procedure to   30
being just one of a range of infertility treatments, consumers have begun to demand more from agencies like Options. They expect to be offered donors who are not just healthy but bright and accomplished and attractive. One recent morning, I attended a matching session at Saint Barnabas Medical Center, in New Jersey, where the members of the egg-donation team were going over the wish lists of various recipients. (Like all the New York-area egg-donation programs, Saint Barnabas practices anonymous donation, in which recipients and donors are matched by nurses and psychologists; the recipients never see a picture of the woman who is chosen for them.) It felt like a good-humored, girls-only swap meet, although the

scarcity of the right kinds of donors was obvious. "She wants Jewish," the program's psychologist said of one would-be recipient, and one of the nurses snorted, "She can wait; she'll be waiting a long time." Someone else asked, "Do we have someone small and dark? And Irish?" Another participant read a wish list of characteristics: "She wants no cat allergies. 'Tall, dark-haired, healthy, athletic, animal-loving.' And a partridge in a pear tree."

Most of the egg-donation professionals I talked to had similar stories of highly specific requests from prospective parents. Dr. Sauer, at Columbia Presbyterian, told me that when he was in charge of an egg-donation program at the University of Southern California, he was approached by a couple from Nebraska, and the husband introduced himself as a former college football player—a Cornhusker. "He had the red pants on and everything," Saucer said. "Because we were the U.S.C. program, he figured that we had very athletic donors, or could get them. He didn't want just a good athlete; he wanted someone who was on one of the actual teams. I said, 'I am not going to go down to the track and find you a donor,' and he got quite indignant." Sauer went on to tell me that he had couples who tried to make special deals, as if there were under-the-counter eggs to be had: "They come in and say, 'I know this is what you usually pay, but if we pay more, will you give us something better?' It's as if they were buying a puppy, or something."

Egg-donor recipients bridle at the suggestion that they are shopping for genes, but the agencies and the programs provide so much personal information about donors that recipients are invited to view eggs as merchandise. After all, most modern parents do everything they can to give a child its best start in life—from taking folic acid while trying to conceive to not drinking during pregnancy to drilling a toddler with flash cards and sending a ten-year-old to tennis camp. So it is not surprising that egg recipients are particularly choosy before conception even takes place. Lyne Macklin, the administrator of an agency in Beverly Hills, the Center for Surrogate Parenting and Egg Donation, told me that there's a great temptation among recipients to engage in a kind of genetic upgrading. "It's like shopping," she said. "If you have the option between a Volkswagen and a Mercedes, you'll select the Mercedes."

It is impossible to determine just how likely a child is to inherit such characteristics as academic ability or athleticism or musicality. Still, would-be parents can play the odds. Robert Plomin, a behavioral geneticist at the University of London, says that a recipient probably ought to pay attention to such characteristics as cognitive ability, which is about fifty per cent heritable. "I generally try to be a scientist and say, 'These are populations and averages, and we can't make very good predictions for an individual,'" he told me. "But I do let friends know that some of these things are heritable."

Egg-donation specialists tend to tell their patients that they should not worry too much about behavioral genetics. Nonetheless, there is some speculation that paying donors high rates might have an effect on the character of the children produced. Robert Jansen, the Australian fertility doctor, told me, "As the price rises and becomes more and more of a motivating factor, and we also appreciate the genetics of personality and character, you start to ask, 'Do you really want to bring up a little girl whose biological mother was someone who decided to charge ten thousand dollars for eggs?'"

Jansen's question suggests a profound anxiety about the new reproductive territory that egg donation has opened up. Egg donation makes it possible, for the first time, for a woman's procreative capacity to be detached from any maternal investment on her part. Though men have always been able to father children they may never meet, the fact that an egg donor might, by semantic equivalence, mother a child she will never know confounds both the dictionary and an ingrained assumption about the maternal instinct.

One day, I asked Schiller whether she had any idea how she would be raising the money for law school if she weren't selling her eggs. "Some idea," she said. "I might be working at Hooters." In an earlier era, Schiller's youth and her fertility would have served her well in the matrimonial marketplace. Because she can now choose an education and a career, deferring marriage and children, her reproductive capital has been made otherwise available—to women who have themselves preferred an education and a career over early childbearing. Schiller told me that she couldn't imagine being ready to have children for at least a decade, if then, and it had occurred to her that she might need reproductive assistance herself one day. "What a sweet irony that would be," she said.

In the years before the birth-control pill and Roe v. Wade, a woman like Schiller might have provided an infertile couple not with eggs but with an actual baby—the product of an unwanted pregnancy, given up for adoption. Indeed, the rising demand for donor eggs—most of which come from white, middle-class women—coincides with a decline in the number of adoptable American infants born to white, middle-class women. Some donors have undergone abortions, and they may see egg donation as a way of making amends. The Options data base features several such women, including Jennifer, a twenty-four-year-old medical assistant. "I had to terminate two pregnancies at ages nineteen and twenty," Jennifer explained. "I felt really bad about it. I want to help someone who cannot have children. I would feel a lot better about my own decisions if I could do that."

The babies who might have resulted from Jennifer's pregnancies would have been highly adoptable (her forebears are European), but her eggs are even more desirable, because they allow a recipient couple to have a baby who is genetically related to one parent. And with egg donation, as opposed to adoption, there is no extraneous birth mother to deal with—as long as Jennifer continues to have no interest in her genetic offspring, that is, and as long as no law is introduced to give donor children the right to track down their genetic mothers.

As the egg-donation industry grows, however, legal changes are expected. "There is currently no controlling federal legislation," Sean Tipton, a spokesman for the American Society for Reproductive Medicine, explains. Donors sign a consent form saying that they are relinquishing any claim to their retrieved eggs. Five states—Florida, North Dakota, Oklahoma, Texas, and Virginia—have passed legislation that releases donors from responsibility for the children born from their eggs. "In most cases, people should be confident that they are giving up those rights," Tipton says. "But it is not clear whether it would survive a court challenge."

Legal scholars expect that, in years to come, lawsuits will be brought   40
by donors who develop regrets about having sold their eggs back in their student days. Karen Synesiou, the co-owner of the Center for Surrogate Parenting and Egg Donation, told me, "If you get an eighteen- or nineteen-year-old who has been stimulated four or five times and her ovaries stop functioning because of all the scarring, she is going to want to sue someone for being infertile." At least one donor has threatened to sue a fertility clinic after being hyperstimulated, but the suit was dropped when the clinic agreed to pay her medical expenses.

Schiller, who as a law student might be expected to be aware of her rights and responsibilities concerning her eggs, seemed vague when I asked her whether she had made any legal arrangement with the couple who had just bought her eggs. She had signed the consent form waiving her rights, she said, but she had not come to any agreement about whether she would have future contact with the family. She seemed to have very little idea of what the couple expected from her; she had never discussed with them whether they planned to tell the child of its origins, and she did not know whether they expected her to be available to the child if it later wanted to know its genetic mother. She wasn't even sure whether they would notify her of a pregnancy, or of a baby's birth, and said that she had never felt that she could ask about these issues. "Ultimately, until it's over and you get paid you feel, 'I had better not say anything,'" she told me.

So far, there has been very little case law in which egg donation plays a role. One notorious case that does involve an egg donor is known as Buzzanca v. Buzzanca. John and Luanne Buzzanca were both infertile, so they obtained an embryo that was left over from an I.V.F. cycle performed on a infertile woman, using a donor egg and her husband's sperm. The embryo was transferred to the womb of a gestational surrogate whom the Buzzancas had hired. During the pregnancy, the Buzzancas separated; shortly after the baby's birth, John claimed that he was exempt from paying child support, because the child was not genetically related to him and had not been born to his wife. A lower court agreed with John Buzzanca that he was not the little girl's parent, but it declined to say who, precisely, was; however, a higher court ruled that John and Luanne were indeed the child's father and mother. The child now lives with Luanne Buzzanca, and she receives child support from John Buzzanca. Some legal scholars have suggested that the original egg donor, who seemed to be unaware that her eggs had been passed on to yet another infertile couple, might have had a claim if she had decided to sue her clinic.

The Buzzanca case has implications not just for the field of assisted reproduction but also for the contemporary cultural definition of parenthood. According to the Buzzanca ruling, parenthood is not a biological category but a conceptual one: its defining characteristic is that of intent. John and Luanne Buzzanca were the child's parents because at one point they had meant to be her parents. This reasoning—the idea that intent trumps biology—makes for some remarkably slippery values. A woman who bears an egg-donor child is encouraged to believe that carrying the fetus is the crucial component of motherhood. But a woman who hires a surrogate to carry her fertilized egg to term for her is encouraged to believe the opposite: that the important thing is the genetic link to the baby, and not the womb out of which the baby came. Biologically, an egg donor's situation is identical to that of a woman who uses a surrogate. But egg donors are encouraged to believe that what makes a woman into a mother is the wish to be a mother—to be what is known in the infertility business as "the social parent."

The American fertility industry is based upon the conviction that a person is the agent of his or her own destiny—that fate and fortune are fashioned, not inflicted. Effective contraception has made it possible for people to believe that all pregnancies can be planned, and that children are chosen. The corollary of that belief is the conviction that choosing to have a child is a right, and that the desire to have one, even when pregnancy is against the odds, should command the utmost attention and effort and resources. The jargon of the reproductive-services industry, which talks about "nontraditional family-building" and "creating families," illustrates this very American idea: that sleeves-rolled-up diligence is what makes people into parents—rather than anything as unreliable as chance, or fate, or luck, or God.

In late June, Schiller finally heard from the couple who had received 45 her eggs four months earlier: the woman had failed to conceive. So far, they hadn't asked her to donate eggs a second time, but they seemed to want to stay in touch, and she wondered whether they might call upon her to repeat the process.

Meanwhile, in the final week of the spring semester, a new advertisement had appeared in the *Columbia Daily Spectator* for a donor who was five feet seven inches tall and had S.A.T. scores of 1300 or more; the ad offered fifty thousand dollars. When we first met, Schiller had told me that she was five feet six; now, she thought, she might be five feet seven, barely. She had contacted the office of the attorney who placed the ad, had sent off a batch of photographs of herself as a baby, as a child, and as an adult, and was waiting to hear whether she would fill the bill.

The attorney was Thomas Pinkerton, the lawyer who had placed the first fifty-thousand-dollar ad, several months earlier. I called Pinkerton at his office in San Diego. He told me that he had started out as a real-estate attorney but that his personal life had redirected his professional life: he and his wife, Darlene, had contracted with his sister for her to carry a surrogate pregnancy for them using Darlene's egg and Pinkerton's sperm. The health department wanted the birth certificate to carry the names of Pinkerton and his sister as the child's parents, but Pinkerton obtained a court order, the first of its kind in San Diego, allowing Darlene to be named as the child's mother.

Pinkerton defended the high fee that his clients were offering by noting that they had been unable to find a donor who met their specifications through the usual agencies and programs. He said that he saw nothing wrong with a client's paying premium rates for hard-to-come-by goods. "People have asked, 'How can a donor make an informed choice about undertaking the risk of going through a medical procedure when there is so much money at stake?'—as if she weren't going to be able to use her mind anymore," Pinkerton said. "But put it in the context of what we are offering other youngsters, such as football players—is that unethical? It is almost an assault on womanhood to say that this woman can't make a decision because there's fifty thousand dollars at stake."

More than two hundred women had responded to Pinkerton's first ad; another hundred had called after the second ad. And, although Pinkerton says that this wasn't his original intention, he is now doing what some in the fertility business had told me they suspected was behind the advertisements all along. He's creating his own Internet data base—a kind of blue-chip directory of donors, which, for a fee, recipients will be able to inspect. Pinkerton has kept the operation small: by mid-July, he said, he was working with ten couples. But he expects it to grow, and he is planning to approach a California business school to assign as a class project the drafting of a business plan for his new agency.

Pinkerton explained that his data base, unlike the on-line agencies, does not list prices for any of the donors. A donor can put herself on the egg market, find out what she's worth, and privately negotiate the fee for her genes—eggBay, so to speak. So far, donors have been settling for considerably less than the fifty-thousand-dollar fee they hoped for when they sent in their original applications; but in theory a donor will be able to command a price even higher than fifty thousand dollars. "We can give a couple access to the data base with the profiles and pictures, and then they can make an offer," Pinkerton said. "They can settle on a figure with her that is totally undirected by us."

As of July, only a month before fall registration, Schiller had not been chosen by one of Pinkerton's recipients, and she had begun to investigate the possibility of putting up her own classified advertisement on one of the Internet's egg-donor sites. She browsed the advertisements that had been placed by couples who were looking for donors. "Gosh, these ads are really sad," she told me. "Most people have to be really desperate before they will even try something like this." There was one couple who had lost many family members in the Holocaust and wanted a Jewish donor to con-

50

tinue the bloodline; another woman had suffered serious damage to her reproductive organs after being in a car accident.

Schiller had recently heard from Columbia's Financial Aid office that she'd be receiving more funds than she expected this academic year, so she hadn't yet decided whether to go through with a fourth donation. But just in case, she had looked into taking a Mensa test in order to have proof of her intelligence, and she had decided one thing: "If someone offers me something really high, and they are an asshole, I won't do it." In any case, Schiller has no regrets about her adventures in the egg marketplace. "It's almost like a hobby now," she said. "This is weird, isn't it? But it is a very interesting experience. I don't think I would trade it for anything."

QUESTIONS

1. Summarize the multiple concerns (medical, ethical, economic, legal) expressed in this essay. How do these concerns overlap with one another?
2. The narrative structure which holds the essay together is Mead's account of Schiller's experience with egg donation; this serves as a framework into which Mead inserts explanations about larger societal issues around the theme. Cindy Schiller's story, however, is not presented chronologically, but rather information from her life is presented when appropriate to the general narrative. Write your own biographical account of Schiller, in chronological order.
3. Why would Mead choose not to explain her information in the order in which it happened? This is the case with respect not only to Schiller's story but also to the history of egg donation; for instance, it is not until after we have been immersed in Schiller's life for a few pages that we learn about "the early days of egg donation" (paragraph 11).
4. How do the large sums of money being made in transactions related to egg donation affect your interpretation of statements by the individuals involved—for instance, the apparently gallant claim by Pinkerton that "it is almost an assault on womanhood to say that this woman can't make a decision because there's fifty thousand dollars at stake"?
5. Mead notes parenthetically, "In the euphemistic parlance of the industry, eggs are 'donated,' never 'sold'"; in addition, recipients offer "gifts" beyond the minimal payment to "donors." We usually presume that the language of "giving" precludes any economic exchange, yet there are often obligations associated with receiving a gift and a necessity to reciprocate in some way. Think of a situation in which you have received a gift which seemed to imply some kind of debt on your part, no matter how "freely" it was given. Write an essay which compares your experience with that of an egg "recipient."
6. Research a local medical institution's practices regarding donation of body parts—organs, eggs, blood, sperm, plasma, and so forth. Does

the institution have written policies on the subject? Is there compensation for the donor? (This is certainly the case in "banks" for sperm and plasma.) Try to speak with someone who has donated in this manner, and write a narrative of his or her account, or relate your own experience if you have made such a donation yourself.

MAKING CONNECTIONS

Imagine a conversation between Mead, Margaret Atwood, (p. 365), and Carol Gilligan (p. 425). How would Gilligan (see "Interviewing Adolescent Girls") or Atwood (see "The Female Body") respond to Mead's essay?

THE STORY OF THE BREAST

Natalie Angier

*Natalie Angier was born in New York City in 1958 and is a gradu-
ate of Barnard College, where she studied both the humanities and
science. After working as a technical writer, she joined the staff of*
Discover *magazine, then became a staff writer at* Time, *and later
an editor at* Savvy. *She has been with the* New York Times *since
1990 and currently serves as the paper's science correspondent.
She won a Pulitzer Prize for reporting in 1991. Angier has also
published two books:* The Beauty and the Beastly: New Views of
the Nature of Life *(1995) and* Woman: An Intimate Geography
(1999), of which the following is an excerpt.

Nancy Burley, a professor of evolution and ecology at the University of
California in Irvine, plays Halloween with birds. She takes male zebra finches
and she accessorizes them. A normal, pre-Burley finch is a beautiful animal,
red of beak and orange of cheek, his chest a zebra print of stripes, his under-
wings polka-dotted in orange, and his eyes surrounded by vertical streaks of
black and white, like the eyes of a mime artist. One thing the zebra finch does
not have is a crest, as some species of birds do. So Burley will give a male a
crest. She will attach a tall white cap of feathers to his head, turning him into
Chef Bird-o-Dee. Or she'll give him a tall red Cat-in-the-Hat cap. His bird
legs are normally a neutral shade of grayish beige, so she gives him flashy an-
klets of red, yellow, lavender, or powder blue. And by altering the visual pith
of him, his finchness, Burley alters his life. As she has shown in a series of
wonderful, amusing, important experiments, female zebra finches have decided opinions about the various accouterments. They love the tall white chef
caps, and they will clamor to mate with a male so haberdashed. Zebra finches
ordinarily couple up and abide by a system of shared parental care of
nestlings, but if a female is paired with a white-hatted male, she gladly works
overtime on child care and allows him to laze — though he doesn't laze but
spends his free time philandering. Call the benighted wife the bird who mistakes a hat for a mate.

But put a male in a tall red cap, and the females turn up their beaks.
No trophy he: you can have him, sister. If a red-capped male manages to
obtain a mate, he ends up being so busy taking care of his offspring that he
has no time for extramarital affairs, and there are no demands for his
moonlighting services anyway.

The opposite holds true for leg bands. Dress a male in white ankle
rings and he's of scant appeal. Put him in red and he's a lovebird.

Zebra finches have no good reason for being drawn to white toques and red socks. We cannot look at the results of Burley's costume experiments and say, Ah, yes, the females are using the white crest as an indicator that the male will be a good father, or that his genes are robust and therefore he's a great catch. A zebra finch with a white crest can hardly be said to bear superior finch genes when he's not supposed to have a crest in the first place. Instead, the unexpected findings offer evidence of the so-called sensory exploitation theory of mate choice. By this proposal, the white hat takes advantage of a neurophysiological process in the zebra finch's brain that serves some other, unknown purpose but that is easily coopted and aroused. The hat stimulates an extant neural pathway, and it lures the female, and the female does not know why, but she knows what she likes. We can understand that impulse, the enticement of an object we deem beautiful. "Human beings have an exquisite aesthetic sense that is its own justification," Burley says. "Our ability to appreciate impressionistic painting cannot be called functional. In my mind, that's what we're seeing with the zebra finches. The preferences are aesthetic, not functional. They don't correlate with anything practical."

Nevertheless, the evidence suggests that if a male finch someday were   5
born with a mutation that gives him a touch of a white thatch, the mutation would spread rapidly through finchdom, possibly becoming accentuated over time, until a bird had the toque by nature that Burley loaned by contrivance. No doubt some researchers in that hypothetical future would assume that the finch's white cap had meaning and was an indicator of zebra finch mettle, and they'd speculate about the epistemology of the trait.

A woman's breasts, I argue, are like Burley's white crests. They're pretty, they're flamboyant, they're irresistible. But they are arbitrary, and they signify much less than we think. This is a contrarian view. Evolutionary theorists have proposed many explanations for the existence of the breast, usually according it a symbolic or functional value, as a signal to men of information they need to know about a potential mate. How can we not give the breast its evolutionary due when it is there in our faces, begging for narrative. "Few issues have been the focus for a wider range of speculation based on fewer facts than the evolutionary origin and physiological function of women's breasts," the biologist Caroline Pond has written. The stories about the breast sound real and persuasive, and they may all have a germ of validity, because we ascribe meaning wherever and however we choose; that is one of the perquisites of being human. As the actress Helen Mirren said in the movie *O Lucky Man*, "All religions are equally true."

Still, I will argue that breasts fundamentally are here by accident. They are sensory exploiters. They say little or nothing about a woman's inherent health, quality, or fecundity. They are accouterments. If we go looking for breasts and for ways to enhance and display our breasts, to make them stand out like unnatural, almost farcical Barbie-doll missile heads, then we are doing what breasts have always done, which is appeal to an irrational aesthetic sense that has no function but that begs to be amused. The ideal breasts are, and always have been, stylized breasts. A woman's breasts welcome illusion and the imaginative opportunities of clothing. They can be enhanced or muted, as a woman chooses, and their very substance suggests as much: they are soft and flexible, clay to play with. They are funny things, really, and we should learn to laugh at them, which may be easier to do if we first take them seriously.

The most obvious point to be made about the human breast is that it is unlike any other bosom in the primate order. The breasts of a female ape or monkey swell only when she is lactating, and the change is usually so modest that it can be hard to see beneath her body hair. Once the mother has weaned her offspring, her breasts flatten back. Only in humans do the breasts inflate at puberty, before the first pregnancy occurs or could even be sustained, and only in humans do they remain engorged throughout life. In fact, the swelling of the breasts in pregnant and lactating women occurs quite independently of pubertal breast development, and in a more uniform manner: a small-breasted woman's breasts grow about as much during pregnancy, in absolute terms, as a busty woman's breasts do, which is why the temporary expansion is comparatively more noticeable on a small-breasted woman. For all women, maternal augmentation results from the proliferation and distention of the cells of the ducts and lobules (the dairy equipment), increased blood flow, water retention, and the milk itself. Small-breasted women have the same amount of lactogenic tissue as large-breasted women do—about a teaspoonful per nonlactating breast—and when they lactate, they can make as much milk. Given the functional nature of lactation, it is under selective pressure to follow fairly standardized rules of behavior.

The growth of the aesthetic breast is another thing altogether. Here, it is development of the fatty and connective tissues of the breast that accounts for its mass. As tissues with few cellular responsibilities or functional restrictions, fat and its fibrous netting can follow the whim of fashion and the consequences of sensory exploitation. They can be enlarged, exaggerated, and accentuated without exacting a great cost to their possessors, at least up to a point. In Philip Roth's novel *Sabbath's Theater*, the following exchange occurs between the eponymous dilettante of the sewer, Mickey Sabbath, and a small-breasted patient in a mental hospital:

"Tits. I understand tits. I have been studying tits since I was thirteen years old. I don't think there's any other organ or body part that evidences so much variation in size as women's tits."

"I *know*," replied Madeline, openly enjoying herself suddenly and beginning to laugh. "And why is that? Why did God allow this enormous variation in breast size? Isn't it amazing? There are women with breasts ten times the size of mine. Or even more. True?"

"That is true."

"People have big noses," she said. "I have a small nose. But are there people with noses ten times the size of mine? Four or five, max. I don't know why God did this to women. . . .

"But I don't think size has to do with milk production," said Madeline. "No, that doesn't solve the problem of what this enormous variation is *for*."

As mad Madeline says, the aesthetic breast that is subject to such wide variation in scale is not the mammalian breast gland that ranks as an organ, a necessary piece of anatomy. On the contrary, the aesthetic breast is nonfunctional to the point of being counterfunctional, which is why it strikes us as so beautiful. We are not enticed by the practical. We understand the worthiness of the practical, but we rarely find it beautiful. The large, nonlactating female breast has so much intrinsic, irrational appeal that it almost sabotages itself. We love the hemispheric breast for itself, independent of, and often in spite of, its glandular role. We love it enough that we can be made squeamish by the sight of a breastfeeding woman. It is not the exposure of the breast in public that makes us uncomfortable, for we welcome an extraordinary degree of décolletage and want to walk toward it, to gaze at it. Nor is it the reminder of our animal nature, for we can eat many things in public and put pieces of food in a baby's mouth — or a bottle of breast milk, for that matter — without eliciting a viewer's discomfort at the patent display of bodily need. Instead, it is the convergence of the aesthetic and the functional that disturbs and irritates us. When we find the image of a breastfeeding mother lovely or appealing, we do so by negating the aesthetic breast in our minds and focusing on the bond between mother and infant, on the miraculous properties that we imagine human milk to have, or on thoughts of warmth, comfort, and love recalled from our childhood. The maternal breast soothes us and invites us to rest. The aesthetic breast arouses us, grabs us by the collar or the bodice, and so it is used on billboards and magazine covers and everywhere we turn. The two conceptual breasts appeal to distinct pathways. One is ancient and logical, the love of mama and mammary. (Sarah Blaffer Hrdy has written: "The Latin term for breasts, *mammae,* derives from the plaintive cry 'mama,' spontaneously uttered by young children from widely divergent linguistic groups and often conveying a single, urgent message, 'suckle me.'") The other pathway is much newer, specific to our species, and it is noisier and more gratuitous. Being strictly human, the aesthetic breast puts on airs and calls itself divine.

Because the display of the beckoning breast is aggressive and ubiqui-   10
tous in the United States, we are said to be unusually, even pathologically, breast-obsessed. In other cultures, including parts of Africa and Asia, breasts are pedestrian. "From my research in China, it's very clear that the breast is much less sexualized there than it is in American culture," Emily Martin, the cultural historian and author of *Flexible Bodies,* said to me. "It's neither hidden nor revealed in any particular way in women's

dress or undergarments. In many villages, women sit in the sun with their breasts exposed, and older women will be out washing clothes with their breasts exposed, and it's all completely irrelevant to erotic arousal." Yet if breast obsession varies in intensity from country to country and era to era, it nonetheless is impressively persistent, and it is not limited to men, or to strictly sexual tableaux. "Everybody loves breasts," Anne Hollander, the author of *Seeing Through Clothes,* told me. "Babies love them, men love them, women love them. The whole world knows that breasts are engines of pleasure. They're great treasures of the human race, and you can't get away from them." The first thing that women did in the fourteenth century, when they broke free of the shapeless drapery of the Christian era, was to flaunt their bosoms. Men shortened their outfits and exposed their legs, women lowered the neckline and tightened the bodice. They pushed their breasts together and up. They took the soft and floppy tissue of the breasts and molded it with corsets and whalebones into firm, projecting globes. "As a fashion gimmick, you can never go wrong with breasts," Hollander says. "They may be deemphasized for a short period, as they were in the sixteenth century, when tiny breasts and thick waists were in vogue, and during the flapper era of the 1920s. But breasts always come back, because we love them so much."

What we love is not the breast per se but the fantasy breast, the aesthetic breast of no practical value. At a recent exhibition of Cambodian sculpture spanning the sixth through fifteenth centuries, I noticed that most of the female deities depicted had breasts that might have been designed by modern plastic surgeons: large, round, and firm. Helen of Troy's breasts were said to be of such flawless, curved, suspended substance that goblets could be cast from their form, as Ezra Pound told us in Canto 120: "How to govern is from Kuan Tze/but the cup of white gold in Petera/Helen's breast gave that." In the art of ancient India, Tibet, Crete, and elsewhere, the cups never runneth over, and women are shown with celestial breasts, zero-gravity planet breasts, the sorts of breasts I've almost never seen in years of using health-club locker rooms. On real women, I've seen breasts as varied as faces: breasts shaped like tubes, breasts shaped like tears, breasts that flop down, breasts that point up, breasts that are dominated by thick, dark nipples and areolae, breasts with nipples so small and pale they look airbrushed. We erroneously associate floppy breasts with older breasts, when in fact the drooping of the breast can happen at any age; some women's breasts are low-slung from the start. Thus the high, cantilevered style of the idealized breast must be considered more than just another expression of a taste for youth.

We don't know why there is such a wide variety of breast sizes, or what exactly controls the growth of the breast, particularly the fat tissue that gives the human breast its bulk. As mammary glands, human breasts follow the standard mammalian pattern. A mammary gland is a modified sweat gland, and milk is highly enriched sweat. Prolactin, the hormone responsible for milk production, predates the evolution of mammals, originally serving to maintain salt and water balance in early vertebrates such as fish—in essence, allowing fish to sweat. In monotremes, the platypus and the spiny anteater, which are considered the most primitive of living mammals, the milk simply seeps from the gland onto the nippleless surface of the mother's skin, rather as sweat does, and is licked off by the young.

Breast tissue begins to develop early, by the fourth week of fetal life. It grows along two parallel milk ridges, ancient mammalian structures that extend from the armpits down to the groin. Males and females both have milk ridges, but only in females do they receive enough hormonal stimulation later in life to achieve complete breastiness. If we were rats or pigs, our twin milk strips would develop into a total of eight teats, to meet the demands of large litters. Mammals such as elephants, cows, goats, and primates, which give birth to only one or two offspring at a time, require only two mammary glands, and so the bulk of the milk strip regresses during fetal development. Among four-legged grazing animals, the teats that grow are located at the hindquarters, where the young can suckle beneath the protective awning of a mother's powerful hind legs and rib cage. In at least one primitive primate, the aye-aye, the twin teats also are situated at the rear end of the mother. But among monkeys, apes, and humans, who either hold their young or carry them clinging to their chests (the better to navigate arboreally), the nipples graced with milk are the uppermost two, closest to the armpits.

Our potential breasts do not entirely abandon us, though. The milk ridge reminds us of our lineage subcutaneously: breast tissue is distributed far more extensively than most of us realize, reaching from the collarbone down to the last two ribs and from the breastbone, in the middle of the chest, to the back of the armpit. In some people the milk ridge expresses itself graphically, as extra nipples or entire extra breasts. Recalling her years as a lingerie saleswoman, an essayist in the *New York Times Magazine* wrote about a customer looking for a bra that would fit her unusual figure. The woman bared her breasts to the essayist, Janifer Dumas. The woman was a modern-day Artemis, the goddess of the hunt, who often is portrayed with multiple breasts. In this case, Artemis had three equal-sized breasts, the standard two on either side of her thorax and the third directly below the left one. Dumas found the perfect item, a "bralette," similar to a sports bra but with a more relaxed fit, no underwire, and a wide elastic band to hug the rib cage. "It occurred to me that this was also the type of bra I sold to women with recent mastectomies," Dumas wrote, "a piece of lingerie designed for comfort, and, as it turned out, able to accommodate more or less."

Primordial breast tissue arises early in embryogenesis, yet the breast is   15 unusual among body parts in that it remains primordial until puberty or later. No other organ, apart from the uterus, changes so dramatically in size, shape, and function as the breast does during puberty, pregnancy, and lactation. It is because the breast must be poised to alter its contours repeatedly throughout adulthood, swelling and shrinking with each new mouth to feed, that it is prone to turning cancerous. The genetic controls that keep cell growth in check elsewhere in the corpus are relaxed in the breast, giving malignancy an easy foothold.

The aesthetic breast develops in advance of the glandular one. Early in adolescence, the brain begins secreting regular bursts of hormones that stimulate the ovaries. The ovaries in turn discharge estrogen, and estrogen encourages the body to lay down fat "depots" in the breast. That adipose tissue is suspended in a gelantinous matrix of connective fibers that extend from the muscle of the chest wall to the underside of the breast skin. Connective tissue can stretch and stretch, to accommodate as much fat as the body inserts between its fibers; the connective tissue's spring gives the breast its bounce. Estrogen is necessary to the aesthetic breasts, but it is not sufficient; the hormone alone does not explain the wide variability in breast size. A woman with large breasts does not necessarily have higher estrogen levels than a small-breasted woman. Rather, the tissue of the breast is more or less responsive to estrogen, a sensitivity determined in part by genetic makeup. Among the sensitive, a very small amount of estrogen fosters an impressive bosom. Estrogen-sensitive women who take birth control pills may discover that they need bigger bras, while the estrogen-insensitive can swallow oral contraceptives by the foilful and find their breasts unmoved. Even some children are extremely sensitive to estrogen. Berton Roueche, the great medical writer, recounted the story of a six-year-old boy who began growing breasts. Eventually, the source of the hypertrophy was traced to his vitamin tablets. A single stamping machine had been used to punch out the vitamins and estrogen pills. "Think of the minute amount of estrogen the stamping machine passed on to the vitamin tablets," Roueche wrote. "And what a profound effect it had." The boy's breasts retreated on cessation of the vitamin tablets, and his parents could breathe again.

Conversely, androgens such as testosterone can inhibit breast adiposity. As we saw earlier, women who are genetically insensitive to androgen may grow very large breasts. Men whose gonads fail to produce enough testosterone sometimes suffer from gynecomastia. Without testosterone to keep breast growth in check, the men's small amount of estrogen has the opportunity to lay down selective depots of fat hurriedly, demonstrating once again that the line between maleness and femaleness is thin—as thin as the fetus's bipotential genital ridge, as thin as the milk ridge in all of us. Yet androgens don't entirely explain discrepancies in breast size among women either. Many women with comparatively high testosterone levels, women whose visible mustaches and abundant armpit hair make it clear that they are not insensitive to the androgens coursing through them, nonetheless have full frontal shelves. Thyroid hormones, stress hormones, insulin, growth hormone—all leave their smudgy fingerprints on mammogenesis. In sum, we don't know what makes the aesthetic breast. We don't have the hormonal recipe for the universal Mae West breast. If science fiction television is any indication, though, in the future, the heartbreak of "micromastia" (plastic-surgeon-speak for small breasts) will be sur-mounted, and if our brains don't get bigger, our breasts surely will. Today, the average nonlactating breast weighs two thirds of a pound and measures about four inches across and two and a half inches from chest wall to nipple tip. The average brassiere size is a 36B, and it has been since the modern bra was invented about ninety years ago. On television shows like *Star Trek,* however, every woman of every race, whether human, Vulcan, Klingon, or Borg, is as bold in bust as in spirit, and no cup less than C will be cast.

Estrogen also helps spur the elaboration of the practical breast, the glandular tissue that presumably will soon secrete its clouded, honied sweat. A series of firm, rubbery ducts and lobes begin threading their way through the fat and ligamentous glue. Each breast usually ends up with be-tween five and nine lobes, where the milk is generated, and each lobe has its independent duct, the conduit that carries the milk to the nipple. The lobes are subdivided into about two dozen lobules, which look like tiny clusters of grapes. The lobes and lobules are distributed fairly evenly throughout the breast, but all the ducts lead to a single destination, the nipple. As the ducts converge on the nipple, curling and bending like snakes or strands of ivy, their diameters widen. The circuitry of lactation follows the hydrodynamic pattern that we recognize from trees, or the veins in a leaf, or the blood vessels in the body. The lobes and lobules are the foliage, the fruits and leaves, while the ducts are the branches, thicken-ing into a braid of trunks. But while in a tree or the body's vasculature the fluid of life is pumped from the widest conduit out to the narrowest vessel or vein, here the milk is generated in each tiny lobular fruit and pulsed to the spacious pipeline below. The ducts perforate the skin of the nipple, and though these portals ordinarily are concealed by the warty folds of the nip-ple tip, when a woman is nursing her nipple balloons out and looks like a watering can, each ductal hole visible and visibly secreting milk.

The ducts and lobules do not fully mature until pregnancy, when they proliferate, thicken, and differentiate. Granular plugs the consistency of ear wax, which normally keep the ducts sealed up, begin breaking down. The lobules sprout microlobules, the alveoli. The dairy farmers commandeer the breast. They push fat out of the way to make more room for them-selves. The breast gains as much as a pound while lactating. The areola, that pigmented bull's-eye surrounding the nipple, also changes markedly in pregnancy. It darkens and seems to creep down the hillock of the breast, like lava spreading slowly from the peak of a volcano. The areola is perme-ated by another set of modified sweat glands, the little goosebumps called Montgomery's glands, and the bumps multiply in the maternal breast and exude lubricating moisture to make the sensation of suckling bearable. After weaning, the lobules atrophy, the ducts regress, the areola retreats, and the fat reclaims dominion over the breast—more or less. Women who breastfeed their children often complain that their breasts never recover their former bounce and bulk. The fat grows lazy and fails to reinfiltrate the spaces from which it was edged out by the gland. The aesthetic breast is a bon vivant, after all, a party favor. For reliability, look to the ducts and lobules. They'll return when needed, and they're not afraid to work up a sweat.

Breasts weigh a few ounces in fact and a few tons in metaphor. As Marilyn Yalom describes admirably in her cultural study *A History of the Breast,* the breast is a communal kiosk, open to all pronouncements and cranks, and the endorsements of the past are easily papered over with the homilies of today. The withered tits of witches and devils represented the wages of lust. In Minoan statues dating from 1600 B.C., priestesses are shown with bare, commanding breasts and snakes wrapped around each arm. The snakes strain their heads toward the viewer, their extended tongues echoing the erect nipples of the figurine, as though to warn that the powerful bosom they bracket might as soon dispense poison as love. The breast is a bralette, able to accommodate more or less. The multi-breasted goddess seen in many cultures projects tremendous strength. So too do the Amazons, those mythical female warriors who lived apart from men, consorting with them once a year solely for the sake of being impregnated, and who reared their daughters but slayed, crippled, or abandoned their sons. The Amazons are most famed for their self-inflicted mastectomies, their willingness to cut off one breast to improve their archery skills and thus to resist conquest by the male hordes surrounding them. For men, Yalom writes, "Amazons are seen as monsters, viragos, unnatural women who have misappropriated the masculine warrior role. The missing breast creates a terrifying asymmetry: one breast is retained to nurture female offspring, the other is removed so as to facilitate violence against men." For women, the Amazon represents an inchoate wish, a nostalgic longing for the future. "The removal of the breast and the acquisition of 'masculine' traits suggests this mythic Amazon's desire to be bisexual, both a nurturing female and an aggressive male, with the nurturance directed exclusively toward other women and the aggression directed exclusively toward men." A softened variant of the Amazon icon occurred in eighteenth-century France, when the figure of Liberty often was shown with one breast clothed, the other bared, her willingness to reveal her breast (or at least her indifference to her temporary state of dishabille) evidence of her commitment to the cause. More recently, women who have had a breast surgically removed for the treatment of cancer have assumed the mantle of the Amazon warrior and proudly, angrily publicized their naked, asymmetrical torsos on magazine covers and in advertisements. Where the breast once was, now there is a diagonal scar, crossing the chest like a bow or a bandolier, alarming, thrilling, and beautiful in its fury.

The breast has been used like a cowbrand, to denote possession. In Rembrandt's famous portrait *The Jewish Bride,* the husband, considerably the elder of the two, is shown with his right hand covering the bride's left breast, claiming her, including her within his gentle, paternal jurisdiction, and her hand reaches up to graze his groping one—though whether as an expression of modesty, concurrence, or hesitation is left gorgeously unclear. In nineteenth-century America, female slaves being put up for auction were photographed barechested, to underscore their status as beasts to be bought. In driving a metaphor home, breasts were beaten, tortured, and mutilated. In the seventeenth century, women accused of witchcraft often had their breasts hacked off before they were burned at the stake. When Anna Pappenheimer, a Bavarian woman who was the daughter of gravediggers and latrine cleaners, was condemned as a witch, her breasts were not merely cut off but stuffed into her mouth and then into the mouths of her two grown sons, a grotesque mockery of Pappenheimer's maternal role.

Early scientists too had to have their say on the breasts. In the eighteenth-century, Linnaeus, the ever-colorful Swedish taxonomist, paid the breast a dubious honor by naming an entire class after it: Mammalia, literally "of the breast," a term of Linnaeus's invention. As Londa Schiebinger has described, Linnaeus could have chosen from other features that mammals were known at the time to have in common. We could have been classified as Pilosa, the hairy ones, or as Aurecaviga, the hollow-eared ones (a reference to the distinctive three-boned structure of the mammalian middle ear), or as bearers of a four-chambered heart (term uncoined and perhaps uncoinable). But despite the derision of some of Linnaeus's contemporaries, we and our fuzzy, viviparous kin became mammals. It was the Enlightenment, and Linnaeus had a point to make, and so again the breast was called upon to service metaphor. Zoologists accepted that humans were a type of animal, as uncomfortable as the notion was and remains. A taxon was needed that would link humans to other species. Whatever feature Linnaeus chose to highlight as the bond between us and them inevitably would become the synecdoche of our beastliness. All mammals are hairy, but men are hairier than women, so Pilosa wouldn't do. The structure of the ear is too dull to merit immortalization through nomenclature. The breast, however, has romance and resonance, and best of all, it is most highly articulated in women. In the same volume in which Linnaeus introduced the term *Mammalia,* he also gave us our species name, *Homo sapiens,* man of wisdom, the category distinguishing humans from all other species. "Thus, within Linnaean terminology, a female characteristic (the lactating mamma) ties humans to brutes, while a traditionally male characteristic (reason) marks our separateness," Schiebinger writes. Thinkers of the Enlightenment advocated the equality and natural rights of all men, and some women of the time, including Mary Wollstonecraft and Abigail Adams, John's wife, argued that women too should be given their due rights—enfranchisement, for example, or the rights to own property and divorce a brutal spouse. The husbands of the Enlightenment smiled with tolerance and sympathy, but they were not prepared to peep over that political precipice. Through zoology and the taxonomic reinforcement of woman's earthiness, rational men found convenient justification for postponing matters of women's rights until woman's reason, her *sapientia,* was fully established. (Interestingly, though, human milk has often been characterized as the purest and most ethereal of body fluids, the least brutish aspect of a woman. . . .)

In the nineteenth century, some scientists used the breast as phrenologists have used the skull, to demarcate and rank the various human races. Certain breasts were more equal than others. The European breast was drawn as a hemisphere standing at full attention—meet the smart and civilized breast. The breast of an African woman was portrayed as flabby and pendulous, like the udder of a goat. In abolitionist literature, illustrations of female slaves gave them high, round, sympathetic breasts—the melanized counterparts to the pop-up breasts of the slaves' tightly cinched mistresses.

Linnaeus hog-tied us to other mammals by our possession of teats, but our breasts, we know, are ours alone. Evolutionary thinkers have known it too, and they have given us a wide selection of justifications for the human breast. As Caroline Pond says, there is little evidence to support any of the theories. We don't have a clue when in human evolution breasts first began their rise. Breasts don't fossilize. We don't know if they appeared before we lost our body hair or after, and in any event we don't know when—or why—we lost our body hair. But breasts are such a prominent feature of a woman's body that scientists keep staring at them, looking for clues. They are baffled by breasts, and they should be.

Men don't have breasts, but they like to stake their claim on breasts, to   25
grope their Jewish bride, and to feel they had a hand in inventing them. We must not be surprised if many evolutionary theories assume that breasts arose to talk to men. By far the most famous explanation in this genre comes from Desmond Morris, the British zoologist, who in 1967 wrote a spectacularly successful book, *The Naked Ape,* in which he presented a metaphor nonpareil, of breasts as buttock mimics. You've probably heard this theory in some form. It's hard to escape it. Like the Rolling Stones, it refuses to retire. As originally conceived, the theory rested on a sequence of assumptions, the first being that men and women needed to form a pair bond—better known as marriage—to raise children. The pair bond required the cultivation of sustained intimacy between partners, which meant intercourse was best done face to face rather than in the anonymous doggy-style position presumed to be the copulatory technique of our prehuman ancestors. To that end, the clitoris migrated forward, to give early women the incentive to seek frontal sex. For the gentlemen, the breast arose as an inspiration to modify their technique, offering a recapitulation ventrally of a body part they had so coveted from behind. In subsequent books, Morris has repeated the theory, illustrating it with photos comparing a good set of female buttocks with a good set of cleavaged knockers.

Maybe he's right about breasts looking somewhat like buttocks, but who's to say that rounded buttocks didn't develop to imitate breasts, or that the two developed in tandem for their intrinsic aesthetic appeal? The high, rounded human buttocks are unlike the flat and narrow rump of many other primates. Morris and others argue that the gluteal hemisphericity surely came first, because the evolution of upright posture demanded greater musculature in the rump. The vertical configuration also created an area where energy could be stored as fat without interfering with basic movements, Timothy Taylor writes in *The Prehistory of Sex*. Moreover, upright posture introduced a need for alluringly shaped female buttocks, Taylor says. When a woman stands up, you can't see her vulva. The presentation of the vulva serves as an important sexual signal in many other primate species. If a woman isn't going to be flashing her vagina, she requires some other sexual signal rearguard, and the buttocks thus became accentuated. To ensure that she caught men's attention coming and going, the woman's breasts soon swelled too. Which is fine, except that women find a high, rounded butt on a man as alluring as a man does on a woman, and women notice it on women, and men on men. Beautiful buttocks are a thing to behold, but they need not have assumed their globular contours to provide a home for a large muscle. Instead, the curviness of the human rump on both sexes could well have been selected as another example of sensory exploitation, and of our preference for the curved and generous over the straight and narrow. The breast might not imitate the buttock so much as the two converge on a common theme.

There are other reasons to be skeptical about the development of breasts as an encouragement to pursue frontal sex. Several other primates, including bonobos and orangutans, also copulate face to face, and the females wear no sexual badges on their chests, no clever replicas of their narrow rumps or swollen vulvas. Nevertheless, they are sought after—in the case of bonobos, many times a day. What is *P. paniscus*'s secret, and does she have a catalogue?

Because breasts, when not serving as visual lures, play an essential role in reproduction, many theorists have assumed that they developed to advertise to men some aspect of a woman's fecundity. Breasts certainly proclaim that a female is of reproductive age, but so do many other things—pubic hair, the widening of the pelvic bone, the wafting of hormonally activated body odors. A woman needs a certain percentage of body fat to sustain a pregnancy. Breasts are two parcels of fat. Perhaps they proclaim that a woman is nutritionally well stocked and so can bear and suckle children, a point that a prehistoric man, surveying the options among a number of calorically borderline women, conceivably would want to know. Yet breasts, for all their prominence, represent a small fraction of the body's total fat mass—4 percent, on average—and their size generally changes less in proportion to a woman's weight gain or loss than other fat depots of the body, like the adipose of the thighs, buttocks, and upper arms; thus breasts fatness is not a great indicator of a woman's health or nutritional status. And as we saw above, breast size has nothing to do with a woman's reproductive or lactational capabilities and so is a poor signal of her maternal worth. Others suggest that breasts evolved to deceive, to confuse a man about a woman's current ovulatory status or whether she is pregnant or not, the better to mask issues of paternity and inhibit the tendency of men to kill infants they know are not their own. Why a man would be attracted to such devious commodities is unclear, unless we assume that he is predisposed for another reason to love the look of a breast.

Women have laid claim to breasts too. Meredith Small recasts the idea of breasts as mobile pantries, but sees them as designed to help women rather than to assure men that they are fertile. "A large breast might be simply a fat storage area for females who evolved under nutritional stress," she writes. "Ancestral humans walked long and far in their search for food, and they needed fat for years of lactation." Again, though, breasts are not the most liquid of fat assets, and they are surprisingly stingy about releasing their energy stores on demand. When a woman is lactating, lipid energy from the hips and thighs is far more readily mobilized than the fat of the breasts, even though the breast fat is much closer to the means of milk production. Helen Fisher proposes that breasts are a woman's pleasure chests, the swollen scaffolding beneath the erotogenic nipples ensuring that the breasts are caressed, sucked, and pressed against for maximum stimulation. Yet not all women have sensitive breasts, nor do they necessarily adore chronic fondling. "I've had a lot of experience in life," says a seventy-five-year-old woman in *Breasts: Women Speak*. "I've come to the conclusion that women get breast cancer because men handle their breasts *too much.*" At the same time, many men have very sensitive nipples, and they only wish women were more inclined to take a lick now and then.

If not for the woman, than maybe for the child. Elaine Morgan, an orig- 30
inal and brave thinker who continues almost single-handedly to push the aquatic ape theory of human evolution, has submitted several breast lines. She believes that humans spent part of their evolutionary development immersed in water, that we are part pinniped, part ape. One excuse for breasts, then, might be that they were Mae Wests, as the British soldiers of World War II called their life jackets—flotation devices that infants could cling to as they nursed. More recently, Morgan has suggested that hairlessness, another presumed legacy of our nautical phase, gave birth to the breast. Young monkeys and apes can cling to their mother's chest hair while they suckle, she says. Human infants have nothing to grab. In addition, they're so helpless, they can't lift their heads up to reach the nipple. The nipple has to come to them. Consequently, the nipple of the human breast is situated lower on the chest than the teat of a monkey is, and it is no longer anchored tightly to the ribs, as it is in monkeys. "The skin of the breast around the nipple becomes more loosely-fitting to make it more maneuverable, leaving space beneath the looser skin to be occupied by glandular tissue and fat," Morgan concludes. "Adult males find the resulting species-specific contours sexually stimulating, but the instigator and first beneficiary of the change was the baby." It's the empty-closet theory of the breast: if it's there, it will be stuffed. Apart from the lack of any evidence to support the aquatic ape theory, the putative benefits of the loosened nipple to nursing are not obvious. A woman must hold her baby to her breast, or prop the baby up with pillows, or strap

the infant in place with a baby sling (which is how the vast majority of women in the developing world nurse their infants). If a mother were to spend much time hunched over a baby in her lap like Daisy the cow, her nipple dangling in the infant's mouth, she might find it difficult ever to straighten back to bipedalism again.

The aesthetic breast won't lift a finger to help you.

QUESTIONS

1. Angier begins her essay with what appears initially to be an unmotivated description of zebra finches and Burley's experiments with them. In paragraph 6 we discover that Angier wishes to present the finches' crests as an analogy to a woman's breasts, the subject of the essay. How are they analogous? Why is she so careful to make this somewhat strained connection?
2. Outline the various evolutionary arguments which Angier responds to at the end of the essay.
3. The essay asserts that breasts are "funny things, really, and we should learn to laugh at them, which may be easier to do if we first take them seriously." Make a list of witticisms, puns ("they're not afraid to work up a sweat"), and other comic moments you discover in the essay. What is the function of humor in Angier's argument?
4. One method of explanation is to break your subject into different categories or concepts in order to clarify the argument. What two major categories of breasts does Angier present? How does this division determine the structure of her argument?
5. "Men don't have breasts." This is true insofar as testosterone keeps "breast growth in check" and prevents lactation from residual milk ridges; yet men's chests have many of the same characteristics that Angier celebrates throughout the essay, including visual appeal and "very sensitive nipples." Write an essay in which you discuss the male chest and its cultural status as an "aesthetic" object.
6. One way to describe "The Story of the Breast" is to say that it attempts to explain how something is inexplicable—a difficult task. Select a topic that you are convinced is essentially inexplicable, and compose an essay which tries to demonstrate this through explanation of failed explanations.

MAKING CONNECTIONS

How would Charles Darwin (p. 576) respond to Natalie Angier's essay? Do you think that Darwin's ideas help to confirm or to deny Angier's explanation? Explain.

THE HE HORMONE

Andrew Sullivan

Born in Godstone, England, in 1963, Andrew Sullivan attended Oxford University and afterward came to the United States to pursue his M.A. and Ph.D. at Harvard. He worked for many years as a staff writer and editor for The New Republic *and is currently a contributing writer for various publications. He has also written two provocative books:* Virtually Normal: An Argument about Homosexuality *(1995), in which he argues in favor of full gay rights, including same-sex marriages; and* Love Undetectable: Notes on Friendship, Sex, and Survival *(1998), in which he reflects on his own status as an HIV-positive gay man. Paradoxically, Sullivan most often casts himself as a political and social conservative; for example, in another essay later in the text (p. 664) he argues against the enactment of hate crimes laws. The following essay originally appeared on April 2, 2000, in the* New York Times Magazine.

It has a slightly golden hue, suspended in an oily substance and injected in a needle about half as thick as a telephone wire. I have never been able to jab it suddenly in my hip muscle, as the doctor told me to. Instead, after swabbing a small patch of my rump down with rubbing alcohol, I push the needle in slowly until all three inches of it are submerged. Then I squeeze the liquid in carefully, as the muscle often spasms to absorb it. My skin sticks a little to the syringe as I pull it out, and then an odd mix of oil and blackish blood usually trickles down my hip.

I am so used to it now that the novelty has worn off. But every now and again the weirdness returns. The chemical I am putting in myself is synthetic testosterone: a substance that has become such a metaphor for manhood that it is almost possible to forget that it has a physical reality. Twenty years ago, as it surged through my pubescent body, it deepened my voice, grew hair on my face and chest, strengthened my limbs, made me a man. So what, I wonder, is it doing to me now?

There are few things more challenging to the question of what the difference between men and women really is than to see the difference injected into your hip. Men and women differ biologically mainly because men produce 10 to 20 times as much testosterone as most women do, and this chemical, no one seriously disputes, profoundly affects physique, behavior, mood and self-understanding. To be sure, because human beings are also deeply socialized, the impact of this difference is refracted through the prism of our own history and culture. But biology, it is all too easy to forget, is at the root of this process. As more people use testosterone medically, as more use testosterone-based steroids in sports and recreation and as more research explores the behavioral effects of this chemical, the clearer the power of that biology is. It affects every aspect of our society, from high divorce rates and adolescent male violence to the exploding cults of bodybuilding and professional wrestling. It helps explain, perhaps better than any other single factor, why inequalities between men and women remain so frustratingly resilient in public and private life. This summer, when an easy-to-apply testosterone gel hits the market, and when more people experience the power of this chemical in their own bodies, its social importance, once merely implicit, may get even harder to ignore.

My own encounter with testosterone came about for a simple medical reason. I am H.I.V.-positive, and two years ago, after a period of extreme fatigue and weight loss, I had my testosterone levels checked. It turned out that my body was producing far less testosterone than it should have been at my age. No one quite knows why, but this is common among men with long-term H.I.V. The usual treatment is regular injection of artificial testosterone, which is when I experienced my first manhood supplement.

At that point I weighed around 165 pounds. I now weigh 185 pounds. My collar size went from a 15 to a 17½ in a few months; my chest went from 40 to 44. My appetite in every sense of that word expanded beyond measure. Going from napping two hours a day, I now rarely sleep in the daytime and have enough energy for daily workouts and a hefty work schedule. I can squat more than 400 pounds. Depression, once a regular feature of my life, is now a distant memory. I feel better able to recover from life's curveballs, more persistent, more alive. These are the long-term effects. They are almost as striking as the short-term ones.   5

Because the testosterone is injected every two weeks, and it quickly leaves the bloodstream, I can actually feel its power on almost a daily basis. Within hours, and at most a day, I feel a deep surge of energy. It is less edgy than a double espresso, but just as powerful. My attention span shortens. In the two or three days after my shot, I find it harder to concentrate on writing and feel the need to exercise more. My wit is quicker, my mind faster, but my judgment is more impulsive. It is not unlike the kind of rush I get before talking in front of a large audience, or going on a first date, or getting on an airplane, but it suffuses me in a less abrupt and more consistent way. In a word, I feel braced. For what? It scarcely seems to matter.

And then after a few days, as the testosterone peaks and starts to decline, the feeling alters a little. I find myself less reserved than usual, and more garrulous. The same energy is there, but it seems less directed toward action than toward interaction, less toward pride than toward lust. The odd thing is that, however much experience I have with it, this lust peak still takes me unawares. It is not like feeling hungry, a feeling you recognize and satiate. It creeps up on you. It is only a few days later that I look back and realize that I spent hours of the recent past socializing in a bar or checking out every potential date who came vaguely over my horizon. You realize more acutely than before that lust is a chemical. It comes; it goes. It waxes; it wanes. You are not helpless in front of it, but you are certainly not fully in control.

Then there's anger. I have always tended to bury or redirect my rage. I once thought this an inescapable part of my personality. It turns out I was wrong. Late last year, mere hours after a T shot, my dog ran off the leash to forage for a chicken bone left in my local park. The more I chased her, the more she ran. By the time I retrieved her, the bone had been consumed, and I gave her a sharp tap on her rear end. "Don't smack your dog!" yelled a burly guy a few yards away. What I found myself yelling back at him is not printable in this magazine, but I have never used that language in public before, let alone bellow it at the top of my voice. He shouted back, and within seconds I was actually close to hitting him. He backed down and slunk off. I strutted home, chest puffed up, contrite beagle dragged sheepishly behind me. It wasn't until half an hour later that I realized I had been a complete jerk and had nearly gotten into the first public brawl of my life. I vowed to inject my testosterone at night in the future.

That was an extreme example, but other, milder ones come to mind: losing my temper in a petty argument; innumerable traffic confrontations; even the occasional slightly too prickly column or e-mail flameout. No doubt my previous awareness of the mythology of testosterone had subtly primed me for these feelings of irritation and impatience. But when I place them in the larger context of my new testosterone-associated energy; and of what we know about what testosterone tends to do to people, then it seems plausible enough to ascribe some of this increased edginess and self-confidence to that biweekly encounter with a syringe full of manhood.

Testosterone, oddly enough, is a chemical closely related to cholesterol. It was first isolated by a Dutch scientist in 1935 from mice testicles and successfully synthesized by the German biologist Adolf Butenandt. Although testosterone is often thought of as the definition of maleness, both men and women produce it. Men produce it in their testicles; women produce it in their ovaries and adrenal glands. The male body converts some testosterone to estradiol, a female hormone, and the female body has receptors for testosterone, just as the male body does. That's why women who want to change their sex are injected with testosterone and develop male characteristics, like deeper voices, facial hair and even baldness. The central biological difference between adult men and women, then, is not that men have testosterone and women don't. It's that men produce much, much more of it than women do. An average woman has 40 to 60 nanograms of testosterone in a deciliter of blood plasma. An average man has 300 to 1,000 nanograms per deciliter. 10

Testosterone's effects start early — really early. At conception, every embryo is female and unless hormonally altered will remain so. You need testosterone to turn a fetus with a Y chromosome into a real boy, to masculinize his brain and body. Men experience a flood of testosterone twice in their lives: in the womb about six weeks after conception and at puberty. The first fetal burst primes the brain and the body, endowing male fetuses with the instinctual knowledge of how to respond to later testosterone surges. The second, more familiar adolescent rush—squeaky voices, facial hair and all—completes the process. Without testosterone, humans would always revert to the default sex, which is female. The Book of Genesis is therefore exactly wrong. It isn't women who are made of men. It is men who are made out of women. Testosterone, to stretch the metaphor, is Eve's rib.

The effect of testosterone is systemic. It engenders both the brain and the body. Apart from the obvious genital distinction, other differences between men's and women's bodies reflect this: body hair, the ratio of muscle to fat, upper-body strength and so on. But testosterone leads to behavioral differences as well. Since it is unethical to experiment with human embryos by altering hormonal balances, much of the evidence for this idea is based on research conducted on animals. A Stanford research group, for example, as reported in Deborah Blum's book "Sex on the Brain," injected newborn female rats with testosterone. Not only did the female rats develop penises from their clitorises, but they also appeared fully aware of how to use them, trying to have sex with other females with merry abandon. Male rats who had their testosterone blocked after birth, on the other hand, saw their penises wither or disappear entirely and presented themselves to the female rats in a passive, receptive way. Other scientists, theorizing that it was testosterone that enabled male zebra finches to sing, injected mute female finches with testosterone. Sure enough, the females sang. Species in which the female is typically more aggressive, like hyenas in female-run clans, show higher levels of testosterone among the females than among the males. Female sea snipes, which impregnate the males, and leave them to stay home and rear the young, have higher testosterone levels than their mates. Typical "male" behavior, in other words, corresponds to testosterone levels, whether exhibited by chromosomal males or females.

Does this apply to humans? The evidence certainly suggests that it does, though much of the "proof" is inferred from accidents. Pregnant women who were injected with progesterone (chemically similar to testosterone) in the 1950's to avoid miscarriage had daughters who later reported markedly tomboyish childhoods. Ditto girls born with a disorder that causes their adrenal glands to produce a hormone like testosterone rather than the more common cortisol. The moving story, chronicled in John Colapinto's book "As Nature Made Him," of David Reimer, who as an infant was surgically altered after a botched circumcision to become a girl, suggests how long-lasting the effect of fetal testosterone can be. Despite a ruthless attempt to socialize David as a girl, and to give him the correct hormonal treatment to develop as one, his behavioral and psychological makeup was still ineradicably male. Eventually, with the help of more testosterone, he became a full man again. Female-to-male transsexuals report a similar transformation when injected with testosterone. One, Susan/Drew Seidman, described her experience in The Village Voice last November. "My sex-drive went through the roof," Seidman recalled. "I felt like I had to have sex once a day or I would die. . . . I was into porn as a girl, but now I'm *really* into porn." For Seidman, becoming a man was not merely physical. Thanks to testosterone, it was also psychological. "I'm not sure I can tell you what makes a man a man," Seidman averred. "But I know it's not a penis."

The behavioral traits associated with testosterone are largely the cliché-ridden ones you might expect. The Big T correlates with energy, self-confidence, competitiveness, tenacity, strength and sexual drive. When you talk to men in testosterone therapy, several themes recur. "People talk about extremes," one man in his late 30's told me. "But that's not what testosterone does for me. It makes me think more clearly. It makes me think more positively. It's my Saint Johnswort."[1] A man in his 20's said: "Usually, I cycle up the hill to my apartment in 12th gear. In the days after my shot, I ride it easily in 16th." A 40-year-old executive who took testosterone for bodybuilding purposes told me: "I walk into a business meeting now and I just exude self-confidence. I know there are lots of other reasons for this, but my company has just exploded since my treatment. I'm on a roll. I feel capable of almost anything."

When you hear comments like these, it's no big surprise that strutting peacocks with their extravagant tails and bright colors are supercharged with testosterone and that mousy little male sparrows aren't. "It turned my life around," another man said. "I felt stronger — and not just in a physical sense. It was a deep sense of being strong, almost spiritually strong." Testosterone's antidepressive power is only marginally understood. It doesn't act in the precise way other antidepressants do, and it probably helps alleviate gloominess primarily by propelling people into greater activity and restlessness, giving them less time to think and reflect. (This may be one reason women tend to suffer more from depression than men.) Like other drugs, T can also lose potency if overused. Men who inject excessive amounts may see their own production collapse and experience shrinkage of their testicles and liver damage.

Individual effects obviously vary, and a person's internal makeup is affected by countless other factors — physical, psychological and external. But in this complex human engine, testosterone is gasoline. It revs you up. A 1997 study took testosterone samples from 125 men and 128 women and selected the 12 with the lowest levels of testosterone and the 15 with the highest. They gave them beepers, asked them to keep diaries and paged them 20 times over a four-day period to check on their actions, feelings, thoughts and whereabouts. The differences were striking. High-testosterone people "experienced more arousal and tension than those low

15

---

[1] *St. Johnswort:* a wildflower or weed used to combat depression. [Eds.]

in testosterone," according to the study. "They spent more time thinking, especially about concrete problems in the immediate present. They wanted to get things done and felt frustrated when they could not. They mentioned friends more than family or lovers."

Unlike Popeye's spinach, however, testosterone is also, in humans at least, a relatively subtle agent. It is not some kind of on-off switch by which men are constantly turned on and women off. For one thing, we all start out with different base-line levels. Some women may have remarkably high genetic T levels, some men remarkably low, although the male-female differential is so great that no single woman's T level can exceed any single man's, unless she, or he, has some kind of significant hormonal imbalance. For another, and this is where the social and political ramifications get complicated, testosterone is highly susceptible to environment. T levels can rise and fall depending on external circumstances—short term and long term. Testosterone is usually elevated in response to confrontational situations—a street fight, a marital spat, a presidential debate—or in highly charged sexual environments, like a strip bar or a pornographic Web site. It can also be raised permanently in continuously combative environments, like war, although it can also be suddenly lowered by stress.

Because testosterone levels can be measured in saliva as well as in blood, researchers like Alan Booth, Allan Mazur, Richard Udry and particularly James M. Dabbs, whose book "Heroes, Rogues and Lovers" will be out this fall, have compiled quite a database on these variations. A certain amount of caution is advisable in interpreting the results of these studies. There is some doubt about the validity of onetime samples to gauge underlying testosterone levels. And most of the studies of the psychological effects of testosterone take place in culturally saturated environments, so that the difference between cause and effect is often extremely hard to disentangle. Nevertheless, the sheer number and scale of the studies, especially in the last decade or so, and the strong behavioral correlations with high testosterone, suggest some conclusions about the social importance of testosterone that are increasingly hard to gainsay.

Testosterone is clearly correlated in both men and women with psychological dominance, confident physicality and high self-esteem. In most combative, competitive environments, especially physical ones, the person with the most T wins. Put any two men in a room together and the one with more testosterone will tend to dominate the interaction. Working women have higher levels of testosterone than women who stay at home, and the daughters of working women have higher levels of testosterone than the daughters of housewives. A 1996 study found that in lesbian couples in which one partner assumes the male, or "butch," role and another assumes the female, or "femme," role, the "butch" woman has higher levels of testosterone than the "femme" woman. In naval medical tests, midshipmen have been shown to have higher average levels of testosterone than plebes. Actors tend to have more testosterone than ministers, according to a 1990 study. Among 700 male prison inmates in a 1995 study, those with the highest T levels tended to be those most likely to be in trouble with the prison authorities and to engage in unprovoked violence. This is true among women as well as among men, according to a 1997 study of 87 female inmates in a maximum security prison. Although high testosterone levels often correlate with dominance in interpersonal relationships, it does not guarantee more social power. Testosterone levels are higher among blue-collar workers, for example, than among white-collar workers, according to a study of more than 4,000 former military personnel conducted in 1992. A 1998 study found that trial lawyers — with their habituation to combat, conflict and swagger — have higher levels of T than other lawyers.

The salient question, of course, is, How much of this difference in aggression and dominance is related to environment? Are trial lawyers naturally more testosteroned, and does that lead them into their profession? Or does the experience of the courtroom raise their levels? Do working women have naturally high T levels, or does the prestige of work and power elevate their testosterone? Because of the limits of researching such a question, it is hard to tell beyond a reasonable doubt. But the social context clearly matters. It is even possible to tell who has won a tennis match not by watching the game, but by monitoring testosterone-filled saliva samples throughout. Testosterone levels rise for both players before the match. The winner of any single game sees his T production rise; the loser sees it fall. The ultimate winner experiences a postgame testosterone surge, while the loser sees a collapse. This is true even for people watching sports matches. A 1998 study found that fans backing the winning side in a college basketball game and a World Cup soccer match saw their testosterone levels rise; fans rooting for the losing teams in both games saw their own T levels fall. There is, it seems, such a thing as vicarious testosterone.

One theory to explain this sensitivity to environment is that testosterone was originally favored in human evolution to enable successful hunting and combat. It kicks in, like adrenaline, in anticipation of combat, mental or physical, and helps you prevail. But a testosterone crash can be a killer too. Toward the end of my two-week cycle, I can almost feel my spirits dragging. In the event of a just-lost battle, as Matt Ridley points out in his book *The Red Queen,* there's a good reason for this to occur. If you lose a contest with prey or a rival, it makes sense not to pick another fight immediately. So your body wisely prompts you to withdraw, filling your brain with depression and self-doubt. But if you have made a successful kill or defeated a treacherous enemy, your hormones goad you into further conquest. And people wonder why professional football players get into postgame sexual escapades and violence. Or why successful businessmen and politicians often push their sexual luck.

Similarly, testosterone levels may respond to more long-term stimuli. Studies have shown that inner-city youths, often exposed to danger in high-crime neighborhoods, may generate higher testosterone levels than unthreatened, secluded suburbanites. And so high T levels may not merely be responses to a violent environment; they may subsequently add to it in what becomes an increasingly violent, sexualized cycle. (It may be no accident that testosterone-soaked ghettos foster both high levels of crime and high levels of illegitimacy.) In the same way, declines in violence and crime may allow T levels to drop among young inner-city males, generating a virtuous trend of further reductions in crime and birth rates. This may help to explain why crime can decline precipitously, rather than drift down slowly, over time. Studies have also shown that men in long-term marriages see their testosterone levels progressively fall and their sex drives subsequently decline. It is as if their wives successfully tame them, reducing their sexual energy to a level where it is more unlikely to seek extramarital outlets. A 1993 study showed that single men tended to have higher levels of testosterone than married men and that men with high levels of testosterone turned out to be more likely to have had a failed marriage. Of course, if you start out with higher T levels, you may be more likely to fail at marriage, stay in the sexual marketplace, see your testosterone increase in response to this and so on.

None of this means, as the scientists always caution, that testosterone is directly linked to romantic failure or violence. No study has found a simple correlation, for example, between testosterone levels and crime. But there may be a complex correlation. The male-prisoner study, for example, found no general above-normal testosterone levels among inmates. But murderers and armed robbers had higher testosterone levels than mere car thieves and burglars. Why is this not surprising? One of the most remarkable, but least commented on, social statistics available is the sex differential in crime. For decades, arrest rates have shown that an overwhelmingly disproportionate number of arrestees are male. Although the sex differential has narrowed since the chivalrous 1930's, when the male-female arrest ratio was 12 to 1, it remains almost 4 to 1, a close echo of the testosterone differential between men and women. In violent crime, men make up an even bigger proportion. In 1998, 89 percent of murders in the United States, for example, were committed by men. Of course, there's a nature-nurture issue here as well, and the fact that the sex differential in crime has decreased over this century suggests that environment has played a part. Yet despite the enormous social changes of the last century, the differential is still 4 to 1, which suggests that underlying attributes may also have a great deal to do with it.

This, then, is what it comes down to: testosterone is a facilitator of risk—physical, criminal, personal. Without the influence of testosterone, the cost of these risks might seem to far outweigh the benefits. But with testosterone charging through the brain, caution is thrown to the wind. The influence of testosterone may not always lead to raw physical confrontation. In men with many options it may influence the decision to invest money in a dubious enterprise, jump into an ill-advised sexual affair or tell an egregiously big whopper. At the time, all these decisions may make some sort of testosteroned sense. The White House, anyone?

The effects of testosterone are not secret; neither is the fact that men have far more of it than women. But why? As we have seen, testosterone is   25 not synonymous with gender; in some species, it is the female who has most of it. The relatively new science of evolutionary psychology offers perhaps the best explanation for why that's not the case in humans. For neo-Darwinians, the aggressive and sexual aspects of testosterone are related to the division of labor among hunter-gatherers in our ancient but formative evolutionary past. This division—men in general hunted, women in general gathered—favored differing levels of testosterone. Women need some testosterone—for self-defense, occasional risk-taking, strength—but not as much as men. Men use it to increase their potential to defeat rivals, respond to physical threats in strange environments, maximize their physical attractiveness, prompt them to spread their genes as widely as possible and defend their home if necessary.

But the picture, as most good evolutionary psychologists point out, is more complex than this. Men who are excessively testosteroned are not that attractive to most women. Although they have the genes that turn women on—strong jaws and pronounced cheekbones, for example, are correlated with high testosterone—they can also be precisely the unstable, highly sexed creatures that childbearing, stability-seeking women want to avoid. There are two ways, evolutionary psychologists hazard, that women have successfully squared this particular circle. One is to marry the sweet class nerd and have an affair with the college quarterback: that way you get the good genes, the good sex and the stable home. The other is to find a man with variable T levels, who can be both stable and nurturing when you want him to be and yet become a muscle-bound, bristly gladiator when the need arises. The latter strategy, as Emma Bovary[2] realized, is sadly more easily said than done.

So over millennia, men with high but variable levels of testosterone were the ones most favored by women and therefore most likely to produce offspring, and eventually us. Most men today are highly testosteroned, but not rigidly so. We don't have to live at all times with the T levels required to face down a woolly mammoth or bed half the village's young women. We can adjust so that our testosterone levels make us more suitable for co-parenting or for simply sticking around our mates when the sexual spark has dimmed. Indeed, one researcher, John Wingfield, has found a suggestive correlation in bird species between adjustable testosterone levels and males that have an active role to play in rearing their young. Male birds with consistently high testosterone levels tend to be worse fathers; males with variable levels are better dads. So there's hope for the new man yet.

From the point of view of men, after all, constantly high testosterone is a real problem, as any 15-year-old boy trying to concentrate on his home-

---

[2]*Emma Bovary:* the heroine of Gustave Flaubert's novel *Madame Bovary* (1857). Married to a good but dull man with a low T-level, she discovers passion with a sensual playboy but is abandoned by him. She falls into debt and, in despair, poisons herself. [Eds.]

work will tell you. I missed one deadline on this article because it came three days after a testosterone shot and I couldn't bring myself to sit still long enough. And from a purely genetic point of view, men don't merely have an interest in impregnating as many women as possible; they also have an interest in seeing that their offspring are brought up successfully and their genes perpetuated. So for the male, the conflict between sex and love is resolved, as it is for the female, by a compromise between the short-term thrill of promiscuity and the long-term rewards of nurturing children. Just as the female does, he optimizes his genetic outcome by a stable marriage and occasional extramarital affairs. He is just more likely to have these affairs than a woman. Testosterone is both cause and effect of this difference.

And the difference is a real one. This is so obvious a point that we sometimes miss it. But without that difference, it would be hard to justify separate sports leagues for men and women, just as it would be hard not to suspect judicial bias behind the fact that of the 98 people executed last year in the United States, 100 percent came from a group that composes a little less than 50 percent of the population; that is, men. When the discrepancy is racial, we wring our hands. That it is sexual raises no red flags. Similarly, it is not surprising that 55 percent of everyone arrested in 1998 was under the age of 25 — the years when male testosterone levels are at their natural peak.

It is also controversial yet undeniable that elevating testosterone levels can be extremely beneficial for physical and mental performance. It depends, of course, on what you're performing in. If your job is to whack home runs, capture criminals or play the market, then testosterone is a huge advantage. If you're a professional conciliator, office manager or teacher, it is probably a handicap. Major League Baseball was embarrassed that Mark McGwire's 1998 season home-run record might have been influenced by his use of androstenedione, a legal supplement that helps increase the body's own production of testosterone. But its own study into andro's effects concluded that regular use of it clearly raises T levels and so improves muscle mass and physical strength, without serious side effects. Testosterone also accelerates the rate of recovery from physical injury. Does this help make sense of McGwire's achievement? More testosterone obviously didn't give him the skill to hit 70 home runs, but it almost certainly contributed to the physical and mental endurance that helped him do so.

Since most men have at least 10 times as much T as most women, it therefore makes sense not to have coed baseball leagues. Equally, it makes sense that women will be underrepresented in a high-testosterone environment like military combat or construction. When the skills required are more cerebral or more endurance-related, the male-female gap may shrink, or even reverse itself. But otherwise, gender inequality in these fields is primarily not a function of sexism, merely of common sense. This is a highly controversial position, but it really shouldn't be. Even more unsettling is the racial gap in testosterone. Several solid studies, published in publications like *Journal of the National Cancer Institute,* show that black men have on average 3 to 19 percent more testosterone than white men. This is

30

something to consider when we're told that black men dominate certain sports because of white racism or economic class rather than black skill. This reality may, of course, feed stereotypes about blacks being physical but not intellectual. But there's no evidence of any trade-off between the two. To say that someone is physically gifted is to say nothing about his mental abilities, as even N.F.L. die-hards have come to realize. Indeed, as Jon Entine points out in his new book, *Taboo,* even the position of quarterback, which requires a deft mix of mental and physical strength and was once predominantly white, has slowly become less white as talent has been rewarded. The percentage of blacks among N.F.L. quarterbacks is now twice the percentage of blacks in the population as a whole.

But fears of natural difference still haunt the debate about gender equality. Many feminists have made tenacious arguments about the lack of any substantive physical or mental differences between men and women as if the political equality of the sexes depended on it. But to rest the equality of women on one physical and psychological equivalence of the sexes is to rest it on sand. In the end, testosterone. This year, for example, Toys "R" Us announced it was planning to redesign its toy stores to group products most likely to be bought by the same types of consumers: in marketing jargon, "logical adjacencies." The results? almost total gender separation. "Girl's World" would feature Easy-Bake Ovens and Barbies; "Boy's World," trucks and action figures. Though Toys "R" Us denied that there was any agenda behind this—its market research showed that gender differences start as young as 2 years old—such a public outcry ensued that the store canceled its plans. Meanwhile, Fox Family Channels is about to introduce two new, separate cable channels for boys and girls, boyzChannel and girlzChannel, to attract advertisers and consumers more efficiently. Fox executives told The Wall Street Journal that their move is simply a reflection of what Nielsen-related research tells them about the viewing habits of boys and girls: that, "in general terms, girls are more interested in entertainment that is relationship-oriented," while boys are "more action-oriented." T anyone? After more than two decades of relentless legal, cultural and ideological attempts to negate sexual difference between boys and girls, the market has turned around and shown that very little, after all, has changed.

Advocates of a purely environmental origin for this difference between the sexes counter that gender socialization begins very early and is picked up by subtle inferences from parental interaction and peer pressure, before being reinforced by the collective culture at large. Most parents observing toddlers choosing their own toys and play patterns can best judge for themselves how true this is. But as Matt Ridley has pointed out, there is also physiological evidence of very early mental differences between the sexes, most of it to the advantage of girls. Ninety-five percent of all hyperactive kids are boys; four times as many boys are dyslexic and learning-disabled as girls. There is a greater distinction between the right and left brain among boys than girls, and worse linguistic skills. In general, boys are better at spatial and abstract tasks, girls at communication. These are generalizations, of course. There are many, many boys who are great linguists and model students, and vice versa. Some boys even prefer, when left to their own devices, to play with dolls as well as trucks. But we are talking of generalities here, and the influence of womb-given testosterone on those generalities is undeniable.

Some of that influence is a handicap. We are so used to associating testosterone with strength, masculinity and patriarchal violence that it is easy to ignore that it also makes men weaker in some respects than women. It doesn't correlate with economic power: in fact, as we have seen, blue-collar workers have more of it than white-collar workers. It gets men into trouble. For reasons no one seems to understand, testosterone may also be an immune suppressant. High levels of it can correspond, as recent studies have shown, not only with baldness but also with heart disease and a greater susceptibility to infectious diseases. Higher levels of prostate cancer among blacks, some researchers believe, may well be related to blacks' higher testosterone levels. The aggression it can foster and the risks it encourages lead men into situations that often wound or kill them. And higher levels of testosterone-driven promiscuity make men more prone to sexually transmitted diseases. This is one reason that men live shorter lives on average than women. There is something, in other words, tragic about testosterone. It can lead to a certain kind of male glory; it may lead to valor or boldness or impulsive romanticism. But it also presages a uniquely male kind of doom. The cockerel with the brightest comb is often the most attractive and the most testosteroned, but it is also the most vulnerable to parasites. It is as if it has sacrificed quantity of life for intensity of experience, and this trade-off is a deeply male one.

So it is perhaps unsurprising that those professions in which this trade-off   35
is most pronounced—the military, contact sports, hazardous exploration, venture capitalism, politics, gambling—tend to be disproportionately male. Politics is undoubtedly the most controversial because it is such a critical arena for the dispersal of power. But consider for a moment how politics is conducted in our society. It is saturated with combat, ego, conflict and risk. An entire career can be lost in a single gaffe or an unexpected shift in the national mood. This ego-driven roulette is almost as highly biased toward the testosteroned as wrestling. So it makes some sense that after almost a century of electorates made up by as many women as men, the number of female politicians remains pathetically small in most Western democracies. This may not be endemic to politics; it may have more to do with the way our culture constructs politics. And it is not to say that women are not good at government. Those qualities associated with low testosterone—patience, risk aversion, empathy—can all lead to excellent governance. They are just lousy qualities in the crapshoot of electoral politics.

If you care about sexual equality, this is obviously a challenge, but it need not be as depressing as it sounds. The sports world offers one way out. Men and women do not compete directly against one another; they have separate tournaments and leagues. Their different styles of physical excellence can be appreciated in different ways. At some basic level, of course, men will always be better than women in many of these contests. Men run faster and throw harder. Women could compensate for this by injecting testosterone, but if they took enough to be truly competitive, they would become men, which would somewhat defeat the purpose.

The harder cases are in those areas in which physical strength is important but not always crucial, like military combat or manual labor. And here the compromise is more likely to be access but inequality in numbers. Finance? Business? Here, where the testosterone-driven differences may well be more subtly psychological, and where men may dominate by discrimination rather than merit, is the trickiest arena. Testosterone-induced impatience may lead to poor decision-making, but low-testosterone risk aversion may lead to an inability to seize business opportunities. Perhaps it is safest to say that unequal numbers of men and women in these spheres is not prima facie evidence[3] of sexism. We should do everything we can to ensure equal access, but it is foolish to insist that numerical inequality is always a function of bias rather than biology. This doesn't mean we shouldn't worry about individual cases of injustice; just that we shouldn't be shocked if gender inequality endures. And we should recognize that affirmative action for women (and men) in all arenas is an inherently utopian project.

Then there is the medical option. A modest solution might be to give more women access to testosterone to improve their sex drives, aggression and risk affinity and to help redress their disadvantages in those areas as compared with men. This is already done for severely depressed women, or women with hormonal imbalances, or those lacking an adequate sex drive, especially after menopause. Why not for women who simply want to rev up their will to power? Its use needs to be carefully monitored because it can also lead to side effects, like greater susceptibility to cancer, but that's what doctors are there for. And since older men also suffer a slow drop-off in T levels, there's no reason they should be cold-shouldered either. If the natural disadvantages of gender should be countered, why not the natural disadvantages of age? In some ways, this is already happening. Among the most common drugs now available through Internet doctors and pharmacies, along with Viagra and Prozac, is testosterone. This summer, with the arrival of AndroGel, the testosterone gel created as a medical treatment for those four to five million men who suffer from low levels of testosterone, recreational demand may soar.

Or try this thought experiment: what if parents committed to gender equity opted to counteract the effect of testosterone on boys in the womb by complementing it with injections of artificial female hormones? That way, structural gender difference could be eradicated from the beginning.

---

[3]prima facie *evidence:* evidence that would establish a fact. [Eds.]

Such a policy would lead to "men and women with normal bodies but identical feminine brains," Matt Ridley posits. "War, rape, boxing, car racing, pornography and hamburgers and beer would soon be distant memories. A feminist paradise would have arrived." Today's conservative cultural critics might also be enraptured. Promiscuity would doubtless decline, fatherhood improve, crime drop, virtue spread. Even gay men might start behaving like lesbians, fleeing the gym and marrying for life. This is a fantasy, of course, but our increasing control and understanding of the scientific origins of our behavior, even of our culture, is fast making those fantasies things we will have to actively choose to forgo.

But fantasies also tell us something. After a feminist century, we may   40
be in need of a new understanding of masculinity. The concepts of manliness, of gentlemanly behavior, of chivalry have been debunked. The New Age bonding of the men's movement has been outlived. What our increasing knowledge of testosterone suggests is a core understanding of what it is to be a man, for better and worse. It is about the ability to risk for good and bad; to act, to strut, to dare, to seize. It is about a kind of energy we often rue but would surely miss. It is about the foolishness that can lead to courage or destruction, the beauty that can be strength or vanity. To imagine a world without it is to see more clearly how our world is inseparable from it and how our current political pieties are too easily threatened by its reality.

And as our economy becomes less physical and more cerebral, as women slowly supplant men in many industries, as income inequalities grow and more highly testosteroned blue-collar men find themselves shunted to one side, we will have to find new ways of channeling what nature has bequeathed us. I don't think it's an accident that in the last decade there has been a growing focus on a muscular male physique in our popular culture, a boom in crass men's magazines, an explosion in violent computer games or a professional wrestler who has become governor. These are indications of a cultural displacement, of a world in which the power of testosterone is ignored or attacked, with the result that it reemerges in cruder and less social forms. Our main task in the gender wars of the new century may not be how to bring women fully into our society, but how to keep men from seceding from it, how to reroute testosterone for constructive ends, rather than ignore it for political point-making.

For my part, I'll keep injecting the Big T. Apart from how great it makes me feel, I consider it no insult to anyone else's gender to celebrate the uniqueness of one's own. Diversity need not mean the equalization of difference. In fact, true diversity requires the acceptance of difference. A world without the unruly, vulnerable, pioneering force of testosterone would be a fairer and calmer, but far grayer and duller, place. It is certainly somewhere I would never want to live. Perhaps the fact that I write this two days after the injection of another 200 milligrams of testosterone into my bloodstream makes me more likely to settle for this colorful trade-off than others. But it seems to me no disrespect to womanhood to say that I am perfectly happy to be a man, to feel things no woman will ever feel to the degree that I feel them, to experience the world in a way no woman ever has. And to do so without apology or shame.

QUESTIONS

1. What sources does Sullivan draw on for this essay? How would you rank them in terms of importance and reliability?
2. How does research on testosterone complicate and challenge the issue of sexual equality? How does Sullivan address this issue? Should we redefine "equality" in matters of sex?
3. Discuss Sullivan's statement that "There is something . . . tragic about testosterone" (paragraph 35). What does he mean? Do you agree? Explain why or why not.
4. Sullivan suggests that one's testosterone level can affect one's job performance (paragraph 30). What would your reaction be if, during a job interview, you were told that a saliva sample to assess your T-level was required? Explain.
5. Consider the stereotypical view of males and females in American culture. Does Sullivan's essay contribute to them, challenge them, complicate them (or all of the above)? Explain.

MAKING CONNECTIONS

In Susan Bordo's essay "Reading the Slender Body" (p. 693), Bordo points out that the image that women have of their bodies is culturally determined. With extreme slenderness as the norm, women are under pressure to lose weight, and to exercise so as to control the margins of their bodies. Are men under similar pressures? How does Sullivan perceive his body? How would Bordo respond to Sullivan's statements about the differences between male and female bodies?

THE MAN WHO MISTOOK
HIS WIFE FOR A HAT

Oliver Sacks

Oliver Sacks was born in London, England, in 1933, and educated in London and Oxford before coming to the United States to complete his education in California and New York. At present he is clinical professor of neurology at Albert Einstein College of Medicine. He is best known, however, for his extraordinary writing on matters related to his medical studies, in such books as Awakenings *(1974),* Seeing Voices: A Journey into the World of the Deaf *(1989),* An Anthropologist on Mars *(1995),* The Island of the Colorblind *(1997), and his national best-seller,* The Man Who Mistook His Wife for a Hat *(1986), in which the following selection appeared. Interested in the art of storytelling as well as in clinical neurology, Sacks subtitled the book in which this essay appeared, "and Other Clinical Tales." He insists that his essays are not just case studies, though they are that, but also tales or fables of "heroes, victims, martyrs, warriors." In his writing, he says, "the scientific and romantic . . . come together at the intersection of fact and fable." Sacks's prose style is lyrical as well as accurate; his explanation of prosopagnosia (perception without recognition) seeks to engage our interest and emotions while it defines and illustrates a syndrome unfamiliar to many readers.*

Dr. P. was a musician of distinction, well known for many years as a singer, and then, at the local School of Music, as a teacher. It was here, in relation to his students, that certain strange problems were first observed. Sometimes a student would present himself, and Dr. P. would not recognize him; or, specifically, would not recognize his face. The moment the student spoke, he would be recognized by his voice. Such incidents multiplied, causing embarrassment, perplexity, fear—and, sometimes, comedy. For not only did Dr. P. increasingly fail to see faces, but he saw faces when there were no faces to see: genially, Magoo-like, when in the street he might pat the heads of water hydrants and parking meters, taking these to be the heads of children; he would amiably address carved knobs on the furniture and be astounded when they did not reply. At first these odd mistakes were laughed off as jokes, not least by Dr. P. himself. Had he not always had a quirky sense of humor and been given to Zen-like paradoxes and jests? His musical powers were as dazzling as ever; he did not feel ill—

he had never felt better; and the mistakes were so ludicrous—and so ingenious—that they could hardly be serious or betoken anything serious. The notion of there being "something the matter" did not emerge until some three years later, when diabetes developed. Well aware that diabetes could affect his eyes, Dr. P. consulted an ophthalmologist, who took a careful history and examined his eyes closely. "There's nothing the matter with your eyes," the doctor concluded. "But there is trouble with the visual parts of your brain. You don't need my help, you must see a neurologist." And so, as a result of this referral, Dr. P. came to me.

It was obvious within a few seconds of meeting him that there was no trace of dementia in the ordinary sense. He was a man of great cultivation and charm who talked well and fluently, with imagination and humor. I couldn't think why he had been referred to our clinic.

And yet there *was* something a bit odd. He faced me as he spoke, was oriented towards me, and yet there was something the matter—it was difficult to formulate. He faced me with his *ears,* I came to think, but not with his eyes. These, instead of looking, gazing, at me, "taking me in," in the normal way, made sudden strange fixations—on my nose, on my right ear, down to my chin, up to my right eye—as if noting (even studying) these individual features, but not seeing my whole face, its changing expressions, "me," as a whole. I am not sure that I fully realized this at the time—there was just a teasing strangeness, some failure in the normal interplay of gaze and expression. He saw me, he *scanned* me, and yet . . .

"What seems to be the matter?" I asked him at length.

"Nothing that I know of," he replied with a smile, "but people seem to   5
think there's something wrong with my eyes."

"But *you* don't recognize any visual problems?"

"No, not directly, but I occasionally make mistakes."

I left the room briefly to talk to his wife. When I came back, Dr. P. was sitting placidly by the window, attentive, listening rather than looking out. "Traffic," he said, "street sounds, distant trains—they make a sort of symphony, do they not? You know Honegger's[1] *Pacific 234?*"

What a lovely man, I thought to myself. How can there be anything seriously the matter? Would he permit me to examine him?

"Yes, of course, Dr. Sacks."   10

I stilled my disquiet, his perhaps, too, in the soothing routine of a neurological exam—muscle strength, coordination, reflexes, tone. . . . It was while examining his reflexes—a trifle abnormal on the left side—that the first bizarre experience occurred. I had taken off his left shoe and scratched the sole of his foot with a key—a frivolous-seeming but essential test of a reflex—and then, excusing myself to screw my ophthalmoscope together, left him to put on the shoe himself. To my surprise, a minute later, he had not done this.

---

[1]*Arthur Honegger* (1892–1955): French composer. [Eds.]

"Can I help?" I asked.

"Help what? Help whom?"

"Help you put on your shoe."

"Ach," he said, "I had forgotten the shoe," adding, *sotto voce,* "The   15
shoe? The shoe?" He seemed baffled.

"Your shoe," I repeated. "Perhaps you'd put it on."

He continued to look downwards, though not at the shoe, with an intense but misplaced concentration. Finally his gaze settled on his foot:
"That is my shoe, yes?"

Did I mis-hear? Did he mis-see?

"My eyes," he explained, and put a hand to his foot. "*This* is my
shoe, no?"

"No, it is not. That is your foot. *There* is your shoe."   20

"Ah! I thought that was my foot."

Was he joking? Was he mad? Was he blind? If this was one of his
"strange mistakes," it was the strangest mistake I had ever come across.

I helped him on with his shoe (his foot), to avoid further complication.
Dr. P. himself seemed untroubled, indifferent, maybe amused. I resumed
my examination. His visual acuity was good: he had no difficulty seeing a
pin on the floor, though sometimes he missed it if it was placed to his left.

He saw all right, but what did he see? I opened out a copy of the *National Geographic Magazine* and asked him to describe some pictures in it.

His responses here were very curious. His eyes would dart from one   25
thing to another, picking up tiny features, individual features, as they had
done with my face. A striking brightness, a color, a shape would arrest his
attention and elicit comment—but in no case did he get the scene-as-a-
whole. He failed to see the whole, seeing only details, which he spotted like
blips on a radar screen. He never entered into relation with the picture as a
whole—never faced, so to speak, *its* physiognomy. He had no sense whatever of a landscape or scene.

I showed him the cover, an unbroken expanse of Sahara dunes.

"What do you see here?" I asked.

"I see a river," he said. "And a little guest-house with its terrace on the
water. People are dining out on the terrace. I see colored parasols here and
there." He was looking, if it was "looking," right off the cover into mid-air
and confabulating nonexistent features, as if the absence of features in the
actual picture had driven him to imagine the river and the terrace and the
colored parasols.

I must have looked aghast, but he seemed to think he had done rather
well. There was a hint of a smile on his face. He also appeared to have decided that the examination was over and started to look around for his hat.
He reached out his hand and took hold of his wife's head, tried to lift it off,
to put it on. He had apparently mistaken his wife for a hat! His wife
looked as if she was used to such things.

I could make no sense of what had occurred in terms of conventional   30
neurology (or neuropsychology). In some ways he seemed perfectly pre-

served, and in others absolutely, incomprehensibly devastated. How could he, on the one hand, mistake his wife for a hat and, on the other, function, as apparently he still did, as a teacher at the Music School?

I had to think, to see him again—and to see him in his own familiar habitat, at home.

A few days later I called on Dr. P. and his wife at home, with the score of the *Dichterliebe* in my briefcase (I knew he liked Schumann),[2] and a variety of odd objects for the testing of perception. Mrs. P. showed me into a lofty apartment, which recalled fin-de-siècle Berlin. A magnificent old Bösendorfer stood in state in the center of the room, and all around it were music stands, instruments, scores. . . . There were books, there were paintings, but the music was central. Dr. P. came in, a little bowed, and, distracted, advanced with outstretched hands to the grandfather clock, but, hearing my voice, corrected himself, and shook hands with me. We exchanged greetings and chatted a little of current concerts and performances. Diffidently, I asked him if he would sing.

"The *Dichterliebe!*" he exclaimed. "But I can no longer read music. You will play them, yes?"

I said I would try. On that wonderful old piano even my playing sounded right, and Dr. P. was an aged but infinitely mellow Fischer-Dieskau,[3] combining a perfect ear and voice with the most incisive musical intelligence. It was clear that the Music School was not keeping him on out of charity.

Dr. P.'s temporal lobes were obviously intact: he had a wonderful musical cortex. What, I wondered, was going on in his parietal and occipital lobes, especially in those areas where visual processing occurred? I carry the Platonic solids in my neurological kit and decided to start with these.   35

"What is this?" I asked, drawing out the first one.

"A cube, of course."

"Now this?" I asked, brandishing another.

He asked if he might examine it, which he did swiftly and systematically: "A dodecahedron, of course. And don't bother with the others—I'll get the icosahedron, too."

Abstract shapes clearly presented no problems. What about faces? I   40 took out a pack of cards. All of these he identified instantly, including the jacks, queens, kings, and the joker. But these, after all, are stylized designs, and it was impossible to tell whether he saw faces or merely patterns. I decided I would show him a volume of cartoons which I had in my briefcase. Here, again, for the most part, he did well. Churchill's cigar, Schnozzle's nose: as soon as he had picked out a key feature he could identify the face. But cartoons, again, are formal and schematic. It remained to be seen how he would do with real faces, realistically represented.

---

[2]*Robert Schumann* (1810–1856): German romantic composer. [Eds.]

[3]*Dietrich Fischer-Dieskau* (b. 1925): German baritone, noted for his interpretations of Schumann. [Eds.]

I turned on the television, keeping the sound off, and found an early Bette Davis film. A love scene was in progress. Dr. P. failed to identify the actress—but this could have been because she had never entered his world. What was more striking was that he failed to identify the expressions on her face or her partner's, though in the course of a single torrid scene these passed from sultry yearning through passion, surprise, disgust, and fury to a melting reconciliation. Dr. P. could make nothing of any of this. He was very unclear as to what was going on, or who was who or even what sex they were. His comments on the scene were positively Martian.

It was just possible that some of his difficulties were associated with the unreality of a celluloid, Hollywood world; and it occurred to me that he might be more successful in identifying faces from his own life. On the walls of the apartment there were photographs of his family, his colleagues, his pupils, himself. I gathered a pile of these together and, with some misgivings, presented them to him. What had been funny, or farcical, in relation to the movie, was tragic in relation to real life. By and large, he recognized nobody: neither his family, nor his colleagues, nor his pupils, nor himself. He recognized a portrait of Einstein because he picked up the characteristic hair and mustache; and the same thing happened with one or two other people. "Ach, Paul!" he said, when shown a portrait of his brother. "That square jaw, those big teeth—I would know Paul anywhere!" But was it Paul he recognized, or one or two of his features, on the basis of which he could make a reasonable guess as to the subject's identity? In the absence of obvious "markers," he was utterly lost. But it was not merely the cognition, the *gnosis,* at fault; there was something radically wrong with the whole way he proceeded. For he approached these faces—even of those near and dear—as if they were abstract puzzles or tests. He did not relate to them, he did not behold. No face was familiar to him, seen as a "thou," being just identified as a set of features, an "it." Thus, there was formal, but no trace of personal, gnosis. And with this went his indifference, or blindness, to expression. A face, to us, is a person looking out —we see, as it were, the person through his *persona,* his face. But for Dr. P. there was no *persona* in this sense—no outward *persona,* and no person within.

I had stopped at a florist on my way to his apartment and bought myself an extravagant red rose for my buttonhole. Now I removed this and handed it to him. He took it like a botanist or morphologist given a specimen, not like a person given a flower.

"About six inches in length," he commented. "A convoluted red form with a linear green attachment."

"Yes," I said encouragingly, "and what do you think it *is,* Dr. P.?"   45

"Not easy to say." He seemed perplexed. "It lacks the simple symmetry of the Platonic solids, although it may have a higher symmetry of its own. . . . I think this could be an inflorescence or flower."

"Could be?" I queried.

"Could be," he confirmed.

"Smell it," I suggested, and he again looked somewhat puzzled, as if I had asked him to smell a higher symmetry. But he complied courteously, and took it to his nose. Now, suddenly, he came to life.

"Beautiful!" he exclaimed. "An early rose. What a heavenly smell!" He started to hum *"Die Rose, die Lillie . . ."* Reality, it seemed, might be conveyed by smell, not by sight. 50

I tried one final test. It was still a cold day, in early spring, and I had thrown my coat and gloves on the sofa.

"What is this?" I asked, holding up a glove.

"May I examine it?" he asked, and, taking it from me, he proceeded to examine it as he had examined the geometrical shapes.

"A continuous surface," he announced at last, "infolded on itself. It appears to have"—he hesitated—"five outpouchings, if this is the word."

"Yes," I said cautiously. "You have given me a description. Now tell me what it is." 55

"A container of some sort?"

"Yes," I said, "and what would it contain?"

"It would contain its contents!" said Dr. P., with a laugh. "There are many possibilities. It could be a change purse, for example, for coins of five sizes. It could . . ."

I interrupted the barmy flow. "Does it not look familiar? Do you think it might contain, might fit, a part of your body?"

No light of recognition dawned on his face.[4] 60

No child would have the power to see and speak of "a continuous surface . . . infolded on itself," but any child, any infant, would immediately know a glove as a glove, see it as familiar, as going with a hand. Dr. P. didn't. He saw nothing as familiar. Visually, he was lost in a world of lifeless abstractions. Indeed, he did not have a real visual world, as he did not have a real visual self. He could speak about things, but did not see them face-to-face. Hughlings Jackson, discussing patients with aphasia and left-hemisphere lesions, says they have lost "abstract" and "propositional" thought—and compares them with dogs (or, rather, he compares dogs to patients with aphasia). Dr. P., on the other hand, functioned precisely as a machine functions. It wasn't merely that he displayed the same indifference to the visual world as a computer but—even more strikingly—he construed the world as a computer construes it, by means of key features and schematic relationships. The scheme might be identified—in an "identi-kit" way—without the reality being grasped at all.

The testing I had done so far told me nothing about Dr. P.'s inner world. Was it possible that his visual memory and imagination were still intact? I asked him to imagine entering one of our local squares from the

---

[4]Later, by accident, he got it on, and exclaimed, "My God, it's a glove!" This was reminiscent of Kurt Goldstein's patient "Lanuti," who could only recognize objects by trying to use them in action.

north side, to walk through it, in imagination or in memory, and tell me the buildings he might pass as he walked. He listed the buildings on his right side, but none of those on his left. I then asked him to imagine entering the square from the south. Again he mentioned only those buildings that were on the right side, although these were the very buildings he had omitted before. Those he had "seen" internally before were not mentioned now; presumably, they were no longer "seen." It was evident that his difficulties with leftness, his visual field deficits, were as much internal as external, bisecting his visual memory and imagination.

What, at a higher level, of his internal visualization? Thinking of the almost hallucinatory intensity with which Tolstoy visualizes and animates his characters, I questioned Dr. P. about *Anna Karenina*. He could remember incidents without difficulty, had an undiminished grasp of the plot, but completely omitted visual characteristics, visual narrative, and scenes. He remembered the words of the characters but not their faces; and though, when asked, he could quote, with his remarkable and almost verbatim memory, the original visual descriptions, these were, it became apparent, quite empty for him and lacked sensorial, imaginal, or emotional reality. Thus, there was an internal agnosia as well.[5]

But this was only the case, it became clear, with certain sorts of visualization. The visualization of faces and scenes, of visual narrative and drama—this was profoundly impaired, almost absent. But the visualization of *schemata* was preserved, perhaps enhanced. Thus, when I engaged him in a game of mental chess, he had no difficulty visualizing the chessboard or the moves—indeed, no difficulty in beating me soundly.

Luria[6] said of Zazetsky that he had entirely lost his capacity to play games but that his "vivid imagination" was unimpaired. Zazetsky and Dr. P. lived in worlds which were mirror images of each other. But the saddest difference between them was that Zazetsky, as Luria said, "fought to regain his lost faculties with the indomitable tenacity of the damned," whereas Dr. P. was not fighting, did not know what was lost, did not indeed know that anything was lost. But who was more tragic, or who was more damned—the man who knew it, or the man who did not?

When the examination was over, Mrs. P. called us to the table, where there was coffee and a delicious spread of little cakes. Hungrily, hum-

65

---

[5] I have often wondered about Helen Keller's visual descriptions, whether these, for all their eloquence, are somehow empty as well? Or whether, by the transference of images from the tactile to the visual, or, yet more extraordinarily, from the verbal and the metaphorical to the sensorial and the visual, she *did* achieve a power of visual imagery, even though her visual cortex had never been stimulated, directly, by the eyes? But in Dr. P.'s case it is precisely the cortex that was damaged, the organic prerequisite of all pictorial imagery. Interestingly and typically he no longer dreamed pictorially—the "message" of the dream being conveyed in nonvisual terms.

[6] *Alexander Luria* (1902–1977): Russian neuropsychologist who worked with victims of traumatic head injuries. [Eds.]

mingly, Dr. P. started on the cakes. Swiftly, fluently, unthinkingly, melodiously, he pulled the plates towards him and took this and that in a great gurgling stream, an edible song of food, until, suddenly, there came an interruption: a loud, peremptory rat-tat-tat at the door. Startled, taken aback, arrested by the interruption, Dr. P. stopped eating and sat frozen, motionless, at the table, with an indifferent, blind bewilderment on his face. He saw, but no longer saw, the table; no longer perceived it as a table laden with cakes. His wife poured him some coffee: the smell titillated his nose and brought him back to reality. The melody of eating resumed.

How does he do anything? I wondered to myself. What happens when he's dressing, goes to the lavatory, has a bath? I followed his wife into the kitchen and asked her how, for instance, he managed to dress himself. "It's just like the eating," she explained. "I put his usual clothes out, in all the usual places, and he dresses without difficulty, singing to himself. He does everything singing to himself. But if he is interrupted and loses the thread, he comes to a complete stop, doesn't know his clothes—or his own body. He sings all the time—eating songs, dressing songs, bathing songs, everything. He can't do anything unless he makes it a song."

While we were talking my attention was caught by the pictures on the walls.

"Yes," Mrs. P. said, "he was a gifted painter as well as a singer. The School exhibited his pictures every year."

I strolled past them curiously—they were in chronological order. All 70 his earlier work was naturalistic and realistic, with vivid mood and atmosphere, but finely detailed and concrete. Then, years later, they became less vivid, less concrete, less realistic and naturalistic, but far more abstract, even geometrical and cubist. Finally, in the last paintings, the canvases became nonsense, or nonsense to me—mere chaotic lines and blotches of paint. I commented on this to Mrs. P.

"Ach, you doctors, you're such Philistines!"[7] she exclaimed. "Can you not see *artistic development*—how he renounced the realism of his earlier years, and advanced into abstract, nonrepresentational art?"

"No, that's not it," I said to myself (but forbore to say it to poor Mrs. P.). He had indeed moved from realism to nonrepresentation to the abstract, yet this was not the artist, but the pathology, advancing—advancing towards a profound visual agnosia, in which all powers of representation and imagery, all sense of the concrete, all sense of reality, were being destroyed. This wall of paintings was a tragic pathological exhibit, which belonged to neurology, not art.

And yet, I wondered, was she not partly right? For there is often a struggle, and sometimes, even more interestingly, a collusion between the powers of pathology and creation. Perhaps, in his cubist period, there

---

[7]*Philistines:* ignorant or smug people who disdain intellectual or artistic values. [Eds.]

might have been both artistic and pathological development, colluding to engender an original form; for as he lost the concrete, so he might have gained in the abstract, developing a greater sensitivity to all the structural elements of line, boundary, contour—an almost Picasso-like power to see, and equally depict, those abstract organizations embedded in, and normally lost in, the concrete.... Though in the final pictures, I feared, there was only chaos and agnosia.

We returned to the great music room, with the Bösendorfer in the center, and Dr. P. humming the last torte.

"Well, Dr. Sacks," he said to me. "You find me an interesting case, I   75
perceive. Can you tell me what you find wrong, make recommendations?"

"I can't tell you what I find wrong," I replied, "but I'll say what I find right. You are a wonderful musician, and music is your life. What I would prescribe, in a case such as yours, is a life which consists entirely of music. Music has been the center, now make it the whole, of your life."

This was four years ago—I never saw him again, but I often wondered about how he apprehended the world, given his strange loss of image, visuality, and the perfect preservation of a great musicality. I think that music, for him, had taken the place of image. He had no body-image, he had body-music: this is why he could move and act as fluently as he did, but came to a total confused stop if the "inner music" stopped. And equally with the outside, the world. . . .[8]

In *The World as Representation and Will*, Schopenhauer[9] speaks of music as "pure will." How fascinated he would have been by Dr. P., a man who had wholly lost the world as representation, but wholly preserved it as music or will.

And this, mercifully, held to the end—for despite the gradual advance of his disease (a massive tumor or degenerative process in the visual parts of his brain) Dr. P. lived and taught music to the last days of his life.

Postscript

How should one interpret Dr. P.'s peculiar inability to interpret, to   80
judge, a glove as a glove? Manifestly, here, he could not make a cognitive judgment, though he was prolific in the production of cognitive hypotheses. A judgment is intuitive, personal, comprehensive, and concrete—we "see" how things stand, in relation to one another and oneself. It was precisely this

---

[8]Thus, as I learned later from his wife, though he could not recognize his students if they sat still, if they were merely "images," he might suddenly recognize them if they *moved*. "That's Karl," he would cry. "I know his movements, his body-music."

[9]*Arthur Schopenhauer* (1788–1860): German philosopher whose work included a theory to explain the life and work of the artist. [Eds.]

setting, this relating, that Dr. P. lacked (though his judging, in all other spheres, was prompt and normal). Was this due to lack of visual information, or faulty processing of visual information? (This would be the explanation given by a classical, schematic neurology.) Or was there something amiss in Dr. P.'s attitude, so that he could not relate what he saw to himself?

These explanations, or modes of explanation, are not mutually exclusive—being in different modes they could coexist and both be true. And this is acknowledged, implicitly or explicitly, in classical neurology: implicitly, by Macrae, when he finds the explanation of defective schemata, or defective visual processing and integration, inadequate; explicitly, by Goldstein, when he speaks of "abstract attitude." But abstract attitude, which allows "categorization," also misses the mark with Dr. P.—and, perhaps, with the concept of "judgment" in general. For Dr. P. *had* abstract attitude—indeed, nothing else. And it was precisely this, his absurd abstractness of attitude—absurd because unleavened with anything else—which rendered him incapable of perceiving identity, or particulars, rendered him incapable of judgment.

Neurology and psychology, curiously, though they talk of everything else, almost never talk of "judgment"—and yet it is precisely the downfall of judgment . . . which constitutes the essence of so many neuropsychological disorders. Judgment and identity may be casualties—but neuropsychology never speaks of them.

And yet, whether in a philosophic sense (Kant's sense),[10] or an empirical and evolutionary sense, judgment is the most important faculty we have. An animal, or a man, may get on very well without "abstract attitude" but will speedily perish if deprived of judgment. Judgment must be the *first* faculty of higher life or mind—yet it is ignored, or misinterpreted, by classical (computational) neurology. And if we wonder how such an absurdity can arise, we find it in the assumptions, or the evolution, of neurology itself. For classical neurology (like classical physics) has always been mechanical—from Hughlings Jackson's mechanical analogies to the computer analogies of today.

Of course, the brain is a machine and a computer—everything in classical neurology is correct. But our mental processes, which constitute our being and life, are not just abstract and mechanical, but personal, as well—and, as such, involve not just classifying and categorizing, but continual judging and feeling also. If this is missing, we become computer-like, as Dr. P. was. And, by the same token, if we delete feeling and judging, the personal, from the cognitive sciences, we reduce them to something as defective as Dr. P.—and we reduce our apprehension of the concrete and real.

---

[10]*Immanuel Kant* (1724–1804): German philosopher; some of his work concerned ethics and moral judgment. [Eds.]

By a sort of comic and awful analogy, our current cognitive neurology   85
and psychology resemble nothing so much as poor Dr. P.! We need the
concrete and real, as he did; and we fail to see this, as he failed to see it.
Our cognitive sciences are themselves suffering from an agnosia essentially
similar to Dr. P.'s. Dr. P. may therefore serve as a warning and parable—
of what happens to a science which eschews the judgmental, the particular,
the personal, and becomes entirely abstract and computational.

It was always a matter of great regret to me that, owing to circumstances beyond my control, I was not able to follow his case further, either
in the sort of observations and investigations described, or in ascertaining
the actual disease pathology.

One always fears that a case is "unique," especially if it has such extraordinary features as those of Dr. P. It was, therefore, with a sense of great
interest and delight, not unmixed with relief, that I found, quite by
chance —looking through the periodical *Brain* for 1956—a detailed description of an almost comically similar case, similar (indeed identical) neu-
ropsychologically and phenomenologically, though the underlying
pathology (an acute head injury) and all personal circumstances were
wholly different. The authors speak of their case as "unique in the documented history of this disorder"—and evidently experienced, as I did,
amazement at their own findings.[11] The interested reader is referred to the
original paper, Macrae and Trolle (1956), of which I here subjoin a brief
paraphrase, with quotations from the original.

Their patient was a young man of 32, who, following a severe automobile accident, with unconsciousness for three weeks, ". . . complained, exclusively, of an inability to recognize faces, even those of his wife and
children." Not a single face was "familiar" to him, but there were three he
could identify; these were workmates: one with an eye-blinking tic, one
with a large mole on his cheek, and a third "because he was so tall and thin
that no one else was like him." Each of these, Macrae and Trolle bring out,
was "recognized solely by the single prominent feature mentioned." In general (like Dr. P.) he recognized familiars only by their voices.

----

[11]Only since the completion of this book have I found that there is, in fact, a
rather extensive literature on visual agnosia in general, and prosopagnosia in particular. In particular I had the great pleasure recently of meeting Dr. Andrew
Kertesz, who has himself published some extremely detailed studies of patients with
such agnosias (see, for example, his paper on visual agnosia, Kertesz 1979). Dr.
Kertesz mentioned to me a case known to him of a farmer who had developed
prosopagnosia and in consequence could no longer distinguish (the faces of) his
cows, and of another such patient, an attendant in a Natural History Museum,
who mistook his own reflection for the diorama of an *ape.* As with Dr. P., and as
with Macrae and Trolle's patient, it is especially the animate which is so absurdly
misperceived. The most important studies of such agnosias, and of visual processing in general, are now being undertaken by A. R. and H. Damasio.

He had difficulty even recognizing himself in a mirror, as Macrae and Trolle describe in detail: "In the early convalescent phase he frequently, especially when shaving, questioned whether the face gazing at him was really his own, and even though he knew it could physically be none other, on several occasions grimaced or stuck out his tongue 'just to make sure.' By carefully studying his face in the mirror he slowly began to recognize it, but 'not in a flash' as in the past—he relied on the hair and facial outline, and on two small moles on his left cheek."

In general he could not recognize objects "at a glance," but would   90 have to seek out, and guess from, one or two features—occasionally his guesses were absurdly wrong. In particular, the authors note, there was difficulty with the *animate.*

On the other hand, simple schematic objects—scissors, watch, key, etc.—presented no difficulties. Macrae and Trolle also note that: "His *topographical memory* was strange: the seeming paradox existed that he could find his way from home to hospital and around the hospital, but yet could not name streets *en route* [unlike Dr. P., he also had some aphasia] or appear to visualize the topography."

It was also evident that visual memories of people, even from long before the accident, were severely impaired—there was memory of conduct, or perhaps a mannerism, but not of visual appearance or face. Similarly, it appeared, when he was questioned closely, that he no longer had visual images in his *dreams.* Thus, as with Dr. P., it was not just visual perception, but visual imagination and memory, the fundamental powers of visual representation, which were essentially damaged in this patient—at least those powers insofar as they pertained to the personal, the familiar, the concrete.

A final, humorous point. Where Dr. P. might mistake his wife for a hat, Macrae's patient, also unable to recognize his wife, needed her to identify herself by a visual *marker,* by ". . . a conspicuous article of clothing, such as a large hat."

QUESTIONS

1. Summarize as clearly as you can the nature of Dr. P.'s problem. What are the symptoms? What seems to have caused them?
2. What conclusions can be drawn from the case of Dr. P. about the way our visual systems work? Using what Sacks himself says and whatever additional conclusions you yourself can draw, what does the case of Dr. P. tell us about the way we see things and what it means to recognize what we see?
3. Sacks has a way of drawing readers into his case studies, of making them concerned about the individuals whose cases he presents. How does he do this? That is, considering him as a writer rather than as a doctor, what aspects of his writing arouse interest and concern? Look at the opening paragraphs of the essay in particular.

4. Is this essay to any degree a story with a plot? Most people find Sacks a very compelling writer. What is it about his way of writing that causes this response? How does he keep readers reading?

5. This essay is not only a single case history and an explanation of some very curious behavior. It also contains or sketches out an argument about the nature of the cognitive sciences—how they should and should not proceed. What is that argument? Do you agree or disagree with the view of cognitive science that Sacks is advocating? Write an essay in which you present his position and develop one of your own on this matter.

6. Write an essay in which you discuss Sacks as a writer and a scientist. Consider such matters as his style of writing, his interest in the arts, his clinical procedures, and the values he expresses or implies in his work. If your instructor wishes, you may look further into his work in order to write this essay.

MAKING CONNECTIONS

Compare Sacks's essay with the reports of John Hersey, "Hatsuyo Naka-mura" (p. 203), and Roy C. Selby Jr. "A Delicate Operation" (p. 295). What elements of a case study do these reports contain? Are they also tales or fables similar to Sacks's essay?

OUR PICTURE OF THE UNIVERSE

Stephen W. Hawking

Stephen W. Hawking (b. 1942), the Lucasian Professor of Mathematics at Cambridge University, is one of the world's leading theoretical physicists. Carl Sagan described the moment in 1974 when he observed "an ancient rite, the investiture of new fellows into the Royal Society, one of the most ancient scholarly organizations on the planet. In the front row a young man in a wheelchair was, very slowly, signing his name in a book that bore on its earliest pages the signature of Isaac Newton. When at last he finished, there was a stirring ovation. Stephen Hawking was a legend even then." Hawking's extraordinary achievements have drawn broad popular admiration in part because he suffers from the serious physical disabilities associated with Lou Gehrig's disease. Hawking is known especially for his work on "black holes" and their implications for a unified theory of physical phenomena. His best-selling book A Brief History of Time *(1988) made his thinking available to the general reader, with over a million copies in print. (In 1992, filmmaker Erroll Morris released a fascinating documentary portrait of Hawking under the same title.) The essay reprinted below is the first chapter of that book, unchanged except for the removal of references to the book as a whole.*

A well-known scientist (some say it was Bertrand Russell) once gave a public lecture on astronomy. He described how the earth orbits around the sun and how the sun, in turn, orbits around the center of a vast collection of stars called our galaxy. At the end of the lecture, a little old lady at the back of the room got up and said: "What you have told us is rubbish. The world is really a flat plate supported on the back of a giant tortoise." The scientist gave a superior smile before replying, "What is the tortoise standing on?" "You're very clever, young man, very clever," said the old lady. "But it's turtles all the way down!"

Most people would find the picture of our universe as an infinite tower of tortoises rather ridiculous, but why do we think we know better? What do we know about the universe, and how do we know it? Where did the universe come from, and where is it going? Did the universe have a beginning, and if so, what happened *before* then? What is the nature of time? Will it ever come to an end? Recent breakthroughs in physics, made possible in part by fantastic new technologies, suggest answers to some of these longstanding questions. Someday these answers may seem as obvious to us as the earth orbiting the sun—or perhaps as ridiculous as a tower of tortoises. Only time (whatever that may be) will tell.

As long ago as 340 B.C. the Greek philosopher Aristotle, in his book *On the Heavens,* was able to put forward two good arguments for believing that the earth was a round sphere rather than a flat plate. First, he realized that eclipses of the moon were caused by the earth coming between the sun and the moon. The earth's shadow on the moon was always round, which would be true only if the earth was spherical. If the earth had been a flat disk, the shadow would have been elongated and elliptical, unless the eclipse always occurred at a time when the sun was directly under the center of the disk. Second, the Greeks knew from their travels that the North Star appeared lower in the sky when viewed in the south than it did in more northerly regions. (Since the North Star lies over the North Pole, it appears to be directly above an observer at the North Pole, but to someone looking from the equator, it appears to lie just at the horizon.) From the difference in the apparent position of the North Star in Egypt and Greece, Aristotle even quoted an estimate that the distance around the earth was 400,000 stadia. It is not known exactly what length a stadium was, but it may have been about 200 yards, which would make Aristotle's estimate about twice the currently accepted figure. The Greeks even had a third argument that the earth must be round, for why else does one first see the sails of a ship coming over the horizon, and only later see the hull?

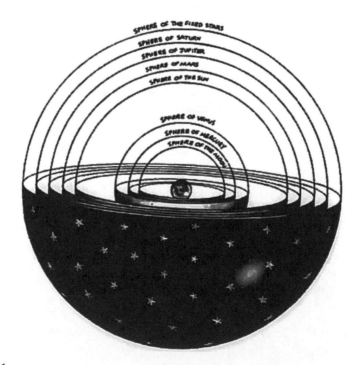

FIGURE 1

Aristotle thought that the earth was stationary and that the sun, the moon, the planets, and the stars moved in circular orbits about the earth. He believed this because he felt, for mystical reasons, that the earth was the center of the universe, and that circular motion was the most perfect. This idea was elaborated by Ptolemy in the second century A.D. into a complete cosmological model. The earth stood at the center, surrounded by eight spheres that carried the moon, the sun, the stars, and the five planets known at the time, Mercury, Venus, Mars, Jupiter, and Saturn (Figure 1). The planets themselves moved on smaller circles attached to their respective spheres in order to account for their rather complicated observed paths in the sky. The outermost sphere carried the so-called fixed stars, which always stay in the same positions relative to each other but which rotate together across the sky. What lay beyond the last sphere was never made very clear, but it certainly was not part of mankind's observable universe.

Ptolemy's model provided a reasonably accurate system for predicting   5
the positions of heavenly bodies in the sky. But in order to predict these positions correctly, Ptolemy had to make an assumption that the moon followed a path that sometimes brought it twice as close to the earth as at other times. And that meant that the moon ought sometimes to appear twice as big as at other times! Ptolemy recognized this flaw, but nevertheless his model was generally, although not universally, accepted. It was adopted by the Christian church as the picture of the universe that was in accordance with Scripture, for it had the great advantage that it left lots of room outside the sphere of fixed stars for heaven and hell.

A simpler model, however, was proposed in 1514 by a Polish priest, Nicholas Copernicus. (At first, perhaps for fear of being branded a heretic by his church, Copernicus circulated his model anonymously.) His idea was that the sun was stationary at the center and that the earth and the planets moved in circular orbits around the sun. Nearly a century passed before this idea was taken seriously. Then two astronomers—the German, Johannes Kepler, and the Italian, Galileo Galilei—started publicly to support the Copernican theory, despite the fact that the orbits it predicted did not quite match the ones observed. The death blow to the Aristotelian/ Ptolemaic theory came in 1609. In that year, Galileo started observing the night sky with a telescope, which had just been invented. When he looked at the planet Jupiter, Galileo found that it was accompanied by several small satellites or moons that orbited around it. This implied that everything did *not* have to orbit directly around the earth, as Aristotle and Ptolemy had thought. (It was, of course, still possible to believe that the earth was stationary at the center of the universe and that the moons of Jupiter moved on extremely complicated paths around the earth, giving the *appearance* that they orbited Jupiter. However, Copernicus's theory was much simpler.) At the same time, Johannes Kepler had modified Copernicus's theory, suggesting that the planets moved not in circles but in ellipses (an ellipse is an elongated circle). The predictions now finally matched the observations.

As far as Kepler was concerned, elliptical orbits were merely an ad hoc hypothesis, and a rather repugnant one at that, because ellipses were clearly less perfect than circles. Having discovered almost by accident that elliptical orbits fit the observations well, he could not reconcile them with his idea that the planets were made to orbit the sun by magnetic forces. An explanation was provided only much later, in 1687, when Sir Isaac Newton published his *Philosophiae Naturalis Principia Mathematica*, probably the most important single work ever published in the physical sciences. In it Newton not only put forward a theory of how bodies move in space and time, but he also developed the complicated mathematics needed to analyse those motions. In addition, Newton postulated a law of universal gravitation according to which each body in the universe was attracted toward every other body by a force that was stronger the more massive the bodies and the closer they were to each other. It was this same force that caused objects to fall to the ground. (The story that Newton was inspired by an apple hitting his head is almost certainly apocryphal. All Newton himself ever said was that the idea of gravity came to him as he sat "in a contemplative mood" and "was occasioned by the fall of an apple.") Newton went on to show that, according to his law, gravity causes the moon to move in an elliptical orbit around the earth and causes the earth and the planets to follow elliptical paths around the sun.

The Copernican model got rid of Ptolemy's celestial spheres, and with them, the idea that the universe had a natural boundary. Since "fixed stars" did not appear to change their positions apart from a rotation across the sky caused by the earth spinning on its axis, it became natural to suppose that the fixed stars were objects like our sun but very much farther away.

Newton realized that, according to his theory of gravity, the stars should attract each other, so it seemed they could not remain essentially motionless. Would they not fall together at some point? In a letter in 1691 to Richard Bentley, another leading thinker of his day, Newton argued that this would indeed happen if there were only a finite number of stars distributed over a finite region of space. But he reasoned that if, on the other hand, there were an infinite number of stars, distributed more or less uniformly over infinite space, this would not happen, because there would not be any central point for them to fall to.

This argument is an instance of the pitfalls that you can encounter in talking about infinity. In an infinite universe, every point can be regarded as the center, because every point has an infinite number of stars on each side of it. The correct approach, it was realized only much later, is to consider the finite situation, in which the stars all fall in on each other, and then to ask how things change if one adds more stars roughly uniformly distributed outside this region. According to Newton's law, the extra stars would make no difference at all to the original ones on average, so the stars would fall in just as fast. We can add as many stars as we like, but they will still always collapse in on themselves. We now know it is impossible to have an infinite static model of the universe in which gravity is always attractive.

It is an interesting reflection on the general climate of thought before the twentieth century that no one had suggested that the universe was expanding or contracting. It was generally accepted that either the universe had existed forever in an unchanging state, or that it had been created at a finite time in the past more or less as we observe it today. In part this may have been due to people's tendency to believe in eternal truths, as well as the comfort they found in the thought that even though they may grow old and die, the universe is eternal and unchanging.

Even those who realized that Newton's theory of gravity showed that the universe could not be static did not think to suggest that it might be expanding. Instead, they attempted to modify the theory by making the gravitational force repulsive at very large distances. This did not significantly affect their predictions of the motions of the planets, but it allowed an infinite distribution of stars to remain in equilibrium—with the attractive forces between nearby stars balanced by the repulsive forces from those that were farther away. However, we now believe such an equilibrium would be unstable: if the stars in some region got only slightly nearer each other, the attractive forces between them would become stronger and dominate over the repulsive forces so that the stars would continue to fall toward each other. On the other hand, if the stars got a bit farther away from each other, the repulsive forces would dominate and drive them farther apart.

Another objection to an infinite static universe is normally ascribed to the German philosopher Heinrich Olbers, who wrote about this theory in 1823. In fact, various contemporaries of Newton had raised the problem, and the Olbers article was not even the first to contain plausible arguments against it. It was, however, the first to be widely noted. The difficulty is that in an infinite static universe nearly every line of sight would end on the surface of a star. Thus one would expect that the whole sky would be as bright as the sun, even at night. Olbers's counterargument was that the light from distant stars would be dimmed by absorption by intervening matter. However, if that happened the intervening matter would eventually heat up until it glowed as brightly as the stars. The only way of avoiding the conclusion that the whole of the night sky should be as bright as the surface of the sun would be to assume that the stars had not been shining forever but had turned on at some finite time in the past. In that case the absorbing matter might not have heated up yet or the light from distant stars might not yet have reached us. And that brings us to the question of what could have caused the stars to have turned on in the first place.

The beginning of the universe had, of course, been discussed long before this. According to a number of early cosmologies and the Jewish/Christian/Muslim tradition, the universe started at a finite, and not very distant, time in the past. One argument for such a beginning was the feeling that it was necessary to have "First Cause" to explain the existence of the universe. (Within the universe, you always explained one event as being caused by some earlier event, but the existence of the universe itself could be explained in this way only if it had some beginning.) Another argument was put forward by St. Augustine in his book *The City of God*. He pointed out that civilization is progressing and we remember who performed this deed or developed that technique. Thus man, and so also perhaps the universe, could not have been around all that long. St. Augustine accepted a date of about 5000 B.C. for the Creation of the universe according to the book of Genesis. (It is interesting that this is not so far from the end of the last Ice Age, about 10,000 B.C. which is when archaeologists tell us that civilization really began.)

Aristotle, and most of the other Greek philosophers, on the other hand,   15
did not like the idea of a creation because it smacked too much of divine intervention. They believed, therefore, that the human race and the world around it had existed, and would exist, forever. The ancients had already considered the argument about progress described above, and answered it by saying that there had been periodic floods or other disasters that repeatedly set the human race right back to the beginning of civilization.

The questions of whether the universe had a beginning in time and whether it is limited in space were later extensively examined by the philosopher Immanuel Kant in his monumental (and very obscure) work, *Critique of Pure Reason,* published in 1781. He called these questions antinomies (that is, contradictions) of pure reason because he felt that there were equally compelling arguments for believing the thesis, that the universe had a beginning, and the antithesis, that it had existed forever. His argument for the thesis was that if the universe did not have a beginning, there would be an infinite period of time before any event, which he considered absurd. The argument for the antithesis was that if the universe had a beginning, there would be an infinite period of time before it, so why should the universe begin at any one particular time? In fact, his cases for both the thesis and the antithesis are really the same argument. They are both based on his unspoken assumption that time continues back forever, whether or not the universe had existed forever. As we shall see, the concept of time has no meaning before the beginning of the universe. This was first pointed out by St. Augustine. When asked: What did God do before he created the universe? Augustine didn't reply: He was preparing Hell for people who asked such questions. Instead, he said that time was a property of the universe that God created, and that time did not exist before the beginning of the universe.

When most people believed in an essentially static and unchanging universe, the question of whether or not it had a beginning was really one of metaphysics or theology. One could account for what was observed equally well on the theory that the universe had existed forever or on the theory that it was set in motion at some finite time in such a manner as to look as though it had existed forever. But in 1929, Edwin Hubble made the landmark observation that wherever you look, distant galaxies are moving rapidly away from us. In other words, the universe is expanding. This means that at earlier times objects would have been closer together. In fact, it seemed that there was a time, about ten or twenty thousand million years ago, when they were all at exactly the same place and when, therefore, the density of the universe was infinite. This discovery finally brought the question of the beginning of the universe into the realm of science.

Hubble's observations suggested that there was a time, called the big bang, when the universe was infinitesimally small and infinitely dense. Under such conditions all the laws of science, and therefore all ability to predict the future, would break down. If there were events earlier than this time, then they could not affect what happens at the present time. Their existence can be ignored because it would have no observational consequences. One may say that time had a beginning at the big bang, in the sense that earlier times simply would not be defined. It should be emphasized that this beginning in time is very different from those that had been considered previously. In an unchanging universe a beginning in time is something that has to be imposed by some being outside the universe; there is no physical necessity for a beginning. One can imagine that God created the universe at literally any time in the past. On the other hand, if the universe is expanding, there may be physical reasons why there had to be a beginning. One could still imagine that God created the universe at the instant of the big bang, or even afterwards in just such a way as to make it look as though there had been a big bang, but it would be meaningless to suppose that it was created *before* the big bang. An expanding universe does not preclude a creator, but it does place limits on when he might have carried out his job!

In order to talk about the nature of the universe and to discuss questions such as whether it has a beginning or an end, you have to be clear about what a scientific theory is. I shall take the simpleminded view that a theory is just a model of the universe, or a restricted part of it, and a set of rules that relate quantities in the model to observations that we make. It exists only in our minds and does not have any other reality (whatever that might mean). A theory is a good theory if it satisfies two requirements: It must accurately describe a large class of observations on the basis of a model that contains only a few arbitrary elements, and it must make definite predictions about the results of future observations. For example, Aristotle's theory that everything was made out of four elements, earth, air, fire, and water, was simple enough to qualify, but it did not make any definite predictions. On the other hand, Newton's theory of gravity was based on an even simpler model, in which bodies attracted each other with a force that was proportional to a quantity called their mass and inversely proportional to the square of the distance between them. Yet it predicts the motions of the sun, the moon, and the planets to a high degree of accuracy.

Any physical theory is always provisional, in the sense that it is only a   20
hypothesis: you can never prove it. No matter how many times the results of experiments agree with some theory, you can never be sure that the next

time the result will not contradict the theory. On the other hand, you can disprove a theory by finding even a single observation that disagrees with the predictions of the theory. As philosopher of science Karl Popper has emphasized, a good theory is characterized by the fact that it makes a number of predictions that could in principle be disproved or falsified by observation. Each time new experiments are observed to agree with the predictions the theory survives, and our confidence in it is increased; but if ever a new observation is found to disagree, we have to abandon or modify the theory. At least that is what is supposed to happen, but you can always question the competence of the person who carried out the observation.

In practice, what often happens is that a new theory is devised that is really an extension of the previous theory. For example, very accurate observations of the planet Mercury revealed a small difference between its motion and the predictions of Newton's theory of gravity. Einstein's general theory of relativity predicted a slightly different motion from Newton's theory. The fact that Einstein's predictions matched what was seen, while Newton's did not, was one of the crucial confirmations of the new theory. However, we still use Newton's theory for all practical purposes because the difference between its predictions and those of general relativity is very small in the situations that we normally deal with. (Newton's theory also has the great advantage that it is much simpler to work with than Einstein's!)

The eventual goal of science is to provide a single theory that describes the whole universe. However, the approach most scientists actually follow is to separate the problem into two parts. First, there are the laws that tell us how the universe changes with time. (If we know what the universe is like at any one time, these physical laws tell us how it will look at any later time.) Second, there is the question of the initial state of the universe. Some people feel that science should be concerned with only the first part; they regard the question of the initial situation as a matter for metaphysics or religion. They would say that God, being omnipotent, could have started the universe off any way he wanted. That may be so, but in that case he also could have made it develop in a completely arbitrary way. Yet it appears that he chose to make it evolve in a very regular way according to certain laws. It therefore seems equally reasonable to suppose that there are also laws governing the initial state.

It turns out to be very difficult to devise a theory to describe the universe all in one go. Instead, we break the problem up into bits and invent a number of partial theories. Each of these partial theories describes and predicts a certain limited class of observations, neglecting the effects of other quantities, or representing them by simple sets of numbers. It may be that this approach is completely wrong. If everything in the universe depends on everything else in a fundamental way, it might be impossible to get close to a full solution by investigating parts of the problem in isolation. Nevertheless, it is certainly the way that we have made progress in the past. The classic example again is the Newtonian theory of gravity, which tells us that the gravitational force between two bodies depends only on one number associated with each body, its mass, but is otherwise independent of what the bodies are made of. Thus one does not need to have a theory of the structure and constitution of the sun and the planets in order to calculate their orbits.

Today scientists describe the universe in terms of two basic partial theories—the general theory of relativity and quantum mechanics. They are the great intellectual achievements of the first half of this century. The general theory of relativity describes the force of gravity and the large-scale structure of the universe, that is, the structure on scales from only a few miles to as large as a million million million million (1 with twenty-four zeros after it) miles, the size of the observable universe. Quantum mechanics, on the other hand, deals with phenomena on extremely small scales, such as a millionth of a millionth of an inch. Unfortunately, however, these two theories are known to be inconsistent with each other—they cannot both be correct. One of the major endeavors in physics today . . . is the search for a new theory that will incorporate them both—a quantum theory of gravity. We do not yet have such a theory, and we may still be a long way from having one, but we do already know many of the properties that it must have. And . . . we already know a fair amount about the predictions a quantum theory of gravity must make.

Now, if you believe that the universe is not arbitrary, but is governed   25
by definite laws, you ultimately have to combine the partial theories into a complete unified theory that will describe everything in the universe. But there is a fundamental paradox in the search for such a complete unified theory. The ideas about scientific theories outlined above assume we are rational beings who are free to observe the universe as we want and to draw logical deductions from what we see. In such a scheme it is reasonable to suppose that we might progress even closer toward the laws that govern our universe. Yet if there really is a complete unified theory, it would also presumably determine our actions. And so the theory itself would determine the outcome of our search for it! And why should it determine that we come to the right conclusions from the evidence? Might it not equally well determine that we draw the wrong conclusion? Or no conclusion at all?

The only answer that I can give to this problem is based on Darwin's principle of natural selection. The idea is that in any population of self-reproducing organisms, there will be variations in the genetic material and upbringing that different individuals have. These differences will mean that some individuals are better able than others to draw the right conclusions about the world around them and to act accordingly. These individuals will be more likely to survive and reproduce and so their pattern of behavior and thought will come to dominate. It has certainly been true in the past that what we call intelligence and scientific discovery has conveyed a survival advantage. It is not so clear that this is still the case: our scientific discoveries may well destroy us all, and even if they don't, a complete unified theory may not make much difference to our chances of survival. However, provided the universe has evolved in a regular way, we might expect that the reasoning abilities that natural selection has given us would be valid also in our search for a complete unified theory, and so would not lead us to the wrong conclusions.

Because the partial theories that we already have are sufficient to make accurate predictions in all but the most extreme situations, the search for the ultimate theory of the universe seems difficult to justify on practical grounds. (It is worth noting, though, that similar arguments could have been used against both relativity and quantum mechanics, and these theories have given us both nuclear energy and the microelectronics revolution!) The discovery of a complete unified theory, therefore, may not aid the survival of our species. It may not even affect our life-style. But ever since the dawn of civilization, people have not been content to see events as unconnected and inexplicable. They have craved an understanding of the underlying order in the world. Today we still yearn to know why we are here and where we came from. Humanity's deepest desire for knowledge is justification enough for our continuing quest. And our goal is nothing less than a complete description of the universe we live in.

QUESTIONS

1. There is a break in the essay after paragraph 18, indicated by extra space between paragraphs. If you had to provide a subtitle for each of the two sections demarcated by that break, what would these subtitles be?

2. What is the function of the anecdote in paragraph 1? Why do you suppose Hawking begins with that story?

3. What is the function of paragraph 2? What kind of sentence structure predominates in this paragraph? Why?

4. The first date mentioned in the essay comes in paragraph 3. Make a list of all the other exact dates that are given, noting the paragraphs in which they appear. Discuss any patterns (or violations of pattern) that you note. What does this list tell you about the organization of the essay?

5. Hawking uses the word *God* with some frequency. How would you describe the notion of God generated by his text? Is it different from your own views? How important is God to Hawking's view of the universe?

6. What is the notion of science that can be derived from Hawking's use of that word? That is, with what definition or concept of science is he working? Is it the same as your own? Discuss.

7. In the latter part of his essay, Hawking takes up the philosophical question of how we can know that we know what we know. Describe and discuss the view that he presents, bringing in any other theories of

knowledge that you have encountered in your studies or reading on the subject.

MAKING CONNECTIONS

Read Carl Sagan's essay, "Can We Know the Universe? Reflections on a Grain of Salt" (p. 178). Are Sagan and Hawking talking about the same universe? Note Sagan's strongest beliefs as expressed in his final paragraphs. Are Sagan and Hawking thinking along the same lines? To what extent does Hawking seem to be answering the challenge that Sagan makes?

The Action of Natural Selection

Charles Darwin

Charles Darwin (1809–1882), British botanist, geologist, and naturalist, is best known for his discovery that natural selection is responsible for changes in organisms during evolution. After an undistinguished academic career and a five-year voyage to South America with a British survey ship, he began keeping his Transmutation Notebooks *(1837–1839), developing the idea of "selection owing to struggle." In 1842 and 1844 he published short accounts of his views and in 1859 published* On the Origin of Species, *which made him famous—even notorious—as the father of the theory of evolution. He preferred to avoid controversy and left the debates over his theories to others whenever possible. But he was a keen observer and continued to study and write on natural history all his life. The essay that follows here is a brief excerpt from* On the Origin of Species, *in which Darwin explains his principle of "natural selection."*

In order to make it clear how, as I believe, natural selection acts, I must beg permission to give one or two imaginary illustrations. Let us take the case of a wolf, which preys on various animals, securing some by craft, some by strength, and some by fleetness; and let us suppose that the fleetest prey, a deer for instance, had from any change in the country increased in numbers, or that other prey had decreased in numbers, during that season of the year when the wolf is hardest pressed for food. I can under such circumstances see no reason to doubt that the swiftest and slimmest wolves would have the best chance for surviving, and so be preserved or selected — provided always that they retained strength to master their prey at this or at some other period of the year, when they might be compelled to prey on other animals. I can see no more reason to doubt this, than that man can improve the fleetness of his greyhounds by careful and methodical selection, or by that unconscious selection which results from each man trying to keep the best dogs without any thought of modifying the breed.

Even without any change in the proportional numbers of the animals on which our wolf preyed, a cub might be born with an innate tendency to pursue certain kinds of prey. Nor can this be thought very improbable; for we often observe great differences in the natural tendencies of our domestic animals; one cat, for instance, taking to catch rats, another mice; one cat,

576

according to Mr. St. John, bringing home winged game, another hares or rabbits, and another hunting on marshy ground and almost nightly catching woodcocks or snipes. The tendency to catch rats rather than mice is known to be inherited. Now, if any slight innate change of habit or of structure benefited an individual wolf, it would have the best chance of surviving and of leaving offspring. Some of its young would probably inherit the same habits or structure, and by the repetition of this process, a new variety might be formed which would either supplant or coexist with the parent-form of wolf. Or, again, the wolves inhabiting a mountainous district, and those frequenting the lowlands, would naturally be forced to hunt different prey; and from the continued preservation of the individuals best fitted for the two sites, two varieties might slowly be formed. These varieties would cross and blend where they met; but to this subject of intercrossing we shall soon have to return. I may add, that, according to Mr. Pierce, there are two varieties of the wolf inhabiting the Catskill Mountains in the United States, one with a light greyhound-like form, which pursues deer, and the other more bulky, with shorter legs, which more frequently attacks the shepherd's flocks.

Let us now take a more complex case. Certain plants excrete a sweet juice, apparently for the sake of eliminating something injurious from their sap: this is effected by glands at the base of the stipules in some Leguminosae, and at the back of the leaf of the common laurel. This juice, though small in quantity, is greedily sought by insects. Let us now suppose a little sweet juice or nectar to be excreted by the inner bases of the petals of a flower. In this case insects in seeking the nectar would get dusted with pollen, and would certainly often transport the pollen from one flower to the stigma of another flower. The flowers of two distinct individuals of the same species would thus get crossed; and the act of crossing, we have good reason to believe (as will hereafter be more fully alluded to), would produce very vigorous seedlings, which consequently would have the best chance of flourishing and surviving. Some of these seedlings would probably inherit the nectar-excreting power. Those individual flowers which had the largest glands or nectaries, and which excreted most nectar, would be oftenest visited by insects, and would be oftenest crossed; and so in the long-run would gain the upper hand. Those flowers, also, which had their stamens and pistils placed, in relation to the size and habits of the particular insects which visited them, so as to favor in any degree the transportal of their pollen from flower to flower, would likewise be favored or selected. We might have taken the case of insects visiting flowers for the sake of collecting pollen instead of nectar; and as pollen is formed for the sole object of fertilization, its destruction appears a simple loss to the plant; yet if a little pollen were carried, at first occasionally and then habitually, by the pollen-devouring insects from flower to flower, and a cross thus effected, although nine-tenths of the pollen were destroyed, it might still be a great gain to the plant; and those individuals which produced more and more pollen, and had larger and larger anthers, would be selected.

When our plant, by this process of the continued preservation or natural selection of more and more attractive flowers, had been rendered highly attractive to insects, they would, unintentionally on their part, regularly carry pollen from flower to flower; and that they can most effectually do this, I could easily show by many striking instances. I will give only one — not as a very striking case, but as likewise illustrating one step in the separation of the sexes of plants, presently to be alluded to. Some holly-trees bear only male flowers, which have four stamens producing rather a small quantity of pollen, and a rudimentary pistil; other holly-trees bear only female flowers; these have a full-sized pistil and four stamens with shrivelled anthers, in which not a grain of pollen can be detected. Having found a female tree exactly sixty yards from a male tree, I put the stigmas of twenty flowers, taken from different branches, under the microscope, and on all, without exception, there were pollen-grains, and on some a profusion of pollen. As the wind had set for several days from the female to the male tree, the pollen could not thus have been carried. The weather had been cold and boisterous, and therefore not favorable to bees, nevertheless every female flower which I examined had been effectually fertilized by the bees, accidentally dusted with pollen, having flown from tree to tree in search of nectar. But to return to our imaginary case: as soon as the plant had been rendered so highly attractive to insects that pollen was regularly carried from flower to flower, another process might commence. No naturalist doubts the advantage of what has been called the "physiological division of labor"; hence we may believe that it would be advantageous to a plant to produce stamens alone in one flower or on one whole plant, and pistils alone in another flower or on one whole plant. In plants under culture and placed under new conditions of life, sometimes the male organs and sometimes the female organs become more or less impotent; now if we suppose this to occur in ever so slight a degree under nature, then as pollen is already carried regularly from flower to flower, and as a more complete separation of the sexes of our plant would be advantageous on the principle of the division of labor, individuals with this tendency more and more increased would be continually favored or selected, until at last a complete separation of the sexes would be effected.

Let us now turn to the nectar-feeding insects in our imaginary case: we may suppose the plant of which we have been slowly increasing the nectar by continued selection, to be a common plant; and that certain insects depended in main part on its nectar for food. I could give many facts, showing how anxious bees are to save time; for instance, their habit of cutting holes and sucking the nectar at the bases of certain flowers, which they can, with a very little more trouble, enter by the mouth. Bearing such facts in mind, I can see no reason to doubt that an accidental deviation in the size and form of the body, or in the curvature and length of the proboscis, &c., far too slight to be appreciated by us, might profit a bee or other insect, so that an individual so characterized would be able to obtain its food more quickly, and so have a better chance of living and leaving descen-

5

dants. Its descendants would probably inherit a tendency to a similar slight deviation of structure. The tubes of the corollas of the common red and incarnate clovers (Trifolium pratense and incarnatum) do not on a hasty glance appear to differ in length; yet the hive-bee can easily suck the nectar out of the incarnate clover, but not out of the common red clover, which is visited by humble-bees alone; so that whole fields of the red clover offer in vain an abundant supply of precious nectar to the hive-bee. Thus it might be a great advantage to the hive-bee to have a slightly longer or differently constructed proboscis. On the other hand, I have found by experiment that the fertility of clover greatly depends on bees visiting and moving parts of the corolla, so as to push the pollen on to the stigmatic surface. Hence, again, if humble-bees were to become rare in any country, it might be a great advantage to the red clover to have a shorter or more deeply divided tube to its corolla, so that the hive-bee could visit its flowers. Thus I can understand how a flower and a bee might slowly become, either simultaneously or one after the other, modified and adapted in the most perfect manner to each other, by the continued preservation of individuals presenting mutual and slightly favorable deviations of structure.

I am well aware that this doctrine of natural selection, exemplified in the above imaginary instances, is open to the same objections which were at first urged against Sir Charles Lyell's[1] noble views on "the modern changes of the earth, as illustrative of geology;" but we now very seldom hear the action, for instance, of the coast-waves, called a trifling and insignificant cause, when applied to the excavation of gigantic valleys or to the formation of the longest lines of inland cliffs. Natural selection can act only by the preservation and accumulation of infinitesimally small inherited modifications, each profitable to the preserved being; and as modern geology has almost banished such views as the excavation of a great valley by a single diluvial wave, so will natural selection, if it be a true principle, banish the belief of the continued creation of new organic beings, or of any great and sudden modification in their structure.

QUESTIONS

1. What does Darwin mean by "natural selection"?
2. The short title of Darwin's major book is often mistakenly given as *The Origin of the Species*. What is the difference between that and the book's correct title, *On the Origin of Species*? Why do you think so many people get it wrong?
3. Why does Darwin "beg permission" in the first sentence? In the same sentence, what does he mean by "imaginary illustrations"? Are they untrue? Explain why or why not.

---

[1]*Sir Charles Lyell* (1797–1875): British geologist. [Eds.]

4. We use the name *bumblebee* for what Darwin (and other English writers before him) called a "humble-bee." Find out something about the word *humble* and about the different kinds of bees. (What is the difference between a hive-bee and a humble-bee, anyway?) For the word *humble*, go to a good dictionary, but don't depend on a dictionary for information about different kinds of bees. Play with the words *humble* and *bumble* to see which of their meanings can be appropriately applied to bees.

5. Darwin's illustrative explanations are excellent examples of process analysis, a type of writing that presents a complicated chain of events as clearly as possible. Select some subject that you know well and that involves an intricate linkage of events. Explain an "imaginary" process taken from that subject. That is, imagine how some little change in an intricate pattern of events would lead to other changes that would cause other changes, until a whole new pattern was established. For example, how would some change in your behavior, appearance, or abilities change the patterns of school and family life around you? Explain the process you imagine as accurately and "scientifically" as you can. Complete your explanation by drawing some conclusion about the principles exemplified by the process you have described.

MAKING CONNECTIONS

Compare Darwin's illustrations of the wolf, the bee, and the flower to James Jeans's explanation in "Why the Sky Is Blue" (p. 505). How are their explanations similar? Are there any striking differences? Explain.

THE LIFE OF THE OTTER

Thom Gunn

Thom Gunn was born in 1929 in Gravesend, England, and received degrees from Cambridge and Stanford universities. For much of his career, he served on the English faculty at the University of California at Berkeley. He published his first volume of poetry, Fighting Terms, *in 1954, and his other collections include* My Sad Captains *(1961),* Touch *(1968),* Jack Straw's Castle *(1976), and* The Man with Night Sweats *(1992), which focused on dealing with the specter of AIDS. Gunn's* Collected Poems *appeared in 1994, and his most recent collection is* Boss Cupid *(2000). In his early poems, Gunn employed strict forms of meter and rhyme (he considered himself a modern-day John Donne), but in later years he began experimenting with looser structures. In subject matter, he has explored topics ranging from violence to biker culture to his own open homosexuality.*

Tucson Desert Museum

From sand he pours himself into deep water,
His other liberty
    in which he swims
Faster than anything that lives on legs,
In wide parabolas   5
     figures of eight
Long loops
    drawn with the accuracy and ease
Of a lithe skater hands behind her back
Who seems to be showing off   10
       but is half lost
In the exuberance of dip and wheel.

The small but long brown beast reaches from play
Through play
    to play   15
     play not as relaxation
Or practice or escape but all there is:
Activity   (hunt, procreation, feeding)
Functional but as if gratuitous.

                   20

Now
    while he flows
        out of a downward curve
I glimpse through glass
        his genitals as neat
As a stone acorn with its two oak leaves   25
Carved in a French cathedral porch,
        relief

Exposed
    crisply detailed
        above the sway   30
Of this firm muscular trunk
        caught in mid-plunge,
Of which the speed contains its own repose
Potency
    set in fur   35
        like an ornament.

QUESTIONS

1. Copy out the entire poem without the line breaks; that is, duplicate the words but present them in a paragraph format, as if the poem were prose. Now read both the verse poem and your paragraph poem aloud. List the differences.
2. Much explaining can be done by comparison, whether explicit or implicit. In this manner, a writer draws upon familiar resources in order to give dimension to the subject he or she depicts. What kinds of comparisons does Gunn make throughout the poem?
3. What kind of beauty does Gunn implicitly praise in this poem?
4. Why is there such a repetitive emphasis on "play" in the middle of the poem? How is "from play" different than "Through play," "to play," and "play not as relaxation / Or practice or escape but all there is"?

MAKING CONNECTIONS

Is "The Life of the Otter" (in capital letters, like a placard in a museum) different from "the life of the [or 'an'] otter"? Write an essay in which you describe your own interaction with an animal. Explain what difference it made whether you observed it in captivity or in "the wild."

ARGUING

Here in "Arguing" you will find authors taking positions on a wide range of controversial subjects—from the issue of cigarette smoking to the status of black English, from the nature of hate to the practices of body management. No matter what their academic fields or professions, these authors energetically defend their stands on the issues and questions they address. But this should come as no surprise. None of us, after all, holds lightly to our beliefs and ideas about what is true or beautiful or good. Indeed, most of us get especially fired up when our views are pitted against the ideas and beliefs of others. So, you will find these authors vigorously engaged in the give-and-take of argument. As a consequence, you will repeatedly find yourself having to weigh the merits of competing positions in a debate or disagreement about some controversial issue.

The distinctive quality of arguing can be seen in the following passage from Daniel Lazare's "Your Constitution Is Killing You":

> The framers, as it turns out, were of two minds where the power of the people was concerned. The Preamble to the Constitution implies a theory of unbounded popular sovereignty in which "we the people" are so powerful that we can "ordain and establish" new constitutions and, in the process, abrogate old ones such as the disastrous Articles of Confederation. The rest of the document implies that "we the people" are so powerless that when it comes to an anachronism such as the Second Amendment, the democratic majority is effectively precluded from changing a Constitution made in the people's name. We the people can move mountains, but we cannot excise one troublesome twenty-seven-word clause. Because we have chained ourselves to a premodern Constitution, we are unable to deal with the modern problem of a runaway gun culture in a modern way. Rather than binding society together, the

effort to force society to conform to the dictates of an outmoded plan of government is tearing it apart. Each new crazed gunman is a symptom of our collective — one might say our constitutional — helplessness. Someday soon, we will have to emancipate ourselves from our eighteenth-century Constitution. The only question is how.

This passage comes one-third of the way into a piece in which Lazare enters the debate on gun control by examining the Second Amendment and the Constitution of which it is a part. He discusses recent arguments about the interpretation of the Second Amendment, which break down into the individualist argument (that individuals have the right to bear arms) versus the collectivist argument (that the right applies only collectively, as to a militia, for example). The most recent judicial ruling is that both individual and collective rights are guaranteed by the Second Amendment. Thus, in order to institute gun control, the amendment would have to be changed. Lazare goes on to declare the Constitution unsuitable for modern times. Now he must provide evidence to argue for this proposition.

It is clear from his opening paragraphs that Lazare is strongly in favor of gun control, and thus his essay is structured on the premise that gun control is necessary. In entering into this hotly debated issue, Lazare's strategy is to attack the document that provides the very foundation of the opposing side's argument. He uses eighteenth-century history as evidence in order to understand how the Second Amendment came about and in order to argue for our emancipation from our present Constitution.

As readers of argumentative writing, we should try to be as impartial as the members of a jury. We should try to set aside any biases or prejudices that we might have about one view or another. Then, we should weigh all the evidence, logic, claims, and appeals for each viewpoint before arriving at a decision about which one we find most convincing. By the same token, as writers of argument we should assume that readers are not likely to be persuaded by a one-sided view of a complex situation. Thus, we should be ready to present a case that not only will support our position, but will respond to the crucial challenges of views that differ from our own. Both as readers and writers, then, we should strive to understand the balanced methods of persuasion that can be found throughout the broad range of argumentative writing.

The Range of Argumentative Writing

Argumentative writing so pervades our lives that we may not even recognize it as such in the many brochures and leaflets that come our way, urging us to vote for one candidate rather than another or to support one cause rather than another. Argumentative writing also figures heavily in newspaper editorials, syndicated columns, and letters to the editor, which are typically given over to debating the pros and cons of one public issue or another, from local taxes to national defense policies. Argument, of course, is fundamental in the judicial process, crucial in the legislative process, and serves the basic aims of the academic world, enabling different ideas and theories to be tested by pitting them against each other. Whatever the field or profession, argument is an important activity in the advancement of knowledge and society.

The broad range of argumentative writing can be understood by considering the kinds of issues and questions that typically give rise to disagreement and debate. The most basic sources of controversy are questions of fact—the who, what, when, and where of things, as well as how much. Intense arguments over questions of fact can develop in any academic or professional field, especially when the facts in question have a significant bearing on the explanation or judgment of a particular subject, body of material, or type of investigation.

Indeed, Elliott Gorn's piece, "Professing History: Distinguishing Between Memory and the Past," concerns the suppression of historical facts in favor of a more noble or easily digestible view of the past, one that is more "marketable." With regard to the American Civil War, Gorn found after reading through "a hundred years of scholarly writing on the topic . . . your head spins with contradictions—the Civil War was an 'irrepressible conflict' and an avoidable one; an ideological war to end slavery and a war that had nothing to do with slavery; a war waged by a rising bourgeoisie against a proto-aristocracy and a war of capitalists fighting each other." So, in a very real sense, the argument in this piece arises over questions of fact as well as questions of how to interpret the facts.

Even when there is no question about the facts themselves, there are likely to be arguments about how to explain the facts. Disagreements of this kind abound across the full range of academic and professional fields. And the arguments inevitably arise out of sharply differing points of view on the facts, as can be seen in Cynthia Ozick's "Who Owns Anne Frank?" Ozick attacks the bowdlerization of Anne Frank's diary, as well as the play and film versions which promote a "sanitized," spiritually uplifting version of the heroine, and ignore "the heavier truth of named and inhabited evil" in her story. Thus Ozick is taking a stand in opposition to the popularized view of Anne Frank.

Differing viewpoints, of course, ultimately reflect differing beliefs and values. The way we view any particular subject is, after all, a matter of personal choice, an outgrowth of what our experience and knowledge have led us to hold as being self-evident. In this sense, beliefs and values are always to some extent at issue in any argumentative situation, even when they remain more or less in the background. But in some cases the conflicting values themselves are so clearly at the heart of the argument that they become a central focus in the debate, as you can see in this well-known passage from the Declaration of Independence:

We hold these truths to be self-evident, that all men are created equal, that they are endowed by their Creator with certain unalienable Rights, that among these are Life, Liberty and the pursuit of Happiness. That to secure these rights, Governments are instituted among Men, deriving their just powers from the consent of the governed. That whenever any Form of Government becomes destructive of these ends, it is the Right of the People to alter or to abolish it, and to institute new Government, laying its foundation on such principles and organizing its powers in such form, as to them shall seem most likely to affect their Safety and Happiness.

In this crucial passage, which comes at the opening of the second paragraph of the Declaration, Thomas Jefferson and his congressional colleagues directly challenged several fundamental assumptions about the rights of people and the sources of governmental power that were then held not only by the British king but also by many British people and others throughout the world. Only in this way was it possible for them to make the compelling case for their ultimate claim that the colonies should be "FREE AND INDEPENDENT STATES . . . absolved from all Allegiance to the British Crown."

Though Jefferson and his colleagues did not outline a new system of government in the Declaration itself, the document does enable us to see that conflicts over beliefs and values can, and often do, have a decisive bearing on questions of policy and planning. For a clear-cut example of how conflicts over beliefs lead to debates over policy, you need only look at Andrew Sullivan's "What's So Bad about Hate." Sullivan notes that "we have created an entirely new offense in American criminal law — a 'hate crime'," but we have only "a remarkably vague idea of what [hate] actually is. President Clinton declared a hate-crime law to be "what America needs in our battle against hate." While most people would respond to the rallying cry to battle against hate, they might have some difficulty in defining just what it is they are to battle against.

Sullivan's strategy is to provide evidence to show how difficult it is to define hate. In the process, he challenges common clichés about hate, such as the belief that "the hate that comes from knowledge is always different from the hate that comes from ignorance," or that hate for a group is worse than hate for a person, a belief that prevents rape from being considered a hate crime. Part of the difficulty of defining hate as a crime is that there are many different kinds of hate. Sullivan cites an authority, psychotherapist Elisabeth Young-Bruehl, who "proposes a typology of the distinct kinds of hate: obsessive, hysterical, and narcissistic." But he concludes that each kind of hate is complicated, and likely to be a combination of various types. He presents a number of different cases as evidence to underscore the difficulty of using *hate crime* as a label.

Just as his argument requires Sullivan to demonstrate the difficulty of defining *hate* and *hate crime,* so every other kind of question imposes on writers a particular set of argumentative obligations. To argue for her reading of Anne Frank's diary as "a conscious literary record of frightened lives in daily peril . . . a story of fear" rather than as an uplifting story, Ozick must draw on the historical facts of Europe in World War II; the textual history of the diary; biographical information about those connected with the diary and its original publication; and the facts surrounding its transformation into a stage play. Susan Bordo draws on medical and social history and on evidence from advertising and film to show how "ideal slenderness" was created and how such an ideal has promoted eating disorders in women. A writer who aims to be persuasive cannot simply assert that something is or is not the case, for readers in general are not willing to be bullied into accepting a particular claim. But they are capable of being reached by civilized and rational methods of persuasion that are appropriate to controversial issues — by evidence, logic, and eloquence.

Methods of Arguing

In any piece of argumentative writing, your primary purpose is to bring readers around to your point of view. Some readers, of course, will agree with you in advance, but others will disagree, and still others will be undecided. So, in planning a piece of argumentative writing, you should begin by examining your material with an eye to discovering the issues that have to be addressed and the points that have to be made to present your case most persuasively to readers, especially those who oppose you or are undecided. This means that you will have to deal not only with issues that you consider relevant, but also with matters that have been raised by your opponents. In other words, you will have to show readers that you have considered both sides of the controversy. In arguing for her interpretation of Anne Frank's diary, Ozick must consider the interpretations she feels falsify Anne Frank's message. Likewise, Lazare must consider various interpretations of the Second Amendment in order to argue for constitutional change.

After you have identified the crucial points to be addressed, you should then select the methods you'll need to make a convincing case with respect to each of the points. Some methods, of course, are imperative no matter what point you are trying to prove. Every piece of argumentation requires that you offer readers evidence to support your position. To do so, you will need to gather and present specific details that bear on each of the points you are trying to make. This basic concern for providing readers with appropriate evidence will lead you inevitably into the activity of reporting. Jefferson, for example, provides a lengthy and detailed list of "injuries" that the king of Great Britain inflicted on the colonies in his attempt to demonstrate the right of the colonies "to throw off such Government." Reporting appropriate evidence constitutes the most basic means of making a persuasive case for any point under consideration. So, any point for which evidence cannot be provided, or for which only weak or limited evidence can be offered, is likely to be much less convincing to readers than one that can be amply and vividly substantiated.

But evidence alone will not be persuasive to readers unless it is brought to bear on a point in a reasonable or logical way. In one of its most familiar forms, induction, logic involves the process of moving from bits of evidence to a generalization or a conclusion that is based on that evidence. For example, Emily Martin, in "The Egg and the Sperm," examines in detail the imagery used in science textbooks and other scientific discourse to demonstrate the use of metaphors based on the notion that men are active and women are passive. Though recent studies show both the egg and the sperm to be active in the process of fertilization, these stereotypes persist, as does a contradicting one of "woman as a dangerous and aggressive threat." This evidence allows Martin to generalize, to make what is called an *inductive leap:* that stereotyped personalization on the level of the cell can lay the foundation for social control of the moment of fertilization.

Deduction, another form of logic, involves the movement from general assumptions or premises to particular conclusions that can be derived from them. For example, having made the general claim that "a long train of abuses" entitles people "to throw off such Government" and having cited, in turn, a long list of abuses that Great Britain had inflicted on the colonies, Jefferson is able to reach the conclusion that the colonies "are Absolved from all Allegiance to the British Crown." Given his initial assumptions about government and the rights of the people, together with his evidence about British abuse of the colonists, Jefferson's deduction seems to be a logical conclusion, as indeed it is. But as in any case of deductive logic, the conclusion is only as convincing as the premises on which it is based. Great Britain, obviously, did not accept Jefferson's premises, so it did not accept his conclusions, logical though they were. Other countries of the time, just as obviously, took a different view of the matter. So, in developing an argument deductively, you need to keep in mind not only the logic of your case, but also the appeal its premises are likely to have for those whom you are most interested in convincing.

As you can see just from the cases of Jefferson, Ozick, and Martin, presenting evidence and using it in a logical way can take a variety of common forms, and all of these forms are likely to be present in subtle and complicated ways in virtually every piece of argumentative writing. Arguing calls on writers to be especially resourceful in developing and presenting their positions. Actually, logic is a necessary—and powerful—tool in every field and profession because it serves to fill in gaps where evidence does not exist or, as in a court case, to move beyond the accumulated evidence to conclusions that follow from it. But like any powerful tool it must be used with care. One weak link in a logical chain of reasoning can lead, after all, to a string of falsehood.

Explanatory techniques, as discussed in the introduction to "Explaining" (p. 323), also can play a role in argument, as you may already have inferred from the passages we have just been discussing. Sullivan's argument about hate is based on his interpretation of key terms, and Ozick's attack on the misreading of Anne Frank's diary relies on causal analysis to make its case. Any piece of argument, in other words, is likely to draw on a wide range of techniques, for argument is always attempting to achieve the complex purpose not only of getting at the truth about something and making that truth intelligible to readers, but also of persuading them to accept it as such.

No matter what particular combination of techniques a writer favors, when carrying out an argument, most save a very telling point or bit of evidence or well-turned phrase for last. Like effective storytellers or successful courtroom lawyers, writers know that a memorable detail makes for a powerful climax. In the pieces that follow in this section, you will see how different writers use the various resources of language to produce some very striking and compelling pieces of argument.

Arts and Humanities

HIROSHIMA

John Berger

After beginning his career as a painter and drawing instructor, John Berger (b. 1926) came to be one of Britain's most influential art critics. He has achieved recognition as a screenwriter, novelist, and documentary writer. As a Marxist, he is concerned with the ideological and technological conditioning of our ways of seeing both art and the world. In Ways of Seeing *(1972), he explores the interrelation between words and images, between verbal and visual meaning. "Hiroshima" first appeared in 1981 in the journal* New Society, *and later in a collection of essays,* The Sense of Sight *(1985). Berger examines how the facts of nuclear holocaust have been hidden through "a systematic, slow and thorough process of suppression and elimination . . . within the reality of politics." Images, rather than words, Berger asserts, can help us see through the "mask of innocence" that evil wears.*

The whole incredible problem begins with the need to reinsert those events of 6 August 1945 back into living consciousness.

I was shown a book last year at the Frankfurt Book Fair. The editor asked me some question about what I thought of its format. I glanced at it quickly and gave some reply. Three months ago I was sent a finished copy of the book. It lay on my desk unopened. Occasionally its title and cover picture caught my eye, but I did not respond. I didn't consider the book urgent, for I believed that I already knew about what I would find within it.

Did I not clearly remember the day—I was in the army in Belfast—when we first heard the news of the bomb dropped on Hiroshima? At how many meetings during the first nuclear disarmament movement had I and others not recalled the meaning of that bomb?

And then, one morning last week, I received a letter from America, accompanying an article written by a friend. This friend is a doctor of philosophy and a Marxist. Furthermore, she is a very generous and warm-hearted woman. The article was about the possibilities of a third world war. Vis-à-vis the Soviet Union she took, I was surprised to read, a position very close to Reagan's. She concluded by evoking the likely scale of destruction which would be caused by nuclear weapons, and then welcomed the positive possibilities that this would offer the socialist revolution in the United States.

It was on that morning that I opened and read the book on my desk. It   5
is called *Unforgettable Fire.*[1]

The book consists of drawings and paintings made by people who were in Hiroshima on the day that the bomb was dropped, thirty-six years ago today. Often the pictures are accompanied by a verbal record of what the image represents. None of them is by a professional artist. In 1974, an old man went to the television center in Hiroshima to show to whomever was interested a picture he had painted, entitled "At about 4 pm, 6th August 1945, near Yurozuyo bridge."

This prompted an idea of launching a television appeal to other survivors of that day to paint or draw their memories of it. Nearly a thousand pictures were sent in, and these were made into an exhibition. The appeal was worded: "Let us leave for posterity pictures about the atomic bomb, drawn by citizens."

Clearly, my interest in these pictures cannot be an art-critical one. One does not musically analyze screams. But after repeatedly looking at them, what began as an impression became a certainty. These were images of hell.

I am not using the word as hyperbole. Between these paintings by women and men who have never painted anything else since leaving school, and who have surely, for the most part, never traveled outside Japan, between these traced memories which had to be exorcised, and the numerous representations of hell in European medieval art, there is a very close affinity.

This affinity is both stylistic and fundamental. And fundamentally it is   10
to do with the situations depicted. The affinity lies in the degree of the multiplication of pain, in the lack of appeal or aid, in the pitilessness, in the equality of wretchedness, and in the disappearance of time.

> I am 78 years old. I was living at Midorimachi on the day of the A-bomb blast. Around 9 am that morning, when I looked out of my window, I saw several women coming along the street one after another towards the Hiroshima prefectural hospital. I realized for the first time, as it is sometimes said, that when people are very much frightened hair really does stand on end. The women's hair was, in fact, standing straight up and the skin of their arms was peeled off. I suppose they were around 30 years old.

Time and again, the sober eyewitness accounts recall the surprise and horror of Dante's verses about the Inferno. The temperature at the center of the Hiroshima fireball was 300,000 degrees centigrade. The survivors are called in Japanese *hibakuska*—"those who have seen hell."

> Suddenly, one man who was stark naked came up to me and said in a quavering voice, "Please help me!" He was burned and swollen all over from the effects of the A-bomb. Since I did not recognize him as my neighbor, I asked who he was. He answered that he was Mr. Sasaki, the son of Mr. Ennosuke Sasaki, who had a lumber shop in Funairi town. That morning he had been doing volunteer labor service, evacuating the houses near the prefectural office in Kato town. He had been burned black all over and had started back to his home in Funairi. He looked miserable—burned and sore, and naked with only pieces of his gaiters trailing behind as he walked. Only the part of his hair covered by his soldier's hat was left, as if he was wearing a bowl. When I touched him, his burned skin slipped off. I did not know what to do, so I asked a passing driver to take him to Eba hospital.

Does not this evocation of hell make it easier to forget that these scenes belonged to life? Is there not something conveniently unreal about hell? The whole history of the twentieth century proves otherwise.

Very systematically in Europe the conditions of hells have been constructed. It is not even necessary to list the sites. It is not even necessary to repeat the calculations of the organizers. We know this, and we choose to forget it.

HOW SURVIVORS SAW IT. A painting by Kazuhiro Ishizu, aged 68

AT THE AIOI BRIDGE, by Sawami Katagiri, aged 76

We find it ridiculous or shocking that most of the pages concerning, for example, Trotsky were torn out of official Soviet history. What has been torn out of our history are the pages concerning the experience of the two atom bombs dropped on Japan.

Of course, the facts are there in the textbooks. It may even be that school children learn the dates. But what these facts mean—and originally their meaning was so clear, so monstrously vivid, that every commentator in the world was shocked, and every politician was obliged to say (whilst planning differently), "Never again"—what these facts mean has now been torn out. It has been a systematic, slow and thorough process of suppression and elimination. This process has been hidden within the reality of politics.

Do not misunderstand me. I am not here using the word "reality" ironically, I am not politically naïve. I have the greatest respect for political reality, and I believe that the innocence of political idealists is often very dangerous. What we are considering is how in this case in the West—not in Japan for obvious reasons and not in the Soviet Union for different reasons—political and military realities have eliminated another reality.

The eliminated reality is both physical—

Yokogawa bridge above Tenma river, 6th August 1945, 8:30 am.
    People crying and moaning were running towards the city. I did not know why. Steam engines were burning at Yokogawa station.
    Skin of cow tied to wire.
    Skin of girl's hip was hanging down.
    "My baby is dead, isn't she?"

and moral.

15

The political and military arguments have concerned such issues as deterrence, defense systems, relative strike parity, tactical nuclear weapons and—pathetically—so-called civil defense. Any movement for nuclear disarmament today has to contend with those considerations and dispute their false interpretation. To lose sight of them is to become as apocalyptic as the Bomb and all utopias. (The construction of hells on earth was accompanied in Europe by plans for heavens on earth.)

What has to be redeemed, reinserted, disclosed and never be allowed to be forgotten, is the other reality. Most of the mass means of communication are close to what has been suppressed.

These paintings were shown on Japanese television. Is it conceivable that the BBC would show these pictures on Channel One at a peak hour? Without any reference to "political" and "military" realities, under the straight title, *This is How It Was, 6th August 1945*? I challenge them to do so.

What happened on that day was, of course, neither the beginning nor   20
the end of the act. It began months, years before, with the planning of the action, and the eventual final decision to drop two bombs on Japan. However much the world was shocked and surprised by the bomb dropped on Hiroshima, it has to be emphasized that it was not a miscalculation, an error, or the result (as can happen in war) of a situation deteriorating so rapidly that it gets out of hand. What happened was consciously and precisely planned. Small scenes like this were part of the plan:

> I was walking along the Hihiyama bridge about 3 pm on 7th August. A woman, who looked like an expectant mother, was dead. At her side, a girl of about three years of age brought some water in an empty can she had found. She was trying to let her mother drink from it.
>
> As soon as I saw this miserable scene with the pitiful child, I embraced the girl close to me and cried with her, telling her that her mother was dead.

There was a preparation. And there was an aftermath. The latter included long, lingering deaths, radiation sickness, many fatal illnesses which developed later as a result of exposure to the bomb, and tragic genetical effects on generations yet to be born.

I refrain from giving the statistics: how many hundreds of thousands of dead, how many injured, how many deformed children. Just as I refrain from pointing out how comparatively "small" were the atomic bombs dropped on Japan. Such statistics tend to distract. We consider numbers instead of pain. We calculate instead of judging. We relativize instead of refusing.

It is possible today to arouse popular indignation or anger by speaking of the threat and immorality of terrorism. Indeed, this appears to be the central plank of the rhetoric of the new American foreign policy ("Moscow is the world-base of all terrorism") and of British policy towards Ireland.

What is able to shock people about terrorist acts is that often their targets are unselected and innocent—a crowd in a railway station, people waiting for a bus to go home after work. The victims are chosen indiscriminately in the hope of producing a shock effect on political decision-making by their government.

The two bombs dropped on Japan were terrorist actions. The calculation was terrorist. The indiscriminacy was terrorist. The small groups of terrorists operating today are, by comparison, humane killers.

Another comparison needs to be made. Today terrorist groups mostly 25 represent small nations or groupings, who are disputing large powers in a position of strength. Whereas Hiroshima was perpetrated by the most powerful alliance in the world against an enemy who was already prepared to negotiate, and was admitting defeat.

To apply the epithet "terrorist" to the acts of bombing Hiroshima and Nagasaki is logically justifiable, and I do so because it may help to reinsert that act into living consciousness today. Yet the word changes nothing in itself.

The first-hand evidence of the victims, the reading of the pages which have been torn out, provokes a sense of outrage. This outrage has two natural faces. One is a sense of horror and pity at what happened; the other face is self-defensive and declares: *this should not happen again (here)*. For some the *here* is in brackets, for others it is not.

The face of horror, the reaction which has now been mostly suppressed, forces us to comprehend the reality of what happened. The second reaction, unfortunately, distances us from that reality. Although it begins as a straight declaration, it quickly leads into the labyrinth of defense policies, military arguments and global strategies. Finally it leads to the sordid commercial absurdity of private fall-out shelters.

This split of the sense of outrage into, on one hand, horror, and, on the other hand, expediency occurs because the concept of evil has been abandoned. Every culture, except our own in recent times, has had such a concept.

That its religious or philosophical bases vary is unimportant. The con- 30 cept of evil implies a force or forces which have to be continually struggled against so that they do not triumph over life and destroy it. One of the very first written texts from Mesopotamia, 1,500 years before Homer, speaks of this struggle, which was the first condition of human life. In public thinking nowadays, the concept of evil has been reduced to a little adjective to support an opinion or hypothesis (abortions, terrorism, ayatollahs).

Nobody can confront the reality of 6th August 1945 without being forced to acknowledge that what happened was evil. It is not a question of opinion or interpretation, but of events.

The memory of these events should be continually before our eyes. This is why the thousand citizens of Hiroshima started to draw on their little scraps of paper. We need to show their drawings everywhere. These terrible images can now release an energy for opposing evil and for the life-long struggle of that opposition.

And from this a very old lesson may be drawn. My friend in the United States is, in a sense, innocent. She looks beyond a nuclear holocaust without considering its reality. This reality includes not only its victims but also its planners and those who support them. Evil from time immemorial has often worn a mask of innocence. One of evil's principal modes of being is *looking beyond* (with indifference) that which is before the eyes.

> August 9th: On the west embankment of a military training field was a young boy four or five years old. He was burned black, lying on his back, with his arms pointing towards heaven.

Only by looking beyond or away can one come to believe that such evil is relative, and therefore under certain conditions justifiable. In reality — the reality to which the survivors and the dead bear witness — it can never be justified.

Note

1. Edited by Japan Broadcasting Corporation, London, Wildwood House, 1981; New York, Pantheon, 1981.

QUESTIONS

1. Berger begins his essay with this powerful sentence: "The whole incredible problem begins with the need to reinsert those events of 6 August 1945 back into living consciousness." What is "the whole incredible problem" as Berger describes and defines it?
2. Berger argues that what happened on August 6, 1945, was "consciously and precisely planned" (paragraph 20). What evidence does he present to support this claim? How does this argument advance his larger purpose?
3. Berger tells his readers that he refrains from giving statistics because "statistics tend to distract" (paragraph 22). What do statistics distance us from understanding about Hiroshima?
4. The content in Berger's essay ranges from thoughts about Hiroshima, to images of hell, to political realities, to terrorist actions, to concepts of evil. How does he connect these various subjects? What is the chain of reasoning?
5. Berger offers various images from the book *Unforgettable Fire*, such as "August 9th: On the west embankment of a military training field was a young boy four or five years old. He was burned black, lying on his back, with his arms pointing towards heaven" (paragraph 33). Look at the various places in the essay where Berger presents such images from *Unforgettable Fire*. What effect does this evidence have on you? How does this evidence strengthen Berger's argument?

6. Spend some time looking at and thinking about the paintings by the survivors, Kazuhiro Ishizu and Sawami Katagiri, reprinted on pages 592 and 593. What do you *see* in these paintings? What do these images represent to you?

MAKING CONNECTIONS

1. Berger insists on closing the distance between ourselves and the essential horror of Hiroshima. Look at some other essays that struggle with issues of distance. Jonathan Swift's "A Modest Proposal" (p. 680) and Alice Walker's "Am I Blue?" (p. 598) would both be examples, but you might propose another. To what an extent is distance an issue in arguing? Compare how two or three arguers handle problems of distance in their essays.

2. One of Berger's strategies in this essay is to challenge and invert popular definitions, as of *terrorism* and *terrorists,* for example (paragraphs 23–26). Similar inversions take place or are hinted at in Jane van Lawick-Goodall's "First Observations" (p. 260) and Alice Walker's "Am I Blue?" (p. 598). In these examples, the inversion involves humans and animals. Write an argument in which you invert the definition of a key term, of *safe* and *unsafe,* for example, or *capitalist* and *communist,* or *fair* and *foul,* or *villain* and *victim.* Experiment with the leverage for arguing that you find in such a radical redefinition.

AM I BLUE?

Alice Walker

Alice Walker (b. 1944) is an essayist, poet, novelist, and short-story writer. The following essay comes from her collection Living by the Word: Selected Writings, 1973–1987 *(1988). About this collection, Walker writes, "In my travels I found many people sitting and thinking thoughts similar to my own. In this study I was taught by these other people, by the art and history of past cultures, by the elements, and by the trees, the flowers, and, most especially, the animals." In the essay reprinted here, Walker questions the distinctions commonly made between human and animal.*

For about three years my companion and I rented a small house in the country that stood on the edge of a large meadow that appeared to run from the end of our deck straight into the mountains. The mountains, however, were quite far away, and between us and them there was, in fact, a town. It was one of the many pleasant aspects of the house that you never really were aware of this.

It was a house of many windows, low, wide, nearly floor to ceiling in the living room, which faced the meadow, and it was from one of these that I first saw our closest neighbor, a large white horse, cropping grass, flipping its mane, and ambling about—not over the entire meadow, which stretched well out of sight of the house, but over the five or so fenced-in acres that were next to the twenty-odd that we had rented. I soon learned that the horse, whose name was Blue, belonged to a man who lived in another town, but was boarded by our neighbors next door. Occasionally, one of the children, usually a stocky teen-ager, but sometimes a much younger girl or boy, could be seen riding Blue. They would appear in the meadow, climb up on his back, ride furiously for ten or fifteen minutes, then get off, slap Blue on the flanks, and not be seen again for a month or more.

There were many apple trees in our yard, and one by the fence that Blue could almost reach. We were soon in the habit of feeding him apples, which he relished, especially because by the middle of summer the meadow grasses—so green and succulent since January—had dried out from lack of rain, and Blue stumbled about munching the dried stalks half-heartedly. Sometimes he would stand very still just by the apple tree, and when one of us came out he would whinny, snort loudly, or stamp the ground. This meant, of course: I want an apple.

It was quite wonderful to pick a few apples, or collect those that had fallen to the ground overnight, and patiently hold them, one by one, up to his large, toothy mouth. I remained as thrilled as a child by his flexible dark lips, huge, cubelike teeth that crunched the apples, core and all, with such finality, and his high, broad-breasted *enormity;* beside which, I felt small indeed. When I was a child, I used to ride horses, and was especially friendly with one named Nan until the day I was riding and my brother deliberately spooked her and I was thrown, head first, against the trunk of a tree. When I came to, I was in bed and my mother was bending worriedly over me; we silently agreed that perhaps horseback riding was not the safest sport for me. Since then I have walked, and prefer walking to horseback riding—but I had forgotten the depth of feeling one could see in horses' eyes.

I was therefore unprepared for the expression in Blue's. Blue was   5
lonely. Blue was horribly lonely and bored. I was not shocked that this should be the case; five acres to tramp by yourself, endlessly, even in the most beautiful of meadows—and his was—cannot provide many interesting events, and once the rainy season turned to dry that was about it. No, I was shocked that I had forgotten that human animals and nonhuman animals can communicate quite well; if we are brought up around animals as children we take this for granted. By the time we are adults we no longer remember. However, the animals have not changed. They are in fact *completed* creations (at least they seem to be, so much more than we) who are not likely *to* change; it is their nature to express themselves. What else are they going to express? And they do. And, generally speaking, they are ignored.

After giving Blue the apples, I would wander back to the house, aware that he was observing me. Were more apples not forthcoming then? Was that to be his sole entertainment for the day? My partner's small son had decided he wanted to learn how to piece a quilt; we worked in silence on our respective squares as I thought . . .

Well, about slavery: about white children, who were raised by black people, who knew their first all-accepting love from black women, and then, when they were twelve or so, were told they must "forget" the deep levels of communication between themselves and "mammy" that they knew. Later they would be able to relate quite calmly, "My old mammy was sold to another good family." "My old mammy was _____." Fill in the blank. Many more years later a white woman would say: "I can't understand these Negroes, these blacks. What do they want? They're so different from us."

And about the Indians, considered to be "like animals" by the "settlers" (a very benign euphemism for what they actually were), who did not understand their description as a compliment.

And about the thousands of American men who marry Japanese, Korean, Filipina, and other non-English-speaking women and of how happy they report they are, "*blissfully,*" until their brides learn to speak English, at which point the marriages tend to fall apart. What then did the men see, when they looked into the eyes of the women they married, before they could speak English? Apparently only their own reflections.

I thought of society's impatience with the young. "Why are they play-   10
ing the music so loud?" Perhaps the children have listened to much of the music of oppressed people their parents danced to before they were born, with its passionate but soft cries for acceptance and love, and they have wondered why their parents failed to hear.

I do not know how long Blue had inhabited his five beautiful, boring acres before we moved into our house; a year after we had arrived—and had also traveled to other valleys, other cities, other worlds—he was still there.

But then, in our second year at the house, something happened in Blue's life. One morning, looking out the window at the fog that lay like a ribbon over the meadow, I saw another horse, a brown one, at the other end of Blue's field. Blue appeared to be afraid of it, and for several days made no attempt to go near. We went away for a week. When we re-turned, Blue had decided to make friends and the two horses ambled or galloped along together, and Blue did not come nearly as often to the fence underneath the apple tree.

When he did, bringing his new friend with him, there was a different look in his eyes. A look of independence, of self-possession, of inalienable *horse*ness. His friend eventually became pregnant. For months and months there was, it seemed to me, a mutual feeling between me and the horses of justice, of peace. I fed apples to them both. The look in Blue's eyes was one of unabashed "this is *it*ness."

It did not, however, last forever. One day, after a visit to the city, I went out to give Blue some apples. He stood waiting, or so I thought, though not beneath the tree. When I shook the tree and jumped back from the shower of apples, he made no move. I carried some over to him. He managed to half-crunch one. The rest he let fall to the ground. I dreaded looking into his eyes—because I had of course noticed that Brown, his partner, had gone—but I did look. If I had been born into slavery, and my partner had been sold or killed, my eyes would have looked like that. The children next door explained that Blue's partner had been "put with him" (the same expression that old people used, I had noticed, when speaking of an ancestor during slavery who had been impregnated by her owner) so that they could mate and she conceive. Since that was accomplished, she had been taken back by her owner, who lived somewhere else.

Will she be back? I asked.   15

They didn't know.

Blue was like a crazed person. Blue *was*, to me, a crazed person. He galloped furiously, as if he were being ridden, around and around his five beautiful acres. He whinnied until he couldn't. He tore at the ground with his hooves. He butted himself against his single shade tree. He looked al-ways and always toward the road down which his partner had gone. And then, occasionally, when he came up for apples, or I took apples to him, he looked at me. It was a look so piercing, so full of grief, a look so *human,* I almost laughed (I felt too sad to cry) to think there are people who do not know that animals suffer. People like me who have forgotten, and daily forget, all that animals try to tell us. "Everything you do to us will happen to you; we are your teachers, as you are ours. We are one lesson" is essentially it, I think. There are those who never once have even considered animals' rights: those who have been taught that animals actually want to be used and abused by us, as small children "love" to be frightened, or women "love" to be mutilated and raped. . . . They are the great-grandchildren of those who honestly thought, because someone taught them this: "Woman can't think" and "niggers can't faint." But most disturbing of all, in Blue's large brown eyes was a new look, more painful than the look of despair: the look of disgust with human beings, with life; the look of hatred. And it was odd what the look of hatred did. It gave him, for the first time, the look of a beast. And what that meant was that he had put up a barrier within to protect himself from further violence; all the apples in the world wouldn't change that fact.

And so Blue remained, a beautiful part of our landscape, very peaceful to look at from the window, white against the grass. Once a friend came to visit and said, looking out on the soothing view: "And it *would* have to be a *white* horse; the very image of freedom." And I thought, yes, the animals are forced to become for us merely "images" of what they once so beautifully expressed. And we are used to drinking milk from containers showing "contented" cows, whose real lives we want to hear nothing about, eating eggs and drumsticks from "happy" hens, and munching hamburgers advertised by bulls of integrity who seem to command their fate.

As we talked of freedom and justice one day for all, we sat down to steaks. I am eating misery, I thought, as I took the first bite. And spit it out.

QUESTIONS

1. Why does Walker begin her argument by setting the scene ("[We] rented a small house in the country . . .") and by leisurely describing the meadow where she first saw Blue?
2. Walker takes great pleasure in describing Blue for her readers. In paragraph 4, she tells us, "I remained as thrilled as a child by his flexible dark lips, huge, cubelike teeth that crunched the apples, core and all, with such finality, and his high, broad-breasted *enormity;* beside which, I felt small indeed." What does Blue represent to Walker? What does she learn from observing him?
3. In paragraph 7, Walker switches from thinking about Blue to thinking about slavery. This kind of transition is the work of the essayist—to link together through language horses, slavery, Indians, and non-

English-speaking women. How does Walker make these various connections? What is her argument?

4. Walker writes in paragraph 18, "And I thought, yes, the animals are forced to become for us merely 'images' of what they once so beautifully expressed. And we are used to drinking milk from containers showing 'contented' cows, whose real lives we want to hear nothing about, eating eggs and drumsticks from 'happy' hens, and munching hamburgers advertised by bulls of integrity who seem to command their fate." How would you respond to this comment? Write a response to Walker's essay in which you argue your position.

5. Some animal rights activists argue that animal rights will emerge as the civil rights movement of the twenty-first century. A central issue in this movement is the question, What distinguishes humans from other animals? Write an essay in which you argue your position on this issue.

MAKING CONNECTIONS

1. Walker's strategies for arguing differ from those of a more formal argument, such as Thomas Jefferson's Declaration of Independence (p. 688). Describe the strategies Walker uses and how they differ from Jefferson's or those of another writer of your choice from this section.

2. Walker's other essay in this volume, "Beauty: When the Other Dancer Is the Self " (p. 42), is categorized as reflective rather than argumentative. Presumably, her approaches to these two essays differ. Compare her two essays. In what passages in "Am I Blue?" do you find Walker most intensely absorbed in arguing? How do those passages stand out? How are they prepared for? Is there an argument embedded in the earlier essay as well? If so, how would you describe it?

WHO OWNS ANNE FRANK?

Cynthia Ozick

One of the country's foremost fiction writers, Cynthia Ozick (b. 1927) grew up in New York City. She graduated from New York University and went on to receive her Ph.D. from Ohio State University. Her novels include Trust *(1966),* The Cannibal Galaxy *(1983), and* The Puttermesser Papers *(1997), and she has also published several collections of short stories. A respected literary critic, Ozick has also served as a visiting lecturer at numerous colleges. Much of her writing focuses on Jewish culture and tradition, and she has written movingly about the aftereffects of the Holocaust. The following essay originally appeared in* The New Yorker *in 1997, shortly before a stage adaptation of Anne Frank's diary was to open on Broadway.*

If Anne Frank had not perished in the criminal malevolence of Bergen-Belsen[1] early in 1945, she would have marked her sixty-eighth birthday last June. And even if she had not kept the extraordinary diary through which we know her it is likely that we would number her among the famous of this century—though perhaps not so dramatically as we do now. She was born to be a writer. At thirteen, she felt her power; at fifteen, she was in command of it. It is easy to imagine—had she been allowed to live—a long row of novels and essays spilling from her fluent and ripening pen. We can be certain (as certain as one can be of anything hypothetical) that her mature prose would today be noted for its wit and acuity, and almost as certain that the trajectory of her work would be closer to that of Nadine Gordimer,[2] say, than to that of Françoise Sagan.[3] As an international literary presence, she would be thick rather than thin. "I want to go on living even after my death!" she exclaimed in the spring of 1944.

This was more than an exaggerated adolescent flourish. She had already intuited what greatness in literature might mean, and she clearly sensed the force of what lay under her hand in the pages of her diary; a conscious literary record of frightened lives in daily peril; an explosive document aimed directly at the future. In her last months, she was assiduously polishing phrases and editing passages with an eye to postwar publication.

---

[1]*Bergen-Belsen:* Nazi concentration camp in World War II. [Eds.]

[2]*Nadine Gordimer* (b. 1923): South African writer critical of apartheid; 1991 Nobel Prize winner. [Eds.]

[3]*Françoise Sagan* (b. 1935): French novelist whose subject matter is less serious than Gordimer's. [Eds.]

Het Achterhuis, as she called her manuscript, in Dutch—"the house be-hind," often translated as "the secret annex"—was hardly intended to be Anne Frank's last word; it was conceived as the forerunner work of a pro-fessional woman of letters.

Yet any projection of Anne Frank as a contemporary figure is an unholy speculation: it tampers with history, with reality, with deadly truth. "When I write," she confided, "I can shake off all my cares. My sorrow disappears, my spirits are revived!" But she could not shake off her capture and annihilation, and there are no diary entries to register and memorialize the snuffing of her spirit. Anne Frank was discovered, seized, and deported; she and her mother and sister and millions of others were extinguished in a program calculated to assure the cruellest and most demonically inventive human degradation. The atrocities she endured were ruthlessly and purposefully devised, from in-dexing by tattoo through systematic starvation to factory-efficient murder. She was designated to be erased from the living, to leave no grave, no sign, no physical trace of any kind. Her fault—her crime—was having been born a Jew, and as such she was classified among those who had no right to exist: not as a subject people, not as an inferior breed, not even as usable slaves. The military and civilian apparatus of an entire society was organized to obliter-ate her as a contaminant, in the way of a noxious and repellent insect. Zyklon B, the lethal fumigant poured into the gas chambers, was, pointedly, a roach poison.

Anne Frank escaped gassing. One month before liberation, not yet six-teen, she died of typhus fever, an acute infectious disease carried by lice. The precise date of her death has never been determined. She and her sis-ter, Margot, were among three thousand six hundred and fifty-nine women transported by cattle car from Auschwitz[4] to the merciless conditions of Bergen-Belsen, a barren tract of mud. In a cold, wet autumn, they suffered through nights on flooded straw in overcrowded tents, without light, sur-rounded by latrine ditches, until a violent hailstorm tore away what had passed for shelter. Weakened by brutality, chaos, and hunger, fifty thou-sand men and women—insufficiently clothed, tormented by lice—suc-cumbed, many to the typhus epidemic.

Anne Frank's final diary entry, written on August 1, 1944, ends intro-spectively—a meditation on a struggle for moral transcendence set down in a mood of wistful gloom. It speaks of "turning my heart inside out, the bad part on the outside and the good part on the inside," and of "trying to find a way to become what I'd like to be and what I could be if . . . if only there were no other people in the world." Those curiously self-subduing ellipses are the diarist's own; they are more than merely a literary effect—they signify a child's muffled bleat against confinement, the last whimper of a prisoner in a cage. Her circumscribed world had a population of eleven—the three Dutch

5

---

[4]*Auschwitz:* Nazi concentration camp in Poland where more than four million people were exterminated in World War II. [Eds.]

protectors who came and went, supplying the necessities of life, and the eight in hiding: the van Daans, their son Peter, Albert Dussel, and the four Franks. Five months earlier, on May 26, 1944, she had railed against the stress of living invisibly—a tension never relieved, she asserted, "not once in the two years we've been here. How much longer will this increasingly oppressive, unbearable weight press down on us?" And, several paragraphs on, "What will we do if we're ever . . . no, I mustn't write that down. But the question won't let itself be pushed to the back of my mind today; on the contrary, all the fear I've ever felt is looming before me in all its horror. . . . I've asked myself again and again whether it wouldn't have been better if we hadn't gone into hiding, if we were dead now and didn't have to go through this misery. . . . Let something happen soon. . . . Nothing can be more crushing than this anxiety. Let the end come however cruel." And on April 11, 1944: "We are Jews in chains."

The diary is not a genial document, despite its author's often vividly satiric exposure of what she shrewdly saw as "the comical side of life in hiding." Its reputation for uplift is, to say it plainly, nonsensical. Anne Frank's written narrative, moreover, is not the story of Anne Frank, and never has been. That the diary is miraculous, a self-aware work of youthful genius, is not in question. Variety of pace and tone, insightful humor, insupportable suspense, adolescent love pangs and disappointments, sexual curiosity, moments of terror, moments of elation, flights of idealism and prayer and psychological acumen—all these elements of mind and feeling and skill brilliantly enliven its pages. There is, besides, a startlingly precocious comprehension of the progress of the war on all fronts. The survival of the little group in hiding is crucially linked to the timing of the Allied invasion. Overhead the bombers, roaring to their destinations, make the house quake; sometimes the bombs fall terrifyingly close. All in all, the diary is a chronicle of trepidation, turmoil, alarm. Even its report of quieter periods of reading and study express the hush of imprisonment. Meals are boiled lettuce and rotted potatoes; flushing the single toilet is forbidden for ten hours at a time. There is shooting at night. Betrayal and arrest always threaten. Anxiety and immobility rule. It is a story of fear.

But the diary in itself, richly crammed though it is with incident and passion, cannot count as Anne Frank's story. A story may not be said to be a story if the end is missing. And because the end is missing, the story of Anne Frank in the fifty years since "The Diary of a Young Girl" was first published has been bowdlerized, distorted, transmuted, traduced, reduced; it has been infantilized, Americanized, homogenized, sentimentalized; falsified, kitschified, and, in fact, blatantly and arrogantly denied. Among the falsifiers have been dramatists and directors, translators and litigators, Anne Frank's own father, and even—or especially--the public, both readers and theatregoers, all over the world. A deeply truth-telling work has been turned into an instrument of partial truth, surrogate truth, or anti-truth. The pure has been made impure—sometimes in the name of the reverse. Almost every hand that has approached the diary with the well-meaning intention of publicizing it has contributed to the subversion of history.

The diary is taken to be a Holocaust document; that is overridingly what it is not. Nearly every edition—and there have been innumerable editions—is emblazoned with words like "a song to life" or "a poignant delight in the infinite human spirit." Such characterizations rise up in the bitter perfume of mockery. A song to life? The diary is incomplete, truncated, broken off—or, rather, it is completed by Westerbork (the hellish transit camp in Holland from which Dutch Jews were deported), and by Auschwitz, and by the fatal winds of Bergen-Belsen. It is here, and not in the "secret annex," that the crimes we have come to call the Holocaust were enacted. Our entry into those crimes begins with columns of numbers: the meticulous lists of deportations, in handsome bookkeepers' handwriting, starkly set down in German "transport books." From these columns—headed, like goods for export, "*Ausgangs-Transporte nach dem Osten*" (outgoing shipments to the east)—it is possible to learn that Anne Frank and the others were moved to Auschwitz on the night of September 6, 1944, in a collection of a thousand and nineteen *Stücke* (or "pieces," another commodities term). That same night, five hundred and forty-nine persons were gassed, including one from the Frank group (the father of Peter van Daan) and every child under fifteen. Anne, at fifteen, and seventeen-year-old Margot were spared, apparently for labor. The end of October, from the twentieth to the twenty-eighth, saw the gassing of more than six thousand human beings within two hours of their arrival, including a thousand boys eighteen and under. In December, two thousand and ninety-three female prisoners perished, from starvation and exhaustion, in the women's camp; early in January, Edith Frank expired.

But Soviet forces were hurtling toward Auschwitz, and in November the order went out to conceal all evidences of gassing and to blow up the crematoria. Tens of thousands of inmates, debilitated and already near extinction, were driven out in bitter cold on death marches. Many were shot. In an evacuation that occurred either on October 28th or on November 2nd, Anne and Margot were dispatched to Bergen-Belsen. Margot was the first to succumb. A survivor recalled that she fell dead to the ground from the wooden slab on which she lay, eaten by lice, and that Anne, heartbroken and skeletal, naked under a bit of rag, died a day or two later.

To come to the diary without having earlier assimilated Elie Wiesel's *Night* and Primo Levi's *The Drowned and the Saved* (to mention two witnesses only), or the columns of figures in the transport books, is to allow oneself to stew in an implausible and ugly innocence. The litany of blurbs—"a lasting testament to the indestructible nobility of the human spirit," "an everlasting source of courage and inspiration"—is no more substantial than any other display of self-delusion. The success—the triumph—of Bergen-Belsen was precisely that it blotted out the possibility of courage, that it proved to be a lasting testament to the human spirit's easy destructibility. "*Hier ist kein Warum*," a guard at Auschwitz warned: here

10

there is no "why," neither question nor answer, only the dark of unreason. Anne Frank's story, truthfully told, is unredeemed and unredeemable.

These are notions that are hard to swallow—so they have not been swallowed. There are some, bored beyond toleration and callous enough to admit it, who are sick of hearing—yet again!—about depredations fifty years gone. "These old events," one of these fellows may complain, "can rake you over only so much. If I'm going to be lashed, I might as well save my skin for more recent troubles in the world." (I quote from a private letter from a distinguished author.) The more common response respectfully discharges an obligation to pity: it is dutiful. Or it is sometimes less than dutiful. It is sometimes frivolous, or indifferent, or presumptuous. But what even the most exemplary sympathies are likely to evade is the implacable recognition that Auschwitz and Bergen-Belsen, however sacramentally prodded, can never yield light.

The vehicle that has most powerfully accomplished this almost universal obtuseness is Anne Frank's diary. In celebrating Anne Frank's years in the secret annex, the nature and meaning of her death has been, in effect, forestalled. The diary's keen lens is helplessly opaque to the diarist's explicit doom—and this opacity, replicated in young readers in particular, has led to shamelessness.

It is the shamelessness of appropriation. Who owns Anne Frank? The children of the world, say the sentimentalists. A case in point is the astonishing correspondence, published in 1995 under the title *Love, Otto*, between Cara Wilson, a Californian born in 1944, and Otto Frank, the father of Anne Frank. Wilson, then twelve-year-old Cara Weiss, was invited by Twentieth Century Fox to audition for the part of Anne in a projected film version of the diary. "I didn't get the part," the middle-aged Wilson writes, "but by now I had found a whole new world. Anne Frank's diary, which I read and reread, spoke to me and my dilemmas, my anxieties, my secret passions. She felt the way I did. . . . I identified so strongly with this eloquent girl of my own age, that I now think I sort of became her in my own mind." And on what similarities does Wilson rest her acute sense of identification with a hunted child in hiding?

> I was miserable being me. . . . I was on the brink of that awful abyss of teenagedom and I, too, needed someone to talk to. . . . (Ironically, Anne, too, expressed a longing for more attention from her father.) . . . Dad's whole life was a series of meetings. At home, he was too tired or too frustrated to unload on. I had something else in common with Anne. We both had to share with sisters who were prettier and smarter than we felt we were. . . . Despite the monumental differences in our situations, to this day I feel that Anne helped me get through the teens with a sense of inner focus. She spoke for me. She was strong for me. She had so much hope when I was ready to call it quits.

A sampling of Wilson's concerns as she matured appears in the interstices of her exchanges with Otto Frank, which, remarkably, date from 1959 until his death, in 1980. For instance: "The year was 1968—etched in my mind. I can't ever forget it. Otis Redding was 'Sittin' on the Dock of the Bay' . . . while we hummed along to 'Hey Jude' by the Beatles." "In 1973–74," she reports, "I was wearing headbands, pukka-shell necklaces, and American Indian anything. Tattoos were a rage"—but enough. Tattoos were the rage, she neglects to recall, in Auschwitz; and of the Auschwitz survivor who was her patient correspondent for more than two decades, Wilson remarks, "Well, what choice did the poor man have? Whenever an attack of 'I-can't-take-this-any-longer' would hit me, I'd put it all into lengthy diatribes to my distant guru, Otto Frank."

That the designated guru replied, year after year, to embarrassing and   15
shabby effusions like these may open a new pathway into our generally obscure understanding of the character of Otto Frank. His responses—from Basel, where he had settled with his second wife—were consistently attentive, formal, kindly. When Wilson gave birth, he sent her a musical toy, and he faithfully offered a personal word about her excitements as she supplied them: her baby sons, her dance lessons, her husband's work on commercials, her freelance writing. But his letters were also political and serious. It is good, he wrote in October, 1970, to take "an active part in trying to abolish injustices and all sorts of grievances, but we cannot follow your views regarding the Black Panthers."[5] And in December, 1973, "As you can imagine, we were highly shocked about the unexpected attack of the Arabs on Israel on Yom Kippur and are now mourning with all those who lost members of their families." Presumably he knew something about losing a family. Wilson, insouciantly sliding past these faraway matters, was otherwise preoccupied, "finding our little guys sooo much fun."

The unabashed triflings of Cara Wilson—whose "identification" with Anne Frank can be duplicated by the thousand, though she may be more audacious than most—point to a conundrum. Never mind that the intellectual distance between Wilson and Anne Frank is immeasurable; not every self-conscious young girl will be a prodigy. Did Otto Frank not comprehend that Cara Wilson was deaf to everything the loss of his daughter represented? Did he not see, in Wilson's letters alone, how a denatured approach to the diary might serve to promote amnesia of what was rapidly turning into history? A protected domestic space, however threatened and endangered, can, from time to time, mimic ordinary life. The young who are encouraged to embrace the diary cannot always be expected to feel the difference between the mimicry and the threat. And (like Cara Wilson) most do not. Natalie Portman, sixteen years old, who will début as Anne Frank in the Broadway revival this December[6] of the famous play based on the diary—a play that has itself

---

[5]*Black Panthers:* a militant black liberation group founded in 1966. [Eds.]
[6]This revival was in 1999. [Eds.]

influenced the way the diary is read—concludes from her own reading that "it's funny, it's hopeful, and she's a happy person."

Otto Frank, it turns out, is complicit in this shallowly upbeat view. Again and again, in every conceivable context, he had it as his aim to emphasize "Anne's idealism," "Anne's spirit," almost never calling attention to how and why that idealism and spirit were smothered, and unfailingly generalizing the sources of hatred. If the child is father of the man—if childhood shapes future sensibility—then Otto Frank, despite his sufferings in Auschwitz, may have had less in common with his own daughter than he was ready to recognize. As the diary gained publication in country after country, its renown accelerating year by year, he spoke not merely about but for its author—and who, after all, would have a greater right? The surviving father stood in for the dead child, believing that his words would honestly represent hers. He was scarcely entitled to such certainty: fatherhood does not confer surrogacy.

Otto Frank's own childhood, in Frankfurt, Germany, was wholly unclouded. A banker's son, he lived untrammelled until the rise of the Nazi regime, when he was already forty-four. At nineteen, in order to acquire training in business, he went to New York with Nathan Straus, a fellow-student and an heir to the Macy's department-store fortune. During the First World War, Frank was an officer in the German military, and in 1925 he married Edith Holländer, a manufacturer's daughter. Margot was born in 1926 and Anneliese Marie, called Anne, in 1929. His characteristically secular world view belonged to an era of quiet assimilation, or, more accurately, accommodation (which includes a modicum of deference), when German Jews had become, at least in their own minds, well integrated into German society. From birth, Otto Frank had breathed the free air of the affluent bourgeoisie.

Anne's childhood, by contrast, fell into shadows almost immediately. She was not yet four when the German persecutions of Jews began, and from then until the anguished close of her days she lived as a refugee and a victim. In 1933, the family fled from Germany to Holland, where Frank had commercial connections, and where he established a pectin business. By 1940, the Germans had occupied the Netherlands. In Amsterdam, Jewish children, Anne among them, were thrown out of the public-school system and made to wear the yellow star. At thirteen, on November 19, 1942, already in hiding, Anne Frank could write:

> In the evenings when it's dark, I often see long lines of good, innocent people accompanied by crying children, walking on and on, ordered about by a handful of men who bully and beat them until they nearly drop. No one is spared. The sick, the elderly, children, babies, and pregnant women—all are marched to their death.

And earlier, on October 9th, after hearing the report of an escape from Westerbork: 20

Our many Jewish friends and acquaintances are being taken away in droves. The Gestapo is treating them very roughly and transporting them in cattle cars to Westerbork. . . . The people get almost nothing to eat, much less to drink, as water is available only one hour a day, and there's only one toilet and sink for several thousand people. Men and women sleep in the same room, and women and children often have their heads shaved. . . . If it's that bad in Holland, what must it be like in those faraway and uncivilized places where the Germans are sending them? We assume that most of them are being murdered. The English radio says they're being gassed.

Perhaps not even a father is justified in thinking he can distill the "ideas" of this alert and sorrowing child, with scenes such as these inscribed in her psyche, and with the desolations of Auschwitz and Bergen-Belsen still ahead. His preference was to accentuate what he called Anne's "optimistical view on life." Yet the diary's most celebrated line (infamously celebrated, one might add) — "I still believe, in spite of everything, that people are truly good at heart" — has been torn out of its bed of thorns. Two sentences later (and three weeks before she was seized and shipped to Westerbork), the diarist sets down a vision of darkness:

I see the world being slowly transformed into a wilderness, I hear the approaching thunder that, one day, will destroy us too, I feel the suffering of millions. . . . In the meantime, I must hold on to my ideals. Perhaps the day will come when I'll be able to realize them!

Because that day never came, both Miep Gies, the selflessly courageous woman who devoted herself to the sustenance of those in hiding, and Hannah Goslar, Anne's Jewish schoolmate and the last to hear her tremulous cries in Bergen-Belsen, objected to Otto Frank's emphasis on the diary's "truly good at heart" utterance. That single sentence has become, universally, Anne Frank's message, virtually her motto — whether or not such a credo could have survived the camps. Why should this sentence be taken as emblematic, and not, for example, another? "There's a destructive urge in people, the urge to rage, murder, and kill," Anne wrote on May 3, 1944, pondering the spread of guilt. These are words that do not soften, ameliorate, or give the lie to the pervasive horror of her time. Nor do they pull the wool over the eyes of history.

Otto Frank grew up with a social need to please his environment and not to offend it; that was the condition of entering the mainstream, a bargain German Jews negotiated with themselves. It was more dignified, and safer, to praise than to blame. Far better, then, in facing the larger postwar world that the diary had opened to him, to speak of goodness rather than destruction: so much of that larger world had participated in the urge to rage. (The diary notes how Dutch anti-Semitism, "to our great sorrow and dismay," was increasing even as the Jews were being hauled away.) After the liberation of the camps, the heaps of emancipated corpses were accusation enough. Postwar sensibility hastened to migrate elsewhere, away from the cruel and the culpable. It was a tone and a mood that affected the diary's reception; it was a mood and a tone that, with cautious yet crucial excisions, the diary itself could be made to support. And so the diarist's dread came to be described as hope, her terror as courage, her prayers of despair as inspiring. And since the diary was now defined as a Holocaust document, the perception of the cataclysm itself was being subtly accommodated to expressions like "man's inhumanity to man," diluting and befogging specific historical events and their motives. "We must not flog the past," Frank insisted in 1969. His concrete response to the past was the establishment, in 1957, of the Anne Frank Foundation and its offshoot the International Youth Center, situated in the Amsterdam house where the diary was composed, to foster "as many contacts as possible between young people of different nationalities, races and religions" — a civilized and tenderhearted goal that nevertheless washed away into do-gooder abstraction the explicit urge to rage that had devoured his daughter.

Otto Frank was merely an accessory to the transformation of the diary from one kind of witness to another kind: from the painfully revealing to the partially concealing. If Anne Frank has been made into what we nowadays call an "icon," it is because of the Pulitzer Prize-winning play derived from the diary — a play that rapidly achieved worldwide popularity, and framed the legend even the newest generation has come to believe in. Adapted by Albert Hackett and Frances Goodrich, a Hollywood husband-and-wife screenwriting team, the theatricalized version opened on Broadway in 1955, ten years after the end of the war, and its portrayal of the "funny, hopeful, happy" Anne continues to reverberate, not only in how the diary is construed but in how the Holocaust itself is understood. The play was a work born in controversy, destined to roil on and on in rancor and litigation. Its tangle of contending lawyers finally came to resemble nothing so much as the knotted imbroglio of Jarndyce vs. Jarndyce, the unending court case of *Bleak House*. Many of the chief figures in the protracted conflict over the Hacketts' play have by now left the scene, but the principal issues, far from fading away, have, after so many decades, intensified. Whatever the ramifications of these issues, whatever perspectives they illumine or defy, the central question stands fast: Who owns Anne Frank?

The hero, or irritant (depending on which side of the controversy one favors), in the genesis of the diary's dramatization was Meyer Levin, a Chicago-born novelist of the social-realist school, the author of such fairly successful works as *The Old Bunch, Compulsion,* and *The Settlers.* Levin began as a man of the left, though a strong anti-Stalinist: he was drawn to proletarian fiction (*Citizens,* about steelworkers), and had gone to Spain in   25 the thirties to report on the Civil War. In 1945, as a war correspondent at-tached to the Fourth Armored Division, he was among the first Americans to enter Buchenwald, Dachau, and Bergen-Belsen. What he saw there was ungraspable and unendurable. "As I groped in the first weeks, beginning to apprehend the monstrous shape of the story I would have to tell," he wrote, "I knew already that I would never penetrate its heart of bile, for the magnitude of this horror seemed beyond human register." The truest telling, he affirmed, would have to rise up out of the mouth of a victim.

His "obsession," as he afterward called it—partly in mockery of the opposition his later views evoked—had its beginning in those repeated scenes of piled-up-bodies as he investigated camp after camp. From then on, he could be said to carry the mark of Abel. He dedicated himself to helping the survivors get to Mandate Palestine, a goal that Britain had made illegal. In 1946, he reported from Tel Aviv on the uprising against British rule, and during the next two years he produced a pair of films on the struggles of the survivors to reach Palestine. In 1950, he published *In Search*, an examination of the effects of the European cataclysm on his ex-perience and sensibility as an American Jew. (Thomas Mann acclaimed the book as "a human document of high order, written by a witness of our fantastic epoch whose gaze remained both clear and steady.") Levin's in-tensifying focus on the Jewish condition in the twentieth century grew more and more heated, and when his wife, the novelist Tereska Torres, handed him the French edition of the diary (it had previously appeared only in Dutch) he felt he had found what he had thirsted after: a voice cry-ing up from the ground, an authentic witness to the German onslaught.

He acted instantly. He sent Otto Frank a copy of *In Search* and in ef-fect offered his services as an unofficial agent to secure British and Ameri-can publication, asserting his distance from any financial gain; his interest, he said, was purely "one of sympathy." He saw in the diary the possibility of "a very touching play or film," and asked Frank's permission to explore the idea. Frank at first avoided reading Levin's book, saturated as it was in passions and commitments so foreign to his own susceptibilities. He was not unfamiliar with Levin's preoccupations; he had seen and liked one of his films. He encouraged Levin to go ahead—though a dramatization, he observed, would perforce "be rather different from the real contents" of the diary. Hardly so, Levin protested: no compromise would be needed; all the diarist's thoughts could be preserved.

The "real contents" had already been altered by Frank himself, and understandably, given the propriety of his own background and of the times. The diary contained, here and there, intimate adolescent musings, talk of how contraceptives work, and explicit anatomical description: "In the upper part, between the outer labia, there's a fold of skin that, on sec-ond thought, looks like a kind of blister. That's the clitoris. Then come the inner labia. . . ." All this Frank edited out. He also omitted passages recording his daughter's angry resistance to the nervous fussiness of her mother ("the most rotten person in the world"). Undoubtedly he better understood Edith Frank's protective tremors, and was unwilling to perpetuate a negative portrait. Beyond this, he deleted numerous expressions of religious faith, a direct reference to Yom Kippur, terrified reports of Germans seizing Jews in Amsterdam. It was prudence, prudishness, and perhaps his own deracinated temperament that stimulated many of these tamperings. In 1991, eleven years after Frank's death, a "definitive edition" of the diary restored everything he had expurgated. But the image of Anne Frank as merry innocent and steadfast idealist—an image the play vividly promoted—was by then ineradicable.

A subsequent bowdlerization, in 1950, was still more programmatic, and crossed over even more seriously into the area of Levin's concern for uncompromised faithfulness. The German edition's translator, Anneliese Schütz, in order to mask or soft-pedal German culpability, went about methodically blurring every hostile reference to Germans and German. Anne's parodic list of house rules, for instance, included "*Use of language:* It is necessary to speak softly at all times. Only the language of civilized people may be spoken, thus no German." The German translation reads, "*Alle Kultursprachen . . . aber leise!*" — "all civilized languages . . . but softly!" "Heroism in the war or when confronting the Germans" is dissolved into "heroism in the war and in the struggle against oppression." ("A book intended after all for sale in Germany," Schütz explained, "cannot abuse the Germans.") The diarist's honest cry, in the midst of a vast persecution, that "there is no greater hostility than exists between Germans and Jews" became, in Schütz's version, "there is no greater hostility in the world than between these Germans and Jews!" Frank agreed to the latter change because, he said, it was what his daughter had really meant: she "by no means measured all Germans by the same yardstick. For, as she knew so well, even in those days we had many good friends among the Germans." But this guarded accommodationist view is Otto Frank's own; it is nowhere in the diary. Even more striking than Frank's readiness to accede to such misrepresentations is the fact that for forty-one years (until a more accurate translation appeared) no reader of the diary in German had ever known an intact text.

In contemplating a dramatization and pledging no compromise, Levin told Frank he would do it "tenderly and with utmost fidelity." He was clear about what he meant by fidelity. In his eyes the diary was conscious testimony to Jewish faith and suffering; and it was this, and this nearly alone, that defined for him its psychological, historical, and metaphysical genuineness, and its significance for the world. With these convictions foremost, Levin went in search of a theatrical producer. At the same time, he was unflagging in pressing for publication; but the work was meanwhile slowly gaining independent notice. Janet Flanner, in her "Letter from Paris" in *The New Yorker* of November 11, 1950, noted the French publication of a book by "a precocious, talented little Frankfurt Jewess"—apparently oblivious of the unpleasant echoes, post-Hitler, of "Jewess." Sixteen English-language publishers on both sides of the Atlantic had already rejected the diary when Levin succeeded in placing it with Valentine Mitchell, a London firm. His negotiations with a Boston house were still incomplete when Doubleday came forward to secure publication rights directly from Frank. Relations between Levin and Frank were, as usual, warm; Frank repeatedly thanked Levin for his efforts to further the fortunes of the diary, and Levin continued under the impression that Frank would support him as the playwright of choice.

If a front-page review in the New York *Times Book Review* can rocket a book to instant sanctity, that is what Meyer Levin, in the spring of 1952, achieved for "Anne Frank: The Diary of a Young Girl." It was an assignment he had gone after avidly. Barbara Zimmerman (afterward Barbara Epstein, a founder of *The New York Review of Books*), the diary's young editor at Doubleday, had earlier recognized its potential as "a minor classic," and had enlisted Eleanor Roosevelt to supply an introduction. (According to Levin, it was ghostwritten by Zimmerman.) Levin now joined Zimmerman and Doubleday in the project of choosing a producer. Doubleday was to take over as Frank's official agent, with the stipulation that Levin would have an active hand in the adaptation. "I think that I can honestly say," Levin wrote Frank, "that I am as well qualified as any other writer for this particular task." In a cable to Doubleday, Frank appeared to agree: "DESIRE LEVIN AS WRITER OR COLLABORATOR IN ANY TREATMENT TO GUARANTEE IDEA OF BOOK." The catch, it would develop, lurked in a perilous contingency: Whose idea? Levin's? Frank's? The producer's? The director's? In any case, Doubleday was already doubtful about Levin's ambiguous role. What if an interested producer decided on another playwright?

What happened next—an avalanche of furies and recriminations lasting years—has lately become the subject of a pair of arresting discussions of the Frank-Levin affair. And if "affair" suggests an event on the scale of the Dreyfus case, that is how Levin saw it: as an unjust stripping away of his rightful position, with implications far beyond his personal predicament. *An Obsession with Anne Frank,* by Lawrence Graver, published by the University of California Press in 1995, is the first study to fashion a coherent narrative out of the welter of claims, counterclaims, letters, cables, petitions, polemics, and rumbling confusions which accompany any examination of the diary's journey to the stage. *The Stolen Legacy of Anne Frank,* by Ralph Melnick, out just now from Yale, is denser in detail and in sources than its predecessor, and more insistent in tone. Both are accomplished works of scholarship that converge on the facts and diverge in their conclusions. Graver is reticent with his sympathies; Melnick is Levin's undisguised advocate. Graver finds no villains; Melnick finds Lillian Hellman.

Always delicately respectful of Frank's dignity and rights—and always mindful of the older man's earlier travail—Levin had promised that he would step aside if a more prominent playwright, someone "world famous," should appear. Stubbornly and confidently, he went on toiling over his own version. As a novelist, he was under suspicion of being unable to write drama. (In after years, when he had grown deeply bitter, he listed, in retaliation, "Sartre, Gorky, Galsworthy, Steinbeck, Wilder!")[7] Though there are many extant drafts of Levin's play, no definitive script is available; both publication and performance were proscribed by Frank's attorneys. A script staged without authorization by the Israel Soldiers' Theatre in 1966 sometimes passes from hand to hand, and reads well: moving, theatrical, actable, professional. This later work was not, however, the script submitted in the summer of 1952 to Cheryl Crawford, one of a number of Broadway producers who rushed in with bids in the wake of the diary's acclaim. Crawford, an eminent co-founder of the Actors Studio, initially encouraged Levin, offering him first consideration and, if his script was not entirely satisfactory, the aid of a more experienced collaborator. Then — virtually overnight — she rejected his draft outright. Levin was bewildered and infuriated, and from then on he became an intractable and indefatigable warrior on behalf of his play — and on behalf, he contended, of the diary's true meaning. In his *Times* review he had summed it up stirringly as the voice of "six million vanished Jewish souls."

Doubleday, meanwhile, sensing complications ahead, had withdrawn as Frank's theatrical agent, finding Levin's presence — injected by Frank — too intrusive, too maverick, too independent and entrepreneurial: fixed, they believed, only on his own interest, which was to stick to his insistence on the superiority of his work over all potential contenders. Frank, too, had begun — kindly, politely, and with tireless assurances of his gratitude to Levin — to move closer to Doubleday's cooler views, especially as urged by Barbara Zimmerman. She was twenty-four years old, the age Anne would have been, very intelligent and attentive. Adoring letters flowed back and forth between them, Frank addressing her as "little Barbara" and "dearest little one." On one occasion he gave her an antique gold pin. About Levin, Zimmerman finally concluded that he was "impossible to deal with in any terms, officially, legally, morally, personally" — a "compulsive neurotic . . . destroying both himself and Anne's play." (There was, of course, no such entity as "Anne's play.")

What had caused Crawford to change her mind so precipitately? She   35
had given Levin's script for further consideration to Lillian Hellman and to the producers Robert Whitehead and Kermit Bloomgarden. All were theatre luminaries; all spurned Levin's work. Frank's confidence in Levin, already much diminished, failed altogether. Advised by Doubleday, he put his trust in the Broadway professionals, while Levin fought on alone.

---

[7]*Jean-Paul Sartre* (1905–1980): French writer; *Maxim Gorky* (1868–1936): Russian writer; *John Galsworthy* (1867–1933): British writer; *John Steinbeck* (1902–1968) and *Thorton Wilder* (1897–1975): American writers. All of them were successful as both playwrights and novelists. [Eds.]

Famous names—Maxwell Anderson, John Van Druten, Carson McCul-
lers—came and went. Crawford herself ultimately pulled out, fearing a
lawsuit by Levin. In the end—with the vigilant Levin still agitating loudly
and publicly for the primacy of his work—Kermit Bloomgarden surfaced
as producer and Garson Kanin as director. Hellman had recommended
Bloomgarden; she had also recommended Frances Goodrich and Albert
Hackett. The Hacketts had a long record of Hollywood hits, from "Father
of the Bride" to "It's a Wonderful Life," and they had successfully scripted
a series of lighthearted musicals. Levin was appalled—had his sacred vision been pushed aside not for the awaited world-famous dramatist but for
a pair of frivolous screen drudges, mere "hired hands"?

The hired hands were earnest and reverent. They began at once to read
up on European history; Judaism, and Jewish practice; they consulted a
rabbi. They corresponded eagerly with Frank, looking to satisfy his expectations. They travelled to Amsterdam and visited 263 Prinsengracht, the
house on the canal where the Franks, the van Daans, and Dussel had been
hidden. They met Johannes Kleiman, who, together with Victor Kugler and
Miep Gies, had taken over the management of Frank's business in order to
conceal and protect him and his family in the house behind. Reacting to
the Hacketts' lifelong remoteness from Jewish subject matter, Levin took
out an ad in the New York *Post* attacking Bloomgarden and asking that
his play be given a hearing. "My work," he wrote, "has been with the Jewish story. I tried to dramatize the Diary as Anne would have, in her own
words. . . . I feel my work has earned the right to be judged by you, the
public." "Ridiculous and laughable," said Bloomgarden. Appealing to the
critic Brooks Atkinson, Levin complained—extravagantly, outrageously—
that his play was being "killed by the same arbitrary disregard that
brought an end to Anne and six million others." Frank stopped answering
Levin's letters; many he returned unopened.

The Hacketts, too, in their earliest drafts, were devotedly "with the Jewish story." Grateful to Hellman for getting them the job, and crushed by
Bloomgarden's acute dislike of their efforts so far, they flew to Martha's
Vineyard weekend after weekend to receive advice from Hellman. "She was
amazing," Goodrich crowed, happy to comply. Hellman's slant—and that
of Bloomgarden and Kanin—was consistently in a direction opposed to
Levin's. Where the diary touched on Anne's consciousness of Jewish fate or
faith, they quietly erased the reference or changed its emphasis. Whatever
was specific they made generic. The sexual tenderness between Anne and the
Young Peter van Daan was moved to the forefront. Comedy overwhelmed
darkness. Anne became an all-American girl, an echo of the perky character
in *Junior Miss*, a popular play of the previous decade. The Zionist aspirations
of Margot, Anne's sister, disappeared. The one liturgical note, a Hanukkah
ceremony, was absurdly defined in terms of local contemporary habits
("eight days of presents"); a jolly jingle replaced the traditional "Rock of
Ages," with its sombre allusions to historic travail. (Kanin had insisted on

something "spirited and gay," so as not to give "the wrong feeling entirely."
"Hebrew," he argued, "would simply alienate the audience.")

Astonishingly, the Nazified notion of "race" leaped out in a line attributed to Hellman and nowhere present in the diary. "We're not the only people that've had to suffer," the Hacketts' Anne says. "There've always been people that've had to . . . sometimes one race . . . sometimes another." This pallid speech, yawning with vagueness, was conspicuously opposed to the pivotal reflection it was designed to betray:

> In the eyes of the world, we're doomed, but if after all this suffering, there are still Jews left, the Jewish people will be held up as an example. Who knows, maybe our religion will teach the world and all the people in it about goodness, and that's the reason, the only reason, we have to suffer. . . . God has never deserted our people. Through the ages Jews have had to suffer, but through the ages they've gone on living, and the centuries of suffering have only made them stronger.

For Kanin, this kind of rumination was "an embarrassing piece of special pleading. . . . The fact that in this play the symbols of persecution and oppression are Jews is incidental, and Anne, in stating the argument so, reduces her magnificent stature." And so it went throughout. The particularized plight of Jews in hiding was vaporized into what Kanin called "the infinite." Reality—the diary's central condition—was "incidental." The passionately contemplative child, brooding on concrete evil, was made into an emblem of evasion. Her history had a habitation and a name; the infinite was nameless and nowhere.

For Levin, the source and first cause of these excisions was Lillian   40
Hellman. Hellman, he believed, had "supervised" the Hacketts, and Hellman was fundamentally political and inflexibly doctrinaire. Her outlook lay at the root of a conspiracy. She was an impenitent Stalinist; she followed, he said, the Soviet line. Like the Soviets, she was anti-Zionist. And, just as the Soviets had obliterated Jewish particularity at Babi Yar, the ravine where thousands of Jews, shot by the Germans, lay unnamed and effaced in their deaths, so Hellman had directed the Hacketts to blur the identity of the characters in the play.

The sins of the Soviets and the sins of Hellman and her Broadway deputies were, in Levin's mind, identical. He set out to punish the man who had allowed all this to come to pass: Otto Frank had allied himself with the pundits of erasure; Otto Frank had stood aside when Levin's play was elbowed out of the way. What recourse remained for a man so affronted and injured? Meyer Levin sued Otto Frank. It was as if, someone observed, a suit were being brought against the father of Joan of Arc. The bulky snarl of courtroom arguments resulted in small satisfaction for Levin: because the structure of the Hacketts' play was in some ways similar to his, the jury detected plagiarism; yet even this limited triumph foundered on the issue of damages. Levin sent out broadsides, collected signatures, summoned a committee of advocacy, lectured from pulpits, took out ads, rallied rabbis and writers (Norman Mailer[8] among them). He wrote *The Obsession,* his grandly confessional *J'Accuse,* rehearsing, in skirmish after skirmish, his fight for the staging of his own adaptation. In return, furious charges flew at him: he was a red-baiter, a McCarthyite.[9] The term "paranoid" began to circulate. Why rant against the popularization and dilution that was Broadway's lifeblood? "I certainly have no wish to inflict depression on an audience," Kanin had argued. "I don't consider that a legitimate theatrical end." (So much for *Hamlet* and *King Lear.*)

Grateful for lightness, reviewers agreed. What they came away from was the charm of Susan Strasberg as a radiant Anne, and Joseph Schildkraut in the role of a wise and steadying Otto Frank, whom the actor engagingly resembled. "Anne is not going to her death; she is going to leave a dent on life, and let death take what's left," Walter Kerr, on a mystical note, wrote in the *Herald Tribune. Variety* seemed relieved that the play avoided "hating the Nazis, hating what they did to millions of innocent people," and instead came off as "glowing, moving, frequently humorous," with "just about everything one could wish for. It is not grim." The *Daily News* confirmed what Kanin had striven for: "Not in any important sense a Jewish play. . . . Anne Frank is a Little Orphan Annie brought into vibrant life." Audiences laughed and were charmed; but they were also dazed and moved.

And audiences multiplied: the Hacketts' drama went all over the world—including Israel, where numbers of survivors were remaking their lives—and was everywhere successful. The play's reception in Germany was especially noteworthy. In an impressive and thoroughgoing essay entitled "Popularization and Memory," Alvin Rosenfeld, a professor of English at Indiana University, recounts the development of the Anne Frank phenomenon in the country of her birth. "The theater reviews of the time," Rosenfeld reports, "tell of audiences sitting in stunned silence at the play and leaving the performance unable to speak or to look one another in the eye." These were self-conscious and thin-skinned audiences; in the Germany of the fifties, theatregoers still belonged to the generation of the Nazi era. (On Broadway, Kanin had unblinkingly engaged Gusti Huber, of that same generation, to play Anne Frank's mother. As a member of the Nazi Actors Guild until Germany's defeat, Huber had early on disparaged "non-Aryan artists.") But the strange muteness in theatres may have derived not so much from guilt or shame as from an all-encompassing compassion; or

---

[8]*Norman Mailer* (b. 1923): combative American writer. [Eds.]

[9]*McCarthyite:* a follower of Joseph McCarthy (1908–1957), Republican senator who crusaded against alleged communist influence within the U.S. government in the early Cold War era. [Eds.]

call it self-pity. "We see in Anne Frank's fate," a German drama critic offered, "our own fate—the tragedy of human existence per se." Hannah Arendt, philosopher and Hitler refugee, scorned such oceanic expressions, calling it "cheap sentimentality at the expense of a great catastrophe." And Bruno Bettelheim, a survivor of Dachau and Buchenwald,[10] condemned the play's most touted line: "If all men are good, there was never an Auschwitz." A decade after the fall of Nazism, the spirited and sanitized young girl of the play became a vehicle for German communal identification—with the victim, not the persecutors—and, according to Rosenfeld, a continuing "symbol of moral and intellectual convenience." The Anne Frank whom thousands saw in seven openings in seven cities "spoke affirmatively about life and not accusingly about her torturers." No German in uniform appeared onstage. "In a word," Rosenfeld concludes, "Anne Frank has become a ready-at-hand formula for easy forgiveness."

The mood of consolation lingers on, as Otto Frank meant it to—and not only in Germany, where, even after fifty years, the issue is touchiest. Sanctified and absolving, shorn of darkness, Anne Frank remains in all countries a revered and comforting figure in the contemporary mind. In Japan, because both diary and play mention first menstruation, "Anne Frank" has become a code word among teen-agers for getting one's period. In Argentina in the seventies, church publications began to link her with Roman Catholic martyrdom. "Commemoration," the French cultural critic Tzvetan Todorov explains, "is always the adaptation of memory to the needs of today."

But there is a note that drills deeper than commemoration: it goes to the idea of identification. To "identify with" is to become what one is not, to become what one is not is to usurp, to usurp is to own—and who, after all, in the half century since Miep Gies retrieved the scattered pages of the diary, really owns Anne Frank? Who can speak for her? Her father, who, after reading the diary and confessing that he "did not know" her, went on to tell us what he thought she meant? Meyer Levin, who claimed to be her authentic voice—so much so that he dared to equate the dismissal of his work, however ignobly motivated, with Holocaust annihilation? Hellman, Bloomgarden, Kanin, whose interpretations clung to a collective ideology of human interchangeability? (In discounting the significance of the Jewish element, Kanin had asserted that "people have suffered because of being English, French, German, Italian, Ethiopian, Mohammedan, Negro, and so on"—as if this were not all the more reason to comprehend and particularize each history.) And what of Cara Wilson and "the children of the world," who have reduced the persecution of a people to the trials of adolescence?

All these appropriations, whether cheaply personal or densely ideological, whether seen as exalting or denigrating, have contributed to the

---

[10]*Dachau, Buchenwald:* Nazi concentration camps. [Eds.]

conversion of Anne Frank into usable goods. There is no authorized version other than the diary itself, and even this has been brought into question by the Holocaust-denial industry—in part a spinoff of the Anne Frank industry—which labels the diary a forgery. One charge is that Otto Frank wrote it himself, to make money. (Scurrilities like these necessitated the issuance, in 1986, of a Critical Edition by the Netherlands State Institute for War Documentation, including forensic evidence of handwriting and ink—a defensive hence sorrowful volume.)

No play can be judged wholly from what is on the page; a play has evocative powers beyond the words. Still, the Hacketts' work, read today, is very much a conventionally well made Broadway product of the fifties, alternating comical beats with scenes of alarm, a love story with a theft, wisdom with buffoonery. The writing is skilled and mediocre, not unlike much of contemporary commercial theatre. Yet this is the play that electrified audiences everywhere, that became a reverential if robotlike film, and that—far more than the diary—invented the world's Anne Frank. Was it the play, or was it the times? The upcoming revival of the Hacketts' dramatization—promising revisions incorporating passages Otto Frank deleted from the diary—will no doubt stimulate all the old quarrelsome issues yet again. But with the Second World War and the Holocaust receding, especially for the young, into distant fable—no different from tales, say, of Attila the Hun—the revival enters an environment psychologically altered from that of the 1955 production. At the same time, Holocaust scholarship—survivor memoirs, oral histories, wave after wave of fresh documentation and analysis—has increased prodigiously. At Harvard, for instance, under the rubric "reception studies," a young scholar named Alex Sagan, a relative of the late astronomer, is examining the ways Anne Frank has been transmuted into, among other cultural manifestations, a heavenly body. And Steven Spielberg's "Schindler's List," about a Nazi industrialist as savior, has left its mark.

It may be, though, that a new production, even now, and even with cautious additions, will be heard in the play's original voice. It was always a voice of good will; it meant, as we say, well—and, financially, it certainly did well. But it was Broadway's style of good will—and that, at least for Meyer Levin, had the scent of ill. For him, and signally for Bloomgarden and Kanin, the most sensitive point—the focus of trouble—lay in the ancient dispute between the particular and the universal. All that was a distraction from the heart of the matter: in a drama about hiding, evil was hidden. And if the play remains essentially as the Hacketts wrote it, the likelihood is that Anne Frank's real history will hardly prevail over what was experienced, forty years ago, as history transcended, ennobled, rarefied. The first hint is already in the air, puffed by the play's young lead: *It's funny, it's hopeful, and she's a happy person.*

Evisceration, an elegy for the murdered. Evisceration by blurb and stage, by shrewdness and naïveté, by cowardice and spirituality, by forgiveness and indifference, by success and money, by vanity and rage, by principle and passion, by surrogacy and affinity. Evisceration by fame, by shame, by blame. By uplift and transcendence. By usurpation.

On Friday, August 4, 1944, the day of the arrest, Miep Gies climbed the   50
stairs to the hiding place and found it ransacked and wrecked. The belea-
guered little band had been betrayed by an informer who was paid seven and
a half guilders—about a dollar—for each person: sixty guilders for the
lot.50 Miep Gies picked up what she recognized as Anne's papers and put
them away, unread, in her desk drawer. There the diary lay untouched, until
Otto Frank emerged alive from Auschwitz. "Had I read it," she said afterward, "I would have had to burn the diary because it would have been too
dangerous for people about whom Anne had written." It was Miep Gies—
the uncommon heroine of this story, a woman profoundly good, a failed savior—who succeeded in rescuing an irreplaceable masterwork. It may be
shocking to think this (I am shocked as I think it), but one can imagine a still
more salvational outcome: Anne Frank's diary burned, vanished, lost—
saved from a world that made of it all things, some of them true, while floating lightly over the heavier truth of named and inhabited evil.

QUESTIONS

1. What is Ozick's purpose in this essay?
2. Why does Ozick say that the diary "cannot count as Anne Frank's
   story"? (paragraph 7)
3. How does Ozick go about defining what the diary is?
4. How does Ozick use the Cara Wilson-Otto Frank material? Why does
   she think Otto Frank is an unreliable interpreter of his daughter's life?
   Do you agree with Ozick's interpretation of Otto Frank? Explain.
5. Ozick details the troubled history of the development of a stage version
   of Anne Frank's story, in which Meyer Levin's version was rejected in
   favor of the Hacketts' version, which finally made it to Broadway in
   1955. Why was this play so popular? Given what you know about
   Meyer Levin's version, do you think it, too, might have achieved similar
   acclaim? Explain.
6. Look again at Ozick's accusations in paragraph 49. Who is being accused?

MAKING CONNECTIONS

Compare the qualities found in Anne Frank's text by Patricia Hampl, John
Berryman, and Cynthia Ozick. How do these qualities compare with those
celebrated by the public, especially after seeing the stage version of the
Diary? What features of writing praised by Ozick, Hampl, and Berryman
can you find in the excerpt from the diary (p. 193)? If you would like to
read the whole diary, be sure to find the "Definitive Edition," published in
1995.

If Black English Isn't a Language, Then Tell Me, What Is?

James Baldwin

James Baldwin was born in Harlem in 1924 and followed his father's vocation, becoming a preacher at the age of fourteen. At seventeen, he left the ministry and devoted himself to writing until his death in 1987. Baldwin's most frequent subject was the relationship between blacks and whites, about which he wrote, "The color of my skin made me automatically an expert." Baldwin himself might also have added that his life's work lay in defining and legitimizing the black voice; like Orwell, Baldwin argued that language is "a political instrument, means, and proof of power." He wrote five novels, a book of stories, one play, and several collections of essays. The following essay on language and legitimacy first appeared in 1979 in the New York Times *and later was included in* The Price of the Ticket: Collected Nonfiction, 1948–1985 *(1985).*

The argument concerning the use, or the status, or the reality, of black English is rooted in American history and has absolutely nothing to do with the question the argument supposes itself to be posing. The argument has nothing to do with language itself but with the role of language. Language, incontestably, reveals the speaker. Language, also, far more dubiously, is meant to define the other—and, in this case, the other is refusing to be defined by a language that has never been able to recognize him.

People evolve a language in order to describe and thus control their circumstances or in order not to be submerged by a situation that they cannot articulate. (And if they cannot articulate it, they are submerged.) A Frenchman living in Paris speaks a subtly and crucially different language from that of the man living in Marseilles; neither sounds very much like a man living in Quebec; and they would all have great difficulty in apprehending what the man from Guadeloupe, or Martinique, is saying, to say nothing of the man from Senegal—although the "common" language of all these areas is French. But each has paid, and is paying, a different price for this "common" language, in which, as it turns out, they are not saying, and cannot be saying, the same things: They each have very different realities to articulate, or control.

What joins all languages, and all men, is the necessity to confront life, in order, not inconceivably, to outwit death: The price for this is the acceptance, and achievement, of one's temporal identity. So that, for example, though it is not taught in the schools (and this has the potential of becoming a political issue) the south of France still clings to its ancient and musical Provençal, which resists being described as a "dialect." And much of the tension in the Basque countries, and in Wales, is due to the Basque and Welsh determination not to allow their languages to be destroyed. This determination also feeds the flames in Ireland for among the many indignities the Irish have been forced to undergo at English hands is the English contempt for their language.

It goes without saying, then, that language is also a political instrument, means, and proof of power. It is the most vivid and crucial key to identity: It reveals the private identity, and connects one with, or divorces one from, the larger, public, or communal identity. There have been, and are, times and places, when to speak a certain language could be dangerous, even fatal. Or, one may speak the same language, but in such a way that one's antecedents are revealed, or (one hopes) hidden. This is true in France, and is absolutely true in England: The range (and reign) of accents on that damp little island make England coherent for the English and totally incomprehensible for everyone else. To open your mouth in England is (if I may use black English) to "put your business in the street." You have confessed your parents, your youth, your school, your salary, your self-esteem, and, alas, your future.

Now, I do not know what white Americans would sound like if there had never been any black people in the United States, but they would not sound the way they sound. *Jazz,* for example, is a very specific sexual term, as in *jazz me, baby,* but white people purified it into the Jazz Age. *Sock it to me,* which means, roughly, the same thing, has been adopted by Nathaniel Hawthorne's descendants with no qualms or hesitations at all, along with *let it all hang out* and *right on! Beat to his socks,* which was once the black's most total and despairing image of poverty, was transformed into a thing called the Beat Generation, which phenomenon was, largely, composed of *uptight,* middle-class white people, imitating poverty, trying to *get down,* to *get with it,* doing their *thing,* doing their despairing best to be *funky,* which we, the blacks, never dreamed of doing—we were funky, baby, like *funk* was going out of style.

Now, no one can eat his cake, and have it, too, and it is late in the day to attempt to penalize black people for having created a language that permits the nation its only glimpse of reality, a language without which the nation would be even more *whipped* than it is.

I say that the present skirmish is rooted in American history, and it is. Black English is the creation of the black diaspora. Blacks came to the United States chained to each other, but from different tribes. Neither could speak the other's language. If two black people, at that bitter hour of the world's history, had been able to speak to each other, the institution of chattel slavery could never have lasted as long as it did. Subsequently, the slave was given, under the eye, and the gun, of his master, Congo Square, and the Bible—or, in other words, and under those conditions, the slave began the formation of the black church, and it is within this unprecedented tabernacle that black English began to be formed. This was not,

5

merely, as in the European example, the adoption of a foreign tongue, but an alchemy that transformed ancient elements into a new language: *A language comes into existence by means of brutal necessity, and the rules of the language are dictated by what the language must convey.*

There was a moment, in time, and in this place, when my brother, or my mother, or my father, or my sister, had to convey to me, for example, the danger in which I was standing from the white man standing just behind me, and to convey this with a speed and in a language, that the white man could not possibly understand, and that, indeed, he cannot understand, until today. He cannot afford to understand it. This understanding would reveal to him too much about himself and smash that mirror before which he has been frozen for so long.

Now, if this passion, this skill, this (to quote Toni Morrison) "sheer intelligence," this incredible music, the mighty achievement of having brought a people utterly unknown to, or despised by "history"—to have brought this people to their present, troubled, troubling, and unassailable and unanswerable place—if this absolutely unprecedented journey does not indicate that black English is a language, I am curious to know what definition of languages is to be trusted.

A people at the center of the western world, and in the midst of so hostile a population, has not endured and transcended by means of what is patronizingly called a "dialect." We, the blacks, are in trouble, certainly, but we are not inarticulate because we are not compelled to defend a morality that we know to be a lie.   10

The brutal truth is that the bulk of the white people in America never had any interest in educating black people, except as this could serve white purposes. It is not the black child's language that is despised. It is his experience. A child cannot be taught by anyone who despises him, and a child cannot afford to be fooled. A child cannot be taught by anyone whose demand, essentially, is that the child repudiate his experience, and all that gives him sustenance, and enter a limbo in which he will no longer be black, and in which he knows that he can never become white. Black people have lost too many black children that way.

And, after all, finally, in a country with standards so untrustworthy, a country that makes heroes of so many criminal mediocrities, a country unable to face why so many of the nonwhite are in prison, or on the needle, or standing, futureless, in the streets—it may very well be that both the child, and his elder, have concluded that they have nothing whatever to learn from the people of a country that has managed to learn so little.

QUESTIONS

1. Baldwin begins his essay by challenging the standard argument concerning black English: "The argument has nothing to do with language itself but with the role of language." What distinctions does Baldwin note be-

tween "language itself" and "the role of language"? Why is this distinction central to his argument?

2. Baldwin's position on black English is at odds with those who would like to deny black English status as a language. Summarize Baldwin's position. Summarize the position of Baldwin's opponents.

3. In paragraph 4, Baldwin writes, "It goes without saying, then, that language is also a political instrument, means, and proof of power." How, according to Baldwin, does language connect or divide one from "public or communal identity"? What evidence does he provide to support this claim that language is a political instrument?

4. Baldwin asks his readers, "What is language?" and thus leads them to define for themselves "what definition of languages is to be trusted" (paragraph 9). Do you find Baldwin's definition and position persuasive? Explain.

5. Reread Baldwin's memorable conclusion. How does he prepare you for this conclusion? What are you left to contemplate?

6. How has Baldwin's essay made you think about your own use of language and the role language plays in your identity? Baldwin makes an important distinction between *dialect* and *language*. Write an essay in which you take a position on the role of language in shaping your identity.

7. Select a dialect with which you are familiar. Analyze the features of this dialect. Write an essay in which you develop a position showing how this dialect reflects the richness of its culture.

MAKING CONNECTIONS

1. Read Alice Walker's essay, "Am I Blue?" (p. 598), paying particular attention to paragraph 17 on Blue's language and to Walker's sense of Blue's power of communication. To what extent does her argument support Baldwin's position on black English?

2. Consider Baldwin's argument about language as a political instrument that forges and reveals identity in relation to the writings of several female writers in "Explaining"—Joan Didion (p. 331), Rebecca Mead (p. 508), and Carol Gilligan (p. 425), in particular. Can you find and describe in those writings evidence of a women's English parallel in some ways to black English? Or is there a men's English you would prefer to describe, drawing on another set of writers? Explain.

POLITICS AND THE ENGLISH LANGUAGE

George Orwell

The rise of totalitarianism in Europe led George Orwell (1903–1950) to write about its causes in his most famous novels, 1984 (1949) and Animal Farm *(1945), and in essays like "Politics and the English Language." In this essay, written in 1946, Orwell tells his readers that "in our time, political speech and writing are largely the defense of the indefensible." He attacks language that consists "largely of euphemism, question begging, and sheer cloudy vagueness." Orwell, like John Berger earlier in this section, is concerned with the ways in which language is often used to conceal unpleasant and horrifying realities.*

Most people who bother with the matter at all would admit that the English language is in a bad way, but it is generally assumed that we cannot by conscious action do anything about it. Our civilization is decadent and our language—so the argument runs—must inevitably share in the general collapse. It follows that any struggle against the abuse of language is a sentimental archaism, like preferring candles to electric light or hansom cabs to aeroplanes. Underneath this lies the half-conscious belief that language is a natural growth and not an instrument which we shape for our own purposes.

Now, it is clear that the decline of a language must ultimately have political and economic causes: it is not due simply to the bad influence of this or that individual writer. But an effect can become a cause, reinforcing the original cause and producing the same effect in an intensified form, and so on indefinitely. A man may take to drink because he feels himself to be a failure, and then fail all the more completely because he drinks. It is rather the same thing that is happening to the English language. It becomes ugly and inaccurate because our thoughts are foolish, but the slovenliness of our language makes it easier for us to have foolish thoughts. The point is that the process is reversible. Modern English, especially written English, is full of bad habits which spread by imitation and which can be avoided if one is willing to take the necessary trouble. If one gets rid of these habits one can think more clearly, and to think clearly is a necessary first step towards political regeneration: so that the fight against bad English is not frivolous and is not the exclusive concern of professional writers. I will come back to this presently, and I hope that by that time the meaning of what I have said here will have become clearer. Meanwhile, here are five specimens of the English language as it is now habitually written.

These five passages have not been picked out because they are especially bad—I could have quoted far worse if I had chosen—but because they illustrate various of the mental vices from which we now suffer. They are a little below the average, but are fairly representative samples. I number them so that I can refer back to them when necessary:

"(1) I am not, indeed, sure whether it is not true to say that the Milton who once seemed not unlike a seventeenth-century Shelley had not become, out of an experience ever more bitter in each year, more alien [*sic*] to the founder of that Jesuit sect which nothing could induce him to tolerate."

> Professor Harold Laski (Essay in *Freedom of Expression*)

"(2) Above all, we cannot play ducks and drakes with a native battery of idioms which prescribes such egregious collocations of vocables as the basic *put up with* for *tolerate* or *put at a loss* for *bewilder*."

> Professor Lancelot Hogben (*Interglossa*)

"(3) On the one side we have the free personality: by definition it is not neurotic, for it has neither conflict nor dream. Its desires, such as they are, are transparent, for they are just what institutional approval keeps in the forefront of consciousness; another institutional pattern would alter their number and intensity; there is little in them that is natural, irreducible, or culturally dangerous. But *on the other* side, the social bond itself is nothing but the mutual reflection of these self-secure integrities. Recall the definition of love. Is not this the very picture of a small academic? Where is there a place in this hall of mirrors for either personality or fraternity?"

> Essay on psychology in *Politics* (New York)

"(4) All the 'best people' from the gentlemen's clubs, and all the frantic fascist captains, united in common hatred of Socialism and bestial horror of the rising tide of the mass revolutionary movement, have turned to acts of provocation, to foul incendiarism, to medieval legends of poisoned wells, to legalize their own destruction of proletarian organizations, and rouse the agitated petty-bourgeoisie to chauvinistic fervour on behalf of the fight against the revolutionary way out of the crisis."

> Communist pamphlet

"(5) If a new spirit *is* to be infused into this old country, there is one thorny and contentious reform which must be tackled, and

that is the humanization and galvanization of the B.B.C. Timidity
here will bespeak cancer and atrophy of the soul. The heart of
Britain may be sound and of strong beat, for instance, but the
British lion's roar at present is like that of Bottom in Shakespeare's
Midsummer Night's Dream—as gentle as any sucking dove. A
virile new Britain cannot continue indefinitely to be traduced in
the eyes or rather ears, of the world by the effete languors of Lang-
ham Place, brazenly masquerading as 'standard English.' When the
Voice of Britain is heard at nine o'clock, better far and infinitely
less ludicrous to hear aitches honestly dropped than the present
priggish, inflated, inhibited, school-ma'amish arch braying of
blameless bashful mewing maidens!"

Letter in Tribune

Each of these passages has faults of its own, but, quite apart from
avoidable ugliness, two qualities are common to all of them. The first is
staleness of imagery: the other is lack of precision. The writer either has a
meaning and cannot express it, or he inadvertently says something else, or
he is almost indifferent as to whether his words mean anything or not. This
mixture of vagueness and sheer incompetence is the most marked characteristic of modern English prose, and especially of any kind of political
writing. As soon as certain topics are raised, the concrete melts into the abstract and no one seems able to think of turns of speech that are not hackneyed: prose consists less and less of *words* chosen for the sake of their
meaning, and more and more of *phrases* tacked together like the sections
of a prefabricated hen-house. I list below, with notes and examples, various of the tricks by means of which the work of prose-construction is habitually dodged:

Dying Metaphors

A newly invented metaphor assists thought by evoking a visual image,   5
while on the other hand a metaphor which is technically "dead" (e.g. *iron
resolution*) has in effect reverted to being an ordinary word and can generally be used without loss of vividness. But in between these two classes
there is a huge dump of worn-out metaphors which have lost all evocative
power and are merely used because they save people the trouble of inventing phrases for themselves. Examples are: *Ring the changes on, take up the
cudgels for, toe the line, ride roughshod over, stand shoulder to shoulder
with, play into the hands of, no axe to grind, grist to the mill, fishing in
troubled waters, on the order of the day, Achilles' heel, swan song, hotbed.*
Many of these are used without knowledge of their meaning (what is a
"rift," for instance?), and incompatible metaphors are frequently mixed, a
sure sign that the writer is not interested in what he is saying. Some
metaphors now current have been twisted out of their original meaning

without those who use them even being aware of the fact. For example, *toe the line* is sometimes written *tow the line*. Another example is *the hammer and the anvil,* now always used with the implication that the anvil gets the worst of it. In real life it is always the anvil that breaks the hammer, never the other way about: a writer who stopped to think what he was saying would be aware of this, and would avoid perverting the original phrase.

Operators or Verbal False Limbs

These save the trouble of picking out appropriate verbs and nouns, and at the same time pad each sentence with extra syllables which give it an appearance of symmetry. Characteristic phrases are: *render inoperative, militate against, make contact with, be subjected to, give rise to, give grounds for, have the effect of, play a leading part (role) in, make itself felt, take effect, exhibit a tendency to, serve the purpose of, etc., etc.* The keynote is the elimination of simple verbs. Instead of being a single word, such as *break, stop, spoil, mend, kill,* a verb becomes a *phrase,* made up of a noun or adjective tacked on to some general-purposes verb such as *prove, serve, form, play, render.* In addition, the passive voice is wherever possible used in preference to the active, and noun constructions are used instead of gerunds (*by examination of* instead of *by examining*). The range of verbs is further cut down by means of the *-ize* and *de-* formation, and the banal statements are given an appearance of profundity by means of the *not un-* formation. Simple conjunctions and prepositions are replaced by such phrases as *with respect to, having regard to, the fact that, by dint of, in view of, in the interests of, on the hypothesis that;* and the ends of sentences are saved from anticlimax by such resounding commonplaces as *greatly to be desired, cannot be left out of account, a development to be expected in the near future, deserving of serious consideration, brought to a satisfactory conclusion,* and so on and so forth.

Pretentious Diction

Words like *phenomenon, element, individual* (as noun), *objective, categorical, effective, virtual, basic, primary, promote, constitute, exhibit, exploit, utilize, eliminate, liquidate,* are used to dress up simple statements and give an air of scientific impartiality to biased judgments. Adjectives like *epoch-making, epic, historic, unforgettable, triumphant, age-old, inevitable, inexorable, veritable,* are used to dignify the sordid processes of international politics, while writing that aims at glorifying war usually takes on an archaic color, its characteristic words being: *realm, throne, chariot, mailed fist, trident, sword, shield, buckler, banner, jackboot, clarion.* Foreign words and expressions such as *cul de sac, ancien régime, deus ex machina, mutatis mutandis, status quo, gleichschaltung, weltanschau-*

ung, are used to give an air of culture and elegance. Except for the useful abbreviations *i.e., e.g.,* and *etc.,* there is no real need for any of the hundreds of foreign phrases now current in English. Bad writers, and especially scientific, political and sociological writers, are nearly always haunted by the notion that Latin or Greek words are grander than Saxon ones, and unnecessary words like *expedite, ameliorate, predict, extraneous, deracinated, clandestine, subaqueous* and hundreds of others constantly gain ground from their Anglo-Saxon opposite numbers.[1] The jargon peculiar to Marxist writing (*hyena, hangman, cannibal, petty bourgeois, these gentry, lackey, flunky, mad dog, White Guard,* etc.) consists largely of words and phrases translated from Russian, German or French; but the normal way of coining a new word is to use a Latin or Greek root with the appropriate affix and, where necessary, the *-ize* formation. It is often easier to make up words of this kind (*deregionalize, impermissible, extramarital, nonfragmentatory* and so forth) than to think up the English words that will cover one's meaning. The result, in general, is an increase in slovenliness and vagueness.

Meaningless Words

In certain kinds of writing, particularly in art criticism and literary criticism, it is normal to come across long passages which are almost completely lacking in meaning.[2] Words like *romantic, plastic, values, human, dead, sentimental, natural, vitality,* as used in art criticism, are strictly meaningless in the sense that they not only do not point to any discoverable object, but are hardly ever expected to do so by the reader. When one critic writes, "The outstanding feature of Mr. X's work is its living quality," while another writes, "The immediately striking thing about Mr. X's work is its peculiar deadness," the reader accepts this as a simple difference of opinion. If words like *black* and *white* were involved, instead of the jargon words *dead* and *living,* he would see at once that language

---

[1]An interesting illustration of this is the way in which the English flower names which were in use till very recently are being ousted by Greek ones, *snapdragon* becoming *antirrhinum, forget-me-not* becoming *myosotis,* etc. It is hard to see any practical reason for this change of fashion: it is probably due to an instinctive turning-away from the more homely word and a vague feeling that the Greek word is scientific.

[2]Example: "Comfort's catholicity of perception and image, strangely Whitmanesque in range, almost the exact opposite in aesthetic compulsion, continues to evoke that trembling atmospheric accumulative hinting at a cruel, an inexorably serene timelessness . . . Wrey Gardiner scores by aiming at simple bull's-eyes with precision. Only they are not so simple, and through this contented sadness runs more than the surface bittersweet of resignation" (*Poetry Quarterly*).

was being used in an improper way. Many political words are similarly abused. The word *Fascism* has now no meaning except in so far as it signifies "something not desirable." The words *democracy, socialism, freedom, patriotic, realistic, justice,* have each of them several different meanings which cannot be reconciled with one another. In the case of a word like *democracy,* not only is there no agreed definition, but the attempt to make one is resisted from all sides. It is almost universally felt that when we call a country democratic we are praising it: consequently the defenders of every kind of régime claim that it is a democracy, and fear that they might have to stop using the word if it were tied down to any one meaning. Words of this kind are often used in a consciously dishonest way. That is, the person who uses them has his own private definition, but allows his hearer to think he means something quite different. Statements like *Marshal Pétain was a true patriot, The Soviet Press is the freest in the world, The Catholic Church is opposed to persecution,* are almost always made with intent to deceive. Other words used in variable meanings, in most cases more or less dishonestly, are: *class, totalitarian, science, progressive, reactionary, bourgeois, equality.*

Now that I have made this catalog of swindles and perversions, let me give another example of the kind of writing that they lead to. This time it must of its nature be an imaginary one. I am going to translate a passage of good English into modern English of the worst sort. Here is a well-known verse from *Ecclesiastes*:

> "I returned and saw under the sun, that the race is not to the swift, nor the battle to the strong, neither yet bread to the wise, nor yet riches to men of understanding, nor yet favor to men of skill; but time and chance happeneth to them all."

Here it is in modern English: 10

> "Objective consideration of contemporary phenomena compels the conclusion that success or failure in competitive activities exhibits no tendency to be commensurate with innate capacity, but that a considerable element of the unpredictable must invariably be taken into account."

This is a parody, but not a very gross one. Exhibit (3), above, for instance, contains several patches of the same kind of English. It will be seen that I have not made a full translation. The beginning and ending of the sentence follow the original meaning fairly closely, but in the middle the concrete illustrations—race, battle, bread—dissolve into the vague phrase "success or failure in competitive activities." This had to be so, because no modern writer of the kind I am discussing—no one capable of using phrases like "objective consideration of contemporary phenomena"—would ever tabulate his thoughts in that precise and detailed way. The whole tendency of modern prose is away from concreteness. Now analyse these two sentences a little more closely. The first contains forty-nine words but only sixty syllables, and all its words are those of everyday life. The second contains thirty-eight words of ninety syllables: eighteen of its words are from Latin roots, and one from Greek. The first sentence contains six vivid images, and only one phrase ("time and chance") that could be called vague. The second contains not a single fresh, arresting phrase, and in spite of its ninety syllables it gives only a shortened version of the meaning contained in the first. Yet without a doubt it is the second kind of sentence that is gaining ground in modern English. I do not want to exaggerate. This kind of writing is not yet universal, and outcrops of simplicity will occur here and there in the worst-written page. Still, if you or I were told to write a few lines on the uncertainty of human fortunes, we should probably come much nearer to my imaginary sentence than to the one from *Ecclesiastes*.

As I have tried to show, modern writing at its worst does not consist in picking out words for the sake of their meaning and inventing images in order to make the meaning clearer. It consists in gumming together long strips of words which have already been set in order by someone else, and making the results presentable by sheer humbug. The attraction of this way of writing is that it is easy. It is easier—even quicker, once you have the habit—to say *In my opinion it is a not unjustifiable assumption that* than to say *I think*. If you use ready-made phrases, you not only don't have to hunt about for words; you also don't have to bother with the rhythms of your sentences, since these phrases are generally so arranged as to be more or less euphonious. When you are composing in a hurry—when you are dictating to a stenographer, for instance, or making a public speech—it is natural to fall into a pretentious, Latinized style. Tags like *a consideration which we should do well to bear in mind* or *a conclusion to which all of us would readily assent* will save many a sentence from coming down with a bump. By using stale metaphors, similes and idioms, you save much mental effort, at the cost of leaving your meaning vague, not only for your reader but for yourself. This is the significance of mixed metaphors. The sole aim of a metaphor is to call up a visual image. When these images clash—as in *The Fascist octopus has sung its swan song, the jackboot is thrown into the melting pot*—it can be taken as certain that the writer is not seeing a mental image of the objects he is naming; in other words he is not really thinking. Look again at the examples I gave at the beginning of this essay. Professor Laski (1) uses five negatives in fifty-three words. One of these is superfluous, making nonsense of the whole passage, and in addition there is the slip *alien* for akin, making further nonsense, and several avoidable pieces of clumsiness which increase the general vagueness. Professor Hogben (2) plays ducks and drakes with a battery which is able to write prescriptions, and, while disapproving of the everyday phrase *put up with*, is unwilling to look *egregious* up in the dictionary and see what it means. (3), if one takes an uncharitable attitude towards it, is simply meaningless:

probably one could work out its intended meaning by reading the whole of the article in which it occurs. In (4), the writer knows more or less what he wants to say, but an accumulation of stale phrases chokes him like tea leaves blocking a sink. In (5), words and meaning have almost parted company. People who write in this manner usually have a general emotional meaning—they dislike one thing and want to express solidarity with another—but they are not interested in the detail of what they are saying. A scrupulous writer, in every sentence that he writes, will ask himself at least four questions, thus: What am I trying to say? What words will express it? What image or idiom will make it clearer? Is this image fresh enough to have an effect? And he will probably ask himself two more: Could I put it more shortly? Have I said anything that is avoidably ugly? But you are not obliged to go to all this trouble. You can shirk it by simply throwing your mind open and letting the ready-made phrases come crowding in. They will construct your sentences for you—even think your thoughts for you, to a certain extent—and at need they will perform the important service of partially concealing your meaning even from yourself. It is at this point that the special connection between politics and the debasement of language becomes clear.

In our time it is broadly true that political writing is bad writing. Where it is not true, it will generally be found that the writer is some kind of rebel, expressing his private opinions and not a "party line." Orthodoxy, of whatever color, seems to demand a lifeless, imitative style. The political dialects to be found in pamphlets, leading articles, manifestos, White Papers and the speeches of under-secretaries do, of course, vary from party to party, but they are all alike in that one almost never finds in them a fresh, vivid, home-made turn of speech. When one watches some tired hack on the platform mechanically repeating the familiar phrases— *bestial atrocities, iron heel, bloodstained tyranny, free peoples of the world, stand shoulder to shoulder*—one often has a curious feeling that one is not watching a live human being but some kind of dummy: a feeling which suddenly becomes stronger at moments when the light catches the speaker's spectacles and turns them into blank discs which seem to have no eyes behind them. And this is not altogether fanciful. A speaker who uses that kind of phraseology has gone some distance towards turning himself into a machine. The appropriate noises are coming out of his larynx, but his brain is not involved as it would be if he were choosing his words for himself. If the speech he is making is one that he is accustomed to make over and over again, he may be almost unconscious of what he is saying, as one is when one utters the responses in church. And this reduced state of consciousness, if not indispensable, is at any rate favorable to political conformity.

In our time, political speech and writing are largely the defense of the indefensible. Things like the continuance of British rule in India, the Russian purges and deportations, the dropping of the atom bombs on Japan, can indeed be defended, but only by arguments which are too brutal for most people to face, and which do not square with the professed aims of political parties. Thus political language has to consist largely of euphemism, question-begging and sheer cloudy vagueness. Defenseless villages are bombarded from the air, the inhabitants driven out into the countryside, the cattle machine-gunned, the huts set on fire with incendiary bullets: this is called *pacification*. Millions of peasants are robbed of their farms and sent trudging along the roads with no more than they can carry: this is called *transfer of population* or *rectification of frontiers*. People are imprisoned for years without trial, or shot in the back of the neck or sent to die of scurvy in Arctic lumber camps: this is called *elimination of unreliable elements*. Such phraseology is needed if one wants to name things without calling up mental pictures of them. Consider for instance some comfortable English professor defending Russian totalitarianism. He cannot say outright, "I believe in killing off your opponents when you can get good results by doing so." Probably, therefore, he will say something like this:

"While freely conceding that the Soviet régime exhibits certain features   15
which the humanitarian may be inclined to deplore, we must, I think, agree that a certain curtailment of the right to political opposition is an unavoidable concomitant of transitional periods, and that the rigors which the Russian people have been called upon to undergo have been amply justified in the sphere of concrete achievement."

The inflated style is itself a kind of euphemism. A mass of Latin words falls upon the facts like soft snow, blurring the outlines and covering up all the details. The great enemy of clear language is insincerity. When there is a gap between one's real and one's declared aims, one turns as it were instinctively to long words and exhausted idioms, like a cuttlefish squirting out ink. In our age there is no such thing as "keeping out of politics." All issues are political issues, and politics itself is a mass of lies, evasions, folly, hatred and schizophrenia. When the general atmosphere is bad, language must suffer. I should expect to find—this is a guess which I have not sufficient knowledge to verify—that the German, Russian and Italian languages have all deteriorated in the last ten or fifteen years, as a result of dictatorship.

But if thought corrupts language, language can also corrupt thought. A bad usage can spread by tradition and imitation, even among people who should and do know better. The debased language that I have been discussing is in some ways very convenient. Phrases like *a not unjustifiable assumption, leaves much to be desired, would serve no good purpose, a consideration which we should do well to bear in mind,* are a continuous temptation, a packet of aspirins always at one's elbow. Look back through this essay, and for certain you will find that I have again and again committed the very faults I am protesting against. By this morning's post I have received a pamphlet dealing with conditions in Germany. The author tells me that he "felt impelled" to write it. I open it at random, and here is almost the first sentence that I see: "(The Allies) have an opportunity not only of achieving a radical transformation of Germany's social and political structure in such a way as to avoid a nationalistic reaction in Germany itself, but at the same time of laying the foundations of a cooperative and unified Europe." You see, he "feels impelled" to write—feels, presumably, that he has something new to say—and yet his words, like cavalry horses answering the bugle, group themselves automatically into the familiar dreary pattern. This invasion of one's mind by ready-made phrases (*lay the foundations, achieve a radical transformation*) can only be prevented if one is constantly on guard against them, and every such phrase anaesthetizes a portion of one's brain.

I said earlier that the decadence of our language is probably curable. Those who deny this would argue, if they produced an argument at all, that language merely reflects existing social conditions, and that we cannot influence its development by any direct tinkering with words and constructions. So far as the general tone or spirit of a language goes, this may be true, but it is not true in detail. Silly words and expressions have often disappeared, not through any evolutionary process but owing to the conscious action of a minority. Two recent examples were *explore every avenue* and *leave no stone unturned*, which were killed by the jeers of a few journalists. There is a long list of flyblown metaphors which could similarly be got rid of if enough people would interest themselves in the job; and it should also be possible to laugh the *not un*-formation out of existence,[3] to reduce the amount of Latin and Greek in the average sentence, to drive out foreign phrases and strayed scientific words, and, in general, to make pretentiousness unfashionable. But all these are minor points. The defense of the English language implies more than this, and perhaps it is best to start by saying what it does not imply.

To begin with it has nothing to do with archaism, with the salvaging of obsolete words and turns of speech, or with the setting up of a "standard English" which must never be departed from. On the contrary, it is especially concerned with the scrapping of every word or idiom which has outworn its usefulness. It has nothing to do with correct grammar and syntax, which are of no importance so long as one makes one's meaning clear, or with the avoidance of Americanisms, or with having what is called a "good prose style." On the other hand it is not concerned with fake simplicity and the attempt to make written English colloquial. Nor does it even imply in every case preferring the Saxon word to the Latin one, though it does imply using the fewest and shortest words that will cover one's meaning. What is above all needed is to let the meaning choose the word, and not the other way about. In prose, the worst thing one can do with words is

---

[3]One can cure oneself of the *not un*-formation by memorizing this sentence: *A not unblack dog was chasing a not unsmall rabbit across a not ungreen field.*

to surrender to them. When you think of a concrete object, you think wordlessly, and then, if you want to describe the thing you have been visualizing you probably hunt about till you find the exact words that seem to fit. When you think of something abstract you are more inclined to use words from the start, and unless you make a conscious effort to prevent it, the existing dialect will come rushing in and do the job for you, at the expense of blurring or even changing your meaning. Probably it is better to put off using words as long as possible and get one's meaning as clear as one can through pictures or sensations. Afterwards one can choose—not simply *accept*—the phrases that will best cover the meaning, and then switch round and decide what impression one's words are likely to make on another person. This last effort of the mind cuts out all stale or mixed images, all prefabricated phrases, needless repetitions, and humbug and vagueness generally. But one can often be in doubt about the effect of a word or a phrase, and one needs rules that one can rely on when instinct fails. I think the following rules will cover most cases:

(i) Never use a metaphor, simile or other figure of speech which you are used to seeing in print.

(ii) Never use a long word where a short one will do.

(iii) If it is possible to cut a word out, always cut it out.

(iv) Never use the passive where you can use the active.

(v) Never use a foreign phrase, a scientific word or a jargon word if you can think of an everyday English equivalent.

(vi) Break any of these rules sooner than say anything outright barbarous.

These rules sound elementary, and so they are, but they demand a deep change of attitude in anyone who has grown used to writing in the style now fashionable. One could keep all of them and still write bad English, but one could not write the kind of stuff that I quoted in those five specimens at the beginning of this article.

I have not here been considering the literary use of language, but merely language as an instrument for expressing and not for concealing or preventing thought. Stuart Chase and others have come near to claiming that all abstract words are meaningless, and have used this as a pretext for advocating a kind of political quietism. Since you don't know what Fascism is, how can you struggle against Fascism? One need not swallow such absurdities as this, but one ought to recognize that the present political chaos is connected with the decay of language, and that one can probably bring about some improvement by starting at the verbal end. If you simplify your English, you are freed from the worst follies of orthodoxy. You cannot speak any of the necessary dialects, and when you make a stupid remark its stupidity will be obvious, even to yourself. Political language— and with variations this is true of all political parties, from Conservatives

20

to Anarchists—is designed to make lies sound truthful and murder respectable, and to give an appearance of solidity to pure wind. One cannot change this all in a moment, but one can at least change one's own habits, and from time to time one can even, if one jeers loudly enough, send some worn-out and useless phrase—some *jackboot, Achilles' heel, hotbed, melting pot, acid test, veritable inferno* or other lump of verbal refuse—into the dustbin where it belongs.

QUESTIONS

1. What is Orwell's position on the ways in which modern writers are destroying the English language?
2. Orwell argues that "thought corrupts language," but he also argues that "language can also corrupt thought" (paragraph 17). What argument is he making? How does language corrupt thought?
3. Orwell writes in paragraph 17, "Look back through this essay, and for certain you will find that I have again and again committed the very faults I am protesting against." Does Orwell, in fact, break his own rules? If so, what might his purpose be in doing so?
4. What sense of himself does Orwell present to his readers? How would you describe his persona, his character?
5. Why do people write badly, according to Orwell? What causes does he identify in his essay? Do you agree with him? Explain.
6. Orwell presents guidelines for good writing in paragraph 19. Take one of your recent essays and analyze how your writing measures up to Orwell's standards.
7. Spend one week developing a list of examples of bad writing from newspapers or popular magazines. Use this material as the basis for an essay in which you develop a thesis to argue your position on politics and language.
8. Written more than fifty years ago, this is probably the best known of all of Orwell's essays. How insightful and current do you find it today? Take five examples from your reading, as Orwell takes from his, and use them as evidence in an argument of your own about the state of contemporary written English. Take your examples from anything you like, including this book—even this question—if you wish. Be careful to choose recent pieces of writing.

MAKING CONNECTIONS

1. Read Orwell's essay, "Shooting an Elephant" (p. 132), in "Reflecting." What do you learn about Orwell, the essayist, from reading these two essays?

2. John Berger (p. 590) and James Baldwin (p. 622), as represented by their essays in this section, are two writers likely to have been influenced by this essay of Orwell's. Choose the essay you responded to more strongly of those two, and write an essay of your own explaining the connections that you find between Orwell and either Berger or Baldwin.

THE INTERFACE CULTURE

Neal Stephenson

Neal Stephenson was born in 1959 in Ft. Meade, Maryland. He graduated from Boston University with a degree in physics, and he had published his first novel by the time he was twenty-five. Not until 1992, however, did he receive wide recognition with Snow Crash, *for which he was hailed as a major cyberpunk novelist. In his mixture of science fiction and virtual reality, Stephenson goes beyond the simply futuristic; as* The Diamond Age *(1995) and, particularly,* Cryptonomicon *(1999) suggest, he is interested in the whole history of technology. The following is from Stephenson's 1999 collection of essays,* In the Beginning . . . Was the Command Line.

A few years ago I walked into a grocery store somewhere and was presented with the following *tableau vivant:* near the entrance a young couple were standing in front of a large cosmetics display. The man was stolidly holding a shopping basket between his hands while his mate raked blister-packs of makeup off the display and piled them in. Since then I've always thought of that man as the personification of an interesting human tendency: not only are we not offended to be dazzled by manufactured images, but we like it. We practically insist on it. We are eager to be complicit in our own dazzlement: to pay money for a theme park ride, vote for a guy who's obviously lying to us, or stand there holding the basket as it's filled up with cosmetics.

I was in Disney World recently, specifically the part of it called the Magic Kingdom, walking up Main Street U.S.A. This is a perfect gingerbread Victorian small town that culminates in a Disney castle. It was very crowded; we shuffled rather than walked. Directly in front of me was a man with a camcorder. It was one of the new breed of camcorders where instead of peering through a viewfinder you gaze at a flat-panel color screen about the size of a playing card, which televises live coverage of whatever the camcorder is seeing. He was holding the appliance close to his face, so that it obstructed his view. Rather than go see a real small town for free, he had paid money to see a pretend one, and rather than see it with the naked eye, he was watching it on television.

And rather than stay home and read a book, I was watching him.

Americans' preference for mediated experiences is obvious enough, and I'm not going to keep pounding it into the ground. I'm not even going to make snotty comments about it—after all, I was at Disney World as a paying customer. But it clearly relates to the colossal success of GUIs,[1] and so I have to talk about it some. Disney does mediated experiences better than anyone. If they understood what OSes[2] are, and why people use them, they could crush Microsoft in a year or two.

In the part of Disney World called the Animal Kingdom there is a new   5 attraction called the Maharajah Jungle Trek. It was open for sneak previews when I was there. This is a complete stone-by-stone reproduction of a hypothetical ruin in the jungles of India. According to its backstory, it was built by a local rajah in the sixteenth century as a game reserve. He would go there with his princely guests to hunt Bengal tigers. As time went on, it fell into disrepair and the tigers and monkeys took it over; eventually, around the time of India's independence, it became a government wildlife reserve, now open to visitors.

The place looks more like what I have just described than any actual building you might find in India. All the stones in the broken walls are weathered as if monsoon rains had been trickling down them for centuries, the paint on the gorgeous murals is flaked and faded just so, and Bengal tigers loll amid stumps of broken columns. Where modern repairs have been made to the ancient structure, they've been done, not as Disney's engineers would do them, but as thrifty Indian janitors would—with hunks of bamboo and rust-spotted hunks of rebar. The rust is painted on, of course, and protected from real rust by a plastic clear-coat, but you can't tell unless you get down on your knees.

In one place you walk along a stone wall with a series of old pitted friezes carved into it. One end of the wall has broken off and settled into the earth, perhaps because of some long-forgotten earthquake, and so a broad jagged crack runs across a panel or two, but the story is still readable: first, primordial chaos leads to a flourishing of many animal species. Next, we see the Tree of Life surrounded by diverse animals. This is an obvious allusion (or, in showbiz lingo, a tie-in) to the gigantic Tree of Life that dominates the center of Disney's Animal Kingdom just as the Castle dominates the Magic Kingdom or the Sphere does Epcot. But it's rendered in historically correct style and could probably fool anyone who didn't have a Ph.D. in Indian art history.

The next panel shows a mustachioed H. sapiens chopping down the Tree of Life with a scimitar, and the animals fleeing every which way. The one after that shows the misguided human getting walloped by a tidal wave, part of a latter-day Deluge presumably brought on by his stupidity.

The final panel, then, portrays the Sapling of Life beginning to grow back, but now Man has ditched the edged weapon and joined the other animals in standing around to adore and praise it.

---

[1]*GUI:* Graphical user interface; the material displayed on a computer monitor's screen, which allows the user to interact with the computer. [Eds.]

[2]*OS:* Operating system, such as Windows or Macintosh. [Eds.]

It is, in other words, a prophecy of the Bottleneck: the scenario, com- 10
monly espoused among modern-day environmentalists, that the world
faces an upcoming period of grave ecological tribulations that will last for
a few decades or centuries and end when we find a new harmonious modus
vivendi[3] with Nature.

Taken as a whole the frieze is a pretty brilliant piece of work. Obviously it's not an ancient Indian ruin, and some person or people now living
deserve credit for it. But there are no signatures on the Maharajah's game
reserve at Disney World. There are no signatures on anything, because it
would ruin the whole effect to have long strings of production credits dangling from every custom-worn brick, as they do from Hollywood movies.

Among Hollywood writers, Disney has the reputation of being a real
wicked stepmother. It's not hard to see why. Disney is in the business of
putting out a product of seamless illusion—a magic mirror that reflects the
world back better than it really is. But a writer is literally talking to his or
her readers, not just creating an ambience or presenting them with something to look at. Just as the command line interface opens a much more direct and explicit channel from user to machine than the GUI, so it is with
words, writer, and reader.

The word, in the end, is the only system of encoding thoughts—the
only medium—that is not fungible, that refuses to dissolve in the devouring torrent of electronic media. (The richer tourists at Disney World wear
t-shirts printed with the names of famous designers, because designs themselves can be bootlegged easily and with impunity. The only way to make
clothing that cannot be legally bootlegged is to print copyrighted and
trademarked words on it; once you have taken that step, the clothing itself
doesn't really matter, and so a t-shirt is as good as anything else. T-shirts
with expensive words on them are now the insignia of the upper class.
T-shirts with cheap words, or no words at all, are for the commoners.)

But this special quality of words and of written communication would
have the same effect on Disney's product as spray-painted graffiti on a
magic mirror. So Disney does most of its communication without resorting
to words, and for the most part, the words aren't missed. Some of Disney's
older properties, such as Peter Pan, Winnie the Pooh, and Alice in Wonderland, came out of books. But the authors' names are rarely if ever mentioned, and you can't buy the original books at the Disney store. If you
could, they would all seem old and queer, like very bad knockoffs of the
purer, more authentic Disney versions. Compared to more recent produc-
tions like *Beauty and the Beast* and *Mulan,* the Disney movies based on
these books (particularly *Alice in Wonderland* and *Peter Pan*) seem deeply
bizarre, and not wholly appropriate for children. That stands to reason,
because Lewis Carroll and J. M. Barrie were very strange men, and such is
the nature of the written word that their personal strangeness shines

---

[3]*modus vivendi:* way of living. [Eds.]

straight through all the layers of Disneyfication like X-rays through a wall. Probably for this very reason, Disney seems to have stopped buying rights to books altogether, and now finds its themes and characters in folk tales, which have the lapidary, timeworn quality of the ancient bricks in the Maharajah's ruins.

If I can risk a broad generalization, most of the people who go to Disney   15
World have zero interest in absorbing new ideas from books. This sounds snide, but listen: they have no qualms about being presented with ideas in other forms. Disney World is stuffed with environmental messages now, and the guides at Animal Kingdom can talk your ear off about biology.

If you followed those tourists home, you might find art, but it would be the sort of unsigned folk art that's for sale in Disney World's African- and Asian-themed stores. In general they only seem comfortable with media that have been ratified by great age, massive popular acceptance, or both. In this world, artists are like the anonymous, illiterate stone carvers who built the great cathedrals of Europe and then faded away into un- marked graves in the churchyard. The cathedral as a whole is awesome and stirring in spite, and possibly because, of the fact that we have no idea who built it. When we walk through it, we are communing not with individual stone carvers but with an entire culture.

Disney World works the same way. If you are an intellectual type, a reader or writer of books, the nicest thing you can say about this is that the execution is superb. But it's easy to find the whole environment a little creepy, because something is missing: the translation of all its content into clear explicit written words, the attribution of the ideas to specific people. You can't argue with it. It seems as if a hell of a lot might be being glossed over, as if Disney World might be putting one over on us, and possibly get- ting away with all kinds of buried assumptions and muddled thinking.

And this is precisely the same as what is lost in the transition from the command line interface to the GUI.

Disney and Apple/Microsoft are in the same business: short-circuiting laborious, explicit verbal communication with expensively designed inter- faces. Disney is a sort of user interface unto itself—and more than just graphical. Let's call it a Sensorial Interface. It can be applied to anything in the world, real or imagined, albeit at staggering expense.

Why are we rejecting explicit word-based interfaces, and embracing   20
graphical or sensorial ones—a trend that accounts for the success of both Microsoft and Disney?

Part of it is simply that the world is very complicated now—much more complicated than the hunter-gatherer world that our brains evolved to cope with—and we simply can't handle all of the details. We have to delegate. We have no choice but to trust some nameless artist at Disney or programmer at Apple or Microsoft to make a few choices for us, close off some options, and give us a conveniently packaged executive summary.

But more importantly, it comes out of the fact that during this century, intellectualism failed, and everyone knows it. In places like Russia and Germany, the common people agreed to loosen their grip on traditional folk-ways, mores, and religion, and let the intellectuals run with the ball, and they screwed everything up and turned the century into an abattoir. Those wordy intellectuals used to be merely tedious; now they seem kind of dangerous as well.

We Americans are the only ones who didn't get creamed at some point during all of this. We are free and prosperous because we have inherited political and value systems fabricated by a particular set of eighteenth-century intellectuals who happened to get it right. But we have lost touch with those intellectuals, and with anything like intellectualism, even to the point of not reading books anymore, though we are literate. We seem much more comfortable with propagating those values to future generations nonverbally, through a process of being steeped in media. Apparently this actually works to some degree, for police in many lands are now complaining that local arrestees are insisting on having their Miranda rights read to them, just like perps in American TV cop shows. When it's explained to them that they are in a different country, where those rights do not exist, they become outraged. *Starsky and Hutch*[4] reruns, dubbed into diverse languages, may turn out, in the long run, to be a greater force for human rights than the Declaration of Independence.

The written word is unique among media in that it is a digital medium that humans can, nonetheless, easily read and write. Humans are conversant in many media (music, dance, painting), but all of them are analog except for the written word, which is naturally expressed in digital form (i.e. it is a series of discrete symbols—every letter in every book is a member of a certain character set, every "a" is the same as every other "a," and so on). As any communications engineer can tell you, digital signals are much better to work with than analog ones because they are easily copied, transmitted, and error-checked. Unlike analog signals, they are not doomed to degradation over time and distance. That is why digital compact disks replaced analog LPs, for example. The digital nature of the written word confers on it exceptional stability, which is why it is the vehicle of choice for extremely important concepts like the Ten Commandments, the Koran, and the Bill of Rights. This is generally thought to be a rather good idea. But the messages conveyed by modern audiovisual media cannot be pegged to any fixed, written set of precepts in that way and consequently they are free to wander all over the place and possibly dump loads of crap into people's minds.

Orlando used to have a military installation called McCoy Air Force   25
Base, with long runways from which B-52s could take off and reach Cuba, or just about anywhere else, with loads of nukes. But now McCoy has been scrapped and repurposed. It has been absorbed into Orlando's civilian airport. The long runways are being used to land 747-loads of tourists from

---

[4]*Starsky and Hutch*: a TV police show, popular in the 1970s. [Eds.]

Brazil, Italy, Russia, and Japan, so that they can come to Disney World and steep in our media for a while.

To traditional cultures, especially word-based ones such as Islam, this is infinitely more threatening than the B-52s ever were. It is obvious, to everyone outside of the United States, that our arch-buzzwords—multiculturalism and diversity—are false fronts that are being used (in many cases unwittingly) to conceal a global trend to eradicate cultural differences. The basic tenet of multiculturalism (or "honoring diversity" or whatever you want to call it) is that people need to stop judging each other—to stop asserting (and, eventually, to stop believing) that this is right and that is wrong, this true and that false, one thing ugly and another thing beautiful, that God exists and has this or that set of qualities.

The lesson most people are taking home from the twentieth century is that, in order for a large number of different cultures to coexist peacefully on the globe (or even in a neighborhood) it is necessary for people to suspend judgment in this way. Hence (I would argue) our suspicion of, and hostility toward, all authority figures in modern culture. As David Foster Wallace has explained in his essay "E Unibus Pluram,"[5] this is the fundamental message of television; it is the message that people absorb, anyway, after they have steeped in our media long enough. It's not expressed in these highfalutin terms, of course. It comes through as the presumption that all authority figures—teachers, generals, cops, ministers, politicians—are hypocritical buffoons, and that hip jaded coolness is the only way to be.

The problem is that once you have done away with the ability to make judgments as to right and wrong, true and false, etc., there's no real culture left. All that remains is clog dancing and macrame. The ability to make judgments, to believe things, is the entire point of having a culture. I think this is why guys with machine guns sometimes pop up in places like Luxor and begin pumping bullets into Westerners. They perfectly understand the lesson of McCoy Air Force Base. When their sons come home wearing Chicago Bulls caps with the bills turned sideways, the dads go out of their minds.

The global anticulture that has been conveyed into every cranny of the world by television is a culture unto itself, and by the standards of great and ancient cultures like Islam and France, it seems grossly inferior, at least at first. The only good thing you can say about it is that it makes world wars and Holocausts less likely—and that is actually a pretty good thing!

The only real problem is that anyone who has no culture, other than   30
this global monoculture, is completely screwed. Anyone who grows up watching TV, never sees any religion or philosophy, is raised in an atmosphere of moral relativism, learns about civics from watching bimbo eruptions on network TV news, and attends a university where postmodernists

---

[5]*E Unibus Pluram:* a play on "e pluribus unum" (out of many, one), the motto of the United States. Wallace's title means "out of one, many." [Eds.]

vie to outdo each other in demolishing traditional notions of truth and quality, is going to come out into the world as one pretty feckless human being. And—again—perhaps the goal of all this is to make us feckless so we won't nuke each other.

On the other hand, if you are raised within some specific culture, you end up with a basic set of tools that you can use to think about and understand the world. You might use those tools to reject the culture you were raised in, but at least you've got some tools.

In this country, the people who run things—who populate major law firms and corporate boards—understand all of this at some level. They pay lip service to multiculturalism and diversity and nonjudgmentalness, but they don't raise their own children that way. I have highly educated, technically sophisticated friends who have moved to small towns in Iowa to live and raise their children, and there are Hasidic Jewish enclaves in New York where large numbers of kids are being brought up according to traditional beliefs. Any suburban community might be thought of as a place where people who hold certain (mostly implicit) beliefs go to live among others who think the same way.

And not only do these people feel some responsibility to their own children, but to the country as a whole. Some of the upper class are vile and cynical, of course, but many spend at least part of their time fretting about what direction the country is going in and what responsibilities they have. And so issues that are important to book-reading intellectuals, such as global environmental collapse, eventually percolate through the porous buffer of mass culture and show up as ancient Hindu ruins in Orlando.

You may be asking: what the hell does all this have to do with operating systems? As I've explained, there is no way to explain the domination of the OS market by Apple/Microsoft without looking to cultural explanations, and so I can't get anywhere, in this essay, without first letting you know where I'm coming from vis-à-vis contemporary culture.

Contemporary culture is a two-tiered system, like the Morlocks and   35 the Eloi in H. G. Wells's *The Time Machine,* except that it's been turned upside down. In *The Time Machine,* the Eloi were an effete upper class, supported by lots of subterranean Morlocks who kept the technological wheels turning. But in our world it's the other way round. The Morlocks are in the minority, and they are running the show, because they understand how everything works. The much more numerous Eloi learn everything they know from being steeped from birth in electronic media directed and controlled by book-reading Morlocks. That many ignorant people could be dangerous if they got pointed in the wrong direction, and so we've evolved a popular culture that is (a) almost unbelievably infectious, and (b) neuters every person who gets infected by it, by rendering them unwilling to make judgments and incapable of taking stands.

Morlocks, who have the energy and intelligence to comprehend details, go out and master complex subjects and produce Disney-like Sensorial Interfaces so that Eloi can get the gist without having to strain their minds or endure boredom. Those Morlocks will go to India and tediously explore a hundred ruins, then come home and build sanitary bug-free versions: highlight films, as it were. This costs a lot, because Morlocks insist on good coffee and first-class airline tickets, but that's no problem, because Eloi like to be dazzled and will gladly pay for it all.

Now I realize that most of this probably sounds snide and bitter to the point of absurdity: your basic snotty intellectual throwing a tantrum about those unlettered philistines. As if I were a self-styled Moses, coming down from the mountain all alone, carrying the stone tablets bearing the Ten Commandments carved in immutable stone—the original command line interface—and blowing his stack at the weak, unenlightened Hebrews worshipping images. Not only that, but it sounds like I'm pumping some sort of conspiracy theory.

But that is not where I'm going with this. The situation I describe here could be bad, but doesn't have to be bad and isn't necessarily bad now.

It simply is the case that we are way too busy, nowadays, to comprehend everything in detail. And it's better to comprehend it dimly, through an interface, than not at all. Better for ten million Eloi to go on the Kilimanjaro Safari at Disney World than for a thousand cardiovascular surgeons and mutual fund managers to go on "real" ones in Kenya. The boundary between these two classes is more porous than I've made it sound. I'm always running into regular dudes—construction workers, auto mechanics, taxi drivers, galoots in general—who were largely aliterate until something made it necessary for them to become readers and start actually thinking about things. Perhaps they had to come to grips with alcoholism, perhaps they got sent to jail, or came down with a disease, or suffered a crisis in religious faith, or simply got bored. Such people can get up to speed on particular subjects quite rapidly. Sometimes their lack of a broad education makes them overapt to go off on intellectual wild-goose chases, but hey, at least a wild-goose chase gives you some exercise. The spectre of a polity controlled by the fads and whims of voters who actually believe that there are significant differences between Bud Lite and Miller Lite, and who think that professional wrestling is for real, is naturally alarming to people who don't. But then countries controlled via the command line interface, as it were, by double-domed intellectuals, be they religious or secular, are generally miserable places to live.

Sophisticated people deride Disneyesque entertainments as pat and saccharine, but if the result of that is to instill basically warm and sympathetic reflexes, at a preverbal level, into hundreds of millions of unlettered mediasteepers, then how bad can it be? We killed a lobster in our kitchen last night and my daughter cried for an hour. The Japanese, who used to be just about the fiercest people on earth, have become infatuated with cuddly, adorable cartoon characters. My own family—the people I know best—is divided about evenly between people who will probably read this essay and people who almost certainly won't, and I can't say for sure that one group is necessarily warmer, happier, or better-adjusted than the other.

40

QUESTIONS

1. Why does Stephenson say that words and written communication "would have the same affect on Disney's product as spray-painted graffiti on a magic mirror" (paragraph 14)?
2. Stephenson finds the absence of "the translation of [Disney World's] content into clear explicit written words" creepy, comparing this feeling with what is lost "in the transition from the command line to the GUI." He asks why we are "rejecting explicit word-based interfaces, and embracing graphical or sensorial ones" (paragraph 20). How does he answer this question? How would you answer it?
3. In the "global anticulture" spread by TV, Stephenson finds the message of being cool, and making no judgments. Why does he think Disney is better than other alternatives (paragraph 39)? Do you agree? Explain.
4. Do you agree with Stephenson's conclusions? Discuss why or why not, with some attention to the tone of this essay.
5. Consider the "values" of a TV show that you watch regularly, or of a theme park that you have visited. Write a defense or a critique of one of these forms of amusement.

MAKING CONNECTIONS

Compare Stephenson's argument regarding mediated experience through an interface with Sherry Turkle's discussion of role-playing in virtual reality in "Constructions and Reconstructions of the Self in Virtual Reality" (p. 492). How might Turkle respond to Stephenson's conclusions?

PROFESSING HISTORY: DISTINGUISHING BETWEEN MEMORY AND THE PAST

Elliott J. Gorn

Historian Elliott J. Gorn (b. 1951) received his undergraduate degree from the University of California at Berkeley and his Ph.D. from Yale. He has taught at Miami University and the University of Alabama, and he is currently at Purdue University. Much of Gorn's research has focused on aspects of popular culture, particularly sports. His books include The Manly Art: Bare-Knuckle Prize Fighting in America *(1986) and* Muhammad Ali: The People's Champ *(1996), and he is a coauthor of* A Brief History of American Sports *(1993). He is completing a study of the turn-of-the-century labor organizer Mary ("Mother") Jones. The following essay originally appeared in the* Chronicle of Higher Education, *a newspaper for college teachers and administrators.*

It's not easy being a historian. Tell people you study literature, and they see you as an arbiter of taste. Scientists help solve the problems of humanity. But historians not only spend inordinate amounts of time with the dead, they work in a field where all the stories have been told, all the questions answered. Joan of Arc is martyred, Hitler invades Czechoslovakia: predictable and depressing.

Of course, it's more complicated than that, but not by much when we face our students each fall. A shadow of frustration crosses their faces: We have to study the Reformation? The Puritans? The Great Depression? Again?

Our nonhistorian colleagues don't help. Friends of mine—especially the lit and cultural-studies types—hold forth on what is wrong with our discipline, and the problem usually comes down to our being "undertheorized." That seems to be a polite term for dumb. Many people in the humanities believe that historians are nothing but mindless empiricists—tweedy, seedy, and dull.

But if you think others are hard on historians, you should watch us brutalize ourselves.

Most graduate students get their first real taste of this in historiography courses. Historiography is simply the study of history writing, of schools of interpretation and criticism, of paradigms and paradigm shifts, of generations of progressive historians, consensus historians, and revision- 5 ist historians, of new social historians and new cultural historians. To a graduate student being initiated into our craft, it seems like a big cat fight.

Aside from the sharp tone some debates take in the pages of scholarly journals, it is the process of open debate that is noteworthy. Take a subject, say the American Civil War, and grind through a hundred years of scholarly writing on the topic. You are left deeply humbled. After much impressive marshaling of evidence and even occasionally fine prose by generations of talented scholars, your head spins with contradictions—the Civil War was an "irrepressible conflict" and an avoidable one; an ideological war to end slavery and a war that had nothing to do with slavery; a war waged by a rising bourgeoisie against a proto-aristocracy and a war of capitalists fighting each other.

Some historians argue more persuasively than others, ask broader questions, use better logic, scour the archives more thoroughly; their side wins for a while. Then the paradigm shifts again, old questions get reformulated, whole new ones come forth. Ideally, budding historians form well-considered opinions about who gets the better of each argument. They might even ponder the larger question of what really drives history—trade flows, capital distribution, class structure, military power, culture, ideology, microbes, environment, chance, God, or, of course, some shifting combination of them all.

For the writer of history, knowledge of historiography presents the largest challenge. Even though we are painfully aware of how fragmented "truth" is, we can only convey so much of that fragmentation and still tell coherent stories. Historiography teaches us that all interpretation is limited by the cultural biases of our times, the skills of the individual historian, the limits of primary sources, the perspectives and blindnesses created by a scholar's social position (yes, race, class, and gender, among other factors). That's why all the hoopla over postmodernism always seemed a bit overblown to many historians. We've been dealing with those issues for a long time; relativism is in our blood.

Still, one cannot suffer Hamlet-like indecision and still write. The stories we tell are constructed, and we know it (though there are a few who still won't admit it). Behind the confident prose and flowing narrative, a good historian is painfully aware of how much has to be left out of the story, how the sources say contradictory things, how compelling other interpretations are, how eagerly our adversaries lie in wait to pounce on our weaknesses, how much must remain untold. We work with those problems as best we can, trying to capture as much nuance and complexity as possible. But, finally, we tell stories in little spaces that necessarily force us to leave out much more than they allow us to include; and we do it because the alternative is to not tell stories at all, at least not historical ones.

It's hard to believe, but good historical practice occasionally gets us in 10 trouble. During the 1990's, historians became embroiled in sticky arguments over subjects like the dropping of the atomic bomb, and the "settling" of the American West. Historians themselves had differed over those issues for years, but no one paid much attention. Then the battleground shifted from obscure scholarly journals to prominent museums, and the debates turned to the distinction between history and memory.

While that is not a hard and fast division, the two are different. Collective memory involves folk or popular notions of the past, which tend to be mythic and usually flattering to those whose past they describe. Memory yields predetermined outcomes—brave men of vision settle the West, brave men of vision defeat the Japanese. Complicate the picture too much, and the feel-good emotions evaporate. Memory necessarily simplifies the past in order to cast it in strong emotional light. Sometimes it reveals less about "what happened" than about what we want to believe happened. More often, memory gets a sliver of the facts and a few atmospherics, then flattens out all the complexity. Memory can be an excellent historical source, but not in the way its creators intend. The film *Titanic,* for example, tells us much more about the United States in 1997 than in 1912.

To return to the Civil War, memory relies on sentiment, on metaphors like "the war of brother against brother"—a sad, sad time it was, since we really were one people after all. The sadness, of course, only makes the reconciliation of North and South sweeter, since the United States emerged from the war a stronger and more unified nation. The metaphors transform a social and political conflict into a family saga.

Historians, by contrast, might disagree with each other, but they tend to see deep social schisms—over economic systems and ideologies, for example—as fundamental to the war and its aftermath. Memory invokes conflict only to dispel it; history sees conflict as endemic to the situation. That is why slavery has little place for Civil War re-enactors. How could everyone have been noble when some held others in bondage, and racism was endemic? And after the war, despite the liberation of four million African-Americans, the problem of race would not go away, because, ultimately, national reunification hinged on disenfranchising, terrorizing, and impoverishing those people. It is difficult to incorporate either slaves or a caste-bound rural proletariat into a warm narrative of national reconciliation. Memory can ignore them; the discipline of history cannot.

But if historians embrace relativism, then isn't memory just one more version of the past, as good as any other? Memory sometimes contains elements of a reasonable interpretation. The problem is that memory does not subject itself to scrutiny. It shuns the rough-and-tumble of scholarly infighting, the questioning of hypotheses, skewering of logic, probing of primary sources. Memory sits serenely above the fray, satisfied in its nostalgia. Both history and memory are ideological, but the former, practiced well, is aware and critical of its own ideological assumptions; memory blithely asserts its untroubled truths.

Historical knowledge, then, is messy stuff, which makes teaching difficult. For the past generation, American historians have emphasized conflict, multiplicity, contingency in their writings. Portraying the historical   15 process as fragmented—going beyond old master narratives to tell stories about groups like immigrants, racial minorities, and workers—creates difficulties in the classroom. If the past is filled with contention, sometimes submerged, sometimes right out in the open, then we must convey the contestedness to our students. One way to do so is to encourage students to be contentious with each other, not to bury their differences but to argue about them. And that means giving up some of the neatness of lectures for the disorderliness of discussions.

Several years ago, two other scholars and I edited an anthology of documents in American history to facilitate that sort of teaching. Each chapter assembled primary sources around a particular episode in American history. Thus, students can read and interpret the words of corporation owners and union leaders from the Great 1877 Railroad Strike; of Lakota Indians and U.S. Cavalry officers from the Battle of Wounded Knee; of Margaret Sanger and Anthony Comstock during the debates over birth control; of civil-rights workers and those who opposed them during Freedom Summer of 1964. In other words, students can learn about the constructedness of historical writing, about historiography.

I remember working on the revisions for the first chapter, which concerns early encounters of Europeans and Native Americans. I was reading Bartolomé de Las Casas's *The Devastation of the Indies*. Las Casas, the first priest ordained in the New World, became the Spanish empire's voice of conscience. Alongside Columbus's journals, we placed Las Casas's descriptions of Spanish soldiers encountering native peoples: "They laid bets as to who, with one stroke of the sword, could split a man in two. . . . They took infants from their mother's breasts . . . and threw them into the rivers. . . . They made some low wide gallows on which the hanged victim's feet almost touched the ground, . . . then set burning wood at their feet and thus burned them alive."

The Devastation of the Indies is a great text to teach, because it raises questions of historical veracity even as it tells an important story. Like all primary sources, Las Casas's account has problems. Disease, not soldiers, killed the vast majority of native peoples. Las Casas slighted the fact that many Native Americans allied themselves with the Spanish in hopes of defeating their tribal enemies. Indeed, *The Devastation of the Indies* was so harsh that it was widely reprinted in France and England as propaganda against Spain. Still, a core of facts remains. Where others celebrated the flowering of a Spanish golden age, Las Casas courageously decried the holocaust that enabled it.

Working on this chapter really depressed me. It was not just the horrifying details of wholesale destruction at the very birth of America. What troubled me as well was my insistence that we include Las Casas in our anthology. What morbid isolation from my countrymen did such an unpatriotic act signify? Why should I rain on Columbus Day parades? Why, when my students seemed happy in a culture whose moral and aesthetic sense was shaped by car and beer commercials, did I feel compelled to cull through dismal texts, and, by anthologizing them, insist that those students become steeped in them, too? Why should I be the one to trouble people, disturb them with 500-year-old stories of atrocity?

It's my job, that's why. For better or worse, I think one of the things I am   20 supposed to do is challenge and even upset students. Not because unhappiness is good in and of itself. Far from it. But, increasingly, Americans are a people without history, with only memory, which means a people poorly prepared for what is inevitable about life—tragedy, sadness, moral ambiguity—and, therefore, a people reluctant to engage difficult ethical issues.

Consumer culture is mostly about denial, about forgetting the past, except insofar as the past is pleasant and, thus, marketable. As historians, we occupy one tiny space where the richness of the past is kept alive, where its complexity is acknowledged and studied, where competing voices can still be heard. One of the most important things historians do is to bear witness to the past, including its horrors, in order to battle the amnesia that would sweep away all that is difficult or repugnant. The distinction between history and memory—that is, the distinction between knowledge of painful things, painfully arrived at, and notions of the past that flatter us with easy myths or cheap emotions—is at the heart of our enterprise.

QUESTIONS

1. What is Gorn arguing for? This essay appeared in a publication that is read primarily by college teachers and administrators. How might students react to it?
2. What does Gorn see as the difference between history and memory, and why does he find it so important?
3. What does Gorn mean when he says that "increasingly, Americans are a people without a history, with only memory . . . a people reluctant to engage difficult ethical issues" (paragraph 20).
4. Gorn says that historical knowledge is "messy stuff, which makes teaching difficult," and he urges teachers to "encourage students to be contentious with each other, not to bury their differences but to argue about them" (paragraph 15). Given your experience as a student in history courses, would you say that this is good advice for teachers? Explain.

MAKING CONNECTIONS

Gorn argues for the importance of teaching works like Bartolomé de las Casas's *The Devastation of the Indies,* which he describes as a text full of "horrifying details" about the Spanish treatment of Native Americans during Spain's golden age of exploration. To show that the birth of America was indeed a bloody one might be considered an "unpatriotic act." Yet he feels that historians must "bear witness to the past, including its horrors." Such texts as de las Casas's force us to revise our glorious heroic myths about the birth of America. Compare Gorn's argument with Cynthia Ozick's ("Who Owns Anne Frank?," p. 603) on the importance of Anne Frank's diary as a historical document.

UNDER THE BED

Jincy Willett

Jincy Willett first published this essay in The Massachusetts Review *in 1983. She has since written a collection of short stories,* Jenny and the Jaws of Life *(1987). In this essay, Willett presents the story of a rape, and in the process she presents an argument on the nature of the tragedy of the event.*

On November 6 of last year, at around 8:15 p.m., I was beaten and raped by a man named Raymond C. Moreau, Jr., who had entered our first floor apartment through a living room window while I was taking a shower. This is neither the most significant event in my life nor the most interesting; nevertheless it is a fact, around which cluster many other facts, and the truth is always worth telling. As I approach forty I am learning to value the truth for its own sake; I discover that most people have little use for it, beyond its practical applications, except as the glue which holds together rickety constructs of theory and opinion. As a rule the brighter and better educated select their facts with great care.

I teach philosophy at our mediocre state junior college. My husband teaches physics at the University. He is the real philosopher, like all good scientists, although, like most good scientists, he amiably resists this description. We self-styled philosophers window shop through metaphysics, epistemology and ethics, until we settle on those views which suit us, and then we tailor them to fit our idiosyncracies. The more cynical among us deliberately choose unpopular or bizarre philosophies the more easily to establish a reputation. My husband is a born verificationist. He does not ask unanswerable questions; he does not whine, or posture, or plead, or shake his fist at the stars. His agnosticism, unlike mine, is consistent throughout, utterly free of petulance and despair. It is he who taught me to hold the truth in such high regard, as he has taught me so many things. He believes in a rational universe. How I love him for that! He is worth a hundred humanists, a thousand priests.

My husband was at an evening seminar on November 6 (or, as we now refer to it, with some humor, "The Night of the Thing") and did not return until 9:00, when I was again alone in the apartment. Of course he blamed himself, especially at first, for having been away, for not coming right home when the seminar concluded. I am very glad he stayed for coffee. Had he interrupted us he would have had to do something, as would Raymond C. Moreau, Jr., who had a gun.

As it happened, and for reasons I shall try to explain, when he came home I was under our double bed, asleep. He did not notice that our television set was missing; there were damp towels on the living room floor, and the bedspread was considerably rumpled, but this did not alarm him so much (for I am not very neat) as the apparent fact of my absence. He was smiling when he opened the front door—I know this, because I am usually there to meet him, and he always smiles—but when he sat on our bed to puzzle out where I might be he was not smiling. I imagine that at that moment he looked his age (he is older than I) and that he let his shoulders sag, and that his expression was blank and vulnerable. I cannot imagine how he looked when, bending down to untie his shoes, he saw the fingertips of my right hand protruding from behind the gray chenille spread. Thank god he has a good heart. He dropped to his knees and took my hand and lifted the spread, at which point I woke up. A farce ensued. (Unfunny, as farces so often are.) I immediately realized, from the way his voice cracked when he called my name, that he was badly frightened, as who wouldn't be; since I did not want to frighten him further I determined not to let him see my face, which was bloody and ugly with bruises. "I'm fine," I said, idiotically, in an exaggerated reasonable tone. "What the hell do you mean," he said, and yanked on my arm. "Come out of there." I braced my other arm against the rail. "I will in a minute. I have to tell you something." Then, unfortunately, and rather horribly, I began to laugh, at the picture we would have made to an impartial observer, at our outlandish dialogue. This is usually called the "hysterical laugh," to distinguish it substantially from genuine laughter. Now my husband—and good for him—wasted no time, but gave the bed a hard sideways push. It flew on well-oiled casters and thumped against wall and windowsill; and for the second time in an hour I was well exposed. A pitiful and wrenching sight I must have been, clutching my old red bathrobe tight around me like a cartoon spinster, hiding my ugly face in the dusty green shag. (To this day a breath of dust makes me flush a little, with artificial shame. The body remembers.) Well, then there was reconciliation, and explanation, and generally the sort of behavior you would expect from lovers to whom such a thing has happened. These events were not extraordinary, except to us, and I shall not record them, here or anywhere else. These are private matters. We are very private people.

Raymond C. Moreau was twenty years old and looked thirty. He had long sand-colored hair, which hung in greasy ropes; small deep-set eyes, I don't know what color; thin lips and receding chin; and a rough, ravaged complexion: the right side of his face especially was seamed and pitted. I gave this information to the police artist and he drew me a picture of Charlie Goodby, a paperboy we had in Worcester when I was a little girl. He—the rapist—wore a soiled yellow windbreaker, an undershirt, beige chinos, and jockey shorts. Obviously he must have worn shoes, but I never noticed. His breath was terrible. He looked, as you would expect, like a bad man and a loser.

During the fifteen or so minutes of our association he said the following:

Get it off. Drop it.

In there, lady.

On the bed.

You got a husband? You all alone, you stupid bitch?   10

Spread them, bitch.

You're all alike. All alike. All alike.

Shut up. I'll kill you.

That's right.

Oh. Love. Love, love love, ahhh, love. Ahhh.   15

Stay there. Stay away from the phone. I'll come back and I'll kill you.

That he said "love, love, love" at the point of orgasm does not, in retrospect, strike me as ironic. On the back of his windbreaker the initials "C H S E" and the numerals "1972" were stencilled in brown. "C H S E 1972" is heavier with implication than "love, love, love." "C H S E 1972," now that I think of it, is eloquent as hell.

He never looked me in the eye. But he did not, I think, purposely avoid my eyes. He was not nervous, or ashamed, or fearful. It just never occurred to him to look there.

I used to be afraid of everything. That is, I was a functioning, relatively happy person with a great deal of fear. Spiders, heights, closed-in places—I had all the phobias in moderation. I never answered the phone without first composing myself for bad news—I always waited a beat before I picked up the receiver. (The ring of a telephone on a late sunny afternoon was particularly menacing to me.) Every time I got on a plane I knew I was going to die; and I was ever aware of the dangers inherent in any form of transportation. If I had to enter a dark room I hurried to the light switch, even though my night vision is excellent. At night I never let my hand or my foot dangle over the side of the bed.

Once or twice a year I would experience a few days of serious dread,   20
touched off by something Walter Cronkite said, or a remark overheard at a sherry hour. Once a colleague mentioned a Roman Catholic legend to the effect that the last Pope would be the first non-Italian. "Then what," I asked him, with a false conspiratorial smile. "The end of the world," he said, and lifted his glass as if to toast this hideous prophecy. Oh, I despised him then, and all the laughing doomsayers, who spread terror all unmindful, precisely because they do not know what terror is. Cassandra[1] never laughed.

It is not that I have ever believed the holocaust inevitable, or even probable; rather, I was forced on some occasions to admit the possibility.

---

[1]*Cassandra:* in Greek mythology, the Trojan princess whose prophecy of the fall of Troy to the Greeks was believed by no one. When the city was conquered, she was raped and eventually murdered. [Eds.]

And on these occasions suicide had a certain appeal for me. I would lie beside my sleeping husband and try to think about a universe purged of human beings—surely there was some comfort in this concept; but then, I would be reminded, there would be no concepts either. A universe of particles, normally neutral: black, a pitiless black whole, with no memories, not even of the finest of us. I kept imagining the moment of purging, the dying, the knowing, and terror froze me so I could not even cry. I feared most that we would see it coming, that we would be spared nothing; that I would be separated from my husband, unable to get to him in time—in the last moments of time; or that we would be together but helpless to end in our own way. Plans must be made, I would think: emergency rations of cyanide. But even then we would not both die at once; one would have to endure alone, for however long it took. . . .

When I had had enough of this I always sought to calm myself, with craven prayer, and with the warmth of my husband's body, and the cool dry cross-grain of his skin; and magically, on the third or fourth sleepless night the terror would slip away.

And other nights, when nothing weighed on me at all, and fearless as a movie hero I lay in wait for sleep, I would suddenly have to rise on one elbow, just like a robot, and strain to hear the sound of my husband breathing; and if I could not be sure of it I would brush and push against him, as though by accident, until I had drawn out a sigh or shaken him into motion.

I was not so much neurotic as superstitious, as though through occasional ritualistic suffering I could save us all. I carefully hid this, and only this, from my husband, my talisman, because I did not want to worry or disappoint him; and if he ever suspected the depth of my perverse irrationality he kindly left me to it.

I am not superstitious now. Whatever else he did to me, Raymond C. Moreau measurably improved the quality of my life. My body sometimes jumps or shrinks from the unexpected casual touch, and this can be awkward. But I know no fear. I don't worry any more.

I used to have a good friend. Regina Montgomery is the only woman outside my family for whom I have ever felt physical affection. She is an Amazon, sturdy and large-breasted, with plain coarse features; she smiles like a big cat and is made beautiful. We are opposites physically, emotionally, politically; she is ten years my junior. She pleased me. She was exotic in her proportions and in her strength; earthy, passionate, intense, everything I was not.

She gave me two weeks to start talking on my own about my experience with Raymond C. Moreau. Actually I did not let her see me the first week, until the marks faded; and when she came to the door it was she, not I, whose eyes were red-rimmed and puffy. I remember she had part of a foil-wrapped fruitcake in her hand, and that she kissed my husband on the cheek and hugged him fiercely—it was so strange to see them embracing, she had always been so shy around him; and that she waited for some sign from me and didn't get it, for she kept her distance, fluttering like a great clumsy bird, saying how wonderful I looked. I was cruel to her, surprising myself; I was bland and cheerful and gracious, serving up the fruitcake, making light, maddening conversation, meticulously avoiding even oblique allusion to the single topic she had come to discuss. Her anxiety, so ingenuously displayed, was as comical as it was touching. I kept thinking that at any moment I would let down, but after awhile she left, unsatisfied and bewildered.

"I understood," she told me after, when we finally had it out. "You couldn't stand to be touched in any way." I let her think this. The truth is, I have a mean streak. Obvious people bring out the worst in me. I was not proud of having tortured her like that; I loved her for her genuine concern, her simple candor, her trust. I made a gift of my confession, describing the attack in detail, answering all her questions. It was not enough for her. "You talk as though this—this horror—happened to someone else. How do you feel? Or don't you even know?" "A total stranger invades my home, hurts me, rapes me, calls me names, turns my life into a melodrama. How do you suppose I feel?" She opened her mouth, shut it again. She had decided, I could see, that I was still not "over it." She would bide her time.

And she watched me closely, obviously, over the next few months, impatiently waiting, I suppose, for me to start drinking, or break into sobs at a faculty meeting, or something like that. Armchair psychoanalysis has always annoyed me, it is such an undisciplined activity. I deeply resented such presumption on the part of a friend.

We went out for wine one afternoon and had an awful fight. Our   30
friendship has not recovered.

"All you can say is, you're not changed, not outraged, not afraid, not anything. Christ, you make it seem like a—an embarrassing *incident!*"

"Or a shaggy dog horror story?" I said, smiling, and poured us wine from our third carafe. Wine makes me happy and reckless.

"But you have changed," said Regina, who was not happy at all. "You're icy. Icy. Not like your old reserve. You've become rude, do you know that? Well, not actively, but I swear you look at people with such—I don't know—contempt—"

"You're just a bad sport," I said, teasing her. The difference in our ages was never more apparent. She was flushed, earnest and drunk, and childishly adamant. "Reggie, look. He just got me on a good day, all right? You know how sometimes a movie will make you cry, and other days you laugh yourself sick—"

"That's disgusting! You were violated! Violence was done to you!"   35

"You say that with such an air of discovery."

"And not just to you. To me. To all women."

"Oh, really?" I was angry now. We had argued the political point before, but this was personal. "Then why don't you tell me about it, Regina? It must have been a ghastly experience."

"You are bitter! You see." She was triumphant.

"Only about you. You want me to be a martyr, a role I find repellent   40
in the extreme. I was victimized, yes, but I am not a victim. And I am not a
symbol. I am not in the symbolizing business."

In the end I said she was no different from Raymond Moreau. Always
willing to take a metaphor and run with it, she stared up at me, stupid and
open-mouthed, trying to understand in what way she had been "raping"
me. I could see clear into her skull. I threw my money down in disgust and
left her there. I had meant only, she thought we were all alike, all alike. All
alike.

I padded on damp feet into the living room, wrapped in a big yellow
towel, another towel on my clean hair. I was going to turn on the television, for the comforting noise. He was winding the cord around its handle;
a nice breeze came in the open window. I said, "Hello." I thought to say,
"I've been expecting you," for this was true; I had been expecting him all
my life. I thought to scream, but then the gun was out. Another woman—
Regina—might have screamed without thinking first. I never do anything
without thinking first.

I let my body have the fear. Bodies are designed to handle fright. It
rippled and shuddered, the heart panicked, the blood scampered in terror. I
watched. Really, it was not so bad. It was nothing like the end of the
world.

He lay me on my back, arranged my legs this way and that, pushed
against me like a vacant idiot child; his belly was soft and slack, it rested
on mine light and warm and unmuscled; when my flesh shrank away it followed, spread thick, a cloying intimate layer of skin and fat. His upper
body he kept to himself, propped up on rosy eczematous elbows. I could
see each row in the machine-weave of his undershirt, the irregular rows of
tiny hairs and diamond-shaped skin segments in his neck and jaw, the arch
of his upper teeth, filigreed with silver. If there is a god, I remember thinking, he certainly attends to detail. He hit my face, alternating open palm
and knuckles, with precise unhurried rhythm; and from my mouth came a
terrible sound, as from a grunting pig. But I did not make the sound. I
could never make a sound like that.

At no time did I need to remind myself that this was happening, and   45
not a dream. There was no feeling of displacement. Nor did I wonder why
he did it. After all, he never wondered about me.

Where is the tragedy here? He did not touch me. Of course, it was unpleasant and wearing, but I have been more deeply hurt by rude bus drivers. It was just a collision of machines.

When he left I was faced with the problem of how to tell my husband.
It does not seem now like such a great problem but then I had been under a
strain and could not think clearly. Once, when I was in college, I was playing bridge with some friends in my dormitory room when a girl from down
the hall—a secretive, nervous girl, a bare acquaintance—shuffled in, in

nightgown and slippers, asked if she could sit and watch. She was very pale, apparently exhausted from crying. She sat still for half an hour, peculiarly ominous but circumspect, until finally, blushing with shame, she confessed, in an offhand way, that she had taken a lot of pills and didn't know what to do. There is just no proper way to inform a roomful of strangers that you have attempted suicide. There is no way at all to tell your husband that you have been raped. Should I stay as I was, naked, unseemly? This seemed a gratuitously cruel method, almost amounting to accusation. Look what's been done to me! I put on my robe and wandered through the apartment, looking for a place to light. Well, I could sit down, on the couch for instance, with a single dim lamp on, and greet him that way — but with what words? For a while I thought seriously of cleaning up, combing my hair; I could stay in shadow, avert my face, never mention it at all. But now my body, which had served me so well, let me down: I was tired and could not even lift a cloth to wash myself. I needed a hiding place, where decisions could be held in abeyance; a place of noncommitment. Intending to rest for only a minute I slid underneath the bed, where the monsters used to be; and there were no monsters there, just me; and I slept without dreaming.

To say the least I have never been effusive or easygoing, but before the rape I got along well enough with my colleagues. There was mutual respect. I have no respect for most of them now; they have shown little for me. We live in an age when self-control, competence, discretion — all are thought abnormal, symptomatic of dysfunction. "But how do you *feel*," they all want to know; their eyes betray them, they are so obvious; some of them dare to ask. "I'm sorry," said our Kant and Leibniz[2] specialist, a man I had always credited with sense. "I'm sorry!" "What for," I asked him, infuriated by his gloomy hangdog look, "are you responsible in some way? Did you once have adolescent rape fantasies? Do you believe in a common consciousness?" Shoddy, second-rate thinkers; bullies. Sentimentalists. *Why, look you now, how unworthy a thing you make of me!*

A police detective came to my office with a high school photograph of Raymond Moreau. After I identified him the detective told me he was dead, shot dead by some woman better prepared than I, a woman with her own gun. (What a stupid criminal was Raymond Moreau!) "Well, that's convenient, isn't it?" I said, and shook his hand. And even he, this stolid, unimaginative fellow, even he paused, surprised, disappointed, waiting for some further response. Tears of relief, perhaps; a primitive whoop of joy.

There are so many like Raymond Moreau.   50

My disgust is not unreasonable. I know, because I have talked to my husband, and he agrees with me. He does urge me, from time to time, not

---

[2]*Immanuel Kant* (1724–1804), German philosopher; *Gottfried Wilhelm Leibniz* (1646–1716), German philosopher. [Eds.]

to be too harsh: they mean no harm, he says. He contends that people usually do the best they can. I suppose he is right, although I do wonder if this is not really a tautology in lush disguise. He has always been a compassionate man. He alone sees me as I am, and loves me as he loves the truth.

We are closer now than ever. We seldom go out; neither of us spends unnecessary time at school. Evenings find us here, laughing, talking into the night. We seem again to have as much to say to each other as when we first were lovers. I have fixed up the apartment quite differently—the bedroom is completely rearranged, with all new linens and a white bedspread and a thick white carpet. (I happen to like white. White does not symbolize.) Often we have picnics, as we did when we were young, only now we hold them indoors on the living room floor; and we drink good wine, '66 burgundies, '61 bordeaux, rich wines of every hue from purple black to brick red. And I have never been so content.

But lately, and too often, as we lie in the dark, I curl away from him, peaceful and fearless, he rises, stealthy, gentle, and leans over me, watching my face; I can feel his breath on my cheek; and I must give him a sign, a sigh, a dreamy moan to ease his mind. Just like a robot he must rise, prompted by my old foolish impulse, unworthy of him, as though by watching he could keep me safe; as though the universe concerned itself with us.

There's the violation. There's the damage, and the tragedy.

QUESTIONS

1. What are Willett's reasons for comparing her friend Regina and the policeman to Raymond Moreau?
2. How does Willett structure her argument?
3. Consider how this essay comments on Willett's opening statement about truth, that "the truth is always worth telling," but that "most people have little use for it."
4. After presenting the facts of the rape, Willett asks, "Where is the tragedy here? . . . It was just a collision of machines" (paragraph 46). What does she mean?
5. Why does Willett refuse to be characterized as a victim? Comment on how the term *victim* is currently used in American society.
6. According to Willett, what, finally, is the tragedy in this case?

MAKING CONNECTIONS

Referring to Elliot Gorn's discussion of facts and interpretation of history (p. 648), comment on Willett's view of facts and truth, and her interpretation of the facts she presents.

THINGS

W. S. Merwin

W. S. Merwin was born in New York City in 1927. A graduate of Princeton University, Merwin spent his early adulthood in Europe studying languages and working as a tutor and translator. He published his first collection of poetry, A Mask for Janus, *in 1952 and has since produced more than twenty subsequent volumes, including* The Lice *(1969), the Pulitzer Prize-winning* The Carrier of Ladders *(1970),* The Vixen *(1996), and* The River Sound *(1999). He is also the author of numerous translations, most recently Dante's* Purgatory *(2000), in addition to essays and memoirs. An active environmentalist, Merwin has lived since the early 1970s on a former pineapple plantation in Hawaii that he has endeavored to return to its natural rainforest state. Of his goals as a poet he has said, "I think there's a kind of desperate hope in poetry now that one really wants, hopelessly, to serve the world. One is trying to say everything that can be said for the things that one loves while there's still time."*

Possessor
At the approach of winter we are there.
Better than friends, in your sorrows we take no pleasure,
We have none of our own and no memory but yours.
We are the anchor of your future.   5
Patient as a border of beggars, each hand holding out its whole treasure,

We will be all the points on your compass.
We will give you interest on yourself as you deposit yourself with us.
Be a gentleman: you acquired us when you needed us,
We do what we can to please, we have some beauty, we are helpless,   10
Depend on us.

QUESTIONS

1. Note the poem's two-part structure. How does it strengthen the rhetorical strategies the things are using to convince the possessor?
2. Why are the things addressing the possessor in this manner?

MAKING CONNECTIONS

Consider your own possessions. What demands do they make upon you? If they could speak, how might they address you?

Social Sciences and Public Affairs

WHAT'S SO BAD ABOUT HATE

Andrew Sullivan

Andrew Sullivan was born in England in 1963 but has been a U.S. resident for many years. A former writer and editor with The New Republic, *he is the author of* Virtually Normal: An Argument about Homosexuality (1995), *which advocates full legal equality for gay men and lesbians, including open service in the military and same-sex marriage. However, on many issues, Sullivan is an outspoken social conservative, as suggested by the following essay, which originally appeared in the* New York Times Magazine *in 1999. More information on Sullivan can be found in the headnote on page 537.*

I

I wonder what was going on in John William King's head two years ago when he tied James Byrd Jr.'s feet to the back of a pickup truck and dragged him three miles down a road in rural Texas. King and two friends had picked up Byrd, who was black, when he was walking home, half-drunk, from a party. As part of a bonding ritual in their fledgling white supremacist group, the three men took Byrd to a remote part of town, beat him and chained his legs together before attaching them to the truck. Pathologists at King's trial testified that Byrd was probably alive and conscious until his body finally hit a culvert and split in two. When King was offered a chance to say something to Byrd's family at the trial, he smirked and uttered an obscenity.

We know all these details now, many months later. We know quite a large amount about what happened before and after. But I am still drawn,

664

again and again, to the flash of ignition, the moment when fear and loathing became hate, the instant of transformation when King became hunter and Byrd became prey.

What was that? And what was it when Buford Furrow Jr., longtime member of the Aryan Nations,[1] calmly walked up to a Filipino-American mailman he happened to spot, asked him to mail a letter and then shot him at point-blank range? Or when Russell Henderson beat Matthew Shepard, a young gay man, to a pulp, removed his shoes and then, with the help of a friend, tied him to a post, like a dead coyote, to warn off others?

For all our documentation of these crimes and others, our political and moral disgust at them, our morbid fascination with them, our sensitivity to their social meaning, we seem at times to have no better idea now than we ever had of what exactly they were about. About what that moment means when, for some reason or other, one human being asserts absolute, immutable superiority over another. About not the violence, but what the violence expresses. About what—exactly—hate is. And what our own part in it may be.

I find myself wondering what hate actually is in part because we have created an entirely new offense in American criminal law—a "hate crime"—to combat it. And barely a day goes by without someone somewhere declaring war against it. Last month President Clinton called for an expansion of hate-crime laws as "what America needs in our battle against hate." A couple of weeks later, Senator John McCain used a campaign speech to denounce the "hate" he said poisoned the land. New York's Mayor, Rudolph Giuliani, recently tried to stop the Million Youth March in Harlem on the grounds that the event was organized by people "involved in hate marches and hate rhetoric."

The media concurs in its emphasis. In 1985, there were 11 mentions of "hate crimes" in the national media database Nexis. By 1990, there were more than a thousand. In the first six months of 1999, there were 7,000. "Sexy fun is one thing," wrote a *New York Times* reporter about sexual assaults in Woodstock '99's mosh pit. "But this was an orgy of lewdness tinged with hate." And when Benjamin Smith marked the Fourth of July this year by targeting blacks, Asians and Jews for murder in Indiana and Illinois, the story wasn't merely about a twisted young man who had emerged on the scene. As the *Times* put it, "Hate arrived in the neighborhoods of Indiana University, in Bloomington, in the early-morning darkness."

But what exactly was this thing that arrived in the early-morning darkness? For all our zeal to attack hate, we still have a remarkably vague idea of what it actually is. A single word, after all, tells us less, not more. For all its emotional punch, "hate" is far less nuanced an idea than prejudice, or bigotry, or bias, or anger, or even mere aversion to others. Is it to stand in for all these varieties of human experience—and everything in between? If

5

---

[1]*Aryan Nations:* an antiminority hate group. [Eds.]

so, then the war against it will be so vast as to be quixotic. Or is "hate" to stand for a very specific idea or belief, or set of beliefs, with a very specific object or group of objects? Then waging war against it is almost certainly unconstitutional. Perhaps these kinds of questions are of no concern to those waging war on hate. Perhaps it is enough for them that they share a sentiment that there is too much hate and never enough vigilance in combating it. But sentiment is a poor basis for law, and a dangerous tool in politics. It is better to leave some unwinnable wars unfought.

II

Hate is everywhere. Human beings generalize all the time, ahead of time, about everyone and everything. A large part of it may even be hardwired. At some point in our evolution, being able to know beforehand who was friend or foe was not merely a matter of philosophical reflection. It was a matter of survival. And even today it seems impossible to feel a loyalty without also feeling a disloyalty, a sense of belonging without an equal sense of unbelonging. We're social beings. We associate. Therefore we disassociate. And although it would be comforting to think that the one could happen without the other, we know in reality that it doesn't. How many patriots are there who have never felt a twinge of xenophobia?

Of course by hate, we mean something graver and darker than this kind of lazy prejudice. But the closer you look at this distinction, the fuzzier it gets. Much of the time, we harbor little or no malice toward people of other backgrounds or places or ethnicities or ways of life. But then a car cuts you off at an intersection and you find yourself noticing immediately that the driver is a woman, or black, or old, or fat, or white, or male. Or you are walking down a city street at night and hear footsteps quickening behind you. You look around and see that it is a white woman and not a black man, and you are instantly relieved. These impulses are so spontaneous they are almost involuntary. But where did they come from? The mindless need to be mad at someone—anyone—or the unconscious eruption of a darker prejudice festering within?

In 1993, in San Jose, Calif., two neighbors—one heterosexual, one homosexual—were engaged in a protracted squabble over grass clippings. (The full case is recounted in *Hate Crimes,* by James B. Jacobs and Kimberly Potter.) The gay man regularly mowed his lawn without a grass catcher, which prompted his neighbor to complain on many occasions that grass clippings spilled over onto his driveway. Tensions grew until one day, the gay man mowed his front yard, spilling clippings onto his neighbor's driveway, prompting the straight man to yell an obscene and common anti-gay insult. The wrangling escalated. At one point, the gay man agreed to collect the clippings from his neighbor's driveway but then later found them dumped on his own porch. A fracas ensued with the gay man spraying the straight man's son with a garden hose, and the son hitting and kick-

10

ing the gay man several times, yelling anti-gay slurs. The police were called, and the son was eventually convicted of a hate-motivated assault, a felony. But what was the nature of the hate: anti-gay bias, or suburban property-owner madness?

Or take the Labor Day parade last year in Broad Channel, a small island in Jamaica Bay, Queens. Almost everyone there is white, and in recent years a group of local volunteer firefighters has taken to decorating a pickup truck for the parade in order to win the prize for "funniest float." Their themes have tended toward the outrageously provocative. Beginning in 1995, they won prizes for floats depicting "Hasidic Park," "Gooks of Hazzard" and "Happy Gays." Last year, they called their float "Black to the Future, Broad Channel 2098." They imagined their community a century hence as a largely black enclave, with every stereotype imaginable: watermelons, basketballs and so on. At one point during the parade, one of them mimicked the dragging death of James Byrd. It was caught on videotape, and before long the entire community was depicted as a caldron of hate.

It's an interesting case, because the float was indisputably in bad taste and the improvisation on the Byrd killing was grotesque. But was it hate? The men on the float were local heroes for their volunteer work; they had no record of bigoted activity, and were not members of any racist organizations. In previous years, they had made fun of many other groups and saw themselves more as provocateurs than bigots. When they were described as racists, it came as a shock to them. They apologized for poor taste but refused to confess to bigotry. "The people involved aren't horrible people," protested a local woman. "Was it a racist act? I don't know. Are they racists? I don't think so."

If hate is a self-conscious activity, she has a point. The men were primarily motivated by the desire to shock and to reflect what they thought was their community's culture. Their display was not aimed at any particular black people, or at any blacks who lived in Broad Channel—almost none do. But if hate is primarily an unconscious activity, then the matter is obviously murkier. And by taking the horrific lynching of a black man as a spontaneous object of humor, the men were clearly advocating indifference to it. Was this an aberrant excess? Or the real truth about the men's feelings toward African-Americans? Hate or tastelessness? And how on earth is anyone, even perhaps the firefighters themselves, going to know for sure?

Or recall H. L. Mencken.[2] He shared in the anti-Semitism of his time with more alacrity than most and was an indefatigable racist. "It is impossible," he wrote in his diary, "to talk anything resembling discretion or judgment into a colored woman. They are all essentially childlike, and even hard experience does not teach them anything." He wrote at another time of the "psychological stigmata" of the "Afro-American race." But it is also true that, during much of his life, day to day, Mencken conducted himself

---

[2]*H. L. Mencken* (1880–1956): American writer, editor, and critic. [Eds.]

with no regard to race, and supported a politics that was clearly integra-
tionist. As the editor of his diary has pointed out, Mencken published
many black authors in his magazine, *The Mercury,* and lobbied on their
behalf with his publisher, Alfred A. Knopf. The last thing Mencken ever
wrote was a diatribe against racial segregation in Baltimore's public parks.
He was good friends with leading black writers and journalists, including
James Weldon Johnson, Walter White and George S. Schuyler, and played
an underappreciated role in promoting the Harlem Renaissance.

What would our modern view of hate do with Mencken? Probably ig-   15
nore him, or change the subject. But, with regard to hate, I know lots of
people like Mencken. He reminds me of conservative friends who oppose
almost every measure for homosexual equality yet genuinely delight in the
company of their gay friends. It would be easier for me to think of them as
haters, and on paper, perhaps, there is a good case that they are. But in real
life, I know they are not. Some of them clearly harbor no real malice toward me or other homosexuals whatsoever.

They are as hard to figure out as those liberal friends who support
every gay rights measure they have ever heard of but do anything to avoid
going into a gay bar with me. I have to ask myself in the same, frustrating
kind of way: are they liberal bigots or bigoted liberals? Or are they neither
bigots nor liberals, but merely people?

III

Hate used to be easier to understand. When Sartre[3] described anti-
Semitism in his 1946 essay "Anti-Semite and Jew," he meant a very specific
array of firmly held prejudices, with a history, an ideology and even a
pseudo-science to back them up. He meant a systematic attempt to demo-
nize and eradicate an entire race. If you go to the Web site of the World
Church of the Creator, the organization that inspired young Benjamin
Smith to murder in Illinois earlier this year, you will find a similarly
bizarre, pseudorational ideology. The kind of literature read by Buford
Furrow before he rained terror on a Jewish kindergarten last month and
then killed a mailman because of his color is full of the same paranoid
loopiness. And when we talk about hate, we often mean this kind of phenomenon.

But this brand of hatred is mercifully rare in the United States. These
professional maniacs are to hate what serial killers are to murder. They
should certainly not be ignored; but they represent what Harold Meyerson,
writing in *Salon,* called "niche haters": cold-blooded, somewhat deranged,
often poorly socialized psychopaths. In a free society with relatively easy
access to guns, they will always pose a menace.

---

[3]*Jean-Paul Sartre* (1905–1980): French philosopher and writer. [Eds.]

But their menace is a limited one, and their hatred is hardly typical of anything very widespread. Take Buford Furrow. He famously issued a "wake-up call" to "kill Jews" in Los Angeles, before he peppered a Jewish community center with gunfire. He did this in a state with two Jewish female Senators, in a city with a large, prosperous Jewish population, in a country where out of several million Jewish Americans, a total of 66 were reported by the F.B.I. as the targets of hate-crime assaults in 1997. However despicable Furrow's actions were, it would require a very large stretch to describe them as representative of anything but the deranged fringe of an American subculture.

Most hate is more common and more complicated, with as many vari-   20 eties as there are varieties of love. Just as there is possessive love and needy love; family love and friendship; romantic love and unrequited love; passion and respect, affection and obsession, so hatred has its shadings. There is hate that fears, and hate that merely feels contempt; there is hate that expresses power, and hate that comes from powerlessness; there is revenge, and there is hate that comes from envy. There is hate that was love, and hate that is a curious expression of love. There is hate of the other, and hate of something that reminds us too much of ourselves. There is the oppressor's hate, and the victim's hate. There is hate that burns slowly, and hate that fades. And there is hate that explodes, and hate that never catches fire.

The modern words that we have created to describe the varieties of hate — "sexism," "racism," "anti-Semitism," "homophobia" — tell us very little about any of this. They tell us merely the identities of the victims; they don't reveal the identities of the perpetrators, or what they think, or how they feel. They don't even tell us how the victims feel. And this simplicity is no accident. Coming from the theories of Marxist and post-Marxist academics, these "isms" are far better at alleging structures of power than at delineating the workings of the individual heart or mind. In fact, these "isms" can exist without mentioning individuals at all.

We speak of institutional racism, for example, as if an institution can feel anything. We talk of "hate" as an impersonal noun, with no hater specified. But when these abstractions are actually incarnated, when someone feels something as a result of them, when a hater actually interacts with a victim, the picture changes. We find that hates are often very different phenomena one from another, that they have very different psychological dynamics, that they might even be better understood by not seeing them as varieties of the same thing at all.

There is, for example, the now unfashionable distinction between reasonable hate and unreasonable hate. In recent years, we have become accustomed to talking about hates as if they were all equally indefensible, as if it could never be the case that some hates might be legitimate, even necessary. But when some 800,000 Tutsis are murdered under the auspices of a Hutu regime in Rwanda, and when a few thousand Hutus are killed in revenge, the hates are not commensurate. Genocide is not an event like a hurricane, in which damage is random and universal; it is a planned and often merciless attack of one group upon another. The hate of the perpetrators is a monstrosity. The hate of the victims, and their survivors, is justified. What else, one wonders, were surviving Jews supposed to feel toward Germans after the Holocaust? Or, to a different degree, South African blacks after apartheid? If the victims overcome this hate, it is a supreme moral achievement. But if they don't, the victims are not as culpable as the perpetrators. So the hatred of Serbs for Kosovars today can never be equated with the hatred of Kosovars for Serbs.

Hate, like much of human feeling, is not rational, but it usually has its reasons. And it cannot be understood, let alone condemned, without knowing them. Similarly, the hate that comes from knowledge is always different from the hate that comes from ignorance. It is one of the most foolish clichés of our time that prejudice is always rooted in ignorance, and can usually be overcome by familiarity with the objects of our loathing. The racism of many Southern whites under segregation was not appeased by familiarity with Southern blacks; the virulent loathing of Tutsis by many Hutus was not undermined by living next door to them for centuries. Theirs was a hatred that sprang, for whatever reasons, from experience. It cannot easily be compared with, for example, the resilience of anti-Semitism in Japan, or hostility to immigration in areas where immigrants are unknown, or fear of homosexuals by people who have never knowingly met one.

The same familiarity is an integral part of what has become known as "sexism." Sexism isn't, properly speaking, a prejudice at all. Few men live without knowledge or constant awareness of women. Every single sexist man was born of a woman, and is likely to be sexually attracted to women. His hostility is going to be very different than that of, say, a reclusive member of the Aryan Nations toward Jews he has never met.

In her book *The Anatomy of Prejudices,* the psychotherapist Elisabeth Young-Bruehl proposes a typology of three distinct kinds of hate: obsessive, hysterical and narcissistic. It's not an exhaustive analysis, but it's a beginning in any serious attempt to understand hate rather than merely declaring war on it. The obsessives, for Young-Bruehl, are those, like the Nazis or Hutus, who fantasize a threat from a minority, and obsessively try to rid themselves of it. For them, the very existence of the hated group is threatening. They often describe their loathing in almost physical terms: they experience what Patrick Buchanan, in reference to homosexuals, once described as a "visceral recoil" from the objects of their detestation. They often describe those they hate as diseased or sick, in need of a cure. Or they talk of "cleansing" them, as the Hutus talked of the Tutsis, or call them "cockroaches," as Yitzhak Shamir[4] called the Palestinians. If you read material from the Family Research Council, it is clear that the group regards

25

---

[4]*Yitzhak Shamir* (b. 1915): former Israeli prime minister. [Eds.]

homosexuals as similar contaminants. A recent posting on its Web site about syphilis among gay men was headlined, "Unclean."

Hysterical haters have a more complicated relationship with the objects of their aversion. In Young-Bruehl's words, hysterical prejudice is a prejudice that "a person uses unconsciously to appoint a group to act out in the world forbidden sexual and sexually aggressive desires that the person has repressed." Certain kinds of racists fit this pattern. White loathing of blacks is, for some people, at least partly about sexual and physical envy. A certain kind of white racist sees in black America all those impulses he wishes most to express himself but cannot. He idealizes in "blackness" a sexual freedom, a physical power, a Dionysian[5] release that he detests but also longs for. His fantasy may not have any basis in reality, but it is powerful nonetheless. It is a form of love-hate, and it is impossible to understand the nuances of racism in, say, the American South, or in British Imperial India, without it.

Unlike the obsessives, the hysterical haters do not want to eradicate the objects of their loathing; rather they want to keep them in some kind of permanent and safe subjugation in order to indulge the attraction of their repulsion. A recent study, for example, found that the men most likely to be opposed to equal rights for homosexuals were those most likely to be aroused by homoerotic imagery. This makes little rational sense, but it has a certain psychological plausibility. If homosexuals were granted equality, then the hysterical gay-hater might panic that his repressed passions would run out of control, overwhelming him and the world he inhabits.

A narcissistic hate, according to Young-Bruehl's definition, is sexism. In its most common form, it is rooted in many men's inability even to imagine what it is to be a woman, a failing rarely challenged by men's control of our most powerful public social institutions. Women are not so much hated by most men as simply ignored in nonsexual contexts, or never conceived of as true equals. The implicit condescension is mixed, in many cases, with repressed and sublimated erotic desire. So the unawareness of women is sometimes commingled with a deep longing or contempt for them.

Each hate, of course, is more complicated than this, and in any one person hate can assume a uniquely configured combination of these types. So there are hysterical sexists who hate women because they need them so much, and narcissistic sexists who hardly notice that women exist, and sexists who oscillate between one of these positions and another. And there are gay-bashers who are threatened by masculine gay men and gay-haters who feel repulsed by effeminate ones. The soldier who beat his fellow soldier Barry Winchell to death with a baseball bat in July had earlier lost a fight to him. It was the image of a macho gay man—and the shame of being bested by him—that the vengeful soldier had to obliterate, even if he

30

---

[5]*Dionysian:* orgiastic. [Eds.]

needed a gang of accomplices and a weapon to do so. But the murderers of Matthew Shepard seem to have had a different impulse: a visceral disgust at the thought of any sexual contact with an effeminate homosexual. Their anger was mixed with mockery, as the cruel spectacle at the side of the road suggested.

In the same way, the pathological anti-Semitism of Nazi Germany was obsessive, inasmuch as it tried to cleanse the world of Jews; but also, as Daniel Jonah Goldhagen shows in his book, *Hitler's Willing Executioners,* hysterical. The Germans were mysteriously compelled as well as repelled by Jews, devising elaborate ways, like death camps and death marches, to keep them alive even as they killed them. And the early Nazi phobia of interracial sex suggests as well a lingering erotic quality to the relationship, partaking of exactly the kind of sexual panic that persists among some homosexual-haters and anti-miscegenation racists. So the concept of "homophobia," like that of "sexism" and "racism," is often a crude one. All three are essentially cookie-cutter formulas that try to understand human impulses merely through the one-dimensional identity of the victims, rather than through the thoughts and feelings of the haters and hated.

This is deliberate. The theorists behind these "isms" want to ascribe all blame to one group in society—the "oppressors"—and render specific others—the "victims"—completely blameless. And they want to do this in order in part to side unequivocally with the underdog. But it doesn't take a genius to see how this approach, too, can generate its own form of bias. It can justify blanket condemnations of whole groups of people—white straight males for example—purely because of the color of their skin or the nature of their sexual orientation. And it can condescendingly ascribe innocence to whole groups of others. It does exactly what hate does: it hammers the uniqueness of each individual into the anvil of group identity. And it postures morally over the result.

In reality, human beings and human acts are far more complex, which is why these "isms" and the laws they have fomented are continually coming under strain and challenge. Once again, hate wriggles free of its definers. It knows no monolithic groups of haters and hated. Like a river, it has many eddies, backwaters and rapids. So there are anti-Semites who actually admire what they think of as Jewish power, and there are gay-haters who look up to homosexuals and some who want to sleep with them. And there are black racists, racist Jews, sexist women and anti-Semitic homosexuals. Of course there are.

IV

Once you start thinking of these phenomena less as the "isms" of sexism, racism and "homophobia," once you think of them as independent psychological responses, it's also possible to see how they can work in a bewildering variety of ways in a bewildering number of people. To take one obvious and sad oddity: people who are demeaned and objectified in society may develop an aversion to their tormentors that is more hateful in its expression than the prejudice they have been subjected to. The F.B.I. statistics on hate crimes throws up an interesting point. In America in the 1990's, blacks were up to three times as likely as whites to commit a hate crime, to express their hate by physically attacking their targets or their property. Just as sexual abusers have often been victims of sexual abuse, and wife-beaters often grew up in violent households, so hate criminals may often be members of hated groups.

Even the Columbine murderers were in some sense victims of hate before 35 they were purveyors of it. Their classmates later admitted that Dylan Klebold and Eric Harris were regularly called "faggots" in the corridors and class-rooms of Columbine High and that nothing was done to prevent or stop the harassment. This climate of hostility doesn't excuse the actions of Klebold and Harris, but it does provide a more plausible context. If they had been black, had routinely been called "nigger" in the school and had then ex-ploded into a shooting spree against white students, the response to the mat-ter might well have been different. But the hate would have been the same. In other words, hate-victims are often hate-victimizers as well. This doesn't mean that all hates are equivalent, or that some are not more justified than others. It means merely that hate goes both ways; and if you try to regulate it among some, you will find yourself forced to regulate it among others.

It is no secret, for example, that some of the most vicious anti-Semites in America are black, and that some of the most virulent anti-Catholic big-ots in America are gay. At what point, we are increasingly forced to ask, do these phenomena become as indefensible as white racism or religious toleration of anti-gay bigotry? That question becomes all the more difficult when we notice that it is often minorities who commit some of the most hate-filled offenses against what they see as their oppressors. It was the mainly gay AIDS activist group Act Up that perpetrated the hateful act of desecrating Communion hosts at a Mass at St. Patrick's Cathedral in New York. And here is the playwright Tony Kushner, who is gay, responding to the Matthew Shepard beating in *The Nation* magazine: "Pope John Paul II endorses murder. He, too, knows the price of discrimination, having de-clared anti-Semitism a sin. . . . He knows that discrimination kills. But when the Pope heard the news about Matthew Shepard, he, too, worried about spin. And so, on the subject of gay-bashing, the Pope and his cardi-nals and his bishops and priests maintain their cynical political silence. . . . To remain silent is to endorse murder." Kushner went on to describe the Pope as a "homicidal liar."

Maybe the passion behind these words is justified. But it seems clear enough to me that Kushner is expressing hate toward the institution of the Catholic Church, and all those who perpetuate its doctrines. How else to interpret the way in which he accuses the Pope of cynicism, lying and mur-der? And how else either to understand the brutal parody of religious voca-tions expressed by the Sisters of Perpetual Indulgence, a group of gay men who dress in drag as nuns and engage in sexually explicit performances in public? Or T-shirts with the words "Recovering Catholic" on them, hot items among some gay and lesbian activists? The implication that someone's religious faith is a mental illness is clearly an expression of contempt. If that isn't covered under the definition of hate speech, what is?

Or take the following sentence: "The act male homosexuals commit is ugly and repugnant and afterwards they are disgusted with themselves. They drink and take drugs to palliate this, but they are disgusted with the act and they are always changing partners and cannot be really happy." The thoughts of Pat Robertson or Patrick Buchanan? Actually that sentence was written by Gertrude Stein,[6] one of the century's most notable lesbians. Or take the following, about how beating up "black boys like that made us feel *good* inside. . . . Every time I drove my foot into his [expletive], I felt better." It was written to describe the brutal assault of an innocent bystander for the sole reason of his race. By the end of the attack, the victim had blood gushing from his mouth as his attackers stomped on his genitals. Are we less appalled when we learn that the actual sentence was how beating up "white boys like that made us feel *good* inside. . . . Every time I drove my foot into his [expletive], I felt better?" It was written by Nathan McCall, an African-American who later in life became a successful journalist at *The Washington Post* and published his memoir of this "hate crime" to much acclaim.

In fact, one of the stranger aspects of hate is that the prejudice expressed by a group in power may often be milder in expression than the prejudice felt by the marginalized. After all, if you already enjoy privilege, you may not feel the anger that turns bias into hate. You may not need to. For this reason, most white racism may be more influential in society than most black racism — but also more calmly expressed.

So may other forms of minority loathing — especially hatred within minorities. I'm sure that black conservatives like Clarence Thomas or Thomas Sowell have experienced their fair share of white racism. But I wonder whether it has ever reached the level of intensity of the hatred directed toward them by other blacks? In several years of being an openly gay writer and editor, I have experienced the gamut of responses to my sexual orientation. But I have only directly experienced articulated, passionate hate from other homosexuals. I have been accused over the years by other homosexuals of being a sellout, a hypocrite, a traitor, a sexist, a racist, a narcissist, a snob. I've been called selfish, callous, hateful, self-hating and malevolent. At a reading, a group of lesbian activists portrayed my face on a poster within the crossfires of a gun. Nothing from the religious right has come close to such vehemence.

I am not complaining. No harm has ever come to me or my property, and much of the criticism is rooted in the legitimate expression of political

40

---

[6]These words were not written by Gertrude Stein. Ernest Hemingway wrote them and attributed them to Stein in *A Moveable Feast* (1964). [Eds.]

differences. But the visceral tone and style of the gay criticism can only be described as hateful. It is designed to wound personally, and it often does. But its intensity comes in part, one senses, from the pain of being excluded for so long, of anger long restrained bubbling up and directing itself more aggressively toward an alleged traitor than an alleged enemy. It is the hate of the hated. And it can be the most hateful hate of all. For this reason, hate-crime laws may themselves be an oddly biased category—biased against the victims of hate. Racism is everywhere, but the already victimized might be more desperate, more willing to express it violently. And so more prone to come under the suspicious eye of the law.

V

And why is hate for a group worse than hate for a person? In Laramie, Wyo., the now-famous epicenter of "homophobia," where Matthew Shepard was brutally beaten to death, vicious murders are not unknown. In the previous 12 months, a 15-year-old pregnant girl was found east of the town with 17 stab wounds. Her 38-year-old boyfriend was apparently angry that she had refused an abortion and left her in the Wyoming foothills to bleed to death. In the summer of 1998, an 8-year-old Laramie girl was abducted, raped and murdered by a pedophile, who disposed of her young body in a garbage dump. Neither of these killings was deemed a hate crime, and neither would be designated as such under any existing hate-crime law. Perhaps because of this, one crime is an international legend; the other two are virtually unheard of.

But which crime was more filled with hate? Once you ask the question, you realize how difficult it is to answer. Is it more hateful to kill a stranger or a lover? Is it more hateful to kill a child than an adult? Is it more hateful to kill your own child than another's? Under the law before the invention of hate crimes, these decisions didn't have to be taken. But under the law after hate crimes, a decision is essential. A decade ago, a murder was a murder. Now, in the era when group hate has emerged as our cardinal social sin, it all depends.

The supporters of laws against hate crimes argue that such crimes should be disproportionately punished because they victimize more than the victim. Such crimes, these advocates argue, spread fear, hatred and panic among whole populations, and therefore merit more concern. But, of course, all crimes victimize more than the victim, and spread alarm in the society at large. Just think of the terrifying church shooting in Texas only two weeks ago.[7] In fact, a purely random murder may be even more terri-

---

[7]*Church shooting:* On September 15, 1999, Larry Gene Ashbrook fired into an evening youth service at Wedgwood Baptist Church in Fort Worth, Texas, killing six people before taking his own life. [Eds.]

fying than a targeted one, since the entire community, and not just a part of it, feels threatened. High rates of murder, robbery, assault and burglary victimize everyone, by spreading fear, suspicion and distress everywhere. Which crime was more frightening to more people this summer: the mentally ill Buford Furrow's crazed attacks in Los Angeles, killing one, or Mark Barton's murder of his own family and several random day-traders in Atlanta, killing 12? Almost certainly the latter. But only Furrow was guilty of "hate."

One response to this objection is that certain groups feel fear more in-   45
tensely than others because of a history of persecution or intimidation. But doesn't this smack of a certain condescension toward minorities? Why, after all, should it be assumed that gay men or black women or Jews, for example, are as a group more easily intimidated than others? Surely in any of these communities there will be a vast range of responses, from panic to concern to complete indifference. The assumption otherwise is the kind of crude generalization the law is supposed to uproot in the first place. And among these groups, there are also likely to be vast differences. To equate a population once subjected to slavery with a population of Mexican immigrants or third-generation Holocaust survivors is to equate the unequatable. In fact, it is to set up a contest of vulnerability in which one group vies with another to establish its particular variety of suffering, a contest that can have no dignified solution.

Rape, for example, is not classified as a "hate crime" under most existing laws, pitting feminists against ethnic groups in a battle for recognition. If, as a solution to this problem, everyone, except the white straight able-bodied male, is regarded as a possible victim of a hate crime, then we have simply created a two-tier system of justice in which racial profiling is reversed, and white straight men are presumed guilty before being proven innocent, and members of minorities are free to hate them as gleefully as they like. But if we include the white straight male in the litany of potential victims, then we have effectively abolished the notion of a hate crime altogether. For if every crime is possibly a hate crime, then it is simply another name for crime. All we will have done is widened the search for possible bigotry, ratcheted up the sentences for everyone and filled the jails up even further.

Hate-crime-law advocates counter that extra penalties should be imposed on hate crimes because our society is experiencing an "epidemic" of such crimes. Mercifully, there is no hard evidence to support this notion. The Federal Government has only been recording the incidence of hate crimes in this decade, and the statistics tell a simple story. In 1992, there were 6,623 hate-crime incidents reported to the F.B.I. by a total of 6,181 agencies, covering 51 percent of the population. In 1996, there were 8,734 incidents reported by 11,355 agencies, covering 84 percent of the population. That number dropped to 8,049 in 1997. These numbers are, of course, hazardous. They probably underreport the incidence of such crimes, but they are the only reliable figures we have. Yet even if they are faulty as an absolute number, they do not show an epidemic of "hate crimes" in the 1990's.

Is there evidence that the crimes themselves are becoming more vicious? None. More than 60 percent of recorded hate crimes in America involve no violent, physical assault against another human being at all, and, again, according to the F.B.I., that proportion has not budged much in the 1990's. These impersonal attacks are crimes against property or crimes of "intimidation." Murder, which dominates media coverage of hate crimes, is a tiny proportion of the total. Of the 8,049 hate crimes reported to the F.B.I. in 1997, a total of eight were murders. Eight. The number of hate crimes that were aggravated assaults (generally involving a weapon) in 1997 is less than 15 percent of the total. That's 1,237 assaults too many, of course, but to put it in perspective, compare it with a reported 1,022,492 "equal opportunity" aggravated assaults in America in the same year. The number of hate crimes that were physical assaults is half the total. That's 4,000 assaults too many, of course, but to put it in perspective, it compares with around 3.8 million "equal opportunity" assaults in America annually.

The truth is, the distinction between a crime filled with personal hate and a crime filled with group hate is an essentially arbitrary one. It tells us nothing interesting about the psychological contours of the specific actor or his specific victim. It is a function primarily of politics, of special interest groups carving out particular protections for themselves, rather than a serious response to a serious criminal concern. In such an endeavor, hate-crime-law advocates cram an entire world of human motivations into an immutable, tiny box called hate, and hope to have solved a problem. But nothing has been solved; and some harm may even have been done.

In an attempt to repudiate a past that treated people differently because of the color of their skin, or their sex, or religion or sexual orientation, we may merely create a future that permanently treats people differently because of the color of their skin, or their sex, religion or sexual orientation. This notion of a hate crime, and the concept of hate that lies behind it, takes a psychological mystery and turns it into a facile political artifact. Rather than compounding this error and extending it even further, we should seriously consider repealing the concept altogether.

To put it another way: Violence can and should be stopped by the government. In a free society, hate can't and shouldn't be. The boundaries between hate and prejudice and between prejudice and opinion and between opinion and truth are so complicated and blurred that any attempt to construct legal and political fire walls is a doomed and illiberal venture. We know by now that hate will never disappear from human consciousness; in fact, it is probably, at some level, definitive of it. We know after decades of education measures that hate is not caused merely by ignorance; and after decades of legislation, that it isn't caused entirely by law.

To be sure, we have made much progress. Anyone who argues that America is as inhospitable to minorities and to women today as it has been in the past has not read much history. And we should, of course, be vigilant that our most powerful institutions, most notably the government, do not actively or formally propagate hatred; and insure that the violent expression of hate is curtailed by the same rules that punish all violent expression.

But after that, in an increasingly diverse culture, it is crazy to expect that hate, in all its variety, can be eradicated. A free country will always mean a hateful country. This may not be fair, or perfect, or admirable, but it is reality, and while we need not endorse it, we should not delude ourselves into thinking we can prevent it. That is surely the distinction between toleration and tolerance. Tolerance is the eradication of hate; toleration is co-existence despite it. We might do better as a culture and as a polity if we concentrated more on achieving the latter rather than the former. We would certainly be less frustrated.

And by aiming lower, we might actually reach higher. In some ways, some expression of prejudice serves a useful social purpose. It lets off steam; it allows natural tensions to express themselves incrementally; it can siphon off conflict through words, rather than actions. Anyone who has lived in the ethnic shouting match that is New York City knows exactly what I mean. If New Yorkers disliked each other less, they wouldn't be able to get on so well. We may not all be able to pull off a Mencken—bigoted in words, egalitarian in action—but we might achieve a lesser form of virtue: a human acceptance of our need for differentiation, without a total capitulation to it.

Do we not owe something more to the victims of hate? Perhaps we do.   55
But it is also true that there is nothing that government can do for the hated that the hated cannot better do for themselves. After all, most bigots are not foiled when they are punished specifically for their beliefs. In fact, many of the worst haters crave such attention and find vindication in such rebukes. Indeed, our media's obsession with "hate," our elevation of it above other social misdemeanors and crimes, may even play into the hands of the pathetic and the evil, may breathe air into the smoldering embers of their paranoid loathing. Sure, we can help create a climate in which such hate is disapproved of—and we should. But there is a danger that if we go too far, if we punish it too much, if we try to abolish it altogether, we may merely increase its mystique, and entrench the very categories of human difference that we are trying to erase.

For hate is only foiled not when the haters are punished but when the hated are immune to the bigot's power. A hater cannot psychologically wound if a victim cannot psychologically be wounded. And that immunity to hurt can never be given; it can merely be achieved. The racial epithet only strikes at someone's core if he lets it, if he allows the bigot's definition of him to be the final description of his life and his person—if somewhere in his heart of hearts, he believes the hateful slur to be true. The only final answer to this form of racism, then, is not majority persecution of it, but minority indifference to it. The only permanent rebuke to homophobia is not the enforcement of tolerance, but gay equanimity in the face of prejudice. The only effective answer to sexism is not a morass of legal proscriptions, but the simple fact of female success. In this, as in so many other things, there is no solution to the problem. There is only a transcendence of it. For all our rhetoric, hate will never be destroyed. Hate, as our predecessors knew better, can merely be overcome.

QUESTIONS

1. Sullivan's argument begins with his title, which contains the premise "hate *is* so bad." Suppose the title ended with a question mark. How might a question affect your reading of the text?
2. In many arguments, the writer begins by defining terms. What problems does Sullivan run into in defining *hate?*
3. Why does Sullivan call the hate-crime law a "facile political artifact" (paragraph 50)? Do you agree with him? Explain.
4. What does Sullivan mean by "A free country will always mean a hateful country"?
5. Sullivan concludes that "hate will never be destroyed . . . [it] can merely be overcome" (paragraph 56). He suggests that we concentrate on achieving toleration rather than tolerance (paragraph 53). What do you think of this conclusion? Does the evidence he presents substantiate his opening premise? Explain.
6. Find a newspaper or newsmagazine account of a recent crime of violence that has been characterized as a "hate crime" and, using some of Sullivan's terms and issues, argue whether the crime may or may not be defined that way.

MAKING CONNECTIONS

For a longer essay, do some further research like that suggested in item 6 above. Assemble a group of news stories detailing violent crimes, and analyze the answers given to the question that is always asked: Why did he/she/they do it? Use your material as the basis for an argument. You may wish to take up Sullivan's questioning of the hate crime law, or you may find your material leads you toward a different thesis.

A Modest Proposal

Jonathan Swift

Jonathan Swift (1667–1745) was born in Dublin, Ireland, of English parents and was educated in Irish schools. A graduate of Trinity College, Dublin, he received a master's degree from Oxford and was ordained a priest in the Church of England in 1695. He was active in politics as well as religion, becoming an editor and pamphlet writer for the Tory party in 1710. After becoming Dean of St. Patrick's Cathedral, Dublin, in 1713, he settled in Ireland and began to take an interest in the English economic exploitation of Ireland, gradually becoming a fierce Irish patriot. By 1724 the English were offering a reward for the discovery of the writer of the Drapier's Letters, *a series of pamphlets secretly written by Swift, attacking the British for their treatment of Ireland. In 1726 Swift produced the first volume of a more universal satire, known to modern readers as* Gulliver's Travels, *which has kept his name alive for 250 years. "A Modest Proposal," his best-known essay on Irish affairs, appeared in 1729.*

A Modest Proposal
for Preventing the Children of Poor People in Ireland
from Being a Burden to Their Parents or Country,
and for Making Them Beneficial to the Public

It is a melancholy object to those who walk through this great town,[1] or travel in the country, when they see the streets, the roads and cabin-doors crowded with beggars of the female sex, followed by three, four, or six children, all in rags, and importuning every passenger for an alms. These mothers, instead of being able to work for their honest livelihood, are forced to employ all their time in strolling, to beg sustenance for their helpless infants, who, as they grow up, either turn thieves for want of work, or leave their dear native country to fight for the Pretender in Spain,[2] or sell themselves to the Barbadoes.[3]

---

[1]*this great town:* Dublin. [Eds.]

[2]*Pretender in Spain:* a Catholic descendant of the British royal family (James I, Charles I, Charles II, and James II) of Stuart. Exiled so that England could be governed by Protestant rulers, the Stuarts lurked in France and Spain, preparing various disastrous schemes for regaining the throne. [Eds.]

[3]*sell themselves to the Barbadoes:* sell themselves as indentured servants, a sort of temporary slavery, to the sugar merchants of the British Caribbean islands. [Eds.]

I think it is agreed by all parties that this prodigious number of children, in the arms, or on the backs, or at the heels of their mothers, and frequently of their fathers, is in the present deplorable state of the kingdom a very great additional grievance; and therefore whoever could find out a fair, cheap, and easy method of making these children sound and useful members of the commonwealth would deserve so well of the public as to have his statue set up for a preserver of the nation.

But my intention is very far from being confined to provide only for the children of professed beggars; it is of a much greater extent, and shall take in the whole number of infants at a certain age who are born of parents in effect as little able to support them as those who demand our charity in the streets.

As to my own part, having turned my thoughts for many years upon this important subject, and maturely weighed the several schemes of other projectors, I have always found them grossly mistaken in their computation. It is true a child just dropped from its dam may be supported by her milk for a solar year with little other nourishment, at most not above the value of two shillings,[4] which the mother may certainly get, or the value in scraps, by her lawful occupation of begging, and it is exactly at one year old that I propose to provide for them, in such a manner as, instead of being a charge upon their parents, or the parish, or wanting food and raiment for the rest of their lives, they shall, on the contrary, contribute to the feeding and partly to the clothing of many thousands.

There is likewise another great advantage to my scheme, that it will prevent those voluntary abortions, and that horrid practice of women murdering their bastard children, alas, too frequent among us, sacrificing the poor innocent babes, I doubt, more to avoid the expense than the shame, which would move tears and pity in the most savage and inhuman breast. 5

The number of souls in Ireland being usually reckoned one million and a half, of these I calculate there may be about two hundred thousand couples whose wives are breeders, from which number I subtract thirty thousand couples who are able to maintain their own children, although I apprehend there cannot be so many under the present distresses of the kingdom, but this being granted, there will remain an hundred and seventy thousand breeders. I again subtract fifty thousand for those women who miscarry, or whose children die by accident or disease within the year. There only remain an hundred and twenty thousand children of poor parents annually born: the question therefore is, how this number shall be reared, and provided for, which as I have already said, under the present situation of affairs is utterly impossible by all the methods hitherto proposed, for we can neither employ them in handicraft or agriculture; we neither build houses (I mean in the country), nor cultivate land: they can very seldom pick up a livelihood by stealing until they arrive at six years old,

---

[4]*shillings:* a shilling used to be worth about one day's labor. [Eds.]

except where they are of towardly parts, although I confess they learn the rudiments much earlier, during which time they can however be properly looked upon only as probationers, as I have been informed by a principal gentleman in the County of Cavan, who protested to me that he never knew above one or two instances under the age of six, even in a part of the kingdom so renowned for the quickest proficiency in that art.

I am assured by our merchants that a boy or girl before twelve years old, is no saleable commodity, and even when they come to this age, they will not yield above three pounds, or three pounds and half-a-crown at most on the Exchange, which cannot turn to account either to the parents or the kingdom, the charge of nutriment and rags having been at least four times that value.

I shall now therefore humbly propose my own thoughts, which I hope will not be liable to the least objection.

I have been assured by a very knowing American of my acquaintance in London, that a young healthy child well nursed is at a year old a most delicious, nourishing and wholesome food, whether stewed, roasted, baked, or boiled, and I make no doubt that it will equally serve in a fricassee, or a ragout.

I do therefore humbly offer it to public consideration, that of the hundred and twenty thousand children already computed, twenty thousand may be reserved for breed, whereof only one fourth part to be males, which is more than we allow to sheep, black-cattle, or swine, and my reason is that these children are seldom the fruits of marriage, a circumstance not much regarded by our savages, therefore one male will be sufficient to serve four females. That the remaining hundred thousand may at a year old be offered in sale to the persons of quality, and fortune, through the kingdom, always advising the mother to let them suck plentifully in the last month, so as to render them plump, and fat for a good table. A child will make two dishes at an entertainment for friends, and when the family dines alone, the fore or hind quarters will make a reasonable dish, and seasoned with a little pepper or salt will be very good boiled on the fourth day, especially in winter.

I have reckoned upon a medium, that a child just born will weigh twelve pounds, and in a solar year if tolerably nursed increaseth to twenty-eight pounds.

I grant this food will be somewhat dear, and therefore very proper for landlords, who, as they have already devoured most of the parents, seem to have the best title to the children.

Infant's flesh will be in season throughout the year, but more plentiful in March, and a little before and after, for we are told by a grave author, an eminent French physician,[5] that fish being a prolific diet, there are more

------

[5]*French physician:* François Rabelais (1494?–1553), physician and satirist known for his *Gargantua and Pantagruel.* [Eds.]

children born in Roman Catholic countries about nine months after Lent than at any other season; therefore reckoning a year after Lent, the markets will be more glutted than usual, because the number of Popish infants is at least three to one in this kingdom, and therefore it will have one other collateral advantage by lessening the number of Papists among us.

I have already computed the charge of nursing a beggar's child (in which list I reckon all cottagers, laborers, and four-fifths of the farmers) to be about two shillings *per annum,* rags included, and I believe no gentleman would repine to give ten shillings for the carcass of a good fat child, which, as I have said, will make four dishes of excellent nutritive meat, when he hath only some particular friend of his own family to dine with him. Thus the Squire will learn to be a good landlord and grow popular among his tenants, the mother will have eight shillings net profit, and be fit for work until she produces another child.

Those who are more thrifty (as I must confess the times require) may flay the carcass; the skin of which artificially dressed, will make admirable gloves for ladies, and summer boots for fine gentlemen.   15

As to our city of Dublin, shambles[6] may be appointed for this purpose, in the most convenient parts of it, and butchers we may be assured will not be wanting, although I rather recommend buying the children alive, and dressing them hot from the knife, as we do roasting pigs.

A very worthy person, a true lover of his country, and whose virtues I highly esteem was lately pleased, in discoursing on this matter to offer a refinement upon my scheme. He said that many gentlemen of this kingdom, having of late destroyed their deer, he conceived that the want of venison might be well supplied by the bodies of young lads and maidens, not exceeding fourteen years of age, nor under twelve, so great a number of both sexes in every county being now ready to starve, for want of work and service: and these to be disposed of by their parents if alive, or otherwise by their nearest relations. But with due deference to so excellent a friend, and so deserving a patriot, I cannot be altogether in his sentiments. For as to the males, my American acquaintance assured me from frequent experience that their flesh was generally tough and lean, like that of our schoolboys, by continual exercise, and their taste disagreeable, and to fatten them would not answer the charge. Then as to the females, it would, I think with humble submission, be a loss to the public, because they soon would become breeders themselves: and besides, it is not improbable that some scrupulous people might be apt to censure such a practice (although indeed very unjustly) as a little bordering upon cruelty, which I confess, hath always been with me the strongest objection against any project, howsoever well intended.

But in order to justify my friend, he confessed that this expedient was put into his head by the famous Psalmanazar, a native of the island Formosa, who came from thence to London, above twenty years ago, and in conversa-

---

[6]*shambles:* slaughterhouses. [Eds.]

tion told my friend that in his country when any young person happened to be put to death, the executioner sold the carcass to persons of quality, as a prime dainty, and that, in his time, the body of a plump girl of fifteen, who was crucified for an attempt to poison the emperor, was sold to his Imperial Majesty's Prime Minister of State, and other great Mandarins of the Court, in joints from the gibbet, at four hundred crowns. Neither indeed can I deny that if the same use were made of several plump young girls in this town who, without one single groat to their fortunes, cannot stir abroad without a chair, and appear at the playhouse and assemblies in foreign fineries, which they never will pay for, the kingdom would not be the worse.

Some persons of a desponding spirit are in great concern about that vast number of poor people, who are aged, diseased, or maimed, and I have been desired to employ my thoughts what course may be taken to ease the nation of so grievous an encumbrance. But I am not in the least pain upon that matter, because it is very well known that they are every day dying, and rotting, by cold, and famine, and filth, and vermin, as fast as can be reasonably expected. And as to the younger laborers they are now in almost as hopeful a condition. They cannot get work, and consequently pine away from want of nourishment, to a degree that if at any time they are accidentally hired to common labor, they have not strength to perform it; and thus the country and themselves are in a fair way of being soon delivered from the evils to come.

I have too long digressed, and therefore shall return to my subject. I think the advantages by the proposal which I have made are obvious and many, as well as of the highest importance.   20

For first, as I have already observed, it would greatly lessen the number of Papists, with whom we are yearly over-run, being the principal breeders of the nation, as well as our most dangerous enemies, and who stay at home on purpose with a design to deliver the kingdom to the Pretender, hoping to take their advantage by the absence of so many good Protestants, who have chosen rather to leave their country than stay at home and pay tithes against their conscience to an idolatrous Episcopal curate.

Secondly, the poorer tenants will have something valuable of their own, which by law may be made liable to distress, and help to pay their landlord's rent, their corn and cattle being already seized, and money a thing unknown.

Thirdly, whereas the maintenance of an hundred thousand children, from two years old, and upwards, cannot be computed at less than ten shillings a piece *per annum,* the nation's stock will be thereby increased fifty thousand pounds *per annum,* besides the profit of a new dish, introduced to the tables of all gentlemen of fortune in the kingdom, who have any refinement in taste, and the money will circulate among ourselves, the goods being entirely of our own growth and manufacture.

Fourthly, the constant breeders, besides the gain of eight shillings sterling *per annum,* by the sale of their children, will be rid of the charge of maintaining them after the first year.

Fifthly, this food would likewise bring great custom to taverns, where   25
the vintners will certainly be so prudent as to procure the best receipts for
dressing it to perfection, and consequently have their houses frequented by
all the fine gentlemen, who justly value themselves upon their knowledge in
good eating; and a skillful cook, who understands how to oblige his guests,
will contrive to make it as expensive as they please.

Sixthly, this would be a great inducement to marriage, which all wise
nations have either encouraged by rewards, or enforced by laws and penalties. It would increase the care and tenderness of mothers towards their
children, when they were sure of a settlement for life, to the poor babes,
provided in some sort by the public to their annual profit instead of expense. We should soon see an honest emulation among the married
women, which of them could bring the fattest child to the market. Men
would become as fond of their wives, during the time of their pregnancy,
as they are now of their mares in foal, their cows in calf, or sows when
they are ready to farrow, nor offer to beat or kick them (as it is too frequent a practice) for fear of a miscarriage.

Many other advantages might be enumerated. For instance, the addition of some thousand carcasses in our exportation of barreled beef; the
propagation of swine's flesh, and improvement in the art of making good
bacon, so much wanted among us by the great destruction of pigs, too frequent at our tables, are no way comparable in taste or magnificence to a
well-grown, fat yearling child, which roasted whole will make a considerable figure at a Lord Mayor's feast, or any other public entertainment. But
this and many others I omit, being studious of brevity.

Supposing that one thousand families in this city would be constant
customers for infants' flesh, besides others who might have it at merry
meetings, particularly weddings and christenings; I compute that Dublin
would take off annually about twenty thousand carcasses, and the rest of
the kingdom (where probably they will be sold somewhat cheaper) the remaining eighty thousand.

I can think of no one objection that will possibly be raised against this
proposal, unless it should be urged that the number of people will be
thereby much lessened in the kingdom. This I freely own, and it was indeed
one principal design in offering it to the world. I desire the reader will observe, that I calculate my remedy *for this one individual Kingdom of* Ireland, *and for no other that ever was, is, or, I think, ever can be upon earth.*
Therefore let no man talk to me of other expedients: *Of taxing our absen-
tees at five shillings a pound: Of using neither clothes, nor household furniture, except what is of our own growth and manufacture: Of utterly
rejecting the materials and instruments that promote foreign luxury: Of
curing the expensiveness of pride, vanity, idleness, and gaming in our
women: Of introducing a vein of parsimony, prudence, and temperance:
Of learning to love our country, wherein we differ even from* Laplanders,
and the inhabitants of Topinamboo: *Of quitting our animosities and fac-
tions, nor act any longer like the* Jews, *who were murdering one another at*

the very moment their city was taken: Of being a little cautious not to sell our country and consciences for nothing: Of teaching landlords to have at least one degree of mercy towards their tenants. Lastly, *of putting a spirit of honesty, industry, and skill into our shopkeepers, who, if a resolution could now be taken to buy only our native goods, would immediately unite to cheat and exact upon us in the price, the measure and the goodness, nor could ever yet be brought to make one fair proposal of just dealing, though often and earnestly invited to it.*

Therefore I repeat, let no man talk to me of these and the like expedients, till he hath at least a glimpse of hope that there will ever be some hearty and sincere attempt to put them in practice.   30

But as to myself, having been wearied out for many years with offering vain, idle, visionary thoughts, and at length utterly despairing of success, I fortunately fell upon this proposal, which as it is wholly new, so it hath something solid and real, of no expense and little trouble, full in our own power, and whereby we can incur no danger in disobliging England. For this kind of commodity will not bear exportation, the flesh being of too tender a consistence to admit a long continuance in salt, *although perhaps I could name a country which would be glad to eat up our whole nation without it.*

After all I am not so violently bent upon my own opinion as to reject any offer, proposed by wise men, which shall be found equally innocent, cheap, easy and effectual. But before some thing of that kind shall be advanced in contradiction to my scheme, and offering a better, I desire the author, or authors, will be pleased maturely to consider two points. First, as things now stand, how they will be able to find food and raiment for a hundred thousand useless mouths and backs? And secondly, there being a round million of creatures in human figure, throughout this kingdom, whose whole subsistence put into a common stock would leave them in debt two millions of pounds sterling; adding those who are beggars by profession, to the bulk of farmers, cottagers, and laborers with their wives and children, who are beggars in effect; I desire those politicians who dislike my overture, and may perhaps be so bold to attempt an answer, that they will first ask the parents of these mortals whether they would not at this day think it a great happiness to have been sold for food at a year old, in the manner I prescribe, and thereby have avoided such a perpetual scene of misfortunes as they have since gone through, by the oppression of landlords, the impossibility of paying rent without money or trade, the want of common sustenance, with neither house nor clothes to cover them from the inclemencies of weather, and the most inevitable prospect of entailing the like, or greater miseries upon their breed for ever.

I profess in the sincerity of my heart that I have not the least personal interest in endeavoring to promote this necessary work, having no other motive than the *public good of my country, by advancing our trade, providing for infants, relieving the poor, and giving some pleasure to the rich.* I have no children by which I can propose to get a single penny; the youngest being nine years old, and my wife past child-bearing.

QUESTIONS

1. A proposal always involves a proposer. What is the character of the proposer here? Do we perceive his character to be the same throughout the essay? Compare, for example, paragraphs 21, 26, and 33.
2. When does the proposer actually offer his proposal? What does he do before making his proposal? What does he do after making his proposal? How does the order in which he does things affect our impression of him and of his proposal?
3. What kinds of counterarguments to his own proposal does this proposer anticipate? How does he answer and refute proposals that might be considered alternatives to his?
4. In reading this essay, most people are quite certain that the author, Swift, does not himself endorse the proposer's idea. How do we distinguish the two of them? What details of style help us make this distinction?
5. Consider the proposer, the counterarguments he acknowledges and refutes, and Swift himself, who presumably does not endorse the proposal. To what extent is Swift's position essentially that which his proposer refutes? To what extent is it still a somewhat different position?
6. To what extent does an ironic essay like this depend on the author and reader sharing certain values without question or reservation? Can you discover any such values explicitly or implicitly present in Swift's essay?
7. Use Swift's technique to write a "modest proposal" of your own about some contemporary situation. That is, use some outlandish proposal as a way of drawing attention to a situation that needs correcting. Consider carefully the character you intend to project for your proposer and the way you intend to make your own view distinguishable from hers or his.

MAKING CONNECTIONS

The power of "A Modest Proposal" lies in the outrageousness of what is proposed and the utterly rational tone in which the proposal is made. Compare the effect of "A Modest Proposal" on the reader with the effect of another argumentative essay. We suggest Neal Stephenson's "The Interface Culture" (p. 639), in which Stephenson fancies he sounds like "your basic snotty intellectual." Why does he say this? What other strategies does he use to try to sway the reader?

THE DECLARATION OF INDEPENDENCE

Thomas Jefferson

Thomas Jefferson (1743–1826) was born in Shadwell, Virginia, attended the College of William and Mary, and became a lawyer. He was elected to the Virginia House of Burgesses in 1769 and was a delegate to the Continental Congress in 1776. When the Congress voted in favor of Richard Henry Lee's resolution that the colonies "ought to be free and independent states," a committee of five members, including John Adams, Benjamin Franklin, and Jefferson, was appointed to draw up a declaration. Jefferson, because of his eloquence as a writer, was asked by this committee to draw up a first draft. Jefferson's text, with a few changes suggested by Franklin and Adams, was presented to the Congress. After a debate in which further changes were made, including striking out a passage condemning the slave trade, the Declaration was approved on July 4, 1776. Jefferson said of it, "Neither aiming at originality of principles or sentiments, nor yet copied from any particular and previous writing, it was intended to be an expression of the American mind."

In Congress, July 4, 1776
The unanimous Declaration of the
thirteen united States of America

When in the Course of human events it becomes necessary for one people to dissolve the political bands which have connected them with another, and to assume among the powers of the earth, the separate and equal station to which the Laws of Nature and of Nature's God entitle them, a decent respect to the opinions of mankind requires that they should declare the causes which impel them to the separation.

We hold these truths to be self-evident, that all men are created equal, that they are endowed by their Creator with certain unalienable Rights, that among these are Life, Liberty and the pursuit of Happiness. That to secure these rights, Governments are instituted among Men, deriving their just powers from the consent of the governed. That whenever any Form of Government becomes destructive of these ends, it is the Right of the People to alter or to abolish it, and to institute new Government, laying its foundation on such principles and organizing its powers in such form, as to them shall seem most likely to affect their Safety and Happiness. Prudence, indeed, will dictate that Governments long established should not be changed for light and transient causes; and accordingly all experience hath shewn that mankind are more disposed to suffer, while evils are sufferable, than to right themselves by abolishing the forms to which they are accustomed. But when a long train of abuses and usurpations, pursuing invariably the same Object evinces a design to reduce them under absolute Despotism, it is their right, it is their duty, to throw off such Government, and to provide new Guards for their future security. Such has been the patient sufferance of these Colonies; and such is now the necessity which constrains them to alter their former Systems of Government. The history of the present King of Great Britain is a history of repeated injuries and usurpations, all having in direct object the establishment of an absolute Tyranny over these States. To prove this, let Facts be submitted to a candid world.

He has refused his Assent to Laws, the most wholesome and necessary for the public good.

He has forbidden his Governors to pass laws of immediate and pressing importance, unless suspended in their operation till his Assent should be obtained; and when so suspended, he has utterly neglected to attend to them.

He has refused to pass other Laws for the accommodation of large districts of people, unless those people would relinquish the right of Representation in the Legislature, a right inestimable to them and formidable to tyrants only. 5

He has called together legislative bodies at places unusual, uncomfortable, and distant from the depository of their Public Records, for the sole purpose of fatiguing them into compliance with his measures.

He has dissolved Representative Houses repeatedly, for opposing with manly firmness his invasions on the rights of the people.

He has refused for a long time, after such dissolutions, to cause others to be elected; whereby the Legislative Powers, incapable of Annihilation, have returned to the People at large for their exercise; the State remaining in the mean time exposed to all the dangers of invasion from without, and convulsions within.

He has endeavored to prevent the population of these States; for that purpose obstructing the Laws for Naturalization of Foreigners; refusing to pass others to encourage their migration hither, and raising the conditions of new Appropriations of Lands.

He has obstructed the Administration of Justice, by refusing his Assent to Laws for Establishing Judiciary Powers. 10

He has made Judges dependent on his Will alone, for the tenure of their offices, and the amount and payment of their salaries.

He has erected a multitude of New Offices, and sent hither swarms of Officers to harass our people, and eat out their substance.

He has kept among us, in times of peace, Standing Armies without the Consent of our legislatures.

He has affected to render the Military independent of and superior to the Civil Power.

He has combined with others to subject us to a jurisdiction foreign to   15
our constitution, and unacknowledged by our laws; giving his Assent to the Acts of pretended Legislation: For quartering large bodies of armed troops among us: For protecting them, by a mock Trial, from punishment for any Murders which they should commit on the Inhabitants of these States: For cutting off our Trade with all parts of the world: For imposing Taxes on us without our Consent: For depriving us in many cases, of the benefits of Trial by Jury: For Transporting us beyond Seas to be tried for pretended offenses: For abolishing the free System of English Laws in a neighboring Province, establishing therein an Arbitrary government, and enlarging its Boundaries so as to render it at once an example and fit instrument for introducing the same absolute rule into these Colonies: For taking away our Charters, abolishing our most valuable Laws and altering fundamentally the Forms of our Governments: For suspending our own Legislatures, and declaring themselves invested with power to legislate for us in all cases whatsoever.

He has abdicated Government here, by declaring us out of his Protection and waging War against us.

He has plundered our seas, ravaged our Coasts, burnt our towns, and destroyed the lives of our people.

He is at this time transporting large Armies of foreign Mercenaries to complete the works of death, desolation and tyranny, already begun with circumstances of Cruelty & Perfidy scarcely paralleled in the most barbarous ages, and totally unworthy the Head of a civilized nation.

He has constrained our fellow Citizens taken Captive on the high Seas to bear Arms against their Country, to become the executioners of their friends and Brethren, or to fall themselves by their Hands.

He has excited domestic insurrections amongst us, and has endeavored   20
to bring on the inhabitants of our frontiers, the merciless Indian Savages, whose known rule of warfare is an undistinguished destruction of all ages, sexes, and conditions.

In every stage of these Oppressions We have Petitioned for Redress in the most humble terms: Our repeated petitions have been answered only by repeated injury. A Prince, whose character is thus marked by every act which may define a Tyrant, is unfit to be the ruler of a free people.

Nor have we been wanting in attention to our British brethren. We have warned them from time to time of attempts by their legislature to extend an unwarrantable jurisdiction over us. We have reminded them of the circumstances of our emigration and settlement here. We have appealed to their native justice and magnanimity, and we have conjured them by the ties of our common kindred to disavow these usurpations, which would inevitably interrupt our connections and correspondence. They too have been deaf to the voice of justice and of consanguinity. We must, therefore, acquiesce in the necessity, which denounces our Separation, and hold them, as we hold the rest of mankind, Enemies in War, in Peace Friends.

We, THEREFORE, the Representatives of the UNITED STATES OF AMERICA, in General Congress, Assembled, appealing to the Supreme Judge of the world for the rectitude of our intentions, do, in the Name, and by Authority of the good People of these Colonies, solemnly publish and declare, That these United Colonies are, and of Right ought to be FREE AND INDEPENDENT STATES; that they are Absolved from all Allegiance to the British Crown, and that all political connection between them and the State of Great Britain, is and ought to be totally dissolved; and that as Free and Independent States; they have full Power to levy War, conclude Peace, contract Alliances, establish Commerce, and to do all the Acts and Things which Independent States may of right do. And for the support of this Declaration, with a firm reliance on the protection of Divine Providence, we mutually pledge to each other our Lives, our Fortunes, and our sacred Honor.

QUESTIONS

1. The Declaration of Independence is frequently cited as a classic deductive argument. A deductive argument is based on a general statement, or premise, that is assumed to be true. What does this document assume that the American colonists are entitled to and on what basis? Look at the reasoning in paragraph 2. What are these truths that are considered self-evident? What does *self-evident* mean?

2. What accusations against the king of Great Britain are the facts presented meant to substantiate? If you were the British king presented with this document, how might you reply to it? Would you attack its premise or reply to its accusations? Or would you do both? (How did George III respond?)

3. To what extent is the audience of the Declaration intended to be the king and people of Great Britain?

4. What other audiences were intended for this document? Define at least two other audiences, and describe how each might be expected to respond.

5. Although this declaration could have been expected to lead to war and all the horrors thereof, it is a most civilized document, showing great respect throughout for certain standards of civility among people and among nations. Define the civilized standards that the declaration assumes. Write an essay that identifies and characterizes the nature and variety of those expectations.

6. Write a declaration of your own, announcing your separation from some injurious situation (an incompatible roommate, a noisy sorority or fraternity house, an awful job, or whatever). Start with a premise,

give reasons to substantiate it, provide facts that illustrate the injurious conditions, and conclude with a statement of what your new condition will mean to you and to other oppressed people.

MAKING CONNECTIONS

1. If Jefferson's declaration is a classic deductive argument, as the first question above suggests, Alice Walker's "Am I Blue?" (p. 598) might stand as a clear example of inductive arguing. Review the structure of her argument. Where does she express her thesis most precisely? Why doesn't she announce it more quickly? What would the Declaration look like if Jefferson had approached it inductively? Write an inductive version of the Declaration of Independence.
2. What if, rather than writing the Declaration of Independence, Jefferson had offered "a modest proposal" to the British king? What do you suppose he would have said? How would he have formulated his argument? Write your own "modest proposal" to the king, addressing him more or less in the manner of Jonathan Swift (p. 680), but drawing on the evidence that Jefferson provides in the Declaration.

READING THE SLENDER BODY

Susan Bordo

Susan Bordo (b. 1947) is a professor of philosophy at the University of Kentucky. Her works include several studies of the French philosopher Rene Descartes, but she is best known for Unbearable Weight: Feminism, Western Culture, and the Body *(1993), an interdisciplinary study of ideas of female body image that was nominated for a Pulitzer Prize. Bordo's most recent book is* The Male Body: A New Look at Men in Public and Private *(1999), "a personal/cultural exploration of the male body from a woman's point of view." Her subjects include eating disorders, cosmetic surgery, sexual harassment, and the evolution of beauty. The following essay was originally published in 1989 in* Body/Politics: Women and the Discourse of Science.

In the late-Victorian era, arguably for the first time in the West, those who could afford to eat well began systematically to deny themselves food in pursuit of an aesthetic ideal.[1] Certainly, other cultures had "dieted." Aristocratic Greek culture made a science of the regulation of food intake, in the service of the attainment of self-mastery and moderation.[2] Fasting, aimed at spiritual purification and domination of the flesh, was an important part of the repertoire of Christian practice in the Middle Ages.[3] These forms of "diet" can clearly be viewed as instruments for the development of a "self" — whether an "inner" self, for the Christians, or a public self, for the Greeks — constructed as an arena in which the deepest possibilities for human excellence might be realized. Rituals of fasting and asceticism were therefore reserved for the select few, aristocratic or priestly in caste, deemed capable of achieving such excellence of spirit. In the late nineteenth century, by contrast, the practices of body management begin to be middle-class preoccupations, and concern with diet becomes attached to the pursuit of an idealized physical weight or shape; it becomes a project in service of "body" rather than "soul." Fat, not appetite or desire, is the declared enemy, and people begin to measure their dietary achievements by the numbers on the scale rather than the level of their mastery of impulse and excess. The bourgeois "tyranny of slenderness" (as Kim Chernin has called it[4]) had begun its ascendancy (particularly over women), and with it the development of numerous technologies — diet, exercise, and, later on, chemicals and surgery — aimed at a purely physical transformation.

Today, we have become acutely aware of the massive and multifaceted nature of such technologies and the industries built around them. To the degree that a popular critical consciousness exists, however, it has been focused largely (and not surprisingly) on what has been viewed as pathological or extreme — on the unfortunate minority who become "obsessed" or go "too far." Television talk shows feature tales of disasters caused by stomach stapling, gastric bubbles, gastrointestinal bypass operations, liquid diets, compulsive exercising. Magazines warn of the dangers of fat-reduction surgery and liposuction. Books and articles about bulimia and anorexia nervosa proliferate. The portrayal of eating disorders by the popular media is often lurid and sensational; audiences gasp at pictures of skeletal bodies or at item-by-item descriptions of the volumes of food eaten during an average binge. Such presentations encourage a "side show" experience of the relationship between the ("normal") audience and those on view ("the freaks"). To the degree that the audience may nonetheless recognise themselves in the behaviour or reported experiences of those on stage, they confront themselves as "pathological" or outside the norm.

Of course, many of these behaviours *are* outside the norm, if only because of the financial resources they require. But preoccupation with fat, diet, and slenderness are not.[5] Indeed, such preoccupation may function as one of the most powerful "normalizing" strategies of our century, ensuring the production of self-monitoring and self-disciplining "docile bodies," sensitive to any departure from social norms, and habituated to self-improvement and transformation in the service of those norms.[6] Seen in this light, the focus on "pathology," disorder, accident, unexpected disaster, and bizarre behaviour obscures the normalizing function of the technologies of diet and body management. For women, who are subject to such controls more profoundly and, historically, more ubiquitously than men, the focus on "pathology" (unless embedded in a political analysis) diverts recognition from a central means of the reproduction of gender.[. . .]

Slenderness and Contemporary Anxiety

In a recent edition of the magazine show *20/20*, several 10-year-old boys were shown some photos of fashion models. The models were pencil thin. Yet the pose was such that a small bulge of hip was forced, through the action of the body, into protuberance — as is natural, unavoidable on any but the most skeletal or the most tautly developed bodies. We bend over, we sit down and the flesh coalesces in spots. These young boys, pointing to the hips, disgustedly pronounced the models to be "fat." Watching the show, I was appalled at the boys' reaction. Yet I couldn't deny that I had also been surprised at my own current perceptions while re-viewing female bodies in movies from the 1970s; what once appeared slender and fit now seemed loose and flabby. *Weight* was not the key element in these changed perceptions — my standards had not come to favour *thinner* bodies—but rather, I had come to expect a tighter, smoother, more "contained" body profile.

The self-criticisms of the anorexic, too, are usually focused on particular soft, protuberant areas of the body (most often the stomach) rather than on the body as a whole. Karen, in *Dying to Be Thin,* tries to dispel what she sees as the myth that the anorexic, even when emaciated, "misperceives" her body as fat:

> I hope I'm expressing myself properly here, because this is important. You have to understand. I don't see my whole body as fat. When I look in the mirror, I don't really see a fat person there. I see certain things about me that are really thin. Like my arms and legs. But I can tell the minute I eat certain things that my stomach blows up like a pig's. I know it gets distended. And it's disgusting. That's what I keep to myself—hug to myself.[7]

Or Barbara:

> Sometimes my body looks so bloated, I don't want to get dressed. I like the way it looks for exactly two days each month: usually, the eighth and ninth days after my period. Every other day, my breasts, my stomach—they're just awful lumps, bumps, bulges. My body can turn on me at any moment; it is an out-of-control mass of flesh.[8]

Much has been made of such descriptions, from both psychoanalytic and feminist perspectives. But for now, I wish to pursue these images of unwanted bulges and erupting stomachs in another direction than that of gender symbolism. I want to consider them as a metaphor for anxiety about internal processes out of control—uncontained desire, unrestrained hunger, uncontrolled impulse. Images of bodily eruption frequently function symbolically in this way in contemporary horror movies—as in recent werewolf films (*The Howling, A Teen-Age Werewolf in London*) and in David Cronenberg's remake of *The Fly.* The original *Fly* imagined a mechanical joining of fly parts and person parts, a variation on the standard "half-man, half-beast" image. In Cronenberg's *Fly,* as in the werewolf genre, a new, alien, libidinous, and uncontrollable self literally bursts through the seams of the victim's old flesh. (A related, frequently copied image occurs in *Alien,* where a parasite erupts from the chest of the human host.) While it is possible to view these new images as technically inspired by special-effects possibilities, I suggest that deeper psycho-cultural anxieties are being given form.

Every year, I present my metaphysics class with Delmore Schwartz's classic poem "The Heavy Bear" [see appendix] as an example of a dualist imagination of self, in which the body is constructed as an alien, unconscious, appetitive force, thwarting and befouling the projects of the soul.

Beginning with an epigraph from Alfred North Whitehead, "The withness of the body," Schwartz's poem makes "the heavy bear who goes with [him]" into "A caricature, a swollen shadow, A stupid clown of the spirit's motive." Last year, for the first time, quite a few students interpreted the poem as describing the predicament of an obese man. This may indicate the increasing literalism of my students. But it also is suggestive of the degree to which the specter of "fat" dominates their imaginations, and codes their generation's anxieties about the body's potential for excess and chaos. In advertisements, the construction of the body as an alien attacker, threatening to erupt in an unsightly display of bulging flesh, is an ubiquitous cultural image. Until the last decade, excess weight was the target of most ads for diet products; today, one is much more likely to find the enemy constructed as bulge, fat, or "flab." "Now" (a typical ad runs), "get rid of those embarrassing bumps, bulges, large stomach, flabby breasts and buttocks. Feel younger, and help prevent cellulite build-up. . . . Have a nice shape with no tummy." To achieve such results (often envisioned as the absolute eradication of body: e.g., "no tummy") a violent assault on the enemy is usually required; bulges must be "attacked" and "destroyed," fat "burned," and stomachs (or, more disgustedly, "guts") must be "busted" and "eliminated." The increasing popularity of liposuction, a far from totally safe technique developed specifically to suck out the unwanted bulges of people of normal weight (it is not recommended for the obese), suggests how far our disgust with bodily bulges has gone. The ideal here is of a body that is absolutely tight, contained, "bolted down," firm (in other words, body that is protected against eruption from within, whose internal processes are under control). Areas that are soft, loose, or "wiggly" are unacceptable, even on extremely thin bodies. Cellulite management, like liposuction, has nothing to do with weight loss, and everything to do with the quest for firm bodily margins.

This perspective helps illuminate an important continuity of meaning between compulsive dieting and bodybuilding in our culture, and reveals why it has been so easy for contemporary images of female attractiveness to oscillate back and forth between a spare "minimalist" look and a solid, muscular, athletic look. The coexistence of these seemingly disparate images does not indicate that a postmodern universe of empty, endlessly differentiating images now reigns. Rather, the two ideals, though superficially very different, are united in battle against a common platoon of enemies: the soft, the loose; unsolid, excess flesh. It is perfectly permissible in our culture (even for women) to have substantial weight and bulk—so long as it is tightly managed. On the other hand, to be slim is simply not enough—so long as the flesh jiggles. Here, we arrive at one source of insight into why it is that the image of ideal slenderness has grown thinner and thinner over the last decade, and why women with extremely slender bodies often still see themselves as "fat." Unless one goes the route of muscle building, it is virtually impossible to achieve a flab-less, excess-less body unless one trims very near to the bone.

Slenderness and the State of the Soul

This "moral" (and, as we shall see, economic) coding of the fat/slender body in terms of its capacities for self-containment and the control of impulse and desire represents the culmination of a developing historical change in the social symbolism of body weight and size. Until the late nineteenth century, the central discriminations marked were those of class, race, and gender; the body indicated one's social identity and "place." So, for example, the bulging stomachs of successful mid-nineteenth-century businessmen and politicians were a symbol of bourgeois success, an outward manifestation of their accumulated wealth.[9] By contrast, the gracefully slender body announced aristocratic status; disdainful of the bourgeois need to display wealth and power ostentatiously, it commanded social space invisibly rather than aggressively, seemingly above the commerce in appetite or the need to eat. Subsequently, this ideal began to be appropriated by the status-seeking middle class, as slender wives became the showpieces of their husbands' success.[10]

Corpulence went out of middle-class vogue at the end of the century (even William Howard Taft, who had weighed over 300 pounds while in office, went on a reducing diet); social power had come to be less dependent on the sheer accumulation of material wealth and more connected to the ability to control and manage the labor and resources of others. At the same time, excess body weight came to be seen as reflecting moral or personal inadequacy, or lack of will.[11] These associations are only possible in a culture of "overabundance" (that is, in a society in which those who control the production of "culture" have more than enough to eat). The moral requirement to diet depends upon the material preconditions that make the *choice* to "diet" an option and the possibility of personal "excess" a reality. Although slenderness has hitherto retained some of its traditional class-associations ("a woman can never be too rich or too thin"), the importance of this equation has eroded considerably over the last decade. Increasingly, the size and shape of the body has come to operate as a marker of personal, internal order (or disorder) — as a symbol for the state of the soul.

Consider one particularly clear example, that of changes in the meaning of the muscled body. Muscularity has had a variety of cultural meanings (until recently largely reserved for male bodies) which have prevented the well-developed body from playing too great a role in middle-class conceptions of attractiveness. Of course, muscles have symbolized masculine power. But at the same time, they have been associated with manual labor and chain-gangs (and thus with lower-class and even criminal status), and suffused with racial meaning (via numerous film representations of sweating, glistening bodies belonging to black slaves and prize-fighters). Given the racial and class biases of our culture, they were associated with the body as material, unconscious, or animalistic. Today, however, the well-muscled body has become a cultural icon; "working out" is a glamorized and sexualized yuppie activity. No longer signifying lower-class status

10

(except when developed to extremes, at which point the old association of muscles with brute, unconscious materiality surfaces once more), the firm, developed body has become a symbol of correct *attitude;* it means that one "cares" about oneself and how one appears to others, suggesting will-power, energy, control over infantile impulse, the ability to "make some-thing" of oneself. "You exercise, you diet," says Heather Locklear, promot-ing Bally Matrix Fitness Centre on television, "and you can do anything you want." Muscles express sexuality, but controlled, managed sexuality that is not about to erupt in unwanted and embarrassing display.[12]

To the degree that the question of class still operates in all this, it relates to the category of social mobility (or lack of it) rather than class *location.* So, for example, when associations of fat and lower-class status exist, they are usually mediated by qualities of attitude or "soul" — fat being perceived as indicative of laziness, lack of discipline, unwillingness to conform, and ab-sence of all those "managerial" abilities that, according to the dominant ide-ology, confer upward mobility. Correspondingly, in popular teen movies such as *Flashdance* and *Vision Quest,* the ability of the (working-class) hero-ine and hero to pare, prune, tighten, and master the body operates as a clear symbol of successful upward aspiration, of the penetrability of class bound-aries to those who have "the right stuff." These movies (as one title explicitly suggests) are contemporary "quest myths"; like their prototype, *Rocky,* they follow the struggle of an individual to attain a personal grail, against all odds, and through numerous trials. But unlike the film quests of a previous era (which sent Mr. Smith to Washington and Mr. Deeds to town to battle the re-spective social evils of corrupt government and big business), *Flashdance* and *Vision Quest* render the hero's and heroine's commitment, will, and spiritual integrity through the metaphors of weight loss, exercise, and tolerance of and ability to conquer physical pain and exhaustion. (In *Vision Quest,* for ex-ample, the audience is encouraged to admire the young wrestler's persever-ance when he ignores the fainting spells and nosebleeds caused by his rigorous training and dieting.)

Not surprisingly, young people with eating disorders often thematize their own experience in similar terms, as in the following excerpt from an interview with a young woman runner:

> Well, I had the willpower. I could train for competition, and I could turn down food any time. I remember feeling like I was on a constant high. And the pain? Sure, there was pain. It was incred-ible. Between the hunger and the muscle pain from the constant workouts? I can't tell you how much I hurt.
>
> You may think I was crazy to put myself through constant, in-tense pain. But you have to remember. I was fighting a battle. And when you get hurt in a battle, you're proud of it. Sure, you may scream inside, but if you're brave and really good, then you take it quietly, because you know it's the price you pay for winning. And I needed to win. I really felt that if I didn't win, I would die . . . all

these enemy troops were coming at me, and I had to outsmart them. If I could discipline myself enough—if I could keep myself lean and strong—then I could win. The pain was just a natural thing I had to deal with.[13]

As in *Vision Quest*, the external context is training for an athletic event. But here, too, that goal becomes subordinated to an internal one. The real battle, ultimately, is with the self. At this point, the limitations of the brief history that I presented in the opening paragraph of this essay are revealed. In that paragraph, the contemporary preoccupation with diet is contrasted to historical projects of body management suffused with moral meaning. In this section, however, I have suggested that examination of even the most "shallow" representations (teen movies) discloses a moral ideology—one, in fact, seemingly close to the aristocratic Greek ideal described by [Michel] Foucault in *The Use of Pleasure*. The central element of that ideal, as Foucault describes it, is an "agonistic relation with the self"—aimed, not at the extirpation of desire and hunger in the interests of 'purity' (as in the Christian strain of dualism), but at a "virile" mastery of desire through constant "spiritual combat."[14]

For the Greeks, however, the "virile" mastery of desire operated within a culture that valorized moderation. The culture of contemporary body-management, struggling to manage desire within a system that is dedicated to the proliferation of desireable commodities, is very different. In cultural fantasies such as *Vision Quest* and *Flashdance*, self-mastery is presented as an attainable and stable state; but . . . the reality of the contemporary agonism of the self is another matter entirely.

NOTES

1. See Keith Walden, "The Road to Fat City: An Interpretation of the Development of Weight Consciousness in Western Society," *Historical Reflections* 12 (3) (1985), pp. 331–73.
2. See Michel Foucault, *The Use of Pleasure* (New York: Random House, 1986).
3. See Rudolph Bell, *Holy Anorexia* (Chicago: University of Chicago Press, 1985); and Carolyn Bynum, *Holy Feast and Holy Fast: The Religious Significance of Food to Medieval Women* (Berkeley: University of California Press, 1987), pp. 31–48.
4. See Kim Chernin, *The Obsession: Reflections on the Tyranny of Slenderness* (New York: Harper & Row, 1981).
5. See Thomas Cash, Barbara Winstead, and Louis Janda, "The Great American Shape-up," *Psychology Today*, April 1986; "Dieting: The Losing Game," *Time*, 20 January 1986, among numerous other general reports.

6. For Foucault on "docile bodies," see *Discipline and Punish* (New York: Vintage, 1979), pp. 135–69. For an application of Foucault's ideas to the practices of diet and fitness, see Walden, "The Road to Fat City." For a Foucauldian analysis of the practices of femininity, see Sandra Bartky, "Foucault, Femininity, and the Modernization of Patriarchal Power," in *Feminism and Foucault,* ed. Irene Diamond and Lee Quinby (Boston: Northeastern University Press, 1988), pp. 61–86.

7. Ira Sacker and Marc Zimmer, *Dying to Be Thin* (New York: Warner, 1987), p. 57.

8. Dalma Heyn, "Body Vision?", *Mademoiselle,* April 1987, p. 213.

9. See Louise Banner, *American Beauty* (Chicago: University of Chicago Press, 1983), pp. 232.

10. Ibid., pp. 53–55.

11. See Walden, *Historical Reflections,* 12 (3), pp. 334–35, 353.

12. I thank Mario Moussa for this point, and for the Heather Locklear quotation.

13. Ira Sacker and Marc Zimmer, op. cit., pp. 149–50.

14. Foucault, *The Use of Pleasure,* pp. 64–70.

Appendix

The Heavy Bear Who Goes with Me

Delmore Schwarz (1913–1966)

"the withness of the body"
— Whitehead

The heavy bear who goes with me,
A manifold honey to smear his face,
Clumsy and lumbering here and there,
The central ton of every place,
The hungry beating brutish one
In love with candy, anger, and sleep,
Crazy factotum, disheveling all,
Climbs the building, kicks the football,
Boxes his brother in the hate-ridden city.

Breathing at my side, that heavy animal,
The heavy bear who sleeps with me,
Howls in his sleep for a world of sugar,
A sweetness intimate as the water's clasp,
Howls in his sleep because the tight-rope
Trembles and shows the darkness beneath,
— The strutting show-off is terrified,
Dressed in his dress-suit, bulge in his pants,
Trembles to think that his quivering meat
Must finally wince to nothing at all.

That inescapable animal walks with me,
Has followed me since the black womb held,
Moves where I move, distorting my gesture,
A caricature, a swollen shadow,
A stupid clown of the spirit's motive,
Perplexes and affronts with his own darkness,

The secret life of belly and bone,
Opaque, too near, my private, yet unknown,
Stretches to embrace the very dear
With whom I would walk without him near,
Touches her grossly, although a word
Would bare my heart and make me clear,
Stumbles, flounders, and strives to be fed
Dragging me with him in his mouthing care,
Amid the hundred million of his kind,
The scrimmage of appetite everywhere.

QUESTIONS

1. Bordo states that the emphasis on pathological conditions such as anorexia and bulimia "obscures the normalizing function of the technologies of diet and body management" (paragraph 3). What does she mean by "normalizing function"? How would you describe a "normal-looking" body?

2. How has the moral coding of the body changed over time (paragraph 9)?

3. We have added Delmore Schwarz's poem, "The Heavy Bear Who Goes with Me," as an appendix. Bordo says that she teaches this poem in her philosophy class as an example of mind-body dualism (paragraph 7), but recently, her students have been interpreting the poem in a literal sense, as being about an obese man. What aspects of the poem might encourage such an interpretation? Try reading the poem in light of Bordo's discussions of control, margins, and moral issues. Which images in the poem best express anxiety about internal processes of control?

4. Bordo's essay was first published in 1990 and was illustrated with advertisements from the late 1980's. Find some recent ads for diet products, health clubs, cosmetic surgeons, and other sources that direct your attention to the improvement of the body. Analyze their content, using Bordo's categories of analysis—thinness, muscularity, control, moral issues, for example—to arrange your material. As you compare the messages of your ads with the ones she cites, you may find you need new categories to work with. Do your ads serve to reinforce her argument? Have attitudes toward the body changed in any ways in the last decade or so? What do your ads want you to think about your body in light of the ideal one they propose? Use your findings to construct an essay in which you come to some conclusion regarding current representations of and attitudes toward the body.

MAKING CONNECTIONS

How does Bordo's essay augment the reflections of Alice Walker ("Beauty: When the Other Dancer Is the Self," p. 42) and Lucy Grealy ("Mirrors," p. 50)? If you wish to complicate the gender issue, consider Andrew Sullivan's "The He Hormone" (p. 537) and his thoughts on the bulking of the male body. Check out some of the growing crop of men's magazines and their advertising pitches to those with less-than-perfect male bodies. Then you can entertain the thesis "Men face just as much pressure to perfect their bodies as women do" — or the opposite.

YOUR CONSTITUTION
IS KILLING YOU

Daniel Lazare

Freelance journalist and writer Daniel Lazare was born in New York City in 1950 and attended the University of Wisconsin and Columbia University. A contributor to the Village Voice, *the* New York Times, *and other periodicals, he is the author of* The Frozen Republic: How the Constitution Is Paralyzing Democracy *(1966). Of that book he has said, "I chose to write about the Constitution simply because it is the most gaping hole in what passes for American political thought. Everyone invokes the constitution and bows his or her head reverently whenever it comes up in conversation. But very few people think about the document in its entirety, much less question why society should be governed by a set of immovable laws dating from the late eighteenth century."*

On June 17, in the aftermath of the massacre at Columbine High School and a similar, if less grisly, incident the following month in Conyers, Georgia, the House of Representatives passed a "juvenile crime bill" steadfast in its refusal to limit the ease with which juveniles can lay their hands on firearms. House Republicans, it was clear, were determined to avoid making any connection between the fact that there are an estimated 240 million guns in the United States, nearly one per person, a number that is increasing by some 5 to 7 million a year, and the increase of violence in our culture. Instead, the problem was that we had forgotten the importance of "family values," that our children had become "spoiled with material things," that we had given in to "liberal relativism." Guns weren't the problem; the problem was "the abandonment of God" in the public sphere.

Representatives Henry Hyde (R., Ill.) and Tom DeLay (R., Tex.) were particularly enthusiastic in their efforts to look beyond guns for a solution. Hyde put the blame on the entertainment industry and tried to push through an amendment to the crime bill that would have made it a jailable offense to sell overtly violent or sexual material to minors. Even when 127 of his fellow Republicans voted against the measure, Hyde refused to let go. "People were misled," he said, "and disinclined to oppose the powerful entertainment industry." DeLay's approach was even more entertaining. At a "God Not Guns" rally, he read aloud an e-mail he claimed to have received that very morning: "The student writes, 'Dear God, Why didn't you stop the shootings at Columbine?' And God writes, 'Dear student, I would have, but I wasn't allowed in school.'" (So much for divine omnipotence.) An hour later DeLay was on the House floor, telling his colleagues that "our school systems teach the children that they are nothing but glorified apes who are evolutionized out of some primordial soup of mud." Other DeLayisms: "We place our children in day-care centers where they learn their socialization skills ... under the law of the jungle ...”; "Our children, who historically have been seen as a blessing from God, are now viewed as either a mistake created when contraception fails or inconveniences that parents try to raise in their spare time." A proposal to allow the display of the Ten Commandments in public schools was subsequently voted into the bill.

Among the further futile gestures housed in a second piece of crime legislation that failed the next day was a measure to reduce the Senate's proposed waiting time for purchases at gun shows and to limit the number of gun shows subject to any waiting period whatsoever. All this despite polls showing two-to-one support for stricter gun control even before Columbine. Two centuries ago, the great fear among the men who drew up the United States Constitution was of a popularly elected legislature falling all over itself to do the public's bidding; today we are witness to a popularly elected body falling all over itself *not* to carry out the democratic will. Why?

The standard liberal response is that the National Rifle Association made them do it. The NRA has used its immense campaign war chest to punish gun-control advocates and stifle dissent. It has twisted and distorted the Constitution. It has cleared a path for troglodytes like Hyde and DeLay. But the real problem is more disconcerting. The reason that Hyde and Co. are able to dominate the gun debate, the reason that the gun lobby is so powerful, is not the NRA but the basis on which the NRA's power rests: i.e., the Second Amendment. The truth about the Second Amendment is something that liberals cannot bear to admit: The right wing is right. The amendment *does* confer an individual right to bear arms, and its very presence makes effective gun control in this country all but impossible.

For decades liberal constitutional scholars have maintained that, contrary to the NRA, the Second Amendment does not guarantee an individual's right to own guns, merely a right to participate in an official state militia. The key phrase, they have argued, is "[a] well regulated Militia," which the introductory clause describes as nothing less than essential to "the security of a free State." A well-regulated militia is not just a goal, consequently, but *the* goal, the amendment's raison d'être. Everything else is subordinate. The right "to keep and bear Arms" is valid only to the degree that it serves that all-important end. There is therefore no *individual* right to bear arms in and of itself, only a *collective* right on the part of the citizens of the states to do so as members of the various official state militias. The right to own the assault weapon of one's choice exists only in the

5

fevered imagination of the National Rifle Association. Its constitutional basis is nil. The only right that the Second Amendment confers is the right to emulate Dan Quayle and join the National Guard.

This is the cheerful, anodyne version of the Second Amendment we're used to from the American Civil Liberties Union and other liberal groups. But as the gun issue has heated up since the Sixties and Seventies, constitutional scholars have taken a second look. The result has been both a renaissance in Second Amendment studies and a remarkable about-face in how it is interpreted. The purely "collectivist" interpretation has been rejected across the board by liberals and conservatives as ahistorical and overly pat. The individualist interpretation, the one that holds that Americans have a right to bear arms whether they're serving in an official state militia or not, has been more or less vindicated. In fact, some academics have gone so far as to compare the NRA's long campaign in behalf of an expansive interpretation of the Second Amendment to the ACLU's long campaign in behalf of an expansive reading of the First. As the well-known constitutional scholar William Van Alstyne put it, "The constructive role of the NRA today, like the role of the ACLU in the 1920s, . . . ought itself not lightly to be dismissed. Indeed, it is largely by the 'unreasonable' persistence of just such organizations in this country that the Bill of Rights has endured." Language like this is what one might expect at some Texas or Colorado gun show, not in the pages of the *Duke Law Journal.*

No less strikingly, the Second Amendment renaissance has also led to a renewed appreciation for the amendment's ideological importance. Previously, scholars were inclined to view the Second Amendment as little more than a historical curiosity, not unlike the Third Amendment, which, as almost no one remembers, prohibits the peacetime quartering of troops in private homes without the owner's consent. Harvard's Laurence Tribe gave the Second Amendment no more than a footnote in the 1988 edition of his famous textbook *American Constitutional Law,* but a new edition, published this August [1999], treats the subject much more extensively. It is now apparent that the amendment, despite its brevity, encapsulates an entire worldview concerning the nature of political power, the rights and duties of citizenship, and the relationship between the individual and the state. It is virtually a constitution-within-the-Constitution, which is undoubtedly why it fuels such fierce passions.

With crazed day traders and resentful adolescents mowing down large numbers of their fellow citizens every few weeks, the implications of this new, toughened-up version of the Second Amendment would seem to be profound. Politically, there's no doubt that it has already had an effect by encouraging the gun lobby to dig in its heels after Littleton, Conyers, the Mark Barton rampage in Atlanta, and the earlier shootings in Kentucky, Arkansas,[1] and else-

---

[1]*Littleton . . . Arkansas:* school shootings involving students as perpetrators. [Eds.]

where. When Joyce Lee Malcolm, professor of history at Bentley College in Waltham, Massachusetts, and the author of a pathbreaking 1994 study, *To Keep and Bear Arms: The Origins of an Anglo-American Right* (Harvard University Press), told a congressional committee a year later that "[i]t is very hard, sir, to find a historian who now believes that it is only a collective right . . . [t]here is no one for me to argue against anymore," it was just the sort of thing that pro-gun forces on Capitol Hill wanted to hear. If it wasn't a sign that God was on their side, then it was a sign that the Constitution was, which in American politics is more or less the same thing.

The judicial impact is a bit harder to assess. Although the Supreme Court has not ruled on the Second Amendment since the 1930s, it has repeatedly upheld gun control measures. But there is evidence that judicial sentiment is beginning to take heed of the academic change of heart. Two years ago, Supreme Court Justice Clarence Thomas indicated that he thought it was time to rethink the Second Amendment; Justice Antonin Scalia apparently thinks so as well. Then, just this past April, two weeks before Eric Harris and Dylan Klebold shot up Columbine High School, a federal judge in a Texas gun case issued a ruling so enthusiastically "individualist" that it was virtually a brief in favor of what is now known in academic circles as the "Standard Model" of the Second Amendment. "The plain language of the amendment," declared Judge Sam R. Cummings, "shows that the function of the subordinate clause [i.e., the portion referring to a well-regulated militia] was not to qualify the right [to keep and bear arms], but instead to show why it must be protected." Rather than mutually exclusive, the collective right to join a state militia and the individual right to own a gun are, according to Cummings, mutually reinforcing. Although anti-gun groups predicted that the decision would soon be overturned, it is clear that a purely collectivist reading is becoming harder and harder to defend; the individualist interpretation, harder and harder to deny.

We have long been in the habit of seeing in the Constitution whatever 10 it is we want to see. Because liberals want a society that is neat and orderly, they tell themselves that this is what the Constitution "wants" as well. This is a little like a nineteenth-century country vicar arguing that the Bible stands for moderation, reform, and other such Victorian virtues when in fact, as anyone who actually reads the text can see, it is filled with murder, mayhem, and the arbitrary vengeance of a savage god. By the same token, the increasingly sophisticated scholarship surrounding the Second Amendment has led to renewed respect for the constitutional text as it is rather than as we would like it to be. The Constitution, it turns out, is not neat and orderly but messy and unruly. It is not modern but pre-modern. It is not the product of a time very much like our own but reflects the unresolved contradictions of a time very different from our own.

Could it be that the Constitution is not the greatest plan on earth, that it contains notions that are repugnant to the modern sensibility? "When we are lost, the best thing for us to do is to look to our Constitution as a beacon of light and a guide to get us through trying times." So declaimed Representative Zoe Lofgren (D., Calif.) during the House impeachment debate last October. Considering how we've all been taught since childhood to revere this document, probably not one American in a thousand would disagree. But what if Zoe Lofgren is wrong—what if the sacred text is seriously, if not fatally, flawed? Could it be that constitutional faith is *not* enough to get us through trying times? In a faith-bound republic like the United States, this is pretty heretical stuff. Yet one of the nice things about the Second Amendment renaissance is the way it forces us to grapple with such heresy. Instead of allowing us to go on blindly trusting in the wisdom of a group of tribal partriarchs known as the Founding Fathers, it compels us to think of ourselves.

The framers, as it turns out, were of two minds where the power of the people was concerned. The Preamble to the Constitution implies a theory of unbounded popular sovereignty in which "we the people" are so powerful that we can "ordain and establish" new constitutions and, in the process, abrogate old ones such as the disastrous Articles of Confederation. The rest of the document implies that "we the people" are so powerless that when it comes to an anachronism such as the Second Amendment, the democratic majority is effectively precluded from changing a Constitution made in the people's name. We the people can move mountains, but we cannot excise one troublesome twenty-seven-word clause. Because we have chained ourselves to a premodern Constitution, we are unable to deal with the modern problem of a runaway gun culture in a modern way. Rather than binding society together, the effort to force society to conform to the dictates of an outmoded plan of government is tearing it apart. Each new crazed gunman is a symptom of our collective—one might say our constitutional—helplessness. Someday soon, we will have to emancipate ourselves from our eighteenth-century Constitution. The only question is how.

Americans tend to give history short shrift; after all, when your Constitution is a timeless masterpiece, who needs to bother with something as boring as the past? But in order to unlock the meaning of the Second Amendment, it is necessary to know a little about the world in which it was created. The most important thing to understand is the eighteenth century's role as the great transitional period. Capitalism, industrialism, the rise of the great metropolis, the creation of new kinds of politics—these were beginning to make themselves felt, and as they did so they were creating shock waves and counter shock waves from one end of the English-speaking world to the other. Urbanization fueled passionate defenses of the old agrarian way of life. A new system of government centered on a prime minister, a cabinet, and an all-powerful House of Commons provoked endless screeds in favor of the old system of checks and balances among a multitude of coequal governing institutions.

This is the source of the great eighteenth-century polarization between what was known as Court and Country—the powerbrokers, influence-wielders, and political fixers on one side, and all those who felt shut out by the new arrangement on the other. Since the 1960s, historians have made immense strides in reconstructing this Anglo-American ideological world. In essence, we now know that it was dominated by fierce controversy over the nature of political power: whether it was harmful or beneficial, oppressive or liberating, whether it should be concentrated in a single legislative chamber or distributed among many. The Country opposition believed passionately in the latter. As a couple of coffeehouse radicals named John Trenchard and Thomas Gordon put it in their hugely popular *Cato's Letters* in the 1720s, "Power is like fire; it warms, scorches, or destroys according as it is watched, provoked, or increased." The solution was to divide power among so many competitive institutions that politicians' "emulation, envy, fear, or interest, always made them spies and checks upon one another." Since power was growing, oppression was growing also. "Patriots," therefore, were continually fighting a rear-guard action against corruption and tyranny, which were forever on the increase.

We can recognize in eighteenth-century beliefs like these such modern   15
U.S. attitudes as the cult of checks and balances, hostility to "big gummint," and the Zoe Lofgrenesque conviction that everything will turn out well so long as we remain true to the constitutional faith of our forefathers. Guns, as it turns out, were also a big part of the eighteenth-century Anglo-American debate. "Standing armies," the great bugaboo of the day, represented concentrated power at its most brutal; the late-medieval institution of the popular militia represented freedom at its most noble and idealistic. Beginning with the highly influential Niccolò Machiavelli, a long line of political commentators stressed the special importance of the popular militias in the defense of liberty. Since the only ones who could defend popular liberty were the people themselves, a freedom-loving people had to maintain themselves in a high state of republican readiness. They had to be strong and independent, keep themselves well armed, and be well versed in the arts of war. The moment they allowed themselves to surrender to the wiles of luxury, the cause of liberty was lost.

Thus, we have Sir Walter Raleigh[2] warning that the first goal of a would-be tyrant is to "unarm his people of weapons, money, and all means whereby they may resist his power." In the mid-seventeenth century, we have the political theorist James Harrington stressing the special importance of an armed yeomanry of self-sufficient small farmers, while in the early eighteenth we have Trenchard and Gordon warning that "[t]he Exercise of despotick Power is the unrelenting War of an armed Tyrant upon his unarmed Subjects." In the 1770s, James Burgh, another writer in this

---

[2]*Sir Walter Raleigh* (1552–1618): English soldier, explorer, writer. [Eds.]

long Country tradition, advised that "[n]o kingdom can be secured [against tyranny] otherwise than by arming the people. The possession of arms is the distinction between a freeman and a slave." A pro-American English radical named Richard Price added in 1784 that

> [T]he happiest state of man is the middle state between the *savage* and the *refined,* or between the wild and the luxurious state. Such is the state of society in CONNECTICUT, and in some others of the *American* provinces; where the inhabitants consist, if I am rightly informed, of an independent and hardy YEOMANRY, all nearly on a level—trained to arms,—instructed in their rights—cloathed in home-spun—of simple manners—strangers to luxury—drawing plenty from the ground—and that plenty, gathered easily by the hand of industry.

This was the Country myth in all its glory, the image of the rough-hewn, liberty-loving "republican" as someone who called no one master, equated freedom and independence, and was not afraid to fight in defense of either or both. Joyce Lee Malcolm points out that where English patriots were content to pay lip service to the importance of arming the people, their cousins across the sea took the notion quite literally. A law passed by the Plymouth Colony in 1623 required "that every freeman or other inhabitant of this colony provide for himselfe and each under him able to beare arms a sufficient musket and other serviceable peece for war." A 1639 law in Newport ordered that "noe man shall go two miles from the Towne unarmed, eyther with Gunn or Sword; and that none shall come to any public Meeting without his weapon." Measures like these were both practical and symbolic. Not only were guns necessary for self-defense but their widespread possession confirmed America's self-image as a homeland of liberty.

Ideas like these do not seem to have abated the least bit during the colonial period; indeed, by the 1770s they were at full boil. By the time British Redcoats faced off against heavily armed colonial irregulars at the Battle of Lexington and Concord in April 1775, it was as if both sides were actors in a political passion play that had been centuries in the making. It was the standing army versus the people's militia, the metropolis versus the hinterlands, centralized imperial power versus the old balanced constitution. Although the militias performed less than brilliantly in the Revolutionary War—Washington, professional soldier that he was, thought that the ragtag volunteer outfits were more trouble than they were worth—the myth lingered on. Americans needed to believe that amateur citizen-soldiers had won the war because their ideology told them that it was only via a popular militia that republican virtue could be established.

It is worth noting that even among those who were skeptical about the militias' military worth, the concept of a people in arms does not seem to have been at all problematic. Although Alexander Hamilton argued against separate state militias at the Constitutional Convention in 1787, for example, he seemed to have had nothing against popular militias per se. In 1788, he argued in *The Federalist Papers* that in the unlikely event that the proposed new national government used what was known at the time as a "select" militia — i.e., an elite corps — to oppress the population at large, the rest of the militia would be more than enough to fight them off. Such "a large body of citizens," he wrote, "little if at all inferior to them in discipline and the use of arms, . . . [would] stand ready to defend their own rights and those of their fellow-citizens." This is one reason why the argument that the Second Amendment confers only a collective right to join the National Guard is specious: today's National Guard is far closer to the eighteenth-century concept of a select militia than to the broad, popular militia the Framers clearly had in mind. And if the Second Amendment was nothing more than a guarantee of a right on the part of the states to organize state militias, it would imply that only the federal government was potentially tyrannical. Yet it is clear from James Madison's writings in *The Federalist Papers* that he saw state governments as potential sources of tyranny as well. Madison wrote that "the advantage of being armed" was one of the things that distinguished Americans from all other nations and helped protect them against abuse of power at all levels of government, federal and state. Anti-federalists quite agreed. Their only quibble was that they demanded a Bill of Rights; they wanted the right to bear arms put in writing for all to see.

The meaning of what is now the Second Amendment becomes clearer   20
still if we take a look at how its wording evolved. Madison's original version, which he drew up in 1789 as a member of the newly created House of Representatives, was on the wordy side but at least had the merit of clarity:

> The right of the people to keep and bear arms shall not be infringed; a well armed and well regulated militia being the best security of a free country; but no person religiously scrupulous of bearing arms shall be compelled to render military service in person.

By reversing the order between the right to bear arms and a well-regulated militia, Madison reversed the priority. Rather than a precondition, his original version suggested that a well-ordered militia was merely one of the good things that flowed from universal gun ownership. A committee to which the amendment was referred, however, changed the order so that the amendment now read,

> A well regulated militia, composed of the body of the people, being the best security of a free State, the right of the people to keep and bear arms shall not be infringed, but no person religiously scrupulous shall be compelled to bear arms.

This was confusing but at least made plain that a militia was essentially synonymous with the people at large. Unfortunately, that notion, too, was lost when the Senate got hold of the amendment and began chopping out words right and left. The reference to "the body of the people" wound up on the cutting-room floor, as did the final clause. The effect was to deprive later generations of an important clue as to what a well-regulated militia actually meant. Although the final version was leaner and more compact, it was also a good deal less clear.

Nonetheless, a few things seem evident. If the Framers were less than explicit about the nature of a well-regulated militia, it was because they didn't feel they had to be. The idea of a popular militia as something synonymous with the people as a whole was so well understood in the eighteenth century that it went without saying, which is undoubtedly why the Senate felt that the reference to "the body of the people" could be safely eliminated. It is also important to note that the flat-out declaration "[t]he right of the people to keep and bear arms shall not be infringed" remained unchanged throughout the drafting process. As Joyce Lee Malcolm has noted, the Second Amendment is a reworking of a provision contained in the English Bill of Rights of 1689. But whereas the English Bill of Rights specified that subjects "may have arms for their defense suitable to their conditions, and as allowed by law," the American version avoided any such restrictions. Since all Americans (or, rather, members of the white male minority) were of the same rank, they possessed the same rights. They could bear arms for any purpose. And since the amendment was now part of the Constitution, the right was not limited by ordinary law but was over and above it. It was the source of law rather than the object. In this regard, as in virtually all others, Americans saw their role as taking ancient liberties and strengthening them so as to render tyranny all the more unlikely.

Although members of the legal academy assume that this is where the discussion ends, they're wrong: it's where the real questions begin. In attempting to nail down the meaning of the Second Amendment, we are therefore forced to recognize that "meaning" itself is problematic, especially across the span of more than two centuries. Once we have finished dissecting the Second Amendment, we are still left with a certain tension that necessarily exists between a well-regulated militia on the one hand and a right to bear arms on the other. One suggests order and discipline, if not government control; the other suggests voluntarism and a welling up from below. Eighteenth-century Country ideology tried to resolve this contradiction by envisioning the popular militia as a place where liberty and discipline would converge, where a freedom-loving people would enjoy the right to bear arms while proving their republican mettle by voluntarily rising to the defense of liberty. But although this certainly sounded nice, a harrowing eight-year war for independence had demonstrated the limits of such voluntarism. No-nonsense Federalists such as Washington and Hamilton recognized that there was no substitute for a professional army, not to mention a strong, centralized nation-state. But they also recognized that they had to get along with elements for whom such ideas were anathema. As a result, they felt they had no choice but to put aside their scruples and promise effective discipline from above *and* spontaneous self-organization from below, strong national government *and* states' rights, as contradictory as those notions might now seem.

The *meaning* of the Second Amendment, therefore, incorporates the con- 25 tradictions in the Founders' thinking. But what's true for the Second Amendment is true for the Constitution as a whole. In June, William Safire rather naively suggested in his *New York Times* column that the solution to the problem of "the Murky Second" was to use the constitutional amending process to clarify its meaning. Did Americans have an unqualified right to bear arms or merely a right to enlist in the National Guard? Since the Founders had "botched" the wording, the solution was simply to fix it. This is indeed logical, but the problem is that the amending process is entirely useless in this instance. Because Article V stipulates that two thirds of each house, plus three fourths of the states, are required to change so much as a comma, as few as thirteen states—representing, by the way, as little as 4.5 percent of the total U.S. population—would be sufficient to block any change. Since no one would have any trouble coming up with a list of thirteen states in the South or the West for whom repealing the sacred Second Amendment would be akin to repealing the four Gospels, the issue is moot.

Since "we the people" are powerless to change the Second Amendment, we must somehow learn to live within its confines. But since this means standing by helplessly while ordinary people are gunned down by a succession of heavily armed maniacs, it is becoming more and more difficult to do so. As a result, politicians from President Clinton on down are forever coming up with ways of reconciling the irreconcilable, of reining in the gun trade without challenging the Second Amendment–fueled gun culture. The upshot is an endless series of ridiculous proposals to ban some kinds of firearms but not others, to limit handgun purchases to one a month, or to provide for background checks at otherwise unregulated traveling gun bazaars. Instead of cracking down on guns, the administration has found it easier to crack down on video games and theater owners who allow sixteen-year-olds to sneak into adult movies. The moral seems to be that guns don't kill people—fart jokes in the R-rated *South Park: Bigger, Longer & Uncut* do.

This is the flip side of the unbounded faith of a Zoe Lofgren[3] or a Barbara Jordan, who famously declared during Watergate, "My faith in the Constitution is whole, it is complete, it is total . . ." If one's faith in the Constitution is total, then one's faith in the Second Amendment is total as

---

[3]*Zoe Lofgren*: congresswoman from California; *Barbara Jordan*: congresswoman from Texas who figured prominently in the investigation of the Watergate scandal of the early 1970s. [Eds.]

well, which means that one places obedience to ancient law above the needs of modern society. Once all the back-and-forth over the meaning of the Second Amendment is finished, the question we're left with is: So what? No one is suggesting that the Founders' thinking on the gun issue is irrelevant, but because they settled on a certain balance between freedom and order, are we obliged to follow suit? Or are we free to strike a different balance? Times change. From a string of coastal settlements, the United States has grown into a republic of 270 million people stretching across the entire North American continent. It is a congested, polluted society filled with traffic jams, shopping malls, and anomic suburbs in which an eighteenth-century right to bear arms is as out of place as silk knee britches and tricornered hats. So why must we subordinate ourselves to a 208-year-old law that, if the latest scholarship is correct, is contrary to what the democratic majority believes is in its best interest? Why can't *we* create the kind of society we want as opposed to living with laws meant to create the kind of society *they* wanted? They are dead and buried and will not be around to suffer the consequences. We the living will.

There is simply no solution to the gun problem within the confines of the U.S. Constitution. As the well-known Yale law professor Akhil Reed Amar put it recently, the Constitution serves to "structure the conversation of ordinary Americans as they ponder the most fundamental and sometimes divisive issues in our republic." In other words, the Constitution's hold on our society is so complete that it controls the way we discuss and debate, even the way we think. Americans are unable to conceive of an alternative framework, to think "outside the box," as the corporate strategists put it. Other countries are free to change their constitutions when it becomes necessary. In fact, with the exception of Luxembourg, Norway, and Great Britain, there is not one advanced industrial nation that has not thoroughly revamped its constitution since 1900. If they can do it, why can't we? Why must Americans remain slaves to the past?

QUESTIONS

1. This essay contains more than one argument, including an argument about the proper interpretation of the Second Amendment to the Constitution. In your own words, summarize that argument. Then, evaluate it. Is it a strong argument? Do you agree with it? Why, or why not?
2. Consider the evidence Lazare offers for his argument about the Second Amendment. Does he look at evidence from more than one side? Does his use of it seem fair and reasonable? Explain.
3. Suppose you were arguing against Lazare in a court of law. Produce the best counterargument you can, either from the evidence he provides or, if your instructor approves, from further research of your own.

4. There is a larger argument in this essay as well, which is advertised (in a catchy, journalistic way) in the title. Make your own summary of this larger argument about the Constitution, then follow the same steps for this argument that you followed for the argument about the Second Amendment. Is one of these arguments stronger than the other? Give reasons for your decision.

5. To what extent does the larger argument (about the Constitution) depend upon the smaller one (about the Second Amendment)?

6. Suppose you accept both of Lazare's arguments. Does this essay suggest any action based on those arguments? Discuss this point thoroughly in class. Is an explicit action recommended? Is a course of action implied? What is Lazare's view of the possibility of further amendments to the Constitution? Do you agree, or not? Why?

MAKING CONNECTIONS

Both Lazare's piece and Robert Frost's "Mending Wall" (p. 730) raise the question of whether the wisdom of our forefathers, as embodied in written or oral texts (the Constitution or "his father's saying"), should be modified. Discuss the positions developed in the two readings. Are they making the same case or different cases? Develop your own case on this issue.

SIFTING THE ASHES

Jonathan Franzen

Jonathan Franzen's (b. 1959) first novel, The Twenty-Seventh City *(1988), was a detective story. He has since written novels dealing with such contemporary issues as environmental pollution, abortion, and religious fundamentalism. This article first appeared in the* New Yorker *with the subtitle "Confessions of a Conscientious Objector in the Cigarette Wars" (1996).*

Cigarettes are the last thing in the world I want to think about. I don't consider myself a smoker, don't identify with the forty-six million Americans who have the habit. I dislike the smell of smoke and the invasion of nasal privacy it represents. Bars and restaurants with a stylish profile — with a clientele whose exclusivity depends in part on the toxic clouds with which it shields itself — have started to disgust me. I've been gassed in hotel rooms where smokers stayed the night before and in public bathrooms where men use the nasty, body-odorish Winston as a laxative. ("Winston tastes bad / Like the one I just had" runs the grammatically unimpeachable parody from my childhood.) Some days in New York it seems as if two-thirds of the people on the sidewalk, in the swirls of car exhaust, are carrying lighted cigarettes; I maneuver constantly to stay upwind. The first casino I ever went to, in Nevada, was a vision of damnation: row upon row of middle-aged women with foot-long faces puffing on foot-long Kents and compulsively feeding silver dollars to the slots. When someone tells me that cigarettes are sexy, I think of Nevada. When I see an actress or an actor drag deeply in a movie, I imagine the pyrenes and phenols ravaging the tender epithelial cells and hardworking cilia of their bronchi, the carbon monoxide and cyanide binding to their hemoglobin, the heaving and straining of their chemically panicked hearts. Cigarettes are a distillation of a more general paranoia that besets our culture, the awful knowledge of our bodies' fragility in a world of molecular hazards. They scare the hell out of me.

Because I'm capable of hating almost every attribute of cigarettes (let's not even talk about cigars), and because I smoked what I believed was my last cigarette five years ago and have never owned an ashtray, it's easy for me to think of myself as nicotine-free. But if the man who bears my name is not a smoker, then why is there again a box fan for exhaust purposes in his living-room window? Why at the end of every workday is there a small collection of cigarette butts in the saucer on the table by this fan?

Cigarettes were the ultimate taboo in the culturally conservative household I grew up in — more fraught, even, than sex or drugs. The year before I was born, my mother's father died of lung cancer. He'd taken up cigarettes as a soldier in the First World War and smoked heavily all his life. Everyone who met my grandfather seems to have loved him, and, much as I may sneer at our country's obsession with health—at the elevation of fitness to godliness and of sheer longevity to a mark of divine favor—the fact remains that if my grandfather hadn't smoked I might have had the chance to know him.

My mother still speaks of cigarettes with loathing. I secretly started smoking them myself in college, perhaps in part because she hated them, and as the years went by I developed a fear of exposure very similar, I'm convinced, to a gay man's fear of coming out to his parents. My mother had created my body out of hers, after all. What rejection of parentage could be more extreme than deliberately poisoning that body? To come out is to announce: this is who I am, this is my identity. The curious thing about "smoker" as a label of identity, though, is its mutability. I could decide tomorrow not to be one anymore. So why not pretend not to be one today? To take control of their lives, people tell themselves stories about the person they want to be. It's the special privilege of the smoker, who at times feels so strongly the resolve to quit that it's as if he'd quit already, to be given irrefutable evidence that these stories aren't necessarily true: here are the butts in the ashtray, here is the smell in the hair.

As a smoker, then, I've come to distrust not only my stories about myself but *all* narratives that pretend to unambiguous moral significance. And it happens that . . . Americans have been subjected to just such a narrative in the daily press, as "secret" documents shed light on the machinations of Big Tobacco, industry scientists step forward to indict their former employers, nine states and a consortium of sixty law firms launch massive liability suits, and the Food and Drug Administration undertakes to regulate cigarettes as nicotine-delivery devices. The prevailing liberal view that Big Tobacco is Evil with a capital "E" is summed up in the *Times'* review of Richard Kluger's excellent new history of the tobacco industry, "Ashes to Ashes." Chiding Kluger for (of all things) his "objectivity" and "impartiality," Christopher Lehmann-Haupt suggests that the cigarette business is on a moral par with slavery and the Holocaust. Kluger himself, impartial or not, repeatedly links the word "angels" with anti-smoking activists. In the introduction to his book he offers a stark pair of options: either cigarette manufacturers are "businessmen basically like any other" or they're "moral lepers preying on the ignorant, the miserable, the emotionally vulnerable, and the genetically susceptible."

My discomfort with these dichotomies may reflect the fact that, unlike Lehmann-Haupt, I have yet to kick the habit. But in no national debate do I feel more out of synch with the mainstream. For all that I distrust American industry, and especially an industry that is vigorously engaged in buying congressmen, some part of me insists on rooting for tobacco. I flinch as I force myself to read the latest health news: SMOKERS MORE LIKELY TO BEAR RETARDED BABIES, STUDY SAYS. I pounce on particularly choice collisions of metaphor and melodrama, such as this one from the *Times:* "The affidavits

5

are the latest in a string of blows that have undermined the air of invincibility that once cloaked the $45 billion tobacco industry, which faces a deluge of lawsuits." My sympathy with cohorts who smoke disproportionately—blue-collar workers, African-Americans, writers and artists, alienated teens, the mentally ill—expands to include the companies that supply them with cigarettes. I think, We're all underdogs now. Wartime is a time of lies, I tell myself, and the biggest lie of the cigarette wars is that the moral equation can be reduced to ones and zeroes. Or have I, too, been corrupted by the weed?

I took up smoking as a student in Germany in the dark years of the early eighties. Ronald Reagan had recently made his "evil empire" speech, and Jonathan Schell was publishing "The Fate of the Earth." The word in Berlin was that if you woke up to an undestroyed world on Saturday morning you were safe for another week; the assumption was that NATO was at its sleepiest late on Friday nights, that Warsaw Pact forces would choose those hours to come pouring through the Fulda Gap, and that NATO would have to go ballistic to repel them. Since I rated my chances of surviving the decade at fifty-fifty, the additional risk posed by smoking seemed negligible. Indeed, there was something invitingly apocalyptic about cigarettes. The nightmare of nuclear proliferation had a counterpart in the way cigarettes—anonymous, death-bearing, missilelike cylinders—proliferated in my life. Cigarettes are a fixture of modern warfare, the soldier's best friend, and, at a time when a likely theater of war was my own living room, smoking became a symbol of my helpless civilian participation in the Cold War.

Among the anxieties best suited to containment by cigarettes is, paradoxically, the fear of dying. What serious smoker hasn't felt the surge of panic at the thought of lung cancer and immediately lighted up to beat the panic down? (It's a Cold War logic: we're afraid of nuclear weapons, so let's build even more of them.) Death is a severing of the connection between self and world, and, since the self can't imagine not existing, perhaps what's really scary about the prospect of dying is not the extinguishment of my consciousness but the extinguishment of the world. The potential deadliness of cigarettes was comforting because it allowed me, in effect, to become familiar with apocalypse, to acquaint myself with the contours of its terrors, to make the world's potential death less strange and so a little less threatening. Time stops for the duration of a cigarette: when you're smoking, you're acutely present to yourself; you step outside the unconscious forward rush of life. This is why the condemned are allowed a final cigarette, this is why (or so the story goes) gentlemen in evening dress stood puffing at the rail as the Titanic went down: it's a lot easier to leave the world if you're certain you've really been in it. As Goethe[1] writes in "Faust," "Presence is our duty, be it only a moment."

---

[1]*Johann Wolfgang Goethe* (1749–1832): German author and scientist, author of the dramatic poem *Faust.* [Eds.]

The cigarette is famously the herald of the modern, the boon companion of industrial capitalism and high-density urbanism. Crowds, hyperkinesis, mass production, numbingly boring labor, and social upheaval all have correlatives in the cigarette. The sheer number of individual units consumed surely dwarfs that of any other manufactured consumer product. "Short, snappy, easily attempted, easily completed or just as easily discarded before completion," the *Times* wrote in a 1925 editorial that Richard Kluger quotes, "the cigarette is the symbol of a machine age in which the ultimate cogs and wheels and levers are human nerves." Itself the product of a mechanical roller called the Bonsack machine, the cigarette served as an opiate for assembly-line workers, breaking up into manageable units long days of grinding sameness. For women, the *Atlantic Monthly* noted in 1916, the cigarette was "the symbol of emancipation, the temporary substitute for the ballot." Altogether, it's impossible to imagine the twentieth century without cigarettes. They show up with Zelig-like[2] ubiquity in old photographs and newsreels, so devoid of individuality as to be hardly noticeable and yet, once noticed, utterly strange.

Kluger's history of the cigarette business reads like a history of American business in general. An industry that in the early eighteen-eighties was splintered into hundreds of small, family-owned concerns had by the turn of the century come under the control of one man, James Buchanan Duke, who by pioneering the use of the Bonsack roller and reinvesting a huge portion of his revenues in advertising, and then by alternately employing the stick of price wars and the carrot of attractive buyout offers, built his American Tobacco Company into the equivalent of Standard Oil or Carnegie Steel. Like his fellow-monopolists, Duke eventually ran afoul of the trust-busters, and in 1911 the Supreme Court ordered the breakup of American. The resulting oligopoly immediately brought out new brands—Camel, Lucky Strike, and Chesterfield—that have vied for market share ever since. To American retailers, the cigarette was the perfect commodity, a staple that generated large profits on a small investment in shelf space and inventory; cigarettes, Kluger notes, "were lightweight and durably packed, rarely spoiled, were hard to steal since they were usually sold from behind the counter, underwent few price changes, and required almost no selling effort."

Since every brand tasted pretty much the same, tobacco companies learned early to situate themselves at the cutting edge of advertising. In the twenties, American Tobacco offered five free cartons of Lucky Strike ("it's toasted") to any doctor who would endorse it, and then launched a campaign that claimed, "20,679 Physicians Say Luckies Are Less Irritating"; American was also the first company to target weight-conscious women ("When tempted to over-indulge, reach for a Lucky instead"). The industry

---

[2]*Zelig:* the protagonist, played by Woody Allen, of Allen's 1984 film *Zelig,* who appears in a number of historical newsreels. [Eds.]

pioneered the celebrity endorsement (the tennis star Bill Tilden: "I've smoked Camels for years, and I never tire of their smooth, rich taste"), radio sponsorship (Arthur Godfrey: "I smoked two or three packs of these things [Chesterfields] every day—I feel pretty good"), assaultive outdoor advertising (the most famous was the "I'd Walk a Mile for a Camel" billboard in Times Square, which for twenty-five years blew giant smoke rings), and, finally, the sponsorship of television shows like "Candid Camera" and "I Love Lucy." The brilliant TV commercials made for Philip Morris—Benson & Hedges smokers whose hundred-millimeter cigarettes were crushed by elevator doors; faux-hand-cranked footage of chambermaids sneaking smokes to the tune of "You've got your own cigarette now, baby"—were vital entertainments of my childhood. I remember, too, the chanted words "Silva Thins, Silva Thins," the mantra for a short-lived American Tobacco product that wooed the female demographic with such appalling copy as "Cigarettes are like girls, the best ones are thin and rich."

The most successful campaign of all, of course, was for Marlboro, an upscale cigarette for ladies which Philip Morris reintroduced in 1954 in a filtered version for the mainstream. Like all modern products, the new Marlboro was designed with great care. The tobacco blend was strengthened so as to survive the muting of a filter, the "flip-top" box was introduced to the national vocabulary, the color red was chosen to signal strong flavor, and the graphics underwent endless tinkering before the final look, including a fake heraldic crest with the motto "*Veni, vidi, vici,*"[3] was settled on; there was even market-testing in four cities to decide the color of the filter. It was in Leo Burnett's ad campaign for Marlboro, however, that the real genius lay. The key to its success was its transparency. Place a lone ranch hand against a backdrop of buttes at sunset, and just about every positive association a cigarette can carry is in the picture: rugged individualism, masculine sexuality, escape from an urban modernity, strong flavors, the living of life intensely. The Marlboro marks our commercial culture's passage from an age of promises to an age of pleasant empty dreams.

It's no great surprise that a company smart enough to advertise as well as this ascended, in just three decades, to a position of hegemony in the industry. Kluger's account of the triumph of Philip Morris is the kind of thing that business schools have their students read for edification and inspiration: to succeed as an American corporation, the lesson might be, do exactly what Philip Morris did. Concentrate on products with the highest profit margin. Design new products carefully, then get behind them and push *hard*. Use your excess cash to diversify into businesses that are structurally similar to your own. Be a meritocracy. Avoid crippling debt. Patiently build your overseas markets. Never scruple to gouge your customers

---

[3]*Veni, vidi, vici:* "I came, I saw, I conquered." [Eds.]

when you see the opportunity. Let your lawyers attack your critics. Be classy—sponsor "The Mahabharata." Defy conventional morality. Never forget that your primary fealty is to your stockholders.

While its chief competitor, R. J. Reynolds, was growing logy and in-bred down in Winston-Salem—sinking into the low-margin discount-cigarette business, diversifying disastrously, and nearly drowning in debt after its leveraged buyout by Kohlberg Kravis Roberts & Company—Philip Morris was becoming the global leader in the cigarette industry and one of the most profitable corporations in the world. By the early nineties, its share of the domestic nondiscount-cigarette market had risen to eighty percent. One share of Philip Morris stock bought in 1966 was worth a hundred and ninety-two shares in 1989 dollars. Healthy, wealthy, and wise the man who quite smoking in '64 and put his cigarette money into Philip Morris common.

The company's spectacular success is all the more remarkable for hav-   15
ing occurred in the decades when the scientific case against cigarettes was becoming overwhelming. With the possible exception of the hydrogen bomb, nothing in modernity is more generative of paradox than cigarettes. Thus, in 1955, when the Federal Trade Commission sought to curb mis-leading advertising by banning the publication of tar and nicotine levels, the ruling proved to be a boon to the industry, by enabling it to advertise filter cigarettes for their implicit safety even as it raised the toxic yields to compensate for the filters. So it went with the 1965 law requiring warning labels on cigarette packs, which preempted potentially more stringent state and local regulations and provided a priceless shield against future liability suits. So it went, too, with the 1971 congressional ban on broadcast ciga-rette advertising, which saved the industry millions of dollars, effectively froze out potential new competitors by denying them the broadcast plat-form, and put an end to the devastating anti-smoking ads then being broadcast under the fairness doctrine. Even such left-handed regulation as the 1982 increase in the federal excise tax benefited the industry, which used the tax as a screen for a series of price increases, doubling the price per pack in a decade, and invested the windfall in diversification. Every forward step taken by government to regulate smoking—the broadcast ban, the ban on in-flight smoking, the welter of local bans on smoking in public places—has moved cigarettes a step further back from the con-sciousness of nonsmoking voters. The result, given the political power of tobacco-growing states, has been the specific exemption of cigarettes from the Fair Labeling and Packaging Act of 1966, the Controlled Substances Act of 1970, the Consumer Product Safety Act of 1972, and the Toxic Sub-stances Act of 1976. In the industry's defense in liability suits, the paradox can be seen in its purest form: because no plaintiff can claim ignorance of to-bacco's hazards—i.e., precisely *because* the cigarette is the most notoriously lethal product in America—its manufacturers cannot be held negligent for selling it. Small wonder that until the Liggett Group broke ranks . . . no ciga-rette maker had ever paid a penny in civil damages.

Now, however, the age of paradox may be coming to an end. As the nation dismantles its missiles, its attention turns to cigarettes. The wall of secrecy that protected the industry is coming down as surely as the Berlin Wall did. The Third Wave is upon us, threatening to extinguish all that is quintessentially modern. It hardly seems an accident that the United States, which is leading the way into the information age, is also in the forefront of the war on cigarettes. Unlike the nations of Europe, which have taken a more pragmatic approach to the smoking problem, taxing cigarettes at rates as high as five dollars a pack, the anti-smoking forces in this country bring to the battle a puritanical zeal. We need a new Evil Empire, and Big Tobacco fills the bill.

The argument for equating the tobacco industry with slave traders and the Third Reich goes like this: because nearly half a million Americans a year die prematurely as a direct consequence of smoking, the makers of cigarettes are guilty of mass murder. The obvious difficulty with the argument is that the tobacco industry has never physically forced anyone to smoke a cigarette. To speak of its "killing" people, therefore, one has to posit more subtle forms of coercion. These fall into three categories. First, by publicly denying a truth well known to its scientists, which was that smokers were in mortal peril, the industry conspired to perpetrate a vast and deadly fraud. Second, by luring impressionable children into a habit very difficult to break, the industry effectively "forced" its products on people before they had developed full adult powers of resistance. Finally, by making available and attractive a product that it knew to be addictive, and by manipulating nicotine levels, the industry willfully exposed the public to a force (addiction) with the power to kill.

A "shocking" collection of "secret" industry documents which was express-mailed by a disgruntled employee of Brown & Williamson to the anti-smoking crusader Stanton A. Glantz, and has now been published by the University of California Press as "The Cigarette Papers," makes it clear that Big Tobacco has known for decades that cigarettes are lethal and addictive and has done everything in its power to suppress and deny that knowledge. "The Cigarette Papers" and other recent disclosures have prompted the Justice Department to pursue perjury charges against various industry executives, and may provide the plaintiffs now suing the industry with positive proof of tortious fraud. In no way, though, are the disclosures shocking. How could anyone who noticed that different cigarette brands have different (but consistent) nicotine levels fail to conclude that the industry can and does control the dosage? What reasonable person could have believed that the industry's public avowals of "doubt" about the deadliness of its products were anything but obligatory, ceremonial lies? If researchers unearthed a secret document proving that Bill Clinton inhaled, would we be shocked? When industry spokesmen impugn the integrity of the Surgeon General and persist in denying the undeniable, they're guilty not so much of fraud as of sounding (to borrow the word of one executive quoted by Kluger) "Neanderthal."

"The simple truth," Kluger writes, "was that the cigarette makers were getting richer and richer as the scientific findings against them piled higher and higher, and before anyone fully grasped the situation, the choice seemed to have narrowed to abject confession and surrender to the health advocates or steadfast denial and rationalization." In the early fifties, when epidemiological studies first demonstrated the link between smoking and lung cancer, cigarette executives did indeed have the option of simply liquidating their businesses and finding other work. But many of these executives came from families that had been respectably trading in tobacco for decades, and most of them appear to have been heavy smokers themselves: unlike the typical heroin wholesaler, they willingly ran the same risks they imposed on their customers. Because they were corporate officers, moreover, their ultimate allegiance was to their stockholders. If having simply stayed in business constitutes guilt, then the circle of those who share this guilt must be expanded to include every individual who held stock in a tobacco company after 1964, either directly or through a pension fund, a mutual fund, or a university endowment. We might also toss in every drugstore and supermarket that sold cigarettes and every publication that carried ads for them, since the Surgeon General's warning, after all, was there for everyone to see.

Once the companies made the decision to stay in business, it was only   20 a matter of time before the lawyers took over. Nothing emerges from "Ashes to Ashes" more clearly than the deforming influence of legal counsel on the actions of the industry. Many industry scientists and some executives appear to have genuinely wished both to produce a safer cigarette and to acknowledge frankly the known risks of smoking. But the industry's attempts to do good were no less paradoxically self-defeating than the government's attempts at regulation. When executives in R. & D. proposed that filtered cigarettes and reduced tar and nicotine yields be marketed as a potential benefit to public health, in-house lawyers objected that calling one brand "safe" or "safer" constituted an admission that other brands were hazardous and thus exposed the maker to liability claims. Likewise, after Liggett had spent millions of dollars developing a substantially less carcinogenic "palladium cigarette" in the seventies, it was treated like contagion by the company's lawyers. Marketing it was bad from a liability standpoint, and developing it and then not marketing it was even worse, because in that case the company could be sued for negligently failing to introduce it. Epic, as the new cigarette was called, was ultimately smothered in legal paper.

Kluger describes an industry in which lawyerly paranoia quickly metastasized into every vital organ. Lawyers coached the executives appearing before congressional committees, oversaw the woefully self-serving "independent" research that the industry sponsored, and made sure that all paperwork connected with studies of addiction or cancer was funneled through outside counsel so that it could be protected under the attorney-client privilege. The result was a weird replication of the dual contradictory

narratives with which I, as a smoker, explain my life: a true story submerged beneath a utilitarian fiction. One longtime Philip Morris executive
quoted by Kluger sums it up like this:

> There was a conflict in the company between science and the law
> that's never been resolved . . . and so we go through this ritual
> dance—what's "proven" and what isn't, what's causal and what's
> just an association—and the lawyers' answer is, "Let's
> stonewall." . . . If Helmut Wakeham [head of R. & D.] had run
> things, I think there would have been some admissions. But he was
> outflanked by the lawyers . . . who . . . were saying, in effect, "My
> God, you can't make that admission" without risking liability ac-
> tions against the company. So there was no cohesive plan—when
> critics of the industry speak of a "conspiracy," they give the com-
> panies far too much credit.

In the inverted moral universe of a tobacco-liability trial, every honest
or anguished statement by an executive is used to prove the defendants'
guilt, while every calculated dodge is used to support their innocence.
There's something very wrong here; but absent a demonstration that
Americans actually swallowed the industry's lies it's far from clear that this
something qualifies as murder.

More damning are recent reports of the industry's recruitment of underage smokers. Lorillard representatives have been observed handing out
free Newports to kids in Washington, D.C.; Philip J. Hilts, in his new
book, "Smokescreen," presents evidence that R. J. Reynolds deliberately
placed special promotional displays in stores and kiosks known to be high-
school hangouts; and the cuddly, penis-faced Joe Camel must rank as one
of the most disgusting apparitions ever to appear in our cultural landscape.
Tobacco companies claim that they are merely vying for market share in
the vital eighteen-to-twenty-four age group, but internal industry documents described by Hilts suggest that at least one Canadian company has
in fact studied how to target entry-level smokers as young as twelve. (According to Hilts, studies have shown that eighty-nine percent of today's
adult smokers picked up the habit before the age of nineteen.) In the opinion of anti-tobacco activists, cigarette advertising hooks young customers
by proffering images of carefree, attractive adult smokers while failing to
hint at the havoc that smoking wreaks. By the time young smokers are old
enough to appreciate the fact of mortality, they're hopelessly addicted.

Although the idea that a manufacturer might willingly stress the down-
side of its products is absurd, I have no doubt that the industry aims its ads
at young Americans. I do doubt, though, whether these ads cause an appre-
ciable number of children to start smoking. The insecure or alienated teen
who lights up for the first time is responding to peer pressure or to the example of grownup role models—movie villains, rock stars, supermodels.
At most, the industry's ads function as an assurance that smoking is a so-

cially acceptable grownup activity. For that reason alone, they should probably be banned or more tightly controlled, just as cigarette-vending machines should be outlawed. Most people who start smoking end up regretting it, so any policy that reduces the number of starters is laudable.

That cigarettes innately appeal to teen-agers, however, is hardly the fault of the manufacturers. In recent weeks, I've noticed several anti-tobacco newspaper ads that offer, evidently for its shock value, the image of a preadolescent girl holding a cigarette. The models are obviously not real smokers, yet, despite their phoniness, they're utterly sexualized by their cigarettes. The horror of underage smoking veils a horror of teen and preteen sexuality, and one of the biggest pleasant empty dreams being pushed these days by Madison Avenue is that a child is innocent until his or her eighteenth birthday. The truth is that without firm parental guidance teen-agers make all sorts of irrevocable decisions before they're old enough to appreciate the consequences—they drop out of school, they get pregnant, they major in sociology. What they want most of all is to sample the pleasures of adulthood, like sex or booze or cigarettes. To impute to cigarette advertising a "predatory" power is to admit that parents now have less control over the moral education of their children than the commercial culture has. Here, again, I suspect that the tobacco industry is being scapegoated—made to bear the brunt of a more general societal rage at the displacement of the family by the corporation.

The final argument for the moral culpability of Big Tobacco is that addiction is a form of coercion. Nicotine is a toxin whose ingestion causes the smoker's brain to change its chemistry in defense. Once those changes have occurred, the smoker must continue to consume nicotine on a regular schedule in order to maintain the new chemical balance. Tobacco companies are well aware of this, and an attorney cited by Kluger summarizes the legal case for coercion as follows: "You addicted me, and you knew it was addicting, and now you say it's my fault." As Kluger goes on to point out, though, the argument has many flaws. Older even than the common knowledge that smoking causes cancer, for example, is the knowledge that smoking is a tough habit to break. Human tolerance of nicotine varies widely, moreover, and the industry has long offered an array of brands with ultra-low doses. Finally, no addiction is unconquerable: millions of Americans quit every year. When a smoker says he wants to quit but can't, what he's really saying is "I want to quit, but I want even more not to suffer the agony of withdrawal." To argue otherwise is to jettison any lingering notion of personal responsibility.

If nicotine addiction were purely physical, quitting would be relatively easy, because the acute withdrawal symptoms, the physical cravings, rarely last more than a few weeks. At the time I myself quit, six years ago, I was able to stay nicotine-free for weeks at a time, and even when I was working I seldom smoked more than a few ultralights a day. But on the day I decided that the cigarette I'd had the day before was my last, I was absolutely flattened. A month passed in which I was too agitated to read a book, too fuzzy-headed even to focus on a newspaper. If I'd had a job at the time, or a family to take care of, I might have hardly noticed the psychological withdrawal. But as it happened nothing much was going on in my life. "Do you smoke?" Lady Bracknell asks Jack Worthing in "The Importance of Being Earnest," and when he admits that he does she replies, "I am glad to hear it. A man should always have an occupation of some kind."

There's no simple, universal reason that people smoke, but of one thing I'm convinced: they don't do it because they're slaves to nicotine. My best guess about my own attraction to the habit is that I belong to a class of people whose lives are insufficiently structured. The mentally ill and the indigent are also members of this class. We embrace a toxin as deadly as nicotine, suspended in an aerosol of hydrocarbons and nitrosamines, because we have not yet found pleasures or routines that can replace the comforting, structure-bringing rhythm of need and gratification that the cigarette habit offers. One word for this structuring might be "self-medication"; another might be "coping." But there are very few serious smokers over thirty, perhaps none at all, who don't feel guilty about the harm they inflict on themselves. Even Rose Cipollone, the New Jersey woman whose heirs in the early eighties nearly sustained a liability judgment against the industry, had to be recruited by an activist. The sixty law firms that have pooled their assets for a class-action suit on behalf of all American smokers do not seem to me substantially less predatory than the suit's corporate defendants. I've never met a smoker who blamed the habit on someone else.

The United States as a whole resembles an addicted individual, with the corporated id going about its dirty business while the conflicted political ego frets and dithers. What's clear is that the tobacco industry would not still be flourishing, thirty years after the first Surgeon General's report, if our legislatures weren't purchasable, if the concepts of honor and personal responsibility hadn't largely given way to the power of litigation and the dollar, and if the country didn't generally endorse the idea of corporations whose ultimate responsibility is not to society but to the bottom line. There's no doubt that some tobacco executives have behaved despicably, and for public-health advocates to hate these executives, as the nicotine addict comes eventually to hate his cigarettes, is natural. But to cast them as moral monsters—a point source of evil—is just another form of prime-time entertainment.

By selling its soul to its legal advisers, Big Tobacco long ago made clear 30
its expectation that the country's smoking problem would eventually be resolved in court. The industry may soon suffer such a devastating loss in a liability suit that thereafter only foreign cigarette makers will be able to afford to do business here. Or perhaps a federal court will undertake to legislate a solution to a problem that the political process has clearly proved itself unequal to, and the Supreme Court will issue an opinion that does for the smoking issue what Brown v. Board of Education did for racial segregation and Roe v. Wade for abortion. "Businessmen are combatants, not

healers," Kluger writes in "Ashes to Ashes," "and when they press against or exceed the bounds of decency in their quest for gain, unhesitant to profit from the folly of others, should the exploited clientele and victimized society expect the perpetrators to restrain themselves out of some sudden divine visitation of conscience? Or must human nature be forcibly corrected when it goes awry?"

Liggett's recent defection notwithstanding, the Medicare suits filed by nine states seem unlikely to succeed as a forcible correction. Kluger notes that these cases arguably amount to "personal injury claims in disguise," and that the Supreme Court has ruled that federal cigarette-labeling laws are an effective shield against such claims. Logically, in other words, the states ought to be suing smokers, not cigarette makers. And perhaps smokers, in turn, ought to be suing Social Security and private pension funds for all the money they'll save by dying early. The best estimates of the nationwide dollar "cost" of smoking, including savings from premature death and income from excise taxes, are negative numbers. If the country's health is to be measured fiscally, an economist quoted by Kluger jokes, "cigarette smoking should be subsidized rather than taxed."

The giant class-action suit filed in New Orleans in March of 1994 represents a more serious threat to Big Tobacco. If a judge concludes that smoking constitutes a social ill on a par with racial segregation, he or she is unlikely to deny standing to the forty-six-million-member "class" represented by the consortium of law firms, and once plaintiffs in a class-action suit are granted standing they almost never lose. The case for regulation of tobacco by the F.D.A is likewise excellent. The modern cigarette is a heavily engineered product, bolstered with a long list of additives, and its nicotine content is manipulable at will. Tobacco companies insist that cigarettes, because no health claims are made for them by the companies, should not be considered a drug. But if nicotine is universally understood to be habit-forming—a central tenet of the industry's liability defense—then the absence of explicit health claims is meaningless. Whether Congress, in its various wafflings, intended cigarettes to be immune from F.D.A. regulation in the first place is, again, a matter that will be decided in court, but a demonstrable history of lies and distortion is sure to weaken the industry's defense.

Ultimately, the belief that the country's century-long love affair with the cigarette can be ended rationally and amicably seems as fond as the belief that there's a painless way to kick nicotine. The first time I quit, I stayed clean for nearly three years. I found I was able to work *more* productively without the distraction and cumulative unpleasantness of cigarettes, and I was happy finally to be the nonsmoker that my family had always taken me to be. Eventually, though, in a season of great personal loss, I came to resent having quit for other people rather than for myself. I was hanging out with smokers, and I drifted back into the habit. Smoking may not look sexy to me anymore, but it still *feels* sexy. The pleasure of carrying the drug, of surrendering to its imperatives and relaxing behind a veil of smoke, is thoroughly licentious. If longevity were the highest good that I could imagine, I might succeed now in scaring myself into quitting. But to the fatalist who values the present more than the future the nagging voice of conscience—of society, of family—becomes just another factor in the mental equilibrium that sustains the habit. "Perhaps," Richard Klein writes in "Cigarettes Are Sublime," "one stops smoking only when one starts to love cigarettes, becoming so enamored of their charms and so grateful for their benefits that one at last begins to grasp how much is lost by giving them up, how urgent it is to find substitutes for some of the seductions and powers that cigarettes so magnificently combine." To live with uncontaminated lungs and an unracing heart is a pleasure that I hope someday soon to prefer to the pleasure of a cigarette. For myself, then, I'm cautiously optimistic. For the body politic, rhetorically torn between shrill condemnation and Neanderthal denial, and habituated to the poison of tobacco money in its legal system, its legislatures, its financial markets, and its balance of foreign trade, I'm considerably less so.

A few weeks ago in Tribeca, in a Magritte-like twilight,[4] I saw a woman in a lighted window on a high floor of a loft apartment building. She was standing on a chair and lowering the window's upper sash. She tossed her hair and did something complicated with her arms which I recognized as the lighting of a cigarette. Then she leaned her elbow and her chin on the sash and blew smoke into the humid air outside. I fell in love at first sight as she stood there, both inside and outside, inhaling contradiction and breathing out ambivalence.

QUESTIONS

1. In publishing this essay with the subtitle "Confessions of a Conscientious Objector in the Cigarette Wars," *The New Yorker* sets it up as confessional, yet we have placed it in the Arguing section of this book. How would you categorize this essay? Is Franzen confessing or arguing or both? Give examples to support your opinion.

2. How does Franzen answer the questions of why he started smoking, why he gave it up, and why he started again? Note how he uses the first question as a frame, returning to it in paragraph 28 to link his own addiction to a national addiction.

3. Consider the symbolic values given the cigarette and cigarette smoking. If giving up cigarettes means, as Richard Klein says, finding "substitutes for some of the seductions and powers that cigarettes so magnificently combine" (paragraph 33), what would you suggest as some possible substitutes?

---

[4]*René Magritte* (1898–1967): French surrealist artist whose twilight skies were sometimes full of hats or umbrellas. [Eds.]

4. The central section of Franzen's essay presents some of the evidence that has been gathered against "Big Tobacco" and its attempts to squelch evidence of how harmful cigarette smoking is. "The argument for equating the tobacco industry with slave traders and the Third Reich" starts in paragraph 17. What does Franzen mean by this comparison?

5. How strong is the evidence Franzen presents for his argument? In what order does he place his evidence? Why do you think he organizes his evidence in this way?

6. Since this article was published, the Food and Drug Administration has decided to regulate tobacco. Do some research on this issue, and report on the implications of such regulation, as well as the issues Franzen raises in paragraph 32.

MAKING CONNECTIONS

Compare Franzen's argument with Andrew Sullivan's in "What's So Bad About Hate" (p. 664). In what ways do the two writers each use personal experience?

MENDING WALL

Robert Frost

Perhaps the most popular and widely acclaimed American poet of the twentieth century, Robert Frost (1874–1963) grew up in Lawrence, Massachusetts. He dropped out of Dartmouth College after less than a semester, later attending Harvard University. For a time an instructor at a private boys' school while living on a farm in New Hampshire, Frost moved his large family to London in 1911, where his first collection of poems, A Boy's Will, *was published in 1913. Its success there led to a growing reputation at home, and Frost returned to the United States in 1915, joining the faculty of Amherst College in 1917. He would go on to win an unprecedented four Pulitzer Prizes for his poetry and to reach a broad audience, both through his published collections and through his lectures and public readings. Frost wrote frequently on the nature and craft of poetry. Among his observations: "There are many other things I have found myself saying about poetry, but the chiefest of these is that it is metaphor, saying one thing and meaning another, saying one thing in terms of another, the pleasure of ulteriority. Poetry is simply made of metaphor."*

Something there is that doesn't love a wall,
That sends the frozen-ground-swell under it,
And spills the upper boulders in the sun;
And makes gaps even two can pass abreast.
The work of hunters is another thing: 5
I have come after them and made repair
Where they have left not one stone on a stone,
But they would have the rabbit out of hiding,
To please the yelping dogs. The gaps I mean,
No one has seen them made or heard them made, 10
But at spring mending-time we find them there.
I let my neighbor know beyond the hill;
And on a day we meet to walk the line
And set the wall between us once again.
We keep the wall between us as we go. 15
To each the boulders that have fallen to each.
And some are loaves and some so nearly balls
We have to use a spell to make them balance:
"Stay where you are until our backs are turned!"

We wear our fingers rough with handling them. 20
Oh, just another kind of outdoor game,
One on a side. It comes to little more:
There where it is we do not need the wall:
He is all pine and I am apple orchard.
My apple trees will never get across 25
And eat the cones under his pines, I tell him.
He only says, "Good fences make good neighbors."
Spring is the mischief in me, and I wonder
If I could put a notion in his head:
"*Why* do they make good neighbors? Isn't it 30
Where there are cows? But here there are no cows.
Before I built a wall I'd ask to know
What I was walling in or walling out,
And to whom I was like to give offense.
Something there is that doesn't love a wall, 35
That wants it down." I could say "Elves" to him,
But it's not elves exactly, and I'd rather
He said it for himself. I see him there
Bringing a stone grasped firmly by the top
In each hand, like an old-stone savage armed. 40
He moves in darkness as it seems to me,
Not of woods only and the shade of trees.
He will not go behind his father's saying,
And he likes having thought of it so well
He says again, "Good fences make good neighbors." 45

QUESTIONS

1. This poem is a reflection with a report inside it and an argument inside it. It is a reflection on the function and meaning of walls, with a report on two neighbors mending their communal wall inside that. Motivated by "Spring," the speaker offers an argument against this particular wall. Is it an argument against walls in general? Explain.
2. Summarize the speaker's argument to his neighbor. Summarize his neighbor's reply. Are the arguments equally simple? Whom do you sympathize with the most? Why?
3. What is the "Something" that doesn't love a wall: nature? entropy? frost? chaos? God? Satan? Discuss your choice.
4. The speaker says mending the wall is a game. Explain what you think he means by that.
5. What does "Good fences make good neighbors" actually mean? Does this apply on a larger scale, to nations as well as to growers of pine and apple trees? Explain why or why not.

6. Discuss walls you know or have heard or read about (China, Berlin, playground, pigpen). Try to develop a theory of the function of walls.

MAKING CONNECTIONS

Look at C. G. Hanzlicek's "Room for Doubt" (p. 773). Does that concept of "room for doubt" apply to the argument of Frost's poem as well? Discuss the way both of these arguments lead from specific situations to larger questions. Does this happen in other arguments in this collection as well? To some more than others? Give examples to support your answer.

Sciences and Technologies

SECRETS OF THE SOFTWARE LICENSE AGREEMENT

David Pogue

David Pogue (b. 1963), a 1985 graduate of Yale with a degree in music, got interested in computers as an aid to composition. He has helped design music software, and he also spent a number of years pursuing a career in musical theater, conducting and composing for the New York stage. When success eluded him, he turned to teaching theater professionals how to use their Macs. He began writing for Macworld *magazine in 1988, and in 1992 he published* Mac for Dummies, *the second of the "for Dummies" books. He has gone on to publish numerous books in this series (including* Music for Dummies), *as well as computer guidebooks and several books of computer humor. He also writes "The Desktop Critic" column for* Macworld, *where the following first appeared.*

Every time you try to install a piece of software or download something from the Internet, you click past a screen of legalese known as the *software license agreement.* You can't get past it without clicking on one of two buttons: Accept or Decline. Nobody actually reads this document, of course. At this point, you blindly click on Accept. After paying $300 or $800 for a piece of software, you just want to get the thing installed.

So I had something of a shock when, seized by a rare wave of boredom, I actually sat down to read one of these things in its entirety. Here's what it said:

"SOFTWARE LICENSE AGREEMENT. We, Microsoft Corporation ("God"), grant you ("powerless supplicant") a nonexclusive license to use the accompanying software (a $300 program on a 50-cent CD—with no printed manual, by the way). You are not permitted to lease, rent,

733

distribute, sublicense, disassemble, reverse-engineer, forward-engineer, sideways-engineer, or dislike the software. In fact, we'd sort of appreciate it if you wouldn't say bad things about the software in public.

"This agreement gives you the right to install one (1) copy of the software on one (1) computer within thirty (30) days of reading this agreement, not because we care how many times you install it, but because we think our customers are idiots who can't understand numbers unless we write them out two (2) times.

"You agree that our installer may spray your System Folder with dozens of extensions, shared libraries, control panels, preference files, fonts, and other crud, without asking first or providing a list of why we put what where. If your computer is unstable as a result, you agree not to investigate allegations that we've entered into a secret conspiratorial cross-promotional relationship with Symantec Corporation, maker of Norton Utilities.

"This software is warranted to become obsolete after six (6) months, at which time the Software Company will offer an upgrade for a reasonable (exorbitant) fee. Such upgrades may also be required when Apple Computer releases a new operating-system version, alters the terms of its developer program, or sneezes. At our sole discretion, we may, in these subsequent upgrades, add RAM[1]-hogging features nobody asked for, change keystroke sequences it's taken you three years to learn, or arbitrarily remove features you've grown to love. You agree to enter this lifelong treadmill of upgrades willingly and happily and not to stumble onto the fact that AppleWorks does most of what our stuff does but at twice the speed, half the cost, and⅟₃₀₀th the RAM.

"Under no circumstances shall we be liable for any incidental, consequential, or future damages arising from the use of this product. In other words, if your kids whip the CD around like a Frisbee or use it as a body-piercing ornament, that's really not our problem.

"This license agreement is effective until terminated—a lot like you, actually. You may terminate the agreement at any time by destroying the software, documents you've created with it, and computers you've run the software on.

"You understand that I'm just an overpaid lawyer, one of 50,000 Silicon Valley legal drones toiling in climate-controlled offices somewhere, and that it doesn't really matter whether or not you accept this agreement. I've got no way of knowing if you're being a good little camper; in the history of software, nobody's ever been prosecuted for installing two (2) or even three (3) copies of this program. In fact, in the history of software, I doubt anyone's even read one of these License Agreements all the way through. I'd be quite surprised, in fact, if you're still reading this one. Nobody ever scrolls down this far. You probably clicked on Accept a long

5

---

[1]*RAM:* random access memory. [Eds.]

time ago and are now confronting a screen full of tool bars with in-
scrutable icons and no labels.

"I never wanted to be a lawyer, you know. My parents pressured me   10
into it. I wanted to be—a lumberjack! No, wait—a novelist. Yeah, that's
it! And this is the perfect publication—100 million copies of this document get distributed every year. Let's see here:

"Heart pounding, Sparrow brushed her long blond hair out of her
eyes. The .45 made a cold, hard companion pressed against the white satin
of her nightgown. As the bombs began to fall on the city, she clutched the
ledge of the skyscraper. 'Don't look down,' she thought. . . ."

QUESTIONS

1. This essay pretends to provide us with an actual SOFTWARE LICENSE
   AGREEMENT. At what point did you realize that there is something
   wrong with this document? How did you know?
2. The document, obviously is a fiction. But sometimes there is truth in fictions. Is there any in this one? Discuss.
3. A fictionalized version of a document can function as an argument.
   Find the argument lurking in this text and repeat it in your own words.
   Who are the targets of this text? What is the point of it?

MAKING CONNECTIONS

Obviously, our lives are full of documents we accept, agree to, and sign
without reading them carefully enough—and they are seldom as entertaining as this one. Think of another such quasi-legal document in your life
(past, present, or future) and produce a version that stands in relation to a
real document as Pogue's text does to a real license agreement. See if you
can generate a similar progression from the plausible but slightly strange to
going way off the deep end.

THE EGG AND THE SPERM
How Science Has Constructed a Romance Based on Stereotypical Male-Female Roles

Emily Martin

Emily Martin (b. 1944) is a professor of anthropology at Johns Hopkins University. She has written The Woman in the Body: A Cultural Analysis of Reproduction *(1987) and* Flexible Bodies: Tracking Immunity in American Culture—From the Days of Polio to the Age of AIDS *(1994). In the following article, which originally appeared in the journal* Signs *(1991), Martin's intent is to expose the cultural stereotypes operative in the so-called scientific language surrounding human reproduction.*

The theory of the human body is always a part of a world-picture. . . . The theory of the human body is always a part of a fantasy.
[JAMES HILLMAN, *The Myth of Analysis*][1]

As an anthropologist, I am intrigued by the possibility that culture shapes how biological scientists describe what they discover about the natural world. If this were so, we would be learning about more than the natural world in high school biology class; we would be learning about cultural beliefs and practices as if they were part of nature. In the course of my research I realized that the picture of egg and sperm drawn in popular as well as scientific accounts of reproductive biology relies on stereotypes central to our cultural definitions of male and female. The stereotypes imply not only that female biological processes are less worthy than their male counterparts but also that women are less worthy than men. Part of

---

Portions of this article were presented as the 1987 Becker Lecture, Cornell University. I am grateful for the many suggestions and ideas I received on this occasion. For especially pertinent help with my arguments and data I thank Richard Cone, Kevin Whaley, Sharon Stephens, Barbara Duden, Susanne Kuechler, Lorna Rhodes, and Scott Gilbert. The article was strengthened and clarified by the comments of the anonymous *Signs* reviewers as well as the superb editorial skills of Amy Gage.

[1]James Hillman, *The Myth of Analysis* (Evanston, Ill.: Northwestern University Press, 1972), 220.

my goal in writing this article is to shine a bright light on the gender stereotypes hidden within the scientific language of biology. Exposed in such a light, I hope they will lose much of their power to harm us.

Egg and Sperm: A Scientific Fairy Tale

At a fundamental level, all major scientific textbooks depict male and female reproductive organs as systems for the production of valuable substances, such as eggs and sperm.[2] In the case of women, the monthly cycle is described as being designed to produce eggs and prepare a suitable place for them to be fertilized and grown—all to the end of making babies. But the enthusiasm ends there. By extolling the female cycle as a productive enterprise, menstruation must necessarily be viewed as a failure. Medical texts describe menstruation as the "debris" of the uterine lining, the result of necrosis, or death of tissue. The descriptions imply that a system has gone awry, making products of no use, not to specification, unsalable, wasted, scrap. An illustration in a widely used medical text shows menstruation as a chaotic disintegration of form, complementing the many texts that describe it as "ceasing," "dying," "losing," "denuding," "expelling."[3]

Male reproductive physiology is evaluated quite differently. One of the texts that sees menstruation as failed production employs a sort of breathless prose when it describes the maturation of sperm: "The mechanisms which guide the remarkable cellular transformation from spermatid to mature sperm remain uncertain. . . . Perhaps the most amazing characteristic of spermatogenesis is its sheer magnitude: the normal human male may manufacture several hundred million sperm per day."[4] In the classic text *Medical Physiology,* edited by Vernon Mountcastle, the male/female, productive/destructive comparison is more explicit: "Whereas the female *sheds* only a single gamete each month, the seminiferous tubules *produce* hundreds of millions of sperm each day" (emphasis mine).[5] The female author of another text marvels at the length of the microscopic seminiferous tubules, which, if uncoiled and placed end to end, "would span almost one-third of a mile!" She writes, "In an adult male these structures produce

[2]The textbooks I consulted are the main ones used in classes for undergraduate premedical students or medical students (or those held on reserve in the library for these classes) during the past few years at Johns Hopkins University. These texts are widely used at other universities in the country as well.

[3]Arthur C. Guyton, *Physiology of the Human Body,* 6th ed. (Philadelphia: Saunders College Publishing, 1984), 624.

[4]Arthur J. Vander, James H. Sherman, and Dorothy S. Luciano, *Human Physiology: The Mechanisms of Body Function,* 3d ed. (New York: McGraw Hill, 1980), 483–84.

[5]Vernon B. Mountcastle, *Medical Physiology,* 14th ed. (London: Mosby, 1980), 2:1624.

millions of sperm cells each day." Later she asks, "How is this feat accomplished?"[6] None of these texts expresses such intense enthusiasm for any female processes. It is surely no accident that the "remarkable" process of making sperm involves precisely what, in the medical view, menstruation does not: production of something deemed valuable.[7]

One could argue that menstruation and spermatogenesis are not analogous processes and, therefore, should not be expected to elicit the same kind of response. The proper female analogy to spermatogenesis, biologically, is ovulation. Yet ovulation does not merit enthusiasm in these texts either. Textbook descriptions stress that all of the ovarian follicles containing ova are already present at birth. Far from being *produced,* as sperm are, they merely sit on the shelf, slowly degenerating and aging like overstocked inventory: "At birth, normal human ovaries contain an estimated one million follicles [each], and no new ones appear after birth. Thus, in marked contrast to the male, the newborn female already has all the germ cells she will ever have. Only a few, perhaps 400, are destined to reach full maturity during her active productive life. All the others degenerate at some point in their development so that few, if any, remain by the time she reaches menopause at approximately 50 years of age."[8] Note the "marked contrast" that this description sets up between male and female: the male, who continuously produces fresh germ cells, and the female, who has stockpiled germ cells by birth and is faced with their degeneration.

Nor are the female organs spared such vivid descriptions. One scientist   5
writes in a newspaper article that a woman's ovaries become old and worn out from ripening eggs every month, even though the woman herself is still relatively young: "When you look through a laparoscope . . . at an ovary that has been through hundreds of cycles, even in a superbly healthy American female, you see a scarred, battered organ."[9]

To avoid the negative connotations that some people associate with the female reproductive system, scientists could begin to describe male and female processes as homologous. They might credit females with "producing" mature ova one at a time, as they're needed each month, and describe males as having to face problems of degenerating germ cells. This degeneration would occur throughout life among spermatogonia, the undifferentiated germ cells in the testes that are the long-lived, dormant precursors of sperm.

But the texts have an almost dogged insistence on casting female processes in a negative light. The texts celebrate sperm production because

---

[6]Eldra Pearl Solomon, *Human Anatomy and Physiology* (New York: CBS College Publishing, 1983), 678.

[7]For elaboration, see Emily Martin, *The Woman in the Body: A Cultural Analysis of Reproduction* (Boston: Beacon, 1987), 27–53.

[8]Vander, Sherman, and Luciano, 568.

[9]Melvin Konner, "Childbearing and Age," *New York ·Times Magazine* (December 27, 1987), 22–23, esp. 22.

it is continuous from puberty to senescence, while they portray egg production as inferior because it is finished at birth. This makes the female seem unproductive, but some texts will also insist that it is she who is wasteful.[10] In a section heading for *Molecular Biology of the Cell*, a best-selling text, we are told that "Oogenesis is wasteful." The text goes on to emphasize that of the seven million oogonia, or egg germ cells, in the female embryo, most degenerate in the ovary. Of those that do go on to become oocytes, or eggs, many also degenerate, so that at birth only two million eggs remain in the ovaries. Degeneration continues throughout a woman's life: by puberty 300,000 eggs remain, and only a few are present by menopause. "During the 40 or so years of a woman's reproductive life, only 400 to 500 eggs will have been released," the authors write. "All the rest will have degenerated. It is still a mystery why so many eggs are formed only to die in the ovaries."[11]

The real mystery is why the male's vast production of sperm is not seen as wasteful.[12] Assuming that a man "produces" 100 million (10^8) sperm per day (a conservative estimate) during an average reproductive life of sixty years, he would produce well over two trillion sperm in his lifetime. Assuming that a woman "ripens" one egg per lunar month, or thirteen per year, over the course of her forty-year reproductive life, she would total five hundred eggs in her lifetime. But the word "waste" implies an excess, too much produced. Assuming two or three offspring, for every baby a woman produces, she wastes only around two hundred eggs. For every baby a man produces, he wastes more than one trillion (10^{12}) sperm.

---

[10]I have found but one exception to the opinion that the female is wasteful: "Smallpox being the nasty disease it is, one might expect nature to have designed antibody molecules with combining sites that specifically recognize the epitopes on smallpox virus. Nature differs from technology, however: it thinks nothing of wastefulness. (For example, rather than improving the chance that a spermatozoon will meet an egg cell, nature finds it easier to produce millions of spermatozoa.)" (Niels Kaj Jerne, "The Immune System," *Scientific American* 229, no. 1 [July 1973]: 53.) Thanks to a *Signs* reviewer for bringing this reference to my attention.

[11]Bruce Alberts et al., *Molecular Biology of the Cell* (New York: Garland, 1983), 795.

[12]In her essay "Have Only Men Evolved?" (in *Discovering Reality: Feminist Perspectives on Epistemology, Metaphysics, Methodology, and Philosophy of Science,* ed. Sandra Harding and Merrill B. Hintikka [Dordrecht, The Netherlands: Reidel, 1983], 45–69, esp. 60–61), Ruth Hubbard points out that sociobiologists have said the female invests more energy than the male in the production of her large gametes, claiming that this explains why the female provides parental care. Hubbard questions whether it "really takes more 'energy' to generate the one or relatively few eggs than the large excess of sperms required to achieve fertilization." For further critique of how the greater size of eggs is interpreted in sociobiology, see Donna Haraway, "Investment Strategies for the Evolving Portfolio of Primate Females," in *Body/Politics,* ed. Mary Jacobus, Evelyn Fox Keller, and Sally Shuttleworth (New York: Routledge, 1990), 155–56.

How is it that positive images are denied to the bodies of women? A look at language — in this case, scientific language — provides the first clue. Take the egg and the sperm.[13] It is remarkable how "femininely" the egg behaves and how "masculinely" the sperm.[14] The egg is seen as large and passive.[15] It does not *move* or *journey,* but passively "is transported," "is swept,"[16] or even "drifts"[17] along the fallopian tube. In utter contrast, sperm are small, "streamlined,"[18] and invariably active. They "deliver" their genes to the egg, "activate the developmental program of the egg,"[19] and have a "velocity" that is often remarked upon.[20] Their tails are "strong" and efficiently powered.[21] Together with the forces of ejaculation, they can "propel the semen into the deepest recesses of the vagina."[22] For this they need "energy," "fuel,"[23] so that with a "whiplashlike motion and strong lurches"[24] they can "burrow through the egg coat"[25] and "penetrate" it.[26]

At its extreme, the age-old relationship of the egg and the sperm takes on a royal or religious patina. The egg coat, its protective barrier, is sometimes called its "vestments," a term usually reserved for sacred, religious dress. The egg is said to have a "corona,"[27] a crown, and to be accompa-

[13]The sources I used for this article provide compelling information on interactions among sperm. Lack of space prevents me from taking up this theme here, but the elements include competition, hierarchy, and sacrifice. For a newspaper report, see Malcolm W. Browne, "Some Thoughts on Self Sacrifice," *New York Times* (July 5, 1988), C6. For a literary rendition, see John Barth, "Night-Sea Journey," in his *Lost in the Funhouse* (Garden City, N.Y.: Doubleday, 1968), 3–13.

[14]See Carol Delaney, "The Meaning of Paternity and the Virgin Birth Debate," *Man* 21, no. 3 (September 1986): 494–513. She discusses the difference between this scientific view that women contribute genetic material to the fetus and the claim of long-standing Western folk theories that the origin and identity of the fetus comes from the male, as in the metaphor of planting a seed in soil.

[15]For a suggested direct link between human behavior and purportedly passive eggs and active sperm, see Erik H. Erikson, "Inner and Outer Space: Reflections on Womanhood," *Daedalus* 93, no. 2 (Spring 1964): 582–606, esp. 591.

[16]Guyton (n. 3), 619; and Mountcastle (n. 5), 1609.

[17]Jonathan Miller and David Pelham, *The Facts of Life* (New York: Viking Penguin, 1984), 5.

[18]Alberts et al., 796.

[19]Ibid., 796.

[20]See, e.g., William F. Ganong, *Review of Medical Physiology,* 7th ed. (Los Altos, Calif.: Lange Medical Publications, 1975), 322.

[21]Alberts et al. (n. 11), 796.

[22]Guyton, 615.

[23]Solomon (n. 6), 683.

[24]Vander, Sherman, and Luciano (n. 4), 4th ed. (1985), 580.

[25]Alberts et al., 796.

[26]All biology texts quoted use the word "penetrate."

[27]Solomon, 700.

nied by "attendant cells."[28] It is holy, set apart and above, the queen to the sperm's king. The egg is also passive, which means it must depend on sperm for rescue. Gerald Schatten and Helen Schatten liken the egg's role to that of Sleeping Beauty: "a dormant bride awaiting her mate's magic kiss, which instills the spirit that brings her to life."[29] Sperm, by contrast, have a "mission,"[30] which is to "move through the female genital tract in quest of the ovum."[31] One popular account has it that the sperm carry out a "perilous journey" into the "warm darkness," where some fall away "exhausted." "Survivors" "assault" the egg, the successful candidates "surrounding the prize."[32] Part of the urgency of this journey, in more scientific terms, is that "once released from the supportive environment of the ovary, an egg will die within hours unless rescued by a sperm."[33] The wording stresses the fragility and dependency of the egg, even though the same text acknowledges elsewhere that sperm also live for only a few hours.[34]

In 1948, in a book remarkable for its early insights into these matters, Ruth Herschberger argued that female reproductive organs are seen as biologically interdependent, while male organs are viewed as autonomous, operating independently and in isolation:

> At present the functional is stressed only in connection with women: it is in them that ovaries, tubes, uterus, and vagina have endless interdependence. In the male, reproduction would seem to involve "organs" only.
>
> Yet the sperm, just as much as the egg, is dependent on a great many related processes. There are secretions which mitigate the urine in the urethra before ejaculation, to protect the sperm. There is the reflex shutting off of the bladder connection, the provision of prostatic secretions, and various types of muscular propulsion. The sperm is no more independent of its milieu than the egg, and yet from a wish that it were, biologists have lent their support to the notion that the human female, beginning with the egg, is congenitally more dependent than the male.[35]

---

[28]A. Beldecos et al., "The Importance of Feminist Critique for Contemporary Cell Biology," *Hypatia* 3, no. 1 (Spring 1988): 61–76.

[29]Gerald Schatten and Helen Schatten, "The Energetic Egg," *Medical World News* 23 (January 23, 1984): 51–53, esp. 51.

[30]Alberts et al., 796.

[31]Guyton (n. 3), 613.

[32]Miller and Pelham (n. 17), 7.

[33]Alberts et al. (n. 11), 804.

[34]Ibid., 801.

[35]Ruth Herschberger, *Adam's Rib* (New York: Pelligrini & Cudaby, 1948), esp. 84. I am indebted to Ruth Hubbard for telling me about Herschberger's work, although at a point when this paper was already in draft form.

Bringing out another aspect of the sperm's autonomy, an article in the journal *Cell* has the sperm making an "existential decision" to penetrate the egg: "Sperm are cells with a limited behavioral repertoire, one that is directed toward fertilizing eggs. To execute the decision to abandon the haploid state, sperm swim to an egg and there acquire the ability to effect membrane fusion."[36] Is this a corporate manager's version of the sperm's activities—"executing decisions" while fraught with dismay over difficult options that bring with them very high risk?

There is another way that sperm, despite their small size, can be made to loom in importance over the egg. In a collection of scientific papers, an electron micrograph of an enormous egg and tiny sperm is titled "A Portrait of the Sperm."[37] This is a little like showing a photo of a dog and calling it a picture of the fleas. Granted, microscopic sperm are harder to photograph than eggs, which are just large enough to see with the naked eye. But surely the use of the term "portrait," a word associated with the powerful and wealthy, is significant. Eggs have only micrographs or pictures, not portraits.

One depiction of sperm as weak and timid, instead of strong and powerful—the only such representation in western civilization, so far as I know—occurs in Woody Allen's movie *Everything You Always Wanted to Know about Sex* *But Were Afraid to Ask*. Allen, playing the part of an apprehensive sperm inside a man's testicles, is scared of the man's approaching orgasm. He is reluctant to launch himself into the darkness, afraid of contraceptive devices, afraid of winding up on the ceiling if the man masturbates.

The more common picture—egg as damsel in distress, shielded only   15
by her sacred garments; sperm as heroic warrior to the rescue—cannot be proved to be dictated by the biology of these events. While the "facts" of biology may not *always* be constructed in cultural terms, I would argue that in this case they are. The degree of metaphorical content in these descriptions, the extent to which differences between egg and sperm are emphasized, and the parallels between cultural stereotypes of male and female behavior and the character of egg and sperm all point to this conclusion.

New Research, Old Imagery

As new understandings of egg and sperm emerge, textbook gender imagery is being revised. But the new research, far from escaping the stereotypical representations of egg and sperm, simply replicates elements of

---

[36]Bennett M. Shapiro, "The Existential Decision of a Sperm," *Cell* 49, no. 3 (May 1987): 293–94, esp. 293.

[37]Lennart Nilsson, "A Portrait of the Sperm," in *The Functional Anatomy of the Spermatozoan*, ed. Bjorn A. Afzelius (New York: Pergamon, 1975), 79–82.

textbook gender imagery in a different form. The persistence of this imagery calls to mind what Ludwik Fleck termed "the self-contained" nature of scientific thought. As he described it, "the interaction between what is already known, what remains to be learned, and those who are to apprehend it, go to ensure harmony within the system. But at the same time they also preserve the harmony of illusions, which is quite secure within the confines of a given thought style."[38] We need to understand the way in which the cultural content in scientific descriptions changes as biological discoveries unfold, and whether that cultural content is solidly entrenched or easily changed.

In all of the texts quoted above, sperm are described as penetrating the egg, and specific substances on a sperm's head are described as binding to the egg. Recently, this description of events was rewritten in a biophysics lab at Johns Hopkins University—transforming the egg from the passive to the active party.[39]

Prior to this research, it was thought that the zona, the inner vestments of the egg, formed an impenetrable barrier. Sperm overcame the barrier by mechanically burrowing through, thrashing their tails and slowly working their way along. Later research showed that the sperm released digestive enzymes that chemically broke down the zona; thus, scientists presumed that the sperm used mechanical *and* chemical means to get through to the egg.

In this recent investigation, the researchers began to ask questions about the mechanical force of the sperm's tail. (The lab's goal was to develop a contraceptive that worked topically on sperm.) They discovered, to their great surprise, that the forward thrust of sperm is extremely weak, which contradicts the assumption that sperm are forceful penetrators.[40] Rather than thrusting forward, the sperm's head was now seen to move mostly back and forth. The sideways motion of the sperm's tail makes the head move sideways with a force that is ten times stronger than its forward movement. So even if the overall force of the sperm were strong enough to mechanically break the zona, most of its force would be directed sideways rather than forward. In fact, its strongest tendency, by tenfold, is to escape by attempting to pry itself off the egg. Sperm, then, must be exceptionally efficient at *escaping* from any cell surface they contact. And the surface of

---

[38]Ludwik Fleck, *Genesis and Development of a Scientific Fact,* ed. Thaddeus J. Trenn and Robert K. Merton (Chicago: University of Chicago Press, 1979), 38.

[39]Jay M. Baltz carried out the research I describe when he was a graduate student in the Thomas C. Jenkins Department of Biophysics at Johns Hopkins University.

[40]Far less is known about the physiology of sperm than comparable female substances, which some feminists claim is no accident. Greater scientific scrutiny of female reproduction has long enabled the burden of birth control to be placed on women. In this case, the researchers' discovery did not depend on development of any new technology. The experiments made use of glass pipettes, a manometer, and a simple microscope, all of which have been available for more than one hundred years.

the egg must be designed to trap the sperm and prevent their escape. Otherwise, few if any sperm would reach the egg.

The researchers at Johns Hopkins concluded that the sperm and egg   20
stick together because of adhesive molecules on the surfaces of each. The egg traps the sperm and adheres to it so tightly that the sperm's head is forced to lie flat against the surface of the zona, a little bit, they told me, "like Br'er Rabbit getting more and more stuck to tar baby the more he wriggles." The trapped sperm continues to wiggle ineffectually side to side. The mechanical force of its tail is so weak that a sperm cannot break even one chemical bond. This is where the digestive enzymes released by the sperm come in. If they start to soften the zona just at the tip of the sperm and the sides remain stuck, then the weak, flailing sperm can get oriented in the right direction and make it through the zona—provided that its bonds to the zona dissolve as it moves in.

Although this new version of the saga of the egg and the sperm broke through cultural expectations, the researchers who made the discovery continued to write papers and abstracts as if the sperm were the active party who attacks, binds, penetrates, and enters the egg. The only difference was that sperm were now seen as performing these actions weakly.[41] Not until August 1987, more than three years after the findings described above, did these researchers reconceptualize the process to give the egg a more active role. They began to describe the zona as an aggressive sperm catcher, covered with adhesive molecules that can capture a sperm with a single bond and clasp it to the zona's surface.[42] In the words of their published account: "The innermost vestment, the *zona pellucida,* is a glyco-protein shell, which captures and tethers the sperm before they penetrate it. . . . The sperm is captured at the initial contact between the sperm tip and the *zona.* . . . Since the thrust [of the sperm] is much smaller than the force needed to break a single affinity bond, the first bond made upon the tip-first meeting of the sperm and *zona* can result in the capture of the sperm."[43]

----

[41]Jay Baltz and Richard A. Cone, "What Force Is Needed to Tether a Sperm?" (abstract for Society for the Study of Reproduction, 1985), and "Flagellar Torque on the Head Determines the Force Needed to Tether a Sperm" (abstract for Biophysical Society, 1986).

[42]Jay M. Baltz, David F. Katz, and Richard A. Cone, "The Mechanics of the Sperm-Egg Interaction at the Zona Pellucida," *Biophysical Journal* 54, no. 4 (October 1988): 643–54. Lab members were somewhat familiar with work on metaphors in the biology of female reproduction. Richard Cone, who runs the lab, is my husband, and he talked with them about my earlier research on the subject from time to time. Even though my current research focuses on biological imagery and I heard about the lab's work from my husband every day, I myself did not recognize the role of imagery in the sperm research until many weeks after the period of research and writing I describe. Therefore, I assume that any awareness the lab members may have had about how underlying metaphor might be guiding this particular research was fairly inchoate.

[43]Ibid., 643, 650.

Experiments in another lab reveal similar patterns of data interpretation. Gerald Schatten and Helen Schatten set out to show that, contrary to conventional wisdom, the "egg is not merely a large, yolk-filled sphere into which the sperm burrows to endow new life. Rather, recent research suggests the almost heretical view that sperm and egg are mutually active partners."[44] This sounds like a departure from the stereotypical textbook view, but further reading reveals Schatten and Schatten's conformity to the aggressive-sperm metaphor. They describe how "the sperm and egg first touch when, from the tip of the sperm's triangular head, a long, thin filament shoots out and harpoons the egg." Then we learn that "remarkably, the harpoon is not so much fired as assembled at great speed, molecule by molecule, from a pool of protein stored in a specialized region called the acrosome. The filament may grow as much as twenty times longer than the sperm head itself before its tip reaches the egg and sticks."[45] Why not call this "making a bridge" or "throwing out a line" rather than firing a harpoon? Harpoons pierce prey and injure or kill them, while this filament only sticks. And why not focus, as the Hopkins lab did, on the stickiness of the egg, rather than the stickiness of the sperm?[46] Later in the article, the Schattens replicate the common view of the sperm's perilous journey into the warm darkness of the vagina, this time for the purpose of explaining its journey into the egg itself: "[The sperm] still has an arduous journey ahead. It must penetrate farther into the egg's huge sphere of cytoplasm and somehow locate the nucleus, so that the two cells' chromosomes can fuse. The sperm dives down into the cytoplasm, its tail beating. But it is soon interrupted by the sudden and swift migration of the egg nucleus, which rushes toward the sperm with a velocity triple that of the movement of chromosomes during cell division, crossing the entire egg in about a minute."[47]

Like Schatten and Schatten and the biophysicists at Johns Hopkins, another researcher has recently made discoveries that seem to point to a more interactive view of the relationship of egg and sperm. This work, which Paul Wassarman conducted on the sperm and eggs of mice, focuses on identifying the specific molecules in the egg coat (the zona pellucida) that are involved in egg-sperm interaction. At first glance, his descriptions seem to fit the model of an egalitarian relationship. Male and female gametes "recognize one another," and "interactions . . . take place between sperm and egg."[48] But the article in *Scientific American* in which those descriptions appear begins with a vignette that presages the dominant motif of their presentation: "It has been

---

[44]Schatten and Schatten (n. 29), 51.

[45]Ibid., 52.

[46]Surprisingly, in an article intended for a general audience, the authors do not point out that these are sea urchin sperm and note that human sperm do not shoot out filaments at all.

[47]Schatten and Schatten, 53.

[48]Paul M. Wassarman, "Fertilization in Mammals," *Scientific American* 259, no. 6 (December 1988): 78–84, esp. 78, 84.

more than a century since Hermann Fol, a Swiss zoologist, peered into his microscope and became the first person to see a sperm penetrate an egg, fertilize it and form the first cell of a new embryo."[49] This portrayal of the sperm as the active party—the one that *penetrates* and *fertilizes* the egg and *produces* the embryo—is not cited as an example of an earlier, now outmoded view. In fact, the author reiterates the point later in the article: "Many sperm can bind to and penetrate the zona pellucida, or outer coat, of an unfertilized mouse egg, but only one sperm will eventually fuse with the thin plasma membrane surrounding the egg proper (*inner sphere*), fertilizing the egg and giving rise to a new embryo."[50]

The imagery of sperm as aggressor is particularly startling in this case: the main discovery being reported is isolation of a particular molecule *on the egg coat* that plays an important role in fertilization! Wassarman's choice of language sustains the picture. He calls the molecule that has been isolated, ZP3, a "sperm receptor." By allocating the passive, waiting role to the egg, Wassarman can continue to describe the sperm as the actor, the one that makes it all happen: "The basic process begins when many sperm first attach loosely and then bind tenaciously to receptors on the surface of the egg's thick outer coat, the zona pellucida. Each sperm, which has a large number of egg-binding proteins on its surface, binds to many sperm receptors on the egg. More specifically, a site on each of the egg-binding proteins fits a complementary site on a sperm receptor, much as a key fits a lock."[51] With the sperm designated as the "key" and the egg the "lock," it is obvious which one acts and which one is acted upon. Could this imagery not be reversed, letting the sperm (the lock) wait until the egg produces the key? Or could we speak of two halves of a locket matching, and regard the matching itself as the action that initiates the fertilization?

It is as if Wassarman were determined to make the egg the receiving partner. Usually in biological research, the *protein* member of the pair of binding molecules is called the receptor, and physically it has a pocket in it rather like a lock. As the diagrams that illustrate Wassarman's article show, the molecules on the sperm are proteins and have "pockets." The small, mobile molecules that fit into these pockets are called ligands. As shown in the diagrams, ZP3 on the egg is a polymer of "keys"; many small knobs stick out. Typically, molecules on the sperm would be called receptors and molecules on the egg would be called ligands. But Wassarman chose to name ZP3 on the egg the receptor and to create a new term, "the egg-binding protein," for the molecule on the sperm that otherwise would have been called the receptor.[52]

25

------

[49]Ibid., 78.

[50]Ibid., 79.

[51]Ibid., 78.

52Since receptor molecules are relatively immotile and the ligands that bind to them relatively motile, one might imagine the egg being called the receptor and the sperm the ligand. But the molecules in question on egg and sperm are immotile

Wassarman does credit the egg coat with having more functions than those of a sperm receptor. While he notes that "the zona pellucida has at times been viewed by investigators as a nuisance, a barrier to sperm and hence an impediment to fertilization," his new research reveals that the egg coat "serves as a sophisticated biological security system that screens incoming sperm, selects only those compatible with fertilization and development, prepares sperm for fusion with the egg and later protects the resulting embryo from polyspermy [a lethal condition caused by fusion of more than one sperm with a single egg]."[53] Although this description gives the egg an active role, that role is drawn in stereotypically feminine terms. The egg *selects* an appropriate mate, *prepares* him for fusion, and then *protects* the resulting offspring from harm. This is courtship and mating behavior as seen through the eyes of a sociobiologist: woman as the hard-to-get prize, who, following union with the chosen one, becomes woman as servant and mother.

And Wassarman does not quit there. In a review article for *Science,* he outlines the "chronology of fertilization."[54] Near the end of the article are two subject headings. One is "Sperm Penetration," in which Wassarman describes how the chemical dissolving of the zona pellucida combines with the "substantial propulsive force generated by sperm." The next heading is "Sperm-Egg Fusion." This section details what happens inside the zona after a sperm "penetrates" it. Sperm "can make contact with, adhere to, and fuse with (that is, fertilize) an egg."[55] Wassarman's word choice, again, is astonishingly skewed in favor of the sperm's activity, for in the next breath he says that sperm *lose* all motility upon fusion with the egg's surface. In mouse and sea urchin eggs, the sperm enters at the *egg's* volition, according to Wassarman's description: "Once fused with egg plasma membrane [the surface of the egg], how does a sperm enter the egg? The surface of both mouse and sea urchin eggs is covered with thousands of plasma membrane-bound projections, called microvilli [tiny "hairs"]. Evidence in sea urchins suggests that, after membrane fusion, a group of elongated microvilli cluster tightly around and interdigitate over the sperm head. As these microvilli are resorbed, the sperm is drawn into the egg. Therefore, sperm motility, which ceases at the time of fusion in both sea urchins and mice, is not required for sperm entry."[56] The section called "Sperm Penetration" more logically would be followed by a section called "The Egg Envelops," rather than "Sperm-Egg Fusion." This would give a parallel—and more accurate—sense that both the egg and the sperm initiate action.

---

molecules. It is the sperm as a cell that has motility, and the egg as a cell that has relative immotility.

[53]Wassarman, 78–79.

[54]Paul M. Wassarman, "The Biology and Chemistry of Fertilization," *Science* 235, no. 4788 (January 30, 1987): 553–60, esp. 554.

[55]Ibid., 557.

[56]Ibid., 557–58. This finding throws into question Schatten and Schatten's description (n. 29 above) of the sperm, its tail beating, diving down into the egg.

Another way that Wassarman makes less of the egg's activity is by describing components of the egg but referring to the sperm as a whole entity. Deborah Gordon has described such an approach as "atomism" ("the part is independent of and primordial to the whole") and identified it as one of the "tenacious assumptions" of Western science and medicine.[57] Wassarman employs atomism to his advantage. When he refers to processing going on within sperm, he consistently returns to descriptions that remind us from whence these activities came: they are part of sperm that penetrate an egg or generate propulsive force. When he refers to processes going on within eggs, he stops there. As a result, any active role he grants them appears to be assigned to the parts of the egg, and not to the egg itself. In the quote above, it is the microvilli that actively cluster around the sperm. In another example, "the driving force for engulfment of a fused sperm comes from a region of cytoplasm just beneath an egg's plasma membrane."[58]

Social Implications: Thinking Beyond

All three of these revisionist accounts of egg and sperm cannot seem to escape the hierarchical imagery of older accounts. Even though each new account gives the egg a larger and more active role, taken together they bring into play another cultural stereotype: woman as a dangerous and aggressive threat. In the Johns Hopkins lab's revised model, the egg ends up as the female aggressor who "captures and tethers" the sperm with her sticky zona, rather like a spider lying in wait in her web.[59] The Schatten lab has the egg's nucleus "interrupt" the sperm's dive with a "sudden and swift" rush by which she "clasps the sperm and guides its nucleus to the center."[60] Wassarman's description of the surface of the egg "covered with thousands of plasma membrane-bound projections, called microvilli" that reach out and clasp the sperm adds to the spiderlike imagery.[61]

These images grant the egg an active role but at the cost of appearing   30
disturbingly aggressive. Images of woman as dangerous and aggressive, the femme fatale who victimizes men, are widespread in Western literature and culture.[62] More specific is the connection of spider imagery with the idea of

---

[57]Deborah R. Gordon, "Tenacious Assumptions in Western Medicine," in *Biomedicine Examined,* ed. Margaret Lock and Deborah Gordon (Dordrecht, The Netherlands: Kluwer, 1988), 19–56, esp. 26.

[58]Wassarman, "The Biology and Chemistry of Fertilization," 558.

[59]Baltz, Katz, and Cone (n. 42 above), 643, 650.

[60]Schatten and Schatten, 53.

[61]Wassarman, "The Biology and Chemistry of Fertilization," 557.

[62]Mary Ellman, *Thinking about Women* (New York: Harcourt Brace Jovanovich, 1968), 140; Nina Auerbach, *Woman and the Demon* (Cambridge, Mass.: Harvard University Press, 1982), esp. 186.

an engulfing, devouring mother.[63] New data did not lead scientists to eliminate gender stereotypes in their descriptions of egg and sperm. Instead, scientists simply began to describe egg and sperm in different, but no less damaging, terms.

Can we envision a less stereotypical view? Biology itself provides another model that could be applied to the egg and the sperm. The cybernetic model—with its feedback loops, flexible adaptation to change, coordination of the parts within a whole, evolution over time, and changing response to the environment—is common in genetics, endocrinology, and ecology and has a growing influence in medicine in general.[64] This model has the potential to shift our imagery from the negative, in which the female reproductive system is castigated both for not producing eggs after birth and for producing (and thus wasting) too many eggs overall, to something more positive. The female reproductive system could be seen as responding to the environment (pregnancy or menopause), adjusting to monthly changes (menstruation), and flexibly changing from reproductivity after puberty to nonreproductivity later in life. The sperm and egg's interaction could also be described in cybernetic terms. J. F. Hartman's research in reproductive biology demonstrated fifteen years ago that if an egg is killed by being pricked with a needle, live sperm cannot get through the zona.[65] Clearly, this evidence shows that the egg and sperm *do* interact on more mutual terms, making biology's refusal to portray them that way all the more disturbing.

We would do well to be aware, however, that cybernetic imagery is hardly neutral. In the past, cybernetic models have played an important part in the imposition of social control. These models inherently provide a way of thinking about a "field" of interacting components. Once the field can be seen, it can become the object of new forms of knowledge, which in turn can allow new forms of social control to be exerted over the components of the field. During the 1950s, for example, medicine began to recognize the psychosocial *environment* of the patient: the patient's family and its psychodynamics. Professions such as social work began to focus on this new environment, and the resulting knowledge became one way to further control the patient. Patients began to be seen not as isolated, individual bodies, but as psychosocial entities located in an "ecological" system: management of "the patient's psychology was a new entrée to patient control."[66]

---

[63]Kenneth Alan Adams, "Arachnophobia: Love American Style," *Journal of Psychoanalytic Anthropology* 4, no. 2 (1981): 157–97.

[64]William Ray Arney and Bernard Bergen, *Medicine and the Management of Living* (Chicago: University of Chicago Press, 1984).

[65]J. F. Hartman, R. B. Gwatkin, and C. F. Hutchison, "Early Contact Interactions between Mammalian Gametes *In Vitro*," *Proceedings of the National Academy of Sciences (U.S.)* 69, no. 10 (1972): 2767–69.

[66]Arney and Bergen, 68.

The models that biologists use to describe their data can have important social effects. During the nineteenth century, the social and natural sciences strongly influenced each other: the social ideas of Malthus about how to avoid the natural increase of the poor inspired Darwin's *Origin of Species*.[67] Once the *Origin* stood as a description of the natural world, complete with competition and market struggles, it could be reimported into social science as social Darwinism, in order to justify the social order of the time. What we are seeing now is similar: the importation of cultural ideas about passive females and heroic males into the "personalities" of gametes. This amounts to the "implanting of social imagery on representations of nature so as to lay a firm basis for reimporting exactly that same imagery as natural explanations of social phenomena."[68]

Further research would show us exactly what social effects are being wrought from the biological imagery of egg and sperm. At the very least, the imagery keeps alive some of the hoariest old stereotypes about weak damsels in distress and their strong male rescuers. That these stereotypes are now being written in at the level of the *cell* constitutes a powerful move to make them seem so natural as to be beyond alteration.

The stereotypical imagery might also encourage people to imagine that   35
what results from the interaction of egg and sperm—a fertilized egg—is the result of deliberate "human" action at the cellular level. Whatever the intentions of the human couple, in this microscope "culture" a cellular "bride" (or femme fatale) and a cellular "groom" (her victim) make a cellular baby. Rosalind Petchesky points out that through visual representations such as sonograms, we are given "*images* of younger and younger, and tinier and tinier, fetuses being 'saved.'" This leads to "the point of viability being 'pushed back' *indefinitely*."[69] Endowing egg and sperm with intentional action, a key aspect of personhood in our culture, lays the foundation for the point of viability being pushed back to the moment of fertilization. This will likely lead to greater acceptance of technological developments and new forms of scrutiny and manipulation, for the benefit of these inner "persons": court-ordered restrictions on a pregnant woman's activities in order to protect her fetus, fetal surgery, amniocentesis, and rescinding of abortion rights, to name but a few examples.[70]

---

[67]Ruth Hubbard, "Have Only Men Evolved?" (n. 12 above), 51–52.

[68]David Harvey, personal communication, November 1989.

[69]Rosalind Petchesky, "Fetal Images: The Power of Visual Culture in the Politics of Reproduction," *Feminist Studies* 13, no. 2 (Summer 1987): 263–92, esp. 272.

[70]Rita Arditti, Renate Klein, and Shelley Minden, *Test-Tube Women* (London: Pandora, 1984); Ellen Goodman, "Whose Right to Life?" *Baltimore Sun* (November 17, 1987); Tamar Lewin, "Courts Acting to Force Care of the Unborn," *New York Times* (November 23, 1987), A1 and B10; Susan Irwin and Brigitte Jordan, "Knowledge, Practice, and Power: Court Ordered Cesarean Sections," *Medical Anthropology Quarterly* 1, no. 3 (September 1987): 319–34.

Even if we succeed in substituting more egalitarian, interactive metaphors to describe the activities of egg and sperm, and manage to avoid the pitfalls of cybernetic models, we would still be guilty of endowing cellular entities with personhood. More crucial, then, than what *kinds* of personalities we bestow on cells is the very fact that we are doing it at all. This process could ultimately have the most disturbing social consequences.

One clear feminist challenge is to wake up sleeping metaphors in science, particularly those involved in descriptions of the egg and the sperm. Although the literary convention is to call such metaphors "dead," they are not so much dead as sleeping, hidden within the scientific content of texts—and all the more powerful for it.[71] Waking up such metaphors, by becoming aware of when we are projecting cultural imagery onto what we study, will improve our ability to investigate and understand nature. Waking up such metaphors, by becoming aware of their implications, will rob them of their power to naturalize our social conventions about gender.

QUESTIONS

1. Summarize Martin's argument. How has she structured it?
2. The first subhead of the essay is "Egg and Sperm: A Scientific Fairy Tale." The implications are that the actions of the egg and sperm constitute a story written by scientists. Why does Martin call it a fairy tale? What fairy tales does it resemble? In the process of your sexual education, what stories were you told?
3. Martin's argument raises the issue of scientific objectivity. Do you think there can be such a thing as a "pure" fact? Or can we only say that one fact is less encumbered by cultural baggage than another fact? What does Martin suggest as the best approach in presenting reproductive facts?
4. Look at some biology textbooks. How is reproduction presented? Are the same or similar "sleeping metaphors" that Martin discusses present in the discussion? What about other bodily processes and functions? Is the male body used as the sole example in discussions of the heart, blood pressure, digestion, or AIDS, for instance?
5. Using the biological information in Martin's essay, write a nonsexist description of the reproductive functions. In your conclusion, reflect on any difficulties you encountered in keeping your cellular entities free of personhood. Switch papers with a classmate to check one another for "sleeping metaphors."
6. Look at a sampling of sex education texts and materials designed for elementary or secondary school students to see if the cultural stereotypes

---

[71]Thanks to Elizabeth Fee and David Spain, who in February 1989 and April 1989, respectively, made points related to this.

Martin warns against are present. What analogies and metaphors do you find being used? Write up your discussion as an argument either for or against the revision of those texts.

MAKING CONNECTIONS

1. Martin's research is an important addition to the argument and issues surrounding stereotyping of the sexes. How does her essay augment the argument in Margaret Atwood's "The Female Body" (p. 365)? What might a Madonna rock video version of a reproductive story be like?
2. Martin warns us to be on the alert for manipulative "sleeping metaphors." Carol Gilligan discusses the metaphors used by adolescent girls (p. 425), and James Jeans relies on analogy to tell his scientific story (p. 505). Are there "sleeping metaphors" lurking in other essays in this text? Discuss.

WOMEN'S BRAINS

Stephen Jay Gould

Stephen Jay Gould (b. 1941) is a professor of biology, geology, and the history of science at Harvard University. He is also a baseball fan and a prolific essayist. In 1974, he began writing "This View of Life," a monthly column for Natural History, *where he has not only explained and defended Darwinian ideas of evolution but also exposed abuses and misunderstandings of scientific concepts and methods. The latest of his many publications is* The Lying Stones of Marrakech: Penultimate Reflections in Natural History *(2000). The following essay appeared in* Natural History *in 1992.*

In the prelude to *Middlemarch*, George Eliot[1] lamented the unfulfilled lives of talented women:

> Some have felt that these blundering lives are due to the inconvenient indefiniteness with which the Supreme Power has fashioned the natures of women: if there were one level of feminine incompetence as strict as the ability to count three and no more, the social lot of women might be treated with scientific certitude.

Eliot goes on to discount the idea of innate limitation, but while she wrote in 1872, the leaders of European anthropometry were trying to measure "with scientific certitude" the inferiority of women. Anthropometry, or measurement of the human body, is not so fashionable a field these days, but it dominated the human sciences for much of the nineteenth century and remained popular until intelligence testing replaced skull measurement as a favored device for making invidious comparisons among races, classes, and sexes. Craniometry, or measurement of the skull, commanded the most attention and respect. Its unquestioned leader, Paul Broca (1824–80), professor of clinical surgery at the Faculty of Medicine in Paris, gathered a school of disciples and imitators around himself. Their work, so meticulous and apparently irrefutable, exerted great influence and won high esteem as a jewel of nineteenth-century science.

Broca's work seemed particularly invulnerable to refutation. Had he not measured with the most scrupulous care and accuracy? (Indeed, he

---

[1]*George Eliot:* pen name of Marianne Evans (1819–1880), British novelist; *Middlemarch* (1871–1872) is considered her greatest work.

had. I have the greatest respect for Broca's meticulous procedure. His numbers are sound. But science is an inferential exercise, not a catalog of facts. Numbers, by themselves, specify nothing. All depends upon what you do with them.) Broca depicted himself as an apostle of objectivity, a man who bowed before facts and cast aside superstition and sentimentality. He declared that "there is no faith, however respectable, no interest, however legitimate, which must not accommodate itself to the progress of human knowledge and bend before truth." Women, like it or not, had smaller brains than men and, therefore, could not equal them in intelligence. This fact, Broca argued, may reinforce a common prejudice in male society, but it is also a scientific truth. L. Manouvrier, a black sheep in Broca's fold, rejected the inferiority of women and wrote with feeling about the burden imposed upon them by Broca's numbers:

> Women displayed their talents and their diplomas. They also invoked philosophical authorities. But they were opposed by *numbers* unknown to Condorcet[2] or to John Stuart Mill.[3] These numbers fell upon poor women like a sledge hammer, and they were accompanied by commentaries and sarcasms more ferocious than the most misogynist imprecations of certain church fathers. The theologians had asked if women had a soul. Several centuries later, some scientists were ready to refuse them a human intelligence.

Broca's argument rested upon two sets of data: the larger brains of men in modern societies, and a supposed increase in male superiority through time. His most extensive data came from autopsies performed personally in four Parisian hospitals. For 292 male brains, he calculated an average weight of 1,325 grams; 140 female brains averaged 1,144 grams for a difference of 181 grams, or 14 percent of the male weight. Broca understood, of course, that part of this difference could be attributed to the greater height of males. Yet he made no attempt to measure the effect of size alone and actually stated that it cannot account for the entire difference because we know, a priori, that women are not as intelligent as men (a premise that the data were supposed to test, not rest upon):

> We might ask if the small size of the female brain depends exclusively upon the small size of her body. Tiedemann has proposed this explanation. But we must not forget that women are, on the average, a little less intelligent than men, a difference which we should not exaggerate but which is, nonetheless, real. We are

---

[2]*Marquis de Condorcet* (1743–1794): French mathematician and revolutionary. [Eds.]
[3]*John Stuart Mill* (1806–1873): British economist and philosopher. [Eds.]

therefore permitted to suppose that the relatively small size of the female brain depends in part upon her physical inferiority and in part upon her intellectual inferiority.

In 1873, the year after Eliot published *Middlemarch,* Broca measured the cranial capacities of prehistoric skulls from L'Homme Mort cave. Here he found a difference of only 99.5 cubic centimeters between males and females, while modern populations range from 129.5 to 220.7. Topinard, Broca's chief disciple, explained the increasing discrepancy through time as a result of differing evolutionary pressures upon dominant men and passive women:

> The man who fights for two or more in the struggle for existence, who has all the responsibility and the cares of tomorrow, who is constantly active in combating the environment and human rivals, needs more brain than the woman whom he must protect and nourish, the sedentary woman, lacking any interior occupations, whose role is to raise children, love, and be passive.

In 1879, Gustave Le Bon, chief misogynist of Broca's school, used these data to publish what must be the most vicious attack upon women in modern scientific literature (no one can top Aristotle). I do not claim his views were representative of Broca's school, but they were published in France's most respected anthropological journal. Le Bon concluded:

> In the most intelligent races, as among the Parisians, there are a large number of women whose brains are closer in size to those of gorillas than to the most developed male brains. This inferiority is so obvious that no one can contest it for a moment; only its degree is worth discussion. All psychologists who have studied the intelligence of women, as well as poets and novelists, recognize today that they represent the most inferior forms of human evolution and that they are closer to children and savages than to an adult, civilized man. They excel in fickleness, inconstancy, absence of thought and logic, and incapacity to reason. Without doubt there exist some distinguished women, very superior to the average man, but they are as exceptional as the birth of any monstrosity, as, for example, of a gorilla with two heads; consequently, we may neglect them entirely.

Nor did Le Bon shrink from the social implications of his views. He was horrified by the proposal of some American reformers to grant women higher education on the same basis as men:

> A desire to give them the same education, and, as a consequence, to propose the same goals for them, is a dangerous chimera. . . .

The day when, misunderstanding the inferior occupations which nature has given her, women leave the home and take part in our battles; on this day a social revolution will begin, and everything that maintains the sacred ties of the family will disappear.

Sound familiar?[4]

I have reexamined Broca's data, the basis for all this derivative pronouncement, and I find his numbers sound but his interpretation ill-founded, to say the least. The data supporting his claim for increased difference through time can be easily dismissed. Broca based his contention on the samples from L'Homme Mort alone—only seven male and six female skulls in all. Never have so little data yielded such far ranging conclusions.

In 1988, Topinard published Broca's more extensive data on the Parisian hospitals. Since Broca recorded height and age as well as brain size, we may use modern statistics to remove their effect. Brain weight decreases with age, and Broca's women were, on average, considerably older than his men. Brain weight increases with height, and his average man was almost half a foot taller than his average woman. I used multiple regression, a technique that allowed me to assess simultaneously the influence of height and age upon brain size. In an analysis of the data for women, I found that, at average male height and age, a woman's brain would weigh 1,212 grams. Correction for height and age reduces Broca's measured difference of 181 grams by more than a third, to 113 grams.

I don't know what to make of this remaining difference because I cannot assess other factors known to influence brain size in a major way. Cause of death has an important effect: degenerative disease often entails a substantial diminution of brain size. (This effect is separate from the decrease attributed to age alone.) Eugene Schreider, also working with Broca's data, found that men killed in accidents had brains weighing, on average, 60 grams more than men dying of infectious diseases. The best modern data I can find (from American hospitals) records a full 100-gram difference between death by degenerative arteriosclerosis and by violence or accident. Since so many of Broca's subjects were elderly women, we may assume that lengthy degenerative disease was more common among them than among the men.

More importantly, modern students of brain size still have not agreed on a proper measure for eliminating the powerful effect of body size. Height is partly adequate, but men and women of the same height do not

10

---

[4]When I wrote this essay, I assumed that Le Bon was a marginal, if colorful, figure. I have since learned that he was a leading scientist, one of the founders of social psychology, and best known for a seminal study on crowd behavior, still cited today (*La psychologie des foules,* 1895), and for his work on unconscious motivation.

share the same body build. Weight is even worse than height, because most of its variation reflects nutrition rather than intrinsic size—fat versus skinny exerts little influence upon the brain. Manouvrier took up this subject in the 1880s and argued that muscular mass and force should be used. He tried to measure this elusive property in various ways and found a marked difference in favor of men, even in men and women of the same height. When he corrected for what he called "sexual mass," women actually came out slightly ahead in brain size.

Thus, the corrected 113-gram difference is surely too large; the true figure is probably close to zero and may as well favor women as men. And 113 grams, by the way, is exactly the average difference between a 5 foot 4 inch and a 6 foot 4 inch male in Broca's data. We would not (especially us short folks) want to ascribe greater intelligence to tall men. In short, who knows what to do with Broca's data? They certainly don't permit any confident claim that men have bigger brains than women.

To appreciate the social role of Broca and his school, we must recognize that his statements about the brains of women do not reflect an isolated prejudice toward a single disadvantaged group. They must be weighed in the context of a general theory that supported contemporary social distinctions as biologically ordained. Women, blacks, and poor people suffered the same disparagement, but women bore the brunt of Broca's argument because he had easier access to data on women's brains. Women were singularly denigrated but they also stood as surrogates for other disenfranchised groups. As one of Broca's disciples wrote in 1881: "Men of the black races have a brain scarcely heavier than that of white women." This juxtaposition extended into many other realms of anthropological argument, particularly to claims that, anatomically and emotionally, both women and blacks were like white children—and that white children, by the theory of recapitulation, represented an ancestral (primitive) adult stage of human evolution. I do not regard as empty rhetoric the claim that women's battles are for all of us.

Maria Montessori did not confine her activities to educational reform for young children. She lectured on anthropology for several years at the University of Rome, and wrote an influential book entitled *Pedagogical Anthropology* (English edition, 1913). Montessori was no egalitarian. She supported most of Broca's work and the theory of innate criminality proposed by her compatriot Cesare Lombroso. She measured the circumference of children's heads in her schools and inferred that the best prospects had bigger brains. But she had no use for Broca's conclusions about women. She discussed Manouvrier's work at length and made much of his tentative claim that women, after proper correction of the data, had slightly larger brains than men. Women, she concluded, were intellectually superior, but men had prevailed heretofore by dint of physical force. Since technology has abolished force as an instrument of power, the era of women may soon be upon us: "In such an epoch there will really be superior human beings, there will really be men strong in morality and in sentiment. Perhaps in this way the reign of women is approaching, when the enigma of her anthropological superiority will be deciphered. Woman was always the custodian of human sentiment, morality and honor."

This represents one possible antidote to "scientific" claims for the con-   15
stitutional inferiority of certain groups. One may affirm the validity of biological distinctions but argue that the data have been misinterpreted by
prejudiced men with a stake in the outcome, and that disadvantaged
groups are truly superior. In recent years, Elaine Morgan has followed this
strategy in her *Descent of Woman,* a speculative reconstruction of human
prehistory from the woman's point of view—and as farcical as more famous tall tales by and for men.

I prefer another strategy. Montessori and Morgan followed Broca's
philosophy to reach a more congenial conclusion. I would rather label the
whole enterprise of setting a biological value upon groups for what it is: irrelevant and highly injurious. George Eliot well appreciated the special
tragedy that biological labeling imposed upon members of disadvantaged
groups. She expressed it for people like herself—women of extraordinary
talent. I would apply it more widely—not only to those whose dreams are
flouted but also to those who never realize that they may dream—but I
cannot match her prose. In conclusion, then, the rest of Eliot's prelude to
Middlemarch:

> The limits of variation are really much wider than anyone would
> imagine from the sameness of women's coiffure and the favorite
> love stories in prose and verse. Here and there a cygnet is reared
> uneasily among the ducklings in the brown pond, and never finds
> the living stream in fellowship with its own oary-footed kind. Here
> and there is born a Saint Theresa, foundress of nothing, whose lov-
> ing heartbeats and sobs after an unattained goodness tremble off
> and are dispersed among hindrances instead of centering in some
> long-recognizable deed.

QUESTIONS

1. In paragraph 3, Gould claims, "Numbers, by themselves, specify nothing. All depends upon what you do with them." What exactly does
   Gould do with numbers?
2. How does Gould's use of numbers differ from what Broca and his followers did with numbers? Specifically, what distinguishes Gould's and
   Broca's methods of calculating and interpreting the facts about
   women's brains?
3. It might also be said, "Quotations, by themselves, specify nothing. All
   depends upon what you do with them." What does Gould do with quotations in this essay?

4. Why do you suppose Gould begins and ends his piece with passages by George Eliot?
5. Why does Gould quote so extensively from Broca and his followers, particularly from Le Bon? What purpose do all of these quotations serve in connection with the points that Gould is trying to make about women's brains and "biological labeling"?
6. Using Gould's essay as a model, write an essay on a subject with which you are familiar, showing how different ways of gathering, calculating, and interpreting numbers have produced significantly different understandings of the subject in question.

MAKING CONNECTIONS

Compare the stereotyping of women's reproductive functions, as presented by Emily Martin in "The Egg and the Sperm" (p. 736), with the stereotyping Gould presents in this essay. What similarities do you find?

ARKS AND GENETIC BOTTLENECKS

Harold J. Morowitz

Biophysicist Harold Morowitz (b. 1927) taught at Yale from 1955 to 1988, then joined the faculty at George Mason University. In his research he focuses on the interface between biology and the information sciences and, more generally, on the thermodynamics of living systems and the origins of life. He has written a number of scholarly works, including The Origin of Cellular Life: Metabolism Recapitulates Biogenesis *(1992), as well as books aimed at a popular audience:* Mayonnaise and the Origins of Life *(1985),* The Thermodynamics of Pizza *(1992), and* The Kindly Dr. Guillotin and Other Essays in Science and Life *(1997), among others. He is also editor-in-chief of the journal* Complexity.

A friend sent me an article that addressed the search for an environmental ethic in the biblical background of the Judeo-Christian tradition. Although the article did not mention it, I began thinking about the major ecological disaster treated in the Bible, the Noachian flood. Most of the planet's terrestrial species were reduced to two members, one male and one female. The rest of the organisms were drowned by the rising waters that covered the earth. This flood, which drove all species to the brink of extinction, resulted from the evil actions of the people of the planet. Moral number one: If we, the inhabitants of the planet, do not behave ourselves, we jeopardize the welfare of all species.

But, alas, Noah must have misunderstood the Lord, for two is most likely an insufficient number of individuals to save a species from extinction after the waters recede. The difficulty has been given the name "the genetic bottleneck." It states that if a species is reduced to a small number of individuals, the amount of genetic variability is so reduced that it is unlikely that the species possesses enough phenotypic variability to survive environmental changes.

Consider that a species is a collection of interbreeding organisms. No two individuals, with the possible exception of identical twins, have the same assortment of genes. Indeed, every individual has paired chromosomes, with two copies of every gene. Often these paired genes are not identical. Nonidentical genes for the same trait occurring at the same locus on a chromosome are designated alleles. The number of allelic forms of a gene may be as few as one or as many as ten or more. All individuals are different as a consequence of the allele(s) they possess at each locus on their chromosomes. A species is therefore both a collection of genetically varied, interbreeding individuals and a common pool of genes that are available for future generations to inherit.

The gene pool, with all of its variability, is considered to be essential to the survival of a species, because one of the trials that all organisms face is a varying environment. This is due to changes of climate as well as to competitor or predator species invading or arising in the habitat. Geological factors due to tectonic shifts, rifts, or other changes may also alter a species' surroundings.

The fitness of a given individual depends on its genome — that is, on which genes from the allelic set it contains at each locus. The more variable the gene pool, the more likely it is that some members of the species will survive any environmental insult, regardless of how severe it is. Conversely, an extremely nonvariable gene pool seems unlikely to result in enough individuals to make it through a crisis.

As a result of these features, most population ecologists feel that when the number of members of a species drops below some critical level, survival in the wild is not possible; intervention, captive breeding, and protected habitats are considered absolutely necessary for survival. Cases in point are the Hawaiian nene and the California condor.

Let us consider the habitat faced by the animals as they step off the ark on Mount Ararat. The receding waters leave little in the way of vegetation for the herbivores. Even if seeds survived the soaking, it will take a long time for plants to grow to the point of providing sufficient food. There are going to be some very hungry herbivores around.

For the rest — the carnivores and the grazers they eat — the situation is going to be even worse. After the hungry lions have eyed the Thompson's gazelles, there are going to be extinct Thompson's gazelles and still hungry lions, who may then turn their attention to the two gnus. Eventually, this could lead to a major species extinction, as a hungry lion has to eat a lot of starving herbivores to keep going. Why didn't the lions evolve into herbivores? With such a small gene pool, they couldn't. It is thus extraordinarily unlikely that the lions could have survived after leaving their temporary home. No I'm afraid the scriptures don't offer much help on the biodiversity problem.

This may be part of our difficulty. We generally operate within an ethic and morality that took shape in a world of relatively low human population, when infant mortality was a major problem and "Be fruitful and multiply" sounded like very good advice. Nowhere do we find hints of biblical overpopulation, although famine was clearly an ever-present threat. Biblical morality is very much about the relationship between individuals or relatively limited groups of individuals. If the Bible says little or nothing about current large-scale problems, it's because they didn't exist in the times of Noah, Moses, or Jesus.

Thus, we now have a world of habitat destruction driven by population pressure, and we are yet urged to be fruitful and multiply, prompted by some religious leaders to reject contraception. We are caught in a time warp, living in one kind of world with an ethical system from an entirely different kind of world. I don't think we can just go back to the good book(s). We're going to have to figure it out for ourselves.

QUESTIONS

1. This essay uses the biblical story of Noah and his Ark to illustrate a scientific principle: the importance of biogenetic diversity. Is the main argument about biodiversity or something else? Summarize the main argument of this essay.
2. Do you understand the biological language used in the first half of this essay? If not, discuss it with your classmates or others, perhaps including your instructor. There is likely to be a biologist somewhere in the crowd.
3. Can you figure out what the last sentence of the essay means? In particular, what does the word *it* refer to? This may take some discussion.
4. Morowitz proposes a certain scenario for the moment when Noah's Ark lands and the animals go ashore. Can you imagine a different scenario? Propose your own.
5. Is there a religious argument here? Discuss.

MAKING CONNECTIONS

1. Robert Coover's "The Brother" (p. 223) also uses the story of Noah. What are the significant similarities and differences between Morowitz's and Coover's uses of the biblical narrative? (You should look at the text in Genesis to see where they started.) Do they take the same attitude toward the original? Is Coover making an argument? Explain.
2. In his last paragraph Morowitz makes a point about our relation to what he calls "an ethical system from an entirely different kind of world." Compare his point to that of Daniel Lazare in "Your Constitution Is Killing You" (p. 704). Is he saying the same thing about the Bible that Lazare is saying about the Constitution? To what extent do they seem to agree with one another? To what extent do you agree with one or both of them? Write an essay in which you work out your own position in relation to such great ethical texts as the Constitution and the Bible.

When Is a Planet Not a Planet?

David H. Freedman

David H. Freedman (b. 1954), a contributing editor at Discover *magazine and* Forbes ASAP, *has also written for* Science, Inc., Wired, *and* Self, *as well as a variety of newspapers and* The Harvard Business Review. *His first book was* Brainmakers: How Scientists Are Moving Beyond Computers to Create a Rival to the Human Brain *(1994), and in 1997 he published* At Large: The Strange Case of the World's Biggest Internet Invasion *(1997), written with Charles C. Mann. The following essay was originally published in the* Atlantic Monthly *in 1998.*

The planet Pluto has been shrinking at an alarming rate for some time now. Well, not actually shrinking—rather, our awareness of how small Pluto is has been growing. Upon its discovery, in 1930, scientists trumpeted that Pluto was about as large as Earth. By the 1960s textbooks were listing it as having a diameter about half that of Earth. In 1978 astronomers discovered that Pluto has a relatively large moon, whose brightness had been mistakenly lumped in with the planet's: when this was taken into account, Pluto was left with a diameter about a sixth that of Earth, or less than half that of Mercury—long considered the runt of the solar system. Seven moons in the solar system are bigger than Pluto.

In addition to being out of place among the planets in terms of size, Pluto has always seemed conceptually lost as well. The four innermost planets are rocky and of modest size; the next four are gas giants. What was a lone, tiny ice ball doing way out at the edge of the solar system? A surprising answer has emerged over the past few years. Pluto, it turns out, is one of at least sixty, and possibly hundreds of thousands of, small, cometlike objects in a belt that extends far beyond the confines of the planets.

This discovery, while providing a scientifically satisfying answer to a long-standing mystery, has also raised a question that has proved to be painful for many astronomers: Is Pluto truly a planet? A growing number of solar-system scientists assert that Pluto's minuteness and its membership in a swarm of like objects mean that it should be classified a "minor planet," as asteroids and comets are. Others are outraged by the idea, insisting that regardless of how its identity has changed, demoting Pluto would dishonor astronomical history and confuse the public. In the end, the debate boils down to this question: What compromises in precision should scientists make in the name of tradition, sentiment, and good public relations?

Leading the assault on Pluto's planethood is Brian Marsden, who for thirty years has been the director of the Central Bureau for Astronomical Telegrams of the International Astronomical Union (IAU), the worldwide nexus for comet and asteroid sightings. Marsden appears to be an unlikely agent of change. In his small office in Cambridge, Massachusetts, he is surrounded by so many teetering piles of paper that he seems to be not sitting in the office so much as embedded in it. Marsden is short and ruddy-faced; his chin and neck are lost to rotundity, and his wispy white hair is arranged in the style of an explosion. But as he makes his case against planet Pluto, his initially soft, stammering, English-accented rumble becomes the resonant boom of an exasperated lecturer. "Pluto has been a long-standing myth that's difficult to kill," he says.

Marsden doesn't have anything against Pluto itself. Quite the contrary: a life spent trying to calculate the complex orbits of the tiniest celestial objects has left him with a fondness for the one planet whose location a hundred years from now cannot be precisely predicted. However, people wouldn't find Pluto's history of planethood quite so deserving of celebration, Marsden says, if they were aware of the circumstances under which that planethood was obtained.

The famous "search for Planet X," which culminated in Pluto's discovery, was the pet project of Percival Lowell, a Boston Brahmin and amateur astronomer who around the turn of the century became obsessed with two notions: that Martians had constructed canals on the surface of their planet, and that tiny, gravity-induced wiggles in the orbits of Uranus and Neptune indicated that a planet with a mass some six times that of Earth lay farther out. Lowell built and endowed an impressive observatory in Flagstaff, Arizona, to prove himself right, but he died in 1916 without having succeeded on either count. The observatory's directors, aware that their institution was something of a laughingstock because of the Martian search, were determined to salvage its reputation by finding the at least marginally less improbable Planet X. They hired a young amateur astronomer by the name of Clyde Tombaugh to do the grunt work involved. Tombaugh proved to be resourceful and diligent beyond all reasonable expectations, and more or less single-handedly picked dim Pluto out of a thick field of stars—a feat that is still considered one of the most impressive in the history of observational astronomy.

Though some leading astronomers of the day, along with Tombaugh himself, suspected from the beginning that the newly discovered object was not the massive Planet X of Lowell's fancy, the observatory directors launched a public-relations blitz designed to link the two inextricably in the public's mind, and also minimized the opportunities for other astronomers to gather contradictory evidence. The observatory withheld news of the discovery for nearly a month, until the seventy-fifth anniversary of Lowell's birth—even while its orbit was carrying Pluto away from clear observability. After the announcement the observatory refused for six weeks more to release the details needed to find Pluto. Lowell's name and prediction were plastered all over the observatory's press releases, though Tombaugh was barely mentioned, and only in later releases. After briefly considering naming the new object for Lowell or his widow, the observatory chose the name Pluto, largely because a symbol for it—P—could be fashioned out of Percival Lowell's initials.

In the ensuing euphoria over the apparent discovery of a new planet (elation was especially pronounced in the United States, where the public was happy to welcome the first "American" planet to the solar system), those voices that questioned Pluto's size were drowned out, and the IAU awarded Pluto official planet status. It wasn't an entirely unreasoned decision. As the observatory argued, Pluto had been found close to where Lowell has predicted Planet X ought to be if it was causing those orbital wiggles (though Tombaugh, skeptical of Lowell's predictions, hadn't focused his search on that area), so it would be quite a coincidence if this new object *wasn't* the enormous Planet X. Besides, if the object was small, it shouldn't have been visible at all so far away from Earth.

Unless, that is, this new object happened to have a highly reflective icy surface, like that of a comet—which eventually proved to be the case. Pluto is much too small to account for the wiggles on which Lowell had based his predictions. Not that that matters, for there *were* no wiggles— the observations that had implied them were erroneous. And even if there had been wiggles, they probably wouldn't have led astronomers to Planet X, because Lowell's calculations were dubious at best. It was sheer coincidence that Pluto happened to be at the predicted spot. And so it was on a staircase of mistakes, hubris, and hype that Pluto was elevated to planethood.

Marsden has publicly questioned Pluto's planethood for nearly two decades. His case picked up steam in the early 1990s, when the astronomers David Jewitt, of the University of Hawaii, and Jane Luu, of Harvard, began spotting cometlike objects just beyond Neptune's orbit. Some followed paths almost exactly like Pluto's highly elliptical and oddly angled loop—an orbit vastly different from those of the eight other planets. Marsden was convinced that the new objects finally explained Pluto's niche in the solar system. "It all fell into place," he says. "Pluto has more in common with comets than it does with planets."

Jewitt and Luu have now discovered sixty objects in what has come to be known as the Kuiper Belt, named after the astronomer Gerard Kuiper, who suggested the existence of such a belt in the 1950s. About a third of them are in Pluto-like orbits, and all of them appear to be, like Pluto, amalgams of ice and rock. As a result, few astronomers now question that Pluto should be regarded as a member of the Kuiper Belt. But does that mean it shouldn't be considered a planet? After all, though Pluto's diameter of approximately 1,400 miles makes it tiny for a planet, it is huge for a Kuiper Belt object; the next largest known member is only about 300 miles across.

Actually, Marsden points out, astronomers have had to ask themselves this sort of question before, and under circumstances that could be seen as clearly establishing a precedent for Pluto. When the small, rocky body later named Ceres was discovered between the orbits of Mars and Jupiter, in 1801, it was proclaimed a planet. A year later a second rocky body was found in a similar orbit; several other discoveries along the same lines soon followed. Even though the approximately 600-mile-wide Ceres is nearly twice the size of the next largest asteroid, it was evident that it was merely the largest member of what we now call the asteroid belt. In 1802 Ceres's planethood was summarily revoked.

Marsden sees little ambiguity in the situation: Pluto should follow Ceres's trail into nonplanethood. "If you are going to call Pluto a planet, there is no reason why you cannot call Ceres a planet," he says. And no one, he points out, is campaigning to have Ceres's planethood restored.

It would help if "planet" had a formal definition against which Pluto could be measured, but none exists. Astronomy got by quite nicely for thousands of years on a we-know-one-when-we-see-one basis. But now that questions about Pluto are forcing the issue, many astronomers find themselves gravitating toward one or the other of two proposed definitions. The first is "a non-moon, sun-orbiting body large enough to have gravitationally 'swept out' almost everything else near its orbit." Among the nine planets Pluto alone fails this test, and it does so spectacularly, owing to the Kuiper Belt. The second is "a non-moon, sun-orbiting body large enough to have gravitationally pulled itself into a roughly spherical shape." Pluto passes this test—but so do Ceres, a half dozen or so other asteroids, and possibly some other members of the Kuiper Belt. "It's very difficult to come up with a physically meaningful definition under which we'd have nine planets," says Hal Levison, an astronomer at the Southwest Research Institute, in Boulder, Colorado.

Does it matter what we call Pluto? Marsden insists that it does. By calling Pluto a planet, he says, astronomers perpetuate a distorted and thoroughly outdated image of a solar system that neatly ends in a ninth planet, rather than trailing off beyond Neptune into a far-reaching and richly populated field of objects. "It gives a misleading impression to the public and particularly to schoolchildren," he says. "We ought to be explaining that there are four giant planets, four terrestrial planets, two belts of minor bodies, and scattered interesting material." 15

At the forefront of those who reject such proposals is the observational astronomer and author David Levy. Levy is about as different from Marsden as two people who are longtime friends and equally esteemed in one field can be. Whereas the Oxford-educated Marsden spends most of his time working out the mathematics of orbits, rarely so much as peeking through a telescope, Levy has for years risen at 4:00 A.M. to nuzzle up to an eyepiece in the cold Arizona desert, hoping to spot new comets. (Among his twenty-one cometary discoveries is Shoemaker-Levy 9, which crashed spectacularly into Jupiter in 1994.) The low-key, amiable Levy is an astronomical Will Rogers[1] to Marsden's excitable don.

Levy opens his case for Pluto by suggesting that it is too big to be called a minor planet, noting that if it rested on Kansas, it would block out the sun over more than half of the United States. He then casts his vote for the "spherical" definition of a planet, conceding that Ceres could sneak in under this rubric. However, Levy is not about to argue that Ceres should be reclassified. "Ceres has been an asteroid for a long time; it's easier to leave things as they are," he says. In any case, he adds, it's a mistake to frame the debate in terms of technical definitions, because something more important than precision is at stake. "This isn't about science, or things," he says. "It's about people."

The person it seems to be most about is Clyde Tombaugh, who died early last year at the age of ninety. Levy dates his own interest in astronomy back to an evening when he was twelve and his father described to him, over the dinner table, how Tombaugh, a twenty-four-year-old observatory assistant without a college degree and literally right off the farm, had carried out his brilliant search. Levy later became very friendly with Tombaugh, and wrote a biography of him. "I promised him I would always argue in favor of Pluto's remaining a planet," he says. "Clyde is gone now, but his wife, Patsy, is still here, and I think changing Pluto's status would be extremely disrespectful."

It would also be disrespectful to the public, Levy argues, and to children in particular. "Kids *like* Pluto," he says. The story of Ceres's demotion isn't relevant, he claims, given that the public has never really thought of Ceres as a planet. Rather, he holds up the case of the brontosaurus. Early in the century paleontologists realized that the apatosaurus and the brontosaurus were actually the same creature; one of them had to go. Taxonomic convention dictates that the first-named species—in this case, the apatosaurus—subsume the second. And so it was that scientists dutifully declared the much-admired brontosaurus nonexistent. "Sure it's a rule, but every kid knows what a brontosaurus is," Levy says. "Why couldn't they have made an exception?" The brontosaurus has, of course, proved unsinkable in common usage. If astronomers ignore Pluto's place in popular culture, Levy warns, then popular culture could ignore them.

Levy further argues that the PR debacle that could result from a demotion of Pluto might well turn around and bite astronomers. One of his biggest concerns is that NASA would decide not to fund the *Pluto Express,* a proposed unmanned flyby mission to Pluto, under consideration for launching around 2003. To Plutophiles, this mission is the ne plus ultra[2] of scientific discovery; there are things we simply cannot know about an 20

---

[1]*Will Rogers* (1879–1935): U.S. comedian known as the "cowboy philosopher." [Eds.]

[2]*ne plus ultra:* the utmost point; highest achievement. [Eds.]

object until we go right on up to it. "I think that downgrading Pluto would kill the mission," Levy says. (For the record, NASA's director, Daniel Goldin, denies that Pluto's planethood or lack thereof would have any effect whatsoever on NASA's plans, and adds that Pluto the Kuiper Belt object is still fundamentally interesting.)

Fortunately for Levy and other supporters of planet Pluto, the Norwegian astronomer Kaare Aksnes is firmly among their number. Aksnes heads the IAU's Working Group for Planetary System Nomenclature, which has the power to force a vote on the question among astronomers worldwide — the only possible route to an official downgrading. Aksnes says he has no interest in putting the matter before the committee — like Levy, he believes that reclassifying Pluto would be a disservice to Tombaugh and to history — and that even if the subject does come up, he has already ensured that it won't garner enough votes to make it out of committee.

But there is reason for Marsden and his like-minded colleagues to take heart as well. There's nothing in the rules to stop the IAU from officially adding the designation "minor planet" to Pluto's label, so that Pluto would enjoy a sort of celestial dual citizenship. In fact, there's some precedent for this: asteroid No. 2060 also became comet 95P when it was observed to have grown a cometary tail. More important, the chairman of the IAU's committee on small bodies' names, the University of Maryland astronomer Michael A'Hearn, is amenable to the idea. Marsden himself is the committee member responsible for assigning minor planets the numbers by which they are officially known, and he has one already picked out for Pluto: asteroid No. 10,000. The committee can only make recommendations, however, and if it does recommend the added label, it can expect a fight when the vote goes before the full body of the IAU. That's because some planet-Pluto boosters regard the dual-citizenship plan the way the National Rifle Association regards proposals to ban assault rifles — as a superficially reasonable step that must be fought tooth and nail because it would give the enemy momentum.

In any case, Pluto doesn't need an official ruling to move into minor planethood. It could happen on a de facto basis, and it probably will. If textbooks begin to present Pluto as a minor planet, the teachers who use those books will almost certainly follow, along with their students. And unlike the generally conservative astronomy community, the textbook industry tends to favor new points of view — if it didn't, there wouldn't be so much need for new textbooks.

Some of the newest astronomy textbooks, in fact, are already openly questioning Pluto's status. William Hartmann, the author of one of the most popular series of astronomy textbooks in the United States, and a recent winner of the American Astronomical Society's Carl Sagan medal for communicating planetary science to the public, refers to Pluto as an "interplanetary body" in his newest books. Though he continues to include Pluto in his table of the planets, to avoid making teachers' lesson plans obsolete, he feels increasingly uncomfortable about doing so. "It's very important in the grand scheme of things for human beings to be able to picture the rest of the universe in the right conceptual terms," he says. "The way we organize things in our heads comes from the names we give those things, and that's particularly important to remember as we teach those names to the next generation."

Many teachers aren't waiting for textbooks to make the jump. I was   25
surprised to learn recently that my twelve-year-old daughter already knows about the debate—it turns out that critically examining Pluto's planetary status is now part of the sixth-grade science curriculum in my town. Dozens of World Wide Web pages address the issue, many of them put up by teachers and students. The inevitable result is that more and more children will grow up thinking of Pluto as the biggest member of a band of icy objects beyond the outermost planet, Neptune. If enough of them become astronomers, the IAU will follow.

Marsden believes, in fact, that this would be the best way for the change to happen. "I am in favor of a more natural evolution, without imposing any edicts," he says.

That seems a reasonable compromise. Even if science can't afford to bend to sentiment, there may be no harm in letting the sentiment die a natural death.

QUESTIONS

1. This is an essay about arguments. Is it also an essay with an argument of its own? If it has one, or if it suggests or implies one, what is it?
2. What are the arguments in favor of dropping Pluto from the status of planet?
3. What are the arguments in favor of keeping Pluto among the planets?
4. Which side, in your judgment, has the better arguments? Why do you take this side? Which side does Freedman seem to favor? How do you know?
5. In this essay, Freedman spends a good deal of time describing the individuals involved. Why do you suppose he does that? What have these individuals got to do with science or with argument? What function do these descriptions have in the essay—either as part of the argument or something else?

MAKING CONNECTIONS

Science, as represented in this essay, seems to have a lot to do with naming. A girl in love once asked, "What's in a name? A rose by any other name would smell as sweet." Marsden asks, "Does it matter what we call

Pluto?" Why are names important in science? Isn't science about things and not about words? Using this and other essays from the science sections of this book, write an essay in which you discuss the importance (or unimportance) of naming in science or in other modes of serious thought. (If you are one of those who believes that science is the only mode of serious thought, then, better stick to science for this essay.)

ON CREATING A WEB SITE

Stuart Moulthrop

Stuart Moulthrop (b. 1957) holds a doctorate from Yale and has taught there as well as at the University of Texas and the Georgia Institute of Technology. He is currently an associate professor at the University of Baltimore, where he teaches creative writing and literature courses and also courses focusing on hypermedia and publication design. He is also emeritus editor of the online journal Postmodern Culture *and a fellow in communication studies at the Royal Melbourne Institute of Technology in Australia. Moulthrop has written a popular work of hypertext fiction,* Victory Garden, *as well as essays and reviews. The following is from one of his Web sites.*

Pillars of Wisdom

What is a well-formed text on the Web?

Axiom of Simplicity
I have no idea how you have set up your browser. My words may come in colors, they may be forced to dress in weird and barbarous fonts, their lines may be broken crazily upon your screen. May the Web grant me the serenity to accept what I cannot design.

Axiom of Familiarity
The screen is but a flickering page. While we work in words, we are still people of the book. Gutenberg lives.

Axiom of Identity
Readers should always know where they are. Let there be no confusion in your places.

Axiom of Verbality
Every picture tells a story—a story of delay, complication, and increased demand on fragile systems. Keep your pictures in reserve. Let the words carry the work.

Axiom of Community
My text has value only insofar as it opens itself to the texts of others. Let there be links.

Axiom of Futurity
We have only this time and these systems. Some day very soon this will all look much better than it does now.

Axiom of Performance
Ignore any of these rules rather than create anything outright barbarous.

QUESTIONS

1. This is not so much an argument as a laying down of the law, the "pillars of wisdom" about Web design, in the form of a set of axioms, like the axioms of geometry. As is proper to a text of wisdom, these come in the form of gnomic, oracular expressions, somewhat like those of a Zen master or guru. Thus, they must be interpreted. Moulthrop is in fact a master of the Web, a kind of guru. Those who wish to rival him will do well to start by examining his axioms. Take them apart and discuss them, one by one.
2. Moulthrop himself has more than one page on the Web. Find his pages and look at them. How would you judge them according to his standards?
3. Find other pages—especially those of your school or people you know. How do they hold up under this kind of scrutiny? Make them available for class discussion in some form.
4. The Axiom of Futurity predicts changes "very soon." Have they already happened? Do you think they should result in any changes to these axioms—such as the Axiom of Verbality? Explain.
5. Imagine yourself as a Webmaster and guru. Make up your own "pillars of wisdom." Try to outdo Moulthrop.
6. Design a Web page for yourself or for some person or entity that needs one. Try to follow these axioms. Discuss the result.

MAKING CONNECTIONS

Moulthrop's Axiom of Perfomance echoes the sixth rule for better writing set forth by George Orwell in "Politics and the English Language" (p. 636). Look at Orwell's other guidelines, referring to the rest of the essay as necessary. How do they compare with Moulthrop's axioms for "a well-formed text on the Web"? Discuss how the different media the two authors are dealing with affects what issues they address and the style and tone of their presentation.

ROOM FOR DOUBT

C. G. *Hanzlicek*

Born in 1943 in Owatonna, Minnesota, C. G. Hanzlicek earned his B.A. at the University of Minnesota and his M.F.A. at the University of Iowa's writing program. He has been on the faculty of the English Department at the University of California, Fresno, since 1966. Hanzlicek's poetry has appeared in a variety of literary magazines, and he has published several collections, including Living in It *(1971),* Calling the Dead *(1982), and* Against Dreaming *(1994). He is also a translator of the German poet Rainer Maria Rilke and of Native American songs. Of his work he has said, "My chief aim as a poet is to write with clarity, total clarity. If I am misunderstood, I have written badly."*

Two boys, using fish heads for bait,
Landed a four-foot angel shark.
Laid out on the pier,
It seemed never to take the right pose
For a serious study of it.   5
Again and again the boys moved it,
Poking fingers into its eye sockets
To drag it across the planks.

It was a creature worth studying:
Broad, blunt snout like a catfish,   10
White lips and belly
Under a black-speckled gray back,
And wide wings like a ray or a skate.
Dianne wanted to say many things,
But only looked out to sea   15
And asked how long sharks live in air.
Oh, a long time, the boys said.

I've heard all the stories
About the sluggish nerves of fish,
But if those stories are true,   20
Why did the shark tremble,
Pound the pier planks with its tail,
Each time forefingers sank
Knuckle-deep into its brow?

To Dianne and me the slaps and shudders   25
Looked a lot like pain.
What the hell, I don't care if they were the crudest reflexes,
With no more feeling behind them
Than ripples rolling out on water
After a dropped stone.   30
What matters is the room for doubt,
The kind of room we all ask for.

QUESTIONS

1. This looks like a report, a narrative about a couple ("Dianne and me")
   watching two boys with a live four-foot shark on a pier. But there is an
   argument in the last half of it. Is the argument a scientific one? Or
   philosophical? Or both? How would you sum it up?
2. The author calls the scientific descriptions of nerve structure in fish
   "stories." What do you think of this characterization? Is it accurate?
   Does he do this for his own persuasive reasons? Could it be useful generally to think of scientific theories as "stories"? Or, to put things the
   other way around, what makes a story "scientific"? Is this poem scientific? In what ways is it or is it not a story you would call scientific?
3. The words *study* and *studying* appear in the first two verse paragraphs.
   What has this text got to say about study and studying?
4. In the second paragraph we are told "Dianne wanted to say many
   things," but we are not told what she wanted to say. What do you suppose she was thinking of saying? Finally, she asks a question and the
   boys answer her. How do that question and the answer make you feel?
   How do you feel in general about what is being reported?
5. The last line changes the focus dramatically, from the pier to "we all."
   This is one of those shifts of focus, like the zoom of a camera, that
   causes us to rethink what we have been seeing and what it means. What
   does it mean, the whole poem and this last line?

MAKING CONNECTIONS

The concept of *room for doubt* is active in some of the other essays in this
section. Would you call it a scientific concept? Write a short essay in which
you consider some of the other texts in "Arguing" in which the question of
room for doubt seems to be opened up or shut down. How important is
room for doubt in thinking and arguing, anyway?

Acknowledgments (continued from copyright page)

Trudy Dittmar. "Pronghorn." From *The North Dakota Quarterly* 62, no. 4. Copyright © 1996 by Trudy Dittmar. Reprinted with the permission of the author.

Rita Dove. "Rosa." From *On the Bus with Rosa Parks*. Copyright © 1999 by Rita Dove. Reprinted with the permission of the author and W.W. Norton & Company, Inc.

Daniel Mark Epstein. "America's No. 1 Song." From *The Atlantic Monthly*, July 1986. Reprinted with permission.

Anne Frank. "At Home, at School, in Hiding." From *The Diary of a Young Girl. The Definitive Edition* edited by Otto H. Frank & Mirjam Pressler, editors, translated by Susan Massotty. Translation copyright © 1995 by Doubleday. Reprinted with the permission of Doubleday, a division of Random House, Inc.

Jonathan Franzen. "Sifting the Ashes." Originally published in *The New Yorker*, May 13, 1996, pp. 40–48. Copyright © 1996 Jonathan Franzen. Reprinted with the permission of the author.

David H. Freedman. "When Is a Planet Not a Planet?" From *The Atlantic Monthly*, February 1998. Reprinted with permission.

Robert Frost. "Mending Wall." From *The Poetry of Robert Frost*, edited by Edward Connery Lathem. Copyright 1923, 1928 by Henry Holt and Company, Inc., renewed 1951, © 1956 by Robert Frost. Reprinted with the permission of Henry Holt and Company LLC.

Henry Louis Gates Jr. "In the Kitchen." From *The New Yorker*, April 18, 1994. Copyright © 1994 by Henry Louis Gates. Reprinted with the permission of the author.

Amy Ghosh. "The Ghosts of Mrs. Gandhi." From *The New Yorker*, July 17, 1995. Copyright © 1995 by Amitov Ghosh. Reprinted with the permission of Aitken, Stone & Wylie, Ltd.

Carol Gilligan. "Interviewing Adolescent Girls." From *Making Connections: The Relational Worlds of Adolescent Girls at Emma Willard School*, edited by Carol Gilligan, Nona Lyons, and Trudy Hammer. Copyright © 1990 by the Presidents and Fellows of Harvard College. Copyright © 1989 by the Emma Willard School, prologue and preface © 1989 by Carol Gilligan. Reprinted with the permission of Harvard University Press.

Malcolm Gladwell. "The Science of Shopping." Originally appeared in *The New Yorker*, November 4, 1996, pp. 66–75. Copyright © 1996 The New Yorker Magazine. Reprinted with the permission of the author.

Louis Gluck. "The Mountain." From *The First Four Books of Poems*. Copyright © 1985 by Louise Gluck. Reprinted with the permission of HarperCollins Publishers, Inc.

Elliott J. Gorn. "Professing History: Distinguishing Between Memory and the Past." From *The Chronicle of Higher Education*, April 20, 2000. Reprinted with the permission of the author.

Stephen Jay Gould. "Women's Brains." From *The Pandas's Thumb: More Reflections in Natural History*. Copyright © 1980 by Stephen Jay Gould. Reprinted with the permission of W.W. Norton & Company, Inc.

Lucy Grealy. "Mirrors." From *Harper's*, February 1993. Copyright © 1993 by *Harper's Magazine*. Reprinted with the permission of *Harper's*. All rights reserved.

Thom Gunn. "The Life of the Otter." From *Collected Poems*. Copyright © 1994 by Thom Gunn. Reprinted with the permission of Farrar, Straus & Giroux, LLC. And Faber & Faber, Ltd.

Patricia Hampl. "Review of *The Diary of a Young Girl*." Originally published in *The New York Times*. Copyright © 1995 by Patricia Hampl. "Reviewing Anne Frank." Copyright © 1997 by Patricia Hampl. Permission granted by Rhoda Weyr Agency, NY.

C.G. Hanzlicek. "Room for Doubt." From *The Cave: Selected and New Poems*. Copyright © 2001. Reprinted with the permission of the University of Pittsburgh Press.

Zöe Tracy Hardy. "What Did You Do in the War, Grandma? A Flashback to August 1945." From *Ms.* Magazine, August 1945. Reprinted with the permission of the author.

Stephen W. Hawking. "Our Picture of the Universe." From *A Brief History of Time*. Copyright © 1988 by Stephen W. Hawking. Used by permission of Bantam Books, a division of Random House, Inc.

Seamus Heaney. "Death of a Naturalist." From *Poems 1969–1975*. Copyright © 1980 by Seamus Heaney. Reprinted with the permission of Farrar, Straus & Giroux, LLC and Faber & Faber, Ltd.

John Hersey. "Hatsuyo Nakamura." Excerpt from *Hiroshima*. Copyright © 1946, © 1985 by John Hersey. Copyright renewed 1973 by John Hersey. Reprinted with the permission of Alfred A. Knopf, a division of Random House, Inc.

Langston Hughes. "Theme for English B." From *The Collected Poems of Langston Hughes*, edited by Arnold Rampersad and David Roessel. Copyright © 1994 by the Estate of Langston Hughes. Reprinted with the permission of Alfred A. Knopf, a division of Random House, Inc.

Pico Iyer. "Where Worlds Collide: In Los Angeles International Airport, the Future Touches Down." From *Harper's*, April 1995. Copyright © 1995 by *Harper's Magazine*. Reprinted with the permission of *Harper's*. All rights reserved.

James Jeans. "Why the Sky Is Blue." Excerpt from *The Stars in Their Courses* by Sir James Jeans. Reprinted with the permission of Cambridge University Press.

Jane Kenyon. "Philosophy in Warm Weather." From *Otherwise: New and Selected Poems*. Copyright © 1993 by Jane Kenyon. Reprinted with the permission of Graywolf Press, St. Paul, Minnesota.

Martin Luther King Jr. "Pilgrimage to Nonviolence." From *Fellowship*, September 1, 1958. Copyright © 1958 by Martin Luther King Jr., copyright renewed 1986 by Coretta Scott King. Reprinted with the permission of The Heirs to the Estate of Martin Luther King Jr., c/o Writers House, Inc. as agent for the proprietors.

Elisabeth Kübler-Ross. "On the Fear of Death." From *On Death and Dying*. Copyright © 1969 by Elisabeth Kübler-Ross. Copyright © 1969 by Elisabeth Kübler-Ross. Reprinted with the permission of Scribner, a division of Simon & Schuster.

Marcus Laffey. "Inside Dope." From *The New Yorker*, February 1, 1999. Copyright © 1999 by Marcus Laffey. Reprinted with the permission of the William Morris Agency.

Philip Larkin. "The Buildings" from *High Windows*. Copyright © 1974 by Philip Larkin. Reprinted with the permission of Farrar, Straus & Giroux, LLC and Faber & Faber, Ltd.

William L. Laurence. "Atomic Bombing of Nagasaki Told by Flight Member." From *The New York Times*, September 9, 1945. Copyright © 1945 by The New York Times Company. Reprinted with permission.

David Lazare. "Your Constitution Is Killing You." From *Harper's*, October 1999. Copyright © 1999 by *Harper's Magazine*. Reprinted with the permission of *Harper's*. All rights reserved.

Barry Lopez. "Wolf Notes" (Editor's title). From *Of Wolves and Men*. Published by Charles Scribner's Sons, 1978. Copyright © 1978 by Barry Holstun Lopez. Reprinted with the permission of Sterling Lord Literistic, Inc.

Emily Martin. "The Egg and the Sperm: How Science Has Constructed a Romance Based on Stereotypical Male-Female Roles." From *Signs: Journal of Women in Culture and Society*, vol. 16, no. 3, pp. 485–501. Copyright © 1991 The University of Chicago Press. Reprinted by permission of the publisher and the author.

Rebecca Mead. "Eggs for Sale." From *The New Yorker*, August 9, 1999. Copyright © 1999 by Rebecca Mead. Reprinted with the permission of the author, c/o The Robbins Office.

W.S. Merwin. "Things." From *The Second Four Books of Poems*. Published by Copper Canyon Press, 1993. Copyright © 1971 by W.S. Merwin. Reprinted with the permission of The Wylie Agency, Inc.

Stanley Milgram. "Some Conditions of Obedience and Disobedience to Authority." From *Human Relations*, vol. 18, no. 1, 1965, pp. 57–76. Copyright © 1972 by Stanley Milgram. Reprinted by permission. All rights controlled by Alexandra Milgram, Literary Executor.

N. Scott Momaday. Excerpt from *The Way to Rainy Mountain*. Copyright © 1969 N. Scott Momaday. First published in *The Reporter*, January 26, 1967. Reprinted with the permission of The University of New Mexico Press.

Monica Moore. "Nonverbal Courtship Patterns in Women: Context and Consequences." From *Ethology and Sociology*, vol. 6, no. 4, 1995. Copyright © 1995 by Monica M. Moore. Reprinted with the permission of the author.

Harold J. Morowitz. "Arks and Genetic Bottlenecks." From *The Kindly Dr. Guillotin and Other Essays*. Copyright © 1997 by Harold J. Morowitz. Reprinted with the permission of Counterpoint Press, a member of Perseus Books, LLC.

Stuart Moulthrop. "On Creating a Web Site." Originally titled "Pillars of Wisdom and Pillars of Folly." Reprinted with the permission of the author.

Farley Mowat. "Observing Wolves." From *Never Cry Wolf*. Copyright © 1963 and renewed 1991 by Farley Mowat Limited. Reprinted with the permission of Little, Brown & Company, Inc.

Vladimir Nabokov. "On Transformation." From *The Atlantic Monthly*, April 2000. Reprinted by arrangement with the Estate of Vladimir Nabokov.

George Orwell. "Shooting an Elephant" and "Politics and the English Language." From *Shooting an Elephant and Other Stories.* Copyright © 1950 by Sonia Brownell Orwell and renewed 1978 by Sonia Pitt-Rivers. Reprinted with permission of Harcourt, Inc. and Bill Hamilton as the Literary Executor of the Estate of the Late Sonia Brownell Orwell and Seeker & Warburg Limited.

Cynthia Ozick. "Who Owns Anne Frank?" From *The New Yorker,* October 6, 1997. Copyright © 1997 by Cynthia Ozick. Reprinted with the permission of Raines & Raines.

David Pogue. "Secrets of the Software License Agreement." From *Macworld.* Reprinted with the permission of *Macworld.*

Sheldon Rampton. "Let Them Eat Nutcake: How Words Make It into the Dictionary." From *Harper's,* November 1998. Copyright © 1998 by *Harper's Magazine.* Reprinted with the permission of *Harper's.* All rights reserved. This article contains a definition for "biosolid" from *Merriam-Webster's Collegiate Dictionary.* Copyright © 2000 by Merriam Webster, Incorporated. Reprinted with the permission of the publishers.

Pattiann Rogers. "The Power of Toads." From *Firekeeper: New and Selected Poems.* Copyright © 1994 by Pattiann Rogers. Reprinted with the permission of Milkweed Editions.

Oliver Sacks. Excerpt from *The Man Who Mistook His Wife for a Hat* (pp. 8–22). Copyright © 1970, 1981, 1983, 1984, 1985 by Oliver Sacks. Reprinted with the permission of Simon & Schuster.

Carl Sagan. "Can We Know the Universe? Reflections on a Grain of Salt." From *Broca's Brain.* Copyright © 1979 by Carl Sagan. Reprinted by permission of the Estate of Carl Sagan.

Delmore Schwarz. "The Heavy Bear Who Goes with Me." From *In Dreams Begin Responsibilities.* Copyright © 1961 by Delmore Schwartz. Reprinted with the permission of New Directions Publishing Corporation.

Roy C. Selby Jr. "A Delicate Operation." From *Harper's,* December 1975. Copyright © 1975 by *Harper's Magazine.* Reprinted with the permission of *Harper's.* All rights reserved.

Richard Selzer. "A Mask on the Face of Death." First published in *Life* magazine. Copyright © 1987 by Richard Selzer. Reprinted with the permission of Georges Borchardt, Inc. for the author. "The Discus Thrower." Excerpt from pages 27–31 in *Confessions of a Knife.* Copyright © 1979 by David Goldman and Janet Selzer, trustees. Reprinted with the permission of Georges Borchardt, Inc. on behalf of the author.

Theodore R. Sizer. "What High School Is." From *Horace's Compromise.* Copyright © 1984 by Theodore R. Sizer. Reprinted with the permission of Houghton Mifflin Company. All rights reserved.

Radcliffe Squires. "A Day in Salamanca." From *Gardens of the World.* Copyright © 1981 by Radcliffe Squires. Reprinted with the permission of Louisiana State University Press.

Neal Stephenson. "The Interface Culture." From *In the Beginning…Was the Command Line.* Copyright © 1999 by Neal Stephenson. Reprinted with the permission of Harper-Collins Publishers, Inc.

Andrew Sullivan. "The He Hormone" and "What's So Bad about Hate." From *The New York Times Magazine,* April 2, 2000, and September 26, 1999. Copyright © 1999, 2000 by Andrew Sullivan. Both reprinted with the permission of The Wylie Agency, Inc.

Margaret Talbot. "The Rorschach Chronicles." From *The New York Times Magazine,* October 17, 1999. Copyright © 1999 by Margaret Talbot. Repinted with the permission of The Wylie Agency, Inc. This piece includes an adaptation of the Comprehensive Personality Profile. Copyright © Wonderlic, Inc. Reprinted with the permission of Wonderlic, Inc., Libertyville, Illinois, 60048.

<www.wonderlic.com>. Also includes a personality assessment quiz adapted from *Behavioral Expressions and Biosocial Bases of Sensation Seeking.* Copyright © 1994. Reprinted with the permission of Cambridge University Press.

Amy Tan. "Mother Tongue." Originally published as "Under Western Eyes" in *The Threepenny Review* (1990), pp. 315–320. Reprinted with the permission of the author and the Sandra Dijkstra Literary Agency.

Lewis Thomas. "The Tucson Zoo." From *Medusa and the Snail: More Notes of a Biology Watcher.* Copyright © 1979 by Lewis Thomas. Reprinted with the permission of Viking Penguin, a division of Penguin Putnam, Inc.

Barbara W. Tuchman. "When Does History Happen?" Originally titled "Can History Be Served Up Hot?" in *The New York Times Book Review,* pp. 1, 28 & 30. Copyright © 1964 by Barbara W. Tuchman. Copyright renewed 1992 by Lester Tuchman. Reprinted with the permission of Russell & Volkening, as agents for the author. "This Is the End of the World: The Black Death." Excerpt from pp. 92–101 in *A Distant Mirror.* Copyright © 1978 by

Barbara W. Tuchman. Reprinted with the permission of Alfred A. Knopf, a division of Random House, Inc.

Sherry Turkle. "Constructions and Reconstructions of the Self in Virtual Reality: Playing in the MUDS." From *Mind, Culture, and Activity: An International Journal*, 1, no. 3 (Summer 1994). Copyright © 1994 by Sherry Turkle. Reprinted with the permission of the author and Lawrence Erlbaum Associates.

Jane van Lawick-Goodall. "First Observations." From *In The Shadow of Man*. Copyright © 1971 by Hugo and Jane van Lawick-Goodall. Reprinted with the permission of Houghton Mifflin Company and Weidenfeld & Nicolson. All rights reserved.

Alice Walker. "Beauty: When the Other Dancer Is the Self." From *In Search of Our Mothers' Gardens: Womanist Prose*. Copyright © 1983 by Alice Walker. "Am I Blue?" from *Living in the Word: Selected Writings 1973–1987*. Copyright © 1986 by Alice Walker. Both reprinted with the permission of Harcourt, Inc.

Jincy Willett. "Under the Bed." First published in *The Massachusetts Review* (Summer 1983). Reprinted with permission.

Patricia J. Williams. "The Death of the Profane: A Commentary on the Genre of Legal Writing." From pp. 44–51 in *The Alchemy of Race and Rights*. Copyright © 1991 by the Presidents and Fellows of Harvard College. Reprinted with the permission of Harvard University Press.

William Carlos Williams. "Spring and All." From *The Collected Poems of William Carlos Williams, Volume II, 1939–1962*, edited by Christopher MacGowan. Copyright © 1955 by William Carlos Williams. Reprinted with the permission of New Directions Publishing Corporation.

Rhetorical Index

Author and Title Index

Research and Writing Online

Whether you want to investigate the ideas behind a thought-provoking essay or conduct in-depth research for a paper, the Web resources for *Fields of Reading* can help you find what you need—and then use it once you find it.

The English Research Room for Navigating the Web

www.bedfordstmartins.com/english_research

The Web brings a flood of information to your screen, but it takes skill to track down the best sources. Not only does *The English Research Room* point you to some reliable starting places for Web investigations, but it also lets you tune up your skills with interactive tutorials.

- Want to improve your skill at searching electronic databases, online catalogs, and the Web? Try the *Interactive Tutorials* for some hands-on practice.
- Need quick access to online search engines, reference sources, and research sites? Explore *Research Links* for some good starting places.
- Have questions on evaluating the sources you find, navigating the Web, or conducting research in general? Consult one of our *Reference Units* for authoritative advice.

Research and Documentation Online for Incorporating Sources

www.bedfordstmartins.com/resdoc

Incorporating sources correctly in a paper is often a challenge, and the Web has made it even more complex. This online version of the popular booklet *Research and Documentation in the Electronic Age,* by Diana Hacker, provides clear advice for the humanities, social sciences, history, and the sciences on

- which Web and library sources are relevant to your topic (with links to Web sources)
- how to integrate outside material into your paper
- how to cite sources correctly, using the appropriate documentation style
- what the format for the final paper should be

INSTRUCTOR'S MANUAL

FIELDS OF
READING

MOTIVES FOR WRITING

Sixth Edition

Nancy R. Comley • David Hamilton • Carl H. Klaus
Robert Scholes • Nancy Sommers

FIELDS OF READING

Motives for Writing

INSTRUCTOR'S MANUAL
SIXTH EDITION

FIELDS OF READING

Motives for Writing

NANCY R. COMLEY
Queens College, CUNY

DAVID HAMILTON
University of Iowa

CARL H. KLAUS
University of Iowa

ROBERT SCHOLES
Brown University

NANCY SOMMERS
Harvard University

BEDFORD/ST. MARTIN'S   Boston ◆ New York

Manufactured in the United States of America.

5 4 3 2 1 0
f e d c b a

For information, write: Bedford/St. Martin's, 75 Arlington Street, Boston, MA 02116 (617-399-4000)

ISBN: 0-312-25816-X

Preface

This manual is meant to help you find your way around *Fields of Reading*, Sixth Edition, and to help you envision some of the ways that the textbook can be put to use in teaching. We begin this manual with the section "Approaches to Teaching from *Fields of Reading*," which introduces the textbook and discusses some ways that it can be used in courses with varying emphases.

Beyond our opening explanations and suggestions, you will find that we have provided answers for all of the reading questions that appear in our text—a discipline that at times compelled us to revise the questions themselves. It may be that you'll think we should also have revised some of our answers. Whatever thoughts and suggestions you have, either for this manual or for *Fields of Reading* itself, we'd welcome hearing about them. Just write us in care of Bedford/St. Martin's, 33 Irving Place, 10th Floor, New York, NY 10003.

Nancy R. Comley
David Hamilton
Carl H. Klaus
Robert Scholes
Nancy Sommers

Contents

EXPLAINING 33

ARGUING 51

APPROACHES TO TEACHING FROM *FIELDS OF READING*

Fields of Reading: Motives for Writing has been designed to suit four basic emphases for selecting and organizing material in college writing courses:

1. Curricular (emphasizing broad academic divisions of learning)
2. Thematic (emphasizing focused topics of study)
3. Rhetorical (emphasizing aims of discourse)
4. Formalistic (emphasizing modes of discourse)

Each of these emphases, distinct as it is, necessarily draws to some extent on one or more of the others, so that the set of four constitutes, in fact, a rich grammar of possibilities for course design. These possibilities, together with the numerous pieces in our collection, suggest a virtually incalculable number of ways in which you can use this book in your courses. For this reason, we will confine ourselves to discussing the basic set of four and leave you to extrapolate some of the permutations and combinations on your own. As you will see, we do not propose to recommend any particular emphasis as being preferable to the others, since you are in the best position to determine the needs of your students. Instead, we will provide a brief description of each method, followed by some ideas about how the readings and apparatus in our collection can be used in each case. Here, then, is a discussion of some approaches you can follow in using material from *Fields of Reading*.

1. *Curricular (emphasizing broad academic divisions of learning).* This emphasis is based on the assumption that students can most effectively be led to develop their academic reading and writing abilities by being given repeated opportunities to read material that reflects the broadly related divisions of learning and professional activity that they will encounter as undergraduates, to write material that takes into account the subject matter and forms that prevail in these academic and professional areas, and in general to think about language use in terms of the ways it is carried on in these broad contexts. Students thus will be encouraged not only to recognize and practice the particular kinds of writing that are affiliated with particular divisions of learning, but also to recognize and develop the qualities that pervade all of the academic and professional areas.

If you wish to follow this emphasis, you can readily do so by focusing on the set of three academic divisions that recur throughout our main table of contents: "Arts and Humanities," "Social Sciences and Public Affairs," and "Sciences and Technologies." You can acquaint your students with this overall approach by having them read the introductory section "For Students," where they will find an explanation of these broad academic divisions as well as a rationale for organizing a college writing course in terms of such categories. Additional perspectives on reading and writing within these broad academic and professional contexts can be found in the four section introductions, particularly the ones devoted to "Reporting" and "Explaining."

In structuring a sequence of reading and writing assignments for this approach, you can divide your course into three main parts, beginning with the arts, followed by the social sciences, and ending with the sciences, immersing your students at length in each broad division. Or you can rotate continuously among the three divisions. Whichever plan you follow, you will probably find it particularly effective to have your students read pieces that will enable them to see how comparable subject matter and situations are handled within each broad division. For example, students might be invited to compare how firsthand observations are written up in each broad area based on their reading of the Frank and Hersey pieces in the "Arts" section of "Reporting," the Mowat and van Lawick-Goodall pieces in the "Social Sciences" section of "Reporting," and the Selzer and Selby pieces in the "Sciences" section of "Reporting." And in connection with their reading, you can have them carry out their own firsthand observations, trying out different ways of writing them up for the various academic divisions or reflecting on how they might have to vary their methods of observation to suit different academic divisions.

2. *Thematic* (*emphasizing focused topics of study*). Given its implicit curricular orientation, this emphasis is necessarily related to the previous one, but rather than working in the context of broad academic divisions, it proceeds according to the assumption that students can most effectively be led to develop their academic reading and writing abilities by being given the opportunity to read and write within the context of focused topics, themes, and issues. This emphasis serves to highlight for students the ways in which particular academic fields or professional areas deal with similar or even identical topics or questions. Teachers who favor this approach will select and organize material to give students a sequence of challenging topics for reading and writing that range across the curriculum.

You can best acquaint your students with this overall approach by having them read the section introductions of "Reflecting," "Reporting," "Explaining," and "Arguing." In each of these introductions, your students will find detailed examples and discussions of how different academic disciplines and different professional fields bring different points of view and thus different ways of writing to deal with the very same subject, topic, or question.

In structuring a sequence of topics, as well as a sequence of matching assignments for a thematic approach, you will find it helpful to consult the Thematic Table of Contents. This guide lists each reading under one or more of the following categories:

> Values and Beliefs
> Cultures in Collision and Contact
> Race and Racism
> The Experience of Women
> Interpreting the Body
> Violence and War
> Life and Death
> Observing Animals
> Understanding the Physical World
> Human Portraits
> Teaching, Learning, and Schooling
> Health, Disease, and Medicine
> Interpreting the Past
>> Anne Frank: Her Place in History
>> The Atomic Bombing of Japan
> Interpreting Current Affairs and Contemporary Human Experience
> Interpreting the Arts and Popular Culture
> Myths and Rituals

3. *Rhetorical* (*emphasizing aims of discourse*). This approach is based on the assumption that students can most effectively be led to develop their academic reading and writing abilities by being oriented to think about language use in terms of various basic purposes served in any academic or professional field (reflecting, reporting, explaining,

2

arguing). Teachers who favor this approach generally select and organize material to give students experience in various aims of discourse. Readings thus are chosen to help students understand the inherent nature of a particular purpose, to help them recognize something of the range of different forms it can assume from one field to another, and by extension to provide students with principles they can apply and models they can adapt in their own writing.

You can acquaint your students with the rationale for this overall view of the purpose by having them read the introductory section "For Students." The new introduction, with an explicit focus on the aims and motives for writing, gives students insight into the motives and purposes of one writer, Patricia Hampl. Then, as you move from one purpose to the next, you can have your students read the section introduction to each particular aim of discourse to prepare them for reading individual selections as well as writing pieces of their own. In putting together a sequence of reading and writing assignments for this approach, you will find it useful to consult the Rhetorical Index, where you will find pieces listed exemplifying all of the important modes of discourse.

4. *Formalistic (emphasizing modes of discourse)*. Given its implicit rhetorical orientation, this emphasis is necessarily related to the previous one, but rather than working in the context of broad rhetorical purposes, it proceeds according to the assumption that students can most effectively be led to develop their academic reading and writing abilities by being given the opportunity to read and write with an eye to the particular forms, modes, and techniques that are used to achieve various academic and professional purposes. Teachers who favor this approach generally select and organize material to give students experience in various modes of discourse. Readings are thus chosen to illustrate particular modes of discourse and thereby to provide students with models that they can adapt to the needs of their own writing.

If you wish to follow this emphasis, you can readily do so by consulting the Rhetorical Index. Within this index, you will find a list that consists of the following twenty-two categories:

Analogy	Illustration
Arguing	Logic
Case Study	Narration
Causal Analysis	Point of View
Comparison and Contrast	Process Analysis
Definition	Purpose
Description	Reflecting
Evidence	Reporting
Explaining	Scientific and Technical Report Format
Explanatory Context	Third Person Perspective
First Person Perspective	Topical Summation

For each of these categories, you will find page references to the points at which the particular mode is discussed in our apparatus as well as references to pieces that exemplify the rhetorical procedure. Thus you can acquaint your students with each mode by having them read about it in our introductory discussions as well as witnessing it at work in exemplary selections. Reading questions and writing assignments that focus on modes of discourse can generally be found among the questions that immediately follow each selection.

Making Connections

Because each of these approaches to teaching *Fields of Reading* encourages the use of comparisons, both among essays in a section and among essays from different sections, we offer a set of questions under the heading "Making Connections" after the questions for study that follow each reading selection.

In these questions, we try to call attention to possibilities for working with pairs and small groups of essays. Sometimes these questions focus on aims and modes of discourse; sometimes they focus more on the content of the essays under discussion.

We have refrained from commenting on these questions here in this manual as we comment in detail on the first set of questions for study. "Making Connections" always follow directly from the earlier study questions and can usually be read in sequence with them. By the time you have worked through the set of questions, you will have plenty of ideas for dealing with the "Making Connections" questions. In any event, they are almost always open-ended. They are for discussion and writing if you choose, and their answers are whatever you and your students find, with conviction, for yourselves.

REFLECTING

Maya Angelou: *Graduation*

1. Students will agree that graduation is an important event anywhere, but discussion of the rituals in Stamps should help them see (especially if they are urban students) the special importance of graduation in a small town like Stamps. Students might also consider the meaning of *important* as it is used in paragraph 5.

2. We might say there are two unplanned events, the first of which inspires the second. Certainly, Donleavy's condescending speech succeeds in taking the joy out of the graduation ceremonies. Students should note the description of audience reactions in paragraphs 42 and 43 and in the writer's thoughts in paragraphs 44 through 47. The feeling of depression is intensified because the writer has so carefully involved the reader in the initial excitement of anticipation. The other unplanned event is Henry Reed's inspiration of the graduation class and his audience, and certainly it is the more important one. Henry's transformation into a leader is all the more interesting because he has been described for us as a polite, soft-spoken, conservative person—outwardly the model, in other words, of what southern whites of that time wished African Americans to be.

3. Donleavy's speech made the writer feel that her people had made no progress since slavery and that "it was awful to be Negro and have no control over my life" (par. 47). But at the end, familiar songs of her people take on meaning for her; she hears the words of these black poets for the first time, She has proudly graduated into membership in "the wonderful, beautiful Negro race" (par. 61) and, we could also say, into an awareness of the power of the language.

4. The movement in this essay might be seen as a change in voice from *they* to *I* to *we,* representing the graduation into and celebration of the writer's membership in her race. The third-person voice in the first five paragraphs presents the general background

of anticipation from a slightly distanced perspective. The movement to the first-person voice helps the reader see and feel the events through the eyes of the writer's youthful persona. During the graduation ceremony, the writer uses both *I* and *we* before the final celebratory use of *we* in the three concluding paragraphs.

5. Students can use Angelou's approach as a model. Remind them to use specific examples as she does to illustrate expectations and attendant excitement and to be equally specific in recording what actually happened. This essay can be simply two paragraphs with expectations in one paragraph and their denouement running parallel in the other, or it can be a more complex structure with more sophisticated development of excitement. In other words, this writing assignment is manageable for basic as well as experienced writers.

6. The structure required by this assignment is also a basically simple one: before and after, or "This is the way I was, then X happened, and this is how I changed." Again, remind students to use specific examples to illustrate the contrast between before and after the turning point.

Alice Walker: *Beauty: When the Other Dancer Is the Self*

1. Dramatic shifts, like film cuts, emphasize contrasts. The writer's intent is not to arouse nostalgia for the past, but to emphasize the difference between—or better, among—the selves that constitute the writer as she is now.

2. The repetition of this phrase emphasizes the point made by the words themselves: despite Walker's vivid memories of the emotional turmoil her injury caused her, those around her saw only continuity in her personality.

3. We start with a two-and-a-half-year-old, the baby of the family who thinks she's "the prettiest" and is admired for being "cute"; then we see the six-year-old Sunday school performer praised not only for her cuteness but for her "sense" and her flawless performance. Then she describes the years after her accident of feeling ugly until, at age fourteen, the "glob" is removed from her eye and she can again raise her head and accept the gaze of others (par. 32). In high school, she is elected "valedictorian, most popular student, and *queen*," the latter honor a validation of her regained prettiness. But many years later, there is the anxiety of being photographed for the cover of a magazine: suppose her blind eye should wander and render her "whatever" rather than "glamorous." It is her child who really validates her mother's beauty by discovering the very special "world" in her mother's blind eye. As paragraph 49 emphasizes, this act joins the inner self and the perceived self as one, "beautiful, whole and free."

4. Walker as perceiver is her harshest critic; in her blind eye is a blemish that she magnifies in others' eyes. Even though others have considered her beautiful (as in high school), it is only when her daughter literally sees beauty in her eye—sees the blemish as a thing of beauty—that Walker can truly accept her own appearance as beautiful. This latter section (pars. 46–49) can be considered as a play on "Beauty is in the eye of the beholder."

5. The subjects of student essays need not be as dramatic as Walker's. A parent's insistence on an unfashionable form of dress, suffering with adolescent facial blemishes, and simply growing out of the stage of being considered "cute" to the not-so-cute preadolescent stage are likely topics. On the other hand, one might suddenly grow into more positive perceptions of self, as Walker's daughter forced her to do.

6. This is an exercise in—or a validation and analysis of—the workings of selective memory as Walker presents them.

1. Grealy learned how to look at herself through her own eyes and to know herself in a way that had previously been unattainable. She had spent many years obsessed with her own image, finding flaws in herself, hiding behind a mask or a scarf, and charting her life by the disfigured self she imagined herself to be. Living without a mirror gave her a "moment of . . . freedom" (par. 47) that allowed her to meet the world with her own face, not the one she imagined the world saw.

2. Grealy believed that her face kept her from getting normal reactions from people, which in turn kept her from happiness. If she could "fix" her face with operations, she would be what she imagined normal people to be: "whole, content, loved" (par. 20).

3. Almost any paragraph will yield wonderful details for students to discuss. Students will understand the power of these details when they try to rewrite the sentences without them.

4. Grealy had hoped that when her face was fixed, her "life and soul" would also be improved. It was comforting to her to imagine that once something was fixed, learned, or acquired, she would always remember the lesson. But as Grealy learns, the most important truths about oneself have to be learned the hard way, through struggle and courage.

5. Grealy's essay is based on personal experience; it is a story of struggle and survival in the face of disease and alienation. Yet while providing the reader with a detailed account of the pain and alienation she felt as a result of her disease and people's ridicule of her, Grealy links her personal experience to history and literature: to the suffering of people in Vietnam and Cambodia and during the Holocaust and to the alienation the characters in Kafka's writing experience.

Additionally, she mentions the love affairs "normal women" must have and the "true identity of the joy [she] was sure everyone but [she] lived with intimately" (par. 23). Yet that is not how "normal" people live. By the end of the essay, she is aware—as evidenced by her first use of the word *we*—that other people suffer as a result of their own images and the images society tries to impose on them.

6. Ask students to brainstorm about moments in their lives when they have come to accept or embrace a simple truth about themselves. How did they learn that truth? What kind of struggle was involved? Encourage students to find some kind of larger meaning or idea to help them shape and organize their essays.

Henry Louis Gates Jr.: *In the Kitchen*

1. "In the Kitchen" is at once the most accurate, appropriate, and suggestive title, given its double-edged reference to both the room where Gates's mother "did hair" and to "the very kinky bit of hair at the back of your head . . . that resisted assimilation." "The Process" is perhaps the most literal-mindedly accurate of the titles, but it lacks the verbal playfulness that pervades the essay. "Straight Hair," given the double-edged implication of "straight," is somewhat suggestive and accurate but not as richly evocative of a bygone era when many black Americans tried to get their hair done "like white people's."

2. Gates's essay is divided into three distinct sections, marked off by space breaks. All three sections are linked by their preoccupation with black hairstyles as emblems of changing black cultural aspirations. The first section is tightly focused on the sights and sounds of Gates's mother doing hair in the family kitchen. The second section, still cen-

tered largely in the kitchen, begins to range more widely in paragraph 14, when Gates explains what "black people" mean by "straight," and again in paragraph 16, when he speculates about the processes and coiffeurs of Frederick Douglass and Phillis Wheatley. The third section leaves home altogether, given its focus on "Nat King Cole's process," which leads to Gates's haunting memory of the time he heard a Cole recording in an Arab restaurant on the island of Zanzibar.

3. No matter what the process—hot irons and/or chemicals and/or homemade concoctions and/or grease and/or stocking caps—each one involves "the application of pressure" and thus is physically oppressive in one way or another, and all are meant to reduce the kinkiness of one's hair in order to make it look more "like white people's." But according to Gates, "a Murrayed-down stocking cap was the respectable version of the process." Although Gates evidently deplores the cultural self-abasement implicit in the process, it takes him back to the warm and loving childhood world of his mother's kitchen.

4. Popular black hairstyles of the past thirty years, such as Afros, dreadlocks, and cornrows, reflect the varied cultural heritages of black Americans—African, Caribbean, and Southern plantation—rather than imitating the look of whites.

5. In Gates's essay, the most important words with specialized meanings are "kitchen," "process," "good," and "bad," the implications of which he explains in paragraphs 5, 8, and 14 and illustrates with detailed examples throughout the essay. Members of each linguistic subgroup acquire an intuitive understanding of their own specialized meanings in the natural course of their daily experience. Individuals who are not members of the group acquire an understanding by reading essays such as Gates's, or by interaction with members of the subgroup who serve as guides to their specialized vocabularies, or by careful observation and inference of contextual meanings.

6. This assignment challenges students to produce a vividly detailed narrative and descriptive essay that is fraught with culturally significant memories. The most effective essays will focus upon specific images and incidents that are resonant with implications.

Frederick Douglass: *Learning to Read and Write*

1. Listing the events of the narrative shows how closely tied Douglass's growing desire for freedom is to his acquisition of reading and writing skills. Students might list these events:

> Mistress begins teaching Douglass to read.
> Mistress, injured by slavery and obedient to Master Hugh, ceases instruction.
> Mistress snatches newspaper away from Douglass.
> Douglass learns to read by befriending white boys.
> He discusses slavery with them and feels the weight of being a slave for life.
> Douglass gets *The Columbian Orator* and reads the dialogue and Sheridan's speech.
> Douglass is able to utter his own thoughts and grows to detest slavery and long for freedom.
> Douglass seeks out talk of slavery and finds the meaning of abolition in the newspaper.
> Douglass helps Irishmen who urge him to escape.
> Douglass plans to wait until he can write.
> Douglass learns to write by watching carpenters, challenging other boys, and copying Master Thomas's work.

2. Douglass describes most fully the scenes that illustrate the effects of slavery on himself and others and his changing attitudes. Events such as his description of his mistress's change in attitude toward him and her snatching the newspaper from him (par. 2) illustrate the slave owner's fear of educated slaves. His feelings after reading Sheridan's speech (par. 6) and the episode with the Irishmen (par. 7) show us why Douglass determined to escape and make poignant his desire for freedom. In such ways Douglass uses description to bring his story to life and to engage readers in his point of view.

3. Douglass argues against slavery throughout his essay, especially in paragraphs 2, 4, 6, and 7. Proof of his argument is given by Douglass's actions and by his descriptions of his feelings. Authorities such as the white boys, *The Columbian Orator*, and the Irish dockworkers provide evidence against slavery. The mistress's transformation supplies evidence against slavery as well, in that it shows how slavery corrupts the slave owner.

4. Sheridan (par. 6) and the Irish dockworkers (par. 7) represent the Irish Catholic situation. The Irish Catholics were a group, like the slaves, who were denied full human rights. This question is useful for a library assignment that can be simple (Who was Richard Brinsley Sheridan, and what did he do?) or extensive (Trace the long history of conflict between the English and the Irish). In comparing the Irish situation to African American slavery, students will have to define what constitutes slavery.

5. To get students started in retelling the story of Master Hugh's wife, "translate" the first paragraph as a class exercise to show students how to put the story into their own words. If the class has not discussed her story as part of the evidence against slavery, this writing assignment should make that point clear.

6. Assuming the persona of Master Hugh's wife is a more challenging assignment than the previous one. It forces students to consider why people owned slaves. Be sure to discuss possible approaches to the assignment in class. Having Master Hugh's wife reflect on the events will be more challenging than having her report them as they occurred, as in diary form.

Amy Tan: *Mother Tongue*

1. After telling her readers that she is "not a scholar of English or literature," Tan goes on to say that she is a "writer . . . someone who has always loved language" (par. 2). Tan is fascinated with the power of language—the ways in which language can "evoke an emotion, a visual image, a complex idea, or a simple truth" (par. 2). Tan knows the English language as a "tool of [her] trade," from the inside out, not from researching it as an object of study, an abstraction, as a scholar might. Tan's disclaimer allows her more latitude and freedom to use her personal experience as evidence.

2. Tan uses the formal, standard English she learned in school and the English she learned from her mother. Her mother's English, Tan's "mother tongue," is a "language of intimacy," the family talk with which she grew up (par. 4). Tan needed to see her mother's English not as something that was broken and needed to be fixed, but as something passionate, full of rhythm and imagery. Embracing both "Englishes" gave Tan a voice of her own, reflecting both the language she learned in school and her mother tongue.

3. Almost every paragraph will yield an example for students. Tan's language is especially evocative when she describes her mother's speech.

4. Tan learned that standard English doesn't offer her the richness of imagery and passionate detail that her mother's colorful English offers. Tan needed to learn not to reject her mother tongue in favor of standard English. She became a writer when she found a voice that could blend her mother's speech with her own.

5. Many students have learned another language at home and will be able to identify with Tan's struggle. This writing assignment offers them an opportunity to think about the ways in which language helps them make sense of their world.

6. Every family has a kind of private language that unites the family and reflects the family's values and beliefs. Students might use the element of language as a lens to look more closely at one aspect of their family life.

Meghan Daum: *My Misspent Youth*

1. "Misspent" often refers to a squandered life, not an overdrawn credit card or a high-priced academic program. Daum's title, compared with her story, has an ambiguous resonance, which suggests that she intends us to understand her story as having serio-comic implications or at least as involving mixed feelings on her part.

2. Daum's indebtedness is so prodigious, especially for a young freelance writer, that it's very difficult to imagine how she will ever be able to improve her financial situation without declaring bankruptcy or writing a best-seller. Her academic and medical indebtedness looms so large that her spending on "ephemeral luxuries" might seem trivial by comparison. Yet the cost of those luxuries almost surely left her unable to afford the health insurance that would have covered most of the $7,000 that she accumulated in dental and medical bills. As the essay unfolds, she gradually comes to seem like an addictive spender, irresistibly drawn to "ephemeral luxuries" and, in general, to living beyond her means.

3. The extraordinarily high cost of Daum's graduate program ($20,000 a year for three years) might well lead students to raise questions about the sociocultural implications of such prohibitively high fees for programs in the arts. Daum herself makes it clear that only "a rich person" (or a scholarship student) can afford such an expensive academic program. Yet her training at Columbia apparently did enable her to obtain freelance assignments and teaching positions that might have been sufficient to cover her living expenses and to begin paying down her academic loans had she not been addicted to so many expensive luxuries. So, there might be grounds for questioning her assertion that all the troubles began with "the first dollar that I put toward my life as a writer in New York. . . ."

4. From the beginning to the end of her piece, it seems clear that Daum is irresistibly drawn not just by the glitter of big city life but by what she refers to in paragraph 3 as "my own romantic notions of life in the big city," which she associates in paragraph 8 with her desire "to live someplace that looked like Mia Farrow's apartment in 'Hannah and Her Sisters'" — in "places where smart people sat around drinking gin and tonics, having interesting conversations, and living, according to my logic, in an authentic way." So one might say that Daum's hunger for what she believed to be the cultural sophistication of big city life was based quite heavily on a fictional version of urbanity.

5. The final paragraph of her piece suggests that Daum has decidedly mixed feelings about her time in New York City. For in one sentence she claims "I might have skipped out on this New York thing altogether and spared myself the financial and psychological disorder." Yet in the very next sentence, she declares that "I've had a very, very good time here." Indeed, throughout the piece, Daum so often swings back and forth in reflecting on her behavior and situation that this essay has a rich array of implications. Thus, it probably should not be interpreted as having a specific theme, thesis, or purpose, except perhaps for Daum's self-evident intention of bearing witness to the incredibly complex predicament that she created for herself as a result of harboring such "romantic notions" about life in the big city.

9

6, 7. Both of these assignments challenge students not only to tell lively and vividly detailed stories about themselves but also to reflect upon their lives in thoughtful detail, much as Daum does throughout her essay.

Louise Glück: *The Mountain*

1. What Glück reveals privately about herself is a very complex sense of her own consciousness—her double awareness, her continuously evolving run of thought and feeling about art and the artist, about herself and her students. The complexity and richness of her inner life is more on display here than anything else, except perhaps for the dazzling highwire act of writing a poem about teaching her students about the artist's life even while she is in the process of delivering them a lecture about it.

2. Glück appears to be an acutely sensitive teacher, so alive to the behavior of her students that she carefully monitors their reactions (and her own behavior) in order to adjust her remarks to the needs of the moment, as she makes clear in lines 17 to 22.

3. The myth of Sisyphus not only conveys "the endless labor" that Glück associates with the artist's and teacher's life, but also the occasional satisfactions that take place when she feels herself not only to be "standing at the top of the mountain" but also to have "added height to the mountain."

4. Glück defies the myth by virtue of having turned her inner reflections into a poem that bears witness to the complexity of her inner life as artist and teacher. Given the fact that the poem is in the present tense, we are constantly tracking Glück's thoughts at the moment they arise in her mind, so it only becomes fully apparent at the end of the poem that she was conscious of writing the poem much earlier in the piece, in lines 14 to 17, when she speaks of "secretly pushing a rock myself, slyly pushing it up the steep face of a mountain."

N. Scott Momaday: *The Way to Rainy Mountain*

1. Momaday's essay is about a pilgrimage that takes place on several levels: a literal journey to his grandmother's house and grave in Oklahoma, a journey in memory back to his grandmother and her history, and a journey back in time to the history of his tribe. Along this "long and legendary way" (par. 14), Momaday is attempting to understand himself and his people, to find his own "small definition made whole and eternal" (par. 13).

2. The essay begins in the present and continually returns to it from excursions to the distant past (Kiowa history), the recent past (Momaday's memories of his grandmother), and the legendary past (the origin of the Big Dipper). The shifting chronology creates a sense of the relationship among these different histories and the way they inform the present.

3. Momaday reports the events of the distant past, the Kiowas' history, but the present and the recent past are evoked through the writer's perceptions. See, for example, the description of the landscape of Rainy Mountain in paragraphs 1, 6, and 13 and the portrait of the author's grandmother and her tribe in paragraphs 9, 11, and 12. In this way the starkness of the destruction of the Kiowas is contrasted with the richness of their culture.

4. The landscape of Rainy Mountain is described in terms of great contrasts: the winter blizzards and the summer heat; the "brittle and brown" grass and the "steaming foliage" (par. 1). It is a lonely and isolated scene, a place where one can hardly imagine human habitation, a landscape in which the force of nature is dominant. One sees "but

one hill or *one* tree or *one* man" (par. 1). Although students may be surprised initially at the final sentence of paragraph 1, the rest of the essay helps to clarify the paradox of a stark and lonely land that stimulates creation. Momaday returns to this theme in his description of Devil's Tower (par. 6), a rock "upthrust against the gray sky as if in the birth of time the core of the earth had broken through its crust and the motion of the world was begun." Students might point to other passages that evoke place, such as the description of houses "like sentinels" in paragraph 10 and the concluding description of the land in paragraphs 13 and 14.

5. Students can begin by describing their own perceptions and memories of a place and then research its history by talking with older family members and people in the community and by reading relevant books and documents. Discussion in small groups might focus on the various ways a writer can interweave past and present events and impressions.

6. In this assignment, students are asked to portray subjects by setting their present environment and way of life beside the events and places of their past. As some of the students will tend to write straight chronologies, you might duplicate a sample student draft so the class can discuss focusing, organizing, and describing versus reporting.

Patricia J. Williams: *The Death of the Profane: A Commentary on the Genre of Legal Writing*

1. Williams wants her readers to realize that the ubiquity of buzzers in New York reflects their power to keep out the "undesirable," society's need to distinguish between desirable and undesirable, and the absolute arbitrary nature of that distinction when based on race. Although law reviews might not consider it verifiable, personal experience can be very powerful in an essay. Williams brings her readers into her personal experience, then guides them to an exploration of public unaccountability and irresponsibility regarding race and racism.

2. Williams's three renditions center around desirability and verifiability. The first telling of the story is personal; it starts in her journal and revolves around her feelings of humiliation and rage, experienced when she was excluded from Benetton's because of her race. As a customer, she was found undesirable. Since Williams felt there was "almost nothing [she] could do, short of physically intruding upon [the salesclerk], that would humiliate him the way he humiliated [her]" (par. 4), it appears she does equate—at least on an emotional level—this kind of discrimination with the assault store owners fear from people of color.

The second rendition revolves around the law journal's perception of her experience as unverifiable. Her rage had been edited out, as had the name of the store and finally all mention of her race because it was "irrelevant."

The third rendition, told at a law-school conference, focuses on the editing process of the law review, which she believes results from "a social text of neutrality" (par. 13). As a result of zealous efforts to eliminate racism and achieve neutrality in the law, reference to race was eliminated. According to Williams, since race is no longer articulated, racism is perceived not to exist. Therefore, the undesirability of people based on race is unverifiable because the "phantom-word" race is never mentioned (par. 13). This allows for further public unaccountability and irresponsibility.

3. The "unverifiable" personal experiences edited out of Williams's essay and the "phantom-word" race relate back to the profane—the sense of the impure, that her story does not belong alongside those who possess "expert" knowledge. Because the genre of legal writing aspires to color blindness, it enforces a standard of neutrality that results in

"an aesthetic of uniformity, in which difference is simply omitted" (par. 13). Williams seems to imply that the genre does not allow for a reality where events sometimes occur because of race and racism. She seems to see a world in which racism is a strong force (like the room in her late godmother's house).

4, 5. You might ask students to break into groups and take different sides of these conversations. When they are finished, ask the groups to summarize their conversations for the class.

6. This exercise is designed to offer students the opportunity to apply the techniques that Williams uses to their own essays.

Langston Hughes: *Theme for English B*

1. The instructor's advice to "let that page come out of you" seems like an invitation for the students to do a piece of expressive writing—i.e., "free writing" that taps their innermost thoughts and feelings without being inhibited by a preoccupation with prescriptive rules of grammar and composition. Although expressive writing and reflective writing both rely heavily on an attention to one's innermost thoughts and feelings, reflective writing tends to be much more self-consciously crafted in the working out of its form and content.

2. The student's direct-address statement in line 18, "Harlem, I hear you," clearly indicates that the "two" speakers he mentions in line 19 refer to himself and to Harlem. The student, in other words, perceives himself to be an embodiment of Harlem, as he has already made clear in lines 17 and 18. So it is that two voices "talk" within this single piece. The somewhat conversational idiom, such as the contractions, and the dominantly I-centered makeup of the sentences seem to be like "talk," as does the free-form quality of the poem, whose lines vary widely in length—sometimes rhyming, sometimes not—as if the form were accidental rather than deliberate.

3. The student's rambling introductory remarks, which move abruptly from a brief personal history to a recap of the route he takes from class to his room at the Y, immediately suggest that he is writing something that comes "out of" him, without the premeditation one might expect in a more carefully reflective piece. Somewhat later on, the associative leap from talking about his personal preferences to reflecting on questions of race suggests the relative freedom of talking on a page compared to the discipline of composing one's thoughts.

4. The poem seems to turn on the question that the student asks in line 20, "Me— who?" The student's self-conscious probing of his identity beyond the given traits of his color leads to his first important recognition that "I guess being colored doesn't make me *not* like / the same things other folks like who are other races." And that insight leads to the student's next important question, "So will my page be colored that I write?" From this point on, the student's carefully developed answers and reflections inevitably lead to the much more confident assertion of his concluding remarks.

Martin Luther King Jr.: *Pilgrimage to Nonviolence*

1. King felt that liberalism was "too sentimental concerning human nature and that it leaned toward a false idealism" (par. 4), while neo-orthodoxy "fell into a mood of anti-rationalism and semifundamentalism, stressing a narrow uncritical biblicism" (par. 6). As he states earlier in paragraph 6, "If liberalism was too optimistic concerning human nature, neo-orthodoxy was too pessimistic."

2. King found useful existentialism's "perception of the anxiety and conflict produced in man's personal and social life by the perilous and ambiguous structure of existence" as well as its conviction "that man's existential situation is estranged from his essential nature" (par. 9). Rauschenbusch argued that religion must be concerned with humanity's social condition in addition to its spiritual condition and thus paved the way for King's application of Christianity to social action.

3. Gandhi's concepts provided the answers to many of King's questions, and the Montgomery experience allowed him to test their applicability. As he states in paragraph 15, "Many issues I had not cleared up intellectually concerning nonviolence were now resolved within the sphere of practical action."

4. Not only did King's personal faith provide the strength to go on with his heroic actions, but also his hopes for a better world depended on the Christian principles he outlines in the final paragraphs of his essay.

5. King's final beliefs are markedly stronger than his original fundamentalism because they are the result of much study, thought, and testing. Though simple (in the best sense of the word), they are infinitely richer for having been through the crucible of thought and experience.

6. King gives succinct and lucid explanations of all the theological and philosophical concepts he uses in an effort to lead his reader through his intellectual pilgrimage.

7. Examples can be found in paragraphs 3, 6, 17, 18, and 19. Such concessions demonstrate King's comprehension of opposing viewpoints (and clarify them for the uninformed reader). This strategy thus ensures presenting what seems to be a fair, even-handed treatment.

8. This question supplies a chance for students to adapt King's method of presentation to their own experiences; responses will of course vary.

9. The students' responses to this question will largely depend on their knowledge of current history and on whether they have an optimistic or pessimistic outlook on life.

Amitov Ghosh: *The Ghosts of Mrs. Ghandi*

1. The title piece probably refers to the several courageous women whom Ghosh encounters in the hours and days immediately following the assassination of Mrs. Ghandi—women who risked their lives to protect others rather than avoiding any kind of political involvement as Ghosh did during most of the violent aftermath.

2. Ghosh explains the paradox most clearly in paragraph 91 when he writes about the dangers and the complex ethical problems of writing about violence: "in such incendiary circumstances, words cost lives, and it is only appropriate that those who deal in words should pay scrupulous attention to what they say. It is only appropriate that they should find themselves inhibited." But to some extent, this explanation is also a rationalization for his long-held silence, a rationalization that he evidently rejects in the following paragraphs.

3. During the first four sections, Ghosh's reminiscence has the appeal of a suspenseful narrative, hinging on the question of how Ghosh, Hari, and Hari's parents and neighbors will surive the violence (or be undone by it). But in the last three sections, the essay turns into an implicit and then overt exploration of the ways that violence can be resisted or prevented, in deeds and words.

4. In each of the incidents that he recalls, Ghosh vividly describes not only the violence but also "the risks that perfectly ordinary people were willing to take for one another." In the first four sections, Ghosh comes across largely as an observer rather than a participant, as someone who follows the model of his literary idol, V. S. Naipaul,

by resisting any kind of political involvement—by refusing to be "a joiner." But Ghosh's role changes drastically in section five when he takes part in the political protest.

5. As Ghosh makes clear in his final paragraph, this essay is in many respects a confessional, an act of expiation: "It is when we think of the world the aesthetic of indifference might bring into being that we recognize the urgency of remembering the stories we have not written." So, in remembering "the ghosts of Mrs. Ghandi," Ghosh bears witness not only to his "horror of violence" but also to his unwitting complicity in "the aesthetic of indifference."

6. An important feature of this assignment is for students to develop their reflections so that they take account of what they were thinking and feeling both at the time of the violent situation and later on. In other words, it is important for them to develop a double view of themselves—as the self remembered and the remembering self.

George Orwell: *Shooting an Elephant*

1. Although he hates his position and the government he serves, Orwell doesn't think much better of the Burmese. He feels that the British empire, for all its faults, "is a great deal better than the younger empires that are going to supplant it" (par. 2). The "white man's burden" here becomes a very real psychological problem.

2. Orwell, as the representative of British imperialism, finds that power can be maintained only by impressing the "natives" but that such power forces the wielder to wear a mask much against his will. Orwell realizes that "I was only an absurd puppet pushed to and fro by the will of those yellow faces behind" (par. 7).

3. Shame and embarrassment overcome Orwell at the end. Though legally in the right, he is morally the fool he tried to avoid becoming in front of the natives. That he could be "glad" a coolie died to save his reputation indicates how reprehensible the imperialist system can be.

4. Orwell's candor adds much to the moral struggle involved in imperialism. Without this tone, the essay would lack psychological tension and the human element.

5. Orwell places his thesis in the middle of the essay (par. 7), where he describes watching the elephant and deciding what to do next. This placement is dramatically effective in that the pressure of the moment seems to force an epiphany on him: "I perceived in this moment that when the white man turns tyrant it is his own freedom that he destroys."

6. A traditional essay dealing with a wider variety of issues concerning imperialism might provide a more comprehensive, even-handed treatment, but it's a harsh critic who'd prefer such an essay over Orwell's. Despite its subjectivity, Orwell's narrative drives home the horror of imperialism much more effectively than many more objective essays could.

7. Orwell's essay provides a concrete example of the extremes to which imperialism can lead and effectively dramatizes the "white man's burden." Though the essay is not overly polemical or propagandistic, it presents an effective argument against imperialism.

8. Most students should be able to find an incident in their own lives (or those of their circle) where the larger social problems of prejudice, sexual or racial discrimination, or inequality were suddenly illuminated by a particular instance.

Zoë Tracy Hardy: *What Did You Do in the War, Grandma? A Flashback to August, 1945*

1. At the beginning of the essay, Hardy accepts war as a bitter but necessary course of action. She reports the war effort in a matter-of-fact manner with little consciousness

of the horrors involved. But after the dropping of the atomic bomb, those horrors haunt her (even causing nightmares) and force her to reevaluate the wisdom of her political leaders.

2. High school physics had filled Hardy with optimistic visions of a world powered by atomic energy, but the "strange new world" (par. 40) that dawns with the dropping of the atomic bomb fills Hardy with dread and pessimistic skepticism.

3. Hardy feels betrayed and outraged—betrayed by political leaders who in truth were "kicking a dead horse—brutally" (as she puts it in par. 52) and outraged at her "final insignificance" (par. 70) in the decision-making process that led to the use of the bomb. Mildred's casual faith in her leaders is unshaken by the bomb, and for that reason Hardy realizes there would always be a gap between her and people like Mildred.

4. There is an interesting parallel between the shedding of her naïveté toward war and toward sex throughout the essay. Hardy learns of new positions, of the existence of prostitutes, and of the differences between sex and the idyllic "Lecture 14" and sex in the real world of war and marriage. In both cases, naïveté is succeeded by maturity, euphemisms by plain speech.

5. Although it begins as a personal reminiscence, the essay concludes with searching questions on the nature of atomic power, the role of the citizen in government affairs, and the naïveté of certain kinds of patriotism. One woman's story becomes the story of countless people whose attitudes were changed by the war.

6. Most students will find Hardy's thoughts as relevant as ever; this is a good topic for classroom discussion.

7. Those students who have already held jobs will find it easier to answer this question than those who have not. Nevertheless, the others should recall a friend's or parent's job that is applicable.

Trudy Dittmar: *Pronghorn*

1. Although Dittmar is a highly sophisticated human being and the pronghorn a wild animal, she empathizes and identifies with pronghorns for several reasons: partly because she sees their beauty as having faded in human eyes, much as she considers her own to be fading; partly because the older pronghorn's defeat and loss of his harem reminds her of a recently failed love affair with a younger man, of her declining powers, and, by implications, of her impending mortality; and partly because she regards her mortal fate, like that of the older pronghorn, as being part of a "long history" that she refers to as "the evolution trail" (par. 32).

2. The numerous experiences that Dittmar tells about in this piece, varied though they are, largely bear witness to the inexorable workings of time, change, and mortality in the lives of human beings and wild creatures alike. Or as Dittmar says in paragraph 23, "It teaches you you can get through it, if there's a way through it, I thought that morning of the antelope. But sometimes there's not a way through it, and when there's not, it teaches that too." Weaving back and forth between her personal story and the pronghorn story, Dittmar gradually brings her essay to bear on the biological truth of things, both about the pronghorn and herself.

3. Anthropomorphizing literally means ascribing human form to nonhuman creatures or things. In ordinary usage, it refers to a tendency to attribute human characteristics or traits to nonhuman beings or to interpret animal behavior in terms of human conduct, as when the old cowboy in the Wyoming saloon characterizes the pronghorn by saying, "All painted up like that and them big eyes bulging out, I always thought they looked like a clown." Dittmar disapproves of anthropomorphizing because it is senti-

mental and unscientific, and because it goes against everything she knows about animals from her training as a wildlife biologist. But during the period she writes about in this essay, given her acute sense of emotional vulnerability, she was evidently unable to resist the temptation to anthropomorphize the pronghorn.

4. Dittmar seems most inclined to anthropomorphize when she is describing the old pronghorn's defeat in paragraphs 16–20 and somewhat later when she is musing upon the subsequent fate of the pronghorn in paragraph 26. She is most like a wildlife biologist in paragraphs 30–31 when she offers a detailed run-down of the pronghorns distinctive characteristics and evolutionary background. Though she never observes herself with the clinical eye of a wildlife biologist, she does tend to look at her behavior somewhat like a psychologist when she discusses the different parts of herself in paragraph 27.

5. In paragraphs 30 to 32, Dittmar looks at the pronghorn and herself in the context of natural evolution, which provides her with the consolatory knowledge that "the illimitable details of life sprang forth continually" from "the dissolution of old bucks and of everything else."

6. This assignment challenges students to find personal significance in the world of nature without sermonizing, sentimentalizing, or anthropomorphizing.

Lewis Thomas: *The Tucson Zoo*

1. The instinctive human hankering for friends (see par. 5) that Thomas perceives in his affectionate reaction to the beavers and otters also provides the link to his discussion of ants, which embody the profoundly social behavior that Thomas celebrates in this piece.

2. Though Thomas's medical training and cellular research schooled him in the scientific method, he worries about its tendency to foster an atomistic, fragmented, and specialized view of things, especially in the first two paragraphs of his essay. But in a surprising reversal of thought prompted by his reflections on the possibility that altruism might be encoded in human DNA, he also recognizes the breathtaking discoveries that may be produced by scientific investigation. So, Thomas might be described as an in-house critic of the scientific establishment.

3. As Thomas makes clear in paragraph 5, he learned nothing new about the otters and beavers, but he did learn something important about himself, "maybe about human beings at large"—that "we are endowed with genes which code out our reaction to beavers and otters, maybe our reaction to each other as well. . . . And the behavior released in us, by such confrontations is, essentially, a surprised affection."

4. Thomas seems to be most scientific in paragraphs 4, 5, and 8, when he is examining his behavior at the zoo and attempting to hypothesize about its possible sources and origins, and in paragraph 9, when he formulates specific questions about the behavior of ants, which could well serve as the basis for scientific investigation. His behavior is least scientific when he is reveling "with pure elation" in the spectacle of the beavers and otters. But the essay itself is probably least scientific when he reflects on the difficulty of making an argument against altruism in paragraph 7.

5. Thomas devotes more detailed attention (and passion) to his reflections on altruism than to anything else in the piece. Yet he eagerly discusses so many other subjects—the reductionism of science, the beavers and otters at play, his elated reaction to the animals, the social behavior of ants, and other topics as well—that it would be misleading to reduce this piece to a single main thesis or purpose.

6. The wording of this assignment is intended to guide students toward a reflective rather than didactic treatment of the subject. Students are specifically invited to explore both their initial and subsequent reactions to a natural event.

Pattiann Rogers: *The Power of Toads*

1. After the first stanza, Rogers offers very little descriptive detail about the toads themselves but much more about the stormy evening. In fact, the remainder of the poem is largely a series of speculative questions about how the toads (or anyone else) might construe all the powerful manifestations of the storm that she evokes in such phrases as "the loin-shaking thunder of the banks," "rising riverlets," "the splitting light, the soaring grey . . . above," "these broken heavens," "the particles of rain descending on the pond," and so on.

2. In the second stanza, Rogers imagines that the toads might think that their croaking calls forth the storm, that "They sing more than songs, creating rain and mist / By their voices." And in the third stanza, she imagines that some toads might even believe their croaking produces the thunder and lightning, causing "The heavens to twist and moan by the continual expansion / Of their lungs."

3. In the fourth stanza, Rogers entertains the possibility that the solipsism of the toads might contain an essential truth about the deep interconnectedness of a rainstorm and love, "And they might be right. . . . Raindrops-finding-earth and coitus could very well / Be known here as one." And in the fifth stanza, she imagines herself and her lover (whom she has evidently been addressing throughout the poem) testing the hypothesis of her fourth stanza — "We could investigate the causal relationship / Between rains and love-by-pondside if we wished."

4. Rogers's celebration of the love-making toads is "scientific" from start to finish in its movement from a detailed observation of natural phenomena (the toads croaking, the sky thundering, and so on) in stanza 1, to hypotheses about the interrelationship of those phenomena in stanzas 2–4, to a proposed testing of the hypothesis in stanza 5. At the same time it is a very witty love poem, whose seductive intention only becomes clear in the final stanza.

Seamus Heaney: *Death of a Naturalist*

1. The vividly detailed descriptive images in the first and third stanzas suggest that Heaney must have been a painstakingly careful observer of life in the flax dam, as he demonstrates in his memory of collecting "jampotfuls of jellied / Specks to range on window-sill at home, / On shelves at school, and wait and watch."

2. Heaney opens his poetic reminiscence with the richly evocative description of the flax dam in order to establish the powerful appeal of that place — the beauty and the mystery — that must have been the source of its initial attraction to him.

3. Heaney's sudden, unexplained focus on the flax dam in line 1, and his obsession with it throughout the rest of the stanza, suggest that he's been so abruptly caught in the hold of a long-past memory that he doesn't even bother to offer any kind of familiar exposition or explanation of what he's up to in writing about the flax dam. The youthful idiom of his references to the "daddy frog" and the "mammy frog" suggest that he is virtually reliving his childhood state of feeling at that point in the poem.

4. The final stanza bears witness to something very much like a coming to knowledge, in which the beautiful images of Heaney's first encounter with the flax dam — "Bubbles gargled delicately, bluebottles / Wove a strong gauze of sound around the smell. / There were dragon-flies, spotted butterflies . . ." — are replaced by "a coarse croaking that I had not heard / Before." So, the violence and ugliness of raw sexuality seem to be what caused him to sicken, turn, and run.

1. When summarizing this scene, students might think about details that are memorable because of their relationship to the rest of the essay. They might note the Haitian guide's comment that he has had contact with prostitutes "like every good Haitian boy" (par. 1) as a striking example of Selzer's argument that societal expectations in Haiti perpetuate the spread of AIDS. Selzer's description of the three "beautiful and young and lively" women might be particularly memorable because of its sharp contrast to the later images of disease and death (par. 2).

Selzer spends so much time with these women because he wants to learn more about the spread of AIDS in Haiti. He describes it at length in his essay because he wants the reader not only to have an intellectual and far-reaching idea of the impact of AIDS on Haiti, but a concrete picture of how individual human beings are both affected and affect the spread of AIDS. These women's attitudes are important because they are typical of attitudes that thwart AIDS prevention.

2. Selzer saw that the doctor could only offer a prescription for a Gatorade-like drink and the phrase "Eat like an ox," ironic because even if the disease did not cause lack of appetite, poverty would prevent patients from buying food (par. 49). He learned that Haiti did not have the resources to provide care for AIDS symptoms. Selzer sensed the futility of the doctor's attempts to combat a fatal disease with such limited resources. At the same time, he witnessed the doctor's willingness to offer what he could and to accept the personal risk of working with AIDS patients, a risk exacerbated by poor conditions (par. 66).

3. The journalist's remark indicates that he blames the American press for Haiti's loss of income from tourism. He asks Selzer not to portray Haiti as a dangerous place to visit. His comment has implications for the prevention of AIDS: it suggests that concern with the economic impact rather than with the health crisis might cause Haitians to downplay the problem and risk, slowing efforts at prevention.

In judging whether Selzer has honored this request, students might consider Selzer's discussion of the source of the AIDS virus. Rather than indict Haiti as "the source of AIDS in the western hemisphere" (par. 103), Selzer considers different possible sources, including the United States. Students should also think about how Selzer's piece would affect their own desire to visit Haiti.

4. Selzer has learned that a country's economic standing in the world and attitudes about a country's economic and social position can affect AIDS care and efforts at prevention. The prostitutes claim that AIDS was "invented by the American government to take advantage of the poor countries" (par. 21), and the Baptist pastor claims that voodoo and the "fornication" of "these people" spread the disease (pars. 80–81). Selzer indicates that this blame thwarts efforts at AIDS prevention and care: the Baptist Mission no longer cares for AIDS patients, and the prostitutes continue in their livelihood. According to Selzer, differences between social classes also affect efforts in treatment. He quotes a doctor who says that change in behavior will only come when "enough heterosexuals of the middle and upper classes die," creating the panic necessary for change (par. 129).

5. To engage the reader, Selzer opens with a detailed description of a scene at the Copacabana. After this first section, the essay is organized in part like a travellogue. His physical journey from one to the other marks the transition from the Baptist Mission Hospital to the general hospital (par. 86). In addition, the whole essay is contained within the two weeks of his trip; the essay ends with his last day in Haiti. Throughout

the essay, Selzer interweaves the specific with the general, beginning with details about his trip to the Copacabana and to the clinic directed by Doctor Pape and ending with a list of statistics about AIDS in Haiti. He juxtaposes different examples to root general facts in individual human experiences and also to make his point about differences in wealth. By following the clean and insular Baptist Mission with the "filthy, crowded, hectic" general hospital (par. 86), Selzer emphasizes the difference between their resources and between the resources of Haiti and of the United States.

6. Students should first think about the meaning of the phrase "the politics of AIDS." They might be able to define this more clearly by identifying points in Selzer's essay where he examines relations of power, particularly of economic power, between countries and between social classes. Their own essays should examine these relations and their effect on AIDS care and prevention. Students might also relate Selzer's reflections about AIDS in Haiti to their experience of the politics of AIDS in their own country.

7. Students should identify both Selzer's position and the elements of his essay that communicate this position. They should think about possible objections and how they would counter those objections. They might also consider how they would balance detailed description of individual cases with the use of statistical evidence in their own version of Selzer's argument.

Carl Sagan: *Can We Know the Universe? Reflections on a Grain of Salt*

1. The essay's opening sentence announces Sagan's emphasis on science as a *way of thinking*, an intellectual method or disposition more than a body of established facts. While science is also a body of knowledge, this knowledge must be continually challengeable, open to criticism and revision, kept fluid rather than accepted as dogma. Scientific thinking is, on the one hand, a matter of formulating questions, advancing hypotheses, and testing the hypothesis against the result of experimentation. But on the other, it has also a large element of the most innocent *wonder*: the ability to ask why things are as they are, even things so apparently simple as a grain of salt. Sagan conceives of his audience as intelligent, curious, and educated—but educated, probably, primarily in the humanities; he tries to acquaint them with the presumably somewhat foreign subject of scientific thinking by drawing out its parallels with aesthetic experience.

2. Sagan poses abstract questions but takes care to provide illustrations (as in pars. 2, 3, and 4) and to use an ordinary example—salt—to illustrate complex ideas. Also, Sagan's enthusiasm for his topic is evident throughout: "It is an astonishing fact . . ." (par. 11); "It is stunning that . . ." (par. 12). Note his emphasis on "passion" and "joy" (par. 11), the opening sentences of paragraph 14, and the concluding paragraph.

3. Sagan, examining a "simple" grain of salt, points out areas where very little is known. In paragraph 6, the equation of the "total number of things knowable by the brain" with only "one percent of the number of atoms in our speck of salt," is designed to challenge the we-know-it-all scientists.

4. Sagan points out that the laws of nature, while they restrict what we might do, "also make the world more knowable" (par. 14). With the brains we have, we could not know a universe with no laws because our brains "require some . . . stability and order" (par. 11). Clearly, Sagan is at ease not knowing it all, as paragraph 15 makes clear: he doesn't want to live in a boring universe.

5, 6, 7. Questions 5 and 6 offer opportunities for personal reflective writing; question 7 provides an opportunity to reflect on an idea.

REPORTING

Anne Frank: *At Home, at School, in Hiding*

1. In paragraph 4, Frank writes of having "everything, except my one true friend," by which she evidently means someone quite special to whom she can confide her most private experiences, her most intimate thoughts and feelings. In keeping with that desire, Frank is intimate with Kitty from start to finish, whether she is talking about how she handles her young suitors, how she copes with her teachers, or how she feels about her impending move to the hideout.

2. Frank's irregular writing habit suggests that she is often so intensely caught up in the experiences of her daily life that she has neither the time nor the inclination to keep in regular touch with her imaginary friend, Kitty. Though Frank is not a regular or methodical diarist, she evidently takes her imaginary friendship seriously enough that she feels obliged to explain herself whenever she goes several days or a week without writing. On such occasions, she usually provides an extensively detailed recap of things in order to bring Kitty up-to-date, as in her entry for July 1.

3. No matter what she is writing about, Frank is always a meticulous observer, alert to all of the important facts of a situation (as in her summary of the anti-Jewish decrees) as well as all of the nuances of human behavior (as in the story of her friendship with Hello). She is so attentive, in fact, that she is able to recall (or reconstruct) the dialogue from an extended conversation with Hello and can produce a detailed floorplan of her family's hideout.

4. Frank comes across in these entries as being a quite complex individual, especially for a thirteen-year-old. She reveals herself by turns to be thoughtfully self-aware of her sometimes frivolous social behavior, playful with her girlfriends, coy and shrewd with her male admirers, daring and witty with her schoolteacher Mr. Keesing, anxious and intensely concerned about the anti-Jewish decrees and her family's perilous situation.

5. Many students will probably be struck by the relatively tame social activities of Frank and her young adolescent compatriots—Ping-Pong, "The Little Dipper Minus Two," and the ice-cream parlor—as well as by the strict parental oversight of her social life. Frank and her friends do, after all, exist in a pre-tech, drug-free, and sexually repressed world. Despite these and other notable differences between Frank's affairs and the lives of her recent American counterparts, they do have in common an intense social consciousness that is a hallmark of young adolescents; it would be well to explore this consciousness in class discussion.

6. Frank's relatively tame social affairs exist within such a menacing political context that it might be interesting to consider the reverse situation, which seems to prevail for many contemporary American youngsters—namely, a convulsive or at least menacing social world in a comparatively tame political context.

7. Most students will probably have little trouble perceiving similarities between apartheid in South Africa and anti-Semitic policies in Nazi Germany, but they might be uncomfortable about seeing the similarities in their own country. Thus it might be useful to have them consider the overtly racist decrees that once existed widely in the United States, as well as the covertly racist policies that still affect various aspects of contemporary American life.

8. A diary that is at once intimate and public—that is, a self-consciously crafted journal—challenges students to be true to themselves while also suiting the interests and needs of a large readership. Such a diary calls for a careful selection, arrangement, and shaping of detail, a lively way with words and anecdotes, an alert ear for how one sounds

in writing, a keen awareness of one's thoughts and feelings, and the skill to tell about them in an engaging style without being either preachy or gushy. This assignment might help students appreciate the remarkable achievement of Anne Frank's diary. It might also encourage them to make something of their own daily experience now and in the future.

John Hersey: *Hatsuyo Nakamura*

1. Through Hatsuyo Nakamura's story, we learn of her suffering and that of others like her, of the Japanese government's neglect of these "explosion-affected persons" (par. 5), of the prejudice of employers against them, and of the effect of radiation sickness (par. 6). We learn of the resignation, the feeling of powerlessness before authority bred into Japanese culture, and of the government's finally being shamed into granting health benefits to the *hibakusha*.

2. Hatsuyo Nakamura is presented to us as a special individual, but at the same time, she represents the many other widowed mothers who survived the blast and struggled to make lives for themselves. To tell her story, Hersey relies, for the most part, on straight reporting of events and uses a minimum of evaluative language. Paragraph 2 provides a good example of this, noting what she saved from the fire, the little money she had, and the shack she rented at the beginning of her "courageous struggle." The facts are enough to affect the reader, who will certainly accept the writer's judgment of courage. The reader feels sorry for her plight, heartened by her will to survive, and glad at her small share of happiness, knowing all the while that most ordinary people can never know what she knows of horror.

3. Hersey sets material from interviews against the background of postwar and current events in Japan. That is, he places his subject in the historical context. Paragraph 5 presents recent history, while paragraph 7 combines material drawn from Nakamura and from the political and cultural history of Japan.

4. As the following list of events indicates, Hersey has arranged his material mainly in chronological order, emphasizing major changes in Nakamura's personal life and setting them in the historical context:

> August 1946 (pars. 1–4): "Weak and destitute," Nakamura reaches her lowest point after being widowed by the war, surviving the bombing, digging out her children, and suffering from radiation sickness. Her resources, saved from the fire, are exhausted. She struggles to survive by sewing and cleaning despite her fatigue. To pay the doctor, she sells her sewing machine (a last link with her husband).
>
> Postwar background and history (pars. 5–7): The *hibakusha* are defined; the prejudice toward them, the A-bomb sickness, and Nakamura's attitude and that of the other survivors are explained.
>
> 1946–52 (pars. 8–13): Nakamura gets wormed, delivers bread, peddles sardines, and collects for the newspapers. She moves to better housing in 1951; her children seem to have avoided radiation sickness. Her shack is converted to a street shop.
>
> 1953 (pars. 14–17): She gets a job at Suyama Chemical, makes mothballs and makes friends, staying there thirteen years.
>
> 1954–57 (pars. 18–23): History is reviewed, including the Lucky Dragon episode, the World Conference Against Atomic and Hydrogen Bombs, and the passage of the A-Bomb Victims Medical Care law. Nakamura avoids "agitation" on these issues. Her son gets a job, gets married, and buys her a new sewing

machine. Her daughter Yaeko leaves and marries. Her daughter Myeko becomes a typist and marries.

1966 (par. 24): Nakamura, now retired, can rest, make dolls, and join a folk dance group.

1967 (par. 25): She goes on the trip to Yasukuni Shrine, finds it crowded, and feels no sense of her husband's spirit.

1975 (pars. 26–29): Japan is booming, Nakamura receives various government pensions, and her children prosper. In May, while dancing at the flower festival to a song of happiness, she collapses, is hospitalized, but insists on going home.

5. The strategy in this writing assignment lies in choosing which events to use and in deciding, on the basis of their importance, how much space to devote to them. Encourage students to work on these decisions after doing their interviews.

6. Here, movement in time must be considered as well as the arrangement of material. Encourage students to consider how the everyday events that involve people take on a new significance in relation to the greater event.

Amanda Coyne: *The Long Good-bye: Mother's Day in Federal Prison*

1. As an observer, Coyne is both involved and detached. Though she has a sister in prison, she is evidently trying to write a carefully detailed reportorial piece about the situation of federally imprisoned women, particularly in relation to their young children and other relatives.

2. By focusing on Mother's Day at the prison, a day when filial ties are emotionally heightened by the circumstances of the occasion, Coyne is able to detail the various ways in which the maternal and familial bonds of imprisoned women are strained and subverted by their incarceration. The ordinary details of day-to-day life in a women's prison are likely to be missing or obscured on a special day such as this.

3. By paying more attention to the other women and children than she does to her sister Jennifer and Jennifer's son, Toby, Coyne is able to document the badly stressed maternal and familial situation of federally imprisoned women and their children without giving an unduly biased amount of attention to the circumstances of her sister. Coyne's detailed account of the nineteen-year-old ex–New York University student enables her to document the irrepressible interest of the prisoners in the accoutrements of their personal and feminine identity.

4. Charity's intense interest in perfume and fashion provides a striking contrast to Ponytail's punishment of the women for wearing short shorts rather than federal shorts. The contrast serves to highlight the extremely repressive conditions of life in this federal prison.

5. Coyne seems to be interested in documenting not only the maternal, familial, and feminine needs of the prisoners themselves, but also the various ways in which those basic human needs are so severely thwarted by the prison system that the children (and other relatives of such women) are clearly seen to be quite badly abused (and innocent) victims of the system. In fact, the hostility (and badly confused feelings) of the children toward their mothers suggests that the prison system might well be an inadvertent breeding ground for criminals of the future.

6. This assignment gives students an opportunity to use the Internet and other periodical indexes as a means of gathering research material on women's prisons and then of analyzing that material to see how other writers perceive and comment on the situation of female prisoners.

7. This assignment, by contrast with the previous one, offers students an opportunity to develop a reportorial piece based entirely on their own firsthand observation. A special challenge of this assignment might be to have students write a report that is as meticulously detailed as Coyne's and that, like Coyne's, is also carefully crafted to make a point about the quality of life in a prison without being preachy or pushy about it.

Jane Kenyon: *Philosophy in Warm Weather*

1. What is the season? How is the weather? How do you know?
2. Her language suddenly has a scientific or mock scientific edge. Have the class paraphrase Kenyon in more colloquial language.
3. The poppy's "shouting" is a metaphor. What is implied about the crow's mental state?
4. The odd conjunction of *Hamlet* and scientific language in the second stanza is worth another look, especially after a reader has taken in the poem.

Robert Coover: *The Brother*

1. Noah's brother is telling the story, but that may not be obvious from the beginning. The point of this question is for readers to notice when and how they catch on to the direction of this story.
2. As readers orient themselves to the story, they should begin to note moments of irony. No, in fact, the speaker will not have that chance again, will he?
3. Surely a reader will notice irony in the story more than once.
4. There is no single answer necessary. A discussion may ensue. The brother's wife is one such detail. Another is his puzzled respect for Noah's singlemindedness. Another is Noah's aloofness from his younger brother, the narrator. We don't think of a brother when we read the Bible story, but we may when we put it in the context of everyday life. Medieval dramatists imagined Noah's wife having to be pulled away from the neighbors while she gossiped with them at the backyard fence. Coover imagines a brother.

Paul Auster: *Auggie Wren's Christmas Story*

1. Auster misses something and then collects himself to try to see better. Explore how this affects his authority in his own story.
2. As Auster learns to see what Wren has been doing, he grants Wren authority for the story that Wren soon tells.
3. This question is open for general discussion. For our part, it's a project more happily considered as an idea than as hundreds of pages of very similar to nearly identical photographs. But the idea is arresting, like so many ideas behind modern and postmodern projects. Perhaps the idea is the project. It is enough for us, as readers.
4. See question 3.
5. You can talk about symmetry or its opposite. Wren's one day is so highly individual that it may call into doubt the efficacy of his larger project. It may seem to suggest that all those snapshots miss the point by blurring the uniqueness of all our days. Or, it may suggest just the opposite: that as Auster really learns to look and see, he, or anyone else, could find in each photograph a story as uncommon as this Christmas tale.

Barbara Tuchman: *"This Is the End of the World": The Black Death*

1. To begin the research for a report on the black plague, students might say that they'd look in the card catalog or for an encyclopedia article with a bibliography. You might ask them to consider the difference between the task of reporting on the black plague in Europe (a large and formidable topic) and reporting on the black plague in London (a more manageable topic). This can lead to a discussion about narrowing topics as well as a discussion about library research. Talking about the composition of such a report should lead to question 2 and the choices Tuchman made in organizing her material.

2. We have reprinted the first quarter of chapter 5. The rest of the chapter discusses at greater length the various effects of the plague mentioned in this introductory section. Tuchman's method is to use numerical data with specific examples to illustrate her general statements. She frequently intersperses her narrative with direct quotations from primary sources. Her general organization might be outlined as follows:

> Paragraphs 1–4: the incident at Messina, introducing a description of the disease and an overview of how lethal it was
>
> Paragraphs 5–8: an overview of how far and fast the disease spread, how many died, and the questionable validity of the count
>
> Paragraphs 9–10: disposal of the bodies, with paragraph 9 making "human" the numbers in paragraph 8; disruption of religious practice
>
> Paragraphs 11–13: death rate in cities, villages, and enclosed places
>
> Paragraphs 14–16: effects of the plague as a calamity that separated people; one example in paragraph 16 of a contrary impulse—the charity of nuns who tended the sick
>
> Paragraphs 17–18: the plague in France—its progress and effects in Normandy, Picardy, Amiens, Tournai, and elsewhere
>
> Paragraph 19: the flight of the rich and the heavy affliction of the poor and the young
>
> Paragraphs 20–21: conditions in the countryside where animals died, crops were untended, and labor was in short supply
>
> Paragraphs 22–26: mortality rates among certain groups: royalty, women, artists, merchants, doctors and clergy, and government officials
>
> Paragraph 27: effects of the plague: lawlessness and debauchery like that during the plague of Athens in 430 B.C.

Subsections are evident in the outline above, and certain subsections are closely related to the topics they follow. Note, for example, paragraphs 9 and 10, which describe the disposal of bodies and the breakdown of religious rites connected with death. The sheer number of corpses, the fear of contagion, and the terror at dying unblessed all help to explain the point made in paragraph 8 about the exaggerated numbers recorded by contemporary chroniclers.

3. The topic of paragraph 20 is the plague's effect on peasants and livestock in the countryside. This topic is related to the statement in the previous paragraph about the poor being more heavily afflicted than the rich. The two main subtopics—the peasants and the animals, domestic and wild—structure the opening and the closing as well as the development of the paragraph. One might say that the last sentence of paragraph 20 neatly completes the first sentence of the paragraph, summing up the horror of the pastoral scene. The first sentence of paragraph 22 refers back to paragraphs 19–21, which discussed the urban poor and the peasants in the countryside. Starting with the one reigning monarch who died, the writer cites other royal deaths and then speculates on

her data: why were most royal victims women? Paragraph 22 ends with Petrarch's literary expression of grief, providing a transition to paragraph 23, which presents deaths in two groups, humanists and merchants.

4. The direct quotations from contemporary observers sum up the topics discussed — and do so more effectively than mere paraphrase could. The reader keeps hearing the voices of the fourteenth century speak for themselves.

5. Tuchman uses individual examples and illustrations to bring to life her facts and figures. For instance, paragraphs 9 and 10 help explain the probable exaggeration of the figures in paragraph 8. In the conclusion of paragraph 11, which reports various death rates, the final image of the deserted village humanizes those previously quoted percentages. Paragraph 14 likewise conveys how hard hit Italy was: it starts with the uncompleted grandeur of a cathedral and concludes with Agnolo di Tura's poignant record of burying his five children "with my own hands." Tuchman is always aware that the study of history includes the small moments as well as the great.

6. As we have already mentioned, Tuchman uses sources to let contemporary observers speak in their own voices, to supply illustrative incidents and anecdotes, and to quote directly to sum up various topics. During class discussion, focusing on one or two representative paragraphs (12, 15, 18, or 19, for example) will show that Tuchman frequently quotes directly from primary sources and paraphrases from them also. In general, Tuchman uses her sources to illustrate her points. What should be stressed in discussion is that her points are distilled from many sources. For example, the opening sentence of paragraph 12, "In enclosed places such as monasteries and prisons, the infection of one person usually meant that of all . . . ," is illustrated by references to five convents and monasteries in the paragraph. In addition, we must consider the other reading Tuchman did in primary and secondary sources (such as Ziegler's *The Black Death*) that also lies behind such a statement.

7. This research assignment can be as small or as ambitious as you wish and as your library permits. A disaster such as the sinking of the *Titanic* or the San Francisco earthquake will be fully documented in books, articles, and newspaper reports. If your community has sustained a disaster in the last twenty-five years, students can interview eyewitnesses, work with local newspaper files, and, in the case of a natural disaster or fire, get a sense of the physical change wrought by the disaster through photographs and visits to the scene.

8. If you plan to assign this question, put some of the major reference works (Campbell, Crawfurd, Deaux, Gasquet, Thompson, and Ziegler) on reserve in the library. You can also suggest that students use general works such as the *Oxford History of England*, *The Cambridge Medieval History*, or a bibliography such as the *Guide to Historical Literature*. The scope of this assignment depends of course on your library's resources and your students' interests.

William L. Laurence: *Atomic Bombing of Nagasaki Told by Flight Member*

1. Students may be struck by the youthfulness of the crew, especially given the momentous nature of their task. The inclusion of Major Sweeney's address in Massachusetts (par. 10) and Laurence's comments to Sergeant Curry that "It's a long way from Hoopeston" (par. 22) emphasize the crew as ordinary American youth who would rather be back at home than out on a bombing mission.

2. Laurence's moral stance is made perfectly clear in paragraph 32: "Does one feel any pity or compassion for the poor devils about to die? Not when one thinks of Pearl Harbor and of the Death March on Bataan." Similarly, in paragraph 29, he predicts what

will happen to a city in Japan, "the land of our enemy." His attitude of just retribution was shared by the majority of Americans. If your students find this fact hard to believe, send them to the library to immerse themselves in newspapers and especially in magazines from 1942 to 1945, paying attention to articles, photographs, and advertisements.

3. Laurence's use of the present tense gives a sense of being with him on that mission, as in paragraphs 1, 10, 21 through 24, 33, and 34. The present tense also expresses his reflection (par. 28) and his anticipation (pars. 30–32) during the mission. He uses the past tense to present preparations for the mission (pars. 3 and 7–9), and from paragraph 35 on, he sticks to the past tense to tell what happened. Notice the switches in tense in paragraphs 28 and 29, showing the movement of his mind.

4. Laurence's report is full of metaphoric language. The bomb is a "man-made meteor" (par. 3), an image that reappears later in paragraph 47. It is "a thing of beauty . . . this 'gadget'" (par. 4), with echoes from Keats and echoes from the kitchen. Later, Laurence calls the bomb a "man-made fireball" (par. 25) and a "black object" (par. 43). Finally, he relies on figurative language to describe the metamorphosis of the blast: it is "born right before our incredulous eyes" (par. 47); its column of smoke forms a living "totem pole . . . with many grotesque masks" (par. 48); this "pillar" spouts a "mushroom top . . . a thousand Old Faithful geysers rolled into one" (par. 49); it resembles "a creature" (par. 50), a "decapitated monster" (par. 51), "a flowerlike form," "a giant mountain of jumbled rainbows," and, last of all, "a monstrous prehistoric creature with a ruff around its neck, a fleecy ruff" (par. 52). Students might consider the various connotations of Laurence's descriptive terms and the mixture of the familiar with the strange, the positive with the negative. In paragraph 52, the last image of the prehistoric monster may suggest to students that human beings have regressed from a civil state through the act of dropping the bomb. Some students, however, may note the interesting mixture of tameness ("ruff") and horror ("monstrous prehistoric creature") in that image and interpret it differently.

5. This writing assignment can be useful for experimenting with time and tense as well as with figurative language. How unfamiliar the event will be to readers, as well as the nature of the event, may well determine the student's need for similes and metaphors.

6. If this assignment is undertaken, students might be referred to Zoë Tracy Hardy's "What Did You Do in the War, Grandma? A Flashback to August, 1945."

W. H. Auden: *The Unknown Citizen*

1. This is a very open-ended question. There are lots of details that sound a little dated or right on target to different readers. What about buying a daily paper, for example?

2. It sounds to us as if Auden was forecasting and envisioned that sort of planning in our future. But now that we are in that future, how accurate was he? Was he predicting still farther ahead?

3. Auden balances prose with verse effects. The lines rhyme, but not in a wholly regular way. Their differing lengths and avoidance of meter tilt the balance toward prose. Here is an opportunity to raise questions from a more literary point of view.

4. One could turn this into a writing assignment very easily: rewrite this poem, in prose most likely, for an unknown woman of the present. It would be a chance to inventory and make explicit student expectations at the present moment.

Farley Mowat: *Observing Wolves*

1. For many students, knowledge of wolves is limited to one species: the Hollywood werewolf. A movie version of *Never Cry Wolf* was released in the fall of 1983, however.

Students may be amused by the report of film reviewer John Noble Wilford that it took two weeks and fifty-seven takes to teach "a wolf named Kolchak to lift its hind leg on cue."

2. Assigning this paragraph before class discussion of the selection will encourage students to read carefully and thoroughly.

3. The narrator has a sense of humor about himself. His careful preparations for observation, reported in paragraphs 2 and 3, are those of the biologist, but his discomfort at being ignored, described in paragraphs 4 and 6, might be considered unscientific. You might ask students whether Mowat's boundary marking results from the scientific method or from human vanity.

4. Students might suggest that Mowat was left to consider the efficiency of wolves, the importance of boundaries, the experience of being stared down by a wolf, the wolf's composure and his own discomfort during this encounter, or other points.

5. Students can find more information in a good encyclopedia. Also, Barry Halstun Lopez's *Of Wolves and Men* (1978) is a fascinating book that questions or modifies some of Mowat's findings.

6. Paragraphs 5 and 12 through 18 present the wolf's actions. Warn students against merely switching from "he" and "the wolf" to "I." Ask them to imagine how a wolf would interpret Mowat's behavior. For example, what does that tired wolf think when he gives Mowat the "brief, sidelong glance" (par. 5)?

7. Ambitious animal lovers may come forth with "A Day in the Life of a Golden Retriever," but a half hour to an hour of animal observation should be sufficient for a short paper. If your community has strict leash laws, students may have to report on the rituals of dogs being walked by their owners (or vice versa).

Jane van Lawick-Goodall: *First Observations*

1. Paragraphs 3, 5, 6, and 8 are some that provide samples of unbiased reporting.

2. The following words from the selection illustrate van Lawick-Goodall's bias toward comparing chimpanzee and human behavior.

Paragraph 3:	obviously listening for a response
	as though in answer
	meet
	youngsters
	excitement
	newcomers
	greeted
Paragraph 4:	hand
	regally . . . clasped
	in greeting
	youngsters . . . games
	happily
	infants . . . tug-of-war
	grooming

3. When she is able to get closer to the chimps, she can recognize a number of different individuals (par. 12), and she names them for humans (or fictional characters) that they remind her of. Her discoveries—that chimps are meat eaters and that they not only use tools but make them—bring the chimps closer to the definition of man as "a creature who 'made tools to a regular and set pattern'" (par. 29).

4. Van Lawick-Goodall observes David Graybeard using a grass stem as a tool to extract termites from their nest. She tests this tool herself and finds that it works. About a week later she observes David Graybeard and Goliath not just using their tools but fashioning them and keeping spares nearby. What she had observed was "the crude beginnings of tool*making*" (par. 28), a skill only man was supposed to possess. Earlier, she had observed the care with which the chimps made their nests each night (par. 5). Their "quite complicated interweaving of the branches" (par. 6) indicates the intelligence and manual ability needed for toolmaking.

5. The *American Heritage Dictionary* defines man as a "member of the only extant species, *Homo sapiens*, distinguished by the ability to communicate by means of organized speech and to record information in a variety of symbolic systems." Students might want to look at recent research in animal communication to see whether man will have to be redefined again.

6. Students can deduce from the article what van Lawick-Goodall actually does (she patiently and carefully observes). They should also consider the physical stamina involved as well as van Lawick-Goodall's attitude toward her subjects.

7. To locate additional information about van Lawick-Goodall, students can consult a periodical index (articles on van Lawick-Goodall have appeared in popular magazines such as *National Geographic*) or social science bibliographies.

8. The suggestion to "look for behavior that is unfamiliar to you" is meant to prevent observing with too knowing an eye. The intention here is for students to discover and report patterns of behavior.

9. Reflecting on the experience of observing is a valuable exercise. It requires students to look at themselves as observers as well as at the process of observing.

10. For this question, students can pair up or work in groups to brainstorm questions that van Lawick-Goodall might have liked to ask her research subjects. When they are done, you might want to ask each group to share its best question with the class.

Rita Dove: *Rosa*

1. Details like "trim name," "sensible coat," and "clean flame of her gaze" are a few.

2. Her bending down to pick up her purse is the one we're thinking of. It's unexpected; it also brings more drama to the confrontation. It recasts Parks as "lady" rather than "protester." Quiet drama.

3. Those two words interpret Parks's behavior. Her "courtesy" in the face of rudeness, or worse, assuming the reader accepts Dove's view of the situation, deepens, complicates, and enriches the moment.

Pico Iyer: *Where Worlds Collide: In Los Angeles International Airport, the Future Touches Down*

1. Iyer's title and subtitle refer to the interactions that take place between people from different cultures with the arrival of each airplane full of new immigrants at the Los Angeles International Airport—interactions prefiguring the global multiculture that Iyer envisions as the result of international travel and international mixing places such as LAX.

2. *They* refers to the groups of recently arrived immigrants from countries and continents around the world—from Central and South America, Africa, India, the Middle East, the Far East, and so on. Iyer refers to these immigrants as "they" and "them" in part to suggest the immediate gulf that exists between new immigrants and American

citizens. The use of *they* also suggests that however varied the immigrants might be, given their country and culture of origin, they collectively constitute the new multiculture and thus might well be subsumed under a collective pronoun.

3. Iyer's essay is so richly detailed with information about the immigrants who arrive at the airport, the people who work there, the airport itself, and the hotels, restaurants, and other businesses located at the airport that he must have spent several days there to gather so much information. Rather than organize his piece methodically in a day-by-day, step-by-step, or part-by-part fashion, Iyer chooses instead to immediately immerse his readers in the continuous and complex flow of life at LAX, beginning with the new immigrants and the array of sights and sounds that they encounter. This lavishly descriptive opening serves as a point of departure for Iyer's first set of reflections on airports as "the new epicenters and paradigms of our dawning post-national age" (par. 8). This descriptive-meditative movement, in turn, sets the pattern for the rest of the essay, in which Iyer spins around the airport and around the theme of his report, each cluster of images leading him into a related set of reflections on LAX, Los Angeles, international airports, or the multicultural future.

4. Iyer is less interested in the physical design or layout of the airport than he is in the rich cultural complexity of the place—in the worlds that collide there. By the same token, he is more interested in the swirling groups of immigrants than he is in any particular person he encounters there. Thus his eye and his mind are always on the move, looking for sights and sounds that will suggest the quality of life at LAX. In fact, only in the last six paragraphs does Iyer linger over anything long enough to offer a detailed and memorable scene or vignette.

5. Iyer seems primarily concerned with reporting on LAX as a means of conceiving it and other international airports as "epicenters and paradigms of our dawning post-national age" (par. 8).

6. This assignment invites students to use Iyer's piece as a model for observing, reporting, and reflecting on an airport, station, or terminal of their choice—not primarily as a physical place to be methodically described, but as a cultural or psychological arena to be vividly detailed and seen as symbolic of the worlds that collide within it. Given Iyer's piece as a model, students should recognize the need to spend several days closely observing the place they choose to write about in order to become so immersed in it that they are filled with a rich body of information to draw on and a rich set of ideas to mull over in their descriptive-meditative observations.

7. This assignment tacitly invites students to adapt the methodology of Iyer's piece to the study of their own college campus. They will have to spend several days looking at it carefully with a fresh eye—as carefully as Iyer looks at LAX, though he already knows it from prior experience—lest they settle for a familiar, rather than fresh, view of their campus.

Barry Lopez: *Wolf Notes*

1. Beginning in the first paragraph, pausing "to inspect a scent mark" and leaving the trail to notice something else are examples. There are others.

2. Again there are many possible details. The description of the wolf's movement in the second paragraph would be a good place to start.

3. It ties him to the world, at least to his neighborhood.

4. Not really a contradiction, but a detail that may seem a bit strange. In paragraph 8 we are told that our wolf will try "unsuccessfully" to mate; in the final paragraph he runs first with one then with two females, and, it would seem, "successfully." But that success, or degree of success, does not depend wholly on mating.

Vladimir Nabokov: *On Transformation*

1. He uses this casual language to bring us toward his subject, to make it less strange. At least that would seem to be a starting point. There are several casual terms, and the text is short. One could easily work this up during class discussion.

2. Apparently it is to allow us to see ourselves as stranger than the strange or even frightening—like many "awful" insects.

Richard Selzer: *The Discus Thrower*

1. Selzer apparently relies on shock value in his writing (obviously in contrast to Dr. Selby). You might ask students what connotations they associate with the word *spy* and which of those connotations are present in the actions of the physician in this piece. This doctor learns by observing his patients—as opposed to the doctor who prefers to look at charts.

2. The present tense allows the reader to participate in the process of spying: observing the last hours of a man who is dying a rather gruesome death. Such immediacy would be lost in the past tense, but students might translate a paragraph or two into the past tense to see how the original effect changes.

3. Again, comparison with Selby's essay might be useful. There the use of the third person objectifies events and participants. Here one of the subjects of Selzer's essay is *his* quest for secrets, perhaps arising from his sense of his limited ability to help this patient. Ask students to rewrite a section in the third person to judge the change that would take place.

4. Certainly, there is compassion present in the doctor's awareness of the man's suffering (pars. 3 and 19) and admiration for the man's defiant gesture and its attendant laughter, as well as his request for shoes. To understand the nurse's attitude, students might consider what she means when she says, "We have to do something about him" (par. 25). There is some suggestion that the nurse is meant to be the "heavy" in this little drama. "The eyes of the head nurse narrow" (par. 35) when she hears the man laugh. Her concern that the man does not eat may be because his not eating makes her look derelict in her duties. She thinks the man hurls his plate because he is "nasty" (par. 27). And the doctor's observation, "I see that we are to be accomplices" (par. 38), suggests a difference in attitude between nurse and doctor.

5. What connotations does *discus thrower* have for your students? They may think of the Olympics, athletes, and competitiveness, especially if they note the care with which the patient, like a well-trained athlete, balances and hefts the plate before throwing (par. 32). The title used here emphasizes the patient as subject, while "Four Appointments with the Discus Thrower" shifts the focus to include the doctor's relationship with the patient.

6. To approach the issue of purpose, you might ask students what they learned from this essay about the following: the doctor-patient relationship, the secrets the doctor as spy wants to know, the hospital as a place to die in, and the patient's attitude toward death.

7. Before students write from the nurse's point of view, you might discuss with your students what a nurse's duties are and how her relationship with her patients is in part determined by her professional relationship with doctors.

8. If your students are fans of the soap "General Hospital," they can contrast the romantic and relatively bloodless picture of television medicine with Selzer's realistic picture of suffering, compassion, and clinical efficiency. Students with hospital experience as patients, workers, or visitors should have their own serious observations to make.

William Carlos Williams: *Spring and All*

1. It begins as a gathering of sentence fragments and only midway through "completes" a sentence. Note how it ends without any punctuation, but then so do all the "poems" in the original printing of the prose/poetry composition of the same title, "Spring and All." The famous "Red Wheel Barrow" also ends without punctuation, though the period is often added when it stands alone in anthologies.

2. The answer leads into interpretation, but it is difficult to ignore the correspondence of the first complete sentence with the stated "approach" of spring to the formerly "lifeless" year.

3. There is a certain gathering of the raw material for a new year.

4. We get Williams's characterization of the young year.

5. Many more terms that we associate with humanity appear in the second half of the poem.

Roy C. Selby Jr.: A *Delicate Operation*

1. If the surgeon did not operate, the woman would become blind. Though it is not explicitly stated, there is the suggestion that if the tumor kept growing, it might affect the blood vessels supplying the brain. The careful laying out of the risks involved invests the procedure with dramatic tension.

2. The writer's purpose would seem to be objectivity; the discourse is similar to that found in medical journals, where the focus is on the procedure rather than the surgeon (and as the title suggests, this is the story of an operation). A first-person approach would tend to make this the story of the surgeon's choices and feelings. To emphasize the difference, ask your students to rewrite a few sentences in the first-person, active voice.

3. Background information is given in the first three paragraphs. Most of the essay is devoted to the operation itself (pars. 4–10). Postoperative events are confined to paragraphs 11 through 12. In paragraph 11, the tension of waiting is reported. Here, we get a sense of how the surgeon felt (anxious and exhausted). In paragraph 12, the report of the patient's condition tells us that the operation was a success. Selby is very careful to explain terms and procedures for a general audience. For example, in paragraph 1 he explains what an EMI scan is; in paragraph 2, he explains angiography and what could result if the undersurface of the brain or the hypothalamus were damaged. He continues to explain terms and procedures unobtrusively throughout.

4. Certainly, paragraphs 7 and 8 might be cited as moments of great tension when the surgeon, unable to collapse the tumor, starts to dissect it without being able to see the arteries and optic nerves. This is the moment of greatest danger to the patient and of greatest demand on the expertise of the surgeon. The writer has invested the procedure with tension by telling the reader what the surgeon could not see. The reader is positioned, as it were, looking over the surgeon's shoulder, following the procedure step by step. Further, the writer's objective, understated approach allows (indeed, almost encourages) the reader to provide the tension.

5. Selby provides an excellent model for discussion of the problem of how much to say when describing procedures for a particular audience. It would be useful for the students to present a paragraph or two of their first draft of this essay to other class members for comments about whether they have included too much or too little explanation.

Update: Brown's article originally appeared in the December 1979 *Atlantic*. In an update in the July 1989 *Atlantic*, Brown reports that "at last count 1,030 families had evacuated the Love Canal area" and that controversy still surrounds the toxicity, illnesses, and deaths of the Love Canal area. According to the environmental Web site EarthBase, in 1990 most of Love Canal was declared suitable for population by the EPA and given the new name Black Creek Village.

1. The poisoning was caused by the Hooker Chemical Company's dumping of toxic wastes for thirty years into Love Canal, an unsuitable receptacle (par. 6). The seepage was looked upon as a "nuisance condition" (par. 12) by the local health department. When the Hooker Company deeded the land to the board of education, the company was vague and secretive about the "remarkable toxicity" (par. 13) of the waste matter. And when the canal started to overflow, plans for remedial drainage were stalled over who would pay the bill and what should be done (par. 18). Nor did the city wish to offend Hooker, a large local employer. State environmental authorities were slow in testing and "appeared to shield the finding" (par. 26) of benzene from the public. Data from the state health department on miscarriages, birth defects, and other illnesses of local residents finally caused the state health commissioner to declare Love Canal "an official emergency" (par. 36). But only those living at the southern end of the canal were told to move, even though those living across the street from them were also suffering similar afflictions. Only after the Love Canal Homeowners Association organized and attracted national attention did relief start to appear (par. 43). Cost was certainly one of the main factors that kept the state from moving swiftly.

2. Brown's information was gathered largely through his own investigations. He provides background information on the building of Love Canal, on the operations of the Hooker Company, and on what chemicals were present and how they affect the human body. He provides case histories of residents' illnesses and birth defects as well as information from the state Department of Environmental Conservation and from the state health department. He interviewed many of the residents, gathered samples of seepage from their homes, and had the samples tested. Thus he was very active in providing evidence to state agencies as well as in informing the public of the conditions at Love Canal.

3. Telling the story of one afflicted family brings the awful nature of this large disaster closer to the reader, who then can absorb it in human terms. Brown uses the narrative strategy of foreshadowing in reporting the ominous events in the Schroeders' lives before the investigation (pars. 3–5 and 7–9). The rest of the article provides the reasons for those events. He returns to the Schroeders and their relatives in paragraphs 20, 21, 24, and 33, thus making their story a subnarrative in the larger story.

4. Some examples of powerful passages are the descriptions of birth defects caused by chemicals in paragraphs 8 and 68, how the chemical waste looked and smelled and what it did to people and the environment in paragraphs 5, 7, and 28, and the effects of dioxin in paragraphs 57 and 63.

5. If you live in an area where a sensational newspaper (like the *New York Post*) and a responsible newspaper (like the *New York Times*) are both available, comparing their treatments of the same news story will be enlightening. Or you can pick up the *Enquirer* at your local supermarket and have students analyze the lack of content in stories with screaming headlines. Such examples should help students imagine a sensational treatment of the Schroeders' story as a contrast to Brown's powerful investigative reporting.

6. If you are fortunate enough to live in a place where the air is clear and the water

is sweet, ask students to find out why this is so and how they can keep it that way. Many students do not know the source of their water supply. They should find out what it is and whether it is near any industries using chemicals or near highways where oil and road salts can wash in. They can find out if the quality of the air they breath is monitored and what is considered an acceptable level of pollution.

Elizabeth Bishop: A Cold Spring

1. There are three other "like" similes: "like movement"; "fell like snow"; and "like Chinese fans." But what of petals burned "*apparently*, by a cigarette-butt"?

2. One can have a field day enumerating the instances of simile sliding toward metaphor: "the violet was flawed on the lawn"; like what? A diamond? A human? And so on.

3. Song-sparrows are "wound up"; a cardinal "cracked a whip." The verb also can be suppressed: the lilac [wears] a cap.

4. Are late springs, in the seasonal sense, also cold ones? Yes, generally so. But *cold* isn't the term, is it? Which leads to the next, rather obvious question:

5. An underlying metaphor seems to be a fresh mountain spring, with spring in the seasonal sense, early, late, or average, likened to it.

Rachel Carson: Undersea

1. Her metaphors and similes, her writing especially as it is thought of as "literary" or "poetic," would seem to be intended to help us bridge the difference in vocabulary.

2. Here is an opportunity to study spatial arrangement as a form of exposition and to apply it to other situations; the explanation of a library is one example.

3. The relative availability of tidal pools seems a likely answer. Carson leads us from the more familiar, from what is easier to inspect, to the more distant and difficult.

4. These seem to be more metaphorical than literal. It's difficult, however, to draw a strict line.

5. Carson seems to have composed for herself a stronger and finally convincing sense of plan, in which case she can set aside for less resolvable sense of paradox.

EXPLAINING

Joan Didion: On Keeping a Notebook

1. Students should note that while Didion's entries do follow a transcription/elaboration/explanation pattern, there are significant differences in her responses to the notebook: some of the entries are explored at great length, often including a full narrative reconstruction of the event and resulting in more general reflections on her note taking; others are cited quickly in sequence, usually to demonstrate that their point is to stir memory. The first passage on "That woman Estelle" opens the piece with a lengthy consideration; the childhood "Arctic night" passage represents her first entry; "dinner with E" provides a moment to ask "Who cares?" about "pointless entries"; an accumu-

lation of short passages leads her to assert that "the point" is to "remember what it was to be me"; two other "FACT"s are initially dismissed as "marginal" but then reconsidered as vehicles of remembering; another paragraph of brief points is followed by the acknowledgment: "not that I should ever use the line, but that I should remember"; a longer anecdote relates a discussion on a California terrace; "So what's new in the whiskey business?" stirs the concluding reflection on aging; and finally, after recalling "that recipe for sauerkraut," she refrains from relating it to her present state.

2. The process of revision seems to be Didion's way of reproducing her own exploration of the issue. In other words, the essay replicates her own contemplation regarding "what is a notebook for," starting with the very first entry, which is initially as enigmatic to her as it is to her readers. In so doing, she leads readers to participate in this sequence of questioning and discovery. Some of her suggestions, in order of presentation are:

- Why did I write it down? In order to remember, of course . . .
- The impulse to write things down is a peculiarly compulsive one . . . useful only accidentally.
- I suppose that it begins or does not begin in the cradle.
- Keepers of private notebooks are . . . lonely and resistant rearrangers of things, anxious malcontents, children affected apparently at birth with some presentiment of loss. [Her mother suggested] that I stop whining and learn to amuse myself by writing down my own thoughts.
- . . . the point of keeping a notebook has never been, nor is it now, to have an accurate factual record of what I have been doing or thinking.
- . . . I tell what some would call lies.
- *How it felt to me:* that is getting closer to the truth about a notebook.
- I sometimes . . . imagine that some thrifty virtue derives from preserving everything observed.
- I imagine . . . that the notebook is about other people. But of course it is not.
- Remember what it was to be me: that is always the point.
- . . . the common denominator . . . is always, transparently, shamelessly, the implacable "I."
- And sometimes even the maker has difficulty with the meaning. . . . is it not just as well to remember that? . . . help me to remember what I am? . . . remember what I am not?
- . . . not that I should ever use the line, but that I should remember. . . .
- I think we are well advised to keep on nodding terms with the people we used to be.
- It is a good idea, then, to keep in touch, and I suppose that keeping in touch is what notebooks are all about.

3. Many of the lines from question 2 could serve as potential titles; see also question 2 following Darwin's essay (p. 576).

4. Paragraph 5 makes the distinction; students should distinguish between the different kinds of "truth" Didion seems to be seeking, for she claims that the vehicle of "the fictitious" actually offers a better sense of her personal truth, "what it was to me."

5. As students share in class what they learned from writing about this question, you may want to ask them to speak more specifically about what they learned about themselves as writers from looking back at past work: How has their writing changed? How has their thinking changed? What do they hope their future selves will be able to say when they look back on their present-day writing?

6. Two of Didion's strongest claims about reasons for keeping notebooks are: "Keepers of private notebooks are a different breed altogether, lonely and resistant rearrangers of things, anxious malcontents, children afflicted apparently at birth with some presentiment of loss" (332) and "our notebooks give us away, for however dutifully we record what we see around us, the common denominator of all we see is always, transparently, shamelessly, the implacable 'I'" (334). Students are likely to respond to some variation of these two ideas and should think about reasons to keep notebooks other than just for the self.

Jan Harold Brunvand: *Urban Legends: "The Boyfriend's Death"*

1. Asking students for their definition of *urban legend* should open up discussion of other terms used in paragraph 1: *folklore, story, oral tradition.* As paragraph 2 makes clear, *urban* refers to literate society, not simply to cities.
2. If students hadn't heard "The Boyfriend's Death" before, it's likely they've heard other urban legends. Whether they'll refer to them as such or cling to the "true story" approach is of interest. Students who live in dorms or who've been to summer camps or other group "sleepover" situations are usually the best sources for urban legends.
3. To this list we might add a whole microwave series, spinoffs from the X in the Oven group. Also, there's the Dead Granny in the Stolen Car, the Naked Lady in the Football Helmet—and on and on.
4. In the wake of publicity about child abuse, cases of children brought up in closets or chained in apartments have come to light. These unfortunately true stories are the stuff legends could derive from. As for proof, is it enough to say that we read it in the *New York Times* or that we saw it (for sixty seconds) on the television news?
5. In paragraphs 5 and 6, Brunvand sets out the general elements of the urban legend:

- The narrative is believable, set in the recent past, involving "normal human beings."
- Credibility is established "from specific details of time and place or from references to source authorities."
- "The story is *true*," occurred recently, and to "someone else . . . quite close to the narrator, or at least 'a friend of a friend.'"

The traditional elements of "The Boyfriend's Death" are set out in paragraph 11.
6. In their response to this question, students should take into consideration the general elements that make up urban legends. You might also encourage students to think carefully about the counterarguments they might encounter and how they can demonstrate knowledge and credibility on their subject.

Theodore R. Sizer: *What High School Is*

1. The report serves several functions. It generates interest; it establishes the writer's authority—his knowledge of the subject; and it supports later generalizations like "the clock is king" (par. 27). The report conveys a critical attitude, partly by its timetable. Encourage your students to find other evaluative elements in the report.
2. This paragraph avoids overt conclusions but underscores the repetitive sameness of Mark's day.
3. The explanatory section (pars. 20–41) is organized around these subtopics:

Paragraphs 20–22: goals of high school
Paragraphs 23–26: traditional organization
Paragraphs 27–29: time schedule
Paragraphs 30–35: subject divisions
Paragraphs 36–39: lack of connection between goals and practice
Paragraphs 40–41: conclusion

In particular, this essay illustrates nicely how to build toward a conclusion. The last paragraph should receive some attention as the goal toward which the text has been moving all along.

4. School's function is not to educate but to pacify—that is the conclusion Sizer reaches. Students should be encouraged to support or to disagree with this conclusion.

5. The report functions in the later explanation to emphasize and document the difference between the pious statements of planners and the actual practices in schools. Without the report, Sizer's explanation would lose force and specificity. Paragraph 23 in particular brings together the two—pointing out that Mark's day shows the true purposes of high school despite the goal statements.

6. We suggest emphasizing Sizer's structure: report followed by explanation. This assignment will work *only* for students whose view or experience of high school is different from Sizer's.

7. Emphasize following Sizer's outline: a typical day followed by a discussion of the relationship between ideals and actuality. Encourage students to select their topics carefully so that they can both present sufficient detail about the typical day and then assess the actual practice.

Daniel Mark Epstein: *America's No. 1 Song*

1. Curious idea, isn't it, that our anthem is wonderfully democratic because no one person can sing it? Have the students trace the emergence of that idea.

2. We take it to be humorous understatement in an ironic air, and in keeping with enough other passages to give a peculiar tone to the whole piece. See the next question.

3. Frankly, we don't know the truth of the matter. We suppose it to be an exaggeration, perhaps we could call it a conceit. The idea is worth entertaining but unlikely to be literally true.

4. That's up to the writer. Few students will be without some memory of pleasure, discomfort, difficulty, embarrassment, or some such feeling in their own encounters with the anthem. How often at the ballpark does one enjoy its singing?

Margaret Atwood: *The Female Body*

1. Atwood begins by questioning the singularity of the topic. She presents her own particular body as the first in a series of ways that female bodies become objectified, or used.

2. The fragmented form of the essay allows Atwood to shift voices and perspectives, giving readers several interpretations of the female body. When she makes surrealist claims, such as "The Female Body is made of transparent plastic" (par. 4), they don't seem as out of place or unbelievable as they would in a formally structured essay. The fragmentation forces readers to make connections and think deeply about the subject matter.

3. In the first paragraph, Atwood presents her perceptions of her own body. Students might use this as a model for in-class writing of a paragraph of their own (preferably objectified) perceptions of their bodies. The "accessories" in the second paragraph are, for the most part, of the sort that are supposed to make the female body more attractive or seductive—though one might well ask what that all-concealing flannel nightie is doing there. The next section presents the female body as an anatomically correct model. The removable reproductive system is worth some comment. Next is a male-female (parental) dialogue on the Barbie issue, and the child's apparent resolution of it. Female students should have lots to say about Barbie, and of course Ken (and maybe G.I. Joe) can be trotted out for comparison. The next sections discuss the female body as commodity, both manufactured and live, and sexual intercourse as mere (anonymous) breeding.

4. Atwood compares the female brain, whose sides converse, and the male brain, whose split sides make men feel cut off by their objectivity. The female body offers "a vision of wholeness" that the male desires and thinks he can capture through possession of the female. Students might consider what is implied by the differences illustrated in paragraph 21: "the void of the universe" versus the leaves, the voices, the woman's offering of tea and cake.

5. You might start students off on this assignment by working on the list of metaphors for the male body in class. Start with the many metaphors for the female body Atwood includes in paragraph 22: "a vision of wholeness, ripeness, like a giant melon" and so on. What metaphors for male bodies come to mind in response to Atwood's list?

John Berryman: *The Development of Anne Frank*

1. While Anne Frank's book has been widely appreciated, Berryman believes that it has been "valued for reasons comparatively insignificant" (par. 1). He finds that no one "has taken her with real seriousness" (par. 3). He compares the intention, or ambition, of Augustine's *Confessions* with that of Frank's *Diary*, stressing the importance of her subject: "the conversion of a child into a person" (par. 4). Pressure forced the "child-adult conversion," and this, coupled with her "exceptional powers of expression" (par. 6), has produced this remarkable book. You may want to discuss Berryman's strategy of comparing a child's writing with that of one of the "greats."

2. Berryman's remark reveals his view of this century as a time not conducive to sanity. His statement implies that to find a sane person at all is a rarity; that Anne Frank kept her sanity in such a grim situation is all the more remarkable. In paragraph 3, he lists the qualities of literary merit in the *Diary* and details his response to Frank through her writing. He repeats later in the paragraph, "One finds her formidable." He explains this comment further in the next paragraph, in comparing her originality and ambition with that of Augustine's *Confessions*. Berryman devotes paragraph 11 to a number of Frank's qualities that he finds admirable.

3. Because Berryman views Anne Frank's experience as a conversion experience, such a view suggests a process with significant stages leading to conversion:

Stage 1 (pars. 14–19): Berryman analyzes the "program" that Anne Frank sets up to deal with the daily problems she confronts, one of which Berryman reads as the tension she feels in her relations with her mother.

Stage 2 (pars. 20–28): Berryman reads Frank's "vision" of her friend Lies, whose fate is in doubt, as one of "love-and-remorse"; Lies actually functions as a screen figure for the real object, Frank's mother. Here, Berryman feels, "the girl is *paying beforehand* . . . for the rebellion against her mother" (par. 28).

37

Stage 3 (pars. 29–33): Frank gives a child's common complaint, "[My mother] doesn't understand me," but her maturity shows in her parallel statement, "I don't understand her either" (par. 30). She decides, "I have to be my own mother" (par. 33).

Stage 4 (pars. 34–35): Here Frank writes of her secret love for Peter Wessel, who along with Peter Van Daan, functions as a screen figure for her father. However, the unsuitability of the father as love object "becomes explicit" (par. 35).

Stage 5 (par. 36): This stage centers around Frank's "intense and miserable attempt to create a post-paternal love object out of the unworthy . . . Peter Van Daan" (par. 36).

Stage 6 (pars. 37–41): Here Frank summarizes the process of her development: "I feel more of a person than a child, I feel quite independent" (par. 39).

4. As for Berryman as a literary critic, he is certainly a sensitive, appreciative reader of Anne Frank's text. His reading of it is partly Freudian, but he avoids the reductiveness that is one of the hazards of that approach. Let your students make the call here. Would they like Berryman as a reader of their own work?

Radcliffe Squires: *A Day in Salamanca*

1. Students will perhaps recognize that reading poetry is less about what is said ("plot") than the manner in which it is said; in this way, rereading a poem resembles the speaker's role, in which the "same" thing happens every time, and the individual moments matter more than the result.

2. "The squint of conspirators" makes it sound as if there were a kind of preconceived plan at work; the boy "chants" his question, which indicates an almost ritualistic act of repetition; "The moment we have all waited for" suggests, once more, a foreknowledge on the part of the priest, students, and speaker.

3. Toward the end, following the moment of recognition that the bird is in fact the boy's pet ("A spoiled princess").

4. Since Squires seems to intend his reader to decipher his meaning, students will need to struggle with this question (poetry's goal is rarely to present some pat moral). Referring to the twentieth century, does he mark it as a century of slaughter, in which there was much "blood-sacrifice" and little "freedom"? Does this comment relate more specifically to a foreigner's presence in Spain, a country that experienced much bloodshed of its own in the civil war of the 1930s?

5. You may want to draw students' attention to the multiple aspects of the poem: the sequence of events and the deeper ideas and meaning that those events capture or symbolize. You might pose the following questions to students: Does their paraphrase capture both aspects of the poem? Are they focusing more on the events or on their interpretation of the events? How does their interpretation of the poem shape the way in which they retell the story?

Sheldon Rampton: *Let Them Eat Nutri-Cake*

1. "Sewage" is generally part of the definition. That seems to set up the problem.

2. This is entirely a matter of opinion, but responses shouldn't be hard to come by.

3. Our notion is that "biosolid" avoids cheap humor. That doesn't rule out other ideas.

4. Again, this may be seen as a matter of opinion, but a case could be made for "biosolid" being more specific.

5. Well, isn't it?

6. An open invitation to survey and reconsider a few words on the more immediate horizons of your students. You could then, if you wanted to make more of a project of it, go back to Rampton's exposition of the steps taken toward introducing a new word into the dictionaries and consider what it would take to make such progress with new terms of students' choice.

Margaret Talbot: *The Rorschach Chronicles*

1. Talbot notes that because what counts as a valued personality trait changes across time, these tests "mirror their cultural moment." Moreover, they reflect the needs of organizations for "people who conformed to their model of the company man or company woman, the team player." The tests, in the end, are perhaps best regarded as historical measures for shifting societal desires, based on a long-standing human inquisitiveness.

2. Paragraph 3 sums this up quite directly: "Modern personality testing . . . is a child of 20th-century research psychology . . . with the help of modern bureaucracies, like corporations and the military, that needed an efficient means of categorizing people by temperament, the better to predict their on-the-job behavior." While part of the initial impetus in the field of psychology was to gain a scientific credibility equivalent to that of medicine, "where personality testing has really taken off lately is not in the doctor's office but in the personnel office." Psychological testing is itself "now a $400-million-a-year industry."

3. Both metaphors are particularly "telltale" because they express a yearning "to endow psychology with some of the status of the hard sciences," as Talbot notes, with the most current technology available to "see through" the body. The tests are thus presented as analogously able to "see through" the mind to a core personality that the subject herself can't see without assistance. The medical metaphors could potentially imply that the tests are a kind of "diagnostic tool" used prior to further treatment (which Talbot praises "[i]n the hands of experienced clinicians"), however, we know that this is not the goal when they are "used very frequently in pre-employment screening."

4. Students may begin their exploration of this question with two quotes from Rorschach: "Modern personality testing . . . is a child of twentieth century research psychology, born of the dream that we can crack the code of human behavior if we only devise the right set of questions" (390) and "personality testing is here to stay—not only because of the many institutions now hooked on it but also because of the deep human curiosity it promises, however teasingly, to satisfy" (395). Students may want to consider not only the "fun" aspect of personality tests but also how scientific advances have led to our culture's desire for definitive answers to complicated and, sometimes, unanswerable questions.

5. Students may want to discuss this issue in the more general context of how people try in many other kinds of situations—such as college admissions interviews, job applications, or examinations—to give the answers the questioner seems to want rather than reveal their "true" selves.

Stanley Milgram: *Some Conditions of Obedience and Disobedience to Authority*

1. Paragraph 3 states the problem Milgram wanted to investigate. Initially, he "conjectured that subjects would not, in general, go above the level of 'Strong Shock'" (par.

68). In fact, the pilot studies indicated *"that subjects would obey authority to a greater extent than we had supposed"* (par. 18), a point that he reexamines from several perspectives at the end of the article (pars. 68–80).

2. In the Postscript, Milgram sums up his conclusion: "With numbing regularity good people were seen to knuckle under the demands of authority and perform actions that were callous and severe" (par. 78). His experiments varying the proximity of the victim and especially of the experimenter indicated that, in general, the closer proximity greatly influenced the subject's behavior.

3. Milgram describes his general procedures in paragraphs 10 through 14. Later, he describes how variations in the procedures developed partially in response to the willingness of subjects to obey. In paragraph 5, with note 4, Milgram recognizes the potential effects of this experiment.

4. Milgram's range of interpretation in paragraphs 28 through 35 includes psychological, physical, and spatial elements apparently derived from examining different assumptions and theoretical positions and from studying his own and other experimental results.

5. The experiments are grouped by the variables they test: immediacy of the victim, closeness of authority, background authority, and others. General comments on tensions fall between the two pairs of quantitative reports.

6. One way of drawing students into a speculative, rather than confessional, discussion would be to ask them to recall incidents involving their treatment by or participation in high school cliques or gangs. See if they can generalize about what holds these groups together, such as the practice of exclusionary tactics, and why members accept the "authority" of the group.

7. This question refers to any interesting problem raised by Milgram's research—he writes that "many subjects cannot find the specific verbal formula that would enable them to reject the role assigned to them by the experimenter" (par. 46). In the context of this experiment, where subjects become so uncomfortable as to experience fits of nervous laughter and even "uncontrollable seizures" (par. 47), students might consider how a lack of words might stand in the way of immediate relief, and what might be appropriate models for these words.

8. You could assign this problem to a few students and ask them to report their findings to the rest of the class.

9. After students have listed their suggested guidelines, you might pair up students and ask them to think of possible objections to one another's guidelines. These pairs, or the class as a whole, could then move to general ethical issues such as whether individual suffering can be justified, especially when it occurs for the sake of public awareness.

10. This assignment requires students to report, explain, and perhaps evaluate their own behavior.

Carol Gilligan: *Interviewing Adolescent Girls*

1. Class responses to this question—which you might present as an in-class writing assignment prior to discussion of the essay—can serve as a verification of Gilligan's findings or as a challenge to them.

2. That classroom dynamics affect learning (and teaching) is no secret, but students seldom get a chance to discuss this.

3. Gail's wall transforms into "a giant block of ice . . . a cube," thus a wall she could melt (par. 4). While to be blocked is a common metaphor, as is the wall, Gail's transformation of it is not so common. She speaks later of a warped perspective (par. 6), of

being "a big sponge" with the ability to "bounce back" (par. 7), stressing resilience here rather than absorption. Gail's image of a "chair casting shadows and making tremendous spokes" (par. 7) shows, as Gilligan says, "how the ordinary can become monumental." It's reminiscent too of the disturbing, threatening shadows found in German expressionist films. For Gail, the repressed can roll up "like a snowball," and she compares her inability to see—her warped perception—to that of Oedipus (par. 10).

4. Discussion might well touch on such issues as mothers and teachers as role models for young women and the difficulty of older women who are caught in marriages or situations in which they've been subservient and who have mixed feelings about such lives for their daughters. Naturally, the range of discussion will vary according to the ages and cultural makeup of class members.

5. What's gender got to do with it? This writing assignment should lay the differences out.

Elisabeth Kübler-Ross: *On the Fear of Death*

1. As Kübler-Ross states, the death of the farmer indicates how old-fashioned customs help both the dying patient and the family accept death and loss (par. 16). She contrasts these customs with those of "a society in which death is viewed as taboo" (par. 18).

2. The writer explains changes in death rates, psychological aspects of dealing with death, customs surrounding death in several cultures, and the reasons why she believes that we try to evade facing death. In addition, she contrasts two extended examples of how people die.

3. Kübler-Ross's purpose is to persuade us to question our personal and cultural attitudes toward death, as paragraphs 27 and 28 indicate. The topics and illustrations preceding these paragraphs suggest her position. She attempts to gain a reader's sympathy with her argument by speaking reasonably and humanely about what she acknowledges to be a frightening topic.

4. Paragraph 2 speaks of the elderly who turn to nonmedical professionals for support, and paragraph 10 describes the emotions "of the child—and the child in us"— who is both guilty and angry when a loved one dies.

5. Whether one is young or old, a patient or a professional like Kübler-Ross, "death is still a fearful, frightening happening, and the fear of death is a universal fear even if we think we have mastered it on many levels" (par. 12).

6. You could suggest that students begin their essays with the narration of someone's death. Many will have never written on this subject before and may have difficulty simply getting down on paper a version of "passing away."

7. This question could invite research on what has been said most recently about euthanasia, pro and con. Students might investigate what sort of legislation is now being considered concerning the rights of the dying and their immediate families.

8. You could assign this essay before the class discussing the Kübler-Ross reading begins. Then give students a change to revise after they've talked and thought about the subject for a while.

Philip Larkin: *The Building*

1. Students may want to look up words the poem uses in less familiar senses ("comb"), words for which they are familiar with the roots or with very similar words ("conceit" and "contravene"), and words that are simply less familiar ("propitiatory").

2. It is a curious rhyme scheme, irregular enough not to be any "scheme" exactly. The rhymes often leap from one stanza to the next. But there is a rhyme for everything, if you allow "caught" with "sort" and "world" with "lulled." Noticing the variety of rhyme, such as "by it" and "quiet," may be of some interest. As for suppositions, something about the desire to be regular enough but not thoroughly regular would be a starting point.

3. This building is a hospital. Students should notice that it is a building where "the porters are scruffy; what keep drawing up / At the entrance are not taxis" (lines 5–6). This is their first clue. Though many people who come here are "at that vague age that claims the end of choice" (20–21) and are preparing to die, others "will be out by lunch, or four" (52).

4. Larkin compares the building to "the handsomest hotel" (line 1), "an airport lounge" (9), and a church (the patients are compared to "the unseen congregations" in line 54 and the building itself to "cathedrals" in line 62). Students may discuss how, in contrast to a hotel, some people never get to leave the hospital. The comparison to an airport lounge picks up on the tension and anxiety that can be silently felt in a hospital waiting room. Like a church, a hospital may offer salvation, but unlike a church, it may not be able to offer redemption for those who are destined to die.

5. References to religion can be found in the following images: people "here to confess that something has gone wrong" (line 22), "a locked church" (41), "the unseen congregations" (54), and "its powers / Outbuild cathedrals" (61–62). The functions of both of these "buildings" are to prepare people to face what we all share and "to transcend / The thought of dying" (61–62).

6. Students will probably vary considerably in which phrase they find most striking, and many may be confused by unfamiliar or unexpected language (such as that mentioned in item 1) or by references to characteristically British streetscapes ("close-ribbed" and "terraced").

Malcolm Gladwell: *The Science of Shopping*

1. This "science" is a form of surveillance, another milestone in the commodification of America through scientific merchandising. Here are some of the terms Paco Underhill uses: *Decompression Zone:* the dead area just inside the door (par. 3); *Invariant Right:* the direction the shopper always turns (pars. 3, 8); *retail anthropology:* the science Underhill has spun off from the ideas of urban anthropologist William Whyte (par. 4); *le facteur bousculade,* or *"butt-brush" theory:* the idea that women jostled on the posterior will not purchase the merchandise they were examining (par. 7); *petting:* touching and fondling the clothes (par. 9); *Zones:* demarcations of depth in a store (par. 10); *wallet carrier:* the father (par. 14); *advocacy:* "what happens when your four-year-old goes over and grabs a bag of cookies that the store has conveniently put on the bottom shelf" (par. 19); *makeup play area:* cosmetic experimentation kiosk (par. 21); *typing:* an attempt to predict purchasing decisions on the basis of demographics (par. 23); *Market Maven:* a shopper who likes to help others shop (par. 24), a subcategory of the type known as Fulfilled (par. 25); *destination items:* basics, like jeans (par. 29); *point of view, or image:* what Calvin Klein and Ralph Lauren want their stores to have (par. 32). Underhill's mother calls him a spy, which is basically what he is and what he does. But then he collates the facts and figures of what he sees in order to make recommendations to his retail clients.

2. The questions here are designed to urge students to consider how one puts together an explanatory essay like this one. Certainly, Gladwell relies most heavily on his inter-

views with Paco Underhill and his viewing of Underhill's videos. But then he goes to talk to retailers and marketing people such as the president of Estée Lauder (pars. 21–22); Claritas and SRI International marketing research firms (pars. 23–25); NBBJ Retail Concepts (pars. 26–27); the president of Banana Republic (par. 28); and representatives of Gap, Calvin Klein, Versace, Donna Karan, Armani, and Ralph Lauren (pars. 30–37). Finally, he looks at the study that inspired Paco Underhill: William Whyte's "The Social Life of Small Urban Spaces" (1980).

3. Gladwell asks if we should "be afraid of Paco Underhill" and notes that we are being researched and watched everywhere. But research shows that shoppers are not pliable or manipulable (par. 18) and that Underhill is teaching sellers to conform to buyers. Worth discussion here is the issue of living in a free, democratic society where we are, paradoxically, almost always under some kind of surveillance. For group discussion, comparing approaches to and strategies for shopping should be fruitful to test the surveillance issue.

4. This assignment encourages students to use Underhill's research methods to write their own essay. They can use this opportunity to test the validity of Underhill's theories and possibly come up with theories of their own.

5. Students should be encouraged to apply Underhill's and Whyte's observations critically. They might imagine that they are being asked, as consultants, to offer recommendations that will enhance the public space they choose.

Monica M. Moore: *Nonverbal Courtship Patterns in Women: Context and Consequences*

1. Discussion here will vary according to the mix or homogeneity of your student population, but everyone should have an opinion on this topic. Moore's subjects are all white, midwestern college students. Your students may, as we suggest in question 2, be able to construct a somewhat different "catalog of nonverbal solicitation behaviors." From watching movies and television, they can also tell which of the "behaviors" can be read universally and whether the topic has been discussed on "Oprah."

2. Many students will have seen this subject discussed on talk shows or in books. Based on what they have seen in these media and on their own observations, students may construct a somewhat different "catalog of nonverbal solicitation behaviors."

3. If students cannot readily think of courtship rituals in the cultures of other countries, you might ask them to consider if differences exist between courtship rituals on California beaches or Manhattan nightclubs. If they have knowledge of how particular religious beliefs affect courtship behavior, they may also bring that into the conversation.

4. Students might consider the limitations of covert observation. You can encourage them to think of other research methods, such as interviews, to use in this situation.

5. The use of the word *fitness* in this context is vague; students may find this question difficult to answer. You might suggest that students consider the term in relation to the relationship that may arise out of the woman's choice, as well as to the biological and evolutionary implications of the term.

6. Students will likely draw mostly on personal observation, experience, and the media to come up with the categories for male behavior.

Marcus Laffey: *Inside Dope*

1. There are a number of references. Students will likely recognize that there is a sense of indifference in such a description of the job as a game ("narcotics is pure tech-

nique") and in its somewhat bleak repetitiveness (see question 2): "We call dealers 'players,' and there are rules as in chess, percentages as in poker, and moves as in schoolyard ball"; "Sometimes you feel like the man on the catwalks over the casino floor." The interchanges between the officers sound like they could be sports announcers calling a play-by-play: "we feel skilled and lucky at once, at the top of our game"; "There are breaks and interruptions, retirements and replacements, but, no matter how often the whistle blows, the game is never over."

2. The sense of this all being a "game" means that it can be, and in fact is, endlessly repeated, as the last paragraph confirms. Early in the essay, Laffey notes, "Most of the spots that we hit are well established, visited by both customers and cops on a regular basis." Additionally, there's a constitutive interdependence between everyone: "In a sense, everybody wants the spot to get busy."

3. The "reading" here recalls that of a sociologist "reading" the social field: recognizing and giving names to patterns of behavior ("there are distinctive addict walks"); offering hypothetical scenarios that stand as representative moments; abstracting from the particular observations to larger generalizations. Laffey makes other references to this kind of analysis: "Even when nothing happens, there is much to interpret"; categorizing the kinds of "stamp brand names."

4. Besides adding an engaging depiction to his narrative, Laffey seems to use this moment (as well as the bubbles rising up, and the incinerator chimney smoking) to suggest the duration of "the wait."

5. These frequent shifts blend the general description of his profession with his own personal involvement; they also serve to draw the reader in as a potential participant.

6. Before students do this writing, you may want to return to what you discussed in question 1 and ask students how Laffey's claim that "the war on drugs is a game for me" frames the tone and the way he includes reflection in the reporting of his day-in-the-life. Students may notice that claims like "The truth is, I am the least of their problems: a night on a cell bench, with prison bologna sandwiches to eat, ranks fairly low amid the hazards of being at the bottom of the criminal food chain" contain a great deal of judgment in them.

Sherry Turkle: *Constructions and Reconstructions of the Self in Virtual Reality*

1. Anecdotes can be very persuasive in that they present a specific instance that seems to offer a coherent wholeness; they also serve to particularize a more general claim. Their danger, of course, is that they may be less representative than they claim to be, and may somewhat misleadingly stand in for argumentation precisely because they have a sheen of "fact" around them. While prose writers seem to be turning more and more frequently to introducing an essay with an anecdote (as perhaps part of a larger turn toward the autobiographical), "anecdotal evidence" in legal argumentation is still treated with understandable suspicion, in that its fabular qualities can mask an otherwise unrepresentative instance.

2. It would appear that the analogy fails to hold with respect to the intent and structure of psychotherapy and MUDs. Whereas in therapy both the patient and the therapist tend to agree upon (and thus focus on) the goal of "'working through' unresolved issues," such work appears to be merely fortuitous in Turkle's examples (that is, it does not appear that participants consciously enter role-playing scenarios with the intent of developing their psyches). Additionally, the patient has a one-on-one relationship with an individual whose training specialized in this "working through," while the MUD par-

ticipant has no such designated guide, professional or not (indeed, the participant only has other participants, which appears to be less like an idealized psychotherapeutic scenario than an analogy to the "ordinary" world).

3. While Turkle seems to hold that the freedom of role-playing games allows for gender indeterminacy, the very fact that the same sexist social dynamics are present (such as "expectation of sexual favors in return for technical assistance"), as are bodily idealizations ("The plain can experience the self-presentation of great beauty; the nerdy can be elegant; the obese can be slender"), should lead students to question whether such role-playing does in fact liberate participants from "constructs" (such as gender) or whether it reconfirms the strength of already existing models, albeit in fantasy form.

4. "second self": through the "evocative power of the computer," a person can have "the opportunity to play an 'aspect of yourself'" embodied "as a separate self in the game space"

"betwixt and between": "both in and not in real life"

"identity workshops": places where someone can "work through" their personal issues

"evocative object": something that "provoke[s] self-reflection and stimulate[s] thought"—in Turkle's essay, this is the computer

Getting students to clarify "virtual," "real," and "ideal" should make them recognize that these terms are not well defined in Turkle's essay; her use of quotation marks throughout the piece often indicates a kind of tentativeness about the appropriateness of the term to the situation.

5. Turkle claims that virtual reality allows participants to "work and rework unresolved personal issues" (494). Students should be able to find the complications and create arguments against this claim through Turkle's own examples. For example, Peter, the graduate student who barely interacts with other human beings, says he plays MUDS so he can talk to people (497). Students should question what gets lost in these virtual interactions and consider the subtleties of real life that a computer cannot simulate. They might want to consider the difference between communicating in the context of a game and in actual life, and the implications and complications that result from these differences.

6. Students who do this assignment should be encouraged to think of generalizations other than the ones Turkle makes and to disagree with her conclusions if appropriate.

James Jeans: Why the Sky Is Blue

1. You might call attention here to Jeans's careful description of what is "familiar"— the waves striking a pier. He devotes a paragraph to this movement, thus establishing the points of correspondence that he uses to explain the lightwaves.

2. Jeans describes how blue lightwaves scatter throughout the sky in the process of struggling through the atmosphere, colliding with obstacles, and changing course again and again.

3. After the analogy is removed, the remaining explanation is straightforward and clear, albeit less easy to visualize.

4. Besides the sea waves, Jeans mentions the regiment of soldiers marching around the tree (par. 1); the prism, the jug of water, and the rainbow (par. 3); and the flash of lightning (par. 4).

5. Because Jeans uses *we*, he places himself with his audience as another person rather than distinguishing himself on a basis such as superior scientific knowledge. The result is a friendlier, less didactic tone than he would have adopted speaking to *you*.

6. Encourage students to develop their analogies as carefully as Jeans does, perhaps even adapting his organizational structure to their topics.

Rebecca Mead: *Eggs for Sale*

1. Students should recognize that the concerns, while distinguishable, are quite thoroughly intertwined. There are unknown health risks that the donor undergoes (possible stroke, other possible long-term side effects including compromised fertility, and a suggested link between fertility drugs and ovarian cancer), in part because she needs the money, although "[a]gencies reject potential donors who say they are doing it just for the money." The couples who can afford the high expenses of purchasing these services are typically upper middle class and white: "People are getting these fair, blue-eyed children, and that does bother me philosophically." While most countries severely limit "trade in gametes and genes" (in fact the United States has some laws against "the commodification of body parts"), there is an escalating market for egg donation, which is leading some doctors, "somewhat belatedly," to express reservations about the commercial trafficking of eggs. There is "no controlling federal legislation" on egg donation at this point, so there will probably be future lawsuits to work through ambiguities about rights and responsibilities regarding what counts as "parenthood" in such circumstances.

2. At some unspecified point, Cindy Schiller's parents were divorced; Schiller's home is in the Southwest. As an undergraduate, Schiller signed up with a donor agency. She first had to undergo "psychological counselling and testing." She twice donated eggs for twenty-five hundred dollars each time, although the second time she suffered from hyper-stimulation. She eventually received a thank-you card from one couple who had a son. Schiller arrived at Columbia in the fall of 1998. Shortly thereafter, she read a notice by a couple seeking a donor. The three of them met at a Broadway café, and quickly agreed to a five thousand dollar price. The following February she heard about the Ivy League newspaper advertisement for donors with specific traits—Schiller was too short. Mead met Schiller for the first time at a pastry shop; Schiller complained of "the whole menopause thing," induced by drugs for her third egg donation. Shortly thereafter she sent for an application from an agency called Options, hoping "to market herself for what might be the last time." During their interaction, Mead listened to a performance by Schiller; asked her how she would raise money were it not for the egg donation ("I might be working at Hooters"); and had a number of discussions with her about other personal, ethical, and legal concerns. In late June of 1999, Schiller heard that the couple who had received her last eggs had not conceived; she was uncertain whether they "might call on her to repeat the process." Another college newspaper ad appeared, which fit Schiller more closely, and she contacted attorney Thomas Pinkerton. By July she had yet to receive an offer through him and was considering her own Internet classified advertisement. She later learned of increased financial aid for school that fall, so she wasn't sure she needed to donate at this point. Regardless, she planned to take a Mensa test for proof of intelligence.

3. Mead creates curiosity about the details of one particular egg donor before making more global statements about egg donation in the United States. This creates a framework for the essay (see question 2), which allows her to move back and forth between the specific and the general.

4. Pinkerton's quote shows how the large sums of money that are involved in egg donations often overshadow the serious medical and ethical issues involved. Women are being encouraged not to consider these issues by being offered a price they cannot refuse. Mead makes it clear that "[t]he United States is the only place in the world in which the rules of the marketplace govern the trade in gametes and genes" (511). Students should think about claims opposed to Pinkerton's, like that of Australian doctor Robert Jansen, who asks, "As the price rises and becomes more and more of a motivating factor, and we also appreciate the genetics of personality and character, you start to ask, 'Do you really want to bring up a little girl whose biological mother was someone who decided to charge ten thousand dollars for eggs?'"(517).

5. Before writing, students should try to identify what egg recipients might feel they "owe" to their donors. Beyond the enormous costs egg recipients pay, Mead also discusses the legal rights of the donor in her relationship with the child and notification of whether her eggs were successfully fertilized (518).

6. Before or after students write their essays, it may be interesting to discuss what they discovered in their research about the differences and similarities between egg donation and organ donation. They should consider medical, ethical, and perhaps legal differences. Ask students how they account for the differences in policy between egg and organ donations on the basis of these other, specific differences.

Natalie Angier: *The Story of the Breast*

1. The analogy is described in paragraphs 6 and 7, her main point being: "a woman's breasts, I argue, are like Burley's white crests . . . they are arbitrary, and they signify less than we think." Most of the work of the essay focuses on emphasizing—even reveling in—the "arbitrary" beauty of the breast and discounting any evolutionary reason for their presence, an admittedly "contrarian view."

2. Angier cites Caroline Pond, who says that "there is little evidence to support any of the theories." Desmond Morris presents breasts as buttock mimics to encourage frontal sex; Timothy Taylor holds that breasts ensure sexual attention when humans became upright (and thus hid the vulva from view); other "theorists have assumed that they developed to advertise to men some aspect of a woman's fecundity." Still "others suggest that breasts evolved to deceive, or to confuse a man about a woman's current ovulatory status or whether she is pregnant or not"; Meredith Small "recasts the idea of breasts as mobile pantries"; Helen Fisher "proposes that breasts are a woman's pleasure chests"; Elaine Morgan suggests that they provide "flotation devices" for infants of aquatic apes.

3. The joking is part of the general light-hearted tone Angier takes toward the breast throughout the essay; it seems that since her main claim is that there's no good explanation for "the aesthetic breast," we should revel in its almost comical variety and inexplicability.

4. She presents a differentiation between the "maternal breast," which lactates and has an anatomical purpose, and "the aesthetic breast," which "is nonfunctional to the point of being counterfunctional, which is why it strikes us as so beautiful." She then alternates her discussion of each of these "types" throughout the essay, sometimes noting their convergence (such as in the breastfeeding mother). After shifting between the two for a number of paragraphs, she devotes a long section in the middle to discussing the anatomical development of the maternal breast before returning to a final discussion of the aesthetic breast, and dismissing functional explanations for this aspect. (See question 2.)

5. Students should note Angier's claim that the breast "is there in our faces, begging for narrative," and that her essay is a series of related narratives about the breast (524). She shows how we endow the female breast with many stories and symbolic associations, like maternal "warmth, comfort, and love" (526). Students should think about what narratives and values the male breast has been associated with: some possibilities are strength, virility, and courage. The aesthetic images the student writer chooses (such as the bare-chested warrior) will determine his or her interpretations.

6. Before students begin to write their own essays, they should articulate all the ways in which Angier tries to explain the inexplicable. The most important technique she uses is to see some value in a variety of explanations, including evolutionary, biological, aesthetic, and culturally specific arguments. Students should see that she does not endorse just one theory but shows how different kinds of explanations partially account for the inexplicable, and they should identify what kinds of argument have been offered for their own inexplicable subjects.

Andrew Sullivan: *The He Hormone*

1. Sullivan refers to numerous research studies, and ordinarily, one would rank such studies as of primary importance. However, in this sort of article for the general reader, the studies are simply referred to without citation. It is possible that Sullivan read some of them, but it is equally possible that he only read about them in one or more of the five books he refers to. Other sources include two very different newspapers: the *Village Voice*, from which he cites a transsexual, and the *Wall Street Journal*, which provides business information on Toys "R" Us. Lastly, he draws on his own experience with testosterone and on interviews with four other men in hormone therapy. Since the studies would seem to validate his own experiences (the most subjective source), we'll rank them first, and second, the books (especially Matt Ridley's *The Red Queen*, which he cites three times); next, the *Wall Street Journal*. The statements from the transsexual, the four men, and Sullivan's reporting of his own experience are subjective, and therefore not as reliable as scientific studies of large groups, but such material is important to an article designed for a popular audience.

2. A high testosterone level is at the root of the biological differences between men and women, and the article presents many of these differences. Thus, in paragraph 31, Sullivan can say, "Since most men have at least 10 times as much T as most women, it therefore makes sense not to have coed baseball leagues." He refers to the plan of Toys "R" Us to separate their toys into a "Girl's World" and a "Boy's World" to make the point that efforts to "negate sexual difference between boys and girls" have brought very little change. He cites politics as a "controversial" area "because it is such a critical arena for the dispersal of power" (par. 35). In our society, "It is saturated with combat, ego, conflict, and risk"—all high-T qualities, and women with their low-T qualities of "patience, risk aversion, [and] empathy" just can't compete. In paragraphs 36 and 37, he suggests alternative approaches to equality, and tells us "we shouldn't be shocked if gender inequality endures" (par. 37). Big T research does seem to prove that men are indeed from Mars.

3. The something "tragic" about testosterone is that it drives men toward the dangerous areas of promiscuity and aggression. High levels of T correspond with baldness, heart disease, and susceptibility to infectious diseases—all of which cause men to live shorter lives than women. Your students may want to discuss the truth or appropriateness of the cockerel metaphor in paragraph 34.

4. You might ask your students what careers they're interested in, and to rank their choices according to Sullivan's high-T and low-T characteristics. Then proceed to the

question of the job interview and the saliva test. Could such a test become as common as testing athletes for drug use?

5. Certainly, the information in Sullivan's essay validates stereotypical views of men as the aggressive hunters and women as the weaker gatherers. Sullivan attempts to palliate this view by injecting some utopian fantasies into his concluding paragraphs, but the final paragraph celebrates Big T and its contribution to an interesting, if unruly, world.

Oliver Sacks: *The Man Who Mistook His Wife for a Hat*

1. Dr. P. cannot recognize or visualize things. He can see, but he cannot put what he sees together in the familiar patterns that humans regularly use. This problem was caused by damage to a particular part of the brain that controls visualization.

2. Most important, we learn that though the eye sees, it is the brain that organizes sight into vision, giving us our world of familiar objects.

3, 4. In the second sentence, the notion of "certain strange problems" rouses the reader's desire for both the strangeness and the solutions. Sacks has a way of presenting behavior at length, with telling detail, before starting any analysis. He also makes a story out of his own gradual realization of the nature and extent of the problem. And he takes pains, from the first sentence on, to characterize the patient, to make us take an interest in this nice, intelligent, artistic man. The meaning of his title, which sounds so bizarre, and the incident from which it is derived are withheld from us until paragraph 29, where they still strike us with considerable force. In short, this essay has many of the qualities of short fiction, with the added element of scientific truthfulness: an unusual and powerful combination.

5. Paragraphs 82 to 85 contain the heart of Sacks's critique of neural science. Here he makes the really startling claim that his science itself seems to suffer from something similar to the same disease as Dr. P. He makes an appeal for science to find a place for feeling and judging as important components of mental life. Students may well agree with this, but they may also feel that these things are not discussable within the boundaries of scientific thought. Obviously, there is no simple position on such a complex matter.

6. What we should be looking for in a student essay such as this one is some ability to see patterns, to select striking illustrations of them, and to consider the strengths and weaknesses of Sacks's special combination of almost fictional writing technique combined with scientific concerns. Since he is an admired and successful writer, students should be able to learn something about writing by looking into the ways in which he has set down the experiences of his case studies. In his writing, he also conveys a manner of interacting with patients that has some of the same qualities as the writing itself—sympathy, creative understanding, interest in striking details. It is obvious for him that science and writing are not opposites but actually support one another. All this can be learned from the two essays in this collection, but reading more of his work should give students even more to work with. Remind students that considering Sacks as both a writer and a scientist is the heart of the assignment.

Stephen W. Hawking: *Our Picture of the Universe*

1. The first section deals with certain high points in the history of Western thought about the universe. The second part is about the nature of scientific theorizing in general and about the problem of a unified theory of the universe in particular.

2. The anecdote functions as a warm-up joke, a way of setting the audience at its ease—but the expression "turtles all the way down" has become an important metaphor in current skeptical thought.

3. The paragraph is dominated by questions ("longstanding questions"). This is a way of stimulating interest in what is coming—possible answers. And, of course, the greatest question, the basis of the whole book—What is time?—is slipped into the last sentence in the paragraph, after we thought all the questions were over.

4. 340 B.C. (par.3), second century A.D. (par. 4), 1514, 1609 (par. 6), 1687 (par. 7), 1691 (par. 9), 1823 (par. 13), 5000 B.C., 10,000 B.C. (par. 14), 1781 (par 16), 1929 (par. 17). The first part of the essay is organized mostly by the chronology of discovery. There are some digressions and some slight alterations, but it is clear that this is the way part one of the essay works. Part two ranges around more, but by avoiding mentioning dates (as he already had done by not dating St. Augustine (fifth century A.D.) in paragraph 16, Hawking deemphasizes this change.

5. See the end of paragraph 18 in particular. Most of the mentions of "God" in this text are attributed to other thinkers, like St. Augustine, but at the end of paragraph 18 Hawking suggests that the theory of an expanding universe would set limits on when "the creator . . . might have carried out his job." See also paragraph 22, where the possibility of an arbitrary god is dismissed.

6. Science for Hawking consists of a set of theories that connects models of the universe to quantities in observations ("with only a few arbitrary elements"—par. 19). See also the first sentence of paragraph 22.

7. Hawking appears to be working with a combination of Popper (par. 20) and Darwin (par. 26). This assignment invites the scientifically oriented student, in particular, to compare theories of knowledge and to express his or her own preference in the matter as cogently and eloquently as possible.

Charles Darwin: *The Action of Natural Selection*

1. By "natural selection," Darwin means the survival of the fittest animals to reproduce.

2. By *the* species, most people mean humans. Egocentrically, they assume the book is about them in particular rather than all species.

3. Darwin is very concerned to convince his readers that he is dealing with realities: facts and truth. He is therefore cautious about introducing illustrations that are meant to be typical but are not reports of specific observations. They are fictions meant to illustrate reality.

4. Bumblebees live in holes in the ground rather than in hollow trees or hives. They are social bees but do not make honeycombs as the honeybees do. Besides referring to the lowly or insignificant, *humble* as a verb has the obsolete meaning of buzzing or humming as a bee does. This question provides an opportunity to work with the dictionary a little and discuss the way words take on meanings. Students should know that there is a lot of guesswork in any dictionary.

5. This is a variation on the basic process-analysis assignment—one that encourages a little imagination.

Thom Gunn: *The Life of the Otter*

1. The breaks in Gunn's lines seem integral to the poem, in that they attempt to capture some of "the exuberance of dip and wheel" seen in the otter's motion. Rewriting a

poem in prose form is always a good way to get students to recognize the significance of lineation, both visually on the page and aurally in recitation.

2. The comparisons range from the directly metaphorical to the implicit association:

"he pours himself" [implied comparison to a liquid]
"swims / Faster than anything that lives on legs" [comparison to other species]
"ease / of a lithe skater" [comparison of motion to a particular kind of human]
"Activity [. . .] / Functional but as if gratuitous" [a kind of self-comparison—his seeming masks what it really is]
"genitals as neat / As a stone acorn" [the comparison to a work in artifice, even more "gratuitous"]
"Potency / set in fur / like an ornament" [again, compressing the comparison between the deeply functional, indeed even primal, quality of the genitals and the apparent non-functional aesthetic beauty]

3. Gunn phrases it in this manner: "Functional but as if gratuitous." The concentration on the genitals in the final lines of the poem emphasize this as the place most necessary yet paradoxically most apparently beautiful in its superfluity. (See answer to question 2.)

4. Again, the poem turns, so to speak, on the sense of the gratuitous as the aesthetic; "play" as a non-functional end in itself.

ARGUING

John Berger: *Hiroshima*

1. "The whole incredible problem," as Berger describes it, is the masking of an event that is evil by "*looking beyond* (with indifference) that which is before the eyes" (par. 33). Statistics and impersonal photos prevent us from seeing the evil nature of the bombing of Hiroshima. To see the reality of the event, we must see the pictures and hear the words of the individuals who survived it. Journalistic accounts distort history by removing its immediacy.

2. Berger emphasizes that "what happened" was begun "months, years before, with the planning of the action, and the eventual final decision to drop two bombs on Japan" (par. 20). He refers here to those who worked on the Manhattan Project and those political and military authorities who decided to employ the bomb. In a sense, Berger need not supply any evidence for this claim. He is simply reminding us that it *was* a calculated decision, "not a miscalculation, an error, or the result . . . of a situation deteriorating so rapidly that it gets out of hand" (par. 20); few would dispute this. Yet Berger feels that we have not fully confronted its implications. He means to call attention to the grotesque irony that so much human "rationality" went into service of such irrational cruelty. Part of the "whole incredible problem" is that our leaders are now capable of coldly, "objectively," contemplating the imposition of similar horrors on entire populations.

3. Berger uses individual incidents rather than statistics to restore the connection between pain and what we call history. For Berger, history is the pain: "We consider

numbers instead of pain. We calculate instead of judging" (par. 22). Statistics distance us from the real evil that caused the suffering at Hiroshima. Morality is ignored when statistics are presented.

4. Berger uses the specific example of Hiroshima to discuss the larger question of political morality. Describing the bombings as terrorist acts, he joins two seemingly disparate kinds of military action: terrorism and "civilized" warfare. Breaking down the distinction between terrorism and supposedly justified wartime tactics, Berger shows that evil exists in the powerful governments that rule today's world but that it is hidden by terms like "defense policies, military arguments and global strategies" (par. 28).

5. Urge your students to avoid platitudes like "sad" or "horrifying" as they consider these individual examples of the bombings. Instead, they might look carefully at each example Berger chooses to include, asking themselves how they differ from one another. What does each image present? What distinguishes one example from another?

6. Again, urge your students to look at the details in these pictures. What patterns do they notice? How do the patterns provide their own way of "reading" the bombings?

Alice Walker: *Am I Blue?*

1. Walker's essay struggles with distance: between human beings and animals, human beings and other human beings, human beings and themselves. Beginning the essay with a leisurely description of her surroundings introduces us to the physical question of distance. The essay also explores various kinds of deception. Walker deceives us into thinking this is a nonargumentative essay when she begins with this vision of serenity. She shows us that the surface seldom reveals the truth, just as the meadow "appeared to run from the end of our dock straight into the mountains" (par. 1) but really was divided from them by a town.

2. Walker enjoys the contrast in size between herself and the horse. It reminds her of her childhood, when she was unafraid of riding, and of her accident, which marks the moment when she decided never to ride again. Most important, the horse teaches Walker the lost art of communicating with animals. She realizes that it is "their nature to express themselves" (par. 5) but that adult human beings ignore animals, seeing them as images rather than as they really are. Walker sees loneliness in Blue's eyes; that vision provokes thoughts of human beings in similar situations of imprisonment.

3. Each of Walker's examples explores how self-deception concerning communication fosters oppression. The white children raised by black mammies conveniently forget their early ability to communicate with them when it is more important that they assert their supremacy by claiming they cannot understand African Americans. The white "settlers" who called Indians animals ignored their ability to communicate with animals, turning them into dumb objects; thinking of the Indians in similar terms, the whites justified their cruelty and thievery. American men who marry non-English-speaking women think they are communicating with them when they really are seeing in their eyes mere reflections of themselves. Society condemns the music of the young because accusing them of transgression upon human rights leaves the facade of their own music of oppression undisturbed.

4. You might encourage your students to establish Walker's distinction between images and expression before they begin their essays. They might ask themselves how a milk carton distorts the "real life" of a cow. What are the larger effects of such distortion?

5. As they prepare to write, your students should discuss the connections Walker makes between herself and Blue. The title of the essay urges us to collapse the distinc-

tions we might make between Walker and the horse, but this involves changing our notion of communication as language to communication through our other senses.

Cynthia Ozick: *Who Owns Anne Frank?*

1. Ozick's purpose may be described in several ways. For example, she is promoting her own interpretations of Anne Frank's story, and in paragraph 10, she sets forth the terms for a historicized reading of the diary. Or one might say she is writing in protest against the forthcoming revival of the Hacketts' version of the play based on the diary.

2. Ozick states that the diary "cannot count as Anne Frank's story . . . because the end is missing" (par. 7). A story isn't a story unless it has an ending, and the diary breaks off in medias res. Ozick implies that if the story of Anne's ending had been written, the diary would not have been misread and used as an instrument to subvert history.

3. Ozick first declares Anne Frank to be a powerful writer and the diary "the forerunner work of a professional woman of letters" and "an explosive document aimed directly at the future" (par. 2). Here, it might be useful for students to read some of the diary and to discuss the question of audience. In paragraph 6, Ozick defines what the diary is *not*: "not a genial document"; not uplifting; "not the story of Anne Frank." However, "The diary is miraculous, a self-aware work of youthful genius"; "a chronicle of trepidation, turmoil, alarm. . . . It is a story of fear." In paragraph 7, Ozick explains that the diary "cannot count as Anne Frank's story" because "the end is missing." Ozick goes on to state that the diary is not "a Holocaust document" because in her definition, Holocaust documents consist of "columns of numbers: the meticulous lists of deportations." Ozick frequently uses the laudatory blurbs promoting the published diary (and later, the dramatic version) in order to refute them, as she does in paragraph 10, where she quotes the blurb: "lasting testament to the indestructible nobility of the human spirit" in order to undercut it by describing Anne's miserable death in Bergen-Belsen (par. 9). She concludes: "the success . . . of Bergen-Belsen was precisely that it blotted out the possibility of courage, that it proved to be a lasting testament to the human spirit's easy destructibility." And thus she can conclude that "Anne Frank's story, truthfully told, is unredeemed and unredeemable."

4. Ozick is pointing out that people can't accept the horror of Anne Frank's death. The difficulty is to accept the "recognition that Auschwitz and Bergen-Belsen . . . can never yield light" (par. 11). It is easier to accept the obtuseness promoted by Anne Frank's diary: "In celebrating Anne Frank's years in the secret annex, the nature and meaning of her death has been, in effect, forestalled. The diary's keen lens is hopelessly opaque to the diarist's explicit doom—and this opacity, replicated in young readers in particular, has led to shamelessness" (par.12). It would be useful here to ask students what Ozick means by "opaque" and "opacity" before going on to discuss her case in point, Cara Wilson, whose correspondence with Otto Frank was published as *Love, Otto* in 1995. Ozick's searing discussion of Wilson's "shabby effusions" serves a larger issue: the "shamelessness of appropriation" and the cheapness of the statement "I identified with . . ." (par. 13). (Note that Ozick returns to "identify with" as appropriation near the end of the essay in paragraphs 45 and 46.) That Otto Frank could "not comprehend that Cara Wilson was deaf to everything the loss of his daughter represented" leads Ozick to conclude that Otto Frank "is complicit in this shallowly upbeat view" (para. 17). For an example of such a view, Ozick quotes the sixteen-year-old actress about to play Anne Frank in a revival of the play: "it's funny, it's hopeful, and she's a happy person." Ozick goes on to compare Otto Frank's "unclouded" childhood with Anne's shadowed life; she pulls out neglected dark passages from the diary that Otto Frank ignores in order to

concentrate on amelioration, "to speak of goodness rather than destruction" so he can resume his middle-class postwar life in the mainstream.

5. In her discussion of the dramatic versions of the diary, Ozick's sympathies clearly lie with Meter Levin, who as a war correspondent was present when Buchenwald, Dachau, and Bergen-Belsen were opened at the end of the war in Europe. The telling of that story, Levin felt, "would have to rise up out of the mouth of a victim" (par. 25). "Obsessed" with his subject, Levin read the diary—by now expurgated by Otto Frank—as a "conscious testimony to Jewish faith and suffering," and in this, according to Ozick, he placed "its main significance for the world" (par. 30). In paragraph 32, Ozick cites two book-length studies that interested students can turn to for more details on the controversy surrounding the Broadway version and the neglect of Levin's version. The "Jewish story" disappears in the hands of the Hacketts and the Broadway producers, and the victimization gets universalized (par. 39). Anne Frank becomes "a Little Orphan Annie brought into vibrant life." Worth discussion: Why was it that "Audiences laughed and were charmed; but they were also dazed and moved" (par. 42)? Point out the explanation in paragraph 43.

6. Eviscerate, according to the *American Heritage Dictionary*, means: "1. to remove the entrails of; disembowel. 2. to take away a vital or essential part of." In this short paragraph (49), "evisceration" is repeated three times in a powerful indictment. We suggest asking students to pick out specific instances of people or events that fit the categories of accusation. For example, the final blow, "[b]y usurpation," can be traced back to paragraph 45 and "to identify with."

James Baldwin: *If Black English Isn't a Language, Then Tell Me, What Is?*

1. Language itself is a device by which human beings communicate with one another. As it is used in human situations, however, language is more than a communicative tool; it is a political construct: "People evolve a language in order to describe and thus control their circumstances or in order not to be submerged by a situation they cannot articulate" (par. 2). The distinction is central to Baldwin because it defines the debate about calling black English a dialect or a language as a debate about the identity of African American people. To call black English a dialect is to compel African Americans "to defend a morality that we know to be a lie" (par. 10). Baldwin contends that white people minimize the role of language in order to demoralize the African American population: "It is not the black child's language that is despised. It is his experience" (par. 11).

2. While his opponents argue that black English is merely a dialect of standard English, Baldwin defines black English as a testament to a history of struggle and a weapon to fight future oppression.

3. Baldwin uses the languages of oppressed people in Ireland, in the Basque countries, and in Wales to defend his position that language is a political instrument. In these countries, arguments about language are arguments about power. Language connects one with power when one speaks the language of the majority, and it divides one from that power when one speaks the language of the oppressed.

4. You might ask your students to look up the word *language* in a dictionary. Comparing that definition to Baldwin's may help them appreciate the distinction Baldwin makes between language and the role of language.

5. The parallelism of the final paragraph emphasizes the severity of Baldwin's critique of those in power in the United States. Ending his paragraph with "a country that has managed to learn so little" (par. 12), Baldwin draws attention to the instructional tone of his essay. He provides the lessons in human understanding and redefinition that are purposefully ignored by the advocates of calling black English a dialect.

6. Your students may need to focus their essays on a specific encounter in which they felt that language played a role in forming their identity. To begin, you might urge them to consider the ways of speaking and listening that they learned in their home environments. How, if at all, did these patterns change when they entered grammar school? High school? College?

7. Suggest that students begin by thinking about the possible dialects around them that they hear but never acknowledge as such. What constitutes a dialect?

George Orwell: *Politics and the English Language*

1. Orwell states that staleness of imagery and lack of precision are destroying the English language. He claims that abstraction is politically dangerous because it reduces the language to senselessness. Perhaps most frightening to Orwell is the fact that obscure diction masks political realities that are too painful to delineate.

2. Language corrupts thought as it anesthetizes the brain. Reading obscure prose teaches one to write obscurely. In the same way, insincere writing, however learned, desensitizes the reader to hypocrisy.

3. By despairing of his ability to avoid all lapses into vagueness, Orwell calls attention to the involuntary nature of the corruption of language. He thereby gives force to his injunction to the reader to be "constantly on guard." Some might say, of course, that if Orwell does not consistently follow his own rules, it may be that the rules are unrealistically strict. Rules (ii) and (iii) in paragraph 19, for instance, would probably, if followed to the letter, make for rather dull prose.

4. Although he presents himself as an expert, by calling attention to his own lapses into obscurity Orwell identifies himself as an individual who wants to reform society — starting with himself. He asks others to follow his advice but does not promise a cure for world problems, only a possible starting point for a solution. His tone is instructional but not insistent or didactic.

5. According to Orwell, people write badly because they hear and read bad writing. Habits are learned, and people are afraid to speak their own minds in clear sentences because they think of proper writing as abstract, Latinate, and obscure. Politicians are particularly bad writers because their words mask harsh realities of pain and oppression.

6. As they analyze their own writing using Orwell's six rules, you might encourage your students to consider their possible reasons (audience, purpose, and so on) for breaking the rules.

7. Students might also consult online magazines or other Internet publications for additional sources and examples.

Neal Stephenson: *The Interface Culture*

1. In paragraph 12, Stephenson claims that "Disney is in the business of putting out a product of seamless illusion — a magic mirror that reflects the world back better than it really is." Graffiti — words — would destroy the illusion. On the other hand, spray-painted graffiti might be transformed into an illusory something-else by such a mirror. Stephenson goes on to develop the consequences of Disney's virtually wordless modes of communication.

2. (Some of us who became computerized through DOS machines weren't altogether happy when our word-processing programs became increasingly iconized and moused!) Stephenson's explanation begins with "the world is very complicated now" and we can't handle all the details, and then moves to the failure of "intellectualism"

in the twentieth century; we Americans, though literate ourselves, prefer to pass on the "values of our intellectual eighteenth-century forefathers "to future generations nonverbally" through media (par. 23). He then discusses the "exceptional stability" of the digital nature of the written word versus the much less stable nature of analog signals such as music, dance, and painting (par. 24). Because "messages conveyed by modern audiovisual media cannot be pegged to any fixed, written set of precepts . . . they are free to wander all over the place and possibly dump loads of crap into people's minds." You may have noticed that this essay is notable for its lack of those helpful transitional words that we are accustomed to finding in more formal arguments. So, we have no clue that paragraphs 25–30 are a sort of "argumeditation" on the "dump loads of crap" issue via the global culture question.

3. In paragraph 25, Stephenson introduces an operative metaphor: the swords into plowshares case of the runways of a former U.S. Air Force "nuke" base now unloading tourists from all over to Disney World. Stephenson works to develop an argument based on "on the one hand but on the other hand" moves: to co-exist peacefully, we need to suspend judgment against others' beliefs; but if you don't judge, then there's no culture left. The global anticulture spread by television seems bad, but it "makes world wars and Holocausts less likely" (par. 29). A person with no other culture than this global one is likely to be a "feckless human being," but one unlikely to nuke someone else (par. 30). "On the other hand, if you are raised within some specific culture," you have a set of tools enabling you "to think about and understand the world," something the power elite of the U.S. understands (pars. 31 and 32). In paragraph 34, Stephenson finally announces the direction of his essay: "Where I'm coming from vis-à-vis contemporary culture." He defines this as a "two-tiered system," and uses a reversal of H. G. Wells's Morlocks and Eloi to exemplify our society, with the technological, book-reading Morlocks controlling the mass of media-directed Eloi. In paragraph 39, Stephenson returns to the "way too busy . . . detail" business and finally comes to a conclusion: "it's better to comprehend [everything] dimly, through an interface, than not at all." How bad is it to get "warm and sympathetic [preverbal] reflexes" from "Disneyesque entertainment"? Ask your students. Worth discussing is Stephenson's somewhat casual approach to the argumentative essay as well as his casual diction.

4. As noted in question 3, Stephenson's approach to argument is rather casual, but some students may be happy with this approach and comfortable with Stephenson's casual diction. Others, however, may find his qualified conclusions troublesome to deal with.

5. Be sure that you preface this writing assignment with a thorough discussion of values and how to read them from TV or theme-based parks. You might have students do group work with particular examples, such as *Buffy the Vampire Slayer* or *The King of Queens*.

Elliott J. Gorn: *Professing History: Distinguishing Between Memory and the Past*

1. This essay, one hopes, will give students a clearer sense of the discipline of history as a contested site, rather than as a monolith, or simply a dry set of textbooks loaded with chronologies. Gorn is urging teachers of history to encourage their students to argue, to ask questions, and to lay bare to them the fact that at times they are only getting part of a complex narrative. Gorn wants students to hear competing voices in order to gain a sense of the many stories out of which a moment in history is comprised. He argues against a reliance on memory, imbued as it is with myth and nostalgia, as a false kind of history.

2. Gorn sets out the differences between history and memory in paragraphs 11–15. We suggest asking students to pull out the major differences and to list them on the board. You might also ask them what "mythic" moments they can come up with regarding American history, such as George Washington and the cherry tree, the first Thanksgiving, and so forth.

Briefly, memory's notions of the past are mythic; the past is simplified and often reflects what we want to believe happened; memory relies on sentiment and embraces nostalgia (see Civil War example, par. 12). History is messy and contentious; given the Civil War, "history sees conflict as endemic," where memory sees simple truths, history sees complexity, contingency.

3. Students may take issue with this statement, but in any case, they should discuss what Gorn means by it. Will introducing a text like Las Casas's *The Devastation of the Indies* make a difference in demythicizing the colonization of the Americas? What stories do your students remember being taught about that moment in history?

4. Some students are likely to have encountered teachers with but one textbook view of history, which they have delivered through lectures. Others may have had teachers like Gorn, who were eager to present students with various, sometimes conflicting views of a period in history. As a writing assignment, the question will produce experiential narrative. Encourage students to incorporate and discuss some of Gorn's points in light of their own experience.

Jincy Willett: *Under the Bed*

1. When Moreau says, "You're all alike," he is attempting to remove Willett's particular identity. He perceives her as an anonymous female body (she notes that he does not look at her eyes or her face). Similarly, Regina wants to remove Willett's identity by making her a symbol; she is disappointed that Willett does not behave as Regina believes a victim should. From Willett's point of view, "she thought we were all alike, all alike" (par. 41). The detective, too, is disappointed at her lack of (proper) response at the news of Moreau's death; again, she does not behave as society believes a rape victim should.

2. She begins with the fact of her rape and the value of telling the truth. She then describes her husband, whom she credits with teaching her to value truth highly. She tells how he found her after the rape, giving the facts, but not all: not their "private matters." In the second section, she describes the rapist and what he said. In the next section, she reflects on her former self and how she has changed from a fearful person to one who is without fear. The fourth section concerns Regina, who "used to be" her good friend, though her opposite "physically, emotionally, politically" (par. 26). Regina finds her changed, but not as Regina would like: "not outraged, not afraid" (par. 31). Willett views Regina's attitude as comparable to Moreau's. In section 5, she provides the physical facts of the rape: his body, his striking her; her not wondering why he did it, her wondering how to tell her husband and finding no words, her hiding under the bed. In the last section, she tells how she has lost respect for her colleagues: they all want to know, "But how do you *feel?*" (par. 48). "We live in an age when self-control, competence, discretion—all are thought abnormal, symptomatic of dysfunction" (par. 48). She says that she is content and that she and her husband seldom go out. In her conclusion, she states the real violation, damage, tragedy: that her husband is now the fearful one.

3. The essay shows that although everyone would profess to having a high regard for truth, this woman's truth of her experience—how she tells it to others—is not considered the "real" truth. Rapes are encoded in particular ways in American culture, and Willett's truth does not conform to those codes.

4. Willett suggests that there was nothing really personal about this encounter: "Nor did I wonder why he did it. After all, he never wondered about me" (par. 45). This is the view of a rationalist. When she says, "It was just a collision of machines," she stresses the impersonality and the dehumanization of the assault. He is a thing that rapes women's bodies. She is a body that happened to be in his path. A tragedy would imply a personal loss; where the personal is absent, there is no tragedy.

5. Willett makes a distinction between being victimized and being a victim. To her, it is a role one assumes for the benefit of society and, in so doing, becomes a symbol: rape victim. Willett believes in the integrity of the individual self; she refuses to act according to the approved codes. One might say that her *body* reacts as a victim's does, or should; she makes a strong point of the dissociation of her mind from her body with regard to the rape and its aftermath. Worth discussion is the degree to which such dissociation is possible. But more to the point is the public's appetite for victim stories and the profits to be made from the media for playing the victim's role. How many types of "abuse" are currently in the news? What are the current forms of victimization playing on Oprah, Geraldo, Jenny, etc., ad nauseam? And why are Americans so attracted to these stories?

6. The tragedy is that her fearfulness has now been transferred to her husband. He is the one hurt, the real victim, she seems to be saying.

W. S. Merwin: *Things*

1. The first stanza sets out what the things now are to the possessor "At the approach of winter" (his advanced age). The stanza break separates present from future, leaving the reader (and the possessor) time to ponder that creepy image: "Patient as a border of beggars." The second stanza projects what the possessions will become, as they entice their owner to invest *all* of himself with them.

2. The false-obsequious, insidious tone of the things that possess their possessor makes clear that they are now everything to him; he will continue to have nothing but them: "as you deposit yourself with us." There is the threat that the possessor himself is becoming a thing, in that he is being overtaken by his possessions.

Andrew Sullivan: *What's So Bad About Hate*

1. If the title read "What's So Bad About Hate?" the reader might assume that Sullivan would be making a case *for* hate or, more probably, that an ironic approach would be used. The present title suggests that Sullivan will challenge most readers to reexamine their assumptions and to renew their convictions that hate is bad, and that its effects on our society must be brought to light. The title does not indicate that Sullivan's argument will take an interesting turn near its conclusion when he targets violence rather than hate.

2. In paragraph 6, Sullivan notes that "we still have a remarkably vague idea of what [hate] actually is." Here he is examining what is meant by "hate crime" in light of the government's having declared war on it (par. 4). He goes on to examine the manifestations of actions that we label as hate (par. 8 and following). *Hate* is a transitive verb: it needs an object. As a noun, the *American Heritage Dictionary* gives us: "Strong dislike; animosity; hatred" or, secondarily, "An object of detestation." But an object is necessary, and it's the psychology operative between the hater and the object that Sullivan considers a mystery, and therefore almost impossible to define.

3. In paragraphs 45 and 46, Sullivan presents figures to show that there is no epidemic of hate crimes: that crimes so designated constitute but a tiny fraction of all reported crimes. The term "hate crime" is, he contends, promoted by "special-interest groups carving out particular protections for themselves" (par. 47). The danger he sees is that this action may "create a future that permanently treats people differently because of the color of their skin, or their sex, religion, or sexual orientation" (par. 48).

4. In paragraph 49, Sullivan states that violence should be the true object of government legislation, because the "boundaries between hate and prejudice and between prejudice and opinion" are so complicated and blurred "that they cannot be effectively legislated against." In a nation as diverse as the United States, "it is crazy to expect that hate . . . can be eradicated" (par. 51). He then goes on to propose toleration as a means of coexistence, rather than tolerance. "We know now that hate will never disappear from human consciousness; in fact, it is probably . . . definitive of it" (par. 49).

5. Sullivan's tolerance-toleration move depends on a definition of terms, and analyzing the difference between these two terms provides a strategy for coexistence. Certainly, Sullivan's suggestion that the "media's obsession with 'hate,' our elevation of it above other social misdemeanors and crimes, may even play into the hands of the pathetic and evil [and their] paranoid loathing" needs discussion (par. 53). You might ask your students to watch the newspaper, and to tune into TV and radio news, noting the occurrence of hate crimes. What was the crime, and who was involved? Surfing the Web should produce a list as well.

Sullivan believes that hate "can merely be overcome." Discuss the final paragraph with your students, making sure they know what is meant by "transcendence."

6. Students may note that the use of the term *hate crime* is becoming quite common. In discussing a particular crime, they should analyze it with Sullivan's definitions and caveats in view.

Jonathan Swift: *A Modest Proposal*

1. The proposer is somewhat deficient in humanitarian sentiment. He is anti-Catholic and anti-Episcopalian, a staunch low-church Protestant (par. 21). He is convinced that people do most things for money (par. 26), though he professes to be motivated that way himself (par. 33).

2. He makes his proposal in paragraph 9. In the earlier paragraphs, he presents himself as a concerned humanitarian, and he describes accurately the terrible economic situation. After stating his proposal, he goes into its details with terrifying rationality and lack of emotion. This order allows us to be implicated more deeply in the situation than if he began with the proposal itself.

3. The counterproposals are mainly included in the italicized lines of paragraph 29. He refutes them simply by scoffing at the idea that anyone would try sincerely to "put them in practice" (par. 30).

4. The absolute taboo against cannibalism and the strong feeling that children should be cherished force us to look for alternatives to the literal meaning. The brutal way that the proposer speaks of people as if they were animals (such as "a child just dropped from its dam" in par. 4) and his pompous references to himself all help to make him repugnant and ridiculous. We credit Swift with the mastery of this obnoxious puppet.

5. Swift seems to believe that some of the rejected remedies in paragraph 29 ought to be tried. We assume that he put them in italics to bring them to people's attention. But he may share some of the proposer's skepticism about the willingness of Ireland's governors to put these ideas into practice.

6. Irony depends heavily on shared values, in this case strong feelings against cannibalism and for the welfare of children.

7. With this assignment, you might caution students to find a proposal that is sufficiently at odds with strongly and generally held values so that no one will be able to take it seriously. In such a proposal, the writer must drive the reader to the ironic interpretation.

Thomas Jefferson: *The Declaration of Independence*

1. The argument in paragraph 2 can be summarized this way:

   a. God created humans with certain rights.
   b. Humans created governments to preserve those rights.
   c. Humans may change governments if they fail to preserve those rights.

Self-evident means that these are axioms, a priori assumptions that are held not to need proof.

2. The accusations against the king boil down to the charge that he is not preserving rights but usurping them, behaving like a despot, a tyrant whose word is law, rather than like a constitutional monarch. A king might reply by questioning the nature of the rights claimed for all men, especially liberty, and perhaps by arguing that governments are designed to protect people from others' taking liberties with them and their property. Certainly, it could be argued that the British were only collecting lawful taxes rather than being despotic in America. King George III, of course, sent in the troops, as rulers like to do.

3. The audience certainly included the British people and Parliament as well as the king. But we must remember that most Americans were British citizens at that time, except slaves, who were not citizens at all but property.

4. The residents of America were the major audience for the document. They were deeply divided and remained so. Many Tories fought on the British side and later settled out of the United States in Canada and the Bahamas. There was an international audience too, especially the French, who finally entered the war decisively on the side of the rebellious colonies.

5. This paper should be an explanation rather than an argument. It requires some careful and perhaps subtle analysis. You might not wish to assign it unless you have confidence in your students' ability to accomplish this.

6. Remind your students to start with a strong enough position. Jefferson worked from God and nature down through men and governments to a particular situation. They should follow his lead. The application of this model to less important matters may produce a comic or parodic effect. Let your students know whether you will approve of such bathos or not.

Susan Bordo: *Reading the Slender Body*

1. It might be a good idea to unpack the whole phrase: "the normalizing function of the technologies of diet and body management." Bordo sees "normalizing" as a major strategy in contemporary culture. The "ideal body" is constructed and promoted by the technologies of film, TV, the fashion industry, and the diet and body management industries. These technologies, which consist of processes, methods, and images they

produce, construct the perfect image or representation of the ideal body, in this case, the slender body. This type of body is seen everywhere, in all forms of media: thus it is accepted as *normal*.

2. The section on "Slenderness and the State of the Soul" outlines the changing concept of the body—the female body, especially. The slender wife becomes the symbol of the husband's success. Excess flesh in our time smacks of those cardinal sins of gluttony and sloth. And, of course, a body that is merely slender isn't enough: it must be in shape, and thus under control. The muscular look that once signified working-class has now achieved middle-class, white-collar status. In paragraph 10, Bordo notes, "the size and shape of the body has come to operate as a marker of personal, internal order (or disorder)—as a symbol for the state of the soul." Control over appetite and the will to work out so as to transform jiggling flesh into well-toned muscles signal an orderly mind, a morally superior person who has won that ancient battle of mind/soul over appetites/body. Extreme believers in this philosophy become anorexics.

3. The controlling metaphor of the bear, the "lumbering" "brutish one," the repetition in lines 10 and 11 of "heavy," "a swollen shadow," all work to bring an image of a large, ungainly body. And the lines "strives to be fed" and "[t]he scrimmage of appetite everywhere" can be construed as one who eats constantly. As far as control is concerned, the "bear" is out of control, engaged in a dangerous tight-rope clown act. His "quivering meat," the "bulge in his pants," signify flesh and emotions out of control as well. There's a lack of firm margins; and the lusts of the flesh, the unsatisfied appetite suggest moral inferiority as well. Of course the poem has more to say than this, especially if one reads it as Bordo hoped her students would: as a twentieth-century entry in the long philosophic and literary tradition of the struggle between mind and body.

4. This assignment does not have to be for or about women only. As a result of the current interest by men in their own bodies, the new crop of male magazines features plenty of angst-producing advertisements featuring pecs and abs. Students can construct categories of analysis from these ads, and the class as a whole can compare the gendered results.

Daniel Lazare: *Your Constitution Is Killing You*

1. The argument is that the "individualist" interpretation is "harder and harder to deny." We think it is a well-made argument. There is new evidence on the topic, however, even as we go to press, in the form of historical studies of gun ownership in America. This evidence seems to run counter to Lazare's argument. The topic is very much alive. You should encourage students to dig into this new material.

2. These are matters of opinion, but it seems like a balanced argument to us.

3. Here is where the latest information will be really important. You should make it clear that this particular argument should be about what the Second Amendment really means, not about one's own opinion on the use of guns.

4. The larger argument is that there is a serious conflict between "obedience to ancient law" and "the needs of modern society"—a conflict that makes us "slaves to the past." There is no right answer to the question of which is stronger, but thinking about the issue should help students to understand both arguments.

5. Heavily, since the smaller argument is the only instance of the outdated nature of the Constitution that is offered. In discussion, one might raise the issue of other features of the Constitution that could also be seen as out of touch with present concerns.

6. The essay offers no solution "within the confines of the Constitution." It also holds out little hope of amending the document. It ends not with suggestions for actions but

with questions. The only course of action implied is changing the Constitution, which Lazare has said is difficult if not impossible. This is not an easy box from which to escape.

Jonathan Franzen: *Sifting the Ashes*

1. Though Franzen's essay reads like a confessional in parts, this reflective part of the essay serves as a frame for his argument against "narratives that pretend to unambiguous moral significance" (par. 5), particularly in relation to the production, distribution, and use of cigarettes.

2. Franzen started smoking in college, perhaps as a form of rebellion against his mother's disapproval: "What rejection of parentage could be more extreme than deliberately poisoning [the body that had been created out of the mother's]?" (par. 4). He then brings in the Cold War anxieties he felt as a student in Germany—with the deadliness of cigarettes perceived as "comforting" because such a quality made a possible apocalypse seem "a little less threatening" (par. 8). Near the end, he returns to his reflections: perhaps cigarettes bring a structure of need and gratification to unstructured lives (par. 28), or perhaps he drifts back to smoking because it *"feels* sexy" (par. 33). Your smoking students should have an opinion on this issue (but forbid them to use the term *cool* and see what happens).

3. You can encourage students to identify particular values that cigarettes symbolize—Franzen's essay suggests individuality and sexuality, for example—then have them suggest substitutes that could also symbolize these values or attributes.

4. Franzen believes that as a nation that does exhibit "puritanical zeal," we need a "new Evil Empire" to vent our wrath upon. Comparing the tobacco industry to Hitler's Third Reich is possible because the large number of people who die prematurely from smoking constitutes mass murder. He then discusses the coercion used in place of force: (1) denying the truth, (2) luring children into the habit, and (3) knowingly selling an addictive product with the power to kill (par. 17).

5. Because no one is ever *forced* to smoke, the guilt of the tobacco companies must be based on coercion. Franzen structures his argument using the three categories set out in paragraph 17. Thus he would consider the tobacco companies' willful (and public) denial of the truth ("that smokers were in mortal peril") and thus their conspiracy to "perpetrate a vast and deadly fraud" as the heaviest, most serious issues. And, of course, perjury, conspiracy, and fraud are legally punishable. The seduction of children through advertising into addiction and the willful exposure of the public to potentially legal addiction are certainly serious offenses but might be construed as ethical and moral offenses rather than legal ones. Franzen also points the finger both at the legislatures that have been bought by Big Tobacco and at tobacco's legal advisers, who continually dissuaded the industry from changes that might have made smoking "safer" for fear of admitting that cigarettes are, indeed, lethal.

6. A lot has happened since this article was published—the big tobacco companies have agreed to a huge settlement to defray states' expenses for smoking-related illnesses. There is more to come, including the issue of the tobacco CEOs' perjury regarding nicotine addiction. And there will be studies of whether these exposures have had any effect on the smoking public in the United States.

Robert Frost: *Mending Wall*

1. It is more an argument about building walls without reflection than an argument against walls in general.

2. The speaker's argument is that in this particular area a wall is not necessary, and that one should think about where to build them. His neighbor's argument is that of folk wisdom — "good fences make good neighbors." The instructor's job in leading this discussion is to encourage a variety of responses and reasons. The poem asks for reflection. The instructor should make sure not to stifle it. Questions about other places where walls are placed inappropriately should help to get things going.

3. All of the above are possibilities. Of course, if it's "frost," then we have to ask about Frost. Once again, the idea is open for discussion. This topic should support a short written assignment.

4. He says it is "just another kind of outdoor game." He means, apparently, that there is nothing much at stake, that the wall is not "necessary."

5. Folk wisdom is often grounded in realities, like all traditional wisdom. It refers to actual borders, of course, like those between nations, but it also refers to staying out of one another's business. The poem suggests that this wisdom may not be adequate to certain situations, that it is a wisdom of "darkness" rather than enlightenment, but it does not deny that it is a kind of wisdom. It opens the question, allows the speaker to say where he stands on it, but does not insist that he is right. It offers a position that it does not require us to take. It just requires us to think about it.

6. This is a question for a written paper. Any good theory will suggest some principles about how and when walls are good or bad things.

David Pogue: *Secrets of the Software License Agreement*

1. This answer should be different for each student. The point is to find out when the student began to feel that something mentioned was not likely to be in any agreement he or she had ever encountered. The word "God" should have set bells ringing. If it didn't, find out why.

2. The discussion might begin with the Microsoft/God analogy and then go on to other things, such as the turn to the personal ("I'm just an overpaid lawyer"), and finally to the sensationalist fiction of the last paragraph.

3. The targets are powerful corporations, especially software manufacturers who sell buggy products and offer little support. Minor targets are lawyers and would-be fiction writers, especially those who are lawyers. There is an argument for actually looking at software agreements, but maybe this text is less an argument than a *jeu d'esprit*, a joke for people who don't read these agreements because they are actually unreadable.

Emily Martin: *The Egg and the Sperm: How Science Has Constructed a Romance Based on Stereotypical Male-Female Roles*

1. Martin proposes to show that "the picture of egg and sperm drawn in popular as well as scientific accounts of reproductive biology relies on stereotypes central to our cultural definitions of male and female. The stereotypes imply not only that female biological processes are less worthy than their male counterparts but also that women are less worthy than men" (par. 1). Her argument is developed in three sections: In the first ("Egg and Sperm: A Scientific Fairy Tale"), by inserting what appears to be an oxymoron in her subtitle, she examines the imagery used by the supposedly objective, factually oriented scientific community to show that the "'facts' of biology" are couched in metaphors generated from the stereotyped notion that males are active, females, passive. In the second section ("New Research, Old Imagery"), she argues that although recent studies show

both egg and sperm to be active, the descriptions persist in replicating stereotypical gender images. In the third section ("Social Implications: Thinking Beyond"), she shows that another dangerous stereotype is present in revisionist accounts: that of "woman as a dangerous and aggressive threat" (par. 29). She warns that "the models that biologists use to describe their data can have important social effects" (par. 33) (e.g., Social Darwinism), stresses the danger of bestowing any kind of "personhood" on "cellular entities" (par. 36), and warns feminists to "wake up" the sleeping metaphors so as to "rob them of their power to naturalize our social conventions about gender" (par. 37).

2. The misrepresentation of scientific facts produces a fairy tale. Of specific fairy tales mentioned, "Sleeping Beauty" is significant, reinforcing the active-passive binary central to male-female stereotyping (par. 10). The sperm's "perilous journey" echoes the myth of the hero's night-sea journey, in which he undergoes various perils before reaching his goal.

3. The issue here is, How objective can science be? Can scientists ever report "just the facts"? Using more egalitarian metaphors, while a step in the right direction, is still a danger: bestowing any kind of personhood on a cellular entity is dangerous, especially to women's abortion rights.

4. The metaphors used in textbooks are an interesting study, and could provide the basis for an analytical argument. You may wish to open up the investigation to textbooks in a variety of disciplines. The types of metaphors used are a signal of the kinds of thinking going on and, as in this case, are revelatory of cultural assumptions in those disciplines.

5. If you are familiar with Laskoff and Johnson's *Metaphors We Live By*, you will realize that our thinking is structured metaphorically and that all language can be considered metaphorical. That metaphors indicative of cultural conditioning will creep into students' descriptions of the reproductive function is a given. One of the values of this writing assignment is their discovery of this fact.

6. Students might also do research about sex education texts and curricula using many of the materials available via the Web.

Stephen Jay Gould: *Women's Brains*

1. Gould uses sophisticated modes of numerical analysis, such as "multiple regression," to refute Broca's simplistic and prejudiced interpretation of numbers. Gould's painstaking analysis of Broca's data epitomizes the "inferential" reasoning that he considers fundamental to science.

2. Broca's method of calculating relies exclusively on raw data concerning the average weight and size of women's brains versus men's brains, without taking into account any of the factors or variables that might account for the differences, such as age, height, disease, and nutrition. Gould, by contrast, takes these and other factors into account in order to demonstrate the dangers of relying on raw, uncorrected data.

3. Gould uses quotations primarily to expose the misogynistic bias of Broca and his followers. The rigorousness of Gould's scientific approach is reflected in the fact that he not only attacks Broca for his chauvinism, but he also chastises Maria Montessori for her reverse discrimination.

4. Both of the passages from George Eliot's prelude to *Middlemarch* fittingly display a far more sophisticated approach to numbers and numerical analysis than Broca and his male followers used. More important, Eliot's reflection, like Gould's analysis, vividly bears witness to the complex ways in which unexamined assumptions about women and women's roles have led to the denigration and victimization of women.

5. Gould's extensive quotations from Broca and his followers not only reveal their misogynistic biases, but also show in each case how those biases distorted their interpretation of the data about women's brains.

6. To fulfill this assignment, students should be advised not to fabricate different ways of gathering, calculating, and interpreting data, but to find examples that they can refute as Gould does, or to find examples of differing interpretations that they can evaluate using Gould's scientific principles and "inferential" methods.

7. Here, as in the preceding assignment, students should be advised to find actual examples that they can evaluate, refute, or both.

Harold J. Morowitz: *Arks and Genetic Bottlenecks*

1. The longest argument is about biodiversity and concludes by saying that the scriptures aren't much help there—which means that the biblical story of Noah and the flood just doesn't match conceptually with scientific biology. According to current science, it couldn't have happened the way the Bible tells it. That argument is then generalized rapidly to a much wider one—namely that the Bible cannot provide ethical guidance for our time because it was written for a time in which our problems did not exist.

2. The key terms are *chromosome, gene pool*, and *allele*. The instructor should be sure to have them clear in her/his own mind before teaching this essay. *Allele*, which is defined in paragraph 3, is probably the one least used in ordinary discourse. If you are asked about it, directing students to the text itself for the definition would (a) show that you know the essay and (b) be pedagogically sound. Student readers should learn to look for help first in the text itself.

3. We suggest letting the discussion be as open as possible. "It" means, we speculate, an ethical system suitable to the conditions of being in which we find ourselves.

4, 5. No right answer to these. Encourage creativity combined with plausibility. There is certainly a secular argument against using ancient moral or religious texts uncritically as solutions for problems that did not exist when they were composed. The argument is that the texts had to be written in ways that were intelligible at the time and adapted to the situation of their readers, which results in certain bits of ethical advice (be fruitful and multiply) becoming unethical in the present context. There are, of course, religious counter-arguments to this position, which should be admitted and given a serious hearing in discussion.

David H. Freedman: *When Is a Planet Not a Planet?*

1. Freedman summarizes Marsden's argument against keeping planet status for Pluto, an argument he seems to approve. He also summarizes Levy's argument for maintaining it, with which he expresses some sympathy. But his own argument is for a reasonable compromise. This argument is based on the idea that in scientific studies, the most adequate concepts will eventually prevail—and those concepts are now being taught in the sixth grade. Therefore, because the truth will prevail, the status of Pluto will change gradually.

2. Marsden's argument is mainly that Pluto's status is accidental and does not fit most of the current definitions or tests for planethood, such as having "swept out its orbit." But this is supported by Sagan's argument that it is important for human beings "to picture the universe in the right conceptual terms." (Any good summary should have these two notions at a minimum.)

3. The arguments range from "Kids *like* Pluto," to the dead Clyde Tombaugh wanted it that way, to the more insidious notion that demoting it could hurt funding for astronomical projects such as the *Pluto Express*. That is, the arguments are either touchy-feely or self-interested–pragmatic in the worst sense.

4. It's a classic case of scientific truth versus Disneyfied mythology and scientific self-interest. Freedman presents it that way and seems very happy that his sixth-grader is learning the right stuff. He also makes it clear that the Norwegian Kaare Asknes will prevent the case from getting a fair hearing, not on scientific grounds but out of loyalty to Tombaugh and "history," which in this case means "mythology."

5. The descriptions give the piece a journalistic liveliness, and it is clear that personalities are having an effect on the debate—call it the Tombaugh effect.

Stuart Moulthrop: *On Creating a Web Site*

1. For each axiom, encourage students to think of specific applications or digital situations in the light of which to evaluate that axiom. In each case, you should begin with some sort of consensus on what is being urged before discussing specific applications of that advice.

2. We think his advice is pretty good. You should always be ready to hear a good critique of it.

3. Students may wish to bring in their own home pages for praise, but make sure they also find some pages they think have flaws—especially flaws by Moulthrop's standards.

4. Higher transmission speeds and greater bandwidth are making pictures more useful, but there is a case to be made that they are often overused, resulting in very cluttered pages. Moulthrop himself uses few images but his home page uses space, color, font selection, and other visual cues to good effect. But his advice about the importance of words is a useful reminder that English teachers can emphasize.

5. Let 'em go in this one, but suggest that the form should follow Moulthrop's—six or seven axioms of one to four lines in length. Brevity is important in this mode. Emphasize this.

6. Encourage frank discussion (maybe in small groups) of what seems strong and what seems weak in each entry. Also encourage explanations about why students couldn't or didn't follow Moulthrop in every instance.

C. G. Hanzlicek: *Room for Doubt*

1. One wants the student's reading here, more than the "right reading," but any discussion should get around to seeing that this is an argument about the application of "scientific" knowledge to questions of ethics or values. Since all science is based on probabilities (we don't know the sun will reappear to us after the night, though the probability is very high), the argument goes, we should be wary of applying those probabilities as if they were certainties. There is also a quasi-Christian argument here about the fallibility of human beings and their need for social judgments that allow for this.

2. These are meant to be open questions. The most interesting one, in our judgment, is "What makes a story scientific?" The answer will have to do with scientific method, objectivity, confirmability, absence of strong contradictory evidence, and acceptance by a community qualified to judge the evidence. The poem does not offer itself as science but as a reminder that science is a web of probabilities, subject to revision, not a fixed body of truth.

3. It suggests that live things are difficult to study but also worthy of study and complicated by their sensitivity to pain inflicted in the course of such study. Very faintly, there are the outlines of a case against vivisection here.

4. There is no way that we will suggest a proper answer for this question. How individual students feel is a matter only they can say, though the instructor should try to draw them out.

5. The poem reminds us of our own frailty, our capacity for suffering, our need for toleration. It suggests that we extend to other creatures some of the tolerance and sympathy we would like for ourselves. This is a variation on the golden rule, but it brings the dead rule to life via the specifically realized situation.

Research and Writing Online

Whether you want to investigate the ideas behind a thought-provoking essay or conduct in-depth research for a paper, the Web resources for *Fields of Reading* can help you find what you need—and then use it once you find it.

The English Research Room for Navigating the Web

www.bedfordstmartins.com/english_research

The Web brings a flood of information to your screen, but it takes skill to track down the best sources. Not only does *The English Research Room* point you to some reliable starting places for Web investigations, but it also lets you tune up your skills with interactive tutorials.

- Want to improve your skill at searching electronic databases, online catalogs, and the Web? Try the *Interactive Tutorials* for some hands-on practice.
- Need quick access to online search engines, reference sources, and research sites? Explore *Research Links* for some good starting places.
- Have questions on evaluating the sources you find, navigating the Web, or conducting research in general? Consult one of our *Reference Units* for authoritative advice.

Research and Documentation Online for Incorporating Sources

www.bedfordstmartins.com/resdoc

Incorporating sources correctly in a paper is often a challenge, and the Web has made it even more complex. This online version of the popular booklet *Research and Documentation in the Electronic Age,* by Diana Hacker, provides clear advice for the humanities, social sciences, history, and the sciences on

- which Web and library sources are relevant to your topic (with links to Web sources)
- how to integrate outside material into your paper
- how to cite sources correctly, using the appropriate documentation style
- what the format for the final paper should be